Marketing Management

Knowledge and Skills   Ninth Edition

J. Paul Peter
University of Wisconsin–Madison

James H. Donnelly, Jr.
University of Kentucky

McGraw-Hill
Irwin

Boston   Burr Ridge, IL   Dubuque, IA   New York   San Francisco   St. Louis
Bangkok   Bogotá   Caracas   Kuala Lumpur   Lisbon   London   Madrid   Mexico City
Milan   Montreal   New Delhi   Santiago   Seoul   Singapore   Sydney   Taipei   Toronto

McGraw-Hill Irwin

MARKETING MANAGEMENT: KNOWLEDGE AND SKILLS

Published by McGraw-Hill/Irwin, a business unit of The McGraw-Hill Companies, Inc., 1221 Avenue of the Americas, New York, NY, 10020. Copyright © 2009, 2007, 2004, 2001, 1998, 1995, 1992, 1989, 1986 by The McGraw-Hill Companies, Inc. All rights reserved. No part of this publication may be reproduced or distributed in any form or by any means, or stored in a database or retrieval system, without the prior written consent of The McGraw-Hill Companies, Inc., including, but not limited to, in any network or other electronic storage or transmission, or broadcast for distance learning.

Some ancillaries, including electronic and print components, may not be available to customers outside the United States.

This book is printed on acid-free paper.

1 2 3 4 5 6 7 8 9 0 WCK/WCK 0 9 8

ISBN   978-0-07-338113-8
MHID   0-07-338113-6

Publisher: *Paul Ducham*
Executive editor: *Doug Hughes*
Editorial assistant: *Devon Raemisch*
Marketing manager: *Katie Mergen*
Project manager: *Dana M. Pauley*
Full service project manager: *Jodi Dowling, Aptara®, Inc.*
Lead production supervisor: *Michael R. McCormick*
Designer: *Matt Diamond*
Photo research coordinator: *Lori Kramer*
Lead media project manager: *Cathy L. Tepper*
Media project manager: *Suresh Babu, Hurix Systems Pvt. Ltd.*
Typeface: *10/12 Times New Roman*
Compositor: *Aptara®, Inc.*
Printer: *Quebecor World Versailles Inc.*

Library of Congress Cataloging-in-Publication Data

Peter, J. Paul.
    Marketing management : knowledge and skills / J. Paul Peter, James H.
  Donnelly, Jr.—9th ed.
      p. cm.
    Includes index.
    ISBN-13: 978-0-07-338113-8 (alk. paper)
    ISBN-10: 0-07-338113-6 (alk. paper)
    1. Marketing—Management.   2. Marketing—Management—Case studies.
  I. Donnelly, James H. II. Title.
  HF5415.13.P387 2009
  658.8—dc22

                                        2008033002

www.mhhe.com

To Gayla

Jim Donnelly

To Rose and Angie

J. Paul Peter

About the Authors

J. Paul Peter

is the James R. McManus–Bascom Professor of Marketing at the University of Wisconsin–Madison. He was a member of the faculty at Indiana State, Ohio State, and Washington University before joining the Wisconsin faculty in 1981. While at Ohio State, he was named Outstanding Marketing Professor by the students, and he has won the John R. Larson Teaching Award at Wisconsin. He has taught a variety of courses including Marketing Management, Marketing Strategy, Consumer Behavior, Marketing Research, and Marketing Theory, among others.

Professor Peter's research has appeared in the *Journal of Marketing,* the *Journal of Marketing Research,* the *Journal of Consumer Research,* the *Journal of Retailing,* and the *Academy of Management Journal,* among others. His article on construct validity won the prestigious William O'Dell Award from the *Journal of Marketing Research,* and he was a finalist for this award on two other occasions. Recently, he was the recipient of the Churchill Award for Lifetime Achievement in Marketing Research, given by the American Marketing Association and the Gaumnitz Distinguished Faculty Award from the School of Business, University of Wisconsin–Madison. He is an author or editor of over 30 books, including *A Preface to Marketing Management,* eleventh edition; *Marketing Management: Knowledge and Skills,* ninth edition; *Consumer Behavior and Marketing Strategy,* eighth edition; *Strategic Management: Concepts and Applications,* third edition; and *Marketing: Creating Value for Customers,* second edition. He is one of the most cited authors in the marketing literature.

Professor Peter has served on the review boards of the *Journal of Marketing, Journal of Marketing Research, Journal of Consumer Research,* and *Journal of Business Research* and was measurement editor for *JMR* and professional publications editor for the American Marketing Association. He has taught in a variety of executive programs and consulted for several corporations as well as the Federal Trade Commission.

James H. Donnelly, Jr.,

is the Thomas C. Simons Professor in the Gatton College of Business and Economics at the University of Kentucky. In 1990 he received the first Chancellor's Award for Outstanding Teaching given at the University. Previously, he had twice received the UK Alumni Association's Great Teacher Award, an award one can only be eligible to receive every 10 years. He has also received two Outstanding Teacher awards from Beta Gamma Sigma, national business honorary. In 1992 he received an Acorn Award recognizing "those who shape the future" from the Kentucky Advocates for Higher Education. In 2001 and 2002 he was selected as "Best University of Kentucky Professor." In 1995 he became one of six charter members elected to the American Bankers Association's Bank Marketing Hall of Fame. He has also received a "Distinguished Doctoral Graduate Award" from the University of Maryland.

During his career he has published in the *Journal of Marketing Research, Journal of Marketing, Journal of Retailing, Administrative Science Quarterly, Academy of Management Journal, Journal of Applied Psychology, Personnel Psychology, Journal of Business Research,* and *Operations Research* among others. He has served on the editorial review board of the *Journal of Marketing.* He is the author of more than a dozen books, which include widely adopted academic texts as well as professional books.

Professor Donnelly is very active in the banking industry where he has served on the board of directors of the Institute of Certified Bankers and the ABA's Marketing Network. He has also served as academic dean of the ABA's School of Bank Marketing and Management.

Preface

Welcome to the ninth edition of *Marketing Management: Knowledge and Skills*. Our goal has always been very clear to us: to enhance students' *knowledge* of marketing management and to advance their *skills* in utilizing this knowledge to develop and maintain successful marketing strategies. *Knowledge enhancement* and/or *skill development* are the purpose of each section included in our book. Our vision always has been *to assemble a complete student resource for marketing management education.* This edition is no exception.

The Present Edition

Our book must continually change because the resources that students and instructors need continually change. Thus, the basic structure of the book continues to evolve and expand, particularly during recent editions. Based on extensive feedback from adoptors and students plus our own intuitions and judgments, we have made numerous changes in this and recent editions.

1. Because the text chapters are an integral part of the book, they have been completely revised and updated. New content has been added throughout. There are new or expanded discussions of the major types of marketing, branding, marketing's role in cross-functional strategic planning, a comparison of data collection techniques in marketing research, the most current psychographic and geographic approaches to segmentation, and a new section on Porter's diamond model of national competitive advantage. We have changed the title of Chapter 6 to "Product and Brand Strategy" to more accurately reflect the content of the chapter.

In this edition we have added 25 new "Marketing Highlights" and deleted numerous others. A popular feature that has received positive feedback from both students and instructors, these highlights are not the usual news items found in many other texts. Instead they present important tools and content that can be used in analyzing marketing cases and problems.

We have carefully selected additional reading for student writing projects and case presentations. Each chapter has additional readings useful for both MBA students as well as undergraduates. Our goal was to make these readings accessible to students at various stages of marketing education.

2. Approximately one-third of the cases in this edition are new. Our search for relevant new cases is indeed an unending challenge. We are very fortunate to be able to add 12 new ones to this edition. The emphasis has always been on well-known companies whenever possible, including both domestic and global companies, high-tech companies, consumer and organizational products, small and large businesses, products and services, and manufacturers and channel members.

We have also made an effort to retain some cases that are popular with instructors and students. These cases can truly be considered "classics." But whether set in 2008 or 1998, these "snapshots in time" enable students to analyze a situation within the time period the case was written and/or to bring the situation up to date with their own research and analysis.

3. An important and valuable student resource updated in this edition is an annotated bibliography of major online databases used in marketing. It is an up-to-date resource for students to use in the analysis of cases, the development of marketing plans, and the analysis of Internet exercises. It is presented in Section IV immediately following the Internet exercises. The Internet exercises have also been revised and updated.

4. Some of the cases include in-class exercises that provide the instructor with opportunities for team building and student participation.

5. For some cases there are accompanying video presentations and discussion questions that can enrich student interest, thinking, analysis, and presentation.

Over the years we have experimented with numerous teaching approaches and philosophies. The structure of this book reflects an evolution from these experiments. Presently, our model includes a six-stage learning approach that includes (1) mastering basic marketing principles, (2) learning approaches and tools for performing marketing analyses, (3) analyzing Internet exercises, (4) analyzing marketing management cases, (5) analyzing strategic marketing cases, and (6) developing marketing plans.

Our six-stage learning approach is the focus of the seven sections of the book. Each section has as its objective either *knowledge enhancement* or *skill development,* or both. The framework and structure of our book is presented in the diagram below and will appear throughout the text to integrate the sections of the book.

Stage 1: Mastering Basic Marketing Principles

It is clearly necessary for students to learn and understand basic definitions, concepts, and marketing logic before they can apply them in the analysis of marketing problems or development of marketing plans. Section I of the book contains 13 chapters that present the essentials of marketing management. One problem we continually face in more advanced case-oriented courses is that most students have long ago discarded or sold their basic marketing texts. Consequently, when they are faced with case problems they have nothing to rely on but their memories. We believe this seriously detracts from the usefulness of case analysis. Thus, we include this section as a reference source for key marketing concepts. Our objective in this section is to focus on material that is relevant primarily for analyzing marketing problems and cases.

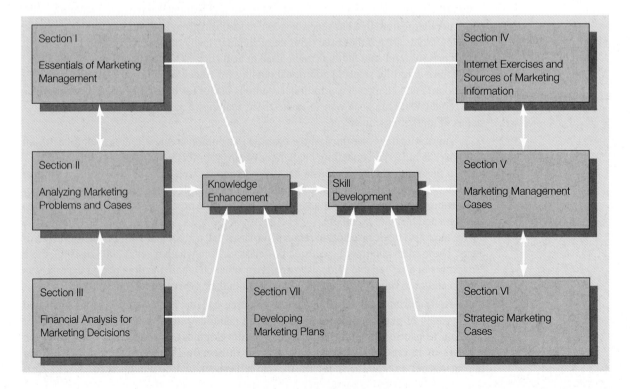

Stage 2: Learning Approaches and Tools for Problem Analysis

The second stage in our approach involves offering students basic tools and approaches for solving marketing problems. Section II, "Analyzing Marketing Problems and Cases," is a widely praised approach to analyzing, writing, and presenting case analyses. Section III, "Financial Analysis for Marketing Decisions," presents some important financial calculations that can be useful in evaluating the financial position of a firm and the financial impact of various marketing strategies. Section IV includes an annotated bibliography of some of the most widely used marketing databases. It will assist students in researching a particular industry or firm and can greatly improve the analysis of cases.

Stage 3: Analyzing Internet Exercises

As a way of introducing students to the challenges of case analysis, some instructors utilize Internet exercises. They find that these exercises are an especially useful way to integrate text material with case work. Accordingly, Section IV provides 11 such exercises. Other instructors, especially those with more advanced marketing students, find their students are fully prepared to tackle case analyses. For these instructors, this section is optional.

Stage 4: Analyzing Marketing Management Cases

It has been our experience that few students have the confidence and experience necessary to analyze complex strategic marketing cases in their first exposure to this type of learning. We believe it is far better for them to apply their skills by analyzing cases for which traditional marketing principles can be applied somewhat directly before they attempt more challenging problems. Accordingly, Section V of the book includes 25 marketing management cases, organized into six groups: market opportunity analysis, product strategy, promotion strategy, distribution strategy, pricing strategy, and social and ethical issues in marketing management. Within each group, cases are sequenced so that later cases contain more information and typically require higher levels of marketing management analysis skills than earlier ones.

Stage 5: Analyzing Strategic Marketing Cases

Once students have developed sufficient skills to provide thoughtful analyses of marketing management cases, they are prepared to tackle strategic marketing cases. These cases go beyond traditional marketing principles and focus on the role of marketing in cross-functional business or organization strategies. Section VI of our book contains 10 such cases. They are sequenced so that the latter cases contain more information and require higher skill levels to analyze them properly.

Stage 6: Developing Marketing Plans

The final stage in our approach involves the development of an original marketing plan. We believe that after a two-course sequence in marketing management, students should be able to do one thing very well and should know that they can do it well: Students should be able to construct a quality marketing plan for any product or service. Section VII provides a framework for developing such a plan. Instructors can consult the *Instructors Manual* that accompanies this book for alternative ways to incorporate this stage into their course.

Flexibility for Instructors

The six-stage process is very flexible and we have found that it can easily be adapted to the needs of students and objectives of instructors. For example, if the course is the first learning experience in marketing, then emphasis could be placed on the first four stages. If students progress well through these stages, then marketing management cases in Section V can be assigned on an individual or group basis.

If the course is for students with one or more courses in marketing or in the capstone marketing course, then major attention should shift to stages 2 through 6. In this instance, Section I becomes a resource for review and reference and the course focuses more on skill development.

Finally, the text can be used for a two-course sequence in marketing management. The first course can emphasize stages 1 through 4 and the second can concentrate on stages 5 and 6.

Acknowledgments

Many talented people contributed to our book in the form of cases and exercises. Our appreciation and thanks go to each one of them. Their names and affiliations appear in the Contents and at the point in the book where their contribution appears. Their work will help others better educate marketing students.

We also must thank the users who responded to our survey. Your assistance was needed as we planned this edition, especially in making the hard choices involved in replacing cases, selecting new cases, and deciding which of the "classic" cases to retain. Again, thanks for your assistance.

We also want to acknowledge those colleagues who provided detailed reviews of previous editions:

Sammy G. Amin
Frostburg State University

Amy Beattie
Champlain College

Andrew Bergstein
Pennsylvania State University

David Bourff
Boise State University

Brad Brooks
Queens College

Carol Bruneau
University of Montana

Richard Campbell
California State University-Bakersfield

Daniel P. Chamberlin
Regent University

V. Glenn Chappell
Meredith College

Henry Chen
University of West Florida

Newell Chiesl
Indiana State University

Pravat K. Choudhury
Howard University

Clare Comm
University of Massachusetts-Lowell

John Considine
LeMoyne College

Robert Cosenza
University of Mississippi

Larry Crowson
University of Central Florida

Rober Cutler
Cleveland State University

Denver D'Rozario
Howard University

Mike Dailey
University of Texas, Arlington

Carl Dresden
Coastal Carolina University

Patricia Duncan
Harris-Stowe State College

Adel I. El-Ansary
University of North Florida

Randall Ewing
Ohio Northern University

Renee Foster
Delta State University

John Gauthier
Gateway Technical College

David Griffith
University of Oklahoma

Angela Hausman
University of Texas-Pan American

Jack Healey
Golden State University

JoAnne S. Hooper
Western Carolina University

Jarrett Hudnall
Mississippi University for Women

Patricia Humphrey
Texas A&M University

Arun K. Jain
University at Buffalo

Wesley H. Jones
University of Indianapolis

Benoy Joseph
Cleveland State University

Dee Anne Larson
Mississippi University for Women

Brian Little
Marshall University

Anne B. Lowery
University of Mobile

Steven Lysonski
Marquette University

ix

Gregory Martin
University of West Florida

Wendy Martin
Judson College

Mary K. McManamon
Lake Erie College

Donald J. Messmer
College of William & Mary

Hudson Nwakanma
Florida A&M University

Elaine Notarantonio
Bryant University

Alphonso Ogbuehi
Bryant University

Thomas L. Parkinson
Moravian College

Hatash Sachdev
Eastern Michigan University

Amit Saini
University of Nebraska-Lincoln

Chris Samfilippo
University of Michigan-Dearborn

William F. Schoell
University of Southern Mississippi

Anusorn M. Singhapakdi
Old Dominion University

Jean Shaneyfelt
Edicon Community College

John Shaw
Providence College

Charlotte Smedberg
Florida Metropolitan University System

R. Mark Smith
Campbell University

Joseph R. Stasio
Merrimack College

Albert J. Taylor
Austin Peay State University

Dillard Tinsley
Austin State University

Joanne Trotter
Gwynedd-Mercy College

David J. Vachon
CSUN

Kevin Webb
Drexel University

Paula Welch
Mansfield University

Dale Wilson
Michigan State University

Mark Young
Winona State University

Finally, we want to acknowledge those colleagues who provided valuable market feedback for this edition:

John Stovall
Georgia Southwestern State University

Amit Saini
University of Nebraska-Lincoln

Shaoming Zou
University of Missouri-Columbia

Robert Cosenza
University of Mississippi

Rodney Stump
Towson University

Mark Toncar
Youngstown State University

Bill Magrogan
National Louis University & Columbia Union College

Cesar Maloles III
California State Univ. East Bay

Ann Little
High Point University

Deborah Salvo
University of St. Thomas

John Wong
Iowa State University

It has always been a pleasure to be McGraw-Hill authors. Professionals like Dana Pauley, project manager, and Devon Raemisch, editorial assistant, supported our efforts with this edition and we are extremely grateful.

Michael Knetter, Dean of the School of Business at the University of Wisconsin, and Devanthan Sudharshan, Dean of the Gatton College of Business and Economics at the University of Kentucky have always supported our efforts.

J. Paul Peter

James H. Donnelly, Jr.

Contents

Section I

Essentials of Marketing Management

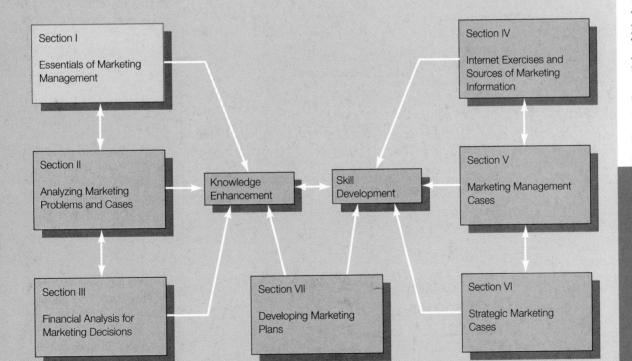

Introduction

1

Strategic Planning and the Marketing Management Process

The purpose of this introductory chapter is to present the marketing management process and outline what marketing managers must *manage* if they are to be effective. In doing so, it will also present a framework around which the remaining chapters are organized. Our first task is to review the organizational philosophy known as the marketing concept, since it underlies much of the thinking presented in this book. The remainder of this chapter will focus on the process of strategic planning and its relationship to the process of marketing planning.

The Marketing Concept

Simply stated, the marketing concept means that *an organization should seek to make a profit by serving the needs of customer groups.* The concept is very straightforward and has a great deal of commonsense validity. Perhaps this is why it is often misunderstood, forgotten, or overlooked.

The purpose of the marketing concept is to rivet the attention of marketing managers on serving broad classes of customer needs (customer orientation), rather than on the firm's current products (production orientation) or on devising methods to attract customers to current products (selling orientation). Thus, effective marketing starts with the recognition of customer needs and then works backward to devise products and services to satisfy these needs. In this way, marketing managers can satisfy customers more efficiently in the present and anticipate changes in customer needs more accurately in the future. This means that organizations should focus on building long-term customer relationships in which the initial sale is viewed as a beginning step in the process, not as an end goal. As a result, the customer will be more satisfied and the firm will be more profitable.

The principal task of the marketing function operating under the marketing concept is not to manipulate customers to do what suits the interests of the firm, but rather to find effective and efficient means of making the business do what suits the interests of customers. This is not to say that all firms practice marketing in this way. Clearly, many firms still emphasize only production and sales. However, effective marketing, as defined in this text, requires that consumer needs come first in organizational decision making.

1. Create customer focus throughout the business.
2. Listen to the customer.
3. Define and nurture your distinctive competence, that is, what your organization does well, better than competitors.
4. Define marketing as market intelligence.
5. Target customers precisely.
6. Manage for profitability, not sales volume.
7. Make customer value the guiding star.
8. Let customers define quality.
9. Measure and manage customer expectations.
10. Build customer relationships and loyalty.
11. Define the business as a service business.
12. Commit to continuous improvement and innovation.
13. Manage the culture of your organization along with strategy and structure.
14. Grow with strategic partners and alliances.
15. Destroy marketing bureaucracy.

Source: See Frederick E. Webster, Jr., "Defining the New Marketing Concept," *Marketing Management* 2, no. 4 (1994), pp. 22–31. For a classic discussion see Robert L. King, "The Marketing Concept: Fact or Intelligent Platitude," *The Marketing Concept in Action,* Proceedings of the 47th National Conference (Chicago, American Marketing Association, 1964), p. 657. Adapted from William O. Bearden, Thomas N. Ingram, and Raymond W. LaForge, *Marketing: Principles and Perspectives,* 5th ed. (Burr Ridge, IL: McGraw-Hill/Irwin, 2007), p. 9.

One qualification to this statement deals with the question of a conflict between consumer wants and societal needs and wants. For example, if society deems clean air and water as necessary for survival, this need may well take precedence over a consumer's want for goods and services that pollute the environment.

What Is Marketing?

Everyone reading this book has been a customer for most of his or her life. Last evening you stopped into a local supermarket to graze at the salad bar, pick up some bottled water and a bag of Fritos corn chips. While you were there, you snapped a $1.00 coupon for a new flavor salad dressing out of a dispenser and tasted some new breakfast potatoes being cooked in the back of the store. As you sat down at home to eat your salad, you answered the phone and someone suggested that you need to have your carpets cleaned. Later on in the evening you saw TV commercials for tires, soft drinks, athletic shoes, and the dangers of smoking and drinking during pregnancy. Today when you enrolled in a marketing course, you found that the instructor has decided that you must purchase this book. A friend has already purchased the book on the Internet. All of these activities involve marketing. And each of us knows something about marketing because it has been a part of our life since we had our first dollar to spend.

Since we are all involved in marketing, it may seem strange that one of the persistent problems in the field has been its definition.[1] The American Marketing Association defines marketing as "an organizational function and a set of processes for creating, communicating, and delivering value to customers and for managing customer relationships in ways that benefit the organization and its stakeholders."[2] This definition takes into account all parties involved in the marketing effort: members of the producing organization, resellers of goods and services, and customers or clients. While the broadness of the definition allows the inclusion of nonbusiness

FIGURE 1.1
Major Types of Marketing

Type	Description	Example
Product	Marketing designed to create exchange for tangible products.	Strategies to sell Gateway computers.
Service	Marketing designed to create exchanges for intangible products.	Strategies by Allstate to sell insurance.
Person	Marketing designed to create favorable actions toward persons.	Strategies to elect a political candidate.
Place	Marketing designed to attract people to places.	Strategies to get people to vacation in national or state parks.
Cause	Marketing designed to create support for ideas, causes, or issues or to get people to change undesirable behaviors.	Strategies to get pregnant women not to drink alcohol.
Organization	Marketing designed to attract donors, members, participants, or volunteers.	Strategies designed to attract blood donors.

exchange processes, the primary emphasis in this text is on marketing in the business environment. However, this emphasis is not meant to imply that marketing concepts, principles, and techniques cannot be fruitfully employed in other areas of exchange as is clearly illustrated in Figure 1.1.

What Is Strategic Planning?

Before a production manager, marketing manager, and personnel manager can develop plans for their individual departments, some larger plan or blueprint for the *entire* organization should exist. Otherwise, on what would the individual departmental plans be based?

In other words, there is a larger context for planning activities. Let us assume that we are dealing with a large business organization that has several business divisions and several product lines within each division (e.g., General Electric, Altria). Before individual divisions or departments can implement any marketing planning, a plan has to be developed for the entire organization.[3] This means that senior managers must look toward the future and evaluate their ability to shape their organization's destiny in the years and decades to come. The output of this process is objectives and strategies designed to give the organization a chance to compete effectively in the future. The objectives and strategies established at the top level provide the context for planning in each of the divisions and departments by divisional and departmental managers.

Strategic Planning and Marketing Management

Some of the most successful business organizations are here today because many years ago they offered the right product at the right time to a rapidly growing market. The same can also be said for nonprofit and governmental organizations. Many of the critical decisions of the past were made without the benefit of strategic thinking or planning. Whether these decisions were based on wisdom or were just luck is not important; they worked for these organizations. However, a worse fate befell countless other organizations. Over three-quarters of the 100 largest U.S. corporations of 70 years ago have fallen from the list. These corporations at one time dominated their markets, controlled vast resources, and had the best-trained workers. In the end, they all made the same critical mistake. Their managements failed to recognize that business strategies need to reflect changing environments

1. It costs a great deal more to acquire a new customer than to keep an old one.
2. Loyal customers buy more from your firm over time.
3. The longer you keep a customer, the more profitable they become over time.
4. It costs less to service loyal customers than new customers.
5. Loyal customers are often excellent referrals for new business.
6. Loyal customers are often willing to pay more for the quality and value they desire.

Source: One of the earliest works on the value of the loyal customer was Frederick F. Reichheld, *The Loyalty Effect,* HBS Press, 1996. Also see Roland T. Rust, Katherine N. Lemon, and Valerie A. Zeithamel, "Return on Marketing: Using Customer Equity to Focus Marketing Strategies," *Journal of Marketing,* January, 2004, pp. 76–89. Adapted from William O. Bearden, Thomas N. Ingram, and Raymond W. LaForge, *Marketing: Principles and Perspectives,* 5th ed. (Burr Ridge, IL: McGraw-Hill/Irwin, 2007), p. 8.

and emphasis must be placed on developing business systems that allow for continuous improvement. Instead, they attempted to carry on business as usual.

Present-day managers are increasingly recognizing that wisdom and innovation alone are no longer sufficient to guide the destinies of organizations, both large and small. These same managers also realize that the true mission of the organization is to provide value for three key constituencies: customers, employees, and investors. Without this type of outlook, no one, including shareholders, will profit in the long run.

Strategic planning includes all the activities that lead to the development of a clear organizational mission, organizational objectives, and appropriate strategies to achieve the objectives for the entire organization. The form of the process itself has come under criticism in some quarters for being too structured; however, strategic planning, if performed successfully, plays a key role in achieving an equilibrium between the short and the long term by balancing acceptable financial performance with preparation for inevitable changes in markets, technology, and competition, as well as in economic and political arenas. Managing principally for current cash flows, market share gains, and earnings trends can mortgage the firm's future. An intense focus on the near term can produce an aversion to risk that dooms a business to stagnation. Conversely, an overemphasis on the long run is just as inappropriate. Companies that overextend themselves betting on the future may penalize short-term profitability and other operating results to such an extent that the company is vulnerable to takeover and other threatening actions.

The strategic planning process is depicted in Figure 1.2. In the strategic planning process the organization gathers information about the changing elements of its environment. Managers from all functional areas in the organization assist in this information-gathering process. This information is useful in aiding the organization to adapt better to these changes through the process of strategic planning. The strategic plan(s)[4] and supporting plan are then implemented in the environment. The end results of this implementation are fed back as new information so that continuous adaptation and improvement can take place.

The Strategic Planning Process

The output of the strategic planning process is the development of a strategic plan. Figure 1.2 indicates four components of a strategic plan: mission, objectives, strategies, and portfolio plan. Let us carefully examine each one.

Organizational Mission

The organization's environment provides the resources that sustain the organization, whether it is a business, a college or university, or a government agency. In exchange for

FIGURE 1.2   The Strategic Planning Process

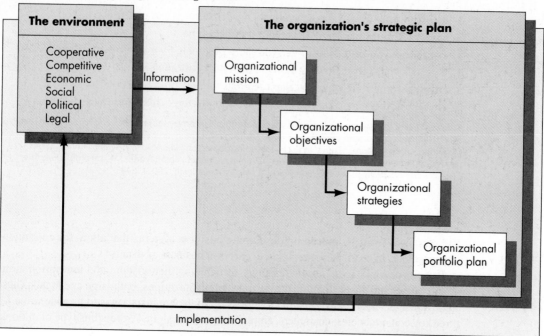

these resources, the organization must supply the environment with quality goods and services at an acceptable price. In other words, every organization exists to accomplish something in the larger environment and that purpose, vision, or mission usually is clear at the organization's inception. As time passes, however, the organization expands, and the environment and managerial personnel change. As a result, one or more things are likely to occur. First, the organization's original purpose may become irrelevant as the organization expands into new products, new markets, and even new industries. For example, Levi Strauss began as a manufacturer of work clothes. Second, the original mission may remain relevant, but managers begin to lose interest in it. Finally, changes in the environment may make the original mission inappropriate, as occurred with the March of Dimes when a cure was found for polio. The result of any or all three of these conditions is a "drifting" organization, without a clear mission, vision, or purpose to guide critical decisions. When this occurs, management must search for a purpose or emphatically restate and reinforce the original purpose.

The mission statement, or purpose, of an organization is the description of its reason for existence. It is the long-run vision of what the organization strives to be, the unique aim that differentiates the organization from similar ones and the means by which this differentiation will take place. In essence, the mission statement defines the direction in which the organization is heading and how it will succeed in reaching its desired goal. While some argue that vision and mission statements differ in their purpose, the perspective we will take is that both reflect the organization's attempt to guide behavior, create a culture, and inspire commitment.[5] However, it is more important that the mission statement comes from the heart and is practical, easy to identify with, and easy to remember so that it will provide direction and significance to all members of the organization regardless of their organizational level.

The basic questions that must be answered when an organization decides to examine and restate its mission are, What is our business? Who is the customer? What do customers

Organization	Mission
Community bank	To help citizens successfully achieve and celebrate important life events with education, information, products, and services.
Skin care products	We will provide luxury skin-care products with therapeutic qualities that make them worth their premium price.
Hotel chain	Grow a worldwide lodging business using total-quality-management (TQM) principles to continuously improve preference and profitability. Our commitment is that *every guest leaves satisfied.*
Mid-size bank	We will become the best bank in the state for medium-size businesses by 2010.

value? and What will our business be?[6] The answers are, in a sense, the assumptions on which the organization is being run and from which future decisions will evolve. While such questions may seem simplistic, they are such difficult and critical ones that the major responsibility for answering them must lie with top management. In fact, the mission statement remains the most widely used management tool in business today. In developing a statement of mission, management must take into account three key elements: the organization's history, its distinctive competencies, and its environment.[7]

1. *The organization's history.* Every organization—large or small, profit or nonprofit—has a history of objectives, accomplishments, mistakes, and policies. In formulating a mission, the critical characteristics and events of the past must be considered.

2. *The organization's distinctive competencies.* While there are many things an organization may be able to do, it should seek to do what it can do best. Distinctive competencies are things that an organization does well—so well in fact that they give it an advantage over similar organizations. For Honeywell, it's their ability to design, manufacture, and distribute a superior line of thermostats.[8] Similarly, Procter & Gamble's distinctive competency is its knowledge of the market for low-priced, repetitively purchased consumer products. No matter how appealing an opportunity may be, to gain advantage over competitors, the organization must formulate strategy based on distinctive competencies.

3. *The organization's environment.* The organization's environment dictates the opportunities, constraints, and threats that must be identified before a mission statement is developed. For example, managers in any industry that is affected by Internet technology breakthroughs should continually be asking, How will the changes in technology affect my customers' behavior and the means by which we need to conduct our business?

However, it is extremely difficult to write a useful and effective mission statement. It is not uncommon for an organization to spend one or two years developing a useful mission statement. When completed, an effective mission statement will be *focused on markets rather than products, achievable, motivating, and specific.*[9]

Focused on Markets Rather than Products   The customers or clients of an organization are critical in determining its mission. Traditionally, many organizations defined their business in terms of what they made ("our business is glass"), and in many cases they named the organization for the product or service (e.g., American Tobacco, Hormel Meats, National Cash Register, Harbor View Savings and Loan Association). Many of these organizations have found that, when products and technologies become obsolete, their mission is no longer relevant and the name of the organization may no longer describe what it does. Thus, a more enduring way of defining the mission is needed. In recent years, therefore, a key feature of mission statements has been an *external* rather than *internal* focus. In other words, the mission statement should focus on the broad class of needs that the organization is seeking to satisfy (external focus), not on the physical product or service that the organization is offering at present (internal focus). These market-driven firms stand out in their ability to continuously anticipate market opportunities and respond before their competitors. Peter Drucker has clearly stated this principle:

> A business is not defined by the company's name, statutes, or articles of incorporation. It is defined by the want the customer satisfies when he buys a product or service. To satisfy the customer is the mission and purpose of every business. The question "What is our business?" can, therefore, be answered only by looking at the business from the outside, from the point of view of customer and market.[10]

While Drucker was referring to business organizations, the same necessity exists for both nonprofit and governmental organizations. That necessity is to state the mission in terms of serving a particular group of clients or customers and meeting a particular class of need.

Achievable   While the mission statement should stretch the organization toward more effective performance, it should, at the same time, be realistic and achievable. In other words, it should open a vision of new opportunities but should not lead the organization into unrealistic ventures far beyond its competencies.

Motivational   One of the side (but very important) benefits of a well-defined mission is the guidance it provides employees and managers working in geographically dispersed units and on independent tasks. It provides a shared sense of purpose outside the various activities taking place within the organization. Therefore, such end results as sales, patients cared for, students graduated, and reduction in violent crimes can then be viewed as the result of careful pursuit and accomplishment of the mission and not as the mission itself.

Specific   As we mentioned earlier, public relations should not be the primary purpose of a statement of mission. It must be specific to provide direction and guidelines to management when they are choosing between alternative courses of action. In other words, "to produce the highest-quality products at the lowest possible cost" sounds very good, but it does not provide direction for management.

Organizational Objectives

Organizational objectives are the end points of an organization's mission and are what it seeks through the ongoing, long-run operations of the organization. The organizational mission is distilled into a finer set of specific and achievable organizational objectives. These objectives must be *specific, measurable, action commitments* by which the mission of the organization is to be achieved.

As with the statement of mission, organizational objectives are more than good intentions. In fact, if formulated properly, they can accomplish the following:

1. They can be converted into specific action.
2. They will provide direction. That is, they can serve as a starting point for more specific and detailed objectives at lower levels in the organization. Each manager will then know how his or her objectives relate to those at higher levels.
3. They can establish long-run priorities for the organization.
4. They can facilitate management control because they serve as standards against which overall organizational performance can be evaluated.

Organizational objectives are necessary in all areas that may influence the performance and long-run survival of the organization. As shown in Figure 1.3 objectives can be established in and across many areas of the organization. The list provided in Figure 1.3 is by no

1. Incomplete—not specific as to where the company is headed and what kind of company management is trying to create.
2. Vague—does not provide direction to decision makers when faced with product/market choices.
3. Not motivational—does not provide a sense of purpose or commitment to something bigger than the numbers.
4. Not distinctive—not specific to our company.
5. Too reliant on superlatives—too many superlatives such as *#1, recognized leader, most successful.*
6. Too generic—does not specify the business or industry to which it applies.
7. Too broad—does not rule out any opportunity management might wish to pursue.

Source: Adapted from Arthur A. Thomson, Jr., A. J. Strickland III, and John E. Gamble, *Crafting and Executing Strategy,* 14th ed. (Burr Ridge, IL: McGraw-Hill/Irwin 2005), p. 21.

Examine, Marketing Highlight 1—3. Do any of the above shortcomings apply to the mission statements in Marketing Highlight 1–3?

means exhaustive. For example, some organizations are specifying the primary objective as the attainment of a specific level of quality, either in the marketing of a product or the providing of a service. These organizations believe that objectives should reflect an organization's commitment to the customer rather than its own finances. Obviously, during the strategic planning process conflicts are likely to occur between various functional departments in the organization. The important point is that management must translate the organizational mission into specific objectives that support the realization of the mission. The objectives may flow directly from the mission or be considered subordinate necessities for carrying out the mission. As discussed earlier, the objectives are specific, measurable, action commitments on the part of the organization.

Organizational Strategies

Hopefully, when an organization has formulated its mission and developed its objectives, it knows where it wants to go. The next managerial task is to develop a "grand design" to get

FIGURE 1.3
**Sample
Organizational
Objectives
(manufacturing firm)**

Area of Performance	Possible Objective
1. Market standing	To make our brands number one in their field in terms of market share.
2. Innovations	To be a leader in introducing new products by spending no less than 7 percent of sales for research and development.
3. Productivity	To manufacture all products efficiently as measured by the productivity of the workforce.
4. Physical and financial resources	To protect and maintain all resources—equipment, buildings, inventory, and funds.
5. Profitability	To achieve an annual rate of return on investment of at least 15 percent.
6. Manager performance and responsibility	To identify critical areas of management depth and succession.
7. Worker performance and attitude	To maintain levels of employee satisfaction consistent with our own and similar industries.
8. Social responsibility	To respond appropriately whenever possible to societal expectations and environmental needs.

Functions	What They May Want to Deliver	What Marketers May Want Them to Deliver
Research and development	Basic research projects	Products that deliver customer value
	Product features	Customer benefits
	Few projects	Many new products
Production/operations	Long production runs	Short production runs
	Standardized products	Customized products
	No model changes	Frequent model changes
	Long lead times	Short lead times
	Standard orders	Customer orders
	No new products	Many new products
Finance	Rigid budgets	Flexible budgets
	Budgets based on return on investment	Budgets based on need to increase sales
	Low sales commissions	High sales commissions
Accounting	Standardized billing	Custom billing
	Strict payment terms	Flexible payment terms
	Strict credit standards	Flexible credit standards
Human resources	Trainable employees	Skilled employees
	Low salaries	High salaries

there. This grand design constitutes the organizational strategies. Strategy involves the choice of major directions the organization will take in pursuing its objectives. Toward this end, it is critical that strategies are consistent with goals and objectives and that top management ensures strategies are implemented effectively. As many as 60 percent of strategic plans have failed because the strategies in them were not well defined and, thus, could not be implemented effectively.[11] What follows is a discussion of various strategies organizations can pursue. We discuss three approaches: (1) strategies based on products and markets, (2) strategies based on competitive advantage, and (3) strategies based on value.

Organizational Strategies Based on Products and Markets   One means to developing organizational strategies is to focus on the directions the organization can take in order to grow. Figure 1.4, which presents the available strategic choices, is a product–market matrix.[12] It indicates that an organization can grow by better managing what it is presently doing or by finding new things to do. In choosing one or both of these paths, it must also decide whether to concentrate on present customers or to seek new ones. Thus, according to Figure 1.4, there are only four paths an organization can take in order to grow.

Market Penetration Strategies   These strategies focus primarily on increasing the sale of present products to present customers. For example:

- Encouraging present customers to use more of the product: "Orange Juice Isn't Just for Breakfast Anymore."
- Encouraging present customers to purchase more of the product: multiple packages of Pringles, instant winner sweepstakes at a fast-food restaurant.
- Directing programs at current participants: A university directs a fund-raising program at those graduates who already give the most money.

Tactics used to implement a market penetration strategy might include price reductions, advertising that stresses the many benefits of the product (e.g., "Milk Is a Natural"), packaging the product in different-sized packages, or making it available at more locations.

FIGURE 1.4
**Organizational
Growth Strategies**

Products Markets	Present Products	New Products
Present customers	Market penetration	Product development
New customers	Market development	Diversification

Other functional areas of the business could also be involved in implementing the strategy in addition to marketing. A production plan might be developed to produce the product more efficiently. This plan might include increased production runs, the substitution of pre-assembled components for individual product parts, or the automation of a process that previously was performed manually.

Market Development Strategies Pursuing growth through market development, an organization would seek to find new customers for its present products. For example:

- Arm & Hammer continues to seek new uses for its baking soda.
- McDonald's continually seeks expansion into overseas markets.
- As the consumption of salt declined, the book *101 Things You Can Do with Salt Besides Eat It* appeared.

Market development strategies involve much, much more than simply getting the product to a new market. Before deciding on marketing techniques such as advertising and packaging, companies often find they must establish a clear position in the market, sometimes spending large sums of money simply to educate consumers as to why they should consider buying the product.

Product Development Strategies Selecting one of the remaining two strategies means the organization will seek new things to do. With this particular strategy, the new products developed would be directed primarily to present customers. For example:

- Offering a different version of an existing product: mini-Oreos, Ritz with cheese.
- Offering a new and improved version of their product: Gillette's latest improvement in shaving technology.
- Offering a new way to use an existing product: Vaseline's Lip Therapy.

Diversification This strategy can lead the organization into entirely new and even unrelated businesses. It involves seeking new products (often through acquisitions) for customers not currently being served. For example:

- Altria, originally a manufacturer of cigarettes, is widely diversified in financial services, Post cereals, Sealtest dairy, and Kraft cheese, among others.
- Brown Foreman Distillers acquired Hartmann Luggage, and Sara Lee acquired Coach Leather Products.
- Some universities are establishing corporations to find commercial uses for faculty research.

Organizational Strategies Based on Competitive Advantage Michael Porter developed a model for formulating organizational strategy that is applicable across a wide variety of industries.[13] The focus of the model is on devising means to gain competitive advantage. Competitive advantage is an ability to outperform competitors in providing something that the market values. Porter suggests that firms should first analyze their industry and then develop either a *cost leadership strategy* or a *strategy based on differentiation*. These general strategies can be used on marketwide bases or in a niche (segment) within the total market.

Using a cost leadership strategy, a firm would focus on being the low-cost company in its industry. They would stress efficiency and offer a standard, no-frills product. They could achieve this through efficiencies in production, product design, manufacturing, distribution, technology, or some other means. The important point is that to succeed, the organization must continually strive to be the cost leader in the industry or market segment it competes in. It must also offer products or services that are acceptable to customers when compared to the competition. Wal-Mart, Southwest Airlines, and Timex Group Ltd. are companies that have succeeded in using a cost leadership strategy.

Using a strategy based on differentiation, a firm seeks to be unique in its industry or market segment along particular dimensions that the customers value. These dimensions might pertain to design, quality, service, variety of offerings, brand name, or some other factor. The important point is that because of uniqueness of the product or service along one or more of these dimensions, the firm can charge a premium price. L. L. Bean, Rolex, Coca-Cola, and Microsoft are companies that have succeeded using a differentiation strategy.

Organizational Strategies Based on Value   As competition increases, the concept of "customer value" has become critical for marketers as well as customers. It can be thought of as an extension of the marketing concept philosophy that focuses on developing and delivering superior value to customers as a way to achieve organizational objectives. Thus, it focuses not only on customer needs, but also on the question, How can we create value for them and still achieve our objectives?

It has become pretty clear that in today's competitive environment it is unlikely that a firm will succeed by trying to be all things to all people.[14] Thus, to succeed firms must seek to build long-term relationships with their customers by offering a unique value that only they can offer. It seems that many firms have succeeded by choosing to deliver superior customer value using one of three value strategies—best price, best product, or best service.

Dell Computers, Costco, and Southwest Airlines are among the success stories in offering customers the best price. Rubbermaid, Nike, Starbucks, and Microsoft believe they offer the best products on the market. Airborne Express, Roadway, Cott Corporation, and Lands' End provide superior customer value by providing outstanding service.

Choosing an Appropriate Strategy

On what basis does an organization choose one (or all) of its strategies? Of extreme importance are the directions set by the mission statement. Management should select those strategies consistent with its mission and capitalize on the organization's distinctive competencies that will lead to a sustainable competitive advantage. A sustainable competitive advantage can be based on either the assets or skills of the organization. Technical superiority, low-cost production, customer service/product support, location, financial resources, continuing product innovation, and overall marketing skills are all examples of distinctive competencies that can lead to a sustainable competitive advantage. For example, Honda is known for providing quality automobiles at a reasonable price. Each succeeding generation of Honda automobiles has shown marked quality improvements over previous generations. Likewise, VF Corporation, manufacturer of Wrangler and Lee jeans, has formed "quick response" partnerships with both discounters and department stores to ensure the efficiency of product flow. The key to sustaining a competitive advantage is to continually focus and build on the assets and skills that will lead to long-term performance gains.

Organizational Portfolio Plan

The final phase of the strategic planning process is the formulation of the organizational portfolio plan. In reality, most organizations at a particular time are a portfolio of businesses, that is, product lines, divisions and schools. To illustrate, an appliance manufacturer may have several product lines (e.g., televisions, washers and dryers, refrigerators, stereos) as well as two divisions, consumer appliances and industrial appliances. A college or university will have numerous schools (e.g., education, business, law, architecture) and several programs within each school. Some widely diversified organizations such as Altria are in numerous unrelated businesses, such as cigarettes, food products, land development, and industrial paper products.

Managing such groups of businesses is made a little easier if resources are plentiful, cash is plentiful, and each is experiencing growth and profits. Unfortunately, providing larger and larger budgets each year to all businesses is seldom feasible. Many are not experiencing growth, and profits and resources (financial and nonfinancial) are becoming more and more scarce. In such a situation, choices must be made, and some method is necessary to help management make the choices. Management must decide which businesses to build, maintain, or eliminate, or which new businesses to add. Indeed, much of the recent activity in corporate restructuring has centered on decisions relating to which groups of businesses management should focus on.

Obviously, the first step in this approach is to identify the various divisions, product lines, and so on that can be considered a "business." When identified, these are referred to as *strategic business units* (SBUs) and have the following characteristics:

- They have a distinct mission.
- They have their own competitors.
- They are a single business or collection of related businesses.
- They can be planned independently of the other businesses of the total organization.

Thus, depending on the type of organization, an SBU could be a single product, product line, or division; a college of business administration; or a state mental health agency. Once the organization has identified and classified all of its SBUs, some method must be established to determine how resources should be allocated among the various SBUs. These methods are known as *portfolio models*. For those readers interested, the appendix of this chapter presents two of the most popular portfolio models, the Boston Consulting Group model and the General Electric model.

The Complete Strategic Plan

Figure 1.2 indicates that at this point the strategic planning process is complete, and the organization has a time-phased blueprint that outlines its mission, objectives, and strategies. Completion of the strategic plan facilitates the development of marketing plans for each product, product line, or division of the organization. The marketing plan serves as a subset of the strategic plan in that it allows for detailed planning at a target market level. This important relationship between strategic planning and marketing planning is the subject of the final section of this chapter.

The Marketing Management Process

Marketing management can be defined as "the process of planning and executing the conception, pricing, promotion, and distribution of goods, services, and ideas to create exchanges with target groups that satisfy customer and organizational objectives."[15] It should be noted that this definition is entirely consistent with the marketing concept, since

FIGURE 1.5
**Strategic Planning
and Marketing
Planning**

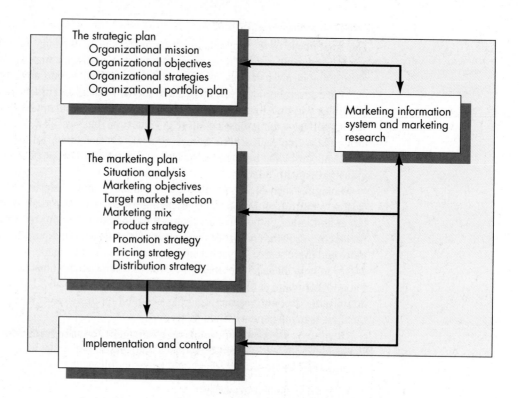

it emphasizes serving target market needs as the key to achieving organizational objectives. The remainder of this section will be devoted to a discussion of the marketing management process according to the model in Figure 1.5.

Situation Analysis

With a clear understanding of organizational objectives and mission, the marketing manager must then analyze and monitor the position of the firm and, specifically, the marketing department, in terms of its past, present, and future situation. Of course, the future situation is of primary concern. However, analyses of past trends and the current situation are most useful for predicting the future situation.

The situation analysis can be divided into six major areas of concern: (1) the cooperative environment; (2) the competitive environment; (3) the economic environment; (4) the social environment; (5) the political environment; and (6) the legal environment. In analyzing each of these environments, the marketing executive must search both for opportunities and for constraints or threats to achieving objectives. Opportunities for profitable marketing often arise from changes in these environments that bring about new sets of needs to be satisfied. Constraints on marketing activities, such as limited supplies of scarce resources, also arise from these environments.

The Cooperative Environment   The cooperative environment includes all firms and individuals who have a vested interest in the firm's accomplishing its objectives. Parties of primary interest to the marketing executive in this environment are (1) suppliers, (2) resellers, (3) other departments in the firm, and (4) subdepartments and employees of the marketing department. Opportunities in this environment are primarily related to methods of increasing efficiency. For example, a company might decide to switch from a competitive bid process of obtaining materials to a single source that is located near the company's plant. Likewise, members of the marketing, engineering, and manufacturing functions may use a teamwork approach to developing new products versus a sequential approach. Constraints consist of such things as unresolved conflicts and shortages of materials. For example, a company manager may believe that a distributor is doing an insufficient job of promoting and selling the product, or a marketing manager may feel that manufacturing is not taking the steps needed to produce a quality product.

The Competitive Environment The competitive environment includes primarily other firms in the industry that rival the organization for both resources and sales. Opportunities in this environment include such things as (1) acquiring competing firms; (2) offering demonstrably better value to consumers and attracting them away from competitors; and (3) in some cases, driving competitors out of the industry. For example, one airline purchases another airline, a bank offers depositors a free checking account with no minimum balance requirements, or a grocery chain engages in an everyday low-price strategy that competitors can't meet. The primary constraints in these environments are the demand stimulation activities of competing firms and the number of consumers who cannot be lured away from competition.

The Economic Environment The state of the macroeconomy and changes in it also bring about marketing opportunities and constraints. For example, such factors as high inflation and unemployment levels can limit the size of the market that can afford to purchase a firm's top-of-the-line product. At the same time, these factors may offer a profitable opportunity to develop rental services for such products or to develop less-expensive models of the product. In addition, changes in technology can provide significant threats and opportunities. For example, in the communications industry, when technology was developed to a level where it was possible to provide cable television using phone lines, such a system posed a severe threat to the cable industry.

The Social Environment This environment includes general cultural and social traditions, norms, and attitudes. While these values change slowly, such changes often bring about the need for new products and services. For example, a change in values concerning the desirability of large families brought about an opportunity to market better methods of birth control. On the other hand, cultural and social values also place constraints on marketing activities. As a rule, business practices that are contrary to social values become political issues, which are often resolved by legal constraints. For example, public demand for a cleaner environment has caused the government to require that automobile manufacturers' products meet certain average gas mileage and emission standards.

The Political Environment The political environment includes the attitudes and reactions of the general public, social and business critics, and other organizations, such as the Better Business Bureau. Dissatisfaction with such business and marketing practices as unsafe products, products that waste resources, and unethical sales procedures can have adverse effects on corporation image and customer loyalty. However, adapting business and marketing practices to these attitudes can be an opportunity. For example, these attitudes have brought about markets for such products as unbreakable children's toys, high-efficiency air conditioners, and more economical automobiles.

The Legal Environment This environment includes a host of federal, state, and local legislation directed at protecting both business competition and consumer rights. In past years, legislation reflected social and political attitudes and has been primarily directed at constraining business practices. Such legislation usually acts as a constraint on business behavior, but again can be viewed as providing opportunities for marketing safer and more efficient products. In recent years, there has been less emphasis on creating new laws for constraining business practices. As an example, deregulation has become more common, as evidenced by events in the airlines, financial services, and telecommunications industries.

Speed of the Process. There is the problem of either being so slow that the process seems to go on forever or so fast that there is an extreme burst of activity to rush out a plan.

Amount of Data Collected. Sufficient data are needed to properly estimate customer needs and competitive trends. However, the law of diminishing returns quickly sets in on the data-collection process.

Responsibility for Developing the Plan. If planning is delegated to professional planners, valuable line management input may be ignored. If the process is left to line managers, planning may be relegated to secondary status.

Structure. Many executives believe the most important part of planning is not the plan itself but the structure of thought about the strategic issues facing the business. However, the structure should not take precedence over the content so that planning becomes merely filling out forms or crunching numbers.

Length of the Plan. The length of a marketing plan must be balanced between being so long that both staff and line managers ignore it and so brief that it ignores key details.

Frequency of Planning. Too frequent reevaluation of strategies can lead to erratic firm behavior. However, when plans are not revised frequently enough, the business may not adapt quickly enough to environmental changes and thus suffer a deterioration in its competitive position.

Number of Alternative Strategies Considered. Discussing too few alternatives raises the likelihood of failure, whereas discussing too many increases the time and cost of the planning effort.

Cross-Functional Acceptance. A common mistake is to view the plan as the proprietary possession of marketing. Successful implementation requires a broad consensus, including other functional areas.

Using the Plan as a Sales Document. A major but often overlooked purpose of a plan and its presentation is to generate funds from either internal or external sources. Therefore, the better the plan, the better the chance of gaining desired funding.

Source: Donald R. Lehmann and Russell S. Winer, *Analysis for Marketing Planning,* 6th ed. (Burr Ridge, IL: McGraw-Hill//Irwin, 2006), chap. 1.

Marketing Planning

The previous sections emphasized that (1) marketing activities must be aligned with organizational objectives and (2) marketing opportunities are often found by systematically analyzing situational environments. Once an opportunity is recognized, the marketing executive must then plan an appropriate strategy for taking advantage of the opportunity. This process can be viewed in terms of three interrelated tasks: (1) establishing marketing objectives, (2) selecting the target market, and (3) developing the marketing mix.

Establishing Objectives   Marketing objectives usually are derived from organizational objectives; in some cases where the firm is totally marketing oriented, the two are identical. In either case, objectives must be specified and performance in achieving them should be measurable. Marketing objectives are usually stated as standards of performance (e.g., a certain percentage of market share or sales volume) or as tasks to be achieved by given dates. While such objectives are useful, the marketing concept emphasizes that profits rather than sales should be the overriding objective of the firm and marketing department. In any case, these objectives provide the framework for the marketing plan.

Selecting the Target Market   The success of any marketing plan hinges on how well it can identify customer needs and organize its resources to satisfy them profitably. Thus, a crucial element of the marketing plan is selecting the groups or segments of potential

Poorly Stated Objectives	Well-Stated Objectives
Our objective is to be a leader in the industry in terms of new product development.	Our objective is to spend 12 percent of sales revenue between 2005 and 2006 on research and development in an effort to introduce at least five new products in 2006.
Our objective is to maximize profits.	Our objective is to achieve a 10 percent return on investment during 2005, with a payback on new investments of no longer than four years.
Our objective is to better serve customers.	Our objective is to obtain customer satisfaction ratings of at least 90 percent on the 2005 annual customer satisfaction survey, and to retain at least 85 percent of our 2005 customers as repeat purchasers in 2006.
Our objective is to be the best that we can be.	Our objective is to increase market share from 30 percent to 40 percent in 2005 by increasing promotional expenditures by 14 percent.

Source: Charles W. Lamb, Jr., Joseph F. Hair, Jr., and Carl McDaniel, *Marketing*, 8th ed. (MASON, OH: Thomson South-Western Publishing Co., 2006), p. 43.

customers the firm is going to serve with each of its products. Four important questions must be answered:

1. What do customers want or need?
2. What must be done to satisfy these wants or needs?
3. What is the size of the market?
4. What is its growth profile?

Present target markets and potential target markets are then ranked according to (1) profitability; (2) present and future sales volume; and (3) the match between what it takes to appeal successfully to the segment and the organization's capabilities. Those that appear to offer the greatest potential are selected. One cautionary note on this process involves the importance of not neglecting present customers when developing market share and sales strategies. A recent study found that for every 10 companies that develop strategies aimed at increasing the number of first-time customers, only 4 made any serious effort to develop strategies geared toward retaining present customers and increasing their purchases.[16] Chapters 3, 4, and 5 are devoted to discussing consumer behavior, industrial buyers, and market segmentation.

Developing the Marketing Mix   The marketing mix is the set of controllable variables that must be managed to satisfy the target market and achieve organizational objectives. These controllable variables are usually classified according to four major decision areas: product, price, promotion, and place (or channels of distribution). The importance of these decision areas cannot be overstated, and in fact, the major portion of this text is devoted to analyzing them. Chapters 6 and 7 are devoted to product and new product strategies, Chapters 8 and 9 to promotion strategies in terms of both nonpersonal and personal selling, Chapter 10 to distribution strategies, and Chapter 11 to pricing strategies. In addition, marketing mix variables are the focus of analysis in two chapters on marketing in special fields, that is, the marketing of services (Chapter 12) and international marketing (Chapter 13). Thus, it should be clear that the marketing mix is the core of the marketing management process.

The output of the foregoing process is the marketing plan. It is a formal statement of decisions that have been made on marketing activities; it is a blueprint of the objectives, strategies, and tasks to be performed.

Implementation and Control of the Marketing Plan

Implementing the marketing plan involves putting the plan into action and performing marketing tasks according to the predefined schedule. Even the most carefully developed plans often cannot be executed with perfect timing. Thus, the marketing executive must closely monitor and coordinate implementation of the plan. In some cases, adjustments may have to be made in the basic plan because of changes in any of the situational environments. For example, competitors may introduce a new product. In this event, it may be desirable to speed up or delay implementation of the plan. In almost all cases, some minor adjustments or fine tuning will be necessary in implementation.

Controlling the marketing plan involves three basic steps. First, the results of the implemented marketing plan are measured. Second, these results are compared with objectives. Third, decisions are made on whether the plan is achieving objectives. If serious deviations exist between actual and planned results, adjustments may have to be made to redirect the plan toward achieving objectives.

Marketing Information Systems and Marketing Research

Throughout the marketing management process, current, reliable, and valid information is needed to make effective marketing decisions. Providing this information is the task of the marketing information system and marketing research. These topics are discussed in detail in Chapter 2.

The Strategic Plan, The Marketing Plan, and Other Functional Area Plans

Strategic planning is clearly a top-management responsibility. In recent years, however, there has been an increasing shift toward more active participation by marketing managers in strategic analysis and planning. This is because, in reality, nearly all strategic planning questions have marketing implications. In fact, the two major strategic planning questions— What products should we make? and What markets should we serve?—are clearly marketing questions. Thus, marketing executives are involved in the strategic planning process in at least two important ways: (1) They influence the process by providing important inputs in the form of information and suggestions relating to customers, products, and middlemen; and (2) they must always be aware of what the process of stategic planning involves as well as the results because everything they do—the marketing objectives and strategies they develop—must be derived from the strategic plan. In fact, the planning done in all functional areas of the organization should be derived from the strategic plan.

Marketing's Role in Cross-Functional Strategic Planning

More and more organizations are rethinking the traditional role of marketing. Rather than dividing work according to function (e.g., production, finance, technology, human resources), they are bringing managers and employees together to participate in *cross-functional teams*. These teams might have responsibility for a particular product, line of products, or group of customers.

Because team members are responsible for all activities involving their products and/or customers, they are responsible for strategic planning. This means that all personnel working in a cross-functional team will participate in creating a strategic plan to serve customers.

FIGURE 1.6   **The Cross-Functional Perspective in Planning**

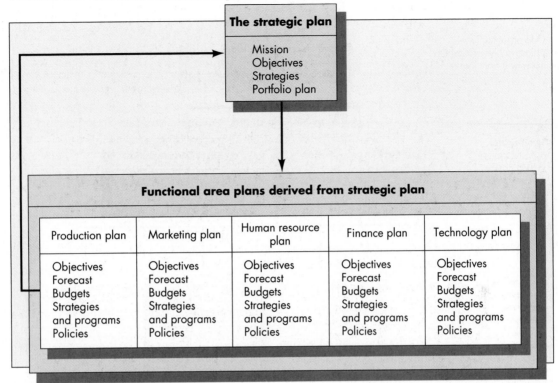

Rather than making decisions independently, marketing managers work closely with team members from production, finance, human resources, and other areas to devise plans that address all concerns. Thus, if a team member from production says, "That product will be too difficult to produce," or if a team member from finance says, "We'll never make a profit at that price," the team members from marketing must help resolve the problems. This approach requires a high degree of skill at problem solving and gaining cooperation.

Clearly the greatest advantage of strategic planning with a cross-functional team is the ability of team members to consider a situation from a number of viewpoints. The resulting insights can help the team avoid costly mistakes and poor solutions. Japanese manufacturers are noted for using cross-functional teams to figure out ways to make desirable products at given target costs. In contrast, U.S. manufacturers traditionally have developed products by having one group decide what to make, another calculate production costs, and yet another predict whether enough of the product will sell at a high enough price.

Thus, in well-managed organizations, a direct relationship exists between strategic planning and the planning done by managers at all levels. The focus and time perspectives will, of course, differ. Figure 1.6 illustrates the cross-functional perspective of strategic planning. It indicates very clearly that all functional area plans should be derived from the strategic plan while at the same time contributing to the achievement of it.

If done properly, strategic planning results in a clearly defined blueprint for management action in all functional areas of the organization. Figure 1.7 clearly illustrates this blueprint using only one organizational objective and two strategies from the strategic plan (above the dotted line) and illustrating how these are translated into elements of the marketing department plan and the production department plan (below the dotted line). Note that in Figure 1.7, all objectives and strategies are related to other objectives and strategies at

FIGURE 1.7   **A Blueprint for Management Action: Relating the Marketing Plan to the Strategic Plan and the Production Plan**

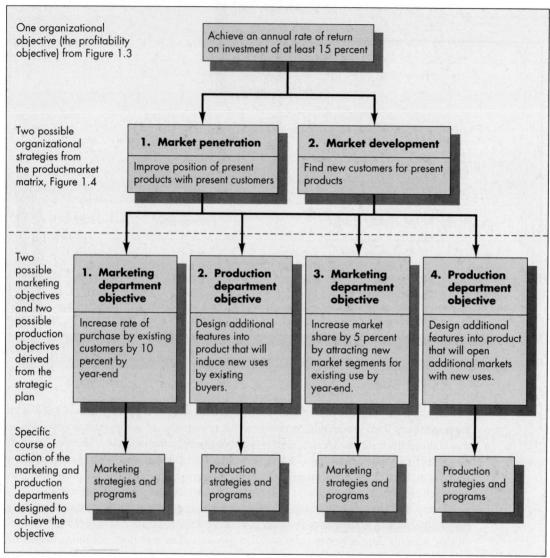

higher and lower levels in the organization: That is, a hierarchy of objectives and strategies exists. We have illustrated only two possible marketing objectives and two possible production objectives. Obviously, many others could be developed, but our purpose is to illustrate the cross-functional nature of strategic planning and how objectives and strategies from the strategic plan must be translated into objectives and strategies for all functional areas including marketing.

Conclusion

This chapter has described the marketing management process in the context of the organization's overall strategic plan. Clearly, marketers must understand their cross-functional role in joining the marketing vision for the organization with the financial goals and manufacturing capabilities of the organization. The greater this ability, the better the likelihood is that the organization will be able to achieve and sustain a competitive advantage, the ultimate purpose of the strategic planning process.

At this point it would be useful to review Figures 1.5, 1.6, and 1.7 as well as the book's Table of Contents. This review will enable you to better relate the content and progression of the material to follow to the marketing management process.

Additional Readings

Christensen, Clayton, M., Scott Cook, and Taddy Hall. "Marketing Malpactice: The Cause and the Cure." *Harvard Business Review,* December 2005, pp. 74–85.

Davenport, James H., and Jeanne C. Harris. *Competing on Analytics.* Boston, MA: HBS Publishing, 2007.

Farris, Paul W., Neil T. Bendle, Phllip E. Pfeifer, and David Reibstein. *Marketing Metrics.* Upper Saddle River, NJ: Wharton School Publishing, 2006.

Kaplan, Robert S., and David P. Norton. "How to Implement a New Strategy without Disrupting Your Organziation." *Harvard Business Review,* March 2006, pp. 100–109.

O'Sullivan, Don, and Andrew V. Abdela. "Marketing Performance Measurement Ability and Performance." *Journal of Marketing,* April 2007, pp. 79–93.

Seiders, Kathleen, and Leonard L. Berry. "Should Business Care about Obesity?" *Sloan Management Review,* Winter 2007, pp. 15–17.

Appendix

Portfolio Models

Portfolio models remain a valuable aid to marketing managers in their efforts to develop effective marketing plans. The use of these models can aid managers who face situations that can best be described as "more products, less time, and less money." More specifically, (1) as the number of products a firm produces expands, the time available for developing marketing plans for each product decreases; (2) at a strategic level, management must make resource allocation decisions across lines of products and, in diversified organizations, across different lines of business; and (3) when resources are limited (which they usually are), the process of deciding which strategic business units (SBUs) to emphasize becomes very complex. In such situations, portfolio models can be very useful.

Portfolio analysis is not a new idea. Banks manage loan portfolios seeking to balance risks and yields. Individuals who are serious investors usually have a portfolio of various kinds of investments (common stocks, preferred stocks, bank accounts, and the like), each with different characteristics of risk, growth, and rate of return. The investor seeks to manage the portfolio to maximize whatever objectives he or she might have. Applying this same idea, most organizations have a wide range of products, product lines, and businesses, each with different growth rates and returns. Similar to the investor, managers should seek a desirable balance among alternative SBUs. Specifically, management should seek to develop a business portfolio that will ensure long-run profits and cash flow.

Portfolio models can be used to classify SBUs to determine the future cash contributions that can be expected from each SBU as well as the future resources that each will require. Remember, depending on the organization, an SBU could be a single product, product line, division, or distinct business. While there are many different types of portfolio models, they generally examine the competitive position of the SBU and the chances for improving the SBU's contribution to profitability and cash flow.

There are several portfolio analysis techniques. Two of the most widely used are discussed in this appendix. To truly appreciate the concept of portfolio analysis, however, we must briefly review the development of portfolio theory.

A Review of Portfolio Theory

The interest in developing aids for managers in the selection of strategy was spurred by an organization known as the Boston Consulting Group (BCG) over 25 years ago. Its ideas, which will be discussed shortly, and many of those that followed were based on the concept of experience curves.

Experience curves are similar in concept to learning curves. Learning curves were developed to express the idea that the number of labor hours it takes to produce one unit of a particular product declines in a predictable manner as the number of units produced increases. Hence, an accurate estimation of how long it takes to produce the 100th unit is possible if the production times for the 1st and 10th units are known. The concept of experience curves was based on this model.

Experience curves were first widely discussed in the Strategic Planning Institute's ongoing Profit Impact of Marketing Strategies (PIMS) study. The PIMS project studies 150 firms with more than 1,000 individual business units. Its major focus is on determining which environmental and internal firm variables influence the firm's return on investment (ROI) and cash flow. The researchers have concluded that seven categories of variables appear to influence the return on investment: (1) competitive position, (2) industry/market environment, (3) budget allocation, (4) capital structure, (5) production processes, (6) company characteristics, and (7) "change action" factors.[17]

The experience curve includes all costs associated with a product and implies that the per-unit costs of a product should fall, due to cumulative experience, as production volume increases. In a given industry, therefore, the producer with the largest volume and corresponding market share should have the lowest marginal cost. This leader in market share should be able to underprice competitors, discourage entry into the market by potential competitors, and, as a result, achieve an acceptable return on investment. The linkage of experience to cost to price to market share to ROI is exhibited in Figure A.1. The Boston Consulting Group's

25

FIGURE A.1   Experience Curve and Resulting Profit

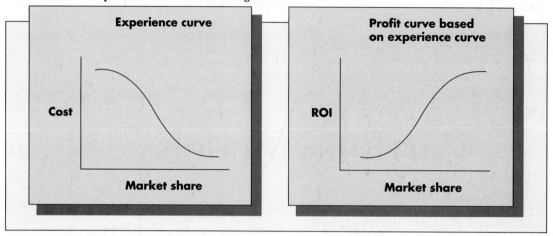

view of the experience curve led the members to develop what has become known as the BCG Portfolio Model.

The BCG Model

The BCG is based on the assumption that profitability and cash flow will be closely related to sales volume. Thus, in this model, SBUs are classified according to their relative market share and the growth rate of the market the SBU is in. Using these dimensions, products are either classified as stars, cash cows, dogs, or question marks. The BCG model is presented in Figure A.2.

* *Stars* are SBUs with a high share of a high-growth market. Because high-growth markets attract competition, such SBUs are usually cash users because they are grow-

ing and because the firm needs to protect their market share position.

* *Cash cows* are often market leaders, but the market they are in is not growing rapidly. Because these SBUs have a high share of a low-growth market, they are cash generators for the firm.

* *Dogs* are SBUs that have a low share of a low-growth market. If the SBU has a very loyal group of customers, it may be a source of profits and cash. Usually, dogs are not large sources of cash.

* *Question marks* are SBUs with a low share of a high-growth market. They have great potential but require great resources if the firm is to successfully build market share.

As you can see, a firm with 10 SBUs will usually have a portfolio that includes some of each of the above. Having

FIGURE A.2
**The Boston
Consulting Group
Portfolio Model**

Relative Market Share

	High	Low
High	Stars	Question marks
Low	Cash cows	Dogs

**Market
Growth
Rate**

developed this analysis, management must determine what role each SBU should assume. Four basic objectives are possible:

1. *Build share.* This objective sacrifices immediate earnings to improve market share. It is appropriate for promising question marks whose share has to grow if they are ever to become stars.
2. *Hold share.* This objective seeks to preserve the SBU's market share. It is very appropriate for strong cash cows to ensure that they can continue to yield a large cash flow.
3. *Harvest.* Here, the objective seeks to increase the product's short-term cash flow without concern for the long-run impact. It allows market share to decline in order to maximize earnings and cash flow. It is an appropriate objective for weak cash cows, weak question marks, and dogs.
4. *Divest.* This objective involves selling or divesting the SBU because better investment opportunities exist elsewhere. It is very appropriate for dogs and those question marks the firm cannot afford to finance for growth.

There have been several major criticisms of the BCG Portfolio Model, revolving around its focus on market share and market growth as the primary indicators of preference. First, the BCG model assumes market growth is uncontrollable.[18] As a result, managers can become preoccupied with setting market share objectives instead of trying to grow the market. Second, assumptions regarding market share as a critical factor affecting firm performance may not hold true, especially in international markets.[19] Third, the BCG model assumes that the major source of

SBU financing comes from internal means. Fourth, the BCG matrix does not take into account any interdependencies that may exist between SBUs, such as shared distribution.[20] Fifth, the BCG matrix does not take into account any measures of profits and customer satisfaction.[21] Sixth, and perhaps most important, the thrust of the BCG matrix is based on the underlying assumption that corporate strategy begins with an analysis of competitive position. By its very nature, a strategy developed entirely on competitive analysis will always be a reactive one.[22] While the above criticisms are certainly valid ones, managers (especially of large firms) across all industries continue to find the BCG matrix useful in assessing the strategic position of SBUs.[23]

The General Electric Model

Although the BCG model can be useful, it does assume that market share is the sole determinant of an SBU's profitability. Also, in projecting market growth rates, a manager should carefully analyze the factors that influence sales and any opportunities for influencing industry sales.

Some firms have developed alternative portfolio models to incorporate more information about market opportunities and competitive positions. The GE model is one of these. The GE model emphasizes all the potential sources of strength, not just market share, and all of the factors that influence the long-term attractiveness of a market, not just its growth rate. As Figure A.3 indicates, all SBUs are classified according to *business strength* and *industry attractiveness*. Figure A.4 presents a list of items that can be used to position SBUs in the matrix.

FIGURE A.3
The General Electric Portfolio Model

Business Strength

		Strong	Average	Weak
Industry Attractiveness	**High**	A	A	B
	Medium	A	B	C
	Low	B	C	C

FIGURE A.4
**Components
of Industry
Attractiveness
and Business
Strength at GE**

Industry Attractiveness	Business Strength
	Market position
Market size	Domestic market share
Market growth	World market share
Profitability	Share growth
Cyclicality	Share compared with leading competitor
Ability to recover from inflation	
World scope	Competitive strengths
	Quality leadership
	Technology
	Marketing
	Relative profitability

Industry attractiveness is a composite index made up of such factors as those listed in Figure A.4. For example: *market size*—the larger the market, the more attractive it will be; *market growth*—high-growth markets are more attractive than low-growth markets; *profitability*—high-profit-margin markets are more attractive than low-profit-margin industries.

Business strength is a composite index made up of such factors as those listed in Figure A.4. Such as *market share*—the higher the SBU's share of market, the greater its business strength; *quality leadership*—the higher the SBU's quality compared to competitors, the greater its business strength; *share compared with leading competitor*—the closer the SBU's share to the market leader, the greater its business strength.

Once the SBUs are classified, they are placed on the grid (Figure A.3). Priority "A" SBUs (often called *the green zone*)

are those in the three cells at the upper left, indicating that these are SBUs high in both industry attractiveness and business strength, and that the firm should "build share." Priority "B" SBUs (often called *the yellow zone*) are those medium in both industry attractiveness and business strength. The firm will usually decide to "hold share" on these SBUs. Priority "C" SBUs are those in the three cells at the lower right (often called the *red zone*). These SBUs are low in both industry attractiveness and business strength. The firm will usually decide to harvest or divest these SBUs.

Whether the BCG model, the GE model, or a variation of these models is used, some analyses must be made of the firm's current portfolio of SBUs as part of any strategic planning effort. Marketing must get its direction from the organization's strategic plan.

Marketing Information, Research, and Understanding the Target Market

Part B

Chapter 2

Marketing Research: Process and Systems for Decision Making

Marketing managers require current, reliable, useful information to make effective decisions. In today's highly competitive global economy, marketers need to exploit opportunities and avoid mistakes if they are to survive and be profitable. Not only is sound marketing research needed, but also a system that gets current, valid information to the marketing decision maker in a timely manner.

   This chapter is concerned with the marketing research process and information systems for decision making. It begins by discussing the marketing research process that is used to develop useful information for decision making. Then, marketing information systems are briefly discussed. The chapter is intended to provide a detailed introduction to many of the important topics in the area, but it does not provide a complete explanation of the plethora of marketing research topics.

The Role of Marketing Research

Marketing research is the process by which information about the environment is generated, analyzed, and interpreted for use in marketing decision making.[1] It cannot be overstated that *marketing research is an aid to decision making and not a substitute for it.* In other words, marketing research does not make decisions, but it can substantially increase the chances that good decisions are made. Unfortunately, too many marketing managers view research reports as the final answer to their problems; whatever the research indicates is taken as the appropriate course of action. Instead, marketing managers should recognize that (1) even the most carefully executed research can be fraught with errors; (2) marketing research does not forecast with certainty what will happen in the future; and (3) they should make decisions in light of their own knowledge and experience, since no marketing research study includes all of the factors that could influence the success of a strategy.

   Although marketing research does not make decisions, it can reduce the risks associated with managing marketing strategies. For example, it can reduce the risk of introducing new products by evaluating consumer acceptance of them prior to full-scale introduction. Marketing research is also vital for investigating the effects of various marketing strategies after they have been implemented. For example, marketing research can examine the effects of a change in any element of the marketing mix on customer perception and behavior.

At one time, marketing researchers were primarily engaged in the technical aspects of research, but were not heavily involved in the strategic use of research findings. Today, however, many marketing researchers work hand-in-hand with marketing managers throughout the research process and have responsibility for making strategic recommendations based on the research.

The Marketing Research Process

Marketing research can be viewed as systematic processes for obtaining information to aid in decision making. There are many types of marketing research, and the framework illustrated in Figure 2.1 represents a general approach to the process. Each element of this process is discussed next.

Purpose of the Research

The first step in the research process is to determine explicitly why the research is needed and what it is to accomplish. This may be much more difficult than it sounds. Quite often a situation or problem is recognized as needing research, yet the nature of the problem is not clear or well defined nor is the appropriate type of research evident. Thus, managers and researchers need to discuss and clarify the current situation and develop a clear understanding of the problem. At the end of this stage, managers and researchers should agree on (1) the current situation involving the problem to be researched, (2) the nature of the problem, and (3) the specific question or questions the research is designed to investigate. This step is crucial since it influences the type of research to be conducted and the research design.

FIGURE 2.1

The Five Ps of the Research Process

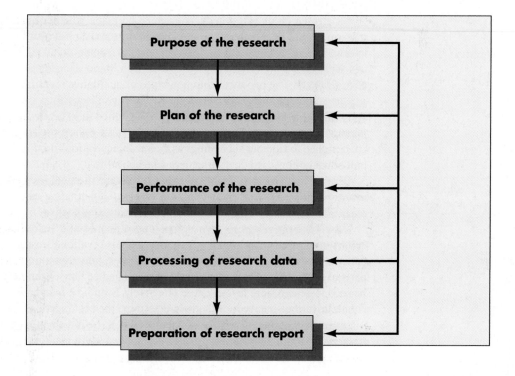

Plan of the Research

Once the specific research question or questions have been agreed on, a research plan can be developed. A research plan spells out the nature of the research to be conducted and includes an explanation of such things as the sample design, measures, and analysis techniques to be used. Three critical issues that influence the research plan are (1) whether primary or secondary data are needed, (2) whether qualitative or quantitative research is needed, and (3) whether the company will do its own research or contract with a marketing research specialist.

Primary versus Secondary Data

Given the information needed and budget constraints, a decision must be made as to whether primary data, secondary data, or some combination of the two is needed. *Primary data* are data collected specifically for the research problem under investigation; *secondary data* are those that have previously been collected for other purposes but can be used for the problem at hand. For example, if a company wanted to know why users of a competitive brand didn't prefer its brand, it may have to collect primary data to find out. On the other hand, if a company wanted to know the population size of key global markets that it might enter, it could find this information from secondary sources. Secondary information has the advantage of usually being cheaper than primary data, although it is not always available for strategy-specific research questions.

There are many sources of secondary data useful for marketing research. Syndicated data providers sell a variety of useful data to companies. Figure 2.2 lists a number of data providers and the type of information they can provide. Government sources, such as the *Statistical Abstracts of the United States* or the *Survey of Current Business,* can provide insights into the economy and industries within it. Trade groups such as the American Medical Association or the National Association of Retail Dealers of America can also be contacted for information relevant to their industries.[2]

Qualitative versus Quantitative Research

Given a research question, a decision must be made whether qualitative or quantitative research would be a better approach. Qualitative research typically involves face-to-face interviews with respondents designed to develop a better understanding of what they think and feel concerning a research topic, such as a brand name, a product, a package, or an advertisement. The two most common types of qualitative research in marketing are focus groups and long interviews. *Focus groups* involve discussions among a small number of individuals led by an interviewer; they are designed to generate insights and ideas. *Long interviews* are conducted by an interviewer with a single respondent for several hours. They are designed to find out such things as the meanings various products or brands have for an individual or how a product influences a person's life.

Quantitative research involves more systematic procedures designed to obtain and analyze numerical data. Four common types of quantitative research in marketing are observation, surveys, experiments, and mathematical modeling.

Observational research involves watching people and recording relevant facts and behaviors. For example, retail stores may use observational research to determine what patterns customers use in walking through stores, how much time they spend in various parts of the store, and how many items of merchandise they examine. This information can be used to design store layouts more effectively. Similarly, many retail marketers do traffic counts at various intersections to help determine the best locations for stores.

Survey research involves the collection of data by means of a questionnaire either by mail, phone, or in person. Surveys are commonly used in marketing research to investigate

FIGURE 2.2   Some Syndicated Data Providers

Company	Syndicated Service	What it Measures
ACNielsen www.acnielsen.com	Scantrack	Provides sales tracking across grocery, drug, and mass merchandisers.
	Homescan	Provides consumer panel service for tracking retail purchases and motivations.
Yahoo! and ACNielsen www.yahoo.com	Internet Confidence Index	Measures (quarterly) the confidence levels in Internet products and services.
Scarborough Research (a service of Arbitron, Inc., and VNU) www.scarborough.com		Provides a syndicated study to print and electronic media, new media companies, outdoor media, sports teams and leagues, agencies, advertisers, and Yellow Pages on local, regional, and national levels—including local market shopping patterns, demographics, media usage, and lifestyle activities.
Millward Brown www.millwardbrown.com	IntelliQuest www.intelliquest.com	Provides studies enabling clients to understand and improve the position of their technology, brands, products, media, or channels.
Information Resources www.infores.com	BehaviourScan	Collects store tracking data used with consumer panel data to track advertising influence in consumer packaged goods.
Nielsen Media Research www.nielsenmedia.com	National People Meter	Provides audience estimates for all national program sources, including broadcast networks, cable networks, Spanish-language networks, and national syndicators.
NOP World www.nopworld.com	Starch Ad Readership Studies	Provides raw readership scores collected via individual depth interview; records the percent of readers who saw the ad and read the copy. The ad is ranked not only against other ads in the issue but also against other ads in its product category over the last two years.
CSA TMO www.csa-fr.com	OPERBAC	Provides continuous tracking of banking insurance and credit purchases in European markets.
DoubleClick www.doubleclick.com	Diameter	Provides online audience measurement services for Web publishers, advertisers, and agencies.
Nielsen//NetRatings www.nielsen-netratings.com		Measures audience data using actual click-by-click Internet user behavior measured through a comprehensive real-time meter installed on individual computers worldwide (home and work).
Taylor Nelson Sofres Intersearch www.tns-i.com	Global eCommerce	Measures e-commerce activity in 27 countries, providing insights into 37 marketplaces via interviews.
J.D. Power Associates www.jdpower.com	PowerReport, PowerGram, etc.	Publishes in-depth analytical reports on automotive, travel, health, and other industries.
MediaMark www.mediamark.com		Supplies multimedia audience research to magazines. television, radio, Internet, and other media, leading national advertisers, and over 450 advertising agencies, including 90 of 100 agencies in the U.S.
Simmons (SMRB) www.smrb.com	National	Provides telephone research that covers important markets critical to advertisers, agencies and media alike—from Kids to Teens, Adults and Hispanics, to Households. 20,000 adults 18 and older.

Source: Donald R. Cooper and Pamela S. Schindler, *Marketing Research* (Burr Ridge, IL: McGraw-Hill/Irwin, 2006), p. 43.

Founded in 1941 in a SoHo loft in New York City, Coach built a reputation for quality leather purses in classic styles. By 1995, however, sales declines had CEO Lew Frankfurt well aware that the company was about to hit the wall. Upscale consumers preferred the offerings of companies like Louis Vuitton, Chanel, Gucci, and newcomer Kate Spade. Coach purses were viewed as conservative, traditional bags, the kind women carried to country clubs, rather than as fun, exciting, sexy, or modern.

To turn the company around, Coach selected new designs using fabric, nylon, and lighter-weight leathers to make the bags trendier. Instead of offering a new collection twice a year, Coach began offering a new collection every month. The company also redesigned its stores and expanded its distribution. It priced its bags at an average of about $200, making them an accessible luxury that appeals both to consumers who have to stretch their budgets to get one and to those who think nothing of spending $700 for Yves Saint Laurent's hot Mombasa bag.

Perhaps the most important change the company made was to select styles based on what consumers thought was cool rather than have designers decide what consumers *should* want. The company spends about $2 million a year on consumer surveys alone. A year before rolling out a product, Coach talks to hundreds of customers, asking for their opinions on every feature of a purse from comfort and strap length to style and color. It asks consumers to rank new designs against existing items. Coach test markets new products in a cross-section of stores around the country. This focus on consumers and understanding what they want sets the company apart in the fashion industry.

Using marketing research and focusing marketing efforts on what customers want paid off handsomely for Coach. Coach stores have annual sales per square foot of $865 compared to traditional retailers, like the Gap, which average $200 to $300. In 2005 Coach earned the number 17 spot on the *BusinessWeek 50* list of top corporate performers. In 2006, Coach's sales grew over 23 percent to $2.11 billion and net income grew over 37 percent to $494 million over the previous year. Clearly, using marketing research that helps Coach understand and deliver products customers want is a profitable strategy for the company.

Sources: Coach.com, April 5, 2007; Diane Brady, "Coach's Split Personality," *BusinessWeek*, November 7, 2005, pp. 60–61; LouAnn Lofton, "Coach's Success Story," Fool.com, June 12, 2003; Amy Tsao, "It's in the Bag for Coach," *BusinessWeek* Online, April 23, 2003; Julia Boorstin, "How Coach Got Hot," *Fortune*, October 28, 2002, pp. 131–134.

customer beliefs, attitudes, satisfaction, and many other issues. Mail surveys are useful for reaching widely dispersed markets but take more time to get responses than telephone surveys; personal surveys involving structured questions are useful but expensive.

Experimental research involves manipulating one variable and examining its impact on other variables. For example, the price of a product could be changed in one test store, while left the same in other stores. Comparing sales in the test store with those in other stores can provide evidence about the likely impact of a price change in the overall market. Experiments are useful for getting a better idea of the causal relationships among variables, but they are often difficult to design and administer effectively in natural settings. Thus, many marketing research experiments are conducted in laboratories or simulated stores to carefully control other variables that could impact results.

Mathematical modeling research often involves secondary data, such as scanner data collected and stored in computer files from retail checkout counters. This approach involves the development of equations to model relationships among variables and uses econometric and statistical techniques to investigate the impact of various strategies and

FIGURE 2.3   **A Comparison of Data Collection Methods Used in Marketing Research**

Method	Advantages	Disadvantages
Focus groups	• Depth of information collected. • Flexibility in use. • Relatively low cost. • Data collected quickly.	• Requires expert moderator. • Questions of group size and acquaintanceships of participants. • Potential for bias from moderator. • Small sample size.
Telephone surveys	• Centralized control of data collection. • More cost-effective than personal interviews. • Data collected quickly.	• Resistance in collecting income, financial data. • Limited depth of response. • Disproportionate coverage of low-income segments. • Abuse of phone by solicitors. • Perceived intrusiveness.
Mail surveys	• Cost-effective per completed response. • Broad geographic dispersion. • Ease of administration. • Data collected quickly.	• Refusal and contact problems with certain segments. • Limited depth of response. • Difficult to estimate nonresponse biases. • Resistance and bias in collecting income, financial data. • Lack of control following mailing.
Personal (in-depth) interviews	• More depth of response than telephone interviews. • Generate substantial number of ideas compared with group methods.	• Easy to transmit biasing cues. • Not-at-homes. • Broad coverage often infeasible. • Cost per contact high. • Data collection time may be excessive.
Mall intercepts	• Flexibility in collecting data, answering questions, probing respondents. • Data collected quickly. • Excellent for concept tests, copy evaluations, other visuals. • Fairly high response rates.	• Limited time. • Sample composition or representativeness is suspect. • Costs depend on incidence rates. • Interviewer supervision difficult.
Internet surveys	• Inexpensive, quickly executed. • Visual stimuli can be evaluated. • Real-time data processing possible. • Can be answered at convenience of respondent.	• Responses must be checked for duplication, bogus responses. • Respondent self-selection bias. • Limited ability to qualify respondents and confirm responses. • Difficulty in generating sample frames for probability sampling.
Projective techniques	• Useful in word association tests of new brand names. • Less threatening to respondents for sensitive topics. • Can identify important motives underlying choices.	• Require trained interviewers. • Cost per interview high.
Observation	• Can collect sensitive data. • Accuracy of measuring overt behaviors. • Different perspective than survey self-reports. • Useful in studies of cross-cultural differences.	• Appropriate only for frequently occurring behaviors. • Unable to assess opinions of attitudes causing behaviors. • May be expensive in data-collection-time costs.

Source: William O. Bearden, Thomas N. Ingram, and Raymond W. LaForge, *Marketing,* 5th ed. (Burr Ridge, IL: McGraw-Hill/Irwin, 2007), p. 134.

tactics on sales and brand choices. Math modeling is useful because it provides an efficient way to study problems with extremely large secondary data sets.

Which of these types of research is best for particular research questions requires considerable knowledge of each of them. Often, qualitative research is used in early stages of investigating a topic to get more information and insight about it. Then, quantitative approaches are used to investigate the degree to which the insights hold across a larger sample or population. Figure 2.3 provides a comparison of a variety of qualitative and quantitative data collection methods.

A. Planning
1. Segmentation: What kinds of people buy our products? Where do they live? How much do they earn? How many of them are there?
2. Demand estimation: Are the markets for our products increasing or decreasing? Are there promising markets that we have not yet reached?
3. Environmental assessment: Are the channels of distribution for our products changing? What should our presence on the Internet be?

B. Problem Solving
1. Product
   a. In testing new products and product-line extensions, which product design is likely to be the most successful? What features do consumers value most?
   b. What kind of packaging should we use?
   c. What are the forecasts for the product? How might we reenergize its life cycle?
2. Price
   a. What price should we charge for our products?
   b. How sensitive to price changes are our target segments?
   c. Given the lifetime value assessments of our segments, should we be discounting or charging a premium to our most valued customers?
   d. As production costs decline, should we lower our prices or try to develop higher-quality products?
   e. Do consumers use price as a cue to value or a cue to quality in our industry?
3. Place
   a. Where, and by whom, are our products being sold? Where, and by whom, should our products be sold?
   b. What kinds of incentives should we offer the trade to push our products?
   c. Are our relationships with our suppliers and distributors satisfactory and cooperative?
4. Promotion
   a. How much should we spend on promotion? How should it be allocated to products and to geographic areas?
   b. Which ad copy should we run in our markets? With what frequency and media expenditures?
   c. What combination of media—newspapers, radio, television, magazines, Internet ad banners—should we use?
   d. What is our consumer coupon redemption rate?

C. Control
1. What is our market share overall? In each geographic area? By each customer type?
2. Are customers satisfied with our products? How is our record for service? Are there many returns? Do levels of customer satisfaction vary with market? With segment?
3. Are our employees satisfied? Do they feel well trained and empowered to assist our customers?
4. How does the public perceive our company? What is our reputation with the trade?

Source: Gilbert A. Churchill, Jr., and Dawn Iacobucci, *Marketing Research: Methodological Foundations,* 9th ed. (Mason, OH: Thomson South-Western, 2005), p. 9.

Company versus Contract Research

Most large consumer goods companies have marketing research departments that can perform a variety of types of research. In addition many marketing research firms, advertising agencies, and consulting companies do marketing research on a contract basis. Some marketing research suppliers have special expertise in a particular type of research that makes them a better choice than doing the research internally. A decision about

Traditional marketing research typically involves identifying possible drivers and then collecting data: for example, increasing couponing (the driver) during spring will increase trial by first-time buyers (the result). Marketing researchers then try to collect information to attempt to verify this relationship.

In contrast, data mining is the extraction of hidden predictive information from large databases. Catalog companies such as Lands' End, Fingerhut, and Spiegel, use data mining to find statistical links that suggest marketing actions. For example, Fingerhut studies about 3,500 variables over the lifetime of a consumer's relationship. It has found that customers who change residences are three times as likely as regular customers to buy tables, fax machines, and decorative products but no more likely to buy jewelry or footwear. So Fingerhut has created a catalog especially targeted at consumers who have recently moved.

Some of these purchase patterns are common sense: Peanut butter and grape jelly purchases are linked and might suggest a joint promotion between Skippy peanut butter and Welch's grape jelly. Other patterns link seemingly unrelated purchases: Supermarkets mined checkout data from scanners and discovered men buying diapers in the evening sometimes buy a six-pack of beer as well. So they placed diapers and beer near each other. Placing potato chips between them increased sales of all three.

Still, the success in data mining ultimately depends on humans—the judgments of the marketing managers and researchers in how to select, analyze, and interpret the information.

Source: Roger A. Kerin, Eric N. Berkowitz, Steven W. Hartley, and William Rudelius, *Marketing*, 8th ed. (Burr Ridge, IL: McGraw-Hill/Irwin, 2006), pp. 222–23.

whether the marketing research department has the ability to do a particular type of research itself or whether all or part of the research should be contracted with a research supplier must be made. In either case, schedules for task completion, the exact responsibilities of all involved parties, and cost need to be considered.

Performance of the Research

Performance of the research involves preparing for data collection and actually collecting them. The tasks at this stage obviously depend on the type of research that has been selected and the type of data needed. If secondary data are to be used, they must be located, prepared for analysis, and possibly paid for. If primary data are to be collected, then observational forms, questionnaires, or other types of measures must be designed, pretested, and validated. Samples must be drawn and interviews must be scheduled or preparations must be made for mailing or phoning selected individuals.

In terms of actual data collection, a cardinal rule is to obtain and record the maximal amount of useful information, subject to the constraints of time, money, and respondent privacy. Failure to obtain and record data clearly can obviously lead to a poor research study, while failure to consider the rights of respondents raises both practical and ethical problems. Thus, both the objectives and constraints of data collection must be closely monitored.

Processing of Research Data

Processing research data includes the preparation of data for analysis and the actual analysis of them. Preparations include such things as editing and structuring data and coding them for analysis. Data sets should be clearly labeled to ensure they are not misinterpreted or misplaced.

The appropriate analysis techniques for collected data depend on the nature of the research question and the design of the research. Qualitative research data consist of interview records that are content analyzed for ideas or themes. Quantitative research data may be analyzed in a variety of ways depending on the objectives of the research.

A critical part of this stage is interpreting and assessing the research results. Seldom, if ever, do marketing research studies obtain findings that are totally unambiguous. Usually, relationships among variables or differences between groups are small to moderate, and judgment and insight are needed to draw appropriate inferences and conclusions. Marketing researchers should always double-check their analysis and avoid overstating the strength of their findings. The implications for developing or changing a marketing strategy should be carefully thought out and tempered with judgment about the overall quality of the study.

Preparation of the Research Report

The research report is a complete statement of everything done in a research project and includes a write-up of each of the previous stages as well as the strategic recommendations from the research. The limitations of the research should be carefully noted. Figure 2.4 illustrates the types of questions marketing researchers and managers should discuss prior to submitting the final research report.

Research reports should be clear and unambiguous with respect to what was done and what recommendations are made. Often research reports must trade off the apparent precision of scientific jargon for everyday language that managers can understand. Researchers should work closely with managers to ensure that the study and its limitations are fully understood.

• Limitations of the Research Process

Although the foregoing discussion presented the research process as a set of simple stages, this does not mean that conducting quality marketing research is a simple task. Many problems and difficulties must be overcome if a research study is to provide valuable information for decision making.[3] For example, consider the difficulties in one type of marketing research, *test marketing*.

The major goal of most test marketing is to measure new product sales on a limited basis where competitive retaliation and other factors are allowed to operate freely. In this way, future sales potential can often be estimated reasonably well. Listed below are a number of problems that could invalidate test marketing study results.

1. Test market areas are not representative of the market in general in terms of population characteristics, competition, and distribution outlets.
2. Sample size and design are incorrectly formulated because of budget constraints.
3. Pretest measurements of competitive brand sales are not made or are inaccurate, limiting the meaningfulness of market share estimates.
4. Test stores do not give complete support to the study such that certain package sizes may not be carried or prices may not be held constant during the test period.

FIGURE 2.4
Eight Criteria for Evaluating Marketing Research Reports

1. Was the type of research appropriate for the research questions?
2. Was the research well designed?
   a. Was the sample studied appropriate for the research questions?
   b. Were measures well developed, pretested, and validated?
   c. Were the data analysis techniques the best ones for the study?
3. Was there adequate supervision of data collection, editing, and coding?
4. Was the analysis conducted according to standards accepted in the field?
5. Do the findings make sense, given the research question and design, and were they considered in light of previous knowledge and experience?
6. Are the limitations of the study recognized and explained in detail?
7. Are the conclusions appropriately drawn or are they over- or understated?
8. Are the recommendations for marketing strategy clear and appropriate?

Marketing researchers have ethical responsibilities to the respondents who provide primary data, clients for whom they work, and subordinates who work under them. Below are a number of ethical responsibilities to these groups.

RESPONSIBILITIES TO RESPONDENTS

1. *Preserving respondent anonymity.* Marketing researchers should ensure that respondents' identities are safe from invasion of privacy.
2. *Avoiding mental stress for respondents.* Marketing researchers should minimize the mental stress placed on respondents.
3. *Avoiding questions detrimental to respondents.* Marketing researchers should avoid asking questions for which the answers conflict with the self-interest of the respondents.
4. *Avoiding the use of dangerous equipment or techniques.* Physical or reputational harm to respondents based on their participation in marketing research should not occur. Respondents should be informed of any other than minimal risks involved in the research and be free to self-determine their participation.
5. *Avoiding deception of respondents.* Respondents should not be deceived about the purpose of the study in most cases. Many consider deception acceptable in research where it is needed to obtain valid results, there is minimal risk to respondents, and respondents are debriefed explaining the real purpose of the study.
6. *Avoiding coercion of respondents.* Marketing researchers should avoid coercing or harassing people to try to get them to agree to be interviewed or fill out questionnaires.

RESPONSIBILITIES TO CLIENTS

1. *Providing confidentiality.* Marketing researchers are obliged not to reveal information about a client to competitors and should carefully consider when a company should be identified as a client.
2. *Providing technical integrity.* Marketing researchers are obliged to design efficient studies without undue expense or complexity and accurately report results.
3. *Providing administrative integrity.* Marketing researchers are obliged to price their work fairly without hidden charges.
4. *Providing guidance on research usage.* Marketing researchers are obliged to promote the correct usage of research and to prevent the misuse of findings.

RESPONSIBILITIES TO SUBORDINATE EMPLOYEES

1. *Creating an ethical work environment.* Marketing research managers are obliged to create an ethical work environment where unethical behavior is not encouraged or overlooked.
2. *Avoiding opportunities for unethical behavior.* Marketing research managers are obliged to avoid placing subordinates in situations where unethical behavior could be concealed but rewarded.

5. Test-market products are advertised or promoted beyond a profitable level for the market in general.
6. The effects of factors that influence sales, such as the sales force, season, weather conditions, competitive retaliation, shelf space, and so forth, are ignored in the research.
7. The test-market period is too short to determine whether the product will be repurchased by customers.

A list of such problems could be developed for any type of marketing research. However, careful research planning, coordination, implementation, and control can help reduce such problems and increase the value of research for decision making.

Marketing Information Systems

Most marketers use computer-based systems to help them gather, sort, store, and distribute information for marketing decisions.[4] A popular form of marketing information system is the marketing decision support system, which is a coordinated collection of data, tools, and techniques involving both computer hardware and software by which marketers gather and interpret relevant information for decision making. These systems require three types of software:

1. Database management software for sorting and retrieving data from internal and external sources.

FIGURE 2.5   Some Information Sources for Marketing Information Systems

Selected Government Sources

American Factfinder	http://factfinder.census.gov/
Economics Statistics Briefing Room	http://www.whitehouse.gov/fsbr/esbr.html
EDGAR Database of Corporate Information (SEC filings)	http://www.sec.gov/edgar.shtml
FedStats	http://www.fedstats.gov/
GPO Access	http://www.gpoaccess.gov/
Stat-USA	http://www.stat-usa.gov/
U.S. Bureau of Labor Statistics	http://www.bls.gov/
U.S. Bureau of the Census	http://www.census.gov/
U.S. Department of Commerce	http://www.commerce.gov/
U.S. Small Business Administration	http://www.sbaonline.sba.gov/
U.S. Patent and Trademark Office	http://www.uspto.gov/
CBDNet (Commerce Business Daily)—government procurement, sales, and contract awards	http://www.cbdnet.access.gpo.gov

Selected Proprietary Sources (with some free information)

Gallup Poll	http://www.gallup.com/poll/
Harris Poll	http://www.harrisinteractive.com/harris_poll/
The Polling Report	http://www.pollingreport.com/
Public Opinion	http://europa.eu.int/comm./public_opinion/
Public Agenda	http://www.publicagenda.org/
Roper Center for Public Opinion Research	http://www.repercenter.uconn.edu
Poll Question Database	http://www.irss.unc.edu/data_archive/pollsearch.html
Forrester Research Reports	http://forrester.com
Roper Reports	http://www.nopworld.com
JD Power Satisfaction Studies	http://www.jdpower.com
Quirk's Marketing Research Review	http://www.quirks.com
Ad Forum	http://www.adforum.com
BizMiner	http://www.bizminer.com

Selected Nonproprietary Sources

Ad* Access	http://scriptorium.lib.duke.edu/adaccess/
Advertising World (ad industry Portal)	http://advertising.utexas.edu/world
American Demographics	http://www.demographics.com
Competia Express (industry portal)	http://www.competia.com/express/
Global Edge	http://www.demographics.com
Kerlins.net Qualitative Research Bibliography	http://kerlins.net/bobbi/research/qualresearch/bibliography/
KnowThis.com Marketing Virtual Library	http://knowthis.com
Marketing and Research Library	http://www.mrlibrary.com/
MarketingPower.com	http://marketingpower.com

Source: Donald R. Cooper and Pamela S. Schindler, *Marketing Research,* Burr Ridge, IL: McGraw-Hill/Irwin, 2006, pp. 122–123.

2. Model base management software that contains routines for manipulating data in ways that are useful for marketing decision making.

3. A dialog system that permits marketers to explore databases and use models to produce information to address their decision-making needs.

Marketing decision support systems are designed to handle information from both internal and external sources. Internal information includes such things as sales records, which can be divided by territory, package size, brand, price, order size, or salesperson; inventory data that can indicate how rapidly various products are selling; or expenditure data on such things as advertising, personal selling, or packaging. Internal information is particularly important for investigating the efficiency and effectiveness of various marketing strategies.

External information is gathered from outside the organization and concerns changes in the environment that could influence marketing strategies. External information is needed concerning changes in global economies and societies, competitors, customers, and technology. Figure 2.5 lists a sample of sources of external information that could be monitored by a marketing information system to help marketers make better decisions. Of course, information from marketing research studies conducted by an organization is also put into marketing information systems to improve marketing strategy development.

Conclusion

This chapter emphasized the importance of marketing research for making sound marketing strategy decisions. The chapter discussed marketing research as a process involving several stages, which include determining the purpose of the research, designing the plan for the research, performing the research, processing the research data, and preparing the research report. Then, marketing information systems were discussed and one type, the marketing decision support system, was explained. Such systems should provide decision makers with the right information, at the right time in the right way, to make sound marketing decisions.

Additional Readings

Churchill, Gilbert A., Jr., and Tom J. Brown. *Basic Marketing Research*. 6th ed. Mason, OH: Thomson South-Western, 2007.

Churchill, Gilbert A., Jr., and Dawn Iacobucci. *Marketing Research: Methodological Foundations*. 9th ed. Mason, OH: Thomson South-Western, 2005.

Cooper, Donald R., and Pamela S. Schindler. *Marketing Research*. Burr Ridge, IL: McGraw-Hill/Irwin, 2006.

McDaniel, Carl, Jr., and Roger Gates. *Marketing Research*. Hoboken, NJ: John Wiley, 2005.

Molhatra, Naresh K. *Marketing Research*. 5th ed. Upper Saddle River, NJ: Pearson Education, 2007.

Parasuraman, A., Dhruv Grewal, and R. Krishnan. *Marketing Research*. 2nd ed. Boston: Houghton Mifflin, 2007.

Zikmund William G., and Barry J. Babin. *Exploring Marketing Research*. 9th ed. Mason, OH: Thomson South-Western, 2007.

Zikmund William G., and Barry J. Babin. *Essentials of Marketing Research*. 3rd ed. Mason, OH: Thomson South-Western, 2007.

Chapter 3

Consumer Behavior

The marketing concept emphasizes that profitable marketing begins with the discovery and understanding of consumer needs and then develops a marketing mix to satisfy these needs. Thus, an understanding of consumers and their needs and purchasing behavior is integral to successful marketing. Unfortunately, there is no single theory of consumer behavior that can totally explain why consumers behave as they do. Instead, there are numerous theories, models, and concepts making up the field. In addition, the majority of these notions have been borrowed from a variety of other disciplines, such as sociology, psychology, anthropology, and economics, and must be integrated to understand consumer behavior.

In this chapter, consumer behavior will be examined in terms of the model in Figure 3.1. The chapter begins by reviewing social, marketing, and situational influences on consumer decision making. These provide information that can influence consumers' thoughts and feelings about purchasing various products and brands. The degree to which this information influences consumers' decisions depends on a number of psychological influences. Two of the most important of these are product knowledge and product involvement, which will then be discussed. The chapter concludes by discussing the consumer decision-making process.

FIGURE 3.1   **An Overview of the Buying Process**

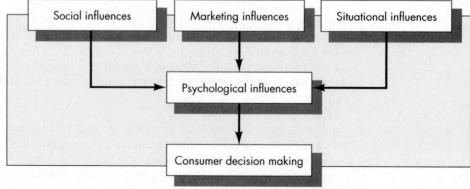

Value	General Features	Relevance to Marketing
Achievement and success activity	Hard work is good; success flows from hard work. Keeping busy is healthy and natural.	Acts as a justification for acquisition of goods ("You deserve it"). Stimulates interest in products that are time-savers and enhance leisure time.
Efficiency and practicality	Admiration of things that solve problems (e.g., save time and effort). People can improve themselves; tomorrow should be better than today.	Stimulates purchase of products that function well and save time. Stimulates desire for new products that fulfill unsatisfied needs; ready acceptance of products that claim to be "new" or "improved."
Material comfort	"The good life."	Fosters acceptance of convenience and luxury products that make life more enjoyable.
Individualism	Being oneself (e.g., self-reliance, self-interest, self-esteem).	Stimulates acceptance of customized or unique products that enable a person to "express his or her own personality."
Freedom	Freedom of choice.	Fosters interest in wide product lines and differentiated products.
External conformity	Uniformity of observable behavior; desire for acceptance.	Stimulates interest in products that are used or owned by others in the same social group.
Humanitarianism	Caring for others, particularly the underdog.	Stimulates patronage of firms that compete with market leaders.
Youthfulness	A state of mind that stresses being "young at heart" and having a youthful appearance.	Stimulates acceptance of products that provide the illusion of maintaining or fostering youthfulness.
Fitness and health	Caring about one's body, including the desire to be physically fit and healthy.	Stimulates acceptance of food products, activities, and equipment perceived to maintain or increase physical fitness.

Source: Leon G. Schiffman and Leslie Lazar Kanuck, *Consumer Behavior*, 9th ed., p. 416, 2007. Reprinted by permission of Pearson Prentice Hall, Inc., Upper Saddle River, NJ.

Social Influences on Consumer Decision Making

Behavioral scientists have become increasingly aware of the powerful effects of the social environment and personal interactions on human behavior. In terms of consumer behavior, culture, social class, and reference group influences have been related to purchase and consumption decisions. It should be noted that these influences can have both direct and indirect effects on the buying process. By direct effects we mean direct communication between the individual and other members of society concerning a particular decision. By indirect effects we mean the influence of society on an individual's basic values and attitudes as well as the important role that groups play in structuring an individual's personality.

Culture and Subculture

Culture is one of the most basic influences on an individual's needs, wants, and behavior, since all facets of life are carried out against the background of the society in which an individual lives. Cultural antecedents affect everyday behavior, and there is empirical support for the notion that culture is a determinant of certain aspects of consumer behavior.

43

Cultural values are transmitted through three basic organizations: the family, religious organizations, and educational institutions; and in today's society, educational institutions are playing an increasingly greater role in this regard. Marketing managers should adapt the marketing mix to cultural values and constantly monitor value changes and differences in both domestic and global markets. To illustrate, one of the changing values in America is the increasing emphasis on achievement and career success. This change in values has been recognized by many business firms that have expanded their emphasis on time-saving, convenience-oriented products.

In large nations such as the United States, the population is bound to lose a significant amount of its homogeneity, and thus subcultures arise. In other words, there are subcultures in the American culture where people have more frequent interactions than with the population at large and thus tend to think and act alike in some respects. Subcultures are based on such things as geographic areas, religions, nationalities, ethnic groups, and age. Many subcultural barriers are decreasing because of mass communication, mass transit, and a decline in the influence of religious values. However, age groups, such as the teen market, baby boomers, and the mature market, have become increasingly important for marketing strategy. For example, since baby boomers (those born between 1946 and 1962) make up about a third of the U.S. population and soon will account for about half of discretionary spending, many marketers are repositioning products to serve them. Snickers candy bars, for instance, used to be promoted to children as a treat but are now promoted to adults as a wholesome between-meals snack.

Social Class

While many people like to think of America as a land of equality, a class structure can be observed. Social classes develop on the basis of such things as wealth, skill, and power. The single best indicator of social class is occupation. However, interest at this point is in the influence of social class on the individual's behavior. What is important here is that different social classes tend to have different attitudinal configurations and values that influence the behavior of individual members. For marketing purposes, four different social classes have been identified.[1]

Upper Americans comprise 14 percent of the population and are differentiated mainly by having high incomes. This class remains the group in which quality merchandise is most prized and prestige brands are commonly sought. Spending with good taste is a priority as are products such as theater; books; investments in art; European travel; household help; club memberships for tennis, golf, and swimming; and prestige schooling for children.

The *middle class* comprises 34 percent of the population, and these consumers want to do the right thing and buy what is popular. They are concerned with fashion and buying what experts in the media recommend. Increased earnings have led to spending on more "worthwhile experiences" for children, including winter ski trips, college education, and shopping for better brands of clothes at more expensive stores. Appearance of the home is important. This group emulates the upper Americans, which distinguishes it from the working class.

The *working class* comprises 38 percent of the population, people who are "family folk" who depend heavily on relatives for economic and emotional support. The emphasis on family ties is only one sign of how much more limited and different working-class horizons are socially, psychologically, and geographically compared to those of the middle class. For them, "keeping up with the times" focuses on the mechanical and recreational, and thus, ease of labor and leisure are what they continue to pursue.

Lower Americans comprise 16 percent of the population and are as diverse in values and consumption goals as are other social levels. Some members of this group are prone to every form of instant gratification known to humankind when the money is available. However, others are dedicated to resisting worldly temptations as they struggle toward what some believe will be a "heavenly reward" for their earthly sacrifices.

For the marketing manager, social class offers some insights into consumer behavior and is potentially useful as a market segmentation variable. However, there is considerable controversy as to whether social class is superior to income for the purpose of market segmentation.

Reference Groups and Families

Groups that an individual looks to (uses as a reference) when forming attitudes and opinions are described as reference groups.[2] Primary reference groups include family and close friends, while secondary reference groups include fraternal organizations and professional associations. A buyer may also consult a single individual about decisions, and this individual would be considered a reference individual.

A person normally has several reference groups or reference individuals for various subjects or different decisions. For example, a woman may consult one reference group when she is purchasing a car and a different reference group for lingerie. In other words, the nature of the product and the role the individual is playing during the purchasing process influence which reference group will be consulted. Reference group influence is generally considered to be stronger for products that are "public" or conspicuous—that is, products that other people see the individual using, such as clothes or automobiles.

As noted, the family is generally recognized to be an important reference group, and it has been suggested that the household, rather than the individual, is the relevant unit for studying consumer behavior.[3] This is because within a household the purchaser of goods and services is not always the user of these goods and services. Thus, it is important for marketing managers to determine not only who makes the actual purchase but also who makes the decision to purchase. In addition, it has been recognized that the needs, income, assets, debts, and expenditure patterns change over the course of what is called the *family life cycle*. The family life cycle can be divided into a number of stages ranging from single, to married, to married with children of different age groups, to older couples, to solitary survivors. It may also include divorced people, both with and without children. Because the life cycle combines trends in earning power with demands placed on income, it is a useful way of classifying and segmenting individuals and families.[4]

Marketing Influences on Consumer Decision Making

Marketing strategies are often designed to influence consumer decision making and lead to profitable exchanges. Each element of the marketing mix (product, price, promotion, place) can affect consumers in various ways.

Product Influences

Many attributes of a company's products, including brand name, quality, newness, and complexity, can affect consumer behavior. The physical appearance of the product, packaging, and labeling information can also influence whether consumers notice a product in-store, examine it, and purchase it. One of the key tasks of marketers is to differentiate their products from those of competitors and create consumer perceptions that the product is worth purchasing.

Price Influences

The price of products and services often influences whether consumers will purchase them at all and, if so, which competitive offering is selected. Stores, such as Wal-Mart, which are perceived to charge the lowest prices, attract many consumers based on this fact alone. For some offerings, higher prices may not deter purchase because consumers believe that the products or services are higher quality or are more prestigious. However,

Marketers know that reference groups can influence both product and brand decisions. They also know that reference group influence varies depending on whether the good is used publicly (a car) or privately (a toothbrush) and whether it is a necessity (a mattress) or a luxury (a sailboat). By examining the nature of products and brands on these two dimensions, the matrix below can be constructed. Marketers could use this matrix to judge how reference group influence should be used in advertising and personal selling efforts. For example, public luxuries could benefit from ads showing owners being admired and complimented for their product and brand selection whereas ads for private necessities might focus more on superior functional performance.

	Necessity	Luxury

Public	**Public necessities**
	Reference group influence
	    Product: Weak
	    Brand: Strong
	Examples: Wristwatch, automobile, man's suit
		Public luxuries
		Reference group influence
		    Product Strong
		    Brand: Strong
		Examples: Golf clubs, snow skis, sailboat, health club

Private	**Private necessities**
	Reference group influence
	    Product: Weak
	    Brand: Weak
	Examples: Mattress, floor lamp, refrigerator
		Private luxuries
		Reference group influence
		    Product: Strong
		    Brand: Weak
		Examples: Plasma TV, trash compactor, ice maker

Source: Adapted from William O. Bearden and Michael J. Etzel, "Reference Group Influences on Product and Brand Purchase Decisions," *Journal of Consumer Research,* September 1982, p. 185 as reported in J. Paul Peter and Jerry C. Olson, *Consumer Behavior and Marketing Strategy,* 8th ed. (Burr Ridge, IL: McGraw-Hill/Irwin, 2008), pp. 342–44.

many of today's value-conscious consumers may buy products more on the basis of price than other attributes.

Promotion Influences

Advertising, sales promotions, salespeople, and publicity can influence what consumers think about products, what emotions they experience in purchasing and using them, and what behaviors they perform, including shopping in particular stores and purchasing specific brands. Since consumers receive so much information from marketers and screen out a good deal of it, it is important for marketers to devise communications that (1) offer consistent messages about their products and (2) are placed in media that consumers in the target market are likely to use. Marketing communications play a critical role in informing consumers about products and services, including where they can be purchased, and in creating favorable images and perceptions.

Place Influences

The marketer's strategy for distributing products can influence consumers in several ways. First, products that are convenient to buy in a variety of stores increase the chances of consumers finding and buying them. When consumers are seeking low-involvement products, they are unlikely to engage in extensive search, so ready availability is important. Second, products sold in exclusive outlets such as Nordstrom may be perceived by consumers as having higher quality. In fact, one of the ways marketers create brand equity—that is, favorable consumer perceptions of brands—is by selling them in prestigious outlets. Third, offering products by nonstore methods, such as on the Internet or in catalogs, can create consumer perceptions that the products are innovative, exclusive, or tailored for specific target markets.

Situational Influences on Consumer Decision Making

Situational influences can be defined as all those factors particular to a time and place of observation that have a demonstrable and systematic effect on current behavior. In terms of purchasing situations, five groups of situational influences have been identified.[5] These influences may be perceived either consciously or subconsciously and may have considerable effect on product and brand choice.

1. *Physical features* are the most readily apparent features of a situation. These features include geographical and institutional location, decor, sounds, aromas, lighting, weather, and visible configurations of merchandise or other material surrounding the stimulus object.

2. *Social features* provide additional depth to a description of a situation. Other persons present, their characteristics, their apparent roles and interpersonal interactions are potentially relevant examples.

3. *Time* is a dimension of situations that may be specified in units ranging from time of day to season of the year. Time also may be measured relative to some past or future event for the situational participant. This allows such conceptions as time since last purchase, time since or until meals or paydays, and time constraints imposed by prior or standing commitments.

4. *Task features* of a situation include an intent or requirement to select, shop for, or obtain information about a general or specific purchase. In addition, task may reflect different buyer and user roles anticipated by the individual. For instance, a person shopping for a small appliance as a wedding gift for a friend is in a different situation than when shopping for a small appliance for personal use.

5. *Current conditions* make up a final feature that characterizes a situation. These are momentary moods (such as acute anxiety, pleasantness, hostility, and excitation) or momentary conditions (such as cash on hand, fatigue, and illness) rather than chronic individual traits. These conditions are considered to be immediately antecedent to the current situation to distinguish the states the individual brings to the situation from states of the individual resulting from the situation. For instance, people may select a certain motion picture because they feel depressed (an antecedent state and a part of the choice situation), but the fact that the movie causes them to feel happier is a response to the consumption situation. This altered state then may become antecedent for behavior in the next choice situation encountered, such as passing a street vendor on the way out of the theater.

Psychological Influences on Consumer Decision Making

Information from group, marketing, and situational influences affects what consumers think and feel about particular products and brands. However, a number of psychological factors influence how this information is interpreted and used and how it impacts the consumer decision-making process. Two of the most important psychological factors are product knowledge and product involvement.[6]

Product Knowledge

Product knowledge refers to the amount of information a consumer has stored in her or his memory about particular product classes, product forms, brands, models, and ways to purchase them. For example, a consumer may know a lot about coffee (product class), ground versus instant coffee (product form), Folgers versus Maxwell House (brand), and various package sizes (models) and stores that sell it (ways to purchase).

Group, marketing, and situational influences determine the initial level of product knowledge as well as changes in it. For example, a consumer may hear about a new Starbucks opening up from a friend (group influence), see an ad for it in the newspaper (marketing influence), or see the coffee shop on the way to work (situational influence). Any of these increase the amount of product knowledge, in this case, a new source for purchasing the product.

The initial level of product knowledge may influence how much information is sought when deciding to make a purchase. For example, if a consumer already believes that Folgers is the best-tasting coffee, knows where to buy it, and knows how much it costs, little additional information may be sought.

Finally, product knowledge influences how quickly a consumer goes through the decision-making process. For example, when purchasing a new product for which the consumer has little product knowledge, extensive information may be sought and more time may be devoted to the decision.

Product Involvement

Product involvement refers to a consumer's perception of the importance or personal relevance of an item. For example, Harley-Davidson motorcycle owners are generally highly involved in the purchase and use of the product, brand, and accessories. However, a consumer buying a new toothbrush would likely view this as a low-involvement purchase.

Product involvement influences consumer decision making in two ways. First, if the purchase is for a high-involvement product, consumers are likely to develop a high degree of product knowledge so that they can be confident that the item they purchase is just right for them. Second, a high degree of product involvement encourages extensive decision making by consumers, which likely increases the time it takes to go through the decision-making process.

Consumer Decision Making

The process by which consumers make decisions to purchase various products and brands is shown in Figure 3.2. In general, consumers recognize a need for a product, search for information about alternatives to meet the need, evaluate the information, make purchases, and evaluate the decision after the purchase. There are three types of decision making, which vary in terms of how complex or expensive a product is and how involved a consumer is in purchasing it.

Extensive decision making requires the most time and effort since the purchase involves a highly complex or expensive product that is important to the consumer. For example, the purchase of a car, house, or computer often involves considerable time and effort comparing alternatives and deciding on the right one. In terms of the number of purchases a consumer makes, extensive decision making is relatively rare, but it is critical for marketers of highly complex or expensive products to understand that consumers are willing to process considerable information to make the best choice. Thus, marketers should provide consumers with factual information that highlights competitive advantages for such high-involvement products.

Limited decision making is more moderate but still involves some time and effort searching for and comparing alternatives. For example, when buying shirts or shorts, consumers may shop several stores and compare a number of different brands and styles.

FIGURE 3.2 **The Consumer Decision-Making Process**

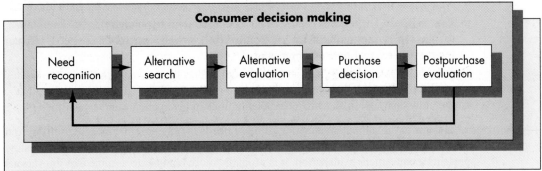

Marketers of products for which consumers usually do limited decision making often use eye-catching advertising and in-store displays to make consumers aware of their products and encourage consumers to consider buying them.

Routine decision making is the most common type and the way consumers purchase most packaged goods. Such products are simple, inexpensive, and familiar; and consumers often have developed favorite brands that they purchase without much deliberation. For example, consumers often make habitual purchases of soft drinks, candy bars, or canned soup without carefully comparing the relative merits of different brands. Marketers of such products need to have them readily available for purchase in a variety of outlets and price them competitively if price is an important criterion to consumers. Marketers of these low-involvement products often use celebrity spokespeople and other non-product-related cues to encourage purchases.

Need Recognition

The starting point in the buying process is the consumer's recognition of an unsatisfied need. Any number of either internal or external stimuli may activate needs or wants and recognition of them. Internal stimuli are such things as feeling hungry and wanting some food, feeling a headache coming on and wanting some Excedrin, or feeling bored and looking for a movie to go to. External stimuli are such things as seeing a McDonald's sign and then feeling hungry or seeing a sale sign for winter parkas and remembering that last year's coat is worn out.

It is the task of marketing managers to find out what needs and wants a particular product can and does satisfy and what unsatisfied needs and wants consumers have for which a new product could be developed. In order to do so, marketing managers should understand what types of needs consumers may have. A well-known classification of needs was developed many years ago by Abraham Maslow and includes five types.[7] Maslow's view is that lower-level needs, starting with physiological and safety needs, must be attended to before higher-level needs can be satisfied. Maslow's hierarchy is described below.

Physiological needs. This category consists of the primary needs of the human body, such as food, water, and sex. Physiological needs will dominate when all needs are unsatisfied. In such a case, none of the other needs will serve as a basis for motivation.

Safety needs. With the physiological needs met, the next higher level assumes importance. Safety needs consist of such things as protection from physical harm, ill health, and economic disaster and avoidance of the unexpected.

Belongingness and love needs. These needs are related to the social and gregarious nature of humans and the need for companionship. This level in the hierarchy is the point of departure from the physical or quasi-physical needs of the two previous levels. Nonsatisfaction of this level of need may affect the mental health of the individual.

Esteem needs. These needs consist of both the need for the self-awareness of importance to others (self-esteem) and actual esteem from others. Satisfaction of these needs leads to feelings of self-confidence and prestige.

Self-actualization needs. This area can be defined as the desire to become more and more what one is, to become everything one is capable of becoming. This means that the individual will fully realize the potentialities of given talents and capabilities.

Maslow assumed that satisfaction of these needs is only possible after the satisfaction of all the needs lower in the hierarchy. While the hierarchical arrangement of Maslow presents a convenient explanation, it is probably more realistic to assume that the various need categories overlap. Thus, in affluent societies, many products may satisfy more than one of these needs. For example, gourmet foods may satisfy both the basic physiological need of hunger as well as esteem and status needs for those who serve gourmet foods to their guests.

Alternative Search

Once a need is recognized, the individual then searches for alternatives for satisfying the need. The individual can collect information from five basic sources for a particular purchase decision.

1. *Internal sources*. In most cases the individual has had some previous experience in dealing with a particular need. Thus, the individual will usually "search" through whatever stored information and experience is in his or her mind for dealing with the need. If a previously acceptable product for satisfying the need is remembered, the individual may purchase with little or no additional information search or evaluation. This is quite common for routine or habitual purchases.

2. *Group sources*. A common source of information for purchase decisions comes from communication with other people, such as family, friends, neighbors, and acquaintances. Generally, some of these (i.e., relevant others) are selected that the individual views as having particular expertise for the purchase decision. Although it may be quite difficult for the marketing manager to determine the exact nature of this source of information, group sources of information often are considered to be the most powerful influence on purchase decisions.

3. *Marketing sources*. Marketing sources of information include such factors as advertising, salespeople, dealers, packaging, and displays. Generally, this is the primary source of information about a particular product. These sources of information will be discussed in detail in the promotion chapters of this text.

4. *Public sources*. Public sources of information include publicity, such as a newspaper article about the product, and independent ratings of the product, such as *Consumer Reports*. Here product quality is a highly important marketing management consideration, since such articles and reports often discuss such features as dependability and service requirements.

5. *Experiential sources*. Experiential sources refer to handling, examining, and perhaps trying the product while shopping. This usually requires an actual shopping trip by the individual and may be the final source consulted before purchase.

The consumer then processes information collected from these sources.[8] However, the exact nature of how individuals process information to form evaluations of products is not fully understood. In general, information processing is viewed as a four-step process in which the individual is (1) exposed to information, (2) becomes attentive to the information, (3) understands the information, and (4) retains the information.[9]

The marketing profession has long recognized the need to uphold its integrity, honor, and dignity. Part of this obligation is to treat customers fairly and honestly. In the American Marketing Association Code of Ethics, a number of issues are concerned with this obligation. Below is a list of some of the Code of Ethics responsibilities that bear directly or indirectly on exchanges with consumers and organizational buyers.

PRODUCT DEVELOPMENT AND MANAGEMENT AREA

Products and services offered should be safe and fit for their intended use.

All substantial risks associated with product or service usage should be disclosed.

Product component substitutions that might materially change the product or impact the buyer's decision should be disclosed.

Extra-cost-added features should be identified.

PROMOTION AREA

Communication about offered products and services should not be deceptive.

False and misleading advertising should be avoided.

High-pressure manipulation or misleading sales tactics should be avoided.

Sales promotions that use deception or manipulation should be avoided.

DISTRIBUTION AREA

The availability of a product should not be manipulated for the purpose of exploitation.

Coercion in the marketing channel should not be used.

Undue influence over the resellers' choice to handle products should be avoided.

PRICING AREA

Price fixing should not be practiced.

Predatory pricing should not be practiced.

The full price associated with any purchase should be disclosed.

Source: Adapted from the American Marketing Association Code of Ethics.

Alternative Evaluation

During the process of collecting information or, in some cases, after information is acquired, the consumer evaluates alternatives on the basis of what he or she has learned. One approach to describing the evaluation process is as follows:

1. The consumer has information about a number of brands in a product class.
2. The consumer perceives that at least some of the brands in a product class are viable alternatives for satisfying a recognized need.
3. Each of these brands has a set of attributes (color, quality, size, and so forth).
4. A set of these attributes is relevant to the consumer, and the consumer perceives that different brands vary in how much of each attribute they possess.
5. The brand that is perceived as offering the greatest number of desired attributes in the desired amounts and desired order will be the brand the consumer will like best.
6. The brand the consumer likes best is the brand the consumer will intend to purchase.[10]

Purchase Decision

If no other factors intervene after the consumer has decided on the brand that is intended for purchase, the actual purchase is a common result of search and evaluation. Actually, a purchase involves many decisions, which include product type, brand, model, dealer selection, and method of payment, among other factors. In addition, rather than purchasing, the consumer may make a decision to modify, postpone, or avoid purchase based on an inhibitor to purchase or a perceived risk.

Traditional risk theorists believe that consumers tend to make risk-minimizing decisions based on their *perceived* definition of the particular purchase. The perception of risk is based on the possible consequences and uncertainties involved. Consequences may range from economic loss, to embarrassment if a new food product does not turn out well, to actual physical harm. Perceived risk may be either functional (related to financial and performance considerations) or psychosocial (related to whether the product will further one's self- or reference-group image). The amount of risk a consumer perceives in a particular product depends on such things as the price of the product and whether other people will see the individual using it.

The perceived risk literature emphasizes that consumers generally try to reduce risk in their decision making. This can be done by either reducing the possible negative consequences or by reducing the uncertainty. The possible consequences of a purchase might be minimized by purchasing in small quantities or by lowering the individual's aspiration level to expect less in the way of results from the product. However, this cannot always be done. Thus, reducing risk by attempting to increase the certainty of the purchase outcome may be the more widely used strategy. This can be done by seeking additional information regarding the proposed purchase. In general, the more information the consumer collects prior to purchase, the less likely postpurchase dissonance is to occur.

Postpurchase Evaluation

In general, if the individual finds that a certain response achieves a desired goal or satisfies a need, the success of this cue-response pattern will be remembered. The probability of responding in a like manner to the same or similar situation in the future is increased. In other words, the response has a higher probability of being repeated when the need and cue appear together again, and thus it can be said that learning has taken place. Frequent reinforcement increases the habit potential of the particular response. Likewise, if a response does not satisfy the need adequately, the probability that the same response will be repeated is reduced.

For some marketers this means that if an individual finds that a particular product fulfills the need for which it was purchased, the probability is high that the individual will repurchase the product the next time the need arises. The firm's promotional efforts often act as the cue. If an individual repeatedly purchases a product with favorable results, loyalty may develop toward the particular product or brand. This loyalty can result in habitual purchases, and such habits are often extremely difficult for competing firms to alter.

Although many studies in the area of buyer behavior center on the buyer's attitudes, motives, and behavior before and during the purchase decision, behavior after the purchase has also been studied. Specifically, studies have been undertaken to investigate postpurchase dissonance, as well as postpurchase satisfaction.

The occurrence of postdecision dissonance is related to the concept of *cognitive dissonance*. This theory states that there is often a lack of consistency or harmony among an individual's various cognitions, or attitudes and beliefs, after a decision has been made—that is, the individual has doubts and second thoughts about the choice made. Further, it is more likely that the intensity of the anxiety will be greater when any of the following conditions exist:

1. The decision is an important one psychologically or financially, or both.
2. There are a number of forgone alternatives.
3. The forgone alternatives have many favorable features.

Influencing Factor	Increasing the Influencing Factor Causes the Search to:
I. Market characteristics	
A. Number of alternatives	Increase
B. Price range	Increase
C. Store concentration	Increase
D. Information availability	Increase
1. Advertising	
2. Point-of-purchase	
3. Sales personnel	
4. Packaging	
5. Experienced consumers	
6. Independent sources	
II. Product characteristics	
A. Price	Increase
B. Differentiation	Increase
C. Positive products	Increase
III. Consumer characteristics	
A. Learning and experience	Decrease
B. Shopping orientation	Mixed
C. Social status	Increase
D. Age and household life cycle	Mixed
E. Product involvement	Mixed
F. Perceived risk	Increase
IV. Situational characteristics	
A. Time availability	Increase
B. Purchase for self	Decrease
C. Pleasant surroundings	Increase
D. Social surroundings	Mixed
E. Physical/mental energy	Increase

Source: Del I. Hawkins, David L. Mothersbaugh, and Roger Best, *Consumer Behavior: Building Marketing Strategy*, 10th ed. (Burr Ridge, IL: Irwin/McGraw-Hill, 2007), p. 548.

These factors can relate to many buying decisions. For example, postpurchase dissonance might be expected to be present among many purchasers of such products as automobiles, major appliances, and homes. In these cases, the decision to purchase is usually an important one both financially and psychologically, and a number of favorable alternatives are usually available.

These findings have much relevance for marketers. In a buying situation, when a purchaser becomes dissonant, it is reasonable to predict such a person would be highly receptive to advertising and sales promotion that support the purchase decision. Such communication presents favorable aspects of the product and can be useful in reinforcing the buyer's wish to believe that a wise purchase decision was made. For example, purchasers of major appliances or automobiles might be given a phone call or sent a letter reassuring them that they have made a wise purchase.

As noted, researchers have also studied postpurchase consumer satisfaction. Much of this work has been based on what is called the *disconfirmation paradigm*. Basically, this approach views satisfaction with products and brands as a result of two other variables.

53

The first variable is the expectations a consumer has about a product before purchase. These expectations concern the beliefs the consumer has about the product's performance.

The second variable is the difference between expectations and postpurchase perceptions of how the product actually performed. If the product performed as well as expected or better than expected, the consumer will be satisfied with the product. If the product performed worse than expected, the consumer will be dissatisfied with it.

One implication of this view for marketers is that care must be taken not to raise prepurchase expectations to such a level that the product cannot possibly meet them. Rather, it is important to create positive expectations consistent with the product's likely performance.[11]

Conclusion

This chapter presented an overview of consumer behavior. Social, marketing, and situational influences on consumer decision making were discussed first, followed by a discussion of two important psychological factors: product knowledge and product involvement. Consumer decision making, which can be extensive, limited, or routine, was viewed as a series of stages: need recognition, alternative search, alternative evaluation, purchase decision, and postpurchase evaluation. Clearly, understanding consumer behavior is a prerequisite for developing successful marketing strategies.

Additional Readings

Blackwell, Rodger D., Paul W. Miniard, and James F. Engel. *Consumer Behavior.* 10th ed. Mason, OH: Thomson South-Western, 2006.

Hawkins, Del I.; David L. Mothersbaugh; and Roger J. Best. *Consumer Behavior: Building Marketing Strategy,* 10th ed. Burr Ridge, IL: McGraw-Hill/Irwin, 2007.

Hoyer, Wayne D., and Deborah J. MacInnis. *Consumer Behavior.* 4th ed. Boston: Houghton Mifflin, 2007.

Peter, J. Paul and Jerry C. Olson. *Consumer Behavior and Marketing Strategy.* 8th ed. Burr Ridge, IL: McGraw-Hill/Irwin, 2008.

Schiffman, Leon G., and Leslie Kanuck. *Consumer Behavior.* 9th ed. Englewood Cliffs, NJ: Prentice Hall, 2007.

Solomon, Michael R. *Consumer Behavior,* 7th ed. Boston: Allyn & Bacon, 2007.

Chapter 4

Business, Government, and Institutional Buying

In the previous chapter we discussed consumer behavior and the decision-making process used to purchase products and services. However, final consumers are not the only purchasers of products and services. Rather, businesses, government agencies, and other institutions buy products and services to maintain their organizations and achieve their organizational objectives. These organizations are major customers for many marketers. In this chapter we discuss the nature of these organizations and offer a general model of the buying process for them. The chapter begins by discussing four categories of organizational buyers and then presents an overview of the organizational buying process.

Categories of Organizational Buyers

Organizational buyers can be classified in many ways. For example, the U.S. government classifies organizations in similar lines of business in the North American Industry Classification System (NAICS, pronounced "knacks"). NAICS provides information about the number of establishments, sales volume, and number of employees in each industry broken down by geographic area. Information on NAICS codes is available online at www.naics.com. In addition, a commercial source, Dun's Business Locator, provides information on over 10 million U.S. businesses. Both of these can provide useful information for organizational marketers seeking organizational buyers. However, for the purpose of this text, it is useful to classify organizational buyers into four categories: These include producers, intermediaries, government agencies, and other institutions. Taken collectively, marketing to producers and intermediaries is called *business-to-business* or *b2b marketing*. Business-to-business marketing has become a topic of increasing interest because it is the major area where Internet marketing has been done profitably.

Producers

These organizational buyers consist of businesses that buy goods and services in order to produce other goods and services for sale. For example, Dell Computer buys computer chips from Intel in order to make computers to be sold to consumers and other organizations. Producers are engaged in many different industries, ranging from agriculture to manufacturing, from construction to finance. Together they constitute the largest segment of organizational buyers. Producers of goods tend to be larger and more geographically concentrated than producers of services.

55

Intermediaries

Marketing intermediaries or resellers purchase products to resell at a profit. This group includes a number of types of resellers such as wholesalers (Grainger) and retailers (Wal-Mart) that buy products from manufacturers and distribute them to consumers and other organizational buyers. Intermediaries also purchase products and services to run their own businesses, such as office supplies and maintenance services. Given their importance to marketing, intermediaries will be discussed in detail in Chapter 10.

Government Agencies

In the United States, government agencies operate at the federal, state, and local levels; there are over 86,000 governmental agencies in this country that purchase machinery, equipment, facilities, supplies, and services. Government agencies account for trillions of dollars worth of buying, and over half of this amount represents purchases by the federal government, making it the world's biggest customer. The governments of other countries also are huge customers for marketers. Marketing to government agencies can be complex since they often have strict purchasing policies and regulations.

Other Institutions

Besides businesses and government agencies, marketers also sell products and services to a variety of other institutions, such as hospitals, museums, universities, nursing homes, and churches. Many of these are nonprofit organizations that purchase products and services to maintain their operations and serve their clientele.

The Organizational Buying Process

Regardless of the type of organization, a buying process is needed to ensure that products and services are purchased and received in a timely and efficient manner. In general, organizations develop a buying process to serve their purchasing needs. Figure 4.1 presents a model of organizational buying that represents some of the common influences and stages in the process.

FIGURE 4.1   **A Model of the Organizational Buying Process**

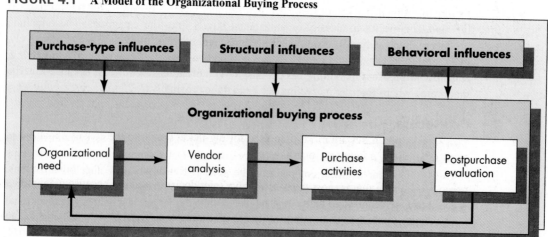

Purchase-Type Influences on Organizational Buying

A major consideration that affects the organizational buying process is the complexity of the purchase that is to be made. Three types of organizational purchase based on their degree of complexity include the straight rebuy, modified rebuy, and new task purchase.[1]

Straight Rebuy

The simplest and most common type of purchase is called a *straight rebuy*. This type of purchase involves routinely reordering from the same supplier a product that has been purchased in the past. Organizations use a straight rebuy when they are experienced at buying the product, have an ongoing need for it, and have regular suppliers of it. In many cases, organizations have computer systems that automatically reorder certain commonly used products. Organizations use this simple approach to purchasing because it is fast and requires relatively few employees.

Straight rebuys are common among organizations that practice *just-in-time inventory*, which is a system of replenishing parts or goods for resale just before they are needed. Such buyers do not have time to hunt around for potential suppliers and solicit bids. Instead they regularly place their orders with a supplier whose quality and timely delivery can be counted on. If a supplier delivers items that are late or of unacceptable quality, these buyers will not have a reserve in inventory to draw on. Therefore, organizations that use just-in-time inventory tend to favor suppliers with a strong commitment to quality.

To retain customers who use straight rebuys, the marketer needs to maintain high-quality products and reliable service so that the customers will continue to be satisfied with their purchases.

Modified Rebuy

When some aspects of the buying situation are unfamiliar, the organization will use a *modified rebuy*. This type of purchase involves considering a limited number of alternatives before making a selection. Organizational buyers follow this approach rather than a straight rebuy when a routine purchase changes in some way; for example, a supplier discontinues a product or stops satisfying the customer, the price of a usual product rises, or a new product becomes available to meet the same need.

In such situations, the organizational buyer considers the new information and decides what changes to make. If the change proves satisfactory and the product is one needed routinely, the buyer may then make it a straight rebuy. Marketers seek to win new organizational customers by giving them reasons to change from a straight rebuy to a modified rebuy in which the marketer's products are considered.

New Task Purchase

Organizations purchase some products only occasionally, especially in the case of large investments such as machinery, equipment, and real estate. In these cases, the organization may use a *new task purchase*. This type of purchase involves an extensive search for information and a formal decision process.

New task purchases are most often used for big-ticket items, so the cost of a mistake is great. Therefore, a new task purchase is time consuming and involves a relatively large number of decision makers, who may consider many alternatives. This is the type of purchase decision that is most likely to involve joint decision making because many kinds of expertise are required to make the best decision.

A new task purchase is an opportunity for the marketer to learn about the needs of the organizations in its target market and to discuss ways to meet organizational needs, such as

FIGURE 4.2   Differences in Types of Organizational Purchases

Purchase Type	Complexity	Time Frame	Number of Suppliers	Applications
Straight rebuy	Simple	Short	One	Frequently purchased, routine products, such as printer paper and toner.
Modified rebuy	Moderate	Medium	Few	Routine purchase that has changed in some way, such as air travel (new fares, flights, destinations).
New task purchase	Complex	Long	Many	Expensive, seldom-purchased products, such as a new location for a department store.

through the use of new products and technology. Figure 4.2 summarizes the differences in the three types of purchases.

Structural Influences on Organizational Buying

The term *structural influences* refers to the design of the organizational environment and how it affects the purchasing process. Three important structural influences on organizational buying are purchasing roles, organization-specific factors, and purchasing policies and procedures.

— Purchasing Roles

It is common in organizational buying for purchases to be made cross-functionally with representatives from different functional departments playing various roles in the process. Taken collectively, these are called the *buying center* and include the following roles:

1. *Initiators,* who start the purchasing process by recognizing a need or problem in the organization. For example, an executive might see a need for faster computers.

2. *Users,* who are the people in the organization who actually use the product, for example, an assistant who would use a new word processor.

3. *Influencers,* who affect the buying decision, usually by helping define the specifications for what is bought. For example, an information systems manager would be a key influencer in the purchase of a new computer system.

4. *Buyers,* who have the formal authority and responsibility to select the supplier and negotiate the terms of the contract. For example, in the purchase of a computer system, the *purchasing agent* would likely perform this role.

5. *Deciders,* who have the formal or informal power to select or approve the supplier that receives the contract. For important technical purchases, deciders may come from R&D, engineering, or quality control.

6. *Gatekeepers,* who control the flow of information in the buying center. Purchasing personnel, technical experts, and assistants can all keep marketers and their information from reaching people performing the other four roles.[2]

When several persons are involved in the organizational purchase decision, marketers may need to use a variety of means to reach each individual or group. Fortunately, it is often easy to find which individuals in organizations are involved in a purchase because such information is provided to suppliers. Organizations do this because it makes suppliers more knowledgeable about purchasing practices, thus making the purchasing process more efficient.[3] Also, a number of firms have developed closer channel relationships that facilitate these transactions.

How Marketing to Organizational Buyers Differs	Example
More variation in buyer–seller relationships	Relationships can be deep and involve several layers of the industry: BASF partners with Gaskell and GM, for example.
Shorter distribution channels	BASF sells fibers *directly* to DuPont for the manufacture of carpet; through distributors to smaller companies. Consumer goods sold through distributors, wholesalers, and retailers.
Greater emphasis on personal selling	BASF salespeople work directly with fire departments to sell the latest fire-fighting chemicals and ensure that they are used properly.
Greater Web integration	BASF uses its *cc-markets* Web site to create a communication space with special customers.
Unique promotional strategies	BASF exhibits at trade shows such as Powder Coatings Europe, a show held every January in Amsterdam.

Source: F. Robert Dwyer and John F. Tanner, *Business Marketing,* 3rd ed. (Burr Ridge, IL: McGraw-Hill/Irwin, 2006), p. 10.

Organization-Specific Factors

Three primary organization-specific factors influence the purchasing process: orientation, size, and degree of centralization. First, in terms of orientation, the dominant function in an organization may control purchasing decisions. For example, if the organization is technology oriented, it is likely to be dominated by engineering personnel, who will make buying decisions. Similarly, if the organization is production oriented, production personnel may dominate buying decisions.

Second, the size of the organization may influence the purchasing process. If the organization is large, it will likely have a high degree of joint decision making for other than straight rebuys. Smaller organizations are likely to have more autonomous decision making.

Finally, the degree of centralization of an organization influences whether decisions are made individually or jointly with others. Organizations that are highly centralized are less likely to have joint decision making. Thus, a privately owned, small company with technology or production orientations will tend toward autonomous decision making, while a large-scale public corporation with considerable decentralization will tend to have greater joint decision making.

Purchasing Policies and Procedures

Organizations typically develop a number of policies and procedures for various types of purchases. These policies and procedures are designed to ensure that the appropriate products and services are purchased efficiently and that responsibility for buying is assigned appropriately. Often a purchasing department will be assigned the task of centralized buying for the whole organization, and individuals within this department will have authority to purchase particular types of products and services in a given price range.

A current trend in many organizations is *sole sourcing,* in which all of a particular type of product is purchased from a single supplier. Sole sourcing has become more popular because organizational buyers have become more concerned with quality and timely delivery and less likely to purchase only on the basis of price. Sole sourcing is advantageous for suppliers because it provides them with predictable and profitable demand and allows them to build long-term relationships with organizational buyers. It is advantageous for organizational buyers because it not only increases timely delivery and quality of supplies but also allows the buyers to work more closely with suppliers to develop superior products that meet their needs and those of their customers. The use of sole sourcing also simplifies the buying process and can make what were formerly modified rebuys into simpler straight rebuys.

Of course, many organizational purchases are more complicated and require policies and procedures to direct the buying process. In many cases, organizations will develop a list of approved vendors from which buyers have authorization to purchase particular products. The buyer's responsibility is to select the vendor that will provide the appropriate levels of quality and service at the lowest cost. These policies and procedures also specify what positions in the purchasing department or buying center have authority to make purchases of different types and dollar amounts.

For large one-time projects, such as the construction of a building, organizations may seek competitive bids for part or all of the project. The development of policies and procedures for handling such purchases is usually complex and involves a number of criteria and committees.

Behavioral Influences on Organizational Buying

Organizational buyers are influenced by a variety of psychological and social factors. We will discuss two of these, personal motivations and role perceptions.

Personal Motivations

Organizational buyers are, of course, subject to the same personal motives or motivational forces as other individuals. Although these buyers may emphasize nonpersonal motives in their buying activities, it has been found that organizational buyers often are influenced by such personal factors as friendship, professional pride, fear and uncertainty (risk), trust, and personal ambitions in their buying activities.

For example, professional pride often expresses itself through efforts to attain status in the firm. One way to achieve this might be to initiate or influence the purchase of goods that will demonstrate a buyer's value to the organization. If new materials, equipment, or components result in cost savings or increased profits, the individuals initiating the changes have demonstrated their value at the same time. Fear and uncertainty are strong motivational forces on organizational buyers, and reduction of risk is often important to them. This can have a strong influence on purchase behavior. Marketers should understand the relative strength of personal gain versus risk-reducing motives and emphasize the more important motives when dealing with buyers.

Thus, in examining buyer motivations, it is necessary to consider both personal and nonpersonal motivational forces and to recognize that the relative importance of each is not a fixed quantity. It will vary with the nature of the product, the climate within the organization, and the relative strength of the two forces in the particular buyer.

Role Perceptions

A final factor that influences organizational buyers is their own perception of their role. The manner in which individuals behave depends on their perception of their role, their commitment to what they believe is expected of their role, the "maturity" of the role type, and the extent to which the institution is committed to the role type.

Different buyers will have different degrees of commitment to their buying role, which will cause variations in role behavior from one buyer to the next. By *commitment* we mean willingness to perform their job in the manner expected by the organization. For example, some buyers seek to take charge in their role as buyer and have little commitment to company

1. Is the need or problem pressing enough that it must be acted on now? If not, how long can action be deferred?
2. What types of products or services could conceivably be used to solve our need or problem?
3. Should we make the item ourselves?
4. Must a new product be designed, or has a vendor already developed an acceptable product?
5. Should a value analysis be performed?
6. What is the highest price we can afford to pay?
7. What trade-offs are we prepared to make between price and other product/vendor attributes?
8. Which information sources will we rely on?
9. How many vendors should be considered?
10. Which attributes will be stressed in evaluating vendors?
11. Should bids be solicited?
12. Should the item be leased or purchased outright?
13. How far can a given vendor be pushed in negotiations? On what issues will that vendor bend the most?
14. How much inventory should a vendor be willing to keep on hand?
15. Should we split our order among several vendors?
16. Is a long-term contract in our interest?
17. What contractual guarantees will we require?
18. How shall we establish our order routine?
19. After the purchase, how will vendor performance be evaluated?
20. How will we deal with inadequate product or vendor performance?

Source: Michael H. Morris, Leyland F. Pitt, and Earl D. Honeycutt, Jr., *Business-to-Business Marketing*, 3rd ed. (Thousand Oaks, CA: Sage Publications, 2001), p. 74.

expectations. The implication for marketers is that such buyers expect, even demand, that they be kept constantly advised of all new developments to enable them to more effectively shape their own role. On the other hand, other buyers may have no interest in prescribing their role activities and accept their role as given to them. Such a buyer is most concerned with merely implementing prescribed company activities and buying policies with sanctioned products. Thus, some buyers will be highly committed to play the role the firm dictates (i.e., the formal organization's perception of their role), while others might be extremely innovative and uncommitted to the expected role performance. Obviously, roles may be heavily influenced by the organizational climate existing in the particular organization.[4]

Organizations can be divided into three groups based on differences in degree of employee commitment. These groups include innovative, adaptive, and lethargic firms. In *innovative firms,* individuals approach their occupational roles with a weak commitment to expected norms of behavior. In an *adaptive organization,* there is a moderate commitment. In a *lethargic organization,* individuals express a strong commitment to traditionally accepted behavior and behave accordingly. Thus, a buyer in a lethargic firm would probably be less innovative in order to maintain acceptance and status within the organization and would keep conflict within the firm to a minimum.

Buyers' perception of their role may differ from the perception of their role held by others in the organization. This difference can result in variance in perception of the actual purchase

1. Avoid the intent and appearance of unethical or compromising practice in relationships, actions, and communications.

2. Demonstrate loyalty to the employer by diligently following the lawful instructions of the employer, using reasonable care and only the authority granted.

3. Refrain from any private or professional business activity that would create a conflict between personal interests and the interests of the employer.

4. Refrain from soliciting or accepting money, loans, credits, or prejudicial discounts and the acceptance of gifts, entertainment, favors, or services from past or potential suppliers that might influence or appear to influence purchasing decisions.

5. Handle confidential or proprietary information belonging to employers or suppliers with due care and proper consideration of ethical and legal ramifications and government regulations.

6. Promote positive supplier relationships through courtesy and impartiality throughout all phases of the purchasing cycle.

7. Refrain from reciprocal agreements that restrain competition.

8. Know and obey the letter and spirit of laws governing the purchasing function and remain alert to the legal ramifications of purchasing decisions.

9. Encourage all segments of society to participate by demonstrating support for small, disadvantaged, and minority-owned businesses.

10. Discourage purchasing's involvement in employer-sponsored programs of personal purchases that are not business related.

11. Enhance the proficiency and stature of the purchasing profession by acquiring and maintaining current technical knowledge and the highest standards of ethical behavior.

12. Conduct international purchasing in accordance with the laws, customs, and practices of foreign countries, consistent with U.S. laws, your organization's policies, and these Ethical Standards and Guidelines.

Source: Institute for Supply Management as reported in F. Robert Dwyer and John F. Tanner, *Business Marketing,* 3rd ed. (Burr Ridge, IL: McGraw-Hill/Irwin, 2006), p. 85.

responsibility held by the buyer. One study involving purchasing agents revealed that, in every firm included in the study, the purchasing agents believed they had more responsibility and control over certain decisions than the other influential purchase decision makers in the firm perceived them as having. The decisions were (1) designing the product, (2) setting a cost for the product, (3) determining performance life, (4) naming a specific supplier, (5) assessing the amount of engineering help available from the supplier, and (6) reducing rejects. This variance in role perception held true regardless of the size of the firm or the significance of the item purchased to the overall success of the firm. It is important, therefore, that the marketer be aware that such perceptual differences may exist and to determine as accurately as possible the amount of control and responsibility over purchasing decisions held by each purchase decision influencer in the firm.

Stages in the Organizational Buying Process

As with consumer buying, most organizational purchases are made in response to a particular need or problem. Ideally, the products or services purchased will meet the organizational need and improve the organization's efficiency, effectiveness, and profits. The organizational buying process can be analyzed as a series of four stages: organizational need, vendor analysis, purchase activities, and postpurchase evaluation.

Organizational Need

Organizations have many needs for products and services to help them survive and meet their objectives. For example, a manufacturer may need to purchase new machinery to increase its production capacity and meet demand; a retailer may need to purchase services from a marketing research firm to better understand its market; a government agency may need to purchase faster computers to keep up with growing demand for its services; a hospital may need to purchase more comfortable beds for its patients. Recognizing these needs, and a willingness and ability to meet them, often results in organizational purchases. For straight rebuys, the purchase process may involve little more than a phone call or a few clicks on a computer to order products and arrange payment and delivery. For modified rebuys or new task purchases, the process may be much more complex.

Vendor Analysis

Organizational buyers must search for, locate, and evaluate vendors of products and services to meet their needs. Searching for and locating vendors is often easy since they frequently make sales calls on organizations that might need their products. Vendors also advertise in trade magazines or on the Internet and have displays at industry trade shows to increase their visibility to organizational buyers. For products and services that the organization has previously purchased, the organization may already have developed a list of approved vendors.

Organizational buyers often use a vendor analysis to evaluate possible suppliers. A *vendor analysis* is the process by which buyers rate each potential supplier on various performance measures such as product quality, on-time delivery, price, payment terms, and use of modern technology. Figure 4.3 presents a sample vendor analysis form that lists a number of purchase criteria and the weights one organization used to compare potential suppliers.

A formal vendor analysis can be used for at least three purposes. First, it can be used to develop a list of approved vendors, all of which provide acceptable levels of products and services. Organizational buyers can then select any company on the list, simplifying the purchase process. Second, a vendor analysis could be used to compare competing vendors; the buyers then select the best one on the basis of the ratings. This could help the organization pare down vendors to a single supplier for which a long-term, sole-sourcing relationship could be developed. Third, a vendor analysis can be done both before and after purchases to compare performance on evaluation criteria and evaluate the process of vendor selection.

Purchase Activities

Straight rebuys may involve a quick order to an approved vendor or sole-source supplier. However, other types of organizational purchases can involve long time periods with extensive negotiations on price and terms and formal contracts stating quality, delivery, and service criteria. The complexity of the product or service, the number of suppliers available, the importance of the product to the buying organization, and pricing all influence the number of purchase activities to be performed and their difficulty. For example, an airline buying a fleet of jumbo jets or a car rental agency buying a fleet of cars may take months or years to negotiate and make purchases. While such buyers may have considerable leverage in negotiating, it should be remembered that these organizations need the products just as badly as the sellers need to sell them. Thus, there is often more collaboration among organizational buyers and sellers than in the consumer market.

Postpurchase Evaluation

Organizational buyers must evaluate both the vendors and the products they purchase to determine whether the products are acceptable for future purchases or whether other

FIGURE 4.3   **Sample Vendor Analysis Form**

Supplier Name: _____   Type of Product: _____

Shipping Location: _____   Annual Sales Dollars: _____

	5 Excellent	4 Good	3 Satisfactory	2 Fair	1 Poor	0 N/A
Quality (45%)						
Defect rates						
Quality of sample	—	—	—	—	—	—
Conformance with quality program	—	—	—	—	—	—
Responsiveness to quality problems	—	—	—	—	—	—
Overall quality	—	—	—	—	—	—
Delivery (25%)						
Avoidance of late shipments						
Ability to expand production	—	—	—	—	—	—
Performance in sample delivery	—	—	—	—	—	—
Response to changes in order size	—	—	—	—	—	—
Overall delivery	—	—	—	—	—	—
Price (20%)						
Price competitiveness						
Payment terms	—	—	—	—	—	—
Absorption of costs	—	—	—	—	—	—
Submission of cost savings plans	—	—	—	—	—	—
Overall price	—	—	—	—	—	—
Technology (10%)						
State-of-the-art components						
Sharing research & development capability	—	—	—	—	—	—
Ability and willingness to help with design	—	—	—	—	—	—
Responsiveness to engineering problems	—	—	—	—	—	—
Overall technology	—	—	—	—	—	—

Buyer: _____   Date: _____

Comments: _____

sources of supply should be found. A comparison of the performance of the vendor and products with the criteria listed on the prior vendor analysis can be useful for this purpose. If the purchase process goes smoothly and products meet price and quality criteria, then the vendor may be put on the approved list or perhaps further negotiations can be made to sole-source with the supplier.

One problem in judging the acceptability of suppliers and products is that different functional areas may have different evaluation criteria. Figure 4.4 presents several functional areas of a manufacturing company and their common concerns in purchasing. Clearly, these concerns should be considered both prior to purchasing from a particular supplier and after purchasing to ensure that every area's needs are being met as well as possible.

FIGURE 4.4
Functional Areas and Their Key Concerns in Organizational Buying

Source: Michael H. Morris, Leyland F. Pitt, and Earl D. Honeycutt, Jr., *Business-to-Business Marketing*, 3rd ed. (Thousand Oaks, CA: Sage Publications, 2001), p. 66.

Functional Areas	Key Concerns
Design and development engineering	Name reputation of vendor; ability of vendors to meet design specifications.
Production	Delivery and reliability of purchases such that interruption of production schedules is minimized.
Sales/marketing	Impact of purchased items on marketability of the company's products.
Maintenance	Degree to which purchased items are compatible with existing facilities and equipment; maintenance service offered by vendor; installation arrangements offered by vendor.
Finance/accounting	Effects of purchases on cash flow, balance sheet, and income statement positions; variances in costs of materials over estimates; feasibility of make-or-buy and lease options to purchasing.
Purchasing	Obtaining lowest possible price at acceptable quality levels; maintaining good relations with vendors.
Quality control	Assurance that purchased items meet prescribed specifications and tolerances, governmental regulations, and customer requirements.

Conclusion

Organizational buyers include individuals involved in purchasing products and services for businesses, government agencies, and other institutions and agencies. The organizational buying process is influenced by whether the purchase is a straight rebuy, modified rebuy, or new task purchase. It is also influenced by people in various purchasing roles, the orientation, size, and degree of centralization of the organization, the organization's purchasing policies and procedures, and individuals' motivations and perceived roles. The organizational buying process can be viewed as a series of four stages ranging from organizational need, to vendor analysis, to purchase activities, to postpurchase evaluation. It is important that companies marketing to organizations understand the influences and process by which organizations buy products and services so their needs can be met fully and profitably.

Additional Readings

Anderson, James C., and James A. Narus. *Business Marketing Management.* 2nd ed. Upper Saddle River, NJ: Prentice Hall, 2004.

Brennan, Ross; Louise E. Canning, and Raymond McDowell. *Business-to-Business Marketing.* Thousand Oaks, CA: Sage, 2007.

Dwyer, F. Robert, and John F. Tanner. *Business Marketing.* 3rd ed. Burr Ridge, IL: McGraw-Hill/Irwin, 2006.

Hutt, Michael D., and Thomas W. Speh. *Business Marketing Management: B2B.* 9th ed. Mason, OH: Thomson South-Western, 2007.

Chapter 5

Market Segmentation

Market segmentation is one of the most important concepts in marketing. In fact, a primary reason for studying consumer and organizational buyer behavior is to provide bases for effective segmentation, and a large portion of marketing research is concerned with segmentation. From a marketing management point of view, selection of the appropriate target market is paramount to developing successful marketing programs.

The logic of market segmentation is quite simple and is based on the idea that a single product item can seldom meet the needs and wants of *all* consumers. Typically, consumers vary as to their needs, wants, and preferences for products and services, and successful marketers adapt their marketing programs to fulfill these preference patterns. For example, even a simple product like chewing gum has multiple flavors, package sizes, sugar contents, calories, consistencies (e.g., liquid centers), and colors to meet the preferences of various consumers. While a single product item cannot meet the needs of all consumers, it can almost always serve more than one consumer. Thus, there are usually *groups of consumers* who can be served well by a single item. If a particular group can be served *profitably* by a firm, it is a viable market segment. In other words, the firm should develop a marketing mix to serve the group or market segment.

 In this chapter we consider the process of market segmentation. We define *market segmentation* as the process of dividing a market into groups of similar consumers and selecting the most appropriate group(s) for the firm to serve. The group or market segment that a company selects to focus on is called a *target market*. We break down the process of market segmentation into six steps, as shown in Figure 5.1. While we recognize that the order of these steps may vary, depending on the firm and situation, there are few if any times when market segmentation analysis can be ignored. In fact, even if the final decision is to "mass market" and not segment at all, this decision should be reached only *after* a market segmentation analysis has been conducted. Thus, market segmentation analysis is a cornerstone of sound marketing planning and decision making.

Delineate the Firm's Current Situation

As emphasized in Chapter 1, a firm must do a complete situational analysis when embarking on a new or modified marketing program. At the marketing planning level, such an analysis aids in determining objectives, opportunities, and constraints to be considered when selecting target markets and developing marketing mixes. In addition, marketing managers must have a clear idea of the amount of financial and other resources that will be available for developing and executing a marketing plan. Thus, the inclusion of this first step in the market segmentation process is intended to be a reminder of tasks to be performed prior to marketing planning.

FIGURE 5.1
A Model of the
Market Segmentation
Process

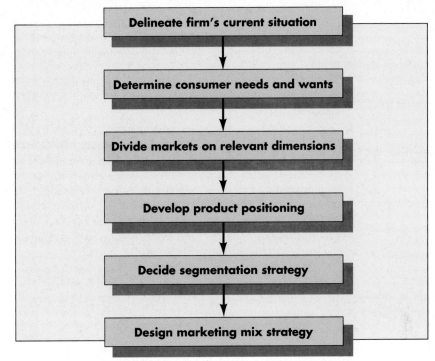

Determine Consumer Needs and Wants

As emphasized throughout this text, successful marketing strategies depend on discovering and satisfying consumer needs and wants. In some cases, this idea is quite operational. To illustrate, suppose a firm has a good deal of venture capital and is seeking to diversify its interest into new markets. A firm in this situation may seek to discover a broad variety of unsatisfied needs. However, in most situations, the industry in which the firm operates specifies the boundaries of a firm's need satisfaction activities. For example, a firm in the communication industry may seek more efficient methods for serving consumers' long-distance telephone needs.

As a practical matter, new technology often brings about an investigation of consumer needs and wants for new or modified products and services. In these situations, the firm is seeking the group of consumers whose needs could best be satisfied by the new or modified product. Further, at a strategic level, consumer needs and wants usually are translated into more operational concepts. For instance, consumer attitudes, preferences, and benefits sought, which are determined through marketing research, are commonly used for segmentation purposes.

Divide Markets on Relevant Dimensions

In a narrow sense, this step is often considered to be the whole of market segmentation (i.e., consumers are grouped on the basis of one or more similarities and treated as a homogeneous segment of a heterogeneous total market). Three important questions should be considered here:

1. Should the segmentation be a priori or post hoc?
2. How does one determine the relevant dimensions or bases to use for segmentation?
3. What are some bases for segmenting consumer and organizational buyer markets?

1. Slower rates of market growth, coupled with increased foreign competition, have fostered more competition, increasing the need to identify target markets with unique needs.

2. Social and economic forces, including expanding media, increased educational levels, and general world awareness, have produced customers with more varied and sophisticated needs, tastes, and lifestyles.

3. Technological advances make it possible for marketers to devise marketing programs that focus efficiently on precisely defined segments of the market.

4. Marketers now find that minority buyers do not necessarily adopt the social and economic habits of the mainstream. For example, many Hispanics speak both Spanish and English and retain much of their culture even as they adapt to U.S. lifestyles, while many others remain in Spanish-speaking enclaves in Hispanic states like Texas and California.

5. Roughly 4 in 10 residents in the United States identify with some segment or niche group that does not reflect the white, heterosexual consumer that historically defined the marketing mainstream.

Source: William O. Bearden, Thomas N. Ingram and Raymond W. LaForge, *Marketing,* Burr Ridge, IL: McGraw-Hill/Irwin, 2007, p. 155.

A Priori versus Post Hoc Segmentation

Real-world segmentation has followed one of two general patterns. An *a priori segmentation* approach is one in which the marketing manager has decided on the appropriate basis for segmentation in advance of doing any research on a market. For example, a manager may decide that a market should be divided on the basis of whether people are nonusers, light users, or heavy users of a particular product. Segmentation research is then conducted to determine the size of each of these groups and their demographic or psychographic profiles.

Post hoc segmentation is an approach in which people are grouped into segments on the basis of research findings. For example, people interviewed concerning their attitudes or benefits sought in a particular product category are grouped according to their responses. The size of each of these groups and their demographic and psychographic profiles are then determined.

Both of these approaches are valuable, and the question of which to use depends in part on how well the firm knows the market for a particular product class. If through previous research and experience a marketing manager has successfully isolated a number of key market dimensions, then an a priori approach based on them may provide more useful information. In the case of segmentation for entirely new products, a post hoc approach may be useful for determining key market dimensions. However, even when using a post hoc approach, some consideration must be given to the variables to be included in the research design. Thus, some consideration must be given to the relevant segmentation dimensions regardless of which approach is used.

Relevance of Segmentation Dimensions

Unfortunately, there is no simple solution for determining the relevant dimensions for segmenting markets. Certainly, managerial expertise and experience are needed for selecting the appropriate dimensions or bases on which to segment particular markets. In most cases, however, at least some initial dimensions can be determined from previous research, purchase trends, and managerial judgment. For instance, suppose we wish to segment the market for all-terrain vehicles. Clearly, several dimensions come to mind for initial consideration, including sex (male), age (18 to 35 years), lifestyle (outdoorsman), and income level (perhaps $30,000 to $80,000). At a minimum, these variables should be included in subsequent segmentation research. Of course, the most market-oriented approach to segmentation is on the basis of what benefits the potential consumer is seeking. Thus, consideration and research of sought benefits are a strongly recommended approach in the marketing literature. This approach will be considered in some detail in the following section.

Bases for Segmentation

A number of useful bases for segmenting consumer and organizational markets are presented in Figure 5.2. This is by no means a complete list of possible segmentation variables but represents some useful bases and categories. Two commonly used approaches for segmenting markets include benefit segmentation and psychographic segmentation. We will discuss these two in some detail. We will also discuss geodemographic segmentation, a recent development with a number of advantages for marketers.

Benefit Segmentation

The belief underlying this segmentation approach is that the benefits people are seeking in consuming a given product are the basic reasons for the existence of true market segments.[1] Thus, this approach attempts to measure consumer value systems and consumer perceptions of various brands in a product class. To illustrate, Russell Haley provided the classic example of a benefit segmentation in terms of the toothpaste market. Haley identified five basic segments, which are presented in Figure 5.3. Haley argued that this segmentation could be very useful for selecting advertising copy, media, commercial length, packaging, and new product design. For example, colorful packages might be appropriate for the sensory segment, perhaps aqua (to indicate fluoride) for the worrier group, and gleaming white for the social segment because of this segment's interest in white teeth.

Calantone and Sawyer also used a benefit segmentation approach to segment the market for bank services.[2] Their research was concerned with the question of whether benefit segments remain stable across time. While they found some stability in segments, there were some differences in attribute importance, size, and demographics at different times. Thus, they argue for ongoing benefit segmentation research to keep track of any changes in a market that might affect marketing strategy.

Benefit segmentation is clearly a market-oriented approach to segmentation that seeks to identify consumer needs and wants and to satisfy them by providing products and services with the desired benefits. It is clearly very consistent with the approach to marketing suggested by the marketing concept.

Psychographic Segmentation

Whereas benefit segmentation focuses on the benefits sought by the consumer, psychographic segmentation focuses on consumer lifestyles. Consumers are first asked a variety of questions about their lifestyles and then grouped on the basis of the similarity of their responses. Lifestyles are measured by asking consumers about their *activities* (work, hobbies, vacations), *interests* (family, job, community), and *opinions* (about social issues, politics, business). The activity, interest, and opinion (AIO) questions are very general in some studies but in others, at least some of the questions relate to specific products.[3]

FIGURE 5.2 Useful Segmentation Bases for Consumer and Organizational Buyer Markets

Consumer Markets

Segmentation Base	Examples of Market Segments
Geographic:	
Continents	Africa, Asia, Europe, North America, South America
Global regions	Southeast Asia, Mediterranean, Caribbean
Countries	China, Canada, France, United States, Brazil
Country regions	Pacific Northwest, Middle Atlantic, Midwest
City, county, or SMSA size	Under 5,000 people; 5,000–19,999, 20,000–49,999, 50,000–99,999; 100,000–249,999; 250,000–499,999; 500,000–999,999; 1,000,000 or over
Population density	Urban, suburban, rural
Climate	Tropical, temperate, cold
Demographic:	
Age	Under 6 years old, 6–12, 13–19, 20–29, 30–39, 40–49, 50–59, 60+
Gender	Male, female
Family size	1–2 persons, 3–4 persons, more than 4 persons
Family life cycle	Single, young married, married with children, sole survivor
Income	Under $10,000 per year, $10,000–$19,999, $20,000–$29,999, $30,000–$39,999, $40,000–$49,999, $50,000–59,999, $60,000–69,999, $70,000+
Education	Grade school or less, some high school, graduated from high school, some college, graduated from college, some graduate work, graduate degree
Marital status	Single, married, divorced, widowed
Social:	
Culture	American, Hispanic, African, Asian, European
Subculture	
Religion	Jewish, Catholic, Muslim, Mormon, Buddhist
Race	European American, Asian American, African American, Hispanic American
Nationality	French, Malaysian, Australian, Canadian, Japanese
Social class	Upper class, middle class, working class, lower class
Thoughts and feelings:	
Knowledge	Expert, novice
Involvement	High, medium, low
Attitude	Positive, neutral, negative
Benefits sought	Convenience, economy, prestige
Innovativeness	Innovator, early adopter, early majority, late majority, laggards, nonadopter
Readiness stage	Unaware, aware, interested, desirous, plan to purchase
Perceived risk	High, moderate, low
Behavior:	
Media usage	Newspaper, magazine, TV, Internet
Specific media usage	*Sports Illustrated, Cosmopolitan, Ebony*
Payment method	Cash, Visa, MasterCard, American Express, check
Loyalty status	None, some, total
Usage rate	Light, medium, heavy
User status	Nonuser, ex-user, current user, potential user
Usage situation	Work, home, vacation, commuting
Combined approaches:	
Psychographics	Achievers, strivers, strugglers
Person/situation	College students for lunch, executives for business dinner
Geodemography	Gray Power, Young Influentials, Blue-Chip Blues

Organizational Buyer Markets

Segmentation Base	Examples of Market Segments
Company size	Small, medium, large relative to industry
Purchase quantity	Small, medium, large account
Product application	Production, maintenance, product component
Organization type	Manufacturer, retailer, government agency, hospital
Location	North, south, east, west sales territory
Purchase status	New customer, occasional purchaser, frequent purchaser, nonpurchaser
Attribute importance	Price, service, reliability of supply

FIGURE 5.3   Toothpaste Market Benefit Segments

	Sensory Segment	Sociable Segment	Worrier Segment	Independent Segment
Principal benefit sought	Flavor and product appearance	Brightness of teeth	Decay prevention	Price
Demographic strengths	Children	Teens, young people	Large families	Men
Special behavioral characteristics	Users of spearmint-flavored toothpaste	Smokers	Heavy users	Heavy users
Brands disproportionately favored	Colgate	Macleans, Ultra Brite	Crest	Cheapest brand
Lifestyle characteristics	Hedonistic	Active	Conservative	Value-oriented

The best-known psychographic segmentation is called VALS™, formerly known as "The Values and Lifestyles Program." Originally developed in the 1970s, it has been redone several times to enhance its ability to explain changing lifestyles and predict consumer behavior. The current VALS system is based on psychological traits that are correlated with purchase behavior. VALS™ is a product of SRI Consulting Business Intelligence.

As shown in Figure 5.4, the VALS™ framework has eight psychographic groups arranged in a rectangle based on two dimensions in the U.S. system. (Japan VALS is

FIGURE 5.4   VALS™ Framework and Segments

Source: SRI Consulting Business Intelligence (SRIC-BI); www.sric-bi.com/VALS.

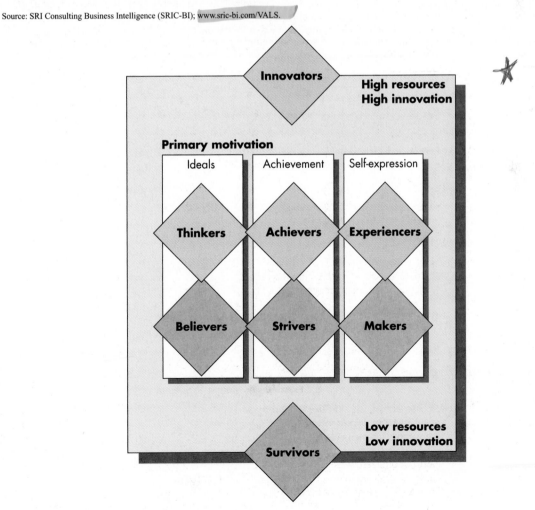

FIGURE 5.4   (continued)

Experiencers.   Experiencers are motivated by self-expression. As young, enthusiastic, and impulsive consumers, Experiencers quickly become enthusiastic about new possibilities but are equally quick to cool. They seek variety and excitement, savoring the new, the offbeat, and the risky. Their energy finds an outlet in exercise, sports, outdoor recreation, and social activities. Experiencers are avid consumers and spend a comparatively high proportion of their income on fashion, entertainment, and socializing. Their purchases reflect the emphasis they place on looking good and having "cool" stuff.

Believers.   Like Thinkers, Believers are motivated by ideals. They are conservative, conventional people with concrete beliefs based on traditional, established codes: family, religion, community, and the nation. Many Believers express moral codes that are deeply rooted and literally interpreted. They follow established routines, organized in large part around home, family, community, and social or religious organizations to which they belong. As consumers, Believers are predictable; they choose familiar products and established brands. They favor American products and are generally loyal customers.

Strivers.   Strivers are trendy and fun loving. Because they are motivated by achievement, Strivers are concerned about the opinions and approval of others. Money defines success for Strivers, who don't have enough of it to meet their desires. They favor stylish products that emulate the purchases of people with greater material wealth. Many see themselves as having a job rather than a career, and a lack of skills and focus often prevents them from moving ahead. Strivers are active consumers because shopping is both a social activity and an opportunity to demonstrate to peers their ability to buy. As consumers, they are as impulsive as their financial circumstance will allow.

Makers.   Like Experiencers, Makers are motivated by self-expression. They express themselves and experience the world by working on it—building a house, raising children, fixing a car, or canning vegetables—and have enough skill and energy to carry out their projects successfully. Makers are practical people who have constructive skills and value self-sufficiency. They live within a traditional context of family, practical work, and physical recreation and have little interest in what lies outside that context. Makers are suspicious of new ideas and large institutions such as big business. They are respectful of government authority and organized labor, but resentful of government intrusion on individual rights. They are unimpressed by material possessions other than those with a practical or functional purpose. Because they prefer value to luxury, they buy basic products.

You can find your VALS classification by filling out a questionnaire on the Internet. The Web address is www.sric-bi.com. The questionnaire takes about 10 minutes to complete, and your lifestyle will take about 10 seconds to compute. You will get a report that includes both your primary and secondary VALS type. The VALS Web site has a lot of information describing the program and different types of VALS segments.

optimized for Japanese consumers.) The vertical dimension segments people based on the degree to which they are innovative and have resources such as income, education, self-confidence, and energy. The horizontal dimension represents primary motivations and includes three different types. Consumers driven by knowledge and principles are motivated primarily by *ideals*. These consumers include the Thinkers and Believers groups. Consumers driven by a goal of demonstrating success to their peers are motivated primarily by *achievement*. These consumers include Achievers and Strivers. Consumers driven by a desire for social or physical activity, variety, and risk taking are motivated primarily by *self-expression*. These consumers include both the Experiencers and Makers. At the top of the rectangle are the Innovators, who have such high resources that they may express any of the three motivations. At the bottom of the rectangle are the Survivors, who live complacently and within their means without a strong primary consumer motivation. Figure 5.4 gives more details about each of the eight groups.[4]

Marketers can purchase research data that show which VALS™ groups are the primary buyers of specific products and services. This information can be used to better focus elements of the marketing mix, such as promotion, on the best target markets.

Geodemographic Segmentation

One problem with many segmentation approaches is that although they identify types or categories of consumers, they do not identify specific individuals or households within a market. Geodemographic segmentation identifies specific households in a market by focusing on local neighborhood geography (such as zip codes) to create classifications of actual, addressable, mappable neighborhoods where consumers live and shop.[5] One geodemographic system created by Claritas, Inc., is called PRIZM NE, which stands for consumers "Potential Ranking Index of ZIP Markets—New Evolution." The system classifies every U.S. neighborhood into one of 15 groups. Each of these groups is further divided into 3 to 6 segments, with a total of 66 distinct segments in this system. Each group and segment is based on zip codes, demographic information from the U.S. Census, and information on product use, media use, and lifestyle preferences. Figure 5.5 shows a sample group with five segments. The PRIZM NE system includes maps of different areas that rank neighborhoods on their potential to purchase specific products and services. The PRIZM NE segmentation is available on major marketing databases from leading providers such as ACNielsen, Arbitron, Gallup, IRI, J. D. Powers, Mediamark, and Nielsen Media Research.

The PRIZM NE system is based on the assumptions that consumers in particular neighborhoods are similar in many respects and that the best prospects are those who actually use a product or other consumers like them. Marketers use PRIZM NE to better understand consumers in various markets, what they are like, where they live, and how to reach them. These data help marketers with target market selection, direct marketing campaigns, site selection, media selection, and analysis of sales potential in various areas.

FIGURE 5.5   PRIZM NE Social Group U1—Urban Uptown

Source: www.claritas.com, April 1, 2006.

Group U1 – Urban Uptown

The five segments in Urban Uptown are home to the nation's wealthiest urban consumers. Members of this social group tend to be affluent to middle class, college educated and ethnically diverse, with above-average concentrations of Asian and Hispanic Americans. Although this group is diverse in terms of housing styles and family sizes, residents share an upscale urban perspective that's reflected in their marketplace choices. Urban Uptown consumers tend to frequent the arts, shop at exclusive retailers, drive luxury imports, travel abroad and spend heavily on computer and wireless technology.

The Urban Uptown group consists of the following segments:

- 04. Young Digerati
- 07. Money and Brains
- 16. Bohemian Mix
- 26. The Cosmopolitans
- 29. American Dreams

04. Young Digerati – Young Digerati are the nation's tech–savvy singles and couples living in fashionable neighborhoods on the urban fringe. Affluent, highly educated and ethnically mixed, Young Digerati communities are typically filled with trendy apartments and condos, fitness clubs and clothing boutiques, casual restaurants and all types of bars–from juice to coffee to microbrew.

07. Money and Brains – The residents of Money & Brains seem to have it all: high incomes, advanced degrees and sophisticated tastes to match their credentials. Many of these citydwellers–predominantly white with a high concentration of Asian Americans–are married couples with few children who live in fashionable homes on small, manicured lots.

16. Bohemian Mix – A collection of young, mobile urbanites, Bohemian Mix represents the nation's most liberal lifestyles. Its residents are a progressive mix of young singles and couples, students and professionals, Hispanics, Asians, African–Americans and whites. In their funky rowhouses and apartments, Bohemian Mixers are the early adopters who are quick to check out the latest movie, nightclub, laptop and microbrew.

26. The Cosmopolitans – These immigrants and descendants of multi–cultural backgrounds in multi-racial, multi-lingual neighborhoods typify the American Dream. Married couples, with and without children, as well as single parents are affluent from working hard at multiple trades and public service jobs. They have big families, which is unusual for social group U1.

29. American Dreams – American Dreams is a living example of how ethnically diverse the nation has become: more than half the residents are Hispanic, Asian or African-American. In these multilingual neighborhoods–one in ten speaks a language other than English–middle-aged immigrants and their children live in middle-class comfort.

Develop Product Positioning

By this time, the firm should have a good idea of the basic segments of the market that could potentially be satisfied with its product. The current step is concerned with positioning the product favorably in the minds of customers relative to competitive products. Several different positioning strategies can be used. First, products can be positioned by focusing on their superiority to competitive products based on one or more attributes. For example, a car could be positioned as less expensive (Hyundai), safer (Volvo), higher quality (Toyota), or more prestigious (Lexus) than other cars. Second, products can be positioned by use or application. For example, Campbell's soup is positioned not only as a lunch item but also for use as a sauce or dip or as an ingredient in main dishes. Third, products can be positioned in terms of particular types of product users. For example, sales for Johnson's Baby Shampoo increased dramatically after the company positioned the product not only for babies but also for active adults who need to wash their hair frequently. Fourth, products can be positioned relative to a product class. For example, Caress soap was positioned by Lever Brothers as a bath oil product rather than as a soap. Finally, products can be positioned directly against particular competitors. For example, Coke and Pepsi and McDonald's and Burger King commonly position directly against each other on various criteria, such as taste. The classic example of positioning is of this last type: Seven-Up positioned itself as a tasty alternative to the dominant soft drink, colas.

One way to investigate how to position a product is by using a *positioning map,* which is a visual depiction of customer perceptions of competitive products, brands, or models. It is constructed by surveying customers about various product attributes and developing dimensions and a graph indicating the relative position of competitors. Figure 5.6 presents a sample positioning map for automobiles that offers marketers a way of assessing whether their brands are positioned appropriately. For example, if Chrysler or Buick wants to be positioned in the minds of consumers as serious competitors to Lexus, then their strategies need to be changed to move up on this dimension. After the new strategies are implemented, a new positioning map could be developed to see if the brands moved up as desired.

FIGURE 5.6
Positioning Map for Automobiles

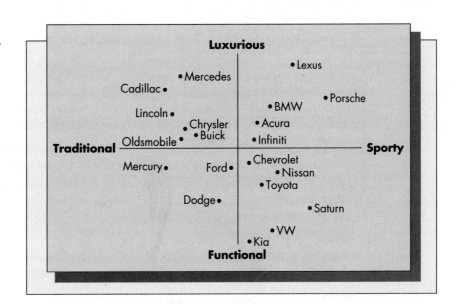

Dividing markets into segments and then selecting the best ones to serve is one of the cornerstones of sound marketing practice. However, there are situations when target marketing has been criticized as being unethical.

- R. J. Reynolds Tobacco Company planned to target African American consumers with a new brand of menthol cigarettes, Uptown. This brand was to be advertised with suggestions of glamour, high fashion, and night life. After criticism for targeting a vulnerable population, the company canceled plans for the brand.
- RJR planned to target white, 18- to 24-year-old "virile" females with a new cigarette brand, Dakota. It was criticized for targeting young, poorly educated, blue-collar women; and although it expanded the market to include males, Dakota failed in test markets and was withdrawn.
- Heileman Brewing Company planned to market a new brand of malt liquor called PowerMaster. Malt liquor is disproportionately consumed by African Americans and in low-income neighborhoods. Criticism of this strategy led the brand to be withdrawn.

One study suggests that whether targeting a group of consumers is unethical depends on two dimensions. The first is the degree to which the product can harm the consumers, and the second is the vulnerability of the group. Thus, to market harmful products to vulnerable target markets is likely to be considered unethical and could result in boycotts, negative word of mouth, and possibly litigation or legislation.

Source: N. Craig Smith and Elizabeth Cooper-Martin, "Ethics and Target Marketing: The Role of Product Harm and Consumer Vulnerability," *Journal of Marketing*, July 1997, pp. 1–20.

Some experts argue that different positioning strategies should be used depending on whether the firm is a market leader or follower and that followers usually should not attempt to position directly against the industry leader.[6] The main point here is that in segmenting markets, some segments might have to be forgone because a market-leading competitive product already dominates in sales and in the minds of customers. Thus, a smaller or less desirable target market may have to be selected since competing with market leaders is costly and not often successful.

Decide Segmentation Strategy

The firm is now ready to select its segmentation strategy. There are four basic alternatives. First, the firm may decide not to enter the market. For example, analysis to this stage may reveal there is no viable market niche for the firm's offering. Second, the firm may decide not to segment but to be a mass marketer. There are at least three situations when this may be the appropriate decision for the firm:

1. The market is so small that marketing to a portion of it is not profitable.
2. Heavy users make up such a large proportion of the sales volume that they are the only relevant target.
3. The brand is the dominant brand in the market, and targeting to a few segments would not benefit sales and profits.

Third, the firm may decide to market to one segment. And fourth, the firm may decide to market to more than one segment and design a separate marketing mix for each. In any case, the firm must have some criteria on which to base its segmentation strategy decisions.

FIGURE 5.7
Selecting Target Markets: Some Questions Marketing Managers Should Answer

In order to select the best target markets, marketing managers must evaluate market segments on a number of dimensions. Below is a list of questions managers should answer before selecting target markets.

Measurability Questions

1. What are the appropriate bases for segmenting this market and are these bases readily measurable?
2. Are secondary data available on these bases so that the market segment can be identified and measured inexpensively?
3. If primary data are needed, is there sufficient return on investment to do the research?
4. Are specific names and addresses of people in this market segment needed; or is general knowledge of their existence, number, and geographic location sufficient?
5. Can purchases of people in this market segment be readily measured and tracked?

Meaningfulness Questions

1. How many people are in this market segment and how frequently will they purchase our product?
2. What market share can we expect in this segment?
3. What is the growth potential of this segment?
4. How strong is competition for this market segment and how is it likely to change in the future?
5. How satisfied are customers in this market segment with current product offerings?

Marketability Questions

1. Can this market segment be reached with our current channels of distribution?
2. If new channels are needed, can we establish them efficiently?
3. What specific promotion media do these people read, listen to, or watch?
4. Can we afford to promote to these people in the appropriate media to reach them?
5. Are people in this market segment willing to pay a price that is profitable for the company?
6. Can we produce a product for this market segment and do so profitably?

Three important criteria on which to base such decisions are that a viable segment must be (1) measurable, (2) meaningful, and (3) marketable.

1. *Measurable*. For a segment to be selected, the firm must be capable of measuring its size and characteristics. For instance, one of the difficulties with segmenting on the basis of social class is that the concept and its divisions are not clearly defined and measured. Alternatively, income is a much easier concept to measure.
2. *Meaningful*. A meaningful segment is one that is large enough to have sufficient sales and growth potential to offer long-run profits for the firm.
3. *Marketable*. A marketable segment is one that can be reached and served by the firm in an efficient manner.

Figure 5.7 offers a list of questions marketing managers should answer when deciding whether a market segment meets these criteria. Segments that do so are viable target markets for the firm's offering. The firm must now give further attention to completing its marketing mix.

Design Marketing Mix Strategy

The firm is now in a position to complete its marketing plan by finalizing the marketing mix or mixes to be used for each segment. Clearly, selection of the target market and designing the marketing mix go hand in hand, and thus many marketing mix decisions should have already been carefully considered. To illustrate, the target market selected may be price sensitive, so some consideration has already been given to price levels, and clearly product positioning has many implications for promotion and channel decisions. Thus, while we place marketing mix design at the end of the model, many of these decisions are made in *conjunction* with target market selection. In the next six chapters of this text, marketing mix decisions will be discussed in detail.

Conclusion

The purpose of this chapter was to provide an overview of market segmentation. Market segmentation was defined as the process of dividing a market into groups of similar consumers and selecting the most appropriate group(s) for the firm to serve. Market segmentation was analyzed as a six-stage process: (1) to delineate the firm's current situation, (2) to determine consumer needs and wants, (3) to divide the market on relevant dimensions, (4) to develop product positioning, (5) to decide segmentation strategy, and (6) to design marketing mix strategy.

Additional Readings

Bolton, Ruth N., and Matthew B. Myers. "Price-Based Global Market Segmentation for Services," *Journal of Marketing,* July 2003, pp. 108–28.

Dickson, Peter R., and James L. Ginter. "Market Segmentation, Product Differentiation, and Marketing Strategy." *Journal of Marketing,* April 1987, pp. 1–10.

Myers, James H. *Segmentation and Positioning for Strategic Marketing Decisions.* Chicago: American Marketing Association, 1996.

Yan kelovich, Daniel, and David Meer. "Rediscovering Market Segmentation," *Harvard Business Review,* February 2006, pp. 122–31.

The Marketing Mix

Chapter

6

Product and Brand Strategy

Product strategy is a critical element of marketing and business strategy, since it is through the sale of products and services that companies survive and grow. This chapter discusses four important areas of concern in developing product strategies. First, some basic issues are discussed, including product definition, product classification, product quality and value, product mix and product line, branding and brand equity, and packaging. Second, the product life cycle and its implications for product strategy are explained. Third, the product audit is reviewed, and finally, three ways to organize for product management are outlined. These include the marketing manager system, brand manager system, and cross-functional teams.

Basic Issues in Product Management

Successful marketing depends on understanding the nature of products and basic decision areas in product management. In this section, we discuss the definition and classification of products, the importance of product quality and value, and the nature of a product mix and product lines. Also considered is the role of branding and packaging.

Product Definition

The way in which the product variable is defined can have important implications for the survival, profitability, and long-run growth of the firm. For example, the same product can be viewed at least three different ways. First, it can be viewed in terms of the *tangible product*—the physical entity or service that is offered to the buyer. Second, it can be viewed in terms of the *extended product*—the tangible product along with the whole cluster of services that accompany it. For example, a manufacturer of computer software may offer a 24-hour hotline to answer questions users may have or to offer free or reduced-cost software updates, free replacement of damaged software, and a subscription to a newsletter that documents new applications of the software. Third, it can be viewed in terms of the *generic product*—the essential benefits the buyer expects to receive from the product. For example, many personal care products bring to the purchaser feelings of self-enhancement and security in addition to the tangible benefits they offer.

From the standpoint of the marketing manager, to define the product solely in terms of the tangible product is to fall into the error of "marketing myopia." Executives who are guilty of committing this error define their company's product too narrowly, since they overemphasize the physical object itself. The classic example of this mistake can be found in railroad passenger

1. An audit of the firm's actual and potential resources
   a. Financial strength
   b. Access to raw materials
   c. Plant and equipment
   d. Operating personnel
   e. Management
   f. Engineering and technical skills
   g. Patents and licenses
2. Approaches to current markets
   a. More of the same products
   b. Variations of present products in terms of grades, sizes, and packages
   c. New products to replace or supplement current lines
   d. Product deletions
3. Approaches to new or potential markets
   a. Geographical expansion of domestic sales
   b. New socioeconomic or ethnic groups
   c. Overseas markets
   d. New uses of present products
   e. Complementary goods
   f. Mergers and acquisitions
4. State of competition
   a. New entries into the industry
   b. Product imitation
   c. Competitive mergers or acquisitions

service. Although no amount of product improvement could have staved off its decline, if the industry had defined itself as being in the transportation business, rather than the railroad business, it might still be profitable today. On the positive side, toothpaste manufacturers have been willing to exercise flexibility in defining their product. For years toothpaste was an oral hygiene product in which emphasis was placed solely on fighting tooth decay and bad breath (e.g., Crest with fluoride). More recently, many manufacturers have recognized the need to market toothpaste as a cosmetic item (to clean teeth of stains), as a defense against gum disease (to reduce the buildup of tartar above the gumline), as an aid for denture wearers, and as a breath freshener. As a result, special-purpose brands have been designed to serve these particular needs, such as Ultra Brite, Close-Up, Aqua-Fresh, Aim, Dental Care, and the wide variety of baking soda, tartar-control formula, and gel toothpastes offered under existing brand names.

In line with the marketing concept philosophy, a reasonable definition of product is that it is *the sum of the physical, psychological, and sociological satisfactions the buyer derives from purchase, ownership, and consumption.* From this standpoint, products are customer-satisfying objects that include such things as accessories, packaging, and service.

Product Classification

A product classification scheme can be useful to the marketing manager as an analytical device to assist in planning marketing strategy and programs. A basic assumption underlying such classifications is that products with common attributes can be marketed in a similar fashion. In general, products are classed according to two basic criteria: (1) end use or market, and (2) degree of processing or physical transformation.

1. *Agricultural products and raw materials.* These are goods grown or extracted from the land or sea, such as iron ore, wheat, and sand. In general, these products are fairly homogeneous, sold in large volume, and have low value per unit or in bulk weight.

2. *Organizational goods.* Such products are purchased by business firms for the purpose of producing other goods or for running the business. This category includes the following:
   a. Raw materials and semifinished goods.
   b. Major and minor equipment, such as basic machinery, tools, and other processing facilities.

      c. Parts or components, which become an integral element of some other finished good.

      d. Supplies or items used to operate the business but that do not become part of the final product.

3. *Consumer goods.* Consumer goods can be divided into three classes:

      a. Convenience goods, such as food, which are purchased frequently with minimum effort. Impulse goods would also fall into this category.

      b. Shopping goods, such as appliances, which are purchased after some time and energy are spent comparing the various offerings.

      c. Specialty goods, which are unique in some way so the consumer will make a special purchase effort to obtain them.

In general, the buying motive, buying habits, and character of the market are different for organizational goods vis-à-vis consumer goods. A primary purchasing motive for organizational goods is, of course, profit. As mentioned in a previous chapter, organizational goods are usually purchased as means to an end and not as an end in themselves. This is another way of saying that the demand for organizational goods is a derived demand. Organizational goods are often purchased directly from the original source with few middlemen, because many of these goods can be bought in large quantities; they have high unit value; technical advice on installation and use is required; and the product is ordered according to the user's specifications. Many organizational goods are subject to multiple-purchase influence, and a long period of negotiation is often required.

The market for organizational goods has certain attributes that distinguish it from the consumer goods market. Much of the market is concentrated geographically, as in the case of steel, auto, or shoe manufacturing. Certain products have a limited number of buyers; this is known as a *vertical market,* which means that (1) it is narrow, because customers are restricted to a few industries; and (2) it is deep, in that a large percentage of the producers in the market use the product. Some products, such as desktop computers, have a *horizontal market,* which means that the goods are purchased by all types of firms in many different industries. In general, buyers of organizational goods are reasonably well informed. As noted previously, heavy reliance is often placed on price, quality control, and reliability of supply source.

In terms of consumer products, many marketing scholars have found the convenience, shopping, and specialty classification inadequate and have attempted either to refine it or to derive an entirely new typology. None of these attempts appears to have met with complete success. Perhaps there is no best way to deal with this problem. From the standpoint of the marketing manager, product classification is useful to the extent that it assists in providing guidelines for developing an appropriate marketing mix. For example, convenience goods generally require broadcast promotion and long channels of distribution as opposed to shopping goods, which generally require more targeted promotion and somewhat shorter channels of distribution.

Product Quality and Value

Quality can be defined as the degree of excellence or superiority that an organization's product possesses.[1] Quality can encompass both the tangible and intangible aspects of a firm's products or services. In a technical sense, quality can refer to physical traits such as features, performance, reliability, durability, aesthetics, serviceability, and conformance to specifications. Although quality can be evaluated from many perspectives, the customer is the key perceiver of quality because his or her purchase decision determines the success of the organization's product or service and often the fate of the organization itself.

Many organizations have formalized their interest in providing quality products by undertaking total-quality management (TQM) programs. TQM is an organizationwide commitment to satisfying customers by continuously improving every business process involved in delivering products or services. Instead of merely correcting defects when they occur, organizations that practice TQM train and commit employees to continually look for ways to do things better so defects and problems don't arise in the first place. The result of this process is higher-quality products being produced at a lower cost. Indeed, the emphasis on quality has risen to such a level that over 70 countries have adopted the ISO 9000 quality system of standards, a standardized approach for evaluating a supplier's quality system, which can be applied to virtually any business.[2]

The term *quality* is often confused with the concept of value. Value encompasses not only quality but also price. *Value* can be defined as what the customer gets in exchange for what the customer gives. In other words, a customer, in most cases, receives a product in exchange for having paid the supplier for the product. A customer's perception of the value associated with a product is generally based both on the degree to which the product meets his or her specifications and the price that the customer will have to pay to acquire the product. Some organizations are beginning to shift their primary focus from one that solely emphasizes quality to one that also equally encompasses the customer's viewpoint of the price/quality trade-off. Organizations that are successful at this process derive their competitive advantage from the provision of customer value. In other words, they offer goods and services that meet or exceed customer needs at a fair price. Recall that Chapter 1 described various strategies based on value.

Product Mix and Product Line

A firm's *product mix* is the full set of products offered for sale by the organization; A product mix may consist of several *product lines,* or groups of products that share common characteristics, distribution channels, customers, or uses. A firm's product mix is described by its width and depth. *Width* of the product mix refers to the number of product lines handled by the organization. For example, one division of General Mills has a widespread mix consisting of five different product lines: ready-to-eat cereals, convenience foods, snack foods, baking products, and dairy products. *Depth* refers to the average number of products in each line. In its ready-to-eat cereals line, General Mills has eight different products. It has five different products in its line of convenience foods. Thus, the organization has a wide product mix and deep product lines.

An integral component of product line planning revolves around the question of how many product variants should be included in the line.[3] Manufacturing costs are usually minimized through large-volume production runs, and distribution costs tend to be lower if only one product is sold, stocked, and serviced. At a given level of sales, profits will usually be highest if those sales have been achieved with a single product. However, many firms offer many product variants.

Organizations offer varying products within a given product line for three reasons. First, potential customers rarely agree on a single set of specifications regarding their "ideal product," differing greatly in the importance and value they place on specific attributes. For example, in the laundry detergent market, there is a marked split between preferences for powder versus liquid detergent. Second, customers prefer variety. For example, a person may like Italian food but does not want to only eat spaghetti. Therefore, an Italian restaurant will offer the customer a wide variety of Italian dishes to choose from. Third, the dynamics of competition lead to multiproduct lines. As competitors seek to increase market share, they find it advantageous to introduce new products that subsegment an existing market segment by offering benefits more precisely tailored to the specific needs of a portion of that segment. For example, Proctor & Gamble offers Jif peanut butter in a low-salt version to target a specific subsegment of the peanut butter market.

All too often, organizations pursue product line additions with little regard for consequences.[4] However, in reaching a decision on product line additions, organizations need to evaluate whether (1) total profits will decrease or (2) the quality/value associated with current products will suffer. If the answer to either of the above is yes, then the organization

A. CLASSES OF CONSUMER GOODS—SOME CHARACTERISTICS AND MARKETING CONSIDERATIONS

Characteristics and Marketing Considerations	Type of Product		
	Convenience	Shopping	Specialty
Characteristics			
Time and effort devoted by consumer to shopping	Very little	Considerable	Cannot generalize; consumer may go to nearby store and buy with minimum effort or may have to go to distant store and spend much time and effort
Time spent planning the purchase	Very little	Considerable	Considerable
How soon want is satisfied after it arises	Immediately	Relatively long time	Relatively long time
Are price and quality compared?	No	Yes	No
Price	Usually low	High	High
Frequency of purchase	Usually frequent	Infrequent	Infrequent
Importance	Unimportant	Often very important	Cannot generalize
Marketing considerations			
Length of channel	Long	Short	Short to very short
Importance of retailer	Any single store is relatively unimportant	Important	Very important
Number of outlets	As many as possible	Few	Few; often only one in a market
Stock turnover	High	Lower	Lower
Gross margin	Low	High	High
Responsibility for advertising	Producer	Retailer	Joint responsibility
Importance of point-of-purchase display	Very important	Less important	Less important
Brand or store name importance	Brand name	Store name	Both
Importance of packaging	Very important	Less important	Less important

Source: Michael J. Etzel, Bruce J. Walker, and William J. Stanton, *Fundamentals of Marketing*, 13th ed. (Burr Ridge IL: McGraw-Hill/Irwin, 2004), pp. 211, 214.

should not proceed with the addition. Closely related to product line additions are issues associated with branding. These are covered next.

Branding and Brand Equity

For some organizations, the primary focus of strategy development is placed on brand building, developing, and nurturing activities.[5] Factors that serve to increase the strength of a brand include[6] (1) product quality when products do what they do very well (e.g., Windex and Easy-Off); (2) consistent advertising and other marketing communications in which brands tell their story often and well (e.g., Pepsi and Visa); (3) distribution intensity whereby customers see the brand wherever they shop (e.g., Marlboro); and (4) brand personality where the brand stands for something (e.g., Disney). The strength of the Coca-Cola brand, for example, is widely attributed to its universal availability, universal awareness, and trademark protection, which came as a result of strategic actions taken by the parent organization.[7]

B. CLASSES OF ORGANIZATIONAL PRODUCTS—SOME CHARACTERISTICS AND MARKETING CONSIDERATIONS

Characteristics and Marketing Considerations	Type of Product				
	Raw Materials	Fabricating Parts and Materials	Installations	Accessory Equipment	Operating Supplies
Example	Iron ore	Engine blocks	Blast furnaces	Storage racks	Paper clips
Characteristics					
Unit price	Very low	Low	Very high	Medium	Low
Length of life	Very short	Depends on final product	Very long	Long	Short
Quantities purchased	Large	Large	Very small	Small	Small
Frequency of purchase	Frequent delivery; long-term purchase contract	Infrequent purchase, but frequent delivery	Very infrequent	Medium frequency	Frequent
Standardization of competitive products	Very much; grading is important	Very much	Very little; custom made	Little	Much
Quantity of supply	Limited; supply can be increased slowly or not at all	Usually no problem	No problem	Usually no problem	Usually no problem
Marketing considerations					
Nature of channel	Short; no middlemen	Short; middlemen for small buyers	Short; no middlemen	Middlemen used	Middlemen used
Negotiation period	Hard to generalize	Medium	Long	Medium	Short
Price competition	Important	Important	Not important	Not main factor	Important
Presale/postsale service	Not important	Important	Very important	Important	Very little
Promotional activity	Very little	Moderate	Sales people very important	Important	Not too important
Brand preference	None	Generally low	High	High	Low
Advance buying contract	Important; long-term contracts used	Important; long-term contracts used	Not usually used	Not usually used	Not usually used

The brand name is perhaps the single most important element on the package, serving as a unique identifier. Specifically, a *brand* is a name, term, design, symbol, or any other feature that identifies one seller's good or service as distinct from those of other sellers. The legal term for brand is *trademark*.[8] A good brand name can evoke feelings of trust, confidence, security, strength, and many other desirable characteristics.[9] To illustrate, consider the case of Bayer aspirin. Bayer can be sold at up to two times the price of generic aspirin due to the strength of its brand image.

1. Microsoft
2. Coca-Cola
3. IBM
4. GE
5. Intel

6. Nokia
7. Walt Disney Co.
8. McDonald's Corp.
9. Toyota Motor Corp.
10. Marlboro

Many companies make use of manufacturer branding strategies in carrying out market and product development strategies. The *line extension* approach uses a brand name to facilitate entry into a new market segment (e.g., Diet Coke and Liquid Tide). An alternative to line extension is brand extension. In *brand extension,* a current brand name is used to enter a completely different product class (e.g., Jello pudding pops, Ivory shampoo).[10]

A third form of branding is *franchise extension* or *family branding,* whereby a company attaches the corporate name to a product to enter either a new market segment or a different product class (e.g., Honda lawnmower, Toyota Lexus). A final type of branding strategy that is becoming more and more common is dual branding. A *dual branding* (also known as joint or cobranding) strategy is one in which two or more branded products are integrated (e.g., Bacardi rum and Coca-Cola, Long John Silver's and A&W Root Beer, Archway cookies and Kellogg cereal, US Airways and Bank of America Visa). The logic behind this strategy is that if one brand name on a product gives a certain signal of quality, then the presence of a second brand name on the product should result in a signal that is at least as powerful as, if not more powerful than, the signal in the case of the single brand name. Each of the preceding four approaches is an attempt by companies to gain a competitive advantage by making use of its or others' established reputation, or both.

Companies may also choose to assign different brand names to each product. This is known as *multibranding* strategy. By doing so, the firm makes a conscious decision to allow the product to succeed or fail on its own merits. Major advantages of using multiple brand names are that (1) the firm can distance products from other offerings it markets; (2) the image of one product (or set of products) is not associated with other products the company markets; (3) the product(s) can be targeted at a specific market segment; and (4) should the product(s) fail, the probability of failure impacting on other company products is minimized. For example, many consumers are unaware that Dreft, Tide, Oxydol, Bold, Cheer, and Dash laundry detergents are all marketed by Procter & Gamble. The major disadvantage of this strategy is that because new names are assigned, there is no consumer brand awareness and significant amounts of money must be spent familiarizing customers with new brands.

Increasingly, companies are finding that brand names are one of the most valuable assets they possess. Successful extensions of an existing brand can lead to additional loyalty and associated profits. Conversely, a wrong extension can cause damaging associations, as perceptions linked to the brand name are transferred back from one product to the other.[11] *Brand equity* can be viewed as the set of assets (or liabilities) linked to the brand that add (or subtract) value.[12] The value of these assets is dependent upon the consequences or results of the marketplace's relationship with a brand. Figure 6.1 lists the elements of brand equity. Brand equity is determined by the consumer and is the culmination of the consumer's assessment of the product, the company that manufactures and markets the product, and all other variables that impact on the product between manufacture and consumer consumption.

Before leaving the topic of manufacturer brands, it is important to note that, as with consumer products, organizational products also can possess brand equity. However, several differences do exist between the two sectors.[13] First, organizational products are usually

FIGURE 6.1
Elements of Brand Equity

Source: David A. Aaker, *Managing Brand Equity.* © 1991, New York, by David A. Aaker. Reprinted with the permission of Free Press, a division of Simon & Schuster. See David A. Aaker, *Building Strong Brands* (New York: Free Press, 1995), for his seminal work on branding as well as David A. Aaker, *Brand Portfolio Strategy: Creating Relevance, Differentiation, Energy, Leverage, and Clarity* (New York: Free Press, 2004). David A. Aaker, *Strategic Market Management* (Hoboken, NJ: John Wiley) 2008, Chapter 9.

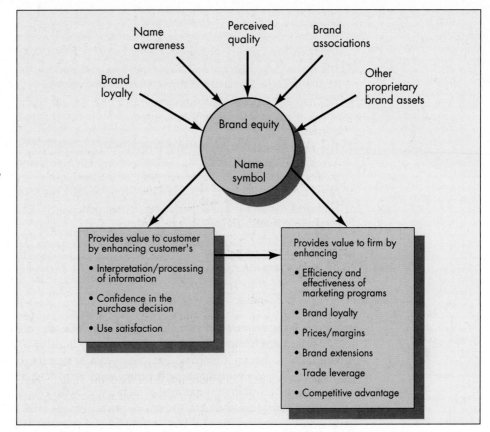

branded with firm names. As a result, loyalty (or disloyalty) to the brand tends to be of a more global nature, extending across all the firm's product lines. Second, because firm versus brand loyalty exists, attempts to position new products in a manner differing from existing products may prove to be difficult, if not impossible. Finally, loyalty to organizational products encompasses not only the firm and its products but also the distribution channel members employed to distribute the product. Therefore, attempts to establish or change brand image must also take into account distributor image.

As a related branding strategy, many retail firms produce or market their products under a so-called private label. For example, Kmart has phased in its own store-brand products to compete with the national brands. There's Nature's Classics, a line of fancy snacks and cookies; Oral Pure, a line of dental care products; Prevail house cleaners; B.E., a Gap-style line of weekend wear; and Benchmark, a line of "made in the U.S.A." tools. Such a strategy is highly important in industries where middlemen have gained control over distribution to the consumer. The growth of the large discount and specialty stores, such as Kmart, Wal-Mart, Target, The Gap, Limited, and others, has accelerated the development of private brands. If a manufacturer refuses to supply certain middlemen with private branded merchandise, the alternative is for these middlemen to go into the manufacturing business, as in the case of Kroger supermarkets.

Private label products differ markedly from so-called generic products that sport labels such as "beer," "cigarettes," and "potato chips." Today's house brands are packaged in distinctively upscale containers. The quality of the products used as house brands equals and sometimes exceeds those offered by name brands. While generic products were positioned as a means for consumers to struggle through recessionary times, private label

1. The name should suggest the product benefits. Names such as Easy Off (oven cleaner) and PowerBook (laptop computer) clearly suggest the benefits of purchasing the product.
2. The name should be memorable, distinctive, and positive. Many automobiles such as Mustang, Eagle, Firebird, and Bronco have strong names.
3. The name should fit the company or product image. Sharp (audio and video functions), Mustard's Last Stand (hot dogs), and Paddy O'Furniture (patio furniture) are some examples.
4. The name should have no legal restrictions. For example, the U.S. Food and Drug Administration discourages the use of word *heart* in food brand names. Also since brand names often need a corresponding address on the Internet, the choice may be complicated because millions of domain names have already been selected.
5. The name should be simple (such as Bold detergent and Sure deodorant), and emotional (Beautiful, Opium, and Obsession perfumes).

Source: Adapted from Roger A. Kerin, Steven W. Hartley, Eric N. Berkowitz, and William Rudelins, *Marketing,* 8th ed. (Burr Ridge, IL: McGraw-Hill/Irwin, 2006). Also see Kevin Lane Keller, *Strategic Brand Management,* 2nd ed. (Upper Saddle River, NJ: Prentice Hall, 2003), chap. 4.

brands are being marketed as value brands, products that are equivalent to national brands but are priced much lower. Private brands are rapidly growing in popularity. For example, it only took JC Penney Company, Inc., five years to nurture its private-label jeans, the Arizona brand, into a powerhouse with annual sales surpassing $500 million.

Consolidation within the supermarket industry, growth of super centers, and heightened product marketing are poised to strengthen private brands even further.[14] However, these gains will not come without a fight from national manufacturers who are undertaking aggressive actions to defend their brands' market share. Some have significantly rolled back prices, while others have instituted increased promotional campaigns. The ultimate winner in this ongoing battle between private (store) and manufacturer (national) brands, not surprisingly, should be the consumer who is able to play off these store brands against national brands. By shopping at a mass merchandiser like Wal-Mart or Walgreens, consumers are exposed to and able to choose from a wide array of both national and store brands, thus giving them the best of both worlds: value and variety.

Packaging

Distinctive or unique packaging is one method of differentiating a relatively homogeneous product. To illustrate, shelf-stable microwave dinners, pumps rather than tubes of toothpaste or bars of soap, and different sizes and designs of tissue packages are attempts to differentiate a product through packaging changes and to satisfy consumer needs at the same time.

In other cases, packaging changes have succeeded in creating new attributes of value in a brand. A growing number of manufacturers are using green labels or packaging their products totally in green wrap to signify low- or no-fat content.[15] Frito-Lay, Quaker Oats, ConAgra, Keebler, Pepperidge Farm, Nabisco, and Sunshine Biscuits are all examples of companies involved in this endeavor.

Finally, packaging changes can make products urgently salable to a targeted segment. For example, the products in the Gillette Series grooming line, including shave cream, razors, aftershave, and skin conditioner, come in ribbed, rounded, metallic-gray shapes, looking at once vaguely sexual and like precision engineering.[16]

Marketing managers must consider both the consumer and costs in making packaging decisions. On one hand, the package must be capable of protecting the product through the channel of distribution to the consumer. In addition, it is desirable for packages to have a convenient size and be easy to open for the consumer. For example, single-serving soups and zip-lock packaging in cereal boxes are attempts by manufacturers to serve consumers better. Hopefully, the package is also attractive and informative, capable of being used as a competitive weapon to project a product's image. However, maximizing these objectives may increase the cost of the product to such an extent that consumers are no longer willing to purchase it. Thus, the marketing manager must determine the optimal protection, convenience, positioning, and promotional strengths of packages, subject to cost constraints.

Product Life Cycle

A firm's product strategy must take into account the fact that products have a life cycle. Figure 6.2 illustrates this life-cycle concept. Products are introduced, grow, mature, and decline. This cycle varies according to industry, product, technology, and market. Marketing executives need to be aware of the life-cycle concept because it can be a valuable aid in developing marketing strategies.

During the introduction phase of the cycle, there are usually high production and marketing costs, and since sales are only beginning to materialize, profits are low or nonexistent. Profits increase and are positively correlated with sales during the growth stage as the market begins trying and adopting the product. As the product matures, profits for the initiating firm do not keep pace with sales because of competition. Here the seller may be forced to "remarket" the product, which may involve making price concessions, increasing product quality, or expanding outlays on advertising and sales promotion just to maintain market share. At some point sales decline, and the seller must decide whether to (1) drop the product, (2) alter the product, (3) seek new uses for the product, (4) seek new markets, or (5) continue with more of the same.

The usefulness of the product life-cycle concept is primarily that it forces management to take a long-range view of marketing planning. In doing so, it should become clear that shifts in phases of the life cycle correspond to changes in the market situation, competition,

FIGURE 6.2
The Product Life Cycle

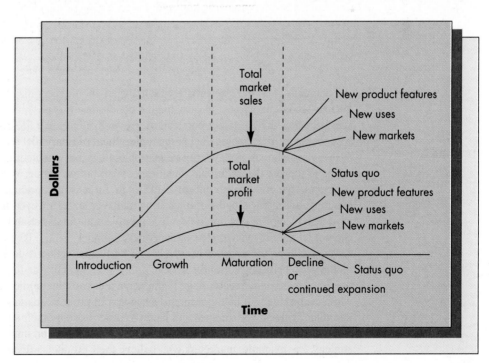

	Life-Cycle Stage			
Strategy Dimension	**Introduction**	**Growth**	**Maturity**	**Decline**
Basic objectives	Establish a market for product type; persuade early adopters to buy	Build sales and market share; develop preference for brand	Defend brand's share of market; seek growth by luring customers from competitors	Limit costs or seek ways to revive sales and profits
Product	Provide high quality; select a good brand; get patent or trademark protection	Provide high quality; add services to enhance value	Improve quality; add features to distinguish brand from competitors' brands	Continue providing high quality to maintain brand's reputation; seek ways to make the product new again
Pricing	Often high to recover development costs; sometimes low to build demand rapidly	Somewhat high because of heavy demand	Low, reflecting heavy competition	Low to sell off remaining inventory or high to serve a niche market
Channels	Limited number of channels	Greater number of channels to meet demand	Greater number of channels and more incentives to resellers	Limited number of channels
Promotion	Aimed at early adopters; messages designed to educate about product type; incentives such as samples and coupons to induce trial	Aimed at wider audience; messages focus on brand benefits; for consumer products, emphasis on advertising	Messages focus on differentiating brand from its competitors' brands; heavy use of incentives such as coupons to induce buyers to switch brands	Minimal, to keep costs down

and demand. Thus, the astute marketing manager should recognize the necessity of altering the marketing mix to meet these changing conditions. It is possible for managers to undertake strategies that, in effect, can lead to a revitalized product life cycle. For example, past advancements in technology led to the replacement of rotary dial telephones by touch-tone, push-button phones. Today, even newer technology has enabled the cordless and cellular phone to replace the traditional touch-tone, push-button phone. When applied with sound judgment, the life-cycle concept can aid in forecasting, pricing, advertising, product planning, and other aspects of marketing management. However, the marketing manager must also recognize that the life cycle is purely a tool for assisting in strategy development and not let the life cycle dictate strategy development.[17]

As useful as the product life cycle can be to managers, it does have limitations that require it to be used cautiously in developing strategy. For one thing, the length of time a product will remain in each stage is unknown and can't be predicted with accuracy. Thus, while each stage will likely occur for a successful product, marketers can't forecast when one stage will end and another will begin in order to adapt their strategies at the appropriate time. Also, they may misjudge when a stage is ending and implement an inappropriate strategy. For example, marketers who believe their products are ending the maturity stage may cut promotion costs and thus push the product into decline, whereas the product might have continued to sell if promotion had been maintained and altered.

Another limitation is that not all products go through the product life cycle in the same way. For example, many products are failures and do not have anything approaching a complete life cycle. Several variations of the life cycle also exist, two of which are fashions and fads.

Fashions are accepted and popular product styles. Their life cycle involves a distinctiveness stage in which trendsetters adopt the style, followed by an emulation stage in which more customers purchase the style to be the trendsetters. Next is the economic stage, in which the style becomes widely available at mass-market prices. Many fashions, such as skirt length and designer jeans, lose popularity, then regain it and repeat the fashion of cycle. The fashion cycle is clearly visible in clothing, cosmetics, tattoos, and body piercing.

Fads are products that experience an intense but brief period of popularity. Their life cycle resembles the basic product life cycle but in a very compressed form. It is usually so brief that competitors have no chance to capitalize on the fad. Some fads may repeat their popularity after long lapses.

Product Adoption and Diffusion

Obviously not all customers immediately purchase a product in the introductory stage of the product life cycle. The shape of the life-cycle curve indicates that most sales occur after the product has been available for awhile. The spread of a product through the population is known as the diffusion of innovation, as illustrated in Figure 6.3, which presents five adopter categories.

The first category is *innovators,* those who are the first to buy a new product. When innovators are consumers, they tend to be people who are venturesome and willing to take risks. When innovators are organizational buyers, they tend to be organizations that seek to remain at the cutting edge through the use of the latest technology and ideas.

If the experience of innovators is favorable, *early adopters* begin to buy. These buyers, who are respected social leaders and above average in education, influence the next group. Influenced by what early adopters have, the rest of the market begins to get interested in the product. The biggest category of buyers is divided into groups called the early majority and late majority. Members of the *early majority* tend to avoid risk and to make purchases carefully. They also have many informal contacts. Members of the *late majority* not only avoid risks, but are cautious and skeptical about new ideas. Eventually, the product becomes

FIGURE 6.3
Adopter Categories

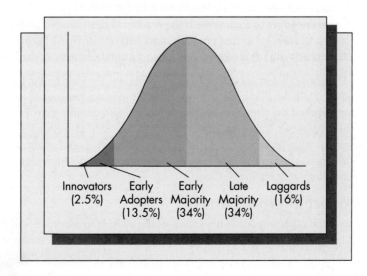

commonplace, and even laggards are ready to buy. *Laggards* are reluctant to make changes and are comfortable with traditional products. They also have a fear of debt, but may eventually purchase a well-established brand.

The Product Audit

The product audit is a marketing management technique whereby the company's current product offerings are reviewed to ascertain whether each product should be continued as is, improved, modified, or deleted. The audit is a task that should be carried out at regular intervals as a matter of policy. Product audits are the responsibility of the product manager unless specifically delegated to someone else.

Deletions

In today's environment, a growing number of products are being introduced each year that are competing for limited shelf space. This growth is primarily due to (1) new knowledge being applied faster, and (2) the decrease in time between product introductions (by a given organization).[18] In addition, companies are not consistently removing products from the market at the same time they are introducing new products. The result is a situation in which too many products are fighting for too little shelf space. One of the main purposes of the product audit is to detect sick products and then bury them. Rather than let the retailer or distributor decide which products should remain, organizations themselves should take the lead in developing criteria for deciding which products should stay and which should be deleted. Some of the more obvious factors to be considered are

> *Sales trends.* How have sales moved over time? What has happened to market share? Why have sales declined? What changes in sales have occurred in competitive products both in our line and in those of other manufacturers?
>
> *Profit contribution.* What has been the profit contribution of this product to the company? If profits have declined, how are these tied to price? Have selling, promotion, and distribution costs risen out of proportion to sales? Does the product require excessive management time and effort?
>
> *Product life cycle.* Has the product reached a level of maturity and saturation in the market? Has new technology been developed that poses a threat to the product? Are more effective substitutes on the market? Has the product outgrown its usefulness? Can the resources used on this product be put to better use?
>
> *Customer migration patterns.* If the product is deleted, will customers of this product switch to other substitute products marketed by our firm? In total, will profits associated with our line increase due to favorable switching patterns?

The above factors should be used as guidelines for making the final decision to delete a product. Deletion decisions are very difficult to make because of their potential impact on customers and the firm. For example, eliminating a product may force a company to lay off some employees. There are other factors to consider as well, such as keeping consumers supplied with replacement parts and repair service and maintaining the goodwill of distributors who have an inventory of the product. The deletion plan should also provide for clearing out of stock in question.

Product Improvement

One of the other important objectives of the audit is to ascertain whether to alter the product in some way or to leave things as they are. Altering the product means changing one or more of its attributes or marketing dimensions. *Attributes* refer mainly to product features,

Instead of abandoning or harvesting an older, mature product, many companies are looking instead to rejuvenate that product and extend its life cycle. The advantages of product rejuvenation include the following:

Less risk. Past experience in all phases of the product's life cycle permits the company to focus on improving business practices instead of formulating completely new, untested methods.

Lower costs. Most, if not all, of the product's start-up costs are now avoided. Plus, prior experience in both marketing and producing the product makes spending more efficient.

Less time. Because the beginning stages of product development have already occurred, the time involved in rejuvenating a product is significantly less than a new venture.

Cheaper market share. The money new products need to invest to create initial brand recognition as well as the lower costs mentioned above can be saved, used to enhance the product offering, or enable the product to be offered at a lower price.

Higher profits. Efficiency, brand recognition, superior product quality, and the ability to have a narrow focus all contribute to lower costs or increased sales, or both, thus increasing the potential for higher profits.

Source: Conrad Berenson and Iris Mohr-Jackson, "Product Rejuvenation: A Less Risky Alternative to Product Innovation," *Business Horizons*, November–December 1994, pp. 51–57. © 1994 by the Foundation for the School of Business at Indiana University. Used with permission. Also see Kevin Lane Keller, *Strategic Brand Management*, 3rd ed. (Upper Saddle River, NJ: Prentice-Hall, 2008), pp. 574–577.

design, package, and so forth. *Marketing dimensions* refer to such things as price, promotion strategy, and channels of distribution.

It is possible to look at the product audit as a management device for controlling the product strategy. Here, control means feedback on product performance and corrective action in the form of product improvement. Product improvement is a top-level management decision, but the information needed to make the improvement decision may come from the consumer or the middlemen. Advertising agencies or consultants often make suggestions. Reports by the sales force should be structured in a way to provide management with certain types of product information; in fact, these reports can be the firm's most valuable product-improvement tool. Implementing a product improvement decision will often require the coordinated efforts of several specialists, plus some research. For example, product design improvement decisions involve engineering, manufacturing, accounting, and marketing. When a firm becomes aware that a product's design can be improved, it is not always clear how consumers will react to the various alterations. To illustrate, in blind taste tests, the Coca-Cola Company found that consumers overwhelmingly preferred the taste of a reformulated, sweeter new Coke over old Coke. However, when placed on the market in labeled containers, new Coke turned out to be a failure due to consumers' emotional attachments to the classic Coke. Consequently, it is advisable to conduct some market tests in realistic settings.

A discussion of product improvement would not be complete without taking into account the benefits associated with benchmarking, especially as they relate to the notion of the extended product, the tangible product along with the whole cluster of services that accompany it.[19] The formal definition of *benchmarking* is the continuous process of measuring products, services, and practices against those of the toughest competitors or companies renowned as leaders. In other words, benchmarking involves learning about best practices from best-performing companies—how they are achieving strong performance. It is an effective tool organizations use to improve on existing products, activities, functions, or processes. Major corporations such as IBM, AT&T, DuPont, Ford, Eastman Kodak,

Miliken, Motorola, and Xerox all have numerous benchmarking studies in progress. For example, IBM has already performed more than 500 benchmarking studies. Benchmarking can assist companies in many product improvement efforts, including (1) boosting product quality, (2) developing more user-friendly products, (3) improving customer order-processing activities, and (4) shortening delivery lead times. In the case of benchmarking, companies can achieve great success by copying others. Thus, by its very nature, benchmarking becomes an essential element in the ongoing product auditing process.

Organizing for Product Management

Whether managing existing products or developing new products (the subject of the next chapter), organizations that are successful have one factor in common: They actively manage both types. Obviously, if a firm has only one product, it gets everyone's attention. But as the number of products grow and the need to develop new products becomes evident, some rational management system is necessary.

Under a *marketing-manager system,* one person is responsible for overseeing an entire product line with all of the functional areas of marketing such as research, advertising, sales promotion, sales, and product planning. This type of system is popular in organizations with a line or lines of similar products or one dominant product line. Sometimes referred to as category management, the marketing manager system is seen as being superior to a brand manager system because one manager oversees all brands within a particular line, thus avoiding brand competition. Organizations such as PepsiCo, Purex, Eastman Kodak, and Levi Strauss use some form of marketing-manager system.

Under a *brand-manager system,* a manager focuses on a single product or a very small group of new and existing products. Typically, this person is responsible for everything from marketing research and package design to advertising. Often called a product-management system, the brand-manager system has been criticized on several dimensions. First, brand managers often have difficulty because they do not have authority commensurate with their responsibilities. Second, they often pay inadequate attention to new products. Finally, they are often more concerned with their own brand's profitability than with the profitability of all of the organization's brands. These criticisms are not aimed at people but at the system itself, which may force brand managers into the above behaviors. Despite its drawbacks, organizations such as RJR Nabisco and Black & Decker have used this system.

Successful *new* products often come from organizations that try to bring all the capabilities of the organization to bear on the problems of customers. Obviously, this requires the cooperation of all the various functional departments in the organization. Thus, the use of *cross-functional teams* has become an important way to manage the development of new products. A *venture team* is a popular method used in such organizations as Xerox, Polaroid, Exxon, IBM, Monsanto, and Motorola. A venture team is a cross-functional team responsible for all the tasks involved in the development of a new product. Once the new product is already launched, the team may turn over responsibility for managing the product to a brand manager or product manager or it may manage the new product as a separate business.

The use of cross-functional teams in product management and new product development is increasing for a very simple reason: Organizations need the contributions of all functions and therefore require their cooperation. Cross-functional teams operate independently of the organization's functional departments but include members from each function. A team might include a member from engineering, marketing, finance, service, and designers. Some organizations even include important outsiders (e.g., parts suppliers) on cross-functional teams. Figure 6.4 presents some important prerequisites for the use of cross-functional teams in managing existing products and developing new products.

FIGURE 6.4
Some Requirements for the Effective Use of Cross-Functional Teams in Product Management and New Product Development

A growing number of organizations have begun using cross-functional teams for product management and new product development. Having representatives from various departments clearly has its advantages, but most important, effective teams must have the nurture and support of management. Some requirements for effective teams are

1. *Commitment of top management and provision of clear goals.* Organizations that successfully use cross-functional teams in product management or development have managers who are deeply committed to the team concept. As a result, high-performance teams have a clear understanding of the product management and development goals of the organization. The importance of these goals encourages individuals to defer their own functional or departmental concerns to team goals.

2. *Trust among members.* For cross-functional teams to work, a high level of trust must exist among members. The climate of trust within a team seems to be highly dependent on members' perception of management's trust of the group as a whole.

3. *Cross-functional cooperation.* If a team is to take responsibility and assume the risk of product development, its members will need detailed information about the overall operation of the organization. It often requires that functional units be willing to share information that previously was not shared with other departments.

4. *Time and training.* Effective cross-functional teams need time to mature. They require massive planning and intense and prompt access to resources, financial and other. Because members have to put aside functional and departmental loyalties and concerns, training is usually necessary.

Conclusion

This chapter has been concerned with a central element of marketing management—product strategy. The first part of the chapter discussed some basic issues in product strategy, including product definition and classification, product quality and value, product mix and product lines, branding and brand equity, and packaging. The product life cycle was discussed as well as the product audit. Finally, three methods of organizing for product management were presented. Although product considerations are extremely important, remember that the product is only one element of the marketing mix. Focusing on product decisions alone, without consideration of the other marketing mix variables, would be an ineffective approach to marketing strategy.

Additional Readings

De Luca, Luigi M., and Kwaku Atuahene-Gima. "Market Knowledge Dimensions and Cross-Functional Collaboration: Examining the Different Routes to Product Innovation Performance." *Journal of Marketing,* January 2007, pp. 95–112.

Gladwell, Malcolm. *The Tipping Point.* NY: Book Bag Books, 2006.

Haigh, David, and Jonathan Knowles. "What's in a Brand?" *Marketing Management,* May/June 2004, pp. 22–28.

Hanlon, Patrick. *Primal Branding.* NY: Free Prees, 2006.

Pullig, Chris, Carolyn J. Simmons, and Richard G. Netemeyer. "Brand Dilution: When Do New Brands Hurt Existing Brands? *Journal of Marketing,* April 2006, pp. 52–64.

Rust, Roland, Debora Viana Thompson, and Rebecca Thompson. "Defeating Feature Fatigue." *Harvard Business Review,* February 2006, pp. 98–109.

Chapter 7

New Product Planning and Development

New products are a vital part of a firm's competitive growth strategy. Leaders of successful firms know that it is not enough to develop new products on a sporadic basis. What counts is a climate of product development that leads to one triumph after another. It is commonplace for major companies to have 50 percent or more of their current sales in products introduced within the last 10 years. For example, the 3M Company derives 30 percent of its revenues from products less than four years old.[1]

Some additional facts about new products are important to remember:

- Many new products are failures. Estimates of new product failures range from 33 percent to 90 percent, depending on industry.
- New product sales grow far more rapidly than sales of current products, potentially providing a surprisingly large boost to a company's growth rate.
- Companies vary widely in the effectiveness of their new product programs.
- A major obstacle to effectively predicting new product demand is limited vision.
- Common elements appear in the management practices that generally distinguish the relative degree of efficiency and success between companies.

In one recent year, almost 22,000 products were introduced in supermarkets, drugstores, mass merchandisers, and health food stores.[2] Of these, only a small percentage (less than 20 percent) met sales goals. The cost of introducing a new brand in some consumer markets can range from $50 million to hundreds of millions of dollars. In addition to the outlay cost of product failures, there are also opportunity costs. These opportunity costs refer not only to the alternative uses of funds spent on product failures but also to the time spent in unprofitable product development.

Product development can take many years. For example, Hills Brothers (now owned by Nestlé) spent 22 years in developing its instant coffee, while it took General Foods (now owned by Altria) 10 years to develop Maxim. However, the success of one new product is no guarantee that additional low-cost brand extensions will be successful. For example, on the positive side, Gillette was able to leverage the research and monies spent on the original Sensor to successfully develop and launch the Sensor razor for women and the Sensor Excel razor. On the negative side, Maxwell House (Altria), Folgers (Procter & Gamble), and Nestlé are still struggling to develop commercially successful lines of fresh whole bean coffee, having been beaten to the punch by smaller companies such as Starbucks, Millstone Coffee, Inc., and Brothers Gourmet Coffees.[3]

Good management, with heavy emphasis on planning, organization, and interaction among the various functional units (e.g., marketing, manufacturing, engineering, R&D), seems to be the key factor contributing to a firm's success in launching new products. The primary reason found for new product failure is an inability on the part of the selling company to match its offerings to the needs of the customer. This inability to satisfy customer needs can be attributed to three main sources: inadequacy of upfront intelligence efforts, failure on the part of the company to stick close to what the company does best, and the inability to provide better value than competing products and technologies.

New Product Strategy

In developing new products, the first question a marketing manager must ask is, In how many ways can a product be new? C. Merle Crawford and Anthony DiBenedetto developed a definition of new products based on the following five different categories:[4]

1. *New-to-the-world products.* Products that are inventions: for example, Polaroid camera, the first car, rayon, the laser printer, in-line skates.
2. *New category entries.* Products that take a firm into a category new to it, but that are not new to the world: for example, P&G's first shampoo, Hallmark gift items.
3. *Additions to product lines.* Products that are line extensions, flankers, and so on, to the firm's current markets, for example, Tide Liquid detergent, Bud Light, Apple's Power Mac.
4. *Product improvements.* Current products made better; virtually every product on the market has been improved, often many times.
5. *Repositionings.* Products that are retargeted for a new use or application; a classic case is Arm & Hammer baking soda, which was repositioned several times as drain deodorant, refrigerator freshener, toothpaste, deodorant, and so on.

The new product categories listed above raise the issue of imitation products, strictly me-too or improved versions of existing products. If a firm introduces a form of dry beer that is new to them but is identical or similar to other beers on the market, is it a new product? The answer is yes, because it is new to the firm. Managers should not get the idea that to imitate is bad and to innovate is good, for most of the best-selling products on the market today are improvements over another company's original invention. The best strategy is the one that will maximize company goals. It should be noted that Crawford and DiBenedetto's categories don't encompass variations such as new to a country, new channel of distribution, packaging improvement, and different resources or method of manufacture, which they consider to be variations of the five categories, especially as these variations relate to additions to product lines.

A second broader approach to the new product question is the one developed by H. Igor Ansoff in the form of growth vectors.[5] This is the matrix first introduced in Chapter 1 that indicates the direction in which the organization is moving with respect to its current products and markets. It is shown again in Figure 7.1.

Market penetration denotes a growth direction through the increase in market share for present product markets. *Product development* refers to creating new products to replace existing ones. Firms using either market penetration or product development strategies are attempting to capitalize on existing markets and combat competitive entry and/or further market incursions. *Market development* refers to finding new customers for existing products. *Diversification* refers to developing new products and cultivating new markets. Firms using market development and diversification strategies are seeking to establish footholds in new markets or preempt competition in emerging market segments.

FIGURE 7.1
Organizational Growth Strategies

Products ⟍ Markets	Present	New
Present	Market penetration	Product development
New	Market development	Diversification

As shown in Figure 7.1, market penetration and market development strategies use present products. A goal of these types of strategies is to either increase frequency of consumption or increase the number of customers using the firm's product(s). A strategic focus is placed on altering the breadth and depth of the firm's existing product lines. Product development and diversification can be characterized as product mix strategies. New products, as defined in the growth vector matrix, usually require the firm to make significant investments in research and development and may require major changes in its organizational structure. Firms are not confined to pursuing a single direction. For example, Miller Brewing Co. has decided four key strategies should dictate its activities for the next decade, including (1) building its premium-brand franchises through investment spending, (2) continuing to develop value-added new products with clear consumer benefits, (3) leveraging local markets to build its brand franchise, and (4) building business globally.[6] Success for Miller depends on pursuing strategies that encompass all areas of the growth vector matrix.

It has already been stated that new products are the lifeblood of successful business firms. Thus, the critical product policy question is not whether to develop new products but in what direction to move. One way of dealing with this problem is to formulate standards or norms that new products must meet if they are to be considered candidates for launching. In other words, as part of its new product policy, management must ask itself the basic question, What is the potential contribution of each anticipated new product to the company?

Each company must answer this question in accordance with its long-term goals, corporate mission, resources, and so forth. Unfortunately, some of the reasons commonly given to justify the launching of new products are so general that they become meaningless. Phrases such as *additional profits, increased growth,* or *cyclical stability* must be translated into more specific objectives. For example, one objective may be to reduce manufacturing overhead costs by using plant capacity better. This may be accomplished by using the new product as an off-season filler. Naturally, the new product proposal would also have to include production and accounting data to back up this cost argument.

In every new product proposal some attention must be given to the ultimate economic contribution of each new product candidate. If the argument is that a certain type of product is needed to keep up with competition or to establish leadership in the market, it is fair to ask, Why? To put the question another way, top management can ask: What will be the effect on the firm's long-run profit picture if we do not develop and launch this or that new product? Policy-making criteria on new products should specify (1) a working definition of the profit concept acceptable to top management, (2) a minimum level or floor of profits, (3) the availability and cost of capital to develop a new product, and (4) a specified time period in which the new product must recoup its operating costs and begin contributing to profits.

It is critical that firms not become solely preoccupied with a short-term focus on earnings associated with new products. For example, in some industrial markets, a 20-year spread has been found between the development and wide-spread adoption of products, on

1. A superior differentiated product that is unique by virtue of features, benefits, quality, and value.
2. A market-driven and customer focused new product development process.
3. Predevelopment work prior to beginning the development process.
4. Clear and early product definition.
5. Appropriate internal organizational structure.
6. A product that is familiar to the company's current products and markets.
7. A new product development process that uses profiles of previous product successes.
8. Controls on the new product development process that ensure sound execution.
9. Sound execution rather than speed.
10. Support for the new product through friendly, courteous, prompt, and efficient customer service.

Source: Based on Robert G. Cooper, "What Distinguishes the Top Performing New Products in Financial Services," *Journal of Product Innovation Management,* September 1994, pp. 281–99; and "The New Product System: The Industry Experience," *Journal of Product Innovation Management,* June 1992, pp. 113–27; and William O. Beardon, Thomas N, Ingram, and Raymond W. LaForge, *Marketing: Principles and Perspectives,* 5th ed. (Burr Ridge, IL: McGraw-Hill/Irwin, 2007), p. 219.

average. Indeed, an advantage that some Japanese firms appear to possess is that their management is free from the pressure of steady improvement in earnings per share that plagues American managers who emphasize short-term profits. Japanese managers believe that market share will lead to customer loyalty, which in turn will lead to profits generated from repeat purchases. Through a continual introduction of new products, firms will succeed in building share. This share growth will then ultimately result in earnings growth and profitability that the stock market will support through higher share prices over the long term.

New Product Planning and Development Process

Ideally, products that generate a maximum dollar profit with a minimum amount of risk should be developed and marketed. However, it is very difficult for planners to implement this idea because of the number and nature of the variables involved. What is needed is a systematic, formalized process for new product planning. Although such a process does not provide management with any magic answers, it can increase the probability of new product success. Initially, the firm must establish some new product policy guidelines that include the product fields of primary interest, organizational responsibilities for managing the various stages in new product development, and criteria for making go-ahead decisions. After these guidelines are established, a process such as the one shown in Figure 7.2 should be useful in new product development.

Idea Generation

Every product starts as an idea. But all new product ideas do not have equal merit or potential for economic or commercial success. Some estimates indicate that as many as 60 or 70 ideas are necessary to yield one successful product. This is an average figure, but it serves to illustrate that new product ideas have a high mortality rate. In terms of money, almost three-fourths of all the dollars of new product expense go to unsuccessful products.

The problem at this stage is to ensure that all new product ideas available to the company at least have a chance to be heard and evaluated. Ideas are the raw materials for product

FIGURE 7.2
The New Product Development Process

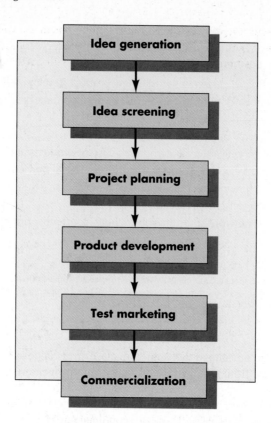

development, and the whole planning process depends on the quality of the idea generation and screening process. Since idea generation is the least costly stage in the new product development process (in terms of investment in funds, time, personnel, and escalation of commitment), it makes sense that an emphasis be placed first on recognizing available sources of new product ideas and then on funneling these ideas to appropriate decision makers for screening.

Top-management support is critical to providing an atmosphere that stimulates new product activity. Many times, great ideas come from some very unusual sources. A top-management structure that is unwilling to take risks will avoid radical new product and other innovation activities and instead concentrate solely on minor areas of improvement such as line extensions. To facilitate top-management support, it is essential that new product development be focused on meeting market needs.

Both technology push and market pull research activities play an important role in new product ideas and development. By taking a broad view of customer needs and wants, basic and applied research (technology push) can lead to ideas that will yield high profits to the firm. For example, Compaq bet millions (and won) on PC network servers in the early 1990s even though business customers said they would never abandon their mainframes. In a similar vein, Chrysler forged ahead with the original minivan despite research showing people disliked the odd-looking vehicle.[7] Marketing, on the other hand, is more responsible for gathering and disseminating information gained from customers and other contacts. This information relates mainly to specific features and functions of the product that can be improved upon or market needs that current products are not satisfying (market pull). For example, product ideas at Rubbermaid often come from employees roaming the aisles at hardware stores and conversations with family and friends.[8] Both technology push and market pull approaches are essential to the generation of new product ideas.

Some firms use mechanisms such as "out-rotation," outsider involvement, and rewards to foster cooperation between design engineers and marketers.[9] Out-rotation involves placing employees in positions that require direct contact with customers, competitors, and other key outside groups. For example, Hewlett-Packard regularly rotates design engineers to retail sales positions on a temporary basis. Other organizations actively involve "outsiders" in planning or reward engineers for making external customer contacts. Regardless of method used, the primary lesson is to keep the communications flow going in all directions throughout the organization.

Idea Screening

The primary function of the idea screening process is twofold: first, to eliminate ideas for new products that could not be profitably marketed by the firm, and second, to expand viable ideas into full product concepts. New product ideas may be eliminated either because they are outside the fields of the firm's interest or because the firm does not have the necessary resources or technology to produce the product at a profit. Generally speaking, the organization has to consider three categories of risk (and its associated risk tolerance) in the idea screening phase prior to reaching a decision:[10]

1. *Strategic risk.* Strategic risk involves the risk of not matching the role or purpose of a new product with a specific strategic need or issue of the organization. If an organization feels it necessary to develop certain types of radical innovations or products new to the company in order to carry out long-term strategies, then management must be willing to dedicate necessary resources and time to pursue these type projects.

2. *Market risk.* Market risk is the risk that a new product won't meet a market need in a value-added, differentiated way. As products are being developed, customer requirements change and new technologies evolve. Management must be willing and able to shift its new product efforts to keep pace with change.

3. *Internal risk.* Internal risk is the risk that a new product won't be developed within the desired time and budget. Up front, management must decide the level of commitment it will extend in terms of time and budgetary expenditures to adequately ensure the completion of specific projects. Concurrently, progress goals must be established so that "proceed" or "do not proceed" decisions can be reached regarding continuation of projects.

In evaluating these risks, firms should not act too hastily in discounting new product ideas solely because of a lack of resources or expertise. Instead, firms should consider forming joint or strategic alliances with other firms. A strategic alliance is a long-term partnership between two organizations designed to accomplish the strategic goals of both parties. Potential benefits to be gained from alliances include (1) increased access to technology, funding, and information; (2) market expansion and greater penetration of current markets; and (3) de-escalated competitive rivalries. Motorola is a company that has prospered by forming numerous joint ventures with both American and foreign companies.[11]

Ideas that appear to have adequate profit potential and offer the firm a competitive advantage in the market should be accepted for further study.

Project Planning

This stage of the process involves several steps. It is here that the new product proposal is evaluated further and responsibility for the project is assigned to a project team. The proposal is analyzed in terms of production, marketing, financial, and competitive factors. A development budget is established, and some preliminary marketing and technical research is undertaken. The product is actually designed in a rough form.

1. Customers
   a. Customer requests
   b. Customer complaints/compliments
   c. Market surveys
   d. Focus groups
2. Competitors
   a. Monitoring competitors' developments
   b. Monitoring testing of competitors' products
   c. Monitoring industry movements
3. Distribution channels
   a. Suppliers
   b. Distributors
   c. Retailers
   d. Trade shows
4. Research and engineering
   a. Product testing
   b. Product endorsement
   c. Brainstorming meetings
   d. Accidental discovery
5. Other internal sources
   a. Management
   b. Sales force
   c. Employee suggestions
   d. Innovation group meetings
   e. Stockholders
6. Other external sources
   a. Consultants
   b. Academic journals
   c. Periodicals and other press

Alternative product features and component specifications are outlined. Finally, a project plan is written up, which includes estimates of future development, production, and marketing costs along with capital requirements and manpower needs. A schedule or timetable is also included. Finally, the project proposal is given to top management for a go or no-go decision.

Various alternatives exist for creating and managing the project teams. Two of the better-known methods are the establishment of a *skunkworks,* whereby a project team can work in relative privacy away from the rest of the organization, and a *rugby* or *relay approach,* whereby groups in different areas of the company are simultaneously working on the project.[12] The common tie that binds these and other successful approaches together is the degree of interaction that develops among the marketing, engineering, production, and other critical staff. The earlier in the process that interactive, cooperative efforts begin, the higher is the likelihood that development efforts will be successful. A key component contributing to the success of many companies' product development efforts relates to the emphasis placed on creating *cross-functional teams* early in the development process. Both of the above methods use cross-functional teams. Members from many different departments come together to jointly establish new product development goals and priorities and to develop new product development schedules. Frequently, marketing and/or sales personnel are called in to lead these teams.[13]

Product Development

At this juncture, the product idea has been evaluated from the standpoint of engineering, manufacturing, finance, and marketing. If it has met all expectations, it is considered a candidate for further research and testing. In the laboratory, the product is converted into a finished good and tested. A development report to management is prepared that spells out in fine detail: (1) results of the studies by the engineering department, (2) required plan design, (3) production facilities design, (4) tooling requirements, (5) marketing test plan; (6) financial program survey, and (7) estimated release date.[14]

Test Marketing

Up until now the product has been a company secret. Now management goes outside the company and submits the product candidate for customer approval. Test-market programs

Participant*	Activity	Participant*	Activity
1. Project Manager	Leader Integrator Translator Mediator Judge Arbitrator Coordinator	4. Strategist	Longer range Managerial Entire program
2. Product champion	Supporter Spokesperson Pusher Won't concede	5. Inventor	Creative scientist Basement inventor Idea source
3. Sponsor	Senior manager Supporter Endorses Assures hearing Mentor Increases output	6. Rationalist 7. Facilitator	Objectivity Reality Reason Financial Boosts productivity

*The participant role may be either formal or informal.

Source: Merle Crawford and Anthony Di Benedetto, *New Products Management,* 8th ed. (Burr Ridge, IL: McGraw-Hill/Irwin, 2007), p. 314.

are conducted in line with the general plans for launching the product. Test marketing is a controlled experiment in a limited geographical area to test the new product or in some cases certain aspects of the marketing strategy, such as packaging or advertising.

The main goal of a test market is to evaluate and adjust, as necessary, the general marketing strategy to be used and the appropriate marketing mix. Additionally, producers can use the early interaction with buyers, occurring in test markets, to begin exploration of issues related to the next generation of product development.[15] Especially in cases where new technologies and markets are emerging, firms can benefit greatly from knowledge gained in test markets. Throughout the test market process, findings are being analyzed and forecasts of volume developed. In summary, a well-done test market procedure can reduce the risks that include not only lost marketing and sales dollars but also capital—the expense of installing production lines or building a new factory. Upon completion of a successful test market phase, the marketing plan can be finalized and the product prepared for launch.

Commercialization

This is the launching step in which the firm commits to introducing the product into the marketplace. During this stage, heavy emphasis is placed on the organization structure and management talent needed to implement the marketing strategy. Emphasis is also given to following up on such things as bugs in the design, production costs, quality control, and inventory requirements. Procedures and responsibility for evaluating the success of the new product by comparison with projections are also finalized.

The Importance of Time

Over the course of the last five years, companies have placed an increasing emphasis on shortening their products' time to market. *Time to market* can be defined as the elapsed

FINANCIAL CRITERIA

    Return on investment (ROI)

    Various profit margin measures

    Sales and sales growth

    Various profit measures

    Payback and payback period

    Internal rate of return (IRR)

    Return on assets (ROA)

    Return on equity (ROE)

    Breakeven and breakeven point

    Share and market share

    Return on sales

    Net present value (NPV)

NONFINANCIAL CRITERIA

Performance of new products

Market share achieved

Satisfaction of customer needs

Other market-related benefits

Strategic issues/fit/synergy

Technical aspects of production

Uniqueness of the new products

Source: Albert L. Page, "Assessing New Product Development Practices and Performance: Establishing Crucial Norms," *Journal of Product Innovation Management,* September 1993, pp. 273–90. 1993 by Elsevier Science Inc. Reprinted by permission of the publisher. Also see Kevin Lane Keller, *Strategic Brand Management,* 3rd ed. (Upper Saddle River, NJ: Prentice-Hall, 2008), chaps. 8–10.

time between product definition and product availability. It has been well documented that companies that are first in bringing their products to market enjoy a competitive advantage both in terms of profits and market share.[16] Successful time-based innovations can be attributed to the use of short production runs, whereby products can be improved on an incremental basis, and the use of cross-functional teams, decentralized work scheduling and monitoring, and a responsive system for gathering and analyzing customer feedback.

Several U.S. companies, including Procter & Gamble, have taken steps to speed up the new product development cycle by giving managers, at the product class and brand family level, more decision-making power. Increasingly, companies are bypassing time-consuming regional test markets, when feasible, in favor of national launches. It is becoming important, more than ever, that firms do a successful job of developing new products right the first time. To accomplish this, companies must have the right people with the right skills and talents in key positions within the new product framework.

Some Important New Product Decisions

In the development of new products, marketers have several important decisions to make about the characteristics of the product itself. These include quality level, product features, product design, and product safety levels.

Quality Level

Both consumers and organizational buyers consider the level of product quality when making purchase decisions for both new and existing products. At a minimum, buyers want products that will perform the functions they are supposed to and do so reasonably well. Some customers are willing to accept lower quality if product use is not demanding and the price is lower. Some homeowners might prefer Sears brand hand tools over the higher-quality Craftsman brand since they are lower priced and may be used only occasionally. Industrial buyers of nuts and bolts for automobiles seldom use the highest quality used in aircraft since cars are used in less demanding situations.

When specialized knowledge is needed to satisfy the needs of customers, cross-functional teams can greatly improve product development success. Such teams bring together complementary skills in one of three areas: technical or functional expertise, problem-solving and decision-making skills, and interpersonal skills.

1. *Technical or functional skills.* It would make little sense for a marketer to design technical specifications for a new type of cellular phone. Likewise, it would make little sense for an engineer to try to guess what features consumers find most important in choosing what type of phone to purchase. In this case, a product development group that consists solely of marketers or engineers would be less likely to succeed than a cross-functional team using the complementary skills of both.

2. *Problem-solving and decision-making skills.* Cross-functional teams possess the ability to identify problems and opportunities the entire organization faces, identify feasible new product alternatives, and make the necessary choices quicker. Most industrial functional units are not able to perform all of these tasks effectively. However, it is likely that the necessary skills are present in a well-chosen cross-functional team and that these skills can be used in the organization's best interests.

3. *Interpersonal skills.* Common understanding and knowledge of problems faced and decisions needed for effective product development cannot arise without effective communication and constructive conflict. What is needed is risk-taking, helpful criticism, objectivity, active listening, support, and recognition of the interests and achievements of others. An effective, cross-functional team is made up of members who, in total, possess all of these skills. Individual members, at various times, will be called on to use their interpersonal skill to move the team forward. The use of the complementary interpersonal skills of team members can lead to extraordinary results for organizations.

In designing new products, marketers must consider what criteria potential customers use to determine their perceptions of quality. While these will vary by product, Figure 7.3 presents eight general criteria.

An important indicator of a number of the criteria listed in Figure 7.3 is the presence and extent of a new product *warranty*. A warranty is the producer's statement of what it will do to compensate the buyer if the product is defective or does not work properly. In many instances, the courts also hold that businesses have implied warranties or unstated promises to compensate buyers if their products fail to perform up to the basic standards of the industry or to the level promised. Certainly an organization that wants to emphasize high quality will offer customers more than implied warranties enforced by the courts.

FIGURE 7.3

Some Criteria for Determining Perceptions of Quality

Source: Adopted from David A. Garvin, "Competing on the Eight Dimensions of Quality," *Harvard Business Review,* November–December 1987. For a discussion of some determinants of quality for service businesses, see chapter 12, "The Marketing of Services."

1. *Performance*—How well does the product do what it is supposed to do?
2. *Features*—Does the product have any unique features that are desirable?
3. *Reliability*—Is the product likely to function well and not break down over a reasonable time period?
4. *Conformance*—Does the product conform to established standards for such things as safety?
5. *Durability*—How long will the product last before it will be worn out and have to be replaced?
6. *Serviceability*—How quickly and easily can any problems be corrected?
7. *Aesthetics*—How appealing is the product to the appropriate senses of sight, taste, smell, feel, and/or sound?
8. *Overall Evaluation*—Considering everything about the product, including its physical characteristics, manufacturer, brand image, packaging, and price, how good is this product?

- *Communicating that something is different about the product.* Successful introductory commercials communicated some point of difference for the new product.
- *Positioning the brand difference in relation to the product category.* Successful commercials positioned their brand's difference within a specific product category. For example, a new breakfast cereal was positioned as the "crispiest cereal" and a new beverage as the "smoothest soft drink."
- *Communicating that the product difference is beneficial to customers.* Nearly all the successful commercials linked a benefit directly to the new product's difference.
- *Supporting the idea that something about the product is different and/or beneficial to consumers.* All the successful commercials communicated support for the product's difference claim or relevance to customers. Support took the form of demonstrations of performance, information supporting a uniqueness claim, endorsements, or testimonials.

Source: Based on research using commercials for new products conducted by Evalucom Inc., and reported in George E. Belch and Michael A Belch, *Advertising and Promotion,* 7th ed. (Burr Ridge, IL: McGraw-Hill/Irwin, 2007), p. 202.

Finally, many marketers offer a guarantee instead of or in addition to a warranty on new products. A *guarantee* is an assurance that the product is as represented and will perform properly. Typically if the product fails to perform, the organization making the guarantee replaces the product or refunds the customer's money. Guarantees imply to some buyers that the manufacturer is confident of the new products' quality.

Product Features

A *product feature* is a fact or particular specification about a product (e.g., "less calories than all other soft drinks," "more vitamin C than any other multiple vitamin"). Marketers select new product features by determining what it is that customers want their products to offer. Effective marketers attempt not only to ask potential customers what they want, but to learn what these customers are likely to need. Such marketers may identify a need for new features that target markets have not yet thought of and may not yet even understand.

Product Design

Many well-designed products are easy to use as intended and pleasing to the senses. Designing new products with both ease of use and aesthetic appeal can be difficult, but it can clearly differentiate a new product from competitors. Good design can add great value to a new product. A well-designed product can please customers without necessarily costing more to make. This is especially likely to happen when the organization uses cross-functional teams to develop its products. If employees from engineering, marketing, and manufacturing work together on what the product will look like and how it will operate, they are more likely to create a design that is easy and economical to make as well as use.

Product Safety

Clearly, new products must have a reasonable level of safety. Safety is both an ethical and practical issue. Ethically, customers should not be harmed by using a product as intended. The practical issue is that when users get harmed by a product, they may stop buying, tell others about their experience, or sue the company that made or sold it.

Some products are inherently dangerous and can result in injury to users. However, it may be so expensive to make them safer that buyers could not afford to buy them. Such products include automobiles, farm equipment and other machinery, and guns. Other products such as patented medicines can harm a small portion of users. Hopefully, the benefits such products offer outweigh their risks.

Causes of New Product Failure

Many new products with satisfactory potential have failed to make the grade for reasons related to execution and control problems. What follows is a brief list of some of the more important causes of new product failures after the products have been carefully screened, developed, and marketed.[17]

1. No competitive point of difference, unexpected reactions from competitors, or both.
2. Poor positioning.
3. Poor quality of product.
4. Nondelivery of promised benefits of product.
5. Too little marketing support.
6. Poor perceived price/quality (value) relationship.
7. Faulty estimates of market potential and other marketing research mistakes.
8. Faulty estimates of production and marketing costs.
9. Improper channels of distribution selected.
10. Rapid change in the market (economy) after the product was introduced.

Some of these problems are beyond the control of management, but it is clear that successful new product planning requires large amounts of reliable information in diverse areas. Each department assigned functional responsibility for product development automatically becomes an input to the information system that the new product decision maker needs. For example, when a firm is developing a new product, it is wise for both engineers and marketers to consider both the kind of market to be entered (e.g., consumer, organizational, international) and specific target segments. These decisions will be of paramount influence on the design and cost of the finished good, which will, of course, directly influence price, sales, and profits.

Need for Research

In many respects it can be argued that the keystone activity of any new product planning system is research—not just marketing research, but technical research as well. Regardless of the way the new product planning function is organized in the company, top management's new product development decisions require data that provide a base for making more intelligent choices. New product project reports ought to be more than a collection of "expert" opinions. Top management has a responsibility to ask certain questions, and the new product planning team has an obligation to generate answers to these questions based on research that provides marketing, economic, engineering, and production information. This need will be more clearly understood if some of the specific questions commonly raised in evaluating product ideas are examined:

1. What is the anticipated market demand over time? Are the potential applications for the product restricted?
2. Can the item be patented? Are there any antitrust problems?
3. Can the product be sold through present channels and the current sales force? What number of new salespersons will be needed? What additional sales training will be required?
4. At different volume levels, what will be the unit manufacturing costs?

5. What is the most appropriate package to use in terms of color, material, design, and so forth?
6. What is the estimated return on investment?
7. What is the appropriate pricing strategy?

While this list is not intended to be exhaustive, it serves to illustrate the serious need for reliable information. Note also that some of the essential facts required to answer these questions can be obtained only through time-consuming and expensive marketing research studies. Other data can be generated in the engineering laboratories or pulled from accounting records. Certain types of information must be based on assumptions, which may or may not hold true, and on expectations about what will happen in the future, as in the case of anticipated competitive reaction or the projected level of sales.

Conclusion

This chapter has focused on the nature of new product planning and development. Attention has been given to the management process required to have an effective program for new product development. It should be obvious that this is one of the most important and difficult aspects of marketing management. The problem is so complex that, unless management develops a plan for dealing with the problem, it is likely to operate at a severe competitive disadvantage in the marketplace.

Additional Readings

Biyalogorsky, Eyal, William Boulding, and Richard Staelin. "Stuck in the Past: Why Managers Persist with New Product Failures." *Journal of Marketing,* April 2006, pp. 108–122.

Carson, Stephen J. "When to Give up Control of Outsourced New Product Development." *Journal of Marketing,* January 2007, pp. 49–66.

Kerber, Ronald L., and Timothy M. Laster. *Strategic Product Creation.* NY: McGraw-Hill, 2007.

Lehman, Donald R., and Russell S. Winer. *Product Management.* 4th ed. Burr Ridge, IL: McGraw-Hill/Irwin, 2005.

Mack, Ben. *Think Two Products Ahead.* NY: John Wiley, 2007.

Chapter 8

Integrated Marketing Communications: Advertising, Sales Promotion, Public Relations, and Direct Marketing

Communicating with customers will be the broad subject of the next two chapters that focus on various elements of promotion. To simplify our discussion, the topic has been divided into two basic categories: nonpersonal communication (Chapter 8) and personal communication (Chapter 9). This chapter also discusses the necessity to integrate the various elements of marketing communication.

Strategic Goals of Marketing Communication

Marketers seek to communicate with target customers for the obvious goal of increased sales and profits. Accordingly, they seek to accomplish several strategic goals with their marketing communications efforts.

Create Awareness

Obviously, we cannot purchase a product if we are not aware of it. An important strategic goal must be to generate awareness of the firm as well as its products. Marketing communications designed to create awareness are especially important for new products and brands in order to stimulate trial purchases. As an organization expands globally, creating awareness must be a critical goal of marketing communications.

Build Positive Images

When products or brands have distinct images in the minds of customers, the customers better understand the value that is being offered. Positive images can even create value for customers by adding meaning to products. Retail stores and other organizations also use communications to build positive images. A major way marketers create positive and distinct images is through marketing communications.

Identify Prospects

Identifying prospects is becoming an increasingly important goal of marketing communications because modern technology makes information gathering much more practical, even in large consumer markets. Marketers can maintain records of consumers who have expressed an interest in a product, then more efficiently direct future communications. Technology now enables marketers to stay very close to their customers. Web sites are used to gather information about prospects, and supermarkets use point-of-sale terminals to dispense coupons selected on the basis of a customer's past purchases.

Build Channel Relationships

An important goal of marketing communications is to build a relationship with the organization's channel members. When producers use marketing communications to generate awareness, they are also helping the retailers who carry the product. Producers may also arrange with retailers to distribute coupons, set up special displays, or hold promotional events in their stores, all of which benefit retailers and wholesalers. Retailers support manufacturers when they feature brands in their ads to attract buyers. Because of such efforts, all members of the channel benefit. Cooperating in these marketing communication efforts can build stronger channel relationships.

Retain Customers

Loyal customers are a major asset for every business. It costs far more to attract a new customer than to retain an existing customer. Marketing communications can support efforts to create value for existing customers. Interactive modes of communication—including salespeople and Web sites—can play an important role in retaining customers. They can serve as sources of information about product usage and new products being developed. They can also gather information from customers about what they value, as well as their experiences using the products. This two-way communication can assist marketers in increasing the value of what they offer to existing customers, which will influence retention.

The Promotion Mix

The promotion mix concept refers to the combination and types of nonpersonal and personal communication the organization puts forth during a specified period.[1] There are five elements of the promotion mix, four of which are nonpersonal forms of communication (advertising, sales promotion, public relations, and direct marketing), and one, personal selling, which is a personal form of communication. Let's briefly examine each one.

1. *Advertising* is a paid form of <u>non</u>personal communications about an organization, its products, or its activities that is transmitted through a mass medium to a target audience. The mass medium might be television, radio, newspapers, magazines, outdoor displays, car cards, or directories.

2. *Sales promotion* is an activity or material that offers customers, sales personnel, or resellers a direct inducement for purchasing a product. This inducement, which adds value to or incentive for the product, might take the form of a coupon, sweepstakes, refund, or display.

3. *Public relations* is a <u>non</u>personal form of communication that seeks to influence the attitudes, feelings, and opinions of customers, noncustomers, stockholders, suppliers, employees, and political bodies about the organization. A popular form is *publicity,* which is a nonpaid form of nonpersonal communication about the organization and its products that is transmitted through a mass medium in the form of a news story. Obviously, marketers seek positive publicity.

4. *Direct marketing* uses direct forms of communication with customers. It can take the form of direct mail, online marketing, catalogs, telemarketing, and direct response advertising. Similar to personal selling, it may consist of an interactive dialog between the marketer and the customer. Its objective is to generate orders, visits to retail outlets, or requests for further information. Obviously, personal selling is a form of direct marketing, but because it is a very personal form of communication, we place it in its own category.

5. *Personal selling* is face-to-face communication with potential buyers to inform them about and persuade them to buy an organization's product. It will be examined in detail in the next chapter.

Obviously, marketers strive for the right mix of promotional elements to ensure that their product is well received. For example, if the product is a new soft drink, promotional effort is likely to rely more on advertising, sales promotion, and public relations (publicity) in order to (1) make potential buyers aware of the product, (2) inform these buyers about the benefits of the product, (3) convince buyers of the product's value, and (4) entice buyers to purchase the product. If the product is more established but the objective is to stabilize sales during a nonpeak season, the promotion mix will likely contain short-run incentives (sales promotions) for people to buy the product immediately. Finally, if the product is a new complex technology that requires a great deal of explanation, the promotional mix will likely focus heavily on personal selling so that potential buyers can have their questions answered.

As seen by the previous examples, a firm's promotion mix is likely to change over time. The mix must be continually adapted to reflect changes in the market, competition, the product's life cycle, and the adoption of new strategies. In essence, the firm should take into account three basic factors when devising its promotion mix: (1) the role of promotion in the overall marketing mix, (2) the nature of the product, and (3) the nature of the market.

Integrated Marketing Communications

In many organizations, elements of the promotion mix are often managed by specialists in different parts of the organization or, in some cases, outside the organization when an advertising agency is used. For example, advertising plans might be developed jointly by the advertising department and the advertising agency; plans for the sales force might be

The importance of integrating marketing communication efforts is widely accepted. While organizations differ on just how fully integrated their efforts are, it is clear that integrated marketing communications is an idea whose time has come. The following are some important differences between a traditional approach to marketing communications and an integrated approach.

Traditional Approach	Integrated Approach
Focus on:	Focus on:
1. Making transactions.	1. Building and nourishing relationships.
2. Customers.	2. All stakeholders in the organization.
3. Independent brand messages.	3. Strategic consistency on brand messages.
4. Mass media—monologue with customers.	4. Interactivity—dialogue with customers.
5. Product claims.	5. Corporate mission marketing.
6. Adjusting prior year's plan.	6. Zero-based campaign planning.
7. Functional department planning and monitoring.	7. Cross-functional planning and monitoring.
8. Communication specialists.	8. Creating core competencies.
9. Mass marketing and customer acquisition.	9. Building and managing databases to retain customers.
10. Stable of agencies.	10. One communication management agency.

Source: Adapted from Tom Duncan and Sandra Moriarity, *Driving Brand Value: Using Integrated Marketing to Manage Profitable Stakeholder Relationships* (New York: McGraw-Hill, 1997), pp. 16–19.

developed by managers of the sales force; and sales promotions might be developed independently of the advertising and sales plans. Thus, it is not surprising that the concept of *integrated marketing communications* has evolved in recent years.

The idea of integrated marketing communications is easy to understand and certainly has a great deal of commonsense validity. But like so many concepts in marketing, it is difficult to implement. The goal of integrated marketing communications is to develop marketing communications programs that coordinate and integrate all elements of promotion—advertising, sales promotion, personal selling, and publicity—so that the organization presents a consistent message. Integrated marketing communication seeks to manage all sources of brand or company contacts with existing and potential customers. Marketing Highlight 8–1 presents the critical aspects of integrated marketing communications and how they differ from the way traditional marketing communications efforts have been managed.

The concept of integrated marketing communication is illustrated in Figure 8.1. It is generally agreed that potential buyers usually go through a process of (1) *awareness* of the product or service, (2) *comprehension* of what it can do and its important features, (3) *conviction* that it has value for them, and (4) *ordering*. Consequently, the firm's marketing communication tools must encourage and allow the potential buyer to experience the various stages. Figure 8.1 illustrates the role of various marketing communication tools for a hypothetical product.

The goal of integrated marketing communication is an important one, and many believe it is critical for success in today's crowded marketplace. As with many management concepts, implementation is slower than many would like to see. Internal "turf" battles within organizations and the reluctance of some advertising agencies to willingly broaden their

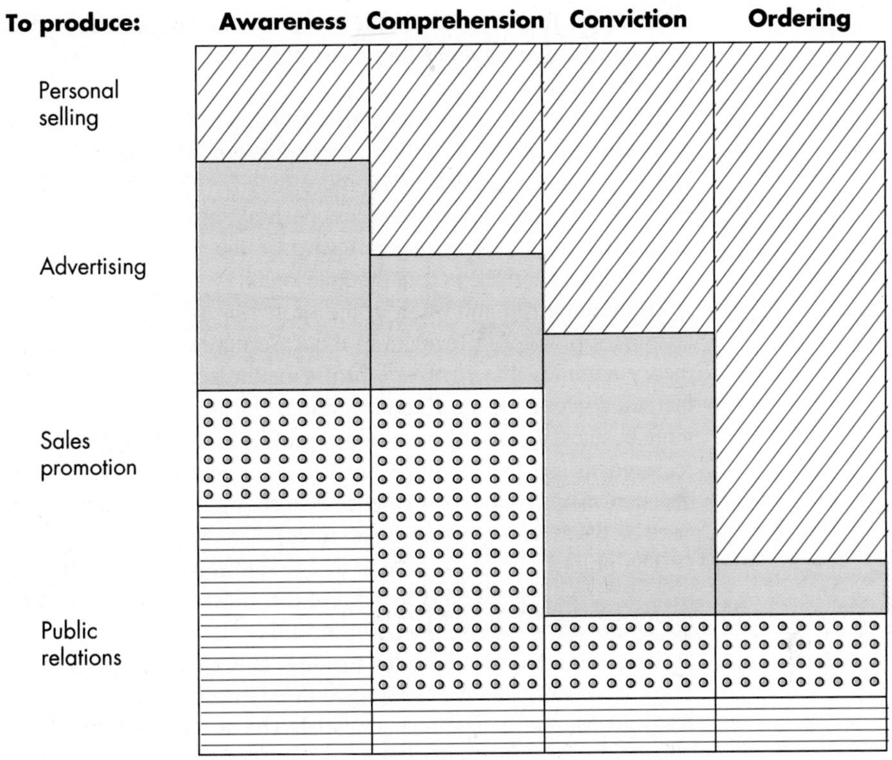

FIGURE 8.1

How Various Promotion Tools Might Contribute to the Purchase of a Hypothetical Product

To produce:	Awareness	Comprehension	Conviction	Ordering
Personal selling				
Advertising				
Sales promotion				
Public relations				

role beyond advertising are two factors that are hindering the successful implementation of integrated marketing communication.

Advertising: Planning and Strategy

Advertising seeks to promote the seller's product by means of printed and electronic media. This is justified on the grounds that messages can reach large numbers of people and make them aware and persuade and remind them about the firm's offerings.

From a marketing management perspective, advertising is an important strategic device for maintaining a competitive advantage in the marketplace. Advertising budgets represent a large and growing element in the cost of goods and services. In a year it is possible for large multiproduct firms to spend $1.5 to $2 billion advertising their products, and it is common to spend $74 to $100 million on one individual brand. Clearly, advertising must be carefully planned.

Objectives of Advertising

There are at least three different viewpoints about the contribution of advertising to the economic health of the firm. The generalist viewpoint is primarily concerned with sales, profits, return on investment, and so forth. At the other extreme, the specialist viewpoint is represented by advertising experts who are primarily concerned with measuring the effects of specific ads or campaigns; here primary attention is given to organizations that offer services that measure different aspects of the effects of advertising such as the Nielsen Index, Starch Reports, Arbitron Index, and Simmons Reports. A middle view, one that might be classified as more of a marketing management approach, understands and appreciates the other two viewpoints but, in addition, sees advertising as a competitive weapon. Emphasis in this approach is given to the strategic aspects of the advertising function.[2]

Building on what was said earlier, objectives for advertising can be assigned that focus on creating *awareness,* aiding *comprehension,* developing *conviction,* and encouraging *ordering.* Within each category, more specific objectives can be developed that take into account time and degree of success desired. Obviously, compared to the large number of people that advertising makes aware of the product or service, the number actually motivated to purchase is usually quite small.

In the long run and often in the short run, advertising is justified on the basis of the revenue it produces. Revenue in this case may refer to either sales or profits. Economic theory assumes that firms are profit maximizers, and the advertising outlays should be increased in every market and medium up to the point where the additional cost of gaining more business equals the incremental profits. Since most business firms do not have the data required to use the marginal analysis approach, they usually employ less-sophisticated decision-making models. Evidence also shows that many managers advertise to maximize sales on the assumption that higher sales mean more profits (which may or may not be true).

The point to be made here is that the ultimate objective of the business advertiser is to make sales and profits. To achieve this objective, customers must purchase and repurchase the advertised product. Toward this end, an approach to advertising is needed that provides for intelligent decision making. This approach must recognize the need for measuring the results of advertising, and these measurements must be as valid and reliable as possible. Marketing managers must also be aware that advertising not only complements other forms of communication but is subject to the law of diminishing returns. This means that for any advertised product, it can be assumed a point is eventually reached at which additional advertising produces little or no additional sales.

Advertising Decisions

In line with what has just been said, the marketing manager must make two key decisions. The first decision deals with determining the size of the advertising budget, and the second deals with how the advertising budget should be allocated. Although these decisions are highly interrelated, we deal with them separately to achieve a better understanding of the problems involved. Today's most successful brands of consumer goods were built by heavy advertising and marketing investment long ago. Many marketers have lost sight of the connection between advertising spending and market share. They practice the art of discounting: cutting ad budgets to fund price promotions or fatten quarterly earnings. Companies employing these tactics may benefit in the short term but may be at a severe competitive disadvantage in the long term.

Marketers at some companies, however, know that brand equity and consumer preference for brands drive market share. They understand the balance of advertising and promotion expenditures needed to build brands and gain share, market by market, regardless of growth trends in the product categories where they compete. For example, Procter & Gamble has built its Jif and Folger's brands from single-digit shares to being among category leaders. In peanut butter and coffee, P&G invests more in advertising and less in discounting than its major competitors. What P&G and other smart marketers such as Kellogg, General Mills, Coke, and PepsiCo hold in common is an awareness of a key factor in advertising: consistent investment spending. They do not raid their ad budgets to increase earnings for a few quarters, nor do they view advertising as a discretionary cost.

Element	Ethical and Legal Concerns
Advertising	• Using deceptive advertising • Reinforcing unfavorable ethnic/racial/sex stereotypes • Encouraging materialism and excessive consumption
Public relations	• Lack of sincerity (paying lip service to worthwhile causes) • Using economic power to gain favorable publicity • Orchestrating news events to present a false appearance of widespread support for the company position
Sales promotion	• Offering misleading consumer promotions • Paying slotting allowances to gain retail shelf space • Using unauthorized mailing lists to reach consumers
Personal selling	• Using high-pressure selling • Failing to disclose product limitations/safety concerns • Misrepresenting product health
Direct marketing communications	• Invading privacy with telemarketing • Using consumer database information without consumers' authorization • Creating economic waste with unwanted direct mail

Source: William O. Bearden, Thomas N. Ingram, and Raymond W. LaForge, *Marketing: Principles and Perspectives,* 5th ed. (Burr Ridge, IL: McGraw-Hill/Irwin, 2007), p. 383.

The Expenditure Question

Most firms determine how much to spend on advertising by one of the following methods.

Percent of Sales

This is one of the most popular rule-of-thumb methods, and its appeal is found in its simplicity. The firm simply takes a percentage figure and applies it to either past or future sales. For example, suppose next year's sales are estimated to be $1 million. Using the criterion of 2 percent of sales, the ad budget would be $20,000. This approach is usually justified by its advocates in terms of the following argument: (1) Advertising is needed to generate sales; (2) a number of cents (i.e., the percentage used) out of each dollar of sales should be devoted to advertising in order to generate needed sales; and (3) the percentage is easily adjusted and can be readily understood by other executives. The percent-of-sales approach is popular in retailing.

Per-Unit Expenditure

Closely related to the above technique is one in which a fixed monetary amount is spent on advertising for each unit of the product expected to be sold. This method is popular with higher-priced merchandise, such as automobiles or appliances. For instance, if a company is marketing color televisions priced at $500, it may decide that it should spend $30 per set on advertising. Since this $30 is a fixed amount for each unit, this method amounts to the same thing as the percent-of-sales method. The big difference is in the rationale used to justify each of the methods. The per-unit expenditure method attempts to determine the retail price by using production costs as a base. Here the seller realizes that a reasonably competitive price must be established for the product in question and therefore attempts to cost out the gross margin. All this means is that, if the suggested retail price is to be $500 and manufacturing costs are $250, a gross margin of $250 is available to cover certain expenses, such as transportation, personal selling, advertising, and dealer profit. Some of these expense items are flexible, such as advertising, while others are nearly fixed, as in the case of transportation.

1. Does the advertising aim at *immediate sales?* If so, objectives might be to

   - Perform the complete selling function.
   - Close sales to prospects already partly sold.
   - Announce a special reason for buying now (price, premium, and so forth).
   - Remind people to buy.
   - Tie in with special buying event.
   - Stimulate impulse sales.

2. Does the advertising aim at *near-term sales?* If so, objectives might be to

   - Create awareness.
   - Enhance brand image.
   - Implant information or attitude.
   - Combat or offset competitive claims.
   - Correct false impressions, misinformation.
   - Build familiarity and easy recognition.

3. Does the advertising aim at building a *long-range consumer franchise?* If so, objectives might be to

   - Build confidence in company and brand.
   - Build customer demand.
   - Select preferred distributors and dealers.
   - Secure universal distribution.
   - Establish a "reputation platform" for launching new brands or product lines.
   - Establish brand recognition and acceptance.

4. Does the advertising aim at helping *increase sales?* If so, objectives would be to

   - Hold present customers.
   - Convert other users to advertiser's brand.
   - Cause people to specify advertiser's brand.
   - Convert nonusers to users.
   - Make steady customers out of occasional ones.
   - Advertise new uses.
   - Persuade customers to buy larger sizes or multiple units.
   - Remind users to buy.
   - Encourage greater frequency or quantity of use.

5. Does the advertising aim at some specific step that leads to a sale? If so, objectives might be to

   - Persuade prospect to write for descriptive literature, return a coupon, enter a contest.
   - Persuade prospect to visit a showroom, ask for a demonstration.
   - Induce prospect to sample the product (trial offer).

6. How important are supplementary benefits of advertising? Objectives would be to

   - Help salespeople open new accounts.
   - Help salespeople get larger orders from wholesalers and retailers.
   - Help salespeople get preferred display space.
   - Give salespeople an entrée.
   - Build morale of sales force.
   - Impress the trade.

7. Should the advertising impart information needed to consummate sales and build customer satisfaction? If so, objectives may be to use

   - "Where to buy it" advertising.
   - "How to use it" advertising.
   - New models, features, package.
   - New prices.
   - Special terms, trade-in offers, and so forth.
   - New policies (such as guarantees).

8. Should advertising build confidence and goodwill for the corporation? Targets may include

   - Customers and potential customers.
   - The trade (distributors, dealers, retail people).
   - Employees and potential employees.
   - The financial community.
   - The public at large.

9. What kind of images does the company wish to build?

   - Product quality, dependability.
   - Service.
   - Family resemblance of diversified products.
   - Corporate citizenship.
   - Growth, progressiveness, technical leadership.

Source: William F. Arens, Michael F. Weigold, and Christian Arens, *Contemporary Advertising,* 11th ed. (Burr Ridge, IL: McGraw-Hill/Irwin, 2008), pp. 624–27 and RL 8–3.

The basic problem with this method and the percentage-of-sales method is that they view advertising as a function of sales, rather than sales as a function of advertising.

All You Can Afford

Here the advertising budget is established as a predetermined share of profits or financial resources. The availability of current revenues sets the upper limit of the ad budget. The only advantage to this approach is that it sets reasonable limits on the expenditures for advertising. However, from the standpoint of sound marketing practice, this method is undesirable because there is no necessary connection between liquidity and advertising opportunity. Any firm that limits its advertising outlays to the amount of available funds will probably miss opportunities for increasing sales and profits.

Competitive Parity

This approach is often used in conjunction with other approaches, such as the percent-of-sales method. The basic philosophy underlying this approach is that advertising is defensive. Advertising budgets are based on those of competitors or other members of the industry. From a strategy standpoint, this is a "followership" technique that assumes that the other firms in the industry know what they are doing and have similar goals. Competitive parity is not a preferred method, although some executives feel it is a safe approach. This may or may not be true depending in part on the relative market share of competing firms and their growth objectives.

The Research Approach

Here the advertising budget is argued for and presented on the basis of research findings. Advertising media are studied in terms of their productivity by the use of media reports and research studies. Costs are also estimated and compared with study results. A typical experiment is one in which three or more test markets are selected. The first test market is used as a control, either with no advertising or with normal levels of advertising. Advertising with various levels of intensity is used in the other markets, and comparisons are made to see what effect different levels of intensity have. The marketing manager then evaluates the costs and benefits of the different approaches and intensity levels to determine the overall budget. Although the research approach is generally more expensive than some other models, it is a more rational approach to the expenditure decision.

The Task Approach

Well-planned advertising programs usually make use of the task approach, which initially formulates the advertising goals and defines the tasks to accomplish these goals. Once this is done, management determines how much it will cost to accomplish each task and adds up the total. This approach is often in conjunction with the research approach.

The Allocation Question

This question deals with the problem of deciding on the most effective way of spending advertising dollars. A general answer to the question is that management's choice of strategies and objectives determines the media and appeals to be used. In other words, the firm's or product division's overall marketing plan will function as a general guideline for answering the allocation question.

From a practical standpoint, however, the allocation question can be framed in terms of message and media decisions. A successful ad campaign has two related tasks: (1) say the right things in the ads themselves, and (2) use the appropriate media in the right amounts at the right time to reach the target market.

Effective advertising should follow a plan. There is no one best way to go about planning an advertising campaign, but in general, marketers should have good answers to the following eight questions:

1. *The management question:* Who will manage the advertising program?
2. *The money question:* How much should be spent on advertising as opposed to other forms of communication?
3. *The market question:* To whom should the advertising be directed?
4. *The message question:* What should the ads say about the product?
5. *The media question:* What types and combinations of media should be used?
6. *The macroscheduling question:* How long should the advertising campaign be in effect before changing ads or themes?
7. *The microscheduling question:* At what times and dates would it be best for ads to appear during the course of the campaign?
8. *The measurement question:* How will the effectiveness of the advertising campaign be measured and how will the campaign be evaluated and controlled?

Message Strategy

The advertising process involves creating messages with words, ideas, sounds, and other forms of audiovisual stimuli that are designed to affect consumer (or distributor) behavior. It follows that much of advertising is a communication process. To be effective, the advertising message should meet two general criteria: (1) It should take into account the basic principles of communication, and (2) it should be predicated upon a good theory of consumer motivation and behavior.

The basic communication process involves three elements: (1) the sender or source of the communication, (2) the communication or message, and (3) the receiver or audience. Advertising agencies are considered experts in the communications field and are employed by most large firms to create meaningful messages and assist in their dissemination. Translating the product idea or marketing message into an effective ad is termed *encoding*. In advertising, the goal of encoding is to generate ads that the audience understands. For this to occur, the audience must be able to *decode* the message in the ad so that the perceived content of the message is the same as the intended content of the message. From a practical standpoint, all this means is that advertising messages must be sent to consumers in an understandable and meaningful way.

Advertising messages, of course, must be transmitted and carried by particular communication channels commonly known as advertising media. These media or channels vary in efficiency, selectivity, and cost. Some channels are preferred to others because they have less "noise," and thus messages are more easily received and understood. For example, a particular newspaper ad must compete with other ads, pictures, or stories on the same page. In the case of radio or TV, while only one firm's message is usually broadcast at a time, other distractions (noise) can hamper clear communications, such as driving while listening to the radio.

The relationship between advertising and consumer behavior is quite obvious. For many products and services, advertising is an influence that may affect the consumer's decision to purchase a particular product or brand. It is clear that consumers are subjected to many selling influences, and the question arises about how important advertising is or can be. In this case, the advertising expert must operate on some theory of consumer behavior. The reader will recall from the discussion of consumer behavior that the buyer was viewed as progressing through various stages from an unsatisfied

NEWSPAPERS

Advantages

1. Flexible and timely.
2. Intense coverage of local markets.
3. Broad acceptance and use.
4. High believability of printed word.

Disadvantages

1. Short life.
2. Read hastily.
3. Small "pass-along" audience.

RADIO

Advantages

1. Mass use (over 25 million radios sold annually).
2. Audience selectivity via station format.
3. Low cost (per unit of time).
4. Geographic flexibility.

Disadvantages

1. Audio presentation only.
2. Less attention than TV.
3. Chaotic buying (nonstandardized rate structures).
4. Short life.

OUTDOOR

Advantages

1. Flexible.
2. Relative absence of competing advertisements.
3. Repeat exposure.
4. Relatively inexpensive.

Disadvantages

1. Creative limitations.
2. Many distractions for viewer.
3. Public attack (ecological implications).
4. No selectivity of audience.

TELEVISION

Advantages

1. Combination of sight, sound, and motion.
2. Appeals to senses.
3. Mass audience coverage.
4. Psychology of attention.

Disadvantages

1. Nonselectivity of audience.
2. Fleeting impressions.
3. Short life.
4. Expensive.

MAGAZINES

Advantages

1. High geographic and demographic selectivity.
2. Psychology of attention.
3. Quality of reproduction.
4. Pass-along readership.

Disadvantages

1. Long closing periods (six to eight weeks prior to publication).
2. Some waste circulation.
3. No guarantee of position (unless premium is paid).

DIRECT MAIL

Advantages

1. Audience selectivity.
2. Flexible.
3. No competition from competing advertisements.
4. Personalized.

Disadvantages

1. Relatively high cost.
2. Consumers often pay little attention and throw it away.

INTERNET

Advantages

1. Interactive.
2. Low cost per exposure.
3. Ads can be placed in interest sections.
4. Timely.
5. High information content possible.
6. New favorable medium.

Disadvantages

1. Low attention getting.
2. Short message life.
3. Reader selects exposure.
4. May be perceived as intruding.
5. Subject to download speeds.

need through and beyond a purchase decision. The end goal of an advertisement and its associated campaign is to move the buyer to a decision to purchase the advertised brand. By doing so, the advertisement will have succeeded in moving the consumer to the trial and repeat purchase stage of the consumer behavior process, which is the end goal of advertising strategy.

The planning of an advertising campaign and the creation of persuasive messages require a mixture of marketing skill and creative know-how. Relative to the dimension of marketing skills, some important pieces of marketing information are needed before launching an ad campaign. Most of this information must be generated by the firm and kept up-to-date. Listed below are some of the critical types of information an advertiser should have.

1. *Who* the firm's customers and potential customers are: their demographic, economic, and psychological characteristics and any other factors affecting their likelihood of buying.
2. *How many* such customers there are.
3. *How much* of the firm's type and brand of product they are currently buying and can reasonably be expected to buy in the short-term and long-term future.
4. *Which* individuals, other than customers and potential customers, *influence* purchasing decisions.
5. *Where* they buy the firm's brand of product.
6. *When* they buy, and frequency of purchase.
7. *Which* competitive brands they buy and frequency of purchase.
8. *How* they use the product.
9. *Why* they buy particular types and brands of products.

Media Mix

Media selection is no easy task. To start with, there are numerous types and combinations of media to choose from. Marketing Highlight 8–5 presents a brief summary of the advantages and disadvantages of some of the major advertising media.

In the advertising industry, a common measure of efficiency or productivity is cost per thousand, or CPMs. This figure generally refers to the dollar cost of reaching 1,000 prospects, and its chief advantage lies in its simplicity and allowance for a common base of comparison between differing media types. The major disadvantage of the use of CPMs also relates to its simplicity. For example, the same commercial placed in two different television programs, having the same viewership and the same audience profile, may very well generate different responses depending on the level of viewer involvement. This "positive effects" theory states that the more the viewers are involved in a television program, the stronger they will respond to commercials. In essence, involving programs produce engaged respondents who demonstrate more favorable responses to advertising messages.

Generally, such measures as circulation, audience size, and sets in use per commercial minute are used in the calculation. Of course, different relative rankings of media can occur, depending on the measure used. A related problem deals with what is meant by "effectively reaching" the prospect.[3] *Reach,* in general, is the number of different targeted audience members exposed at least once to the advertiser's message within a predetermined time frame. Just as important as the number of different people exposed (reach) is the number of times, on average, that they are exposed to an advertisement within a given time period. This rate of exposure is called *average frequency.* Since marketers all have budget constraints, they must decide whether to increase reach at the expense of average frequency or average frequency at the expense of reach. In essence, the marketer's dilemma is to develop a media schedule that both (1) exposes a sufficient number of targeted customers (reach) to the firm's product and (2) exposes them enough times (average frequency) to the product to produce the desired effect. The desired effect can come in the form of reaching goals associated with any or all of the categories of advertising objectives (the prospect becomes aware of the product, takes action, etc.) covered earlier in the chapter.

Sales Promotion

Over the past two decades, the popularity of sales promotion has been increasing. Two reasons for this increased popularity are undoubtedly the increased pressure on management for short-term results and the emergence of new purchase tracking technology. For example, many supermarket cash registers are now equipped with a device that dispenses coupons to a customer at the point of purchase. The type, variety, and cash amount of the coupon will vary from customer to customer based on their purchases. In essence, it is now possible for the Coca-Cola Company to dispense coupons only to those customers who purchase Pepsi Cola, thus avoiding spending promotional dollars on already-loyal Coke drinkers. Figure 8.2 presents some popular targets of sales promotion and the methods used.

Push versus Pull Marketing

Push and pull marketing strategies comprise the two options available to marketers interested in getting their product into the hands of customers. They are illustrated in Figure 8.3. *Push strategies* involve aiming promotional efforts at distributors, retailers, and sales personnel to gain their cooperation in ordering, stocking, and accelerating the sales of a product. For example, a local rock band may visit local DJs seeking air play for their record, offer distributors special prices to carry the CD, and offer retailers special allowances for putting up posters or special counter displays. These activities, which are usually in the form of price allowances, distribution allowances, and advertising dollar allowances, are designed to "push" the CD toward the customer.[4]

Pull strategies involve aiming promotional efforts directly at customers to encourage them to ask the retailer for the product. In the past few years drug manufacturers have begun to advertise prescription drugs directly to consumers. Customers are encouraged to "Ask Your Doctor" about Viagra or Paxil. These activities, which can include advertising and sales promotion, are designed to "pull" a product through the channel from manufacturer to buyer.

FIGURE 8.2 **Example of Sales Promotion Activities**

Source: William D. Perreault, Jr. and E. Jerome McCarthy, *Basic Marketing: A Global Managerial Approach,* 15th ed. Irwin/McGraw-Hill, 2005, chap. 14.

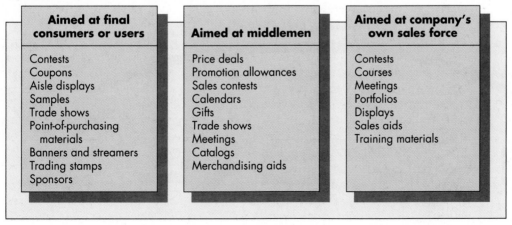

Aimed at final consumers or users	Aimed at middlemen	Aimed at company's own sales force
Contests	Price deals	Contests
Coupons	Promotion allowances	Courses
Aisle displays	Sales contests	Meetings
Samples	Calendars	Portfolios
Trade shows	Gifts	Displays
Point-of-purchasing materials	Trade shows	Sales aids
Banners and streamers	Meetings	Training materials
Trading stamps	Catalogs	
Sponsors	Merchandising aids	

PROCEDURES FOR EVALUATING SPECIFIC ADVERTISEMENTS

1. *Recognition tests.* Estimate the percentage of people claiming to have read a magazine who recognize the ad when it is shown to them (e.g., Starch Message Report Service).
2. *Recall tests.* Estimate the percentage of people claiming to have read a magazine who can (unaided) recall the ad and its contents (e.g., Gallup and Robinson Impact Service, various services for TV ads as well).
3. *Opinion tests.* Potential audience members are asked to rank alternative advertisements as most interesting, most believable, best liked.
4. *Theater tests.* Theater audience is asked for brand preferences before and after an ad is shown in context of a TV show (e.g., Schwerin TV Testing Service).

PROCEDURES FOR EVALUATING SPECIFIC ADVERTISING OBJECTIVES

1. *Awareness.* Potential buyers are asked to indicate brands that come to mind in a product category. A message used in an ad campaign is given and buyers are asked to identify the brand that was advertised using that message.
2. *Attitude.* Potential buyers are asked to rate competing or individual brands on determinant attributes, benefits, and characterizations using rating scales.

PROCEDURES FOR EVALUATING MOTIVATIONAL IMPACT

1. *Intention to buy.* Potential buyers are asked to indicate the likelihood they will buy a brand (on a scale from "definitely will not" to "definitely will").
2. *Market test.* Sales changes in different markets are monitored to compare the effects of different messages, budget levels.

Source: Joseph Guiltinan and Gordon Paul, *Marketing Management,* 6th ed., © 1997, New York, McGraw-Hill, Inc., p. 274. Reproduced by permission of The McGraw-Hill Companies.

FIGURE 8.3   **Push versus Pull Strategies in Marketing Communications**

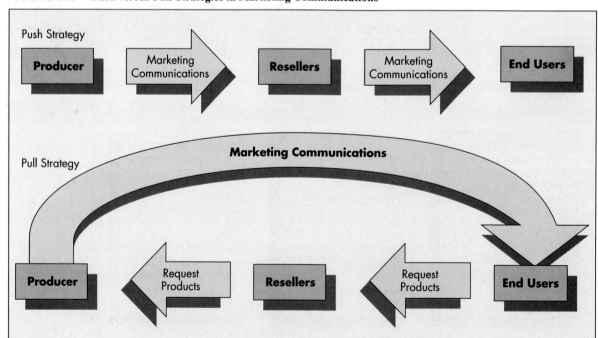

Trade Sales Promotions

Trade promotions are those promotions aimed at distributors and retailers of products who make up the distribution channel. The major objectives of trade promotions are to (1) convince retailers to carry the manufacturer's products, (2) reduce the manufacturer's inventories and increase the distributor's or retailer's inventories, (3) support advertising and consumer sales promotions, (4) encourage retailers either to give the product more favorable shelf space or to place more emphasis on selling the product, and (5) serve as a reward for past sales efforts.

Promotions built around price discounts and advertising or other allowances are likely to have higher distributor/retailer participation levels than other type promotions because a direct economic incentive is attached to the promotion.[5] The importance attached to individual types of promotions may vary by the size of distributor/retailer. For example, small retailers do not consider contests, sweepstakes, and sales quotas as being important to their decision to participate in promotions; getting the full benefit of such promotions is difficult due to their size. Marketers must keep in mind that not all distributors or retailers will have the same reaction to promotions offered. The manufacturer must carefully consider differences in attitudes when designing and implementing trade promotion programs.

Consumer Promotions

Consumer promotions can fulfill several distinct objectives for the manufacturer. Some of the more commonly sought-after objectives include (1) inducing the consumer to try the product, (2) rewarding the consumer for brand loyalty, (3) encouraging the consumer to trade up or purchase larger sizes of a product, (4) stimulating the consumer to make repeat purchases of the product, (5) reacting to competitor efforts, and (6) reinforcing and serving as a complement to advertising and personal selling efforts.

Figure 8.4 presents a brief description of some of the most commonly used forms of consumer promotion activities.

What Sales Promotion Can and Can't Do

Advocates of sales promotion often point to its growing popularity as a justification for the argument that we don't need advertising; sales promotion itself will suffice. Marketers should bear in mind that sales promotion is only one part of a well-constructed integrated marketing communications program. While sales promotion is proven to be effective in achieving the objectives listed in the previous sections, there are several compelling reasons why it should not be used as the sole promotional tool. These reasons include sales promotion's inability (1) to generate long-term buyer commitment to a brand in many cases; (2) to change, except on a temporary basis, declining sales of a product; (3) to convince

FIGURE 8.4
Some Commonly Used Forms of Consumer Promotions

• *Sampling.*	Customers are offered regular trial sizes of the product either free or at a nominal price.
• *Price deals.*	Customers are offered discounts from the product's regular price.
• *Bonus packs.*	Additional amounts of the product are given to buyers when they purchase the product.
• *Rebates and refunds.*	Customers are given reimbursements for purchasing the product either on the spot or through the mail.
• *Sweepstakes and contests.*	Prizes are available either through chance selection or games of skill.
• *Premiums.*	A reward or gift can come from purchasing a product.
• *Coupons.*	Probably the most familiar and widely used of all consumer promotions, now often available at point of purchase.

WHEN DIRECTED AT CONSUMERS

1. To obtain the trial of a product.
2. To introduce a new or improved product.
3. To encourage repeat or greater usage by current users.
4. To bring more customers into retail stores.
5. To increase the total number of users of an established product.

WHEN DIRECTED AT SALESPEOPLE

1. To motivate the sales force.
2. To educate the sales force about product improvements.
3. To stabilize a fluctuating sales pattern.

WHEN DIRECTED AT RESELLERS

1. To increase reseller inventories.
2. To obtain displays and other support for products.
3. To improve product distribution.
4. To obtain more and better shelf space.

buyers to purchase an otherwise unacceptable product; and (4) to make up for a lack of advertising or sales support for a product. In addition, promotions can often fuel the flames of competitive retaliation far more than other marketing activities. When the competition gets drawn into the promotion war, the effect can be a significant slowing of the sharp sales increases predicted by the initiator of the promotion. Worse yet, promotions can often devalue the image of the promoted brand in the consumer's eyes.

The dilemma marketers face is how to cut back on sales promotions without losing market share to competitors. In an effort to overcome this problem, some consumer products companies are instituting new pricing policies to try to cut back on the amount of sales promotions used. For example, Procter & Gamble and General Mills have instituted everyday low-price strategies for many of their products. The intent of this type of policy is to give retailers a lower list price in exchange for cutting trade promotions. While the net cost of the product to retailers remains unchanged, retailers are losing promotional dollars that they controlled. In many situations, although trade allowances are supposed to be used for encouraging retail sales, it is not uncommon for retailers to take a portion of the trade allowance money as profit. The rationale behind companies' (such as Procter & Gamble and General Mills) efforts to cut back on trade and other promotions is (1) not to force brand-loyal customers to pay unusually high prices when a product isn't on special; (2) to allow consumers to benefit from a lower average shelf price, since retailers will no longer have discretion over the use of allowance dollars; and (3) to improve efficiencies in manufacturing and distribution systems because retailers will lose the incentive to do heavy forward buying of discounted items.

In addition to developing pricing policies to cut back on short-term promotions, some consumer products companies are starting to institute *frequency marketing programs* in which they reward consumers for purchases of products or services over a sustained period of time.[6] These programs are not technically considered sales promotions due to their ongoing nature. Frequency marketing originated in 1981 when American Airlines launched its frequent-flyer program with the intention of securing the loyalty of business travelers.

| | Marketing Objective | | |
Consumer Reward Incentive	Induce trial	Customer retention/loading	Support IMC program/ build brand equity
Immediate	• Sampling • Instant coupons • In-store coupons • In-store rebates	• Price-off deals • Bonus packs • In- and on-package free premiums • Loyalty programs	• Events • In- and on-package free premiums
Delayed	• Media- and mail-delivered coupons • Mail-in refunds and rebates • Free mail-in premiums • Scanner- and Internet-delivered coupons	• In- and on-package coupons • Mail-in refunds and rebates • Loyalty programs	• Self-liquidating premiums • Free mail-in premiums • Contests and sweepstakes • Loyalty programs

Source: George E. Belch and Michael A. Belch, *Advertising and Promotion*, 7th ed. (Burr Ridge, IL: McGraw-Hill/Irwin, 2007), p. 525.

Public Relations

As noted earlier in the chapter, public relations is a nonpersonal form of communication that tries to influence the overall image of the organization and its products and services among its various stakeholder groups. Public relations managers prefer to focus on communicating positive news about the organization, but they must also be available to minimize the negative impacts of a crisis or problem. We have already noted that the most popular and frequently used public relations tool is publicity. There are several forms of publicity:

1. *News release.* An announcement regarding changes in the organization or the product line, sometimes called a *press release.* The objective is to inform members of the media of a newsworthy event in the hope that they will convert it into a story.
2. *News conference.* A meeting held for representatives of the media so that the organization can announce major news events such as new products, technologies, mergers, acquisitions, and special events, or, in the case of a crisis or problem, present its position and plans for dealing with the situation.
3. *Sponsorship.* Providing support for and associating the organization's name with events, programs, or even people such as amateur athletes or teams. Besides publicity, sponsorship can also include advertising and sales promotion activities. Many organizations sponsor sporting events, art festivals, and public radio and television programs.
4. *Public service announcements.* Many nonprofit organizations rely on the media to donate time for advertising for contributions and donors. Many nonprofit organizations cannot afford the cost of advertising or in some cases are prohibited from doing so.

Direct Marketing

We already know that with direct marketing the organization communicates directly with customers either online or through direct mail, catalogs, direct response advertising, or personal selling (the subject of the next chapter).

Direct marketing methods are certainly not new. In fact, several of them will be discussed later in the book as methods of nonstore retailing. What is new is the ability to design and use them more efficiently and effectively because of the availability of computers and databases. Technology has clearly been the catalyst in the tremendous growth in direct marketing activities in the last decade. Because of technology, it is now possible for marketers to customize communication efforts and literally create one-to-one connections and dialogues with customers. This would be especially true for those organizations that have successfully implemented an integrated marketing communications program.

Another obvious catalyst for growth in direct marketing has been consumers' increased use of the Internet for purchasing many types of products. The projected growth rates for online expenditures continue to rise. As growth continues in the number of households with Internet access and in the number of businesses with Web sites and product or service offerings via the Internet, it will likely fuel even greater growth in direct marketing.

For the American consumer facing a "poverty of time," direct marketing offers many benefits. In addition to saving time, consumers often save money, get better service, and enjoy increased privacy; many even find it entertaining. For the marketer, sales revenues are the obvious benefit but not the only one. Direct marketing activities are often very effective in generating sales leads when a customer asks for more information about a product or service and can also increase store traffic when potential buyers are encouraged to visit a dealership or retail store.

Conclusion

This chapter has been concerned with integrated marketing communications. Remember that advertising and sales promotion are only two of the ways by which sellers can affect the demand for their product. Advertising and sales promotion are only part of the firm's promotion mix, and in turn, the promotion mix is only part of the overall marketing mix. Thus, advertising and sales promotion begin with the marketing plan and not with the advertising and sales promotion plans. Ignoring this point can produce ineffective and expensive promotional programs because of a lack of coordination with other elements of the marketing mix.

Additional Readings

Arens, William. *Contemporary Advertising.* 8th ed. Burr Ridge, IL: McGraw-Hill/Irwin, 2007.

Belch, George E., and Michael A. Belch. *Advertising and Promotion: An Integrated Marketing Communication's Perspective.* 7th ed. Burr Ridge, IL: McGraw-Hill/Irwin, 2007.

Biehal, Gabriel, and Daniel A. Shenin. "The Influence of Corporate Messages on Product Portfolio." *Journal of Marketing,* April 2007, pp. 12–25.

Khermouch, Gerry. "The Top 5 Rules of the Ad Game." *Business Week,* January 20, 2003, pp. 72–73.

Prins, Remco, and Peter C. Verhoef. "Marketing Communication Drivers of Adoption Timing of a New E-Service among Existing Customers." *Journal of Marketing,* April 2007, pp. 169–83.

Shultz, Don E. "IMC Receives More Appropriate Definition." *Marketing News,* September 15, 2004, pp. 8–9.

Appendix

Major Federal Agencies Involved in Control of Advertising

Agency	Function
Federal Trade Commission	Regulates commerce between states; controls unfair business practices; takes action on false and deceptive advertising; most important agency in regulation of advertising and promotion.
Food and Drug Administration	Regulatory division of the Department of Health, Education, and Welfare; controls marketing of food, drugs, cosmetics, medical devices, and potentially hazardous consumer products.
Federal Communications Commission	Regulates advertising indirectly, primarily through the power to grant or withdraw broadcasting licenses.
Postal Service	Regulates material that goes through the mails, primarily in areas of obscenity, lottery, and fraud.
Alcohol and Tobacco Tax Division	Part of the Treasury Department; has broad powers to regulate deceptive and misleading advertising of liquor and tobacco.
Grain Division	Unit of the Department of Agriculture responsible for policing seed advertising.
Securities and Exchange Commission	Regulates advertising of securities.

Information Source	Description
Patent Office	Regulates registration of trademarks.
Library of Congress	Controls protection of copyrights.
Department of Justice	Enforces all federal laws through prosecuting cases referred to it by other government agencies.

Chapter 9

Personal Selling, Relationship Building, and Sales Management

Personal selling, unlike advertising or sales promotion, involves direct relationships between the seller and the prospect or customer. In a formal sense, personal selling can be defined as a two-way flow of communication between a potential buyer and a salesperson that is designed to accomplish at least three tasks: (1) identify the potential buyer's needs; (2) match those needs to one or more of the firm's products or services; and (3) on the basis of this match, convince the buyer to purchase the product.[1] The personal selling element of the promotion mix can encompass diverse forms of direct interaction between a salesperson and a potential buyer, including face-to-face, telephone, written, and computer communication. The behavioral scientist would most likely characterize personal selling as a type of personal influence. Operationally, it is a complex communication process, one still not fully understood by marketers.

Importance of Personal Selling

The importance of the personal selling function depends partially on the nature of the product. As a general rule, goods that are new and different, technically complex, or expensive require more personal selling effort. The salesperson plays a key role in providing the consumer with information about such products to reduce the risks involved in purchase and use. Insurance, for example, is a complex and technical product that often needs significant amounts of personal selling. In addition, many organizational products cannot be presold, and the salesperson has a key role to play in finalizing the sale.

It is important to remember that, for many companies, the salesperson represents the customer's main link to the firm. In fact, to some, the salesperson is the company. Therefore, it is imperative that the company take advantage of this unique link. Through the efforts of the successful salesperson, a company can build relationships with customers that continue long beyond the initial sale. It is the salesperson who serves as the conduit through which information regarding product flaws, improvements, applications, or new uses can pass from the customer to the marketing department. To illustrate the importance of using salespeople as an information resource, consider this fact: In some industries, customer information serves as a major source for up to 90 percent of new product and process ideas.

Along with techniques described in the previous chapter, personal selling provides the push needed to get middlemen to carry new products, increase their amount of goods purchased, and devote more effort in merchandising a product or brand.

In summary, personal selling is an integral part of the marketing system, fulfilling two vital duties (in addition to the core sales task itself): one for customers and one for companies.[2] First, the salesperson dispenses knowledge to buyers. Lacking relevant information, customers are likely to make poor buying decisions. For example, computer users would not learn about new equipment and new programming techniques without the assistance of computer sales representatives. Doctors would have difficulty finding out about new drugs and procedures were it not for pharmaceutical salespeople. Second, salespeople act as a source of marketing intelligence for management. Marketing success depends on satisfying customer needs. If present products don't fulfill customer needs, then profitable opportunities may exist for new or improved products. If problems with a company's product exist, then management must be quickly apprised of the fact. In either situation, salespeople are in the best position to act as the intermediary through which valuable information can be passed back and forth between product providers and buyers.

The Sales Process

Personal selling is as much an art as it is a science. The word *art* is used to describe that portion of the selling process that is highly creative in nature and difficult to explain. This does not mean there is little control over the personal selling element in the promotion mix. It does imply that, all other things equal, the trained salesperson can outsell the untrained one.

Before management selects and trains salespeople, it should have an understanding of the sales process. Obviously, the sales process will differ according to the size of the company, the nature of the product, the market, and so forth, but some elements are common to almost all selling situations. For the purposes of this text, the term *sales process* refers to two basic factors: (1) the objectives the salesperson is trying to achieve while engaged in selling activities; and (2) the sequence of stages or steps the salesperson should follow in trying to achieve the specific objectives (the relationship-building process).

Objectives of the Sales Force

Much like the concepts covered in the previous chapter, personal selling can be viewed as a strategic means to gain competitive advantage in the marketplace. For example, most organizations include service representatives as part of their sales team to ensure that customer concerns with present products are addressed and remedied at the same time new business is being solicited.

In a similar manner, marketing management understands that while, ultimately, personal selling must be justified on the basis of the revenue and profits it produces, other categories of objectives are generally assigned to the personal selling function as part of the overall promotion mix.[3] These objectives are

1. *Information provision.* Especially in the case of new products or customers, the salesperson needs to fully explain all attributes of the product or service, answer any questions, and probe for additional questions.
2. *Persuasion.* Once the initial product or service information is provided, the salesperson needs to focus on the following objectives:
   - Clearly distinguish attributes of the firm's products or services from those of competitors.
   - Maximize the number of sales as a percent of presentations.

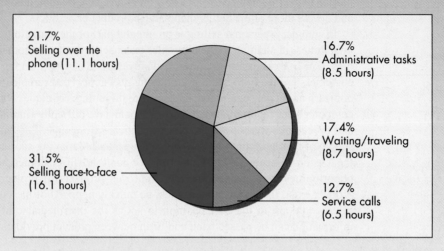

21.7%
Selling over the
phone (11.1 hours)

16.7%
Administrative tasks
(8.5 hours)

17.4%
Waiting/traveling
(8.7 hours)

31.5%
Selling face-to-face
(16.1 hours)

12.7%
Service calls
(6.5 hours)

Source: Roger Kerin, Steven W. Hartley, Eric Berkowitz, and William Rudelins, *Marketing,* 8th ed., (Burr Ridge, IL: McGraw-Hill/Irwin, 2007), p. 532.

- Convert undecided customers into first-time buyers.
- Convert first-time customers into repeat purchasers.
- Sell additional or complementary items to repeat customers.
- Tend to the needs of dissatisfied customers.

3. *After-sale service.* Whether the sale represents a first-time or repeat purchase, the salesperson needs to ensure the following objectives are met:

- Delivery or installation of the product or service that meets or exceeds customer expectations.
- Immediate follow-up calls and visits to address unresolved or new concerns.
- Reassurance of product or service superiority through demonstrable actions.

The Sales Relationship-Building Process

For many years, the traditional approach to selling emphasized the first-time sale of a product or service as the culmination of the sales process. As emphasized in Chapter 1, the marketing concept and accompanying approach to personal selling view the initial sale as merely the first step in a long-term relationship-building process, not as the end goal. As we shall see later in this chapter, long-term relationships between the buyer and seller can be considered partnerships because the buyer and seller have an ongoing, mutually beneficial affiliation, with each party having concern for the other party's well-being.[4] The relationship-building process, which is designed to meet the objectives listed in the previous section, contains six sequential stages (Figure 9.1). These stages are (1) prospecting, (2) planning the sales call, (3) presentation, (4) responding to objections, (5) obtaining commitment/closing the sale, and (6) building a long-term relationship. What follows is a brief description of each of the stages.

Prospecting

The process of locating potential customers is called *prospecting.* The prospecting activity is critical to the success of organizations in maintaining or increasing sales volume.

FIGURE 9.1
The Sales Relationship-Building Process

Source: Adapted from material discussed in Barton A. Weitz, Stephen B. Castleberry, and John F. Tanner, *Selling: Building Partnerships,* 6th ed. (Burr Ridge, IL: Irwin/McGraw-Hill, 2007), p. 171.

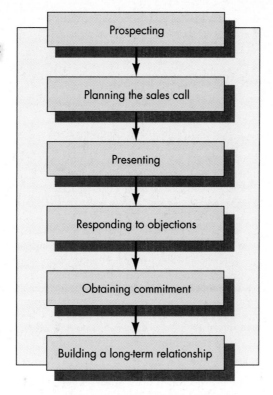

Continual prospecting is necessary for several reasons, including the fact that customers (1) switch to other suppliers, (2) move out of the organization's market area, (3) go out of business because of bankruptcy, (4) are acquired by another firm, or (5) have only a one-time need for the product or service. In addition, the organization's buying contracts with present customers may be replaced and organizations that wish to grow must increase their customer base. Prospecting in some fields is more important than in others. For example, a stockbroker, real estate agent, or partner in an accounting firm with no effective prospecting plan usually doesn't last long in the business. In these positions, it may take as many as 100 contacts to gain 10 prospects who will listen to presentations from which one to two sales may result. On the other hand, a Procter & Gamble sales representative in a certain geographic area would likely know all the potential retailers for Crest toothpaste.

The prospecting process usually involves two major activities that are undertaken on a continual, concurrent basis. First, prospects must be located. When names and addresses of prospects are not available, as is usually the case when firms enter new markets or a new salesperson is hired, they can be generated by randomly calling on businesses or households or by employing mass appeals (through advertising). This process, called *random lead generation,* usually requires a high number of contacts to gain a sale. A *lead* is a potential prospect that may or may not have the potential to be a true prospect, a candidate, to whom a sale could be made.

For most professional, experienced salespeople, a more systematic approach to generating leads from predetermined target markets is used. This approach, aptly named *selected-lead searching,* uses existing contacts and knowledge to generate new prospects. In general, the best source of prospects is referrals from satisfied customers. The more satisfied one's customers are, the higher the quality of leads a salesperson will receive from them. Marketing Highlight 9–2 lists some common sources of leads and how they are used to generate new contacts.

Source	How Used
Satisfied customers	Current and previous customers are contacted for additional business and leads.
Endless chain	Salesperson attempts to secure at least one additional lead from each person he or she interviews.
Center of influence	Salesperson cultivates well-known, influential people in the territory who are willing to supply lead information.
Promotional activities	Salesperson ties into the company's direct mail, telemarketing, and trade shows to secure and qualify leads.
Lists and directories	Salesperson uses secondary data sources, which can be free or fee-based.
Canvassing	Salesperson tries to generate leads by calling on totally unfamiliar organizations.
Spotters	Salesperson pays someone for lead information.
Telemarketing	Salesperson uses phone and/or telemarketing staff to generate leads.
Sales letters	Salesperson writes personal letters to potential leads.
Other sources	Salesperson uses noncompeting salespeople, people in his or her own firm, social clubs, and so forth, to secure lead information.

Source: Adapted from material discussed in Barton A. Weitz, Stephen B. Castleberry, and John F. Tanner, *Selling: Building Partnerships,* 6th ed. (Burr Ridge, IL: Irwin/McGraw-Hill, 2007), p. 174.

The second step in the prospecting process involves screening. Once leads are generated, the salesperson must determine whether the prospect is a true prospect. This qualifying process usually entails gathering information, which leads to answering five questions:

1. Does the lead have a want or need that can be satisfied by the purchase of the firm's products or services?
2. Does the lead have the ability to pay?
3. Does the lead have the authority to pay?
4. Can the lead be approached favorably?
5. Is the lead eligible to buy?

Depending on the analysis of answers to these questions, the determination of whether a lead is a true prospect can be made. In seeking and qualifying leads, it is important to recognize that responsibility for these activities should not be totally assumed by individual salespeople. Rather, companies should develop a consistent, organized program, recognizing that the job of developing prospects belongs to the entire company, not just the sales force.

Planning the Sales Call

Salespeople will readily admit that their number one problem is getting through the door for an appointment with a prospect. Customers have become sophisticated in their buying strategies. Consequently, salespeople have to be equally sophisticated in developing their selling strategies.

While a full discussion on the topic of planning sales calls is beyond the scope of this text, what follows are brief descriptions of some key areas of knowledge salespeople should possess prior to embarking on sales calls.

1. They should have thorough knowledge of the company they represent, including its past history. This includes the philosophy of management as well as the firm's basic operating policies.

	Production	Sales	Marketing	Partnering
Time Period	Before 1930	1930 to 1960	1960 to 1990	After 1990
Objective	Making sales	Making sales	Satisfying customer needs	Building relationships
Orientation	Short-term seller needs	Short-term seller needs	Short-term customer needs	Long-term customer and seller needs
Role of Salesperson	Provider	Persuader	Problem solver	Value creator
Activities of Salespeople	Taking orders, delivering goods	Aggressively convincing buyers to buy products	Matching available offerings to buyer needs	Creating new alternatives, matching buyer needs with seller capabilities

Source: Barton A. Weitz, Stephen B. Castleberry, and John F. Tanner, *Selling: Building Relationships,* 6th ed. (Burr Ridge, IL: McGraw-Hill/Irwin, 2007), p. 35.

2. They should have thorough knowledge of their products and/or product lines. This is particularly true when selling organizational products. When selling very technical products, many firms require their salespeople to have training as engineers.

3. They should have good working knowledge of competitors' products. This is a vital requirement because the successful salesperson will have to know the strengths and weaknesses of those products that are in competition for market share.

4. They should have in-depth knowledge of the market for their merchandise. *The market* here refers not only to a particular sales territory but also to the general market, including the economic factors that affect the demand for their goods.

5. They should have accurate knowledge of the buyer or the prospect to whom they are selling. Under the marketing concept, knowledge of the customer is a vital requirement.

Presenting

Successful salespeople have learned the importance of making a good impression. One of the most important ways of improving the buyer's impression is for the salesperson to be well prepared in the knowledge areas discussed above. Some salespeople actually develop a checklist of things to take to the presentation so that nothing is forgotten. Just as important is the development of good interpersonal skills; they are a key ingredient of effective selling. Salespeople who can adapt their selling style to individual buyer needs and styles have a much stronger overall performance than less-flexible counterparts.

Responding to Objections

To assume the buyer will passively listen and positively respond to a sales presentation by placing an immediate order would be unrealistic. Salespeople can expect to hear objections

133

(issues or concerns raised by the buyer) at any time during the presentation and subsequent relationship. Objections can be raised when the salesperson attempts to secure appointments, during the presentation, when the salesperson attempts to obtain commitment, or during the after-sale follow-up.

When sales prospects raise an objection, it is a sign that they are not ready to buy and need an acceptable response to the objection before the buying decision can be made. In response to an objection, the salesperson should not challenge the respondent. Rather, the salesperson's objective should be to present the necessary information so that the prospect is able to make intelligent decisions based on that information.

Obtaining Commitment

At some point, if all objections have been resolved, the salesperson must ask for commitment. It's a rare moment when a customer will ask to buy. Consequently, knowing how and when to close a sale is one of a salesperson's most indispensable skills.

It should be noted that not all sales calls end in commitment, a successful closing. If commitment is not obtained, salespeople should analyze the reasons and determine whether (1) more sales calls are necessary to obtain commitment; or (2) currently, there just does not exist a good match between customer needs and seller offerings. If the salesperson determines that more calls are necessary, then he or she should leave the meeting with a clear action plan, which is agreeable to the customer, for the next visit.

Building a Long-Term Relationship

Focusing on building and maintaining long-term relationships with customers has become an important goal for salespeople. As marketers realize that it can take five times as much to acquire a new customer than to service an existing one, the importance of customer retention and relationship building has become very clear.[5] Terry Vavra focuses on the value of current customers to the organization and has developed the concept of *aftermarketing,* which focuses the organization's attention on providing continuing satisfaction and reinforcement to individuals or organizations that are past or current customers. The goal of aftermarketing is to build lasting relationships with customers.[6] Successful aftermarketing efforts require that many specific activities be undertaken by the salesperson and others in the organization. These activities include

1. Establishing and maintaining a customer information file.
2. Monitoring order processing.
3. Ensuring initial proper use of the purchased product or service.
4. Providing ongoing guidance and suggestions.
5. Analyzing customer feedback and responding quickly to customer questions and complaints.
6. Continually conducting customer satisfaction research and responding to it.

As seen by the preceding discussion, there are no magic secrets of successful selling. The difference between good salespeople and mediocre ones is often the result of training plus experience. Training is no substitute for experience; the two complement each other. The difficulty with trying to discuss the selling job in terms of basic principles is that experienced, successful salespeople will always be able to find exceptions to these principles.

Relationships Can Lead to Partnerships

When the interaction between a salesperson and a customer does not end with the sale, the beginnings of a relationship are present. Many salespeople are finding that building relationships and even partnering with customers is becoming increasingly important.

1. *Improved sales productivity.* When the product or system being purchased is for the whole organization, different specialists handle different parts of the job. This usually results in a more effective and efficient sales process.
2. *More flexibility and quicker decisions.* To thrive in today's increasingly competitive markets, buying organizations often require selling organizations to produce small runs of tailored products on a very tight schedule. Cross-functional sales teams enable sellers to be more flexible because all functional units are involved in the sales process, which also enables the seller to make quicker decisions in response to buyer demands.
3. *Better decisions.* In most cases, the use of cross-functional teams composed of individuals with varied backgrounds in the company will lead to more innovative forms of thought and superior decisions than would be the case of an individual acting alone. Improved decisions would benefit both the buyer and the seller.
4. *Increased customer satisfaction.* The ultimate measure of the success of cross-functional sales teams comes with increased customer satisfaction, cemented relationships, and repeat business. The energy, flexibility, and commitment associated with cross-functional sales teams have led many organizations to adopt the approach.

When a buyer and a salesperson have a close personal relationship, they both begin to rely on each other and communicate honestly. When each has a problem, they work together to solve it. Such market relationships are known as *functional relationships.* An important trust begins to exist between each party. As with any relationship, each often gives and takes when the situation calls for it in order to keep the relationship intact. The reader may have such a relationship with a long-term medical or dental practitioner or hair cutter.

When organizations move beyond functional relationships, they develop *strategic partnerships,* or *strategic alliances.* These are long-term, formal relationships in which both parties make significant commitments and investments in each other in order to pursue mutual goals and to improve the profitability of each other. While a functional relationship is based on trust, a strategic partnership or alliance moves beyond trust. The partners in the relationship actually invest in each other. Obviously, the reasons for forming strategic partnerships vary. Some do it to create joint opportunities (banks, insurance companies, and brokerage firms), to gain access to new markets (United Parcel Service of America (UPS) and Mail Boxes Etc.), to develop new technology or exploit joint opportunities (IBM and Apple), or to gain a marketing advantage over competitors (United Airlines and Starbucks Coffee, American Airlines and Career Track).

People Who Support the Sales Force

In many instances, sales personnel will require some assistance at various stages of the sales process. These support personnel do not seek the order. Their purpose is to focus on the long-term relationship and increase the likelihood of sales in the long run.

Missionary salespeople are used in certain industries such as pharmaceuticals to focus solely on promotion of existing products and introduction of new products. They may call on physicians to convince them to prescribe a new drug or on pharmacies to convince them to promote a new cold remedy with a large display during the cold and flu season.

A *technical sales specialist* supports the sales staff by providing training or other technical assistance to the prospect. This individual may follow up an expression of interest to the salesperson from a prospect, especially when the product is to be used to solve certain technical problems of the buyer. Some organizations will provide training

1. *Ego strength:* A healthy self-esteem that allows one to bounce back from rejection.
2. *A sense of urgency:* Wanting to get it done now.
3. *Ego drive:* A combination of competitiveness and self-esteem.
4. *Assertiveness:* The ability to be firm, lead the sales process, and get one's point across confidently.
5. *Willingness to take risk:* Willingness to innovate and take a chance.
6. *Sociable:* Outgoing, talkative, friendly, and interested in others.
7. *Abstract reasoning:* Ability to understand concepts and ideas.
8. *Skepticism:* A slight lack of trust and suspicion of others.
9. *Creativity:* The ability to think differently.
10. *Empathy:* The ability to place oneself in someone else's shoes.

Source: Research conducted by Sales and Marketing Management involving 209 salespeople representing 189 companies in 37 industries and reported in George E. Belch and Michael A. Belch, *Advertising and Promotion,* 7th ed. (Burr Ridge, IL: McGraw-Hill/Irwin, 2007), p. 583.

to the front-line staff of the buying organization who will be expected to sell the product to their customers.

Finally, when the product is extremely high priced and is being sold to the whole organization, *cross-functional sales teams* are often used. Since products increase in technical complexity, and units of the buying organization require specialized knowledge before a buying decision can be made, team selling has increased in popularity. For example, a manufacturer's sales team might be made up of people from sales, engineering, customer service, and finance, depending on the needs of the customer. A bank's sales team might consist of people from the commercial lending, investments, small business, and trust departments.

Managing the Sales and Relationship-Building Process

Every personal sale can be divided into two parts: the part done by the salespeople and the part done for the salespeople by the company. For example, from the standpoint of the product, the company should provide the salesperson with a product skillfully designed, thoroughly tested, attractively packaged, adequately advertised, and priced to compare favorably with competitive products. Salespeople have the responsibility of being thoroughly acquainted with the product, its selling features, and points of superiority and possess a sincere belief in the value of the product. From a sales management standpoint, the company's part of the sale involves the following:

1. Efficient and effective sales tools, including continuous sales training, promotional literature, samples, trade shows, product information, and adequate advertising.
2. An efficient delivery and reorder system to ensure that customers will receive the merchandise as promised.
3. An equitable compensation plan that rewards performance, motivates the salesperson, and promotes company loyalty. It should also reimburse the salesperson for all reasonable expenses incurred while doing the job.
4. Adequate supervision and evaluation of performance as a means of helping salespeople do a better job not only for the company but for themselves as well.

The Sales Management Task

Marketing managers and sales managers must make some very important decisions regarding how the sales force should be organized. Most companies organize their sales efforts either by geography, product, or customer. These are illustrated in Figure 9.2.

In a *geographic structure,* individual salespeople are assigned geographic territories to cover. A salesperson calls on all prospects in the territory and usually represents all of the company's products. A geographic structure provides the practical benefit of limiting the distance each salesperson must travel to see customers and prospects.

In a *product structure,* each salesperson is assigned to prospects and customers for a particular product or product line. A product structure is useful when the sales force must have specific technical knowledge about products in order to sell effectively. However, this structure can result in a duplication of sales efforts because more than one salesperson can call on the same customer. Consequently, it tends to be expensive.

A *customer structure* assigns a salesperson or selling team to serve a single customer or single type of customer. This structure works best when different types of buyers have large or significantly different needs. When this structure involves devoting all of a salesperson's time to a single customer, it is expensive but can result in large sales and satisfied customers.

In a variation of the customer structure, a company may employ *major account management,* or the use of team selling to focus on major customers to establish long-term relationships.[7] Procter & Gamble, whose sales force used to be organized by product, has shifted to major account management. Assigning resources to particular customers has proved to be more flexible and customer focused for the company.

FIGURE 9.2
Organizing the Sales Force

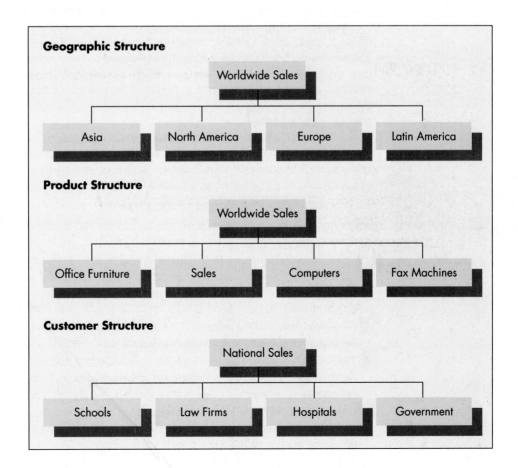

The customer-organized structure is well suited for the use of cross-functional teams. However, geographic and product territories can also be effective. The key is that sales management and the sales force must concentrate on learning and meeting customers' wants and needs better than competitors do.

Controlling the Sales Force

There are two obvious reasons why it is critical that the sales force be properly controlled. First, personal selling can be the largest marketing expense component in the final price of the product. Second, unless the sales force is somehow directed, motivated, and audited on a continual basis, it is likely to be less efficient than it is capable of being. Controlling the sales force involves four key functions: (1) forecasting sales, (2) establishing sales territories and quotas, (3) analyzing expenses, and (4) motivating and compensating performance.

Forecasting Sales

Sales planning begins with a forecast of sales for some future period or periods. From a practical standpoint, these forecasts are made on a short-term basis of a year or less, although long-range forecasts of one to five years are made for purposes other than managing the sales force, such as financing, production, and development. Generally speaking, forecasting is the marketing manager's responsibility. In large firms, because of the complexity of the task, it is usually delegated to a specialized unit, such as the marketing research department. Forecast data should be integrated into the firm's marketing information system for use by sales managers and other executives. For many companies, the sales forecast is the key instrument in the planning and control of operations.

The *sales forecast* is an estimate of how much of the company's output, either in dollars or in units, can be sold during a specified future period under a proposed marketing plan and under an assumed set of economic conditions. A sales forecast has several important uses: (1) It is used to establish sales quotas; (2) it is used to plan personal selling efforts as well as other types of promotional activities in the marketing mix; (3) it is used to budget selling expenses; and (4) it is used to plan and coordinate production, logistics, inventories, personnel, and so forth.

Sales forecasting has become very sophisticated in recent years, especially with the increased availability of computer software. It should be mentioned, however, that a forecast is never a substitute for sound business judgment. At the present time no single method of sales forecasting gives uniformly accurate results with infallible precision. Outlined next are some commonly used sales forecasting methods.[8]

1. *Jury of executive opinion method.* This combines and averages the views of top management representing marketing, production, finance, purchasing, and administration.
2. *Sales force composite method.* This is similar to the first method in that it obtains the combined views of the sales force about the future outlook for sales. In some companies all salespeople, or district managers, submit estimates of the future sales in their territory or district.
3. *Customer expectations method.* This approach involves asking customers or product users about the quantity they expect to purchase.
4. *Time-series analysis.* This approach involves analyzing past sales data and the impact of factors that influence sales (long-term growth trends, cyclical fluctuations, seasonal variations).
5. *Correlation analysis.* This involves measuring the relationship between the dependent variable, sales, and one or more independent variables that can explain increases or decreases in sales volumes.

6. *Other quantitative techniques.* Numerous statistical and mathematical techniques can be used to predict or estimate future sales. Two of the more important techniques are (*a*) growth functions, which are mathematical expressions specifying the relationship between demand and time; and (*b*) simulation models, in which a statistical model of the industry is developed and programmed to compute values for the key parameters of the model.

Establishing Sales Territories and Quotas

The establishment of sales territories and sales quotas represents management's need to match personal selling effort with sales potential (or opportunity). Soundly designed sales territories can improve how the market is served.[9] It is much easier to pinpoint customers and prospects and to determine who should call on them when the market is geographically divided than when the market is considered a large aggregate of potential accounts. The geographic segments should represent small clusters of customers or prospects within some physical proximity. Implied here is the notion that there are some distinct economic advantages to dividing the market into smaller segments. Salespeople restricted to a geographic area are likely to get more sales in the territory. Instead of simply servicing the "easy" and larger accounts, they are prone to develop small accounts. Of course, there are criteria other than geography for establishing territories. One important criterion is product specialization. In this case, salespeople are specialists relative to particular product or customer situations.

The question of managing sales territories cannot be discussed meaningfully without saying something about sales quotas. In general, quotas represent goals assigned to salespeople. As such, quotas provide three main benefits. First, they provide incentives for salespeople. For example, the definite objective of selling $500,000 worth of computer equipment is more motivating to most salespeople than the indefinite charge to go out and sell computer equipment. Sales bonuses and commissions based on quotas can also be motivational. Second, quotas provide a quantitative standard against which the performance of individual sales representatives or other marketing units can be measured. They allow management to pinpoint individuals and units that are performing above average and those experiencing difficulty. Third, quotas can be used not only to evaluate salespersons' performances but also to evaluate and control their efforts. As part of their job, salespeople are expected to engage in various activities besides calling on established accounts. These activities might include calling on new accounts, collecting past-due accounts, and planning and developing sales presentations. Activity quotas allow the company to monitor whether salespeople are engaging in these activities to the extent desired.

Sales quotas represent specific sales goals assigned to each territory or unit over a designated time period. The most common method of establishing quotas for territories is to relate sales to forecasted sales potential. For example, if the Ajax Drug Company's territory M has an estimated industry sales potential for a particular product of $400,000 for the year, the quota might be set at 25 percent of that potential, or $100,000. The 25 percent figure represents the market share Ajax estimates to be a reasonable target. This $100,000 quota may represent an increase of $20,000 in sales over last year (assuming constant prices) that is expected from new business.

In establishing sales quotas for its individual territories or sales personnel, management needs to take into account three key factors. First, all territories will not have equal potential and, therefore, compensation must be adjusted accordingly. Second, all salespeople will not have equal ability and assignments may have to be made accordingly. Third, the sales task in each territory may differ from time period to time period. For instance, the nature of some territories may require that salespeople spend more time seeking new accounts, rather than servicing established accounts, especially in the case of so-called new territories. The point to be made here is that quotas can vary, not only by territory but also by assigned tasks. The effective sales manager should assign quotas not only for dollar sales but also for each major

Marketing Highlight 9–6 Effort- and Results-Oriented Measures for Evaluating Salespeople

EFFORT-ORIENTED MEASURES

1. Number of sales calls made.
2. Number of maintenance-repairs-operations (MRO) calls made.
3. Number of complaints handled.
4. Number of checks on reseller stocks.
5. Uncontrollable lost job time.
6. Number of inquiries followed up.
7. Number of demonstrations completed.

RESULTS-ORIENTED MEASURES

1. Sales volume (total or by product or model).
2. Sales volume as a percentage of quota.
3. Sales profitability (dollar gross margin or contribution).
4. Number of new accounts.
5. Number of stockouts.
6. Number of distributors participating in programs.
7. Number of lost accounts.
8. Percentage volume increase in key accounts.
9. Number of customer complaints.
10. Distributor sales-inventory ratios.

Source: Adapted from Thomas N. Ingram, Raymond W. Laforge, and Charles H. Schwepker, Jr., *Sales Management: Analysis and Decision Making,* 6th ed. (Mason, OH: Thomson Southwestern, 2006), chap. 15; and Thayer C. Taylor, "SFA: The Newest Orthodoxy," *Sales and Marketing Management,* February 1993, pp. 26–28.

selling function. Figure 9.3 is an example of how this is done for the Medi-test Company, where each activity is assigned a quota and a weight reflecting its relative importance.

Analyzing Expenses

Sales forecasts should include a sales expense budget. In some companies, sales expense budgets are developed from the bottom up. Each territorial or district manager submits

FIGURE 9.3
Medi-test Company Sales Activity Evaluation

Territory: Southern
Salesperson: Marsha Smith

Functions	(1) Quota	(2) Actual	(3) Percent (2 ÷ 1)	(4) Weight	(5) Score (3 × 4)
Sales volume					
Old business	$380,000	$300,000	79	0.7	55.3
New business	$ 20,000	$ 20,000	100	0.5	50.0
Calls on prospects					
Doctors	20	15	75	0.2	15.0
Druggists	80	60	75	0.2	15.0
Wholesalers	15	15	100	0.2	20.0
Hospitals	10	10	100	0.2	20.0
				2.0	175.3

Performance index = 175.3

estimates of expenses and forecasted sales quotas. These estimates are usually prepared for a period of a year and then broken down into quarters and months. The sales manager then reviews the budget requests from the field offices and from staff departments.

Motivating and Compensating Performance

An important task for the sales manager is motivating and compensating the sales force. These two tasks are major determinants of sales force productivity. Managing people is always a challenge and involves personal interaction with members of the sales force, time in the field visiting customers, free-flowing communication with the sales force, either by e-mail or telephone, and providing feedback on a regular basis as well as coaching and developing incentive programs through which job promotions or increased earnings can be achieved.[10]

There are two basic types of compensation: salary and commission. *Salary* usually refers to a specific amount of monetary compensation at an agreed rate for definite time periods. *Commission* is usually monetary compensation provided for each unit of sales and expressed as a percentage of sales. The base on which commissions are computed may be volume of sales in units of product, gross sales in dollars, net sales after returns, sales volume in excess of a quota, or net profits. Very often, several compensation approaches are combined. For example, a salesperson might be paid a base salary, a commission on sales exceeding a volume figure, and a percentage share of the company's profits for that year.

In addition to straight dollar compensation, there are numerous other forms of incentives that can be used to motivate the sales force. Some of these types of incentives and their potential performance outcomes are listed in Figure 9.4.

FIGURE 9.4
Types of Incentives and Their Possible Performance Outcomes

Source: Some of the material was adapted from Gilbert A. Churchill Jr., Neil M. Ford, and Orville C. Walker, *Sales Force Management,* 5th ed. (Burr Ridge, IL: Irwin/McGraw-Hill, 1997), p. 490.

Types of Incentives

- Positive feedback on salesperson performance evaluation.
- Company praise (e.g., recognition in a newsletter).
- Bonus (e.g., cash, merchandise, or travel allowances).
- Salary increase.
- Pay for performance for specific new product idea.
- Paid educational allowance.
- Earned time off.
- Fringe benefits.
- Stock options.
- Vested retirement plan.
- Profit sharing.

Performance Outcomes

- Sell a greater dollar volume.
- Increase sales of more profitable products.
- Push new products.
- Push selected items at designated seasons.
- Achieve a higher degree of market penetration by products, kinds of customers, or territories.
- Increase the number of calls made.
- Secure large average orders.
- Secure new customers.
- Service and maintain existing business.
- Reduce turnover of customers.
- Achieve full-line (balanced) selling.
- Reduce direct selling costs.
- Submit reports and other data promptly.

Conclusion

This chapter has attempted to outline and explain the personal selling aspect of the promotion mix. An emphasis was placed on describing the importance of the relationship-building aspect of the personal selling process. For organizations that wish to continue to grow and prosper, personal selling plays an integral part in the marketing of products and services. As long as production continues to expand through the development of new and highly technical products, personal selling will continue to be an important part of marketing strategy.

Additional Readings

Futrell, Charles M. *ABC's of Relationship Selling through Service.* 9th ed., Burr Ridge, IL: McGraw-Hill, 2007.

Gonzalez, Gabriel R., Douglas Hoffman, and Thomas N. Ingram. "Improving Relationship Selling through Failure Analysis and Recovery Efforts: A Framework and Call to Action." *Journal of Personal Selling and Sales Management.* Spring 2005, pp. 24–32.

Hunter, Gary K., and William D. Perreault. "Making Sales Technology Effective." *Journal of Marketing,* January 2007, pp. 16–34.

Keiningham, Timothy, and Terry Vavra. *The Customer Delight Principle.* New York: McGraw-Hill, 2001.

Payne, Adrian, and Pennie Frow. "A Strategic Framework for Customer Relationship Management." *Journal of Marketing,* October 2005, pp. 167–76.

Stevens, Howard, and Theodore Kinni. *Achieve Sales Results.* Avon, MA: Platinum Press, 2007.

10

Distribution Strategy

Channel of distribution decisions involve numerous interrelated variables that must be integrated into the total marketing mix. Because of the time and money required to set up an efficient channel, and since channels are often hard to change once they are set up, these decisions are critical to the success of the firm.

This chapter is concerned with the development and management of channels of distribution and the process of goods distribution in complex, highly competitive, and specialized economies. It should be noted at the outset that channels of distribution provide the ultimate consumer or organizational buyer with time, place, and possession utility. Thus, an efficient channel is one that delivers the product when and where it is wanted at a minimum total cost.

The Need for Marketing Intermediaries

A *channel of distribution* is the combination of institutions through which a seller markets products to the user or ultimate consumer. The need for other institutions or intermediaries in the delivery of goods is sometimes questioned, particularly since the profits they make are viewed as adding to the cost of the product. However, this reasoning is generally fallacious, since producers use marketing intermediaries because the intermediary can perform functions more cheaply and more efficiently than the producer can. This notion of efficiency is critical when the characteristics of advanced economies are considered.

For example, the U.S. economy is characterized by heterogeneity in terms of both supply and demand. In terms of numbers alone, there are over 7 million establishments with employees comprising the supply segment of the economy, and there are nearly 110 million households making up the demand side. Clearly, if each of these units had to deal on a one-to-one basis to obtain needed goods and services, and there were no intermediaries to collect and disperse assortments of goods, the system would be totally inefficient. Thus, the primary role of intermediaries is to bring supply and demand together in an efficient and orderly fashion.

Classification of Marketing Intermediaries and Functions

There are a great many types of marketing intermediaries, many of which are so specialized by function and industry that they need not be discussed here. Figure 10.1 presents the major types of marketing intermediaries common to many industries. Although there is some overlap in this classification, these categories are based on the marketing

FIGURE 10.1

Major Types of Marketing Intermediaries

Source: Based on Peter D. Bennett, ed., *Dictionary of Marketing Terms,* 2d ed. (Chicago: American Marketing Association, 1995).

Middleman—an independent business concern that operates as a link between producers and ultimate consumers or organizational buyers.

Merchant middleman—a middleman who buys the goods outright and takes title to them.

Agent—a business unit that negotiates purchases, sales, or both but does not take title to the goods in which it deals.

Wholesaler—a merchant establishment operated by a concern that is primarily engaged in buying, taking title to, usually storing and physically handling goods in large quantities, and reselling the goods (usually in smaller quantities) to retailers or to organizational buyers.

Retailer—a merchant middleman who is engaged primarily in selling to ultimate consumers.

Broker—a middleman who serves as a go-between for the buyer or seller. The broker assumes no title risks, does not usually have physical custody of products, and is not looked upon as a permanent representative of either the buyer or the seller.

Manufacturers' agent—an agent who generally operates on an extended contractual basis, often sells within an exclusive territory, handles noncompeting but related lines of goods, and possesses limited authority with regard to prices and terms of sale.

Distributor—a wholesale middleman especially in lines where selective or exclusive distribution is common at the wholesaler level in which the manufacturer expects strong promotional support; often a synonym for wholesaler.

Jobber—a middleman who buys from manufacturers and sells to retailers; a wholesaler.

Facilitating agent—a business firm that assists in the performance of distribution tasks other than buying, selling, and transferring title (i.e., transportation companies, warehouses, etc.)

functions performed; that is, various intermediaries perform different marketing functions and to different degrees. Figure 10.2 is a listing of the more common marketing functions performed in the channel.

It should be remembered that whether or not a manufacturer uses intermediaries to perform these functions, the functions have to be performed by someone. In other words, the managerial question is not whether to perform the functions, but who will perform them and to what degree.

FIGURE 10.2

Major Functions Performed in Channels of Distribution

Source: Roger A. Kerin, Eric N. Berkowitz, Steven W. Hartley, and William Rudelius, *Marketing,* 8th ed. (Burr Ridge, IL: McGraw-Hill/Irwin, 2006), p. 398.

Transactional Function

Buying: Purchasing products for resale or as an agent for supply of a product.

Selling: Contacting potential customers, promoting products, and soliciting orders.

Risk taking: Assuming business risks in the ownership of inventory that can become obsolete or deteriorate.

Logistical Function

Assorting: Creating product assortments from several sources to serve customers.

Storing: Assembling and protecting products at a convenient location to offer better customer service.

Sorting: Purchasing in large quantities and breaking into smaller amounts desired by customers.

Transporting: Physically moving products to customers.

Facilitating Function

Financing: Extending credit to customers.

Grading: Inspecting, testing, or judging products, and assigning them quality grades.

Marketing information and research: Providing information to customers and suppliers, including competitive conditions and trends.

Channels of Distribution

As previously noted, a channel of distribution is the combination of institutions through which a seller markets products to the user or ultimate consumer. Some of these links assume the risks of ownership; others do not. The conventional channel of distribution patterns for consumer goods markets are shown in Figure 10.3.

Some manufacturers use a *direct channel,* selling directly to a market. For example, Gateway 2000 sold computers through the mail without the use of other intermediaries. Using a direct channel, called *direct marketing,* increased in popularity as marketers found that products could be sold directly using a variety of methods. These include direct mail, telemarketing, direct-action advertising, catalog selling, cable selling, online selling, and direct selling through demonstrations at home or place of work. These will be discussed in more detail later in this chapter.

In other cases, one or more intermediaries may be used in the distribution process. For example, Hewlett-Packard sells its computers and printers through retailers such as Best Buy and Office Max. A common channel for consumer goods is one in which the manufacturer sells through wholesalers and retailers. For instance, a cold remedy manufacturer may sell to drug wholesalers who, in turn, sell a vast array of drug products to various retail outlets. Small manufacturers may also use agents, since they do not have sufficient capital for their own sales forces. Agents are commonly used intermediaries in the jewelry industry. The final channel in Figure 10.3 is used primarily when small wholesalers and retailers are involved. Channels with one or more intermediaries are referred to as *indirect channels*.

In contrast to consumer products, the direct channel is often used in the distribution of organizational goods. The reason for this stems from the structure of most organizational markets, which often have relatively few but extremely large customers. Also, many organizational products, such as computer systems, need a great deal of presale and postsale service. Distributors are used in organizational markets when there is a large number of buyers but each purchases a small amount of a product. As in the consumer market, agents are used

FIGURE 10.3   **Conventional Channels of Distribution of Consumer Goods**

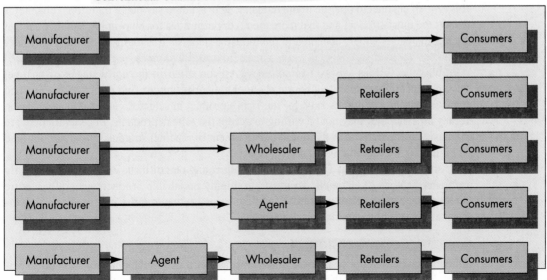

FIGURE 10.4   Conventional Channels of Distribution for Organizational Goods

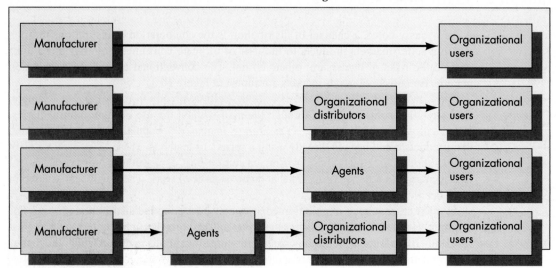

in organizational markets in cases where manufacturers do not wish to have their own sales forces. Such an arrangement may be used by small manufacturers or when the market is geographically dispersed. The final channel arrangement in Figure 10.4 may also be used by a small manufacturer or when the market consists of many small customers. Under such conditions, it may not be economical for sellers to have their own sales organization.

Selecting Channels of Distribution

Given the numerous types of channel intermediaries and functions that must be performed, the task of selecting and designing a channel of distribution may at first appear to be overwhelming. However, in many industries, channels of distribution have developed over many years and have become somewhat traditional. In such cases, the producer may be limited to this type of channel to operate in the industry. This is not to say that a traditional channel is always the most efficient and that there are no opportunities for innovation. But the fact that such a channel is widely accepted in the industry suggests it is highly efficient. A primary constraint in these cases and in cases where no traditional channel exists is that of *availability* of the various types of middlemen. All too often in the early stages of channel design, executives map out elaborate channel networks only to find out later that no such independent intermediaries exist for the firm's product in selected geographic areas. Even if they do exist, they may not be willing to accept the seller's products. In general, there are six basic considerations in the initial development of channel strategy. These are outlined in Figure 10.5.

It should be noted that for a particular product any one of these characteristics greatly influences choice of channels. To illustrate, highly perishable products generally require direct channels, or a firm with little financial strength may require intermediaries to perform almost all of the marketing functions.

Specific Considerations

The above characteristics play an important part in framing the channel selection decision. Based on them, the choice of channels can be further refined in terms of

FIGURE 10.5   General Considerations in Channel Planning

1. **Customer characteristics.**
   a. Number.
   b. Geographic dispersion.
   c. Preferred channels and outlets for purchase.
   d. Purchasing patterns.
   e. Use of new channels (e.g., online purchasing).
2. **Product characteristics.**
   a. Unit value.
   b. Perishability.
   c. Bulkiness.
   d. Degree of standardization.
   e. Installation and maintenance services required.
3. **Intermediary characteristics.**
   a. Availability.
   b. Willingness to accept product or product line.
   c. Geographic market served.
   d. Marketing functions performed.
   e. Potential for conflict.
   f. Potential for long-term relationship.
   g. Competitive products sold.
   h. Financial condition.
   i. Other strengths and weaknesses.
4. **Competitor characteristics.**
   a. Number.
   b. Relative size and market share.
   c. Distribution channels and strategy.
   d. Financial condition and estimated marketing budget.
   e. Size of product mix and product lines.
   f. Overall marketing strategy employed.
   g. Other strengths and weaknesses.
5. **Company characteristics.**
   a. Relative size and market share.
   b. Financial condition and marketing budget.
   c. Size of product mix and product lines.
   d. Marketing strategy employed.
   e. Marketing objectives.
   f. Past channel experience.
   g. Marketing functions willing to perform.
   h. Other strengths and weaknesses.
6. **Environmental characteristics.**
   a. Economic conditions.
   b. Legal regulations and restrictions.
   c. Political issues.
   d. Global and domestic cultural differences and changes.
   e. Technological changes.
   f. Other opportunities and threats.

(1) distribution coverage required, (2) degree of control desired, (3) total distribution cost, and (4) channel flexibility.

Distribution Coverage Required

Because of the characteristics of the product, the environment needed to sell the product, and the needs and expectations of the potential buyer, products will vary in the intensity of distribution coverage they require. Distribution coverage can be viewed along a continuum ranging from intensive to selective to exclusive distribution.

Intensive Distribution   Here the manufacturer attempts to gain exposure through as many wholesalers and retailers as possible. Most convenience goods require intensive distribution based on the characteristics of the product (low unit value) and the needs and expectations of the buyer (high frequency of purchase and convenience).

Selective Distribution   Here the manufacturer limits the use of intermediaries to the ones believed to be the best available in a geographic area. This may be based on the service organization available, the sales organization, or the reputation of the intermediary. Thus, appliances, home furnishings, and better clothing are usually distributed selectively. For appliances, the intermediary's service organization could be a key factor, while for better clothing and home furnishings, the intermediary's reputation would be an important consideration.

Exclusive Distribution   Here the manufacturer severely limits distribution, and intermediaries are provided exclusive rights within a particular territory. The characteristics of the product are a determining factor here. Where the product requires certain specialized selling effort or investment in unique facilities or large inventories, this arrangement is usually selected. Retail paint stores are an example of such a distribution arrangement.

THE PERFECT INTERMEDIARY

1. Has access to the market that the manufacturer wants to reach.
2. Carries adequate stocks of the manufacturer's products and a satisfactory assortment of other products.
3. Has an effective promotional program—advertising, personal selling, and product displays. Promotional demands placed on the manufacturer are in line with what the manufacturer intends to do.
4. Provides services to customers—credit, delivery, installation, and product repair—and honors the product warranty conditions.
5. Pays its bills on time and has capable management.

THE PERFECT MANUFACTURER

1. Provides a desirable assortment of products—well designed, properly priced, attractively packaged, and delivered on time and in adequate quantities.
2. Builds product demand for these products by advertising them.
3. Furnishes promotional assistance to its middlemen.
4. Provides managerial assistance for its middlemen.
5. Honors product warranties and provides repair and installation service.

THE PERFECT COMBINATION

1. Probably doesn't exist.

Degree of Control Desired

In selecting channels of distribution, the seller must make decisions concerning the degree of control desired over the marketing of the firm's products. Some manufacturers prefer to keep as much control over their products as possible. Ordinarily, the degree of control achieved by the seller is proportionate to the directness of the channel. One Eastern brewery, for instance, owns its own fleet of trucks and operates a wholly owned delivery system direct to grocery and liquor stores. Its market is very concentrated geographically, with many small buyers, so such a system is economically feasible. However, all other brewers in the area sell through distributors.

When more indirect channels are used, the manufacturer must surrender some control over the marketing of the firm's product. However, attempts are commonly made to maintain a degree of control through some other indirect means, such as sharing promotional expenditures, providing sales training, or other operational aids, such as accounting systems, inventory systems, or marketing research data on the dealer's trading area.

Total Distribution Cost

The total distribution cost concept has developed out of the more general topic of systems theory. The concept suggests that a channel of distribution should be viewed as a total system composed of interdependent subsystems, and that the objective of the system (channel) manager should be to optimize total system performance. In terms of distribution costs, it generally is assumed that the total system should be designed to minimize costs, other things being equal. The following is a representative list of the major distribution costs to be minimized:

1. Transportation.
2. Order processing.

3. Cost of lost business (an opportunity cost due to inability to meet customer demand).
4. Inventory carrying costs, including:
    a. Storage-space charges.
    b. Cost of capital invested.
    c. Taxes.
    d. Insurance.
    e. Obsolescence and deterioration.
5. Packaging.
6. Materials handling.

The important qualification to the total-cost concept is the statement "other things being equal." The purpose of the total-cost concept is to emphasize total system performance to avoid suboptimization. However, other important factors must be considered, not the least of which are level of customer service, sales, profits, and interface with the total marketing mix.

Channel Flexibility

A final consideration relates to the ability of the manufacturer to adapt to changing conditions. To illustrate, much of the population has moved from inner cities to suburbs, and thus buyers make most of their purchases in shopping centers and malls. If a manufacturer had long-term exclusive dealership with retailers in the inner city, the ability to adapt to this population shift could have been severely limited.

Managing a Channel of Distribution

Once the seller has decided on the type of channel structure to use and selected the individual members, the entire coalition should operate as a total system. From a behavioral perspective, the system can be viewed as a social system since each member interacts with the others, each member plays a role vis-à-vis the others, and each has certain expectations of the other. Thus, the behavioral perspective views a channel of distribution as more than a series of markets or participants extending from production to consumption.

Relationship Marketing in Channels

For many years in theory and practice, marketing has taken a competitive view of channels of distribution. In other words, since channel members had different goals and strategies, it was believed that the major focus should be on concepts such as power and conflict. Research interests focused on issues concerning bases of power, antecedents and consequences of conflict, and conflict resolution.

More recently, however, a new view of channels has developed. Perhaps because of the success of Japanese companies in the 1980s, it was recognized that much could be gained by developing long-term commitments and harmony among channel members. This view is called *relationship marketing*, which can be defined as "marketing with the conscious aim to develop and manage long-term and/or trusting relationships with customers, distributors, suppliers, or other parties in the marketing environment."[1]

It is well documented in the marketing literature that long-term relationships throughout the channel often lead to higher-quality products with lower costs. These benefits may account for the increased use of vertical marketing systems.[2]

Vertical Marketing Systems

To this point in the chapter the discussion has focused primarily on conventional channels of distribution. In conventional channels, each firm is relatively independent of the other

FIGURE 10.6
**Major Types of
Vertical Marketing
Systems**

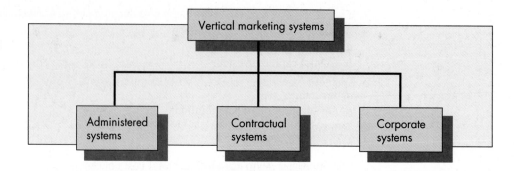

members in the channel. However, one of the important developments in channel management in recent years is the increasing use of vertical marketing systems.

Vertical marketing systems are channels in which members are more dependent on one another and develop long-term working relationships in order to improve the efficiency and effectiveness of the system. Figure 10.6 shows the major types of vertical marketing systems, which include administered, contractual, and corporate systems.[3]

Administered Systems

Administered vertical marketing systems are the most similar to conventional channels. However, in these systems there is a higher degree of interorganizational planning and management than in a conventional channel. The dependence in these systems can result from the existence of a strong channel leader such that other channel members work closely with this company in order to maintain a long-term relationship. While any level of channel member may be the leader of an administered system, Wal-Mart, Kmart, and Sears are excellent examples of retailers that have established administered systems with many of their suppliers.

Contractual Systems

Contractual vertical marketing systems involve independent production and distribution companies entering into formal contracts to perform designated marketing functions. Three major types of contractual vertical marketing systems are the retail cooperative organization, wholesaler-sponsored voluntary chain, and various franchising programs.

In a retail cooperative organization, a group of independent retailers unite and agree to pool buying and managerial resources to improve competitive position. In a wholesaler-sponsored voluntary chain, a wholesaler contracts with a number of retailers and performs channel functions for them. Usually, retailers agree to concentrate a major portion of their purchasing with the sponsoring wholesaler and to sell advertised products at the same price. The most visible type of contractual vertical marketing systems involves a variety of franchise programs. Franchises involve a parent company (the franchisor) and an independent firm (the franchisee) entering into a contractual relationship to set up and operate a business in a particular way. Many products and services reach consumers through franchise systems, including automobiles (Ford), gasoline (Mobil), hotels and motels (Holiday Inn), restaurants (McDonald's), car rentals (Avis), and soft drinks (Pepsi). In fact, some analysts predict that within the next 10 years, franchises will account for 50 percent of all retail sales.

Corporate Systems

Corporate vertical marketing systems involve single ownership of two or more levels of a channel. A manufacturer's purchasing wholesalers or retailers is called *forward*

A franchise is a means by which a producer of products or services achieves a direct channel of distribution without wholly owning or managing the physical facilities in the market. In effect, the franchisor provides the franchisee with the franchisor's knowledge, manufacturing, and marketing techniques for a financial return.

INGREDIENTS OF A FRANCHISED BUSINESS

Six key ingredients should be included within a well-balanced franchise offered to a franchisee. These are given in order of importance.

- *Technical knowledge* in its practical form is supplied through an intensive course of study.
- *Managerial techniques* based on proven and time-tested programs are imparted to the franchisee on a continuing basis, even after the business has been started or taken over by the franchisee.
- *Commercial knowledge* involving prescribed methods of buying and selling is explained and codified. Most products to be obtained, processed, and sold to the franchisee are supplied by the franchisor.
- *Financial instruction* on managing funds and accounts is given to the franchisee during the indoctrination period.
- *Accounting controls* are set up by the franchisor for the franchisee.
- *Protective safeguards* are included in the intensive training of the franchisee for employees and customers, including the quality of the product, as well as the safeguards for assets through adequate insurance controls.

ELEMENTS OF AN IDEAL FRANCHISE PROGRAM

- *High gross margin.* In order for the franchisee to be able to afford a high franchise fee (which the franchisor needs), it is necessary to operate on a high gross margin percentage. This explains the widespread application of franchising in the food and service industries.
- *In-store value added.* Franchising works best in those product categories in which the product is at least partially processed in the store. Such environments require constant on-site supervision—a chronic problem for company-owned stores using a hired manager. Owners simply are willing to work harder over longer hours.
- *Secret processes.* Concepts, formulas, or products that the franchisee can't duplicate without joining the franchise program.
- *Real estate profits.* The franchisor uses income from ownership of property as a significant revenue source.
- *Simplicity.* The most successful franchises have been those that operate on automatic pilot: All the key decisions have been thought through, and the owner merely implements the decisions.

Source: Partially adapted from Philip D. White and Albert D. Bates, "Franchising Will Remain Retailing Fixture, but Its Salad Days Have Long Since Gone," *Marketing News*, February 17, 1984, p. 14; and Scott Shane and Chester Spell, "Factors for New Franchise Success," *Sloan Management Review*, Spring 1998, pp. 43–50. Also see Stephen Spinelli, Jr., Robert M. Rosenberg, and Sue Birley, *Franchising* (Upper Saddle River, NJ: Prentice-Hall PTR, 2004).

integration. Wholesalers or retailers' purchasing channel members above them is called *backward integration.* Firms may choose to develop corporate vertical marketing systems in order to compete more effectively with other marketing systems, to obtain scale economies, and to increase channel cooperation and avoid channel conflict.

Wholesaling

As noted, wholesalers are merchants that are primarily engaged in buying, taking title to, usually storing and physically handling goods in large quantities, and reselling the goods (usually in smaller quantities) to retailers or to industrial or business users.[4] Wholesalers are also called *distributors* in some industries, particularly when they have exclusive distribution rights, such as in the beer industry. Other wholesalers that do not take title to goods are called *agents, brokers,* or *manufacturers' representatives* in various industries. There are over 890,000 wholesalers in the United States.

Wholesalers create value for suppliers, retailers, and users of goods by performing distribution functions efficiently and effectively. They may transport and warehouse goods, exhibit them at trade shows, and offer advice to retailers concerning which lines of products are selling best in other areas. Producers use wholesalers to reach large markets and extend geographic coverage for their goods. Wholesalers may lower the costs for other channel members by efficiently carrying out such activities as physically moving goods to convenient locations, assuming the risk of managing large inventories of diverse products, and delivering products as needed to replenish retail shelves.

While producers may actively seek out wholesalers for their goods, wholesalers also try to attract producers to use their services. To do so, they may offer to perform all the distribution functions or tailor their services to include only the functions that producers do not have the ability to perform effectively. Naturally, wholesalers especially seek producers of major brands for which sales and profit potential are likely to be the greatest. Wholesalers may compete with other wholesalers to attract producers by offering lower costs for the functions they perform. Wholesalers with excellent track records that do not carry directly competing products and brands, that have appropriate locations and facilities, and that have relationships with major retail customers can more easily attract manufacturers of successful products. Also, wholesalers that serve large markets may be more attractive since producers may be able to reduce the number of wholesalers they deal with and thereby lower their costs. Long-term profitable producer–wholesaler relationships are enhanced by trust, doing a good job for one another, and open communication about problems and opportunities.

Wholesalers also need to attract retailers and organizational customers to buy from them. In many cases, wholesalers have exclusive contracts to distribute products in a particular trading area. For popular products and brands with large market shares, the wholesaler's task is simplified because retailers want to carry them. For example, distributors of Coke and Pepsi can attract retailers easily because the products sell so well and consumers expect to find them in many retail outlets. Retail supermarkets and convenience stores would be at a competitive disadvantage without these brands.

However, for new or small market-share products and brands, particularly those of less well-known manufacturers, wholesalers may have to do considerable marketing to get retailers to stock them. Wholesalers may get placement for such products and brands in retail stores because they have previously developed strong long-term working relationships with them. Alternatively, wholesalers may have to carefully explain the marketing plan for the product, why it should be successful, and why carrying the product will benefit the retailer.

While there are still many successful wholesalers, the share of products they sell is likely to continue to decrease. This is because large retail chains such as Wal-Mart have gained such market power that they can buy directly from manufacturers and bypass wholesalers altogether. The survival of wholesalers depends on their ability to meet the needs of both manufacturers and retailers by performing distribution functions more efficiently and effectively than a channel designed without them.

BENEFITS FOR MANUFACTURERS

- Provide the ability to reach diverse geographic markets cost effectively.
- Provide information about retailers and end users in various markets.
- Reduce costs through greater efficiency and effectiveness in distribution functions performed.
- Reduce potential losses by assuming risks and offering expertise.

BENEFITS FOR RETAILERS

- Provide potentially profitable products otherwise unavailable for resale in retail area.
- Provide information about industries, manufacturers, and other retailers.
- Reduce costs by providing an assortment of goods from different manufacturers.
- Reduce costs through greater efficiency in distribution functions performed.

BENEFITS FOR END USERS

- Increase the product alternatives available in local markets.
- Reduce retail prices by the efficiency and effectiveness contributed to the channel.
- Improve product selection by providing information to retailers about the best products to offer end users.

Store and Nonstore Retailing

As noted, retailers are merchants who are primarily engaged in selling to ultimate consumers. The more than 3.2 million retailers in the United States can be classified in many ways. For example, they are broken down in the North American Industry Classification System (NAICS) codes into eight general categories and a number of subcategories based on the types of merchandise they sell.[5]

Marketers have a number of decisions to make to determine the best way to retail their products. For example, decisions have to be made about whether to use stores to sell merchandise, and if so, whether to sell through company-owned stores, franchised outlets, or independent stores or chains. Decisions have to be made about whether to sell through nonstore methods, such as the Internet, and if so, which methods of nonstore retailing should be used. Each of these decisions brings about a number of others such as what types of stores to use, how many of them, what locations should be selected, and what specific types of nonstore retailing to use.

Store Retailing

Over 90 percent of retail purchases are made through stores. This makes them an appropriate retail method for most types of products and services. Retailers vary not only in the types of merchandise they carry but also in the breadth and depth of their product assortments and the amount of service they provide. In general, *mass merchandisers* carry broad product assortments and compete on two bases. Supermarkets (Kroger) and department stores (Macy's) compete with other retailers on the basis of offering a good selection in a number of different categories, whereas supercenters (Wal-Mart Supercenters), warehouse clubs (Costco), discount stores (Wal-Mart), and off-price retailers (T.J. Maxx) compete more on the basis of offering lower prices on products in their large assortments.

Manufacturers of many types of consumer goods must get distribution in one or more types of mass merchandisers to be successful.

Specialty stores handle deep assortments in a limited number of product categories. Specialty stores include limited-line stores that offer a large assortment of a few related product lines (The Gap), single-line stores that emphasize a single product (Batteries Plus), and category killers (Circuit City), which are large, low-priced limited-line retail chains that attempt to dominate a particular product category. If a product type is sold primarily through specialty stores and sales are concentrated in category killer chains, manufacturers may have to sell through them to reach customers.

Convenience stores (7-Eleven) are retailers whose primary advantages to consumers are location convenience, close-in parking, and easy entry and exit. They stock products that consumers want to buy in a hurry, such as milk or soft drinks, and charge higher prices for the purchase convenience. They are an important retail outlet for many types of convenience goods.

In selecting the types of stores and specific stores and chains to resell their products, manufacturers (and wholesalers) have a variety of factors to consider. They want stores and chains that reach their target market and have good reputations with consumers. They want stores and chains that handle distribution functions efficiently and effectively, order large quantities, pay invoices quickly, display their merchandise well, and allow them to make good profits. Selling products in the right stores and chains increases sales, and selling in prestigious stores can increase the equity of a brand and the price that can be charged. The locations of retail stores, the types of people who shop at them, and the professionalism of the salespeople and clerks who work in them all affect the success of the stores and the products they sell. In addition to the merchandise offered, store advertising, and price levels, the characteristics of the store itself—including layout, colors, smells, noises, lights, signs, and shelf space and displays—influence the success of both the stores and the products they offer.

Nonstore Retailing

Although stores dominate sales for most products, there are still opportunities to market products successfully in other ways. Five nonstore methods of retailing include catalogs and direct mail, vending machines, television home shopping, direct sales, and electronic exchanges.[6]

Catalogs and Direct Mail

As shown in Figure 10.7, catalogs and direct mail dominate nonstore retailing. The advantages of this type of nonstore retailing for marketers are that consumers can be targeted effectively and reached in their homes or at work, overhead costs are decreased, and assortments of specialty merchandise can be presented with attractive pictures and in-depth descriptions of features and benefits. Catalogs can also remain in homes or offices for a lengthy time period, making available potential sales. Catalogs can offer specialty products for unique markets that are geographically dispersed in a cost-effective manner. Although consumers cannot experience products directly as they can in stores, catalog retailers with reputations for quality and generous return policies can reduce consumers' risks. For example, Levenger, which sells pens, desks, and "other tools for serious readers," sends consumers a postage-paid label to return unwanted merchandise. Many consumers enjoy the time savings of catalog shopping and are willing to pay higher prices to use it.

Vending Machines

Vending machines are a relatively limited method of retail merchandising, and most vending machine sales are for beverages, food, and candy. The advantages for marketers include the following: They are available for sales 24 hours a day, they can be placed in a variety of

FIGURE 10.7
Annual Nonstore Retail Sales

Source: Adapted from Michael Levy and Barton A. Weitz, *Retailing Management,* 5th ed. (Burr Ridge, IL: McGraw-Hill/Irwin. 2004), pp. 57–62. Reproduced with permission from The McGraw-Hill Companies.

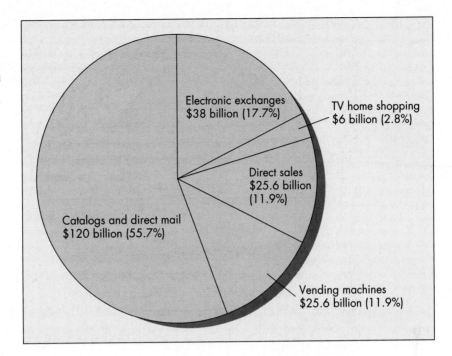

high-traffic locations, and marketers can charge higher prices. While uses of vending machines for such things as airline insurance and concert and game tickets are not unusual, this method has limited potential for most products.

Television Home Shopping

Television home shopping includes cable channels dedicated to shopping, infomercials, and direct-response advertising shown on cable and broadcast networks. Home Shopping Network and QVC are the leaders in this market, and the major products sold are inexpensive jewelry, apparel, cosmetics, and exercise equipment. While this method allows better visual display than catalogs, potential customers must be watching at the time the merchandise is offered; if not, they have no way of knowing about the product or purchasing it.

Direct Sales

Direct sales are made by salespeople to consumers in their homes or offices or by telephone. The most common products purchased this way are cosmetics, fragrances, decorative accessories, vacuum cleaners, home appliances, cooking utensils, kitchenware, jewelry, food and nutritional products, and educational materials. Avon, Mary Kay, and Tupperware are probably the best-known retail users of this channel. Salespeople can demonstrate products effectively and provide detailed feature and benefit information. A limitation of this method is that consumers are often too busy to spend their time this way and do not want to pay the higher prices needed to cover the high costs of this method of retailing.

Electronic Exchange

Electronic exchanges or Internet marketing involves customers collecting information, shopping, and purchasing from Web sites on the Internet. Electronic exchange has had its greatest success in business-to-business marketing, although it accounts for only about 10 percent of business-to-business commerce. In the business-to-consumer market, electronic exchange is the fastest-growing type of nonstore retailing. However, sales in this

When developing commercial Web sites, it is important to consider what customers experience when searching for information, evaluating alternative products, and purchasing them. Below are some basic questions that Web site designers should consider.

INFORMATION SEARCH

1. Ease of navigation—is it easy to move throughout the Web site?
2. Speed of page downloads—does each page load quickly enough?
3. Effectiveness of search features—are search features returning the information users are looking for?
4. Frequency of product updates—is product information updated often enough to meet user needs?

EVALUATION OF ALTERNATIVES

1. Ease of product comparisons—is it easy to compare different products offered on the Web site?
2. Product descriptions—are product descriptions accurate, clear, and comprehensive enough to allow customers to make informed decisions?
3. Contacting customer service representatives—are customer service phone numbers easy to locate?
4. In-stock status—are out-of-stock products flagged before the customer proceeds to the checkout process?

PURCHASE

1. Security and privacy issues—do users feel comfortable transmitting personal information?
2. Checkout process—are users able to move through the checkout process in a reasonable amount of time?
3. Payment options—are payment options offered that nonbuyers desire?
4. Delivery options—are delivery options offered that nonbuyers desire?
5. Ordering instructions—are ordering instructions easy to understand?

Source: Based on Douglas K. Hoffman and John E. G. Bateson, *Services Marketing: Concepts, Strategies, and Cases.* 3rd ed. (Mason, OH: Thomson South Western, 2006), p. 86.

market are still a small portion of the sales in traditional retail stores. In fact, Wal-Mart's sales in its traditional stores are far greater than the total of all business-to-consumer exchanges on the Internet taken collectively.

Initially, many analysts thought that electronic exchange would become a leading source of commerce because of its potential to reduce costs for marketers and prices for customers. However, these analysts may have overestimated the ability of electronic exchange to do so; marketing functions in a channel still have to be performed although, admittedly, some of them can be done more efficiently using this method. For example, order-taking and processing can be done more efficiently and accurately by electronic means.

Figure 10.8 lists some of the advantages and disadvantages of the electronic exchange for marketers. In examining this figure, it is important to recognize that there are some differences in the advantages and disadvantages depending on whether the marketer is a small, entrepreneurial venture or a large, established company. Since electronic exchange offers low-entry barriers, this is an advantage for a small company that wants to get into a market and compete for business with less capital. However, for large, established companies, this is less of an advantage since they have the capital to invest; low-entry barriers create more competition for them from smaller companies.

FIGURE 10.8
Electronic Commerce: Advantages and Disadvantages for Marketers

---

Advantages for Marketers

Reduces the need for stores, paper catalogs, and salespeople; can be cost efficient.
Allows good visual presentation and full description of product features and benefits.
Allows vast assortments of products to be offered efficiently.
Allows strategic elements, such as product offerings, prices, and promotion appeals, to be changed quickly.
Allows products to be offered globally in an efficient manner.
Allows products to be offered 24 hours a day, 365 days a year.
Fosters the development of one-on-one, interactive relationships with customers.
Provides an efficient means for developing a customer database and doing online marketing research.

Disadvantages for Marketers

Strong price competition often squeezes profit margins.
Low entry barriers lead some e-marketers to overemphasize order-taking and not develop sufficient infrastructure for order fulfillment.
Customers must go to the Web site rather than having marketers seek them out via salespeople and advertising; advertising their Web sites is prohibitively expensive for many small e-marketers.
Limits the market to customers who are willing and able to purchase electronically; many countries still have a small population of computer-literate people.
Not as good for selling touch-and-feel products as opposed to look-and-buy products unless there is strong brand/store/site equity (Dell computers/Wal-Mart/Amazon.com) or the products are homogeneous (books, CDs, plane tickets, etc.).
Often less effective and efficient in business-to-consumer markets than in business-to-business markets.

Similarly, large companies with established names and brand equity can more easily market products that customers would ordinarily want to examine before purchase (touch-and-feel products) than can smaller companies with less brand equity. For example, companies like Lands' End, J.C. Penney, and Wal-Mart are more successful in attracting customers electronically because customers know the companies and their offerings better and perceive less risk in purchasing from them than from a new or unknown electronic marketer. This does not mean that newer companies that sell only by electronic means cannot compete for business. Companies such as Amazon.com and Priceline.com have created well-known Web sites and have generated considerable sales. However, as with most dot.com businesses, generating profits has been difficult for them.

In sum, while electronic exchange has not met the growth expectations of many marketers, it is an established alternative for marketing some products and services. It does provide customers with a wealth of product information and product assortments that are readily available. Many electronic marketers have found ways to deliver superior customer value and become profitable and many others are close to doing so.[7]

Conclusion

This chapter introduced the distribution of goods and services in a complex, highly competitive, highly specialized economy. It emphasized the vital need for marketing intermediaries to bring about exchanges between buyers and sellers in a reasonably efficient manner. The chapter examined various types of intermediaries and the distribution functions they perform as well as topics in the selection and management of distribution channels. Finally, both wholesaling and store and nonstore retailing were discussed.

Additional Readings

Chopra, Sunil, and Peter Meindl. *Supply Chain Management.* 2nd ed. Upper River Saddle, NJ: Prentice Hall, 2004.

Coughlin, Anne T.; Erin Anderson; Louis W. Stern; and Adel I. El-Ansary. *Marketing Channels.* 7th ed. Upper Saddle River, NJ: Prentice Hall, 2006.

Levy, Michael, and Burton A. Weitz. *Retailing Management.* 6th ed. Burr Ridge, IL: Irwin/McGraw-Hill, 2007.

Rosenbloom, Bert. *Marketing Channels: A Management View.* 7th ed. Mason, OH: Tomson South-Western, 2004.

Simchi-Levi, David; Philip Kaminsky, and Edith Simchi-Levi. *Designing and Managing the Supply Chain.* 3rd ed. Burr Ridge, IL: McGraw-Hill, 2008.

11

Pricing Strategy

One of the most important and complex decisions a firm has to make relates to pricing its products or services. If consumers or organizational buyers perceive a price to be too high, they may purchase competitive brands or substitute products, leading to a loss of sales and profits for the firm. If the price is too low, sales might increase, but profitability may suffer. Thus, pricing decisions must be given careful consideration when a firm is introducing a new product or planning a short- or long-term price change.

This chapter discusses demand, supply, and environmental influences that affect pricing decisions and emphasizes that all three must be considered for effective pricing. However, as will be discussed in the chapter, many firms price their products without explicitly considering all of these influences.

Demand Influences on Pricing Decisions

Demand influences on pricing decisions concern primarily the nature of the target market and expected reactions of consumers to a given price or change in price. There are three primary considerations here: demographic factors, psychological factors, and price elasticity.

Demographic Factors

In the initial selection of the target market that a firm intends to serve, a number of demographic factors are usually considered. Demographic factors that are particularly important for pricing decisions include the following:

1. Number of potential buyers.
2. Location of potential buyers.
3. Position of potential buyers (organizational buyers or final consumers).
4. Expected consumption rates of potential buyers.
5. Economic strength of potential buyers.

These factors help determine market potential and are useful for estimating expected sales at various price levels.

Psychological Factors

Psychological factors related to pricing concern primarily how consumers will perceive various prices or price changes. For example, marketing managers should be concerned with such questions as these:

1. Will potential buyers use price as an indicator of product quality?
2. Will potential buyers be favorably attracted by odd pricing (e.g. 99¢, $3,999)?

Small changes in price can lead to large differences in net income. For example, at Coca-Cola, a 1 percent improvement in the price received for its products would result in a net income boost of 6.4 percent; at Fuji Photo, 16.7 percent; at Nestlé, 17.5 percent; at Ford, 26 percent; and at Philips, 28.7 percent. In some companies, a 1 percent improvement in the price received would be the difference between a profit and a significant loss. Given the cost structure of large corporations, a 1 percent boost in realized price yields an average net income gain of 12 percent. In short, when setting pricing objectives and developing pricing strategies, it's worth the effort to do pricing research to see what prices consumers are willing to pay and still feel they are receiving good value.

Source: Based on Robert J. Dolan and Hermann Simon, *Power Pricing: How Managing Price Transforms the Bottom Line* (New York: Free Press, 1996), p. 4. Also see Kent B. Monroe, *Pricing: Making Profitable Decisions*, 3rd ed. (Burr Ridge, IL: McGraw-Hill/Irwin, 2003), Chapter 12.

3. Will potential buyers perceive the price as too high relative to the service the product gives them or relative to competition?
4. Are potential buyers prestige oriented and therefore willing to pay higher prices to fulfill this need?
5. How much will potential buyers be willing to pay for the product?

While psychological factors have a significant effect on the success of a pricing strategy and ultimately on marketing strategy, answers to the above questions may require considerable marketing research. In fact, a review of buyers' subjective perceptions of price concluded that very little is known about how price affects buyers' perceptions of alternative purchase offers and how these perceptions affect purchase response.[1] However, some tentative generalizations about how buyers perceive price have been formulated. For example, research has found that persons who choose high-priced items usually perceive large quality variations within product categories and see the consequences of a poor choice as being undesirable. They believe that quality is related to price and see themselves as good judges of product quality. In general, the reverse is true for persons who select low-priced items in the same product categories. Thus, although information on psychological factors involved in purchasing may be difficult to obtain, marketing managers must at least consider the effects of such factors on their desired target market and marketing strategy.[2]

There are three types of psychological pricing strategies. First there is *prestige pricing*, in which a high price is charged to create a signal that the product is exceptionally fine. Prestige pricing is commonly used for some brands of cars, clothing, perfume, jewelry, cosmetics, wine and liquor, and crystal and china. Second, there is *odd pricing*, or odd-even pricing, in which prices are set a few dollars or a few cents below a round number. For example, Frito-Lay's potato chips are priced at 69 cents a bag rather than 70 cents to encourage consumers to think of them as less expensive (60 some-odd cents) rather than 70 cents. Hertz economy cars are rented for $129 rather than $130 to appear less expensive. Third, there is *bundle pricing*, in which several products are sold together at a single price to suggest a good value. For example, travel agencies offer vacation packages that include travel, accommodations, and entertainment at a single price to connote value and convenience for customers.

Price Elasticity

Both demographic and psychological factors affect price elasticity. Price elasticity is a measure of consumers' price sensitivity, which is estimated by dividing relative changes in the quantity sold by the relative changes in price:

$$e = \frac{\text{Percent change in quantity demanded}}{\text{Percent change in price}}$$

Although price elasticity is difficult to measure, two basic methods are commonly used to estimate it. First, price elasticity can be estimated from historical data or from price/-quantity data across different sales districts. Second, price elasticity can be estimated by sampling a group of consumers from the target market and polling them concerning various price/quantity relationships. Both of these approaches provide estimates of price elasticity; but the former approach is limited to the consideration of price changes, whereas the latter is often expensive and there is some question as to the validity of subjects' responses. However, even a crude estimate of price elasticity is a useful input to pricing decisions.[3]

Supply Influences on Pricing Decisions

For the purpose of this text, supply influences on pricing decisions can be discussed in terms of three basic factors. These factors relate to the objectives, costs, and nature of the product.

Pricing Objectives

Pricing objectives should be derived from overall marketing objectives, which in turn should be derived from corporate objectives. Since it is traditionally assumed that business firms operate to maximize profits in the long run, it is often thought that the basic pricing objective is solely concerned with long-run profits. However, the profit maximization norm does not provide the operating marketing manager with a single, unequivocal guideline for selecting prices. In addition, the marketing manager does not have perfect cost, revenue, and market information to be able to evaluate whether or not this objective is being reached. In practice, then, many other objectives are employed as guidelines for pricing decisions. In some cases, these objectives may be considered as operational approaches to achieve long-run profit maximization.

Research has found that the most common pricing objectives are (1) pricing to achieve a target return on investment, (2) stabilization of price and margin, (3) pricing to achieve a target market share, and (4) pricing to meet or prevent competition.

Cost Considerations in Pricing

The price of a product usually must cover costs of production, promotion, and distribution, plus a profit for the offering to be of value to the firm. In addition, when products are priced on the basis of costs plus a fair profit, there is an implicit assumption that this sum represents the economic value of the product in the marketplace.

Cost-oriented pricing is the most common approach in practice, and there are at least three basic variations: markup pricing, cost-plus pricing, and rate-of-return pricing. *Markup pricing* is commonly used in retailing: A percentage is added to the retailer's invoice price to determine the final selling price. Closely related to markup pricing is *cost-plus pricing,* in which the costs of producing a product or completing a project are totaled and a profit amount or percentage is added on. Cost-plus pricing is most often used to describe the pricing of jobs that are nonroutine and difficult to "cost" in advance, such as construction and military weapon development.

Rate-of-return or *target pricing* is commonly used by manufacturers. With this method, price is determined by adding a desired rate of return on investment to total costs. Generally, a break-even analysis is performed for expected production and sales levels and a rate

There are two common pricing strategies at the retail level: EDLP, which stands for "everyday low pricing," and high/low, which means that the retailer charges prices that are sometimes above competitors' but promotes frequent sales that lower prices below them. Four successful U.S. retailers—Home Depot, Wal-Mart, Office Depot, and Toys 'R' Us—have adopted EDLP, while many fashion, grocery, and drug stores use high/low. Below is a list of the advantages of each of these pricing strategies.

ADVANTAGES OF EDLP

- *Assures customers of low prices.* Many customers are skeptical about initial retail prices. They have become conditioned to buying only on sale—the main characteristic of a high/low pricing strategy. The EDLP strategy lets customers know that they will get the same low prices every time they patronize the EDLP retailer. Customers don't have to read the ads and wait for items they want to go on sale.

- *Reduces advertising and operating expenses.* The stable prices caused by EDLP limit the need for the weekly sale advertising used in the high/low strategy. In addition, EDLP retailers do not have to incur the labor costs of changing price tags and signs and putting up sales signs.

- *Reduces stockouts and improves inventory management.* The EDLP approach reduces the large variations in demand caused by frequent sales with large markdowns. As a result, retailers can manage their inventories with more certainty. Fewer stockouts mean more satisfied customers, higher sales, and fewer rain checks.

ADVANTAGES OF HIGH/LOW

- *Increases profits through price discrimination.* High/low pricing allows retailers to charge higher prices to customers who are not price sensitive and are willing to pay the "high" price and lower prices to price-sensitive customers who will wait for the "low" sale price.

- *Sales create excitement.* A "get them while they last" atmosphere often occurs during a sale. Sales draw a lot of customers, and a lot of customers create excitement. Some retailers augment low prices and advertising with special in-store activities like product demonstrations, giveaways, and celebrity appearances.

- *Sells merchandise.* Sales allow retailers to get rid of slow-selling merchandise.

Source: Based on Michael Levy and Barton A. Weitz, *Retailing Management,* 6th ed. (Burr Ridge, IL: McGraw-Hill/Irwin, 2007), p. 418.

of return is added on. For example, suppose a firm estimated production and sales to be 75,000 units at a total cost of $300,000. If the firm desired a before-tax return of 20 percent, the selling price would be $(300,000 + 0.20 \times 300,000) \div 75,000 = \$4.80$.

Cost-oriented approaches to pricing have the advantage of simplicity, and many practitioners believe that they generally yield a good price decision. However, such approaches have been criticized for two basic reasons. First, cost approaches give little or no consideration to demand factors. For example, the price determined by markup or cost-plus methods has no necessary relationship to what people will be willing to pay for the product. In the case of rate-of-return pricing, little emphasis is placed on estimating sales volume. Even if it were, rate-of-return pricing involves circular reasoning, since unit cost depends on sales volume but sales volume depends on selling price. Second, cost approaches fail to reflect competition adequately. Only in industries where all firms use this approach and have similar costs and markups can this approach yield similar prices and minimize price competition. Thus, in many industries, cost-oriented pricing could lead to severe price competition, which could eliminate smaller firms. Therefore, although costs are a highly important consideration in price decisions, numerous other factors need to be examined.

The following formulas are used to calculate break-even points in units and in dollars:

$$BEP_{(in\ units)} = \frac{FC}{(SP - VC)}$$

$$BEP_{(in\ dollars)} = \frac{FC}{1 - (VC/SP)}$$

where

FC = Fixed cost

VC = Variable cost

SP = Selling price

If, as is generally the case, a firm wants to know how many units or sales dollars are necessary to generate a given amount of profit, profit (P) is simply added to fixed costs in the formulas. In addition, if the firm has estimates of expected sales and fixed and variable costs, the selling price can be solved for. (A more detailed discussion of break-even analysis is provided in the financial analysis section of this book.)

Product Considerations in Pricing

Although numerous product characteristics can affect pricing, three of the most important are (1) perishability, (2) distinctiveness, and (3) stage in the product life cycle.

Perishability

Some products, such as fresh meat, bakery goods, and some raw materials are physically perishable and must be priced to sell before they spoil. Typically, this involves discounting the products as they approach being no longer fit for sale. Products can also be perishable in the sense that demand for them is confined to a specific time period. For example, high fashion and fad products lose most of their value when they go out of style and marketers have the difficult task of forecasting demand at specific prices and judging the time period of customer interest. While the time period of interest for other seasonal products, such as winter coats or Christmas trees, is easier to estimate, marketers must still determine the appropriate price and discount structure to maximize profits and avoid inventory losses or carrying costs.

Distinctiveness

Marketers try to distinguish their products from those of competitors and if successful, can often charge higher prices for them. While such things as styling, features, ingredients, and service can be used to try to make a product distinctive, competitors can copy such physical changes. Thus, it is through branding and brand equity that products are commonly made distinctive in customers' minds. For example, prestigious brands like Rolex, Tiffany's, and Lexus can be priced higher in large measure because of brand equity. Of course, higher prices also help create and reinforce the brand equity of prestigious products.

Life Cycle

The stage of the life cycle that a product is in can have important pricing implications. With regard to the life cycle, two approaches to pricing are skimming and penetration price policies. A *skimming* policy is one in which the seller charges a relatively high price on a new product. Generally, this policy is used when the firm has a temporary monopoly and when demand for the product is price inelastic. In later stages of the life cycle, as competition moves in and other market factors change, the price may then be lowered. Digital watches and calculators are examples of this. A *penetration* policy is one in which the seller charges a relatively low price on a new product. Generally, this policy is used when the firm expects competition to move in rapidly and when demand for the product is, at least in the short run, price elastic. This policy is also used to obtain large economies of scale and as a major instrument for rapid creation of a mass market. A low price and profit margin may also discourage competition. In later stages of the life cycle, the price may have to be altered to meet changes in the market.

Environmental Influences on Pricing Decisions

Environmental influences on pricing include variables that the marketing manager cannot control. Two of the most important of these are competition and government regulation.

Competition

In setting or changing prices, the firm must consider its competition and how competition will react to the price of the product. Initially, consideration must be given to such factors as

1. Number of competitors.
2. Market shares, growth, and profitability of competitors.
3. Strengths and weaknesses of competitors.
4. Likely entry of new firms into the industry.
5. Degree of vertical integration of competitors.
6. Number of products sold by competitors.
7. Cost structure of competitors.
8. Historical reaction of competitors to price changes.

These factors help determine whether the firm's selling price should be at, below, or above competition. Pricing a product at competition (i.e., the average price charged by the industry) is called *going-rate pricing* and is popular for homogeneous products, since this approach represents the collective wisdom of the industry and is not disruptive of industry harmony. An example of pricing below competition can be found in *sealed-bid pricing,* in which the firm is bidding directly against competition for project contracts. Although cost and profits are initially calculated, the firm attempts to bid below competitors to obtain the job contract. A firm may price above competition because it has a superior product or because the firm is the price leader in the industry.

Government Regulations

Prices of certain goods and services are regulated by state and federal governments. Public utilities are examples of state regulation of prices. However, for most marketing managers, federal laws that make certain pricing practices illegal are of primary consideration in pricing decisions. The list below is a summary of some of the more important legal constraints on pricing. Of course, since most marketing managers are not trained as lawyers, they usually seek legal counsel when developing pricing strategies to ensure conformity to state and federal legislation.

1. Price fixing is illegal per se. Sellers must not make any agreements with competitors or distributors concerning the final price of the goods. The Sherman Antitrust Act is the primary device used to outlaw horizontal price fixing. Section 5 of the Federal Trade Commission Act has been used to outlaw price fixing as an unfair business practice.

2. Deceptive pricing practices are outlawed under Section 5 of the Federal Trade Commission Act. An example of deceptive pricing would be to mark merchandise with an exceptionally high price and then claim that the lower selling price actually used represents a legitimate price reduction.

3. Price discrimination that lessens competition or is deemed injurious to it is outlawed by the Robinson-Patman Act (which amends Section 2 of the Clayton Act). Price discrimination is not illegal per se, but sellers cannot charge competing buyers different prices for essentially the same products if the effect of such sales is injurious to competition. Price differentials can be legally justified on certain grounds, especially if the price differences reflect cost differences. This is particularly true of quantity discounts.

4. Promotional pricing, such as cooperative advertising, and price deals are not illegal per se; but if a seller grants advertising allowances, merchandising service, free goods, or special promotional discounts to customers, it must do so on proportionately equal terms. Sections 2(d) and 2(e) of the Robinson-Patman Act are designed to regulate such practices so that price reductions cannot be granted to some customers under the guise of promotional allowances.[4]

A General Pricing Model

It should be clear that effective pricing decisions involve considerations of many factors, and different industries may have different pricing practices. Although no single model will fit all pricing decisions, Figure 11.1 presents a general model for developing prices for products and services.[5] While all pricing decisions cannot be made strictly on the basis of this model, it does break pricing strategy into a set of manageable stages that are integrated into the overall marketing strategy.

Set Pricing Objectives

Given a product or service designed for a specific target market, the pricing process begins with a clear statement of the pricing objectives. These objectives guide the pricing strategy and should be designed to support the overall marketing strategy. Because pricing strategy has a direct bearing on demand for a product and the profit obtained, efforts to set prices must be coordinated with other functional areas. For example, production will have to be able to meet demand at a given price, and finance will have to manage funds flowing in and out of the organization at predicted levels of production.

Evaluate Product–Price Relationships

As noted, the distinctiveness, perishability, and stage of the life cycle a product is in all affect pricing. In addition, marketers need to consider what value the product has for customers and how price will influence product positioning. There are three basic value positions. First, a product could be priced relatively high for a product class because it offers value in the form of high quality, special features, or prestige. Second, a product could be priced at about average for the product class because it offers value in the form of good quality for a reasonable price. Third, a product could be priced relatively low for a product class because it offers value in the form of acceptable quality at a low price. A Porsche or Nike Air Jordans are examples of the first type of value; a Honda Accord or Keds tennis shoes are examples of the second; and Hyundai cars and private label canvas shoes are examples of the third. Setting prices so that targeted customers will perceive products to offer greater value than competitive offerings is called *value pricing*.

In addition, research is needed to estimate how much of a particular product the target market will purchase at various price levels—price elasticity. This estimate provides

FIGURE 11.1
A General Pricing Model

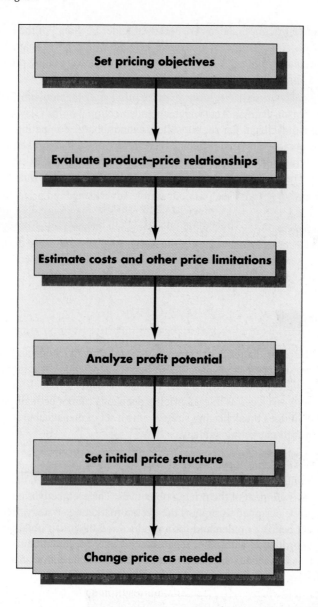

valuable information about what the target market thinks about the product and what it is worth to them.

Estimate Costs and Other Price Limitations

The costs to produce and market products provide a lower bound for pricing decisions and a baseline from which to compute profit potential. If a product cannot be produced and marketed at a price to cover its costs and provide reasonable profits in the long run, then it should not be produced in its designed form. One possibility is to redesign the product so that its costs are lower. In fact, some companies first determine the price customers are willing to pay for a product and then design it so that it can be produced and marketed at a cost that allows targeted profits.

Other price limitations that need to be considered are government regulations and the prices that competitors charge for similar and substitute products. Also, likely competitive

1. *Base pricing strategies on sound research.* Although a recent study found that few companies do serious pricing research, it is a must for sound pricing strategies. Research is needed to understand the factors that influence supply and demand.

2. *Continuously monitor pricing decisions.* Pricing should be treated as a process of developing prices and changing them as needed rather than an annual budgeting exercise. Price decisions define an organization's value image in the eyes of customers and competitors.

3. *Recognize that buyers may have difficulty in computing price differences.* Buyers do not constantly monitor the prices of many products and will not necessarily quickly recognize the value in a price deal.

4. *Recognize that customers evaluate prices comparatively.* Behavioral pricing research suggests that customers compare prices and price deals relative to internal or external reference prices rather than just evaluating them in an absolute sense. An internal reference price is the price a customer has in mind for a product and an external reference price is one the customer has seen in advertising, a catalog, or on a store sign or price tag.

5. *Recognize that buyers typically have a range of acceptable prices.* Buyers often have an upper and lower threshold or range of acceptable prices rather than only one acceptable price they are willing to pay.

6. *Understand the importance of relative price to buyers.* The relative price of a product compared to competitive offerings or to what a buyer previously paid for it may be more important than the absolute price asked.

7. *Understand the importance of price information.* Price information can affect preferences and choices for different models in a product line or for competitive offerings, particularly when buyers cannot easily evaluate product quality.

8. *Recognize that price elasticities vary.* Price elasticities vary according to the direction of a price change, and buyers are generally more sensitive to price increases than to price decreases. Thus, it is easier to lose sales to current customers by increasing prices than it is to gain sales from new buyers by reducing them.

Source: Based on Kent B. Monroe and Jennifer L. Cox, "Pricing Practices That Endanger Profits," *Marketing Management,* September/October 2001, pp. 42–46.

reactions that could influence the price of a new product or a price change in an existing one need to be considered.

Analyze Profit Potential

Analysis in the preceding stages should result in a range of prices that could be charged. Marketers must then estimate the likely profit in pricing at levels in this range. At this stage, it is important to recognize that it may be necessary to offer channel members quantity discounts, promotional allowances, and slotting allowances to encourage them to actively market the product. *Quantity discounts* are discounts for purchasing a large number of units. *Promotional allowances* are often in the form of price reductions in exchange for the channel member performing various promotional activities, such as featuring the product in store advertising or on in-store displays. *Slotting allowances* are payments to retailers to get them to stock items on their shelves. All of these can increase sales but also add marketing cost to the manufacturer and affect profits.

Set Initial Price Structure

Since all of the supply, demand, and environmental factors have been considered, a marketer can now set the initial price structure. The price structure takes into account the price to various channel members, such as wholesalers and retailers, as well as the recommended price to final consumers or organizational buyers.

Change Price as Needed

There are many reasons why an initial price structure may need to be changed. Channel members may bargain for greater margins, competitors may lower their prices, or costs may increase with inflation. In the short term, discounts and allowances may have to be larger or more frequent than planned to get greater marketing effort to increase demand to profitable levels. In the long term, price structures tend to increase for most products as production and marketing costs increase.

Conclusion

Pricing decisions that integrate the firm's costs with marketing strategy, business conditions, competition, demand, product variables, channels of distribution, and general resources can determine the success or failure of a business. This places a very heavy burden on the price maker. Modern-day marketing managers cannot ignore the complexity or the importance of price management. Pricing strategies must be continually reviewed and must take into account that the firm is a dynamic entity operating in a very competitive environment. There are many ways for money to flow out of a firm in the form of costs, but often there is only one way to bring in revenues and that is by the price-product mechanism.

Additional Readings

Mazumdar, Tridib; S. P. Raj, and Indrajit Sinha. "Reference Price Research: Review and Propositions." *Journal of Marketing,* October 2005, pp. 84–102.

Monroe, Kent B. *Pricing: Making Profitable Decisions.* 3d ed. New York: McGraw-Hill, 2003.

Nagle, Thomas T., and John Hogan. *The Strategy and Tactics of Pricing.* 4th ed. Englewood Cliffs, NJ: Prentice Hall, 2006.

Winer, Russell S. *Pricing.* Cambridge, MA: Marketing Science Institute, 2005.

Part D

Marketing in Special Fields

12

The Marketing of Services

Over the course of the past 40 years, the fastest-growing segment of the American economy has not been the production of tangibles but the performance of services. Spending on services has increased to such an extent that today it captures more than 50 cents of the consumer's dollar. In addition, the service sector in the United States produces a balance-of-trade surplus and is expected to be responsible for all net job growth in the forseeable future.[1] The dominance of the service sector is not limited to the United States. The service sector accounts for more than half the GNP and employs more than half the labor force in most Latin American and Caribbean countries. Over the course of the next decade, the service sector will spawn whole new legions of doctors, nurses, medical technologists, physical therapists, home health aids, and social workers to administer to the needs of an aging population, along with armies of food servers, child care providers, and cleaning people to cater to the wants of two-income families. Also rising to the forefront will be a swelling class of technical workers, including computer engineers, systems analysts, and paralegals.

Many marketing textbooks still devote little attention to program development for the marketing of services, especially those in the rapidly changing areas of health care, finance, and travel. This omission is usually based on the assumption that the marketing of products and services is basically the same, and, therefore, the techniques discussed under products apply as well to the marketing of services. Basically, this assumption is true. Whether selling goods or services, the marketer must be concerned with developing a marketing strategy centered on the four controllable decision variables that comprise the marketing mix: the product (or service), the price, the distribution system, and promotion. In addition, the use of marketing research is as valuable to service marketers as it is to product marketers. However, because services possess certain distinguishing characteristics, the task of determining the marketing mix ingredients for a service marketing strategy may raise different and more difficult problems than those encountered in marketing products.

The purpose of this chapter is fourfold. First, the reader will become acquainted with the special characteristics of services and their strategy implications. Second, key concepts associated with providing quality services will be discussed. Third, obstacles will be described that in the past impeded and still continue to impede development of services marketing. Finally, current trends and strategies of innovation in services marketing will be explored. With this approach, the material in the other chapters of the book can be integrated to give a better understanding of the marketing of services.

Before proceeding, some attention must be given to what we refer to when using the term *services*. Probably the most frustrating aspect of the available literature on services is that the definition of what constitutes a service remains unclear. The fact is that no common definition and boundaries have been developed to delimit the field of services. The American Marketing Association has defined services as follows:[2]

1. *Service products,* such as a bank loan or home security, that are intangible, or at least substantially so. If totally intangible, they are exchanged directly from producer to user, cannot be transported or stored, and are almost instantly perishable. Service products are often difficult to identify, since they come into existence at the same time they are bought and consumed. They are composed of intangible elements that are inseparable; they usually involve customer participation in some important way, cannot be sold in the sense of ownership transfer, and have no title. Today, however, most products are partly tangible and partly intangible, and the dominant form is used to classify them as either goods or services (all are products). These common, hybrid forms, whatever they are called, may or may not have the attributes just given for totally intangible services.

2. *Services,* as a term, is also used to describe activities performed by sellers and others that accompany the sale of a product and that aid in its exchange or its utilization (e.g., shoe fitting, financing, an 800 number). Such services are either presale or postsale and supplement the product but do not comprise it.

The first definition includes what can be considered almost pure services, such as insurance, banking, entertainment, airlines, health care, telecommunications, and hotels; the second definition includes such services as wrapping, financing an automobile, providing warranties on computer equipment, and the like because these services exist in connection with the sale of a product or another service. This suggests that marketers of goods are also marketers of services. For example, one could argue that McDonald's is not in the hamburger business. Its hamburgers are actually not very different from those of the competition. McDonald's is in the service business.

More and more manufacturers are also exploiting their service capabilities as stand-alone revenue producers. For example, General Motors, Ford, and Chrysler all offer financing services. Ford and General Motors have extended their financial services offerings to include a MasterCard, which offers discounts on purchases of their automobiles.

The reader can imagine from his or her own experience that some purchases are very tangible (a coffeemaker) while others are very much intangible (a course in marketing). Others have elements of both (lunch on a flight from New York to Chicago). In other words, in reality there is a goods–service continuum, with many purchases including both tangible goods and intangible services. Figure 12.1 illustrates such a continuum. On the goods side of the continuum, the buyer owns an object after the purchase. On the services side of the continuum, when the transaction is over, the buyer leaves with an experience and a feeling. When the course in marketing is over or the flight from New York to Chicago is completed, the student or passenger leaves with a feeling.

The examples of services on the right side of Figure 12.1 are mostly or entirely intangible. They do not exist in the physical realm. They cannot appeal to the five senses.

FIGURE 12.1
The Goods–Service Continuum

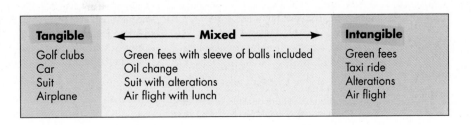

Tangible	← ———— Mixed ———— →	Intangible
Golf clubs	Green fees with sleeve of balls included	Green fees
Car	Oil change	Taxi ride
Suit	Suit with alterations	Alterations
Airplane	Air flight with lunch	Air flight

Important Characteristics of Services

Services possess several unique characteristics that often have a significant impact on marketing program development. These special features of services may cause unique problems and often result in marketing mix decisions that are substantially different from those found in connection with the marketing of goods. Some of the more important of these characteristics are intangibility, inseparability, perishability and fluctuating demand, a client relationship, customer effort, and uniformity. They are presented in Figure 12.2.

Intangibility

The obvious basic difference between goods and services is the intangibility of services, and many of the problems encountered in the marketing of services are due to intangibility. To illustrate, how does an airline make tangible a trip from Philadelphia to San Francisco? These problems are unique to service marketing.

The fact that many services cannot appeal to a buyer's sense of touch, taste, smell, sight, or hearing before purchase places a burden on the marketing organization. For example, hotels that promise a good night's sleep to their customers cannot actually show this service in a tangible way. Obviously, this burden is most heavily felt in a firm's promotional program, but, as will be discussed later, it may affect other areas. Depending on the type of service, the intangibility factor may dictate use of direct channels because of the need for personal contact between the buyer and seller. Since a service firm is actually selling an idea or experience, not a product, it must tell the buyer what the service will do because it is often difficult to illustrate, demonstrate, or display the service in use. For example, the hotel must somehow describe to the consumer how a stay at the hotel will leave the customer feeling well rested and ready to begin a new day.

The above discussion alludes to two strategy elements firms should employ when trying to overcome the problems associated with service intangibility. First, tangible aspects associated with the service should be stressed. For example, advertisements for airlines should emphasize (through text and visuals) the newness of the aircraft, the roominess of the

FIGURE 12.2 **Unique Characteristics Distinguishing Services from Goods**

Characteristic	Services	Goods
Intangibility	The customer owns only memories, outcomes, or feelings such as an airline flight, greater knowledge or styled hair.	The customer owns objects that can be used, resold, or given to others.
Inseparability	Services often cannot be separated from the person providing them. They are often produced and consumed at the same time.	Goods are usually produced and sold by different people.
Perishability	Services can be used only at the time they are offered. They cannot be inventoried, stored, or transported.	Goods can be placed in inventory for use at another time.
Client Relationship	Services often involve a long-term personal relationship between buyer and seller.	Goods often involve an impersonal short-term relationship although in many instances relationship strength and duration are increasing.
Customer Effort	Customers are often heavily involved in the production.	Customer's involvement may be limited to buying the completed product and using it.
Uniformity	Because of inseparability and high involvement on the part of the buyer, each service may be unique, with the quality likely to vary.	Variations in quality and variance from standards can be corrected before customers purchase products.

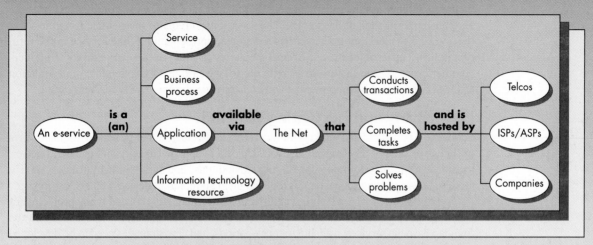

cabin, and the friendliness of the flight attendants. Second, end benefits resulting from completion of the service encounter should be accentuated. In the case of air travel, an individual's ability to make an important meeting or arrive home in time for a special occasion could be the derived benefit.

Inseparability

In many cases, a service cannot be separated from the person of the seller. In other words, the service must often be produced and marketed simultaneously. Because of the simultaneous production and marketing of most services, the main concern of the marketer is usually the creation of time and place utility. For example, the bank teller produces the service of receiving a deposit and markets other appropriate bank services at the same time. Many services, therefore, are tailored and not mass produced. Often, because a company's employees are "the company" at the point of contact, they must be given wide latitude and assistance in determining how best to tailor a specific service to meet customer needs.

The implication of inseparability on issues dealing with the selection of channels of distribution and service quality is quite important. Inseparable services cannot be inventoried, and thus direct sale is the only feasible channel of distribution. Service quality cannot sometimes be completely standardized due to the inability to completely mechanize the service encounter. However, some industries, through innovative uses of technology, have been able to overcome or, at least, alleviate challenges associated with the inseparability characteristic.

For example, in the financial services industry, automated teller machines (ATMs) and home banking, through use of computers and telephones, have contributed greatly to eliminating the need for the customer to directly interact with a bank teller. Further, many banks are developing computer applications to allow tellers and other service representatives to think like expert problem solvers. These applications allow for platform banking, a means of enabling bank representatives in any location to bring up on a screen all the information the bank has about the customer. Every face-to-face contact with a customer can mean an opportunity to make a sale and, more importantly, further the relationship with the customer. Of course, the bank representative is still of critical importance as the one who might recognize by the customer's expression or words that this visit is not the appropriate time to be marketing additional services.

173

In addition to technology, tangible representations of the service can serve to overcome the inseparability problem. For example, in the insurance industry, a contract serves as the tangible representation of the service. The service itself remains inseparable from the seller (insurance provider), but the buyer has a tangible representation of the service in the form of a policy. This enables the use of intermediaries (agents) in the marketing of insurance. Another example is in the use of a credit card—the card itself is a tangible representation of the service that is being produced and consumed each time the card is being used.

Perishability and Fluctuating Demand

Services are perishable and markets for most services fluctuate either by season (tourism), days (airlines), or time of day (movie theaters). Unused telephone capacity and electrical power; vacant seats on planes, trains, buses, and in stadiums; and time spent by catalog service representatives waiting for customers to reach them all represent business that is lost forever.

The combination of perishability and fluctuating demand has created many problems for marketers of services. Specifically, in the areas of staffing and distribution, avenues must be found to have the services available for peak periods, and new strategies need to be developed to make use of the service during slack periods. Some organizations are attempting to cope with these problems through the use of pricing strategy. *Off-peak pricing* consists of charging different prices during different times or days in order to stimulate demand during slow periods. Discounts given for weekend calling, Saturday night stay-overs, early-bird dinners, or winter cruises are all examples of efforts service providers make to redistribute demand.

Other organizations are dealing with issues related to peak period demand through the use of technology. To illustrate, a well-designed voice mail system allows companies and callers to cut down on missed phone calls, eliminates long waits on hold, and delivers clear, consistent messages. In the catalog industry, automated call routing (ACR) is used to route incoming calls to available service representatives in the order in which they were received. Finally, in the utilities industry, many electric utilities no longer have to generate capacity that will meet peak electrical demand. Instead, they rely on buying unused power from other utilities in other regions of the country.

Client Relationship

In the marketing of a great many services, a client relationship, as opposed to a customer relationship, exists between the buyer and the seller. In other words, the buyer views the seller as someone who has knowledge that is of value. Examples of this type of relationship are the physician-patient, college professor–student, accountant–small business owner, and broker-investor. The buyer, many times, abides by the advice offered or suggestions provided by the seller, and these relationships may be of an ongoing nature. Also, since many service firms are client-serving organizations, they may approach the marketing function in a more professional manner, as seen in health care, finance, and legal, governmental, and educational services.

Professionals face at least two marketing challenges. First, in many cases, fear or hostility is brought to the transaction because the customer is uncertain about how genuine the professional's concern for his or her satisfaction is. For example, many unpleasant reasons exist for consulting doctors, lawyers, bankers, or even visiting a college professor. These could include having surgery, being sued, having to take out a loan, or doing poorly on an exam. Second, even high-quality service delivery by the professional can lead to dissatisfied customers. For a physician, the ability to provide high-quality medical care may be overshadowed by a brusque, unfriendly personality. For a college professor, the demand on students to contact or visit him or her only during office hours, coupled with students' own hectic work schedules, can diminish the impact of the professor's classroom presentations. It is vitally important that the professional service provider strive to build long-term positive relationships with clients.

Type of Service	Type of Customer	Principal Expectations
Automobile repair	Consumers	*Be competent.* Fix it right the first time.
		Explain things. Explain why the customer needs the suggested repairs—provide an itemized list.
		Be respectful. "Don't treat me like an idiot."
Automobile insurance	Consumers	*Keep me informed.* "I shouldn't have to learn about insurance law changes from the newspaper."
		Be on my side. "I don't want them to treat me like I am a criminal just because I have a claim."
		Play fair. "Don't drop me when something goes wrong."
		Protect me from catastrophe. "Make sure my estate is covered in the event of a major accident."
		Provide prompt service. "I want a fast settlement of my claims."
Hotel	Consumers	*Provide a clean room.* "Don't have a deep-pile carpet that can't be completely cleaned . . . You can literally see germs down there."
		Provide a secure room. Good deadbolts and a peephole on the door.
		Treat me like a guest. "It is almost like they're looking you over to decide whether or not they're going to let you have a room."
		Keep your promise. "They said the room would be ready at the promised time, but it wasn't."
Property and casualty insurance	Business customers	*Fulfill obligations.* Pay up.
		Learn my business and work with me. "I expect them to know me and my company."
		Protect me from catastrophe. Cover risk exposure so there is no single big loss.
		Provide prompt service. Fast claim service.
Equipment repair	Business customers	*Share my sense of urgency.* Speed of response. "One time I had to buy a second piece of equipment because of the huge downtime with the first piece."
		Be prepared. Have all the parts ready.
Truck and tractor rental/leasing	Business customers	*Keep the equipment running.* Have equipment working all the time—that is the key.
		Be flexible. "The leasing company should have the leasing flexibility to rent us equipment when we need it."
		Provide full service. Get rid of all the paperwork and headaches.

Source: A. Parasuraman, Leonard L. Berry, and Valarie A. Zeithaml, "Understanding Customer Expectations of Service," *Sloan Management Review,* Spring 1991, pp. 39–48.

Customer Effort

Customers are often involved to a relatively great degree in the production of many types of service. In some restaurants you clean your table. You may carry your luggage to a cart parked next to a baggage compartment of the plane. If you wish to enjoy an exhibit at a local art museum, you must walk around the facility and pay careful attention to what is on display. If an organization purchases the services of an advertising agency, employees will have to work with the agency, review its ideas, and make the final selections.

Obviously, not every service requires the same degree of customer effort. Your effort with a credit card service may be little beyond taking it from your wallet to make a purchase and writing a check once a month to pay the bill.

Uniformity

The quality of services can vary more than the quality of goods. Producers of goods have procedures to prevent, identify, and correct defects. If these procedures are working, customers are unlikely to purchase defective products. This is not the case with most services. Because they are often human performances and often customized to the needs of the buyer, quality can vary. Each trip to the bank or airline flight or university course can be a different experience. Many service jobs such as nursing, teaching, and career counseling require a positive attitude; how employees feel influences their performance.

Providing Quality Services

In today's increasingly competitive environment, quality service is critical to organizational success. Unlike products in which quality is often measured against standards, service quality is measured against performance.[3] Since services are frequently produced in the presence of a customer, are labor intensive, and are not able to be stored or objectively examined, the definition of what constitutes good service quality can be difficult and, in fact, continually changes in the face of choices.[4] Customers determine the value of service quality in relation to available alternatives and their particular needs. In general, problems in the determination of good service quality are attributable to differences in the expectations, perceptions, and experiences regarding the encounter between the service provider and consumer. These gaps can be classified as follows:

1. The gap between consumer expectations and management perceptions of consumer expectations.
2. The gap between management perceptions of consumer expectations and the firm's service quality specifications.
3. The gap between service quality specifications and actual service quality.
4. The gap between actual service delivery and external communications about the service.

In essence, the customer perceives the level of service quality as being a function of the magnitude and direction of the gap between expected service and perceived service. Management of a company may not even realize that they are delivering poor-quality service due to differences in the way managers and consumers view acceptable quality levels. To overcome this problem and to avoid losing customers, firms must be aware of the determinants of service quality. A brief description of these determinants follows.

1. *Tangibles* include the physical evidence of the service. For example, employees are always visible in a hotel lobby dusting, emptying ash trays, or otherwise cleaning up. Likewise, clean, shiny, up-to-date medical equipment or aircraft are examples of tangible elements.
2. *Reliability* involves the consistency and dependability of the service performance. For example, does a bank or phone company always send out accurate customer statements? Likewise, does the plumber always fix the problem on his or her first visit?
3. *Responsiveness* concerns the willingness or readiness of employees or professionals to provide service. For example, will a physician see patients on the same day they call in to say they are ill? Will a college professor return a student's call the same day?

4. *Assurance* refers to the knowledge and competence of service providers and the ability to convey trust and confidence. This determinant encompasses the provider's name and reputation; possession of necessary skills; and trustworthiness, believability, and honesty. For example, a bank will guarantee same-day loan processing; a doctor is highly trained in a particular specialty.

5. *Empathy* refers to the service provider's efforts to understand the customer's needs and then to provide, as best as possible, individualized service delivery. For example, flight attendants on a customer's regular route learn what type of beverages the customer drinks and what magazines the customer reads.

Each of the determinants on the previous page plays an important role in how the customer views the service quality of a firm. Turning service quality into a powerful competitive weapon requires continuously striving for service superiority—consistently performing above the adequate service level and capitalizing on opportunities for exceeding the desired service level. Relentless efforts to continually improve service performance may well be rewarded by improvements in customer attitudes toward the firm: from customer frustration to customer preference to customer loyalty. What should be obvious is that to be successful, a service firm must have both an effective means to measure customer satisfaction and dedicated employees to provide high-quality service.

Customer Satisfaction Measurement

As mentioned above, satisfied customers can become loyal customers. Service quality and customer satisfaction are of growing concern to business organizations throughout the world, and research on these topics generally focuses on two key issues: (1) understanding the expectations and requirements of the customer, and (2) determining how well a company and its major competitors are succeeding in satisfying these expectations and requirements.[5]

As such, an organization's approach to measuring service quality through customer satisfaction measurement (CSM) and effectively implementing programs derived from results of such studies can spell the difference between success and failure. Research on market leaders' CSMs found they had the following aspects in common:

1. Marketing and sales employees were primarily responsible (with customer input) for designing CSM programs and questionnaires.

2. Top management and the marketing function championed the programs.

3. Measurement involved a combination of qualitative and quantitative research methods that primarily included mail questionnaires, telephone surveys, and focus groups.

4. Evaluations included both the company's and competitors' satisfaction performance.

5. Results of all research were made available to employees, but not necessarily to customers.

6. Research was performed on a continual basis.

7. Customer satisfaction was incorporated into the strategic focus of the company via the mission statement.

8. There was a commitment to increasing service quality and customer satisfaction from employees at all levels within the organization.

The Importance of Internal Marketing

Properly performed customer satisfaction research can yield a wealth of strategic information about customers, the sponsoring company, and competitors. However, service quality goes beyond the relationship between a customer and a company. Rather, as shown by the last aspect listed, it is the personal relationship between a customer and the particular employee that the customer happens to be dealing with at the time of the service encounter that ultimately determines service quality. The importance of having customer-oriented, front-line people cannot be overstated.[6] If frontline service personnel are unfriendly, unhelpful, uncooperative, or uninterested in the customer, the customer will tend to project that same attitude to the company as a whole. The character and personality of an organization reflects the character and personality of its top management. Management must develop programs that will stimulate employee commitment to customer service. To be successful, these programs must contain five critical components:

1. *A careful selection process in hiring frontline employees.* To do this, management has to clearly define the skills the service person must bring to the job.[7] For example, Fairfield Inn often considers as many as 25 candidates for each housekeeping or front-desk position.[8]

2. *A clear, concrete message* that conveys a particular service strategy that frontline people can begin to act on. People delivering service need to know how their work fits in the broader scheme of business operations.[9] They need to have a cause because servicing others is just too demanding and frustrating to be done well each day without one.[10]

3. *Significant modeling by managers,* that is, managers demonstrating the behavior that they intend to reward employees for performing. For example, some airline executives regularly travel economy class to talk to customers and solicit ideas for improvement.[11]

4. *An energetic follow-through process,* in which managers provide the training, support, and incentives necessary to give the employees the capability and willingness to provide quality service.[12]

5. *An emphasis on teaching employees to have good attitudes.* This type of training usually focuses on specific social techniques, such as eye contact, smiling, tone of voice, and standards of dress.

However, organizing and implementing such programs will only lead to temporary results unless managers practice a strategy of internal marketing. We define *internal marketing* as the continual process by which managers actively encourage, stimulate, and support employee commitment to the company, the company's goods and services, and the company's customers. Emphasis should be placed on the word *continual.* Managers who consistently pitch in to help when needed, constantly provide encouragement and words of praise to employees, strive to help employees understand the benefits of performing their jobs well, and emphasize the importance of employee actions on both company and employee results are practitioners of internal marketing. In service marketing, successful internal marketing efforts, leading to employee commitment to service quality, are a key to success.

Federal Express serves as a prime example of the benefits accruing to a company that successfully practices internal marketing.[13] Federal Express is the first service organization to win the Malcolm Baldrige National Quality Award. The company's motto is "people, service, and profits." Behind its purple, white, and orange planes and uniforms are self-managing work teams, gainsharing plans, and empowered employees seemingly consumed with providing flexible and creative services to customers with varying needs. Federal Express is a high-involvement, horizontally coordinated organization that encourages employees to use their judgment above and beyond the rulebook.

Overcoming the Obstacles in Service Marketing

The factors of intangibility and inseparability, as well as difficulties in coming up with objective definitions of acceptable service quality, make comprehension of service marketing difficult. However, in view of the size and importance of services in our economy, considerable innovation and ingenuity are needed to make high-quality services available at convenient locations for consumers as well as businesspeople. In fact, the area of service marketing probably offers more opportunities for imagination and creative innovation than does goods marketing. Unfortunately, many service firms still lag in the area of creative marketing. Even today, those service firms that have done a relatively good job have been slow in recognizing opportunities in all aspects of their marketing programs. Four reasons, connected to past practices, can be given for the lack of innovative marketing on the part of service marketers: (1) a limited view of marketing, (2) a lack of strong competition, (3) a lack of creative management, and (4) no obsolescence.

Limited View of Marketing

Because of the nature of their service, many firms depended to a great degree on population growth to expand sales. A popular example here is the telephone company, which did not establish a marketing department until 1955. It was then that the company realized it had to be concerned not only with population growth but also with meeting the needs of a growing population. Increases in educational levels and the standard of living also bring about the need for new and diversified services.

Service firms must meet these changing needs by developing new services and new channels and altering existing channels to meet the changing composition and needs of the population. For many service industries, growth has come as a result of finding new channels of distribution. For example, some banks and other financial service companies were able to grow and tap into new markets by establishing limited-service kiosks in malls and supermarkets. Airlines have successfully brought in a whole new class of travelers by offering advance-purchase discounted fares. Traditionally, users of these fares either drove or used other means of transportation to reach their destination.

While many service firms have succeeded in adopting a marketing perspective, others have been slow to respond. It was not until deregulation of the telecommunications industry took place in 1984 that the telephone companies began taking a broadened view of marketing. Even today, critics point to the obsession with inventing new technology versus using current technology in meeting customer needs as a weakness of these companies.

Limited Competition

A second major cause of the lack of innovative marketing in many service industries was the lack of competition. Many service industries such as banking, railroads, and public utilities have, throughout most of their histories, faced very little competition; some have even been regulated monopolies. Obviously, in an environment characterized by little competition, there was not likely to be a great deal of innovative marketing. However, two major forces have changed this situation. First, in the past two decades the banking, financial services, railroad, cable, airline, telecommunications industries, and utilities have all been deregulated in varying degrees. With deregulation has come a need to be able to compete effectively. Second, service marketing has taken on an international focus. Today, many foreign companies are competing in domestic service markets. Foreign interests own several banks, many hotels (including Holiday Inn), and shares in major airlines (including Northwest and US Airways). Likewise, American companies are expanding overseas as markets open up. For example, Merrill Lynch & Co. purchased Smith New Court PLC, a large British security firm, to become the world's largest brokerage firm.

Noncreative Management

For many years, the managements of service industries have been criticized for not being progressive and creative. Railroad management has long been criticized for being slow to innovate. More recently, however, railroads have become leading innovators in the field of

On the Internet, you cannot have a more convenient location than your competition. Everyone is just a click away. It is critical that it is easy to do business with your company in order to attract and retain customers. Following are some ways to improve e-service.

1. A customer should be able to buy something in seven clicks or less beginning from the home page. Many experts believe the ideal should be four clicks.

2. Images should load quickly. Research shows that eight seconds is the longest people will wait before they move on to another site.

3. From a product section of your site, customers should be able to get from your home page to a product page in that section in one click.

4. Shopping should be easy. Searching, browsing, checking out, returning items, and getting assistance from a live person must be simple.

5. Customers should have the choice to register their personal information (e.g., address and credit card information) or to enter this information each time they purchase.

6. A customer should be able to check out in no more than three steps.

7. Delivery should be on time.

Source: Ron Zemke, *E-Service: 24 Ways to Keep Your Customers—When the Competition Is Just a Click Away* (New York: Amazon, 2001).

freight transportation, introducing such innovations as piggyback service and containerization, and in passenger service, introducing luxury overnight accommodations on trains with exotic names such as the Zephyr. Some other service industries, however, have been slow to develop new services or to innovate in the marketing of their existing services. In fact, as a whole, U.S. firms lag behind their Japanese and German competitors not only in collecting customer satisfaction data but also in designing services that address customers' needs.[14]

No Obsolescence

A great advantage for many service industries is the fact that many services, because of their intangibility, are less subject to obsolescence than goods. While this is an obvious advantage, it has also led some service firms to be sluggish in their approach to marketing. Manufacturers of goods may constantly change their marketing plans and seek new and more efficient ways to produce and distribute their products. Since service firms are often not faced with obsolescence, they often failed to recognize the need for change. This failure has led to wholesale changes in many industries as new operators who possessed marketing skills revolutionized the manner in which the service is performed and provided. Many barbershops and hair dressers have gone out of business due to an inability to compete against hairstyling salons. Many accountants have lost clients to tax preparation services, such as H&R Block, that specialize in doing one task well and have used technology, including Internet filing services, to their advantage. Likewise, the old, big movie house has become a relic of the past as entrepreneurs realized the advantages to be gained from building and operating theater complexes that contain several minitheaters in or near suburban malls.

The Service Challenge

Despite traditional thinking and practices on the part of many marketing managers and writers concerning the similarities between the operation of manufacturing and services organizations, the past decade has seen the growth of many innovative ways of meeting the service challenge. The service challenge is the quest to (1) constantly develop new services that will better meet customer needs, (2) improve on the quality and variety of existing services, and (3) provide and distribute these services in a manner that best serves the customer. This next section illustrates the challenges facing companies in various service industries and examples of marketing strategies they employ to meet the service challenge.

Banking

"Banking is vital to a healthy economy. Banks are not." This is the message that a banking expert delivered to a group of his peers.[15] Needless to say, the days when banking was considered a dead-end career, but one that offered stable employment for marketers, are long gone. Perhaps banking best exemplifies the changes that are taking place as service organizations strive to become practitioners of the "marketing concept." Buy or be bought is the new watchword in the banking industry, which is experiencing the biggest wave of consolidation in its history.

Banking is becoming an increasingly technology-driven business. The main reason is that more and more financial services, from loans to credit cards, are being marketed through computers and telephones instead of through branches. Banks large enough to afford big technology investments can reach customers nationwide even though their physical franchise may be limited. For example, most consumers possess credit cards from banks they have never physically visited. Further, the advent of new electronic delivery systems (via computer) for consumer and small-business banking could, within the next decade, greatly reduce the number of branch banks needed. To prevent a loss of a large portion of their customer base, many of the leading banks, such as Chase Manhattan and Citibank, are aligning themselves with software and hardware manufacturers to develop home banking systems.

Banks have also learned the value of bundling services. Many now offer an account that combines checking, savings, credit card, and auto loan features. Benefits to the customer include free ATM transactions, interest-bearing checking accounts, no-fee credit cards, and the convenience of one-stop banking. In addition, they offer preapproved auto loans and cash-flow statements. Most banks also target some marketing activities toward senior citizens, which may include discount coupons for entertainment, travel newsletters, and lower monthly minimum required balances.

Competition between banks and other financial institutions will continue to intensify. The survivors will be those that have best mastered the art of services marketing.

Health Care

The distribution of health care services is of vital concern. In health care delivery, the inseparability characteristic presents more of a handicap than in other service industries because users (patients) literally place themselves in the hands of the seller. Although direct personal contact between producer and user is often necessary, new and more efficient means of distribution seem to be evolving.

Up until the past few decades, medical care has been traditionally associated with the solo practice, fee-for-service system. Recently, several alternative delivery systems have been developed, most notably the health maintenance organization (HMO). This type of delivery system stresses the creation of group health care clinics using teams of salaried health practitioners (physicians, pharmacists, technicians, and so forth) that serve a specified, enrolled membership on a prepaid basis. The primary benefits to the customer (patient) from membership in an HMO are (1) the ability to have all ailments treated at one facility, (2) payment of a fixed fee for services, and (3) the encouragement of preventive versus remedial treatments. The success of the HMO concept in traditional medical care has inspired similar programs to be developed for dental and eye care.

In the pharmaceutical field, Chronimed of Minnetonka, Minnesota, has focused on providing great customer service as its avenue to success.[16] The company supplies 100,000 patients across the United States with specialized medications that local pharmacies can't afford to stock. Chronimed's skill is twofold. First, it provides needed drugs by mail to organ transplant recipients and patients with diabetes or AIDS. Second, it employs a team of 50 pharmacists and assistants who provide much-needed information about the medications they dispense, such as details about drug interaction and side effects. As evidenced by the above examples, health care companies, regardless of the specific area in which they compete, are becoming more and more market oriented as they try to differentiate their offerings from those of the competition.

Insurance

In recent years, the insurance industry has exploded with new product and service offerings. Not too long ago, customers were faced with limited options in choosing life, hospital, or auto insurance. Now there is a wide array of insurance policies to choose from, including universal life policies, which double as retirement savings; nursing care insurance; reversible mortgages, which allow people to take equity from their house while still living in it; and other offerings aimed at serving an aging population. To illustrate, Prudential Insurance Company offers a program whereby terminally ill policyholders are allowed to withdraw funds against the face value of their policy while still alive. In addition to insurance services, most insurance companies now offer a full range of financial services, including auto loans, mortgages, mutual funds, and certificates of deposit.

Distribution of insurance services has also been growing. The vending machines found in airports for flight insurance have been finding their way into other areas. Travel auto insurance is now available in many motel chains and through the AAA. Group insurance written through employers and labor unions also has been extremely successful. In each instance, the insurance industry has used intermediaries to distribute its services.

Travel

The travel industry, most notably the airlines, has been a leader in the use of technology. Computerized reservation systems allow customers to book plane tickets from home or work. Nearly all airlines are using Internet sites to dispense flight and fare information. Airlines are in the midst of implementing ticketless travel programs in which passengers purchase tickets, select their seats, and pick up boarding passes and luggage tags at machines resembling ATMs.[17] Technology has also allowed airlines to make strategic pricing decisions through the use of yield management. In yield management, certain seats on aircraft are discounted and certain ones aren't. Through the use of elaborate computer programs, managers are able to determine who their customer segments are and who is likely to purchase airline tickets when and to where.

Despite its success in employing technology to attract additional customers and offer added convenience, the airline industry has operated in somewhat dire straits, plagued by problems associated with overcapacity, high labor costs, and low perceived service quality. The decade of the 90s could be considered the most turbulent ever encountered by U.S. commercial airlines.[18] During this time, some airlines either went out of business (Midway, Eastern, and Pan Am) or were in and out of bankruptcy proceedings (Continental, America West, and TWA); and most others operated at a loss. In the early 2000s, both United Airlines and Delta Airlines faced bankruptcy.

A notable exception to the fate that befell most carriers is Southwest Airlines, which has finally convinced its peers that a carrier can be consistently profitable by offering cheap fares on short-distance routes. Now, big carriers such as Continental and United have created their own Southwest look-alikes to supplement their long-haul, full-service, high-fare

"I'm a nice customer. You all know me. I'm the one who never complains, no matter what kind of service I get.

"I'll go into a restaurant, and I'll sit while the waitress gossips with a friend and never bothers to look to see if my hamburger is ready to go. Sometimes a party who came in after I did gets my hamburger, but I don't say a word in complaint when the waitress tells me, 'Oh, I'm sorry. I'll order another for you.' I just wait.

It's the same when I go to a bank. I don't throw my weight around. I try to be thoughtful of the other person. If I get poor service I'm as polite as can be. I don't believe rudeness in return is the answer.

"The other day I stopped in at the neighborhood gas station. I waited for almost five minutes before the attendant took care of me. And when he did, he spilled gas and wiped the car windows with an oily rag. I didn't expect him to thank me for stopping by—and he didn't. Naturally, I didn't complain about the service.

"I never kick. I never nag. I never criticize. And I wouldn't dream of making a scene, as I've seen some people do in public places. I think that's uncalled for. No, I'm the nice customer. And I'll tell you what else I am.

"I'm the customer who never comes back!

"In fact, a nice customer like me, multiplied by others of my kind, can just about ruin a business. There are a lot of nice people in the world, just like me. When we get pushed far enough, we go on down the street to another store, another bank, where they're smart enough to hire help who have been trained to appreciate nice customers.

"He laughs loudest, they say, who laughs last. I laugh when I see you frantically spending your money on expensive advertising to get me back, when you could have had me in the first place for a few kind words and a smile and some good services.

"I don't care what business you're in. Maybe you live in a different town; maybe I've never heard of you. But if you're going broke or your business is bad, maybe there are enough people like me, who do know you. I'm your customer who never comes back."

Source: Unknown.

operations. Southwest's secret to success (which other airlines may or may not be able to imitate) is the high level of employee morale everyone associated with the company exhibits. This has come as a direct result of upper management's internal marketing efforts.

Implications for Service Marketers

The preceding sections emphasized the use of all components of the marketing mix. Many service industries have been criticized for an overdependence on advertising. The overdependence on one or two elements of the marketing mix is a mistake that service marketers cannot afford. The sum total of the marketing mix elements represents the total impact of the firm's marketing strategy. The slack created by severely restricting one element cannot be compensated by heavier emphasis on another, since each element in the marketing mix is designed to address specific problems and achieve specific objectives.

Services must be made available to prospective users, which implies distribution in the marketing sense of the word. The revised concept of the distribution of services points out that service marketers must distinguish conceptually between the production and distribution of services. The problem of making services more widely available must not be ignored.

The above sections also pointed out the critical role of new service development. In several of the examples described, indirect distribution of the service was made possible because "products" were developed that included a tangible representation of the service. This development facilitates the use of intermediaries, because the service can now be separated from the producer. In addition, the development of new services paves the way for companies to expand and segment their markets. With the use of varying service bundles, new technology, and alternative means of distributing the service, companies are now able to practice targeted marketing.

Conclusion

This chapter has dealt with the complex topic of service marketing. While the marketing of services has much in common with the marketing of products, unique problems in the area require highly creative marketing management skills. Many of the problems in the service area can be traced to the intangible and inseparable nature of services and the difficulties involved in measuring service quality. However, considerable progress has been made in understanding and reacting to these difficult problems, particularly in the area of distribution. In view of the major role services play in our economy, it is important for marketing practitioners to better understand and appreciate the unique problems of service marketing.

Additional Readings

Barlow, Janelle, and Paul Steward. *Branded Customer Service.* San Francisco, CA: Berrett Koehler, 2006.

Berry, Leonard L. *Discovering the Soul of Service.* New York: Free Press, 2000.

Berry, Leonard L., and Kent D. Seltman. "Building a Strong Services Brand: Lessons from Mayo Clinic." *Business Horizons* 50 (2007), pp. 199–209.

Fullerton, Sam. *Sports Marketing.* Burr Ridge, IL: McGraw-Hill/Irwin, 2007.

Gronroos, Christian. *Service Management and Marketing.* 3rd ed., New York: John Wiley and Sons, 2007.

Hoffman, K. Douglas, and John E. G. Bateson. *Services Marketing.* Mason, OH: Thomson South-Western, 2006.

Shuman, Jeffrey, Twombly, Janice, and David Rottenberg. *Everyone Is a Customer.* Chicago: Dearbon Trade Publishing, 2002.

Chapter

13

Global Marketing

A growing number of U.S. corporations have transversed geographical boundaries and become truly multinational in nature. For most other domestic companies, the question is no longer, Should we go international? Instead, the questions relate to when, how, and where the companies should enter the international marketplace. The past 15 years have seen the reality of a truly world market unfold.

Firms invest in foreign countries for the same basic reasons they invest in their own country. These reasons vary from firm to firm but fall under the categories of achieving offensive or defensive goals. Offensive goals are to (1) increase long-term growth and profit prospects; (2) maximize total sales revenue; (3) take advantage of economies of scale; and (4) improve overall market position. As many American markets reach saturation, American firms look to foreign markets as outlets for surplus production capacity, sources of new customers, increased profit margins, and improved returns on investment. For example, the ability to expand the number of locations of McDonald's restaurants in the United States is becoming severely limited. Yet, on any given day, only 0.5 percent of the world's population visits McDonald's. Indeed, in the recent past, of the 50 most profitable McDonald's outlets, 25 were located in Hong Kong. For PepsiCo, the results are similar. Its restaurant division operates over 10,000 Kentucky Fried Chicken, Pizza Hut, and Taco Bell outlets abroad.

Multinational firms also invest in other countries to achieve defensive goals. Chief among these goals are the desire to (1) compete with foreign companies on their own turf instead of in the United States, (2) gain access to technological innovations that are developed in other countries, (3) take advantage of significant differences in operating costs between countries, (4) preempt competitors' global moves, and (5) avoid being locked out of future markets by arriving too late.

Such well-known companies as Zenith, Pillsbury, Shell Oil, CBS Records, and Firestone Tire & Rubber are now owned by non-U.S. interests. Since 1980, the share of the U.S. high-tech market held by foreign products has grown from less than 8 percent to over 25 percent. In such diverse industries as power tools, tractors, television, and banking, U.S. companies have lost the dominant position they once held. By investing solely in domestic operations or not being willing to adapt products to foreign markets, U.S. companies are more susceptible to foreign incursions. For example, there has been a great uproar over Japan's practice of not opening up its domestic automobile market to U.S. companies. However, as of the end of the 90s, a great majority of the American cars shipped to Japan still had the steering wheel located on the left side of the vehicle—the opposite of where it should be for the Japanese market.

In many ways, marketing globally is the same as marketing at home. Regardless of which part of the world the firm sells in, the marketing program must still be built around a sound product or service that is properly priced, promoted, and distributed to a carefully analyzed target market. In other words, the marketing manager has the same controllable decision variables in both domestic and nondomestic markets.

Although the development of a marketing program may be the same in either domestic or nondomestic markets, special problems may be involved in the implementation of marketing programs in nondomestic markets. These problems often arise because of the environmental differences that exist among various countries that marketing managers may be unfamiliar with.

In this chapter, marketing management in a global context will be examined. Methods of organizing global versus domestic markets, global market research tasks, methods of entry strategies into global markets, and potential marketing strategies for a multinational firm will be discussed. In examining each of these areas, the reader will find a common thread—knowledge of the local cultural environment—that appears to be a major prerequisite for success in each area.

With the proper adaptations, many companies have the capabilities and resources needed to compete successfully in the global marketplace. To illustrate, companies as diverse as Kellogg's, Avon, Eli Lilly, and Sun Microsystems all generate a large percentage of their sales from foreign operations. Smaller companies can also be successful. For example, Nemix, Inc., of Bell Gardens, California, is a franchisee of Church's Fried Chicken. Small by world standards, this company has succeeded in developing a fully vertical operation in Poland, doing everything from raising chickens to operating restaurants.[1]

The Competitive Advantage of Nations

As each year passes, it becomes more and more clear that some industries and companies succeed on a global scale while others do not. Harvard Business School professor Michael Porter introduced what he calls the "diamond" of national advantage to explain a nation's competitive advantage and why some companies and industries become global business leaders. Figure 13.1 presents Porter's model. The diamond presents four factors that determine the competitive advantage or disadvantage of a nation.

1. *Factor conditions.* The nation's ability to turn its natural resources, skilled labor, and infrastructure into a competitive advantage.

FIGURE 13.1
Porter's Diamond of National Advantage

Source: Michael E. Porter, *The Competitive Advantage of Nations* (New York: Fress Press, 1990), pp. 577–615.

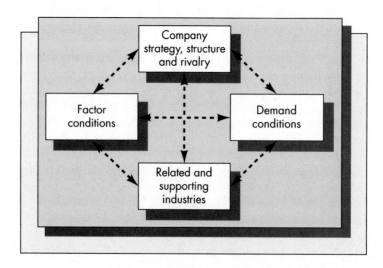

2. *Demand conditions.* The nature of domestic demand and the sophistication of domestic customers for the industry's product or service.

3. *Related and supporting industries.* The existence or absence in the country of supplier and related industries that are also internationally competitive.

4. *Company strategy, structure, and rivalry.* The conditions in the nation that govern how companies are created, organized, and managed, and how intensely they compete domestically.

Before Porter developed his model, he studied companies in more than 100 industries. While the most successful companies differed in many ways and employed different strategies, a very important common theme emerged: A company that succeeds on a global scale, first succeeded in intense domestic competition. His model is a dynamic model and illustrates how over time, a nation can build up and maintain its competitive advantage in any industry.

Organizing for Global Marketing

When compared with the tasks it faces at home, a firm attempting to establish a global marketing organization faces a much higher degree of risk and uncertainty. In a foreign market, management is often less familiar with the cultural, political, and economic situation. Many of these problems arise as a result of conditions specific to the foreign country. Managers are also faced with the decisions concerning how to organize the multinational company.

Problems with Entering Foreign Markets

While numerous problems could be cited, attention here will focus on those that firms most often face when entering foreign markets.

Cultural Misunderstanding

Differences in the cultural environment of foreign countries may be misunderstood or not even recognized because of the tendency for marketing managers to use their own cultural values and priorities as a frame of reference. Some of the most common areas of difference lie in the way dissimilar cultures perceive time, thought patterns, personal space, material possessions, family roles and relationships, personal achievement, competitiveness, individuality, social behavior, and other interrelated issues.[2] Another important source of misunderstandings is in the perceptions of managers about the people with whom they are dealing. Feelings of superiority can lead to changed communication mannerisms.

American managers must make the necessary efforts to learn, understand, and adapt to the cultural norms of the managers and customers they deal with in other parts of the world. Failure to do so will result in missed market opportunities.

On the other hand, companies should not shy away from attempting to enter global markets because conventional wisdom says that products and service will not succeed in some regions purely due to cultural reasons. For example, PepsiCo's Pepsi division entered into a $500 million offensive to try to grab a larger share of the $6 billion Brazilian soft-drink market.[3] Understanding the dramatic changes that had taken place in Brazil, Pepsi repositioned itself as the choice of a new Brazil. Advertisements for the Pepsi brand feature young people enumerating recent changes in Brazil, such as the devaluation of its currency in 1999. Does this campaign sound familiar? It should since it's a takeoff on the popular "Pepsi, the choice of a new generation" theme used in the United States. Actions taken by PepsiCo's Frito-Lay unit serve as another example of a successful adaptation to cultural differences.[4] In China, Frito-Lay introduced its popular Cheetos snack food. The

BODY LANGUAGE

- Standing with your hands on your hips is a gesture of defiance in Indonesia.
- Carrying on a conversation with your hands in your pockets makes a poor impression in France, Belgium, Finland, and Sweden.
- Shaking your head from side to side means yes in Bulgaria and Sri Lanka.
- Crossing your legs to expose the sole of your shoe is really taboo in Muslim countries. In fact, to call a person a "shoe" is a deep insult.

PHYSICAL CONTACT

- Patting a child on the head is a grave offense in Thailand or Singapore, since the head is revered as the location of the soul.
- In an Oriental culture, touching another person is considered an invasion of privacy; in Southern European and Arabic countries, it is a sign of warmth and friendship.

PROMPTNESS

- Be on time when invited for dinner in Denmark or in China.
- In Latin countries, your host or business associate would be surprised if you arrived at the appointed hour.

EATING AND COOKING

- It is rude to leave anything on your plate when eating in Norway, Malaysia, or Singapore.
- In Egypt, it is rude *not* to leave something.
- In Italy and Spain, cooking is done with oil.
- In Germany and Great Britain, margarine and butter are used.

OTHER SOCIAL CUSTOMS

- In Sweden, nudity and sexual permissiveness are quite all right, but drinking is really frowned on.
- In Spain, there is a very negative attitude toward life insurance. By receiving insurance benefits, a wife feels that she is profiting from her husband's death.
- In Western European countries, many consumers still are reluctant to buy anything (other than a house) on credit. Even for an automobile, they will pay cash.

Source: William J. Stanton, Michael J. Etzel, and Bruce J. Walker, *Fundamentals of Marketing,* 13th ed. (Burr Ridge IL: McGraw-Hill/Irwin, 2004), p. 544.

twist to this effort lies in the fact that the Chinese are not big consumers of dairy products. In China, Cheetos are cheeseless, instead consisting of flavors such as "Savory American Cream" and "Zesty Japanese Steak." As a result of these and other adaptations, it's no wonder that PepsiCo ranks among the leaders in the global food and beverage industry.

Political Uncertainty

Governments are unstable in many countries, and social unrest and even armed conflict must sometimes be reckoned with. Other nations are newly emerging and anxious to seek their independence. These and similar problems can greatly hinder a firm seeking to establish its position in foreign markets. For example, at the turn of the century, firms scaled back their investment plans in Russia due to, among other reasons, (1) a business environment plagued by mobsters, (2) politics badly corrupted by the botched invasion of Chechnya, and (3) an economy troubled by runaway inflation and a plummeting ruble.[5] This is not to say investment in Russia is a poor choice. Rather, in situations like this, caution must be used and companies must have a keen understanding of the risks involved in undertaking sizable investments.

Import Restrictions

Tariffs, import quotas, and other types of import restrictions hinder global business. These are usually established to promote self-sufficiency and can be a huge roadblock for the multinational firm. For example, a number of countries, including South Korea, Taiwan, Thailand, and Japan, have placed import restrictions on a variety of goods produced in America, including telecommunications equipment, rice, wood products, automobiles, and produce. In other cases, governments may not impose restrictions that are commonly adhered to in the United States. For example, Chrysler pulled out of a proposed investment deal in China, worth billions of dollars, because the Chinese government refused to protect its right to limit access to technological information.

Exchange Controls and Ownership Restrictions

Some nations establish limits on the amount of earned and invested funds that can be withdrawn from it. These exchange controls are usually established by nations that are experiencing balance-of-payment problems. In addition, many nations have a requirement that the majority ownership of a company operating there be held by nationals. These and other types of currency and ownership regulations are important considerations in the decision to expand into a foreign market. For example, up until a few years ago, foreign holdings in business ventures in India were limited to a maximum of 40 percent. Once this ban was lifted, numerous global companies such as Sony, Whirlpool, JVC, Grundig, Panasonic, Kellogg's, Levi Strauss, Pizza Hut, and Domino's rushed to invest in this market.[6]

Economic Conditions

As noted earlier, nations' economies are becoming increasingly intertwined, and business cycles tend to follow similar patterns. However, there are differences, mainly due to political upheaval or social changes, and these may be significant. In determining whether to invest, marketers need to perform in-depth analyses of a country's stage of economic development, the buying power of its populace, and the strength of its currency. For example, when the North American Free Trade Agreement (NAFTA) was signed, many American companies rushed to invest in Mexico, building production facilities and retail outlets. These companies assumed that signing the agreement would stabilize Mexico's economy. In the long term, these investments may pay off. However, many companies lost millions of dollars there due to the devaluation of the peso. Indeed, the crash of the peso caused the retail giant Wal-Mart to scale back a $1 billion investment project to open stores throughout Mexico.

Organizing the Multinational Company

There are two kinds of global companies—the multidomestic corporation and the global corporation.[7] The *multidomestic company* pursues different strategies in each of its foreign markets. It could have as many different product variations, brand names, and advertising campaigns as countries in which it operates. Each overseas subsidiary is autonomous. Local managers are given the authority to make the necessary decisions and are held accountable for results. In effect, the company competes on a market-by-market basis. Honeywell and General Foods are U.S. firms that have operated this way.

The *global company,* on the other hand, views the world as one market and pits its resources against the competition in an integrated fashion. It emphasizes cultural similarities across countries and universal consumer needs and wants rather than differences. It standardizes marketing activities when there are cultural similarities and adapts them when the cultures are different. Since there is no one clear-cut way to organize a global company,

City	Rank in 2000	Projected Rank in 2015
Tokyo, Japan	1	1
Mexico City, Mexico	2	4
New York, U.S.	3	6
São Paulo, Brazil	4	5
Mumbai (Bombay), India	5	2
Kolkata (Calcutta), India	6	7
Shanghai, China	7	10
Buenos Aires	8	8
Delhi, India	9	3
Los Angeles, U.S.	10	9

Source: *The World Almanac and Book of Facts,* 2007.

three alternative structures are normally used: (1) worldwide product divisions, each responsible for selling its own products throughout the world; (2) divisions responsible for all products sold within a geographic region; and (3) a matrix system that combines elements of both of these arrangements. Many organizations, such as IBM, Caterpillar, Timex, General Electric, Siemens, and Mitsubishi, are structured in a global fashion.

Most companies are realizing the need to take a global approach to managing their businesses. However, recognizing the need and actually implementing a truly global approach are two different tasks. For some companies, industry conditions dictate that they take a global perspective. The ability to actually implement a global approach to managing international operations, however, largely depends on factors unique to the company. Globalization, as a competitive strategy, is inherently more vulnerable to risk than a multidomestic or domestic strategy, due to the relative permanence of the organizational structure once established.

In determining whether or not to globalize a particular business, managers should look first at their industry.[8] Market, economic, environmental, and competitive factors all influence the potential gains to be realized by following a global strategy. Factors constituting the external environment that are conducive to a global strategy are:

1. *Market factors.* Homogeneous market needs, global customers, shorter product life cycles, transferable brands and advertising, and the ability to globalize distribution channels.
2. *Economic factors.* Worldwide economies of scale in manufacturing and distribution, steep learning curves, worldwide sourcing efficiencies, rising product development costs, and significant differences in host-country costs.
3. *Environmental factors.* Improving communications, favorable government policies, and the increasing speed of technological change.
4. *Competitive factors.* Competitive interdependencies among countries, global moves of competitors, and opportunities to preempt a competitor's global moves.[9]

Many of the reasons given in the first part of the chapter about why a domestic company should become a multinational can also be used to support the argument that a firm should take a global perspective. This is because the integration of markets is forcing companies that wish to remain successful not only to become multinationals but also to take a global perspective in doing so. In the past, companies had the option of remaining domestic or going multinational due to the separation of markets. This is no longer the case.

Growth in global markets has created opportunities for building global brands. The advantages are many and so are the pitfalls. Here are 10 commandments that marketers can use when planning a global branding campaign.

1. *Understand similarities and differences in the global branding landscape.* The best brands retain consistency of theme and alter specific elements to suit each country.
2. *Don't take shortcuts in brand building.* Build brands in new markets from the "bottom up."
3. *Establish marketing infrastructure.* Most often, firms adopt or invest in foreign partners for manufacturing and distribution.
4. *Embrace integrated marketing communications.* Because advertising opportunities may be more limited, marketers must use other forms of communication such as sponsorship and public relations.
5. *Establish brand partnerships.* Most global brands have marketing partners ranging from joint venture partners to franchisees and distributors who provide access to distribution.
6. *Balance standardization and customization.* Know what to standardize and what to customize.
7. *Balance global and local control.* This is very important in the following areas: organization structure, entry strategies, coordination processes, and mechanisms.
8. *Establish operable guidelines.* Set the rules about how the brand will be positioned and marketed.
9. *Implement a global brand equity measurement system.* The ideal measurement system provides complete, up-to-date information on the brand and on all its competitors to the appropriate decision makers.
10. *Leverage brand elements.* If the meanings of the brand name and all related trademarked identifiers are clear, they can be an invaluable source of brand equity worldwide.

Source: Kevin Lane Keller, "The Ten Commandments of Global Branding," *MBA Bullet Point,* October 3–16, 2000, p. 3, and Kevin Lane Keller, *Strategic Brand Management,* 3rd ed. (Upper Saddle River, NJ: Prentice-Hall, 2008), chap. 14.

Several internal factors can either facilitate or impede a company's efforts to undertake a global approach to marketing strategies. These factors and their underlying dimensions are

1. *Structure.* The ease of installing a centralized global authority and the absence of rifts between present domestic and international divisions or operating units.
2. *Management processes.* The capabilities and resources available to perform global planning, budgeting, and coordination activities, coupled with the ability to conduct global performance reviews and implement global compensation plans.
3. *Culture.* The ability to project a global versus national identity, a worldwide versus domestic commitment to employees, and a willingness to tolerate interdependence among business units.
4. *People.* The availability of employable foreign nationals and the willingness of current employees to commit to multicountry careers, frequent travel, and having foreign superiors.

Overall, whether a company should undertake a multidomestic or global approach to organizing its international operations will largely depend on the nature of the company and its products, how different foreign cultures are from the domestic market, and the company's ability to implement a global perspective. Many large brands have failed in their quest to go global. The primary reason for this failure is rushing the process. Successful global brands carefully stake out their markets, allowing plenty of time to develop their overseas marketing efforts and evolve into global brands.

Indeed, in many cases, firms do not undertake either purely multidomestic or global approaches to marketing. Instead, they develop a hybrid approach whereby these global brands carry with them the same visual identity, the same strategic positioning, and the same advertising. In addition, local characteristics are factored in. Regardless of the approach undertaken, management and organizational skills that emphasize the need to handle diversity are the critical factors that determine the long-term success of any company's endeavors in the global marketplace.

Programming for Global Marketing

In this section of the chapter, the major areas in developing a global marketing program will be examined. As mentioned at the outset, marketing managers must organize the same controllable decision variables that exist in domestic markets. However, many firms that have been extremely successful in marketing in the United States have not been able to duplicate their success in foreign markets.

Global Marketing Research

Because the risks and uncertainties are so high, marketing research is equally important in foreign markets and in domestic markets and probably more so. Many companies encounter losing situations abroad because they do not know enough about the market.[10] They don't know how to get the information or find the cost of collecting the information too high. To be successful, organizations must collect and analyze pertinent information to support the basic go/no-go decision before getting to the issues addressed by conventional market research. Toward this end, in attempting to analyze foreign consumers and markets, at least four organizational issues must be considered.

Population Characteristics

Population characteristics are one of the major components of a market, and significant differences exist between and within foreign countries. If data are available, the marketing manager should be familiar with the total population and with the regional, urban, rural, and interurban distribution. Other demographic variables, such that the number and size of families, education, occupation, and religion, are also important. In many markets, these variables can have a significant impact on the success of a firm's marketing program. For example, in the United States, a cosmetics firm can be reasonably sure that the desire to use cosmetics is common among women of all income classes. However, in Latin America the same firm may be forced to segment its market by upper-, middle-, and lower-income groups, as well as by urban and rural areas. This is because upper-income women want high-quality cosmetics promoted in prestige media and sold through exclusive outlets. In some rural and less prosperous areas, cosmetics must be inexpensive; in other rural areas, women do not accept cosmetics.

Ability to Buy

To assess the ability of consumers in a foreign market to buy, four broad measures should be examined: (1) gross national product or per capita national income, (2) distribution of income, (3) rate of growth in buying power, and (4) extent of available financing. Since each of these vary in different areas of the world, the marketing opportunities available must be examined closely.

Many consumer goods companies have sought growth by expanding into global markets. For U.S. companies, this is sound strategy since 95 percent of the world's population and two-thirds of its purchasing power are located outside their country. The potential for success in global markets is enhanced when companies carefully research and analyze consumers in foreign countries, just as it is in domestic markets. Below are some suggestions for companies seeking to successfully market to global consumers.

- Research the cultural nuances and customs of the market. Be sure that the company and brand name translate favorably in the language of the target country, and if not, consider using an abbreviation or entirely different brand name for the market. Consider using marketing research firms or ad agencies that have detailed knowledge of the culture.
- Determine whether the product can be exported to the foreign country as is or whether it has to be modified to be useful and appealing to targeted consumers. Also, determine what changes need to be made to packaging and labeling to make the product appealing to the market.
- Research the prices of similar products in the target country or region. Determine the necessary retail price to make marketing it profitable in the country, and research whether a sufficient number of consumers would be willing to pay that price. Also, determine what the product has to offer that would make consumers willing to pay a higher price.
- On the basis of research, decide whether the targeted country or region will require a unique marketing strategy or whether the same general strategy can be used in all geographic areas.
- Research the ways consumers purchase similar products in the targeted country or region and whether the company's product can be sold effectively using this method of distribution. Also, determine if a method of distribution not currently being used in the country could create a competitive advantage for the product.
- Pretest integrated marketing communication efforts in the targeted country to ensure not only that messages are translated accurately but also that subtle differences in meaning are not problematic. Also, research the effectiveness of planned communication efforts.

Marketing consumer goods successfully in global markets requires a long-term commitment because it may take time to establish an identity in new markets. However, with improving technology and the evolution of a global economy, both large and small companies have found global marketing both feasible and profitable.

Source: Dom Del Prete, "Winning Strategies Lead to Global Marketing Success," *Marketing News,* August 18, 1997, pp. 1, 2. Also see Philip R. Cateora and John L. Graham, *International Marketing,* 12th ed. (Burr Ridge, IL: McGraw-Hill/Irwin, 2005), chap. 8.

Willingness to Buy

The cultural framework of consumer motives and behavior is integral to the understanding of the foreign consumer. If data are available, cultural values and attitudes toward the material culture, social organizations, the supernatural, aesthetics, and language should be analyzed for their possible influence on each of the elements in the firm's marketing program. It is easy to see that such factors as the group's values concerning acquisition of material goods, the role of the family, the positions of men and women in society, and the various age groups and social classes can have an effect on marketing because each can influence consumer behavior.

In some areas tastes and habits seem to be converging, with different cultures becoming more and more integrated into one homogeneous culture, although still separated by national boundaries. This appears to be the case in Western Europe, where consumers are developing into a mass market. This convergence obviously will simplify the task for a marketer in this region. However, cultural differences still prevail among many areas of the world and strongly influence consumer behavior. Marketing organizations may have to do primary research in many foreign markets to obtain usable information about these issues.

Differences in Research Tasks and Processes

In addition to the dimensions mentioned above, the processes and tasks associated with carrying out the market research program may also differ from country to country. Many market researchers count on census data for in-depth demographic information. However, in foreign countries the market researcher is likely to encounter a variety of problems in using census data. These include[11]

1. *Language.* Some nations publish their census reports in English. Other countries offer census reports only in their native language; some do not take a census.

2. *Data content.* Data contained in a census vary from country to country and often omit items of interest to researchers. For example, most foreign nations do not include an income question on their census. Others do not include such items as marital status or education levels.

3. *Timeliness.* The United States takes a census every 10 years. Japan and Canada conduct one every five years. However, some northern European nations are abandoning the census as a data-collection tool and instead are relying on population registers to account for births, deaths, and changes in marital status or place of residence.

4. *Availability in the United States.* If a researcher requires detailed household demographics on foreign markets, the cost and time required to obtain the data will be significant. Unfortunately, census data for many countries do not exist. For some it will be difficult to obtain, although data about others can be found on the Internet.

Global Product Strategy

Global marketing research can help determine whether (1) there is an unsatisfied need for which a new product could be developed to serve a foreign market or (2) there is an unsatisfied need that could be met with an existing domestic product, either as is or adapted to the foreign market. In either case, product planning is necessary to determine the type of product to be offered and whether there is sufficient demand to warrant entry into a foreign market.

Most U.S. firms would not think of entering a domestic market without extensive product planning. However, some marketers have failed to do adequate product planning when entering foreign markets. An example of such a problem occurred when American manufacturers began to export refrigerators to Europe. The firms exported essentially the same models sold in the United States. However, the refrigerators were the wrong size, shape, and temperature range for some areas and had weak appeal in others—thus failing miserably. Although adaptation of the product to local conditions may have eliminated this failure, this adaptation is easier said than done. For example, even in the domestic market, overproliferation of product varieties and options can dilute economies of scale. This dilution results in higher production costs, which may make the price of serving each market segment with an adapted product prohibitive.

The solution to this problem is not easy. In some cases, changes need not be made at all or, if so, can be accomplished rather inexpensively. In other cases, the sales potential of the particular market may not warrant expensive product changes. For example, Pepsi's Radical Fruit line of juice drinks was introduced without adaptation on three continents. On the other hand, U.S. companies wishing to market software in foreign countries must undertake painstaking and costly efforts to convert the embedded code from English to foreign languages. This undertaking severely limits the potential markets where individual software products can be profitably marketed. In any case, management must examine these product-related problems carefully prior to making foreign market entry decisions.

Global Distribution Strategy

The role of the distribution network in facilitating the transfer of goods and titles and in the demand stimulation process is as important in foreign markets as it is at home. Figure 13.2 illustrates some of the most common channel arrangements in global marketing. The continuum ranges from no control to almost complete control of the distribution system by manufacturers.

The channel arrangement where manufacturers have the least control is shown at the left in Figure 13.2. These are the most indirect channels of distribution. Here manufacturers sell to resident buyers, export agents, or export merchants located in the United States. In reality, these are similar to some domestic sales, since all the marketing functions are assumed by intermediaries.

Manufacturers become more directly involved and, hence, have greater control over distribution, when they select agents and distributors located in foreign markets. Both perform similar functions, except that agents do not assume title to the manufacturers' products, while distributors do. If manufacturers should assume the functions of foreign agents or distributors and establish their own foreign branch, they greatly increase control over their global distribution system. Manufacturers' effectiveness will then depend on their own administrative organization rather than on independent intermediaries. If the foreign branch sells to other intermediaries, such as wholesalers and retailers, as is the case with most consumer goods, manufacturers again relinquish some control. However, since the manufacturers are located in the market area, they have greater potential to influence these intermediaries. For example, Volkswagen, General Motors, Anheuser-Busch, and Procter & Gamble have each made substantial investments in building manufacturing facilities in Brazil. These investments allow the companies to begin making direct sales to dealers and retailers in the country.

The channel arrangement that enables manufacturers to exercise a great deal of control is shown at the right in Figure 13.2. Here, manufacturers sell directly to organizational buyers

FIGURE 13.2
Common Distribution Channels for Global Marketing

Source: Betty J. Punnett and David A. Ricks, *International Business,* p. 257. Reproduced with the permission of South-Western College Publishing. Copyright © 1992 PWS-Kent Publishing Co. All rights reserved.

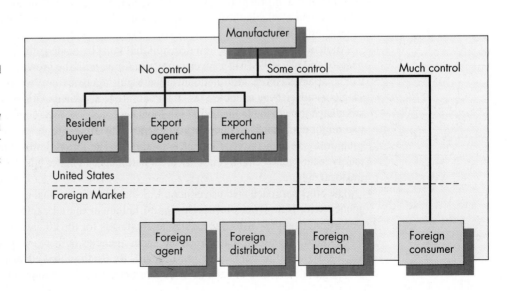

or ultimate consumers. Although this arrangement is most common in the sale of organizational goods, some consumer goods companies have also pursued this arrangement.

Global Pricing Strategy

In domestic markets, pricing is a complex task. The basic approaches used in price determination in foreign markets are the same as those discussed earlier in the chapter on pricing. However, the pricing task is often more complicated in foreign markets because of additional problems associated with tariffs, antidumping laws, taxes, inflation, and currency conversion.

Import duties are probably the major constraint for global marketers and are encountered in many markets. Management must decide whether import duties will be paid by the firm or the foreign consumer, or whether they will be paid by both. This and similar constraints may force the firm to abandon an otherwise desirable pricing strategy or may force the firm out of a market altogether.

Another pricing problem arises because of the rigidity in price structures found in many foreign markets. Many foreign intermediaries are not aggressive in their pricing policies. They often prefer to maintain high unit margins at the expense of low sales volume rather than develop large sales volume by means of lower prices and smaller margins per unit. Many times this rigidity is encouraged by legislation that prevents retailers from cutting prices substantially at their own discretion. These are only a few of the pricing problems foreign marketers encounter.

Global Advertising and Sales Promotion Strategy

When expanding their operations into the world marketplace, most firms are aware of the language barriers that exist and realize the importance of translating their messages into the proper idiom. However, numerous other issues must be resolved as well, such as selecting appropriate media and advertising agencies in foreign markets.

There are many problems in selecting media in foreign markets. Often the media that are traditionally used in the domestic market are not available. For example, it was not until recently that national commercial TV became a reality in the former Soviet Union. If media are available, they may be so only on a limited basis or they may not reach the potential buyers. In addition to the problem of availability, other difficulties arise from the lack of accurate media information. There is no rate and data service or media directory that covers all the media available throughout the world. Where data are available, their accuracy is often questionable.

Another important promotion decision that must be made is the type of agency used to prepare and place the firm's advertisements. Along with the growth in multinational product companies, more multinational advertising agencies are available. Among the top 15 global advertising agencies, less than half are U.S. owned. Alliances and takeovers have stimulated growth in the formation of global agencies. The U.S. company can take either of two major approaches to choosing an agency. The first is to use a purely local agency in each area where the advertisement is to appear. The rationale for this approach is that a purely local agency employing only local nationals can better adapt the firm's message to the local culture.

The other approach is to use either a U.S.-based multinational agency or a multinational agency with U.S. offices to develop and implement the ad campaign. For example, the Coca-Cola Company uses one agency to create ads for the 80 nations in which Diet Coke is marketed. The use of these so-called super agencies is increasing (annual growth rates averaged over 30 percent in the last decade). By using global advertising agencies, companies are able to take advantage of economies of scale and other efficiencies. However,

Rank	Advertiser	Headquarters	Ad Spending (Millions US Dollars)		
			Outside the U.S.	U.S.	Worldwide
1.	Procter & Gamble Co.	Cincinnati, Ohio	$4,350	$3,572	$7,922
2.	Unilever	London/Rotterdam	2,859	603	3,462
3.	L'Oreal	Paris, France	1,878	768	2,646
4.	Toyota Motor Corp.	Toyota City, Japan	1,510	1,098	2,608
5.	Nestlé	Vevey, Switzerland	1,401	498	1,899
6.	Ford Motor Co.	Dearborn, Michigan	1,155	1,643	2,798
7.	Coca-Cola Co.	Atlanta, Georgia	1,128	379	1,507
8.	General Motors	Detroit, Michigan	1,120	2,798	3,918
9.	Volkswagen	Wolfsburg, Germany	1,037	418	1,455
10.	PSA Peugeot Citroen	Paris, France	1,032	0	1,032

Source: "Top Ten Global Advertisers," *Advertising Age,* November 14, 2005, p. 81.

global agencies are not without their critics. Many managers believe that small, local agencies in emerging markets take a more entrepreneurial and fresher approach to advertising than do global agencies. Much discussion has developed over which approach is best, and it appears that both approaches can be used successfully.

The use of sales promotion can also lead to opportunities and problems for marketers in foreign markets. Sales promotions often contain certain characteristics that are more attractive than other elements of the promotion mix.[12] In less-wealthy countries, consumers tend to be even more interested in saving money through price discounts, sampling, or premiums. Sales promotion can also be used as a strategy for bypassing restrictions on advertising placed by some foreign governments. In addition, sales promotion can be an effective means for reaching people who live in rural locations where media support for advertising is virtually nonexistent.

Entry and Growth Strategies for Global Marketing

A major decision facing companies that desire either to enter a foreign market or pursue growth within a specific market relates to the choice of entry or growth strategy. What type of strategy to employ depends on many factors, including the analysis of market opportunities, company capabilities, the degree of marketing involvement and commitment the company is willing to make, and the amount of risk that the company is able to tolerate.[13] A company can decide to (1) make minimal investments of funds and resources by limiting its efforts to exporting; (2) make large initial investments of resources and management effort to try to establish a long-term share of global markets; or (3) take an incremental approach whereby the company starts with a low-risk mode of entry that requires the least financial and other resource commitment and gradually increases its commitment over time. All three approaches can be profitable. In general, a company can initially enter a global market and, subsequently, pursue growth in the global marketplace in six ways:

1. *Exporting.* Exporting occurs when a company produces the product outside the final destination and then ships it there for sale. It is the easiest and most common approach for a company making its first international move. Exporting has two distinct advantages. First, it

197

avoids the cost of establishing manufacturing operations in the host country; second, it may help a firm achieve experience-curve and location economies. By manufacturing the product in a centralized location and exporting it to other national markets, the firm may be able to realize substantial scale economies from its global sales volume. This method is what allowed Sony to dominate the global TV market. The major disadvantages related to exporting include (1) the sometimes higher cost associated with the process, (2) the necessity of the exporting firm to pay import duties or face trade barriers, and (3) the delegation of marketing responsibility for the product to foreign agents who may or may not be dependable.

2. *Licensing.* Companies can grant patent rights, trademark rights, and the right to use technological processes to foreign companies. This is the most common strategy for small and medium-size companies. The major advantage to licensing is that the firm does not have to bear the development costs and risks associated with opening up a foreign market. In addition, licensing can be an attractive option in unfamiliar or politically volatile markets. The major disadvantages are that (1) the firm does not have tight control over manufacturing, marketing, and strategy that is required for realizing economies of scale; and (2) there is the risk that foreign companies may capitalize on the licensed technology. RCA Corporation, for example, once licensed its color TV technology to a number of Japanese firms. These firms quickly assimilated the technology and used it to enter the U.S. market.

3. *Franchising.* Franchising is similar to licensing but tends to involve longer-term commitments. Also, franchising is commonly employed by service firms, as opposed to manufacturing firms. In a franchising agreement, the franchisor sells limited rights to use its brand name in return for a lump sum and share of the franchisee's future profits. In contrast to licensing agreements, the franchisee agrees to abide by strict operating procedures. Advantages and disadvantages associated with franchising are primarily the same as with licensing except to a lesser degree. In many cases, franchising offers an effective mix of centralized and decentralized decision making.

4. *Joint ventures.* A company may decide to share management with one or more collaborating foreign firms. Joint ventures are especially popular in industries that call for large investments, such as natural gas exploration and automobile manufacturing. Control of the joint venture may be split equally, or one party may control decision making. Joint ventures hold several advantages. First, a firm may be able to benefit from a partner's knowledge of the host country's competitive position, culture, language, political systems, and so forth. Second, the firm gains by sharing costs and risks of operating in a foreign market. Third, in many countries, political considerations make joint ventures the only feasible entry mode. Finally, joint ventures allow firms to take advantage of a partner's distribution system, technological know-how, or marketing skills. For example, General Mills teamed up with CPC International in an operation called International Dessert Partners to develop a major baking and dessert-mix business in Latin America. The venture combines General Mills' technology and Betty Crocker dessert products with CPC's marketing and distribution capabilities in Latin America. The major disadvantages associated with joint ventures are that (1) a firm may risk giving up control of proprietary knowledge to its partner; and (2) the firm may lose the tight control over a foreign subsidiary needed to engage in coordinated global attacks against rivals.

5. *Strategic alliances.* Although some consider strategic alliances a form of joint venture, we consider them a distinct entity for two reasons. First, strategic alliances are normally partnerships that two or more firms enter into to gain a competitive advantage on a worldwide versus local basis. Second, strategic alliances are usually of a much longer-term nature than are joint ventures. In strategic alliances, the partners share long-term goals and pledge almost total cooperation. Strategic alliances can be used to reduce manufacturing costs, accelerate technological diffusion and new product development, and overcome legal

and trade barriers.[14] The major disadvantage associated with formation of a strategic alliance is the increased risk of competitive conflict between the partners.

6. *Direct ownership.* Some companies prefer to enter or grow in markets either through establishment of a wholly owned subsidiary or through acquisition. In either case, the firm owns 100 percent of the stock. The advantages to direct ownership are that the firm has (1) complete control over its technology and operations, (2) immediate access to foreign markets, (3) instant credibility and gains in the foreign country when acquisitions are the mode of entry or growth, and (4) the ability to install its own management team. Of course, the primary disadvantages of direct ownership are the huge costs and significant risks associated with this strategy. These problems may more than offset the advantages depending upon the country entered.

Regardless of the choice of methods used to gain entry into and grow within a foreign marketplace, companies must somehow integrate their operations. The complexities involved in operating on a worldwide basis dictate that firms decide on operating strategies. A critical decision that marketing managers must make relates to the extent of adaptation of the marketing mix elements for the foreign country in which the company operates. Depending on the area of the world under consideration and the particular product mix, different degrees of standardization/adaptation of the marketing mix elements may take place. As a guideline, standardization of one or more parts of the marketing mix is a function of many factors that individually and collectively affect companies' decision making.[15] It is more likely to succeed under the following conditions:

- When markets are economically similar.
- When worldwide customers, not countries, are the basis for segmenting markets.
- When customer behavior and lifestyles are similar.
- When the product is culturally compatible across the host country.
- When a firm's competitive position is similar in different markets.
- When competing against the same competitors, with similar market shares, in different countries, rather than competing against purely local companies.
- When the product is an organizational and high-technology product rather than a consumer product.
- When there are similarities in the physical, political, and legal environments of home and host countries.
- When the marketing infrastructure in the home and host countries is similar.

The decision to adapt or standardize marketing should be made only after a thorough analysis of the product-market mix has been undertaken. The company's end goal is to develop, manufacture, and market the products best suited to the actual and potential needs of the local (wherever that may be) customer and to the social and economic conditions of the marketplace. There can be subtle differences from country to country and from region to region in the ways a product is used and what customers expect from it.

Conclusion

The world is truly becoming a global market. Many companies that avoid operating in the global arena are destined for failure. For those willing to undertake the challenges and risks necessary to become multinational corporations, long-term survival and growth are likely outcomes. The purpose of this chapter was to introduce the reader to the opportunities, problems, and challenges involved in global marketing.

Additional Readings

Cateora, Philip A., and John L. Graham. *International Marketing.* 12th ed., Burr Ridge, IL: McGraw-Hill/Irwin, 2005.

Erdem, Tulin, Joffe Swait, and Ana Valenzuela. "Brands as Signals: A Cross Country Validation Study." *Journal of Marketing,* January 2006, pp. 34–49.

Friedman, Thomas L. *The World Is Flat.* New York: Farrar, Straus, and Giroux, 2005.

Ghemawat, Pankaj. "Regional Strategies for Global Leadership." *Harvard Business Review,* December 2005, pp. 98–109.

McEwen, William, Xiaoguang Fang, Zhang Chuanping, and Richard Bunkholder. "Inside the Mind of the Chinese Consumer." *Harvard Business Review,* March 2006, pp. 66–77.

Steenkamp, Jan-Benedict E. M., and Inge Geyskens. "How Country Characteristics Affect the Perceived Value of Web Sites." *Journal of Marketing,* July 2006, pp. 136–50.

Section II

Analyzing Marketing Problems and Cases

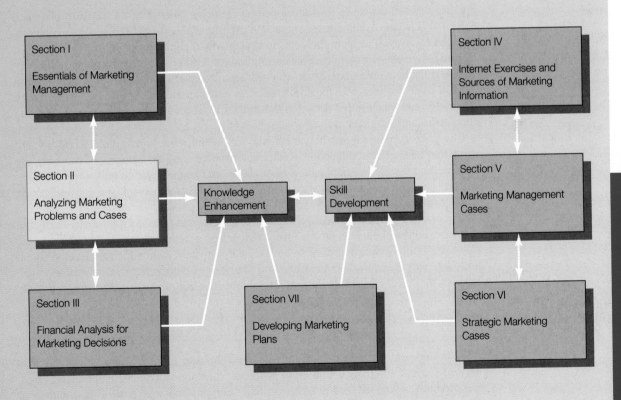

Case studies help bridge the gap between classroom learning and the practice of marketing management. They provide us with an opportunity to develop, sharpen, and test our analytical skills at

- Assessing situations.
- Sorting out and organizing key information.
- Asking the right questions.
- Defining opportunities and problems.
- Identifying and evaluating alternative courses of action.
- Interpreting data.
- Evaluating the results of past strategies.
- Developing and defending new strategies.
- Interacting with other managers.
- Making decisions under conditions of uncertainty.
- Critically evaluating the work of others.
- Responding to criticism.

Source: David W. Cravens, Charles W. Lamb, Jr., and Victoria L. Crittenden, *Strategic Marketing Management Cases,* 7th ed., (Burr Ridge, IL: McGraw-Hill/Irwin, 2002), p. 671.

The use of business cases was developed by faculty members of the Harvard Graduate School of Business Administration in the 1920s. Case studies have been widely accepted as one effective way of exposing students to strategic marketing processes.

Basically, cases represent detailed descriptions or reports of business problems. They are often written by a trained observer who was actually involved in the firm or organization and had some dealings with the problems under consideration. Cases generally entail both qualitative and quantitative data that the student must analyze to determine appropriate alternatives and solutions.

The primary purpose of the case method is to introduce a measure of realism into marketing management education. Rather than emphasizing the teaching of concepts, the case method focuses on application of concepts and sound logic to real-world business problems. In this way, students learn to bridge the gap between abstraction and application and to appreciate the value of both.

The primary purpose of this section is to offer a logical format for the analysis of case problems. Although there is no one format that can be successfully applied to all cases, the following framework is intended to be a logical sequence from which to develop sound analyses. This framework is presented for analysis of comprehensive marketing cases; however, the process should also be useful for shorter marketing cases, incidents, and problems.

A Case Analysis Framework

A basic approach to case analysis involves a four-step process. First, the problem is defined. Second, alternative courses of action are formulated to solve the problem. Third, the alternatives are analyzed in terms of their strengths and weaknesses. And fourth, an alternative is accepted and a course of action is recommended. This basic approach is quite useful for students well versed in case analysis, particularly for shorter cases or incidents. However, for the newcomer, this framework may be oversimplified. Thus, the following expanded framework and checklists are intended to aid students in becoming proficient in case and problem analysis.

1. Analyze and Record the Current Situation

Whether the analysis of a firm's problems is done by a manager, student, or paid business consultant, the first step is to analyze the current situation. This does not mean writing up a history of the firm but entails the type of analysis described below. This approach is useful not only for getting a better grip on the situation but also for discovering both real and potential problems—central concerns of any case analysis.

Phase 1: The Environment

The first phase in analyzing a marketing problem or case is to consider the environment in which the firm is operating. The environment can be broken down into a number of different components such as the economic, social, political, and legal areas. Any of these may contain threats to a firm's success or opportunities for improving a firm's situation.

Phase 2: The Industry

The second phase involves analyzing the industry in which the firm operates. A framework provided by Michael Porter includes five competitive forces that need to be considered to do a complete industry analysis.[1] The framework is shown in Figure 1 and includes rivalry among existing competitors, threat of new entrants, and threat of substitute products. In addition, in this framework, buyers and suppliers are included as competitors because they can threaten the profitability of an industry or firm.

While rivalry among existing competitors is an issue in most cases, analysis and strategies for dealing with the other forces can also be critical. This is particularly so when a firm is considering entering a new industry and wants to forecast its potential success. Each of the five competitive forces is discussed below.

Rivalry among Existing Competitors   In most cases and business situations a firm needs to consider the current competitors in its industry in order to develop successful strategies. Strategies such as price competition, advertising battles, sales promotion offers, new product

FIGURE 1   Competitive Forces in an Industry

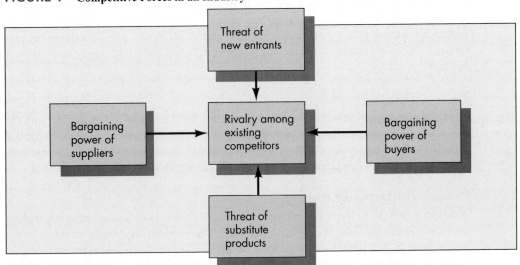

Source: Adapted from Michael E. Porter, "Industry Structure and Competitive Strategy: Keys to Profitability," *Financial Analysts Journal,* July–August 1980, p. 33.

introductions, and increased customer service are commonly used to attract customers from competitors.

To fully analyze existing rivalry, it is important to determine which firms are the major competitors and what are their annual sales, market share, growth profile, and strengths and weaknesses. Also, it is useful to analyze their current and past marketing strategies to try to forecast their likely reactions to a change in a competitive firm's strategy. Finally, it is important to consider any trends or changes in government regulation of an industry or changes in technology that could affect the success of a firm's strategy.

Threat of New Entrants   It is always possible for firms in other industries to try to compete in a new industry. New entrants are more likely in industries that have low entry barriers. *Entry barriers* include such things as a need for large financial resources, high brand equity for existing brands in an industry, or economies of scale obtained by existing firms in an industry. Also, existing firms in an industry may benefit from experience curves; that is, their cumulative experience in producing and marketing a product may reduce their per-unit costs below those of inexperienced firms. In general, the higher the entry barriers, the less likely outside firms are to enter an industry. For example, the entry barriers for starting up a new car company are much higher than for starting up an online software company.

Threat of Substitute Products   In a broad sense, all firms in an industry compete with industries producing substitute products. For example, in cultures where bicycles are the major means of transportation, bicycle manufacturers compete with substitute products such as motor scooters and automobiles. Substitutes limit the potential return in an industry by placing a ceiling on the prices a firm in the industry can profitably charge. The more attractive the price–performance alternative offered by substitutes, the tighter the lid on industry profits. For example, the price of candy, such as Raisinets chocolate-covered raisins, may limit the price that can be charged for granola bars.

Bargaining Power of Suppliers   Suppliers can be a competitive threat in an industry because they can raise the price of raw materials or reduce their quality. Powerful suppliers can reduce the profitability of an industry or firm if companies cannot raise their prices to cover price increases by suppliers. Also, suppliers may be a threat because they may forward integrate into an industry by purchasing a firm that they supply or other firms in the industry.

Bargaining Power of Buyers   Buyers can compete with an industry by forcing prices down, bargaining for higher quality or more services, and playing competitors off against each other. All these tactics can lower the profitability of a firm or industry. For example, because Wal-Mart sells such a large percentage of many companies' products, it can negotiate for lower prices than smaller retailers can. Also, buyers may be a threat because they may backward integrate into an industry by purchasing firms that supply them or other firms in the industry.

Phase 3: The Organization

The third phase involves analysis of the organization itself not only in comparison with the industry and industry averages but also internally in terms of both quantitative and qualitative data. Key areas of concern at this stage are such factors as objectives, constraints, management philosophy, financial condition, and the organizational structure and culture of the firm.

Phase 4: The Marketing Strategy

Although there may be internal personnel or structural problems in the marketing department that need examination, typically an analysis of the current marketing strategy is the next phase. In this phase, the objectives of the marketing department are analyzed in comparison with those of the firm in terms of agreement, soundness, and attainability. Each element of the marketing mix as well as other areas, such as marketing research and

A common criticism of prepared cases goes something like this: "You repeated an awful lot of case material, but you really didn't analyze the case." Yet, at the same time, it is difficult to verbalize exactly what *analysis* means—that is, "I can't explain exactly what it is, but I know it when I see it!"

This is a common problem since the term *analysis* has many definitions and means different things in different contexts. In terms of case analysis, one thing that is clear is that analysis means going beyond simply describing the case information. It includes determining the implications of the case information for developing strategy. This determination may involve careful financial analysis of sales and profit data or thoughtful interpretation of the text of the case.

One way of thinking about analysis involves a series of three steps: synthesis, generalizations, and implications. A brief example of this process follows.

The high growth rate of frozen pizza sales has attracted a number of large food processors, including Pillsbury (Totino's), Quaker Oats (Celeste), American Home Products (Chef Boy-ar-dee), Nestlé (Stouffer's), General Mills (Saluto), and H. J. Heinz (La Pizzeria). The major independents are Jeno's, Tony's, and John's. Jeno's and Totino's are the market leaders, with market shares of about 19 percent each. Celeste and Tony's have about 8 to 9 percent each, and the others have about 5 percent or less.

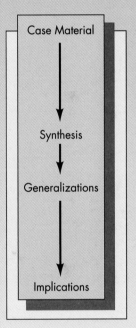

Case Material

↓

Synthesis

↓

Generalizations

↓

Implications

The frozen pizza market is a highly competitive and highly fragmented market.

In markets such as this, attempts to gain market share through lower consumer prices or heavy advertising are likely to be quickly copied by competitors and thus tend not to be very effective.

Lowering consumer prices and spending more on advertising are likely to be poor strategies. Perhaps increasing freezer space in retail outlets could be effective (this might be obtained through trade discounts). A superior product, for example, better-tasting pizza, microwave pizza, or increasing geographic coverage of the market, may be better strategies for obtaining market share.

Note that none of the three analysis steps includes any repetition of the case material. Rather, they all involve abstracting a meaning of the information and, by pairing it with marketing principles, coming up with the strategic implications of the information.

information systems, is analyzed in terms of whether it is internally consistent, synchronized with the goals of the department and firm, and focused on specific target markets. Although cases often are labeled in terms of their primary emphasis, such as "pricing" or "advertising," it is important to analyze the marketing strategy and entire marketing mix, since a change in one element will usually affect the entire marketing program.

In performing the analysis of the current situation, the data should be analyzed carefully to extract the relevant from the superfluous. Many cases contain information that is not relevant to the problem; it is the analyst's job to discard this information to get a clearer picture of the current situation. As the analysis proceeds, a watchful eye must be kept on each phase to determine (1) symptoms of problems, (2) current problems, and (3) potential problems. Symptoms of problems are indicators of a problem but are not problems in and of themselves. For example, a symptom of a problem may be a decline in sales in a particular sales territory. However, the problem is the root cause of the decline in sales—perhaps the field representative quit making sales calls and is relying on phone orders only.

The following is a checklist of the types of questions that should be asked when performing the analysis of the current situation.

Checklist for Analyzing the Current Situation

Phase 1: The Environment

1. What is the state of the economy and are there any trends that could affect the industry, firm, or marketing strategy?
2. What are current trends in cultural and social values and how do these affect the industry, firm, or marketing strategy?
3. What are current political values and trends and how do they affect the industry, firm, or marketing strategy?
4. Is there any current or pending federal, state, or local legislation that could change the industry, firm, or marketing strategy?
5. Overall, are there any threats or opportunities in the environment that could influence the industry, firm, or marketing strategy?

Phase 2: The Industry

1. What industry is the firm in?
2. Which firms are the major competitors in the industry and what are their annual sales, market share, and growth profile?
3. What strategies have competitors in the industry been using and what has been their success with them?
4. What are the relative strengths and weaknesses of competitors in the industry?
5. Is there a threat of new competitors coming into the industry and what are the major entry barriers?
6. Are there any substitute products for the industry and what are their advantages and disadvantages compared to this industry's products?
7. How much bargaining power do suppliers have in this industry and what is its impact on the firm and industry profits?
8. How much bargaining power do buyers have in this industry and what is its impact on the firm and industry profits?

Phase 3: The Organization

1. What are the objectives of the organization? Are they clearly stated? Attainable?
2. What are the strengths of the organization? Managerial expertise? Financial? Copyrights or patents?
3. What are the constraints and weaknesses of the organization?
4. Are there any real or potential sources of dysfunctional conflict in the structure of the organization?
5. How is the marketing department structured in the organization?

Phase 4: The Marketing Strategy

1. What are the objectives of the marketing strategy? Are they clearly stated? Are they consistent with the objectives of the firm? Is the entire marketing mix structured to meet these objectives?
2. What marketing concepts are at issue in the current strategy? Is the marketing strategy well planned and laid out? Is the strategy consistent with sound marketing principles? If the strategy takes exception to marketing principles, is there a good reason for it?

3. To what target market is the strategy directed? Is it well defined? Is the market large enough to be profitably served? Does the market have long-run potential?

4. What competitive advantage does the marketing strategy offer? If none, what can be done to gain a competitive advantage in the marketplace?

5. What products are being sold? What are the width, depth, and consistency of the firm's product lines? Does the firm need new products to fill out its product line? Should any product be deleted? What is the profitability of the various products?

6. What promotion mix is being used? Is promotion consistent with the products and product images? What could be done to improve the promotion mix?

7. What channels of distribution are being used? Do they deliver the product at the right time and right place to meet customer needs? Are the channels typical of those used in the industry? Could channels be made more efficient?

8. What pricing strategies are being used? How do prices compare with similar products of other firms? How are prices determined?

9. Are marketing research and information systematically integrated into the marketing strategy? Is the overall marketing strategy internally consistent?

The relevant information from this preliminary analysis is now formalized and recorded. At this point the analyst must be mindful of the difference between facts and opinions. Facts are objective statements, such as financial data, whereas opinions are subjective interpretations of facts or situations. The analyst must make certain not to place too much emphasis on opinions and to carefully consider any variables that may bias such opinions.

Regardless of how much information is contained in the case or how much additional information is collected, the analyst usually finds that it is impossible to specify a complete framework for the current situation. At this point, assumptions must be made. Clearly, since each analyst may make different assumptions, it is critical that assumptions be explicitly stated. When presenting a case, the analyst may wish to distribute copies of the assumption list to all class members. This avoids confusion about how the analyst perceives the current situation, and others can evaluate the reasonableness and necessity of the assumptions.

2. Analyze and Record Problems and Their Core Elements

After careful analysis, problems and their core elements should be explicitly stated and listed in order of importance. Finding and recording problems and their core elements can be difficult. It is not uncommon when reading a case for the first time for the student to view the case as a description of a situation in which there are no problems. However, careful analysis should reveal symptoms, which lead to problem recognition.

Recognizing and recording problems and their core elements is most critical for a meaningful case analysis. Obviously, if the root problems are not explicitly stated and understood, the remainder of the case analysis has little merit because the true issues are not being dealt with. The following checklist of questions is designed to assist in performing this step of the analysis.

Checklist for Analyzing Problems and Their Core Elements

1. What is the primary problem in the case? What are the secondary problems?

2. What proof exists that these are the central issues? How much of this proof is based on facts? On opinions? On assumptions?

3. What symptoms are there that suggest these are the real problems in the case?

4. How are the problems, as defined, related? Are they independent or are they the result of a deeper problem?

5. What are the ramifications of these problems in the short run? In the long run?

3. Formulate, Evaluate, and Record Alternative Courses of Action

This step is concerned with the question of what can be done to resolve the problem defined in the previous step. Generally, a number of alternative courses of action are available that could potentially help alleviate the problem condition. Three to seven are usually a reasonable number of alternatives to work with. Another approach is to brainstorm as many alternatives as possible initially and then reduce the list to a workable number.

Sound logic and reasoning are very important in this step. It is critical to avoid alternatives that could potentially alleviate the problem, but would create a greater new problem or require greater resources than the firm has at its disposal.

After serious analysis and listing of a number of alternatives, the next task is to evaluate them in terms of their costs and benefits. Costs are any output or effort the firm must exert to implement the alternative. Benefits are any input or value received by the firm. Costs to be considered are time, money, other resources, and opportunity costs; benefits are such things as sales, profits, brand equity, and customer satisfaction. The following checklist provides a guideline of questions to be used when performing this phase of the analysis.

Checklist for Formulating and Evaluating Alternative Courses of Action

1. What possible alternatives exist for solving the firm's problems?
2. What limits are there on the possible alternatives? Competence? Resources? Management preference? Ethical responsibility? Legal restrictions?
3. What major alternatives are now available to the firm? What marketing concepts are involved that affect these alternatives?
4. Are the listed alternatives reasonable, given the firm's situation? Are they logical? Are the alternatives consistent with the goals of the marketing program? Are they consistent with the firm's objectives?
5. What are the financial and other costs of each alternative? What are the benefits? What are the advantages and disadvantages of each alternative?
6. Which alternative best solves the problem and minimizes the creation of new problems, given the above constraints?

4. Select and Record the Chosen Alternative and Implementation Details

In light of the previous analysis, the alternative is now selected that best solves the problem with a minimum creation of new problems. It is important to record the logic and reasoning that precipitated the selection of a particular alternative. This includes articulating not only why the alternative was selected but also why the other alternatives were not selected.

No analysis is complete without an action-oriented decision and plan for implementing the decision. The accompanying checklist indicates the type of questions that should be answered in this stage of analysis.

Checklist for Selecting and Implementing the Chosen Alternative

1. What must be done to implement the alternative?
2. What personnel will be involved? What are the responsibilities of each?
3. When and where will the alternative be implemented?
4. What will be the probable outcome?
5. How will the success or failure of the alternative be measured?

Pitfalls to Avoid in Case Analysis

Following is a summary of some of the most common errors analysts make when analyzing cases. When evaluating your analysis or those of others, this list provides a useful guide for spotting potential shortcomings.

1. *Inadequate definition of the problem.* By far the most common error made in case analysis is attempting to recommend courses of action without first adequately defining or understanding the core problems. Whether presented orally or in a written report, a case analysis must begin with a focus on the central issues and problems represented in the case situation. Closely related is the error of analyzing symptoms without determining the root problem.

2. *The search for "the answer."* In case analysis, there are usually no clear-cut solutions. Keep in mind that the objective of case studies is learning through discussion and exploration. There is usually no one "official" or "correct" answer to a case. Rather, there are usually several reasonable alternative solutions.

3. *Not enough information.* Analysts often complain there is not enough information in some cases to make a good decision. However, there is justification for not presenting *all* of the information in a case. As in real life, a marketing manager or consultant seldom has all the information necessary to make an optimal decision. Thus, reasonable assumptions have to be made, and the challenge is to find intelligent solutions in spite of the limited information.

4. *Use of generalities.* In analyzing cases, specific recommendations are necessarily not generalities. For example, a suggestion to increase the price is a generality; a suggestion to increase the price by $1.07 is a specific.

5. *A different situation.* Analysts sometimes exert considerable time and effort contending that "If the situation were different, I'd know what course of action to take" or "If the marketing manager hadn't already fouled things up so badly, the firm wouldn't have a problem." Such reasoning ignores the fact that the events in the case have already happened and cannot be changed. Even though analysis or criticism of past events is necessary in diagnosing the problem, in the end, the present situation must be addressed and decisions must be made based on the given situations.

6. *Narrow vision analysis.* Although cases are often labeled as a specific type of case, such as "pricing," "product," and so forth, this does not mean that other marketing variables should be ignored. Too often analysts ignore the effects that a change in one marketing element will have on the others.

7. *Realism.* Too often analysts become so focused on solving a particular problem that their solutions become totally unrealistic. For instance, suggesting a $1 million advertising program for a firm with a capital structure of $50,000 is an unrealistic solution.

8. *The marketing research solution.* A quite common but unsatisfactory solution to case problems is marketing research; for example, "The firm should do this or that type of marketing research to find a solution to its problem." Although marketing research may be helpful as an intermediary step in some cases, marketing research does not solve problems or make decisions. In cases where marketing research is recommended, the cost and potential benefits should be fully specified in the case analysis.

9. *Rehashing the case material.* Analysts sometimes spend considerable effort rewriting a two- or three-page history of the firm as presented in the case. This is unnecessary since the instructor and other analysts are already familiar with this information.

10. *Premature conclusions.* Analysts sometimes jump to premature conclusions instead of waiting until their analysis is completed. Too many analysts jump to conclusions upon first reading the case and then proceed to interpret everything in the case as justifying their conclusions, even factors logically against it.

A useful approach to gaining an understanding of the situation an organization is facing at a particular time is called *SWOT analysis.* SWOT stands for the organization's *strengths* and *weaknesses* and the *opportunities* and *threats* it faces in the environment. Below are some issues an analyst should address in performing a SWOT analysis.

POTENTIAL RESOURCE STRENGTHS AND COMPETITIVE CAPABILITIES

- A powerful strategy.
- Core competencies in _____.
- A distinctive competence in _____.
- A product that is strongly differentiated from those of rivals.
- Competencies and capabilities that are well matched to industry key success factors.
- A strong financial condition; ample financial resources to grow the business.
- Strong brand-name image/company reputation.
- An attractive customer base.
- Economy of scale and/or learning and experience curve advantages over rivals.
- Proprietary technology/superior technological skills/important patents.
- Superior intellectual capital relative to key rivals.
- Cost advantages over rivals.
- Strong advertising and promotion.
- Product innovation capabilities.
- Proven capabilities in improving production processes.
- Good supply chain management capabilities.
- Good customer service capabilities.
- Better product quality relative to rivals.
- Wide geographic coverage and/or strong global distribution capability.
- Alliances/joint ventures with other firms that provide access to valuable technology, competencies, and/or attractive geographic markets.

POTENTIAL RESOURCE WEAKNESSES AND COMPETITIVE DEFICIENCIES

- No clear strategic direction.
- Resources that are not well matched to industry key success factors.
- No well-developed or proven core competencies.
- A weak balance sheet; too much debt.
- Higher overall unit costs relative to key competitors.
- Weak or unproven product innovation capabilities.
- A product/service with ho-hum attributes or features inferior to those of rivals.
- Too narrow a product line relative to rivals.
- Weak brand image or reputation.
- Weaker dealer network than key rivals and/or lack of adequate global distribution capability.

Communicating Case Analyses

The final concern in case analysis deals with communicating the results of the analysis. The most comprehensive analysis has little value if it is not communicated effectively. Case analyses are communicated through two primary media—the written report and the oral presentation.

- Behind on product quality, R&D, and/or technological know-how.
- In the wrong strategic group.
- Losing market share because _____.
- Lack of management depth.
- Inferior intellectual capital relative to leading rivals.
- Subpar profitability because _____.
- Plagued with internal operating problems or obsolete facilities.
- Behind rivals in e-commerce capabilities.
- Short on financial resources to grow the business and pursue promising initiatives.
- Too much underutilized plant capacity.

POTENTIAL MARKET OPPORTUNITIES

- Openings to win market share from rivals.
- Sharply rising buyer demand for the industry's product.
- Serving additional customer groups or market segments.
- Expanding into new geographic markets.
- Expanding the company's product line to meet a broader range of customer needs.
- Utilizing existing company skills or technological know-how to enter new product lines or new businesses.
- Online sales.
- Integrating forward or backward.
- Falling trade barriers in attractive foreign markets.
- Acquiring rival firms or companies with attractive technological expertise or capabilities.
- Entering into alliances or joint ventures that can expand the firm's market coverage or boost its competitive capability.
- Openings to exploit emerging new technologies.

POTENTIAL EXTERNAL THREATS TO A COMPANY'S WELL-BEING

- Increasing intensity of competition among industry rivals—may squeeze profit margins.
- Slowdowns in market growth.
- Likely entry of potent new competitors.
- Loss of sales to substitute products.
- Growing bargaining power of customers or suppliers.
- A shift in buyer needs and tastes away from the industry's product.
- Adverse demographic changes that threaten to curtail demand for the industry's product.
- Vulnerability to industry driving forces.
- Restrictive trade policies on the part of foreign governments.
- Costly new regulatory requirements.

Source: Arthur A. Thompson, Jr., A. J. Strickland III, and John E. Gamble, *Crafting and Executing Strategy*, 14th ed. (Burr Ridge, IL: McGraw-Hill/Irwin, 2005), p. 95.

The Written Report

Since the structure of the written report will vary by the type of case analyzed, the purpose of this section is not to present a "one and only" way of writing up a case; it is to present some useful generalizations to aid analysts in case write-ups.

A good written report starts with an outline that organizes the structure of the analysis in a logical manner. The following is a general outline for a marketing case report.

1. Read the case quickly to get an overview of the situation.
2. Read the case again thoroughly. Underline relevant information and take notes on potential areas of concern.
3. Review outside sources of information on the environment and the industry. Record relevant information and the source of this information.
4. Perform comparative analysis of the firm with the industry and industry averages.
5. Analyze the firm.
6. Analyze the marketing program.
7. Record the current situation in terms of relevant environmental, industry, firm, and marketing strategy parameters.
8. Make and record necessary assumptions to complete the situational framework.
9. Determine and record the major issues, problems, and their core elements.
10. Record proof that these are the major issues.
11. Record potential courses of action.
12. Evaluate each initially to determine constraints that preclude acceptability.
13. Evaluate remaining alternatives in terms of costs and benefits.
14. Record analysis of alternatives.
15. Select an alternative.
16. Record alternative and defense of its selection.
17. Record the who, what, when, where, how, and why of the alternative and its implementation.

I. **Title Page**
II. **Table of Contents**
III. **Executive Summary** (one- to two-page summary of the analysis and recommendations)
IV. **Situation Analysis**
    A. *Environment*
        1. Economic conditions and trends
        2. Cultural and social values and trends
        3. Political and legal issues
        4. Summary of environmental opportunities and threats
        5. Implications for strategy development
    B. *Industry*
        1. Classification and definition of industry
        2. Analysis of existing competitors
        3. Analysis of potential new entrants
        4. Analysis of substitute products
        5. Analysis of suppliers
        6. Analysis of buyers
        7. Summary of industry opportunities and threats
        8. Implications for strategy development
    C. *Organization*
        1. Objectives and constraints
        2. Financial condition
        3. Management philosophy
        4. Organizational structure

      5. Organizational culture

      6. Summary of the firm's strengths and weaknesses

      7. Implications for strategy development

    D. *Marketing strategy*

      1. Objectives and constraints

      2. Analysis of sales, profits, and market share

      3. Analysis of target market(s)

      4. Analysis of marketing mix variables

      5. Summary of marketing strategy's strengths and weaknesses

      6. Implications for strategy development

  V. Problems Found in Situation Analysis

    A. *Statement of primary problem(s)*

      1. Evidence of problem(s)

      2. Effects of problem(s)

    B. *Statement of secondary problem(s)*

      1. Evidence of problem(s)

      2. Effects of problem(s)

  VI. Strategic Alternatives for Solving Problems

    A. *Description of strategic alternative 1*

      1. Benefits of alternative 1

      2. Costs of alternative 1

    B. *Description of strategic alternative 2*

      1. Benefits of alternative 2

      2. Costs of alternative 2

    C. *Description of strategic alternative 3*

      1. Benefits of alternative 3

      2. Costs of alternative 3

 VII. Selection of Strategic Alternative and Implementation

    A. *Statement of selected strategy*

    B. *Justification for selection of strategy*

    C. *Description of implementation of strategy*

VIII. Summary

  IX. Appendices

    A. *Financial analysis*

    B. *Technical analysis*

Writing the case report entails filling out the details of the outline in prose form. Of course, not every case report requires all the headings listed above, and different headings may be required for some cases. Like any other skill, it takes practice to determine the appropriate headings and approach for writing particular cases. However, good case reports flow logically from topic to topic, are clearly written, are based on solid situation analysis, and demonstrate sound strategic thinking.

The Oral Presentation

Case analyses are often presented by an individual or team. As with the written report, a good outline is critical, and it is often useful to hand out the outline to each class member. Although there is no best way to present a case or to divide responsibility between team members, simply reading the written report is unacceptable because it encourages boredom and interferes with all-important class discussion.

The use of visual aids can be quite helpful in presenting class analyses. However, simply presenting financial statements contained in the case is a poor use of visual media. On the other hand, graphs of sales and profit curves can be more easily interpreted and can be quite useful for making specific points.

Oral presentation of cases is particularly helpful to analysts for learning the skill of speaking to a group. In particular, the ability to handle objections and disagreements without antagonizing others is a skill worth developing.

Conclusion

From the discussion it should be obvious that good case analyses require a major commitment of time and effort. Individuals must be highly motivated and willing to get involved in the analysis and discussion if they expect to learn and succeed in a course where cases are used. Persons with only passive interest who perform "night before" analyses cheat themselves out of valuable learning experiences that can aid them in their careers.

Additional Readings

Aaker, David A. *Strategic Market Management*. 8th ed. Hoboken, NJ: Wiley, 2008.

Cravens, David W; Charles W. Lamb, Jr.; and Victoria L. Crittenden. *Strategic Marketing Management Cases*. 7th ed. Burr Ridge, IL: McGraw-Hill/Irwin, 2002, Appendix B.

Kevin, Roger A., and Robert A. Peterson. *Strategic Marketing Problems*. 11th ed. Upper Saddle River, NJ: Prentice Hall, 2007.

Section III

Financial Analysis for Marketing Decisions

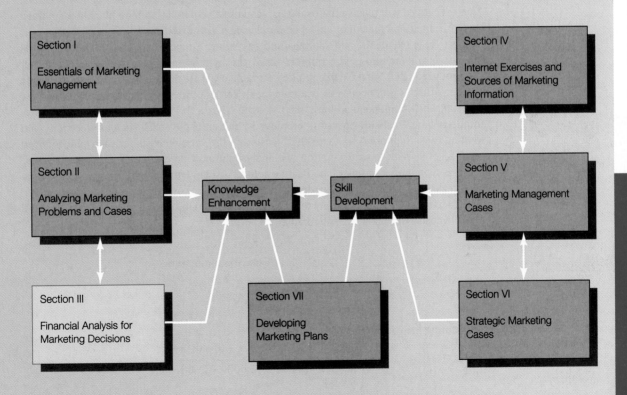

Financial Analysis

Financial analysis is an important aspect of strategic marketing planning and should be an integral part of marketing problem and case analysis. In this section, we present several financial tools that are useful for analyzing marketing problems and cases. First, we investigate break-even analysis, which is concerned with determining the number of units or dollar sales, or both, necessary to break even on a project or to obtain a given level of profits. Second, we illustrate net present value analysis, which is a somewhat more sophisticated tool for analyzing marketing alternatives. Finally, we investigate ratio analysis, which can be a useful tool for determining the financial condition of the firm, including its ability to invest in a new or modified marketing program.

Break-Even Analysis

Break-even analysis is a common tool for investigating the potential profitability of a marketing alternative. The *break-even point* is that level of sales in either units or sales dollars at which a firm covers all of its costs. In other words, it is the level at which total sales revenue just equals the total costs necessary to achieve these sales.

To compute the break-even point, an analyst must have or be able to obtain three values. First, the analyst needs to know the selling price per unit of the product (*SP*). For example, suppose the Ajax Company plans to sell its new electric car through its own dealerships at a retail price of $5,000. Second, the analyst needs to know the level of fixed costs (*FC*). Fixed costs are all costs relevant to the project that do not change regardless of how many units are produced or sold. For instance, whether Ajax produces and sells 1 or 100,000 cars, Ajax executives will receive their salaries, land must be purchased for a plant, a plant must be constructed, and machinery must be purchased. Other fixed costs include such things as interest, lease payments, and sinking fund payments. Suppose Ajax has totaled all of its fixed costs and the sum is $1.5 million. Third, the analyst must know the variable costs per unit produced (*VC*). As the name implies, variable costs are those that vary directly with the number of units produced. For example, each car Ajax produces involves costs for raw materials and components to build the car, such as batteries, electric motors, steel bodies, and tires; labor costs for operating employees; and machine costs, such as electricity and welding rods. Suppose Ajax totals these costs and the variable costs for each car produced equal $3,500. With this information, the analyst can now determine the break-even point, which is the number of units that must be sold to just cover the cost of producing the cars. The break-even point is determined by dividing total fixed costs by the *contribution margin*. The contribution margin is simply the difference between the selling price per unit (*SP*) and variable costs per unit (*VC*). Algebraically,

$$BEP_{\text{(in units)}} = \frac{\text{Total fixed costs}}{\text{Contribution margin}}$$

$$= \frac{FC}{SP - VC}$$

Substituting the Ajax estimates,

$$BEP_{\text{(in units)}} = \frac{1,500,000}{5,000 - 3,500}$$

$$= \frac{1,500,000}{1,500}$$

$$= 1,000 \text{ units}$$

In other words, the Ajax Company must sell 1,000 cars to just break even (i.e., for total sales revenue to cover total costs).

Alternatively, the analyst may want to know the break-even point in terms of dollar sales volume. Of course, if the preceding analysis has been done, one could simply multiply the $BEP_{\text{(in units)}}$ times the selling price to determine the break-even sales volume (i.e., 1,000 units $\times$ \$5,000/unit = \$5 million). However, the $BEP_{\text{(in dollars)}}$ can be computed directly, using the formula below:

$$BEP_{\text{(in dollars)}} = \frac{FC}{1 - \dfrac{VC}{SP}}$$

$$= \frac{1,500,000}{1 - \dfrac{3,500}{5,000}}$$

$$= \frac{1,500,000}{1 - .7}$$

$$= \$5,000,000$$

Thus, Ajax must produce and sell 1,000 cars, which equals \$5 million sales, to break even. Of course, firms do not want to just break even but want to make a profit. The logic of break-even analysis can easily be extended to include profits (P). Suppose Ajax decided that a 20 percent return on fixed costs would make the project worth the investment. Thus, Ajax would need 20% $\times$ \$1,500,000 = \$300,000 before-tax profit. To calculate how many units Ajax must sell to achieve this level of profits, the profit figure (P) is added to fixed costs in the above formulas. (We will label the break-even point as BEP' to show that we are now computing unit and sales levels to obtain a given profit level.) In the Ajax example:

$$BEP'_{\text{(in units)}} = \frac{FC + P}{SP - VC}$$

$$= \frac{1,500,000 + 300,000}{5,000 - 3,500}$$

$$= \frac{1,800,000}{1,500}$$

$$= 1,200 \text{ units}$$

In terms of dollars,

$$BEP'_{\text{(in dollars)}} = \frac{FC + P}{1 - \dfrac{VC}{SP}}$$

$$= \frac{1,500,000 + 300,000}{1 - \dfrac{3,500}{5,000}}$$

$$= \frac{1,800,000}{1 - .7}$$

$$= \$6,000,000$$

Thus, Ajax must produce and sell 1,200 cars (sales volume of $6 million) to obtain a 20 percent return on fixed costs. Analysis must now be directed at determining whether a given marketing plan can be expected to produce sales of at least this level. If the answer is yes, the project would appear to be worth investing in. If not, Ajax should seek other opportunities.

Net Present Value Analysis

The profit-oriented marketing manager must understand that the capital invested in new products has a cost. It is a basic principle in business that whoever wishes to use capital must pay for its use. Dollars invested in new products could be diverted to other uses—to pay off debts, pay dividends to stockholders, or buy U.S. Treasury bonds that would yield economic benefits to the corporation. If, on the other hand, all of the dollars used to finance a new product have to be borrowed from lenders outside the corporation, interest has to be paid on the loan.

One of the best ways to analyze the financial aspects of a marketing alternative is *net present value* analysis. This method employs a discounted cash flow, which takes into account the time value of money and its price to the borrower. The following example will illustrate this method.

To compute the net present value of an investment proposal, the cost of capital must be estimated. The cost of capital can be defined as the required rate of return on an investment that would leave the owners of the firm as well off as if the project was not undertaken. Thus, it is the minimum percentage return on investment that a project must make to be worth undertaking. There are many methods of estimating the cost of capital. However, because these methods are not the concern of this text, we will simply assume that the cost of capital for the Ajax Corporation has been determined to be 10 percent.[1] Again, it should be noted that once the cost of capital is determined, it becomes the minimum rate of return required for an investment—a type of cutoff point. However, some firms in selecting their new product investments select a minimum rate of return that is above the cost of capital figure to allow for errors in judgment or measurement.

The Ajax Corporation is considering a proposal to market instant-developing movie film. After conducting considerable marketing research, sales were projected to be $1 million per year. In addition, the finance department compiled the following information concerning the projects:

New equipment needed	$700,000
Useful life of equipment	10 years
Depreciation	10% per year
Salvage value	$100,000
Cost of goods and expenses	$700,000 per year
Cost of capital	10%
Tax rate	50%

To compute the net present value of this project, the net cash flow for each year of the project must first be determined. This can be done in four steps:

1. Sales − Cost of goods and expenses = Gross income or

$$\$1,000,000 - 700,000 = \$300,000$$

2. Gross income − Depreciation = Taxable income or

$$\$300,000 - (10\% \times 600,000) = \$240,000$$

3. Taxable income − Tax = Net income or

$$\$240,000 - (50\% \times 240,000) = \$120,000$$

4. Net income + Depreciation = Net cash flow or

$$\$120,000 + 60,000 = \$180,000 \text{ per year}$$

Because the cost of capital is 10 percent, this figure is used to discount the net cash flows for each year. To illustrate, the $180,000 received at the end of the first year would be discounted by the factor $1/(1 + 0.10)$, which would be $180,000 \times 0.9091 = \$163,638$; the $180,000 received at the end of the second year would be discounted by the factor $1/(1 + 0.10)^2$, which would be $180,000 \times 0.8264 = \$148,752$, and so on. (Most finance textbooks have present value tables that can be used to simplify the computations.) The table that follows shows the present value computations for the 10-year project. It should be noted that the net cash flow for year 10 is $280,000 because there is an additional $100,000 inflow from salvage value.

Thus, at a discount rate of 10 percent, the present value of the net cash flow from new product investment is greater than the $700,000 outlay required, and so the decision can be considered profitable by this standard. Here the net present value is $444,560, which is the difference between the $700,000 investment outlay and the $1,144,560 discounted cash

Year	Net Cash Flow	0.10 Discount Factor	Present Value
1	$ 180,000	0.9091	$ 163,638
2	180,000	0.8264	148,752
3	180,000	0.7513	135,234
4	180,000	0.6830	122,940
5	180,000	0.6209	111,762
6	180,000	0.5645	101,610
7	180,000	0.5132	92,376
8	180,000	0.4665	83,970
9	180,000	0.4241	76,338
10	280,000	0.3855	107,940
Total	$1,900,000		$1,144,560

flow. The *present value ratio* is nothing more than the present value of the net cash flow divided by the cash investment. If this ratio is 1 or larger than 1, the project would be profitable for the firm to invest in.

There are many other measures of investment worth, but only one additional method will be discussed. It is the very popular and easily understood payback method. *Payback* refers to the amount of time required to pay back the original outlay from the cash flows. Staying with the example, the project is expected to produce a stream of cash proceeds that is constant from year to year, so the payback period can be determined by dividing the investment outlay by this annual cash flow. Dividing $700,000 by $180,000, the payback period is approximately 3.9 years. Firms often set a maximum payback period before a project will be accepted. For example, many firms refuse to take on a project if the payback period exceeds three years.

This example should illustrate the difficulty in evaluating marketing investments from a profitability or economic worth standpoint. The most challenging problem is that of developing accurate cash flow estimates because there are many possible alternatives, such as price of the product and channels of distribution, and the consequences of each alternative

Years	8%	10%	12%	14%	16%	18%
1	.9259	.9091	.8929	.8772	.8621	.8475
2	.8573	.8264	.7972	.7695	.7432	.7182
3	.7938	.7513	.7118	.6750	.6407	.6086
4	.7350	.6830	.6355	.5921	.5523	.5158
5	.6806	.6209	.5674	.5194	.4761	.4371
6	.6302	.5645	.5066	.4556	.4104	.3704
7	.5835	.5132	.4523	.3996	.3538	.3139
8	.5403	.4665	.4039	.3506	.3050	.2660
9	.5002	.4241	.3606	.3075	.2630	.2255
10	.4632	.3855	.3220	.2697	.2267	.1911

must be forecast in terms of sales volumes, selling costs, and other expenses. In spite of all the problems, management must evaluate the economic worth of new product and other decisions, not only to reduce some of the guesswork and ambiguity surrounding marketing strategy development but also to reinforce the objective of making profits.

Ratio Analysis

Firms' income statements and balance sheets provide a wealth of information that is useful for developing marketing strategies. Frequently, this information is included in marketing cases, yet analysts often have no convenient way of interpreting the financial position of the firm to make sound marketing decisions. Ratio analysis provides the analyst an easy and efficient method for investigating a firm's financial position by comparing the firm's ratios across time or with ratios of similar firms in the industry or with industry averages.

Ratio analysis involves four basic steps:

1. Choose the appropriate ratios.
2. Compute the ratios.
3. Compare the ratios.
4. Check for problems or opportunities.

1. Choose the Appropriate Ratios

The five basic types of financial ratios are (1) liquidity ratios, (2) asset management ratios, (3) profitability ratios, (4) debt management ratios, and (5) market value ratios.[2] While calculating ratios of all five types is useful, liquidity, asset management, and profitability ratios provide information that is most directly relevant for marketing decision making. Although many ratios can be calculated in each of these groups, we have selected two of the most commonly used and readily available ratios in each group to illustrate the process.

Liquidity Ratios   One of the first considerations in analyzing a marketing problem is the liquidity of the firm. *Liquidity* refers to the ability of the firm to pay its short-term obligations. If a firm cannot meet its short-term obligations, there is little that can be done until this problem is resolved. Simply stated, recommendations to increase advertising, to do marketing research, or to develop new products are of little value if the firm is about to go bankrupt.

1. http://finance.yahoo.com/. Input the company symbol to receive financial ratios and other useful information. Under the "Company" heading, "Key statistics," "Competitors," and "Industry" are most useful for comparative ratio analyses.
2. *Annual Statement Studies.* Published by Robert Morris Associates, this work includes 11 financial ratios computed annually for over 150 lines of business. Each line of business is divided into four size categories.
3. *Industry Norms and Key Business Ratios.* Published by Dun & Bradstreet, this work provides a variety of industry ratios.
4. *Almanac of Business and Industrial Financial Ratios.* The almanac, published by Prentice Hall, Inc., lists industry averages for 22 financial ratios. Approximately 170 businesses and industries are listed.
5. *Quarterly Financial Report for Manufacturing Corporations.* This work, published jointly by the Federal Trade Commission and the Securities and Exchange Commission, contains balance-sheet and income-statement information by industry groupings and by asset-size categories.
6. Trade associations and individual companies often compute ratios for their industries and make them available to analysts.

The two most commonly used ratios for investigating liquidity are the *current ratio* and the *quick ratio* (or "acid test"). The current ratio is determined by dividing current assets by current liabilities and is a measure of the overall ability of the firm to meet its current obligations. A common rule of thumb is that current ratio should be about 2:1.

The quick ratio is determined by subtracting inventory from current assets and dividing the remainder by current liabilities. Since inventory is the least liquid current asset, the quick ratio deals with assets that are most readily available for meeting short-term (one-year) obligations. A common rule of thumb is that the quick ratio should be at least 1:1.

Asset Management Ratios   Asset management ratios investigate how well the firm handles its assets. For marketing problems, two of the most useful asset management ratios are concerned with *inventory turnover* and *total asset utilization.* The inventory turnover ratio is determined by dividing sales by inventories.[3] If the firm is not turning its inventory over as rapidly as other firms, it suggests that too much money is being tied up in unproductive or obsolete inventory. In addition, if the firm's turnover ratio is decreasing over time, it suggests that there may be a problem in the marketing plan, because inventory is not being sold as rapidly as it had been in the past. One problem with this ratio is that, since sales usually are recorded at market prices and inventory usually is recorded at cost, the ratio may overstate turnover. Thus, some analysts prefer to use cost of sales rather than sales in computing turnover. We will use cost of sales in our analysis.

A second useful asset management ratio is total asset utilization. It is calculated by dividing sales by total assets and is a measure of how productively the firm's assets have been used to generate sales. If this ratio is well below industry figures, it suggests that the firm's marketing strategies are less effective than those of competitors or that some unproductive assets need to be eliminated.

Profitability Ratios   Profitability is a major goal of marketing and is an important measure of the quality of a firm's marketing strategies. Two key profitability ratios are *profit margin on sales* and *return on total assets.* Profit margin on sales is determined by dividing profit before tax by sales. Serious questions about the firm and marketing plan should be raised if profit margin on sales is declining across time or is well below other firms in the industry.

FIGURE 1   Balance Sheet and Income Statement for Ajax Home Computer Company

Ajax Home Computer Company
Balance Sheet
March 31, 2008
(in thousands)

Assets		Liabilities and Stockholders' Equity	
Cash	$ 30	Trade accounts payable	$ 150
Marketable securities	40	Accrued	.25
Accounts receivable	.200	Notes payable	.100
Inventory	...430	Accrued income tax	40
Total current assets	...700	Total current liabilities	.315
Plant and equipment	.1,000	Bonds	.500
Land	.500	Debentures	.85
Other investments	...200	Stockholders' equity	.1,500
Total assets	$2,400	Total liabilities and stockholders' equity	$2,400

Ajax Home Computer Company
Income Statement
for the 12-Month Period Ending March 31, 2008
(in thousands)

Sales	$3,600
Cost of sales	
Labor and materials	2,000
Depreciation	.200
Selling expenses	.500
General and administrative expenses	80
Total cost	2,780
Net operating income	.820
Less interest expense	
Interest on notes	.20
Interest on debentures	.200
Interest on bonds	...300
Total interest	.520
Profit before tax	.300
Federal income tax (@40%)	...120
Net profit after tax	$ 180

Return on total assets is determined by dividing profit before tax by total assets. This ratio is the return on the investment for the entire firm.

2. Compute the Ratios

The next step in ratio analysis is to compute the ratios. Figure 1 presents the balance sheet and income statement for the Ajax Home Computer Company. These six ratios can be calculated from the Ajax balance sheet and income statement as follows:

Liquidity ratios:

$$\text{Current ratio} = \frac{\text{Current assets}}{\text{Current liabilities}} = \frac{700}{315} = 2.2$$

$$\text{Quick ratio} = \frac{\text{Current assets} - \text{Inventory}}{\text{Current liabilities}} = \frac{270}{315} = .86$$

Asset management ratios:

$$\text{Inventory turnover} = \frac{\text{Cost of sales}}{\text{Inventory}} = \frac{2,780}{430} = 6.5$$

$$\text{Total asset utilization} = \frac{\text{Sales}}{\text{Total assets}} = \frac{3,600}{2,400} = 1.5$$

Profitability ratios:

$$\text{Profit margin on sales} = \frac{\text{Profit before tax}}{\text{Sales}} = \frac{300}{3,600} = 8.3\%$$

$$\text{Return on total assests} = \frac{\text{Profit before tax}}{\text{Total assets}} = \frac{300}{2,400} = 12.5\%$$

3. Compare the Ratios

While rules of thumb are useful for analyzing ratios, it cannot be overstated that comparison of ratios is always the preferred approach. The ratios computed for a firm can be compared in at least three ways. First, they can be compared over time to see if there are any favorable or unfavorable trends in the firm's financial position. Second, they can be compared with the ratios of other firms of similar size in the industry. Third, they can be compared with industry averages to get an overall idea of the firm's relative financial position in the industry.

Figure 2 provides a summary of the ratio analysis. The ratios computed for Ajax are presented along with the median ratios for firms of similar size in the industry and the industry median. The median is often reported in financial sources, rather than the mean, to avoid the strong effect of outliers.[4]

4. Check for Problems or Opportunities

The ratio comparison in Figure 2 suggests that Ajax is in reasonably good shape financially. The current ratio is above the industry figures, although the quick ratio is slightly below them. However, the high inventory turnover ratio suggests that the slightly low quick ratio should not be a problem, since inventory turns over relatively quickly. Total asset utilization is slightly below industry averages and should be monitored closely. This, coupled with the slightly lower return on total assets, suggests that some unproductive assets should be eliminated or that the production process needs to be made more efficient. While the problem could be ineffective marketing, the high profit margin on sales suggests that marketing effort is probably not the problem.

FIGURE 2
Ratio Comparison for Ajax Home Computer Company

	Ajax	Industry Firms Median ($1–10 Million in Assets)	Overall Industry Median
Liquidity ratios			
Current ratio	2.2	1.8	1.8
Quick ratio	.86	.9	1.0
Asset management ratios			
Inventory turnover	6.5	3.2	2.8
Total assets utilization	1.5	1.7	1.6
Profitability ratios			
Profit margin	8.3%	6.7%	8.2%
Return on total assets	12.5%	15.0%	14.7%

Conclusion

This section has focused on several aspects of financial analysis that are useful for marketing decision making. The first, break-even analysis, is commonly used in marketing problem and case analysis. The second, net present value analysis, is quite useful for investigating the financial impact of marketing alternatives, such as new product introductions or other long-term strategic changes. The third, ratio analysis, is a useful tool sometimes overlooked in marketing problem solving. Performing a ratio analysis as a regular part of marketing problem and case analysis can increase the understanding of the firm and its problems and opportunities.

Additional Readings

Brealey, Richard A., Stewart C. Myers, and Geoffrey A. Hirt. *Fundamentals of Corporate Finance.* 5th ed. Burr Ridge, McGraw-Hill, 2007.

Ross, Stephen A.; Randolph W. Westerfield; and Jeffrey F. Jaffe. *Corporate Finance.* 7th ed. Burr Ridge, IL: Irwin/McGraw-Hill, 2005.

Ross, Stephen A.; Randolph W. Westerfield; and Bradford D. Jordan. *Fundamentals of Corporate Finance.* 7th ed. Burr Ridge, IL: Irwin/McGraw-Hill, 2006.

Section IV

Internet Exercises and Sources of Marketing Information

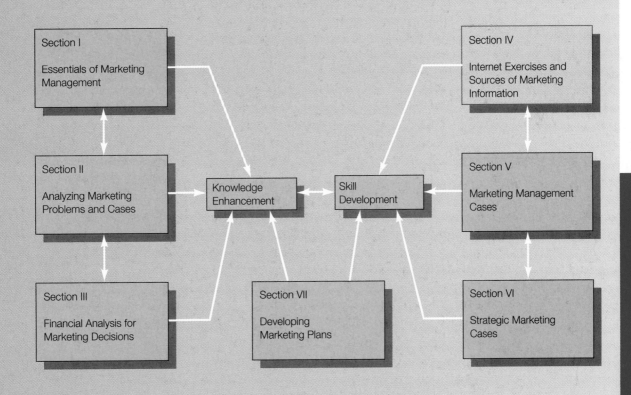

Internet Exercises

Charles Heath *University of Kentucky*

Exercise 1

Corporate Web Sites

Major corporations have Web sites. For the most part, the primary purpose of the corporate Web site is to communicate with the company's current and potential customers, investors, and channel partners. Because Web sites are used to attract new business, they are a good place to determine what the corporation sees as its mission and primary purpose.

For this assignment, visit the following corporate Web sites to find the business information requested.

IBM, http://www.ibm.com   Cisco Systems, http://www.cisco.com

Microsoft, http://www.microsoft.com   Ben and Jerry's, http://www.benjerry.com

1. Look for a statement of mission.
2. Investigate their company's history and changes over time.
3. Look for what the company claims to be its strengths (what are managers selling to investors) and distinctive competencies.
4. Identify organizational objectives. Does the firm make statements resembling those in Figure 1-3, in Chapter One?
5. Look at product lines and business units.

Exercise 2

Online versus Offline Retail Experiences

The growth of e-commerce has brought about a whole new shopping experience. It is easy to see that shopping online is different from shopping at a traditional "brick and mortar" store. But how is it different? What are companies doing to make the shopping experience similar and/or different?

Pick two retail sites on the Web that have famous "real world" counterparts. Examples:

Barnes and Noble, http://www.bn.com   Macy's, http://www.macys.com

Best Buy, http://www.bestbuy.com   Nordstrom, http://shop.nordstrom.com

Bloomingdales,   Office Max,
http://www.bloomingdales.com   http://www.officemax.com

Circuit City, http://www.circuitcity.com   Sears, http://www.sears.com

CVS Pharmacy, http://www.cvs.com   Target Stores, http://www.target.com

Eddie Bauer,   Toys R Us, http://www.toysrus.com
http://www.eddiebauer.com
                                             Victoria's Secret,
The Gap Online, http://www.gap.com   http://www.victoriassecret.com

JCPenny, http://www.jcp.com   Wal-Mart, http://www.walmart.com

1. Compare shopping at the virtual retailer to the physical version. What about the shopping experience is similar?
2. Now, contrast the two experiences. What does the online store offer that the brick and mortar store cannot? What does the brick and mortar store offer that the virtual store cannot?
3. What value does the online site add to the retailer as a corporation?
4. Now visit Kroger, http://www.kroger.com, or Jewel-Osco, http://www.jewelosco.com. What is different about the online presence of this store as compared to the two other retailers you visited earlier? What is the same? Why do you think both types of store

have chosen their particular strategy? If you were the CEO of either Kroger or Jewel, how would you utilize your Web presence?

Exercise 3

Consumer Decision-Making Process

When consumers make a purchase, they progress through a series of behaviors. The consumer decision-making (CDM) process describes those behaviors and the activities that take place at each stage. In order to increase sales, marketers are looking at the five stages and trying to find ways to influence consumers as they progress through the CDM process.

The Internet is the most recent tool that marketers are using to influence consumers. Discuss the impact of the Internet on the five stages of the CDM process. What happens differently, or how does the Internet use these processes to sell more efficiently?

Need Recognition

During the first stage, the consumer recognizes a need that can be satisfied by a purchase. In what ways are Internet marketers attempting to trigger consumers' recognition of needs? What are some things that Amazon.com, http://www.amazon.com, is doing to activate need recognition?

Alternative Search

Once consumers realize a need, they begin to search for potential ways to satisfy that need by finding information about the alternatives. Information is available from five primary sources of information: internal, group, marketing, public, and experimental sources. How can the Internet provide information for consumers? Which of the sources can the Internet influence? What impact does the information available at Edmunds, http://www.edmunds.com, have on consumers' alternative search?

Alternative Evaluation

Consumers next evaluate all the viable alternatives that can satisfy the need and compare them against each other. Consumers purchase the brand that best satisfies the need. Many times comparing products is difficult because of complex product features, numerous available choices, and physical distance between products in stores. Visit PriceRunner, http://www.pricerunner.com, and select any product category of your choice. How does this Web site help consumers compare product alternatives?

Purchase Decision

The consumer decides to make a purchase of the intended brand, purchase a different brand, or postpone the purchase. The Internet plays a major role in consumers' purchase decisions. What are some Internet features that influence purchase decisions? Revisit Amazon.com and discuss some of the ways the site influences the consumer's purchase decision. What role does UPS [http://www.ups.com] play in the purchase decision? Visit the site of Paypal, http://www.paypal.com, and discuss the role of digital cash, credit cards, cash, and checking accounts on the purchase decision.

Postpurchase Evaluation

The consumer reviews the purchase and the entire purchase process for the product. If consumers have doubts or second thoughts about a purchase, they experience postpurchase dissonance. What are Internet marketers doing online to help customers avoid dissonance? Go to the Ford Web site, [http://www.ford.com]. If you had a problem with the purchase of a Ford Explorer, what does the site do to help you alleviate or avoid dissonance? How does EBay.com, http://www.ebay.com, allow consumers to review the purchase process?

Exercise 4

Discovering Product Assortments Online

Most companies manufacture a wide range of products that they then offer to consumers. How companies that offer multiple products and product lines manage those offerings is of extreme importance to the overall success of the company.

Using the Internet, visit one of these corporate sites:

Proctor & Gamble, http://www.pg.com

Kraft Foods, http://www.kraft.com/default.htm

Gillette.com, http://www.gillette.com

General Motors, http://www.gm.com

General Mills, http://www.generalmills.com

Browse through the site and find where product offerings are discussed. How has the firm defined its product mix? How many different product lines does it offer? Discuss both the breadth and depth of the product mix. Pick three products and identify what type of product they are (convenience, shopping, or specialty) and why the company produces that type of product.

Exercise 5

Brand Equity on the Internet

Branding issues are of extreme importance to manufactures, traditional retailers, and customers. The growth of the Internet has increased the importance of a strong product brand name, especially due to trust and security issues. The brand name is used to differentiate products in both traditional and online retail situations.

Pick a company from the list below and write a few words that describe your thoughts about the company whose Web site you are about to visit:

Apple, http://www.apple.com

Baldwin Pianos, http://www.baldwinpiano.com

Ben and Jerry's, http://www.benjerry.com

Coke, http://www.coke.com

Fender Guitars, http://www.fender.com

IBM, http://www.ibm.com/ebusiness/

L.L. Bean, http://www.llbean.com

McDonald's, http://www.mcdonalds.com

Metropolitan Museum of Art, http://www.metmuseum.org

MTV, http://www.mtv.com

Ragu, http://www.eat.com

Reebok, http://www.reebok.com

Starbucks, http://www.starbucks.com

Target, http://www.target.com

Now, browse the company's Web site and get a good feeling for what information is presented at the site, how the site is organized, the theme, color scheme, images, and so on. Answer these questions:

1. What is the main purpose for the Web site?
2. What messages is the Web site trying to convey?
3. What did you think about the company before visiting the Web site, and how does your perception compare to the message conveyed by the Web site? Does the Web material match what you thought or is it different?
4. What is it about the Web site that is helping the company build brand equity?

Exercise 6

The Impact of Communities on Marketing

Communities are areas online where consumers who share interests gather and interact. A number of virtual areas function as a community through discussion lists, chat rooms, and message boards. The unique properties of online communities offer marketers opportunities to reach their customers in ways that never existed before.

1. Go to the Amazon.com, http://www.amazon.com/ home page and surf around. Describe the various attempts at building community that exist on the site. How does Amazon use reference groups to influence consumers at the Web site?
2. Visit the message boards at iVillage.com, http://www.ivillage.com, or WebMD, http://www.webmd.com, and pick a topic. How might a company benefit by advertising in a community? What would be the difference between sponsorship and advertising?
3. Take a tour of GM's Owner Center at the GM Web site, http://www.gm.com, by clicking on the Owner Center link on the navigation bar at the top of the page. What are some ways that a company can use community to develop new products or change existing ones?

Exercise 7

Pricing Issues on the Internet

One of the easiest places to see the impact of the Internet on marketing is by looking at its effect on pricing decisions and consumers' perceptions of prices. Since its inception, the World Wide Web (WWW) has developed the reputation as being *the* place to shop to get the lowest prices.

1. Why has this reputation developed?
2. Why might it be possible to charge lower prices online?
3. Are products really cheaper?

To answer this last question, choose two products and find them for sale online (books, CDs, and software work very well). Calculate the total price that would be charged to your credit card, then go to a "brick and mortar" retailer and find prices for the same product there. Make your comparisons.

1. Where is the cheapest place to buy the products that you have selected?
2. What costs are involved in determining where to buy your product?
3. Are there any nonfinancial costs to shopping online? To offline shopping?

Exercise 8

Selecting the Internet as a Distribution Channel

One very important decision that marketers need to make is which channels of distribution to use for its products or services. Four primary considerations need to be analyzed before making the distribution choice:

1. Distribution coverage required
2. Degree of control desired
3. Total distribution cost
4. Channel flexibility

Discuss the implications of using the Internet on these four considerations. To help analyze the possible implications of the Internet on these elements, visit the following sites and consider how each company distributes its products differently than traditional manufacturers do.

Dell Computers, http://www.dell.com

Gateway Computers, http://www.gateway.com

Peapod Groceries, http://www.peapod.com

Amazon.com, http://www.amazon.com/

Also visit the following sites and think about the role they play in the new breed of channel intermediaries:

Federal Express (FedEx), http://www.fedex.com

United Parcel Service (UPS), http://www.ups.com/us

Roadway Express, http://www.roadway.com

Yahoo.com, http://www.yahoo.com

IBM eBusiness, http://www.ibm.com/ebusiness/

Exercise 9

Internet Advertising

Marketers need to decide the best possible way to get the message about their products to those consumers who would be interested in making a purchase. Advertising is one of the most popular methods for companies to use to deliver their product messages. However, the marketing communications manager must not only decide where to advertise but also how to communicate the message. Advertising can accomplish four primary objectives:

1. Awareness
2. Comprehension
3. Conviction
4. Ordering

Discuss how Internet advertising can be used to accomplish these four objectives.

Awareness—Visit both Buy.com, http://www.buy.com, and Amazon.com, http://www.amazon.com/. What features of their home pages are attempting to trigger awareness in the consumer? Is one more effective at generating awareness?

Comprehension—Go to the Sony Web site, http://www.sony.com, select electronics, electronics again, then chose televisions from the drop-down list. How does this site help comprehension of the product offering?

Conviction—Go to CDnow.com, http://www.cdnow.com, and select the artist and title of your choice. What does CDnow do to try to convince customers to purchase a CD?

Ordering—Go to Google.com, http://www.google.com, and search for glasses. Notice the different ways that Google sells advertising space. How are sponsored links different form TV ads and magazine ads for a consumer who wants to order the product?

Exercise 10

The Adaptation of Services to the Internet

The way that services are offered to consumers is changing drastically because of the impact of the Internet. How have the following industries had to change to adapt to this technological change?

Banking—Go to the US Bank home page, http://www.usbank.com, and select Internet banking from the home page. Take a look at Citibank, http://www.citibank.com, eMortgages.com, http://www.emortgages.com, and Lending Tree, http://www.lendingtree.com.

Healthcare—Visit one of the following prescription drug sites: Viagra, http://www.viagra.com, Rogaine, http://www.rogaine.com, or Prozac, http://www.prozac.com. Try one of these sites: Dentists.com, http://www.dentists.com, Ask a Nurse, http://www. askanurse.com, or WebMD.com, http://www.webmd.com.

Insurance—Log on to Instant Quote, http://www.instantquote.com, and click on "how it works." How does this compare to the "old" way of buying insurance?

Travel—Visit one of the following travel sites: Cheaptickets.com, http://www.cheaptickets.com, Travelocity.com, http://www.travelocity.com, Expedia, http://www.expedia.com. How have the growth of these online reservation sites affected the travel agencies? What role do travel agencies *now* play in the marketplace?

Exercise 11

Marketing Communications Techniques in the Internet Age

A blog (Web log) is personal, contemporary, and sometimes interactive publishing of information on the Internet. Blogging has become an extremely popular activity on the Internet today. Blogs exist for every interest, every product, and every company. Many major companies have actively incorporated blogging into their marketing communications strategies.

Visit these corporate blogs:

Avon Romance Publishing (warning: adult themes), http://www. avonromanceblog.blogspot.com/

Garmin, http://garmin.blogs.com/

Google, http://googleblog.blogspot.com/

Harvard Law School, http://blogs.law.harvard.edu/

Southwest Airlines, http://www.blogsouthwest.com/

Visit these consumer-based blogs:

Gizmodo, the gadgets blog, http://Gizmodo.com/

Fast Food News, http://www.foodfacts.info/blog/

Strange New Products, http://www.strangenewproducts.com/

Cars! Cars! Cars! http://carscarscars.blogs.com/

1. How can the content of consumer blogs affect companies?
2. What marketing communications purposes would a company-supported blog serve?
3. How can companies use the content of blogs to help accomplish corporate objectives?
4. How might blogging by employees adversely affect a company? An employee?

Internet Sources of Marketing Information

Charles Heath *University of Kentucky*

Thousands of sites on the World Wide Web (WWW) can contain information about a company you are researching. For example, a search conducted on Google in June 2007 found 658,000,000 Web pages that contain the word "Microsoft"! That's up from 47,200,000 Web pages when searched in 2005. A similar search found over 7 million pages for Monsanto, a life sciences company. Though far fewer results, it would be impossible to search 7 million Web sites for information about the corporate subject of your marketing plan. More importantly, a very small percentage of those pages contain information that would be of any use!

This section is designed to provide you with a list of sources that would be helpful in finding the information necessary to write an insightful marketing plan. Different levels of information will be available about a company at these sites. To begin your search, visit your own library's Web site and see if they offer a tutorial on doing business research on the Internet. One commercial site is Researching Companies Online [http://www.learnweb-skills.com/company/index.html]. It is very broad, covers many topics, and is a bit dated (circa 2004), but it may prove useful in getting you started. The business resource librarian at your university's library will be another very valuable resource! Please look beyond *this* list during your research and utilize other sources as well. Hopefully this list will help you save hours of time and eliminate the frustration sometimes associated with searching the Internet! Some of these sites may require you to register in order to use the useful parts of their sites.

Corporate Web Sites

The place to begin looking for information about a company is its Web site. The Web site can provide a wealth of information about what the company is doing in the marketplace and includes access to annual reports, press releases, and in some cases, dedicated space for student projects. Remember that corporate Web sites are also designed to attract investors and provide a great deal of investment level information for that purpose. Don't expect to find any company secrets though!

The vast majority of corporate sites have bought their own corporation domain name, such as www.microsoft.com, www.abc.com, and www.ibm.com. Others use abbreviated versions of their company name. Procter & Gamble, for example, is www.pg.com, and Ben and Jerry's is www.benjerry.com.

Search Engines and Directories

The enormous growth of the Web has placed a growing strain on the ability of search engines to adequately represent the total number of Web pages. Today the key to using search engines is efficiency not volume. For tips on understanding how search engines work and improving your search skills, visit "Web Searching Tips" on SearchEngineWatch.com, http://searchenginewatch.com/showPage.html?page=facts.

www.wikipedia.com—Though not exactly a directory, Wikipedia has become a favorite destination for students researching a topic. It is invaluable in that almost all topics are covered, but one must remember that content is written by unknown contributors and is often inaccurate, incomplete, or biased. Use it to get a base, then move on to more in-depth research.

www.altavista.com—This directory provides tons of possible results and has a new easy-to-use search tool.

www.google.com—Started as a project at Stanford, it is now the Web's leading search destination.

www.yahoo.com—The Internet's best directory, Yahoo! offers categorized and indexed results.

If you aren't satisfied with these three, pay a visit to "Top 100 Alternative Search Engines," http://www.readwriteweb.com/archives/top_100_alternative_search_engines_feb07.php, by Charles Knight. One hundred not enough? Try Mashable's list of "140+ Search Engines and Directories," http://mashable.com/2007/10/23/140-search-engines/, by Patric Herber.

Government Sites

The government, at both federal and state levels, collects a great deal of information about companies and industries. This information has always been available in the government references section of your university library. Now, the government has done an admirable job of creating access to this information via Internet sources. Here are a few of the useful government sites:

www.census.gov—The Census bureau details economic and social descriptors. It includes a handy population tool on the front page.

www.commerce.gov—The Commerce Department Web site contains useful legislative information pertinent to the external environment.

www.dol.gov—The Department of Labor home page links to a great deal of labor information, including the Bureau of Labor Statistics.

www.fedstats.gov—Fedstats offers statistics from over 100 federal agencies at one location.

www.loc.gov—The Library of Congress is a vault of information about many subjects.

www.cia.gov—The CIA Web site features the *World Factbook,* an excellent resource for international information.

www.sec.gov—Quarterly and annual financial reports that must be filed with the SEC can be accessed here through the EDGAR database.

Business Publications

Since business publications focus their reporting on the business world, they are an excellent source for information about companies and today's marketplace. Almost all of the major business publications have Web sites that include stories from the current issue as well as some archives that can be searched. A few of the sites do require a membership to search their archives. These are among the more important business news sites:

www.adage.com—The world of advertising is at your mouse click with *Advertising Age's* Web site.

www.adweek.com—This is the home of *Adweek* and links to its partners *Brandweek* and *Mediaweek.*

www.barrons.com—*Barrons* online presents some market information for free and full-text versions of the print version to subscribers.

www.brandweek.com—Information covering the top brands, including the strategies to promote them and the people who create them can be found here.

www.business2.com—The Web version of the e-commerce magazine features Internet-related issues.

www.businessweek.com—Some of the articles are subscription only, but this site includes some good free information as well.

www.demographics.com—*American Demographics* magazine and its wealth of statistical data can be found here.

www.forbes.com—This is the place for access to the type of news, articles, and information that *Forbes* is known for.

www.pathfinder.com—Links not only to the *Time* magazine home page, but also to *Fortune* and *Money* home pages are here. On the *Fortune* site, follow the *Fortune* 500 link for company profiles, financial information, and industry comparisons.

www.salesandmarketing.com—The popular sales publication offers articles online. However, a magazine subscription is needed to search the archives.

www.sportsbusinessjournal.com—Street & Smith's *Sports Business Journal* is the leading edge of sports marketing information if you are a subscriber or register.

www.thomasregister.com—Information about thousands of U.S. companies, including contact information, can be located at this site.

www.usnews.com—More than just college rankings, the online version of the *US News and World Report* is a wealth of information.

Newspapers

Major newspapers also have a presence on the World Wide Web. Since they focus exclusively on news, they are an excellent online source of business information. While the major newspapers carry a good deal of national information, more regionalized newspapers focus on the business news in their immediate geographic region. Matching a company's headquarters with its local newspaper may result in more information than looking only at the large national papers.

National Papers

www.usatoday.com—America's newspaper has a user-friendly site that contains all the major business news.

www.wsj.com—THE business newspaper is a subscription-based service that has archives of its articles online. It might be a good idea to subscribe while you are in college.

www.newsindex.com—This news only search engine looks through more than 250 newspapers online and retrieves all matches to your search request.

Large City Papers

www.nyt.com—*The New York Times* maintains its class and informative content online.

www.chicagotribune.com—The Windy City's newspaper makes it easy to search and find corporate information.

www.washingtonpost.com—From the nation's capital, the *Washington Post* is rich in politically based business news.

International Papers

www.sunday-times.co.uk—Get an international flavor by searching through London's source of business information.

www.financialtimes—If you want international business information, you must look at the *Financial Times*.

Regional Papers

http://dir.yahoo.com/News_and_Media/Newspapers/By_Region/U_S_States/—This site lists regional newspapers by the state in which they are published.

General Business Sites

In addition to print media and newspapers, a number of Web sites provide researchers and investors with timely and in-depth business information. These sites provide news headlines and also allow the researcher to search the site using keywords.

www.bloomberg.com—A leading provider of market information, Bloomberg.com is a great source for business news, market data, and specific company information.

www.cnnmoney.com—A joint venture between the news network CNN and *Money* magazine, this site provides up-to-the-minute information about the marketplace and companies.

www.dailystocks.com—The Web's first and largest stock research site is a great way to get a feel for a company and their activities. Many additional links track stock movements and news.

www.fool.com—Home of the Motley Fool, this site gives you access to a great deal of information, once you register.

globaledge.msu.edu—The Michigan State University Center for International Business Education and Research (CIBER) maintains a directory of international Web resources.

www.hoovers.com—Possibly the best business information site on the Web, this site provides great information from Hoovers' business search function plus a business directory that links the researcher to even more business information.

knowledge.wharton.upenn.edu—You'll get access to articles and studies about many business topics—after you sign up for free.

www.marketwatch.com—Dow Jones provides business and investment news.

moneycentral.msn.com/investor—The investing page on MSN's Money section contains both market and corporate information.

www.msnbc.com—This joint venture between Microsoft and NBC Television has both event news and business information.

www.reuters.com—Reuters is a leading source of business information with a market focus.

Yahoo! Industry News—If you are doing a report on a specific industry, this page will guide you to all the recent news stories.

Internet Marketing Reference Sites

This collection of sites provides information about Internet marketing or e-commerce issues both B-to-B (business-to-business) and B-to-C (business-to-consumer).

www.ClickZ.com—ClickZ has numerous articles that focus on business use of the Internet. The stats page is particularly useful.

www.cnet.com—CNET central is an online information mecca. Information includes personal technology reviews, corporate news stories, downloads, and more.

www.ecommercetimes.com—Here you'll find *E-Commerce Times* offers "The Front Page" and "Everything You Need to Know about Doing Business Online."

www.emarketer.com—eMarketer.com offers good e-commerce information.

www.fastcompany.com—*Fast Company* and its magazine counterpart focus on the e-commerce field.

www.interactiveage.com—*Interactive Age* provides information about the technical side of the Internet.

www.jupiterresearch.com—This home of Jupiter's research projects offers tantalizing information, but registration and even purchase is necessary to reach it.

www.netb2b.com—Look here for business-to-business information for marketing and e-commerce strategists.

www.redherring.com—Red Herring has business information with a tech twist. Some of it is free information, but more in-depth information requires a subscription.

www.wired.com—*Wired News* contains information about business, culture, politics, and technology.

www.zdnet.com—ZDNet provides business information that focuses on technology firms and advances.

Compilation Sites

The following are sites that have been created and maintained as resources for business-based research.

UM Document Center, http://www.lib.umich.edu/govdocs/stats.html—The University of Michigan's Document Center maintains a listing of Web-based statistical resources including housing, labor, consumers, agriculture, and more.

Public Register's Annual Report Service, http://www.prars.com/—You can visit corporate Web sites or call their investor relations for an annual report or you can visit PRARS and they will send you free copies of annual reports—completely *free* with no printing costs or shipping costs!

Wall Street Executive Library, http://www.executivelibrary.com/—A compilation of business Web sites even larger than *this* one is available here.

Section V

Marketing Management Cases

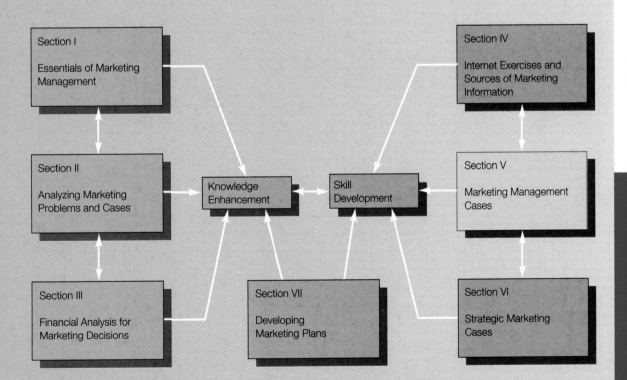

Section I — Essentials of Marketing Management

Section II — Analyzing Marketing Problems and Cases

Section III — Financial Analysis for Marketing Decisions

Knowledge Enhancement

Section VII — Developing Marketing Plans

Skill Development

Section IV — Internet Exercises and Sources of Marketing Information

Section V — Marketing Management Cases

Section VI — Strategic Marketing Cases

Note to the Student

The primary emphasis of the cases in this section is on marketing as a functional business or organizational area. As such, much of the analysis in these cases involves research and selection of appropriate target markets and the development and management of marketing mix variables.

We have divided these cases into six groups to help focus your analysis. These six groups include cases dealing with market opportunity analysis, product strategy, promotion strategy, distribution strategy, pricing strategy, and selected issues in marketing management. However, keep in mind that regardless of how the case is classified, you should not become too focused on a single issue or marketing mix variable and ignore other elements of marketing strategy.

Market Opportunity Analysis

1

McDonald's Corporation in the New Millennium

J. Paul Peter and Ashish Gokhale *University of Wisconsin–Madison*

Jack Greenberg, CEO of McDonald's Corporation, stared into the clear September skies thinking about the "Big Mac Attack." At one time, the term was an advertising slogan referring to a craving for a McDonald's Big Mac burger. However, "Big Mac Attack" now referred to McDonald's earnings declines in the late 1990s and early 2000s. Dynamic market expansion, new products, and special promotional strategies had made McDonald's Corporation a leader of the fast-food industry. However, sales growth in the United States had slowed to below the industry average in recent years. Jack Greenberg was trying to decide on a set of appropriate strategies for the future in order to reverse the declines and to stay ahead of competition.

The Fast-Food Industry

Years of profit drains and flat sales are driving fast-food chains to find new marketing strategies to compete in a mature market. While McDonald's and most other hamburger

J. Paul Peter is James R. McManus–Bascom Professor in Marketing and Ashish Gokhale was a Project Assistant at the University of Wisconsin–Madison.

© Pierre Roussel/Liason/Getty Images

chains continue discounting and offering a variety of new products to attract customers, they also seek to shed their "cheap and greasy" image with new store designs. Major competitors in the hamburger segment of the fast-food industry in order of annual sales are McDonald's, Burger King, Wendy's, and Hardee's.

Since these chains recognize the importance of drive-through customers (65 percent of sales), they are all trying to increase the speed of drive-through delivery. Strategies include using timers to encourage employees to prepare and deliver food faster, training employees in faster food preparation methods, having separate kitchens and food preparation facilities for drive-through customers, and even windshield responders that automatically bill customers. Drive-through sales are expected to grow three times faster than on-premise sales. It is estimated that increasing drive-through efficiency by 10 percent increases average fast-food restaurant sales by $54,000. The average fast-food restaurant has sales of about $560,000 per year.

Another segment of the fast-food industry is comprised of a number of nonhamburger fast-food restaurants. Major players in this segment include Pizza Hut, KFC (Kentucky Fried Chicken), and Taco Bell. Sales in these restaurants have grown faster than hamburger chains in recent years. A growing trend is the move by customers to nonhamburger sandwiches. Subway dominates the market with more than 13,200 U.S. outlets. Prepared meals and sandwiches available in supermarkets, convenience stores, and gas stations are competitors as are the variety of microwave meals available to consumers.

Another trend is the recognition of the importance of heavy users of fast-food restaurants. It is estimated that heavy users comprise 20 percent of customers but account for 60 percent of all visits. Some of these customers visit fast-food restaurants 20 times per month and spend up to $40 per day in them. Heavy users have been described as single males, under 30 years of age, who have working class jobs, love loud music, don't read much, and hang out with friends.

A major change in the fast-food industry is the increase in the fast-casual segment that includes restaurants like Boston Market, Panera Bread Company, and Atlanta Bread Company. These chains offer deli sandwiches and meals that are more upscale than traditional fast food, served in nicer restaurants with more comfortable surroundings, but faster than in traditional restaurants. It is estimated that the fast-casual sector is growing from 15 to 20 percent per year, while growth in the quick service sector is only about 2 percent a year. "People are willing to pay a couple dollars more for a better dining experience, yet don't want to sacrifice the convenience of quick service. Fast-casual combines all the elements for what the on-the-go consumer—which seems to be almost everyone these days—is looking for," said one analyst.[1]

Americans are eating out less often compared to previous years and eating habits are changing.[2] Though the recession is a major reason why folks aren't eating out as much at upscale restaurants, it's another story at fast-food restaurants. Many younger consumers are getting tired of fast food and are thinking about their health. There seems to be a growing dissatisfaction with the quality aspect of the McDonald's and Burger Kings of the world. It's not just young adults who are turning away from fast food. Baby boomers are also looking for "better" alternatives and fast food is not as appealing to this large group who frequently eat out.

McDonald's Corporation

McDonald's systemwide sales for 2001 were over $40 billion, but net income shrunk 17 percent to $1.64 billion, as shown in the exhibit. McDonald's U.S. market share remained above that of competitors, but grew more slowly. Its share was up 2.2 percent in 2000 compared to 2.7 percent growth for Burger King Corp. and 2.5 percent for Wendy's International.[3]

EXHIBIT   McDonald's Corporation Summary of Financial Data 1997–2001

Dollars in Millions, Except per Share Data	2001	2000	1999	1998	1997
Franchised sales	$ 24,838	24,463	23,830	22,330	20,863
Company-operated sales	$ 11,040	10,467	9,512	8,895	8,136
Affiliated sales	$ 4,752	5,251	5,149	4,754	4,639
Total Systemwide Sales	$ 40,630	40,181	38,491	35,979	33,638
Total revenues	$ 14,870	14,243	13,259	12,421	11,409
Operating income	$ 2,697	3,330	3,320	2,762	2,808
Income before taxes	$ 2,330	2,882	2,884	2,307	2,407
Net income	$ 1,637	1,977	1,948	1,550	1,642
Cash provided by operations	$ 2,688	2,751	3,009	2,766	2,442
Capital expenditures	$ 1,906	1,945	1,868	1,879	2,111
Free cash flow	$ 782	806	1,141	887	331
Treasury stock purchases	$ 1,090	2,002	933	1,162	765
Financial position at year end					
Total assets	$ 22,535	21,684	20,983	19,784	18,242
Total debt	$ 8,918	8,474	7,252	7,043	6,463
Total shareholders' equity	$ 9,488	9,204	9,639	9,465	8,852
Shares outstanding IN MILLIONS	1,280.7	1,304.9	1,350.8	1,356.2	1,371.4
Total Systemwide Restaurants	30,093	28,707	26,309	24,513	22,928

[1]Mitchell Speiser, analyst at Lehman Brothers.
[2]Harris Interactive, December 2001.
[3]Kate MacArthur, *Advertising Age,* Mar. 18, 2002.

Looking for hits to reverse earnings declines, McDonald's accelerated plans for "New Tastes Menu" items.[4] Products for limited-time offers included a fried chicken sandwich of tenderloin strips under the Chicken Selects name, a new grilled chicken sandwich, a brownie, a pork tenderloin sandwich, and a Philly cheese steak sandwich. Facing competitors' chicken sandwiches, like Wendy's Spicy Chicken Filet and Burger King's Chicken Whopper, McDonald's put chicken menu items at the forefront of its offerings. The chain also added a chicken-honey biscuit item to its menu. Other entries included a breakfast steak burrito similar to an existing sausage version, hot dog McNuggets for kids, and an Italian-style burger similar to the Chicken Parmesan. The McRib sandwich was reintroduced.

McDonald's advertising message focused on tasty and nutritious food, friendly folks, and fun. The company invested heavily in advertising its product and improving its public image. McDonald's annual Charity Christmas Parade in Chicago and its Ronald McDonald House charity provided the company with a positive corporate image. Much of its promotional budget was spent on games, giveaways and deals, including Monopoly II, Scrabble, a Kraft salad dressing give-away, Happy Meals, plush toys, in-store kid videos, and various Big Mac–related deals.

McDonald's opened its first domestic McCafe with the expectation that the gourmet coffee shop would move it closer to its goal of doubling sales at existing U.S. restaurants over the next decade.[5] The 32-seat McCafe occupies a 900-square-foot space that shares an entrance with a traditional McDonald's restaurant. The menu features a selection of specialty drinks, including cappuccinos, lattes, teas, and fruit smoothies served via a limited service front counter. Enhancing the coffee bar is a glass display case filled with a variety of high-end cakes, pastries, cookies and soft pretzels. Customers can place carryout orders that are packaged in disposable containers. If patrons opt to dine in the cafe, all drinks and food items are served on china with stainless steel flatware. McCafe originated in Australia in 1993 and has grown to more than 300 units in 17 countries. The gourmet coffee concept was created to be placed within or adjacent to existing McDonald's restaurants. McDonald's estimates that the new concept will boost sales by 15 percent. At McCafe, cappuccino drinks start at $2.49 featuring a coffee imported from Italy. The drink menu includes specialty coffees, listed as "Caramel Cream Steamer," "French Vanilla" and "Milky Way." The pastries, including tiramisu, cheesecake, apple tart and muffins, range in price from $1.59 to $2.59. Many of the items are baked on-site and the others are prepared daily by various local suppliers. In addition to three on-premise bakers, the cafe has a staff of 15 with about six employees working each shift. Created to enhance an upscale coffee shop environment, the cafe's decor features lace curtains, mahogany accents, a leather couch, an antique mirror, wall sconces, and fresh flowers.

Major Competitors in the Hamburger Segment

McDonald's has three major competitors in the hamburger segment. These include Burger King, Hardee's and Wendy's. Both Burger King and Wendy's have had small gains in market share while Hardee's lost share.

Burger King Corp.

Burger King Corp., in its ongoing effort to increase sales and market share, offered a new salad line and a permanent array of value-priced offerings, endeavors already under way at its fast-food competitors. The nation's number 2 burger chain, hoping to show signs of a

[4]Bob Sperber, *Brandweek,* Mar. 11, 2002.
[5]*Nation's Restaurant News,* May 14, 2001.

turnaround in order to expedite its pending separation from parent Diageo PLC of London, debuted more than 10 new or improved products, including the Chicken Whopper, which officials said stimulated sales growth. The menu overhaul is one part of a major turnaround strategy engineered by Burger King's chairman and chief executive, John Dasburg, who joined the chain in 2000.

As part of BK's sweeping transformation program, restaurant operators had to make extensive kitchen and drive-through upgrades. The Chicken Whopper, which debuted in 2001, generated "an enormous amount of trial" that led to double-digit same-store-sales growth at restaurants. Burger King is developing a more permanent marketing strategy and moving away from its previous tactical approach, which revolved around the monthly changes in menu items and deals.

Hardee's

Hardee's parent, CKE Restaurants Inc., owns or franchises 2,784 Hardee's and 112 Taco Bueno restaurants and showed a 15 percent decline in net income in a recent quarter. The chain posted year-to-year quarterly declines of 4.8 percent in company-owned same-store sales. The efforts to reverse slowing but continuing sales erosion at Hardee's, the industry's number 4 burger chain, had dominated management's attention in its conversion of Hardee's to a format called "Star Hardee's."

The company attempted to reverse sliding sales by introducing new items on the menu and joining the price-promotion burger wars. The company tested individual item discounts at most of Hardee's company-owned units. Franchisees in selected markets offered sandwiches bundled with regular-sized French fries and a soft drink for $2.99. Other new Hardee's sales-spiking tactics included its midpriced sandwich option, the Famous Bacon Cheeseburger for $1.59, and a new Croissant Sunrise breakfast sandwich for $1.79. The chain hoped to increase breakfast sales by at least 2 percent; currently breakfast items account for approximately 10 percent of Hardee's sales.

CKE also owns or franchises 878 upscale fast-food chains, Carl's Jr. It rolled out a premium sandwich product that had first debuted on the Hardee's menu in 1994 and recently was second only to the Carl's Jr.'s $3.99 sirloin steak sandwich in trial markets.

Wendy's International

Wendy's has had the strongest same-store-sales gains of the major burger chains in recent years. Chain officials and Wall Street analysts attributed at least part of the growth to Wendy's line of four upscale salads called "Garden Sensations." The nation's No. 3 burger chain holds an enviable position—analysts consistently rank it ahead of chief rivals in quality, customer satisfaction, innovation, and unit-level sales. Citing Wendy's planned 30 percent boost in media outlays to an estimated $308 million in 2002 and its strong focus on in-store operations, one analyst stated, "This one-two punch looks like a formidable foe for rival chains to face this year."[6] Wendy's same-store sales were expected to grow 3 percent in 2002, eclipsing the 2 percent projections for Tricon Global Restaurants' Taco Bell and KFC, and a 1 percent to 2 percent projection for McDonald's Corp.

Wendy's product line includes four core menu items: burgers, chicken sandwiches, its value menu, and its Garden Sensations salads. The salad line is designed to provide custom taste comparable to salads offered by casual-dining chains and includes the $3.99 Chicken BLT, Taco Supremo, Mandarin Chicken, and $2.99 Spring Mix salads. The Garden Sensations line was expected to contribute 5 percent to total Wendy's sales.[7]

[6]Mark Kalinowski, restaurant analyst for Salomon Smith Barney.
[7]Merrill Lynch analyst Peter Oakes, January 2002.

Major Competition in the Nonhamburger Segment

The gradual shift of consumer preference toward hamburger substitutes has created strong competitors for McDonald's. Three of the major competitors offering nonhamburger fast foods are Pizza Hut, Kentucky Fried Chicken, and Taco Bell.

Pizza Hut

Pizza Hut dominates the pizza segment with 22 percent of all restaurant pizza sales in the country, with Domino's lagging far behind with about 11 percent of sales. Papa John's has steadily expanded to the point where it is the country's fourth largest pizza chain behind Little Caesars.

Pizza Hut is owned by Tricon Global Restaurants, which also owns KFC and Taco Bell. It scored a major success with its P'Zone, a portable, calzone-like item that company officials call "the pizza that actually sold out in test market."[8] The $70 million national product launch featured the P'Zone for $5.99, or two for $10.99. Each pie is made with a 12-inch traditional crust, a layer of sliced mozzarella cheese and a choice of three different ingredient combinations: pepperoni; a mixture of meats that includes pepperoni, sausage, beef and ham; or sausage with green peppers and red onions. The P'Zone exceeded expectations and drove same-store sales up 7 percent to 8 percent. Pizza Hut's latest effort was called "a well-executed, differentiated, yet value-oriented product that would drive traffic and sales over the next several periods"[9] by one industry analyst.

KFC

KFC (Kentucky Fried Chicken) operates 11,000 global outlets of which 5,400 are in the United States. Its recent strategies included a "Kids Lap Top Pack" meal program to attract more kids and families to its food offerings. KFC planned to introduce the meals as part of its new product lineup for 2002.[10] Roughly 80 percent of KFC's domestic stores signed up to offer the kids' meals, which featured more food and variety of choices. The meals are priced at $2.99 and offer 18 different food combinations. The kids' meal containers, designed to open as a laptop computer, featured colorfully illustrated interactive puzzles and games. The idea built upon the latest batch of kids' meals launched previously, which introduced an education theme with crossword puzzles, word searches, and mazes. KFC took away the staple of most kids meals—the plastic toy—after company research found that children, especially older ones, were not interested in them. Instead, the new meals included stickers or a paper-based prize. The chain doesn't expect the new meal to generate substantial returns immediately. "This is about brand building; it's not about building sales today,"[11] said a company spokesperson.

Other new products at KFC for 2002 included a meal of three spicy Blazin' Crispy Strips with a choice of side and a biscuit priced at $2.99 and the Blazin' Buffalo Twister sandwich and a beverage in the price range of $2.29 to $2.79. In fiscal 2001, KFC led its sister brands, Pizza Hut and Taco Bell, in same-store sales at U.S. company-owned stores, posting growth of 3 percent.

[8]Amy Zuber, *Nation's Restaurant News,* Feb. 11, 2002.
[9]John Ivankoe of J. P Morgan Securities in New York.
[10]Cynthia Koplos, KFC's director of marketing.
[11]Cynthia Koplos, KFC's director of marketing.

Taco Bell

The dramatic rebound in sales at Taco Bell and a 19 percent increase in 2001 profits were due to a strategy shift to higher-priced products, like the Grilled Stuft Burrito and Chicken Quesadilla.[12] Taco Bell's success with high-priced offerings proved that the brand could leverage its strengths to bring up the average meal price, as well as appeal to light and medium users.[13] Taco Bell planned to add more grilled extensions with higher quality tortillas, beef and beans, and sell them at non-discounted prices. Officials said Taco Bell would continue to experiment with ingredients, such as fish and pork, that are unique to fast food.

McDonald's Future

Jack Greenberg recognized the difficult task the company faced in trying to grow sales, market share and profits in a fiercely competitive industry. He recognized the strengths of competitors in the burger segment but also knew that other providers of fast food and other meals were quick to take advantage of changes in customer preferences and tastes. He knew he had to counter attack the "Big Mac Attack" and find market opportunities for McDonald's.

Discussion Questions

1. How are customer tastes changing in the fast-food industry? What impact do these changes have on McDonald's?
2. How well are these changes in customer tastes and preferences being reflected in competitive strategies in the industry?
3. What are McDonald's strengths and weaknesses and what conclusions do you draw about its future?
4. Should McDonald's develop a separate strategy for the heavy user segment of the fast food industry?
5. What should Jack Greenberg do to grow sales, profits, and market share at McDonald's?

---

[12]Amy Zuber, *Nation's Restaurant News,* Feb. 25, 2002.
[13]Salomon Smith Barney analyst Mark Kalinowski.

Case

2

South Delaware Coors, Inc.

James E. Nelson and Eric J. Karson *University of Colorado*

Larry Brownlow was just beginning to realize the problem was more complex than he thought. The problem, of course, was giving direction to Manson and Associates regarding which research should be completed by February 20, 1989, to determine market potential of a Coors beer distributorship for a two-county area in southern Delaware. With data from this research, Larry would be able to estimate the feasibility of such an operation before the March 5 application deadline. Larry knew his decision on whether or not to apply for the distributorship was the most important career choice he had ever faced.

Larry Brownlow

Larry was just completing his M.B.A. and, from his standpoint, the Coors announcement of expansion into Delaware could hardly have been better timed. He had long ago decided the best opportunities and rewards were in smaller, self-owned businesses and not in the jungles of corporate giants. Because of a family tragedy some three years ago, Larry found himself in a position to consider small business opportunities such as the Coors distributorship. Approximately $500,000 was held in trust for Larry, to be dispersed when he reached age 30. Until then, Larry and his family lived on an annual trust income of about $40,000. It was on this income that Larry decided to leave his sales engineering job and return to graduate school for his M.B.A.

The decision to complete a graduate program and operate his own business had been easy to make. While he could have retired and lived off investment income, Larry knew such a life would not be to his liking. Working with people and the challenge of making it on his own, Larry thought, were far more preferable to enduring an early retirement.

Larry would be 30 in July, about the time money would actually be needed to start the business. In the meantime, he had access to about $15,000 for feasibility research. While

This case was written by Professor James E. Nelson and doctoral student Eric J. Karson, University of Colorado. This case is intended for use as a basis for class discussion rather than to illustrate either effective or ineffective administrative decision making. Some data are disguised. © by the Business Research Division, College of Business and Administration and the Graduate School of Business Administration, University of Colorado, Boulder, Colorado 80309–0419.

there certainly were other places to spend the money, Larry and his wife agreed the opportunity to acquire the distributorship could not be overlooked.

Coors, Inc.

Coors's history dates back to 1873, when Adolph Coors built a small brewery in Golden, Colorado. Since then, the brewery has prospered and become the fourth-largest seller of beer in the country. Coors's operating philosophy could be summed up as "hard work, saving money, devotion to the quality of the product, caring about the environment, and giving people something to believe in." Company operation is consistent with this philosophy. Headquarters and most production facilities are still located in Golden, Colorado, with a new Shenandoah, Virginia, facility aiding in nationwide distribution. Coors is still family operated and controlled. The company issued its first public stock, $127 million worth of nonvoting shares, in 1975. The issue was received enthusiastically by the financial community despite its being offered during a recession.

Coors's unwillingness to compromise on the high quality of its product is well known both to its suppliers and to its consuming public. Coors beer requires constant refrigeration to maintain this quality, and wholesalers' facilities are closely controlled to ensure proper temperatures are maintained. Wholesalers are also required to install and use aluminum can recycling equipment. Coors was one of the first breweries in the industry to recycle its cans.

Larry was aware of Coors's popularity with many consumers in adjacent states. However, Coors's corporate management was seen by some consumers to hold antiunion beliefs (because of a labor disagreement at the brewery some 10 years ago and the brewery's current use of a nonunion labor force). Some other consumers perceived the brewery to be somewhat insensitive to minority issues, primarily in employment and distribution. The result of these attitudes—plus many other aspects of consumer behavior—meant that Coors's sales in Delaware would depend greatly on the efforts of the two wholesalers planned for the state.

Manson Research Proposal

Because of the press of his studies, Larry had contacted Manson and Associates in January for their assistance. The firm was a Wilmington-based general research supplier that had conducted other feasibility studies in the south Atlantic region. Manson was well known for the quality of its work, particularly with respect to computer modeling. The firm had developed special expertise in modeling population and employment levels for cities, counties, and other units of area for periods of up to 10 years into the future.

Larry had met John Rome, senior research analyst for Manson, and discussed the Coors opportunity and appropriate research extensively in the January meeting. Rome promised a formal research proposal (Exhibits 1 and 2) for the project, which Larry now held in his hand. It certainly was extensive, Larry thought, and reflected the professionalism he expected. Now came the hard part, choosing the more relevant research from the proposal, because he certainly couldn't afford to pay for it all. Rome had suggested a meeting for Friday, giving Larry only two more days to decide.

Larry was at first overwhelmed. All the research would certainly be useful. He was sure he needed estimates of sales and costs in a form allowing managerial analysis, but what data in what form? Knowledge of competing operations' experience, retailer support, and consumer acceptance also seemed important for feasibility analysis. For example, what if consumers were excited about Coors and retailers indifferent or the other way around? Finally, several of the studies would provide information that could be useful in later

EXHIBIT 1 **Manson and Associates Research Proposal**

Mr. Larry Brownlow
1198 West Lamar
Chester, PA 12345

January 16, 1989

Dear Larry:

It was a pleasure meeting you last week and discussing your business and research interests in Coors wholesaling. After further thought and discussion with my colleagues, the Coors opportunity appears even more attractive than when we met.

Appearances can be deceiving, as you know, and I fully agree some formal research is needed before you make application. Research that we recommend would proceed in two distinct stages and is described below:

Stage One Research Based on Secondary Data and Manson Computer Models:

Study A: National and Delaware per Capita Beer Consumption for 1988–1992.
   Description: Per capita annual consumption of beer for the total population and population aged
      21 and over is provided in gallons.
   Source: Various publications, Manson computer model
   Cost: $1,000

Study B: Population Estimates for 1985–1995 for Two Delaware Counties in Market Area.
   Description: Annual estimates of total population and population aged 21 and over is provided for
      the period 1985–1995.
   Source: U.S. Bureau of Census, Sales Management Annual Survey of Buying Power, Manson
      computer model
   Cost: $1,500

Study C: Coors Market Share Estimates for 1990–1995.
   Description: Coors market share for the two-county market area based on total gallons consumed
      is estimated for each year in the period 1990–1995. This data will be projected from Coors's
      nationwide experience.
   Source: Various publications, Manson computer model
   Cost: $2,000

Study D: Estimated Liquor and Beer Licenses for the Market Area, 1990–1995.
   Description: Projections of the number of on-premise sale operations and off-premise sale
      operations is provided.
   Source: Delaware Department of Revenue, Manson computer model
   Cost: $1,000

Study E: Beer Taxes Paid by Delaware Wholesalers for 1987 and 1988 in the Market Area.
   Description: Beer taxes paid by each of the six presently operating competing beer wholesalers is
      provided. This can be converted to gallons sold by applying the state gallonage tax rate (6 cents
      per gallon).
   Source: Delaware Department of Revenue
   Cost: $200

Study F: Financial Statement Summary of Wine, Liquor, and Beer Wholesalers for Fiscal Year 1986.
   Description: Composite balance sheets, income statements, and relevant measures of performance
      provided for 510 similar wholesaling operations in the United States is provided.
   Source: Robert Morris Associates Annual Statement Studies 1987 ed.
   Cost: $49.50

(continued)

EXHIBIT 1   Manson and Associates Research Proposal   (*concluded*)

Stage Two Research Based on Primary Data:

Study G: Consumer Study
  Description: Study G involves focus group interviews and a mail questionnaire to determine
    consumer past experience, acceptance, and intention to buy Coors beer. Three focus
    group interviews would be conducted in the two counties in the market area. From these
    data, a mail questionnaire would be developed and sent to 300 adult residents in the
    market area, utilizing direct questions and semantic differential scale to measure attitudes
    toward Coors beer, competing beers, and an ideal beer.
  Source: Manson and Associates
  Cost: $6,000

Study H: Retailer Study
  Description: Group interviews would be conducted with six potential retailers of Coors beer in
    one county in the market area to determine their past beer sales and experience and their
    intention to stock and sell Coors. From these data, a personal interview questionnaire would
    be developed and executed at all appropriate retailers in the market area to determine
    similar data.
  Source: Manson and Associates
  Cost: $4,800

Study I: Survey of Retail and Wholesale Beer Prices
  Description: Study I involves in-store interviews with a sample of 50 retailers in the market area
    to estimate retail and wholesale prices for Budweiser, Miller Lite, Miller, Busch, Bud Light,
    Old Milwaukee, and Michelob.
  Source: Manson and Associates
  Cost: $2,000

Examples of the form of final report tables are attached [Exhibit 2]. This should give you a better idea of the data you will receive.

  As you can see, the research is extensive and, I might add, not cheap. However, the research as outlined will supply you with sufficient information to make an estimate of the feasibility of a Coors distributorship, the investment for which is substantial.

  I have scheduled 9:00 next Friday as a time to meet with you to discuss the proposal in more detail. Time is short, but we firmly feel the study can be completed by February 20, 1989. If you need more information in the meantime, please feel free to call.

Sincerely,

John

John Rome

Senior Research Analyst

EXHIBIT 2 **Examples of Final Research Report Tables**

(A) National and Delaware Resident Annual Beer Consumption per Capita, 1988–1992 (Gallons)

	U.S. Consumption		Delaware Consumption	
Year	Based on Entire Population	Based on Population over Age 21	Based on Entire Population	Based on Population over Age 21
1988				
1989				
1990				
1991				
1992				

Source: Study A.

(B) Population Estimates for 1986–1996 for Two Delaware Counties in Market Area

	Entire Population					
County	1986	1988	1990	1992	1994	1996
Kent						
Sussex						

	Population Age 21 and Over					
County	1986	1988	1990	1992	1994	1996
Kent						
Sussex						

Source: Study B.

(C) Coors Market Share Estimates for 1990–1995

Year	Market Share (%)
1990	
1991	
1992	
1993	
1994	
1995	

Source: Study C.

(D) Liquor and Beer License Estimates for Market Area for 1990–1995

Type of License	1990	1991	1992	1993	1994	1995
All beverages						
Retail beer and wine						
Off-premises beer only						
Veterans beer and liquor						
Fraternal						
Resort beer and liquor						

Source: Study D.

(E) Beer Taxes Paid by Beer Wholesalers in the Market Area, 1987 and 1988

Wholesaler	1987 Tax Paid ($)	1988 Tax Paid ($)
A		
B		
C		
D		
E		
F		

Source: Study E.

Note: Delaware beer tax is 6 cents per gallon.

EXHIBIT 2   Examples of Final Research Report Tables   *(continued)*

(F) Financial Statement Summary for 510 Wholesalers of Wine, Liquor, and Beer in Fiscal Year 1986

Assets	Percentage
Cash and equivalents	
Accounts and notes receivable net	
Inventory	
All other current	
Total current	
Fixed assets net	
Intangibles net	
All other noncurrent	____
Total	100.0

Ratios
Quick
Current
Debts/worth

Liabilities	Percentage
Notes payable—short-term	Sales/receivables
Current maturity long-term debt	Cost sales/inventory
Accounts and notes payable—trade	Percentage profit before taxes
Accrued expenses	based on total assets
All other current	
Total current	
Long-term debt	
All other noncurrent	
Net worth	____
Total liabilities and net worth	100.0
Income Data	
Net sales	100.0
Cost of sales	
Gross profit	
Operating expenses	
Operating profit	
All other expenses net	____
Profit before taxes	

Source: Study F (Robert Morris Associates, © 1987)

Interpretation of Statement Studies Figures

RMA recommends that Statement Studies data be regarded only as general guidelines and not as absolute industry norms. There are several reasons why the data may not be fully representative of a given industry:

1. The financial statements used in the *Statement Studies* are not selected by any random or statistically reliable method. RMA member banks voluntarily submit the raw data they have available each year, with these being the only constraints: (a) The fiscal year-ends of the companies reported may not be from April 1 through June 29, and (b) their total assets must be less than $100 million.

2. Many companies have varied product lines; however, the *Statement Studies* categorize them by their primary product Standard Industrial Classification (SIC) number only.

3. Some of our industry samples are rather small in relation to the total number of firms in a given industry. A relatively small sample can increase the chances that some of our composites do not fully represent an industry.

4. There is the chance that an extreme statement can be present in a sample, causing a disproportionate influence on the industry composite. This is particularly true in a relatively small sample.

5. Companies within the same industry may differ in their method of operations which in turn can directly influence their financial statements. Since they are included in our sample, too, these statements can significantly affect our composite calculations.

6. Other considerations that can result in variations among different companies engaged in the same general line of business are different labor markets; geographical location; different accounting methods; quality of products handled; sources and methods of financing; and terms of sale.

For these reasons, RMA does not recommend the Statement Studies figures be considered as absolute norms for a given industry. Rather the figures should be used only as general guidelines and in addition to the other methods of financial analysis. RMA makes no claim as to the representativeness of the figures printed in this book.

(continued)

EXHIBIT 2   Examples of Final Research Report Tables   (continued)

(G) Consumer Questionnaire Results

	Yes	No			Yes	No
Consumed Coors in the Past:	%	%	**Usually Buy Beer at:**			%

Attitudes toward Coors:	%
Strongly like	
Like	
Indifferent/no opinion	
Dislike	
Strongly dislike	
Total	100.0

Usually Buy Beer at:	
Liquor stores	
Taverns and bars	
Supermarkets	
Corner grocery	
Total	100.0

Weekly Beer Consumption:	%
Less than 1 can	
1–2 cans	
3–4 cans	
5–6 cans	
7–8 cans	
9 cans and over	
Total	100.0

Features Considered Important When Buying Beer:	%
Taste	
Brand Name	
Price	
Store location	
Advertising	
Carbonation	
Other	
Total	100.0

Intention to Buy Coors:	%
Certainly will	
Maybe will	
Not sure	
Maybe will not	
Certainly will not	
Total	100.0

Semantic Differential Scale—Consumers*

	Extremely	Very	Somewhat	Somewhat	Very	Extremely	
Masculine	___	___	___	___	___	___	Feminine
Healthful	___	___	___	___	___	___	Unhealthful
Cheap	___	___	___	___	___	___	Expensive
Strong	___	___	___	___	___	___	Weak
Old-fashioned	___	___	___	___	___	___	New
Upper-class	___	___	___	___	___	___	Lower-class
Good taste	___	___	___	___	___	___	Bad taste

Source: Study G.
*Profiles would be provided for Coors, three competing beers, and an ideal beer.

(H) Retailer Questionnaire Results

Brands of Beer Carried:	%
Budweiser	
Miller Lite	
Miller	
Busch	
Bud Light	
Old Milwaukee	
Michelob	

Beer Sales:	%
Budweiser	
Miller Lite	
Miller	
Busch	
Bud Light	
Old Milwaukee	
Michelob	
Others	
Total	100.0

(continued)

EXHIBIT 2   Examples of Final Research Report Tables   (concluded)

Semantic Differential Scale—Retailers*

	Extremely	Very	Somewhat	Somewhat	Very	Extremely	
Masculine	___	___	___	___	___	___	Feminine
Healthful	___	___	___	___	___	___	Unhealthful
Cheap	___	___	___	___	___	___	Expensive
Strong	___	___	___	___	___	___	Weak
Old-fashioned	___	___	___	___	___	___	New
Upper-class	___	___	___	___	___	___	Lower-class
Good taste	___	___	___	___	___	___	Bad taste

Intention to Sell Coors: % _____

Certainly will
Maybe will
Not sure
Maybe will not
Certainly will not   _____
   Total   100.0

Source: Study G.

*Profiles would be provided for Coors, three competing beers, and an ideal beer.

(I) Retail and Wholesale Prices for Selected Beers in the Market Area

Beer	Wholesale* Six-Pack Price (dollars)	Retail† Six-Pack Price (dollars)
Budweiser		
Miller Lite		
Miller		
Busch		
Bud Light		
Old Milwaukee		
Michelob		

Source: Study I.
*Price that the wholesaler sold to retailers.
†Price that the retailer sold to consumers.

months of operation in the areas of promotion and pricing, for example. The problem now appeared more difficult than before!

It would have been nice, Larry thought, to have had some time to perform part of the suggested research himself. However, there was just too much in the way of class assignments and other matters to allow him that luxury. Besides, using Manson and Associates would give him research results from an unbiased source.

Investing and Operating Data

Larry was not completely in the dark regarding investment and operating data for the distributorship. In the past two weeks he had visited two beer wholesalers in his hometown of Chester, Pennsylvania, who handled Anheuser-Busch and Miller beer, to get a feel for their operations and marketing experience. It would have been nice to interview a Coors wholesaler, but Coors management had strictly informed all of their distributors to provide no information to prospective applicants.

While no specific financial data was discussed, general information had been provided in a cordial fashion because of the noncompetitive nature of Larry's plans. Based on his conversations, Larry made the following estimates:

Inventory		$240,000
Equipment		
Delivery trucks	$150,000	
Forklift	20,000	
Recycling and miscellaneous equipment	20,000	
Office equipment	10,000	
Total equipment		200,000
Warehouse		320,000
Land		40,000
Total investment		$800,000

A local banker had reviewed Larry's financial capabilities and saw no problem in extending a line of credit on the order of $400,000. Other sources also might loan as much as $400,000 to the business.

As a rough estimate of fixed expenses, Larry planned on having four route salespeople, a secretary, and a warehouse manager. Salaries for these people and himself would run about $160,000 annually plus some form of incentive compensation he had yet to determine. Other fixed or semifixed expenses were estimated at:

Equipment depreciation	$35,000
Warehouse depreciation	15,000
Utilities and telephone	12,000
Insurance	10,000
Personal property taxes	10,000
Maintenance and janitorial	5,600
Miscellaneous	2,400
	$90,000

According to the wholesalers, beer in bottles and cans outsold keg beer by a three-to-one margin. Keg beer prices at the wholesale level were about 45 percent of prices for beer in bottles and cans.

Meeting

The entire matter deserved much thought. Maybe it was a golden opportunity, maybe not. The only thing certain was that research was needed, Manson and Associates was ready, and Larry needed time to think. Today is Tuesday, Larry thought—only three days until he and John Rome would get together for direction.

Case **3**

IVEY

Richard Ivey School of Business
The University of Western Ontario

Ruth's Chris: The High Stakes of International Expansion

Allen H. Kupetz and Ilon Alon *University of Western Ontario*

> "Well, I was so lucky that I fell into something that I really, really love. And I think that if you ever go into business, you better find something you really love, because you spend so many hours with it . . . it almost becomes your life."

> Ruth Fertel, 1927–2002
> Founder of Ruth's Chris Steak House

In 2006, Ruth's Chris Steak House (Ruth's Chris) was fresh off a sizzling initial public offering (IPO). Dan Hannah, vice president for business development since June 2004, was responsible for the development of a new business strategy focused on continued growth of franchise and company-operated restaurants. He also oversaw franchisee relations. Now a public company, Ruth's Chris had to meet Wall Street's expectations for revenue growth. Current stores were seeing consistent incremental revenue growth, but new restaurants were critical and Hannah knew that the international opportunities offered a tremendous upside.

With restaurants in just five countries including the United States, the challenge for Hannah was to decide where to go to next. Ruth's Chris regularly received inquiries from would-be franchisees all over the world, but strict criteria—liquid net worth of at least U.S. $1 million, verifiable experience within the hospitality industry, and an ability and desire to develop multiple locations—eliminated many of the prospects. And the cost of a franchise—a U.S. $100,000 per restaurant franchise fee, a 5 percent of gross sales royalty fee, and a 2 percent of gross sales fee as a contribution to the national advertising campaign—eliminated some qualified prospects. All this was coupled with a debate within Ruth's Chris senior management team about the need and desire to grow its international business. So where was Hannah to look for new international franchisees and what countries would be best suited for the fine dining that made Ruth's Chris famous?

The House that Ruth Built

Ruth Fertel, the founder of Ruth's Chris, was born in New Orleans in 1927. She skipped several grades in grammar school, and later entered Louisiana State University in Baton Rouge at the age of 15 to pursue degrees in chemistry and physics. After graduation, Fertel landed a job teaching at McNeese State University. The majority of her students were football players who not only towered over her, but were actually older than she was. Fertel taught for two semesters. In 1948, the former Ruth Ann Adstad married Rodney Fertel who lived in Baton Rouge and shared her love of horses. They had two sons, Jerry and Randy. They opened a racing stable in Baton Rouge. Ruth Fertel earned a thoroughbred trainer's license, making her the first female horse trainer in Louisiana. Ruth and Rodney Fertel divorced in 1958.

In 1965, Ruth Fertel spotted an ad in the *New Orleans Times-Picayune* selling a steak house. She mortgaged her home for $22,000 to purchase Chris Steak House, a 60-seat restaurant on the corner of Broad and Ursuline in New Orleans, near the fairgrounds racetrack. In September of 1965, the city of New Orleans was ravaged by Hurricane Betsy just a few months after Fertel purchased Chris Steak House. The restaurant was left without power, so she cooked everything she had and brought it to her brother in devastated Plaquemines Parish to aid in the relief effort.

In 1976, the thriving restaurant was destroyed in a kitchen fire. Fertel bought a new property a few blocks away on Broad Street and soon opened under a new name, "Ruth's Chris Steak House," since her original contract with former owner, Chris Matulich, precluded her from using the name Chris Steak House in a different location. After years of failed attempts, Tom Moran, a regular customer and business owner from Baton Rouge, convinced a hesitant Fertel to let him open the first Ruth's Chris franchise in 1976. It opened on Airline Highway in Baton Rouge. Fertel reluctantly began awarding more and more franchises. In the 1980s, the little corner steak house grew into a global phenomenon with restaurants opening every year in cities around the nation and the world (see Figure 1). Fertel became something of an icon herself and was dubbed by her peers "*The First Lady of American Restaurants.*"

Ruth's Chris grew to become the largest fine dining steak house in the United States (see Exhibit 1) with its focus on an unwavering commitment to customer satisfaction and its broad selection of USDA Prime grade steaks (USDA Prime is a meat grade label that refers to evenly distributed marbling that enhances the flavor of the steak). The menu also included premium quality lamb chops, veal chops, fish, chicken and lobster. Steak and seafood combinations and a vegetable platter were also available at selected restaurants. Dinner entrees were generally priced between $18 to $38. Three company-owned restaurants were open for lunch and offered entrees generally ranging in price from $11 to $24. The Ruth's Chris core menu was similar at all of its restaurants. The company occasionally

FIGURE 1   Ruth's Chris Restaurant Growth by Decade

Source: Ruth's Chris Steak House files.

Decade	New Restaurants (total)	New Restaurants (company-owned)	New Restaurants (franchises)
1965–1969	1	1	0
1970–1979	4	2	2
1980–1989	19	8	11
1990–1999	44	19	25
2000–2005	25	12	13
	93[2]	42	51

introduced new items as specials that allowed the restaurant to offer its guests additional choices, such as items inspired by Ruth's Chris New Orleans heritage.[1]

In 2005, Ruth's Chris enjoyed a significant milestone, completing a successful IPO that raised more than $154 million in new equity capital. In its 2005 annual report, the company said it had plans "to embark on an accelerated development plan and expand our footprint through both company-owned and franchised locations." In 2005 restaurant sales grew to a record $415.8 million from 82 locations in the United States and 10 international locations including Canada (1995, 2003), Hong Kong (1997, 2001), Mexico (1993, 1996, 2001) and Taiwan (1993, 1996, 2001). As of December 2005, 41 of the 92 Ruth's Chris restaurants were company owned and 51 were franchisee owned, including all 10 of the international restaurants (see Exhibit 2).

Ruth's Chris's 51 franchisee-owned restaurants were owned by just 17 franchisees, with five new franchisees having the rights to develop a new restaurant, and the three largest franchisees owning eight, six, and five restaurants respectively. Prior to 2004, each franchisee entered into a 10-year franchise agreement with three 10-year renewal options for each restaurant. Each agreement granted the franchisee territorial protection, with the option to develop a certain number of restaurants in their territory. Ruth's Chris's franchisee agreements generally included termination clauses in the event of nonperformance by the franchisee.[3]

A World of Opportunities

As part of the international market selection process, Hannah considered four standard models (see Figure 2):

1. Product development—new kinds of restaurants in existing markets
2. Diversification—new kinds of restaurants in new markets
3. Penetration—more of the same restaurants in the same market
4. Market development—more of the same restaurants in new markets

Ruth's Chris never seriously considered the product development model (new kinds of restaurants in existing markets). It had built a brand based on fine dining steak houses and,

---

[1]Ruth's Chris Steak House 2005 Annual Report, p. 7.

[2]Due to damage caused by Hurricane Katrina, Ruth's Chris was forced to temporarily close its restaurant in New Orleans, Louisiana.

[3]Ruth's Chris Steak House 2005 Annual Report, p. 10.

FIGURE 2
**Restaurant Growth
Paths***

*This diagram is based on
Ansoff's Product/Market Matrix,
first published in "Strategies
for Diversification," *Harvard
Business Review,* 1957.

	Restaurant Brands	
	Existing	**New**
Existing **Market** **New**	**Penetration** (more restaurants) *Same market, same product* **Market development** (new markets) *New markets,) same product*	**Product development** (new bands) *Same market, new product* **Diversification** (new brands for new market) *New product, new market*

with only 92 stores, the company saw little need and no value in diversifying with new kinds of restaurants.

Ruth's Chris also never seriously considered the diversification model (new kinds of restaurants in new markets). In only four international markets, Hannah knew that the current fine dining steak house model would work in new markets without the risk of brand dilution or brand confusion.

The penetration model (more of the same restaurants in the same market) was already underway in a small way with new restaurants opening up in Canada. The limiting factor was simply that fine dining establishments would never be as ubiquitous as quick service restaurants (that is, fast food) like McDonald's. Even the largest cities in the world would be unlikely to host more than five to six Ruth's Chris Steak Houses.

The market development model (more of the same restaurants in new markets) appeared the most obvious path to increased revenue. Franchisees in the four international markets—Canada, Hong Kong, Mexico, and Taiwan—were profitable and could offer testimony to would-be franchisees of the value of a Ruth's Chris franchise.

With the management team agreed on a model, the challenge shifted to market selection criteria. The key success factors were well-defined:

- *Beef-eaters:* Ruth's Chris was a steak house (though there were several fish items on the menu) and, thus, its primary customers were people who enjoy beef. According to the World Resources Institute, in 2002 there were 17 countries above the mean per capita of annual beef consumption for high-income countries (93.5 kilograms—see Exhibit 3).[4]

- *Legal to import U.S. beef:* The current Ruth's Chris model used only USDA Prime beef, thus it had to be exportable to the target country. In some cases, Australian beef was able to meet the same high U.S. standard.

- *Population/high urbanization rates:* With the target customer being a well-to-do beef-eater, restaurants needed to be in densely populated areas to have a large enough pool. Most large centers probably met this requirement.

- *High disposable income:* Ruth's Chris is a fine dining experience and the average cost of a meal for a customer ordering an entrée was over $70 at a Ruth's Chris in the United States. While this might seem to eliminate many countries quickly, some

[4]World Resources Institute, "Meat Consumption: Per Capita (1984–2002)," retrieved on June 7, 2006 from http://earthtrends.wri.org/text/agriculture-food/variable-193.html.

countries (e.g. China) have such large populations that even a very small percentage of people with high disposable income could create an appropriate pool of potential customers.

- *People go out to eat:* This was a critical factor. If well-to-do beef-eaters did not go out to eat, these countries had to be removed from the target list.
- *Affinity for U.S. brands:* The name "Ruth's Chris" was uniquely American as was the Ruth Fertel story. Countries that were overtly anti-United States would be eliminated from—or at least pushed down—the target list. One measure of affinity could be the presence of existing U.S. restaurants and successful franchises.

What should Ruth's Chris Do Next?

Hannah had many years of experience in the restaurant franchising business, and thus had both personal preferences and good instincts about where Ruth's Chris should be looking for new markets. "Which markets should we enter first?" he thought to himself. Market entry was critical, but there were other issues too. Should franchising continue to be Ruth's Chris's exclusive international mode of entry? Were there opportunities for joint ventures or company-owned stores in certain markets? How could he identify and evaluate new potential franchisees? Was there an opportunity to find a global partner/brand with which to partner?

Hannah gathered information from several reliable U.S. government and related Web sites and created the table in Exhibit 4. He noted that many of his top prospects currently did not allow the importation of U.S. beef, but he felt that this was a political (rather than a cultural) variable and thus could change quickly under the right circumstances, especially with what he felt was the trend toward ever more free trade. He could not find any data on how often people went out to eat or a measure of their affinity toward U.S. brands. Maybe the success of U.S. casual dining restaurants in a country might be a good indicator of how its citizens felt toward U.S. restaurants. With his spreadsheet open, he went to work on the numbers and began contemplating the future global expansion of the company.

"If you've ever had a filet this good, welcome back."

Ruth Fertel, 1927–2002
Founder of Ruth's Chris Steak House

EXHIBIT 1 **Fine Dining Steak Houses by Brand in the United States (2005)**

Source: Ruth's Chris Steak House files.

Company Name	Number of Restaurants
Ruth's Chris	92
Morton's	66
Fleming's	32
Palm	28
Capital Grille	22
Shula's	16
Sullivan's	15
Smith & Wollensky	11
Del Frisco	6

EXHIBIT 2   **Ruth's Chris Locations in the United States (2005)**

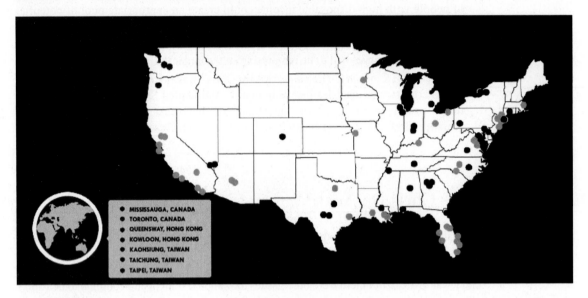

● MISSISSAUGA, CANADA
● TORONTO, CANADA
● QUEENSWAY, HONG KONG
● KOWLOON, HONG KONG
● KAOHSIUNG, TAIWAN
● TAICHUNG, TAIWAN
● TAIPEI, TAIWAN

◉ Company - owned

● Franchisee - owned

Source: Ruth's Chris Steak House files.

EXHIBIT 3   **Meat consumption per Capita* (in kilograms)**

Region/Classification	2002	2001	2000	1999	1998	Growth Rate 1998–2002
World	39.7	38.8	38.6	38.0	37.7	5.31%
Asia (excluding Middle East)	27.8	26.9	26.6	25.7	25.4	9.45
Central America/Caribbean	46.9	45.7	44.8	42.9	41.3	13.56
Europe	74.3	72.5	70.5	70.6	73.1	1.64
Middle East/North Africa	25.7	25.7	26.0	25.1	24.7	4.05
North America	123.2	119.1	120.5	122.2	118.3	4.14
South America	69.7	68.4	69.1	67.6	64.2	8.57
Sub-Saharan Africa	13.0	12.9	13.1	12.8	12.6	3.17
Developed countries	80.0	78.0	77.2	77.3	77.6	3.09
Developing countries	28.9	28.1	28.0	27.1	26.6	8.65
High-income countries	93.5	91.9	92.0	92.2	90.9	2.86
Low-income countries	8.8	8.6	8.4	8.3	8.2	7.32
Middle-income countries	46.1	44.6	43.9	42.7	42.3	8.98

*World Resources Institute, "Meat Consumption: Per Capita (1984–2002)," retrieved on June 7, 2006 from http://earthtrends.wri.org/text/agriculture-food/variable-193.html.

EXHIBIT 4   **Data Table**

Country	Per Capita Beef Consumption (kg)	Population (1,000s)	Urbanization Rate (%)	Per Capita GDP (PPP in US$)
Argentina	97.6	39,921	90%	$13,100
Bahamas	123.6	303	89	20,200
Belgium	86.1	10,379	97	31,400
Brazil	82.4	188,078	83	8,400
Chile	66.4	16,134	87	11,300
China	52.4	1,313,973	39	6,800
Costa Rica	40.4	4,075	61	11,100
Czech Rep	77.3	10,235	74	19,500
France	101.1	60,876	76	29,900
Germany	82.1	82,422	88	30,400
Greece	78.7	10,688	61	22,200
Hungary	100.7	9,981	65	16,300
Ireland	106.3	4,062	60	41,000
Israel	97.1	6,352	92	24,600
Italy	90.4	58,133	67	29,200
Japan	43.9	127,463	65	31,500
Kuwait	60.2	2,418	96	19,200
Malaysia	50.9	24,385	64	12,100
Netherlands	89.3	16,491	66	30,500
Panama	54.5	3,191	57	7,200
Poland	78.1	38,536	62	13,300
Portugal	91.1	10,605	55	19,300
Russia	51	142,893	73	11,100
Singapore	71.1	4,492	100	28,100
South Africa	39	44,187	57	12,000
South Korea	48	48,846	80	20,400
Spain	118.6	40,397	77	25,500
Switzerland	72.9	7,523	68	32,300
Turkey	19.3	70,413	66	8,200
UAE/Dubai	74.4	2,602	85	43,400
U.K.	79.6	60,609	89	30,300
United States	124.8	298,444	80	41,800
Vietnam	28.6	84,402	26	2,800

Source: World Resources Institute, "Meat Consumption: Per Capita (1984–2002)," retrieved on June 7, 2006 from http://earthtrends.wri.org/text/agriculture-food/variable-193.html and World Bank Key Development Data & Statistics, http://web.worldbank.org/WBSITE/EXTERNAL/DATASTATISTICS/0,,contentMDK:20535285~menuPK:232599~pagePK:64133150~piPK:64133175~theSitePK:239419,00.html, retrieved on June 7, 2006.

4

Coach Inc.: Is Its Advantage in Luxury Handbags Sustainable?

John E. Gamble *University of South Alabama*

In the six years following its October 2000 initial public offering (IPO), Coach Inc.'s net sales had grown at a compounded annual rate of 26 percent and its stock price had increased by 1,400 percent as a result of a strategy keyed to "accessible" luxury. Coach created the "accessible" luxury category in ladies' handbags and leather accessories by matching key luxury rivals on quality and styling, while beating them on price by 50 percent or more. Not only did Coach's $200–$500 handbags appeal to middle income consumers wanting a taste of luxury, but affluent consumers with the means to spend $2,000 or more on a handbag regularly snapped up its products as well. By 2006, Coach had become the best-selling brand of ladies' luxury handbags and leather accessories in the United States with a 25 percent market share and was the second best-selling brand of such products in Japan with an 8 percent market share. Beyond its winning combination of styling, quality, and pricing, the attractiveness of Coach retail stores and high levels of customer service provided by its employees contributed to its competitive advantage.

Much of the company's growth in net sales was attributable to its rapid growth in company-owned stores in the United States and Japan. Coach stores ranged from prominent flagship stores on Rodeo Drive and Madison Avenue to factory outlet stores. In fact, Coach's factory stores had achieved higher comparable store growth during 2005 and 2006 than its full-price stores. At year-end 2006, comparable store sales in Coach factory stores had increased by 31.9 percent since year-end 2005, while comparable store sales for Coach full price stores experienced a 12.3 percent year-over-year increase. In 2006 Coach products were sold in 218 full-price company-owned stores, 86 factory stores, 900 U.S. department stores, 118 locations in Japan, and 108 international locations outside Japan.

Going into 2007, the company's executives expected to sustain its impressive growth through monthly introductions of fresh new handbag designs and the addition of retail locations in the United States, Japan, and rapidly growing luxury goods markets in Asia. The company planned to add three to five factory stores per year to eventually reach 105 stores in the United States., add 30 full-price stores per year in the United States to reach

300, and add at least 10 stores per year in Japan to reach as many as 180 stores. The company also expected its licensed international distributors to open new locations in Hong Kong and mainland China. Other growth initiatives included strategic alliances to bring the Coach brand to such additional luxury categories as women's knitwear and fragrances. Only time would tell if Coach's growth could be sustained and its advantage would hold in the face of new accessible luxury lines recently lauched by such industry elites as Giorgio Armani, Dolce & Gabbana, and Gianni Versace.

Company History

Coach was founded in 1941 when Miles Cahn, a New York City leather artisan, began producing ladies' handbags. The handbags crafted by Cahn and his family in their SoHo loft were simple in style and extremely resilient to wear and tear. Coach's classic styling and sturdy construction proved popular with discriminating consumers and the company's initial line of 12 unlined leather bags soon developed a loyal following. Over the next 40 years, Coach was able to grow at a steady rate by setting prices about 50 percent lower than those of more luxurious brands, adding new models, and establishing accounts with retailers such as Bloomingdale's and Saks Fifth Avenue. The Cahn family also opened company-owned stores that sold Coach handbags and leather accessories. After 44 years of family management, Coach was sold to diversified food and consumer goods producer, Sara Lee.

Sara Lee's 1985 acquisition of Coach left the handbag manufacturer's strategy and approach to operations more or less intact. The company continued to build a strong reputation for long-lasting, classic handbags. However, by the mid-1990s, the company's performance began to decline as consumers developed a stronger preference for stylish French and Italian designer brands such as Gucci, Prada, Louis Vuitton, Dolce & Gabbana, and Ferragamo. By 1995, annual sales growth in Coach's best-performing stores fell from 40 percent to 5 percent as the company's traditional leather bags fell out of favor with consumers.

In 1996, Sara Lee made 18-year Coach veteran Lew Frankfort head of its listless handbag division. Frankfort's first move was to hire Reed Krakoff, a top Tommy Hilfiger designer, as Coach's new creative director. Krakoff believed new products should be based upon market research rather designers' instincts about what would sell. Under Krakoff, Coach conducted extensive consumer surveys and held focus groups to ask customers about styling, comfort, and functionality preferences. The company's research found consumers were looking for edgier styling, softer leathers, and leather-trimmed fabric handbags. Once prototypes had been developed by a team of designers, merchandisers, and sourcing specialists, hundreds of previous customers were asked to rate prototype designs against existing handbags. The prototypes that made it to production were then tested in selected Coach stores for six months before a launch was announced. The design process developed by Krakoff also allowed Coach to launch new collections every month. Prior to his arrival, Coach introduced only two collections per year.

Frankfort's turnaround plan also included a redesign of the company's flagship stores to complement Coach's contemporary new designs. Frankfort abandoned the stores' previous dark, wood paneled interiors in favor of minimalist architectural features that provided a bright and airy ambiance. The company also improved the appearance of its factory stores, which carried test models, discontinued models, and special lines that sold at discounts ranging from 15 percent to 50 percent. Such discounts were made possible by the company's policy of outsourcing production to 40 suppliers in 15 countries. The outsourcing agreements allowed Coach to maintain a sizeable pricing advantage relative to other luxury handbag brands in its full price stores as well. Handbags sold in Coach full-price stores ranged from $200–$500, which was well below the $700–$800 entry-level price charged by other luxury brands.

Coach's attractive pricing enabled it to appeal to consumers who would not normally consider luxury brands, while the quality and styling of its products were sufficient to satisfy traditional luxury consumers. In fact, a *Women's Wear Daily* survey found that Coach's quality, styling, and value mix was so powerful that affluent women in the United States ranked Coach ahead of much more expensive luxury brands such as Hermes, Ralph Lauren, Prada, and Fendi.[1] By 2000, the changes to Coach's strategy and operations allowed the brand to build a sizable lead in the "accessible luxury" segment of the leather handbags and accessories industry and made it a solid performer in Sara Lee's business lineup. With the turnaround successfully executed, Sara Lee management elected to spin off Coach through an IPO in October 2000 as part of a restructuring initiative designed to focus the corporation on food and beverages.

Coach Inc.'s performance proved to be stellar as an independent, public company. The company's annual sales had increased from $500 million in 1999 to more than $2.1 billion in 2006. Its earnings over the same timeframe improved from approximately $16.7 million to $494 million. By late 2006, Coach Inc.'s share price had increased nearly 15 times from the 2000 IPO price. Exhibit 1 presents income statements for Coach Inc. for fiscal 1999 through fiscal 2006. Its balance sheets for fiscal 2005 and fiscal 2006 are presented in Exhibit 2. Coach's market performance between its October 2000 IPO date and December 2006 is presented in Exhibit 3.

Overview of the Global Luxury Goods Industry in 2006

The world's most well-to-do consumers spent more than $105 billion on luxury goods such as designer apparel, fine watches and writing instruments, jewelry, and select quality leather goods in 2005. The global luxury goods industry was expected to grow by 7 percent during 2006 to reach $112 billion. Italian luxury goods companies accounted for 27 percent of industry sales in 2005, while French luxury goods companies held a 22 percent share of the market, Swiss companies owned a 19 percent share, and U.S. companies accounted for 14 percent of the luxury goods industry.

Growth in the luxury goods industry had been attributed to increasing incomes and wealth in developing countries in Eastern Europe and Asia and changing buying habits in the United States. Although traditional luxury consumers in the United States ranked in the top 1 percent of wage earners with household incomes of $300,000 or better, a growing percentage of luxury goods consumers earned substantially less, but still aspired to own products with higher levels of quality and styling. The growing desire for luxury goods by middle-income consumers was thought to be a result of a wide range of factors, including effective advertising and television programming that glorified conspicuous consumption. The demanding day-to-day rigor of a two-income household was another suggested factor because it led middle-income consumers to reward themselves with luxuries.

An additional factor contributing to rising sales of luxury goods was the growth of big box discounters such as Wal-Mart and Target. Discounters' low prices on everyday items had facilitated a "Trade up, trade down"[2] shopping strategy, whereby consumers could buy necessities at very low prices and then splurge on indulgences ranging from premium vodka to $4,000 Viking stoves. The combined effect of such factors had allowed spending on luxury goods to grow at four times the rate of overall spending in the United States.

[1]"How Coach Got Hot," *Fortune*, 146, no. 8 (October 28, 2002).
[2]As quoted in "Stores Dancing Chic to Chic, *Houston Chronicle*, May 6, 2006.

EXHIBIT 1   Coach Inc.'s Consolidated Statements of Income, 1999–2006 (in thousands, except share amounts)

	2006	2005	2004	2003	2002	2001	2000	1999
Net sales	$2,111,501	$1,710,423	$1,321,106	$953,226	$719,403	$600,491	$537,694	$500,944
Cost of sales	472,622	399,652	331,024	275,797	236,041	218,507	220,085	226,190
Gross profit	1,638,879	1,310,771	990,082	677,429	483,362	381,984	317,609	274,754
Selling, general and administrative expenses	874,275	738,208	584,778	458,980	362,211	275,727	261,592	248,171
Reorganization costs					3,373	4,569		7,108
Operating income	764,604	572,563	405,304	218,449	117,778	101,688	56,017	19,475
Interest income (expense), net	32,623	15,760	3,192	1,059	(299)	(2,258)	(387)	(414)
Income before provision for income taxes and minority interest	797,227	588,323	408,496	219,508	117,479	99,430	55,630	19,061
Provision for income taxes	302,950	216,070	152,504	81,219	41,695	35,400	17,027	2,346
Minority interest, net of tax		13,641	18,043	7,608	184			
Net income	$494,277	$358,612	$237,949	$130,681	$75,600	$64,030	$38,603	$16,715
Net income per share*								
Basic	$1.30	$0.95	$0.64	$0.36	$0.21	$0.20	$0.14	$0.06
Diluted	$1.27	$0.92	$0.62	$0.35	$0.21	$0.19	$0.14	$0.06
Shares used in computing net income per share:								
Basic	379,635	378,670	372,120	359,116	352,192	327,440	280,208	280,208
Diluted	388,495	390,191	385,558	371,684	363,808	337,000	280,208	280,208

*The two-for-one stock splits in April 2005, October 2003 and July 2002 have been retroactively applied to all prior periods.

Source: Coach Inc. 10-Ks.

EXHIBIT 2   Coach Inc.'s Balance Sheets, Fiscal 2005–Fiscal 2006 (in thousands)

ASSETS	July 1, 2006	July 2, 2005
Cash and cash equivalents	$143,388	$154,566
Short-term investments	394,177	228,485
Trade accounts receivable, less allowances of $6,000 and $4,124, respectively	84,361	65,399
Inventories	233,494	184,419
Deferred income taxes	78,019	50,820
Prepaid expenses and other current assets	41,043	25,671
Total current assets	974,482	709,360
Long-term investments		122,065
Property and equipment, net	298,531	203,862
Goodwill	227,811	238,711
Indefinite life intangibles	12,007	12,088
Deferred income taxes	84,077	54,545
Other noncurrent assets	29,612	29,526
Total assets	$1,626,520	$1,370,157
LIABILITIES AND STOCKHOLDERS' EQUITY		
Accounts payable	$79,819	$64,985
Accrued liabilities	261,835	188,234
Revolving credit facility		12,292
Current portion of long-term debt	170	150
Total current liabilities	341,824	265,661
Deferred income taxes	31,655	4,512
Long-term debt	3,100	3,270
Other liabilities	61,207	40,794
Total liabilities	$437,786	$314,237
Stockholders' equity		
Preferred stock: (authorized 25,000,000 shares; $0.01 par value) none issued		
Common stock: (authorized 1,000,000,000 shares; $0.01 par value) issued and outstanding 369,830,906 and 378,429,710 shares, respectively	$3,698	$3,784
Additional paid-in-capital	775,209	566,262
Retained earnings	417,087	484,971
Accumulated other comprehensive (loss) income	(7,260)	903
Total stockholders' equity	$1,188,734	$1,055,920
Total liabilities and stockholders' equity	$1,626,520	$1,370,157

Source: Coach Inc. 2006 10-K.

EXHIBIT 3 **Performance of Coach Inc.'s Stock Price, 2000–2006**

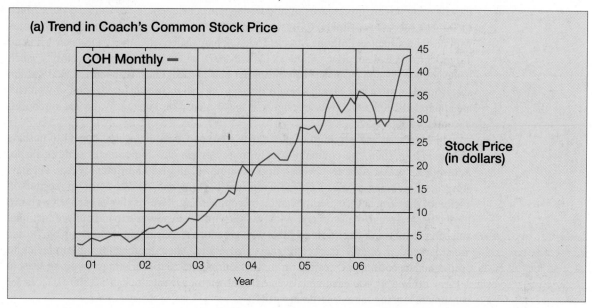

(a) Trend in Coach's Common Stock Price

(b) Performance of Coach's Stock Price Versus the S&P 500 Index

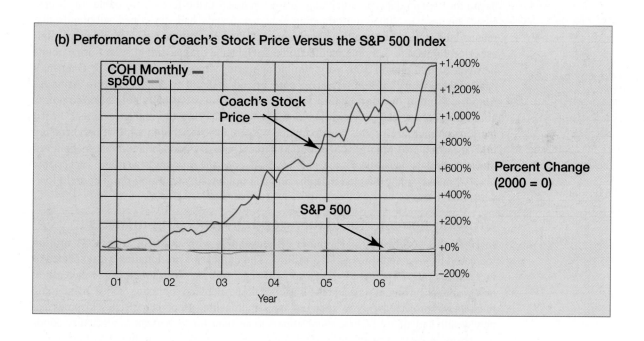

Both retailers and luxury goods manufacturers had altered their strategies in response to the changing buying preferences of middle-income consumers in the United States. Much of Target's success was linked to its merchandising strategy that focused on relationships with designers such as Philippe Starck, Todd Oldham, Michael Graves, and Isaac Mizrahi. Target's growth had not gone unnoticed by Wal-Mart, which in 2004 began to closely watch haute couture fashion trends for inspiration for new apparel lines. Wal-Mart hosted fashion shows in Manhattan and Miami's South Beach to launch its Metro 7 collection of women's apparel in fall 2005. Exsto was a designer-inspired menswear line that Wal-Mart introduced in summer 2006.

Wal-Mart also had begun to evaluate new store concepts that might appeal to upscale consumers. In 2006, the company was testing a stylish new Supercenter store in Plano, Texas, that stocked gourmet cheeses, organic produce, and 1,200 different wines. The new store also included a Wi-Fi coffee shop and a sushi bar. A Wal-Mart spokesperson explained the company's experimentation by commenting, "We've always been a top choice for the budget-minded customers. What we're trying to do now is expand our product line, and sell products more relevant to folks who are more discerning in their shopping."[3] Like Wal-Mart, other middle market retailers had altered their merchandising strategies to accommodate consumers' desires for luxury. During the 2006 Christmas shopping season, J. Crew offered $1,400 cashmere overcoats and Home Depot stocked $2,800 HDTVs for consumers looking for extraordinary gifts.

Manufacturers of the finest luxury goods sought to exploit middle-income consumers' desire for such products by launching "diffusion lines" that offered "affordable" or "accessible" luxury.[4] In 2006, most leading designer brands had developed subbrands that retained the styling and quality of the marquee brand, but sold at considerably more modest price points. For example, while Dolce & Gabbana dresses might sell at price points between $1,000 and $1,500, very similar appearing dresses under Dolce & Gabbana's "affordable luxury" brand—D&G—were priced at $400 to $600. Giorgio Armani's Emporio Armani line and Gianni Versace's Versus lines typically sold at price points about 50 percent less than similar-looking items carrying the marquee labels. Profit margins on marquee brands approximated 40 percent–50 percent, while most diffusion brands carried profit margins of about 20 percent. Luxury goods manufacturers believed diffusion brands' lower profit margins were offset by the growing size of the "accessible luxury" market and protected margins on such products by sourcing production to low-wage countries.

Growing demand for luxury goods in emerging markets

In 2004, the worldwide total number of households with assets of at least $1 million increased by 7 percent to reach 8.3 million. The number of millionaires was expected to increase another 23 percent by 2009 to reach 10.2 million. With much of the increase in new wealth occurring in Asia and the Eastern Europe, demand for luxury goods in emerging markets was projected to grow at annual rates approaching 10 percent. Rising incomes and new wealth had allowed Chinese consumers to account for 11 percent of all luxury goods purchases in 2004. The Chinese market for luxury goods was predicted to increase to 24 percent of global revenues by 2014, which would make it the world's largest market for luxury goods. In 2006, a number of prestigious Western retailers such as Saks Fifth Avenue had opened retail stores in China to build a first mover advantage in the growing market. Similarly, most luxury goods companies had opened stores in China's largest cities with Louis Vuitton operating 12 stores in 10 cities in 2006.

---

[3]Ibid.

[4]"Some Fashion Houses Bolster Lower Priced Lines," *The Wall Street Journal,* September 25, 2006.

Luxury goods producers were also opening retail stores in India, which was another rapidly growing market for luxury goods. In 2005, approximately 50,000 households earned more than 10 million rupees (approximately $250,000) and were the backbone of India's $500 million luxury goods market. The number of households in India with annual incomes over 10 million rupees was expected to double by 2010. As of 2006, Versace, Louis Vuitton, Dior, Chanel, Hugo Boss, and Tommy Hilfiger had opened retail locations in India. Gucci and Giorgio Armani had announced plans to open flagship stores in India by 2008. LVMH, which was the parent company of Louis Vuitton, Givenchy, Fendi, and others, planned to expand its network of 50 stores in 18 Indian cities to 100 luxury stores in 23 cities by 2008.

Counterfeiting

In 2006, more than $500 billion worth of counterfeit goods were sold in countries throughout the world. European and American companies that produced highly sought after branded products were most vulnerable to counterfeiting, with fakes plaguing almost every industry. Fake Rolex watches or Ralph Lauren Polo shirts had long been a problem, but by the mid-2000s, counterfeiters were even making knockoffs of branded auto parts and prescription drugs. Counterfeiting had become so prevalent that the Global Congress on Combating Counterfeiting estimated that 9 percent of all goods sold worldwide were not genuine. The European Union's trade commission categorized the problem as "nothing short of an economic crisis."[5] Interpol believed in 2005 that terrorist organizations such as al Qaeda commonly used counterfeiting to fund their activities since fake brands were as profitable as drugs and because there was very little risk of being prosecuted if caught. About two-thirds of all counterfeit goods were produced by manufacturers in China.

One problem in combating counterfeiting was the demand for knockoffs. In the United States, China, and Europe, vendors and consumers who traded in outdoor street markets knowingly bought and sold fakes and had little reservations about doing so. Using Great Britain as an illustration of the problem, experts estimated that 100 million fake luxury goods were sold in Britain in 2005 and that one in eight adult Britons had purchased a fake in the past year. The European Union and the Chinese government took a step toward combating piracy in 2005 with the signing of an agreement that would fine owners of outdoor bazaars in China if vendors were caught selling counterfeit goods. In addition, the agreement called for landlords to terminate the lease of any vendor caught selling counterfeit goods a second time. The Chinese government convicted more than 5,500 individuals of intellectual property rights crimes in 2005. However, many piracy and counterfeiting experts believed the problem would not subside until the Chinese government adopted a zero tolerance policy against fakes.

Coach's Strategy and Industry Positioning

In 2006, Coach Inc. designed and marketed ladies handbags, leather accessories such as key fobs, belts, electronics accessories, and cosmetics cases, and outerwear such as gloves, hats, and scarves. Coach also designed and marketed leather business cases and luggage. The company entered into a licensing agreement with the Movado Group in 1998 to make Coach-branded watches available in Coach retail stores. Coach entered into a similar agreement with the Jimlar Corporation in 1999 that gave Jimlar the right to manufacture and market Coach-branded ladies footwear. In 2006, Coach footwear was available in 500

[5]As quoted in "Gumshoe's Intuition: Spotting Counterfeits at Port of Antwerp," *The Wall Street Journal,* December 14, 2006, A1.

locations in the United States, including department stores and Coach retail stores. Marchon Eyewear became a licensee for Coach branded eyewear and sunglasses in 2003. Coach sunglasses were sold in Coach retail stores, department stores, and specialty eyewear stores. Coach frames for prescription glasses were sold through Marchon's network of optical retailers.

Handbags accounted for 67 percent of Coach's 2006 sales, while women's accessories accounted for 23 percent of the company's sales, men's accessories accounted for 2 percent of sales, and outerwear made up 2 percent of 2006 net sales. Business cases and luggage each accounted for 1 percent of company 2006 revenues. Royalties from Coach's licensing agreements with Movado, Jimlar, and Marchon accounted for 1 percent, 2 percent, and 1 percent of the company's 2006 net sales, respectively.

Coach held a 25 percent share of the U.S. luxury handbag market and was the second best-selling brand of luxury handbags in Japan with an 8 percent market share. Through 2006, Coach had focused on Japan and the United States since those two countries ranked numbers 1 and 2, respectively, in global luxury goods spending. Coach's sales in Japan had increased from $144 million in 2002 to more than $420 million in 2006, while the company's market share in the United States had more than doubled from the 12 percent it held in 2002.

Approach to Differentiation

The market research design process developed by Executive Creative Director Reed Krakoff provided the basis of Coach's differentiated product line, but the company's procurement process that selected only the highest quality leathers and its sourcing agreements with quality offshore manufacturers were additional contributors to the company's reputation for high quality. Monthly product launches enhanced the company's voguish image and gave consumers reason to make purchases on a regular basis. The company's market research found its best customers visited a Coach store once every two months and made a purchase every seven months. In 2006, the average Coach customer purchased four handbags per year, which had doubled since 2002. Lew Frankfort said the increase was attributable to monthly product launches that "increase the frequency of consumer visits" and women's changing style preference of "using bags to complement their wardrobes in the same way they used to use shoes."[6] A retail analyst agreed with Frankfort's assessment of the importance of frequent product introductions, calling it "a huge driver of traffic and sales [that] has enabled them to capture the . . . customer who wants the newest items and fashions."[7] Seventy percent of Coach's 2006 sales came from products introduced within the fiscal year.

The aesthetic attractiveness of Coach's full price stores, which were designed by an in-house architectural group under the direction of Krakoff, further enhanced the company's luxury image. A 2006 survey of 2,000 wealthy shoppers by the Luxury Group ranked Coach store environments tenth among luxury brands. The surveyed shoppers found little differences among the 10 highest-rated store atmospheres, with number 1 Louis Vuitton scoring 88.1 out of 100, number 2 Hermes scoring 87.9, Armani and Gucci scoring 86, Versace, Ferragamo, and Prada all scoring 85, and Burberry and Coach tying at 84 out of 100.

Coach sought to make customer service experiences an additional differentiating aspect of the brand. Coach had agreed since its founding to refurbish or replace damaged handbags, regardless of the age of the bag. In 2006, the company provided store employees with regular customer service training programs and scheduled additional personnel during peak

---

[6]As quoted in "Fashions Keep Retailer Busy," *Investor's Business Daily*, February 10, 2005, p. A04.
[7]Ibid.

shopping periods to ensure that all customers were attended to satisfactorily. Through the company's Special Request service, customers were allowed to order merchandise for home delivery if the particular handbag or color wasn't available during a visit to a Coach store.

Retail Distribution

Coach channels of distribution included direct-to-consumer channels and indirect channels. Direct-to-consumer channels included full price stores in the United States, factory stores in the United States, Internet sales, catalog sales, and stores in Japan. Wholesale accounts with department stores in the United States and in international markets outside Japan represented the company's indirect sales. Exhibit 4 provides selected financial data for Coach Inc. by channel of distribution.

EXHIBIT 4   Selected Financial Data for Coach Inc. by Channel of Distribution, Fiscal 2004–Fiscal 2006 (in thousands)

Fiscal 2006

	Direct-to-Consumer	Indirect	Corporate Unallocated*	Total
Net sales	$1,610,691	$500,810		$2,111,501
Operating income (loss)	717,326	313,689	(266,411)	764,604
Income (loss) before provision for income taxes and minority interest	717,326	313,689	(233,788)	797,227
Depreciation and amortization expense	43,177	5,506	16,432	65,115
Total assets	$743,034	$91,247	792,239	$1,626,520
Additions to long-lived assets	$70,440	$6,036	57,400	$133,876

Fiscal 2005

	Direct-to-Consumer	Indirect	Corporate Unallocated*	Total
Net sales	$1,307,425	$402,998		$1,710,423
Operating income (loss)	548,520	243,276	(219,233)	572,563
Income (loss) before provision for income taxes and minority interest	548,520	243,276	(203,473)	588,323
Depreciation and amortization expense	37,275	4,362	8,763	50,400
Total assets	$646,788	$69,569	$653,800	$1,370,157
Additions to long-lived assets	$70,801	$4,778	$19,013	$94,592

Fiscal 2004

	Direct-to-Consumer	Indirect	Corporate Unallocated*	Total
Net sales	$1,002,737	$318,369		$1,321,106
Operating income (loss)	403,884	178,390	(176,970)	405,304
Income (loss) before provision for income taxes and minority interest	403,884	178,390	(173,778)	408,496
Depreciation and amortization expense	30,054	3,509	6,537	40,100
Total assets	$328,530	$64,770	$666,979	$1,060,279
Additions to long-lived assets	$57,589	$3,884	$12,186	$73,659

Breakdown of Coach Inc.'s Unallocated Corporate Expenses, 2004–2006 (in thousands)

	Fiscal Year Ended		
	July 1, 2006	July 2, 2005	July 3, 2004
Production variances	$14,659	$11,028	$12,581
Advertising, marketing and design	(91,443)	(70,234)	(56,714)
Administration and information systems	(148,846)	(125,217)	(102,682)
Distribution and customer service	(40,781)	(34,810)	(30,155)
Total corporate unallocated	($266,411)	($219,233)	($176,970)

Source: Coach Inc. 2006 10-K.

In the United States, Coach products could be found in approximately 900 department stores, 218 Coach full price stores, and 86 Coach factory outlet stores. U.S. consumers could also order Coach products through either the company's Web site or its printed catalog. The company mailed about 4.1 million catalogs to strategically selected households in the United States during 2006 and placed another 3.5 million catalogs in Coach retail stores for customers to pick up during a store visit. Sales from catalogs were incidental since the catalogs were primarily used to build brand awareness, promote store traffic, and help shoppers evaluate styles before visiting a Coach retail store. Coach's Web site accomplished the same goals as its catalogs, but had become a significant contributor to overall sales. In 2006, the Web site had 40 million unique visitors and generated $54 million in net sales. The company also sent promotional e-mails to 55 million selected customers in 2006.

Full Price Stores   Coach's full price U.S. retail stores accounted for 54 percent of Coach's 2006 net sales. Beginning in 2003, full price stores were divided into three categories—core locations, fashion locations, and flagship stores. Under Coach's tiered merchandising strategy, the company's flagship stores carried the most sophisticated and highest-priced items, while core stores carried widely demanded lines. The company's fashion locations tended to stock a blend of Coach's best-selling lines and chic specialty bags. By 2006, the company had successfully graduated many core locations to fashion locations. Management believed Coach had remaining opportunities in the United States to move core stores to fashion stores and fashion stores to flagship stores.

Coach's site selection process placed its core and fashion stores in upscale shopping centers and downtown shopping areas, while flagship stores were restricted to high-profile fashion districts in cities such as New York, Chicago, Beverly Hills, and San Francisco. Even though flagship stores were "a beacon for the brand"[8] as Frankfort described them, the company had been very prudent in the number of flagship stores it operated since such stores, by definition, were required to be located on the world's most expensive parcels of real estate.

Factory Stores   Coach's factory stores in the United States were generally located 50 or more miles from its full price stores and made up about 19 percent of the company's 2006 net sales. About 75 percent of factory store inventory was produced specifically for Coach's factory stores, while the remaining 25 percent was made up of overstocked items and discontinued models. Coach's 10 percent to 50 percent discounts offered in factory stores allowed the company to maintain a year-round full-price policy in full price stores. Coach CEO Lew Frankfort believed discounted prices were critical to success in retailing since 80 percent of women's apparel sold in the United States was bought on sale or in a discount store. "Women in the U.S. have been trained to expect to be able to find a bargain if they either go through the hunt . . . or are willing to buy something after the season," said Frankfort.[9]

Coach had found that there was very little overlap between shoppers in full-price stores and factory stores. The company's market research found the typical full-price store shopper was a 35-year-old, college-educated, single or newly married working woman. The typical factory store shopper was a 45-year-old, college-educated, married, professional woman with children. The average annual spending in a Coach store by full-price shoppers was $1,100. Factory store shoppers spent about $770 annually on Coach products, with 80 percent spent in factory stores and 20 percent spent in a full-price store. The 80:20 ratio of spending also applied to full-price store customers. A retail analyst characterized the

---

[8]As quoted in "Coach's Split Personality," *Business Week,* November 7, 2005.
[9]As quoted in "Coach Sales Strategy Is in the Bag," *Financial Times,* April 18, 2006, p. 22.

difference between the two types of Coach customers as "one wants fashion first and the other is a discount shopper . . . There is no question it is a very different mindset."[10] Coach had found that its full-price customers and factory store customers were equally brand loyal.

Coach's factory stores had outperformed full-price stores in terms of comparable store sales growth during 2005 and 2006, with comparable factory store sales increasing by 31.9 percent during 2006 and comparable full price store sales increasing by 12.3 percent during the year. The company's impressive overall growth in comparable store sales was attributable, to some degree, to its policy of charting sales for every store and every type of merchandise on a daily basis. During holiday shopping periods, management received sales updates two or three times per day. The frequent updates allowed management to shift production to the hottest selling items to avoid stockouts.

The company's top-performing factory store during 2005 was its Woodbury Common outlet store located about 50 miles outside New York City. The store's 2005 sales of $20 million and estimated 2006 sales of $25 million made it as productive as the company's Madison Avenue flagship store. Some degree of Coach's success with its outlet stores resulted from its strategy that valued factory stores as much as full-price stores. The company was committed to providing factory store customers with service and quality equal to that provided to full-price customers. A May 2006 *Consumer Reports* review of outlet stores rated Coach number 1 in terms of merchandise quality and customer service.

At year-end 2006, Lew Frankfort stated that the company would add three to five factory stores per year until it reached 105 and 30 full-price stores per year to reach 300. Long-term, Frankfort believed North America could support 400 full-price Coach stores. Frankfort did not want factory outlet stores to grow too rapidly since "Our destiny lies in our ability to grow full-price stores."[11] Some analysts were worried that Coach's highly successful factory stores might some day dilute its image. A Luxury Institute analyst described the dilemma faced by Coach and luxury diffusion brands by commenting "To be unique and exclusive you cannot be ubiquitous."[12] Exhibit 5 shows Coach's growth in retail stores by type and geographic region between 2001 and 2006.

U.S. Wholesale   Wholesale sales of Coach products to U.S. department stores increased by 23 percent during 2006 to reach $232 million. Department stores were becoming less relevant in U.S. retailing with the average consumer spending less time in malls and shopping in fewer stores during visits to malls. The share of the U.S. retail market held by department stores declined from about 30 percent in 1990 to approximately 20 percent in 2000. However, handbags and accessories remained a better performing product category for such retailers. Coach had eliminated 500 department store accounts between 2002 and 2006. Macy's, Bloomingdale's, Lord and Taylor, Marshall Fields, Filene's, Dillards, Nordstrom, Saks Fifth Avenue, and Parisian were the highest-volume department store sellers of Coach merchandise in 2006.

International Markets

International Wholesale   Coach's wholesale distribution in international markets involved department stores, free-standing retail locations, shop-in-shop locations, and specialty retailers in 18 countries. The company's largest international wholesale accounts were the DFS Group, Lotte Group, Shila Group, Tasa Meng Corporation, and

---

[10]Ibid.

[11]As quoted in "Coach's Split Personality."

[12]As quoted in "Expansion into U.S.: Extending the Reach of the Exclusive Lifestyle Brands," *Financial Times*, July 8, 2006, p. 17.

EXHIBIT 5 Coach Inc.'s Retail Stores by Geographic Region, Fiscal 2001–Fiscal 2006

North America

Full-price company-owned stores	2006	2005	2004	2003	2002	2001
	218	193	174	156	138	121
Net increase vs. prior year	25	19	18	18	17	15
Percentage increase vs. prior year	11.5%	9.8%	10.3%	11.5%	12.3%	12.4%
Retail square footage	562,553	490,925	431,617	363,310	301,501	251,136
Net increase vs. prior year	71,628	59,308	68,307	61,809	50,365	42,077
Percentage increase vs. prior year	12.7%	12.1%	15.8%	17.0%	16.7%	16.8%
Average square footage	2,581	2,544	2,481	2,329	2,185	2,076

Factory stores	2006	2005	2004	2003	2002	2001
	86	82	76	76	74	68
Net increase vs. prior year	4	6	0	2	6	5
Percentage increase vs. prior year	4.7%	7.3%	0.0%	2.6%	8.1%	7.4%
Factory square footage	281,787	252,279	231,355	232,898	219,507	198,924
Net increase vs. prior year	29,508	20,924	(1,543)	13,391	20,583	16,414
Percentage increase vs. prior year	10.5%	8.3%	(0)	5.7%	9.4%	8.3%
Average square footage	3,277	3,077	3,044	3,064	2,966	2,925

Coach Japan

Total locations	2006	2005	2004	2003	2002	2001
	118	103	100	93	83	76
Net increase vs. prior year	15	3	7	10	7	6
Percentage increase vs. prior year	12.7%	2.9%	7.0%	10.8%	8.4%	7.9%
Total square footage	194,375	161,632	119,291	102,242	76,975	63,371
Net increase vs. prior year	32,743	42,341	17,049	25,267	13,604	7,229
Percentage increase vs. prior year	16.8%	26.2%	14.3%	24.7%	17.7%	11.4%
Average square footage	1,647	1,569	1,193	1,099	927	834

Other International

	2006	2005	2004	2003	2002	2001
International freestanding stores	21	14	18	n.a.	n.a.	n.a.
International department store locations	63	58	70	n.a.	n.a.	n.a.
Other international locations	24	22	27	n.a.	n.a.	n.a.
Total international wholesale locations	108	94	115	n.a.	n.a.	n.a.

n.a. Not available
Source: Coach Inc. 10-Ks.

EXHIBIT 6 Coach Inc.'s Net Sales and Assets by Geographic Region, Fiscal 2004–Fiscal 2006 (in thousands)

Source: Coach Inc. 2006 10-K.

	United States	Japan	Other International	Total
Fiscal 2006				
Net sales	$1,574,285	$420,509	$116,707	$2,111,501
Long-lived assets	266,190	298,087	3,684	567,961
Fiscal 2005				
Net sales	$1,253,170	$372,326	$84,927	$1,710,423
Long-lived assets	314,919	288,338	2,995	606,252
Fiscal 2004				
Net sales	$982,668	$278,011	$60,427	1,321,106
Long-lived assets	280,938	55,487	2,384	338,809

Imaginex. The largest portion of sales by these companies was to traveling Japanese consumers. Coach's largest wholesale country markets were Korea, Hong Kong, Taiwan, Singapore, Japan, Saudi Arabia, Australia, Mexico, Thailand, Malaysia, the Caribbean, China, New Zealand, and France. In 2006, international wholesale accounts amounted to $147 million.

Coach Japan   Coach products in Japan were sold in shop-in-shop department store locations, full-price Coach stores, and Coach factory stores. The company had 118 retail locations in Japan in 2006 although company managers believed Japan could support as many as 180 retail outlets. Coach's expansion plan for Japan called for at least 10 new stores annually, which would more than double its number of flagship stores to 15. Coach management believed the increase in stores would allow the company to increase its market share in Japan to 15 percent. The number of Coach retail locations in Japan and other international markets for 2001 through 2006 is presented in Exhibit 5. Coach Inc.'s sales and assets by geographic region are provided in Exhibit 6.

Coach's Strategic Options in 2007

Going into 2007, Lew Frankfort's key growth initiatives involved store expansion in the United States, Japan, Hong Kong, and mainland China, increasing sales to existing customers to drive comparable store growth, and creating alliances to exploit the Coach brand in additional luxury categories. The company's managers believed there was an opportunity to double the number of full-price retail stores in North America and increase the number of North American factory stores by a third. Also the company believed Japan could support approximately 70 additional Coach stores. Licensed distributors in Hong Kong operated 13 locations there and planned to open at least 10 locations on mainland China by 2007.

The company's second growth initiative was to increase same-store sales through continued development of new styles, the development of new usage collections, and the exploitation of gift-giving opportunities. The company had recently begun to prewrap items during holiday shopping periods and had created a new section of its Web site for gift-givers. Coach.com's gift guide recommended items that might appeal to women based upon their needs. For example, the Web site recommended handbags preferred by professional women, handbags for formal events, items for fashion-oriented teens, and essential handbags.

During late 2006, Coach launched a women's knitwear collection through a strategic alliance with Lutz & Patmos. The leather and fur trimmed cashmere and wool knits ranged from $300 to $1,500. The company also entered into an agreement with a division of the

Estee Lauder Company for the development of a fragrance that would be sold in Coach stores beginning in spring 2007.

For the first quarter of fiscal 2007, Coach's comparable store sales for full price stores increased by 16 percent relative to the same period in 2006. Coach factory stores achieved year-over-year comparable store sales growth of 27.1 percent. The company's indirect sales improved by 11 percent between the first quarter of 2006 and the first quarter of fiscal 2007. Operating income during the first quarter of 2007 increased by 36 percent, while operating margins improved by 340 basis points to reach 35.7 percent. Lew Frankfort attributed the company's continuing sales and profit growth to 19 new store openings in the United States, new handbag collections such as Coach Signature Stripe, Chelsea, Hamptons silhouettes, and Legacy lifestyle, and the increased assortment of gifts under $100 geared to price-sensitive holiday shoppers. The company's stock provided nearly a 35 percent return to shareholders during the 2006 calendar year. The challenge for Lew Frankfort and other key Coach executives was to defend against competitive attack from French and Italian luxury goods makers and sustain the impressive growth rate the company had achieved since its 2000 IPO.

5

Panera Bread Company

Arthur A. Thompson *The University of Alabama*

As Panera Bread Company headed into 2007, it was continuing to expand its market presence swiftly. The company's strategic intent was to make great bread broadly available to consumers across the United States. It had opened 155 new company-owned and franchised bakery-cafés in 2006, bringing its total to 1,027 units in 36 states. Plans were in place to open another 170 to 180 café locations in 2007 and to have nearly 2,000 Panera Bread bakery-cafés open by the end of 2010. Management was confident that Panera Bread's attractive menu and the dining ambience of its bakery-cafés provided significant growth opportunity, despite the fiercely competitive nature of the restaurant industry.

Already Panera Bread was widely recognized as the nationwide leader in the specialty bread segment. In 2003, Panera Bread scored the highest level of customer loyalty among quick-casual restaurants, according to a study conducted by TNS Intersearch.[1] J. D. Power and Associates' 2004 restaurant satisfaction study of 55,000 customers ranked Panera Bread highest among quick-service restaurants in the Midwest and Northeast regions of the United States in all categories, which included environment, meal, service, and cost. In 2005, for the fourth consecutive year, Panera Bread was rated among the best of 121 competitors in the Sandleman & Associates national customer satisfaction survey of more than 62,000 consumers. Panera Bread had also won "best of" awards in nearly every market across 36 states.

Company Background

In 1981, Louis Kane and Ron Shaich founded a bakery-café enterprise named Au Bon Pain Company Inc. Units were opened in malls, shopping centers, and airports along the East Coast of the United States and internationally throughout the 1980s and 1990s; the company prospered and became the dominant operator within the bakery-café category. In 1993, Au Bon Pain Company purchased Saint Louis Bread Company, a chain of 20 bakery-cafés located in the St. Louis, Missouri, area. Ron Shaich and a team of Au Bon Pain managers then spent considerable time in 1994 and 1995 traveling the country and studying the market for fast-food and quick-service meals. They concluded that many patrons of fast-food chains like McDonald's, Wendy's, Burger King, Subway, Taco Bell, Pizza Hut, and

[1]According to information in Panera Bread's press kit; the results of the study were reported in a 2003 *Wall Street Journal* article.

KFC could be attracted to a higher-quality, quick-dining experience. Top management at Au Bon Pain then instituted a comprehensive overhaul of the newly acquired Saint Louis Bread locations, altering the menu and the dining atmosphere. The vision was to create a specialty café anchored by an authentic, fresh-dough artisan bakery and upscale quick-service menu selections. Between 1993 and 1997, average unit volumes at the revamped Saint Louis Bread units increased by 75 percent, and over 100 additional Saint Louis Bread units were opened. In 1997, the Saint Louis Bread bakery-cafés were renamed Panera Bread in all markets outside St. Louis.

By 1998, it was clear that the reconceived Panera Bread units had connected with consumers. Au Bon Pain management concluded the Panera Bread format had broad market appeal and could be rolled out nationwide. Ron Shaich believed that Panera Bread had the potential to become one of the leading fast-casual restaurant chains in the nation. Shaich also believed that growing Panera Bread into a national chain required significantly more management attention and financial resources than the company could marshal if it continued to pursue expansion of both the Au Bon Pain and Panera Bread chains. He convinced Au Bon Pain's board of directors that the best course of action was for the company to go exclusively with the Panera Bread concept and divest the Au Bon Pain cafés. In August 1998, the company announced the sale of its Au Bon Pain bakery-café division for $73 million in cash to ABP Corporation; the transaction was completed in May 1999. With the sale of the Au Bon Pain division, the company changed its name to Panera Bread Company. The restructured company had 180 Saint Louis Bread and Panera Bread bakery-cafés and a debt-free balance sheet.

Between January 1999 and December 2006, close to 850 additional Panera Bread bakery-cafés were opened, some company-owned and some franchised. Panera Bread reported sales of $829.0 million and net income of $58.8 million in 2006. Sales at franchise-operated Panera Bread bakery-cafés totaled $1.2 billion in 2006. A summary of Panera Bread's recent financial performance is shown in Exhibit 1.

The Panera Bread Concept and Strategy

The driving concept behind Panera Bread was to provide a premium specialty bakery and café experience to urban workers and suburban dwellers. Its artisan sourdough breads made with a craftsman's attention to quality and detail and its award-winning bakery expertise formed the core of the menu offerings. Panera Bread specialized in fresh baked goods, made-to-order sandwiches on freshly baked breads, soups, salads, custom roasted coffees, and other café beverages. Panera's target market was urban workers and suburban dwellers looking for a quick-service meal and a more aesthetically pleasing dining experience than that offered by traditional fast food restaurants.

In his letter to shareholders in the company's 2005 annual report, Panera chairman and CEO Ron Shaich said:

> We think our continued commitment to providing crave-able food that people trust, served in a warm, community gathering place by associates who make our guests feel comfortable, really matters. When this is rooted in our commitment to the traditions of hand-crafted, artisan bread, something special is created. As we say here at Panera, it's our Product, Environment, and Great Service (PEGS) that we count on to deliver our success—year in and year out.

Panera Bread's distinctive menu, signature café design, inviting ambience, operating systems, and unit location strategy allowed it to compete successfully in five submarkets of the food-away-from-home industry: breakfast, lunch, daytime "chill out" (the time between breakfast and lunch and between lunch and dinner when customers visited its bakery-cafés

EXHIBIT 1 Selected Consolidated Financial Data for Panera Bread, 2002–2006 ($ in millions, except for per share amounts)

	2006	2005	2004	2003	2002
Income Statement Data					
Revenues:					
Bakery-café sales	$666,141	$499,422	$362,121	$265,933`	$212,645
Franchise royalties and fees	61,531	54,309	44,449	36,245	27,892
Fresh dough sales to franchisees	101,299	86,544	72,569	61,524	41,688
Total revenues	828,971	640,275	479,139	363,702	282,225
Bakery café expenses:					
Food and paper products	197,182	142,675	101,832	73,885	63,370
Labor	204,956	151,524	110,790	81,152	63,172
Occupancy	48,602	37,389	26,730	18,981	15,408
Other oprating expenses	92,176	70,003	51,044	36,804	27,971
Total bakery café expenses	542,916	401,591	290,396	210,822	169,921
Fresh dough costs of sales to franchisees	85,618	75,036	65,627	54,967	38,432
Depreciation and amortization	44,166	33,011	25,298	18,304	13,794
General and administrative expenses	59,306	46,301	33,338	28,140	24,986
Preopening expenses	6,173	3,241	2,642	1,531	1,051
Total costs and expenses	738,179	559,180	417,301	313,764	248,184
Operating profit	90,792	81,095	61,838	49,938	34,041
Interest expense	92	50	18	48	32
Other (income) expense, net	(1,976)	(1,133)	1,065	1,592	467
Provision for income taxes	33,827	29,995	22,175	17,629	12,242
Net income	$ 58,849	$ 52,183	$ 38,430*	$ 30,669	$ 21,300
Earnings per share					
Basic	$1.88	$1.69	$1.28	$1.02	$0.74
Diluted	1.84	1.65	1.25	1.00	0.71
Weighted average shares outstanding					
Basic	31,313	30,871	30,154	29,733	28,923
Diluted	32,044	31,651	30,768	30,423	29,891
Balance Sheet Data					
Cash and cash equivalents	$ 52,097	$ 24,451	$ 29,639	$ 42,402	$ 29,924
Investments in government securities	20,025	46,308	28,415	9,019	9,149
Current assets	127,618	102,774	58,220	70,871	59,262
Total assets	542,609	437,667	324,672	256,835	195,431
Current liabilities	109,610	86,865	55,705	44,792	32,325
Total liabilities	144,943	120,689	83,309	46,235	32,587
Stockholders' equity	397,666	316,978	241,363	193,805	151,503
Cash Flow Data					
Net cash provided by operating activities	$104,895	$110,628	$ 84,284	$ 73,102	$ 46,323
Net cash used in investing activities	(90,917)	(129,640)	(102,291)	(66,856)	(40,115)
Net cash provided by financing activities	13,668	13,824	5,244	6,232	5,664
Net (decrease) increase in cash and cash equivalents	27,646	(5,188)	(12,763)	12,478	11,872

*After adjustment of $239,000 for cumulative effect of accounting change.

Sources: 2006 10-K report, pp. 36–38, 2005 10-K report, pp. 16–17; 2003 10-K report, pp. 29–31; and company press release, February 8, 2007.

to take a break from their daily activities), light evening fare for eat-in or take-out, and take-home bread. In 2006, Panera began enhancing its menu in ways that would attract more diners during the evening meal hours. Management's long-term objective and strategic intent was to make Panera Bread a nationally recognized brand name and to be the

EXHIBIT 2 Selected Operating Statistics, Panera Bread Company, 2000–2006

	2006	2005	2004	2003	2002	2001	2000
Revenues at company operated stores (in millions)	$ 666.1	$ 499.4	$ 362.1	$ 265.9	$ 212.6	$ 157.7	$ 125.5
Revenues at franchised stores (in millions)	$1,245.5	$1,097.2	$ 879.1	$ 711.0	$ 542.6	$ 371.7	$ 199.4
Systemwide store revenues (in millions)	$1,911.6	$1,596.6	$1,241.2	$ 976.9	$ 755.2	$ 529.4	$ 324.9
Average annualized revenues per company-operated bakery-café (in millions)	$ 1.967	$ 1.942	$ 1.852	$ 1.830	$ 1.764	$ 1.636	$ 1.473
Average annualized revenues per franchised bakery-café (in millions)	$ 2.074	$ 2.016	$ 1.881	$ 1.860	$ 1.872	$ 1.800	$ 1.707
Average weekly sales, company-owned cafés	$ 37.833	$ 37,348	$ 35,620	$35,198	$33,924	$31,460	$28,325
Average weekly sales, franchised cafés	$ 39,894	$ 38,777	$ 36,171	$35,777	$35,997	$34,607	$32.832
Comparable bakery-café sales percentage increases*							
Company-owned	3.9%	7.4%	2.9%	1.7%	4.1%	5.8%	8.1%
Franchised	4.1%	8.0%	2.6%	(0.4)%	6.1%	5.8%	10.3%
Systemwide	4.1%	7.8%	2.7%	0.2%	5.5%	5.8%	9.1%
Company-owned bakery-cafés open at year-end	391	311	226	173	132	110	90
Franchised bakery-cafés open at year-end	636	566	515	429	346	259	172
Total bakery-cafés open	1,027	877	741	602	478	369	262

*The percentages for comparable store sales are based on annual changes at stores open at least 18 months.
Sources: Company 10-K reports 2000, 2001, 2003, 2005, and 2006; company press releases, January 4, 2007, and February 8, 2007.

dominant restaurant operator in the specialty bakery-café segment. According to Scott Davis, Panera's senior vice president and chief concept officer, the company was trying to succeed by "being better than the guys across the street" and making the experience of dining at Panera so attractive that customers would be willing to pass by the outlets of other fast-casual restaurant competitors to dine at a nearby Panera Bread bakery-café.[2] Davis maintained that the question about Panera Bread's future was not *if* it would be successful but *by how much*.

Management believed that its concept afforded growth potential in suburban markets sufficient to expand the number of Panera bread locations by 17 percent annually through 2010 (see Exhibits 3 and 4) and to achieve earnings per share growth of 25 percent annually. Panera Bread's growth strategy was to capitalize on Panera's market potential by opening both company-owned and franchised Panera Bread locations as fast as was prudent. So far, franchising had been a key component of the company's efforts to broaden its market penetration. Panera Bread had organized its business around company-owned bakery-café operations, the franchise operations, and fresh dough operations; the fresh bread unit supplied dough to all Panera Bread stores, both company-owned and franchised.

[2]As stated in a presentation to securities analysts, May 5, 2006.

EXHIBIT 3   Areas of High and Low Market Penetration of Panera Bread Bakery-Cafés, 2006

High Penetration Markets			Low Penetration Markets		
Area	Number of Panera Bread Units	Population per Bakery-Café	Area	Number of Panera Bread Units	Population per Bakery-Café
St. Louis	40	67,000	Los Angeles	17	1,183,000
Columbus, OH	19	83,000	Miami	2	1,126,000
Jacksonville	12	98,000	Northern California	10	1,110,000
Omaha	12	101,000	Seattle	5	860,000
Cincinnati	26	108,000	Dallas/Fort Worth	10	590,000
Pittsburgh	25	142,000	Houston	12	335,000
Washinton D.C./Northern Virginia	26	152,000	Philadelphia	25	278,000

Untapped Markets

New York City	Phoenix	Austin
Salt Lake City	Tucson	San Antonio
Memphis	District of Columbia	Green Bay/Appleton
New Orleans	Spokane	Shreveport
Atlantic City	Baton Rouge	Toronto
Albuquerque	Little Rock	Vancouver

Source: Panera Bread management presentation to securities analysts, May 5, 2006

EXHIBIT 4   Comparative U.S. Market Penetration of Selected Restaurant Chains, 2006

Restaurant Chain	Number of Locations	Population per Location
Subway	19,965	15,000
McDonald's	13,727	22,000
Starbucks Coffee	7,700	39,000
Applebee's	1,800	166,000
Panera Bread	910	330,000

Note: Management believed that a 17 percent annual rate of expansion of Panera Bread locations through 2010 would result in 1 café per 160,000 people.
Source: Panera Bread management presentation to securities analysts, May 5, 2006.

Panera Bread's Product Offerings and Menu

Panera Bread's signature product was artisan bread made from four ingredients—water, natural yeast, flour, and salt; no preservatives or chemicals were used. Carefully trained bakers shaped every step of the process, from mixing the ingredients, to kneading the dough, to placing the loaves on hot stone slabs to bake in a traditional European-style stone deck bakery oven. Exhibit 5 shows Panera's lineup of breads.

The Panera Bread menu was designed to provide target customers with products built on the company's bakery expertise, particularly its 20-plus varieties of bread baked fresh throughout the day at each café location. The key menu groups were fresh baked goods, made-to-order sandwiches and salads, soups, light entrées, and café beverages. Exhibit 6 shows a sampling of the items on a typical Panera Bread menu.

The menu offerings were regularly reviewed and revised to sustain the interest of regular customers, satisfy changing consumer preferences, and be responsive to various seasons of the year. The soup lineup, for example, changed seasonally. Product development was

EXHIBIT 5   Panera's Lineup of Bread Varieties, 2006

Sourdough

Panera's signature sourdough bread that featured a golden, crackled crust and firm, moderately structured crumb with a satisfying, tangy flavor. *Available in Baguette, Loaf, XL Loaf, Roll and Bread Bowl.*

Asiago Cheese

Chunks of Asiago cheese were added to the standard sourdough recipe and baked right in, with more Asiago cheese sprinkled on top. *Available in Demi and Loaf.*

Focaccia

A traditional Italian flatbread made with Panera's artisan starter dough, olive oil, and chunks of Asiago cheese. *Available in three varieties—Asiago Cheese, Rosemary & Onion and Basil Pesto.*

Nine Grain

Made with cracked whole wheat, rye, corn meal, oats, rice flour, soy grits, barley flakes, millet, and flaxseed plus molasses for a semisweet taste. *Available in Loaf.*

Tomato Basil

A sourdough-based bread made with tomatoes and basil, topped with sweet walnut streusel. *Available in XL Loaf.*

Cinnamon Raisin

A light raisin bread with a swirl of cinnamon, sugar and molasses. *Available in Loaf.*

Artisan Sesame Semolina

Made with enriched durum and semolina flours to create a golden yellow crumb, topped with sesame seeds. *Available in Loaf and Miche.*

Artisan Multigrain

Nine grains and sesame, poppy and fennel seeds blended with molasses, topped with rolled oats. *Available in Loaf.*

Artisan French

Made with Panera's artisan starter to create a nutty flavor with a wine-like aroma. *Available in Baguette and Miche.*

Whole Grain

A moist, hearty mixture of whole spelt flour, millet, flaxseed and other wheat flours and grains, sweetened with honey and topped with rolled oats. *Available in loaf, miche and baguette.*

White Whole Grain

A new bread created especially for Panera Kids sandwiches; a sweeter alternative to the whole Grain bread with a thin, caramelized crust sweetened with honey and molasses. *Available in Loaf.*

French

A classic French bread characterized by a thin, crackly crust, slightly sweet taste and a lighter crumb than our sourdough. *Available in Baguette, Loaf, XL Loaf and Roll.*

Ciabatta

A flat, oval-shaped loaf with a delicate flavor and soft texture; made with Panera's artisan starter and a touch of olive oil. *Available in Loaf.*

Honey Wheat

A mild wheat bread with tastes of honey and molasses; the soft crust and crumb made it great for sandwiches. *Available in Loaf.*

Rye

Special nature leavening, unleached flour, and chopped rye kernels were used to create a delicate rye flavor. *Available in Loaf.*

Sunflower

Made with honey, lemon peel, and raw sunflower seeds and topped with sesame and honey-roasted sunflower seeds. *Available in Loaf.*

Artisan Three Seed

The addition of sesame, poppy, and fennel seeds created a sweet, nutty, anise-flavored bread. *Available in Demi.*

Artisan Three Cheese

Made with Parmesan, Romano, and Asiago cheeses and durum and semolina flours. *Available in Demi, Loaf and Miche.*

Artisan Stone-Milled Rye

Made with Panera's artisan starter, chopped rye kernels, and caraway seeds, topped with more caraway seeds. *Available in Loaf and Miche.*

Artisan Country

Made from artisan starter with a crisp crust and nutty flavor. *Available in loaf, miche and demi.*

Lower-Card Pumpkin Seed

Made from Panera's artisan starter dough, pumpkin seeds and flax meal to create a subtle, nutty flavor. *Available in Loaf.*

Lower-Carb Italian Herb

Made from Panera's artisan starter dough, roasted garlic, dried herbs and sesame seed topping. *Available in Loaf.*

Source: www.panerabread.com (accessed July 28, 2006).

EXHIBIT 6   Sample Menu Selections, Panera Bread Company, 2006

Bakery
Loaves of Bread (22 varieties)
Bagels (11 varieties)
Cookies (5 varieties)
Scones (5 varieties)
Cinnamon Rolls, Pecan Rolls
Croissants
Coffee Cakes
Muffins (5 varieties)
Artisan and Specialty Pastries (8 varieties)
Brownies (3 varieties)
Mini-Bundt Cakes (3 varieties)

Signature Sandwiches
Pepperblue Steak
Garden Veggie
Tuscan Chicken
Asiago Roast Beef
Italian Combo
Bacon Turkey Bravo
Sierra Turkey
Turkey Romesco
Mediterranean Veggie

Café Sandwiches
Smoked Turkey Breast
Chicken Salad
Tuna Salad
Smoked Ham and Cheese

Hot Panini Sandwiches
Turkey Artichoke
Frontega Chicken
Smokehouse Turkey
Portobello and Mozzarella

Baked Egg Souffles
Four Cheese
Spinach and Artichoke
Spinach and Bacon

Soups
Broccoli Cheddar
French Onion
Baked Potato
Low Fat Chicken Noodle
Cream of Chicken and Wild Rice
Boston Clam Chowder
Low Fat Vegetarian Garden Vegetable
Low Fat Vegetarian Black Bean
Vegetarian Roasted Red Pepper and Lentil
Tuscan Chicken and Ditalini
Tuscan Vegetable Ditalini

Hand Tossed Salads
Asian Sesame Chicken
Fandango
Greek
Caesar
Grilled Chicken Caesar
Bistro Steak
Classic Café
California Mission Chicken
Fuji Apple Chicken
Strawberry Poppyseed and Chicken
Grilled Salmon Salad

Side Choices
Portion of French Baguette
Portion of Whole Grain Baguette
Kettle-cooked or Baked Chips
Apple

Panera kids
Grilled Cheese
Peanut Butter and Jelly
Kids Deli

Beverages
Coffee
Hot and Iced Teas
Sodas
Bottled Water
Juice
Organic Milk
Organic Chocolate Milk
Hot Chocolate
Orange Juice
Organic Apple Juice
Espresso
Cappuccino
Lattes
Mango Raspberry Smoothie

Source: Sample menu posted at www.panerabread.com (accessed July 29, 2006).

focused on providing food that customers would crave and trust to be tasty. New menu items were developed in test kitchens and then introduced in a limited number of the bakery-cafés to determine customer response and verify that preparation and operating procedures resulted in product consistency and high quality standards. If successful, they were then rolled out systemwide. New product rollouts were integrated into periodic or seasonal menu rotations, which Panera referred to as "Celebrations."

Panera recognized in late 2004 that significantly more customers were conscious about eating "good" carbohydrates, prompting the introduction of whole grain breads. In 2005, several important menu changes were made. Panera introduced a new line of artisan sweet goods made with gourmet European butter, fresh fruit toppings, and appealing fillings; these new artisan pastries represented a significantly higher level of taste and upgraded quality. To expand its breakfast offerings and help boost morning-hour sales, Panera introduced egg soufflés baked in a flaked pastry shell. And, in another health-related move, Panera switched to the use of natural, antibiotic-free chicken in all of its chicken-related sandwiches and salads. During 2006, the chief menu changes involved the addition of light entrées to jump-start dinner appeal; one such menu addition was crispani (a pizzalike topping on a thin crust). In 2006, evening-hour sales represented 20 percent of Panera's business.

Panera Fresh Catering

In 2004–2005, Panera Bread introduced a catering program to extend its market reach into the workplace, schools, parties, and gatherings held in homes. Panera saw catering as an opportunity to grow lunch and dinner sales with making capital investments in additional physical facilities. By the end of 2005, catering was generating an additional $80 million in sales for Panera Bread. Management foresaw considerable opportunity for future growth of Panera's catering operation.

Marketing

Panera's marketing strategy was to compete on the basis of providing an entire dining experience rather than by attracting customers on the basis of price only. The objective was for customers to view dining at Panera as being a good value—meaning high-quality food at reasonable prices—so as to encourage frequent visits. Panera Bread performed extensive market research, including the use of focus groups, to determine customer food and drink preferences and price points. The company tried to grow sales at existing Panera locations through menu development, product merchandising, promotions at everyday prices, and sponsorship of local community charitable events.

Historically, marketing had played only a small role in Panera's success. Brand awareness had been built on customers' satisfaction with their dining experience at Panera and their tendency to share their positive experiences with friends and neighbors. About 85 percent of consumers who were aware that there was a Panera Bread bakery-café in their community or neighborhood had dined at Panera on at least one occasion.[3] The company's marketing research indicated that 57 percent of consumers who had "ever tried" dining at Panera Bread had been customers in the past 30 days. This high proportion of trial customers to repeat customers had convinced management that getting more first-time diners into Panera Bread cafés was a potent way to boost store traffic and average weekly sales per store.

[3]As cited in Panera Bread's presentation to securities analysts on May 5, 2006.

Panera's research also showed that people who dined at Panera Bread very frequently or moderately frequently typically did so for only one part of the day. Yet 81 percent indicated "considerable willingness" to try dining at Panera Bread at other parts of the day.[4]

Franchise-operated bakery-cafés were required to contribute 0.7 percent of their sales to a national advertising fund and 0.4 percent of their sales as a marketing administration fee and were also required to spend 2.0 percent of their sales in their local markets on advertising. Panera contributed similar amounts from company-owned bakery-cafés toward the national advertising fund and marketing administration. The national advertising fund contribution of 0.7 percent had been increased from 0.4 percent starting in 2006. Beginning in fiscal 2006, national advertising fund contributions were raised to 0.7 percent of sales, and Panera could opt to raise the national advertising fund contributions as high as 2.6 percent of sales.

In 2006, Panera Bread's marketing strategy had several elements. One element aimed at raising the quality of awareness about Panera by continuing to feature the caliber and appeal of its breads and baked goods, by hammering the theme "food you crave, food you can trust," and by enhancing the appeal of its bakery-cafés as a neighborhood gathering place. A second marketing initiative was to raise awareness and boost trial of dining at Panera Bread at multiple meal times (breakfast, lunch, "chill out" times, and dinner). Panera avoided hard-sell or in-your-face marketing approaches, preferring instead to employ a range of ways to softly drop the Panera Bread name into the midst of consumers as they moved through their lives and let them "gently collide" with the brand; the idea was to let consumers "discover" Panera Bread and then convert them into loyal customers by providing a very satisfying dining experience. The third marketing initiative was to increase perception of Panera Bread as a viable evening meal option and to drive early trials of Panera for dinner (particularly among existing Panera lunch customers).

Franchise Operations

Opening additional franchised bakery-cafés was a core element of Panera Bread's strategy and management's initiatives to achieve the company's growth targets. Panera Bread did not grant single-unit franchises, so a prospective franchisee could not open just one bakery-café. Rather, Panera Bread's franchising strategy was to enter into franchise agreements that required the franchise developer to open a number of units, typically 15 bakery-cafés in six years. Franchisee candidates had to be well capitalized, have a proven track record as excellent multiunit restaurant operators, and agree to meet an aggressive development schedule. Applicants had to meet eight stringent criteria to gain consideration for a Panera Bread franchise:

- Experience as a multiunit restaurant operator.
- Recognition as a top restaurant operator.
- Net worth of $7.5 million.
- Liquid assets of $3 million.
- Infrastructure and resources to meet Panera's development schedule for the market area the franchisee was applying to develop.
- Real estate experience in the market to be developed.
- Total commitment to the development of the Panera Bread brand.
- Cultural fit and a passion for fresh bread.

---

[4]Ibid.

The franchise agreement typically required the payment of a franchise fee of $35,000 per bakery-café (broken down into $5,000 at the signing of the area development agreement and $30,000 at or before a bakery-café opened) and continuing royalties of 4–5 percent on sales from each bakery-café. Franchise-operated bakery-cafés followed the same standards for in store operating standards, product quality, menu, site selection, and bakery-café construction as did company-owned bakery-cafés. Franchisees were required to purchase all of their dough products from sources approved by Panera Bread. Panera's fresh dough facility system supplied fresh dough products to substantially all franchise-operated bakery-cafés. Panera did not finance franchisee construction or area development agreement payments or hold an equity interest in any of the franchise-operated bakery-cafés. All area development agreements executed after March 2003 included a clause allowing Panera Bread the right to purchase all bakery-cafés opened by the franchisee at a defined purchase price, at any time five years after the execution of the franchise agreement.

Exhibit 7 shows estimated costs of opening a new franchised Panera Bread bakery-café. As of 2006, the typical franchise-operated bakery-café averaged somewhat higher average weekly and annual sales volumes than company-operated cafés (see Exhibit 2), was equal to or slightly more profitable, and produced a slightly higher return on equity investment than company-operated cafés (partly because many franchisees made greater use of debt in financing their operations than did Panera, which had no long-term debt at all).[5] During the 2003–2006 period, in four unrelated transactions, Panera purchased 38 bakery-cafés from franchisees.

Panera provided its franchisees with market analysis and site selection assistance, lease review, design services and new store opening assistance, a comprehensive 10-week initial training program, a training program for hourly employees, manager and baker certification, bakery-café certification, continuing education classes, benchmarking data regarding costs and profit margins, access to company developed marketing and advertising programs, neighborhood marketing assistance, and calendar planning assistance. Panera's

EXHIBIT 7 **Estimated Initial Investment for a Panera Bread Bakery-Café, 2007**

Investment Category	Actual or Estimated Amount	To Whom Paid
Franchise fee	$35,000	Panera
Real property	Varies according to site and local real estate market conditions	
Leasehold improvements	$350,000 to $1,250,000	Contractors
Equipment	$250,000 to $300,000	Equipment vendors, Panera
Fixtures	$60,000 to $90,000	Vendors
Furniture	$50,000 to $70,000	Vendors
Consultant fees and municipal impact fees (if any)	$20,000 to $120,000	Architect, engineer, expeditor, others
Supplies and inventory	$19,000 to $24,175	Panera, other suppliers
Smallwares	$24,000 to $29,000	Suppliers
Signage	$20,000 to $72,000	Suppliers
Additional funds (for working capital and general operating expenses for 3 months)	$175,000 to $245,000	Vendors, suppliers, employees, utilities, landlord, others
Total	$1,003,000 to $2,235,175, plus real estate and related costs	

Source: www.panerabread.com (accessed February 9, 2007).

[5]Ibid.

surveys of its franchisees indicated high satisfaction with the Panera Bread concept, the overall support received from Panera Bread, and the company's leadership. The biggest franchisee issue was the desire for more territory. In turn, Panera management expressed satisfaction with the quality of franchisee operations, the pace and quality of new bakery-café openings, and franchisees' adoption of Panera Bread initiatives.[6]

As of April 2006, Panera had entered into area development agreements with 42 franchisee groups covering 54 markets in 34 states; these franchisees had commitments to open 423 additional franchise-operated bakery-cafés. If a franchisee failed to develop bakery-cafés on schedule, Panera had the right to terminate the franchise agreement and develop its own company-operated locations or develop locations through new area developers in that market. As of mid-2006, Panera Bread did not have any international franchise development agreements but was considering entering into franchise agreements for several Canadian locations (Toronto and Vancouver).

Site Selection and Café Environment

Bakery-cafés were typically located in suburban, strip mall, and regional mall locations. In evaluating a potential location, Panera studied the surrounding trade area, demographic information within that area, and information on competitors. Based on analysis of this information, including the use of predictive modeling using proprietary software, Panera developed projections of sales and return on investment for candidate sites. Cafés had proved successful as freestanding units, as both in-line and end-cap locations in strip malls, and in large regional malls.

The average Panera bakery-café was approximately 4,600 square feet. The great majority of the locations were leased. Lease terms were typically for 10 years with one, two, or three 5-year renewal option periods thereafter. Leases typically entailed charges for minimum base occupancy, a proportionate share of building and common-area operating expenses and real estate taxes, and a contingent percentage rent based on sales above a stipulated sales level. The average construction, equipment, furniture and fixture, and signage cost for the 66 company-owned bakery-cafés opened in 2005 was $920,000 per bakery-café after landlord allowances.

Each bakery-café sought to provide a distinctive and engaging environment (what management referred to as "Panera Warmth"), in many cases using fixtures and materials complementary to the neighborhood location of the bakery-café. In 2005–2006, the company had introduced a new G2 café design aimed at further refining and enhancing the appeal of Panera bakery-cafés as a warm and appealing neighborhood gathering place (a strategy that Starbucks had used with great success). The G2 design incorporated higher-quality furniture, cozier seating areas and groupings, and a brighter, more open display case. Many locations had fireplaces to further create an alluring and hospitable atmosphere that patrons would flock to on a regular basis, sometimes for a meal, sometimes to meet friends and acquaintances for a meal, sometimes to take a break for a light snack or beverage, and sometimes to just hang out with friends and acquaintances. Many of Panera's bakery-cafés had outdoor seating, and virtually all cafés featured free wireless high-speed (Wi-Fi) Internet access—Panera considered free Wi-Fi part of its commitment to making its bakery-cafés open community gathering places where people could catch up on some work, hang out with friends, read the paper, or just relax. All Panera cafés used real china and stainless silverware instead of paper plates and plastic utensils.

[6]Ibid.

Bakery-Café Supply Chain

Panera had invested about $52 million in a network of 17 regional fresh dough facilities (16 company-owned and one franchise-operated) to supply fresh dough daily to both company-owned and franchised bakery-cafés. These facilities, totaling some 313,000 square feet, employed about 830 people who were largely engaged in preparing the fresh doughs, a process that took about 48 hours. The dough-making process began with the preparation and mixing of Panera's all-natural starter dough, which then was given time to rise; other all-natural ingredients were then added to create the different bread and bagel varieties (no chemicals or preservatives were used). Another period of rising then took place. Next the dough was cut into pieces, shaped into loaves or bagels, and readied for shipment in fresh dough form. There was no freezing of the dough, and no partial baking was done at the fresh dough facilities. Each bakery-café did all of the baking itself, using the fresh doughs delivered daily. The fresh dough facilities manufactured about 50 different products, with 11 more rotated throughout the year.

Distribution of the fresh bread and bagel doughs was accomplished through a leased fleet of about 140 temperature-controlled trucks operated by Panera personnel. Trucks on average delivered dough to six bakery-cafés, with trips averaging about 300 miles (but in some cases extending to as much as 500 miles—management believed the optimal trip length was about 300 miles). The fresh dough was sold to both company-owned and franchised bakery-cafés at a delivered cost not to exceed 27 percent of the retail value of the product. Exhibit 8 provides financial data relating to each of Panera's three business segments: company-operated bakery-cafés, franchise operations, and fresh dough facilities. The sales and operating profits associated with the fresh doughs supplied to company-operated bakery cafés are included in the revenues and operating profits of the company-owned bakery-café segment. The sales and operating profits of the fresh dough facilities segment shown in Exhibit 8 all represent transactions with franchised bakery-cafés.

Management claimed that the company's fresh-dough-making capability provided a competitive advantage by ensuring consistent quality and dough-making efficiency. It was more economical to concentrate the dough-making operations in a few facilities dedicated to that function than it was to have each bakery-café equipped and staffed to do all of its baking from scratch.

Panera obtained ingredients for its doughs and other products manufactured at the fresh dough facilities from a variety of suppliers. While some ingredients used at the fresh dough facilities were sourced from a single supplier, there were numerous suppliers of each ingredient and Panera could obtain ingredients from another supplier when necessary. Panera contracted externally for the supply of sweet goods to its bakery-cafés. In November 2002, it entered into a cost-plus agreement with Dawn Food Products Inc. to provide sweet goods for the period 2003–2007. Sweet goods were completed at each bakery-café by professionally trained bakers—completion entailed finishing with fresh toppings and other ingredients and baking to established artisan standards.

Panera had arrangements with independent distributors to handle the delivery of sweet goods and other materials to bakery-cafés. Virtually all other food products and supplies for retail operations, including paper goods, coffee, and smallwares, were contracted for by Panera and delivered by the vendors to the designated distributors for delivery to the bakery-cafés. Individual bakery-cafés placed orders for the needed supplies directly from a distributor two to three times per week. Franchise-operated bakery-cafés operate under individual contracts with one of Panera's three primary independent distributors or other regional distributors.

EXHIBIT 8 Business Segment Information, Panera Bread Company, 2003–2006 ($ in thousands)

	2006	2005	2004	2003
Segment revenues:				
Company bakery-café operations	$666,141	$499,422	$362,121	$265,933
Franchise operations	61,531	54,309	44,449	36,245
Fresh dough operations	159,050	128,422	103,786	93,874
Intercompany sales eliminations	(57,751)	(41,878)	(31,217)	(32,350)
Total revenues	$828,971	$640,275	$479,139	$363,702
Segment operating profit:				
Company bakery-café operations	$123,225	$ 97,831	$ 71,725	$ 55,111
Franchise operations	54,160	47,652	39,149	32,132
Fresh dough operations	15,681	11,508	6,942	6,557
Total segment operating profit	$193,066	$156,991	$117,816	$ 93,800
Depreciation and amortization:				
Company bakery-café operations	$ 32,741	$ 23,345	$ 17,786	$ 12,256
Fresh dough operations	7,097	6,016	4,356	3,298
Corporate administration	4,328	3,650	3,156	2,750
Total	$ 44,166	$ 33,011	$ 25,298	$ 18,304
Capital expenditures				
Company bakery-café operations	$ 86,743	$ 67,554	$ 67,374	$ 33,670
Fresh dough operations	15,120	9,082	9,445	8,370
Corporate administration	7,433	5,420	3,610	3,721
Total capital expenditures	$109,296	$ 82,056	$ 80,429	$ 45,761
Segment assets				
Company bakery-café operations	$374,795	$301,517	$204,295	$147,920
Franchise operations	3,740	2,969	1,778	1,117
Fresh dough operations	59,919	37,567	39,968	33,442
Other assets	104,155	95,614	78,631	74,356
Total assets	$542,609	$437,667	$324,672	$256,835

Sources: Company 10-K reports, 2004, 2005, and 2006.

Competition

According to the National Restaurant Association, sales at the 925,000 food service locations in the United States were forecast to be about $511 billion in 2006 (up from $308 billion in 1996), and account for 47.5 percent of consumers' food dollars (up from 25 percent in 1955). Commercial eating places accounted for about $345 billion of the projected $511 billion in total food service sales, with the remainder divided among drinking places, lodging establishments with restaurants, managed food service locations, and other types of retail, vending, recreational, and mobile operations with food service capability. The U.S. restaurant industry had about 12.5 million employees in 2006, served about 70 billion meals and snack occasions, and was growing about 5 percent annually.[7] Just over 7 out of 10 eating and drinking places in the United States were independent single-unit establishments with fewer than 20 employees.

Even though the average U.S. consumer ate 76 percent of meals at home, on a typical day, about 130 million U.S. consumers were food service patrons at an eating establishment—sales at commercial eating places averaged close to $1 billion daily. Average household expenditures for food away from home in 2004 were $2,434, or $974 per person. In 2003, unit sales averaged $755,000 at full-service restaurants and $606,000 at

[7]Information posted at www.restaurant.org (accessed August 1, 2006).

limited-service restaurants; however, very popular restaurant locations achieved annual sales volumes in the $2.5 million to $5 million range. The profitability of a restaurant location ranged from exceptional to good to average to marginal to money-losing.

The restaurant business was labor-intensive, extremely competitive, and risky. Industry members pursued differentiation strategies of one variety of another, seeking to set themselves apart from rivals via pricing, food quality, menu theme, signature menu selections, dining ambience and atmosphere, service, convenience, and location. To further enhance their appeal, some restaurants tried to promote greater customer traffic via happy hours, lunch and dinner specials, children's menus, innovative or trendy dishes, diet-conscious menu selections, and beverage/appetizer specials during televised sporting events (important at restaurants/bars with big screen TVs). Most restaurants were quick to adapt their menu offerings to changing consumer tastes and eating preferences, frequently featuring heart-healthy, vegetarian, organic, low-calorie, and/or lowcarb items on their menus. It was the norm at many restaurants to rotate some menu selections seasonally and to periodically introduce creative dishes in an effort to keep regular patrons coming back, attract more patrons, and remain competitive.

Consumers (especially those who ate out often) were prone to give newly opened eating establishments a trial, and if they were pleased with their experience to return, sometimes frequently—loyalty to existing restaurants was low when consumers perceived there were better dining alternatives. It was also common for a once-hot restaurant to lose favor and confront the stark realities of a dwindling clientele, forcing it to either reconceive its menu and dining environment or go out of business. Many restaurants had fairly short lives; there were multiple causes for a restaurant's failure—a lack of enthusiasm for the menu or dining experience, inconsistent food quality, poor service, a bad location, meal prices that patrons deemed too high, and superior competition by rivals with comparable menu offerings.

While Panera Bread competed with specialty food, casual dining, and quick-service restaurant retailers—including national, regional, and locally owned restaurants—its closest competitors were restaurants in the so-called fast-casual restaurant category. Fast-casual restaurants filled the gap between fast-food and casual, full-table-service dining. A fast-casual restaurant provided quick-service dining (much like fast-food enterprises) but were distinguished by enticing menus, higher food quality, and more inviting dining environments; typical meal costs per guest were in the $7–$12 range. Some fast-casual restaurants had limited table service and some were self-service (like fast-food establishments). Exhibit 9 provides information on prominent national and regional chains that were competitors of Panera Bread.

EXHIBIT 9   **Representative Fast-Casual Restaurants Chains and Selected Full-Service Restaurant Chains in the United States, 2006**

Company	Number of Locations, 2005–2006	Select 2005 Financial Data	Key Menu Categories
Atlanta Bread Company	160 bakery-cafés in 27 states	Not available (privately held company)	Fresh-baked breads, waffles, salads, sandwiches, soups, wood-fired pizza and pasta (select locations only), baked goods, desserts
Applebee's Neighborhood Grill and Bar	1,730+ locations in 49 states, plus some 70 locations in 16 other countries	2005 revenues of $1.2 billion; average annual sales of $2.5 million per location; alcoholic beverages accounted for about 12 percent of sales	Beef, chicken pork, seafood, and pasta entrées plus appetizers, salads, sandwiches, a selection of Weight Watchers branded menu alternatives, desserts, and alcoholic beverages

(continued)

EXHIBIT 9   *Continued*

Company	Number of Locations, 2005–2006	Select 2005 Financial Data	Key Menu Categories
Au Bon Pain	190 company-owned and franchised bakery-cafés in 23 states; 222 locations internationally	Systemwide sales of about $245 million in 2005	Baked goods (with a focus on croissants and bagels), soups, salads, sandwiches and wraps, and coffee drinks
Baja Fresh	300+ locations across the United States	A subsidiary of Wendy's International	Tocos, burritos, quesadilla, fajitas, salads, soups, sides, and catering services
Bruegger's	260 bakery-cafés in 17 states	2005 revenues of $155.2 million; 3,500 full-time employees	Several varieties of bagels and muffins, sandwiches, salads, and soups
California Pizza Kitchen*	190+ locations in 27 states and 5 other countries	2005 revenues of $480 million; average annual sales of $3.2 million per location	Signature California-style hearth-baked pizzas; creative salads, pastas, soups and sandwiches; appetizers; desserts, beer, wine, coffees, teas, and assorted beverages
Chili's Grill and Bar* (a subsidiary of Brinker International**)	1,074 locations in 49 states and 23 countries	Average revenue per meal of ≈12.00; average capital investment of $2.4 million per location	Chicken, beef, and seafood entrées, steaks, appetizers, salads, sandwiches, desserts, and alcoholic beverages (13.6 percent of sales)
Chipotle Mexican Grill	500+ locations (all company-owned)	2005 sales of $628 million; 13,000 employees	A selection of gourmet burritos and tocos
Corner Bakery Café (a subsidiary of Brinker International**)	90 locations in 8 states and District of Columbia	Average revenue per meal of ≈ $7.44; average capital investment of $1.7 million per location	Breakfast selections (egg scramblers, pastries, mixed berry parfaits); lunch/diner selections (hot and cold sandwiches, salads, soups, and desserts); catering (≈ 21 percent of sales)
Cracker Barrel	527 combination retail stores and restaurants in 42 states	Restaurant sales of $2.1 billion in 2005; average restaurant sales of $3.3 million	Two menus (breakfast and lunch/dinner); named "Best Family Dining Chain" for 15 consecutive years
Culver's	330 locations in 16 states	Not available (a privately held company)	Signature hamburgers served on buttered buns, fried battered cheese curds, value dinners (chicken, shrimp, cod with potato and slaw), salads, frozen custard, milkshakes, sundaes, and fountain drinks
Fazoli's	380 locations in 32 states	Not available (a privately held company)	Spaghetti and meatballs, fettuccine Alfredo, lasagna, ravioli, submarinos and panini sandwiches, salads, and breadsticks
Fuddruckers	200+ locations in the Unites States and 6 Middle Eastern countries	Not available (a privately held company)	Exotic hamburgers (the feature menu item), chicken and fish sandwiches, French fries and other sides, soups, salads, desserts
Jason's Deli	150 locations in 20 states	Not available (a privately held company)	Sandwiches, extensive salad bar, soups, loaded potatoes, desserts; catering services, party trays, and box lunches
McAlister's Deli	200+ locations in 18 states	Not available (a privately held company)	Deli sandwiches, loaded baked potatoes, soups, salads, and desserts, plus sandwich trays and lunch boxes

(continued)

EXHIBIT 9 (*concluded*)

Company	Number of Locations, 2005–2006	Select 2005 Financial Data	Key Menu Categories
Moe's Southwest Grill	200+ location in 35 states	Not available (a privately held company)	Tex-Mex foods prepared fresh— tacos, burritos, fajitas, quesadillas, nachos, salads, chips and salsa
Noodles & Company	120+ urban and suburban locations in 16 states	Not available (a privately held company)	Asian, Mediterranean and American noodle/pasta entrées, soups and salads
Nothing But Noodles	39 locations in 20 states	Not available (a privately held company)	Starters, a wide selections of American and Italian pastas, Asian dishes with noodles, pasta-less entrées, soups, salads, and desserts
Qdoba Mexican Grill	280+ locations in 40 states	A subsidiary of Jack in the Box, Inc.; Jack in the Box had 2005 revenues of $2.5 billion, 2,300+ Jack in the Box and Qdoba locations, and 44,600 employees	Signature burritos, a "Naked Burrito" (a burrito served in a bowl without the fortilla), nontraditional taco salads, three-cheese nachos, five signature salsas, and a Q-to-Go Hot Taco Bar catering alternative
Rubio's Fresh Mexican Grill	150 locations in 5 western states	2005 revenues of $141 million; average sales of $960,000 per location	Signature fish tacos; chicken beef, and pork tacos; burritos and quesadillas; salads; proprietary salsas; sides; and domestic and imported beers
Starbucks	7,500+ company-operated and licensed locations in the United States, plus ≈3,000 international locations	2005 revenues of $6.4 billion; estimated retail sales of $1.1 million per company-operated location	Italian-style espresso beverages, teas, sodas, juices, assorted pastries and confections; some locations offer sandwiches and salads

*Denotes a full-service restaurant.
**Brinker International was a multiconcept restaurant operator with over 1,500 restaurants including Chili's Grill & Bar, Chili's Too, Corner Bakery Café, Romano's Macaroni Grill, On the Border Mexican Grill & Cantina, and Maggiano's Little Italy. Brinker had 2005 sales of $3.9 billion.
Sources: Company Web sites and en.wikipedia.org/wiki/Fast_casual_restaurant (accessed August 2, 2006).

Product Strategy

Case

6

Starbucks—Early 2008

J. Paul Peter *University of Wisconsin–Madison*

© Davis Barber/Photo Edit

Starbucks Corporation is the world's largest coffee retailer and has continued its phenomenal success into 2008. The company has won a variety of awards for its work in setting coffee-buying guidelines that are environmentally, socially, and economically responsible and for being one of the most admired companies in the United States. In one

J. Paul Peter is James R. Mc Manus–Bascom Professor in Marketing at the University of Wisconsin–Madison. All information in this case is taken from public sources including starbucks.com.

recent year it donated over $36 million in cash and products and nearly 400,000 hours of community volunteer work. Exhibit 1 summarizes its growth in revenues, earning, and stores in recent years. However, the company made some serious strategic errors and faced increasingly strong competition causing its stock price to fall from $36 to $18 per share in early 2008.

Starbucks was started in Seattle, Washington, in 1971 when three young men decided to try their hand at selling gourmet coffee. They were betting that consumers would pay $1.50 for a cup of their coffee compared to 40 cents for a generic coffee offered elsewhere. By 2008 there were more than 15,000 Starbucks coffeehouses in 44 countries worldwide.

EXHIBIT 1 **Starbucks Growth in Revenue, Earnings, and Number of Stores**

Source: www.Starbucks.com.

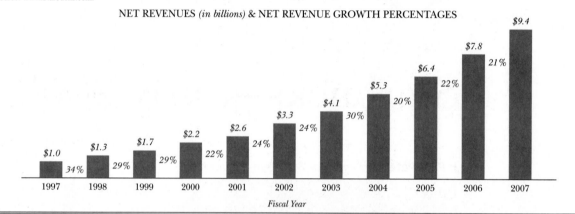

NET REVENUES *(in billions)* & NET REVENUE GROWTH PERCENTAGES

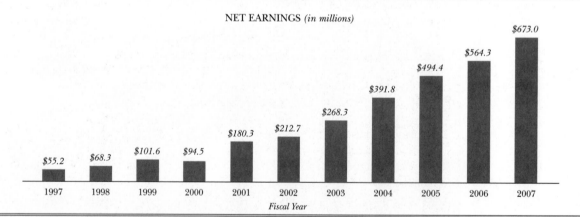

NET EARNINGS *(in millions)*

STORES OPEN AT YEAR END
(Company-operated and licensed stores)

☐ International
■ United States

Starbucks long-term goal is to have 30,000 stores worldwide. Store locations are selected for high traffic and high visibility. Over 33 million customers visit a Starbucks coffeehouse each week worldwide.

A recent study found that there are over 166 million coffee drinkers in the United States, and the number of them has increased steadily since the mid-1990s. A significant trend in U.S. coffee drinking has been the increase in the amount of coffee drinking in the out-of-home segment. For example, coffee drinkers aged 25–29 increased their out-of-home coffee consumption from 42 to 66 percent in a recent year and 30–59-year-olds from 33 to 46 percent. Coffee drinkers 60 and older increased their out-of-home consumption from 14 to 20 percent in the same year. Of the out-of-home segment, the biggest increase was among those who drink their coffee at work. However, while more consumers are drinking coffee in the workplace, they are increasingly getting their coffee from outside the office. This means the percentage of at-work coffee being sourced from within the workplace has declined dramatically.

Starbucks has made coffee drinking a social phenomenon by offering consumers a comfortable atmosphere in which to drink a premium beverage while either chatting with friends, reading a newspaper or magazine, or working on their laptops. Howard Schultz, chairman of Starbucks, believes that the company has created a "third place" between home and work where people can go for personal time out or to relax with friends. Whereas many of these people previously would have stopped in a bar for a beer, they now frequent Starbucks for coffee.

Schultz also attributes the company's success to the 172,000 employees working worldwide. Starbucks' employee training program churns out "baristas" by educating classes of 300 to 400 in courses such as "Brewing the Perfect Cup at Home" and "Coffee Knowledge." They are taught to remind customers who buy Starbucks coffee beans to brew at home to purchase new beans weekly and that tap water might not be sufficient for brewing really good coffee. They are also encouraged to share their feelings about working at Starbucks. Employees are given guidelines for maintaining and enhancing self-esteem, learning how to listen and acknowledge customer comments, and knowing when to ask for help. If the annual barista turnover of 60 percent compared to 140 percent for hourly wage earners in the fast-food industry is any indication of the quality of its training programs, Starbucks seems to have made progress in developing employee loyalty. Most of Starbucks employees have some education beyond high school, and their average age is 26. Eligible employees qualify for a comprehensive benefits package, including stock options and health, medical, dental, and vision coverage. Concern for employees is one of Starbucks guiding principles, as shown in Exhibit 2.

Starbucks' product line includes more than 30 blends and single-origin coffees, handcrafted espresso and blended beverages, Tazo teas, a line of bottled Frappuccino coffee drinks and Starbucks DoubleShot. In addition it offers an exclusive line of Starbucks Barista home espresso machines, coffee brewers and grinders, freshly baked pastries, a line of super-premium ice cream, a line of premium chocolate, sandwiches, salad, coffee mugs and coffee accessories, compact discs, and assorted gift items. It also offers a highly successful Starbucks Card, a reloadable stored-value card, which allows consumers to prepay the purchase of Starbucks products. The card can then be used and reloaded with funds when needed either at a Starbucks store or at Starbucks.com. This card has been hugely successful with over 27 million cards in use and over $400 million in sales in the first quarter of 2008 alone. The card is so successful it is being launched internationally with initial rollouts in Japan and Greece. The card provides convenience to customers but does not offer any discount for prepayment. In fact, Starbucks does not discount any of its products or offer special prices or sales.

Starbucks also has licensing agreements for its products with a number of other companies. For example, it has an agreement with Pepsi-Cola Company to produce and distribute

EXHIBIT 2 Starbucks' Mission Statement and Guiding Principles

Establish Starbucks as the premier purveyor of the finest coffee in the world while maintaining our uncompromising principles while we grow.
The following six guiding principles will help us measure the appropriateness of our decisions:
–Provide a great work environment and treat each other with respect and dignity.
–Embrace diversity as an essential component in the way we do business.
–Apply the highest standards of excellence to the purchasing, roasting and fresh delivery of our coffee.
–Develop enthusiastically satisfied customers all of the time.
–Contribute positively to our communities and our environment.
–Recognize that profitability is essential to our future success.

Environmental Mission Statement

Starbucks is committed to a role of environmental leadership in all facets of our business.
–We fulfill this mission by a commitment to:
–Understanding of environmental issues and sharing information with our partners.
–Developing innovative and flexible solutions to bring about change.
–Striving to buy, sell and use environmentally friendly products.
–Recognizing that fiscal responsibility is essential to our environmental future.
–Instilling environmental responsibility as a corporate value.
–Measuring and monitoring our progress for each project.
–Encouraging all partners to share in our mission.

Source: www.Starbucks.com.

bottled Starbucks products and one with Kraft Foods, Inc., to distribute Starbucks coffee beans and ground coffees and packaged tea products in grocery and warehouse club stores. It has an agreement with Dreyer's Grand Ice Cream, Inc., to develop and distribute Starbucks line of superpremium ice cream and one with Jim Beam Brands Inc. to manufacture and market a Starbucks premium liqueur product. It has an alliance with SYSCO Corporation to distribute its coffee and tea products to institutional food services for health care accounts, office coffee distributors, hotels, restaurants, airlines, and other retailers.

Starbucks Corporation is a very successful company. However, its stock price recently dropped, which can be attributed to a variety of factors. First, the success of Starbucks encouraged competitors to focus on coffee products and new restaurants. For example, McDonald's Corporation has greatly improved its sales and profits by putting increased emphasis on the quality of its coffee. The growth in the number of café-style coffeehouses and restaurants, like Panera Bread, also hurt Starbucks' same-store sales.

Second, while growing the number of stores rapidly has fueled growth in revenue and earnings, it also makes Starbucks so available that it may not be as special to consumers as it once was. Not too long ago, the arrival of a Starbucks store was a major event, a recognition that a town or neighborhood was worthy of the chic Seattle-based chain. However, in recent years, every street corner, airport concourse, and roadside rest stop in America seemed to attract a Starbucks. Recognition of the over-saturation problem is one reason why Starbucks decided to place its emphasis on store growth in international markets where its business remains robust. It also closed 100 underperforming locations in the United States.

Finally, in its attempts to be more efficient, Starbucks may have reduced the quality of the purchase and use experience. For example, by using flavor-locked packaging for its coffees, the fresh-ground-coffee aroma was lost, not to mention the sound of beans being scooped and ground onsite. By adding hot sandwiches and bakery products to compete with McDonald's, Starbucks became more of a fast-food restaurant than a coffeehouse in the minds of some consumers. By trading comfy, stuffed chairs for plastic and selling a variety of games and other products, the quality of the coffee-drinking experience was reduced for many consumers. By adding drive-throug windows and speeding up service, many consumers may have started to view Starbucks coffee as a commodity rather than something special and its employees as order-takers rather than knowledgeable coffee experts.

Discussion Questions

1. What is Starbucks' product?
2. What advantages does McDonald's have in competing with Starbucks for coffee sales?
3. What changes in society helped Starbucks become successful?
4. What strategic factors account for Starbucks' long-term success in building brand equity?
5. What are the advantages of the Starbucks Card to the company and to customers?
6. What recommendations do you have to improve Starbucks competitive position?
7. Evaluate Starbucks' mission statement and guiding principles. What do they suggest about the company?

Case 7

easyCar.com

John J. Lawrence *University of Idaho*

Luis Solis *University of Idaho Instituto de Empresa*

> At easyCar we aim to offer you outstanding value for money. To us value for money means a reliable service at a low price. We achieve this by simplifying the product we offer, and passing on the benefits to you in the form of lower prices.[1]

This was the stated mission of car rental company easyCar.com. EasyCar was a member of the EasyGroup family of companies, founded by the flamboyant Greek entrepreneur Stelios Haji-Ioannou, who was known simply as Stelios to most. Stelios founded low-cost air carrier easyJet.com in 1995 after convincing his father, a Greek shipping billionaire, to loan him the £5 million (note: in January 2003, £1 = €1.52 = U.S.$1.61) needed to start the business.[2] EasyJet was one of the early low-cost, no frills air carriers in the European market. It was built upon a foundation of simple point-to-point flights, booked over the Internet, and the aggressive use of yield management policies to maximize the revenues it derived from its assets. The company proved highly successful, and as a result Stelios had expanded this business model to industries with similar characteristics as the airline industry. EasyCar, founded in 2000 on a £10 million investment on the part of Stelios, was one of these efforts.

EasyCar's approach, built on the easyJet model, was quite different from the approaches used by the traditional rental car companies. EasyCar rented only a single vehicle type at each location it operated, while most of its competitors rented a wide variety of vehicle types.

EasyCar did not work with agents—over 95 percent of its bookings were made through the company's Web site, with the remainder of bookings being made directly through the company's phone reservation system (at a cost to the customer of €0.95 per minute for the call). Most rental car companies worked with a variety of intermediaries, with their own Web sites accounting for less than 10 percent of their total booking.[3] And like easyJet, easyCar managed prices in an attempt to have its fleet rented out 100 percent of the time and to generate the maximum revenue from its rentals. EasyCar's information system constantly evaluated projected demand and expected utilization at each site, and adjusted price accordingly. Because of its aggressive pricing, easyCar was able to achieve a fleet utilization

---

This case was prepared by John J. Lawrence of the University of Idaho and Luis Solis of the Instituto de Empresa as a basis for class discussion.

[1] EasyCar.com Web site

[2] "The Big Picture—An Interview with Stelios," *Sunday Herald* (UK), March 16, 2003.

[3] "Click to Fly," *Economist,* 13 May 2004.

rate in excess of 90 percent[4]—much higher than other major rental car companies. Industry leader Avis Europe, for example, had a fleet utilization rate of 68 percent.[5]

It was January 2003. EasyCar had broken even in the fiscal year ending September 2002[6] on revenues of £27 million.[7] This represented a significant improvement over 2001, when easyCar had lost £7.5 million on revenues of £18.5 million.[8] While pleased that the company had broken even in only its third year of operation, Stelios set aggressive financial goals for easyCar for the next two years. Plans called for quadrupling revenues in the next two years in preparation for a planned initial public offering in the second half of 2004. EasyCar's goal was to reach £100 million in revenue and £10 million in profit for the year 2004. The £100 million revenue goal and £10 million profit goal were felt necessary to obtain the desired return from an IPO. It was thought that with this level of performance, the company might be worth about £250 million.[9] In order to achieve these financial goals, the company was pushing to open an average of two new sites a week through 2003 and 2004 to reach a total of 180 sites by the end of 2004.[10]

The Rental Car Industry in Western Europe

The Western European rental car industry consisted of many different national markets that were only semi-integrated. While there were many companies that competed within this European rental car industry, a handful of companies held dominant positions, either across a number of national markets or within one or a few national markets. Industry experts saw the sector as ripe for consolidation.[11] Several international companies—notably Avis, Europcar, and Hertz—had strong positions across most major European markets. Within most countries, there was also a primarily national or regional company that had a strong position in its home market and perhaps moderate market share in neighboring markets. Sixt was the market leader in Germany, for example, while Atesa (in partnership with National) was the market leader in Spain. Generally these major players accounted for more than half of the market. In Germany, for example, Sixt, Europcar, Avis and Hertz had a combined 60 percent of the €2.5 billion German rental car market.[12] In Spain, the top five firms accounted for 60 percent of the €920 million Spanish rental car market. Generally, these top firms targeted both business and vacation travelers and offered a wide range of vehicles for rent. Exhibit 1 provides basic information on these market-leading companies.

In addition to these major companies, many smaller rental companies operated in each market. In Germany, for example, there were over 700 smaller companies,[13] while in Spain there were more than 1,600 smaller companies. Many of these smaller companies operated at only one or a few locations and were particularly prevalent in tourist locations. A number of brokers also operated in the sector, like Holiday Autos. Brokerage companies did not

[4]E. Simpkins, "Stelios Isn't Taking It Easy," *Sunday Telegraph* (UK), December 15, 2002.

[5]Avis Europe PLC 2002 annual report, p. 10, at ir.avis-europe.com/avis/reports on August 16, 2004.

[6]E. Simpkins, "Stelios Isn't Taking It Easy."

[7]"Marketing: Former eBay UK Chief Lands Top easyCar Position," *Financial Times Information Limited,* January 9, 2003.

[8]T. Burt, "EasyCar Agrees Deal with Vauxhall," *Financial Times,* April 30, 2002, p. 24.

[9]N. Hodgson, "Stelios Plans easyCar Float," *Liverpool Echo,* September 24, 2002.

[10]E. Simpkins, "Stelios Isn't Taking It Easy."

[11]"Marketing Week: Don't Write off the Car Rental Industry," *Financial Times Information Limited,* September 26, 2002.

[12]"EasyCar Set to Shake up German Car Rental Market," European Intelligence Wire, February 22, 2002.

[13]Ibid.

EXHIBIT 1   Information on easyCar's Major European Competitors

	easyCar	Avis Europe	Europcar	Hertz	Sixt
Number of rental outlets	46	3100	2,650	7,000	1,250
2002 fleet size	7,000	120,000	220,000	700,000	46,700
Number of countries	5	107	118	150	50
Largest market	UK	France	France	U.S.	Germany
Who owns company	EasyGroup/ Stelios Haji-Ioannou	D'Ieteren (Belgium) is majority shareholder	Volkswagen AG	Ford Motor Company	Publicly traded
European revenues	€41 million	€1.25 billion	€1.12 billion	€910 million	€600 million
Company Web site	www.easycar.com	www.avis-europe.com	www.europcar.com	www.hertz.com	ag.sixt.com

Source: Information in this table came from each company's Web site and online annual reports. European revenues are for vehicle rental in Europe and are estimated based on market share estimates for 2001 from Avis Europe's website.

own their own fleet of cars but basically managed the excess inventory of other companies and matched customers with rental companies with excess fleet capacity.

Overall, the rental car market could be thought of as composed of two broad segments: a business segment and a tourist/leisure segment. Depending on the market, the leisure segment represented somewhere between 45 and 65 percent of the overall market, and a large part of this segment was very price conscious. The business segment made up the remaining 35 to 55 percent of the market. It was less price sensitive than the tourist segment and more concerned about service quality, convenience, and flexibility.

The Growth of EasyCar

EasyCar opened its first location in London, on April 20, 2000 under the name EasyRentacar. In the same week, easyCar opened locations in Glasgow and Barcelona. All three locations were popular easyJet destinations. Vehicles initially could be rented for as low as €15 per day plus a one-time car preparation fee of €8. Each of these locations had a fleet consisting entirely of Mercedes A-class vehicles. It was the only vehicle that easyCar rented at the time.

EasyCar had signed a deal with Mercedes, amidst much fanfare, at the Geneva Motor Show earlier in the year to purchase a total of 5,000 A-class vehicles. The vehicles, which came with guaranteed buy-back terms, cost easyCar's parent company a little over £6 million.[14] Many in the car rental industry were surprised by the choice, expecting easyCar to rely on less expensive models.[15] In describing the acquisition of the 5000 Mercedes vehicles, Stelios had said:

> The choice of Mercedes reflects the easyGroup brand. EasyRentacar will use brand new Mercedes cars in the same way that easyJet uses brand new Boeing aircraft. We do not compromise on the hardware, we just use innovation to substantially reduces costs. The car hire industry is where the airline industry was five years ago, a cartel feeding off the corporate client. EasyRentacar will provide a choice for consumers who pay out of their own pockets and who will not be ripped off for traveling mid-week.[16]

EasyCar quickly expanded to other locations, focusing first on those locations that were popular with easyJet customers, including Amsterdam, Geneva, Nice, and Malaga. By July 2001, a little over a year after its initial launch, easyCar had fleets of Mercedes A-class vehicles in 14 locations in the UK, Spain, France, and the Netherlands. At this point, easyCar

[14]N. Hodgson, "Stelios Plans easyCar Float."

[15]A. Felsted, "EasyCar Courts Clio for Rental Fleet," *Financial Times,* February 11, 2002, p. 26.

[16]EasyCar.com Web site news release, March 1, 2000.

secured £27 million from a consortium of Bank of Scotland Corporate Banking and NBGI Private Equity to further expand its operations. The package consisted of a combination of equity and loan stock.

While easyCar added a few sites in the second half of 2001 and early 2002, volatile demand in the wake of the September 11 attacks forced easyCar to roll out new rental locations somewhat slower than originally expected.[17] Growth accelerated, however, in spring 2002. Between May 2002 and January 2003, easyCar opened 30 new locations, going from 18 sites to a total of 48 sites. This acceleration in growth also coincided with a change in easyCar's policy regarding the makeup of its fleet. By May 2002, easyCar's fleet consisted of 6,000 Mercedes A-class vehicles across 18 sites. Beginning in May, however, easyCar began to stock its fleet with other types of vehicles. It still maintained its policy of only offering a single vehicle at each location, but now the vehicle the customer received depended on the location. The first new vehicle easyCar introduced was the Vauxhall Corsa. According to Stelios,

> Vauxhall Corsas cost easyCar £2 a day less than Mercedes A-Class so we can pass this saving on to customers. Customers themselves will decide if they want to pay a premium for a Mercedes. EasyGroup companies benefit from economies of scale where relevant but we also want to create contestable markets among our suppliers so that we can keep the cost to our customers as low as possible.[18]

By January 2003, easyCar was also using Ford Focuses (four locations), Renault Clios (three locations), Toyota Yarises (three locations), and Mercedes Smart cars (two locations), in addition to the Vauxhall Corsas (seven locations) and the Mercedes A-class vehicles (28 locations). Plans called for a further expansion of the fleet, from the 7,000 vehicles that easyCar had in January to 24,000 vehicles across 180 rental sites by the end of 2004.[19]

In addition to making vehicles available at more locations, easyCar had also changed its policies for 2003 to allow rentals for as little as one hour, and with as little as one hour's notice of rental. By making this change, Stelios felt that easyCar could be a serious competitor to local taxis, buses, trains, and even car ownership. EasyCar expected that if it made car rental simple enough and cheap enough, some people living in traffic-congested European cities who only use their car occasionally would give up the costs and hassles of car ownership and simply hire an easyCar when they needed a vehicle. Tapping into this broader transportation market would help the company reach its ambitious future sales goals.

Facilities

EasyCar had facilities in a total of 17 cities in five European countries, as shown in Exhibit 2. It primarily located its facilities near bus and train stations in the major European cities, seeking out sites that offered lower lease costs. It generally avoided prime airport locations, as the cost for space at and, in some cases, near airports was significantly higher than most other locations. When easyCar did locate near an airport, it generally chose sites off the airport, in order to reduce the cost of the lease. Airport locations also tended to require longer hours to satisfy customers arriving on late flights or departing on very early flights. EasyCar kept its airport locations open 24 hours a day, whereas its other locations were generally only open from 7 A.M. to 11 P.M.

The physical facilities at all locations were kept to a minimum. In many locations, easyCar leased space in an existing parking garage. Employees worked out of a small, self-contained

---

[17]T. Burt, "EasyCar Agrees Deal with Vauxhall."

[18]EasyCar.com Web site news release, May 2, 2002.

[19]"Marketing Week: EasyCar Appoints Head of European Marketing," *Financial Times Information Limited*, January 9, 2003.

EXHIBIT 2
EasyCar Locations in January 2003

Source: EasyCar.com Web site January 2003.

Country	City	Number	Number Near an Airport
France	Nice	1	1
France	Paris	8	0
Netherlands	Amsterdam	3	1
Spain	Barcelona	2	0
Spain	Madrid	2	0
Spain	Majorca	1	1
Spain	Malaga	1	1
Switzerland	Geneva	1	1
UK	Birmingham	2	0
UK	Bromley	1	0
UK	Croydon	1	1
UK	Glasgow	2	1
UK	Kingston-Upon-Thames	1	0
UK	Liverpool	2	1
UK	London	15	0
UK	Manchester	2	1
UK	Waterford	1	0
Total	5 Countries, 17 Cities	46	9

cubicle within the garage. The cubicle, depending on the location, might be no more than 15 square meters, and included little more than a small counter and a couple of computers at which staff processed customers as they came to pick up or return their vehicles. EasyCar also leased a number of spaces within the garage for its fleet of cars. However, because easyCar's vehicles were rented 90 percent of the time, the number of spaces required at an average site, which had a fleet of about 150 cars, was only 15–20 spaces.[20] To speed up the opening of new sites, easyCar had equipped a number of vans with all the needed computer and telephone equipment to run a site.[21] From an operational perspective, it could open a new location by simply leasing 20 or so spaces in a parking garage, hiring a small staff, driving a van to the location, and adding the location to the company's Web site. Depending on the fleet size at a location, easyCar typically had only one or two people working at a site at a time.

Vehicle Pickup and Return Processes

Customers arrived at a site to pick up a vehicle within a prearranged one-hour time period. Each customer selected this time slot when he or she booked the vehicles. EasyCar adjusted the first day's rental price based on the pickup time. Customers who picked their cars up earlier in the day or at popular times were charged more compared to customers picking up their cars later in the day or at less busy times. Customers were required to bring a printed copy of their contract, along with the credit card they used to make the booking and identification. Given the low staffing levels, customers occasionally had to wait 30 minutes or more to be processed and receive their vehicles, particularly at peak times of the day. Processing a customer began with the employee accessing the customer's contract online. If the customer was a new easyCar customer to the site, the basic policies and possible additional charges were briefly explained. The employee then made copies of the customer's identification and credit card and took a digital photo of the customer. The customer was charged an €80 refundable deposit, signed the contract, and was on the way.

[20]E. Simpkins, "Stelios Isn't Taking It Easy."
[21]Ibid.

All vehicles were rented with more or less empty fuel tanks with the exact level dependent on how much gasoline was left in the vehicle when the previous renter returned it. Customers were provided with a small map of the immediate area around the rental site, showing the location and hours of nearby gas stations. Customers could return vehicles with any amount of gas in them as long as the "low-fuel" indicator light in the vehicle was not on. Customers who returned vehicles with the low-fuel indicator light on were charged a fueling fee of €16.

Customers were also expected to return the vehicle within a prearranged one-hour time period, which they also selected at the time of booking. While customers did not have to worry about refueling the car before returning it, they were expected to thoroughly clean the car. This clean car policy had been implemented in May 2002 as a way to further reduce the price customers could pay for their vehicle. Prior to this change, all customers paid a fixed preparation fee of €11 each time they rented a vehicle (up from the €8 preparation fee when the company started operations in 2000). The new policy reduced this up-front preparation fee to €4 but required customers to either return the vehicle clean or pay an additional cleaning fee of €16. In order to avoid any misunderstanding about what it meant by a clean car, easyCar provided customers with an explicit description of what constituted a clean car, both for the interior and the exterior of the car. This included that it had to be apparent that the exterior of the car had been washed prior to returning the vehicle. The map that customers were provided when they picked up their cars that showed nearby gas stations also showed nearby car washes where they could clean the car before returning it. While easyCar had received some bad press in relation to the policy,[22] 85 percent of customers returned their vehicles clean as a result of the policy.

When a customer returned the vehicle, an easyCar employee would check to make sure that the vehicle was clean, undamaged, and that the low-fuel indicator light was not on. The employee would also check the kilometers driven. The customer would then be notified of any additional charges. These charges would be subtracted from the €80 deposit and the difference refunded to the customer's credit card (or, if additional charges exceeded the €80 deposit, the customer's credit card would be charged the difference).

Pricing

EasyCar clearly differentiated itself from its competitors with its low price. In addition, pricing also played a key role in easyCar's efforts to achieve high utilization of its fleet of cars. EasyCar advertised prices as low as €5 per day plus a per-rental preparation fee of €4. Prices, however, varied by the location and dates of the rental, when the booking was made, and what time the car was to be picked up and returned. EasyCar's systems constantly evaluated projected demand and expected utilization at each site and adjusted price accordingly. Achieving the €5 per day rate usually required customers to book well in advance, and these rates were typically only available on weekdays. Weekend rates, when booked well in advance, typically started a few euros higher than the weekday rates. As a given rental date approached, however, the price typically went up significantly as easyCar approached 100 percent fleet utilization for that day. Rates could literally triple overnight if there was sufficient booking activity. Generally, however, easyCar's price was less than half that of its major competitors. EasyCar, unlike most other rental car companies, required customers to pay in full at the time of booking, and once a booking was made, it was nonrefundable.

EasyCar's base price covered only the core rental of the vehicle—the total price customers paid was in many cases much higher and depended on how the customer reserved, paid for,

---

[22]J. Hyde, "Travel View: Clearing up on the Extras," *The Observer* (UK), July 7, 2002.

used, and returned the vehicle. EasyCar's price was based on customers booking through the company's Web site and paying for their rental with their easyMoney credit card. EasyMoney was the easyGroup's credit and financial services company. Customers who chose to book through the company's phone reservation system were charged an additional €0.95 a minute for the call, and those who used other credit cards were charged €5 extra. All vehicles had to be paid for by a credit or debit card—cash was not accepted. The base rental price allowed customers to drive vehicles 100 kilometers per day—additional kilometers were charged at a rate of €0.12 per kilometer. In addition, customers were expected to return their cars clean and on time. Customers who returned cars that did not meet easyCar's standards for cleanness were charged a €16 cleaning fee. Those who returned their cars late were immediately charged €120 and subsequently charged an additional €120 for each 24-hour period in which the car was not returned. EasyCar explained the high late fee as representing the cost that it would likely incur in providing another vehicle to the next customer. Customers wishing to make any changes to their bookings were also charged a change fee of €16. Changes could be made either before the rental started or during the rental period, but were limited to changing the dates, times, and location of the rental and were subject to the prices and vehicle availability at the time the change was being made. If the change resulted in an overall lower price for the rental, however, no refund was provided for the difference.

Beginning in 2003, all customers were also required to purchase loss/damage insurance for an additional charge of €4 a day that eliminated the customer's liability for loss or damage to the vehicle (excluding damage to the tires or windshield of the vehicle). Through 2002, customers were able to choose whether or not to purchase additional insurance from easyCar to eliminate any financial liability in the event that the rental vehicle was damaged. The cost of this insurance had been €6 a day, and approximately 60 percent of easyCar's customers purchased this optional insurance. Those not purchasing this insurance had either assumed the liability for the first €800 in damages personally, or had their own insurance through some other means (e.g., some credit card companies provide this insurance to their cardholders at no additional charge for short-term rentals paid for with the credit card).

EasyCar's Web site attempted to make all these additional charges clear to customers at the time of their booking. EasyCar had received a fair amount of bad press when it first opened for business after many renters complained about having to pay undisclosed charges when they returned their cars.[23] In response, easyCar had revamped its Web site in an effort to make these charges more transparent to customers and to explain the logic behind many of these charges.

Promotion

EasyCar's promotional efforts had through 2002 focused primarily on posters and press advertising. Posters were particularly prevalent in metro systems and bus and train stations in cities were easyCar had operations. All this advertising focused on easyCar's low price. According to founder Stelios:

> You will never see an advert for an easy company offering an experience—it's about price. If you create expectations you can't live up to then you will ultimately suffer as a result.[24]

In 2002, easyCar spent £1.43 million on such advertising.[25]

EasyCar also promoted itself by displaying its name, phone number, and Web site address prominently on the doors and rear window of its entire fleet of vehicles, and took advantage

---

[23]J. Stanton, "The Empire That's Easy Money," *Edinburgh Evening News,* November 26, 2002.
[24]"The big picture—an interview with Stelios."
[25]"Marketing Week: EasyCar Appoints Head of European Marketing."

of free publicity when the opportunity presented itself. An example of seeking out such publicity occurred when Hertz complained that easyCar's comparative advertising campaign in the Netherlands that featured the line "The best reason to use easyCar.com can be found at hertz.nl" violated Dutch law that required comparative advertising to be exact, not general. In response, Stelios and a group of easyCar employees, dressed in orange boiler suits and with a fleet of easyCar vehicles, protested outside the Hertz Amsterdam office with signs asking "What is Hertz frightened of?"[26]

In an effort to help reach its goal of quadrupling sales in the next two years, easyCar had hired Jennifer Mowat for the new position of commercial director to take over responsibility for easyCar's European marketing. Mowat had previously been eBay's UK country manager and had recently completed an MBA in Switzerland. Previously, Stelios and easyCar's managing director, Andrew Fitzmaurice, had handled the marketing function themselves.[27] As part of this stepped-up marketing effort, easyCar also planned to double its advertising budget for 2003, to £3 million, and to begin to advertise on television. The television advertising campaign was to feature easyCar's founder, Stelios.[28]

Legal Challenges

EasyCar faced several challenges to its approaches. The most significant dealt with a November 2002 ruling made by the Office of Fair Trading (OFT) that easyCar had to grant customers seven days from the time they made a booking to cancel their booking and receive a full refund. The OFT was a UK governmental agency that was responsible for protecting UK consumers from unfair and/or anticompetitive business practices. The ruling against easyCar was based on the 2000 Consumer Protection Distance Selling Regulations. These regulations stipulated that companies that sell at a distance (e.g., by Internet, phone) must provide customers with a seven-day cooling-off period, during which time customers can cancel their contracts with the company and receive a full refund. The law exempted accommodation, transportation, catering, and leisure service companies from this requirement. The OFT's ruling concluded that easyCar did not qualify as a transportation service company because the consumers had to drive themselves, and as such they were not receiving a transport service, just a car.[29]

EasyCar had appealed the OFT's decision to the UK High Court on the grounds that it was indeed a transportation service company and was entitled to an exemption from this requirement. EasyCar was hopeful that it would eventually win this legal challenge. EasyCar had argued that this ruling would destroy the company's book-early-pay-less philosophy and could lead to a tripling of prices.[30] Chairman Stelios was quoted as saying:

> It is very serious. My fear is that as soon as we put in the seven-day cooling off periods our utilization rate will fall from 90 percent to 65 percent. That's the difference between a profitable company and an unprofitable one.[31]

EasyCar was also concerned that prolonged legal action on this point could interfere with its plans for a 2004 IPO.

---

[26]EasyCar.com Web site news release, April 22, 2002.

[27]"Marketing Week: EasyCar Appoints Head of European Marketing."

[28]"Campaigning: EasyGroup Appoints Publicis for easyCar TV Advertising Brief," *Financial Times Information Limited,* January 31, 2003.

[29]J. Macintosh, "EasyCar Sues OFT Amid Threat to Planned Flotation," *Financial Times,* November 22, 2002, p. 4.

[30]"Marketing Week: EasyCar Appoints Head of European Marketing."

[31]J. Mackintosh, "EasyCar Sues OFT Amid Threat to Planned Flotation."

OFT, for its part, had also applied to the UK High Court for an injunction to make the company comply with the ruling. Other rental car companies were generally unconcerned about the ruling, as few offered big discounts for early bookings or nonrefundable bookings.[32]

EasyCar's new policy of posting the pictures of customers whose cars were 15 days or more overdue was also drawing legal criticism. EasyCar had recently received public warnings from lawyers that this new policy might violate data protection, libel, privacy, confidentiality, and human rights laws.[33] Of particular concern to some lawyers was the possibility that easyCar might post the wrong person's picture, given the large number of customers the company dealt with.[34] Such a mistake could open the company to costly libel suits. The policy of posting the pictures of overdue customers on the easyCar Web site, initiated in November 2002, was designed to reduce the losses associated with customers renting a vehicle and never returning it. The costs were significant, according to Stelios:

> These cars are expensive, £15,000 each, and we have 6,000 of them. At any given time we are looking for as many as several tens which, are overdue. If we don't get one back, it's a write-off. We are writing off an entire car, and its uninsurable.[35]

Stelios was also convinced of the legality of the new policy. In a letter to the editor responding to the legal concerns raised in the press, Stelios said:

> From a legal perspective, we have been entirely factual and objective and are merely reporting the details of the overdue car and the person who collected it. In addition, our policy is made very clear in our terms and conditions and the photo is taken both overtly and with the consent of the customer. . . . I estimate the total cost of overdue cars to be 5 percent of total easyCar costs, or 50p on every car rental day for all customers. In 2004, when I intend to float easyCar, this cost will amount to £5 million unless we can reduce our quantity of overdue cars.[36]

In the past, easyCar had simply provided pictures to police when a rental was 15 or more days overdue. It was hoped that posting the picture would both discourage drivers from not returning vehicles and shame those drivers who currently had overdue cars into returning them. In fact, the first person who easyCar posted to its Web site did indeed return his car two days later. The vehicle was 29 days late.[37]

The Future

At the end of 2002, Stelios had stepped down as the CEO of easyJet so that he could devote more of his time to the other easyGroup companies, including easyCar. He had three priorities for the new year. One was to turn around a money-losing easyInternetCafe business, which Stelios had described as "the worst mistake of my career."[38] The 22-store chain had lost £80 million in the last two years. A second was to oversee the planned launch of another new easyGroup business, easyCinema, in spring 2003. And the third was to oversee the rapid expansion of the easyCar chain, so that it would be ready for an initial public offering in the second half of 2004.

---

[32]Ibid.

[33]B. Sherwood, & A. Wendlandt. "EasyCar May Be in Difficulty over Naming Ploy," *Financial Times*, November 14, 2002, p. 2.

[34]Ibid.

[35]"e-business: Internet Fraudsters Fail to Steal Potter Movie's Magic & Other News," *Financial Times Information Limited*, November 19, 2002.

[36]S. Haji-Ioannou, "Letters to the Editor: Costly Effect of Late Car Return," *Financial Times*, November 16, 2002, p. 10.

[37]M. Hookham, "How Stelios Nets Return of His Cars," *Daily Post* (Liverpool, UK), November 14, 2002.

[38]S. Bentley, "The Worst Mistake of My Career, By Stelios" *Financial Times*, December 24, 2002.

8

Pfizer, Inc., Animal Health Products[1]— Industry Downturns and Marketing Strategy

Jakki Mohr, and

Sara Streeter, MBA *University of Montana*

Gail Oss, Territory Manager of Pfizer, Inc., Animal Health Group in western Montana and southeastern Idaho, was driving back to her home office after a day of visiting cattle ranchers in her territory. The combination of the spring sunshine warming the air and the snow-capped peaks of the Bitterroot Mountains provided a stunningly beautiful backdrop for her drive. But the majestic beauty provided little relief to her troubled thoughts.

The NAFTA agreement with Canada and Mexico had hit local ranchers particularly hard. The influx of beef cattle into the U.S. market from these countries, as well as beef from other countries (e.g., Australia) that entered the United States via more lenient import restrictions in Mexico, had wreaked havoc over the past year. Prices of beef had declined precipitously from the prior year. Ranchers in the past had retained sufficient reserves to come back from a bad year, but this year, things were particularly bad. The prices being offered for the calves by the feedlot operators were, in many cases, less than the costs of raising those calves. Ranchers' objectives had changed from making some modest income off their cattle operations to minimizing their losses.

In this environment, ranchers were actively seeking ways to cut costs. Gail sold high-quality animal health products, oftentimes at a premium price. One way in which ranchers could cut costs was either to scrimp on animal healthcare products, such as vaccines and

[1]Some of the information in this case has been modified to protect the proprietary nature of firms' marketing strategies. The case is intended to be used as a basis for class discussion rather than to illustrate either effective or ineffective marketing strategies.

antibiotics, or to switch to a lower-cost alternative. The current environment posed a particularly severe threat, not only to Gail's company, but also to her very livelihood. Gail had spent a substantial amount of time and effort cultivating long-term relationships with many of these ranchers—many of whom she had had to convince of her credibility, given her gender. Given the time and effort she had spent cultivating these relationships, as well as the camaraderie she felt with her customers, she did not want to see the ranchers in her territory go under. Ranching was an important part of the history of Montana; many ranchers had ties to the land going back generations. They took pride in producing the food for many tables in the U.S. and other areas of the world. Gail felt that Pfizer could use its fairly significant resources in a very influential manner to help these ranchers. Merely lowering the price on her products (if that was even possible) was merely a band-aid solution to the problem.

As part of Gail's weekly responsibilities, she communicated via an automated computer system to her sales manager, Tom Brooks, (also in Montana) and to the marketing managers at headquarters (in Exton, Pennsylvania). She knew she needed to report the severity of the situation, but more importantly, she wanted to encourage headquarters to take the bull by the horns, so to speak. So, she was pondering the message she would write that evening from her kitchen table.

Industry Background

The supply chain (Exhibit 1) for beef begins with the cow/calf producer (the commercial rancher). Commercial ranchers are in the business of breeding and raising cattle for the purpose of selling them to feedlots. Ranchers keep a herd of cows that are bred yearly. The calves are generally born in the early spring, weaned in October, and shipped to feedlots generally in late October/early November. The ranchers' objectives are to minimize death loss in their herd and to breed cows that give birth to low birth-weight calves (for calving ease), produce beef that will grade low choice by having a good amount of marbling, and produce calves that gain weight quickly. Success measures include conception rate of cows exposed to bulls, live birth rates, birth weights, weaning weights, death loss, and profitability. By the time a rancher sells his calves to the feedlot, the name of the game is pounds. The rancher generally wants the biggest calves possible by that time.

Within a commodity market, basic laws of supply and demand are influenced by those in a position to control access to the markets. Four meatpackers controlled roughly 80 percent of the industry. Meatpackers have acted as an intermediary between the meat consumer and the meat producer. This situation has not facilitated a free flow of information throughout the supply chain, and therefore, the industry has not been strongly consumer focused.

Exhibit 2 traces the market share for beef, pork, and poultry from 1970–1997 and projects changes in the market through 2003. The market share for beef has fallen from 44 percent in 1970 to 32% in 1997, a 27% drop.

Some of the reasons for the decline included

- Changes in consumer lifestyles (less time spent in preparing home-cooked meals); an interesting statistic is that two-thirds of all dinner decisions are made on the same day and of those, three-quarters don't know what they're going to make at 4:30 PM.
- Health/nutritional issues (dietary considerations involving cholesterol, fat content, food-borne diseases, etc.).
- Switching to alternative meat products.

EXHIBIT 1
Supply Chain for Beef

Cow/Calf Producers → Feedlot → Meat Packer → Customers (food service, retail, etc.)

EXHIBIT 2
Per Capita Meat Consumption % Market Share (Retail Weight)

Source: USDA & NCBA.

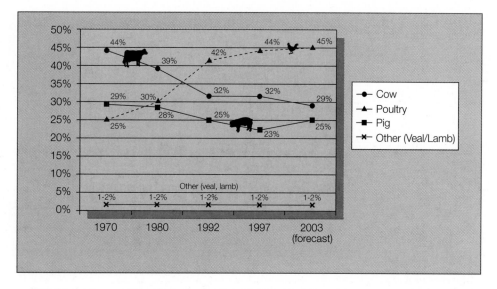

In addition, the pork and poultry industries had done a better job of marketing their products. During 1997, the number of new poultry products (for example, stuffed chicken entrees, gourmet home meal replacements) introduced to the market increased 13 percent from the prior year, compared to an increase of only 3.5 percent for new beef products. And, retail pricing for beef remained stubbornly high (although this high price did not translate into higher prices of the calves on a per-weight basis to the ranchers, as discussed subsequently).

Based upon historical data, shown in Exhibit 3, the beef production cycle spans a 12-year period in which production levels expand and contract. As Exhibit 3 shows, the amount of beef produced (bars in the chart, millions of pounds on the left-hand scale) increased through the mid-90s—despite the declining beef consumption in the United States shown in the prior figure. This relationship between production and consumption is consistent with other commodity markets, where an inverse relationship between supply and demand exists.

Some of the reasons for increased beef production in the mid-90s included

- Herd liquidation: low cattle prices, coupled with the high cost of feed, drove some producers out of business.
- Improved genetics and animal health/nutrition increased production yields; indeed, although cow numbers had decreased by 10 percent since 1985 (as noted by Exhibit 4), productivity per cow increased by 29 percent.
- Export of beef increased sevenfold since 1985 (to 2 billion pounds); key markets include Japan (54 percent of export volume); Canada (16 percent); Korea (11 percent), and Mexico (9 percent).

Exhibit 3 also shows that the price the ranchers received for their beef cattle varied inversely with production (right-hand scale). Although calf prices were expected to rise slightly through the late 90s/early 2000s, the prices paid were still far below the relatively high prices consumers paid at retail. One of the reasons given for the relatively low prices paid to ranchers on a per-pound basis for their calves was the high degree of concentration at the meat packer level of the supply chain. As noted previously, four packing houses controlled access to the market. Some ranchers believed this gave the packing houses near-monopoly power in setting prices (both for what they would pay feedlot operators for the

EXHIBIT 3
Beef Production and Price

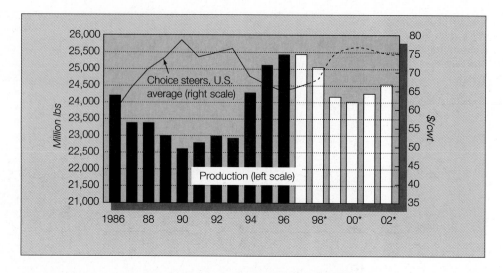

calves, and in charging prices to their downstream customers (e.g., the grocery store chains). Although the U.S. government had investigated the possibility of collusion among packers, the evidence was not sufficient to draw any firm conclusions.

To further complicate matters, the NAFTA agreement passed in 1989 had given open access to the U.S. markets from Mexican and Canadian ranchers. The lowering of trade barriers, coupled with weakness in the Canadian dollar and the Mexican peso, made imported livestock cheap, compared to U.S.-grown animals. As a result, thousands of head of cattle came streaming across the borders. The flow was heaviest from Canada.

During the summer of 1998, ranchers had been quite vocal in drawing attention to the influx of cattle from Canada. Local governments were somewhat responsive to their concerns. Indeed, trucks carrying Canadian cattle had been turned back at the U.S./Canadian border for minor infractions, such as licensing. In addition, the trucks were consistently pulled over for inspections. A private coalition of ranchers, calling itself the Ranchers-Cattlemen Action Legal Foundation (R-CALF) filed three separate petitions with the U.S. International Trade Commission (ITC) on October 1, 1998, two against Canada and one against Mexico, asking for U.S. government trade investigations. The group requested that antidumping duties be levied on meat or livestock imports from the two countries. The Montana Stockgrowers Association had been an early and steadfast supporter of R-CALF.

The ITC determined that there was evidence to support the charge that Canadian cattle imports were causing material injury to U.S. domestic cattle producers. The Department of Commerce began to collect information on Canadian subsidies and prices at which Canadian cattle are sold in Canada and in the United States. In the case against Mexico, the ITC determined that there was no indication that imports of live cattle from Mexico were causing "material injury" to the domestic industry in the U.S. Dissatisfied with the response, R-CALF decided to appeal the case to the Court of International Trade.

Ranchers were doing what they could to minimize the impact of the NAFTA agreement on their livelihoods; however, some could not sustain their operations in light of the lower cattle prices. The number of cattle operations was declining. In many cases, smaller ranchers were selling out to their larger neighbors. This reality was reflected in the cattle inventory statistics, shown in Exhibit 4. The number of cattle kept by U.S. ranchers had declined from a high of approximately 132 million head in 1975, to just under 100 million head in 1998. As noted previously, improvements in genetics and animal health and nutrition allowed ranchers to increase production yields, even with fewer head.

EXHIBIT 4   **Total U.S. Inventory**

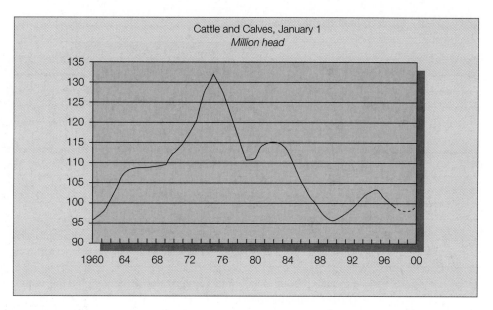

Additional Industry Changes

Some of the changes that had occurred in the poultry and pork industries, including more ready-to-eat products and branded products, were expected to diffuse into the cattle industry. Industry analysts believed that the beef industry would need to develop products that could be more easily prepared, and to develop branded products that consumers could recognize and rely upon for quality and convenience. In addition, industry analysts believed that the beef industry would need to improve the quality of its products (in terms of more consistent taste and tenderness), as currently only 25 percent of the beef produced met quality targets.

The development of branded beef would require a tracking system from "birth-to-beef" in the supply chain. Such tracking would allow standardized health, quality, and management protocols, as well as improved feedback through the entire production model. This change would also necessitate the producers being more closely linked to the feedlots to improve the quality of the beef. Branded beef production would move the industry from a cost-based (production) model to a value-added model. Better coordination along the supply chain would insure an increased flow of information from the consumer to the producer. Alliances between the cow/calf producer and the feedlots would allow ranchers to better track the success of their calves (based on health and weight gain). Such data could allow the ranchers to further improve the genetics of their herd by tracking which cow/bull combinations had delivered the higher-yield calves. As part of these trends, some degree of integration or vertical coordination will occur in the beef industry. Ranchers will need to participate in order to ensure market access for their product. Ranchers will have to think beyond the boundaries of their own ranches.

Pfizer Animal Health Group

Pfizer Inc. is a research-based, diversified health care company with global operations. Pfizer Animal Health is one of the corporation's three major business groups (the other two being the Consumer Health Care Group and U.S. Pharmaceuticals). The Animal Health

EXHIBIT 5   **Pfizer Animal Health Organization**

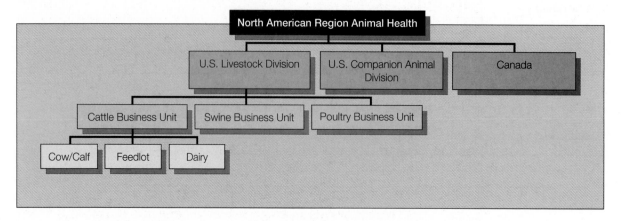

Products Group accounted for roughly 12 percent of the company's revenues in 1998 (Pfizer Annual Report).

Pfizer Animal Health products are sold to veterinarians and animal health distributors in more than 140 countries around the world for use by livestock producers and horse and pet owners; the products are used in more than 30 animal species. Pfizer Animal Health is committed to providing high-quality, research-based health products for livestock and companion animals. The company continues to invest significant dollars for research and development. As a result, Pfizer has many new animal health products in its research pipeline, a number of which have already been introduced in some international markets and will become available in the United States in the next several years.

As Exhibit 5 shows, the Animal Health Group is divided into a North America Region with a U.S. Livestock Division, a U.S. Companion Animal Division (cats, dogs, etc.), and Canada. The Cow/Calf Division falls under the Cattle Business Unit within the Livestock Division. That Division is organized further by product type (Wood Mackenzie Report).

The marketing managers for each cattle market segment work closely with product managers and sales managers to ensure timely, accurate information back from the field. Territory managers responsible for all sales activities report to an Area Sales Manager, who in turn reports to the national sales and marketing manager. Territory managers are typically compensated on a roughly 80 percent salary/20 percent commission basis. This percentage would vary by salesperson by year: in a good year the commission might be a much higher percentage of overall earnings, while in a bad year, the salary component might be a greater percentage of the salesperson's overall earnings.

Marketing Strategy

Pfizer's Cow/Calf Division offers a full range of products to cattle ranchers, including vaccines for both newborn calves and their mothers, medications (for example, dewormers, antidiarrheals), and antibiotics (for pneumonia and other diseases). Pfizer's sophisticated research-and-development system resulted in a number of new and useful products for the market. For example, Pfizer developed a long-lasting dewormer that was simply poured along the cow's back. This technology was a significant time-saver for the rancher, eliminating the need to administer either an oral medication or an injection. Moreover, Pfizer had been the first company to come up with a modified-live and killed virus vaccine, a significant technological breakthrough that provided safety for pregnant animals and the efficacy of a modified-live virus.

Pfizer offered a diverse product line to cow/calf ranchers. Some of Pfizer's key product lines are compared to those of competitors in Exhibit 6.

Pfizer segmented ranchers in the cow/calf business on the basis of herd size, as shown in Exhibit 7.

"Hobbyists" are so called because in many cases, these ranchers run their cattle as a sideline to some other job. "Traditionalists'" main livelihood is their cattle operation. The "Business" segment operations are large ranches, owned either by a family or a corporation.

Pfizer's extensive network of field sales representatives visits the ranchers to inform them about new and existing products. Time spent with accounts was typically allocated on the basis of volume of product purchased.

Pfizer positioned its products on the combination of superior science (resulting from its significant R&D efforts) and high-quality production/quality control techniques. For example, although other companies in the market (particularly generics) used similar formulations in their products, on occasion they did not have good quality control in the production line, resulting in batches of ineffective vaccines and recalls. Pfizer backed its products completely with a Technical Services Department. If ranchers had any kind of health or nutritional problem with their herds, they could call on a team of Pfizer technical specialists who would work with the local veterinarian, utilizing blood and other diagnostics to identify the problem and suggest a solution.

Pfizer also was very involved in the cattle industry itself. Each territory manager was given an annual budget that included discretionary funds to be spent in his/her territory to sponsor industry activities such as seminars on herd health, stock shows, 4-H, and so forth. Gail Oss, for example, chose to spend a significant portion of her discretionary funds sponsoring meetings and conferences for the Montana Stockgrower's Association, which might include a veterinarian or a professor from the Extension Office of a state university speaking on issues pertinent to ranchers.

The majority of Pfizer's trade advertising was focused on specific products and appeared in cattle industry publications, such as *Beef Magazine* and *Bovine Veterinarian.* One ad read, "More veterinarians are satisfied with [Pfizer's] Dectomax Pour-On," and went on to describe veterinarians' superior satisfaction and greater likelihood of recommending Dectomax compared to a key competitor, Ivomec:

> Eighty-four percent of veterinarians who recommended Dectomax Pour-On said they were satisfied or very satisfied with its performance—compared to only 51 percent who were satisfied or very satisfied with Ivomec Eprinex Pour-On. . . . If choosing only between Dectomax and Ivomec, over three out of four veterinarians would choose to recommend Dectomax Pour-On.

Another ad read, "Calf Health Program Boosts Prices by Up to $21 More per Head." The data in the copy-intensive ad highlighted that "cow-calf producers enrolled in value-added programs like Pfizer Select Vaccine programs are being rewarded for their efforts with top-of-the-market prices." Such programs are based on a consistent program of vaccinating animals with specific products, and they provide optimal disease protection. The programs result in cattle that perform more consistently and predictably in terms of weight gain and beef quality—resulting in higher prices at sale time.

Although the territory managers called on ranchers (as well as the veterinarians, distributors, and dealers) in their territories, they sold no product directly to ranchers. Ranchers could buy their animal health products from either a local veterinarian or a distributor or dealer (such as a feed-and-seed store). The percentage of product flowing through vets or distributors and dealers varied significantly by region. In areas where feedlots (versus

EXHIBIT 6 Comparison of Product Lines

Company	Pfizer	American Home Products (Fort Dodge)	Bayer	Merial
Sales and Profitability	10-year average annual sales growth increase of 3.8%; average for global veterinary market is 6.9%. Profit rate in 1997 was 8.4%. Market share in 1997 was 15.3%	10-year average annual sales growth increase of 7.8%; average for global veterinary market is 6.9%. Profit rate in 1997 was 11.0%; market share was 9.0%	10-year average annual sales growth increase of 10.2%; average for global veterinary market is 6.9%. Profit rate in 1997 was 16.8%; market share was 10.9%.	10-year average annual sales growth increase of 11.9%; average for global veterinary market is 6.9%. Profit rate in 1997 was 22.8%; market share was 16.4%.
Bovine Diseases Covered by Product Range	IBR; P1–3; BVD; BRSV; leptospira; rotavirus; coronavirus; campylobacter; clostridia; E.Coli; pasteurellosis; haemophilus.	Pasteurellosis; enterotoxaemia; chlamydia; salmonella; IBR; P1–3; brucellosis; rabies; E.Coli; anaplasmosis; tetanus; BVD; BRSV; leptospirosis; trichomonas; campylobacter; papilloma; haemophilus	IBR; FMD; IPV; P1–3; balanoposthitis; clostridia; haemophilus; BRSV; BVD; leptospira; E.Coli; rhinotracheitis; campylobacter.	Foot and mouth; rabies; brucellosis; paratuberculosis; rhinotracheitis; rotavirus; coronavirus; colibaccillosis; parainfluenza; BVD; aglactia; foot rot; black leg; IBR; leptospira; clostridia; pasteurella; BRSV; E.Coli.
Significant Products for Cattle	Comprehensive product line; anti-infectives have formed basis of product line for many years; vaccine businesses also very important; also sells a performance enhancer, virginiamycin; parasiticides, led by Dectomax, starting to make significant impact on sales; Valbazen anthelmintic; broad range of general pharmaceuticals.	Predominantly a vaccine company; antibiotics centered on anti-mastitis products; anti-infectives based on penicillins, tetracyclines, sulphonamides and quinolones; parasiticides led by Cydectin; main products in general pharmaceuticals are anabolic implants for muscle growth.	Product range biased towards parasiticides, particularly ectoparasiticides, and antibiotics; overall product range is diverse; some mastitis anti-microbials; wide range of pharmaceuticals, but sales value of each product is limited; focus is more towards companion animal market.	Most important product sector is parasiticides, with product range dominated by Ivermectin, which was the first endectocide to reach the market; success of Ivermectin has drawn strong competition; remainder of product range made up primarily of anthelmintics and a range of general pharmaceuticals and vaccines.
Strengths	Strong manufacturing capabilities based on fermentation expertise and capacity; global marketing coverage supported by strategic local manufacture;	Leading global vaccine business; good international exposure; comprehensive vaccine product range; potential for growth through Cydectin.	Growing market in expanding companion animal sector; solid in-house manufacturing supported by global distribution capability;	Leading veterinary vaccine company with broad product portfolio; strong line of new product introductions; good companion animal

(continued)

EXHIBIT 6 *(concluded)*

Company	Pfizer	American Home Products (Fort Dodge)	Bayer	Merial
	strong range of new products in early commercialization; broad product range with strength in companion animals.		business focused on key market areas.	business; global distribution network; strength in parasiticides and vaccines sectors.
Weaknesses	North America still dominates turnover; high proportion of sales due to off-patent products; heavily dependent on performance of livestock markets.	Business with disparate parts requiring strong central focus; except for vaccines, product range is dominated by commodity products; R&D likely to be reduced.	Underweight in USA; lack of critical mass in biologicals; no blockbuster product in North American market; narrow anti-infectives product portfolio; current R&D emphasis away from new product discovery.	Specialist pharmaceutical product line, not significantly involved in livestock sectors; aging anti-infectives portfolio; Ivermectin subject to intense competition.
% of R&D to Sales*	5	3	3	2
Position on Quality vs. Price†	5	3.5	3	3
Price Support of Distibution Channel‡	2	4	3	3

* Specific ratios are considered proprietary. Hence, a general rating scale is used where 5 means a higher percentage of R&D/Sales and 1 is a lower percentage.
† 5 = Focus on Quality only; 1 = Focus on Low Price only
‡ 5 = Strong emphasis on SPIFs (Special Promotional Incentive Funds) and price-related trade promotions; 1 = low emphasis
Source: This information is taken from the Wood MacKenzie Animal Health Market Review and its Veterinary Company Profiles, both done on a worldwide basis.

EXHIBIT 7
Pfizer Market Segments, 1998

Segment	# of Cattle	# of Operations	% of National Cattle Inventory
Hobbyist	<100	808,000	50%
Traditionalist	100–499	69,000	36%
Business	500+	5,900	14%

cow/calf ranchers) were the predominant customers, 95 percent of the product might flow through distributors. In areas where ranchers are the predominant customers, vets might sell 50 percent of the product, depending upon customer preferences.

Vets were particularly important given that the overwhelming majority of ranchers said that the person they trusted the most when it came to managing the health of their herd was their veterinarian. Pfizer capitalizes on this trust in the vet in its marketing program. When the vet consults and recommends a Pfizer product to a rancher, the vet gives the rancher a coded coupon which may be redeemed at either a vet clinic or supply house. When the coupon is sent back to Pfizer for reimbursement, the vet is credited for servicing that product, regardless of where the product is purchased.

Pfizer offers some trade promotions to vets and distributors, including volume rebate programs, price promotions on certain products during busy seasonal periods, and so forth. However, Pfizer's competitors oftentimes gave much more significant discounts and SPIFs to distributors. As a result, when a rancher went to a distributor to buy a product the vet had recommended, the distributor might switch the rancher to a similar product for which the distributor was making more profit. If it was a Pfizer product the vet had recommended, the distributor might switch the rancher to a competitor's product. Pfizer had historically avoided competing on the basis of such promotional tactics, feeling instead that redirecting such funds back into R&D resulted in better long-term benefits for its customers.

So, as Gail pondered these various facets of the company's market position and strategies, she decided to take a strong stance in her weekly memo. It was time to cut the bull.

Discussion Questions

1. Evaluate the trends affecting the cattle ranching industry.

2. To what degree is a high quality/premium price position a strength or a liability during an industry downturn? What are the various ways Pfizer could handle this situation?

3. Evaluate the various dimensions of Pfizer's marketing strategy: market segmentation and positioning; product/price; distribution; trade advertising and trade promotion; personal selling; public relations and sponsorships. What makes sense and what doesn't? Why or why not?

4. Would Pfizer benefit from a relationship marketing focus? How would its marketing strategy need to be modified to take such a focus?

5. When an industry is in decline, to what extent should a supplier be involved in ensuring its customers' livelihoods?

Case 9

IVEY

Richard Ivey School of Business
The University of Western Ontario

The Launch of the Sony Playstation 3[1]

David Wesley and Gloria Barczak *Northeastern University*

"The PlayStation 3 was the most successful launch in Sony's history."
—Jack Tretton, president and chief executive officer
of Sony Computer Entertainment of America.[2]

In the days leading up to the November 17, 2006 launch of the PlayStation 3 (PS3), enthusiasts lined city blocks for the privilege of spending $600 for the most powerful video game console ever created. Its predecessor, the acclaimed PlayStation 2 (PS2), had already become the world's best-selling video game console with more than 100 million units sold. The unprecedented display of enthusiasm for the PS3 suggested that Sony had another winner on its hands.[3] The company projected sales of six million PS3 consoles worldwide by March 2007,[4] a level that the PS2 took almost a year to reach.[5]

[1]This case has been written on the basis of published sources only. Consequently, the interpretation and perspectives presented in this case are not necessarily those of Sony Computer Entertainment of America or any of its employees.

[2]"Battle Station," *Electronic Gaming Monthly,* March 2007, p.64.

[3]"PS3 'To Win Console War'," *Personal Computer World,* January 25, 2007.

[4]"Sony Ships 1 Million PS3s in Japan, Seen Missing Target," *EWeek,* January 16, 2007.

[5]"Cumulative Production Shipments of Hardware / PlayStation 2," Sony Computer Entertainment Inc. Business Data, www.scei.co.jp/corporate/data/bizdataps2_e.html, accessed April 18, 2007.

At the core of the PS3 was an IBM "cell" processor, touted by Sony as a "supercomputer on a chip."[6] "The Cell outperforms many of the latest PC processors and delivers up to ten times the performance of a typical home computer," stated a company press release.

> In terms of real-world application, it means incredibly detailed and interactive environments, more enemies, larger battles, and hyper-realistic game play. The increased processing power of the Cell also means developers for the first time can create games closer to actual intelligence instead of artificial intelligence, giving them the ability to closely mimic human reasoning and movement.[7]

Sony's initial euphoria was short-lived, however. By February 2007, more than a third of PS3 consoles remained unsold, and some retailers reported a higher number of returns than sales.[8] Consumers said they felt let down by Sony. The PS3 looked no better than Microsoft's Xbox 360, they complained, even though the Xbox 360 had already been on the market for more than a year, and sold for $200 less than the PS3. Customers also lamented the PS3's lack of interesting games, spotty support for PlayStation 2 games, and uninspiring online capabilities. Meanwhile, Nintendo's inexpensive and quirky Wii console had become all the rage, despite its underpowered processor and comparatively basic graphics.

Company Background

Sony Corporation was founded in Tokyo, in 1945, as the Tokyo Telecommunications Engineering Corporation. After building Japan's first tape recorder, the company convinced Bell Laboratories to license its new transistor technology. At a time when transistors were used primarily in military applications, Sony was one of the first companies to successfully apply the technology to consumer radios. By the late 1950s, Sony had become one of the world's leading producers of radios. The company later expanded into televisions, stereos, and other home entertainment products. In 2006, Sony had an annual net income of $1 billion on $64.5 billion in revenues.

Product Innovation

Sony had a long history of product innovation that had resulted in well-known brands, such as Betamax, Trinitron, and Walkman. The company was also very protective of its intellectual property and was therefore reluctant to license its technologies to competitors. As a result, Sony products often lost market share to inferior technologies offered by competitors.

The Betamax videotape format was the one of the more infamous examples of a superior product that failed to win consumer acceptance. Introduced in 1975, Betamax tapes were smaller and provided higher definition video than the competing VHS format introduced by JVC the following year. However, Sony was unwilling to adapt the technology to accommodate longer play times because doing so would degrade the video quality. Consumers, however, preferred longer recording times over higher definition images. Moreover, Sony Betamax players were significantly more expensive than the VHS players being produced by third-party manufacturers under license from JVC. In 1988, Sony abandoned the format and began manufacturing VHS players.[9]

---

[6]John C. Dvorak, "Sony's New PlayStation 3 Game Machine Will Use an Advanced 2-teraflop CPU Being Developed Jointly by IBM, Sony, and Toshiba, *PC Magazine,* March 22, 2005, p.53.

[7]"Cell Broadband Engine Fact Sheet," *Sony Computer Entertainment Inc. Press Release,* October 23, 2006.

[8]"Battle Station," *Electronic Gaming Monthly,* March 2007, p.70.

[9]Marc Wielage, "The Rise and Fall of Beta," *Videofax,* Spring 1988, pp. 28–29.

A more celebrated brand was the Walkman portable music player, which Sony introduced in 1979. The Walkman was a portable music player that played standard audio cassettes and was capable of sound reproduction on par with much larger players. The brand dominated the portable music market in the 1980s and for much of the 1990s. By the mid-1990s, portable music had moved from cassettes to CDs. The digital technology used in music CDs reproduced sounds with higher quality at lower cost. As a result, Sony's competitors were able to introduce a large number of inexpensive portable CD players. Nevertheless, the Sony CD Walkman continued to enjoy strong market share.

When digital music became popular in the late 1990s, Sony opted to promote its own proprietary ATRAC format over the more popular mp3 standard.[10] In early 2005, Ken Kutaragi, chairman and chief executive officer (CEO) of Sony Computer Entertainment, admitted that Sony employees were frustrated by the company's unwillingness to support other formats.[11] All the same, Sony continued to promote ATRAC for its Walkman and other Sony electronics products. The decision allowed Sony's rivals to capture most of the portable music market.

The iPod, introduced by Apple in 2001, became the fastest selling portable music player in history with 100 million units sold by 2007. The Walkman, by comparison, took a decade to reach the 100 million mark.[12] The iPod supported at least seven different audio formats, including standard mp3 and Microsoft WAV, in addition to video and data. Apple also provided its easy-to-use iTunes music software as a free download for users of both Macintosh and Windows computers.[13]

Although iTunes was originally developed as an interface for the iPod, anyone could use it to organize, purchase and play music, as well as to copy and burn music CDs. By early 2007, Apple had sold more than 2.5 billion songs, 50 million television shows and 1.3 million movies through its iTunes music store.[14] Lastly, iTunes acted both as an interface for the free distribution of audio files, known as Podcasts, and as a conduit for online radio stations.

To counter the trend toward lower fidelity digital music, Sony launched its Super Audio Compact Disc (SACD), an audio format that greatly improved the sound fidelity of recorded music and, through proprietary copy protection technologies, prevented unauthorized copying of music content. However, Sony's copy protection schemes significantly added to manufacturing costs and made SACD systems incompatible with most stereos.[15] In the end, Sony found few electronics manufacturers willing to accept its restrictive licensing terms, and few consumers willing to invest in expensive proprietary stereo equipment. In 2004, after being on the market for four years, SACD had a market share of less than 0.5 percent of U.S. music sales.[16] The following year, sales of lower fidelity online music more than tripled to $1.1 billion, representing a market share of 6 percent of total U.S. music sales.[17]

[10]"Sony PSP: How Well Does the PlayStation Portable Play Music?" www.*about.com,* accessed March 16, 2007.

[11]"Proprietary Worries Delayed New Sony Products, Top Executive Admits," *The Globe and Mail,* January 21, 2005, p. B12.

[12]"100 Million iPods Sold Since 2001," *San Francisco Chronicle,* April 10, 2007, p. C1.

[13]www.apple.com/ipod, accessed April 9, 2007.

[14]"Apple Sells 100 million iPods," *eWeek,* April 9, 2007.

[15]"SACD Is Dead," ultraaudio.com/opinion/20050401.htm, April 1, 2005, accessed April 5, 2007.

[16]"DVD-Audio Sales Five Times Higher Than SACD Sales," highfidelityreview.com/news/news.asp?newsnumber=18483611 April 22, 2004, accessed April 5, 2007.

[17]"Digital Music Sales Triple in 2005," *PC World,* January 20, 2006, p. 8.

In 2005, Sony's copy protection schemes resulted in one of the most notorious scandals to hit the music industry. Without informing its customers, Sony installed what was known as a rootkit on many of its music CDs. When the CD was inserted into a drive on a Windows computer, the rootkit software installed itself on the computer. The software not only disabled the owner's ability to copy music, it also opened the computer to a number of serious security risks and in some cases allowed Sony to remotely monitor the user's actions.

Sony was later found to be in violation of the laws of the United States and several other countries. In early 2007, Sony settled charges by the U.S. Federal Trade Commission after it agreed to provide compensation and remedies to consumers.[18] However, the scandal became a lightning rod for the growing movement against proprietary and protected media and caused irreparable harm to Sony's reputation within the music industry. Nevertheless, Sony continued to seek new ways to prevent consumers from copying digital media. For example, in early 2007, the company distributed 25 million DVDs with a new copy protection technology, known as the Advanced Regional Copy Control Operating Solution (ARccOS). However, ARccOS unintentionally prevented movies from being played on many DVD players, including at least one Sony-branded player. This time, Sony immediately offered to send free replacement discs to affected consumers.[19]

One of Sony's most successful brands was Trinitron, a superior television technology patented by Sony in the 1960s. Trinitron's ability to produce higher quality color images quickly established Sony as the category leader. As a result, consumers were often willing to pay a premium for Trinitron-branded televisions. More importantly, Trinitron televisions were capable of displaying every standard video format, including over-the-air broadcasts, digital and analog cable, standard and progressive scan DVD, VHS, computers and, more recently, both Blu-ray and HD-DVD high-definition video disc formats. Later, Trinitron became one of the most popular technologies used in computer CRT monitors. It was sold under license by most major computer manufacturers, including Apple, Dell, and IBM.[20]

Sony continued to enjoy strong market share in Trinitron televisions and monitors well after its patent expired in 1996. In 2006, Sony continued to lead the market in televisions. "Sony's leadership position in television has been consistent over the past few years," noted Steve Baker of NPD, a market research firm. "What makes this performance impressive is the number of competitors in the TV space continues to grow at a staggering pace."[21]

To meet the growing demand for high-definition video content, Sony developed a high-capacity proprietary DVD player, known as Blu-ray. Blu-ray was one of two competing technologies that offered a much higher definition than standard DVDs. The other was HD-DVD, a format developed by Toshiba. PlayStation 3 consoles had built-in support for Blu-ray content, in contrast to Microsoft's Xbox 360, which supported HD-DVD through an optional external drive. Although Blu-ray discs had a higher capacity than HD-DVD, the video quality was comparable. However, Blu-ray players were more costly to manufacture and sold for nearly twice the price of comparable HD-DVD players. Yet, most major movie studios supported either Blu-ray or both formats.[22]

[18]"Sony BMG Settles FTC Charges," *Federal Trade Commission News Release,* ftc.gov/opa/2007/01/sony.shtm, January 30, 2007, accessed April 5, 2007.

[19]"Sony Replaces Some Copy-Protected DVDs," *blogs.pcworld.com/staffblog/archives/004150.html,* April 18, 2007, accessed June 28, 2007.

[20]"Superior Quality of Trinitron TV Screens Leads to Computer Display Applications," www.sony.net/Fun/SH/1-25/h1.html, accessed April 3, 2007.

[21]"Sony Takes TV Market Share Lead," *TWICE (This Week in Consumer Electronics),* January 12, 2007.

[22]"Universal Backs Out of Blu-ray," *PC Magazine,* September 19, 2006.

Video Gaming

In the 1980s and early 1990s, the video game market was dominated by Nintendo and Atari. Sony entered the market originally as a supplier of components for the Nintendo Entertainment System (NES) home console. However, when Nintendo failed to introduce new technologies that would considerably improve the gaming experience, Sony decide to seize the opportunity.

When Sony launched its $299 PlayStation console in 1995, it was one of the first to use 32-bit three-dimensional graphics.[23] Sony offered developers a number of incentives, including higher margins and advanced development tools. Even before the console was launched, Sony entered into development partnerships with 164 Japanese software companies.[24] By 2005, the PlayStation had become the most popular console in history with sales of more than 100 million units and a library of more than 7,000 games.[25]

Sony launched the PlayStation 2 (PS2) in 2000 with a price of $299. Not only could the PS2 play existing PlayStation games, newly developed games were able to take advantage of the console's more advanced graphical and processing capabilities as well as its ability to deliver enhanced content through a built-in DVD drive. The "emotion engine" processor was specifically designed to enhance 3-D full-motion video, and it was several times more powerful than processors used in most personal computers at the time.[26] Although production delays marred the initial launch, once production caught up with demand, sales remained solid. By 2007, the PS2 had surpassed the original PlayStation as the bestselling console in history.[27]

In 2003, Sony introduced a handheld gaming device known as the PlayStation Portable (PSP). In true Sony fashion, the PSP was the most advanced portable console on the market, in terms of both graphics and processing power. It also supported playback of full-length movies and digital music.[28] The PSP proved less successful than Sony's home consoles. In addition to costing nearly twice as much as competing handheld devices from Nintendo, the PSP had a limited number of innovative game titles. Many were games that had been ported from home consoles, and few took advantage of the unique capabilities of portable gaming. In contrast, the $129 Nintendo DS had two screens and a touch pen that allowed gamers to interact with the console in unique ways. The PSP fared just as poorly as a music player. Its built-in memory could not hold even one album in mp3 format, and purchasing additional proprietary memory from Sony proved just as expensive as purchasing a new Apple iPod.

---

[23]The first console to offer these capabilities was the 3DO Player, launched in 1993 by the 3DO Company of California. The 3DO also played music, video, and karaoke CDs, and could serve as home computer with Internet capabilities. However, the $700 unit was deemed too expensive by consumers who saw its primary function as a video game machine. By 1996, 3DO was forced out of the market. 3DO Interactive Multiplayer FAQ, classicgaming.com/museum/faqs/3dofaq.shtml, June 10, 2000, accessed June 26, 2007.

[24]"Sony Has Some Very Scary Monsters in the Works," *Business Week,* May 23, 1994 p. 116.

[25]www.scei.co.jp/corporate/data/bizdataps2_e.html, accessed March 9, 2007.

[26]"The Sony Emotion Engine: Will PlayStation2 Replace Your PC?" *archives.cnn.com/2000/TECH/computing/02/01/emotion.engine.idg/,* February 1, 2000, accessed June 28, 2007.

[27]"Cumulative Production Shipments of PlayStation2," *Sony Computer Entertainment Inc. Business Data,* available at www.scei.co.jp/corporate/data/bizdataps2_e.html, accessed April 10, 2007.

[28]"From Sony, a Hand-Held Entertainment Center," *The New York Times,* May 13, 2004, p. 7.

The PlayStation 3

As early as 2005, Ken Kutaragi, chairman and CEO of Sony Computer Entertainment, pledged to deliver a machine with twice the processing power of the PS3's nearest competitor, Microsoft's Xbox 360.[29] Like the Xbox 360, the target market for the PlayStation 3 was 18- to 35-year-old male gamers with above-average education and a high degree of comfort with new technology.[30]

Technical problems related to the console's built-in Blu-ray drive caused Sony to delay manufacturing and push back the initial launch from spring 2006 to fall 2006.[31] Despite the delayed release, Sony was unable to manufacture the anticipated one million consoles needed to meet market demand.[32] By the time the PS3 was launched in North America on November 17, 2006, retailers had fewer than 200,000 units to distribute. Kaz Hirai, president and group chief operating officer (COO) of Sony Computer Entertainment, recognized the problem, but tried to downplay its importance over the longer term:

> We are going to ramp up production and try to get as many units into the hands of consumers as possible for the launch. That is also why we strategically decided to delay the European launch [until Spring 2007], so that we could concentrate more on the Japanese and North American markets. But the most important thing for us is providing compelling software for the long term, so that six or seven years from now we can have a platform that consumers can embrace and enjoy.[33]

Sony attempted to mitigate the shortage by air freighting consoles directly from Japan. "We will continue to utilize airfreight delivery for the PlayStation 3 to assure a steady stream of systems for North American consumers through the end of the year," Sony assured retailers in an official statement.

> And while initial day-one launch shipment goals weren't achievable due to early manufacturing issues, those problems have been resolved and we do remain focused on having one million PS3s in the pipeline by December 31, 2006.[34]

Sony supported the launch of the PS3 with a $150 million advertising campaign that aimed to convince potential customers to hold off purchasing a new system until after the holiday season instead of purchasing an Xbox 360 or Wii. The slogan "Play Beyond," originally developed for the Electronic Entertainment Expo (E3) 2006 trade show by Sony's advertising agency TBWA, continued to be used throughout the prelaunch period. However, it quickly became the target of popular Internet spoofs by gamers protesting the high cost of the console. One spoof, titled "Pay Beyond" became widely circulated on the Internet (see Exhibit 1). TBWA campaign director Rob Schwartz expressed concern over the negativity surrounding the upcoming launch. "Sometimes I feel like a character in a video game, like everybody's shooting at me," he joked.[35]

In New York City, Sony celebrated the launch with free food and live performances by Ludacris, Charles Q. Murphy, and other well-known performers.[36] Elsewhere, enthusiastic

[29]"Sony Claims PlayStation 3 Performance Edge," *Electronic Engineering Times,* May 23, 2005, p. 33.

[30]"Sony Gets Its Game On," *Daily Variety,* May 10, 2006, p. 1.

[31]"It's a Gaming Console! It's an Entertainment Hub!" *Fast Company,* December 2005, p. 41.

[32]"'06 Had Sony Singing the Blues," *Electronic Engineering Times,* December 28, 2006, p. 8.

[33]"Interview with Kaz Hirai," available at games.kikizo.com/news/200610/009_p2.asp, October 3, 2006, accessed April 9, 2007.

[34]"Sony Responds to NPD Figures," 1up.com/do/newsStory?cId=3155762, December 8, 2006, accessed April 9, 2007.

[35]"Sony Needs a Home Run with the PS3," Fortune money.cnn.com/magazines/fortune/fortune_archive/2006/11/13/8393083/index.htm, October 31, 2006, accessed June 28, 2007.

[36]Wii Got Game in Console Face-off, *The New York Post,* November 16, 2006.

EXHIBIT 1   **Sony Billboard and "Pay Beyond" Spoof**

Source: www.Kotaku.com, accessed June 8, 2007.

gamers camped out for as long as several days in front of retail stores in an often futile at-tempt to secure one of the few consoles allocated to each retail store. Many stores stayed open past midnight, and lines often stretched around city blocks. Across the United States, extra police had to be called in to control unruly crowds that had gathered in front of shops.[37] In the days that followed, consoles sold for well over $2,000 on eBay.

When Sony launched the European PlayStation 3 in March 2007, it experienced none of the problems encountered during the North American release. Instead, it was plagued by a different problem, namely lack of demand. In the United Kingdom alone, retailers canceled more $20 million worth of orders in the days leading up to the launch. In an at-tempt to generate positive publicity, on launch day, Sony gave a free high-definition tele-vision valued at more than $4,000 to the first 125 people to purchase a PS3[38] "People knew that we have a huge level of stock and that meant that there wasn't the usual level of hysteria that you get with a stock shortage," explained Alan Duncan, marketing director for Sony Computer Entertainment UK. "For us, we just wanted to say to the people who did make the effort, 'Thank you very much.'"[39]

Pricing

The Sony PlayStation 3 was the most expensive console ever launched, with a price tag of $600, or $500 for a stripped-down version with a smaller hard drive and no wireless mod-ule. Nevertheless, Sony lost between $240 and $306 on each console sold (see Exhibit 2). In fact, the basic console cost Sony almost as much to make as the premium model. Sony saved only $11 by using a smaller hard drive and $15.50 by eliminating the wireless adap-tor.[40] Microsoft had also initially lost $126 on each Xbox 360 it sold. However, by the end of 2006, lower component costs and operational efficiencies helped bring the console's cost to $323, earning Microsoft a gross margin of $76 on each unit sold.[41]

Despite Sony's willingness to subsidize each console purchase, many users complained that the PS3 cost $200 more than the Xbox 360. Some also criticized Sony's decision to not include the video cables needed to take advantage of the console's graphics capabilities and to eliminate rumble (a vibration feedback feature).[42] According to Sony, eliminating rum-ble was a "strategic decision" aimed at reducing costs. "The issue is trying to isolate the vi-bration feature from the motion sensors," Hirai claimed.

> It is a balancing act to be able to present the controller to the consumer at an affordable price. We have one controller in the box, but many consumers will want to go out and get an extra controller. If isolating the vibration from the sensing means that the controllers are going to be expensive, then we're doing the consumer a huge disservice.[43]

Skeptics, however, claimed that the decision had more to do with a lawsuit in which Sony was found guilty of infringing on a rumble patent registered by Immersion Corporation and

[37]"PlayStation Craze: Lucky Few Got Game," *The Boston Herald,* November 18, 2006, p. 5.

[38]"Sony PS3 Hit by £10m in Cancellations," *Brand Republic Daily News,* brandrepublic.com/BrandRepublicNews/News/646182/Sony-PS3-hit-10m-cancellations/ March 27, 2007, accessed June 28, 2007.

[39]"Q&A: Sony UK's Alan Duncan," gamespot.com/news/6168115.htm, March 30, 2007, accessed April 12, 2007.

[40]"Sony Taking Big Hit on Each PS3 Sold; Xbox 360 in the Black," arstechnica.com/news.ars/post/20061116-8239.html, November 16, 2006, accessed March 21, 2007.

[41]Ibid.

[42]"Battle Station," *Electronic Gaming Monthly,* March 2007, p. 67.

[43]"Hirai: Motion Sensing Beats Rumble," games.kikizo.com/news/200610/009.asp, October 3, 2006, accessed June 13, 2007.

EXHIBIT 2   Sony Playstation 3 Manufacturing Cost (60 Gb Model)

Source: "Sony Taking Big Hit on Each PS3 Sold; Xbox 360 in the Black," www.arstechnica.com/news.ars/post/20061116-8239.html, November 16, 2006, accessed March 21, 2007.

Miscellaneous Manufacturing Components	$148.00
Reality Synthesizer	129.00
Blu-ray Drive	125.00
Cell CPU	89.00
I/O Bridge Controller	59.00
SATA Hard Drive	54.00
XDR RAM	48.00
Power Supply	37.50
Case	33.00
Emotion Engine/Graphics Synthesizer	27.00
Motherboard and cooling	22.00
Wireless Module	15.50
Memory Board	5.00
Bluetooth	4.10
Other Miscellaneous Components	4.75
Manufacturing Expense	40.00
Total Cost	840.85

ordered to pay $90.7 million in damages. Immersion Corporation also challenged Sony's claim that it would be costly to isolate the vibration and motion sensors. "The two signals can be differentiated using filtering and other techniques," it noted.[44] For example, Nintendo spent approximately $5 on each controller to include both rumble and motion-sensing features.[45]

Tretton defended the console's higher cost relative to competitors. "I would point out a couple of things," he said.

> Historically our platforms have staying power. Not three years, not five years, but 10 years. So are you making an investment for the next 45 days, the next year, the next five years, or 10 years? The PS3 has the best gaming experience of any platform that's ever shipped, with great gaming, free online play, Blu-ray movie playback, the ability to go online and surf the Internet, the ability to download your pictures and videos and the ability to rip your music.[46]

> I think the consumers that get their hands on a PlayStation 3 clearly see the value and not only want to buy one for $599, in some instances they're willing to pay ridiculous prices to buy one on eBay.[47]

Although consoles did indeed sell for more than $2,000 on eBay during the first few days of the U.S. launch, prices quickly plummeted to just over $1,000. By early 2007, auction prices for new PS3 consoles were near or below suggested retail. With the end of the holiday rush, retail stores began to report an excess build-up of stock. "Customers are disappointed," one retailer complained.

> They are telling us that too many of the launch games are also available on the Xbox 360, and first-party titles aren't innovative enough for them. We have 24 PS3s in stock right now and we're getting more returns than we are selling systems.[48]

[44]"Immersion Offers to Rumble PS3," ps3.ign.com/articles/713/713259p1.html, June 19, 2006.

[45]"The Motion Sensing Accelerometer and the Rumble Pack Cost Nintendo Approximately $2.50 Each: Wii will Rock You," *Fortune*, June 11, 2007, pp.82–92.

[46]"Battle Station," *Electronic Gaming Monthly*, March 2007.

[47]"SCEA CEO Says PS3 Will Be 'Difficult to Cost Reduce'," dailytech.com/article.aspx?newsid=5810, January 23, 2007, accessed March 7, 2007.

[48]"Battle Station," *Electronic Gaming Monthly*, March 2007, p. 70.

With stand-alone Blu-ray players costing as much or more than the PS3, some felt that Blu-ray capability alone justified the extra cost. Others were not so sure. "The decision to make the PS3 a Trojan horse for Sony's high-def Blu-ray disc technology could be backfiring," one analyst suggested. "Unless you convince consumers that this extra feature is something they truly want, they'll only view it as an added expense."[49]

Pundits took opposite sides in the debate over whether Microsoft or Sony had the best strategy. On one side, the release of the Xbox 360 a year in advance of Sony would give Microsoft a considerable head start over its rival. Microsoft could then attract core gamers who were unwilling to wait for the PlayStation 3 and build up a library of quality titles. Conversely, Sony would have a year to learn from Microsoft's mistakes and adapt its console more to the needs of customers.

"Content Is King"

Every console manufacturer understood that one of the keys to success was having a library of quality game titles to offer consumers. Consider the Sega Dreamcast. When the Sega console was launched in 1999, it was far ahead of its time. Hardcore gamers were so enthusiastic, that for several months after its release, the Dreamcast was almost impossible to find on store shelves. Yet, the Dreamcast proved a failure and eventually had to be withdrawn from the market. In the book *Smartbomb,* video games journalists Heather Chaplin and Aaron Ruby reflected on the Dreamcast's demise. The Dreamcast was "awesome," they observed, "and many gamers still refer to it as one of the best consoles ever built."

> There are a dozen stories about consoles that were ahead of their time. . . . The Dreamcast was discontinued after only two years, because Sega simply couldn't get enough machines into people's homes and couldn't establish a library of games quickly enough.[50]

The lessons of the Dreamcast and other consoles were not lost on Hirai. "Compelling entertainment content" was the most important feature of any entertainment device, he explained a few weeks before the launch of the PS3:

> We all know—it's a cliché but it's a truism—that content is king. The most important thing for us is being able to provide a platform for content creators to really get excited about, so that they can take full advantage of what we bring to them in terms of a technological palette. The PlayStation 3 really brings so much more in terms of the raw processing power and so much more in terms of storage capacity with the Blu-ray drive. [51]

Nevertheless, the PlayStation 3 launched with only 15 titles, the majority of which were franchise games that had previously been available for the Xbox 360. Among the handful of exclusive titles, *Resistance: Fall of Man* quickly became the console's bestselling title. It was also its most violent, garnering a "mature" rating from the Entertainment Software Review Board (ESRB) for intense violence, blood and gore, and strong language.[52]

Although Sony praised *Resistance* as its highest-ranking and best-selling title, users were less enthusiastic. Professional reviewers called it "mostly unoriginal," a first-person shooting game that borrowed heavily from previously successful games for other platforms.[53] In

---

[49]Ibid.

[50]Heather Chaplin and Aaron Ruby, *Smartbomb: The Quest for Art, Entertainment, and Big Bucks in the Videogame Revolution,* Algonquin, Chapel Hill, NC, 2005, p. 225.

[51]"Interview with Kaz Hirai," games.kikizo.com/news/200610/009_p2.asp, October 3, 2006, accessed February 21, 2007.

[52]Mature-rated games were considered suitable for ages 17 and older.

[53]"Review of Resistance: Fall of Man," gamespot.com/ps3/action/insomniacshooter/review.html?om_act=convert&om_clk=gssummary&tag=summary;review, November 15, 2006, accessed February 20, 2007.

EXHIBIT 3   Sony Press Release

PLAYSTATION®3 system
FACT SHEET

Building on its more than 10 years as the leader and innovator in the gaming industry, Sony Computer Entertainment ushers in a new era in gaming and home entertainment with the launch of the PLAYSTATION®3(PS3™) system. This revolutionary computer entertainment system will serve as a platform for consumers to enjoy next generation entertainment in the home for years to come.

The PS3™ system is powered by the Cell Broadband Engine™, a revolutionary microprocessor that leapfrogs the performance of existing processors giving the PS3 system supercomputer-like power and performance that up until now, game developers have only dreamt about. Every PS3 system is equipped with a built-in Blue-ray™ Disc player so users can enjoy high-definition gaming and movies. Blue-ray offers developers unprecedented storage capacity so they can fully express their creativity and pristine picture quality at 1080p, the highest-definition resolution available today. The PS3 system supports a broad range of displays from conventional or standard TVs to the latest full HD (1080i/1080p) flat panel displays.

The PS3 system also comes standard with Giga-bit Ethernet and a pre-installed upgradeable Hard Disk Drive (HDD) so users can download a variety of content as well as access on-line games and services over the network.

The PS3 system features the new SIXAXIS™ wireless controller which was built by refining the popular PlayStation® controller, the de facto standard in gaming with several hundred million units sold worldwide. The new SIXAXIS controller features breakthrough technology and a highly sensitive motion-sensing system so users are able to maneuver the controller as a natural extension of their bodies in real-time and with high-precision.

The PS3 system is backwards compatible so users can still enjoy virtually their entire PS one™ and PlayStation®2 computer entertainment system games as well as their CDs and DVDs.

Source: Sony Computer Entertainment of America, December 18, 2006.

contrast, the Xbox 360 boasted 12 titles that were ranked higher than *Resistance,* including several similar style shooting games. Even the Nintendo Wii, a console which had been on the market for about as long as the PS3, had higher ranking titles.[54]

Tretton defended Sony's lineup of launch titles. In his opinion, the company's track record for bestselling titles spoke for itself:

> Take a look back at the debuts of all the past consoles to compare launch lineups. We have published thousands of great games for all our PlayStation platforms over the years, selling billions of units. That won't suddenly change for the PS3. You can expect a steady flow of exceptional titles for the PS3 for years to come.[55]

Sony advertised that the PS3 would be "backward compatible" with virtually all of the "thousands of great games" (see Exhibit 3). In reality, only a few titles worked properly on

[54]www.gamespot.com, accessed February 20, 2007.
[55]"Battle Station," *Electronic Gaming Monthly,* March 2007.

the system. Sony eventually provided an update that resolved most compatibility issues, but not soon enough for many consumers who believed that the company should have been more upfront about compatibility issues.[56]

Software Development

The complexity of the advanced graphics engines and processors utilized in the Xbox 360 and PS3 significantly increased the burden on software developers who sought to take advantage of these features. Development cycles stretched from 12 months for the previous generation consoles to up to 36 months for Xbox 360 and PS3 titles.[57] As a result, fewer game developers were willing to stake their future on a single platform, preferring instead to spread their development costs over several platforms. For some developers, there was no other option. "When companies try to create these vast games that consumers really want," explained Shigeru Miyamoto, director and general manager of Nintendo Entertainment Analysis and Development, "they try and use every last bit of technology to create really incredible games." Miyamoto, an industry veteran who famously developed the original Donkey Kong, Mario Brothers, and Zelda games, believed that "the development cost is going to be so high that they'll never be able to recoup it from sales."[58] Cross-platform licensing was one way to reduce that risk.

Microsoft's solution was to create a core set of developer tools, known as XNA, that allowed code to be shared across different Microsoft platforms.[59] As a result, games developed for personal computers, such as *Final Fantasy XI* by Square Enix, could be more easily ported to the Xbox 360. Whereas *Final Fantasy* took about six months to port to the Xbox 360, Square Enix estimated that it could take up to three years and cost several million dollars to completely rewrite the code for the PS3.[60]

When Microsoft created the original Xbox, it too was similar to Microsoft personal computers (PCs), and for this reason some developers believed it "would kill the PlayStation 2." The simplicity of the Xbox, they contended, made it a console "that gamers and game developers would die for," while the PlayStation 2, with its proprietary processor and unique operating system, created programming challenges that would take years to sort through. Instead, most developers chose the PS2 over the Xbox despite the technical challenges.[61] By 2006, the PS2 had a library of approximately 8,000 titles worldwide and a market share of 51 percent, compared to 34 percent for the Xbox and 15 percent for the Nintendo Gamecube.[62]

Average unit costs could be broken into several categories (see Exhibit 4). Art, design and programming accounted for nearly half of the total retail cost of a next generation video game, while the remainder went to marketing, distribution and retail markup. Increasingly detailed computer-generated graphics and animation, much of which mirrored

[56]"PS3 Updated to 1.50," *IGN News* (ps3.ign.com/articles/758/758306p1.html), January 24, 2007, accessed April 12, 2007

[57]"Product Development," *THQ 2006 Annual Report,* June 7, 2006.

[58]From an interview published on N-Europe (n-europe.com/news.php?nid=4563,) May 22 2003, accessed March 20, 2007.

[59]"Sony and Microsoft Take the Next-Gen Battle to the Japanese Front," *Electronic Gaming Monthly,* October 1, 2005, p. 18.

[60]"Square Enix Working on PS3, Vista MMORPG," gamespot.com/news/6147946.html, April 19, 2006, accessed March 5, 2007.

[61]Chaplin and Ruby, *Smartbomb,* p. 231.

[62]"Microsoft Bets Console Can Draw in Non-gamers," *USA Today* (usatoday.com/tech/gaming/2005-11-12-xbox360-ambition_x.htm), November 12, 2005, accessed June 28, 2007.

EXHIBIT 4 **Video Game per Unit Cost Next Generation Console Estimates**

Source: Forbes.com

Art and design	$15	25 %
Programming and engineering	$12	20 %
Retail markup	$12	20 %
Console license fee	$7	12 %
Marketing	$4	7 %
Market development fund	$3	5 %
Manufacturing and packaging	$3	5 %
Third-party licensing	$3	5 %
Publisher profit	$1	2 %
Total Retail Cost	$60	100 %

the special effects work normally associated with Hollywood studios, had the most impact on development costs. Programming costs, which included basic game play, artificial intelligence and online services, also increased.[63]

Retail markup on a $60 title was about $12. Of this, *Forbes* estimated a net earnings contribution of only $1 per title sold at large retailers, such as Best Buy and Circuit City.

The Nintendo Wii, on the other hand, was a much simpler system. Development costs were likewise lower. Brian Farrell, CEO of THQ Inc., one of the world's leading game developers, noted:

> One of the things we like about the Wii is that development costs are nowhere near what they are on the PS3 and Xbox 360. It wasn't a whole new programming environment. So we had a lot of tools and tech that work in that environment. Costs could be as little as a third of the high-end next-generation titles. Maybe the range is a quarter to a half.[64]

As a result, Nintendo was able to boast a number of exclusive titles for the launch of the Wii, including highly rated games, such as *Zelda: Twilight Princess* and *WarioWare: Smooth Moves*. It also allowed Nintendo to include its popular *Wii Sports* title free with each console.

Better Looking Games?

Although Hirai recognized the challenges of having the same content released on multiple platforms, he felt the PS3 offered advantages over other consoles.

> When you compare the PlayStation 3 version of a game to any other version of the same game, it's a completely different entertainment experience. It is an exclusive entertainment experience for consumers enjoying a game on the PS3 as compared to any other console.[65]

In his opinion, the PS3's photorealistic graphics and advanced processing ability would revolutionize gaming in ways never before seen. Therefore, when the console failed to live up to those expectations, many consumers turned their backs on Sony. By early 2007, returns outstripped sales, and store shelves became overstocked with unsold consoles.

Sony was dismayed by the amount of negative press the PS3 had received (see Exhibit 5). Some blamed Sony for delivering a console that did not live up to the prelaunch hype. Even

---

[63]"Why Gears of War Costs $60," *Forbes* (www.forbes.com/2006/12/19/ps3-xbox360-costs-tech-cx_rr_game06_1219expensivegames.html), December 19, 2006, accessed June 28, 2007.

[64]"Wii Dev Costs Fraction of PS3's, 360's," gamespot.com/wii/driving/cars/news.html?sid=6149154, May 5, 2006, accessed February 20, 2007.

[65]"Interview with Kaz Hirai," games.kikizo.com/news/200610/009_p2.asp, October 3, 2006, accessed February 21, 2007.

EXHIBIT 5   News Headlines

"Sony's PlayStation 3 Is Not Worth the Hype"
The PlayStation 3 goes on sale in the U.S. today, but I wouldn't recommend buying one, not even for the regular price, which is plenty expensive without the import markup.

Time, November 17, 2006

"Enthusiasts Warn Masses, Don't Believe the Hype"
Is Sony's new PlayStation 3 worth getting pumped full of lead? The answer: not likely, since software programmers for the new gaming system want to fire a few rounds into the machine themselves.

Boston Herald, November 18, 2006

"Will PlayStation 3 Be the New Betamax?"
Sony's Blu-ray technology is hot stuff. But, as it found out back in the 1980s, technical superiority doesn't always guarantee success.

The Independent (UK), November 26, 2006

"Glitches a New-tech Byproduct"
The race to get first-generation concepts to market often means they're available before all the bugs have been worked out. Tyson J. Carter slept through a hailstorm as he camped outside a Target store to nab a PlayStation 3 last month. But the deluge of woe began when he got Sony Corp.'s $600 video game console home.

Los Angeles Times, December 18, 2006

"The HD War Wages On"
Blu-ray vs. HD DVD is more than PlayStation 3 vs. Xbox 360. Why? Because people would rather play with their Wii.

Toronto Sun (Canada), January 7, 2007

"Sony Ships 1 Million PS3s in Japan, Seen Missing Target"
Japan's Sony said it has shipped 1 million PlayStation 3 game consoles in Japan, but speculation is rising that the company would fall far short of its 6 million global shipment target by March.

EWeek, January 16, 2007

"Hobbled by Disappointing Sales and a Loss at the Game Unit, Sony's Profit Drops 5%"
The dip in Sony's quarterly earnings released early Tuesday underscores what many analysts call the biggest single challenge now facing the recovering Japanese electronics conglomerate: the shaky start of its long-awaited PlayStation 3 game console.

The New York Times, January 31, 2007

the editors of the *Official PlayStation Magazine*, a periodical that normally advocated on Sony's behalf, said they felt let down by Sony's "promises for better looking games." In their view, the PS3 offered few advantages over the Xbox 360:

> Blu-ray. The Cell Processor. The RSX graphics chip. The PS3 was supposed to be the most insanely advanced gaming machine ever created. It was supposed to be able to deliver visuals well beyond anything capable on console or PC. According to Sony, the next generation wasn't supposed to begin until PS3 arrived. So why is it, then, that all these PS3 games look just the same as they do on the Xbox 360?[66]

Tretton believed that many journalists simply did not understand the needs of gamers. Instead, they targeted Sony because of its undisputed position as the market leader. "Because we're in that leadership position, there are a lot of expectations thrust upon us, and some of them are a little unrealistic," he asserted:

> I did an interview with *Time* magazine, and the guy did his first interview ever on the games industry, and touched his first machine two days before that. I would argue that *Time* magazine may not be plugged in to the consumer or the gamer. All I can talk to is the people that we've attempted to sell PlayStation 3s to, and we've attempted to sell PlayStation 3s to a million people, and they have bought them as quickly as we can get them out to them. . . . I'll look at what gets written in the press for just what it is: an attempt to try to create headlines and sell newspapers.[67]

[66]"What the Cell Is Going On?" *The Official Sony PlayStation Magazine*
(1up.com/do/feature?cId=3155393), November 28, 2006, accessed June 28, 2007.
[67]"Battle Station," *Electronic Gaming Monthly*, March 2007, p.66.

Product Sales

Although initial sales were promising, by early 2007, the PS3 had dropped to fourth place in the United States (see Exhibit 6). Worldwide, the Nintendo Wii outsold the PS3 by a ratio of two to one, and total global PS3s sales through to March 2007 numbered 1.5 million units, compared to 5 million units of the Nintendo Wii and more than 10 million units of the Xbox 360.[68]

Most games analysts believed that the success of the PS3 would ultimately depend more on Sony's ability to bring quality game titles to the platform than on raw performance. "The real issue for Sony is whether they can get back the momentum they had with PS2," declared one. "The only thing that is going to drive that is the number of titles available."[69] At the end of the day, the PlayStation was "still the world's most successful gaming brand ever."[70] In the minds of some experts, that would be enough for the PS3 to eventually surpass its competitors.

Tretton blamed "society" and its penchant to support underdogs for the PS3's problems. If the console were to fall to third place, "people would have a warm spot in their hearts for the good old days of PlayStation," he asserted.

> I think in time we'll be able to migrate the vast majority of the audience we've established with PlayStation 2 to PlayStation 3.[71]

EXHIBIT 6
Monthly U.S. Sales of Video Game Hardware

Source: NPD Funworld. Cited in "NPD: $1.25B in US Game Sales Kick off '07," gamespot.com/wii/action/thelegendofzelda/news.html?sid=6166199, February 21, 2007, accessed March 16, 2007.

		Units Sold		
Company	Platform	November 2006	December 2006	January 2007
Nintendo	Wii	476,000	604,200	435,503
Sony	PlayStation 2	664,000	1,400,000	299,352
Microsoft	Xbox 360	511,000	1,100,000	294,000
Sony	PlayStation 3	197,000	490,700	243,554
Nintendo	DS	918,000	1,600,000	239,000
Sony	PSP	412,000	953,200	211,000
Nintendo	Game Boy Advance	641,000	850,000	179,000
Nintendo	Game Cube	70,000	64,000	24,000

[68]"Sony PS3 Hit by £10m in Cancellations," *Brand Republic Daily News,* brandrepublic.com/BrandRepublicNews/News/646182/Sony-PS3-hit-10m-cancellations/ March 27, 2007, accessed June 28, 2007.

[69]"Gamers Get Set for PlayStation 3," *BBC News,* March 22, 2007.

[70]"PlayStation 3 launched in Europe," *BBC News,* March 23, 2007.

[71]"Battle Station," *Electronic Gaming Monthly,* March 2007, p.66

10

Snacks to Go

JoAnn K. Linrud *Central Michigan University*

Jill Harms's half-year tenure as Assistant Category Manager for the Nuts, Natural Snacks and Cookies Category at Sathers, Inc. had been exciting. The variety of tasks in her category had been a challenge partly because Sathers management had targeted the Nuts, Natural Snacks and Cookies Category for growth, and partly because she had been given full responsibility for the category from the first day she had started at Sathers. That meant that she directly reported to Mike Halverson, Director of Marketing.

Her focus on this Friday in mid-July of 1995 was the recommendation she would make to Mike on Monday concerning Snacks to Go, the snack nuts product line introduced earlier in the year. After a fast start, sales had lagged. Now, with lackluster market-monitoring reports on her desk, Jill was being asked to decide the line's fate. As she thought about possible alternatives for the product line, she knew she could commission a new round of research. But pressures were mounting to improve the line's performance—soon—or drop the line completely.

Background

History

As if the economic woes of the Great Depression weren't enough, in 1936 John Sathers' grocery store in Round Lake, Minnesota, burned to the ground. With a tenacity of spirit that wouldn't allow him to give up, he instead began to distribute cookies in bulk to area grocers, adding other products as time passed. Ten years later, his son Kenneth joined the business, after serving as a bomber pilot in WWII. Kenneth implemented the philosophy of value by selling packages of cookies and other products such as almond bark, four packages for $1.00, to grocers in a five-county area. Sathers serviced their accounts with a sales force that personally took orders, delivered product, and stocked shelves. A turning point came when a number of salesmen left the organization, leaving Sathers shorthanded. As a stop-gap measure, Sathers management offered discounts to the customers who would order by telephone and stock their own shelves. Consequently, Sathers became an early entrant in the field of telephone marketing.

In the 1960s Kenneth Sathers initiated the "pegboard" display: hanging cellophane bags with paper headers. Distributed in 10 states by this time, Sathers' candy caught the eye of some regional Kmart managers, who were at that time responsible for making buying decisions for their own stores. Kenneth convinced these Kmarts to carry two bags of candy for $1.00, Sathers' original "Two for One." Success in these stores led to the capture of the entire Kmart account by 1972. So began national distribution of the Sathers line of packaged candy.

Still emphasizing repackaging (called "rebagging" by some in the trade), Sathers purchased a nut roasting operation in the 1960s, expanding the product line beyond cookies and candy. Further acquisitions included a New Orleans manufacturing plant from American Candy Company in 1985, and an additional candy manufacturing operation in the later 1980s. Sathers acquired Powell's Inc., a Hopkins, Minnesota, candy manufacturer and distributor with over 340 employees and revenues of about $30 million in 1991, bringing the company's total employees to 1,500 and its in-house production to 50 percent, well toward its goal of 80 percent. The Powell's acquisition also netted Sathers a film-printing business, Flex-o-Print, which would increase their packaging capabilities.

In 1992, Sathers upgraded its Round Lake packaging facility with a robotics operation. By 1993, Sathers' $135 million in sales marked the tenth straight year of sales gains. In 1994, Sathers broadened the product line produced in the Hopkins operation. That year also brought the acquisition of the assets of North Star Candy Company, a Wisconsin-based niche candy marketer.

To manage the change from distributor to manufacturer, Sathers hired a professional management team, headed by Howard Kosel, who came to Sathers as president in 1980. He assumed the CEO duties when William S. Bradfield joined the organization as executive vice president in 1989. Bradfield became COO and president in 1991, positions he continued to hold. Michael Halverson was brought in as director of marketing, a newly created position, in 1992. Mr. Halverson instituted the category manager organizational design for his department; some category managers' positions were unfilled. (See the Marketing Organizational Chart in Exhibit 1.) Over the years, ownership had passed to four grandsons of John Sathers. Although their management style was "hands-off," a family atmosphere pervaded the Round Lake facility.

Operations

In 1995, Sathers manufactured and distributed bag candy, nuts, natural snacks, and cookies, sold through over 50,000 drug, convenience, grocery, variety, and discount stores worldwide. Sathers grouped its products into six categories: general candy, seasonal candy, nuts and natural snacks, cookies, international, and private label candy. (See Exhibit 2 for a description of each category.)

Hanging bag candy was Sathers' mainstay; the "Two for $1.00" Value Line generated up to 50 percent of the vertically integrated company's $150 million in revenues. Sathers employed approximately 1,500 people in its manufacturing plants in Hopkins, a Minneapolis suburb, and New Orleans, and in its distribution centers in Chattanooga, Pittston, Pennsylvania, and Round Lake, and at Flex-o-Print, at Rogers, just north of Minneapolis.

The 350,000 square foot facility at Round Lake (population 463, in the southwestern part of Minnesota) was command central for all operations, including the telemarketing arm and the fleet of trucks used for distribution in the U.S. and Canada. The plant was equipped with a $5 million robotics packaging operation to run 10 lines using the latest robotics and vision inspection system, ending with robotics palletization. The system gave Sathers state-of-the-art efficiency in packaging and quality control. Round Lake also had a computerized telemarketing system for calling each customer every three weeks to track existing accounts, take orders, and monitor new business efforts.

The Sathers truck fleet capped its distribution system with over 300 trucks running at almost 100 percent efficiency, carrying finished product out and supplies in. The system enabled Sathers to complete delivery in about half the time of typical truck delivery, allowing

EXHIBIT 1   Marketing Organizational Chart

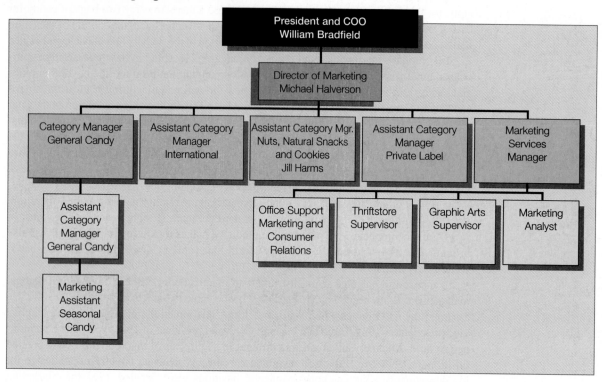

EXHIBIT 2   Sathers Product Categories

Category	Description
General Candy	• 119 items in the 2/$1.00 line (chocolate candy, licorice, jelly/gummy candy, mint candy, kiddie candy, coconut candy, hard candy, caramel candy, traditional candy, sugar-free candy, Hispanic candy) • 70 items in the profit-advantage line • 25 items in the 2/$3.00 line in the traditional "peg board" hanging bags • 85 different candy products offered in bulk • Other package alternatives including prepacked shippers and large lay-down bag candy
Seasonal Candy	• Many products in the general candy lines, offered in special packages and priced for seasonal product movement
Nuts and Natural Snacks	• 24 items in the 2/$1.00 line (such as Salted-in-the-shell, Sunflower Seeds and Peanuts, Spanish Peanuts, Banana Chips, Mixed Nuts, Aloha Mix, Trail Mix, Pineapple Tidbits, Red and Natural Pistachios, etc.) • 23 items in the profit-advantage line • Over 30 items offered in bulk
Cookies	• 16 items in the 2/$1.00 line (such as Chocolate Covered Regal Graham Cookies, Coco Chip Cookies, Oatmeal Raisin Cookies, Fig Bars, Striped Shortbread Cookies, Sandwich Crèmes, etc.) • Sugar-free wafers in four flavors with separate counter and floor displays
International	• Sales of candy, nuts, and natural snacks to 30 accounts in countries such as Mexico, Canada, Saudi Arabia, Panama, Uruguay, and countries in the Caribbean
Private Label Candy	• Sales of candy, nuts, and natural snacks to 12 accounts of national and regional drug and discount stores.

customers to minimize inventory. Sales were to confections distributors, retail chain distribution centers, and some direct store-door delivery accounts. And, while Sathers did very little consumer promotions, it heavily supported retailers and distributors' efforts to sell to retailers. For example, Sathers provided point-of-purchase signage and racks, product re-order tags, product samples, and detailed instructions for product display, order, and reorder. Sathers paid no slotting allowances.

Candy Market

Candy consumption, in general, was on the rise in the United States, from 16 pounds per capita in 1986 to almost 22 pounds in 1994, with a retail market of $12 to $15 billion. Reasons for the growth varied. Candy was often treated as a reward, even in (and because of) troubled economic times. Value lines were likely to do better in recessions. Some experts believed that the growth had occurred at a time of increasing health-consciousness because people were eating better overall, so they were more willing to reward themselves. About 80 percent of consumer candy decisions were made at the retail store.

The candy market could be divided into two parts: chocolate and nonchocolate. Since chocolate candy made up 60 percent of all confection sales, Sathers competed with other nonchocolate producers for the remaining shelf space. "[The nonchocolate category] is a tough game," according to Jan Kitt, a sales and marketing consultant who specializes in candy. "Good hard candy tastes the same no matter who makes it. It's very difficult to get a point of difference . . . Since candy is a commodity business, distribution is the name of the game. If the product is out there, it will be purchased. The more it's available, the more people will buy it. That stands more true for confection than for any other category." Of all suppliers of confections, gum, and snacks to U.S. convenience stores in 1991, Sathers ranked twelfth, according to the *ICC/Accutracks Convenience Store Report,* ahead of Cornnuts, Inc., and E. J. Brach Corp. And Sathers ranked seventh of all nonchocolate brands, ahead of Tootsie Roll. After-tax profit margins in the candy industry ranged from 2 to 5 percent.

Sathers' Strategy for Success

Competitors and the trade recognized Sathers' competitive advantages. "There are a lot of rebaggers, but Sathers' strength is in distributing the product," according to Kenneth McCarley, of the Winona Division of Brock Candy Company of Chattanooga, a competitor. Another competitor, Ron Meyer of Shari Candies, Inc. (Mankato, Minnesota) recognized Sathers as a "very well-run company whose business has been built on service." Keith Canning of Pine State Tobacco and Candy (Augusta, Maine) called Sathers "the single most successful company we've brought on in the last five years. The penetration they've had in the East has been nothing short of phenomenal. You can't go into a store in this area and not see it." And Dave McElhatten, a candy buyer for Kmart, pointed to Sathers' creativity: "They're always looking for new products. They're very good at innovation."[1]

Sathers' strategy for success was built on offering a price point, exemplified by the "Two for $1.00" Value Line, and building a distribution network based on service. Sathers' President William Bradfield pointed out that value, to Sathers, "doesn't only mean more product for the money. It includes product quality, variety, availability, price, packaging, and quantity. . . . The consumer value is the driving force of the company. We have a very real mindset that whatever we do has to add value for the customer."[2]

Vice President of Operations Charlie Mayer echoed the idea. "The path we've taken has been a tremendous advantage because we control the product from start to finish.

---

[1]Laurie Fink, "Sweet Success," *Corporate Report—Minnesota,* March, 1992, pp. 28–32.

[2]"It's in the Bag: Hanging Bag Candy Manufacturer Sathers, Inc." *U.S. Distribution Journal,* (July 15, 1994), pp. 42–43.

Everything in this company revolves around service to the customer first because that's what distribution is. That has been the cornerstone of the development of this company."[3]

Building on that cornerstone, William Bradfield identified Sathers' goals. "We have a very simple formula—be profitable, continue to grow, with a focus on candy." Sathers' strategy for the 21st century will be to "continue to develop our position in nuts, natural snacks and cookies, but we will dominantly be a candy manufacturer."

The Snacks to Go Product Line

Development of Snacks to Go

When Jill arrived at Sathers as an assistant category manager and was given responsibility for the Snacks to Go line in January of 1995, progress in developing the line was well underway. The idea for a snack nuts product in a ziplock package for "on the go" consumers was initiated in early 1994. The aim in developing the line was to become one of the first in the industry to introduce a ziplock package filled with nuts and natural snacks, while achieving Sathers' company objective of developing the nuts and natural snacks category.

To explore the feasibility of using a ziplock bag closing for snack nuts, Sathers had contacted Zip-Pak, the originator of the ziplock zipper bag closing, to learn more about ziplock zippers. Zip-Pak provided information from a 1989 Food Packaging Research Study of 300 food shoppers in four U.S. cities conducted by an independent research firm. The study revealed that most consumers who preferred resealable packaging would switch brands and pay more for the food protection, convenience, and freshness that resealable packaging offered. Over half of the respondents preferred nuts in resealable packaging, and of those who ate nuts often, most believed that it was important to preserve the freshness of the food, to keep it from drying out and becoming stale, and that the package should be easy to open and close.

In general, consumers appeared to have positive responses to the idea of resealable packages. With that information, the next step was to gain knowledge of consumers' snack nuts consumption. To do that, Sathers commissioned a nationally recognized marketing research firm to conduct focus groups and personal interviews. Sathers believed such analysis would offer greater depth about usage patterns than other research types, such as mail or telephone surveys, for instance.

1. Focus Groups—Phase 1

The firm conducted two focus groups in June 1994 to explore positioning and package themes. Qualifying participants for these focus groups, conducted in Chicago, had purchased nuts for snacking within the past three months, at a drug, convenience, or discount store, from a stand-up display, pouch, or hanging bag, jar or can, and were between 18 and 44 years old. Objectives of the research included determining attitudes toward snacking and the role of nuts in snacking; attitudes toward and usage of packaged nuts; awareness, attitudes, and imagery of packaged nut brands; opinions regarding packaging formats; reactions to the ziplock concept and execution; reactions to three selected positionings: "freshness," "convenience," and "health"; reactions to three package designs; and interest in a microwaveable snack nut product sold in convenience stores.

Results revealed that these focus group participants snacked every day, eating both salty and sweet snacks. While snacking, for them, was often solitary, nuts were associated with parties, as well as with routine snacking, and were chosen for their taste, convenience, and protein. Disadvantages of nuts as a snack included being fattening, greasy, more expensive,

[3]Susan Tiffany, "Sathers Secures Niche as Manufacturer," *Candy Industry,* July 1995, pp. 51–57.

and containing harmful oils. There was no "right time" for snacking on nuts; purchase was often driven by mood and a coupon or sale, and included a variety of nut types, rather than just one type. Snack nuts were purchased in discount, grocery, and convenience stores, as planned and impulse purchases.

In terms of package format, the advantage of cans and jars was their resealability, while bags were more portable, more appropriate for one or several snacks, and more easily disposed of when finished. However, they were often easy to spill and not resealable. A ziplock closing for snack nuts was seen as a clear advantage, with a primary benefit of preventing spilling. A larger bag that could be resealed for a later snack could also yield a cost savings. The "convenience" positioning, therefore, captured the essence of the portability concept. While "freshness" was an appealing concept, most of these respondents did not have problems with stale nuts. Because of their high fat content, snack nuts were not seen as being "healthy." Consequently, the ideal packaged snack nuts product would be convenient, easy to open and seal, fresh, portable, and a healthier alternative to "typical" snacks. A microwaveable snack nut product was not appealing to these consumers.

Packaging designs viewed by these focus groups corresponded with the three positioning alternatives, "freshness," "convenience," and "health." These packages were larger and more colorful than the traditional Sathers' "Two for $1.00" header package. Participants seemed to prefer the new lively package, considering it to be more eye-catching, to communicate a better quality, fresher product, and perhaps to be more successful at upgrading the image of the "Two for $1.00" package.

While Planters, Fisher, and Evon's were the most recognized, better quality brands, the respondents exhibited little brand loyalty within the snack nuts category. Purchase of an unknown brand was more likely, however, if the consumer could see the product through a film or cellophane "window." The participants' attitudes towards brands revealed that Sathers was either not well recognized or was known for candy. Respondents' perceptions were drawn from the Sathers' "Two for $1.00" package, Planters' Mr. Peanut, and Fisher's colorful foil packages and advertising. A projective technique used to ascertain brand impressions resulted in the following profiles:

Sathers: unsophisticated, plain, common, not necessarily downscale, but thrifty/frugal.

Planters: conservative/traditional/classic, stable, ranging between affluent and middle class, aged 50s.

Fisher: trendy, sophisticated, affluent, aged 30s to 40s.

2. Focus Groups—Phase 2

The research firm conducted a second set of two focus groups in Tampa in August, 1994, to gauge reactions to revised positioning and packaging designs and to assess ziplock packaging for Sathers. The qualifying characteristics for these participants were the same as before; the purposes were the same, except for the addition of an objective about attitudes toward salt, and the omission of the "microwaveable" objective.

Tampa participants' responses about snacking in general and snack nuts in particular were very similar to the Chicago groups' responses. However, brand was more important for these consumers. They purchased from a small set of "known" brands (Planters, Eagle, and Fisher, most often) partly because of their confidence that better-known brands were fresher, a concern in the hot, humid Florida climate. Planters' quality image was favored for its duration in the marketplace, availability, and advertisements. A projective technique resulted in these brand impressions:

Sathers (based on the traditional "Two for $1.00" package): Younger group members suggested a teenaged, downscale male. Older members suggested a 20–40 year old male or female, unsophisticated and nondescript.

Planters: older gentleman who enjoys the finer things in life and has finances to pay for them;

Fisher: upscale, young, trendy male or female.

Members of these groups were also more particular about package format features. Determination of freshness came from a package with evidence of air in the bag (vacuum sealed) and a clear product-viewing area (more important for unknown brands). Flashy, brightly colored packages appealed more to younger respondents. Reactions to the concept and execution of a ziplock package closing were universally favorable.

Tampa respondents preferred the "freshness" positioning concept over the "convenience" concept. Ideal positioning, however, would include both, plus being easy to open and close, economical, and a healthier alternative to "typical" snacks.

The Tampa residents viewed somewhat different package executions than the Chicago groups, since the designs were modified on the basis of the Chicago groups' responses. Of four executions, all larger and more brightly colored than the traditional Sathers "Two for $1.00" package, more preferred a lively white and green Snacks to Go package with nut cartoon characters, a design that they believed to be more attention-getting and that upgraded the image of the brand. Some expressed concern that the window didn't reveal enough of the product within.

While the presence of salt was a concern, particularly among the 35–44 year old consumers, most agreed that salt was an important ingredient in snack nuts. "Lightly salted" nuts were viewed favorably; most group members did not purchase "salt substitute" products.

3. Personal Interviews

To enhance and crystallize these findings, an additional research effort was conducted in September 1994 by the same research firm. In this investigation, 76 respondents completed personal interviews at two locations in Chicago. Respondent qualifications were identical to the earlier studies, with the exception of extending the upper age limit to 54. These respondents answered questions about the ziplock features and the Snacks to Go name, and they rated three different package executions:

Green package with red letters.

Blue package with graduated darkening of the blue.

Green package with yellow letters.

The blue package rated highest on a Five-point like–dislike scale. In addition, it was also chosen as the best at gaining attention, conveying a quality product, and conveying a premium-priced product. Again, the ziplock was overwhelmingly rated as a good idea. Over 80 percent liked the Snacks to Go name. In a comparison of the blue Snacks to Go package with competitive brands' packages, Planters outperformed Sathers, but Sathers was rated higher than the Fisher package.

The Snacks to Go Program

With these three research reports to guide their decision making, Jill and Mike Halverson developed the program for introducing Snacks to Go in the spring of 1995.

Products

Products chosen for the Snacks to Go line were the top two items in the Sathers snack nuts line (Salted-in-the-shell Sunflower Seeds and Shelled Roasted Sunflower Nuts) and the top two items in the Natural Snacks line (Trail Mix and California Mix). The main selling point would be the ziplock package closing feature, which would appeal to active 18–44 year olds. To accommodate their on-the-go lifestyle, the product would be available in convenience stores. To ensure freshness, a "nitrogen flushing" procedure would be used before sealing the packages. Some products, particularly Shelled Roasted Sunflower Nuts, had a tendency to spoil when exposed to oxygen. In packaging, "nitrogen flushing" would remove the oxygen from the package, preserving freshness and ensuring a longer shelf life. The process would not be necessary for nonroasted products, such as Trail Mix, California Mix, and Salted-in-the-shell Sunflower Seeds.

Packaging for the four items, identical but for the item names, consisted of a 9.5" by 6" film package, bright blue in the center graduated to dark blue at the bottom. (See Exhibit 3.) A bright yellow band crossed the upper portion of the package; "Snacks to Go" was printed in large yellow letters across the center blue portion. Below the letters, on the left side were two cashew nut cartoon characters wearing helmets, one driving a sporty red cartoon car, the other on in-line skates, depicting "on the go" activities. To the right of the characters was a clear window, approximately 2" by 1.5" to display the contents, above which read the item name in a half-inch band, black letters on white background.

The brand name "Sathers" was emblazoned in half-inch red letters on the yellow band near the package top, beside a red banner proclaiming "NEW! Resealable Package." At the very top, a red stripe crossed the package, with the words "ZIP-PAK" and "Resealable Packaging" identifying the closing feature in white letters. The package backside contained directions for opening and resealing the zipper, nutrition facts, ingredients, distribution information, a guarantee and thank you message from Sathers, a bar code and a repeat of the cashew character in the red sports car.

These packages were designed to hang on a state-of-the-art tubular blue metal display rack approximately 5' high by 18" wide, in a three-by-four format: three facings of an item in a row with four rows, approximately six bags deep. The top of the display repeated the yellow-on-blue "Snacks to Go" name and art, with "Sathers" and "ZIP-PAK" in somewhat smaller letters. The rack would hold six cases of product (72 packages, 18 of each product).

Pricing

Because the ziplock closing feature required a minimum package size, the price points for the four items were chosen to remain competitive. Expected retailer and distributor combined margins for all items were around 30 percent. Suggested retail price for California Mix (6.25 oz.), Trail Mix (7.0 oz.), and Shelled Roasted Sunflower Nuts (9.0 oz.) would be $1.49, while Salted-in-the-shell Sunflower Seeds (6.25 oz.), would be sold at $.89. A $.99 price point was considered for all four packages, but it was not profitable to produce the smaller package with a ziplock closing that the $.99 price point would have required. Suggested retail prices were not printed on the packages.

Promotion and Distribution

Sathers account executives would be responsible for introducing the Snacks to Go program to convenience store distributors and large retailers with their own warehouses. Incentives included a $3.00 per rack spiff for all distributor salespeople who gained placement in stores. There was a $.20 per case allowance for distributors who met their quota, established by Sathers. The blue tubular rack (at a cost of approximately $60 each to Sathers) would be supplied free to the retailer.

Sales incentives for the account executives were designed to successfully motivate the sales force during the roll-out period of the new program. As such, both individual and regional performance would be rewarded. Each salesperson participating in the program would be provided with realistic sales quotas by his or her regional sales manager. Over the four-month duration of the program, case sales by salesperson (as a percent of quota) and regional sales would be posted on a tally board. At the end of the fourth month, all salespersons achieving quota would earn a choice of a Sony Watchman TV or a Sony portable CD player. The salesperson with the highest sales, as a percentage over quota, would receive a weekend

EXHIBIT 3   The Snacks to Go Product Line

EXHIBIT 4A
**Snacks to Go Sell
Sheet**

Introducing...

SATHERS,   has created a brand new innovation in the nut and snack market. **SATHERS**,   line of fresh roasted nuts are now available in convenient resealable zip lock packages. Eat some now ... save some for later!

- Your customers will love the convenience of a resealable and spill-proof package.
- Your impulse sales will soar with the colorful and bold graphics.
- The unique and dynamic floorstand will attract consumers to the Snacks to Go™ display.
- The Snacks to Go™ zip lock package will provide a fresh snack every time you use it!
- We offer a variety of four different items: California Mix, Trail Mix, Salted-in-Shell Sunflower Seeds and Sunflower Nuts

Item Code	Description	Case Pack	SRP
5200	Shelled Roasted Sunflower Nuts	12	$1.49
5201	Trail Mix	12	$1.49
5202	California Mix	12	$1.49
5203	Salted-in-Shell Sunflower Seeds	12	$ .89
3420	Floorstand (Provided by Sathers with program participation)		

SATHERS   Round Lake, Minnesota 56167

(895)

The National Value Line,

F-191-A

getaway package worth $500. For an entire region achieving quota, a special event, such as a team outing at an Atlanta Braves baseball game, would be offered.

To assist the sales force, supplementary support materials and a direct mail kit were provided. The printed support materials included a brochure outlining the key features of the program and the bold graphics of the packaging. In addition, a sell sheet, line art (an artist's rendering of what the display rack would look like), a planogram (a diagram of product packages to be displayed on the rack, per the contract), and a contract were designed to aid in the selling effort to distributors (see Exhibits 4a–4d). The contract was

SNACKS TO GO LINE ART

binding between Sathers and the retailer; among other specifications, it stated that the rack would be used exclusively for Snacks to Go product. The direct mail kit included a large sample of the Snacks to Go ziplock package, a sales flier, and an introduction letter to the distributor's buyer to familiarize accounts with the program and prepare them for the salesperson's visit. No consumer promotions were planned.

The Roll-Out

While convenience stores throughout the nation were the eventual outlet through which Sathers would market Snacks to Go, convenience stores in the Southeast region were targeted for the March to June program roll-out. Specifically, this included Oklahoma, Arkansas, Louisiana, Mississippi, Tennessee, Alabama, Georgia, North and South Carolina, Virginia, Florida, and part of Texas. Although the entire snack nut category's heaviest concentration of sales was in the Northeast, the Southeast was a stronger area for the Sathers

EXHIBIT 4C
Snacks to Go
Planogram

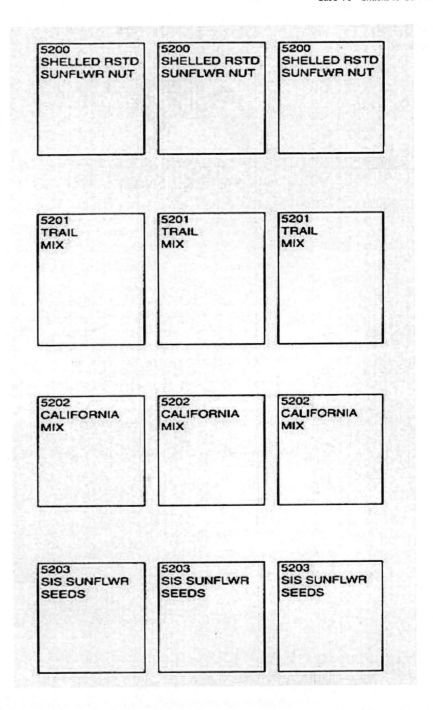

brand. Competition in the Southeast would come mostly from Planters (with 1994 market share of 35.2 percent), Fisher (3.8 percent), and Eagle (2.6 percent). Private labels accounted for 19.2 percent market share. The remainder of the market was composed of many small, regional brands. David and Sons was known in the sunflower seeds and sunflower nuts categories. The Snacks to Go line would be competitively priced (see Exhibit 5). There was some seasonality in the snack food market. Generally, presentations to distributors were made six months in advance to obtain seasonally-appropriate distribution. Snack food presentations often began in January.

EXHIBIT 4D
Snacks to Go
Contract

SATHERS® SNACKS TO GO PROGRAM

Sathers Inc. (hereinafter referred to as "Sathers") and _____
_____, the participating customer (hereinafter referred to as the "Participant"), agree to the
following:

1. Sathers will supply Participant with the merchandising floorstand attached as Exhibit A as specified below at no charge to the Participant.

2. Participant will order sufficient quantities of open stock Sathers Snacks to Go™ (zip lock bags) on an ongoing basis to fill and maintain distribution of Sathers Snacks to Go™ (zip lock bags) on the floorstands.

3. Participant will display only Sathers Snacks to Go™ (zip lock bags) products on the floorstand. The merchandising floorstands remain the property of Sathers Inc.

4. If the floorstand becomes damaged or additional stands are needed, Participant agrees to contact their Sathers sales representative immediately.

5. Floorstands will be set to a planogram agreed to by Participant and Sathers.

This contract becomes effective on the day signed and will remain in effect until cancelled by either the Participant or Sathers.

Participant:
Number of stands per store:

Number of stores:

Total floorstands requested:

Signature:

Date:

Sathers Inc.

Signature:

Title:

Date:

HEADQUARTERS: WHITE COPY / SALES: YELLOW COPY / PARTICIPANT: PINK COPY   S-221 (295)

One hundred ten distributor accounts in the southeast region were selected, to be sold by seven account executives and a regional sales manager. The goal for this region was to have 10,000 cases and 1,200 display racks placed by June 30, with sales of $650,000 by December 1, 1995. The initial presentation to the Sathers sales force occurred February 27, at the American Wholesale Marketers Association trade show. Through March and April the sales force introduced the Snacks to Go program to their targeted accounts. All accounts had been presented by the end of May, with product completely placed by the end of June.

EXHIBIT 5
Price Comparisons

Brand	Weight in Oz.	Price	Price per Oz.
Sunflower Seeds			
Planters	2.0	.33	.11
SATHERS	6.25	.89	.1424
David & Son*	6.25	.89	.1424
Evons	2.75	.50	.1818
Fisher	3.25	.69	.212
Sunflower Kernels			
SATHERS	9.0	1.49	.1655
David & Son*	10.0	1.99	.199
Planters	3.75	.75	.20
Trail Mix			
SATHERS	7.0	1.49	.2128
Evons	2.0	.50	.25
Planters (Fruit & Nut)*	3.0	1.09	.3633
California Mix			
Golden Stream	12.0	2.59	.2158
SATHERS	6.25	1.49	.2384
Harmony	4.0	.99	.2475
Evons*	2.0	.50	.25
Fisher	2.5	.97	.388

*Dominant brand in category, nationwide.

Performance

Beginning with initial placement, the sales force tracked sales of the targeted accounts with weekly performance checks, usually on Monday. The Snacks to Go line had achieved good distributor placement at the outset, building upon the strength of the Sathers distribution network. Of the 110 targeted accounts, 50 percent took initial placement. And while weekly case sales showed slow movement in March and into April, by mid-April sales picked up and showed dramatic increases through May. By June, however, case sales had slowed again. While initial placement with distributors had been good, none of the distributors took the program for all their stores. Just 26 distributors placed reorders.

The June sales report showed that sales had slowed to 5 to 6 packages per week per store, very slow movement indeed compared to about 25 packages per week for Sathers' "Two for $1.00" brand. Fewer than 8,000 cases had been sold, and fewer than 800 racks had been placed. (See Exhibit 6 for sales charts.) In consultation with Mike Halverson, Jill had extended the promotional program for another month.

June's slow sales were doubly disappointing when added to the packaging problem Jill had faced. In April, she had been alerted to a problem with the Shelled Roasted Sunflower Nuts package. After carefully inspecting the packages, she'd discovered that the film package had air leaks, which allowed oxygen to mix with the product, causing the product to spoil and the shelf life, which had originally been one year, to deteriorate. While all new product had been packaged with a new, more resilient film and distributed, about 2,000 cases of the old product had already been sold.

So, at the end of June, seeking specific reasons for the declining sales, Jill had asked for a quick internal study of snack nuts consumers in convenience stores where Snacks to Go

EXHIBIT 6
Weekly Case Sales Patterns for Snacks to Go Products

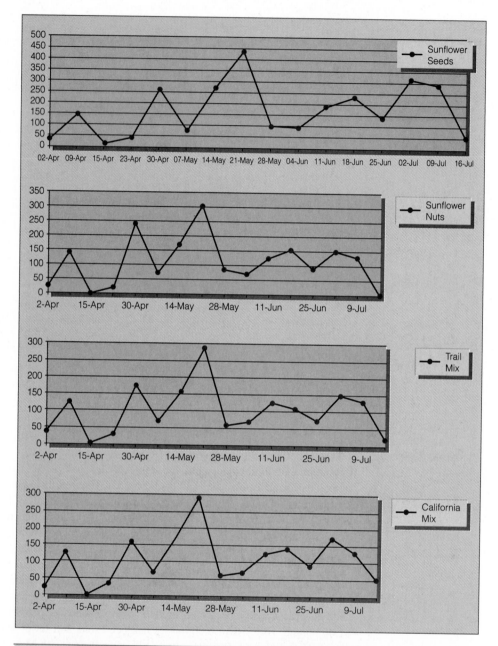

EXHIBIT 7
Convenience Store Survey Results*

Demographics: (Of 57 labeled surveys)

	White Male	White Female	Black Male	Black Female	Hispanic Female
Teenager	6	3			
20s and 30s	14	7	6		3
40s+	9	6	1	2	

Results: (Of 72 total respondents)

Percent who did not recognize the ziplock closing feature: 69%

Percent who wanted a change in the variety of products: 21

Percent who thought the ziplock was worth paying more money for: 65

EXHIBIT 7
(concluded)

Interviewer's Comments:

It seems to be the teenagers and the travelers who are most likely to buy this package.
Everyone liked the colorful graphics and were attracted mostly by the bright colors.
A lot of people mentioned that they would like to see candy in a ziplock bag.
It was mentioned several times that the top of the package was sort of boring.
The product in the window seems to be drowning out the characters, hard to see them.

*This was a mall-intercept survey of consumers in one convenience store where the Snacks to Go line was sold.

EXHIBIT 8
Comments from
Distributors'
Surveys*

Positive comments:

- Packaging, nice rack system.
- Likes package, likes rack.
- Rack and packaging looked very good at spring show.
- The rack was very nice, packaging was nice, looked good.
- Ziplock/unpriced.
- Ziplocks, rack system.
- Graphics/rack and unpriced.
- Good concept, but not sure if its niche is drug outlets, perhaps better in food stores.
- New concept.
- All the items are top-selling items.
- Ziplock bag.
- Package stands out, is attractive.
- Love the package.
- Rack was easy to put together, and had all contents needed.
- Love the ziplock feature; attraction is the graphics and design of the display; very bright graphics is eye catching.
- Chain retailers feel ziplock differentiates program from others and helps sales.

Negative comments:

- Too many facings on racks, because it is selling so slow retailers are putting other items on the rack. Need more items to fill rack.
- $1.49 too high, $1.29 better. Rack too large for 4 items.
- Consumer doesn't realize it is a resealable bag. Resealable needs to be more prominent.
- It is not selling.
- Market is very competitive, thus hard to get good selling numbers. Program is average selling at best.
- Add pistachios.
- If Sathers were a guaranteed product everyone would order more when a new product is introduced and avoid running out of a good selling item.
- $.89 OK, $1.49 too high, should be $.99.
- Package geared towards kids, but good package.
- $.89 OK, $1.49 too high, recommend $.99.
- Would like one retail price; would like to see different variety, some candy in the bags; already so many nut/snack competitors. Other suggestions: banana chips, sesame sticks, chocolates.
- Add ziplock gummies to mix.

*These comments were offered by the 21 distributors who returned the survey. Additionally, they reported that some convenience stores utilized the rack, while others placed the Snacks to Go products "in line," on the shelf with other snack products. Of those that did use the rack, some placed it near the front of the store, some near the back, some near the pop cooler, and some in other locations within the store.

had been distributed, and a poll of distributors in the Southeast region. The results, which she'd just reviewed, were not encouraging (see Exhibits 7 and 8).

Mike Halverson was anticipating her review and recommendation. What would she tell him? She could commission a new round of research, which should include store tests at grocery and drug stores, in addition to convenience stores, to monitor case sales by product type. But this would take 10 weeks, at a minimum, and cost approximately $30,000. Or, she could suggest a different approach to marketing the product. She'd have to give more thought to exactly what she would change: additional trade promotions? price changes? additional design changes? How about a product change—a switch to candy? But, would that be consistent with the Snacks to Go concept and William Bradfield's charge to develop the snack nuts category? Finally, she knew she could recommend dropping the line completely. That would be a tough decision; would it be giving up too soon?

It was a mixed blessing that the company was closing at 2:30 this Friday, Jill thought, as she packed the sales and research study reports into her briefcase. It was going to be a long weekend of careful thinking about what she'd recommend to Mike on Monday morning for the future of the Snacks to Go product line.

Promotion Strategy

11

Wind Technology

Ken Manning *University of South Carolina*

Jakki J. Mohr *University of Montana*

Kevin Cage, general manager of Wind Technology, sat in his office on a Friday afternoon watching the snow fall outside his window. It was January 1991 and he knew that during the month ahead he would have to make some difficult decisions regarding the future of his firm, Wind Technology. The market for the wind profiling radar systems that his company designed had been developing at a much slower rate than he had anticipated.

The Situation

During Wind Technology's 10-year history, the company had produced a variety of weather-related radar and instrumentation. In 1986, the company condensed its product mix to include only wind-profiling radar systems. Commonly referred to as wind profilers, these products measure wind and atmospheric turbulence for weather forecasting, detection of wind direction at NASA launch sites, and other meteorological applications (i.e., at universities and other scientific monitoring stations). Kevin had felt that this consolidation would position the company as a leader in what he anticipated to be a high-growth market with little competition.

Wind Technology's advantages over Unisys, the only other key player in the wind-profiling market, included the following: (1) The company adhered stringently to specifications and quality production; (2) Wind Technology had the technical expertise to provide

This case was prepared by Ken Manning of the University of South Carolina and Jakki J. Mohr, University of Montana. This case is intended for use as a basis for class discussion rather than to illustrate either effective or ineffective administrative decision making. Some data are disguised. All rights reserved.

full system integration. This allowed customers to order either basic components or a full system including software support; (3) Wind Technology's staff of meteorologists and atmospheric scientists provided the customer with sophisticated support, including operation and maintenance training and field assistance; (4) Finally, Wind Technology had devoted all of its resources to its wind-profiling business. Kevin believed that the market would perceive this as an advantage over a large conglomerate like Unisys.

Wind Technology customized each product for individual customers as the need arose; the total system could cost a customer from $400,000 to $5 million. Various governmental entities, such as the Department of Defense, NASA, and state universities had consistently accounted for about 90 percent of Wind Technology's sales. In lieu of a field sales force, Wind Technology relied on top management and a team of engineers to call on prospective and current customers. Approximately $105,000 of their annual salaries was charged to a direct selling expense.

The Problem

The consolidation strategy that the company had undertaken in 1986 was partly due to the company being purchased by Vaitra, a high-technology European firm. Wind Technology's ability to focus on the wind-profiling business had been made possible by Vaitra's financial support. However, since 1986 Wind Technology had shown little commercial success, and due to low sales levels, the company was experiencing severe cash-flow problems. Kevin knew that Wind Technology could not continue to meet payroll much longer. Also, he had been informed that Vaitra was not willing to pour more money into Wind Technology. Kevin estimated that he had from 9 to 12 months (until the end of 1991) in which to implement a new strategy with the potential to improve the company's cash flow. The new strategy was necessary to enable Wind Technology to survive until the wind-profiler market matured. Kevin and other industry experts anticipated that it would be two years until the wind-profiling market achieved the high growth levels that the company had initially anticipated.

One survival strategy that Kevin had in mind was to spin off and market component parts used in making wind profilers. Initial research indicated that, of all the wind-profiling system's component parts, the high-voltage power supply (HVPS) had the greatest potential for commercial success. Furthermore, Kevin's staff on the HVPS product had demonstrated knowledge of the market. Kevin felt that by marketing the HVPS, Wind Technology could reap incremental revenues, with very little addition to fixed costs. (Variable costs would include the costs of making and marketing the HVPS. The accounting department had estimated that production costs would run approximately 70 percent of the selling price, and that 10 percent of other expenses—such as top management direct-selling expenses—should be charged to the HVPS.)

High-Voltage Power Supplies

For a vast number of consumer and industrial products that require electricity, the available voltage level must be transformed to different levels and types of output. The three primary types of power supplies include linears, switchers, and converters. Each type manipulates electrical current in terms of the type of current (AC or DC) and/or the level of output (voltage). Some HVPS manufacturers focus on producing a standardized line of power supplies, while others specialize in customizing power supplies to the user's specifications.

High-voltage power supplies vary significantly in size and level of output. Small power supplies with relatively low levels of output (under 3 kV)[1] are used in communications

[1]kV (kilovolt): 1,000 volts.

equipment. Medium-sized power supplies that produce an output between 3 and 10 kV are used in a wide range of products including radars and lasers. Power supplies that produce output greater than 10 kV are used in a variety of applications, such as high-powered X rays and plasma-etching systems.

Background on Wind Technology's HVPS

One of Wind Technology's corporate strategies was to control the critical technology (major component parts) of its wind-profiling products. Management felt that this control was important since the company was part of a high-technology industry in which confidentiality and innovation were critical to each competitor's success. This strategy also gave Wind Technology a differential advantage over its major competitors, all of whom depended on a variety of manufacturers for component parts. Wind Technology had successfully developed almost all of the major component parts and the software for the wind profiler, yet the development of the power supply had been problematic.

To adhere to the policy of controlling critical technology in product design (rather than purchasing an HVPS from an outside supplier), Wind Technology management had hired Anne Ladwig and her staff of HVPS technicians to develop a power supply for the company's wind-profiling systems. Within six months of joining Wind Technology, Anne and her staff had completed development of a versatile power supply which could be adapted for use with a wide variety of equipment. Some of the company's wind-profiling systems required up to 10 power supplies, each modified slightly to carry out its role in the system.

Kevin Cage had delegated the responsibility of investigating the sales potential of the company's HVPS to Anne Ladwig since she was very familiar with the technical aspects of the product and had received formal business training while pursuing an MBA. Anne had determined that Wind Technology's HVPS could be modified to produce levels of output between 3 and 10 kV. Thus, it seemed natural that if the product was brought to market, Wind Technology should focus on applications in this range of output. Wind Technology also did not have the production capabilities to compete in the high-volume, low-voltage segment of the market, nor did the company have the resources and technical expertise to compete in the high-output (10 kV +) segment.

The Potential Customer

Power supplies in the 3–10 kV range could be used to conduct research, to produce other products, or to place as a component into other products such as lasers. Thus, potential customers could include research labs, large end-users, OEMs, or distributors. Research labs each used an average of three power supplies; other types of customers ordered a widely varying quantity.

HVPS users were demanding increasing levels of reliability, quality, customization, and system integration. *System integration* refers to the degree to which other parts of a system are dependent upon the HVPS for proper functioning, and the extent to which these parts are combined into a single unit or piece of machinery.

Anne had considered entering several HVPS market segments in which Wind Technology could reasonably compete. She had estimated the domestic market potential of these segments at $237 million. To evaluate these segments, Anne had compiled growth forecasts for the year ahead and had evaluated each segment in terms of the anticipated level of customization and system integration demanded by the market. Anne felt that the level of synergy between Wind Technology and the various segments was also an important consideration in selecting a target market. Exhibit 1 summarizes this information. Anne believed that if the product was produced, Wind Technology's interests would be best served by selecting only one target market on which to concentrate initially.

EXHIBIT 1   **HVPS Market Segments in the 3–10 kV Range**

Application	Forecasted Annual Growth (%)	Level of Customization/ Level of System Integration*	Synergy Rating**	Percent of $237 Million Power Supply Market***
General/univ. laboratory	5.40	Medium/medium	3	8
Lasers	11.00	Low/medium	4	10
Medical equipment	10.00	Medium/medium	3	5
Microwave	12.00	Medium/high	4	7
Power modulators	3.00	Low/low	4	25
Radar systems	11.70	Low/medium	5	12
Semiconductor	10.10	Low/low	3	23
X-ray systems	8.60	Medium/high	3	10

*The level of customization and system integration generally in demand within each of the applications is defined as low, medium, or high.
**Synergy ratings are based on a scale of 1 to 5; 1 is equivalent to a very low level of synergy and 5 is equivalent to a very high level of synergy. These subjective ratings are based on the amount of similarities between the wind-profiling industry and each application.
***Percentages total 100 percent of the $237 million market in which Wind Technology anticipated it could compete.
Note: This list of applications is not all-inclusive.

EXHIBIT 2   **Competitor Profile (3–10 kV range)**

Company	Gamma	Glassman	Kaiser	Maxwell*	Spellman
Approximate annual sales	$2 million	$7.5 million	$3 million		$7 million
Market share	1.00%	3.00%	1.50%		2.90%
Price**	$5,830	$5,590	$6,210	$5,000–$6,000	$6,360
Delivery	12 weeks	10 weeks	10 weeks	8 weeks	12 weeks
Product customization	No	Medium	Low	Medium	Low
System integration experience	Low	Low	Low	Medium	Low
Customer targets	Gen. lab.	Laser	Laser	Radar	Capacitors
	Space	Medical	Medical	Power mod.	Gen. lab.
	Univ. lab.	X ray	Microwave	X ray	Microwave
			Semiconductor	Medical equip.	X ray

*Maxwell was in the final stages of product development and stated that the product would be available in the spring. Maxwell anticipated that the product would sell in the $5,000–$6,000 range.
**Price quoted for an HVPS with the same specifications as the "standard" model developed by Wind Technology.

Competition

To gather competitive information, Anne contacted five HVPS manufacturers. She found that the manufacturers varied significantly in terms of size and marketing strategy (see Exhibit 2). Each listed a price in the $5,500–$6,500 range on power supplies with the same features and output levels as the HVPS that had been developed for Wind Technology. After she spoke with these firms, Anne had the feeling that Wind Technology could offer the HVPS market superior levels of quality, reliability, technical expertise, and customer support. She optimistically believed that a one-half percent market share objective could be achieved the first year.

Promotion

If Wind Technology entered the HVPS market, they would require a hard-hitting, thorough promotional campaign to reach the selected target market. Three factors made the selection of elements in the promotion mix especially important to Wind Technology: (1) Wind Technology's poor cash flow, (2) the lack of a well-developed marketing department, and (3) the need to generate incremental revenue from sales of the HVPS at a minimum cost. In fact, a rule of thumb

EXHIBIT 3 **Trade Publications**

Trade Publication	Editorial	Cost per Color Insertion (1 page)	Circulation
Electrical manufacturing	For purchasers and users of power supplies, transformers, and other electrical products.	$4,077	35,168 nonpaid
Electronic component news	For electronics OEMs. Products addressed include work stations, power sources, chips, etc.	$6,395	110,151 nonpaid
Electronic manufacturing news	For OEMs in the industry of providing manufacturing and contracting of components, circuits, and systems.	$5,075	25,000 nonpaid
Design news	For design OEM's covering components, systems, and materials.	$8,120	170,033 nonpaid
Weatherwise	For meteorologists covering imaging, radar, etc.	$1,040	10,186 paid

Note: This is a partial list of applicable trade publications. Standard Rate and Data Service lists other possible publications.

used by Wind Technology was that all marketing expenditures should be about 9 to 10 percent of sales. Kevin and Anne were contemplating the use of the following elements:

1. Collateral Material

Sales literature, brochures, and data sheets are necessary to communicate the product benefits and features to potential customers. These materials are designed to be (1) mailed to customers as part of direct-mail campaigns or in response to customer requests, (2) given away at trade shows, and (3) left behind after sales presentations.

Because no one in Wind Technology was an experienced copywriter, Anne and Kevin considered hiring a marketing communications agency to write the copy and to design the layout of the brochures. This agency would also complete the graphics (photographs and artwork) for the collateral material. The cost for 5,000 pieces (including the 10 percent markup for the agency) was estimated to be $5.50 each.

2. Public Relations

Kevin and Anne realized that one very cost-efficient tool of promotion is publicity. They contemplated sending out new product announcements to a variety of trade journals whose readers were part of Wind Technology's new target market. By using this tool, interested readers could call or write to Wind Technology, and the company could then send the prospective customers collateral material. The drawback of relying too heavily on this element was very obvious to Kevin and Anne—the editors of the trade journals could choose not to print Wind Technology's product announcements if their new product was not deemed newsworthy.

The cost of using this tool would include the time necessary to write the press release and the expense of mailing the release to the editors. Direct costs were estimated by Wind Technology to be $500.

3. Direct Mail

Kevin and Anne were also contemplating a direct-mail campaign. The major expenditure for this option would be buying a list of prospects to whom the collateral material would be mailed. Such lists usually cost around $5,000, depending upon the number of names and the list quality. Other costs would include postage and the materials mailed. These costs were estimated to be $7,500 for a mailing of 1,500.

4. Trade Shows

The electronics industry had several annual trade shows. If they chose to exhibit at one of these trade shows, Wind Technology would incur the cost of a booth, the space at the show, and the travel and incidental costs of the people attending the show to staff the booth. Kevin and Anne estimated these costs at approximately $50,000 for the exhibit, space, and materials, and $50,000 for a staff of five people to attend.

5. Trade Journal Advertising

Kevin and Anne also contemplated running a series of ads in trade journals. Several journals they considered are listed in Exhibit 3, along with circulation, readership, and cost information.

6. Personal Selling

(a) Telemarketing (Inbound/Inside Sales).[2] Kevin and Anne also considered hiring a technical salesperson to respond to HVPS product inquiries generated by product announcements, direct mail, and advertising. This person's responsibilities would include answering phone calls, prospecting, sending out collateral material, and following up with potential customers. The salary and benefits for one individual would be about $50,000.

(b) Field Sales Closing of sales for the HVPS might require some personal selling at the customer's location, especially if Wind Technology pursued the customized option. Kevin and Anne realized that potentially this would provide them with the most incremental revenue, but it also had the potential to be the most costly tool. Issues such as how many salespeople to hire, where to position them in the field (geographically), and so on, were major concerns. Salary plus expenses and benefits for an outside salesperson were estimated to be about $80,000.

Decisions

As Kevin sat in his office and perused the various facts and figures, he knew that he would have to make some quick decisions. He sensed that the decision about whether or not to proceed with the HVPS spin-off was risky, but he felt that not to do something to improve the firm's cash flow was equally risky. Kevin also knew that if he decided to proceed with the HVPS, Wind Technology could position it in a number of segments in that market. He mulled over which segment appeared to be a good fit for Wind Technology's abilities (given Anne's recommendation that a choice of one segment would be best). Finally, Kevin was concerned that if they entered the HVPS market, promotion for their product would be costly, further exacerbating the cash flow situation. He knew that promotion would be necessary, but the exact mix of elements would have to be designed with financial constraints in mind.

---

[2]"Inbound" refers to calls that potential customers make to Wind Technology, rather than "outbound," in which Wind Technology calls potential customers (i.e., solicits sales).

12

Mountain Dew: Selecting New Creative

Douglas B. Holt *Oxford University*

Standing at the front of a PepsiCo conference room, Bill Bruce gestured enthusiastically, pointing to the sketches at his side. Bruce, a copywriter and executive creative director, headed up the creative team on the Mountain Dew account for PepsiCo's advertising agency, BBDO New York. In fact, it was Bruce who devised the famous "Do the Dew" campaign that had catapulted Mountain Dew to the number 3 position in its category. With his partner, art director Doris Cassar, Bruce had developed 10 new creative concepts for Mountain Dew's 2000 advertising to present to PepsiCo management. Gathered in the room to support Bruce and Cassar were BBDO senior executives Jeff Mordos (chief operating officer), Cathy Israelevitz (senior account director), and Ted Sann (chief creative officer). Each of the three executives had over a decade of experience working on Mountain Dew. Representing PepsiCo were Scott Moffitt (Marketing Director, Mountain Dew), Dawn Hudson (chief marketing officer, and a former senior ad agency executive), and Gary Rodkin (chief executive officer, Pepsi Cola North America).

Scott Moffitt scribbled notes as he listened to Bruce speak. Moffitt and the brand managers under him were charged with day-to-day oversight of Mountain Dew marketing. These responsibilities included brand strategy, consumer and sales promotions, packaging, line extensions, product changes, and sponsorships. But for Moffitt and the senior managers above him, the most important decisions of the year were made in conference rooms with BBDO creatives. Each of the ads would cost over a million dollars to produce. But the production costs were minor compared to the $55 million media budget that would be committed to air these spots. Historically, PepsiCo management had learned that selecting the right creative was one of the most critical decisions they made in terms of impact on sales and profits.

Mountain Dew had carried PepsiCo's soft drink revenues during the 1990s as cola brands struggled. But now the "*Do the Dew*" campaign was entering its eighth year, a long stretch by any consumer goods baseline. Many other brands were now sponsoring the same alternative sports that Mountain Dew had relied upon to boost its image. And teens were gravitating to new activities and new music that Dew's competitors had successfully exploited in their branding activities. Figuring out how to keep the campaign working hard to maintain the brand's relevance with its target consumers had become a chief preoccupation of senior management at both PepsiCo and BBDO. At the same time, key competitors were raising their ad budgets as competition in both the carbonated soft drink (CSD) and noncarbonated drinks categories was heating up, sending Dew sales below targets. Choosing the right ads to maximize the impact of Mountain Dew's relatively small media budget was a make-or-break decision.

PepsiCo and BBDO

PepsiCo was widely considered to be one of the most sophisticated and aggressive marketing companies in the world. In North America, the company had three divisions, each with category-leading brands. Pepsi and Mountain Dew were the number 2 and 3 soft drinks. Frito-Lay dominated the salty-snack category with Ruffles, Lay's, Doritos, and Cheetos. And the company had recently acquired Tropicana, the leading juice brand. In 2000, PepsiCo had acquired the SoBe line of teas and "functional" drinks from South Beach Beverages, which it operated as a stand-alone subsidiary.

BBDO was one of the 10 largest ad agencies in the world, with worldwide billings of about $15 billion. Of the largest full-service agencies, BBDO was particularly renowned for the quality of its creative work. The roster of the New York office, BBDO New York, included many high-powered clients such as General Electric, Visa, M&M/Mars, Charles Schwab, and FedEx. Their top 10 accounts had been BBDO clients for an average of 32 years. BBDO's relationship with PepsiCo dated to breakthrough campaigns for Pepsi in the 1960s. BBDO took over Mountain Dew from Ogilvy & Mather in 1974 and had held the account ever since. In 1998, PepsiCo hired Uniworld, the largest African-American owned ad agency in the United States, to develop a separate Mountain Dew campaign targeted to African Americans.

The Carbonated Soft Drinks Category

As in most other countries, in the United States soft drink consumption was ubiquitous. And, until recently, soft drinks had meant cola. The retail carbonated soft drinks (CSD) category had long been dominated by the two cola giants, Coke and Pepsi. In the so-called cola wars of the 1960s and 70s, Pepsi directly attacked Coke with taste tests and with advertising designed to make Pepsi the hipper and more stylish "choice of the new generation," implying that Coke was a drink for older and less "with it" people. The soft drink category, and colas in particular, boomed throughout the 1970s and 1980s as people substituted away from coffee to soft drinks as a source of caffeine. The industry also consolidated as once-important brands (RC Cola, Orange Crush, A&W Root Beer) faded into the background. By the 1990s, three companies controlled all of the major national brands: The Coca-Cola Company (Coke, Diet Coke, Sprite), PepsiCo (Pepsi, Diet Pepsi, Mountain Dew), and Cadbury-Schweppes (Dr. Pepper and 7-UP).

CSDs were a promotion-intensive category. In most grocery stores, Coke and Pepsi controlled a great deal of shelf space and displays. They had so much clout that their bottlers were able to choose how to stock the shelves and what to display. Impulse purchase displays had become an important source of incremental volume. A substantial and increasing share of volume came from convenience stores, where most purchases were of single servings purchased for immediate consumption. The major brands ran seasonal promotions, such as "under the cap" games in which every tenth bottle had a free bottle give-away written under the cap. More junior brand managers spent considerable time developing and implementing these promotions.

Product, promotion, packaging, and pricing innovations were constant though usually incremental, quickly diffusing throughout the category. In the last decade, one of the major innovations in the category had been the 20-ounce single serve bottle, usually priced at $.99 and sold as an impulse purchase. The margins on this bottle were higher than the 12-packs or 2-liter bottles. Also, all of the large brands introduced 24-pack cases sold to heavy users. Brand managers worked to keep package design contemporary. For example, at PepsiCo, both Pepsi and Mountain Dew had substantial make-overs in the 1990s resulting in richer and more vibrant colors and simplified graphics. Other brands, including 7-UP and Sprite also executed similar packaging redesigns.

For most of the twentieth century, PepsiCo and The Coca-Cola Company competed fiercely, each responding in tit-for-tat fashion to the other's successes. Pepsi rolled out lemon-lime Slice in the 1980s to compete against Sprite, but soon withdrew support for that brand. Recently it was rumored that the company was plotting yet another new lemon-lime introduction. In the 1970s, Coca-Cola introduced Mr. Pibb to attack Dr. Pepper and Mello-Yello as a me-too competitor against Mountain Dew. With Mountain Dew's national success in the 1990s, Coca-Cola launched a second frontal assault, introducing another copy-cat brand called Surge. In addition, both companies had launched other new products without much success: Coke had flopped with OK Cola (the cynical retro cola), and Fruitopia (the neo-hippie fruit beverage). PepsiCo had similar problems with the introduction of Crystal Pepsi (the clear crisp cola), though it was able to establish Pepsi One as a niche brand.

In the 1990s, cola growth slowed and the "flavor" CSDs did very well. Sprite, Mountain Dew, and Dr. Pepper all enjoyed great success, although 7-UP continued to struggle (See Exhibit 1). In 1999, however, all CSD sales suffered as a result of customers' sticker shock to a category-wide 5 percent retail price increase, and also a trend toward experimentation with noncarbonated drinks and bottled water as substitutes for soft drinks. Sports drinks were led by Gatorade, tea and juice blends by Snapple, Arizona, and SoBe, and the highly caffeinated "energy" drinks by Red Bull. These drinks, sometimes termed "functional" or "alternative," often included a stimulant (caffeine or similar substance) and plant extracts reputed to have medicinal value (ginko, guarana, St. Johns Wort, ginseng). Many of these drinks were launched by small companies with grass-roots marketing efforts focused on music and sports sponsorships, on-site promotions, and nontraditional distribution (e.g., sandwich shops for Snapple, record stores for Red Bull). Industry rumors were circulating that Coca-Cola, Anheuser-Busch, PepsiCo, and Cadbury-Schweppes were working aggressively to develop functional drinks to tap into this growing segment.

Advertising and Branding

Over many decades, Coca-Cola had become "America's drink" (and later the preferred drink in many countries around the world) through advertising that conveyed that Coke served as a social elixir. Coke promoted the idea that the drink brought people together in friendship around ideas that people in the nation cared about. From 1995 onward, Coke had struggled as it experimented with a variety of new branding ideas. Pepsi rose to the rank of Coke's loyal opposition in the 1960s with the successful "The Pepsi Generation" ad campaign, in which the brand harnessed the ideas and passions of the 1960s counterculture.

EXHIBIT 1   CSD Sales/Share (Million cases/Percent market)

Source: Maxwell Report

	1990		1991		1992		1993		1994		1995		1996		1997		1998		1999 (Est.)	
	Sales	Share	Sales	Share	Sales	Share	Sales	Share	Sales	Share	Sales	Share	Sales	Share	Sales	Share	Sales	Share	Sales	Share
Coke	1,565.5	20.1	1,597.9	20.1	1,613.9	20.1	1,680.4	20.2	1,776.7	20.4	1,868.6	20.8	1,929.2	20.8	1,978.2	20.6	2,037.5	20.6	2,018.0	20.3
Pepsi	1,370.0	17.6	1,338.0	16.9	1,327.3	16.5	1,305.9	15.7	1,310.0	15.0	1,344.3	15.0	1,384.6	14.9	1,391.5	14.5	1,399.8	14.2	1,371.8	13.8
Diet Coke	726.9	9.3	741.2	9.3	732.6	9.1	740.6	8.9	767.6	8.8	793.0	8.8	811.4	8.7	819.0	8.5	851.8	8.6	843.0	8.5
Diet Pepsi	490.0	6.3	500.0	6.3	509.5	6.4	491.5	5.9	511.2	5.9	521.4	5.8	541.5	5.8	523.5	5.5	529.7	5.4	503.0	5.1
Sprite	295.0	3.8	313.1	3.9	328.1	4.1	357.6	4.3	396.3	4.5	460.3	5.1	529.8	5.7	598.0	6.2	651.8	6.6	671.5	6.8
Dr. Pepper	364.8	4.7	385.3	4.9	414.0	5.2	445.6	5.4	485.1	5.6	515.0	5.7	536.8	5.8	566.8	5.9	599.4	6.1	630.0	6.3
Mountain Dew	300.0	3.9	327.5	4.1	351.1	4.4	387.6	4.7	455.0	5.2	509.6	5.7	535.6	5.8	605.2	6.3	665.1	6.7	705.0	7.1
7-UP	211.5	2.7	207.7	2.6	211.3	2.6	209.9	2.5	221.5	2.5	219.9	2.5	217.7	2.3	216.7	2.3	210.9	2.1	204.9	2.1
Surge															69.0		51.8		26.7	
Mello Yello	42.9		49.5		59.5		64.0		64.6		61.6		59.0		46.6		42.4		41.6	

EXHIBIT 2   Advertising Spending: Television Media
(Major CSDs, $MM)

Source: Competitive Media Reports.

	1990	1991	1992	1993	1994	1995	1996	1997	1998	1999	2000 (Est.)
Coke	$157.4	$139.9	$168.1	$131.1	$161.5	$124.7	$199.8	$156.8	$140.4	$167.7	$208.3
Pepsi	129.8	141.3	137.8	144.0	120.6	133.1	98.1	133.1	140.5	165.9	159.6
Mountain Dew	12.9	20.0	25.9	29.1	30.3	38.3	40.4	43.1	50.3	45.0	55.9
Sprite	32.0	36.1	27.5	26.9	36.0	54.6	57.9	60.6	56.2	69.9	87.7
Dr. Pepper	32.2	49.3	50.1	52.8	61.5	65.4	67.9	81.0	86.8	102.4	106.8
7-UP	38.8	37.4	23.7	29.4	27.3	23.2	33.1	38.7	27.0	38.7	45.1
Surge	0.0	0.0	0.0	0.0	0.0	0.0	0.0	15.5	21.0	19.6	0.2

More recently, Pepsi used celebrities—particularly musicians such as Michael Jackson, Madonna, Faith Hill, Ricky Martin, and Mary J. Blige—to convey the idea that Pepsi was an expression of youth attitudes. Nonetheless, the Pepsi brand also had struggled to maintain sales in the 1990s.

7-UP was successful in the 1970s branding against the colas as the "uncola" in ads that used a charismatic Jamaican actor to describe the purity and naturalness of 7-UP in a tropical setting. Similarly, the sweet cherry-cola concoction Dr Pepper challenged the audience to "be a Pepper" with well-received dance numbers that encouraged consumers to do their own thing rather than follow the masses in drinking cola. From the late 1980s onward, 7-UP faded as the brand was used as a cash cow with ever-shrinking media investments. Meanwhile, Mountain Dew rose from its regional status to become a major "flavor" brand. The three major flavor brands dominated different geographic areas: Dr Pepper dominated Texas and the rest of the deep South, Mountain Dew dominated rural areas, particularly in the Midwest and Southeast, and Sprite dominated urban-ethnic areas.

Category advertising spending exceeded $650 million (see Exhibit 2). PepsiCo spent substantially less as a percentage of sales than its competitors. Instead, the company relied on exceptional creativity to make the advertising work harder for less cost. PepsiCo viewed the creative development process as a key organizational competency, a strategic weapon that was central to their financial success.

Mountain Dew Brand History

Mountain Dew was invented by the Hartman Beverage Company in Knoxville, Tennessee, in the late 1940s. The bright yellow-green drink in the green bottle packed a powerful citrus flavor, more sugar and more caffeine than other soft drinks, and less carbonation so that it could be drunk quickly. The drink became a favorite on the Eastern seaboard, through Kentucky, Tennessee, and eventually spread up through the Great Lakes states (skirting the big cities) and into the Northern Plains of Minnesota and the Dakotas. PepsiCo, amazed by Dew's success in what brand managers would come to call the "NASCAR belt" (the stock car racing circuit that drew rural men as its primary audience), and in need of a "flavor" soft-drink to round out its line-up, purchased Mountain Dew in 1964.

PepsiCo originally assigned Mountain Dew to the Ogilvy & Mather ad agency. The strategy for the new brand extrapolated from Dew's origins and existing packaging. The beverage's heart-pumping caffeine and sugar rush were linked to its backwoods heritage to produce the idea of a comic "hillbilly" character named Willie who drank Mountain Dew to "get high" on the soft drink equivalent of moonshine liquor. The tagline, "Yahoo! Mountain Dew!" was accompanied by "Thar's a bang in ever' bottle."

In 1973 PepsiCo assigned the brand to BBDO, its agency of record for Pepsi. For two decades client and agency worked to expand the brand's reach from America's hinterlands into the suburbs and cities of the major metropolitan areas. The major campaign of the 1970s—"Hello Sunshine"—sought to tie Mountain Dew's distinctive product characteristics to a set of backcountry recreational images. The yellow-green product and strong citrus flavor are represented over and over by the gleaming sun sparkling in beautiful natural settings. The product name is represented in virtually every ad by mountains, dew drops reflecting in the sun, and condensed drops on cans to represent dew. The energizing effects of the caffeine and sugar are toned down and now are a refreshing part of an active outdoor lifestyle. Often the ads featured casual coed athletic activities that always ended in a plunge into a rural pond or creek.

This campaign pulled the Mountain Dew brand into more contemporary terrain, but it was still too rural to get much traction in the suburbs. So in the 1980s, PepsiCo directly targeted suburban teenagers with a new campaign called "Country Cool." The creative idea was to marry the popular athletic endeavors of suburban kids (cool) with Mountain Dew's active rural lifestyle (country), all punctuated by the refreshing Dew plunge. Ads featured male teens performing on skateboards, mountain bikes, and BMX bikes. A new tune was crafted for the occasion: "Being cool you'll find is a state of mind. Your refreshing attitude. Things get hot. Cool is all you got. Dewin' it country cool. So chill on out; when the heat comes on. With a cool, smooth Mountain Dew. Dewin' it Country Cool. Mountain Dew. Dewin' it Country Cool."

BBDO jettisoned the "country" component of the campaign in 1991 to build an entire campaign around athletic stunts. This advertising departed dramatically from anything that BBDO had produced in the previous 16 years. The spots featured daredevil maneuvers of sports like windsurfing, rollerblading, motocross cycling, and paragliding. The closely framed shots, which put the viewer in the middle of the action, also suggested excitement and energy. The spots were set to aggressive rock music rather than studio jingles. In 1992, a new song called "Get Vertical" was introduced with the lyrics "Ain't no doubt about the power of dew, got the airborne thrust of rocket fuel."

Cultural Trends

PepsiCo and BBDO managers paid close attention to cultural trends. They were particularly focused on track music and sports trends since these activities were so central to youth culture.

Music

Three musical trends dominated the airwaves in the 1990s. Rap music exploded to become the most popular genre in the country. At first, gangsta rap, which flaunted misogynistic and violent lyrics, was said to represent the reality of life in the "hood" (the American ghetto). From 1992 onward, gangsta rap broke out with a lighter sound and slightly less aggressive lyrics, sometimes called gangsta-lite, that made the music much more accessible while maintaining the forbidding connotations. By 1993, media coverage of the travails of celebrity rappers like Snoop Doggy Dog and Tupac Shakur ruled not only the music magazines but *People* and *Newsweek*. Rap music, and the hip-hop lifestyle of which it was a part, permeated teen life. MTV's program *Yo! MTV Raps* and specialty magazines like *The Source* and *Vibe* became mainstream cultural venues. By 1999, rap remained very popular amongst male teens, especially in urban areas, though its Top 40 appeal had subsided somewhat.

At roughly the same time, the alternative rock music scene, which throughout the 1980s existed as a small subcultural scene found mostly on college campuses, also exploded. Two Seattle bands—Nirvana and Pearl Jam—put CDs at the top of the charts with aggressive and emotive music that combined equal parts punk and heavy metal. The media tagged this music "grunge" and anointed Seattle as grunge headquarters. Grunge was marketed heavily by the culture industries—music labels put out dozens of grunge bands, films that displayed the grunge attitude appeared, and fashion runways and J.C. Penney's stores were clogged with flannel shirts and clothes that had the look of the vintage Salvation Army gear that was the uniform of the grunge scene. Grunge faded in its influence in part due to the death of its most talented lead actor when Nirvana's Kurt Cobain committed suicide in 1995.

Later in the 1990s, techno music began making significant inroads into American youth culture. Invented in the 1980s as "house music" in low-budget studios of Chicago and Detroit, this beat-driven dance music became the lifeblood of dance parties called "raves" in places like London and the Spanish island of Ibiza. Raves quickly spread throughout continental Europe and beyond. Raves were all-night dancing marathons often set up in warehouses, exotic outdoor locales, and other improvised spaces. Raves attracted young people, mostly teens, who danced for hours at a time, not in pairs, but in free-form groups. The highly rhythmic music and long-winded dancing combined to produce for some fans an ecstatic trance-like state. The music was produced almost entirely by disk jockeys sampling records with tape loops and other electronic tricks. Many subgenres have since emerged that mix and match musical styles from around the world. Part of the scene was a drug called ecstasy, a drug that induces promiscuous affection, sensory overload, and euphoria. And, to keep the energy flowing all night, the dancers demanded energizing drinks. In particular, an enterprising Austrian company marketed Red Bull, a drink that was once an Asian hangover cure, as a rave stimulant. Either straight or mixed with vodka, Red Bull became the rave drink of choice. Raves diffused rather late to the United States, but proved to be most popular in the major metropolitan areas.

Sports

The so-called "alternative sports" took off in the early 1990s. Teen enthusiasts transformed casual hobby activities—mountain biking, skateboarding, paragliding, BMX biking, and inline skating—into highly technical, creative, and often dangerous sports. Snowboarding became an overnight hit with teens. Bungee jumping was a fad that disappeared quickly. As these sports became increasingly risky and creative, they began to attract spectators. So-called extreme sports—skiing down extremely steep terrain or jumping off tall buildings with a parachute—were covered by ESPN. ESPN also aggressively promoted circuits and tournaments to professionalize these new sports, which culminated in the Extreme Games in 1994, a nontraditional Olympics of sorts. Mountain Dew was one of the founding lead sponsors of the Extreme Games, which later became the X Games. Later, NBC followed with the Gravity Games, and MTV also began to cover these sports. Grunge music, more aggressive styles of rap, and various hybrids were prominent aural expressions of these sports.

GenX Ethos

During the 1990s, teens and young adults evinced a growing cynicism toward the dominant work-oriented values of the previous generation and toward corporations more generally. They found that working hard to get ahead in terms of salary and occupational prestige was harder to swallow in an era of corporate reengineering. Their cynicism also extended to corporations themselves and their marketing efforts. As this cohort became increasingly knowledgeable about how marketing worked and increasingly jaded about why brands were popular, they were not interested in listening to "sales messages" that tried to persuade them into believing a particular brand of soft drink or beer was cool. Instead, these youth adopted a campy interest in non-trendy products, television programs, and music of previous eras.

As these odd new tastes became commercialized in programming like Nickelodeon cable channel's "Nick at Nite" series—which featured less-than-notable programming from the 1950s–1970s—"retro" was born.

The Do the Dew Campaign

In 1992, senior management at PepsiCo sensed an opportunity to increase business on Diet Mountain Dew. Diet Mountain Dew's distribution was limited mostly to the rural regions where the brand was strongest, even though regular Dew was now a national brand. Diet Mountain Dew performed very well on product tests versus other diet drinks in the category because the heavy citrus flavor did a better job of masking the undesirable taste of the artificial sweetener. So PepsiCo allocated money for incremental advertising to support an effort to expand Diet Mountain Dew distribution. Bill Bruce, then a junior copywriter working on several brands, was assigned to the project. The strategy statements that guided the initial creative idea and subsequent spots in the campaign are reported in Exhibit 3. Bruce came up with the "Do Diet Dew" tag line (which soon evolved into "Do the Dew" to support the entire brand) and several new ideas to embellish what BBDO had begun with the Get Vertical campaign.

The first breakthrough ad of the new campaign, *Done That,* features a hair-raising shot of a guy jumping off the edge of a cliff to take a free-fall toward the narrow canyon's river bottom, set to throbbing grunge music. This was the first ad to feature the "Dew Dudes"— four young guys who are witnessing the daredevil stunts presented in the ad and commenting on them. *Done That* became a huge hit, capturing the country's imagination. The ad was widely parodied and the phrase "been there, done that" entered the vernacular. For 1994 and 1995, BBDO produced three carbon-copy "pool-outs"[1] of *Done That.* By 1995, after two years of these ads, consumer interest in the creative was fading fast. According to Jeff Mordos, if the creative hadn't moved to another idea that year, consumers' flagging interest and the potential of a revolt by PepsiCo bottlers likely would have forced PepsiCo to develop an entirely new campaign.

For 1995, three of four spots produced relied upon different creative ideas. One of these spots, *Mel Torme,* became the second hit of the campaign. The spot was a parody featuring the aging Vegas lounge singer Mel Torme, tuxedo-clad atop a Vegas hotel crooning "I Get a Kick out of You," with lyrics altered to incorporate Mountain Dew references. He impresses the Dew Dudes with a base jump of his own. Similar ads followed. In *007,* a teenage James Bond engages in a frenetic pursuit scene with typical Bond stunts, accompanied by the familiar Bond theme music. The Dew Dudes are not impressed until Bond comes upon a Mountain Dew vending machine. In *Training,* brash tennis star Andre Agassi performs extreme stunts as training exercises, and then plays an extreme game of tennis with the Dew Dudes as his coaches.

In 1997, BBDO came up with two breakthrough spots. The director of Nirvana's classic music video "Smells Like Teen Spirit" was hired to direct *Thank Heaven,* which mimics a music video. The spot stars the lead singer of an alternative rock band called Ruby. She sings a punked-up version of the classic song "Thank Heaven for Little Girls," in which the grunge style suggests the "little girls" of old have been replaced by the feminine brand of

---

[1]The noun *pool-out* is derived from a verb that is particular to the advertising business—"to pool out." The idea is to develop a pool of ads that are all closely related derivations from the same creative idea. Some advertisers feel that pools deliver a more consistent campaign while others feel that the ads become too formulaic when they are so similar. Regardless, there is a great temptation when an ad breaks through and becomes a hit to develop pool-outs to extend the popularity.

EXHIBIT 3   Mountain Dew Brand Communications Strategies (1993–1999)

Source: PepsiCo

	Objective	Strategy	Target	Executional Direction
1993–94	Increase awareness and trial of Mountain Dew	You can have the most thrilling, exciting, daring experience but it will never compete with the experience of a Mt. Dew	Male teens/young adults	• Distinct campaign with Dew equity consistency • Leverage "full tilt taste" and "rush" as point of difference
1995	Distinguish Mt. Dew within the competitive environment through contemporary communication of the trademark's distinct, historical positioning	You can have the most thrilling, exciting, daring experience but it will never compete with the experience of a Mt. Dew	Bull's eye: 18 yr. old leading edge male Broad 12–29 year olds	• Shift to a unified trademark focus modeled after "Do Diet Dew" • Explore outdoor settings • Predominant male, mid-20's casting • Preserve balance between "outlandish" and "realistic" actions/sports
1996	Optimize Dew's positioning equity among the target in a highly relevant and contemporary manner	(You can have the most thrilling, exciting, daring experience but . .) there's nothing more intense than slamming a Mt. Dew	Bull's eye: 18 yr. old leading-edge male Broad: 12–29 year olds	• Bring "Do the Dew" trademark campaign to the next level
1997	Optimize Dew's positioning equity among the target in a highly relevant and contemporary manner • Strengthen brand perceptions among AA • Encourage product trial where familiarity is low	(You can have the most thrilling, exciting, daring experience but . .) there's nothing more intense than slamming a Mt. Dew	Bull's eye: 18 yr. old leading-edge male Broad: 12–29 year olds	• Continue "Do the Dew" trademark campaign and encompass the Mt. Dew experience
1998	Build badge value and authentic, true Icon status for Mt. Dew in the world of youth-targeted consumer goods	Associate Mt. Dew with thrilling and exhilarating adventures in a light-hearted manner	Bull's eye: 18 yr. old leading-edge male Broad: 12–29 male/female	• Evolve the "Do the Dew" campaign against core target with fresh and relevant copy • Develop ethnically-targeted "cross-appeal" spot • Enhance product perception
1999	Optimize relevance of Dew's positioning among the target	Associate Mt. Dew with the exhilarating intensity of life's most exciting, fun adventures	Male Teens (16 yr. old epicenter) • Invite teen girls while continuing as male CSD • Maintain cross-over appeal among 20–39 year olds	• Develop pool of "Do the Dew" executions • Explore other metaphors beyond alternative sports to express "exhilarating intensity" • One execution should have AA/urban relevance • Communicate quenching • Inclusion of water-greenery elements not mandatory

aggressiveness presented in the ad. *Jackie Chan* deploys the Hong Kong movie star's patented martial arts with humorous stunts into the campaign's jaded, "seen it already" motif. The ad begins in the midst of what seems like a classic chase scene from a Chan film with lots of harrowing action. When Chan faces down his enemy, the Dew Dudes magically appear as Confucian wisemen who assist Chan with cans of Mountain Dew.

Other ads produced were significantly less effective. *Scream,* a high-speed amalgam of extreme sports shots that are organized to answer the lead-in question—"What is a Mountain Dew?"—did not fare well. And *Michael Johnson,* a spot developed to broaden Dew's appeal in the African-American community, did not meet the company's expectations.

By 1998, PepsiCo managers worried that the advertising was becoming too predictable. In particular, they were concerned that the use of alternative sports was becoming less impactful due to oversaturation. Many other brands, including companies like Bagel Bites, AT&T, Gillette Extreme Deodorant, and Slim Jims beef jerky snacks, were now major sponsors of alternative sports. To keep the campaign fresh, they needed to find alternative ways to express Mountain Dew's distinctive features. *Parking Attendant,* produced in 1999, was a solid effort at advancing toward an alternative expression. The spot features a parking attendant who takes liberties when parking a BMW handed off by a stuffy businessman. The kid drives as if in a police chase, flying from one building to another, accompanied by a frenetic surf instrumental that had been featured in Quentin Tarantino's *Pulp Fiction* a few years prior.

Mountain Dew Market Research

Mountain Dew's distinctive demographic profile reflected the brand's historic popularity in the NASCAR belt (see the Brand Development Index Map in Exhibit 4 and lifestyle analysis in Exhibit 5a). And Mountain Dew had much lower penetration of the total population than its major competitors. But its consumers were the most loyal in the category. Mountain Dew had the highest "gatekeeping" rating of all CSDs—it was the drink that mothers tried the hardest to keep out of the stomachs of their children. Periodically, the PepsiCo research department fielded a major study to assess the "health" of the brand, and to direct any fine-tuning. A 1997 "brand fitness" study profiled the status of the Dew brand versus its major competitors (Exhibits 6a–d).

PepsiCo monitored both the effectiveness of individual ads, as well as the cumulative impact of advertising on the overall health of the Mountain Dew brand. The contribution made by a single ad toward building brand equity was notoriously challenging to measure. Both quantitative and qualitative research provided data from which managers make useful inferences. But Pepsi managers had yet to find a research method that was accurate enough to rely upon to provide definitive judgments on ad effectiveness. PepsiCo routinely gathered a wide variety of data that hinted at an ad's impact. In addition to formal research, managers monitored "talk value" or "buzz"—the extent to which the ad has been picked up by the mass media. In particular, *The Tonight Show* and David Letterman were useful barometers. Feedback from the Mountain Dew Web site, unofficial Web sites, and the brand's 800 number were important gauges as well. In addition, PepsiCo carefully monitored how the salesforce and bottlers responded to the ads, since they were getting direct feedback from their customers. PepsiCo managers used all these data as filters. But, ultimately, the evaluation of advertising rested on managerial judgement. Based on their past experience with the brand and with advertising across many brands, managers made a reasoned evaluation.

However, PepsiCo managers did rely on market research to assess the cumulative impact of advertising on the brand. Because many other factors—especially pricing and retail display activity—had an immediate short-term impact on sales, it was often difficult to draw causal relationships between advertising and sales. But advertising campaigns do directly

EXHIBIT 4 **Mountain Dew Brand Development Index Map**

Source: BBDO New York

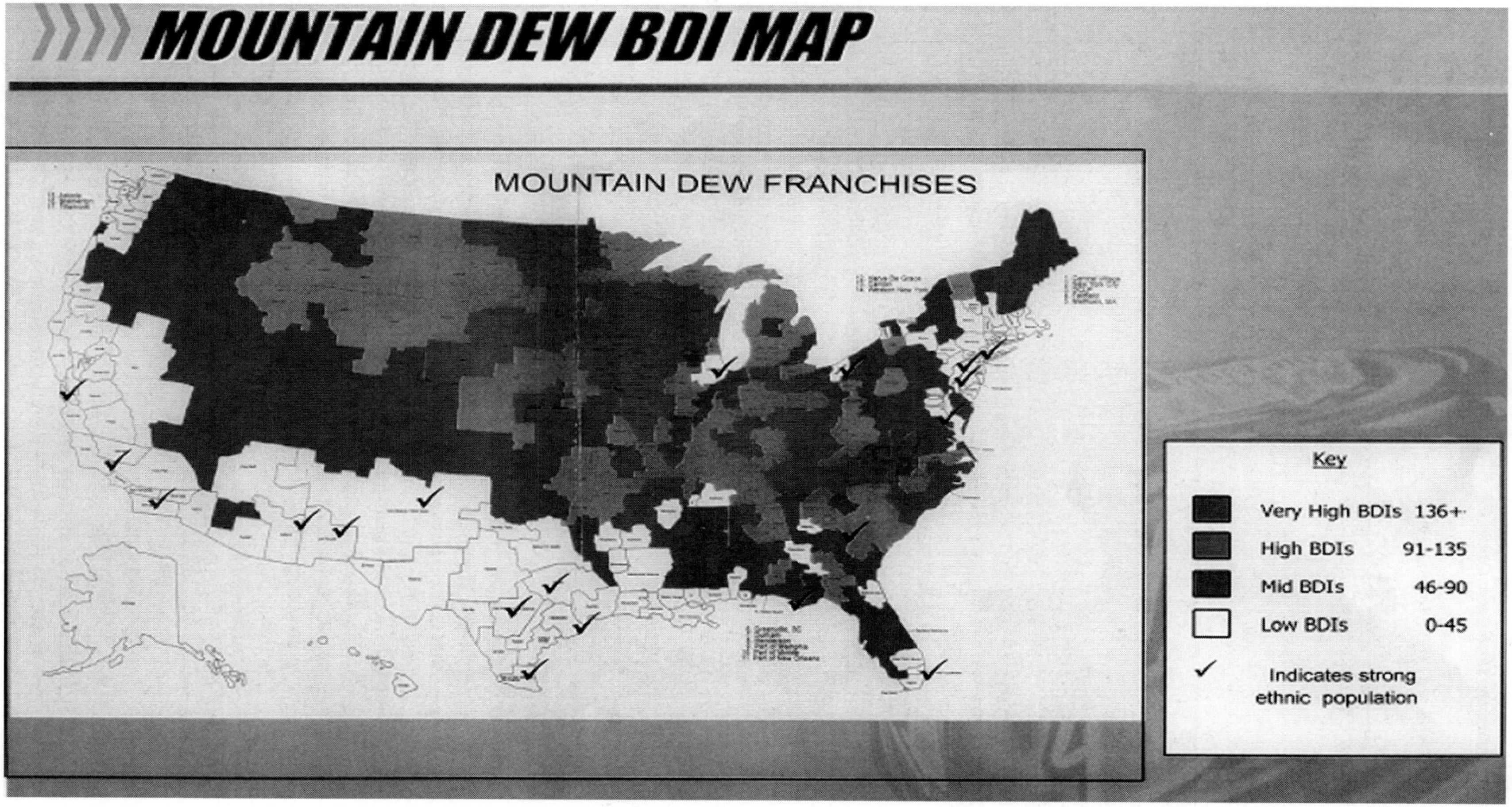

MOUNTAIN DEW BDI MAP

MOUNTAIN DEW FRANCHISES

Key

■	Very High BDIs 136+
■	High BDIs 91–135
■	Mid BDIs 46–90
□	Low BDIs 0–45
∕	Indicates strong ethnic population

EXHIBIT 5A **Spectra Lifestyle Analysis**

Source: AC Nielsen Product Library 11/97 to 11/99.

Mountain Dew Consumption Index

Lifestage

Spectra Lifestyle	18–34 W/Kids	18–34 W/O Kids	35–54 W/Kids	35–54 W/O Kids	55–64	65+	Total Lifestyle
Upscale Suburbs	82	77	101	56	45	13	64
Traditional Families	118	121	160	79	42	35	96
Mid Upscale Suburbs	101–	111	108	71	64	18	66
Metro Elite	139	85	141	47	47	21	72
Working Class Towns	237	139	242	121	67	42	139
Rural Towns & Farms	225	153	212	141	91	39	140
Mid Urban Melting Pot	148	104	97	52	49	31	74
Downscale Rural	309	142	291	127	87	43	158
Downscale Urban	99	98	107	73	55	32	76
Total Lifestage	171	112	165	83	61	31	100

impact how the brand is perceived. And these perceptions, in turn, drive sales. So PepsiCo had assembled a set of what they termed key performance indicators (KPIs), intermediate measures that were directly impacted by advertising and that had been proven to significantly impact sales. Managers tracked KPIs, also referred to as *brand health* measures, both for teens and for 20–39 year olds. But managers were particularly concerned with brand health amongst teens because at this age soft drink consumers often moved from experimenting with a variety of drinks to becoming loyal lifetime drinkers of a single soda. The latest study, conducted in the spring of 1999, reported Mountain Dew's teen KPIs. Dew improved 6 points on "Dew Tastes Better" (to 48 percent versus a year ago). Unaided brand awareness had dropped 5 points (to 39 percent). "For someone like me" had increased 5 points (to 53 percent). And "Dew Drinkers are Cool" increased 5 points (to 64 percent).

2000 Planning

In 1999, Mountain Dew became the third largest carbonated soft drink at retail, overtaking Diet Coke. However, part of this success in gaining share had to do with the sustained weakness of Pepsi and Coke. In 1999, the problems that the colas were facing seemed to be spreading to Mountain Dew, Sprite, and Dr. Pepper. All of the leading CSDs began to show real weakness as alternative noncarbonated drinks began to attract a great deal of trial, especially amongst teens. While Mountain Dew sales began to lag, all of the "brand health" indicators remained strong. And the advertising continued to significantly outperform competition. In planning for 2000, Moffitt and his senior management were particularly concerned with two dilemmas:

- How to keep the "Do the Dew" campaign working hard to build the brand given that extreme sports were becoming overexposed.
- How to respond to the growing threat of non-CSDs, especially Gatorade and the new highly caffeinated and sugary energy drinks like Red Bull.

A detailed strategy statement was developed by Moffitt's team at Pepsi-Cola North America, in conjunction with the account team at BBDO New York led by Cathy Israelevitz. This strategy was boiled down to a single sentence to focus the development of new

EXHIBIT 5B   Lifestyle Glossary

Source: AC Nielsen Product Library 11/97 to 11/99.

Upscale Suburbs

"The American Dream," a nice house in a nice suburban neighborhood. College-educated executives and professionals who index high on travel, eating out, playing golf, going to health clubs, buying imported cars, watching/reading business and news. Low African American and Hispanic. High income.

Traditional Families

Like Upscale Suburbs, but lower socioeconomic level. Mix of lower level administrators and professionals with well-paid blue-collar. Index high on gardening, DIY home improvement, driving SUVs, camping, classic rock, sports radio. Low African American and Hispanic. Mid-high income.

Mid/Upscale Suburbs

Live in first-generation suburbs that are now part of the urban fringe. Lower income than Traditional Families, but more college-educated and white collar. Index high on baseball fans, casino gambling using Internet, attending live theatre, reading science and technology, listening/watching news. Low African American and Hispanic. Mid-high income.

Metro Elite

Younger and more urban, college-educated, ethnically diverse. Very attuned to new fashions. Geographically mobile. Index high on health clubs, bars and night clubs, fashion magazines, VH-1, music, film, computers. Middle income.

Working Class Towns

Well-paid blue collar families living in suburbs of smaller cities. Index high on auto racing, fishing, hunting, country music, camping, televised sports. Own trucks or minivans. Low African American and Hispanic. Middle income.

Rural Towns & Farms

Small towns mostly in the middle of the country, dominated by blue-collar and agricultural work. Index high on rodeos, fishing, woodworking, chewing tobacco, wrestling, camping, country music, TV movies, USA and TNN channels. Don't read magazines and newspapers. Low African American. Lower income.

Mid-Urban Melting Pot

Urban multiethnic neighborhoods. Old European ethnic enclaves and new Asian immigrants, mixed with African-American and Hispanic neighborhoods. Index high on menthol cigarettes, dance music, boxing, pro basketball, lottery, Home Shopping Network, heavy TV viewing, urban contemporary radio. Lower income, low college, service industries.

Downscale Rural

Poor rural areas in Appalachia, throughout the South, and the Plains States. This socially conservative and religious area is sometimes called "the Bible belt." While indexing high African American, these are very segregated neighborhoods with little racial mixing. Lowest on education, occupation, income, housing. Index high on trucks, chewing tobacco, belonging to veteran's club, target shooting, tractor pulls, country music, fishing and hunting., daytime drama TV programs.

Downscale Urban

Same socioeconomic profile as Downscale Rural but very different cultural profile, more similar to Mid-Urban Melting Pot. Mostly African American and Hispanic urban neighborhoods.

creative: *Symbolize that drinking Mountain Dew is an exhilarating experience.* This document was used to brief Bruce and his creative team (Exhibit 7).

Super Bowl

In addition to these strategic issues, Moffitt had to consider carefully where these ads would be broadcast. Mountain Dew's national media plan focused on a younger audience. Typical buys would include MTV, *The Simpsons,* and ESPN during alternative sports broadcasts. However, with its long run of sales increases in the 1990s, Mountain Dew was becoming less of a niche brand. Partly in recognition of this expanding customer base and partly to celebrate within the company Dew's arrival as the third most popular CSD, top management decided to feature Mountain Dew rather than Pepsi during the Super Bowl.

EXHIBIT 6A
Brand Imagery—
Mountain Dew

Source: BBDO New York.

Product Imagery

*Too sweet
Most entertaining ads
Fun to drink
Intense experience
Lots of flavor

When need energy boost
In mood for something different
*At a sporting event

User Imagery (54%)

Psychographic Imagery

Adventurous
Wild
Active
Daring
*Courageous
Exciting
Free-spirited
Rebellious
Spontaneous
Athletic
Youthful
Cool
Hip
*Out-going

EXHIBIT 6B
Brand Imagery—
Surge

Source: BBDO New York

Product Imagery

*Can't relate to ads
*Low quality product
*Not always available
Unique
Intense experience
*Tastes artificial

When need energy boost
In mood for something
different

User Imagery (49%)

Psychographic Imagery

Wild
Rebellious
Daring
Adventurous
Active
Up-to-date
Athletic
*Trendy
Youthful
*Leading-edge
Exciting
Spontaneous
Individualistic
*Powerful
Hip
In style

EXHIBIT 6C
Brand Imagery—
7 UP

Source: BBDO New York

Product Imagery

*Least fattening
Lowest calories
Low in sodium
*Too little flavor
*Not sweet enough
*Not filling
*Healthy/good for you
Most refreshing

User Imagery (48%)

Psychographic Imagery

Sensitive
Relaxed
Peaceful
*Healthy
Feminine
Kind
*Nurturing

(Nice)
(Loyal)
(Cooperative)

EXHIBIT 6D
Brand Imagery—
Sprite

Source: BBDO New York

Product Imagery

Lowest calories
Most refreshing
*Thirst quenching
*Goes down easy
Low in sodium

In a nice restaurant
*After exercise/sports

(In the evening)
(In the morning)

User Imagery (56%)

Psychographic Imagery

Feminine
Sensitive
Peaceful
*Nice
Relaxed
Free-spirited
*Cooperative
*Friendly
*Happy
Kind

(Innovative)

EXHIBIT 7
Mountain Dew FY 2000 Brand Communications Strategy

Source: PepsiCo

Objective: Expand appeal of Mountain Dew to new users while reinforcing it among current users
Positioning: To <u>18 year old males</u>, who embrace excitement, adventure and fun, Mountain Dew is the great tasting carbonated soft drink that <u>exhilarates like no other</u> because it is <u>energizing</u>, <u>thirst-quenching</u>, and has a <u>one-of-a-kind citrus flavor</u>.
Communication Strategy: Symbolize that drinking Mountain Dew is an exhilarating experience.
Target: Male Teens—18 year-old epicenter

- Ensure appeal amongst 20–39 year olds (current users)
- Drive universal appeal (white, African-American, Hispanic, and other ethnic)

Product Benefits	Emotional Benefits	Personality
Energizing	Exhilaration	Irreverent
Quenching	Excitement	Daring
Great Taste		Fun

The Super Bowl had for decades been a hugely influential event for advertisers. The game drew the biggest audience of the year and the ads received an amazing amount of attention. In recent years, the frenzy around the advertising had grown disproportionately to the game itself. The media paid almost as much attention to the ads shown as to the teams and players. The networks interviewed the advertisers and the stars of the ads, and even replayed the ads on their programs. So a Super Bowl ad now had a huge ripple effect in free public relations. In addition, the Super Bowl was an extremely important contest for advertisers and especially for ad agencies. To "win" the Super Bowl (to be voted the top ad in the *USA Today* Ad Meter poll reported in the newspaper the following day) was a prestigious honor within the industry. Finally, Super Bowl ads provided a powerful sales tool to motivate retailers and distributors. PepsiCo and other grocery products advertisers used their annual Super Bowl advertising to sell in retail displays.

Super Bowl advertising, as a result, had become a distinctive genre within advertising. The demographically diverse audience demanded advertising with hooks that were easily understood. Insider humor did not work. While MTV ads could talk in a colloquial language to teens, Super Bowl ads could not afford this luxury. Second, the heated competition to win the affection of the audience had led to "big" productions that would stand out against an ever-more impressive set of competitors.

The New Creative

Bruce and Cassar had just finished presenting 10 new ad concepts for PepsiCo to evaluate. For each concept, PepsiCo managers were given a "storyboard"—a script and a set of rough pencil sketches that depicted the most important scenes. Bruce and Cassar talked through each storyboard to help the client imagine how the ad would look if it were produced. The storyboard served as the skeletal outline of the ad. The creatives put flesh on these bones by describing in detail the characters, the action, how the scene is depicted, and the music. Of the 10 new concepts, Moffitt and his senior managers hoped to select three ads to produce. The two best ads would run on the Super Bowl and then all three ads would be broadcast throughout 2000. It was already October, so there was barely enough time to produce the ads presented to get them on the Super Bowl. Asking Bruce to try again was not an option. The 10 initial concepts were quickly whittled down to five finalists.

1. *Labor of Love.* A humorous spot about the birth of a Dew drinker. The doctor in the delivery room calls out "code green" and retreats to catch with a baseball mitt the baby as it shoots out of its mother like a cannon.

2. *Cheetah.* One of the Dew Dudes chases down a cheetah on a mountain bike. The cheetah, running on the African plain, has stolen his Dew and he wants it back. He tackles the cat, pulls the can out of the cat's stomach, but finds that it's empty and full of holes.

3. *Dew or Die.* The Dew Dudes are called in to foil the plot of an evil villain who is threatening to blow up the planet. Performing daredevil maneuvers down a mountain, they get sidetracked in a ski lodge with some girls, but accidentally save the world anyway, powered by a spilled can of Dew.

4. *Mock Opera.* A parody of the Queen song *Bohemian Rhapsody* sung by the Dew Dudes who mock the cover of the original Queen album. The ad portrays the story of the altered lyrics: alternative sports action in which the athletes just miss cans of Dew as they shoot by.

5. *Showstopper.* A take-off on an extravagantly choreographed production number that mimics a Buzby Berkeley musical/dance film from the 1930s. The dancers are silver-clad BMX riders and skateboarders who perform for the Dew Dudes posing as directors.

PepsiCo viewed the evaluation of new creative as the most challenging aspect of brand management. Unlike decisions on new product ideas, consumer promotions, or product improvements, there was no market research or marketplace data to guide the decision. Junior managers typically did not sit in the agency presentations as they were not yet seasoned enough to judge creative work. PepsiCo believed that managers first had to gain knowledge of how advertising worked to build brands through years of seasoning and tutorials on several of the company's brands. So Scott Moffitt was the most junior person in the room. The skills and judgment that he demonstrated would be key to moving up the ladder at PepsiCo.

Bill Bruce finished presenting his last storyboard and scanned the room to lock eyes with the PepsiCo executives who would be deciding the fate of his ideas. Scott Moffitt didn't return the gaze. Instead he looked anxiously at his superiors, knowing that the spotlight would next focus on him. This was his chance to prove himself not only to PepsiCo senior management, but also to BBDO. BBDO's senior managers had become influential advisors, whom PepsiCo's top marketing executives routinely relied upon to help guide branding decisions. With six years of experience under his belt, this was Moffitt's chance to earn their respect as a contributing member to these critical discussions. Moffitt was eager to make a strong impression with nuanced and well-reasoned evaluations. Following longstanding protocol in packaged goods companies, the junior manager at the table gets the first crack at evaluating the creative. Moffitt cleared his throat, complimented Bruce on the high quality of the new work he had presented, and began his evaluation.

Case

13

Red Bull

**Richard R. Johnson, Jordan Mitchell, Paul W. Farris,
and Ervin Shames** *University of Virginia*

"We don't bring the product to the people. We bring the people to the product."[1]

—Dietrich Mateschitz, Founder, Red Bull GmbH

By any measure, Red Bull was a runaway success. Sales of Red Bull, a nonalcoholic, carbonated energy drink, reached 1.9 billion cans in 120 countries in 2004.[2] Red Bull had been a forerunner in establishing the worldwide energy-drink category estimated at more than $4.7 billion,[3] enjoying approximately half of the worldwide market share.[4] Since the company's 1997 U.S. debut, Red Bull had emerged as the seventh-leading carbonated soft drink company in terms of market share, growing by 45 percent to achieve sales of 30 million cases (see **Table 1**).[5] Hundreds of companies had entered the segment in hopes that they would rush the "Bull" and grab a piece of the lucrative market. Only a handful of enterprises such as Hansen Natural, with their drink called Monster, and Rockstar with a beverage of the same name, were able to challenge Red Bull's dominant market position by offering double the size at the same price. Along with small upstarts, Coca-Cola and Pepsi were eager to increase their lagging positions in the energy-drink sphere. Coca-Cola had entered the category in 2000 with its brand KMX, but it had failed to win over consumers. In early 2005, Coca-Cola launched a new energy-drink brand called Full Throttle to fight back. Pepsi had purchased the South Beach Beverage Company (SoBe) and had launched Amp under the Mountain Dew brand to etch out a competitive position.

This case was written from public sources by Richard R. Johnson and revised by Jordan Mitchell under the supervision of Paul W. Farris, Landmark Communications Professor of Business Administration, and Ervin Shames, Visiting Lecturer in Business Administration. It was written as a basis for class discussion rather than to illustrate effective or ineffective handling of an administrative situation. Copyright © 2002 by the University of Virginia Darden School Foundation, Charlottesville, VA. All rights reserved. *To order copies, send an e-mail to sales@dardenbusinesspublishing.com. No part of this publication may be reproduced, stored in a retrieval system, used in a spreadsheet, or transmitted in any form or by any means—electronic, mechanical, photocopying, recording, or otherwise—without the permission of the Darden School Foundation.* Rev. 07/05.

[1]"Selling Energy—Red Bull," *Economist,* (May 11, 2002).

[2]"Canada Prepares for Energy Drink Surge," *Globe and Mail* March 24, 2005.

[3]"The World Market for Soft Drinks," *Euromonitor,* September 2004, table 82, 39.

[4]"Hansen Natural Analyst Report," Adams Harkness, May 4, 2005, p. 4.

[5]"Beverage Digest," www.beveragedigest.com (accessed June 30, 2005).

TABLE 1   Top 10 U.S. Carbonated Soft Drink Companies, 2004.

Company	2004 Market Share	2004 Cases (millions)	Volume % Change
Coca-Cola Co.	43.1	4414.8	−1.0%
Pepsi-Cola Co.	31.7	3241.7	+0.4%
Cadbury Schweppers	14.5	1485.9	+2.3%
Cott Corp.	5.5	564.9	+18.2%
National Beverage	2.4	249.4	+2.2%
Big Red	0.4	41.5	−0.5%
Red Bull	0.3	30.0	+45.0%
Hansen Natural	0.2	20.2	+56.6%
Monarch Co.	0.1	9.8	+7.6%
Rockstar	0.1	9.7	+154.5%
Private Label/Other	1.7	171.5	−11.2%
Total	100.0	10,239.4	+1.0%

Source: "Maxwell Ranks Soft Drink Industry for 2004," Beverage Digest.

It looked as though the energy-drink segment would continue growing, with some analysts predicting the U.S. market to double at $3.5 to $4 billion by 2009. Some also predicted that Coca-Cola and Pepsi would force consolidation. How could Red Bull maintain its leadership position in a maturing category? Could the company survive the onslaught of competition, or was Red Bull a sitting duck?

Background

While touring Thailand in the early 1980s, Austrian businessman Dietrich Mateschitz took note of a Thai energy drink called Krating Daeng (or "red bull") that had become a popular pick-me-up or stimulant, especially amongst blue-collar workers. Believing that such a drink would be popular in Europe, Mateschitz made a deal with TC Pharmaceuticals, owners of Krating Daeng, that gave him the international rights to the drink in exchange for a 51 percent share in his Red Bull company.[6] Mateschitz adapted the taste of the drink to suit the western palate, and replaced the Thai bottle with a slim silver 250 ml. (8.3 oz.) can featuring a logo with two red bulls about to collide head-on in the foreground, and a yellow sun in the background. Beneath the logo appeared the words "energy drink."

As the name implies, energy drinks were designed to give the body a jolt of energy Red Bull alleged that its product contained several energy-boosting ingredients, including taurine glucoronolactone, and caffeine. Taurine is an amino acid occurring naturally in the body that acts as a metabolic transmitter with detoxifying qualities, but whose levels can drop as a result in situations of high stress or physical exertion. Glucoronolactone, like taurine, also has a detoxifying effect and can help eliminate harmful substances from the body. Caffeine a known stimulant, acts on the brain and circulatory system, and a single 250 ml. can of Red Bull contained 80 milligrams, a level of caffeine equivalent to a cup of coffee. Coca-Cola had 34 milligrams in each 12-ounce can.[7] The combination

[6]Acharn Terry Fredrickson, "About Business," *Bangkok Post,* October 18, 2000, http://www.bangkokpost.net/education/site2000/bcoc1800.htm (accessed September 12, 2002).
[7]Kerry A. Dolan. "The Soda with Buzz," *Forbes,* March 28, 2005.

**A Red Bull Flügtag participant prepares to launch a
homemade chicken-craft into an Austrian lake**

of these ingredients, along with carbohydrates in the form of glucose and sucrose as well as various vitamins, formed a beverage that, according to Red Bull, created the following effects:

- Increased physical endurance.
- Improved reaction speed and concentration.
- Increased mental alertness (to stay awake).
- Improved overall feeling of well-being.
- Stimulated metabolism and increased stamina.

The company captured these attributes in the phrase "Red Bull stimulates body and mind."[8]

Product Introduction in Austria

Red Bull faced challenges even before the product debuted. The company's ability to make claims regarding Red Bull's performance benefits was restricted under Austria's laws for "traditional foods." Arguing that its product contained characteristics from all three of Austria's food and drug categories—traditional, dietary, and pharmaceutical—but did not belong in any one, Red Bull successfully lobbied the government to create a new classification, "functional foods." This category required extensive documentation to support health-benefit claims, which created a significant entry barrier that had the effect of keeping away competitors for five years following Red Bull's launch.[9]

Red Bull finally debuted in 1987 in Mateschitz's home country of Austria. The product was positioned not for specific occasions, but rather for a range of occasions. With the flexible brand positioning "Revitalizes Body and Mind," Red Bull touted itself as suitable for such occasions as these:

- When a long day is over, and a long night starts.
- On long sleep-inducing motorways.
- During intensive working days when the date planner is filling up, and your energy reserves are emptying out.

---

[8]Red Bull Web site: http://www.redbull.com/faq/index.html (accessed September 12, 2002).
[9]Kevin Lane Keller, "Red Bull: Branding Brand Equity in New Ways," *Strategic Brand Management and Best Practice in Branding Cases.* 2nd Ed. (Upper Saddle River: Prentice Hall, 2003), 53–72.

- Prior to demanding athletic activities, or in a performance drop during a game . . . [along with water].
- Before tests and exams, when there's no time to sleep.
- Or as first-aid after a long party night.[10]

Red Bull provided tips for the best use of its product during athletic events lasting more than an hour: "The best way to achieve the full effect of Red Bull is to drink 1–2 cans about 30–45 minutes before the end of the competition, for example, before the final spurt phase of bike racing or long distance running, at halftime in soccer, rugby, basketball, and volleyball matches, and before the final set in tennis, squash, or table tennis."[11]

Early adopters of Red Bull included people attending clubs and rave parties, as well as truckers and students. Norbert Kraihamer, the company's global director of marketing and sales, explained:

> There are five user categories: students, drivers, clubber, business people, and sports people. Forget about age, where do they shop and when do they use it? Well, drivers use it on petrol forecourts. Clubbers use it in pubs and clubs, students use it in pubs and clubs and around campuses. We say we only have two dimensions: people who are mentally fatigued and people who are physically fatigued, or both. . . . I find loyal customers as soon as I can convince them that the product works. If they experience that the product keeps them awake, in a good mood, focused, vigilant, then they'll buy again. That's one of our secrets. If you do it right, you'll be getting up to 75% or even 80% re-purchase rate.[12]

In nightspots, Red Bull was often used as a mixer. A common combination was Red Bull and vodka, sometimes called a Smirnoff Bull. Another combination, called a shambles, featured Red Bull and champagne. Other mixers included gin, whisky, or, in southern Germany, beer. Kraihamer clarified that the company was not opposed to its product being used as a mixer, but that "over time we must make sure that the product is regarded as much more than a mixer. This is not a drink for a restaurant, this is a nutritional item."[13]

In line with selling Red Bull as a nutritional item, the company charged up to four times more per ounce than average soft drink prices, or $1.99 to $3 per 250 ml. can, and deliberately set prices at least 10 percent above competing energy drinks to maintain a premium image. Kraihamer noted, "We are much more expensive than [cola]. This is OK because ours is an efficiency product, so we can charge this price premium, which is the secret of its success."[14]

Red Bull's strategy for market entry relied heavily on word-of-mouth and "seeding." The company targeted a select handful of hip and trendy clubs, bars, and stores, allowing trendsetters the first opportunity to sample its product in hopes that they would become influencers and generate buzz. The company limited availability of the product during the seeding process. After six months of seeding, Red Bull introduced its product to locations surrounding the "in" seeding locations, thus making it easier for the consumer to purchase the brand. The final step was to enter supermarkets, thus reaching the mass market.[15]

Red Bull also targeted specific celebrities, including sports figures and entertainers, and sponsored sporting events ranging from Formula One racing to extreme skiing to soapbox races to the "Flügtag," where participants launched homemade flying objects off of a ramp

---

[10]Red Bull Web site: http://www.redbull.com/product/ingredients/index.html, (accessed September 17, 2002).

[11]Claire Phoenix, "Red Bull—Fact and Function," *Softdrinksworld*, February 2001, pp. 26–35.

[12]Phoenix "Red Bull."

[13]Ibid.

[14]Dolan, "The Soda with Buzz."

[15]Keller, "Red Bull."

into a lake. In late 2004, the company purchased the Jaguar Formula One racing team, re-naming it after the Red Bull brand. With estimates that the team would cost $100 million per year to run while only bringing in $70 million in revenues,[16] some industry savants questioned Red Bull's move. Mateschitz explained:

> As the CEO of Red Bull I have hard responsibilities. I cannot spend any marketing money, any budgets, any sponsorship by Red Bull on behalf of my personal passions, likes, or dis-likes. So the decision to be involved in motor sports is all good for the brand, a good market-ing decision. If you then in addition gain personal satisfaction, all the better. But the underlying decision has to be a purely rational rather than an emotional decision.[17]

Unlike any other major beverage company's marketing plan, Red Bull bought its tradi-tional advertising last. Their approach was to plan a media push only when the market had matured, thus reinforcing, rather than introducing, the brand. As Red Bull's vice president of marketing noted, "Media is not a tool that we use to establish the market. It is a critical part. It's just later in the development."[18] Red Bull invested 65 percent of sales in its early days in marketing, and entering 2005, continued to spend 30 percent of sales on marketing.[19]

Red Bull employed the slogan "Red Bull Verleiht Flüüügel" ("Red Bull Gives You Wii-ings") in its advertising. With the assistance of a colleague, Mateschitz created Red Bull's "adult cartoon" advertisement, which featured one character with an energy deficiency and another with a solution: Red Bull. One ad featured a dentist and Count Dracula. The den-tist tells Dracula that he'll have to remove the Count's teeth, to which Dracula replies that without his teeth he will not be able to drink blood: "But without fresh blood my body will wither and my mind will fade." The dentist proposes a solution: "One revitalizing Red Bull and you'll be prince of the night again." A picture of the Red Bull can appears, along with the copy, "Red Bull Energy Drink. Vitalizes Body and Mind." The dentist then samples the drink, delivers the punchline, "You know, Red Bull gives you *wiiing*," then sprouts wings and flies away. The animated spots transcended specific target groups, enabling the com-pany to establish a wide consumer base.[20]

Red Bull Mystique

Several experts argued that Red Bull achieved its cult following in part due to the rumors sur-rounding the product. One false rumor suggested that taurine, a key ingredient in Red Bull, was derived from bull testicles. Another falsity claimed that the drink was an aphrodisiac. Yet amongst the outright falsehoods circulated about Red Bull were a few grains of truth, includ-ing the partially correct rumor that Red Bull was banned in Europe. The drinks were banned in Denmark, Norway, Sweden, and France after health officials believed that the consump-tion of Red Bull was linked to deaths.[21] Cans of Red Bull in several countries bore labels warning against mixing the drink with alcohol. Across the Atlantic, sales of Red Bull were not permitted in Canada for several years, leading to cross-border smuggling of the product.[22] However, in 2004, health officials in Canada approved the sale of energy drinks with warning labels recommending that quantities should not surpass 500 ml. (16.6 oz.) per day.

[16]Dolan, "The Soda with Buzz."

[17]Alan Henry, "Motor Racing: Red Bull Puts Fizz Back into the Grid. . . .," *The Guardian,* March 1, 2005, p. 29.

[18]Kenneth Hein, "A Bull's Market," *Brandweek,* May 28, 2001, p. 21.

[19]Phoenix, "Red Bull."

[20]Keller, "Red Bull."

[21]"Canada Prepares for Energy Drink Surge," *Globe and Mail,* March 24, 2005.

[22]Ibid.

A research team from the Loughborough University Sleep Research Centre conducted a study to verify Red Bull's controversial claims of its product's ability to increase concentration, reaction time, and endurance. They tested the product on fatigued drivers. Their results indicated that one can of Red Bull was effective in reducing sleepiness and that two cans of Red Bull could eliminate fatigue altogether for 90 minutes.[23]

Missteps in the U.K. Market

Red Bull faced a challenge when considering expansion in Europe in the mid-1990s. Most countries within what is now the European Union, of which Austria was not yet a member, had a list of allowable food ingredients, and taurine was not on the list. However, Red Bull was able to enter through Scotland and then the United Kingdom, as Scotland only maintained a list of ingredients *not* approved for use in food, and taurine was not on that list. This entry point enabled access to certain other European markets (see **Table 2**).[24]

The U.K. sports and energy market consisted of two segments at the time of Red Bull's entry in 1995. The first segment consisted of refreshment energy drinks. Market leader Lucozade, originally launched in 1927, offered several variants and sizes, and had built a reputation for offering energy through glucose. The second segment, sports drinks, was created by the introduction of Lucozade Sport in 1990. This segment consisted of isotonic drinks designed to enhance physical performance and provide rapid replenishment by boosting absorption of fluid, minerals, and sugar.[25]

Red Bull changed its traditional market-entry strategy as it launched its product in the United Kingdom. First, the company marketed Red Bull as a sports drink instead of as a stimulation drink as in Austria. This was a significant decision considering Lucozade's domination of the sports-drink market and consumers' preestablished notions of what a sports drink should be. Second, rather than pursuing the word-of-mouth strategy, Red Bull sold its product immediately through mass-market channels, such as chain stores, in hopes that consumers would choose Red Bull over the other products on the shelf. Kraihamer commented, "The U.K. team started from the wrong end . . . they were wrong, they totally

TABLE 2   **Red Bull Early Market Entries**

Source: Claire Phoenix.

1987	Austria	1996	Belgium
1992	Hungary		Greece
1993	Scotland		New Zealand
1994	Germany		Portugal
	Slovenia		Romania
1995	Baltic States		Spain
	Czech Republic		Sweden
	Netherlands	1997	Ireland
	Poland		South Africa
	Russia		U.S.A.
	Slovakia	1998	Brazil
	Switzerland		Finland
	U.K.		Italy
		1999	Australia

[23]Phoenix, "Red Bull."

[24]Keller, "Red Bull."

[25]"UK Energy and Sports Drinks—Space . . . The Final Frontier." *Softdrinksworld,* February 2001, pp. 36–43.

misunderstood how to create a customer base." Third, the marketing mix used in Austria, including the ironic advertising with the cartoon commercial and the sporting-event links, was ignored in favor of a billboard-focused campaign in the United Kingdom. The company chose a new slogan for the U.K. campaign: "You should never underestimate what Red Bull can do for you."[26] By the end of 1996, Red Bull's share of the sports- and energy-drink market stood at less than 2 percent[27] One industry expert referred to Red Bull's U.K. experience as "an expensive disaster."[28]

The U.K. management team was replaced following this disappointing showing. The new management team repositioned Red Bull as a functional energy (or stimulation) drink, thus creating a new third segment in the U.K. sports- and energy-drink market. They also returned to the company's traditional method of building markets through word-of-mouth. Further, they replaced the U.K. slogan with what had worked in Austria. As Kraihamer explained of the U.K. slogan, "'You should never underestimate what Red Bull can do for you,' was far too long and misunderstood, whereas the 'It gives you wiiings' slogan as we now know works at all levels and on a worldwide scale."[29]

From Failure to Success in the United Kingdom

Following these changes, Red Bull was positioned for success in the United Kingdom. Red Bull's volume tripled in 1998, and then quadrupled in 1999 to sales of 170 million cans—and then climbed another 50 percent in 2000 to 260 million cans.[30] By 2004, Red Bull had become the third-leading soft drink by value in the United Kingdom, trailing only Coca-Cola and Pepsi. The brand held a 62 percent share of the growing "functional-energy" segment of the sports- and energy-drink market.[31] Red Bull achieved significant market penetration amongst the 14–19 and 20–29 year old age groups (see Figure 1). Red Bull proved popular for social occasions, with 32 percent saying that they drank Red Bull in pubs and bars at night, and 13 percent indicating that Red Bull was their favorite drink during that time.

Kraihamer credited Red Bull's premium price as part of the brand's success in the United Kingdom.

If you have a product and the consumer recognizes the benefit, you are going to create a large consumer base. . . . If the product doesn't do anything and is eight times, five times, whatever

FIGURE 1 Red Bull Market Penetration, 2000

Source: Red Bull College: Kevin Lane Keller.

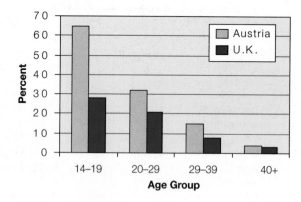

[26]Phoenix, "Red Bull."

[27]Keller, "Red Bull."

[28]Phoenix, "Red Bull."

[29]Ibid.

[30]Ibid.

[31]"The European Market for Energy & Sports Drinks to 2006," Mindbranch.com, (accessed June 30, 2005).

more expensive than a normal soft drink, what will people say? Very often I have the impression that all of our so-called competitors have never understood that. They think it is a fashion thing or that it is all a hype issue—which it is not.

Kraihamer continued, "We need people to hate us. As soon as we run out of haters, we have to create a foundation for haters because we lose our sharp image."[32]

America: A Bull Market?

Red Bull was introduced to the U.S. market in 1997. The company launched the product in a handful of targeted geographic areas, or "cells," instead of launching nationwide. As Kraihamer described:

> Our intention was never to go to the States and say "We are launching Red Bull. . . ." We chose small market cells. Santa Cruz was the first test market. Then we went to parts of San Francisco. After that we went to Santa Monica—our home base in the U.S. Our concept works better, the smaller the community we go into, because we are word-of-mouth people. In a huge area nobody hears you. In a small area you get the message across quite quickly. So we worked in the United States with the principle of healthy cells. When one small cell became a success story, we moved on to the next cell. . . . [T]hese cells are becoming bigger and bigger. But initially it was towns or parts of towns.[33]

Red Bull maintained its strategy of appearing first in trendy on-premise locations. Markus Pichler, executive vice president of Strategic Planning for Red Bull North America, explained, "We go to on-premise accounts [versus retailers] first, because the product gets a lot of visibility and attention. It goes faster to deal with individual accounts, not big chains and their authorization process. In clubs, people are open to new things."[34] A distributor commented, "They only select five accounts in an area instead of all of them. It could be a boards-and-blades store or an underage disco. . . . If a [bar next door asks for it], they'll say, 'You can't have it yet.'"[35]

In addition to its emphasis on sampling events at hip nightspots, Red Bull sponsored several dozen alterna-athletes, and underwrote many extreme sports competitions. One such event was the Red Bull Huckfest ski and snowboard competition in Utah. Said Pichler, "We find consumers there, early adopters."[36] Other events included cliff diving in Hawaii, street luge in San Francisco, paragliding in Chicago, and hang gliding in Aspen." The fourth Red Bull Music Academy, held in New York City in 2001, featured a collection of 60 club deejays from around the world gathered to learn the tricks of the turntable trade from master deejays. The deejays were under no obligation to promote Red Bull when they returned to their respective clubs, but the company hoped that they would mention Red Bull when telling others of their trip, and credit the company for its support of the scene.[37] The Red Bull Music Academy toured around the world in diverse locations such as London, Sao Paule, Cape Town, and Rome.

In total, Red Bull spent $600 million on worldwide advertising and marketing, which represented 30 percent of sales. In contrast, Coca-Cola spent 9 percent on advertising, albeit on sales of $20 billion.[38] Some industry observers believed that measured media accounting for only about 18 percent of Red Bull's total marketing.[39] A Red Bull spokesperson, disputing

---

[32]Phoenix, "Red Bull."

[33]Ibid.

[34]Hein, "A Bull's Market."

[35]Kenneth Hein. "Red Bull Charging Ahead." *Brandweek,* October 15, 2001, p. 438.

[36]"Red Bull Charging Ahead."

[37]Ibid.

[38]Kerry A. Dolan, "The Soda with Buzz," *Forbes* March 28, 2005.

[39]Hein, "A Bull's Market."

the figure, admitted that, "the perception that these events don't cost much to produce is good for us. We don't want to be seen as having lots of money to spend. But it's not as easy and inexpensive as people think."[40] Giving insight into Red Bull's strategy of highly specific use of electronic media, Kraihamer commented, "After 11 o'clock, we are much more likely to find our target audience. With cinema, we never just buy a media plan; we always choose to go with certain films—extreme action films or highly sophisticated cult films. . . ."[41]

The Soft Drink and Functional Drinks Market

The global soft-drink market was estimated at nearly U.S. $300 billion and accounted for approximately 11 trillion U.S. fluid ounces.[42] The soft-drink market generally included the following classifications: carbonated soft drinks (40 percent of market), bottled water (35 percent), fruit/vegetable juice (12 percent, ready-to-drink tea (4.5 percent), ready-to-drink coffee (0.9 percent), Asian specialty drinks (2.7 percent), concentrates (0.8 percent), and functional drinks (3 percent). **Exhibit 1** shows the growth of each segment within the global soft-drink market.

Functional drinks encompassed three main rubrics: sports drinks, energy drinks, and elixirs (a beverage with curing properties). Led by Pepsi's Gatorade[43] and Coca-Cola's Aquarius, the sports-drink category grew at a compound annual growth rate of 9.5 percent over the past five years, and dominated the functional drinks sector representing 77 percent of the volume. The sports-drink segment was considered to be relatively more mature than other functional drinks such as energy drinks and elixirs. Gatorade, for example, had been on the U.S. market since the 1960s, but continued to grow through product development and aggressive marketing. Euromonitor estimated that sports drinks would grow at an average rate of 5 percent on a global basis until 2008.[44] Some industry observers believed that sports drinks and elixirs containing healthier ingredients such as vitamins and electrolytes would outperform energy drinks, as consumers demanded more healthy alternatives.

EXHIBIT 1   **Global Volume of Soft Drinks Market by Category**

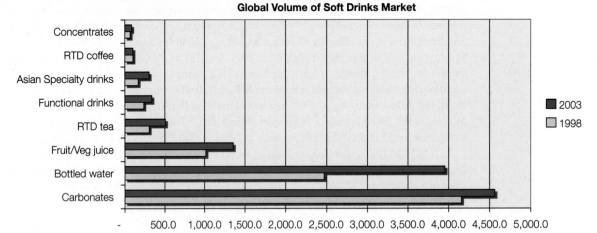

[40]Ibid.

[41]Phoenix, "Red Bull."

[42]"The World Market for Soft Drinks," *Euromonitor*, September 2004, Table 80, 39.

[43]Gatorade was developed by Quaker Oats. Pepsi purchased Quaker Oats in 2001.

[44]"The World Market for Soft Drinks," *Euromonitor*, September 2004, Table 95, 43.

Competition Abounds

By 2001, Red Bull had captured 65 percent of the $275 million new energy-drink market that it helped to create.[45] Around that time, Anheuser-Busch launched 180, Coke introduced KMX, and Pepsi brought to market both Mountain Dew Amp and SoBe Adrenaline Rush, all as competitors to Red Bull. Other entrants included Snapple Venom, Arizona Extreme Energy, Blue Ox, Bomba Energy, Dark Dog, Red Alert, Deezel, Power Horse USA, Go-Go Energy, and Hemp Soda.[46] Still, Red Bull maintained its position as the leader of the pack.[47] Kraihamer, speaking of Red Bull's competitors at the time, commented:

> I think they perceive it all as a micro-market thing. . . . This is peanuts. It's keeping some marketing people busy, but they don't realize the true potential. They might become competitors in time, but I think it is to our advantage that we are small.[48]

By 2005, the landscape for energy drinks had changed significantly. The U.S. energy-drink market was estimated between $1.6 and $2.0 billion in 2004 with growth hovering between 58 percent and 73 percent[49] Red Bull's U.S. overall market share (including all points of distribution) had dropped from 75 percent in 1998 to 47 percent in 2005.[50] Several competitors had been successful in growing their distribution networks and appealing to consumers through innovative communication. **Exhibit 2** shows key competitors' volumes in the U.S. energy-drinks market.

EXHIBIT 2 **Top Energy Brands in the United States**

Top 12 Energy Brands In U.S. Food, Drug and Mass Channels-Period Ending Dec 2004						
Brand	Sales $	YoY Change	Share $	*Volume Sales oz.*	YoY Change	Share %
Red Bull	$ 155,728,144	71.0%	60.3%	*700,026,495*	73.5%	49.6%
Rockstar	$ 22,797,562	125.4%	8.8%	*189,600,224*	127.2%	13.4%
Monster (Hansen)	$ 16,268,929	223.1%	6.3%	*139,289,344*	228.0%	9.9%
SoBe Adrenaline Rush (Pepsi)	$ 15,231,377	15.7%	5.9%	*67,769,376*	15.3%	4.8%
Amp (Mountain Dew)	$ 14,191,741	14.7%	5.5%	*63,349,544*	13.6%	4.5%
SoBe No Fear (Pepsi)	$ 10,108,871	190.3%	3.9%	*79,767,944*	187.0%	5.6%
Hansen (Hansen Energy)	$ 3,130,313	−13.1%	1.2%	*15,669,595*	−3.7%	1.1%
KMX (Coca-Cola)	$ 1,917,185	−63.7%	0.7%	*8,985,793*	−64.8%	0.6%
EAS Piranha (Abbot Labs)	$ 1,555,390	100.7%	0.6%	*7,821,674*	60.0%	0.6%
Lost (Hansen)	$ 1,401,335	n/a	0.5%	*11,765,080*	n/a	0.8%
Rush (Monarch)	$ 1,245,518	202.1%	0.5%	*9,480,658*	282.2%	0.7%
Fuze Omega	$ 1,207,002	629.9%	0.5%	*10,910,017*	684.3%	0.8%
Other	$ 13,459,817		5.2%	*107,986,527*		7.6%
Energy Category	$ 258,243,184	61.1%	100.0%	*1,412,422,272*	70.0%	100.0%

Source: Information Resources Inc. as cited in Hansen Natural Analyst Report, Adams Harkness, May 4, 2005, p. 7. Data is for food, drug and mass only and excludes Wal-Mart, club, food service, bar and convenience-store channels.
NOTE: These volumes likely represent between 15 and 25% of the overall volume sold in the U.S. in the energy drinks sector.

[45]Walker.

[46]Kenneth Hein. "Necessity and Invention," *Brandweek,* February 19, 2001, p. 22.

[47]Sweeney, "Red Bull."

[48]Phoenix, "Red Bull."

[49]Adams Harkness; Scott Leith, "The Buzz on Energy Drinks: Coke, Pepsi, and Tiny Firms Vie for Sip of Caffeine-Packed Beverage Market," *Atlanta Journal-Constitution,* April 8, 2005, p. F-1.

[50]Dolan, "The Soea with Buzz."

Hansen Natural

A Red Bull alterna-athlete competes in the 2000 X Games in San Francisco

California's Hansen Natural had first competed against Red Bull in 1997 in the United States when the company launched Hansen Energy drink. Lacking targeted advertising to energy-drink consumers such as sports enthusiasts, college students, and truckers, Hansen's energy product did not make a dent in the Red Bull-dominated market. In 2002, the company came back with Monster, packaged in black cans with neon-accented claw marks.

The cans were double the volume of Red Bull's cans and were offered to distributors for a comparable price, resulting in a $1.99 price to the final consumer.[51] The company also used its own staff to assist the 300 independent distributors restock the product in convenience-store refrigerators.[52]

Hansen supported the launch with its slogan "Unleash the Beast," and sent out teams of Monster "ambassadors" to distribute samples at motocross, surfing, and skateboarding competitions as well as concerts and beach parties. The company was a sponsor of the Vans Warped music tour and in 2005, the company created the "Monster Army," a sponsored group of professional athletes.

Largely driven by the success of the Monster brand, Hansen experienced sales increases of 162 percent in 2004. This propelled Monster to second place, capturing an 18 percent market share of the energy-drinks segment. Hansen's CEO Rodney Sacks bubbled over with enthusiasm at the results, "These are the new soft drinks of the world."[53]

Hansen had a slew of new product releases, such as Joker, exclusively for Circle-K stores: Rumba, a juice with high caffeine content, and Lost, a name that Hansen had licensed from a leading skateboarding, surfing, and snowboarding apparel brand.[54]

Other Upstarts

A number of other entrepreneurial ventures had challenged Red Bull's leadership. Rock Star, based in Las Vegas, launched its energy beverage in 2001, and occupied third place in the U.S. market with 16 percent share. Rock Star's primary consumers were teenage males. The company promoted its brand through associations with celebrities and music events. In 2005, the company inked a deal with Coca-Cola whereby Rock Star would pay fees for Coca-Cola to distribute the product throughout the United States.[55]

It was estimated that more than 1,000 products from hundreds of different small enterprises had attempted to break through the noise by launching their own energy drinks, often focusing on a specific subset of consumers. For instance, extreme sports enthusiasts were targeted by not only Red Bull and Monster, but also Go Fast! and Fuze, whereas video game junkies were targeted by BAWLS and Guarana. Three brands—Crunk!!.. Pimp Juice, and DefCon 3—were focused on the hip-hop market, and consumers interested in Jewish

[51]Christopher Palmeri, "Hansen Natural; Charging at Red Bull with a Brawny Energy Brew." *BusinessWeek,* June 6, 2005, p. 74.

[52]Palmeri, "Hansen Natural."

[53]Ibid.

[54]Adams Harkness.

[55]"Food Brief—Coca-Cola Co. Deal Is Reached to Distribute another Firm's Energy Drink," *The Wall Street Journal,* April 29, 2005, p. A-11.

mysticism were singled out with the product Kaballah energy drink.[56] Kaballah even signed pop-icon Madonna to endorse the product.[57]

The Two Giants: Coca-Cola and Pepsi

In early 2005, Coca-Cola released Full Throttle, its second energy drink, after its first energy brand KMX captured only 0.9 percent of the U.S. market.[58] Full Throttle was marketed in 16 oz. black cans with bright lettering set to a backdrop of dramatic flames. Coca-Cola planned on using its wide distribution system, supported by promotions such as giveaways at Monster Truck Jams and motorcycles shows. A Coca-Cola spokesperson explained that the target for Full Throttle was different from that of the club-goers and extreme-sports people who typically consumed energy drinks: "We are speaking to the guy's guy."[59] A Red Bull spokesperson seemed unconcerned: "Movement by the bigger players onto the scene really just validates the category."[60]

Pepsi's position was distinct from Coca-Cola's as they had gained more market share with Mountain Dew Amp and two SoBe products called No Fear and Adrenaline Rush. SoBe, a short form for South Beach Beverage Company, was founded in 1996 and was purchased by Pepsi in 2001 for an estimated $400 million.[61] To spur on sales, SoBe had partnered with the national convenience store 7-11 for a cobranded SoBe Slurpee.

The Canned-Coffee Category: A Threat?

Regular coffee served hot was a mainstay throughout the world with an estimated 500 billion cups served each year. In the United States, per capita consumption was about seven pounds a year, whereas Scandinavian countries topped the worldwide list, consuming more than 20 pounds per capita per year.[62] More than half of Americans were estimated to drink coffee daily, consuming an average of 3.4 cups per day.[63]

Several packaged-goods companies were looking to offer innovative ready-to-drink cold-coffee products. Pepsi, for example, had introduced the coffee-flavored Pepsi Kona as a test product in the mid-1990s, but never launched it due to lackluster results. Later, Pepsi teamed up with Starbucks to introduce Mazagran, a carbonated coffee-based drink that was sold at select Starbucks locations, but Mazagran was never released nationally. The Pepsi–Starbucks partnership continued, and together the companies launched Starbucks Frappuccino iced coffee and Starbucks DoubleShot espresso drink, which held 90 percent of the noncarbonated, ready-to-drink coffee segment as of 2005.[64]

In other countries, companies were experimenting with a fusion of coffee, milk, and energy drinks. Backed by a Nestlé venture-capital fund, and Austrian executive who helped introduce

---

[56]Burt Helm, "The Sport of Extreme Marketing," *BusinessWeek* March 14, 2005, p. 14.

[57]Adam Hellinker, "Madonna to Give Cult Drink a Boost," *Express on Sunday,* February 6, 2005, p. 17.

[58]Gillian Wee, "Coca-Cola Seeks Swig of Revved-Up Energy Drink Market," *Knight Ridder/Tribune Business News,* February 5, 2005.

[59]Ibid.

[60]Ibid.

[61]Hoovers Company Capsule, www.hoovers.com, (accessed June 29, 2005).

[62]Nation Master Statistics, www.nationmaster.com, (accessed July 7, 2005).

[63]Roast and Post Coffee Company, www.realcoffee.co.uk, (accessed July 7, 2005).

[64]Christina Cheddar Berk, "Coca-Cola Seeks to Refresh Product Line With New Items," *Dow Jones Newswires,* January 11, 2005.

Red Bull to the United States was launching his own brand called Returnity in Europe—a milk-based product deemed to be a "brain shake."[65] In Australia, the milk brand Dare launched a coffee, guarana, and milk drink with the appeal that it could be used to replace real coffee or energy drinks. A representative commented on the approach to the end consumers, "[We want to] touch them through their passion points—reach out through credible links to music, entertainment, fashion, sports, technology, and sex. The entire marketing mix will drive the brand's outlaw personality and encapsulate the 24–7, nonstop living theme."[66]

Even Red Bull Beverages Co. in Thailand (the producer of Red Bull) was preparing for the Thai relaunch of a canned-coffee version of Krating Daeng in the summer of 2005.[67]

Looking Ahead

Red Bull estimated it would sell 1 billion cans in the United States in 2005. Based on per-capita consumption, many believed that there was room for Red Bull to grow. Kraihamer had explained the per-capita targets as Red Bull was growing:

> In the best markets today, we can achieve a potential of 10 per person—ten cans per head, per year. We don't know if we can achieve a potential 15 or 20 per person, but I believe so.[68]

It was estimated that in the United States, Red Bull had moved from 0.4 cans per person in 2001 to 2.5 cans per person in 2004. While further growth opportunities appeared significant since the energy-drinks segment was still growing rapidly, Red Bull needed to overcome several challenges. One analyst gave this view of the competitive situation:

> Market-leader Red Bull is also a very strong competitor, but focused on the 8 oz. can category (particularly in liquor establishments), while Hansen and Rock Star focus their energy efforts on 16 oz. cans at retail. While Coke and Pepsi are obviously the dominant beverage players in the U.S. and have had some success in energy (more so Pepsi than Coke) with their respective Full Throttle and SoBe brands, we doubt that their success has met internal expectations. Coke's first effort under the KMX brand was clearly a failure. If brands such as Monster and Rock Star continue to grow north of $100 million each with strong sales per point of distribution, we would expect the big players to consolidate the fast-growing brands.[69]

Analysts with *BevNet*, a Web site and industry newsletter tracking the entire beverage industry, shared their opinion of how Red Bull fits into the market as of 2005:

> Red Bull faces some potential bumps in the road in the coming 24 months. First, the product has completely oversaturated the market—Red Bull is in just about anywhere that you can fit a mini-cooler, as well as mass merchandisers, bike shops, bars, etc., etc., etc. This could result in Red Bull becoming passé by removing the "cool" factor that made the brand so successful. Second, while other companies are improving formulations, flavors, and packaging, Red Bull stays the same. Will consumers find something that truly works better? Third, from our point of view Red Bull has a less-than-stellar industry reputation—and many people are praying for their demise as a result. Finally, given that Red Bull is a one-trick pony (compared to others such as Coke and Pepsi), the party is in serious jeopardy if sales start to slump, a price war starts, or over-energy-drink health concerns start to proliferate. Overall, tremendous brand power right now, but does it have true staying power to last another five years as number one?

[65]Dagmar Mussey, "Nestle Introduces European 'Brain Shake,'" *Advertising Age* June 6, 2005, p. 20.
[66]"Dare Shoots into Energy Drinks Market with a New Coffee Product." *B&T Weekly*, February 3, 2005.
[67]"Thailand: Red Bull Changes Aim to Coffee Drinks," *Thai News Service*, June 20, 2005.
[68]Phoenix, "Red Bull."
[69]Adams Harkness.

In response to extending the brand's reach, Red Bull was testing an herbal tea drink named Carpe Diem in Los Angeles and was considering using the name to launch an international fast-food concept served in edible potato containers. As well, the company was about to release a quarterly magazine touching upon the key themes of the Red Bull lifestyle such as extreme sports, the clubbing life, and music.[70]

"We have the next hundred years in front of us,"[71] stated Mateschitz about the brand's future. He then offered up his opinion on why consumers would continue drinking Red Bull: "We created the market. If you appreciate the product, you want the real one, the original. Nobody wants to have a Rolex made in Taiwan or Hong Kong."[72]

[70]Dolan, "The Soda with Buzz."
[71]Ibid.
[72]Ibid.

14

IVEY

Richard Ivey School of Business
The University of Western Ontario

"Hips Feel Good"— Dove's Campaign for Real Beauty

David Wesley *Northeastern University*

Kerstin Dunleavy, brand manager for Unilever's Dove line, was both excited and concerned about her meeting the next morning with Unilever's senior management. She was about to make one of the most important presentations of her career, one that involved taking the successful relaunch of Dove beauty products to the next level.

Dunleavy had already helped mastermind the original turnaround of Unilever's Dove line, which some believed had already been a career-maker for her. She, however, knew that the real test would come as phase two became operational. Only then would she truly be able to establish her reputation as a premier brand manager in the ultra-competitive beauty industry.

Without doubt, Unilever had placed a heavy load on Dunleavy's shoulders. As she gathered her thoughts, she wondered what the next month would hold as Dove rolled out the second phase of the relaunch in September 2006. She placed a call to her assistant executive brand manager and marketing advisor, Michael B. Allen. "Tomorrow I will be laying out the specifics of phase two of the relaunch," she reminded him.

> Things are looking good right now. The self-esteem issues we have focused on have resonated with our target audience. I want it to continue, but I am not so sure about our next move. I want it to continue in the right way.
>
> If the competition copies our strategy, we will just become one of them. Remember that a difference that doesn't stand out is not a difference. Let's go over what has happened in the past two years one more time to make sure we understand how we got here.

Allen agreed that societal marketing had both benefited the brand and helped customers feel good about themselves. He replied,

> Our business has been to sell products, not to satisfy our customers or cure society's ills. But now we know that we can do both. As long as we keep listening to customers, there is no reason why we can't continue to stand out and distinguish ourselves from our competitors.

Background

Unilever was one of the largest consumer products companies in the world with annual revenues of approximately $50 billion and a staff of 250,000. The company's product lines were organized into four main areas: Cooking and Eating, Beauty and Style, Healthy Living, and Around the House.

Unilever employed a global marketing strategy that was adapted to suit individual cultures and the unique requirements of its subsidiaries. The company's branding policies had been considerably modified in recent years. In 2004, its "Path to Growth" strategy reduced the number of products from 1,600 to 400. The company's brand strategy was also modified to emphasize product brand names, while a newly designed Unilever logo adorned its packages (see Exhibit 1).

EXHIBIT 1   **Unilever Logo and Symbols**

Sun

Our primary natural resource. All life begins with the sun—the ultimate symbol of vitality. It evokes Unilever's origins in Port Sunlight and can represent a number of our brands. Flora, Slim Fast and Omo all use radiance to communicate their benefits.

Hand

A symbol of sensitivity, care and need. It represents both skin and touch. The flower represents fragrance. When seen with the hand, it represents moisturizers or cream.

Bee

Represents creation, pollination, hard work and bio-diversity. Bees symbolize both environmental challenges and opportunities.

DNA

The double helix, the genetic blueprint of life and a symbol of bio-science. It is the key to a healthy life. The sun is the biggest ingredient of life, and DNA the smallest.

Hair

A symbol of beauty and looking good. Placed next to the flower it evokes cleanliness and fragrance; placed near the hand it suggests softness.   *(continued)*

EXHIBIT 1 (*continued*)

Palm tree

A nurtured resource. It produces palm oil as well as many fruits—coconuts and dates—and also symbolizes paradise.

Sauces or spreads

Represents mixing or stirring. It suggests blending in flavors and adding taste.

Bowl

A bowl of delicious-smelling food. It can also represent a ready meal, hot drink or soup.

Spoon

A symbol of nutrition, tasting and cooking.

Spice & flavors

Represents chili or fresh ingredients.

Fish

Represents food, sea or fresh water.

Sparkle

Clean, healthy and sparkling with energy.

Bird

A symbol of freedom. It suggests a relief from daily chores, and getting more out of life.

Tea

A plant or an extract of a plant, such as tea. Also a symbol of growing and farming.

Lips

Represent beauty, looking good and taste.

Ice cream

A treat, pleasure and enjoyment.

(*continued*)

EXHIBIT 1   (*concluded*)

Recycle
Part of our commitment to sustainability.

Particles
A reference to science, bubbles and fizz.

Frozen
The plant is a symbol of freshness, the snowflake represents freezing. A transformational symbol.

Container
Symbolizes packaging–a pot of cream associated with personal care.

Heart
A symbol of love, care and health.

Clothes
Represent fresh laundry and looking good.

Wave & Liquid
Symbolizes cleanliness, freshness and vigor. A reference to clean.

Along with the new public image came a new corporate mission. Titled "Vitality," it proclaimed:

> We meet everyday needs for nutrition, hygiene, and personal care with brands that help people feel good, look good and get more out of life.[1]

Development of Dove

Dove was originally developed in the United States as a nonirritating skin cleaner for pretreatment use on burns and wounds during World War II. In 1957, the basic Dove bar was reformulated as a beauty soap bar. It was the first beauty soap to use mild, nonsoap ingredients plus moisturizing cream to avoid drying the skin, the way soap can.

[1]"Vitality", *Unilever Magazine,* 132, (2004), p. 19.

In the 1970s, an independent clinical study found Dove to be milder than 17 leading bar soaps. Based on the results of that study, the company launched a promotional campaign that highlighted the soap's mildness.

Between 1990 and 2004, Dove expanded its product line to include body wash, facial cleansers, moisturizers, deodorants, and hair care products. In 2005, revenues from Unilever's Dove product line reached $3 billion.

Competition

The beauty industry was highly competitive with many well-supported brands and products. There were few secrets within the industry, and products were in many ways similar. As such, marketing and communications were as critical to a product's success as new product development. For example, the Body Shop line of beauty care products emphasized social and environmental responsibility as well as all-natural products, thereby appealing to the psyche of the emotionally influenced buyer. As the importance of situational influences increased, marketers began to shift their emphasis from product-related variables to consumer-related variables.[2]

Modernizing the Brand Image

In 2003, the management of Unilever met to discuss the future of the Dove brand. Even though the company's growing product line was available in 40 countries, sales of its flagship Dove brand were in decline since market share was being lost to competitors.

To understand the reasons for the decline, the company undertook a focused brand analysis under the direction of the Ernest Dichter Institute, a Zürich-based market research firm. The result of the brand audit was revealing. Consumers appreciated Dove both for its natural ingredients and its reliability as a moisturizer. However, on a more emotional level, the brand felt dated and old-fashioned.

Although Dove's brand image did not resonate with consumers, those who used it recognized the quality of the products. For Unilever it was clear that the Dove brand needed a new image, and to that end, management laid out the following targets:

*   Increase market share through improvement of the brand image.
*   Develop an outstanding marketing campaign.
*   Retain the functional strengths of the brand.

Dove needed to evolve into a modern and desirable brand, while at the same time standing out against the myriad other products offered by Unilever's competitors (see Exhibit 2). With that goal in mind, Unilever created a global team under the direction of Kerstin Dunleavy, global brand manager for Dove, to develop a new brand strategy for Dove beauty care products.

The Dove Research Study

Before setting out to design a new marketing strategy, Dunleavy's team sought to first understand the relationship of women to beauty, without specifically focusing on beauty care products. They wanted to answer four basic questions:

*   What do women mean by beauty?
*   How happy are they with their own beauty?

[2]A *situational influence* is a temporary force that influences behavior, usually associated with the immediate purchasing environment. Dimensions of situational influence include the time when purchases are made, the physical surroundings, and the emotional state or mood of the purchaser. Where consumers buy are the physical surroundings. How consumers buy refers to the terms of the purchase. Conditions under which consumers buy relates to states and moods.

EXHIBIT 2   Examples of Competitor Advertisements

Sources: Garnier, Nivea and Jergens (Center for Interactive Advertising, University of Texas, Austin), L'Oreal Communication.

- How does a woman's sense of her own beauty affect her well-being?
- What influence does mass media and pop culture have on the perception of ideal beauty?

To find answers for these questions, the company turned to StrategyOne, a global research firm that worked with experts from Massachusetts General Hospital, the Harvard University Program in Aesthetics and Well Being, and the London School of Economics.

Between February and June 2004, StrategyOne surveyed 3,200 women from Argentina, Brazil, Canada, France, Italy, Japan, the Netherlands, Portugal, Spain, the United Kingdom and the United States. The results of the survey were presented in a paper titled, "The Real Truth about Beauty: A Global Report."[3] The report showed a wide disparity between the ideal of beauty portrayed in the media and the perception of beauty as understood by women themselves. The following were the most notable observations.

- Only 2 percent of women described themselves as beautiful.
- 47 percent said they were overweight—a trend that increases with age.
- 68 percent believed that the media and advertising set an unrealistic standard of beauty that most women can never achieve.
- 75 percent wished that the media would portray more diverse measures of physical attractiveness, such as size, shape, and age.
- 77 percent said that beauty could be achieved through attitude, spirit, and other attributes that have nothing to do with physical appearance.
- 48 percent strongly agreed with the statement: "When I feel less beautiful, I feel worse about myself in general."
- 45 percent believed that women who are more beautiful have greater opportunities in life.
- 26 percent have considered plastic surgery, a result that varied considerably by country. For example, 54 percent of Brazilian participants have considered cosmetic surgery.

Aside from the perceived need for cosmetic surgery, the results were remarkably consistent from country to country. For Susie Orbach, a feminist psychotherapist and writer who coauthored the report, the problem was clear. She explained:

> Most of the images we see of women bear little relationship to reality. Overwhelmingly, beauty is defined as tall, thin and young. It is a very limited definition that is presented as the norm, although it is anything but—it excludes most women and encourages them to be unnecessarily self-critical as most of us fall far short of the images of perfection that we are bombarded with daily.[4]

Based on the results of the report, Dunleavy's team perceived an opportunity to redefine beauty in a way that Unilever's competitors had ignored. The team presented its findings to Unilever's executive board along with a strategy to relaunch Dove using new and unconventional ideals of beauty. True beauty could be found in many forms, sizes, and ages, they explained. Dove had to integrate this idea in its own brand image and spark discussions by attention-seeking campaigns. The team wanted to choose "real" women for the ensuing advertising campaigns, women who were not "treated" via retouching, the type of women one might encounter every day.

---

[3]Nancy Etcoff et al., "The Real Truth about Beauty: A Global Report: Findings of the Global Study on Women, Beauty and Well-Being," September 2004, available at www.campaignforrealbeauty.com/uploadedfiles/dove_white_paper_final.pdf.

[4]"Vitality," *Unilever Magazine*, 132, (2004), p. 9.

The functional advantages of a high-quality product were to be retained. At the same time, it was considered essential to differ significantly in the emotional positioning from Unilever's main competitors. In contrast to competitors such as Nivea, L'Oreal, and Garnier, emphasis was not to be placed on perfect looks of top models but on the ethical aspect of beauty. The moral concern was to boost the self-confidence of women. The products were to be derived from this starting point. According to Dunleavy, the brand and not the single products were to be in the foreground. The emotional ties to the target group needed to be strengthened.

Some members of the executive board expressed concern that taking such an unconventional approach to beauty might expose the company to unnecessary risk. After all, if portraying regular women in beauty advertising was such a good idea, why hadn't anyone tried it? Eventually the board decided to support the effort noting that the risk was outweighed by the need to turn around the flagging Dove brand. In Dunleavy's mind, it was the strength of the supporting data presented in the StrategyOne report that finally swayed the vote of the more reticent board members in favor of the real women campaign.

The Campaign for Real Beauty

The campaign was launched with a mandate from Unilever to increase revenues by a lofty 80 percent, an undertaking that would be supported by an advertising budget of approximately $27 million in Europe alone. Unilever worked closely with the advertising firm Ogilvy & Mather to rebrand Dove.

The "Campaign for Real Beauty" began in earnest in September 2004, with the launch of the Web site campaignforrealbeauty.com. Women went online to cast their votes and join the beauty debate in chat rooms. Confessions, philosophical questions, and rants showed that nerves were being struck.[5] Statements such as "My mommy taught me to believe in myself and to feel good about who I am" were prominently displayed on the site, along with opportunities for potential customers to share their views about the concept of beauty (see Exhibit 3).

The main target group was 30- to 39-year-old women, who had not yet tried any skin-firming products. Although the broader target group included any women who used body lotions and creams, Dove expected to experience significant gains among women over age 30, a time when signs of age appear, skin is increasingly less firm, and cellulite forms.

Based on the results of the StrategyOne research, the Dove team believed that beauty could be reflected in different shapes, sizes, and ages, and that "real beauty can be genuinely stunning." Dunleavy explained:

> With the Dove beauty philosophy, we're not saying that the stereotypical Claudia Schiffer view of beauty isn't great—it is—we simply want to broaden the definition of beauty.

That definition was reflected in a new brand mission statement, "to make more women feel beautiful every day, by widening today's stereotypical view of beauty and inspiring women to take great care of themselves.

The Advertising Campaign: What Is Beauty?

When Unilever launched its ground-breaking advertising campaign in Europe, the core message stated, "No models—but firm curves." Ads featured a group of women of different ages, shapes, and racial backgrounds, dressed only in bras and knickers, animated and laughing among themselves and clearly happy to be themselves. Models for the ads were chosen by well-trained assistants in a "street casting" in order to achieve a great acceptance

[5]"Dove's Flight of Fancy," *Marketing Magazine* (Ireland), April 2006, www.marketing.ie, accessed April 16, 2007.

EXHIBIT 3 Campaign for Real Beauty Online Discussion Forum

Source: www.campaignforrealbeauty.com, accessed February 26, 2007.

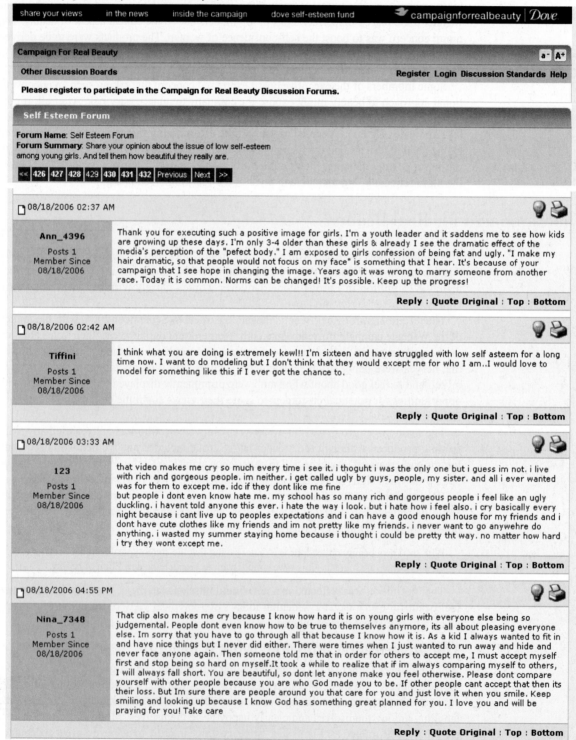

EXHIBIT 4   Tick Box ADS

Source: Unilever

☐ 44 and hot?
☐ 44 and not?

Can women be hotter at 40 than 20? Join the beauty debate.

campaignforrealbeauty.com *Dove.*

☐ grey?
☐ gorgeous?

Why can't more women feel glad to be grey? Join the beauty debate.

campaignforrealbeauty.com *Dove.*

among the observers. When the campaign was later rolled out in other countries, different models were chosen to reflect local cultural differences.

Some ads asked viewers to make a choice. For example, one featured a 96-year-old woman named Irene and asked "wrinkled or wonderful?" followed by the question "Will society ever accept the beauty of old age?" Another ad featured a heavy-set woman named Tabatha, and asked "oversized or outstanding?" followed by the question, "Does true beauty only squeeze into a size 6?" (See Exhibit 4 for two other ads in the series.) At the campaignforrealbeauty Web site, Internet users could cast votes for the ads or join online debates in the forums section.

The company supplemented traditional television and magazine-based beauty advertising with outdoor advertising, such as billboards, posters and signs. Billboards specifically provided a presence that made it easy for journalists to report about the campaign (see Exhibit 5). When the campaign was later rolled out in the United States, an electronic billboard was erected in Times Square that asked bystanders to text message their responses to a beauty question posed by the Dove ads and see their votes counted instantly in the debate. It was the first-ever outdoor mobile marketing event in the United States.

The promotional mix was supported by an unprecedented amount of public relations that built as Ogilvy & Mather coaxed the news media to cover the launch of the campaign and to create debate around Western society's concepts of beauty. The objective was to provoke public attention with a controversial message. To foster discussion, Unilever partnered with American Women in Radio and Television, a nonprofit organization that sought to advance the impact of women in the electronic media by educating, advocating, and acting as a resource to its members. "It was to be the talk of town," noted Sebastian Munden, managing director for Home and Personal Care of Unilever.

The Results

Early results were dramatic. Massive media coverage that included as many as 800 newspaper and magazine articles, many of which featured high-profile debates, helped to nearly quadruple sales of Dove-branded products. Market share increased in six European core markets from an average of 7.4 percent in 2003 to 13.5 percent by the end of 2004.[6] Traffic on the company Web site quickly reached 4,000 visitors a day.

In 2005, a new brand audit by Millward Brown, a market research company, showed a significant image shift. The brand gained attributes such as "open," "active" and "self-confident," and existing characteristics for the skin-firming series, such as "fun," "energetic" and "confident," strengthened further (see Exhibit 6). The turnaround was no less than remarkable. Dove was seen not only as a top-quality brand but also as an industry expert in cosmetics and beauty. Moreover, for the first time, the brand was able to break into the premium segment of the market. For its part, Ogilvy & Mather won the Grand Effie Award from the New York American Marketing Association in 2006, for the "most significant achievement in marketing communications."[7]

Realbeauty

Many girls developed low self-esteem from insecurities about their looks. As a direct result, some failed to reach their full potential later in life. To help these girls, Dove simultaneously established a "Self-Esteem Fund" to support local initiatives. "We've made it mandatory that every country launching the campaign links up with an association that's in line with the Dove Self-Esteem Fund," explained Dunleavy.[8] For example, one program titled "uniquely ME!" partnered with U.S. Girl Scout troops to help build self-confidence in girls aged 8 to 14, largely in economically disadvantaged communities.

Unilever also sought to address eating disorders in young females, which research had shown to be directly linked to low self-esteem. The company focused on girls between the ages of 8 and 17. Unilever hired Ogilvy & Mather to develop a 45-second commercial for the 2006 Super Bowl football championship, considered by many to be the most important television advertising event of the year. The commercial suggested ways adults could make a difference in how girls felt about themselves. "All throughout the spot, the voices for the

---

[6]"Medaillenflut für deutsche Agenturen, *Horizont*," October 6, 2005, p. 34.

[7]"Dove's 'The Campaign for Real Beauty,' Created by Ogilvy & Mather Wins the 2006 Grand Effie Award," Company Press Release, June 8, 2006.

[8]"Vitality," *Unilever Magazine,* 132, (2004), p. 11.

EXHIBIT 5 Outdoor Advertising

Source: Unilever

EXHIBIT 6 **Brand Audit 2005 by Millward Brown**

Note: Pre-Ads were surveyed from November to December 2003. During/After Ads were surveyed from March to July 2004.
Source: Millward Brown International Research, Agreeing Before and After Dove Communications Strategy, "Firming Lotion."

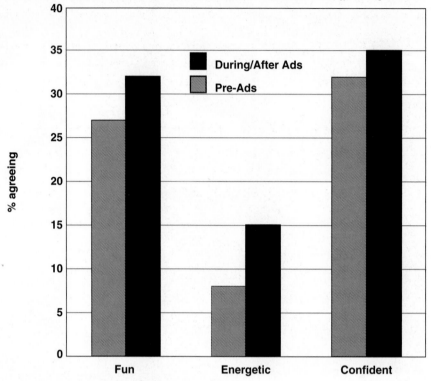

members of the Girl Scouts of Nassau County Chorus from Long Island, New York, can be heard singing a version of True Colors."[9]

In Canada and Germany, similar projects were launched under the name "Body Talk," "a program to inform and educate young schoolgirls about perceptions of beauty, helping boost their self-esteem."[10] Further ideas for projects were collected in seminars with teachers in order to include Body Talk messages effectively into teaching subjects.

Another activity was a mother–daughter workbook, designed by the U.S. Girl Scouts, in cooperation with the team that developed the original "Real Truth about Beauty" report. The free workbook could be used together by mother and daughter, and it supported mothers in their efforts to encourage communication in the family and to help their daughters improve their self-esteem.

Finally, Unilever needed to improve communication about Dove products so that statements in advertisements appeared more sincere.

Next Steps

Dunleavy's mind was working at warp speed. The more she thought, the more questions she had. While the first steps of the relaunch were clearly successful, she knew it would not be enough to satisfy Unilever. She sincerely believed that customer-based marketing was

[9]"Super Bowl Spot Launches Multi-Tiered Effort Encouraging Girls to Feel More Confident, Recognize Their Unique Beauty," Campaignforrealbeauty.com, January 27, 2006, available at http://sev.prnewswire.com/advertising/20060127/NYF01927012006-1.html, accessed August 28, 2006.

[10]"How Real Curves Can Grow Your Brand," *Viewpoint Online Magazine,* Ogilvy.com, April 2005, available at http://www.ogilvy.com/uploads/koviewpoint/dove.pdf, accessed August 28, 2006.

paramount. Unilever had quality, well-positioned products. Keeping them there would be the real test.

The next step of the relaunch was set to commence in September. Dunleavy wondered how to maintain the brand's momentum while continuing to take advantage of the stubborn portrayal of flawless beauty by competitors. She also wondered whether the competition would try to imitate Dove's success by launching similar campaigns. In the world of marketing, the reward for success is typically more and better competition. What should Dove do to prepare for the next phase?

Conclusion

Dunleavy and Allen joked about how much was riding on their next series of strategic moves. "I believe we are doing what needs to be done," noted Allen.

> Our customers are our customers. That may sound a little silly, but I know that we are making a difference beyond just making good products. We make good products and we sell them in a manner that is fair and honest. Our promotional work has been cutting edge and I believe it has changed the industry's approach to the portrayal of what is real beauty. Let's listen to the research and combine it with what we have learned in the past two years.

"Tomorrow morning I am going to be asking for some substantial resources to keep this thing going," Dunleavy added.

> We need to be aware of what we need and why we need it. Do me a favor. Be ready with specifics as we lay out the plan. You can brief me later.

Case

15

IKEA's Global Strategy: Furnishing the World

Paul Kolesa

IKEA is a furniture manufacturer and retailer, well known throughout the world for its knockdown furniture. Its large retail stores in the blue-and-yellow colors of the Swedish flag are located on the outskirts of major cities, attracting shoppers who are looking for modern designs at good value. The low-cost operation relies on buyers with automobiles to carry the disassembled furniture in packaged kits and assemble the pieces at home.

The IKEA case is interesting because it shows how even retailers can go global once the key competitive advantages of the offering are standardized. The case focuses on the American entry, which posed barriers IKEA had not encountered before and which forced adaptation of some features.

IKEA, the Swedish furniture store chain virtually unknown outside of Scandinavia 25 years ago, has drawn large opening crowds to its stores as it has pushed into Europe, Asia, and North America. Along the way it has built something of a cult following, especially among young and price-conscious consumers. But the expansion was not always smooth and easy, for example, in Germany and Canada, and it was particularly difficult in the United States.

Company Background

IKEA was founded in 1943 by Ingvar Kamprad to serve price-conscious neighbors in the province of Smaland in southern Sweden. Early on, the young entrepreneur hit upon a

This case was prepared by Paul Kolesa for class analysis and discussion.

winning formula, contracting with independent furniture makers and suppliers to design furniture that could be sold as a kit and assembled in the consumer's home. In return for favorable and guaranteed orders from IKEA, the suppliers were prohibited from selling to other stores. Developing innovative modular designs whose components could be mass produced and venturing early into eastern Europe to build a dedicated supplier network, IKEA could offer quality furniture in modern Scandinavian designs at very low prices. By investing profits in new stores, the company expanded throughout Scandinavia in the 1950s.

Throughout the following years, the IKEA store design and layout remained the same; IKEA was basically a warehouse store. Because the ready-to-assemble "knockdown" kits could be stacked conveniently on racks, inventory was always large, and instead of waiting for the store to deliver the furniture, IKEA's customers could pick it up themselves. Stores were therefore located outside of the big cities, with ample parking space for automobiles. Inside, an assembled version of the furniture was displayed in settings along with other IKEA furniture. The purchaser could decide on what to buy, obtain the inventory tag number, and then either find the kit on the rack, or, in the case of larger pieces, have the kit delivered through the back door to the waiting car.

This simple formula meant that there were relatively few sales clerks on the floor to help customers sort through the more than 10,000 products stocked. The sales job consisted mainly of making sure that the assembled pieces were attractively displayed, that clear instructions were given as to where the kits could be found, and that customers did not have to wait too long at the checkout lines. IKEA's was a classic "cash-and-carry" approach, except that credit cards were accepted.

This approach, which trims costs to a minimum, is dependent on IKEA's global sourcing network of more than 2,300 suppliers in 67 countries. Because IKEA's designers work closely with suppliers, savings are built into all its products from the outset. Also since the same furniture is sold all around the world, IKEA reaps huge economies of scale from the size of its stores and the big production runs necessary to stock them. Therefore, IKEA is able to match rivals on quality while undercutting them up to 30 percent on price.

To draw the customers to the distant stores, the company relies on word-of-mouth, limited advertising, and its catalogues. These catalogues are delivered free of charge in the mailboxes of potential customers living in the towns and cities within reach of a store. The catalogues depict the merchandise not only as independent pieces of furniture but also together in actual settings of a living room, bedroom, children's room, and so on. This enables the company to demonstrate its philosophy of creating a "living space," not just selling furniture. It also helps the potential buyer visualize a complete room and simplifies the planning of furnishing a home. It also shows how IKEA's various components are stylistically integrated into a complete and beautiful whole. Even though furniture is hardly high-tech, the philosophy is reminiscent of the way high-tech producers, such as mobile phone makers, attempt to develop add-on features that fit their particular brand and not others.

As the company has grown, the catalogue has increased in volume and in circulation. By 2003, the worldwide circulation of the 360-page catalogue reached over 130 million, making it the world's largest printed publication distributed for free. In 2003 the catalogue was distributed in 36 countries and 28 languages, showing more than 3,000 items from storage solutions and kitchen renovation ideas to office furniture and bedroom furnishings.

Sales totaled about 12.2 billion U.S. dollars in 2003, with a net profit margin around 6–7 percent. Of this, Europe accounted for over 80 percent of revenues, with Asia accounting for 3 percent, and North America 15 percent. The huge stores are relatively few in number—only 175 worldwide but growing rapidly—and the company employs about

EXHIBIT 1
IKEA Sales Data

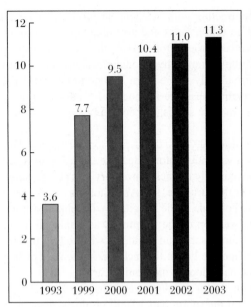

Turnover for the IKEA Group:

Sales for the IKEA Group for the financial year 2003 (1 September 2002 – 31 August 2003) totaled 11.3 billion euro (12.2 billion USD).

76,000 people around the world (see Exhibits 1 and 2). Many of the stores have only one expatriate Swedish manager at the top, sufficient to instill the lean Ingvar Kamprad and IKEA ethos in the local organization.

Although the firm remains private, it continues to innovate and reorganize itself. For instance, fast decision making is aided by a management structure that is as flat as the firm's knockdown furniture kits, with only four layers separating IKEA's chief executive from its checkout workers. In 1992 IKEA abolished internal budgets and now each region must merely keep below a fixed ratio of costs to turnover.

European Expansion

In the 1960s and 70s, as modern Scandinavian design became increasingly popular, expansion into Europe became a logical next step. The company first entered the German-speaking regions of Switzerland, thereby testing itself in a small region similar to Scandinavia. Yet expansion so far away from Sweden made it necessary to develop new suppliers, which meant that Kamprad traveled extensively, visiting potential suppliers and convincing them to become exclusive IKEA suppliers. Once the supply chain was established, the formula of consumer-assembled furniture could be used. After some resistance from independent furniture retailers who claimed that the furniture was not really "Swedish," since much of it came from other countries, IKEA's quality/price advantage proved irresistible even to fastidious Swiss consumers.

The next logical target was Germany, much bigger than Switzerland, but also culturally close to IKEA's roots. In Germany, well-established and large furniture chains were formidable foes opposed to the competitive entry and there were several regulatory obstacles. The opening birthday celebration of the first store in 1974 outside Cologne was criticized because in German culture birthdays should be celebrated only every 25 years. The use of the Swedish flag and the blue-yellow colors was challenged because the IKEA subsidiary was an incorporated German company (IKEA GmbH). The celebratory breakfast was mistitled because no eggs were served. Despite these rearguard actions from the established German retailers, IKEA GmbH became very successful,

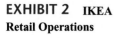

**EXHIBIT 2   IKEA
Retail Operations**

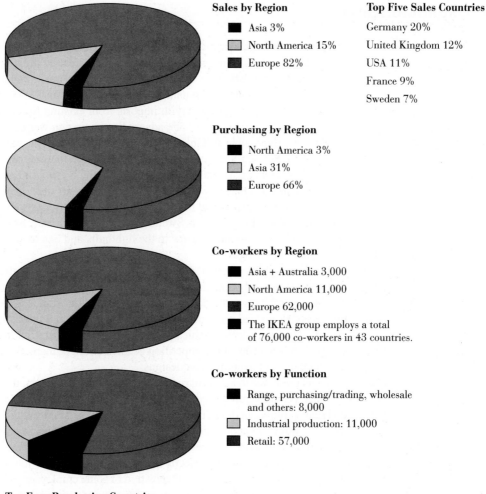

Sales by Region

■ Asia 3%
□ North America 15%
■ Europe 82%

Top Five Sales Countries

Germany 20%
United Kingdom 12%
USA 11%
France 9%
Sweden 7%

Purchasing by Region

■ North America 3%
□ Asia 31%
■ Europe 66%

Co-workers by Region

■ Asia + Australia 3,000
□ North America 11,000
■ Europe 62,000
■ The IKEA group employs a total
  of 76,000 co-workers in 43 countries.

Co-workers by Function

■ Range, purchasing/trading, wholesale
  and others: 8,000
□ Industrial production: 11,000
■ Retail: 57,000

Top Four Purchasing Countries

China 18%
Poland 12%
Sweden 9%
Italy 7%

and was thus accepted, being voted German marketer of the year in 1979. The acceptance of IKEA's way of doing business was helped by the fact that IKEA had enlarged the entire market by its low prices, and some of the established retailers adopted the same formula in their own operations.

To get the stores abroad started, Kamprad usually sent a team of three or four managers who could speak the local language and had experience in an existing IKEA store. This team hired and trained the sales employees, organized the store layout, and established the sales and ordering routines. Although the tasks were relatively simple and straightforward, IKEA's lean organizational strategies meant that individual employees were assigned greater responsibilities and more freedom than usual in more traditional retail stores. Although this was not a problem in Europe and Japan (where its Japanese-sounding name also was an advantage), it was a problem in the United States.

Canadian Entry

To prepare for eventual entry into the United States, IKEA first expanded into Canada. The Canadian market was close to the U.S. market, and creating the supply network for Canada would lay the foundation for what was needed for the much larger U.S. market. Drawing upon a successful advertising campaign and positive word-of-mouth, and by combining newly recruited local suppliers with imports from existing European suppliers, the Canadian entry was soon a success. The advertising campaign was centered around the slogan, "IKEA: The impossible furniture store from Sweden," which was supported by a cartoon drawing of a moose's head, complete with antlers. The moose symbol had played very well in Germany, creating natural associations "with the north," and also creating an image of fun and games that played well in the younger segments the company targeted. The Canadians responded equally well to the slogan and the moose, as well as to IKEA's humorous cartoonlike ads poking fun at its Swedish heritage ("How many Swedes does it take to screw in a lightbulb? Two—one to screw in the lightbulb, and one to park the Volvo"), which became often-heard jokes.

The United States presented a much different challenge, as it offered a much larger market with a dispersed population, great cultural diversity, and strong domestic competition. The initial problems centered around which part of the United States to attack first. While the east coast seemed more natural, with its closer ties to Europe, the California market on the west coast was demographically more attractive. But trafficking supplies to California would be a headache, and competition seemed stronger there, with the presence of established retailers of Scandinavian designs.

Then, there was the issue of managing the stores. In Canada, the European management style had been severely tested. The unusually great independence and authority of each individual employee in the IKEA system had been welcomed, but the individuals often asked for more direction and specific guidance. For example, the Swedish start-up team would say to an employee, "You are in charge of the layout of the office furniture section of the store," and consider this a perfectly actionable and complete job description. This seemed to go against the training and predisposition of some employees, who came back with questions such as, "How should this piece of furniture be displayed?" IKEA's expansion team suspected that the situation would be possibly even more difficult in the United States. The team also wondered if the same slogan and the moose symbol would be as effective in the United States as it had been in Germany and Canada.

Entry Hurdles in the United States

From the outset IKEA had succeeded despite breaking many of the standard rules of international retailing: enter a market only after exhaustive study; cater to local tastes as much as possible; and tap into local expertise through acquisitions, joint ventures, or franchising. Although breaking these rules had not hurt IKEA in Europe, the firm got into some trouble in America with its initial seven stores; six on the east coast and one in California. Many people visited the stores, looked at the furniture, and left empty-handed, citing long queues and nonavailable stock as chief complaints.

IKEA managers believed that their most pressing problem in entering the U.S. market was the creation of a stable supply chain. By taking an incremental approach, starting with a few stores on the east coast including an initial one outside Philadelphia, IKEA managers believed that they had ensured a smooth transition from the eastern United States, with its relative proximity to European suppliers, and its Canadian beachhead. Although the store in southern California was much farther away, its large market and customer demographics—young and active—favored IKEA's modern designs and assemble-it-yourself strategy. The California entry was also precipitated by the emergence of a local imitator, "Stør," which had opened ahead of IKEA, capitalizing on the word-of-mouth generated by IKEA'S new concept.

IKEA's early effort had problems because of less adaptation to the American market than customers desired. For example, IKEA decided not to reconfigure its bedroom furniture to the different dimensions used in the American market. As a result, the European-style beds sold by IKEA were slightly narrower and longer than standard American beds, and customers' existing mattresses and sheets did not fit the beds. Even though IKEA stocked European-sized sheets in the stores, bed sales remained very slow. IKEA ended up re-designing about a fifth of its American product range and sales immediately increased by around 30–40 percent.

The American suppliers, whom IKEA gradually recruited to reduce the dependence on imports, also proved in need of upgrading and instruction in IKEA's way of producing furniture. IKEA sent its people to the suppliers' plants, providing technical tips about more efficient methods and helping the suppliers shop around for better-quality or lower-price materials. Now IKEA produces about 45 percent of the furniture sold in its American stores locally, up from 15 percent just a few years earlier. In turn this has helped the firm cut prices in its American stores for three years running. The American difficulties also highlighted how growth could lead to quality problems in managing its increasingly complex global supply chain, so IKEA began conducting random checks.

Other adaptations to the American market proved just as successful. For instance, new cash registers were installed to speed throughput by 20 percent, with the goal of eliminating long checkout lines. Store layout was altered to conform more with American aesthetics and shopping styles. A more generous return policy than in Europe was instituted and a next-day delivery service was implemented.

Promotion

While some managers helped establish the supply side of the stores, IKEA's marketing staff was busy with the promotional side of the business. Store locations had generally disadvantaged IKEA relative to competitors. Because of the huge size of the stores (typically around 200,000 square feet), the need to keep a large inventory so that customers could get the purchased furniture immediately, and the amount of land needed for parking around each store, most stores were located in out-of-the-way places—next to the airport in New Jersey in one case and in a shopping mall 20 miles south of Washington, DC, in another. Thus, advertising was needed to make potential customers aware of store locations. It was thought that lower prices and selection would do the rest—positive word-of-mouth had proven the best advertising in most other markets.

But in the United States' competitive retail climate IKEA found that more focused media advertising was needed. As one manager stated: "In Europe you advertise to gain business; in the United States you advertise to stay in business." The diversity of the consumers made word-of-mouth less powerful than in ethnically more homogeneous countries. Management decided that a strong slogan and unique advertising message were going to be necessary to really bring awareness close to the levels in other countries.

The Moose symbol of IKEA (see Exhibit 3), although successful in Germany and Canada, was considered strange and too provincial for the U.S. market and would project the wrong image especially in California. Instead IKEA, in collaboration with its New York–based advertising agency Deutsch, developed a striking slogan that combined the

EXHIBIT 3

down-home touch of the company philosophy with the humorous touch of the Moose: "It's a big country. Someone's got to furnish it" (see Exhibit 4).

Following the success of this advertising strategy, the company ventured further to establish itself as a pioneering store and to attract new kinds of customers. IKEA and Deutsch developed a series of eight TV advertising spots that featured people at different transitional stages in their lives, when they were most likely to be in the market for furniture. One spot featured a young family who had just bought a new house, another a couple whose children had just left home, and so on. IKEA even developed one spot that featured a homosexual couple, two men talking about furnishing their home. It was a daring step, applauded by most advertising experts and impartial observers. The campaign had a positive impact on IKEA's image—and on IKEA's sales. The company has continued the trend. One 30-second TV spot showed a divorced woman buying furniture for the first time on her own.

EXHIBIT 4

It's a big country.
Someone's got to furnish it.

The privately held company won't reveal income figures, but it is successful in each of the market areas where it has located its U.S. stores. It is credited with being partly responsible for a shift in furniture buying behavior in the United States. Choosing furniture has become a matter of personality, lifestyle, and emotions in addition to functionality. IKEA's managers like that—they want IKEA to be associated with the "warmest, most emotional furniture in the world."

Discussion Questions

1. What are IKEA's firm-specific advantages? Country-specific advantages?
2. What are the cultural factors that make expansion abroad in retailing difficult? What has made it possible in IKEA's case?
3. Describe how IKEA's expansion has reenergized mature markets around the world and changed the competitive situation.
4. How does the TV advertising campaign initiated by IKEA overcome the entry barrier of high advertising expenditures?
5. Should IKEA expand further in the United States or focus on other countries?

Sources: Case compiled by Paul Kolesa from Rita Martenson, "Innovations in International Retailing," University of Gothenburg, Sweden: Liber, 1981; "Furnishing the World," *The Economist,* November 19, 1994, pp. 79–80; Richard Stevenson, "IKEA's New Realities: Recession and Aging Consumers," *The New York Times,* April 25, 1993, p. F4; Kate Fitzgerald, "IKEA Dares to Reveal Gays Buy Tables Too," *Advertising Age,* March 12, 1994, pp. 3, 41; Vito Pilieci. "The IKEA Catalogue: Swedish for Massive Circulation," *Calgary Herald,* August 27, 2003, p. C1.

Blockbuster Entertainment Corporation

James A. Kidney *Southern Connecticut State University*

Introduction

Seated at his desk in a rented two-story stucco executive office building in downtown Fort Lauderdale, Florida, H. Wayne Huizenga prepared to announce record revenues and net income for his chain of Blockbuster Video stores. His mid-April 1992 announcement would attribute those results to "increasing market penetration, gains in same-store revenue, and continued emphasis on cost control and increased productivity."[1] As Blockbuster Entertainment Corporation's Chairman of the Board and Chief Executive Officer, he also prepared to announce that it was now possible to pay a cash dividend to the company's 8,000 stockholders—something that had not been done before.

At the end of 1991, having achieved a 13 percent share of market, the company announced that its goal was to reach a 20 percent share of the U.S. home video market and have 3,000 Blockbuster Video stores operating in North America by 1995.[2] In some of its most mature markets, such as Atlanta, Chicago, Dallas, Detroit, and South Florida, that would mean market shares well in excess of 30 percent. Such a high share of market has been rare in specialty retailing. However, Blockbuster was the only U.S. video rental chain operating on a nationwide basis. Its next largest competitor was a regional chain, less than one-tenth its size.

This case was prepared by Dr. James A. Kidney, Management Department, School of Business, Southern Connecticut State University, New Haven, CT 06515.

[1]Corporate news release dated April 21, 1992.

[2]The total population of video rental stores operating throughout the United States ranged between 25,000 and 29,000, and turnover of individual store locations was quite high during the late 1980s and early 1990s.

External Challenges and Opportunities

As Huizenga optimistically pondered the company's strategic situation over the next five to seven years, there were several interesting external challenges and opportunities lurking on the horizon:

- With a higher market share than all of its 300 closest competitors combined, how much further could the company's market penetration grow?
- Could any significant technological changes in home entertainment alter the video rental industry's attractiveness?
- What were the future implications of Philips Electronics N.V.'s recent investment in Blockbuster stock?

Company History

David P. Cook, a 31-year-old Texas entrepreneur, founded the company in December 1982 as Cook Data Services, Inc., a provider of software and computer services to the oil and gas industries. Facing a sagging market for such services, Cook decided to switch over to a new, rapidly growing niche in specialty retailing—video rental stores. Cook's first store was opened during 1985, and the present corporate name was adopted one year later. From the outset, Cook recognized that an innovative superstore concept would draw many customers away from typical mom-and-pop rental stores and that well-designed computerized information systems would be advantageous for inventory planning and control as well as for customer information.

The typical mom-and-pop store had a spartan, nondescript atmosphere; short hours; a selection of fewer than 3,000 titles stressing recent hits; and empty boxes to be brought to a clerk who would have to find appropriate tapes—provided they were then in stock. Many mom-and-pops obtained significant rental revenues from X-rated videos, and that occasionally created an unwholesome image.

In comparison, Cook's idea was to have a family-oriented atmosphere with an extensive selection of children's videos, longer, more convenient hours, improved layout, quality service, faster check-in/check-out, state-of-the-art real time computer information systems, and a thoroughly trained professional staff.

Attracting Huizenga's Attention

After only two years of operation, Blockbuster's latent potential attracted the attention of Huizenga. By that time, Cook owned 8 stores and franchised 11 more in the Dallas area. Huizenga, then 48 years old, was restless, looking for a way to come back from early retirement, after having successfully made a small fortune from several companies.

Huizenga's previous experience had been in building up businesses in a variety of dissimilar industries, such as trash bin rentals and garbage hauling, dry cleaning, lawn care, portable toilet rentals, water cooler rentals and sale of bottled water. His most notable success was Waste Management, Inc., which he had honed into the world's largest waste collection and disposal company.

There was a common denominator running throughout his past entrepreneurial ventures. Each had rendered relatively basic services, had repeat customers, required little employee training, earned a steady cash flow, and was able to expand within an industry filled with small, undercapitalized competitors. Usually, the fragmented industries he entered were ripe for consolidation, because greater firm size led to economies of scale in marketing, distribution, computerized information systems, and/or potential clout in purchasing products and services.

Expansion and Acquisition of Store Locations

During 1987 Huizenga and a couple of close business associates bought out Blockbuster's founders and franchise holders for $18 million, and soon thereafter began acquiring small regional chains, such as Southern Video Partnership and Movies to Go. To help him run the new business, Huizenga hired several former upper level managers from McDonald's Corporation. His upper management group adopted the view that Blockbuster's target audience should be very similar to McDonald's broad-based restaurant clientele. Thus, Blockbuster's national expansion of its retail business was based upon McDonald's well-established growth philosophy, namely: blitz major markets, add stores quickly, use franchising to speed the process of obtaining managerial talent and operating capital, and never admit that the market is saturated.

Facing a rapid rise in VCR ownership, management tried to combine careful planning with opportunistic risk taking. An aggressive acquisition program was financed by new equity capital, in order to avoid burdensome long-term debt. Over the following four years, additional regional chains, such as Video Library Inc., Major Video Corp., Oklahoma Entertainment Inc., Vector Video Inc., Video Superstores Venture L.P., and Erol's Inc. were eagerly gobbled up.

A major international thrust was launched in early 1992, with the acquisition of Cityvision plc, the largest home video retailer in the U.K. Operating under the "Ritz" name and enjoying a 20 percent share of market, this firm had roughly 800 small stores and was considered to be an underperformer.

Around the same time, several Blockbuster Video stores were opened in Japan in a joint venture with Fujita & Co., a retailer running over 800 McDonald's restaurants and holding a stake in Toys 'R' Us Japan, Ltd. Jointly they hoped to open 1,000 stores over the next 10 years.

Describing the hectic, and occasionally disorganized, rush to add store locations Huizenga explained, "We felt we had to go fast because we had nothing proprietary. We had to get the locations in each area before somebody else moved in. It was a mistake, but it turned out okay. We have the locations, the people are trained, and the customers are ours. Now if somebody else comes in, they have to take it away from us."[3]

Blockbuster Video's Profile as of 1992

Blockbuster Video was a membership only club, serving more than 29 million members worldwide, who rented more than 1 million of the company's videocassettes daily. Without incurring any membership fees, patrons were provided with bar-coded membership cards which allowed for speedy computerized check-out from the issuing store. Cards were sometimes honored at other locations in the chain as well. By requiring personal photo identification and an application for membership, rather than dealing with anonymous walk-ins, the rental store was able to secure an extra measure of control over tapes which left the premises. A major credit card also had to be presented, so that the store could charge members for lost or damaged inventory.

[3] *The New York Times Business World Magazine,* June 9, 1991.

EXHIBIT 1
Blockbuster Entertainment Corporation (Number of Blockbuster video stores, by ownership type)

Source: Blockbuster's 1991 Annual Report and 1992 press releases.

Date	Company	Franchised	Total
December 31, 1985	1	0	1
December 31, 1986	19	0	19
December 31, 1987	112	126	238
December 31, 1988	341	248	589
December 31, 1989	561	518	1,079
December 31, 1990	787	795	1,582
December 31, 1991	1,025	1,003	2,028
March 31, 1992	1,805	1,024	2,829

Note: The surge in company stores during the first quarter of 1992 is attributable to the Cityvision plc acquisition.

The typical Blockbuster Video store was located in a free-standing building of approximately 6,000 square feet (560 square meters) and was open from 10:00 A.M. to midnight, seven days per week, 365 days per year. The atmosphere was bright and wholesome. Aisles were clearly marked and divided into more than 30 categories to distribute customer traffic and encourage browsing. Video boxes with tapes inside were openly displayed within easy reach. Similar categories were placed adjacent to one another, thereby increasing the potential for increased rentals. Blockbuster's superstores typically carried a comprehensive selection of 10,000 prerecorded videocassettes, consisting of more than 8,000 titles. The strongest months for video store rentals tended to be December through March and June through August, with Hollywood's release schedule being a crucial variable.

Blockbuster Video stores proudly claimed to offer "More Movies Than Anyone in the World." Additionally, their relatively weak, fragmented rivals were seldom able to match Blockbuster's advertising clout and wide array of attractions, such as computer-driven movie selection aids; a three-evening rental policy; an attractive overnight pricing policy for new hit releases which improved turnover and in-stock positions; a state-of-the-art management information system that tracked rentals and market trends; microwave popcorn and other snack foods; promotional tie-ins with Domino's Pizza, Pepsi-Cola, Pizza Hut, Subway, U.S. Air, and Universal Studios; drop-off boxes for fast returns; and publicity from an annual Blockbuster Bowl football game. Nevertheless, some competitors clearly differentiated themselves from Blockbuster by offering lower prices, reservations, home delivery, or hard core "adult" videos.

As of March 31, 1992, there were 2,829 Blockbuster Video stores, worldwide, up from 19 just five years earlier (Exhibit 1).

Locations and Operations

By the first quarter of 1992, 68 percent of Blockbuster's stores were located in 46 of America's 50 states, with the remaining 32 percent located in Austria, Australia, Canada, Chile, Guam, Japan, Mexico, Puerto Rico, Spain, the United Kingdom, and Venezuela. Nearly all of the company's retail, distribution, and administrative facilities were rented under noncancellable operating leases, which in most cases contained renewal options. Blockbuster employed approximately 12,500 individuals.

There had historically tended to be a 50–50 balance between company-owned and franchised locations. Although franchising remained beneficial in foreign countries, where local partners made it easier to conduct business, franchising within the U.S. became less essential once the company had an ample cash flow and employed many competent people who could help manage ongoing growth.

The usual initial investment (i.e., franchise fee, inventory, equipment, and start-up capital) for a franchised location ranged from $700,000 to $1,000,000. Annual operating costs

EXHIBIT 2
Blockbuster
Entertainment
Corporation (selected
annual financial data)

Source: Blockbuster's 1991
Annual Report and Standard &
Poor's Stock Report.

	1991	1990	1989	1988	1987
Income Data (million $)					
Systemwide revenue	1,520	1,133	663	284	98
Company revenue	868	633	402	136	43
Operating costs & expenses	714	514	326	110	37
Operating income	154	119	76	26	6
Net income	94	69	44	17	3
Depreciation & amortization	189	124	76	22	5
Cash flow	283	193	120	39	8
Balance Sheet Data (million $)					
Total assets	804	608	417	235	105
Cash & cash equivalents	48	49	40	9	7
Current assets	163	116	93	39	27
Current liabilities	164	110	83	49	17
Long-term debt	134	169	118	39	22
Shareholders' equity	483	315	208	124	59
Per Share Data ($)					
Earnings per share	.56	.42	.28	.12	.04
Tangible book value	2.35	1.65	1.18	.75	.41
Stock price—high	15.12	13.37	10.81	6.25	2.63
Stock price—low	7.75	6.75	4.87	1.06	.75
Common Stock and Equivalents (millions)					
Average shares outstanding	168	162	155	142	75

Notes: Systemwide revenues include franchise store revenues, while company revenues do not. Operating costs and expenses include depreciation and amortization. Cash flow is net income plus depreciation and amortization. Tangible book value excludes cost of purchased businesses in excess of market value of tangible assets acquired (unamortized goodwill).

per location fell in the $400,000 to $500,000 range. Franchisees were provided extensive guidelines for site selection, store design and product selection, as well as customer service, and management training programs. In addition, the company furnished national and local advertising and promotional programs for the entire system. Franchisees paid royalties and other fees for those services and also routinely paid Blockbuster Entertainment for videocassette inventories, computer hardware, and software.

For a typical Blockbuster Video store, cash flow payback on initial store investment occurred rapidly—generally in under three years. The average new store attained monthly revenues of $70,000 within 12 months of the opening date.

Systemwide revenues, for company-owned and franchise-owned operations combined, as well as other selected financial data are shown in Exhibit 2.

Sources of Revenues

During 1991, 5 percent of company revenues were derived from franchise royalties and fees, 20 percent from product sales mainly to franchisees, and 75 percent from rentals. Other than low-priced used products, outright sales of home videos were never emphasized prior to late 1991, because the largest sellers were highly competitive national discount chains like Wal-Mart and Kmart. As a growing portion of consumer spending went towards videocassette and laser disc purchases, it became logical for video rental stores to begin taking the sell-through market more seriously.

EXHIBIT 3
Estimated and Projected Annual U.S. Movie Revenues, by Viewing Method ($ billions)

Source: Blockbuster's 1991 Annual Report.

Viewing Method	1990	1995	2000
Video	10.3	15.2	19.3
Movie theater	5.1	6.9	7.4
Pay cable (premium channels)	5.1	6.2	7.6
Pay-per-view	.01	0.5	2.0
Total	20.6	28.8	36.3

Mr. Joseph Baczko, who headed the highly successful International Division of Toys 'R' Us, Inc. for eight years, was hired in 1991 as Blockbuster's new president and chief operating officer. To carry out a process of "retailizing" as well as internationalizing the company, he brought several executives with significant retailing experience into the firm. Promotional and display efforts to stimulate sell-through transactions were given added emphasis under Baczko's direction. Given his background in toys, he was interested in treating child oriented movies, such as *Batman, Bambi, The Little Mermaid,* and *101 Dalmatians,* mainly as sell-through rather than rental products. Blockbuster's stores also began renting Nintendo and Sega Genesis video game products.

Industry Environment

Rentals and sales of home videos in the United States amounted to a mere $700 million in 1982. By 1991, domestic revenue for the video rental industry reached $11 billion, and Americans were spending more than twice as much to watch movies at home as they did to watch them in movie theaters. Within the marketplace for prerecorded videocassettes, movies accounted for more than 80 percent of rental revenues and at least 50 percent of dollars spent on purchases. Blockbuster Entertainment estimated that the U.S. video rental market for movies would reach $19.3 billion by the turn of the century (Exhibit 3).

In 1980, the percentage of U.S. households owning at least one television set reached 98 percent and remained at that level thereafter. By 1995, analysts expected there would be almost 100 million households in the U.S., and 98 percent of them were likely to own at least one color TV set. Blockbuster Entertainment expected 91 percent of those TV-owning households also to own VCRs (Exhibit 4), with more than 35 percent of them owning at least two machines.

VCR ownership in Europe also was growing rapidly, with household penetration rates in individual countries lagging behind those of the United States anywhere from two to five years. Total 1991 worldwide spending for home video rental and sales was $21.2 billion (Exhibit 5). Licensing, sale, and rental practices differed from one product/market to another, and in some countries most of the television viewing population remained unaware that movie videos could be rented instead of being purchased.

Movie Production and Distribution

Approximately 390 to 450 new feature films were released annually in the United States. Eight of the largest distributors accounted for more than 90 percent of movie theater film rentals in the United States and Canada. Most of them, such as Paramount, Universal, Warner, Fox, Columbia, and Disney, had been in business for more than 50 years. Leading producers and distributors of videos were usually subsidiaries of large companies that owned other leisure-time businesses. Large distributors also had prime access to international channels for distributing American-made films in foreign countries. Musical,

EXHIBIT 4
Estimated and Projected VCR and Cable TV Penetration among U.S. TV Owning Households (millions of TV owning households, percent with VCRs, percent with cable TV, and percent with additional pay-per-view or pay cable services, by year)

Source: Blockbuster's 1991 Annual Report, the Universal Almanac, and author's estimates.

Year	No. of TV Owning Households	Percent with VCR	Cable	Pay Cable
1980	76	1	20	7
1981	78	3	22	10
1982	82	6	30	16
1983	83	10	34	19
1984	84	17	39	24
1985	85	30	43	26
1986	86	42	46	27
1987	87	53	48	26
1988	89	62	49	27
1989	90	68	53	29
1990	92	72	56	29
1991	92	77	58	30
1992	93	82	61	31
1993	95	86	64	32
1994	96	89	67	34
1995	97	91	70	36

Note: From 1982 through 1995, it's assumed that 98 percent of all U.S. households own televisions.

EXHIBIT 5
Estimated Population, Home Video Spending, VCR Penetration and Basic Cable Penetration by Country, as of 1991

Sources: Blockbuster's 1991 Annual Report, *This Business of Television*, and 1992 *World Almanac*.

Country	Population (millions)	Video Spending ($ billions)	VCRs (% of households)	Cable (% of households)
Australia	17	0.7	70	0
Canada	27	1.2	65	69
France	56	0.7	40	10
Germany	79	0.7	46	32
Italy	58	0.6	38	1
Japan	124	2.6	70	20
United Kingdom	57	1.4	70	2
United States	250	11.0	75	57
Others	4,732	2.3	n.a.	n.a.
Worldwide total	5,400	21.2	n.a.	n.a.

Note: n.a. = not available

cultural, educational, exercise, instructional, and documentary videos tended to be handled by smaller distributors.

The time span from the point when work began on a new movie to the point when its revenue stream was largely realized often was five years or longer. Over that period, producers and distributors attempted to play out their products in a manner which gave them an optimum revenue stream.

By 1991, home video had become a major ancillary source of revenue for movie studios. For example, *Nothing but Trouble* (directed by Dan Aykroyd, 1991) grossed $8.5 million in box office receipts. The studio's share was roughly 50 percent. When released on videocassette, the same movie earned an additional $9.6 million in revenue for the studio.[4]

The sequence of each film's release depended on the nature of individual deals made by the distributor. Domestic release usually occurred somewhat ahead of international release.

[4]Source: Blockbuster Entertainment 1991 Corp. Annual Report.

A typical major studio's United States release tended to be rolled out in the following illustrative manner:

Theatrical showings: January through April, 1992

Home video: Midsummer, 1992

Airline: Midsummer, 1992

Pay-per-view: Latesummer or fall, 1992

Pay cable (premium channels): Winter, 1992–93

If attractively priced, popular movies that were developed for young children were likely to achieve a sell-through market of 1.5 million or more copies. Movies that had been adult hits at the box office within the latest year were the ones most in demand for rentals, and 100,000 to 500,000 copies of them were generally sold, mostly to video rental stores. Assuming a $3 charge per rental, it normally took anywhere from 13 to 19 rentals to recover a store's initial investment in a hit movie tape.

Distributors set high initial suggested retail prices (roughly $80 to $100 on box office hits) for videotaped films they expected consumers to rent and low prices (roughly $20 to $30) for those they expected consumers to buy. Each videocassette cost distributors about $2 to manufacture and $2 to market. Wholesale prices paid by Blockbuster were generally 55 to 65 percent of suggested retail prices.

Wholesalers

Despite the fact that movies were the mainstay of the home video business, Blockbuster Entertainment traditionally purchased its movie rental inventory from wholesalers rather than film distributors. Having achieved nationwide scope, the company could decide to bypass regional wholesalers and purchase its movies more economically directly from motion picture distributors.

Technological Threats

During the decade from 1982 through 1991 Americans purchased 1.2 billion prerecorded and 2.2 billion blank videocassettes. They also built up a $32 billion investment in VCR equipment. This burgeoning consumer commitment to VCR technology seemed to assure long-range demand for videocassettes. Nevertheless, the ease of duplicating and pirating videocassettes was a matter of some concern to movie producers. As laser discs began to attract a modest following, rentals and sales of video discs were being added to many video store's product offerings.

No one knew precisely when new types of home entertainment might begin to undermine home videotape viewing. Cable television was expected to become a more and more serious threat. Even though three out of five TV-owning households subscribed to cable service as of 1991, only one-third of those subscribers had access to movies on pay cable (e.g. HBO, Showtime, Cinemax, The Disney Channel, The Movie Channel) or pay-per-view channels.

Employing "addressable technology," pay-per-view service allowed customers to call in and have a movie, concert, or sporting event broadcast on their TV for a fee. Being transaction based, pay-per-view depended upon impulse buying. It was sold by direct mailings, advertisements, bill stuffers, and 24 hour "barker" promotional channels.

In 1992, sporting events generated almost twice as much pay-per-view business as other alternatives. As pay-per-view's market potential continued to develop, the summer of 1992 was regarded as an important psychological turning point. Cable operators were seeking broadcasting rights for live coverage of the Olympic Games in Atlanta, Georgia, hoping that such coverage would significantly boost the number of new subscribers for pay-per-view services.

While viewers had to watch pay-per-view at a scheduled time, this service certainly provided greater convenience than having to make two round trips to a video store. The competitive threat was moderated by the fact that most new movies were released on videocassettes before they appeared on pay-per-view services or pay cable. However, that disparity could disappear rapidly if movie distributors were enticed by cable's potential for licensing and revenue sharing arrangements.

Interactive Television

Over the long-term, advances in satellite and cable television technology and entry of regional telephone companies into the electronic home delivery arena were other potential concerns within the U.S. market. With new developments in fiber optics and digital signal compression, expansion to 500 channels could become feasible for video delivery systems. Thus, there was a possibility that "video-on-demand" could become a reality on cable or telephone systems by the mid 1990s.

Anticipating major advances in communications, IBM and Time Warner Corp. had begun discussing ways to combine data processing and transmitting expertise with cable TV systems, TV shows, and movies. IBM believed interactive television would eventually encroach upon a wide array of existing entertainment and information product/markets, including catalog shopping, broadcast and cable advertising, home video, information services, theater, video games, electronic messaging, videoconferencing, photography, records, tapes, and CDs. Furthermore, the Federal Communications Commission (FCC) had allocated a portion of the broadcast spectrum to interactive television and intended to award licenses to investors who could serve large markets.

Nervous Investors

Had the video rental market remained extremely fragmented, it might not have become so large and well-established. Some industry watchers predicted that Blockbuster's success in becoming a high-quality specialty retail chain might impair the development of innovative competing technologies for accessing home entertainment.

Recognizing that other forms of retailing were withstanding competition from television, Baczko made the following point, "Home shopping has not taken the store away, and pay-per-view is not going to do so to video. I don't think you can ever beat a retailing environment."[5]

Nevertheless, newspaper reports of questionable depreciation accounting practices, bankruptcy filings by sizable video retailers, and media hype of future electronic home delivery systems, from time to time stirred predictions of impending disaster for the video rental industry. Consequently, Blockbuster's common stock attracted speculators and short sellers, and the market price per share plunged every so often as frightened investors hastily bailed out to "take profits" or "stop losses." For example, the price per share reached a high of $15.125 and a low of $7.75 on the New York Stock Exchange during the first half of 1991.

---

[5] *The New York Times,* February 21, 1992.

EXHIBIT 6
Philips Electronics N.V., Net Sales by Product Sector and Geographical Area (mMillions of guilders)

Source: Philips' 1991 Annual Report.

	1991	1990
Product Sector		
Lighting	7,351	7,026
Consumer products	26,861	25,856
Professional products and systems	12,510	12,400
Components and semiconductors	7,844	7,953
Miscellaneous	2,420	2,529
Net sales	56,986	55,764
Geographical Area		
Netherlands	3,206	3,604
Rest of Europe	30,433	30,366
U.S.A. and Canada	12,833	11,819
Latin America	3,142	3,361
Africa	730	772
Asia	5,565	4,770
Australia and New Zealand	1,077	1,072
Net sales	56,986	55,764

Note: On December 31, 1991 and 1990, respectively, one U.S. dollar equaled 1.71 and 1.69 Dutch guilders.

Strategic Alliance with Philips Electronics

During 1992, an intriguing strategic alliance began to emerge between Blockbuster Entertainment Corp. and Philips Electronics, N.V. Headquartered in the Netherlands, Philips was the world's second largest consumer electronics company after Japan's Matsushita Electric Industrial Co. Philips' decision to purchase 13 million newly issued common shares (nearly 7.2 percent of outstanding shares) of Blockbuster suggested that the two companies might be heading toward a close working relationship.[6]

In 1991 consumer products accounted for 47 percent of Philips' $33 billion in sales revenues. The early 1990s found the U.S., Canada, Australia, the United Kingdom, and Japan all experiencing economic downturns and declining consumer confidence. Stagnant demand and bloody price wars were curbing profits throughout the consumer electronics industry. Battered by stagnant demand and stiff price competition from its Japanese competitors, Philips reported a $3 billion loss in 1990. Philips' new President, Jan D. Timmer, was struggling to slash the payroll, close inefficient plants, and divest unprofitable operations. A streamlining and restructuring process initiated by Timmer provided a $210 million profit on sales of $33 billion in 1991. Recent sales data are shown in Exhibit 6.

Some analysts, suspecting that Huizenga might be ready to move on to another new venture, speculated that Philips might be interested in acquiring a controlling interest in Blockbuster Entertainment Corp. Others expressed doubts that outright ownership and management of a captive group of rental stores would serve Philips' best interest.

Having pioneered such consumer electronics products as the videocassette recorder, audio compact disc, digital compact cassette, and high-definition television, Philips had long been a superior technological leader. Marketing agility and competitive pricing had never been Philips' strengths. Philips conceivably might be aiming for a reliable international retail base for rapid, broad distribution of future hardware and software products.

---

[6]These funds have been used by Blockbuster to help pay for the Cityvision plc acquisition.

Philips owned 51 percent of Super Club Holding & Finance S.A., a poorly performing music and video retail chain. With store locations in Europe and the United States, Super Club might benefit from a tie-in with Blockbuster. Philips also owned 80 percent of Polygram, one of the three largest music publishing, production, marketing, and distribution companies in the world, and a major European manufacturer of compact discs. Recognizing the increasingly complementary natures of the audio and video fields, Polygram had begun producing and distributing filmed entertainment, as part of its strategy to become a multicultural, global entertainment company.

Philips' Multimedia Systems

Potentially even more relevant were Philips' plans for a new Imagination Machine. Philips had developed a new Compact Disk Interactive (CD-I) entertainment system that could turn the family TV into a terminal through which one could play regular music CDs, view photo CD disks, and interact with programs rather than just watch them. Touted as the "VCR of the 21st century," Philips' Imagination Machine was one of the products that Timmer was counting on heavily to revive depressed earnings. Blending text, full-motion video, and stereo-quality sound, it called up sports statistics during live broadcasts, displayed digital snapshots, played karaoke sing-along disks, used Nintendo's new games and played movies and music videos. While CD-I had been promoted primarily to the consumer market, it was also highly suited to the educational market.

Philips utilized a special format for its CD-ROM, which was supported by several other electronics firms as well. Commodore, Apple, Toshiba, and Tandy were offering multimedia equipment with different CD formats. Sony and Panasonic (Matsushita) had not yet revealed the type of standard they might support. Having witnessed the VHS/Beta wars of the late 1970s, Philips recognized the need to insure that its CD-I standard won out over its rivals. Ultimately, the availability of appealing multimedia software would help determine which compact disc standard would dominate.

Potential New Undertakings

As Blockbuster entered numerous foreign markets, its employees started to acquire increasing familiarity with markets for movies and home entertainment within many different cultures and political jurisdictions. Blockbuster's increasing knowledge of ways to formalize and expand global rental markets could help foster widespread acceptance of the rental concept for expensive multimedia CDs, such as encyclopedias, music libraries, and games. Blockbuster could thus become a leading worldwide distributor of a new generation of home entertainment products, perhaps selling and/or renting Philips' Imagination Machines and CDs.

Reacting to investor skepticism a year earlier, Huizenga had optimistically asserted, "We have the best locations in town. We've got a plain vanilla box. We can sell shoes there if we want to. Maybe we'll build a music store that's green and white. We could call it Chartbusters."[7] Such remarks indicate that someday Blockbuster Entertainment Corporation could be attracted to retailing opportunities elsewhere within the diverse, yet more and more intertwined, marketplace for home entertainment products.

[7] *The New York Times Business World Magazine,* June 9, 1991.

17

eBay: In a League by Itself

Louis Marino and Patrick Kreiser *The University of Alabama*

On September 20, 2000, eBay's top management surprised the financial community by announcing ambitious objectives of $3 billion in annual revenues by year-end 2005, a gross margin target above 80 percent, and target operating margins of 30–35 percent. Given that eBay's 2000 annual revenues were only $400 million, the $3 billion annual revenue target implied a compound annual growth rate of 50 percent from the end of 2000 through 2005—an objective some analysts criticized as too aggressive. Other analysts, however, wondered if the revenue target was ambitious enough, since online auction sales were forecast to reach $54.3 billion by 2007 and since eBay was far and away the dominant player in the online auction market.

But in early 2004 eBay was well on its way to meeting the 2005 goals it set for itself in 2000. In January 2004, eBay reported 2003 revenues of $2.17 billion and a gross margin of 81 percent. If the company could grow its revenues by 40 percent in 2004, it could reach its $3 billion annual revenue goal a year ahead of the 2005 target date. However, analysts were becoming increasingly concerned about whether eBay could sustain its phenomenal growth (see Exhibit 1), given that almost one-third of all U.S. Internet users were already registered on eBay and that eBay could expect stiffening competition from other ambitious online auction sites and e-tailers as it pursued its growth initiatives.

Building on the vision of its founder, Pierre Omidyar (pronounced oh-*mid*-ee-ar), eBay was initially conceived as an online marketplace that would facilitate a person-to-person trading community based on a democratized, efficient market in which everyone could have equal access through the same medium, the Internet. Leveraging a unique business model and the growing popularity of the Internet, eBay had dominated the online auction market since its beginning in the mid-1990s and had grown its business to include over 94.9 million registered users from more than 150 countries heading into 2004. The auction site's diverse base of registered users in early 2004—which ranged from high school and college students looking to make a few extra dollars, to Fortune 500 companies such as IBM selling excess inventory, to large government agencies like the U.S. Postal Service selling undeliverable parcels—differed greatly from its original user base of individuals and small companies.

EXHIBIT 1   **Selected Indicators of eBay's Growth, 1996–2003**

	1996	1997	1998	1999	2000	2001	2002	2003
Number of registered users (in millions)	0.041	0.341	2.2	10.0	22.0	42.4	61.7	94.9
Active users (in millions)	NA	NA	NA	NA	NA	18.0	27.7	41.2
Gross merchandise sales (in millions)	$7	$95	$745	$2,800	$5,400	$9,300	$14,900	$24,000
Number of auctions listed (in millions)	0.29	4.4	33.7	129	264	423	638	971

EXHIBIT 2   **Estimated Growth in Global E-Commerce 1999–2004**

	1999	2000	2001	2002	2003	2004
Estimated value of e-commerce transactions	$170 billion	$657 billion	$1.23 billion	$2.23 trillion	$3.98 trillion	$6.79 trillion

Source: Forrester Research.

The Growth of E-Commerce and Online Auctions

The concepts underlying the Internet were first conceived in the 1960s, but it wasn't until the 1990s that the Internet garnered widespread use and became a part of everyday life. The *Computer Industry Almanac* estimated that by the end of 2002 there were approximately 665 million Internet users worldwide in over 150 countries and that number would grow to over 1 billion users worldwide by 2005.[1] While the top 15 countries accounted for more than 70 percent of the computers in use, slightly less than one-fourth of these Internet users (160.7 million) resided in the United States, and the United States' share as a percentage of total Internet users worldwide was falling. The highest areas of Internet usage growth were expected to be in developing countries in Asia, Latin America, and Eastern Europe with increasing access through new technologies such as Web-enabled cell phones. However, it was expected that total growth rates would not exceed 20 percent annually in the future.

Forrester Research forecast that worldwide e-commerce revenues would be $6.79 trillion in 2004 and that online retail would grow at a 19 percent annual rate between 2003 and 2008 to reach $229.9 billion, of which 25 percent, or $57.5 billion, was expected to come from online auction sales. It was also predicted that North America would account for 51.5 percent of total e-commerce sales in 2004, with the Asia-Pacific region accounting for 24.3 percent, Western Europe accounting for 22.5 percent, and Latin America accounting for 12.1 percent of total sales. Within the business-to-consumer segment, eBay's primary area of operation, U.S. e-commerce accounted for over 65 percent of all Internet transactions in 1999 but was expected to account for only about 38 percent in 2003 and potentially less in the future, due to rapid expansion in other parts of the world. Asia was expected to grow especially rapidly following the 2001 decision to include China in the World Trade Organization. In 2002, Germany, the United Kingdom, France, and Italy accounted for 70 percent of the e-commerce revenues in Western Europe, but this share was expected to decline as business-to-business e-commerce in Europe was expected to triple from 2003 to 2006. Exhibit 2 displays the expected total growth in worldwide e-commerce between 1999 and 2004.

[1]www.c-i-a.com, press releases, April 2001 and July 2001.

Key Success Factors in Online Retailing

It was relatively easy to create a Web site that functioned like a retail store; the more significant challenge was for an online retailer to generate traffic to the site in the form of both new and returning customers. To reach new customers, some online retailers partnered with search engines—such as Google, MySimon, or StreetPrices—that allowed customers to compare prices for a given product from many retailers. Other tactics employed to build traffic included direct e-mail, online advertising at portals and content-related sites, and some traditional advertising such as print and television advertising. For customers who found their way to a site, most online retailers endeavored to provide extensive product information, include pictures of the merchandise, make the site easily navigable, and have enough new things happening at the site to keep customers coming back. (A site's ability to generate repeat visitors was known as *stickiness.*) For new Internet users, retailers had to help them overcome their nervousness about using the Internet itself to shop for items customers generally bought in stores. Web sites had to appease concerns about the possible theft of credit card numbers and the possible sale of personal information to marketing firms. Online retailing also had severe limitations in the case of those goods and services people wanted to see in person to verify their quality. From the retailer's perspective, there was the issue of collecting payment from buyers who wanted to use checks or money orders instead of credit cards.

Online Auctions

The first known auctions were held in Babylon around 500 BC. In AD 193, the entire Roman Empire was put up for auction after the emperor Pertinax was executed. Didius Julianus bid 6,250 drachmas per royal guard and was immediately named emperor of Rome. However, Julianus was executed only two months later, suggesting that he may have been the first-ever victim of the winner's curse (bidding more than the good would cost in a nonauction setting).

Auctions have endured throughout history for several reasons. First, they give sellers a convenient way to find a buyer for something they would like to dispose of. Second, auctions are an excellent way for people to collect difficult-to-find items, such as certain Beanie Babies or historical memorabilia, that have a high value to them personally. Finally, auctions are one of the "purest" markets that exist for goods, in that they bring buyers and sellers into contact to arrive at a mutually agreeable price. As technological advances led to the advent and widespread adoption of the Internet, this ancient form of trade found a new medium.

Online auctions worked in essentially the same way as traditional auctions, the only difference being that the auction process occurred over the Internet rather than at a specific geographic location with buyers and sellers physically present. There are three basic categories of online auctions:

1. *Business-to-business* auctions, typically involving equipment and surplus merchandise.
2. *Business-to-consumer* auctions, in which businesses sold goods and services to consumers via the Internet. Many such auctions involved companies interested in selling used or discontinued goods, or liquidating unwanted inventory.
3. *Person-to-person* auctions, which gave interested sellers and buyers the opportunity to engage in competitive bidding.

Since eBay's pioneering of the person-to-person online auction process in 1995, the number of online auction sites on the Internet had grown to well over 2,750 by the end of 2001. Forrester Research predicted that 6.5 million customers would use online auctions in 2002.

Online auction operators could generate revenue in four principal ways:

1. Charging sellers for listing their good or service.
2. Charging a commission on all sales.
3. Selling advertising on their Web sites.
4. Selling their own new or used merchandise via the online auction format.

More recently, however, online auction sites had also added a fifth revenue-generation option that allowed buyers to purchase the desired good without waiting for an auction to close:

5. Selling their own goods or allowing other sellers to offer their goods in a fixed-price format.

Most sites charged sellers either a fee or a commission and sold advertising to companies interested in promoting their goods or services to users of the auction site.

Online Auction Users

Participants in online auctions could be grouped into six categories: (1) bargain hunters, (2) hobbyist/collector buyers, (3) professional buyers, (4) casual sellers, (5) hobbyist/collector sellers and (6) power and corporate sellers.

Bargain Hunters

Bargain hunters viewed online auctions primarily as a form of entertainment; their objective usually was to find a great deal. Bargain hunters were thought to make up only 8 percent of active online users but 52 percent of eBay visitors. To attract repeat visits from bargain hunters, industry observers said, sites must appeal to them on both rational and emotional levels, satisfying their need for competitive pricing, the excitement of the search, and the desire for community.

Hobbyist and Collector Buyers

Hobbyists and collectors used auctions to search for specific goods that had a high value to them personally. They were very concerned with both price and quality. Collectors prized eBay for its wide variety of product offerings.

Professional Buyers

As the legitimacy of online auctions grew, a new type of buyer began to emerge: the professional buyer. Professional buyers covered a broad range of purchasers, from purchasing managers acquiring office supplies to antiques and gun dealers purchasing inventory. Like bargain hunters, professional buyers were looking for a way to help contain costs; and like hobbyists and collectors, some professional buyers were seeking unique items to supplement their inventory. The primary difference between professional buyers and other types, however, was their affiliation with commercial enterprises. With the growth of online auction sites dedicated to business-to-business auctions, professional buyers were becoming an increasingly important element of the online auction landscape.

Casual Sellers

Casual sellers included individuals who used eBay as a substitute for a classified ad listing or a garage sale to dispose of items they no longer wanted. While many casual sellers listed only a few items, some used eBay to raise money for some new project.

Hobbyist and Collector Sellers

Sellers who were hobbyists or collectors typically dealt in a limited category of goods and looked to eBay as a way to sell selected items in their collections to others who might want them. Items ranged from classic television collectibles, to hand-sewn dolls, to coins and stamps. The hobbyists and collectors used a range of traditional and online outlets to reach their target markets. A number of the sellers used auctions to supplement their retail operations, while others sold exclusively through online auctions and in fixed-price formats such as Half.com.

Power and Corporate Sellers

Power sellers were typically small to medium-sized businesses that favored eBay as a primary distribution channel for their goods and often sold tens of thousands of dollars' worth of goods every month on the site. One estimate suggested that while these power sellers accounted for only 4 percent of eBay's population, they were responsible for 80 percent of eBay's total business.[2] Individuals who were power sellers could often make a full-time job of the endeavor.

As with the evolution of buyers, commercial enterprises were becoming an increasingly important part of the online auction industry. These commercial enterprises generally achieved power-seller status relatively rapidly. On eBay, for example, some of the new power sellers were familiar names such as IBM, Compaq, and the U.S. Postal Service (which sells undeliverable items on eBay under the user name usps-mrc).

Pierre Omidyar and the Founding of eBay

Pierre Omidyar was born in Paris, France, to parents who had left Iran decades earlier. The family emigrated to the United States when Omidyar's father began a residency at Johns Hopkins University Medical Center. Omidyar attended Tufts University, where he met his future wife, Pamela Wesley, who came to Tufts from Hawaii to get a degree in biology. Upon graduating in 1988, the couple moved to California, where Omidyar, who had earned a bachelor of science degree in computer science, joined Claris, an Apple Computer subsidiary in Silicon Valley, and wrote a widely used graphics application, MacDraw. In 1991, Omidyar left Claris and cofounded Ink Development (later renamed eShop), which became a pioneer in online shopping and was eventually sold to Microsoft in 1996. In 1994 Omidyar joined General Magic as a developer services engineer and remained there until mid-1996, when he left to pursue full-time development of eBay.

Internet folklore has it that eBay was founded solely to allow Pamela to trade Pez dispensers with other collectors. While Pamela was certainly a driving force in launching the initial Web site, Pierre had long been interested in how one could establish a marketplace to bring together a fragmented market. Pierre saw eBay as a way to create a person-to-person trading community based on a democratized, efficient market where everyone could have equal access through the same medium, the Internet. Pierre set out to develop his marketplace and to meet both his and Pamela's goals. In 1995 he launched the first online auction under the name of Auctionwatch at the domain name of www.eBay.com. The name *eBay* stood for "electronic Bay area," coined because Pierre's initial concept was to attract neighbors and other interested San Francisco Bay area residents to the site to buy and sell items of mutual interest. The first auctions charged no fees to either buyers or sellers and contained mostly computer equipment (and no Pez dispensers). Pierre's fledgling venture generated $1,000 in revenue the first month and an additional $2,000 the second. Traffic grew rapidly, however, as word about the site spread in the Bay area and a community of collectors emerged, using the site to trade and chat—even some marriages resulted from exchanges in eBay chat rooms.[3]

By February 1996, the traffic at Pierre Omidyar's site had grown so much that his Internet service provider informed him that he would have to upgrade his service. When

[2]Claire Tristram, " 'Amazoning' Amazon," www.contextmag.com, November 1999.
[3]Quentin Hardy, "The Radical Philanthropist," *Forbes,* May 1, 2000, p. 118.

Omidyar compensated for this by charging a listing fee for the auction and saw no decrease in the number of items listed, he knew he was on to something. Although he was still working out of his home, Omidyar began looking for a partner and in May asked his friend Jeffrey Skoll to join him in the venture. While Skoll had never cared much about money, his Stanford master of business administration degree provided the firm with the business background that Omidyar lacked. With Omidyar as the visionary and Skoll as the strategist, the company embarked on a mission to "help people trade practically anything on earth."

Their concept for eBay was to "create a place where people could do business just like in the old days—when everyone got to know each other personally, and we all felt we were dealing on a one-to-one basis with individuals we could trust."

In eBay's early days, Omidyar and Skoll ran the operation alone, using a single computer to serve all of the pages. Omidyar served as CEO, chief financial officer, and president, while Skoll functioned as copresident and director. It was not long until Omidyar and Skoll grew the company to a size that forced them to move out of Pierre Omidyar's living room, due to the objections of Pamela, and into Skoll's living room. Shortly thereafter, the operations moved into the facilities of a Silicon Valley business incubator for a time until the company settled in its current facilities in San Jose, California. Exhibits 3 and 4 present eBay's recent financial statements.

eBay's Transition to Professional Management

From the beginning Pierre Omidyar intended to hire a professional manager to serve as the president of eBay: "[I would] let him or her run the company so . . . [I could] go play," he said.[4] In 1997 both Omidyar and Skoll agreed that it was time to locate an experienced professional to function as CEO and president. In late 1997 eBay's headhunters came up with a candidate for the job: Margaret (Meg) Whitman, then general manager for Hasbro, Inc.'s preschool division. Whitman had received her bachelor of arts degree in economics from Princeton and her master of business administration from the Harvard Business School; her first job was in brand management at Procter & Gamble. Her experience also included serving as the president and CEO of FTD, the president of Stride Rite Corporation's Stride Rite Division, and the senior vice president of marketing for the Walt Disney Company's consumer products division.

When first approached by eBay, Whitman was not especially interested in joining a company that had fewer than 40 employees and less than $6 million in revenues the previous year. It was only after repeated pleas that Whitman agreed to meet with Omidyar in Silicon Valley. After a second meeting, Whitman realized the company's enormous growth potential and agreed to give eBay a try. According to Omidyar, Meg Whitman's experience in global marketing with Hasbro's Teletubbies, Playskool, and Mr. Potato Head brands made her "the ideal choice to build upon eBay's leadership position in the one-to-one online trading market without sacrificing the quality and personal touch our users have grown to expect."[5] In addition to convincing Whitman to head eBay's operations, Omidyar had been instrumental in helping bring in other talented senior executives and in assembling a capable board of directors. Notable members of eBay's board of directors included Scott Cook, the founder of Intuit, a highly successful financial software company, and Fred D. Anderson, executive vice president and chief financial officer of Apple.

---

[4]"Billionaires of the Web," *Business 2.0,* June 1999.
[5]eBay press release, May 7, 1998.

EXHIBIT 3   eBay's Income Statements, 1996–2002 (In thousands, except per share figures)

	1996	1997	1998	1999	2000	2001	2002	2003
Net revenues	$32,051	$41,370	$86,129	$224,724	$431,424	$748,821	$1,214,100	$2,165,096
Cost of net revenues	6,803	8,404	16,094	57,588	95,453	134,816	213,876	416,058
Gross profit	$25,248	$32,966	$70,035	$167,136	$335,971	$614,005	$1,000,224	$1,749,038
Operating expenses:								
Sales and marketing	$13,139	$15,618	$35,976	$96,239	$166,767	$253,474	$349,650	$567,565
Product development	28	831	4,640	24,847	55,863	75,288	104,636	159,315
General and administrative	5,661	6,534	15,849	43,919	73,027	105,784	171,785	304,703
Patent litigation expense	—	—	—	0	—	—	—	29,965
Payroll taxes on stock options	—	—	0	0	2,337	2,442	4,015	9,590
Amortization of acquired intangibles	—	—	805	1,145	1,443	36,591	15,941	50,659
Merger-related costs	—	—	0	4,359	1,550	0	0	0
Total operating expenses	$18,828	$22,983	$57,270	$170,509	$300,977	$473,579	$646,027	$1,119,797
Income (loss) from operations	$6,420	$9,983	$12,765	$(3,373)	$34,994	$140,426	$354,197	$629,241
Interest and other income (expense), net	(2,607)	(1,951)	1,799	23,833	46,337	41,613	49,209	37,803
Interest expense	—	—	(2,191)	(2,319)	(3,374)	(2,851)	(1,492)	(4,314)
Impairment of certain equity investments	—	—	0	0	0	(16,245)	(3,781)	(1,230)
Income before income taxes and minority interest	$3,813	$8,032	$12,373	$18,141	$77,957	$162,943	$398,133	$661,500
Provision for income taxes	(475)	(971)	(4,789)	(8,472)	(32,725)	(80,009)	(145,946)	(206,738)
Minority interests in consolidated companies	—	—	(311)	(102)	3,062	7,514	(2,296)	(7,578)
Net income	$3,338	$7,061	$7,273	$9,567	$48,294	$90,448	$249,891	$447,184
Net income per share:								
Basic	$0.39	$0.29	$0.07	$0.04	$0.19	$0.34	$0.43	$0.69
Diluted	0.07	0.08	0.03	0.04	0.17	0.32	0.43	0.67
Weighted-average shares:								
Basic	8,490	24,428	104,128	217,674	251,776	268,971	574,992	638,288
Diluted	45,060	84,775	233,519	273,033	280,346	280,595	585,640	656,657

Source: Company financial documents.

EXHIBIT 4 eBay's Consolidated Balance Sheets, 1997–2003 (In thousands)

	Year Ended December 31						
	1997	1998	1999	2000	2001	2002	2003
Assets							
Current assets:							
Cash and cash equivalents	$3,723	$37,285	$219,679	$201,873	$523,969	$1,109,313	$1,381,513
Short-term investments	1,024	40,401	181,086	354,166	199,450	89,690	340,576
Accounts receivable, net		12,425	36,538	67,163	101,703	131,453	225,871
Funds receivable						41,014	79,893
Other current assets	220	7,479	22,531	52,262	58,683	96,988	118,029
Total current assets	$4,967	$97,590	$459,834	$675,464	$883,805	$1,468,458	$2,145,882
Long-term investments					286,998	470,227	934,171
Restricted cash and investments					129,614	134,644	127,432
Property and equipment, net	652	44,062	111,806	125,161	142,349	218,028	601,785
Goodwill					187,829	1,456,024	1,719,311
Investments			373,988				
Deferred tax assets			5,639		21,540	84,218	
Intangible and other assets, net		7,884	12,675	23,299	26,394	292,845	291,553
Total assets	$5,619	$149,536	$963,942	$1,182,403	$1,678,529	$4,040,226	$5,820,134
Liabilities and stockholders' equity							
Current liabilities:							
Accounts payable	$252	$9,997	$31,538	$31,725	$33,235	$47,424	$64,633
Funds payable and amounts due to customers						50,396	106,568
Accrued expenses and other current liabilities		6,577	32,550	60,882	94,593	199,323	356,491
Deferred revenue and customer advances	128	973	5,997	12,656	15,583	18,846	28,874
Debt and leases, current portion	258	4,047	12,285	15,272	16,111	2,970	2,840
Income taxes payable	169	1,380	6,455	11,092	20,617	67,265	87,870
Deferred tax liabilities, current		1,682					
Other current liabilities	128	5,981	7,632	5,815			
Total current liabilities	$1,124	$24,656	$88,825	$137,442	$180,139	$386,224	$647,276
Debt and leases, long-term portion	305	18,361	15,018	11,404	12,008	13,798	124,476
Deferred tax liabilities, long-term					3,629	27,625	79,238
Other liabilities	157			6,549	15,864	22,874	33,494
Minority interests					37,751	33,232	39,408
Total liabilities	$1,586	$48,998	$111,475	$168,643	$249,391	$483,753	$923,892
Series B redeemable convertible preferred stock and Series B warrants	3,018						
Total stockholders' equity	1,015	100,538	852,467	1,013,760	1,429,138	3,556,473	4,896,242
	$5,619	$149,536	$963,942	$1,182,403	$1,678,529	$4,124,444	$5,820,134

Source: Company financial documents.

How an eBay Auction Worked

eBay endeavored to make it very simple to buy and sell goods. In order to sell or bid on goods, users first had to register at the site. Once they registered, users selected both a user name and a password. Unregistered users were able to browse the Web site but were not permitted to bid on any goods or list any items for auction.

On the Web site, search engines helped customers determine what goods were currently available. When registered users found an item they desired, they could choose to enter a single bid or to use automatic bidding (called proxy bidding). In automatic bidding the customer entered an initial bid sufficient to make him or her the high bidder, and then the bid would be automatically increased as others bid for the same object until the auction ended and either the bidder won or another bidder surpassed the original customer's maximum specified bid. Regardless of which bidding method they chose, users could check bids at any time and either bid again, if they had been outbid, or increase their maximum amount in the automatic bid. Users could choose to receive e-mail notification if they were outbid.

Once the auction had ended, the buyer and seller were each notified of the winning bid and were given each other's e-mail address. The parties to the auction would then privately arrange for payment and delivery of the good.

Fees and Procedures for Sellers

Buyers on eBay were not charged a fee for bidding on items, but sellers were charged an insertion fee and a "final value" fee; they could also elect to pay additional fees to promote their listing. Listing, or insertion, fees ranged from 30 cents for auctions with opening bids, minimum values, or reserve prices of between $0.01 and $0.99, to $4.80 for auctions with opening bids, minimum values, or reserve prices of $500 and up. Final value fees ranged from 1.25 to 5 percent of the final sale price and were computed according to a graduated fee schedule in which the percentage fell as the final sales price rose. As an example, in a basic auction with no promotion, if the item had brought an opening bid of $200 and eventually sold for $1,500, the total fee paid by the seller would be $35.48—the $3.60 insertion fee plus $31.88. The $31.88 was based on a fee structure of 5 percent of the first $25 (or $1.25), 2.5 percent of the additional amount between $25.01 and $1,000 (or $24.38), and 1.25 percent of the additional amount between $1,000.01 and $1,500 (or $6.25). Auction fees varied for special categories of goods such as passenger vehicles in eBay Motors that were charged a $40 transaction fee when the first successful bid was placed and a $100 insertion fee for residential, commercial, and other real estate.

Sellers could also customize items by adding photographs and featuring their item in a gallery. Sellers could indicate a photograph in the item's description if they posted the photograph on a Web site and provided eBay with the appropriate Web address. Items could be showcased in the Gallery section with a catalog of pictures rather than text. A seller who used a photograph in his or her listing could have this photograph included in the Gallery section for 25 cents or featured there for $19.95. A Gallery option was available in all categories of eBay, but fees varied between categories and the prominence of the gallery. For example, a simple gallery listing cost 25 cents, whereas a featured gallery listing, which included a periodic listing in the featured section above the general gallery, cost $19.95. In the eBay Motors gallery, options could cost as much as $99.95.

To make doing business on eBay more attractive to potential sellers, the company introduced several features. To receive a minimum price for an auction, the seller could specify an opening bid or set a reserve price on the auction. If the bidding did not top the reserve price, the seller was under no obligation to sell the item to the highest bidder and could relist the item at no additional cost. For items with a reserve price between $0.01 and $49.99, the fee was $1.00; between $50.00 and $199.99, the fee was $2.00; and for over $200, the fee was 1 percent of the reserve price. If the seller wished, he or she could also set a Buy It Now price that allowed bidders to pay a set amount for a listed item. The fee for this service was $1.00. If the Buy It Now price was met, the auction would end immediately.

As of June 11, 2001, new sellers at eBay were required to provide both a credit card number and bank account information to register. While eBay admitted that these requirements are extreme, it argued that they helped protect everyone in the community against fraudulent sellers and ensured that sellers were of legal age and were serious about listing the item on eBay.

How Transactions Were Completed

Under the terms of eBay's user agreement, if a seller received one or more bids above the stated minimum, or reserve, price, the seller was obligated to complete the transaction, although eBay had no enforcement power beyond suspending a noncompliant buyer or seller from using the company's service. In the event the buyer and seller were unable to complete the transaction, the seller notified eBay, which then credited the seller the amount of the final value fee.

When an auction ended, the eBay system validated that the bid fell within the acceptable price range. If the sale was successful, eBay automatically notified the buyer and seller via e-mail; the buyer and seller could then either work out the transaction details independent of eBay or use eBay's checkout and payment services to complete the transaction. In its original business model, at no point during the process did eBay take possession of either the item being sold or the buyer's payment. In an effort to increase revenues, eBay expanded its offerings to facilitate buyers' payments by first offering services that accepted credit card payments and electronic funds transfers on behalf of the seller and then purchasing PayPal, the leading third-party online payment facilitator in 2003. To make selling easier, eBay also had alliances with two leading shippers, the U.S. Postal Service and United Parcel Service (UPS). Both of these shippers had centers on eBay that would allow sellers to calculate postage and to print postage-paid labels. However, the buyer and seller still had to independently arrange shipping terms, with buyers typically paying for shipping. Items were sent directly from the buyer to the seller unless an independent escrow service was arranged to help ensure security.

To encourage sellers to use eBay's ancillary services the company offered an automated checkout service to help expedite communication, payment, and delivery between buyers and sellers.

Feedback Forum

In early 1996 eBay pioneered a feature called Feedback Forum to build trust among buyers and sellers and to facilitate the establishment of reputations within its community. Feedback Forum encouraged individuals to record comments about their trading partners. At the completion of each auction, both the buyer and seller were allowed to leave positive, negative, or neutral comments about each other. Individuals could dispute feedback left about them by annotating comments in question.

By assigning values of +1 for a positive comment, 0 for a neutral comment, and −1 for a negative comment, each trader earned a ranking that was attached to his or her user name. A user who had developed a positive reputation over time had a color-coded star symbol displayed next to his or her user name to indicate the amount of positive feedback. The highest ranking a trader could receive was "over 100,000," indicated by a red shooting star. Well-respected high-volume traders could have rankings well into the thousands.

Users who received a sufficiently negative net feedback rating (typically a −4) had their registrations suspended and were thus unable to bid on or list items for sale. Buyers could review a person's feedback profile before deciding to bid on an item listed by that person or before choosing payment and delivery methods. A sample user profile is shown in Exhibit 5.

EXHIBIT 5   A Sample Feedback Forum Profile

home | pay | sign out | services | site map | help ⑦

| Browse | Search | Sell | My eBay | Community | Powered By IBM |

← Back to My eBay   Home > Services > Feedback Forum > **Member Profile**   Why does this page look different?

Member Profile: nuggett12 (50 ★)

		Recent Ratings:				
Feedback Score:	**50**		Past Month	Past 6 Months	Past 12 Months	Member since: May-17-99
Positive Feedback:	**100%**					Location: United States
		➕ positive	0	16	21	▪ ID History
Members who left a positive:	50					▪ Items for Sale
Members who left a negative:	0	⊙ neutral	0	0	0	
All positive feedback received:	56	➖ negative	0	0	0	
Learn about what these numbers mean.		Bid Retractions (Past 6 months): 0				Contact Member

All Feedback Received | From Buyers | From Sellers | Left for Others

56 feedback received by nuggett12   page 1 of 3

Comment	From	Date / Time	Item #
➕ Super transaction! Lightning FAST payment! Thanks! Come back again soon :)	Seller fussypants (fpdotcomm@aol.com) (1382 ★)	Jan-06-04 18:25	2976322019
➕ FAST PAYMENT!! GREAT EBAY'R!! THANKS!!	Seller cheribook (cheriberri5@aol.com) (645 ★)	Dec-11-03 10:35	2207627646
➕ Very prompt and courteous buyer, great to deal with, Thanks!	Seller network482 (sales@shopoem.com) (11742 ⭐)	Nov-28-03 01:04	3057703028
➕ Very prompt and courteous buyer, great to deal with, Thanks!	Seller network482 (sales@shopoem.com) (11742 ⭐)	Nov-28-03 01:04	3058162337
➕ very good transaction	Seller hoefken@earthlink.net (hoefken@earthlink.net) (35 ⭐) no longer a registered user	Nov-27-03 11:48	3061637655
➕ FAST PAY!!! EXCELLENT!!! PLEASURE TO DO BUSINESS WITH! AAAA+++++	Seller rafaelos (lancergroup@yahoo.com) (3907 ★)	Nov-25-03 08:22	2966729737
➕ Very prompt and courteous buyer, great to deal with, Thanks!	Seller network482 (sales@shopoem.com) (11742 ⭐)	Nov-14-03 08:38	3058162328
➕ Very prompt and courteous buyer, great to deal with, Thanks!	Seller network482 (sales@shopoem.com) (11742 ⭐)	Nov-14-03 08:38	3057561133
➕ a+	Seller mountainairvideo (firebaseutah@aol.com) (1817 ★) 🔧	Nov-10-03 11:12	243650630174
➕ Quick payment, and easy to deal with. Fine buyer!	Seller dumbells101 (91 ★)	Oct-27-03 06:29	2863059214
➕ A very easy and fast transaction. Couldn't ask for a better buyer.	Seller cornshedprofits (1459 ★)	Oct-05-03 03:05	243633243888
➕ Fast payment enjoed working with you.....	Seller mmddaa@msn.com (82 ★)	Sep-21-03 20:35	3627701979
➕ Smooth transaction!	Seller phoenix_trading_co (23518 ⭐)	Sep-02-03 13:47	3044087884
➕ Smooth transaction!	Seller phoenix_trading_co (23518 ⭐)	Sep-02-03 13:42	3044088621
➕ Great seller! Delivered promptly! Smooth transaction.	Buyer bama-tarheels (3)	Aug-25-03 11:44	2188695578
⊙ Prompt payment and good communication	Seller rjpedigo (35 ⭐)	Aug-17-03 14:53	3040479706
➕ I highly recommend this seller.	Buyer jessievanderhoff (6)	Jul-21-03 11:48	3033456370
➕ Customer is A+! We appreciate your business and fast payment!	Seller restaurant.com (100851 ⭐)	Apr-14-03 13:14	2922961668
➕ Customer is A+! We appreciate your business and fast payment!	Seller restaurant.com (100851 ⭐)	Apr-14-03 13:14	2922958665
➕ Worthwhile in every way. A+	Seller genuine_oem (29204 ⭐)	Feb-10-03 21:41	1949802659
➕ EXCELLENT eBayer, GREAT customer service, DEFFINATELY do bus. with again! AAAA++	Buyer brendon800 (81 ★)	Feb-09-03 18:01	2156921953
➕ Very understanding. I Would have great confidence buying from this seller.	Buyer longinternational (142 ⭐)	Feb-01-03 18:44	2156940759
➕ Item as described & functioning. Shipping excellent. Will do business again!	Buyer brkidsman (11 ⭐)	Dec-10-02 07:25	1789511721
⊙ AN EXAMPLE OF A GOOD EBAYER _ HIGHLY RECOMMENDED _ AAAAAAA++++++	Seller shilito34 (1338 ★)	Oct-03-02 15:12	1772433194
➕ Super quick payment and very patient. My apologies for being late...	Seller dane_mel (107 ⭐)	Sep-13-02 09:00	243518255865

Source: www.ebay.com, February 4, 2004.

The terms of eBay's user agreement prohibited actions that would undermine the integrity of the Feedback Forum, such as leaving positive feedback about oneself through other accounts or leaving multiple negative comments about someone else through other accounts. The Feedback Forum had several automated features designed to detect and prevent some forms of abuse. For example, feedback posted from the same account, positive or negative, could not affect a user's net feedback rating by more than one point, no matter how many comments an individual made. Furthermore, a user could make comments only about his or her trading partners in completed transactions. Prior to 2004, once a feedback comment was made, it could not be altered. However, as of February 9, 2004, the system was changed in response to suggestions by community members to all users to mutually withdraw feedback about each other. Withdrawn feedback would no longer impact a user's feedback rating.

The company believed its Feedback Forum was extremely useful in overcoming users' initial hesitancy about trading over the Internet, since it reduced the uncertainty of dealing with an unknown trading partner. However, there was growing concern among sellers and bidders that feedback might be positively skewed, as many eBayers chose not to leave negative feedback for fear of unfounded retribution that could damage their carefully built reputations.

eBay's Strategy to Sustain Its Market Dominance

Meg Whitman assumed the helm of eBay in February 1998 and began acting as the public face of the company. In an effort to stay in touch with her customers, Whitman hosted an auction on eBay herself. She found the experience so enlightening that she required all of eBay's managers to sell on eBay. Pierre Omidyar stepped back to become chairman of eBay's board of directors and focused his time and energy on overseeing eBay's strategic direction and growth, business model and site development, and community advocacy. Jeff Skoll, who became the vice president of strategic planning and analysis, concentrated on competitive analysis, new business planning and incubation, the development of the organization's overall strategic direction, and supervision of customer support operations.

The Move to Go Public

eBay's initial public offering (IPO) took place on September 24, 1998, with a starting price of $18 per share. The IPO exceeded that price and closed the day up 160 percent at $47. The IPO generated $66 million in new capital for the company and was recognized by several investing publications. The success of the September 1998 offering led eBay to issue a follow-up offering in April 1999 that raised an additional $600 million. As a qualification to the IPOs, eBay's board of directors retained the right to issue as many as 5 million additional shares of preferred stock with no further input from the current shareholders in case of a hostile takeover attempt.

eBay's Business Model

According to eBay's Meg Whitman, the company could best be described as a dynamic, self-regulating economy. Its business model was based on creating and maintaining a person-to-person trading community in which buyers and sellers could readily and conveniently exchange information and goods. The company's role was to function as a value-added facilitator of online buyer–seller transactions by providing a supportive infrastructure that enabled buyers and sellers to come together in an efficient and effective manner. Success depended not only on the quality of eBay's infrastructure but also on the quality and quantity of buyers and sellers attracted to the site; in management's view, this entailed maintaining a compelling trading environment, a number of trust and safety programs, a cost-effective and convenient trading experience, and strong community affinity.

EXHIBIT 6   **Share of eBay Transaction Revenue Growth, 2001–2008**

	2001(a)	2002(a)	2003(e)	2004(e)	2005(e)	2006(e)	2007(e)	2008(e)
U.S.	62.8%	48.0%	31.7%	39.1%	31.7%	32.5%	32.5%	32.7%
International	32.6	36.9	34.6	35.9	41.6	42.0	38.7	38.7
Payments	4.7	15.1	33.8	25.0	26.7	25.5	28.8	28.6
	100.0%	100.0%	100.0%	100.0%	100.0%	100.0%	100.0%	100.0%

By developing the eBay brand name and increasing the customer base, eBay endeavored to attract a sufficient number of high-quality buyers and sellers necessary to meet the organization's goals. The online auction format meant that eBay carried zero inventory and could operate a marketplace without the need for a traditional sales force.

eBay's business model was built around three profit centers: the domestic business (auction operations within the United States), international business (auction operations outside of the United States), and payments (e.g., PayPal). It was estimated that, in 2003, U.S. operations accounted for 31.7 percent of revenue growth, international's share was 34.6 percent, and the remaining 33.8 percent was from payments (see Exhibit 6).

Specific elements of eBay's business model that the company particularly recognized as key to its success included:[6]

1. The fact that it was the largest online trading forum, with a critical mass of buyers, sellers, and items listed for sale.

2. Its compelling and entertaining trading environment, which had strong values, established rules, and procedures that facilitated communication and trade between buyers and sellers.

3. Established trust and safety programs such as SafeHarbor. This program provided guidelines for trading, aided in resolving disputes, and warned and suspended (both temporarily and permanently) users who violated eBay's rules.

4. Cost-effective, convenient trading.

5. Strong community affinity.

6. An intuitive user interface that was easy to understand, arranged by topics, and fully automated.

In implementing its business model, eBay employed three main competitive tactics. First, it sought to build strategic partnerships in all stages of its value chain, creating an impressive portfolio of over 250 strategic alliances with companies such as America Online (AOL), Yahoo, IBM, Compaq, and Walt Disney. Second, it actively sought customer feedback and made improvements on the basis of this information. Third, it actively monitored both its external and internal environments for developing opportunities. One way eBay executives kept in touch with internal trends was by hosting online town hall meetings and by visiting cities with large local markets. The feedback gained from these meetings was used to adopt and adjust practices to keep customers satisfied.

eBay's Strategy

eBay's strategy to sustain growth rested on five key elements:[7]

1. *Broaden the existing trading platform* within existing product categories, across new product categories, through geographic expansion, both domestic and international, and through introduction of additional pricing formats such as fixed price sales.

---

[6]Company 10K filing with the Securities and Exchange Commission, March 3, 2001, pp. 4–6.
[7]eBay company 10K, filed March 28, 2001.

2. *Foster eBay community affinity* by instilling a vibrant, loyal eBay community experience, seeking to maintain a critical mass of frequent buyers and sellers with a vested interest in the eBay community.

3. *Enhance features and functionality* by continually updating and enhancing the features and functionality of the eBay and Half.com Web sites to ensure continuous improvement in the trading experience.

4. *Expand value-added services* to include end-to-end personal trading service by offering a variety of pre- and post-trade services to enhance the user experience and make trading easier.

5. *Continue to develop U.S. and international markets* that employ the Internet to create an efficient trading platform in local, national, and international markets that can be transformed into a seamless, truly global trading platform.

Broadening the Existing Trading Platform

Efforts intended to broaden the eBay trading platform concentrated on growing the content within current categories, broadening the range of products offered according to user preferences, and developing regionally targeted offerings. Growth in existing product categories was facilitated by deepening the content within the categories through the use of content-specific chat rooms and bulletin boards as well as targeted advertising at trade shows and in industry-specific publications.

To broaden the range of products offered, eBay developed new product categories, introduced specialty sites, and developed eBay stores. Over 2,000 new categories were added between 1998 and 2000, and by 2003 eBay offered over 27,000 categories of items (greatly expanded from the original 10 categories in 1995). Ten of these categories had gross merchandise sales of over $1 billion, including eBay Motors ($7.5 billion), Consumer Electronics ($2.6 billion), Computers ($2.4 billion), Books/Movies/Music ($2.0 billion), Clothing and Accessories ($1.8 billion), Sports ($1.8 billion), Collectibles ($1.5 billion), Toys ($1.5 billion), Home and Garden ($1.3 billion), and Jewelry and Gemstones ($1.3 billion).

Significant new product categories and specialty sites developed since eBay's early days included:

- *eBay Motors,* which began as a category and was developed when eBay noticed that an increasing number of automobile transactions were taking place on its site. In 2002, eBay Motors sold more than $3 billion worth of vehicles and parts and was the largest online marketplace for buying and selling autos as of mid-2003. According to Meg Whitman, "One month, we saw the miscellaneous category had a very rapid growth rate, and someone said we have to find out what's going on. It was the buying and selling of used cars. So we said, maybe what we should do is give these guys a separate category and see what happens. It worked so well that we created eBay Motors."[8] In partnership with AutoTrader.com this category was later expanded to a specialty site.

- *The LiveAuctions specialty site,* which allowed live bidding via the Internet for auctions occurring in brick-and-mortar auction houses around the world. Through an alliance with Icollector.com, eBay users had access to more than 300 auction houses worldwide. Auction houses that participated in this agreement were well rewarded, as more than 20 percent of their sales went to online bidders. One auction broadcast on the LiveAuctions site, held in February 2001, featured items from a rare Marilyn Monroe collection including a handwritten note from Monroe that listed her reasons for divorcing her first husband.

[8]"Q&A with eBay's Meg Whitman," *BusinessWeek E.Biz,* December 3, 2001.

- *The eBay Business marketplace,* launched in 2002, which allowed business-related items to be sold in one location. Items such as office technology, wholesale lots, and marketplace services were offered at this destination. By the end of 2002, over 500,000 items were listed in eBay Business each week and more than $1 billion in annualized gross merchandise sales occurred across these categories.
- *eBay's Real Estate category,* launched to foster eBay's emerging real estate marketplace. The offerings within this category were significantly enhanced by eBay's August 2001 acquisition of Homesdirect, which specialized in the sale of foreclosed properties owned by government agencies such as Housing and Urban Development and the Department of Veterans Affairs (formerly known as the Veterans Administration). The company estimated that a parcel of land was sold through the Real Estate category every 45 minutes during 2002.

Other notable moves to broaden the platform included the following:

- The Application Program Interface (API) and Developers Program was launched to allow other companies to use eBay's commerce engine and technology to build new sites.
- Starting in 1999, eBay launched over 60 regional sites to offer a more local flavor to eBay's offerings. These regional sites focused on the 50 largest metropolitan areas in the United States. Regional auction sites were intended to encourage the sale of items that were prohibitively expensive to ship, items that tended to have only a local appeal, and items that people preferred to view before purchasing. To supplement the regional sites, in mid-2001 eBay began offering sellers the option of having their items listed in a special seller's area in the classified sections of local newspapers. Sellers could highlight specific items, their eBay store, or their user ID in these classifieds.
- In June 2001 eBay introduced eBay stores to complement new offerings, to make it easier for sellers to build loyalty and for buyers to locate goods from specific sellers and to prevent sellers from driving bidders to the seller's own Web site. In an eBay store the entirety of a seller's auctions would be listed in one convenient location. These stores could also offer a fixed-price option from a seller and the integration of a seller's Half.com listings with their auction listings. While numerous sellers of all sizes moved to take advantage of eBay stores, the concept was especially appealing to large retailers such as IBM, Hard Rock Café, Sears, and Handspring that were moving to take advantage of eBay's reach and distribution power.
- In May 2002 eBay reached an agreement with Accenture to develop a service intended to allow large sellers to more efficiently sell their products. These sellers were able to use a wide range of tools, such as high-volume listing capabilities, expanded customer service and support, and payment and fulfillment processes.
- A fixed-price format was established through the acquisition of Half.com and allowed eBay to compete more directly with online sellers such as Amazon.com. Half.com was a fixed-price, person-to-person format that enabled buyers and sellers to trade books, CDs, movies and video games at prices starting at generally half of the retail price. Like eBay, Half.com offered a feedback system that helped buyers and sellers to build a solid reputation. eBay intended to eventually fully integrate both Half.com's listings and the feedback system into eBay's current site.

Fostering eBay Community Affinity

From its founding, eBay considered developing a loyal, vivacious trading community to be a cornerstone of its business model. This community was nurtured through open and honest communication and was built on five basic values that eBay expected its members to honor:

> We believe people are basically good.
>
> We believe everyone has something to contribute.

We believe that an honest, open environment can bring out the best in people.

We recognize and respect everyone as a unique individual.

We encourage you to treat others the way that you want to be treated.[9]

The company recognized that these values could not be imposed by fiat. According to Omidyar,

> As much as we at eBay talk about the values and encourage people to live by those values, that's not going to work unless people actually adopt those values. The values are communicated not because somebody reads the Web site and says, "Hey, this is how we want to treat each other, so I'll just start treating people that way." The values are communicated because that's how they're treated when they first arrive. Each member is passing those values on to the next member. It's little things, like you receive a note that says, "Thanks for your business."[10]

Consistent with eBay's desire to stay in touch with its customers and be responsive to their needs, the company flew in 10 new sellers every few months to hold group meetings known as Voice of the Customer. The company noted that 75–80 percent of new features were originally suggested by community members.

An example of eBay values in action took place when eBay introduced a feature that referred losing bidders to similar auctions from other eBay sellers, eliciting a strong outcry from the community. Sellers demanded to know why eBay was stealing their sales, and one longtime seller went so far as to auction a rare eBay jacket so that he could use the auction as a forum to complain about "eBay's new policy of screwing the folks who built them."[11] This caught the attention of Omidyar and Whitman, who met with the seller in his home for 45 minutes. After the meeting eBay changed its policy.

Recognizing that many new users might not get the most out of their eBay experience, and hoping to introduce new entrepreneurs to the community, the company created eBay University in August 2000. The university traveled across the country to hold two-day seminars in various cities. These seminars attracted between 400 and 500 people, who each paid $25 for the experience. Courses offered ranged from freshmen-level classes that introduced buying and selling on eBay to graduate-level classes that taught the intricacies of bulk listing and competitive tactics. eBay University was so successful that the company partnered with Evoke Communications to offer an online version of the classes. While community members gained knowledge from these classes, so did eBay. The company kept careful track of questions and concerns and used them to uncover areas that needed improvement.

A second important initiative to make the eBay community more inclusive was aimed at the fastest-growing segment of the U.S. population, adults 50 and older. In an effort to bridge the digital divide for seniors, eBay launched the Digital Opportunity Program for Seniors and set a goal of training and bringing online 1 million seniors by 2005. Specific elements of this plan included partnering with SeniorNet, the leading nonprofit computer technology trainer of seniors, and donating $1 million to this organization for training and establishing 10 new training facilities by 2005, developing a volunteer program for training seniors, and creating a specific area on eBay for Senior Citizens (www.ebay.com/seniors).

To foster a sense of community among eBay users, the company employed tools and tactics designed to promote both business and personal interactions between consumers, to foster trust between bidders and sellers, and to instill a sense of security among traders. Interactions between community members were facilitated through the creation of chat rooms based on personal interests. These chat rooms allowed individuals to learn about their chosen collectibles and to exchange information about items they collected.

---

[9]http://pages.ebay.com/help/community/values.html, January 1, 2002.

[10]"Q&A with eBay's Meg Whitman."

[11]Ibid.

To manage the flow of information in the chat rooms, eBay employees went to trade shows and conventions to seek out individuals who had knowledge about and a passion for either a specific collectible or a category of goods. These enthusiasts would act as community leaders or ambassadors; they were never referred to as employees but were compensated $1,000 a month to host online discussions with experts.

Although personal communication between members fostered a sense of community, as eBay's community grew from "the size of a small village to a large city" additional measures were necessary to ensure a continued sense of trust and honesty among users.[12] One of eBay's earliest trust-building efforts was the 1996 creation of the Feedback Forum, described earlier.

Unfortunately, the Feedback Forum was not always sufficient to ensure honesty and integrity among traders. eBay estimated that far less than 1 percent of the millions of auctions completed on the site involved some sort of fraud or illegal activity, but some users, like Clay Monroe, disagreed. Monroe, a Seattle-area trader of computer equipment, estimated that "ninety percent of the time everybody is on the up and up . . . [but] . . . ten percent of the time you get some jerk who wants to cheat you." Fraudulent or illegal acts perpetrated by sellers included misrepresentation of goods; trading in counterfeit goods or pirated goods that infringed on others' intellectual property rights; failure to deliver goods paid for by buyers; and shill bidding, whereby sellers would use a false bidder to artificially drive up the price of a good. Buyers could manipulate bids by placing an unrealistically high bid on a good to discourage other bidders and then withdraw their bid at the last moment to allow an ally to win the auction at a bargain price. Buyers could also fail to deliver payment on a completed auction.

Recognizing that fraudulent activities represented a significant danger to eBay's future, management took the Feedback Forum a step further in 1998 by launching the SafeHarbor program to provide guidelines for trade, provide information to help resolve user disputes, and respond to reports of misuse of the eBay service. The SafeHarbor initiative was expanded in 1999 to provide additional safeguards and to actively work with law enforcement agencies and members of the trading community to make eBay more secure. New elements of SafeHarbor included:

- Free insurance, with a $25 deductible for transactions under $200 and further protection for buyers and sellers who used PayPal.
- Cooperation with local law enforcement agencies to identify and prosecute fraudulent buyers and sellers.
- Enhancements to the Feedback Forum such as listing whether the user was a buyer or a seller in a transaction.
- A partnership with SquareTrade, an online dispute resolution service.
- A partnership with Escrow.com to promote the use of escrow services on purchases over $500.
- A new class of verified eBay users with an accompanying icon.
- Easy access to escrow services.
- Tougher policies relating to nonpaying bidders and shill bidders.
- Clarification of which items were not permissible to list for sale (such as items associated with Nazi Germany, the Ku Klux Klan, or other groups that glorified hate, racial intolerance, or racial violence).
- A strengthened antipiracy and anti-infringement program known as the Verified Rights Owner program (VeRO), and the introduction of dispute resolution services.

---

[12]Tristram, "'Amazoning' Amazon."

The use of verified buyer and seller accounts was viewed as especially significant because it allowed eBay to ensure that suspended users did not open new eBay accounts under different names. User information was verified through Atlanta-based Equifax, Inc. To further ensure that suspended users didn't register new accounts with different identities, eBay partnered with Infoglide to use a similarity search technology to examine new registrant information.

To implement these new initiatives, eBay increased the number of positions in its Safe-Harbor department from 24 to 182, including full-time employees and independent contractors. It also organized the department around the functions of investigations, community watch, and fraud prevention. The investigations group was responsible for examining reported trading violations and possible misuses of eBay. The fraud prevention group mediated customer disputes over such things as the quality of the goods sold. If a written complaint of fraud was filed against a user, eBay generally suspended the alleged offender's account, pending an investigation. Despite all of these initiatives, innovative thieves were developing new ways to cheat honest bidders and sellers as quickly as eBay could identify and ban them from the system, and many eBayers still viewed this as one of the most significant threats to the eBay community.

The community watch group worked with over 100 industry-leading companies, ranging from software publishers to toy manufactures to apparel makers, to protect intellectual property rights. To ensure that illegal items were not being sold and sale items listed did not violate intellectual property rights, this SafeHarbor group automated daily keyword searches on auction content. Offending auctions were closed and the seller was notified of the violation. Repeated violations resulted in suspension of the seller's account.

As eBay expanded its categories to include Great Collections and the new automobile categories, new safeguards were introduced to meet the unique needs of these areas. In the eBay Great Collections category, the company partnered with Collector's Universe to offer authentication and grading services for specific products such as trading cards, coins, and autographs. In the automobile area, one of eBay's fastest-growing segments, eBay partnered with Saturn to provide users with access to a nationwide automobile brand and offered a free limited one-month or 1,000-mile warranty, free purchase insurance up to $20,000 with a $500 deductible, and a special escrow service (Secure Pay) designed for the needs of automotive buyers and sellers.

Expanding Value-Added Services

Since its earliest days, eBay had realized that to be successful, its service had to be both easy to use and convenient to access. Recognizing this, the company continuously sought to add services to fill these needs by offering a variety of pre- and post-trade services to enhance the user experience and provide an end-to-end trading experience.

Early efforts in this direction included alliances with:

- Leading shipping services (USPS and UPS).
- Two companies that helped guarantee that buyers would get what they paid for (Tradesafe and I-Escrow).
- The world's largest franchiser of retail business, communications, and postal service centers (Mailboxes, Etc.).
- The leader in multicarrier Web-based shipping services for e-commerce (iShip.com).

To facilitate person-to-person credit card payments, eBay acquired PayPal, a company that specialized in transferring money from one cardholder to another, in October 2002. Using the newly acquired capabilities of PayPal, eBay was able to offer sellers the option of accepting credit card payments from other eBay users. At the end of 2002, PayPal was available to users in 38 countries, including the United States. eBay's objective was to make credit card payment a "seamless and integrated part of the trading experience."[13] The company expected that net revenues from the payments segment of PayPal would be approximately $300 to $310 million in 2003.

Developing U.S. and International Markets

As competition increased in the online auction industry, eBay began to seek growth opportunities in international markets in an effort to create a global trading community. While international buyers and sellers had been trading on eBay for some time, there were no facilities designed especially for the needs of these community members. In entering international markets, eBay considered three options: it could build a new user community from the ground up, acquire a local organization, or form a partnership with a strong local company. In realizing its goals of international growth, eBay employed all three strategies.

In late 1998, eBay's initial efforts at international expansion into Canada and the United Kingdom relied on building new user communities. The first step in establishing these communities was creating customized home pages for users in those countries. These home pages were designed to provide content and categories locally customized to the needs of users in specific countries, while providing them with access to a global trading community. Local customization in the United Kingdom was facilitated through the use of local management, grassroots and online marketing, and participation in local events.[14] In February 1999 eBay partnered with PBL Online, a leading Internet company in Australia, to offer a customized Australian and New Zealand eBay home page. When the site went live in October 1999, transactions were denominated in Australian dollars and, while buyers could bid on auctions anywhere in the world, they could also search for items located exclusively in Australia. Further, local chat boards were designed to facilitate interaction between Australian users, and country-specific categories, such as Australian coins and stamps as well as cricket and rugby memorabilia, were offered.

To further expand its global reach, eBay acquired Germany's largest online person-to-person trading site, Alando.de AG, in June 1999. eBay's management handled the transition of service in a manner calculated to be smooth and painless for Alando.de AG's users. While users would have to comply with eBay rules and regulations, the only significant change for Alando.de AG's 50,000 registered users was that they would have to go to a new URL to transact their business.

To establish an Asian presence, in February 2000 eBay formed a joint venture with NEC to launch eBay Japan. According to the new CEO of eBay Japan, Merle Okawara, an internationally renowned executive, NEC was pleased to help eBay in leveraging the tried-and-trusted eBay business model to provide Japanese consumers with access to a global community of active online buyers and sellers. In customizing the site to the needs of Japanese users, eBay wrote the content exclusively in Japanese and allowed users to bid in yen. The site had over 800 categories ranging from internationally popular categories (such as computers, electronics, and Asian antiques) to categories with a local flavor (such as Hello Kitty, Pokémon, and pottery). The eBay Japan site also debuted a new merchant-to-person concept known as Supershops, which allowed consumers to bid on items listed by companies.

In 2001, eBay expanded into South Korea through an acquisition of a majority ownership position in the country's largest online trading service, Internet Auction Co. Ltd., and into Belgium, Brazil, Italy, France, the Netherlands, Portugal, Spain, and Sweden through the acquisition of Europe's largest online trading platform, iBazar. Further expansion in 2001 included the development of a local site in Singapore, and an equity-based alliance

---

[13]eBay press release, May 18, 1999.
[14]eBay 10K, filed March 30, 2000.

with the leading online auction site for the Spanish and Portuguese-speaking communities in Latin America, MercadoLibre.com, that would give eBay access to Argentina, Chile, Colombia, Ecuador, Mexico, Uruguay, and Venezuela.

At the end of 2003 eBay had a presence in 28 countries, including Australia, Austria, Belgium, Canada, China (through an investment in the Chinese company Eachnet), France, Germany, Ireland, Italy, the Netherlands, New Zealand, Singapore, South Korea, Spain, Sweden, Switzerland, Taiwan, Great Britain, and Latin America (through an investment in MercadoLibre.com) and held the top online auction position in every country except Taiwan, where it was a close number two to Yahoo. eBay perceived this rapid international expansion as one of the keys to attaining its goal of having $3 billion in annual revenues by 2005. Growth opportunities were especially appealing in Asia (due to rapid increases in Internet access) and Europe. The company's international business grew by 165 percent in 2002, and its largest international markets were Germany (where 75 percent of eBay users were classified as active users), the United Kingdom, and South Korea. At the end of 2002, the company said:

> [We are] going to invest heavily in international expansion, to tap the huge potential that appears to be the hallmark of Germany, the UK, and Korea and so many of the other markets that we've entered. And we're going to do all of this with the same financial discipline we have always shown by staying true to our strategy of balancing returns with appropriate investment to capitalize on the company's long-term opportunities.[15]

How eBay's Auction Site Compared with Those of Rivals

Auction sites varied in a number of respects: their inventory, the bidding process, extra services and fees, technical support, functionality, and sense of community. Since its inception eBay had gone to great lengths to make its Web site intuitive, easy to use by both buyers and sellers, and reliable. Efforts to ensure ease of use ranged from narrowly defining categories (to allow users to quickly locate desired products) to introducing services designed to personalize a user's eBay experience. Two specific services developed by eBay and launched in 1998 to increase personalization were My eBay and About Me. My eBay gave users centralized access to confidential, current information regarding their trading activities. From his or her My eBay page a user could view information pertaining to his or her current account balances with eBay; feedback rating; the status of any auctions in which he or she was participating, as either a buyer or a seller; and auctions in favorite categories. In October, eBay introduced the About Me service, which allowed users to create customized home pages that could be viewed by all other eBay members and could include elements from the My eBay page such as user ratings or items the user had listed for auction, as well as personal information and pictures. This service not only increased customer ease of use but also contributed to the sense of community among the traders; one seller stated that the About Me service "made it easier and more rewarding for me to do business with others."[16] New features and services added in 2000 included new listing functions that could make an auction stand out, including Highlight and Feature Plus, as well as a feature that allowed sellers to cross-list their products in two categories, a tool to set prequalification guidelines for bidders, a new imaging and photo hosting service that made it easier for sellers to include pictures of their goods, and the introduction of the Buy It Now tool.

Throughout its history eBay had struggled to balance its explosive growth with its technological infrastructure. To counter several significant service outages the company had faced in its early days, eBay hired Maynard Webb, a premier software engineer and troubleshooter who was working at Gateway Computer. Webb took swift action, forming alliances with key vendors such as Sun, IBM, and Microsoft, and outsourcing its technology

---

[15]2002 eBay annual report.

[16]Ann Pearson, in an eBay press release dated October 15, 1998.

EXHIBIT 7   **Performance Metrics for Online Auction Firms**

	Customer Experience Metrics				
	Reliability		Efficiency		Consistency
	Percent Error Rate	Average Transaction Length (seconds)	Minimum Transaction Length (seconds)	Maximum Transaction Length (seconds)	Variability of Transaction Length (seconds)
Amazon Auctions	0.52	5.68	3.39	47.1	3.6
BidVille	0.62	3.90	.05	71.1	3.77
eBay	3.97	13.20	7.34	97.5	6.01
ePier	1.02	7.29	4.7	83	5.99
uBid	11.76	5.95	3.05	185	8.39
Yahoo Auctions	2.38	10.94	2.97	112	4.37

Source: Benchmark Study of Online Auction Performance August–September 2003, www.empirix.com.

and Web site operations to Exodus Communications and Abovenet. These outsourcing agreements were intended to allow Exodus and Abovenet to "manage network capacity and provide a more robust backbone" while eBay focused on its core business.[17] While eBay still experienced minor outages when it changed or expanded services (for example, a system crash coincided with the introduction of the original 22 regional Web sites), system downtime decreased. However, the stability of the system under eBay's explosive growth and continuous introduction of new features was a continuing management concern.

In 2003 Empirix conducted a benchmark study of online auction site performance that measured key performance metrics for six leading auction sites. This study included three customer experience metrics: efficiency (how long transactions were in seconds), consistency (how much the transaction lengths varied), and reliability (how often transactions were completed successfully). Results indicated that Amazon.com had the best performance, BidVille had the shortest transaction length, and eBay's Web applications were slower and more error prone than rivals' (see Exhibit 7).

eBay's Main Competitors

eBay considered the ability to attract buyers, the volume of transactions and selection of goods, customer service, and brand recognition to be the most important competitive factors in the online auction industry. In addition to these principal factors, eBay was also attempting to compete along several other dimensions: sense of community, system reliability, reliability of delivery and payment, Web site convenience and accessibility, level of service fees, and quality of search tools.[18]

Early in eBay's history the company's main rivals could be considered classified advertisements in newspapers, garage sales, flea markets, collectibles shows, and other venues such as local auction houses and liquidators. As eBay's product mix and selling techniques evolved, the company's range of competitors did as well. The broadening of eBay's product mix beyond collectibles to include practical household items, office equipment, toys, and so on brought the company into more direct competition with brick-and-mortar retailers, import/export companies, and catalog and mail order companies. Further, with the acquisition of Half.com, the introduction of eBay stores, and the growing percentage of fixed-price and Buy It Now sales as a percentage of eBay's revenue, eBay considered itself to be competing in a broad sense with a number of other online retailers, such as Wal-Mart, Kmart, Target, Sears, JCPenney, and Office Depot. In competing with these larger sellers, eBay began to adopt some of their tools, such as the use of gift certificates. The company also felt that it was competing with a number of specialty retailers, such as Christie's (antiques), KB Toys (toys),

[17]eBay press release, October 8, 1999.
[18]Ibid.

EXHIBIT 8

Customer Service Rankings (Scores out of 100)

Sector/Company	1999	2000	2001	2002
E-commerce				
E-commerce retail	NA	78	77	83
Yahoo, Inc.	74	73	76	78
Amazon.com, Inc.	NA	84	84	88
Online Auctions Overall	NA	72	74	77
eBay	NA	80	82	82
uBid, Inc.	NA	67	69	70
Portals/search engines				
Yahoo, Inc.	74	73	76	78
Google, Inc.	NA	NA	80	82
Retail				
Overall retail	73.3	72.9	74.8	74.6
Target	74	73	77	78
Sears	71	73	76	75
Wal-Mart	72	73	75	74

Source: American Customer Satisfaction Index, www.theacsi.org.

Blockbuster (movies), Dell (computers), Foot Locker (sporting goods), Ticketmaster (tickets), and Home Depot (tools).[19] In 2003 eBay begin experiencing competition from new sources, including portals (such as Yahoo) and search providers (such as Google and Overture) that sought to become primary launch pads for online shopping. Exhibit 8 displays eBay's customer service rankings as compared to a variety of rivals' customer service rankings.

eBay management saw traditional competitors as inefficient because their fragmented local and regional nature made it expensive and time-consuming for buyers and sellers to meet, exchange information, and complete transactions. Moreover, the competitors suffered from three other deficiencies: (1) They tended to offer limited variety and breadth of selection as compared to the millions of items available on eBay, (2) they often had high transaction costs, and (3) they were information inefficient in the sense that buyers and sellers lacked a reliable and convenient means of setting prices for sales or purchases. By the same token, eBay's management saw its online auction format as competitively superior to these rivals because (1) it facilitated buyers and sellers meeting, exchanging information, and conducting transactions; (2) it allowed buyers and sellers to bypass traditional intermediaries and trade directly, thus lowering costs; (3) it provided global reach to greater selection and a broader base of participants; (4) it permitted trading at all hours and provided continuously updated information; and (5) it fostered a sense of community among individuals with mutual interests.

Even with the strengthening competition, analysts estimated that eBay controlled approximately 85 percent of the consumer-to-consumer online auction market and 64 percent of total online auction revenue share. The most significant competitors to eBay's auction business included Amazon Auctions, Yahoo Auctions, and uBid. Two of the smaller competitors in the online auction industry included BidVille (an auction site with no listing fees and no final value fees) and ePier (60,000 members as of January, 2004). Both of these had closely copied eBay's look and fee structure and touted themselves as "alternatives to eBay."

Amazon.com Auctions

Amazon.com's business strategy was to "be the world's most customer-centric company where customers can find and discover anything they may want to buy online."[20] With its customer base of 35 million users in over 150 countries and a very well-known brand name, Amazon.com

---

[19]eBay 10Q annual report, November 14, 2001.

[20]2000 Amazon annual report.

EXHIBIT 9
Operating Results

Year	Income or (Loss) from Operations (in millions)
1996	$(6.2)
1997	(31.0)
1998	(124.5)
1999	(720.0)
2000	(863.9)
2001	(412.3)
2002	64.1
2003	400.0 (est)

was considered the closest overall competitive threat to eBay, especially as eBay expanded its business model beyond its traditional auction services. Analysts estimated that Amazon.com had a 5–7 percent share of all online retail sales, but Hitwise, an Internet competitive intelligence service, found that for the week ending September 20, 2003, eBay had a 93.6 percent share of all Web traffic to auction sites while Amazon.com had only a 1.1 percent share.

Amazon was created in July 1995 as an online bookseller and had rapidly transitioned into a full-line, one-stop-shopping retailer with a product offering that included books, music, toys, electronics, tools and hardware, lawn and patio products, video games, software, and a mall of boutiques (called z-shops). Amazon.com was the Internet's number one music, video, and book retailer. One of the distinctive features customers appreciated about Amazon.com was the extensive reviews available for each item. These product reviews were written both by professionals and by regular users who had purchased a specific product. The company's 2003 net sales were estimated between $6.2 and $6.7 billion, up almost 58.9 percent from 2002. In 2002 Amazon.com generated its first profit from operations—$64.1 million—and in 2003 operating profits increased substantially from 2002 (as seen in Exhibit 9). One significant weakness analysts noted in Amazon's financials was that the company's free shipping policies, put in place to draw more customers, had a significant, negative impact on net income.

By 2003 Amazon's management felt that it was time to strike a better balance between cost control and growth in executing a strategy intended to enhance Amazon's position as leader in retail e-commerce. An indication of the company's success was the rise in Amazon's customer base from 14 million to 20 million during 2000 and to 35 million by 2003. The company invested more than $300 million in infrastructure in 1999 and opened two international sites, www.amazon.co.uk (the United Kingdom) and www.amazon.de (Germany), and later added www.amazon.ca (Canada), www. amazon.co.jp (Japan) and www.amazon.fr (France). These sites, along with Amazon.com, were among the most popular online retail domains in Europe. By 2004 international sales had grown to over $2 billion from just $168 million in 1999 and accounted for 38 percent of all Internet sales.

Some analysts felt that in expanding its position both internationally and abroad Amazon had conceded the top spot in online auction to eBay and was looking to explore other avenues. Amazon often used strategic alliances to support its innovative expansion initiatives. For example, the company had agreements with Borders Books to allow customers to pick up Amazon.com book orders in-store, as well as e-commerce partnerships with Ashford.com, Drugstore.com, CarsDirect.com, and Sotheby's (a leading auction house for art, antiques, and collectibles), and opened a co-branded toy and video game store online with Toysrus.com. During 2003, the company announced an agreement with the band Pearl Jam to sell the group's music directly to fans through Amazon's Advantage program. By 2003 Amazon.com had over 550,000 active third-party sellers on its site and 350 branded sellers, most of them selling through shops rather than auctions. These third-party sellers accounted for over 22 percent of U.S. sales. To further expand the company's reach, in September 2003 Amazon established an independent unit called A9 that was charged with creating the best shopping search tool for Amazon's use and for use by other companies and third-party Web sites. To compete with eBay's fixed-price formats, Amazon began including links on product pages that allowed customers to view identical new and used items from third-party sellers.

uBid.com

uBid's mission statement was to "be the most recognized and trusted business-to-consumer marketplace, consistently delivering exceptional value and service to its customers and supplier partners."[21] According to the company, "uBid delivers to the customer both the cost savings of an auction and the customer care of popular brand name retail e-commerce sites, making uBid a destination point for consumer share of wallet as they capitalize on the benefits of this high performance hybrid business model."[22] As such, uBid considered itself to be in direct competition with eBay, although a distant second, especially to that portion of eBay's business that was derived from large corporations and smaller companies wanting to sell their products through an auction format. The company's business model centered on offering brand-name merchandise, often refurbished and closeout, at a deep discount in a relatively broad range of categories from leading brand-name manufacturers such as Sony, Hewlett-Packard, IBM, Compaq, AMD, Minolta, and over 1,000 other suppliers. Categories included Computer and Office; Consumer Electronics; Music, Movies & Games; Jewelry & Gifts; Travel & Events; Home & Garden; Sports; Toys & Hobbies; Apparel; Collectibles; and Everything Else. The merchandise was offered in both an online auction format in which prices started at $1.00 and through uBid's fixed-price superstore. The merchandise was sourced from corporate partners and from uBid's own operations, which included a 400,000-square-foot warehouse and refurbishment center, and their current parent company Petters Group Worldwide, and from small and medium-sized companies who were members of uBid's Certified Merchant Program. Although uBid had offered consumer-to-consumer auctions at one time, the company had discontinued this option as of 2002 due to the costs associated with policing fraud and concerns over product quality.

Founded in April 1997, uBid offered an initial public offering on the Nasdaq in December 1998. The company had experienced significantly increased revenues every year since its inception through 2000, but it had never captured the share of the auction market that its founders hoped was possible, although it at one time had a 14.7 percent share of revenues in the online auction market. In mid-2000 uBid was sold to CGMI Networks, and then it was sold again to Petters Group Worldwide in 2003. With each sale the number of workers employed by uBid fell and the product mix was changed in an attempt to find a niche market that would insulate the company from the competitive power of eBay.

Yahoo Auctions

Yahoo.com, the first online navigational guide to the Web, launched Yahoo Auctions in 1998. Yahoo.com offered services to nearly 200 million users every month in North America, Europe, Asia, and Latin America. The Web site was available in 24 countries and 12 languages. Yahoo reported net revenues of $1.11 billion in 2000 (up 88 percent from 1999) and net income of $290 million. Yahoo's user base grew from 120 million to over 180 million during 2000. In December 2000 Yahoo's traffic increased to an average of 900 million page views per day (up 94 percent from 1999). Yahoo had entered into numerous alliances and marketing agreements to generate additional traffic at its site and was investing in new technology to improve the site's performance and attractiveness.

Its auction services were provided to users free of charge in the early days, and the number of auctions listed on Yahoo increased from 670,000 to 1.3 million during the second

---

[21]www.ubid.com/about/companyinfo.asp.
[22]Ibid.

half of 1999. However, when Yahoo decided to start charging users a listing fee in January 2001, listings fell from over 2 million to about 200,000.[23] Yahoo Auctions also offered many extra services to its users. For example, the Premium Sellers Program was designed to reward the sellers that were consistently at the top of their category. These Premium Sellers were allowed enhanced promotions, premium placement, and direct access to customer support. In recognition of the fall in listings due to the listing fee instituted in January, Yahoo Auctions announced a revamped performance-based pricing model for its U.S. auctions in November 2001. In this system, which was relatively similar to eBay's, listing fees were reduced and sellers were charged according to the value of an item sold. In response to this change the number of listings rose to more than 500,000 by December 7, 2001.

While Yahoo had significant reach throughout the world, including over 25 local auction sites internationally, by 2004 Yahoo Auctions had reduced its international operations from 16 countries to 7 (Brazil, Canada, Hong Kong, Japan, Mexico, Singapore, and Taiwan). In 2002 alone Yahoo conceded its auction sites in France, Germany, Italy, Spain, and the United Kingdom and Ireland and promoted eBay's sites in each of those countries via banner ads and text links. In 2003 Yahoo sold its Australian site as well. However, in 2004 Yahoo began offering auctions in China through a joint venture with a dominant Chinese Web portal, Sina, indicating that it had not completely abandoned the international auction market. Further reinforcing Yahoo's commitment to online retail, in July 2003 Yahoo acquired Overture, which was the leading provider of commercial search as of the end of the first quarter of 2003 with more than 88,000 advertisers globally as well as an extensive affiliate distribution network. Many of the sellers who advertised on Overture also advertised on eBay, and some analysts estimated that the amount of sales by merchants through the combination of Yahoo's and Overture's offerings would total between one-half to two-thirds of that available on eBay.

eBay's New Challenges

Heading into 2004 eBay was the undisputed leader in the online auction industry. To reach this enviable position, eBay had to overcome a number of hurdles. Throughout its history, eBay faced each new challenge with an eye on its founding values and an ear for community members. Omidyar said, "What we do have to be cautious of, as we grow, is that our core is the personal trade, because the values are communicated person-to-person. It can be easy for a big company to start to believe that it's responsible for its success. Our success is really based on our members' success. They're the ones who have created this, and they're the ones who will create it in the future. If we lose sight of that, then we're in big trouble."[24] The company applied this perspective in response to significant customer concerns regarding the growing presence of corporate sellers on eBay.

Omidyar and Whitman recognized the importance of eBay's culture and were aware of the potential impact rapid growth and the evolution of the product line could have on this valued asset. When asked about the importance of the culture Omidyar said, "If we lose that, we've pretty much lost everything."[25] Whitman agreed with the importance of eBay's culture, but she did not see the influx of larger retailers and liquidators as a significant problem. Even as these sellers grew to account for 5 percent of eBay's total business in 2004 (from 1 percent in 2001), these large sellers received no favorable treatment. Whitman stated, "There are no special deals. I am passionate about creating this level playing field."[26]

[23]Troy Wolverton , "eBay Seeks to Sail into New Territory," CNET News.com, July 19, 2001.

[24]"Q&A with eBay's Pierre Omidyar," *BusinessWeek E.Biz*, December 3, 2001.

[25]"The People's Company," *BusinessWeek E.Biz*, December 3, 2001.

[26]"Queen of the Online Flea Market," Economist.com, December 30, 2003.

While smaller sellers applauded this view, some larger sellers viewed these policies as overly restrictive.

Heading into 2004, eBay faced two fundamental challenges:

1. How could eBay continue to grow at its current pace given the maturing of its domestic market?

2. As eBay's business model evolved to include more fixed-price sales, could it transfer its competitive advantage in the online auction industry into the more general area of online retail?

Continued Growth

By virtually any measure, eBay's growth had been outstanding. However, this impressive track record, coupled with the progress the company had made in reaching its stated goals, had created high expectations among investors. These lofty expectations began to cause some concern among analysts as eBay's domestic core market of online auction sales began to show some warning signals. For example, in 2003 the average conversion rate (the number of auctions that were completed successfully) was approximately 51 percent, a rate that had held steady over the last two years. However, supply imbalances threatened this key metric. In many categories, as the number of sellers grew, supply was beginning to outstrip demand. One of the few categories in which demand outstripped supply was eBay Motors, which had an average of 11 bids from seven unique users for each sale. Further, almost half of eBay's registered users were from the United States and represented almost one-third of all U.S. Internet users. With the U.S. online auction market maturing and eBay maintaining the dominant market share, analysts were concerned with how much more penetration eBay could achieve.

In response to these concerns, eBay cited new trends indicating that even in the United States the company was reaching new customers and had room to grow. One of the trends eBay saw as particularly promising was the increasing use of eBay's 28,000 registered Trading Assistants and the emergence of drop-off eBay consignment services. Trading Assistants were experienced eBay sellers who, for a fee, would help users sell their items on eBay. Extending this service, drop-off consignment services began to spring up as early as 2000. These consignment services, such as AuctionDrop, QuickDrop, and Picture-It-Sold, would take physical possession of a customer's items, typically those with an eBay value of over $50, and sell them on eBay for a fee equal to between 30 and 40 percent of the item's final sale price. The company was encouraged by these activities because they reached sellers who would not normally use the Internet.

eBay also challenged the theory that the maturity of its markets was based on the company's total market penetration in key categories. For example, eBay argued that it had significant market opportunity in areas such as eBay Motors, where its $6.7 billion in gross merchandise sales accounted for less than 1 percent of the value of all vehicles sold in the United States. Based on this model, none of eBay's largest categories had a market penetration of 5 percent (see Exhibit 10).

Evolution of the Business Model

There was little concern that any company could seriously threaten eBay in its core auction business in the near future, but with the increasing use of tools such as gift certificates, the growing importance of fixed-price sales, the purchase of Half.com, and the growing popularity of Buy It Now, eBay came into more direct competition with retailers such as Amazon.com, with e-commerce solutions, and with the likes of Microsoft. Some analysts also thought that search engines such as Google that were directing customers to clients who paid to have their sites prominently featured in the search engine's results would also become a competitor in the near future, but Meg Whitman dismissed this possibility, saying, "We see Google and Yahoo search and MSN search . . . as actually enablers of our business,"

EXHIBIT 10
eBay's Largest
Auction Categories,
by Annualized Gross
Merchandise Sales, as
Fourth Quarter 2003
(In millions)

	Fourth-Quarter 2003	Market Penetration
Motors	$7,500	< 1%
Consumer electronics	2,600	1–4%
Computers	2,400	1–3%
Books, movies, music	2,000	~ 3%
Clothing and accessories	1,800	< 1%
Sports	1,800	2–5%
Collectibles	1,500	2–3%
Toys	1,500	~ 5%
Home and garden	1,100	< 1%

Source: Corporate reports, Lehman Brothers estimates, www.lehman.com.

she said. "We think both natural search and paid search are allies of ours."[27] When asked about how the evolution of eBay's business model influenced the company's sphere of competition, Whitman said,

> If we were a retailer, we'd be the 27th-largest in the world. So our sellers are competing [with retailers] for consumer dollars. If you're thinking about buying a set of golf clubs or a tennis racket or a jacket or a pair of skis, you decide whether you're going to do that at eBay, at Wal-Mart, a sporting-goods store, or Macy's. I would define our competition more broadly than ever before.[28]

The threat of these competitors increased as fixed-price sales comprised an ever-increasing percentage of eBay's total sales and growth. By the end of 2003, fixed-price trading accounted for 28 percent of eBay's gross merchandise sales (the dollar value of merchandise sold) and was expected to experience continued growth throughout the foreseeable future.

The Future

Heading into 2004, eBay was almost certain to reach the aggressive growth targets it had set for itself in 2000—and its stock price reflected this belief (see Exhibit 11). In fact, most analysts forecast that eBay would meet these goals a year early. The main question that plagued investors was, How would the company continue its phenomenal growth rate? In considering future moves eBay had a few issues to address. First, how should it prioritize its efforts? Was additional expansion in the international markets the highest priority? If so, where? Alternatively, should eBay focus on further broadening its offerings to include more categories, more specialty sites, and more sellers? How much emphasis should be put on fixed-price options? If the company chose to continue expanding its fixed-price offerings, how could it position itself vis-à-vis established online retailers, and how could it defend itself against new, more diverse competitors such as paid search engines?

Finally, eBay was facing increasing dissatisfaction by some of its largest corporate sellers. Some corporate sellers were experiencing significant difficulty with selling a large volume of goods on the site while maintaining a sufficient profit margin. According to Walt Shill, the former chief of Return-Buy, a company that liquidated unsold merchandise for electronics retailers and manufacturers, eBay didn't have enough buyer demand to absorb significant quantities of a single good, such as a specific brand and model of a digital camera, in a short period

[27]Ben Berkowitz, "eBay to Experiment Again with Local Auction Sites," www.usatoday.com, February 24, 2004.
[28]"Meg Whitman on eBay's Self-Regulation," *BusinessWeek Online*, August 18, 2003.

EXHIBIT 11
eBay's Stock Price Performance, March 2003–February 2004

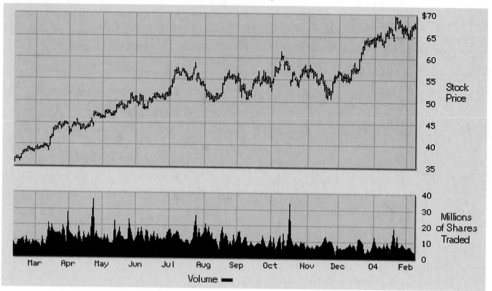

Source: www.bigcharts.com, February 9, 2004.

of time, as eBay was "two inches deep and miles wide."[29] Whitman acknowledged this problem and stated that, for sellers wishing to "move a thousand of the same computer in a day, eBay may not be one of the most effective channels."[30] This problem, coupled with eBay's fairness policy, was causing many large sellers such as Motorola and Circuit City to abandon selling on eBay and to search for additional sales outlets. According to Scott Wingo, CEO of ChannelAdvisor, a leading provider of auction and marketplace management software that was partially owned by eBay, eBay would need to reconsider its level-playing-field policy, which prohibited giving special perks or fee discounts to big sellers if it wanted to attract large businesses and keep growing at its current rate.[31]

When eBay posted its 2003 results in early 2004, it was apparent to most industry observers that it would easily reach its stated goals a year early. Perhaps the only significant concern among analysts and investors was whether eBay could continue its growth without stretching itself too thin, especially given Meg Whitman's philosophy, as evinced in the following statement:

> You really need to do things 100 percent. Better to do 5 things at 100 percent than 10 things at 80 percent. Because the devil in so much of this is in the detail and while we have to move very, very fast, I think you are not well served by moving incredibly rapidly and not doing things that well.[32]

[29]Nick Wingfield, "As eBay Grows, Site Disappoints Some Big Vendors," *The Wall Street Journal,* February 26, 2004.

[30]Ibid.

[31]Ibid.

[32]"What's Behind the Boom at eBay?" *BusinessWeek Online,* May 21, 1999.

Case

18

Wal-Mart Stores, Inc.: A New Set of Challenges

Arthur A. Thompson *The University of Alabama*

In early 2004, Wal-Mart's president and CEO, H. Lee Scott, was bullish not only about Wal-Mart's growth prospects but also about its ability to deal with critics who were challenging the company's seemingly virtuous business model of relentlessly wringing cost efficiencies out of its supply chain and providing customers with everyday low prices. Scott and other members of Wal-Mart's highly regarded management team, as well as members of founder Sam Walton's family, could look with justifiable pride on the company's remarkable journey from humble beginnings in the 1960s as a folksy discount retailer in the boondocks of Arkansas to what in 2004 was a $260 billion retailing juggernaut in the early stages of globalizing its operations from its headquarters in Bentonville, Arkansas (which was now served by two daily nonstop flights to New York's LaGuardia Airport). Wal-Mart's growth over the past four decades was unprecedented:

	1962	1970	1980	1990	2000	2004
Sales	$1.4 million	$31 million	$1.2 billion	$26 billion	$191 billion	$256 billion
Profits	$112,000	$1.2 million	$41 million	$1 billion	$6.3 billion	$9.0 billion
Stores	9	32	276	1,528	4,188	4,906

Just as unprecedented was Wal-Mart's impact on general merchandise retailing and the attraction its stores had to shoppers. During 2003, about 140 million people in 11 countries shopped Wal-Mart's almost 4,700 stores every week. More than half of American shoppers visited a Wal-Mart at least once a month, and one-third went once a week—in 2002 an estimated 82 percent of American households made at least one purchase at Wal-Mart.[1] Since the early 1990s, the company had gone from dabbling in supermarket sales to taking the number 1 spot in grocery retailing worldwide. In the United States, Wal-Mart was the biggest employer in 21 states, and it employed 1.4 million people worldwide, far more than any other company.[2] It was the largest retailer in Canada and Mexico, as well as in the

[1]Anthony Bianco and Wendy Zellner, "Is Wal-Mart Too Powerful?" *BusinessWeek,* October 6, 2003, p. 102.

[2]Jerry Useem, "One Nation Under Wal-Mart," *Fortune,* March 3, 2003, p. 66.

United States and the world as a whole. On November 28, 2003, Wal-Mart set a one-day sales record of $1.52 billion in the United States and over $1.6 billion worldwide—figures bigger than the gross domestic products of 36 countries.

Wal-Mart's performance and prominence in the retailing industry had resulted in numerous awards. By the turn of the century, it had been named "Retailer of the Century" by *Discount Store News,* made the *Fortune* magazine lists of "Most Admired Companies in America" and "100 Best Companies to Work for in America," and been included on the *Financial Times'* "Most Respected in the World" list. In 2000, Wal-Mart was ranked fifth on *Fortune*'s list of the "Global Most Admired Companies." In 2002, Wal-Mart became number 1 on the *Fortune* 500 list of the largest companies in America and also on *Fortune*'s Global 500 list. Wal-Mart topped *Fortune*'s 2003 list of "Most Admired Companies in America" and was recognized as the "Largest Corporate Cash Giver" by *Forbes* magazine based on the *Chronicle of Philanthropy*'s survey of sales and cash donations for 2002—Wal-Mart's cash contributions to some 80,000 organizations increased in 2002 to $136 million, up 17 percent from 2001; in addition, customers and associates raised another $70 million at Wal-Mart's stores and clubs. Wal-Mart received the 2002 Ron Brown Award, the highest presidential award recognizing outstanding achievement in employee relations and community initiatives. In 2003, American Veterans Awards gave Wal-Mart its "Corporate Patriotism Award."

Wal-Mart's success had made the Walton family (Sam Walton's heirs and living relatives) the wealthiest in the world—in 2003, five Walton family members controlled about 1.75 billion shares of Wal-Mart stock worth about $93 billion. Increases in the value of Wal-Mart's stock over the years had made hundreds of Wal-Mart employees, retirees, and shareholders millionaires or multimillionaires. Since 1970, when Wal-Mart shares were first issued to the public, the company's stock had split 11 times. A $1,650 investment in Wal-Mart stock in 1970 (100 shares purchased at the initial offer price of $16.50) equated to 204,800 shares worth $10.8 million as of December 2003.

Company Background

Sam Walton graduated from the University of Missouri in 1940 with a degree in economics and took a job as a management trainee at J. C. Penney Company. His career with Penney's ended with a call to military duty in World War II. When the war was over, Walton decided to purchase a franchise and open a Ben Franklin retail variety store in Newport, Arkansas, rather than return to Penney's. Five years later, when the lease on the Newport building was lost, Walton decided to relocate his business in Bentonville, Arkansas, where he bought a building and opened Walton's 5 & 10 as a Ben Franklin–affiliated store. By 1960 Walton was the largest Ben Franklin franchisee, with nine stores.

In 1961 Walton started to become concerned about the long-term competitive threat to variety stores posed by the emerging popularity of giant supermarkets and discounters. An avid pilot, he took off in his plane on a cross-country tour to study the changes in stores and retailing trends, then put together a plan for a discount store of his own. Walton went to Chicago to try to interest Ben Franklin executives in expanding into discount retailing; when they turned him down, he decided to go forward on his own because he believed deeply in the retailing concept of offering significant price discounts to expand sales volumes and increase overall profits. The first Wal-Mart Discount City opened July 2, 1962, in Rogers, Arkansas. The store was successful, and Walton quickly began to look for opportunities to open stores in other small towns and to attract talented people with retailing experience to help him grow the business. Although he started out as a seat-of-the-pants merchant, he had great instincts, was quick to learn from other retailers' successes and failures, and was adept at garnering ideas for improvements from employees and promptly trying them out. Sam Walton incorporated his business as Wal-Mart Stores in 1969. When the company went public in 1970 and sold 300,000 shares at $16.50 each to help finance its rapid growth, it had 38 stores and sales of $44.2 million. In 1979, with 276 stores, 21,000 employees, and operations in 11 states, Wal-Mart became the first company to reach $1 billion in sales in such a short time.

As the company grew, Sam Walton proved to be an effective and visionary leader. His folksy demeanor and his talent for motivating people, combined with a very hands-on management style and an obvious talent for discount retailing, produced a culture and a set of values and beliefs that kept Wal-Mart on a path of continuous innovation and rapid expansion. Moreover, Wal-Mart's success and Walton's personable style of leadership generated numerous stories in the media that cast the company and its founder in a positive light. As Wal-Mart emerged as the premier discount retailer in the United States in the 1980s, an uncommonly large cross-section of the American public came to know who Sam Walton was and to associate his name with Wal-Mart. Sam Walton's folksy personality, unpretentious manner, and interest in people and their feelings caused people inside and outside the company to hold him in high esteem. Regarded by many as "the entrepreneur of the century" and "a genuine American folk hero," he enjoyed a reputation of being not only a community-spirited man who was concerned for his employees but also a devoted family man who epitomized the American dream and demonstrated the virtues of hard work.

Just before Sam Walton's death in 1992, his vision was for Wal-Mart to become a $125 billion company by 2000. But his handpicked successor, David D. Glass, beat that target by almost two years. Under Glass's leadership (1988–2000), Wal-Mart's sales grew at an average annual compound rate of 19 percent, pushing revenues up from $20.6 billion to $165 billion. When David Glass retired in January 2000, H. Lee Scott was chosen as Wal-Mart's third president and CEO. In the four years that Scott had been CEO, Wal-Mart's sales had grown over $100 billion, matching the company's growth in its first 35 years. Even though there were Wal-Mart stores in all 50 states and 10 foreign countries in 2004, Scott and other senior executives believed there were sufficient domestic and foreign growth opportunities to permit the company to grow at double-digit rates for the foreseeable future and propel Wal-Mart's revenues past $500 billion by 2010.

Exhibit 1 provides a summary of Wal-Mart's financial and operating performance for the 1993–2004 fiscal years.

Yet, while a report by the prominent Boston Consulting Group said, "The world has never known a company with such ambition, capability, and momentum," in 2003 there were growing signs that the continued growth and influence of the "Beast of Bentonville" was breeding a backlash among competing retailers, organized labor, community activists, and so-called cultural progressives. Wal-Mart was drawing increasing flak from organized labor about the company's low wages and antiunion posture. It was confronting some 6,000 lawsuits on a variety of issues, including one claiming that it discriminated against female employees.

Wal-Mart's Strategy

The hallmarks of Wal-Mart's strategy were multiple store formats, low everyday prices, wide selection, a big percentage of name-brand merchandise, a customer-friendly store environment, low operating costs, innovative merchandising, a strong emphasis on customer satisfaction, disciplined expansion into new geographic markets, and in many cases using acquisitions to enter foreign markets. On the outside of every Wal-Mart store in big letters was the message "We Sell for Less." The company's advertising tag line reinforced the low-price theme: "Always low prices. Always." Major merchandise lines included housewares, consumer electronics, sporting goods, lawn and garden items, health and beauty aids,

EXHIBIT 1   **Financial and Operating Summary, Wal-Mart Stores, Fiscal Years 1993–2004 (In billions, except earnings per share data)**

	Fiscal Year Ending January 31					
	2004	2003	2002	2001	2000	1993
Financial and operating data						
Net sales	$256.3	$244.5	$217.8	$191.3	$165.0	$55.5
Net sales increase	12%	12%	14%	16%	20%	26%
Domestic comparable store sales increase*	5%	5%	6%	5%	8%	11%
Cost of sales	198.7	191.8	171.6	150.3	129.7	44.2
Operating, selling, general and administrative expenses	44.9	41.0	36.2	31.6	27.0	8.3
Interest costs, net	0.8	0.9	1.2	1.2	0.8	0.3
Net income	$ 9.0	$ 8.0	$ 6.7	$ 6.3	$ 5.4	$ 2.0
Earnings per share of common stock (diluted)	$2.07	$1.81	$1.49	$1.40	$1.20	$0.44
Balance sheet data						
Current assets	$ 34.2	$30.5	$27.9	$26.6	$24.4	$10.2
Net property, plant, equipment, and capital leases	55.2	51.9	45.8	40.9	36.0	9.8
Total assets	104.9	94.7	83.5	78.1	70.3	20.6
Current liabilities	37.4	32.6	27.3	28.9	25.8	6.8
Long-term debt	17.5	16.6	15.7	12.5	13.7	3.1
Long-term obligations under capital leases	3.0	3.0	3.0	3.2	3.0	1.8
Shareholders' equity	43.6	39.3	35.1	31.3	25.8	8.6
Financial ratios						
Current ratio	0.9	0.9	1.0	0.9	0.9	1.5
Return on assets	8.6%	9.2%	8.5%	8.7%	9.5%	11.1%
Return on shareholders' equity	20.6%	21.6%	20.1%	22.0%	22.9%	25.3%
Other year-end data						
Number of domestic Wal-Mart Discount stores	1,478	1,568	1,647	1,736	1,801	1,848
Number of domestic Wal-Mart Supercenters	1,471	1,258	1,066	888	721	34
Number of domestic Sam's Clubs	538	525	500	475	463	256
Number of domestic Neighborhood Markets	64	49	31	19	7	—
Number of international stores	1,355	1,288	1,170	1,070	1,004	10

*Defined as sales at stores open a full year that have not been expanded or relocated in the past 12 months.

Source: Wal-Mart annual reports for 2003 and 2004.

apparel, home fashions, paint, bed and bath goods, hardware, jewelry, automotive repair and maintenance, toys and games, and groceries.

Multiple Store Formats

In 2004, Wal-Mart was seeking to meet customers' needs with four different retail concepts: Wal-Mart discount stores, Supercenters, neighborhood markets, and Sam's Clubs:

- *Discount stores*—These stores ranged from 40,000 to 125,000 square feet, employed an average of 150 people, and offered as many as 80,000 different items, including family apparel, automotive products, health and beauty aids, home furnishings, electronics, hardware, toys, sporting goods, lawn and garden items, pet supplies, jewelry, housewares, prescription drugs, and packaged grocery items. Discount stores had sales in the $30 to $50 million range, depending on store size and location.

- *Supercenters*—Supercenters, which Wal-Mart started opening in 1988 to meet a demand for one-stop family shopping, joined the concept of a general merchandise discount store with that of a full-line supermarket. They ranged from 109,000 to 220,000 square feet, employed between 200 and 550 associates, had about 36 general merchandise departments, and offered up to 150,000 different items, at least 30,000 of which were grocery products. In addition to the value-priced merchandise offered at discount stores and a large supermarket section with 30,000+ items, Supercenters contained such specialty shops as vision centers, tire and lube expresses, a fast-food restaurant, portrait studios, one-hour photo centers, hair salons, banking, and employment agencies. Typical Supercenters had annual sales in the $80–$100 million range.

- *Sam's Clubs*—A store format that Wal-Mart launched in 1983, Sam's was a cash-and-carry, members-only warehouse that carried about 4,000 frequently used, mostly brand-name items in bulk quantities along with some big-ticket merchandise. The product lineup included fresh, frozen, and canned food products, candy and snack items, office supplies, janitorial and household cleaning supplies and paper products, apparel, CDs and DVDs, and an assortment of big-ticket items (TVs, tires, large and small appliances, watches, jewelry, computers, camcorders, and other electronic equipment). Stores were approximately 110,000 to 130,000 square feet in size, with most goods displayed in the original cartons stacked in wooden racks or on wooden pallets. Many items stocked were sold in bulk quantity (five-gallon containers, bundles of a dozen or more, and economy-sized boxes). Prices tended to be 10–15 percent below the prices of the company's discount stores and Supercenters since merchandising costs and store operation costs were lower. Sam's was intended to serve small businesses, churches and other religious organizations, beauty salons and barber shops, motels, restaurants, offices, local schools, families, and individuals looking for great prices on large-volume quantities or big-ticket items. Annual member fees were $30 for businesses and $35 for individuals—there were 46 million members in 2003. Sam's stores employed about 125 people each and had annual sales averaging $63 million. A number of Sam's stores were located adjacent to a Supercenter or discount store.

- *Neighborhood markets*—Neighborhood markets—the company is newest store format, launched in 1998—were designed to appeal to customers who just needed groceries, pharmaceuticals, and general merchandise. They were always located in markets with Wal-Mart Supercenters so as to be readily accessible to Wal-Mart's food distribution network. Neighborhood Markets ranged from 42,000 to 55,000 square feet, employed 80–100 people each, and featured fresh produce, deli foods, fresh meat and dairy items, health and beauty aids, one-hour photo and traditional photo developing services, drive-through pharmacies, stationery and paper goods, pet supplies, and household supplies—about 28,000 items in total.

Domestically, during 2004 Wal-Mart planned to open approximately 50 to 55 new discount stores, 220 to 230 new Supercenters, 25 to 30 new neighborhood markets, and 35 to 40 new Sam's Clubs. Relocations or expansions of existing discount stores accounted for approximately 140 of the new Supercenters, and approximately 20 of the Sam's Clubs were relocations or expansions.

Internationally, Wal-Mart planned to open 130 to 140 units in the 10 countries where it already had stores; of these, 30 were expected to be relocations or expansions. In 2004 Wal-Mart expected to spend $18 million to open three new stores in eastern China, an area where French retailer Carrefour (the world's second largest retailer behind Wal-Mart) and Germany's Metro AG had stores; Wal-Mart had opened 31 stores in 15 cities across the country since 1996.

Exhibit 2 shows the number of Wal-Mart stores in each state and country. There were still many locations in the United States that were underserved by Wal-Mart stores. Inner-city

EXHIBIT 2
Wal-Mart's Store
Count, January 2003

State	Discount Stores	Super centers	Sam's Clubs	Neighborhood Markets
Alabama	34	49	9	2
Alaska	6	0	3	0
Arizona	24	17	10	0
Arkansas	35	43	4	6
California	133	0	30	0
Colorado	17	29	14	0
Connecticut	27	2	3	0
Delaware	3	3	1	0
Florida	66	87	37	1
Georgia	42	61	20	0
Hawaii	6	0	1	0
Idaho	5	11	1	0
Illinois	81	33	27	0
Indiana	42	42	14	0
Iowa	27	24	7	0
Kansas	29	23	6	0
Kentucky	34	41	5	0
Louisiana	35	47	12	0
Maine	12	9	3	0
Maryland	32	5	13	0
Massachusetts	41	1	3	0
Michigan	48	14	22	0
Minnesota	34	9	12	0
Mississippi	21	41	5	1
Missouri	56	58	14	0
Montana	5	6	1	0
Nebraska	10	11	3	0
Nevada	11	7	5	0
New Hampshire	19	6	4	0
New Jersey	30	0	8	0
New Mexico	6	18	5	0
New York	52	22	18	0
North Carolina	47	52	17	0
North Dakota	8	0	2	0
Ohio	70	28	26	0
Oklahoma	41	40	7	12
Oregon	24	3	0	0
Pennsylvania	50	43	20	0
Rhode Island	8	0	1	0
South Carolina	22	37	9	0
South Dakota	6	4	2	0
Tennessee	33	57	15	2
Texas	117	155	68	24
Utah	6	15	7	1
Vermont	4	0	0	0
Virginia	21	52	13	0
Washington	29	6	2	0
West Virginia	8	20	3	0
Wisconsin	49	20	11	0
Wyoming	2	7	2	0
U.S. totals	1,568	1,258	525	49

(continued)

EXHIBIT 2
(concluded)

	Discount Stores	Super centers	Sam's Clubs	Neighborhood Markets
International/ Worldwide				
Argentina	0	11	0	0
Brazil	0	12	8	2[a]
Canada	213	0	0	0
China	0	20	4	2
Germany	0	94	0	0
S. Korea	0	15	0	0
Mexico	472[b]	75	50	0
Puerto Rico	9	1	9	33[c]
United Kingdom	248[d]	10	0	0
International totals	942	238	71	37
Grand totals	2,510	1,496	596	86

[a]Brazil includes Todo Dias.

[b]Mexico includes 118 Bodegas, 50 Suburbias, 44 Superamas, and 260 Vips.

[c]Puerto Rico includes 33 Amigos.

[d]United Kingdom includes 248 ASDA Stores.

sections of New York City had no Wal-Mart stores of any kind because ample space with plenty of parking was unavailable at a reasonable price. Wal-Mart's first Supercenter in all of California opened in 2003 at a three-story location in downtown Los Angeles that had escalators sized for shopping carts. There were no Supercenters in New Jersey, Rhode Island, Vermont, or Hawaii, and only 1 in Massachusetts and 2 in Connecticut (versus 155 in Texas, 87 in Florida, 58 in Missouri, 52 in North Carolina, 49 in Alabama, and 47 in Louisiana).

Wal-Mart's various domestic and international stores were served by 108 regional general merchandise and food distribution centers. Five additional distribution centers averaging over 1 million square feet of space were planned for 2004.

Wal-Mart's Geographic Expansion Strategy

One of the most distinctive features of Wal-Mart's domestic strategy was the manner in which it expanded outward into new geographic areas. Whereas many chain retailers achieved regional and national coverage quickly by entering the largest metropolitan centers before trying to penetrate less-populated markets, Wal-Mart always expanded into adjoining geographic areas, saturating each area with stores before moving into new territory. New stores were usually clustered within 200 miles of an existing distribution center so that daily deliveries could be made cost-effectively; new distribution centers were added as needed to support store expansion into additional areas. In the United States, the really unique feature of Wal-Mart's geographic strategy had involved opening stores in small towns surrounding a targeted metropolitan area before moving into the metropolitan area itself—an approach Sam Walton had termed "backward expansion." Wal-Mart management believed that any town with a shopping-area population of 15,000 or more was big enough to support a Wal-Mart Discount Store and that towns of 25,000 could support a Supercenter. Once stores were opened in towns around the most populous city, Wal-Mart would locate one or more stores in the metropolitan area and begin major market advertising.

By clustering new stores in a relatively small geographic area, Wal-Mart could spread advertising expenses for breaking into a new market across all the area stores, a tactic the company used to keep its advertising costs under 1 percent of sales (compared to 2 or 3 percent for other discount chains). Don Soderquist, Wal-Mart's retired senior vice chairman, explained why the company preferred its backward expansion strategy:

> Our strategy is to go into smaller markets first before we hit major metro areas because you've got a smaller population base to convince over. So you begin to get the acceptance in smaller markets and the word begins to travel around and people begin to travel further and further to get to your stores.[3]

In the small towns Wal-Mart entered, it was not unusual for a number of local businesses that carried merchandise similar to Wal-Mart's lines to fail within a year or two of Wal-Mart's arrival. Wal-Mart's low prices tended to attract customers away from apparel shops, general stores, pharmacies, sporting goods stores, shoe stores, hardware stores, supermarkets, and convenience stores operated by local merchants. The "Wal-Mart effect" in small communities was so potent that it had spawned sometimes fierce local resistance to the entry of a new Wal-Mart among both local merchants and area residents wanting to preserve the economic vitality of their downtown areas and protect against the invasion of what they considered to be an unsightly Wal-Mart store and parking lot. Consulting firms formed that specialized in advising local retailers on how to survive the opening of a Wal-Mart.

For the past several years, Wal-Mart had been driving hard to expand its geographic base of stores outside the United States through a combination of new store construction and acquisition. Acquisition of general merchandise or supermarket chains had been a part of Wal-Mart's entry and/or store expansion strategy in Canada, Mexico, Brazil, Japan, Puerto Rico, China, and Great Britain. International sales accounted for 16.7 percent of total sales in fiscal 2003, and the percentage was expected to rise in the coming years. Wal-Mart stores in China had some of the highest traffic counts of any stores in the world. Wal-Mart's entry into Japan via minority ownership of Japan's fifth largest supermarket chain, Seiyu, had stirred a retailing revolution among Japanese retailers to improve their merchandising, cut their costs, lower their prices, and streamline their supply chains. Prior to buying a minority stake in Seiyu in 2002 (with an option to increase its ownership to 67 percent by 2007), Wal-Mart had studied the Japanese market for four years. It planned to spend most of 2003–2004 getting Seiyu stores and its Japanese supply chain ready for a full-scale assault on penetrating the Japanese market with a lineup of both supermarket and general merchandise products. Sales at Wal-Mart's nearly 1,300 international stores averaged about $31 million per store in fiscal 2003; the company's international division had 2003 total sales of $40.7 billion (up 15 percent) and operating profits of $2.0 billion (up almost 56 percent).

But as Wal-Mart grew more global, management intended to "remain local" in terms of the goods it carried and in some of the ways it operated. Most store managers and senior managers in its foreign operations were natives of the countries where Wal-Mart operated; many had begun their careers as hourly employees. Wal-Mart did, however, have a program that allowed stores in different areas to exchange best practices.

Everyday Low Prices

While Wal-Mart did not invent the concept of everyday low pricing, it had done a better job than any other discount retailer in executing the strategy. The company was widely seen by consumers as being the lowest-priced general merchandise retailer in its market. Recent studies showed that prices of its grocery items were 8 to 27 percent below those of such leading supermarket chain competitors as Kroger (which used the City Market brand in the states west of the Mississippi), Safeway, and Albertson's, after making allowances for specials and loyalty cards. In-store services were also bargain-priced—customers could wire money for a flat $12.95 (versus a fee of $50 to wire $1,000 at Western Union) and could

---

[3]*Discount Store News,* December 18, 1989, p. 162.

purchase money orders for 46 cents (versus 90 cents charged by the U.S. Postal Service). Wal-Mart touted its low prices on its storefronts ("We Sell for Less"), in advertising, on signs inside its stores, and on the logos of its shopping bags. Some economists believed that Wal-Mart's everyday low prices had reduced inflationary pressures economywide, allowing all U.S. consumers to benefit from the Wal-Mart effect. The well-known financier Warren Buffet said, "You add it all up and they have contributed to the financial well-being of the American public more than any other institution I can think of."[4]

Merchandising Innovations

Wal-Mart was unusually active in testing and experimenting with new merchandising techniques. From the beginning, Sam Walton had been quick to imitate good ideas and merchandising practices employed by other retailers. According to the founder of Kmart, Sam Walton "not only copied our concepts; he strengthened them. Sam just took the ball and ran with it."[5] Wal-Mart prided itself on its "low threshold for change," and much of management's time was spent talking to vendors, employees, and customers to get ideas for how Wal-Mart could improve. Suggestions were actively solicited from employees. Most any reasonable idea was tried; if it worked well in stores where it was first tested, then it was quickly implemented in other stores. Experiments in store layout, merchandise displays, store color schemes, merchandise selection (whether to add more upscale lines or shift to a different mix of items), and sales promotion techniques were always under way. Wal-Mart was regarded as an industry leader in testing, adapting, and applying a wide range of cutting-edge merchandising approaches. In 2003 Wal-Mart was testing the merits of an in-store candy department featuring an assortment mainly targeted to children, with bulk candy from Brach's, Jelly Belly, and M&M, plus a wide range of novelty and licensed items and coin-operated kiddie rides.

Advertising

Wal-Mart relied less on advertising than most other discount chains did. The company distributed only one or two circulars per month and ran occasional TV ads, relying primarily on word of mouth to communicate its marketing message. Wal-Mart's advertising expenditures ran about 0.3 percent of sales revenues, versus 1.5 percent for Kmart and 2.3 percent for Target. Wal-Mart spent $676 million on advertising in fiscal 2003, $618 million in fiscal 2002, and $574 million in fiscal 2001. Wal-Mart's spending for radio and TV advertising was said to be so low that it didn't register on national ratings scales. Most Wal-Mart broadcast ads appeared on local TV and local cable channels. Wal-Mart did no advertising for its Sam's Club stores. The company often allowed charities to use its parking lots for their fund-raising activities.

Distribution

Over the years, Wal-Mart's management had turned the company's centralized distribution systems into a competitive edge—the company's low distribution costs and cost-effective supply chain management practices were a big reason why its prices were low. Wal-Mart got an early jump on competitors in distribution efficiency because of its rural store locations. Whereas other discount retailers relied on manufacturers and distributors to ship directly to their mostly metropolitan-area stores, Wal-Mart found that its rapid growth during the 1970s was straining suppliers' ability to use independent trucking firms to make frequent and timely deliveries to its growing number of rural store locations. To improve the delivery of merchandise to its stores, the company in 1980 began to build its own centralized distribution centers and to supply stores from these centers with daily deliveries by its own truck fleet. Wal-Mart added new distribution centers when new outlying stores could no longer be reliably and economically supported from an existing center.

[4]As quoted in Useem, "One Nation Under Wal-Mart," p. 68.
[5]As quoted in Bill Saporito, "What Sam Walton Taught America," *Fortune,* May 4, 1992, p. 105.

The Competitive Environment

Discount retailing was an intensely competitive business. Competition among discount retailers centered on pricing, store location, variations in store format and merchandise mix, store size, shopping atmosphere, and image with shoppers. Wal-Mart's primary competitors were Kmart and Target in general merchandise retailing, and in superstores that also included a full-line supermarket Super Target stores and Super Kmart stores. Wal-Mart also competed against category retailers like Best Buy and Circuit City in electronics; Toys "R" Us in toys; Goody's in apparel; Bed, Bath, and Beyond in household goods; and Kroger, Albertson's, and Safeway in groceries.

Surveys of households comparing Wal-Mart with Kmart and Target indicated that Wal-Mart had a strong competitive advantage. According to *Discount Store News:*

> When asked to compare Wal-Mart with Kmart and Target, the consensus of households is that Wal-Mart is as good or better. For example, of the households with a Wal-Mart in the area, 59 percent said that Wal-Mart is better than Kmart and Target; 33 percent said it was the same. Only 4 percent rated Wal-Mart worse than Kmart and Target . . . When asked why Wal-Mart is better, 55 percent of the respondents with a Wal-Mart in their area said lower/better prices . . . Variety/selection and good quality were the other top reasons cited by consumers when asked why Wal-Mart is better. Thirty percent said variety; 18 percent said good quality.[6]

The two largest competitors in the warehouse club segment were Costco and Sam's Clubs; BJ's Wholesale Club, a smaller East Coast chain, was the only other major U.S. player in this segment.[7] For the year ended August 31, 2003, Costco had U.S. sales of $34.4 billion at 312 stores versus $32.9 billion at 532 stores for Sam's. The average Costco store generated annual revenues of $112 million, almost double the $63 million average at Sam's. Costco catered to affluent households with upscale tastes and located its stores in mostly urban areas. Costco's 42 million members averaged 11.4 store visits annually and spent an average of $94 per visit, which compared favorably with averages of 8.5 visits and expenditures of $78 at Sam's. Costco was the nation's biggest retailer of fine wines ($600 million annually) and roasted chickens (55,000 rotisserie chickens a day). While its product line included food and household items, sporting goods, vitamins, and various other merchandise, its big attraction was big-ticket luxury items (diamonds and plasma TVs) and the latest gadgets at bargain prices (Costco capped its markups at 14 percent). Costco had beaten Sam's in being the first to sell fresh meat and produce (1986 versus 1989), to introduce private-label items (1995 versus 1998), and to sell gasoline (1995 versus 1997). Costco offered its workers good wages and fringe benefits (full-time hourly workers made about $40,000 after four years).

Wal-Mart's rapid climb to become the largest supermarket retailer had triggered heated price competition in the aisles of most supermarkets. Wal-Mart's three major rivals—Kroger, Albertson's, and Safeway—along with a host of smaller regional supermarket chains, were scrambling to cut costs, narrow the price gap with Wal-Mart, and otherwise differentiate themselves so as to retain their customer base and grow revenues. Continuing increases in the number of Wal-Mart Supercenters meant that the majority of rival supermarkets would be within 10 miles of a Supercenter by 2010. Wal-Mart had recently concluded that it took fewer area residents to support a Supercenter than the company had thought; management believed that Supercenters in urban areas could be as little as four miles apart and still attract sufficient store traffic. Kroger had announced plans to cut its

---

[6]*Discount Store News,* December 18, 1989, p. 168.

[7]The information in this paragraph is drawn from John Helyar, "The Only Company Wal-Mart Fears," *Fortune,* November 24, 2003, pp. 158–66.

costs by $500 million by January 31, 2004, to put it in better position to match Wal-Mart's lower prices on grocery items. Supermarket industry observers were speculating that either Albertson's (which was already closing underperforming stores and struggling to maintain current revenues) or Safeway (which had its hands full trying to digest a series of acquisitions of regional supermarket chains) would not survive a coming shakeout among the weaker supermarket competitors.

Wal-Mart's Approaches to Strategy Execution

To implement and execute its strategy, Wal-Mart put heavy emphasis on getting the lowest possible prices from its suppliers, forging close working relationships with key suppliers in order to capture win–win cost savings throughout its supply chain, keeping its internal operations lean and efficient, paying attention to even the tiniest details in store layouts and merchandising, making efficient use of state-of-the-art technology, and nurturing a culture that thrived on hard work, constant improvement, and pleasing customers, especially passing cost savings on to customers in the form of low prices.

Wal-Mart's Use of Cutting-Edge Technology

Wal-Mart began using computers to maintain inventory control on an item basis in its distribution centers and stores in 1974. Wal-Mart began testing point-of-sale scanners in 1981 and then committed to systemwide use of scanning bar codes in 1983—a move that improved checkout times by 25–30 percent. In 1984, Wal-Mart developed a computer-assisted merchandising system that allowed each store to tailor the product mix to its own market circumstances and sales patterns. Between 1985 and 1987 Wal-Mart installed the nation's largest private satellite communication network, which allowed two-way voice and data transmission between headquarters, the distribution centers, and the stores and one-way video transmission from Bentonville's corporate offices to distribution centers and to the stores; the system was less expensive than the previously used telephone network. The video system was used regularly by company officials to speak directly to all employees at once.

In 1989 Wal-Mart established direct satellite links with about 1,700 vendors supplying close to 80 percent of the goods sold by Wal-Mart; these links allowed the use of electronic purchase orders and instant data exchanges. Wal-Mart also used the satellite system's capabilities to develop a credit card authorization procedure that took five seconds, on average, to authorize a purchase, speeding up credit check-out by 25 percent compared to the prior manual system. In the early 1990s, through pioneering collaboration with Procter & Gamble, Wal-Mart instituted an automated reordering system that notified suppliers as their items moved through store checkout lanes; this allowed suppliers to track sales and inventories of their products (so they could plan production and schedule shipments accordingly).

Throughout the 1990s Wal-Mart continued to invest in information technology and online systems, usually being a first-mover among retailers in upgrading and improving its capabilities as new technology was introduced. By 2003 the company had developed and deployed sophisticated information technology systems and online capability that not only gave it real-time access to detailed figures on most any aspect of its operations but also made it a leader in cost-effective supply chain management. It could track the movement of goods through its entire value chain—from the sale of items at the cash register backward to stock on store shelves, in-store backup inventory, distribution center inventory, and shipments en route. Moreover, Wal-Mart collaborated with its suppliers to develop data-sharing capabilities aimed at streamlining the supply of its stores, avoiding both stockouts and excess inventories, identifying slow-selling items that might warrant replacement, and spotting ways to squeeze costs out of the supply chain. The company's Retail Link system allowed suppliers to track their wares through Wal-Mart's value chain, get hourly sales figures for each item, and monitor gross margins on each of their products (Wal-Mart's actual selling price less what it paid the supplier).

In mid-2003 Wal-Mart informed its suppliers that they would have to convert to electronic product code (EPC) technology based on radio frequency identification (RFID) systems by 2005. EPCs involved a new product numbering standard that went beyond identifying products. Every single item that rolled off a manufacturing line was embedded with an electronic tag containing a unique number. EPCs offered users significant time savings and enhanced their ability to update online databases—identifying where and when a case or pallet of goods arrived, for example—in supply chain logistics applications. EPC tags could be read by RFID scanners when brought into range of a tag reader—unlike bar codes, they did not have to be directly in the line of sight of the scanner. Wal-Mart's management expected that EPC scanning would eventually be built into warehouse bin locations and store shelves, allowing the company to locate and track items throughout the supply chain in real time. With EPC and RFID capability, every single can of soup or DVD or screwdriver in Wal-Mart's supply chain network or on its store shelves could then be traced back to where and when it was made, where and when it arrived at the store, and where and when it was sold (or turned up missing). Further, EPCs linked to an online database provided a secure way of sharing product-specific information with supply chain partners. Wal-Mart management believed that EPC technology, in conjunction with the expanding production of RFID-capable printers/encoders, had the potential to revolutionize the supply chain by providing more accurate information about product movement, stock rotation, and inventory levels; it was also seen as a significant tool for preventing theft and dealing with product recalls. An IBM study indicated that EPC tagging would reduce stockouts by 33 percent, while an Accenture study showed that EPC/RFID technology could boost worker productivity by 5 percent and shrink working capital and fixed capital requirements by 5 to 30 percent.

The attention Wal-Mart management placed on using cutting-edge technology and the astuteness with which it deployed this technology along its value chain to enhance store operations and continuously drive down costs had, over the years, resulted in Wal-Mart's being widely regarded as having the most cost-effective, data-rich information technology systems of any major retailer in the world. So powerful had Wal-Mart's influence been on retail supply chain efficiency that its competitors (and many other retailers as well) had found it essential to follow Wal-Mart's lead and pursue "Wal-Martification" of their retail supply chains.[8]

Relationships with Suppliers

Wal-Mart was far and away the biggest customer of virtually all of its suppliers (see Exhibit 3). Wal-Mart's scale of operation allowed it to bargain hard with suppliers and get their bottom prices. It looked for suppliers who were dominant in their category (thus providing strong brand-name recognition), who could grow with the company, who had full product lines (so that Wal-Mart buyers could both cherry-pick and get some sort of limited exclusivity on the products the company chose to carry), who had the long-term commitment to R&D to bring new and better products to retail shelves, and who had the ability to become more efficient in producing and delivering what it supplied.

Procurement personnel spent a lot of time meeting with vendors and understanding their cost structure. By making the negotiation process transparent, Wal-Mart buyers soon learned whether a vendor was doing all it could to cut down its costs and quote Wal-Mart an attractively low price. Wal-Mart's purchasing agents were dedicated to getting the lowest

[8]Paul Lightfoot, "Wal-Martification," *Operations and Fulfillment,* June 1, 2003, posted at www.opsandfulfillment.com.

EXHIBIT 3 **The Scale of Wal-Mart's Purchases from Selected Suppliers and its Market Shares in Selected Product Categories**

Supplier	Percent of Total Sales to Wal-Mart	Product Category	Wal-Mart's U.S. Market Share*
Tandy Brands Accessories	39%	Dog food	36%
Dial	28	Disposable diapers	32
Del Monte Foods	24	Photographic film	30
Clorox	23	Shampoo	30
Revlon	20–23	Paper towels	30
RJR Tobacco	20	Toothpaste	26
Procter & Gamble	17	Pain remedies	21
		CDs, DVDs, and videos	15–20
		Single-copy sales of magazines	15
Although sales percentages were not available, Wal-Mart was also the biggest customer of Disney, Campbell Soup, Kraft, and Gillette.		Although market shares were not available, Wal-Mart was also the biggest seller of toys, guns, diamonds, detergent, video games, socks, and bedding.	

*Based on sales through food, drug, and mass merchandisers.

Sources: Jerry Useem, "One Nation Under Wal-Mart," *Fortune,* March 3, 2003, p. 66; and Anthony Bianco and Wendy Zellner, "Is Wal-Mart Too Powerful?" *BusinessWeek,* October 6, 2003, p. 102.

prices they could, and they did not accept invitations to be wined or dined by suppliers. The marketing vice president of a major vendor told *Fortune* magazine:

> They are very, very focused people, and they use their buying power more forcefully than anybody else in America. All the normal mating rituals are verboten. Their highest priority is making sure everybody at all times in all cases knows who's in charge, and it's Wal-Mart. They talk softly, but they have piranha hearts, and if you aren't totally prepared when you go in there, you'll have your ass handed to you.[9]

All vendors were expected to offer their best price without exception; one consultant that helped manufacturers sell to retailers observed, "No one would dare come in with a half-ass price."[10]

Even though Wal-Mart was tough in negotiating for absolute rock-bottom prices, the price quotes it got were still typically high enough to allow suppliers to earn a profit. Being a Wal-Mart supplier generally meant having a stable and dependable enough sales base to operate production facilities in a cost-effective manner. Moreover, once Wal-Mart decided to source from a vendor, then it worked closely with the vendor to find *mutually beneficial* ways to squeeze costs out of the supply chain. Every aspect of a supplier's operation got scrutinized—how products were developed, what they were made of, how costs might be reduced, what data Wal-Mart could supply that would be useful, how sharing data online could prove beneficial, and so on. Nearly always, as they went through the process with Wal-Mart personnel, suppliers saw ways to prune costs or otherwise streamline operations in ways that enhanced their profit margins. In 1989 Wal-Mart became the first major retailer to embark on a program urging vendors to develop products and packaging that would not harm the environment. In addition, Wal-Mart expected its vendors to contribute ideas about how to make its stores more fun insofar as their products were concerned. The maker of Power Rangers products, for example, had created the world's largest inflatable structure—a 5,000-cubic-foot moon—which toured Wal-Mart parking lots.[11] Coca-Cola had routed its Los-Angeles-to-Atlanta Olympic Torch Run past as many Wal-Mart stores as

[9]As quoted in *Fortune,* January 30, 1989, p. 53.
[10]As quoted in Useem, "One Nation Under Wal-Mart," p. 68.
[11]Ibid., p. 74.

possible. Those suppliers that were selected as "category managers" for such product groupings as lingerie or pet food or school supplies were expected to educate Wal-Mart on everything that was happening in their respective product category.

Some 200 vendors had established offices in Bentonville to work closely with Wal-Mart on a continuing basis—most were in an area referred to locally as "Vendorville." Vendors were encouraged to voice any problems in their relationship with Wal-Mart and to become involved in Wal-Mart's future plans. Top-priority projects ranged from using more recyclable packaging to working with Wal-Mart on merchandise displays and product mix to tweaking the just-in-time ordering and delivery system to instituting automatic reordering arrangements to coming up with new products with high customer appeal. Most recently, one of Wal-Mart's priorities was working with vendors to figure out how to localize the items carried in particular stores and thereby accommodate varying tastes and preferences of shoppers in different areas where Wal-Mart had stores. Most vendor personnel based in Bentonville spent considerable time focusing on which items in their product line were best for Wal-Mart, where they ought to be placed in the stores, how they could be better displayed, what new products ought to be introduced, and which ones ought to be rotated out.

A 2003 survey conducted by Cannondale Associates found that manufacturers believed Wal-Mart was the overall best retailer with which to do business—the fifth straight year in which Wal-Mart was ranked number one.[12] Target was ranked second, and Costco was ranked seventh. The criteria for the ranking included such factors as clearest company strategy, best store branding, best buying teams, most innovative consumer marketing/merchandising, best supply chain management practices, best overall business fundamentals, and best practice management of individual product categories. One retailing consultant said, "I think most [suppliers] would say Wal-Mart is their most profitable account."[13] While this might seem surprising because of Wal-Mart's enormous bargaining clout, the potentially greater profitability of selling to Wal-Mart stemmed from the practices of most other retailers to demand that suppliers pay sometimes steep slotting fees to win shelf space and their frequent insistence on supplier payment of such extras as in-store displays, damage allowances, handling charges, penalties for late deliveries, rebates of one kind or another, allowances for advertising, and special allowances on slow-moving merchandise that had to be cleared out with deep price discounts; further, most major retailers expected to be courted with Super Bowl tickets, trips to the Masters golf tournament, fancy dinners at conventions and trade shows, or other perks in return for their business. All of these extras represented costs that suppliers had to build into their prices. At Wal-Mart everything was boiled down to one price number, and no "funny-money" extras ever entered into the deal.[14]

Most suppliers viewed Wal-Mart's single bottom-line price and its expectation of close coordination as a win–win proposition, not only because of the benefits of cutting out all the funny-money costs and solidifying their relationship with a major customer but also because what they learned from the collaborative efforts and mutual data-sharing often had considerable benefit in the rest of their operations. Many suppliers, including Procter & Gamble, liked Wal-Mart's supply chain business model so well that they had pushed their other customers to adopt similar practices.[15]

Wal-Mart's Standards for Suppliers

In the 1990s Wal-Mart began establishing standards for its suppliers, with particular emphasis on foreign suppliers that had a history of problematic wages and working conditions. Management believed that suppliers' practices regarding workers' hours; child labor;

---

[12]Reported in a *DSN Retailing Today Online* editorial by Tony Lisanti, November 10, 2003.
[13]As quoted in Useem, "One Nation Under Wal-Mart," p. 74.
[14]Ibid.
[15]Ibid.

discrimination based on race, religion, or other factors; workplace safety, and compliance with local laws and regulations could be attributed to Wal-Mart and could affect its reputation with customers and shareholders. To mitigate the potential for being adversely affected by the manner in which its suppliers conducted their business, Wal-Mart had established a set of supplier standards and set up an internal group to see that suppliers were conforming to the published ethical standards and business practices of Wal-Mart itself.

The company's supplier standards had been through a number of changes as the concerns of Wal-Mart management evolved over time. Suppliers' factories were monitored regularly, and in February 2003 Wal-Mart took direct control of foreign factory audits. Wal-Mart had factory certification teams based in offices in Dubai, Singapore, India, and China; the offices were staffed with more than 100 Wal-Mart employees dedicated to monitoring foreign factory compliance with the company's supplier standards. All suppliers were asked to sign a document certifying their compliance with the standards and were required to post a version of the supplier standards in both English and the local language in each production facility servicing Wal-Mart.

Distribution Center Operations

Throughout the 1980s and 1990s, Wal-Mart had pursued a host of efficiency-increasing actions at its distribution centers. The company had been a global leader in automating its distribution centers and expediting the transfer of incoming shipments from manufacturers to its fleet of delivery trucks, which made daily deliveries to surrounding stores. Prior to automation, bulk cases received from manufacturers had to be opened by distribution center employees and perhaps stored in bins, then picked and repacked in quantities needed for specific stores, and finally loaded onto trucks for delivery to Wal-Mart stores—a manual process that was error-prone and sometimes slow. Using state-of-the-art technology, Wal-Mart had automated many of the labor-intensive tasks, gradually creating an ever-more-sophisticated and cost-efficient system of conveyors, bar-coding, and handheld computers, along with other devices with the capability to quickly sort incoming shipments from manufacturers into smaller, store-specific quantities and route them to waiting trucks to be sent to stores to replenish sold merchandise. Often, incoming goods from manufacturers being unloaded at one section of the warehouse were immediately sorted into store-specific amounts and conveyed directly onto waiting Wal-Mart trucks headed for those particular stores—a large portion of the incoming inventory was in a Wal-Mart distribution center an average of only 12 hours. Distribution center employees had access to real-time information regarding the inventory levels of all items in the center and used the different bar codes for pallets, bins, and shelves to pick up items for store orders. Handheld computers also enabled the packaging department to get accurate information about which items to pack for which store and what loading dock to convey them to.

Truck Fleet Operations

Wal-Mart operated a fleet of 3,500+ company-owned trucks to get goods from its 100+ distribution centers to its almost 5,000 stores. Wal-Mart hired only experienced drivers who had driven more than 300,000 accident-free miles with no major traffic violations. Distribution centers had facilities where drivers could shower, sleep, eat, or attend to personal business while waiting for their truck to be loaded. A truck dispatch coordinator scheduled the dispatch of all trucks according to the available time of drivers and estimated driving time between the distribution center and the designated store. Drivers were expected to pull their trucks up to the store dock at the scheduled time (usually late afternoon or early evening) even if they arrived early; trucks were unloaded by store personnel during nighttime hours, with a two-hour gap between each new truck delivery (if more than one was scheduled for the same night).

In instances where it was economical, Wal-Mart trucks were dispatched directly to a manufacturer's facilities, picked up goods for one or more stores, and delivered them directly, bypassing the distribution center entirely. Manufacturers that supplied certain high-volume items or even a number of different items sometimes delivered their products in truckload lots directly to some or many of Wal-Mart's stores.

Store Construction and Maintenance

Wal-Mart management worked at getting more mileage out of its capital expenditures for new stores, store renovations, and store fixtures. Ideas and suggestions were solicited from vendors regarding store layout, the design of fixtures, and space needed for effective displays. Managers had open-air offices that could be furnished economically, and store designs featured a maximum of display space that could be rearranged and refurbished easily. Wal-Mart claimed that the design and aisle width at its new Supercenters would accommodate 100 million shoppers a week. Because Wal-Mart insisted on a high degree of uniformity in the new stores it built, the architectural firm Wal-Mart employed was able to use computer modeling techniques to turn out complete specifications for 12 or more new stores a week. Moreover, the stores were designed to permit quick, inexpensive construction as well as to allow for low-cost maintenance and renovation. All stores were renovated and redecorated at least once every seven years. If a given store location was rendered obsolete by the construction of new roads or the opening of new shopping locations, then the old store was abandoned in favor of a new store at a more desirable site. In 2003, Wal-Mart stores were being expanded or relocated at the rate of 100–200 annually.

In keeping with the low-cost theme for facilities, Wal-Mart's distribution centers and corporate offices were also built economically and furnished simply. The offices of top executives were modest and unpretentious. The lighting, heating, and air-conditioning controls at all Wal-Mart stores were connected via computer to Bentonville headquarters, allowing cost-saving energy management practices to be implemented centrally and freeing store managers from the time and worry of trying to hold down utility costs. Wal-Mart mass-produced a lot of its displays in-house, not only saving money but also cutting the time needed to roll out a new display concept to as little as 30 days. The company also had a group that disposed of used fixtures and equipment via auctions at the store sites where the surplus existed—a calendar of upcoming auctions was posted on the company's Web site.

Wal-Mart's Approach to Providing Superior Customer Service

Wal-Mart tried to put some organization muscle behind its pledge of "Satisfaction Guaranteed" and do things that would make customers' shopping experience at Wal-Mart pleasant. Store managers challenged store associates to practice what Sam Walton called "aggressive hospitality." A "greeter" was stationed at store entrances to welcome customers with a smile, thank them for shopping at Wal-Mart, assist them in getting a shopping cart, and answer questions about where items were located. Clerks and checkout workers were trained to be courteous and helpful and to exhibit a "friendly, folksy attitude." All store associates were called on to display the "10-foot attitude" and commit to a pledge of friendliness: "I solemnly promise and declare that every customer that comes within ten feet of me, I will smile, look them in the eye, and greet them." Wal-Mart's management stressed five themes in training and supervising store personnel:

1. Think like a customer.
2. Sell what customers want to buy.
3. Provide a genuine value to the customer.
4. Make sure the customer has a good time.
5. Exceed the customer's expectations.

In all stores, efforts were made to present merchandise in easy-to-shop shelving and displays. Floors in the apparel section were carpeted to make the department feel homier and to make shopping seem easier on customers' feet. Store layouts were constantly scrutinized to improve shopping convenience and make it easier for customers to find items. Store employees wore blue vests to make it easier for customers to pick them out from a distance. Fluorescent lighting was recessed into the ceiling to create a softer impression than exposed fluorescent lighting strips. Yet nothing about the decor conflicted with Wal-Mart's low-price image; retailing consultants considered Wal-Mart to be very adept at sending out an effective mix of signals concerning customer service, low prices, quality merchandise, and friendliness. Wal-Mart's management believed that the effort the company put into making its stores more user-friendly and inviting caused shoppers to view Wal-Mart in a more positive light. A reporter for *Discount Store News* observed:

> The fact is that everything Wal-Mart does from store design to bar coding to lighting to greeters-regardless of how simple or complex—is implemented only after carefully considering the impact on the customer. Virtually nothing is done without the guarantee that it benefits the customer in some way . . . As a result Wal-Mart has been able to build loyalty and trust among its customers that is unparalleled among other retail giants.[16]

The Culture at Wal-Mart in 2003

Wal-Mart's culture in 2003 continued to be deeply rooted in Sam Walton's business philosophy and leadership style. Mr. Sam, as he had been fondly called, had been not only Wal-Mart's founder and patriarch but also its spiritual leader—and still was in many respects. Four key core values and business principles underpinned Sam Walton's approach to managing:[17]

- Treat employees as partners, sharing both the good and bad about the company so that they will strive to excel and participate in the rewards. (Wal-Mart fostered the concept of partnership by referring to all employees as "associates," a term Sam Walton had insisted on from the company's beginnings because it denoted a partnerlike relationship.)
- Build for the future, rather than just immediate gains, by continuing to study the changing concepts that are a mark of the retailing industry and be ready to test and experiment with new ideas.
- Recognize that the road to success includes failing, which is part of the learning process rather than a personal or corporate defect or failing. Always challenge the obvious.
- Involve associates at all levels in the total decision-making process.

Sam Walton practiced these principles diligently in his own actions and insisted that other Wal-Mart managers do the same. Up until his health failed badly in 1991, he spent several days a week visiting the stores, gauging the moods of shoppers, listening to employees discuss what was on their minds, learning what was or was not selling, gathering ideas about how things could be done better, complimenting workers on their efforts, and challenging them to come up with good ideas.

The values, beliefs, and practices that Sam Walton instilled in Wal-Mart's culture and that still carried over in 2003 were reflected in statements made in his autobiography:

> Everytime Wal-Mart spends one dollar foolishly, it comes right out of our customer's pockets. Everytime we save a dollar, that puts us one more step ahead of the competition— which is where we always plan to be.

> One person seeking glory doesn't accomplish much; at Wal-Mart, everything we've done has been the result of people pulling together to meet one common goal.

> I have always been driven to buck the system, to innovate, to take things beyond where they've been.

---

[16]*Discount Store News,* December 18, 1989, p. 161.
[17]Sam Walton with John Huey, *Sam Walton: Made in America* (New York: Doubleday, 1992), p. 12.

We paid absolutely no attention whatsoever to the way things were supposed to be done, you know, the way the rules of retail said it had to be done.

My role has been to pick good people and give them the maximum authority and responsibility.

I'm more of a manager by walking and flying around, and in the process I stick my fingers into everything I can to see how it's coming along . . . My appreciation for numbers has kept me close to our operational statements, and to all the other information we have pouring in from so many different places.

The more you share profit with your associates—whether it's in salaries or incentives or bonuses or stock discounts—the more profit will accrue to your company. Why? Because the way management treats the associates is exactly how the associates will then treat the customers. And if the associates treat the customers well, the customers will return again and again.

The real challenge in a business like ours is to become what we call servant leaders. And when they do, the team—the manager and the associates—can accomplish anything.

There's no better way to keep someone doing things the right way than by letting him or her know how much you appreciate their performance.

I like my numbers as quickly as I can get them. The quicker we get that information, the quicker we can act on it.

The bigger we get as a company, the more important it becomes for us to shift responsibility and authority toward the front lines, toward that department manager who's stocking the shelves and talking to the customer.

We give our department heads the opportunity to become real merchants at a very early stage of the game . . . we make our department heads the managers of their own businesses . . . We share everything with them: the costs of their goods, the freight costs, the profit margins. We let them see how their store ranks with every other store in the company on a constant, running basis, and we give them incentives to want to win.

We're always looking for new ways to encourage our associates out in the stores to push their ideas up through the system . . . Great ideas come from everywhere if you just listen and look for them. You never know who's going to have a great idea.

A lot of bureaucracy is really the product of some empire builder's ego . . . We don't need any of that at Wal-Mart. If you're not serving the customers, or supporting the folks who do, we don't need you.

I believe in always having goals, and always setting them high . . . The folks at Wal-Mart have always had goals in front of them. In fact, we have sometimes built real scoreboards on the stage at Saturday morning meetings.

You can't just keep doing what works one time, because everything around you is always changing. To succeed, you have to stay out in front of that change.[18]

Walton's success flowed from his cheerleading management style, his ability to instill the principles and management philosophies he preached into Wal-Mart's culture, the close watch he kept on costs, his relentless insistence on continuous improvement, and his habit of staying in close touch with both consumer and associates. It was common practice for Walton to lead cheers at annual shareholder meetings, store visits, managers' meetings, and company events. His favorite was the Wal-Mart cheer:

Give me a W!

Give me an A!

Give me an L!

---

[18]Ibid., pp. 10, 12, 47, 63, 115, 128, 135, 140, 213, 226–229, 233, 246, 249–254, and 256.

Give me a Squiggly!

   (Here, everybody sort of does the twist.)

Give me an M!

Give me an A!

Give me an R!

Give me a T!

What's that spell?

Wal-Mart!

Whose Wal-Mart is it?

My Wal-Mart!

Who's number one?

The Customer! Always!

In 2003, the Wal-Mart cheer was still a core part of the Wal-Mart culture and was used throughout the company at meetings of store employees, managers, and corporate gatherings in Bentonville to create a "whistle while you work" atmosphere, loosen everyone up, inject fun and enthusiasm, and get sessions started on a stimulating note. While the cheer seemed corny to outsiders, once they saw the cheer in action at Wal-Mart they came to realize its cultural power and significance. And much of Sam Walton's cultural legacy remained intact in 2003, most especially among the company's top decision makers and longtime managers. As a *Fortune* writer put it:

> Spend enough time inside the company—where nothing backs up a point better than a quotation from Walton scripture—and it's easy to get the impression that the founder is orchestrating his creation from the beyond.[19]

The Three Basic Beliefs Underlying the Wal-Mart Culture in 2003

Wal-Mart top management stressed three basic beliefs that Sam Walton had preached since 1962:

1. *Treat individuals with respect and dignity*—Management consistently drummed the theme that dedicated, hardworking, ordinary people who teamed together and who treated each other with respect and dignity could accomplish extraordinary things. Throughout company literature, comments could be found referring to Wal-Mart's "concern for the individual." Such expressions as "Our people make the difference," "We care about people," and "People helping People" were used repeatedly by Wal-Mart executives and store managers to create and nurture a family-oriented atmosphere among store associates.

2. *Provide service to customers*—Management stressed that the company was nothing without its customers. Management emphasized that, to satisfy customers and keep them coming back again and again, the company had to build their trust in its pricing philosophy—Wal-Mart customers had to always find the lowest prices with the best possible service. One of the standard Wal-Mart mantras preached to all associates was that the customer was boss. Associates in stores were urged to observe the rule regarding the "10-foot attitude."

3. *Strive for excellence*—The concept of striving for excellence stemmed from Sam Walton's conviction that prices were seldom as low as they needed to be and that product quality was seldom as high as customers deserved. The thesis at Wal-Mart was that new ideas and ambitious goals made the company reach further and try harder—the process of finding new and innovative ways to push boundaries and constantly improve

---

[19]Useem, "One Nation Under Wal-Mart," p. 72.

made the company better at what it did and contributed to higher levels of customer satisfaction. Wal-Mart managers at all levels spent much time and effort motivating associates to offer ideas for improvement and to function as partners. It was reiterated again and again that every cost counted and that every worker had a responsibility to be involved.

These three beliefs were supplemented by several supporting cultural themes and practices:

- Go all-out to exceed customers' expectations and make sure that customers have a good time shopping at Wal-Mart. Every associate repeatedly heard "The customer is boss and the future depends on you."
- Practice Sam Walton's 10 rules for building a business. Management had distilled much of Sam Walton's business philosophy into 10 rules (see Exhibit 4); these were reiterated

EXHIBIT 4   Sam Walton's 10 Rules for Building a Business

Rule 1: Commit to your business. Believe in it more than anybody else. I think I overcame every single one of my personal shortcomings by the sheer passion I brought to my work. I don't know if you're born with this kind of passion, or if you can learn it. But I do know you need it. If you love your work, you'll be out there every day trying to do it the best you possibly can, and pretty soon everybody around will catch the passion from you—like a fever.

Rule 2: Share your profits with all your Associates, and treat them as partners. In turn, they will treat you as a partner, and together you will all perform beyond your wildest expectations. Remain a corporation and retain control if you like, but behave as a servant leader in a partnership. Encourage your Associates to hold a stake in the company. Offer discounted stock, and grant them stock for their retirement. It's the single best thing we ever did.

Rule 3: Motivate your partners. Money and ownership alone aren't enough. Constantly, day-by-day, think of new and more interesting ways to motivate and challenge your partners. Set high goals, encourage competition, and then keep score. Make bets with outrageous payoffs. If things get stale, cross-pollinate; have managers switch jobs with one another to stay challenged. Keep everybody guessing as to what your next trick is going to be. Don't become too predictable.

Rule 4: Communicate everything you possibly can to your partners. The more they know, the more they'll understand. The more they understand, the more they'll care. Once they care, there's no stopping them. If you don't trust your Associates to know what's going on, they'll know you don't really consider them partners. Information is power, and the gain you get from empowering your Associates more than offsets the risk of informing your competitors.

Rule 5: Appreciate everything your Associates do for the business. A paycheck and a stock option will buy one kind of loyalty. But all of us like to be told how much somebody appreciates what we do for them. We like to hear it often, and especially when we have done something we're really proud of. Nothing else can quite substitute for a few well-chosen, well-timed, sincere words of praise. They're absolutely free—and worth a fortune.

Rule 6: Celebrate your successes. Find some humor in your failures. Don't take yourself so seriously. Loosen up, and everybody around you will loosen up. Have fun. Show enthusiasm—always. When all else fails, put on a costume and sing a silly song. Then make everybody else sing with you. Don't do a hula on Wall Street. It's been done. Think up your own stunt. All of this is more important, and more fun, than you think, and it really fools the competition. "Why should we take those cornballs at Wal-Mart seriously?"

Rule 7: Listen to everyone in your company. And figure out ways to get them talking. The folks on the front lines—the ones who actually talk to the customer—are the only ones who really know what's going on out there. You'd better find out what they know. This really is what total quality is all about. To push responsibility down in your organization, and to force good ideas to bubble up within it, you must listen to what your Associates are trying to tell you.

Rule 8: Exceed your customers' expectations. If you do, they'll come back over and over. Give them what they want—and a little more. Let them know you appreciate them. Make good on all your mistakes, and don't make excuses—apologize. Stand behind everything you do. The two most important words I ever wrote were on that first Wal-Mart sign, "Satisfaction Guaranteed." They're still up there, and they have made all the difference.

Rule 9: Control your expenses better than your competition. This is where you can always find the competitive advantage. For 25 years running—long before Wal-Mart was known as the nation's largest retailer—we ranked No. 1 in our industry for the lowest ratio of expenses to sales. You can make a lot of different mistakes and still recover if you run an efficient operation. Or you can be brilliant and still go out of business if you're too inefficient.

Rule 10: Swim upstream. Go the other way. Ignore the conventional wisdom. If everybody else is doing it one way, there's a good chance you can find your niche by going in exactly the opposite direction. But be prepared for a lot of folks to wave you down and tell you you're headed the wrong way. I guess in all my years, what I heard more often than anything was: a town of less than 50,000 population cannot support a discount store for very long.

Source: www.walmartstores.com, accessed December 18, 2003.

to associates and used at meetings to guide decision making and the crafting and executing of Wal-Mart's strategy.

- Observe the Sundown Rule: Answer requests by sundown on the day they are received. Management believed this working principle had to be taken seriously in a busy world in which people's job performance depended on cooperation from others.

Wal-Mart's culture had unusually deep roots at the headquarters complex in Bentonville. The numerous journalists and business executives who had been to Bentonville and spent much time at Wal-Mart's corporate offices uniformly reported being impressed with the breadth, depth, and pervasive power of the company's culture. Jack Welch, former CEO of General Electric and a potent culture builder in his own right, noted that "the place vibrated" with cultural energy. There was little evidence that the culture in Bentonville was any weaker in 2003 than it had been 12 years earlier when Sam Walton personally led the culture-building, culture-nurturing effort.

But Wal-Mart executives nonetheless were currently facing a formidable challenge in sustaining the culture in the company's distribution centers and especially in its stores. Annual turnover rates in Wal-Mart's stores were running about 45 percent in 2002–2003 and had run as high as 70 percent in 1999 when the economy was booming and the labor market was tight. Such high rates of turnover among the company's worldwide workforce of 1.4 million, coupled with the fact that Wal-Mart would need to add another 800,000 new employees from 2004 to 2008 (including 47,000 management positions) to staff its new stores and distribution centers, made keeping the culture intact outside Bentonville a Herculean task. No other company in all of business history had been confronted with cultural indoctrination of so many new employees in so many locations in such a relatively short time.

Soliciting Ideas from Associates

Associates at all levels were expected to be an integral part of the process of making the company better. Wal-Mart store managers usually spent a portion of each day walking around the store checking on how well things were going in each department, listening to associates' comments, soliciting suggestions, discussing how improvements could be made, and praising associates who were doing a good job. Store managers frequently asked associates what needed to be done better in their department and what could be changed to improve store operations. Associates who believed that a policy or procedure detracted from operations were encouraged to challenge and change it. Task forces to evaluate ideas and plan out future actions to implement them were common, and it was not unusual for the person who developed the idea to be appointed the leader of the group. An assistant store manager explained the importance of getting employees to suggest ways to boost sales:

> We are encouraged to be merchants. If a sales clerk, a checker or a stockman believes he can sell an item and wants to promote it, he is encouraged to go for it. That associate can buy the merchandise, feature it, and maintain it as long as he can sell it.[20]

That same assistant store manager, when he accidentally ordered four times as many Moon Pies for an in-store promotion as intended, was challenged by the store manager to be creative and figure out a way to sell the extra inventory. The assistant manager's solution was to create the first World Championship Moon Pie Eating Contest, held in the store's parking lot in the small town of Oneonta, Alabama. The promotion and contest drew thousands of spectators and was so successful that it became an annual store event.

Listening to employees was a very important part of each manager's job. All of Wal-Mart's top executives relied on a concept known as management by walking around; they visited stores, distribution centers, and support facilities regularly, staying on top of what

[20]*Discount Store News,* December 18, 1989, p. 83.

was happening and listening to what employees had to say about how things were going. Senior managers at Wal-Mart's Bentonville headquarters believed that visiting stores and listening to associates was time well spent because a number of the company's best ideas had come from Wal-Mart associates—Wal-Mart's use of people greeters at store entrances was one of those ideas.

Compensation and Incentives

New hourly associates at U.S. Wal-Mart stores were paid anywhere from $1 to $6 above the minimum wage, depending on the type of job, and could expect to receive a raise within the first year at one or both of the semiannual job evaluations. Typically, at least one raise was guaranteed in the first year if Wal-Mart planned to keep the individual on the staff. The other raise depended on how well the associate worked and improved during the year. At the store level, only the store manager was salaried; all other associates, including the department managers, were considered hourly employees. A 2003 study by *Forbes* found that Wal-Mart employees earned an average hourly wage of $7.50, which translated to an annual income of $18,000. Store clerks generally earned the least—one study showed that sales clerks earned an average of $8.23 an hour and $13,861 annually in 2001.[21] Workers that unloaded trucks and stocked store shelves could earn anywhere from $25,000 to $50,000.

Part-time jobs were most common among sales clerks and checkout personnel in the stores where customer traffic varied appreciably during days of the week and months of the year. New full-time and part-time associates became eligible for health care benefits after a six-month wait and a one-year exclusion for preexisting conditions. As of 2003, about 60 percent of the roughly 800,000 U.S. Wal-Mart associates signed up for coverage (compared with an average of 72 percent for the whole retailing industry); many Wal-Mart associates did not sign up for health care coverage because another household member already had family coverage at his or her place of employment. Worker premiums for coverage were as little as $13 every two weeks with an annual deductible of $1,000, but associates could opt for plans with a higher premium and a lower deductible.[22] The health care benefit package covered 100 percent of most major medical expenses above $1,750 in employee out-of-pocket expenses and entailed no lifetime cap on medical cost coverage (a feature offered by fewer than 50 percent of U.S. employers). The company's health benefits also included dental coverage, short- and long-term disability, an illness protection plan, and business travel accident insurance. But to help control its health care costs for associates, Wal-Mart's plan did not pay for flu shots, eye exams, child vaccinations, chiropractic services, and certain other treatments allowed in the plans of many companies; further, Wal-Mart did not pay any health care costs for retirees. Due to Wal-Mart management's recent efforts to control costs for health care benefits, the company's health care costs compared very favorably with those of other organizations:[23]

	Average Cost per Eligible Employee	
	2001	2002
U.S. employees of a cross-section of large, medium, and small companies	$4,924	$5,646
Employees of wholesale/retail stores	4,300	4,834
Wal-Mart employees (estimated)	3,000	3,500

[21]According to documents filed in a lawsuit against the company and cited in Bianco and Zellner, "Is Wal-Mart Too Powerful?" p. 102.
[22]Bernard Wysocki Jr. and Ann Zimmerman, "Wal-Mart Cost-Cutting Finds a Big Target in Health Benefits," *The Wall Street Journal,* September 30, 2003, p. A16.
[23]Ibid., p. A1.

Wal-Mart's package of fringe benefits for full-time employees (and some part-time employees) also included:

- Vacation and personal time.
- Holiday pay.
- Jury duty pay.
- Medical and bereavement leave.
- Military leave.
- Maternity/paternity leave.
- Confidential counseling services for associates and their families.
- Child care discounts for associates with children (through four national providers).
- GED reimbursement/scholarships for associates and their spouses.

Wal-Mart associates received 10 percent off selected merchandise and Sam's Club associates received a Sam's Club membership card at no cost.

According to management, some 60 percent of associates indicated that a major reason they joined Wal-Mart was the benefits. In addition to compensation and fringe benefits, Wal-Mart had installed an extensive system of incentives that allowed associates to share monetarily in the company's success.

The Profit-Sharing Plan

Wal-Mart maintained a profit-sharing plan for full- and part-time associates; individuals were eligible after one year and 1,000 hours of service. Annual contributions to the plan were tied to the company's profitability and were made at the sole discretion of management and the board of directors. Employees could contribute up to 15 percent of their earnings to their 401(k) accounts. Wal-Mart's contribution to each associate's profit-sharing account became vested at the rate of 20 percent per year beginning the third year of participation in the plan. After seven years of continuous employment the company's contribution became fully vested; however, if the associate left the company prior to that time, the unvested portions were redistributed to all remaining employees. The plan was funded entirely by Wal-Mart, and most of the profit-sharing contributions were invested in Wal-Mart's common stock. The company had contributed more than $2.7 billion toward associates' profit-sharing and 401(k) accounts since 1972. Company contributions to the plan totaled $98.3 million in 1991, $129.6 million in 1992, and $166 million in 1993 but had risen significantly over the last decade—annual contributions to 401(k) and profit-sharing worldwide amounted to $663 million in fiscal 2003, $555 million in fiscal 2002, and $486 million in fiscal 2001. Associates could begin withdrawals from their account upon retirement or disability, with the balance paid to family members upon death.

Stock Purchase and Stock Option Plans

A stock purchase plan was adopted in 1972 to allow eligible employees a means of purchasing shares of common stock through regular payroll deduction or annual lump-sum contribution. Prior to 1990, the yearly maximum under this program was $1,500 per eligible employee; starting in 1990 the maximum was increased to $1,800 annually. The company contributed an amount equal to 15 percent of each participating associate's contribution. Longtime employees who had started participating in the early years of the program had accumulated stock worth over $100,000. About one-fourth of Wal-Mart's employees participated in the stock purchase plan in 1993, but this percentage had since declined because many new employees opted not to participate.

In addition to regular stock purchases, certain employees qualified to participate in stock option plans; options expired 10 years from the date of the grant and could be exercised in nine annual installments. In 2003 there were over 59 million shares reserved for issuance under stock option plans. The value of options granted in recent years was substantial: $96 million (1990), $128 million (1991), $143 million (1992), and $235 million (1993).

Sales Contests and Other Incentive Programs

Associate incentive plans were in place in every store, club, distribution center, and support facility. Associates received bonuses for "good ideas," such as how to reduce shoplifting or how to improve merchandising. Wal-Mart instituted a shrinkage bonus in 1980. If a store held losses from theft and damage below the corporate goal, every associate in that store was eligible to receive up to $200. As a result, Wal-Mart's shrinkage ran about 1 percent, compared to an industry average of 2 percent. One of Wal-Mart's most successful incentive programs involved in-store sales contests that allowed departments within the store to do a special promotion and pricing on items they themselves wanted to feature. Management believed these contests boosted sales, breathed new life into an otherwise slow-selling item, and helped keep associates thinking about how to help bolster sales. In 1999 (the most recent year for which data were available), Wal-Mart paid $500 million in incentive bonuses based on store and individual performance to 525,000 full- and part-time employees.

On the basis of data provided by Wal-Mart associates, *Fortune* had included Wal-Mart on its list of the "100 Best Companies to Work For" for four of the six years from 1998 to 2003. Wal-Mart was the largest U.S. employer of African Americans and Hispanics.

However, in 2003, Wal-Mart was faced with a federal lawsuit filed by six female employees claiming that the company discriminated against women in pay, promotions, training, and job assignments—plaintiffs' attorneys were seeking class-action status for the lawsuit on behalf of all past and present female workers at Wal-Mart's U.S. stores and wholesale clubs. According to data from various sources, while two-thirds of Wal-Mart's hourly employees were women, less than 15 percent held store manager positions. There were also indications of pay gaps between male and female employees. The differences increased up the corporate ladder for the same positions, beginning with full-time hourly women employees making 6.2 percent less than their male counterparts, and female senior vice presidents making 50 percent less than men in the same position. According to a study conducted by the plaintiffs as part of their discrimination lawsuit and based on an analysis of Wal-Mart's payroll data, female workers at Wal-Mart between 1996 and 2001 earned 4.5 to 5.6 percent less than men doing similar jobs and with similar experience levels. The pay gap allegedly widened higher up the management ladder. The study found that male management trainees made an average of $23,175 a year, compared with $22,371 for women trainees. At the senior vice president level, the average male made $419,435 a year, whereas the four female senior vice presidents earned an average of $279,772.

Training

Top management was committed to providing all associates state-of-the-art training resources and development time to help achieve career objectives. The company had a number of training tools in place, including classroom courses, computer-based learning, distance learning, corporate intranet sites, mentor programs, satellite broadcasts, and skills assessments. In November 1985 the Walton Institute of Retailing was opened in affiliation with the University of Arkansas. Within a year of its inception every Wal-Mart manager from the stores, the distribution facilities, and the general office was expected to take part in special programs at the Walton Institute to strengthen and develop the company's managerial capabilities.

Management Training

Wal-Mart store managers were hired in one of three ways. Hourly associates could move up through the ranks from sales to department manager to manager of the check lanes into store management training—more than 65 percent of Wal-Mart's managers had started out as hourly associates. Second, people with outstanding merchandising skills at other retail companies were recruited to join the ranks of Wal-Mart managers. And third, Wal-Mart recruited college graduates to enter the company's training program. Store management trainees went through an intensive on-the-job training program of almost 20 weeks and then were given responsibility for an area of the store. Trainees who progressed satisfactorily and showed leadership and job knowledge were promoted to an assistant manager, which included further training in various aspects of retailing and store operations. Given Wal-Mart's continued store growth, above-average trainees could progress to store manager within five years. Through bonuses for sales increases above projected amounts and company stock options, the highest-performing store managers earned well into six figures annually.

Associate Training

Wal-Mart did not provide a specialized training course for its hourly associates. Upon hiring, an associate was immediately placed in a position for on-the-job-training. From time to time, training films were shown in associates' meetings. Store managers and department managers were expected to train and supervise the associates under them in whatever ways were needed. As one associate put it, "Mostly you learn by doing. They tell you a lot; but you learn your job every day."

Respect for the individual, one of the company's three core values, was reinforced throughout the training process for both managers and associates. Wal-Mart had been ranked among *Training* magazine's "Top Training 100" companies in 2001 and 2002.

Meetings and Rapid Response

The company used meetings both as a communication device and as a culture-building exercise. In Bentonville, there were Friday merchandising meetings and Saturday-morning meetings at 7:30 AM to review the week. The weekly merchandising meeting included buyers and merchandising staff headquartered in Bentonville and various regional managers who directed store operations.

David Glass, Wal-Mart's former CEO, explained the purpose of the Friday merchandise meetings:

> In retailing, there has always been a traditional, head-to-head confrontation between operations and merchandising. You know, the operations guys say, "Why in the world would anybody buy this? It's a dog, and we'll never sell it." Then the merchandising folks say, "There's nothing wrong with that item. If you guys were smart enough to display it well and promote it properly, it would blow out the doors." So we sit all these folks down together every Friday at the same table and just have at it.
>
> We get into some of the doggonedest, knock-down drag-outs you have ever seen. But we have a rule. We never leave an item hanging. We will make a decision in that meeting even if it's wrong, and sometimes it is. But when the people come out of that room, you would be hard-pressed to tell which ones oppose it and which ones are for it. And once we've made that decision on Friday, we expect it to be acted on in all the stores on Saturday. What we guard against around here is people saying, "Let's think about it." We make a decision. Then we act on it.[24]

At the Saturday-morning meetings—a Wal-Mart tradition since 1961—top officers, merchandising and regional managers, and other Bentonville headquarters' staff (about 100 people in all) gathered to exchange ideas on how well things were going and talk about any problems relating to the week's sales, store performance, special promotion items, store construction, distribution centers, transportation, supply chain activities, and so on. As with the Friday merchandise meetings, decisions were made about what actions needed to be taken.

---

[24]Walton with Huey, *Sam Walton*, pp. 225–26.

The store meetings and the Friday/Saturday meetings in Bentonville, along with the in-the-field visits by Wal-Mart management, created a strong bias for action. A *Fortune* reporter observed, "Managers suck in information from Monday to Thursday, exchange ideas on Friday and Saturday, and implement decisions in the stores on Monday."[25]

Wal-Mart's Future: Mounting Flak from Several Directions

Sam Walton had engineered the development and rapid ascendancy of Wal-Mart to the forefront of the retailing industry—the discount stores and Sam's Clubs were strategic moves that he directed. His handpicked successor, David Glass, had directed the hugely successful move into Supercenters and grocery retailing, as well as presiding over the company's growth into the world's largest retailing enterprise; the neighborhood market store format also came into being during his tenure as CEO. H. Lee Scott, Wal-Mart's third CEO, had the challenge of globalizing Wal-Mart operations and continuing the long-term process of saturating the U.S. market with Supercenters and adding other types of stores in those areas that were underserved.

But as 2003 unfolded, it was apparent that Scott had to deal with a growing number of issues and obstacles that were being thrown in Wal-Mart's path, some of which were embarrassing or threatening. Not only was the company faced with over 6,000 active lawsuits, ranging from antitrust and consumer issues to torts claims (like a customer suffering injury from falling in a store or being in a collision with a Wal-Mart truck). A couple of the lawsuits had potentially serious consequences—like the one alleging the company discriminated against women, which had potential to turn into the largest sex-bias class action ever, and a second alleging that associates were forced to work unpaid overtime. But Wal-Mart was also getting flak from other quarters, forcing management to devote more time and attention to putting out brushfires than to growing and operating the business (as had been the case during the David Glass era):

- Wal-Mart had to temporarily stop selling guns at its 118 stores across California following what California's attorney general said were hundreds of violations of state laws. Investigations by California authorities revealed that six Wal-Mart stores had released guns before the required 10-day waiting period, failed to verify the identity of buyers properly, sold illegally to felons, and committed other violations. Wal-Mart cooperated with governmental officials and agreed to immediately suspend firearms sales until corrective action could be taken and store associates properly trained on state firearms laws.

- In New York, Wal-Mart had run afoul of the state's 1988 toy weapons law. The toy guns Wal-Mart sold had an orange cap at the end of the barrel but otherwise looked real, thus violating New York laws banning toy guns with realistic colors such as black or aluminum and not complying with New York's requirement that toy guns have unremovable orange stripes along the barrel. Investigators from the state attorney general's office shopped 10 Wal-Marts in New York state from Buffalo to Long Island and purchased toy guns that violated the law at each of them. The president of New York's State Police Investigators Union said, "Without clear markings, it is extremely difficult to tell the difference between a toy gun and a real weapon." Wal-Mart acknowledged that its toy guns did not have all of the state-required markings, but the company maintained that it need only comply with federal law, which requires an orange cap on the end of the barrel. Wal-Mart had sold more than 42,000 toy guns in the state during the past two and a half years. If the state of New York prevailed in its halt of toy gun sales at Wal-Mart, it could seek damages equal to $1,000 for each illegal toy gun sold since April 1, 1997.

[25]Saporito, "What Sam Walton Taught America," p. 105.

- Immigration authorities were investigating certain Wal-Mart managers for knowingly hiring janitorial contractors who were using illegal immigrants to clean stores. In a series of predawn raids on October 23, 2003, federal agents had arrested nearly 250 illegal immigrants after cleaning shifts at 61 Wal-Mart stores in 21 states; agents also searched a manager's office at Wal-Mart's Bentonville headquarters and took 18 boxes of documents relating to cleaning contractors dating back to March 2000.[26] Federal officials reportedly had wiretaps showing that Wal-Mart officials knew its contractors were furnishing illegal cleaning crews. Several weeks later, Wal-Mart was notified that it had been included in a federal grand jury probe of the contractors. Wal-Mart, however, was indignant about the charges, saying that Wal-Mart managers at many levels knew about the problem of illegal workers in its stores and had been cooperating with federal authorities in the investigations for almost three years. Wal-Mart indicated that it had helped federal investigators tape conversations between some of its store managers and employees of the cleaning contractors suspected of using illegal immigrants; that it revised its written contracts with cleaning contractors in 2002 to include language that janitorial contractors were complying with all federal, state, and local employment laws (because of the information developed in 2001); and that it had begun bringing all janitorial work in-house rather than outsourcing such services in 2003 because outsourcing was more expensive—in October 2003 fewer than 700 Wal-Mart stores used outside cleaning contractors, down from almost half in 2000.

- United Food and Commercial Workers (UFCW) was exerting all the pressure it could to force Wal-Mart to raise its wages and benefits for associates to levels that would be comparable to union wages and benefits at unionized supermarket chains. A UFCW spokeswoman in Southern California, where union members were striking supermarket chains to protest efforts to trim health care costs, said:

  > Their productivity is becoming a model for taking advantage of workers, and our society is doomed if we think the answer is to lower our standards to Wal-Mart's level. What we need to do is to raise Wal-Mart to the standard we have set using the supermarket industry as an example so that Wal-Mart does not destroy our society community by community.[27]

Wal-Mart's labor costs were said to be 20 percent less than those at unionized supermarkets.[28] In Dallas, 20 supermarkets had closed once Wal-Mart had saturated the area with its Supercenters. According to one source, for every Wal-Mart Supercenter opened in the next five years, two other supermarkets would be forced to close, thus casting some doubt on whether Wal-Mart's entry into a community resulted in a net increase in jobs and tax revenues.[29] One trade publication estimated that Wal-Mart's plans to open more than 1,000 Supercenters in the United States in the 2004–2008 period would boost Wal-Mart's grocery and related revenues from $82 billion to $162 billion, thus increasing its market share in groceries from 19 percent to 35 percent and its share of pharmacy and drugstore-related sales from 15 percent to 25 percent.[30]

- Opponents of "big-box" retailers had battled against Wal-Mart's efforts to locate new stores in such states as Vermont and California. Oakland officials had recently voted to limit stores with full-service supermarkets to 100,000 square feet or 2.5 acres—a

[26]Ann Zimmerman, "After Huge Raid on Illegals, Wal-Mart Fires Back at U.S.," *The Wall Street Journal,* December 19, 2003, pp. A1, A10.

[27]As quoted in Lorrie Grant, "Retail Giant Wal-Mart Faces Challenges on Many Fronts," *USA Today,* November 11, 2003, p. B2.

[28]Bianco and Zellner, "Is Wal-Mart Too Powerful?" p. 103.

[29]Ibid.

[30]Ibid., p. 108.

move deliberately aimed at blocking Wal-Mart's plan to open 187,000-square-foot Supercenters in the Oakland area. In Contra Costa County, near San Francisco, county supervisors enacted an ordinance prohibiting any retail outlet larger than 90,000 square feet from devoting more than 5 percent of its floor space to food or other non-taxable goods—Wal-Mart gathered enough signatures to force a referendum in March 2004, but the referendum lost due mainly to certain tactics Wal-Mart employed as opposed to citizens' rejection of Wal-Mart Supercenters.[31] Restrictive zoning codes, vocal opponents of big-box retailers (most of whom were desirous of protecting local businesses from the competition of Wal-Mart's everyday low prices), high land costs in urbanized areas, and combative labor unions were major reasons why in 2003 Wal-Mart had more stores in rural and less urbanized areas compared to major metropolitan areas. Saturating major metropolitan areas with Supercenters, Sam's Clubs, and neighborhood markets was crucial to Wal-Mart's strategy of sustaining its double-digit growth rate in the United States.

- An article by newspaper reporter Jon Talton in the August 17, 2003 issue of Phoenix's *Arizona Republic* slammed Wal-Mart on several fronts:

  Fair play is a heartland value. But Wal-Mart is known for clear-cutting the retail landscape. Competing national stores won't even consider locating within three miles of a Wal-Mart Supercenter, and local retailers go out of business. Suppliers are bullied for "everyday low prices," with the result being that many have been forced from business.

  Speaking of fair, you're the nation's largest employer, with a million "associates." But relatively few work 40-hour weeks, and a union cashier at Safeway or Albertson's can make twice as much as one of your checkers. Nor is it easy for someone making seven bucks an hour to afford your "pay-for-it-yourself" benefits.

- Wal-Mart had been criticized for refusing to stock CDs or DVDs with parental warning stickers (mostly profanity-laced hip-hop music) and for either pulling certain racy magazines (*Maxim, Stuff,* and *FHM*) from its shelves or obscuring their covers. Critics contended that Wal-Mart made no effort to survey shoppers about how they felt about such products but rather that it responded in ad hoc fashion to complaints lodged by a relative handful of customers and by conservative outside groups.[32] Wal-Mart had also been the only one of the top 10 drugstore chains to refuse to stock Preven, a morning-after contraceptive introduced in 1999, because company executives did not want its pharmacists to have to grapple with the moral dilemma of abortion.

- In Colorado, the UFCW accused Wal-Mart of harassing workers to keep them from joining its local in Denver and elsewhere. According to the complaint filed with the National Labor Relations Board, Wal-Mart managers at a Denver store threatened, intimidated, and illegally monitored employees who were organizing. Similar complaints had previously been filed in Florida and Texas. A Wal-Mart spokesman denied the charge concerning the Denver store and noted that similar complaints at other locations had been dismissed without a hearing. Even so, Wal-Mart, which had an official policy of being strongly opposed to unionization, had seen the number of complaints about its efforts to prevent unionization grow in recent years—so far, 17 complaints had been filed in 12 states.

A Web site called Walmartwatch.com had sprung up to collect and publicize reports of misbehavior and wrongful conduct on the part of Wal-Mart management and the company's growing economic power and influence. A union-affiliated Web site (www.nlcnet.org), run by the National Labor Committee, was also disseminating anti–Wal-Mart information.

[31]Ibid.

[32]Ibid., pp. 104, 106.

H. Lee Scott was understandably concerned about the raft of issues that threatened to mar Wal-Mart's reputation and raise questions about the company's efforts to secure the lowest prices for its customers. He recognized that the company's size and market standing made it an attractive target for critics; as he put it, "In the past we were judged by our aspirations. Now, we're going to be judged by our exceptions."[33] Scott had launched his own investigations into the sex-bias claims and the use of illegal workers and vowed that there would be zero tolerance on Wal-Mart's part for misbehavior:

> Wal-Mart does not and will not tolerate illegal workers in any capacity. Whatever we find, we would be shocked if a Wal-Mart executive were ever involved in the hiring of illegal workers.
>
> What we can't do is give people the fuel to attack us. I have a responsibility that is twofold: to make sure we're not doing the wrong thing, and to make sure that we are trying to communicate that this is a quality company.[34]

However, despite concerns in some quarters over Wal-Mart's growing size and economic influence, Scott believed the company could grow to be two or three times its present size.

[33]Useem, "One Nation Under Wal-Mart," p. 78.
[34]Grant, "Retail Giant Wal-Mart Faces Challenges on Many Fronts," p. B1.

Pricing Strategy

19

Schwinn Bicycles

J. Paul Peter *University of Wisconsin–Madison*

Inside a plain, brown building in Boulder, Colorado, is a shrine to an American icon: the Schwinn bicycle. Some mud-caked from daily use, some shiny museum pieces—dozens of bikes stand atop file cabinets and lean against cubicles. Amid the spokes and handlebars, a group of zealots is working to pull off the turnaround of the century in the bike business. Brimming with energy, they're determined to resurrect the best known brand on two wheels. But as Schwinn celebrates its 100th anniversary, its management team faces a long uphill climb. Just two years ago, once-mighty Schwinn had a near-death experience in bankruptcy court. Now it's trying to rise to the top of the crowded mountain bike market.

For years, Schwinn was the top U.S. brand with as much as 25 percent of the market. Now, it has less than 5 percent of the $2.5 billion annual retail bike market. The new Schwinn will sell about 400,000 redesigned bikes—many of them Asian-made models—that sell for $200 to $400 retail, the lower end of the adult bike market. Those models are catching on. But the turnaround won't be a success unless Schwinn persuades cyclists to fork over $700 or more for its newer bikes. Below are market shares of manufacturers for bikes retail-priced $400 and up:

Trek	24%
Cannondale	12%
Specialized	12%
Schwinn	7%

This case prepared by J. Paul Peter of the University of Wisconsin–Madison.
Source: Patrick McGeehan, "Biking Icon Wants to Lose Training Wheels," *USA Today,* August 8, 1995, pp. 1B, 2B; "Hard Pedaling Powers Schwinn Uphill in Sales, Toward Profits," *Chicago Tribune,* June 22, 1995, p. 2N; " 'New Schwinn' Bike Has Gone Full Cycle," *Chicago Tribune,* May 16, 1995, p. 3N.

Giant	6%
Diamondback	6%
GT	6%
Scott	4%
Mongoose	3%
Pro Flex	3%

The mass market for low-priced bikes and those made for children is dominated by three U.S. manufacturers: Huffy, Murray, and Roadmaster. The mass market accounts for about 8.5 million of the 12 million bikes sold in the nation annually.

Schwinn's history as a maker of sturdy, low-cost bikes is no longer the asset it once was. Many under-30 cyclists see Schwinns as the bikes their parents rode. They prefer trendier mountain bikes, with their padded seats, upright handlebars, fat tires and additional gears for climbing.

"We have an image challenge," admits Schwinn Marketing Director Gregg Bagni. That's clear from a walk around the University of Colorado campus a half-mile away. Outside dorms and classrooms, racks are filled with bikes made by Trek Bicycle, Specialized Bicycle Components, Cannondale and Giant. Waterloo, Wisconsin-based Trek is the leader. This year it expects about $300 million in revenue on sales of more than 900,000 bikes.

"When I was a kid, if you had a Schwinn, you were the luckiest kid in the world," says Scott Montgomery, a Cannondale marketing chief. "Ask a college kid now and they'll say, 'Oh, Schwinn? They're toast.'"

For decades, the Schwinn brand, synonymous with durability, ruled the road. Generations of kids clamored for the company's Excelsiors, Phantoms, Sting-Rays and 10-speed Varsitys. "Schwinn used to be number one and you could hardly find number two," says industry consultant Bill Fields. But in the late '70s and early '80s, cyclists veered off the road into the woods and mountains. Schwinn ignored the mountain bike craze for most of the '80s. By 1992, two-thirds of bikes sold were mountain bikes and Schwinn was in bankruptcy court. Unable to pay lenders or suppliers, the descendants of company founder Ignaz Schwinn sold the company to the Zell/Chilmark Investment fund for $43 million. Zell/Chilmark appointed new management and funded the company, Scott Sports Group, with an additional $7 million.

So far, the Schwinn turnaround is being attempted on a shoestring. Schwinn's workforce shrank from 300 employees to about 180 when the company was reorganized and moved from Chicago to Boulder. The move west was calculated to attract young workers plugged into the mountain-biking community. Once assembled, the managers focused on product design. They had inherited a Schwinn line whose only mountain bikes were priced at the low end of the bike-shop range, between $200 and $400.

"Previous management wouldn't believe anybody would buy a $1,500 mountain bike with the Schwinn name on it," one Schwinn executive stated. Now, Schwinn is emblazoned on everything from $100 kids' bikes to $2,500 mountain bikes. Its top-of-the-line, American-made Homegrown model starts at $1,750. One of its hottest products is a decidedly low-tech, retro-style, one-speed Cruiser with a wide seat and balloon tires. It's selling fast in Sunbelt states for up to $250. The Cruiser appeals to retirees and snowbirds in beach communities and to college students who call them "bar bikes" because they are ridden to bars and back.

"They want to position this company as high-end, high-tech," says Cannondale's Montgomery. "And what they've got is this traditional, old-fashioned Harley-Davidson type of product. That's their greatest marketing challenge."

Today's bike business is quite different from the one Schwinn dominated so long ago. Exclusive dealerships like Schwinn uses are disappearing, being replaced by independent bike shops. The typical bike shop carries four brands, so Schwinn bikes are subjected to side-by-side comparisons with competing products. Some of the other brands, such as Trek and Cannondale, have built reputations for cutting-edge technology. Cannondale makes aluminum-frame bikes in U.S. plants, and Trek, a pioneer in carbon fiber frames, is moving production back from Taiwan. All but a few thousand Schwinns are made in Asia.

"Handmade in the USA is a tremendous marketing feature," says Brett Hahn, manager of Yeti Cycles in Durango, Colorado. "Bottom line: Mountain biking is a U.S. sport." Yeti makes hundreds of frames for Schwinn's top-of-the-line Homegrown models. Schwinn is considering buying Yeti or another U.S. manufacturer.

Discussion Questions

1. What are the strengths and weaknesses of Schwinn?
2. What opportunities and threats does the company face?
3. How important is it for mountain bikes to be made in America?
4. Evaluate Schwinn's strategy of selling bikes for prices from $100 to $2,500.
5. Evaluate Zell/Chilmark's decision to invest $50 million in Schwinn. What did it get for its money? Calculate the breakeven point and the payback period for this investment given the following assumptions: Schwinn has 4 percent of the retail bike market; Schwinn bikes are marked up an average of 20 percent at retail; Schwinn has a 25 percent profit margin on its bikes.
6. Noting that 80 percent of Trek's sales are for bikes priced $400 and over, how many bikes does Schwinn sell in this category?

Case 20

Toyota

Brian Brenner and Chester Dawson* *BusinesssWeek*

YOI KANGAE, YOI SHINA! That's Toyota-speak for "Good thinking means good products." The slogan is emblazoned on a giant banner hanging across the company's Takaoka assembly plant, an hour outside the city of Nagoya. Plenty of good thinking has gone into the high-tech ballet that's performed here 17 hours a day. Six separate car models—from the Corolla compact to the new youth-oriented Scion xB—glide along on a single production line in any of a half-dozen colors. Overhead, car doors flow by on a conveyor belt that descends to floor level and drops off the right door in the correct color for each vehicle. This efficiency means Takaoka workers can build a car in just 20 hours.

The combination of speed and flexibility is world class (Exhibit 1). More important, a similar dance is happening at 30 Toyota plants worldwide, with some able to make as many as eight different models on the same line. That is leading to a monster increase in productivity and market responsiveness—all part of the company's obsession with what President Fujio Cho calls "the criticality of speed."

Remember when Japan was going to take over the world? Corporate America was apoplectic at the idea that every Japanese company might be as obsessive, productive, and well-managed as Toyota Motor Corp. We know what happened next: One of the longest crashes in business history revealed most of Japan Inc. to be debt-addicted, inefficient, and clueless. Today, 13 years after the Nikkei peaked, Japan is still struggling to avoid permanent decline. World domination? Hardly.

Except in one corner. In autos, the Japanese rule (Exhibit 2). And in Japan, one company—Toyota—combines the size, financial clout, and manufacturing excellence needed to dominate the global car industry in a way no company ever has. Sure, Toyota, with $146 billion in sales, may not be tops in every category. GM is bigger—for now. Nissan Motor Co. makes slightly more profit per vehicle in North America, and its U.S. plants are more efficient. Both Nissan and Honda have flexible assembly lines, too. But no car company is as strong as Toyota in so many areas.

Of course, the carmaker has always moved steadily forward: Its executives created the doctrine of *kaizen*, or continuous improvement (Exhibit 3). "They find a hole, and they plug it," says auto-industry consultant Maryann Keller. "They methodically study problems, and they solve them." But in the past few years, Toyota has accelerated these gains, raising the bar for the entire industry. Consider:

- Toyota is closing in on Chrysler to become the third-biggest carmaker in the U.S. Its U.S. share, rising steadily, is now above 11 percent.

*With Kathleen Kerwin in Detroit, Christopher Palmeri in Los Angeles, and Paul Magnusson in Washington

EXHIBIT 1 Global Push

Toyota's on the offensive around the globe. Here's a look at its worldwide operations:

North America

SALES: 1.94 million

Toyota's products keep gaining on the Big Three's models, while Lexus is a luxury leader. Toyota employs 35,000 people and runs 10 factories in the region, and has 11.2% of the U.S. market.

Europe

SALES: 756,000

Has a 4.4% market share, led by the **Yaris** compact and a new **Avensis** with a cleaner diesel engine. Plans to boost production in Britain and France. Lexus though, is struggling.

Southwest Asia

SALES: 268,000

Builds cars in Bangladesh, India, Pakistan, and Turkey. The durable **Qualis** SUV is a big hit in India, and Toyota plans to start building transmissions there in mid-2004.

Southeast Asia

SALES: 455,000

Assembles cars in seven countries and is expanding its factories in Thailand and Indonesia. Plans to export trucks, engines, and components from the region to 80 countries.

South America

SALES: 97,000

Builds cars in Argentina, Brazil, Colombia, and Venezuela. Regionwide revenues fell 10% last year because of economic troubles in Argentina, but sales in Brazil grew after the launch of a new **Corolla.**

Africa

SALES: 140,000

Has manufacturing plants in Kenya and South Africa. Last year, it saw sales across the continent jump 10.5%, thanks to a new **Corolla** sedan and **Prado** SUV.

China

SALES: 58,000

Playing catch-up with rivals Volkswagen and GM. In April, it agreed with FAW to make the **Land Cruiser, Corolla, and Crown.** Share today is about 1.5%, but Toyota wants 10% by 2010.

Japan

SALES: 1.68 million

Has maintained 40% plus market share for five years running. New models this year include the **Sienta** compact minivan, the sportier **Wish** minivan, and a revamped **Harrier** SUV.

Data: Toyota Motor, 2002 sales figures.

EXHIBIT 2 Way Ahead of the Pack

Data: Bloomberg Financial Markets, Harbour & Associates, J.D. Power & Associates, Toyo Keizai, Dresden Kleinwort, Burnham Securities. Research assistance by Susan Zegel.

	Market Cap*	Operating Profit*	Hours per Vehicle†	Defects‡
Toyota	$110	$12.7	21.83	196
Nissan	54	7.5	16.83	258
Honda	40	6.1	22.27	215
DaimlerChrysler	38	5.7	28.04†	311
GM	24	3.8	24.44	264
Ford	22	3.6	26.14	287

*Billions. †Average assembly time (North America). ‡Problems per 100 vehicles on year 2000 models.

- At its current rate of expansion, Toyota could pass Ford Motor Co. in mid-decade as the world's number 2 auto maker. The number 1 spot—still occupied by General Motors Corp., with 15 percent of the global market—would be the next target. President Cho's goal is 15 percent of global sales by 2010, up from 10 percent today. "They dominate wherever they go," says Nobuhiko Kawamoto, former president of Honda Motor Co. "They try to take over everything."

- Toyota has broken the Japanese curse of running companies simply for sales gains, not profit. Its operating margin of 8 percent plus (versus 2 percent in 1993) now dwarfs those of Detroit's Big Three. Even with the impact of the strong yen, estimated 2003 profits of $7.2 billion will be double 1999's level. On November 5, the company reported profits of $4.8 billion on sales of $75 billion for the six months ended Sept. 30. Results like that have given Toyota a market capitalization of $110 billion—more than that of GM, Ford, and DaimlerChrysler combined (Exhibit 4).

- The company has not only rounded out its product line in the United States with sport-utility vehicles, trucks, and a hit minivan, but it also has seized the psychological advantage in the market with the Prius, an eco-friendly gasoline-electric car. "This is going to be a real paradigm shift for the industry," says board member and top engineer Hiroyuki Watanabe. In October, when the second-generation Prius reached U.S. showrooms, dealers got 10,000 orders before the car was even available.

EXHIBIT 3   Kaizen in Action

Toyota stresses constant improvement, or *kaizen*, in everything it does. Here's how the company revamped the 2004 Sienna minivan after the previous generation got disappointing reviews.

- The 3.3-liter, 230 hp engine is bigger and more powerful than before, but it gets slightly better gas mileage.
- Now has five-speed transmission instead of four.
- The 2004 is nimbler with a turning diameter of 36.8 feet–3.2 feet shorter than the previous model.
- At $23,495, it's $920 cheaper than the 2003.
- Third-row seats fold flat into the floor. On the older model they had to be removed to maximize cargo space.
- The new model is longer and wider than the 2003, with more headroom, leg room, and 12% more cargo space.

Camry

Bland? Sure, as bland as the bread and butter it is to Toyota. This reliable family sedan has been America's top-selling car in five of the past six years.
$19,560–$25,920

Prius

A funky-looking and earth-friendly gas-electric hybrid that gets 55 mpg—but offers the power and roominess of a midsize sedan.
$20,510

Scion xB

An attempt to be hip and edgy included underground marketing for this new car aimed at young people. Sales have been double Toyota's forecasts.
$14,165–$14,965

Yaris

The snub-nosed compact is Toyota's top-seller in Europe. Its Euro-styling has made it a hit in Japan too, where it's known as the Vitz. $11,787–$14,317

Tundra

This full-size pickup has built a loyal following as it has grown in bulk and power. A Double Cab model due in November will up the ante.
$16,495–$31,705*

Lexus RX330

The first Lexus built in North America, this luxury SUV boasts a smooth, car-like ride and nimble handling. It has been Lexus' U.S. sales leader.
$35,700–$37,500

*Doesn't include Double cab model, which isn't yet priced.
Data: Toyota Motor; *BusinessWeek*, Edmunds.com Inc.

EXHIBIT 4
Toyota's Money Machine

Data: Toyota Motor Corp., Lehman Brothers Inc.

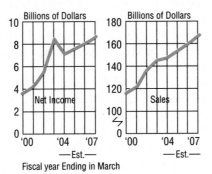

Fiscal year Ending in March

- Toyota has launched a joint program with its suppliers to radically cut the number of steps needed to make cars and car parts. In the past year alone, the company chopped $2.6 billion out of its $113 billion in manufacturing costs without any plant closures or layoffs. Toyota expects to cut an additional $2 billion out of its cost base this year.

- Toyota is putting the finishing touches on a plan to create an integrated, flexible, global manufacturing system. In this new network, plants from Indonesia to Argentina will be designed both to customize cars for local markets and to shift production to quickly satisfy any surges in demand from markets worldwide. By tapping, say, its South African plant to meet a need in Europe, Toyota can save itself the $1 billion normally needed to build a new factory.

If Cho gets this transformation right, he'll end up with an automotive machine that makes the Americans and Germans quake. Cost-cutting and process redesign will chop out billions in expenses. That will keep margins strong and free up cash to develop new models and technologies such as the Prius, to invest in global manufacturing, and to invade markets such as Europe and China. New models and new plants will build share, which will build more clout. And if there's a hiccup—well, there's a cash-and-securities hoard of $30 billion. "This is a company that does not fear failure," says Cho.

Roadblocks?

Can anything stop Toyota? There are some potential roadblocks. Toyota doesn't always get it right: Its early attempts at the youth market, minivans, and big pickup trucks all disappointed. It remains dependent on the U.S. business for some 70 percent of earnings. Its Lexus luxury sedans are losing ground to BMW, though Lexus' strong SUV sales are keeping the division in the game. The average Toyota owner is about 46, a number the company must lower or risk going the way of Buick. And most of Toyota's big sellers aren't exactly head-turners.

Meanwhile, Toyota's rivals are hardly sitting still. GM is finishing up a $4.3 billion revamp of Cadillac, and a revival is in the works: Overall GM quality is on an upswing too. "Toyota is a good competitor, but they're not unbeatable," says GM Chairman G. Richard Wagoner Jr. Over at Nissan, CEO Carlos Ghosn doubts Toyota's big bet on hybrids will pay off. "There will be no revolution," he predicts. And Detroit's Big Three are praying that a strong yen will batter Toyota. If the yen sticks at 110 to the dollar over the next 12 months, Toyota could see its pretax profits shrink by $900 million.

A strengthening yen might have hammered Toyota in the 1980s, and it will certainly have an impact next year. But today, three decades after starting its global push, Toyota can't be accused of needing a cheap yen to subsidize exports. Since starting U.S. production in 1986, Toyota has invested nearly $14 billion there. What's more, many of its costs are now set in dollars: Last year, Toyota's purchases of parts and materials from 500 North American suppliers came to $19 billion—more than the annual sales of Cisco Systems Inc. or Oracle Corp. The U.S. investment is an enormous natural hedge against the yen. "About 60 percent of what we sold here, we built here," Toyota Chairman Hiroshi Okuda said in a Sept. 10 speech in Washington.

Better for Toyota, those cars are also among the industry's biggest money-makers. Take SUVs: Ten years ago, Toyota had a puny 4 percent share. Today, it owns nearly 12 percent of that high-margin segment with eight models ranging from the $19,000 RAV4 to the $65,000 Lexus LX 470—and makes as much as $10,000 on each high-end model it sells. The company is steadily robbing Ford, Chrysler, and GM of their primacy in the cutthroat U.S. SUV market and has largely sat out the latest round of rebates: Toyota's average incentive per car this fall is just $647, compared with $3,812 at GM and $3,665 at Ford, according to market watcher Edmunds.com. This is one war of attrition where Detroit is clearly outgunned.

Toyota's charge into SUVs indicates a new willingness to play tough in the United States, which it considers vital to its drive for a global 15 percent share. "The next era is full-size trucks and luxury, environmental, and youth cars," predicts James E. Press, chief operating officer at Toyota Motor Sales USA Inc. Toyota is already intent on boosting its 4.5 percent market share in pickups, the last profit refuge of the Big Three. Toyota is building an $800 million plant in San Antonio, Tex., that will allow it to more than double its Tundra output, to some 250,000 trucks a year by 2006, with rigs powerful and roomy enough to go head to head with Detroit's biggest models.

Toyota plans to extend its early lead in eco-cars by pushing the Prius and adding a hybrid Lexus RX 330 SUV next summer. The Lexus will get as much as 35 miles per gallon, compared with roughly 21 mpg for a conventional RX 330. And Toyota is vigorously attacking the youth market with the $14,500 Scion xB compact, which surprised Toyota-bashers with its angular, minimalist design. Since the Scion's U.S. launch in California in June, Toyota has sold nearly 7,700 of them, 30 percent better than forecast. Toyota Vice President James Farley says three out of four buyers of the brand had no intention of buying a Toyota when they started looking. "That's exactly why we started the Scion," he says.

The Scion is evidence that Toyota's growing cash cushion gives it the means to revamp its lackluster designs. When Cho traveled through Germany in 1994, he recalls being asked: Why are Toyota cars so poorly styled? Part of the problem, says Cho, is that too many Toyotas were designed with Japanese consumers in mind and then exported. Some worked; some flopped.

These days, design teams on the West Coast of the United States, in southern France, and back home compete for projects. That has paid off with models such as the Yaris, Toyota's best seller in Europe, where the company now has a 4.4 percent share, compared with less than 3 percent a decade ago. The Yaris was designed by a Greek, Sotiris Kovos, then imported successfully to Japan because of its "European" look. "Toyota has finally recognized that buyers want to feel like they have some level of style," says Wesley Brown, a consultant with auto researcher Iceology. The redesigned Solara sports coupe is getting high grades, too: A V-shape line flowing up from the grille gives it a more muscular silhouette, and its interior is 20 percent roomier than before.

Toyota Man

Leading Toyota to this new level of global vigor is Cho. He's Toyota Man personified: Self-effacing, ever smiling, but an executive whose radar seems to pick up every problem and opportunity. "Cho understands as much as anyone I've ever seen what's actually happening on the factory floor," says manufacturing consultant Ronald E. Harbour, whose firm's annual report on productivity is the industry bible.

That feel for the factory didn't come naturally. The 66-year-old company lifer studied law, not business, at the prestigious University of Tokyo and could have easily ended up as a faceless bureaucrat at the Ministry of Finance. But Cho learned the car business—and clearly learned it well—at the knee of Taichi Ohno, the creator of the legendary Toyota Production System, a series of in-house precepts on efficient manufacturing that changed the industry. Ohno, a brilliant but notoriously hot-headed engineer, lectured Cho about the need to be flexible and to look forward.

That advice is something Cho found invaluable when he was tapped to oversee the 1988 launch of Toyota's key U.S. plant in Georgetown, Ky., now the company's biggest U.S. factory and the maker of the Camry sedan. The good-natured and unpretentious Cho regularly worked the plant floor, making sure to shake hands with each line worker at Christmas to show his appreciation. He spoke at Rotary Club meetings and stopped to make small talk with the folks in Georgetown.

Given Toyota's booming U.S. sales in the late 1990s, few inside the company were surprised when Cho won the top job. Yet equally few had any clue that the new president was about to unleash so many powerful changes. Like his predecessor Okuda, Cho had long been frustrated by Toyota's glacial decision-making process and cultural insularity. Those had led to missed opportunities, such as when product planners at headquarters in Japan resisted calls from their U.S. colleagues to build an eight-cylinder pickup truck. Cho is rectifying that deficiency with a vengeance with the San Antonio plant.

Then three years ago, as Ghosn—"le cost killer"—was slashing billions at rival Nissan and cutting its supplier ranks in half, Cho had a revelation: If Nissan could do it, Toyota could do it better. The resulting program, called Construction of Cost Competitiveness for the 21st Century, or CCC21, taps into the company's strengths across the board to build cars more efficiently. It's also turning many operations inside out.

No Detail Too Small

Toyota has always valued frugality. It still turns down the heat at company-owned employee dormitories during working hours and labels its photocopy machines with the cost per copy to discourage overuse. But cost-cutting was often a piecemeal affair. With CCC21, Cho set a bold target of slashing prices on all key components for new models by 30 percent, which meant working with suppliers and Toyota's own staff to ferret out excess. "Previously, we tried to find waste here and there," says Cho. "But now there is a new dimension of proposals coming in."

EXHIBIT 5
Deciphering Toyota-Speak
A handy glossary for understanding the company's vernacular.

Kaizen	PDCA	Obeya
Continuous improvement. Employees are given cash rewards for ferreting out glitches in production and devising solutions.	Plan, do, check, action. Steps in the development cycle aimed at quick decision-making in a task such as designing a car.	Literally, "big room," Regular face-to-face brainstorming sessions among engineers, designers, marketers, and suppliers.
Pokayoke	**CCC21**	**GBL**
Mistake-proofing. Use of sensors to detect missing parts or improper assembly. Robots alert workers to errors by flashing lights.	Construction of Cost Competitiveness for the 21st century. A three-year push to slash costs of 170 components that account for 90% of parts expenses.	Global Body Line. A manufacturing process that holds auto frames together for welding with one brace instead of the 50 braces previously required.

In implementing CCC21, no detail is too small. For instance, Toyota designers took a close look at the grip handles mounted above the door inside most cars. By working with suppliers, they managed to cut the number of parts in these handles to five from 34, which helped cut procurement costs by 40 percent. As a plus, the change slashed the time needed for installation by 75 percent—to three seconds. "The pressure is on to cut costs at every stage," says Takashi Araki, a project manager at parts maker Aisin Seiki Co.

Just as Cho believes he can get far more out of suppliers, he thinks Toyota can make its workers vastly more productive. This is classic *kaizen,* but these days it has gone into overdrive (Exhibit 5). In the middle of the Kentucky plant, for instance, a *Kaizen* Team of particularly productive employees works in a barracks-like structure. The group's sole job is coming up with ways to save time and money. Georgetown employees, for instance, recommended removing the radiator support base—the lower jaw of the car—until the last stage of assembly. That way, workers can step into the engine compartment to install parts instead of having to lean over the front end and risk straining their backs. "We used to have to duck into the car to install something," explains Darryl Ashley, 41, a soft-spoken Kentucky native who joined Toyota nine years ago.

In Cambridge, Ontario, Cho is going even further: He's determined to show the world that Toyota can meet its own highest standards of excellence anywhere in its system. It was once company doctrine that Lexus could only be made in Japan. No longer. Production of the RX 330 SUV started in Cambridge on Sept. 26. If the Canadian hands can deliver the same quality as their Japanese counterparts, Toyota will be able to chop shipping costs by shifting Lexus production to the market where the bulk of those cars are sold (Exhibit 6).

The Japanese bosses put the Canadians through their paces. The 700 workers on the RX 330 line trained for 12 weeks, including stints in Japan for 200 of them. There, the Canadians managed to beat Japanese teams in quality assessment on a mock Lexus line. Cambridge has taken Toyota's focus on *poka-yoke,* or foolproofing measures, to another level. The plant has introduced "Circle L" stations where workers must double- and triple-check parts that customers have complained about—anything from glove boxes to suspension systems. "We know that if we can get this right, we may get to build other Lexus models," says Jason Birt, a 28-year-old Lexus line worker.

The Cambridge workers are aided by a radical piece of manufacturing technology being rolled out to Toyota plants worldwide. The system, called the Global Body Line, holds vehicle frames in place while they're being welded, using just one master brace instead of the dozens of separate braces required in a standard factory. No big deal? Perhaps, but the system is half as expensive to install. Analysts say it lets Toyota save 75 percent of the cost of refitting a production line to build a different car, and it's key to Toyota's ability to make multiple models on

EXHIBIT 6
Lexus: Still Looking for Traction in Europe

Source: Brian Bremner and Chester Dawson, "Can Anything Stop Toyota?" *Business-Week* November 17, 2003, 114–122.

When Dirk Lindermann was looking for a new luxury sedan last summer, he considered Mercedes and BMW before settling on a $40,000, black Audi A4. Lexus, though, didn't even enter into the game. "Lexus has no personality," says the 40-year-old Berlin advertising executive.

That's a problem for Toyota Motor Corp. The company's smooth-driving Lexus sedans sprinted from zero to luxury-market leader in the U.S. during the 1990s, overtaking German rivals Mercedes and BMW—as well as Cadillac and Lincoln—by offering better quality and service at a lower price. But Lexus is going nowhere fast in Europe: After 12 years in showrooms, last year it registered sales of just 21,156 cars—down 11% from 2001—compared with more than 234,000 in the U.S.

Toyota itself is fast shedding any *arriviste* stigma in the Old World. Since it began producing cars on the Continent in the '90s, European sales are up nearly 60%, to 734,000. Now it wants to crack the high-end with a renewed push for Lexus. The goal is to triple sales of the six Lexus models Toyota offers there by 2010, to at least 65,000 cars. "The potential in

Europe for Lexus is every bit as great as in the U.S.," says Stuart McCullough, director of Lexus Europe.

To make Lexus a success, though, Toyota needs to establish it as a separate brand. Until now, the car has been sold in Europe mainly through Toyota's 250 dealerships, along with the far less lustrous Yaris, Corolla, and Avensis models. So Toyota is trying to set up dealerships that offer luxury-car buyers the kind of white-glove service they demand. "Lexus has to establish its own heritage, not just chase BMW and Mercedes," says Tadashi Arashima, president and chief executive of Toyota Motor Marketing Europe.

Will image-conscious Europeans warm up to Lexus if the cars are sold in tony showrooms? In Spain, where exclusive Lexus dealerships have been operating since 2000, sales are up 9% so far this year, though the brand sold just 969 vehicles in the country. "We've been able to show that these cars can compete with the big German brands in quality and also offer a lot more in terms of price," says Jorge Merino, head of sales at Axel, a three-year-old Lexus dealership in Madrid.

One big selling point is Lexus' six-year warranty. And the carmaker includes three years of free checkups, maintenance, and roadside assistance. That compares with a standard guarantee of two years at most luxury brands. "I like BMW and Mercedes, but I have a feeling I may get more for my money with Lexus," says Ignacio Redondo, a legal consultant in Madrid who drives a Saab 900 but is mulling a new Lexus for the first time.

Harder, though, will be conforming to the European concept of luxury. Americans love comfort, size and dependability, while Europeans think luxury means attention to detail and brand heritage. "The biggest selling point for Lexus is that it doesn't break down," says Philipp Rosengarten, analyst at Global Insight Inc.'s automotive group. That's not enough to succeed in Europe. Instead, Lexus needs to create a desire to own the car—and even with plush dealerships and extended warranties, it has kilometers to go before reaching that goal.

By Gail Edmondson in Frankfurt, and Karen Nickel Anhalt in Berlin with Paulo Prada in Madrid.

---

a single line. Better yet, the brace increases the rigidity of the car early in production, which boosts the accuracy of welds and makes for a more stable vehicle. "The end results are improved quality, shortened welding lines, reduced capital investment, and less time to launch new vehicles," says Atsushi Niimi, president of Toyota Motor Manufacturing North America.

Cho and his managers are not just reengineering how Toyota makes its cars—they want to revolutionize how it creates products. With the rise of e-mail and teleconferencing, teams of designers, engineers, product planners, workers, and suppliers rarely all convened in the same place. Under Cho, they're again required to work face to face, in a process Toyota calls obeya—literally, "big room." This cuts the time it takes to get a car from the drawing board to the showroom. It took only 19 months to develop the 2003 Solara. That's better than 22 months for the latest Sienna minivan, and 26 months for the latest Camry—well below the industry average of about three years.

If all this sounds like Toyota is riding a powerful growth wave, well, it is. While Cho is as mild-mannered and modest as they come, the revolution he has kicked off is anything but. Toyota is in the midst of a transformative makeover—and if Cho succeeds, the entire global auto industry is in for one, too.

Case

21

Cowgirl Chocolates

John J. Lawrence, Linda J. Morris, and Joseph J. Geiger *University of Idaho*

Marilyn looked at the advertisement—a beautiful woman wearing a cowboy hat in a watering trough full of hot and spicy Cowgirl Chocolate truffles (see Exhibit 1). The ad would appear next month in the March/April edition of *Chile Pepper* magazine, the leading magazine for people who like fiery foods. The ad, the first ever for the business, cost $3,000 to run and Marilyn wondered if it would be her big mistake for 2001. Marilyn allowed herself one $3,000–$6,000 mistake a year in trying to get her now four-year old business to profitability. Two years ago, it was the pursuit of an opportunity to get her product into Great Britain on the recommendation of the owner of a British biscuit company who loved her chocolates. Despite significant effort and expense, she could not convince anyone in Great Britain to carry her chocolates. Last year it was her attempt to use a distributor for the first time. It was a small, regional distributor, and she had provided $5,000 worth of product and had never gotten paid. She eventually got half her product back, but by the time she did it had limited remaining shelf life and she already had enough new stock on hand to cover demand. She ended up giving most of what she got back away.

Marilyn knew it took time to make money at something. She was now an internationally celebrated ceramicist, but it had taken 20 years for her ceramic art to turn a profit. She also knew, however, that she could not wait 20 years for her foray into chocolates to make money, especially not at the rate that she was currently losing money. Last year, despite not paying herself a salary and occasionally bartering her art for services, the small business's revenues of $30,000 did not come close to covering her $50,000+ in expenses. While her art for a long time did not make money, it did not lose that kind of money either. Her savings account was slowly being depleted as she loaned the company money. She knew that the product was excellent—it had won numerous awards from the two main fiery food competitions in the United States—and her packaging was also excellent and had won awards itself. She just was not sure how to turn her award-winning products into a profitable business.

This case was prepared by the authors for the sole purpose of providing material for class discussion. It is not intended to illustrate either effective or ineffective handling of a managerial situation. The authors thank Marilyn Lysohir for her cooperation and assistance with this project.

EXHIBIT 1   **Cowgirl Chocolate Ad to Appear in *Chile Pepper* Magazine**

spicy chocolate truffles and more • www.cowgirlchocolates.com • toll free 888.882.4098

Company History

Cowgirl Chocolates was started in Moscow, Idaho, in 1997 by Marilyn Lysohir and her husband, Ross Coates. Marilyn and Ross were both artists. Marilyn was an internationally known ceramicist and lecturer; Ross was also a sculptor and a professor of fine arts at a nearby university. They had started publishing a once-a-year arts magazine in 1995 called *High Ground*. *High Ground* was really a multimedia product—each edition contained more than simply printed words and pictures. For example, past editions had included such things as vials of Mount St. Helen's ash, cassette tapes, seeds, fabric art, and chocolate bunnies in addition to articles and stories. One edition was even packaged in a motion picture canister. With a total production of about 600 copies, however, *High Ground* simply would not pay for itself. But the magazine was a labor of love for Marilyn and Ross, and so they sought creative ways to fund the endeavor. One of the ways they tried was selling hot and spicy chocolate truffles.

The fact that Marilyn and Ross turned to chocolate was no random event. Marilyn's first job, at age 16, was at Daffin's Candies in Sharon, Pennsylvania. The business's owner, Pete Daffin, had been an early mentor of Marilyn's and had encouraged her creativity. He even let her carve a set of animals, including an 8-foot tall chocolate bunny, for display. Her sculptures proved irresistible to visiting youngsters, who would take small bites out of the sculptures. It was at this point that Marilyn realized the power of chocolate.

In addition to loving chocolate, Marilyn loved things hot and spicy. She also was aware that cayenne and other chilies had wonderful health properties for the heart. But it was her brother who originally gave her the idea of combining hot and spicy with chocolate. Marilyn considered her brother's idea for a while, and could see it had possibilities, so she started experimenting in her kitchen. She recruited neighbors, friends and acquaintances to try out her creations. While a few people who tried those early chocolates were not so sure that combining hot and spicy with chocolate made sense, many thought the chocolates were great. Encouraged, and still searching for funding for *High Ground,* Marilyn found a local candy company to produce the chocolates in quantity, and she and her husband established Cowgirl Chocolates.

The name itself came from one friend's reaction the first time she tasted the chocolates—the friend exclaimed "these are cowboy chocolates!" Marilyn agreed that there was a certain ruggedness to the concept of hot and spicy chocolates that matched the cowboy image, but thought that *Cowgirl* Chocolates was a more appropriate name for her company. Marilyn found the picture of May Lillie that would become the Cowgirl Chocolate logo in a book about cowgirls. May Lillie was a turn of the century, pistol-packing cowgirl, and Marilyn loved the picture of May looking down the barrel of a pistol because May looked so tough. And it certainly was not hard to envision May adopting the Cowgirl Chocolate motto—Sissies Stay Away. That motto had come to Marilyn when a group of friends told her that they really did not like her hot and spicy chocolates. Marilyn was a little disappointed and hurt, and thought to herself "well, sissies stay away, if you don't like them, don't eat them."

The Product

Cowgirl chocolate sold its hot and spicy creations in three basic forms: individually wrapped truffles, chocolate bars, and a hot caramel dessert sauce. The individually wrapped truffles were available in a variety of packaging options, with most of the packaging designed to set Cowgirl Chocolates apart. The truffles could be purchased in gift boxes, in drawstring muslin bags, and in a collectible tin. According to Marilyn, this packaging made them "more than a candy—they become an idea, an experience, a gift." The truffles were also available in a plain plastic bag over Cowgirl Chocolate's Web site for customers who just wanted the chocolate and did not care about the fancy packaging. The chocolate bars and truffles were offered in several flavors. The chocolate bars were available in either orange espresso or lime tequila crunch. The truffles were available in plain chocolate, mint, orange, lime tequila, and espresso. The plain chocolate, mint, and orange truffles were packaged in gold wrappers, while the lime tequila truffles were packaged in green wrappers. The espresso truffles were the hottest, about twice as hot as the other varieties, and were wrapped in a special red foil to give customers some clue that these were extra hot. Cowgirl Chocolates' full line of product offerings are described in Exhibit 2 and are shown in Exhibit 3.

EXHIBIT 2   Cowgirl Chocolate Product Offerings with Price and Cost Figures

Item	Approximate Percentage of Total Revenues	Suggested Retail Price[1]	Wholesale Price[1]	Total Item Cost (a + b)	Cost of Chocolate or Sauce (a)	Cost of Product Packaging[2] (b)
Spicy Chocolate Truffle Bars (available in 2 flavors: orange-espresso or lime tequila crunch)	50%	$2.99	$1.50	$1.16	$1.04	$0.12
1/4-pound Muslin Bag (13 truffles in a drawstring muslin bag—available in 3 flavors: assorted hot, lime-tequila, and mild-mannered)	16%	$6.95	$3.50	$2.35	$1.69	$0.66
1/2-pound Tin (assorted hot & spicy truffles in a collectable tin)	12%	$14.95	$7.50	$4.78[3]	$3.25	$1.53
Hot Caramel Dessert Sauce (9.5 oz. Jar)	10%	$5.95	$3.50	$2.50	$2.00	$0.50
Sampler Bag (4 assorted hot truffles in a small drawstring muslin bag)	7%	$2.95	$1.50	$0.97	$0.52	$0.45
1/4-pound Gift Box (assorted hot truffles or mild-mannered truffles in a fancy gift box with gift card)	~ 1%	$8.95	$4.50	$2.95	$1.69	$1.26
1-pound Gift Box (assorted hot truffles or mild-mannered truffles in a fancy gift box with gift card)	~ 1%	$24.95	$12.95	$9.05	$6.37	$2.68
Gift Bucket (tin bucket containing 1/4-pound gift box, 2 truffle bars and 1 jar of caramel sauce)	~ 1%	$39.95	$20.95	$11.02	$5.77	$5.25
Gift Basket (made of wire and branches and containing 1/2-pound tin, 2 truffle bars, 1 jar of caramel sauce and a T-shirt)	~ 1%	$59.95	$30.95	$23.06	$15.29[3]	$7.77
Nothing Fancy (1-pound assorted hot truffles or mild-mannered truffles in a plastic bag)	~ 1%	$19.50	N.A.	$7.42	$6.37	$1.05

[1]Approximately 1/3 of sales were retail over the Cowgirl Chocolate website, the remaining 2/3 of sales were to wholesale accounts (i.e., to other retailers).
[2]Packaging cost includes costs of container (bags, tins, or boxes), labels, and individual truffle wrapping. Packaging cost assumes Marilyn packs the items and does not include the packing & labeling fee charged by Seattle Chocolates if they do the packing ($1.00 per 1/2 pound tin or 1 pound box; $0.75 per 1/4 pound box; $0.25 per 1/4 pound bag; $0.20 per sampler bag).
[3]This cost includes the cost of the T-shirt.

EXHIBIT 3
Picture of Cowgirl
Chocolate Products
& Packaging

Marilyn was also in the process of introducing "mild-mannered" truffles. Mild-mannered truffles were simply the same fine German chocolate that Marilyn started with to produce all of her chocolates, but without the spice. Marilyn had chosen silver as the wrapper color for the mild-mannered truffles. While she took kidding from friends about how this did not fit with the company's motto—Sissies Stay Away—which was integrated into the company's logo and printed on the back of company t-shirts and hats, she had decided that even the sissies deserved excellent chocolate. Further, she thought that having the mild-mannered chocolate might allow her to get her product placed in retail locations that had previously rejected her chocolates as being too spicy. Marilyn was the first to admit that her chocolates packed a pretty good kick that not everybody found to their liking. She had developed the hot and spicy chocolates based primarily on her own tastes and the input of friends and acquaintances. She had observed many peoples' reactions upon trying her hot and spicy chocolates at trade shows and at new retail locations, and while many people liked her chocolates, the majority found at least some of the varieties to be too hot. In general, men tended to like the hotter truffles much more than women did. Marilyn knew her observations were consistent with what information was available on the fiery foods industry—only approximately 15 percent of American consumers were currently eating hot and spicy foods and men were much more inclined to eat hot and spicy foods than were women. In addition to introducing "mild-mannered" chocolates, Marilyn was also thinking about introducing a chocolate with a calcium supplement aimed at woman concerned about their calcium intake.

All of Cowgirl Chocolate's chocolate products were sourced from Seattle Chocolates, a Seattle-based company that specialized in producing European-style chocolate confections wrapped in an elegant package fit for gift giving. Seattle Chocolates obtained all of its raw chocolate from world-renowned chocolate producer Schokinag of Germany. Seattle Chocolates sold its own retail brand plus provided private label chocolate products for a variety of companies including upscale retailers like Nieman Marcus and Nordstroms. Seattle Chocolates was, at least relative to Cowgirl Chocolates, a large company with annual sales in excess of $5 million. Seattle Chocolates took Cowgirl Chocolates on as a private label customer because they liked and were intrigued by the company's product and owners, and they had made some efforts to help Cowgirl Chocolates along the way. Seattle Chocolates provided Cowgirl Chocolates with a small amount of its table space at several important trade shows and produced in half batches for them. A half batch still consisted of 150 pounds of a given variety of chocolate, which was enough to last Cowgirl Chocolates for six months at 2000 sales rates. Marilyn hoped that she could one day convince Seattle Chocolates to manage the wholesale side of Cowgirl Chocolates, but Seattle Chocolates simply was not interested in taking this on at the present time, at least in part because they were not really sure where the market was for the product. Marilyn also knew she would need to grow sales significantly before Seattle Chocolates would seriously consider such an arrangement, although she was not sure exactly how much she would have to grow sales before such an arrangement would become attractive to Seattle Chocolates.

The chocolate bars themselves cost Cowgirl Chocolates $1.04 per bar while the individual chocolate truffles cost $0.13 per piece. Seattle Chocolates also performed the wrapping and packing of the product. The chocolate bar wrappers cost $0.06 per bar. The wrapper design of the bars had recently been changed to incorporate dietary and nutritional information. While such information was not required, Marilyn felt it helped convey a better image of her chocolates. The change had cost $35 to prepare the new printing plates. Including the materials, wrapping the individual truffles cost $0.02 per piece.

The distinctive muslin bags, collector tins and gift boxes also added to the final product cost. The muslin bags cost $0.35 each for the quarter-pound size and $0.32 each for the sampler size. The tamperproof seals for the bags cost an additional $0.05/bag. The minimum bag order was 500 bags. As with the chocolate bar wrappers, Cowgirl Chocolate had to buy the printing plates to print the bags. The plates to print the bags, however, cost $250 per plate. Each color of each design required a separate plate. Each of her three quarter-pound bag styles (assorted, lime-tequila, and mild-mannered) had a three-color design. One plate that was used to produce the background design was common to all three styles of bags, but each bag required two additional unique plates. There was also a separate plate for printing the sampler bags. Marilyn was planning to discontinue the separate lime-tequila bag, and just include lime-tequila truffles in the assorted bag as a way to cut packaging costs. The lime-tequila bags had been introduced a year ago, and while they sold reasonably well, they also appeared to mostly cannibalize sales of the assorted bags.

The collectible tins cost $0.80 each, and the labels for these tins cost $0.19 per tin. The tape used to seal the tins cost $0.04 per tin. The minimum order for the tins was for 800 units. The company that produced the tins had recently modified the tin design slightly to reduce the chance that someone might cut themselves on the edge of the can. Unfortunately, this change had resulted in a very small change to the height of the can, which left Cowgirl Chocolate with labels too big for the can. Each label currently had to be trimmed slightly to fit on the can. The alternative to this was to switch to a smaller label. This would require purchasing a new printing plate at a cost of about $35 and might require the purchase of a new printing die (the die holds the label while it is printed), which would cost $360. Marilyn also had hopes of one day being able to get her designs printed directly on the tins. It would make for even nicer tins and save the step of having to adhere the labels to the tins. The minimum order for such tins, however, was 15,000 units.

The gift boxes, including all of the associated wrapping, ribbon, and labels, cost about $1.70 per box. The gift boxes did not sell nearly as well as the tins or bags and were available primarily through Cowgirl Chocolates Web site. Marilyn was still using and had a reasonable inventory of boxes from a box order she had placed three years ago.

Marilyn currently had more packaging in inventory than she normally would because she had ordered $5,000 worth in anticipation of the possibility of having her product placed in military PX stores at the end of 2000. Seattle Chocolates had been negotiating to get its product into these stores, and there had been some interest on the part of the PX stores in also having Cowgirl Chocolate products. Given the six- to eight-week lead time on packaging, Marilyn had wanted to be positioned to quickly take advantage of this opportunity if it materialized. While Marilyn was still hopeful this deal might come about, she was less optimistic than she had been at the time she placed the packaging order.

Marilyn was concerned that the actual packing step was not always performed with the care it should be. In particular, she was concerned that not enough or too many truffles ended up in the bags and tins, and that the seals on these containers, which made the packages more tamper resistant, were not always applied correctly. Each quarter-pound bag and gift box was supposed to contain 13 individual truffles, each half-pound tin was supposed to contain 25 individual truffles, and each one-pound gift box was supposed to contain 49 individual truffles. The tins, in particular, had to be packed pretty tightly to get 25 truffles into them. Marilyn had done some of the packing herself at times, and wondered if she would not be better off hiring local college or high school students to do the packing for her to insure that the job was done to her satisfaction. It could also save her some money, as Seattle Chocolates charged her extra for packing the tins and bags. The tins, in particular, were expensive because of the time it took to apply the labels to the top and side of the tin and because of the extra care it took to get all 25 truffles into the tin. Seattle Chocolates charged $1.00 per tin for this step.

Marilyn made the caramel sauce herself with the help of the staff in a commercial kitchen in Sandpoint, Idaho, about a 2½-hour drive north of Moscow. She could make 21 cases of 12 jars each in one day, but including the drive it took all day to do. As with the chocolate, she used only the best ingredients, including fresh cream from a local Moscow dairy. Marilyn figured her costs for the caramel sauce at about $2.50 per jar, which included the cost of the ingredients, the jars, the labeling and the cost of using the Sandpoint kitchen. That figure did not include any allowance for the time it took her to make the sauce or put the labels on the jars. She was considering dropping the caramel sauce from her product line because it was a lot of work to produce and she was not sure she really made any money on it after her own time was factored in. She had sold 70 cases of the sauce in 2000, however, so she knew there was some demand for the product. She was considering the possibility of only offering it at Christmas time as a special seasonal product. She was also looking into the possibility of having a sauce company in Montana make it for her. The company produced caramel, chocolate, and chocolate-caramel sauces that had won awards from the fancy food industry trade association. Marilyn thought the sauces were quite good, although she did not like their caramel sauce as much as her own. The company would sell her 11 oz. jars of any of the sauces, spiced up to Marilyn's standards, for $2.75 per jar. Marilyn would have to provide the labels, for which she would need to have new label designs made to match the jar style the company was set up for, and she would also have to pay a shipping cost of $70–$90 per delivery. The company requested a minimum order size of 72 cases, although the company's owner had hinted that they might be willing to produce in half batches initially.

All of Cowgirl Chocolate's products had won awards, either in the annual Fiery Food Challenges sponsored by *Chile Pepper* magazine or the Scovie Award Competitions sponsored by *Fiery Foods* magazine (the Scovie awards are named after the Scovie measure of heat). All in all, Cowgirl Chocolates had won 11 awards in these two annual competitions. Further, the truffles had won first place in the latest Fiery Food Challenge and the caramel sauce won first place in the latest Scovie competition. The packaging, as distinctive as the chocolate itself, had also won several awards, including the 2000 Award for Excellence for Package Design from American Corporate Identity.

Distribution and Pricing

Marilyn's attempts to get her chocolates into the retail market had met with varying degrees of success. She clearly had been very successful in placing her product in her hometown of Moscow, Idaho. The Moscow Food Co-op was her single best wholesale customer, accounting for 10 percent–15 percent of her annual sales. The Co-op sold a wide variety of natural and/or organic products and produce. Many of its products, like Cowgirl Chocolates, were made or grown locally. The Co-op did a nice job of placing her product in a visible shelf location and generally priced her product lower than any other retail outlet. The Co-op sold primarily the chocolate bars, which it priced at $2.35, and the quarter-pound muslin bags of truffles, which it priced at $5.50. This compared to the suggested retail prices of $2.99 for the bars and $6.99 for the bags. The product was also available at three other locations in downtown Moscow: Wild Women Traders, a store that described itself as a "lifestyle outfitter" and that sold high-end women's clothing and antiques; Northwest Showcase, a store that sold locally produced arts and crafts; and Bookpeople, an independent bookstore that catered to customers who liked to spend time browsing an eclectic offering of books and drinking espresso before making a book purchase.

Marilyn was unsure how many of these local sales were to repeat purchasers who really liked the product and how many were to individuals who wanted to buy a locally made product to give as a gift. She was also unsure how much the Co-op's lower prices boosted the sales of her product at that location. At the Co-op, her product was displayed with other premium chocolates from several competitors, including Seattle Chocolates' own branded chocolate bars, which were priced at $2.99. Marilyn knew the Seattle Chocolate bars were clearly comparable in chocolate quality (although without the spice and cowgirl image). Some of the other competitors' comparably sized bars were priced lower, at $1.99, and some smaller bars were priced at $1.49. While these products were clearly higher in quality than the inexpensive chocolate bars sold in vending machines and at the average supermarket checkout aisle, they were made with a less expensive chocolate than she used and were simply not as good as her chocolates. Marilyn wondered how the price and size of the chocolate bar affected the consumer's purchase decision, and how consumers evaluated the quality of each of the competing chocolate bars when making their purchase.

Outside of Moscow, Marilyn had a harder time getting her product placed onto store shelves and getting her product to move through these locations. One other Co-op, the Boise Food Co-op, carried her products, and they sold pretty well there. Boise was the capital of Idaho and the state's largest city. The Boise Museum of Fine Arts gift shop also carried her product in Boise, although the product did not turn over at this location nearly as well as it did at the Boise Co-op. Other fine art museums, gift shops in places like Missoula, Montana, Portland, Oregon, and Columbus, Ohio, carried Cowgirl Chocolates and Marilyn liked having her product in these outlets. She felt that her reputation as an artist helped her get her product placed in such locations, and the product generally sold well in these locations. She thought her biggest distribution coup was getting her product sold in the world-renowned Whitney Museum in New York City. She felt that the fact that it was sold there added to the product's panache. Unfortunately, the product did not sell there particularly well and it was dropped by the museum. The museum buyer had told Marilyn that she simply thought it was too hot for their customers. Another location in New York City, the Kitchen Market, did much better. The Kitchen Market was an upscale restaurant and gourmet food take-out business. The Kitchen Market was probably her steadiest wholesale customer other than the Moscow Co-op. The product also sold pretty well at the few similar gourmet markets where she had gotten her product placed, like Rainbow Groceries in Seattle and the Culinary Institute of America in San Francisco.

Marilyn had also gotten her product placed in a handful of specialty food stores that focused on hot and spicy foods. Surprisingly, she found, the product had never sold well in these locations. Despite the fact that the product had won the major fiery food awards, customers in these shops did not seem to be willing to pay the premium price for her product.

She had concluded that if her product was located with similarly priced goods, like at the Kitchen Market in New York City, it would sell, but that if it stood out in price then it did not sell as well. Marilyn was not sure, however, just how similarly her product needed to be priced compared to other products the store sold. It seemed clear to her that her $14.95 half-pound tins were standing out in price too much in the hot and spicy specialty stores that thrived on selling jars of hot sauce that typically retailed for $2.99 to $5.99. Marilyn wondered how her product might do at department stores that often sold half-pound boxes of "premium" chocolates for as little as $9.95. She knew her half-pound tins contained better chocolate, offered more unique packaging and logo design, and did not give that "empty feeling" that the competitor's oversized boxes did, but wondered if her product would stand out too much in price in such retail locations.

Several online retailers also carried Cowgirl Chocolates, including companies like Salmon River Specialty Foods and Sam McGee's Hot Sauces, although sales from such sites were not very significant. Marilyn had also had her product available through Amazon.com for a short time, but few customers purchased her product from this site during the time it was listed. Marilyn concluded that customers searching the site for music or books simply were not finding her product, and those who did simply were not shopping for chocolates.

Marilyn also sold her products retail through her own Web site. The Web site accounted for about one-third of her sales. She liked Web-based sales, despite the extra work of having to process all the small orders, because she was able to capture both the wholesale and retail profits associated with the sale. She also liked the direct contact with the retail customers, and frequently tossed a few extra truffles into a customer's order and enclosed a note that said "a little extra bonus from the head cowgirl." Marilyn allowed customers to return the chocolate for a full refund if they found it not to their liking. Most of her sales growth from 1999 to 2000 had come from her Web site.

The Web site itself was created and maintained for her by a small local Internet service provider. It was a fairly simple site. It had pages that described the company and its products and allowed customers to place orders. It did not have any of the sophisticated features that would allow her to use it to capture information to track customers. Although she did not know for sure, she suspected that many of her Internet sales were from repeat customers who were familiar with her product. She included her Web site address on all of her packaging and had listed her site on several other sites, such as saucemall.com and worldmall.com, that would link shoppers at these sites to her site. Listing on some of these sites, such as saucemall.com, was free. Listing on some other sites cost a small monthly fee—for the worldmall.com listing, for example, she paid $25/month. Some sites simply provided links to her site on their own. For example, one customer had told her she had found the Cowgirl Chocolate site at an upscale shopping site called Style365.com. She was not sure how much traffic these various sites were generating on her site, and was unsure how best to attract new customers to her website aside from these efforts.

Marilyn had attempted to get her product into a number of bigger name, upscale retailers, like Dean & Delucca and Coldwater Creek. Dean and Delucca was known for its high-end specialty foods, and the buyers for the company had seemed interested in carrying Cowgirl Chocolates, but the owner had nixed the idea because he found the chocolates too spicy. One of the buyers had also told Marilyn that the owner was more of a chocolate purist or traditionalist who did not really like the idea of adding cayenne pepper to chocolate. Marilyn had also tried hard to get her product sold through Coldwater Creek, one of the largest catalog and online retailers in the country that sold high-end women's apparel and gifts for the home. Coldwater Creek was headquartered just a couple of hours north of Moscow in Sandpoint, Idaho. Like Dean & Delucca, Coldwater Creek had decided that the chocolate was too spicy. Coldwater Creek had also expressed some reservations about carrying food products other than at its retail outlet in Sandpoint. Marilyn hoped that the introduction of mild-mannered Cowgirl Chocolates would help get her product into sites like these two.

Promotion

Marilyn was unsure how best to promote her product to potential customers given her limited resources. The ad that would appear in *Chile Pepper* magazine was her first attempt at really advertising her product. The ad itself was designed to grab readers' attention and pique their curiosity about Cowgirl Chocolates. Most of the ads in the magazine were fairly standard in format. They provided a lot of information and images of the product packed into a fairly small space. Her ad was different—it had very little product information and utilized the single image of the woman in the watering trough. It was to appear in a special section of the magazine that focused on celebrity musicians like Willie Nelson and The Dixie Chicks.

Other than the upcoming ad, Marilyn's promotional efforts were focused on trade shows and creating publicity opportunities. She attended a handful of trade shows each year. Some of these were focused on the hot and spicy food market, and it was at these events that she had won all of her awards. Other trade shows were more in the gourmet food market, and she typically shared table space at these events with Seattle Chocolates. She always gave away a lot of product samples at these trade shows, and had clearly won over some fans to her chocolate. But while these shows occasionally had led to placement of her product in retail locations, at least on a trial basis, they had as yet failed to land her what she would consider to be a really high volume wholesale account.

Marilyn also sought ways to generate publicity for her company and products. Several local newspapers had carried stories on her company in the last couple of years, and each time something like that would happen, she would see a brief jump in sales on her Web site. *The New York Times* had also carried a short article about her and her company. The day after that article ran, she generated sales of $1,000 through her Web site. More publicity like *The New York Times* article would clearly help. The recently released movie *Chocolat* about a woman who brings spicy chocolate with somewhat magical powers to a small French town was also generating some interest in her product. A number of customers had inquired if she used the same pepper in her chocolates as was used in the movie. Marilyn wondered how she might best capitalize on the interest the movie was creating in spicy chocolates. She thought that perhaps she could convince specialty magazines like *Art & Antiques* or regional magazines like *Sunset Magazine* or even national magazines like *Good Housekeeping* to run stories on her, her art, and her chocolates. But she only had so much time to divide between her various efforts. She had looked into hiring a public relations firm, but had discovered that this would cost something on the order of $2,000/month. She did not expect that any publicity a public relations firm could create would generate sufficient sales to offset this cost, particularly given the limited number of locations where people could buy her chocolates. Marilyn was considering trying to write a cookbook as a way to generate greater publicity for Cowgirl Chocolates. She always talked a little about Cowgirl Chocolates when she gave seminars and presentations about her art, and thought that promoting a cookbook would create similar opportunities. The cookbook would also feature several recipes using Cowgirl Chocolate products.

In addition to being unsure how best to promote her product to potential customers, Marilyn also wondered what she should do to better tap into the seasonal opportunities that presented themselves to sellers of chocolate. Demand for her product was somewhat seasonal, with peak retail demand being at Christmas and Valentine's Day. But she was clearly not seeing the Christmas and Valentine sales of other chocolate companies. Seattle Chocolates, for example, had around three-quarters of its annual sales in the fourth quarter, whereas Cowgirl Chocolate sales in the second half of 2000 were actually less than in the first half. Likewise, while Cowgirl Chocolates experienced a small increase in demand around Valentine's Day, it was nowhere near the increase in demand that other chocolate companies experienced. Marilyn did sell some gift buckets and baskets through her Web site, and these were more popular at Christmas and Valentine's Day. The Moscow Co-op had also sold some of these gift baskets and buckets during the 2000 Christmas season. Marilyn knew that the gift basket industry in the United States was pretty large, and that the industry even had its own trade publication called the *Gift Basket Review*. But she was not sure if gift baskets were the best way to generate sales at these two big holidays and thought that she could probably be doing more. One other approach to spur these seasonal sales that she was planning to try was to buy lists of e-mail addresses, that would allow her to send out several e-mails promoting her products right before Valentine's Day and Christmas. She had talked to the owners of a jewelry store about sharing the expense of this endeavor and they had tentative plans to purchase 10,000 e-mail addresses for $300.

What Next?

Marilyn looked again at the advertisement that would be appearing soon in *Chile Pepper* Magazine. The same friend who had helped her with her award winning package design had helped produce the ad. It would clearly grab people's attention, but would it bring customers to her products in the numbers she needed?

Next to the ad sat the folder with what financial information she had. Despite having little training in small business accounting and financial management, Marilyn knew it was important to keep good records. She had kept track of revenues and expenses for the year, and she had summarized these in a table (see Exhibit 4). Marilyn had shared this revenue and cost information with a friend with some experience in small business financial management, and the result was an estimated income statement for the year 2000 based upon the unaudited information in Exhibit 4. The estimated income statement, shown in Exhibit 5, revealed that Cowgirl had lost approximately $6,175 on operations before taxes. Combining the information in Exhibits 4 and 5, it appeared that the inventory had built up to approximately $16,848 by December 31, 2000. Marilyn had initially guessed she had $10,000 worth of product and packaging inventory, about twice her normal level of inventory, between what was stored in her garage turned art studio turned chocolate warehouse and what was stored for her at Seattle Chocolates. But the financial analysis indicated that she either had more inventory than she thought or that she had given away more product than she originally thought. Either way, this represented a significant additional drain on her resources—in effect cash expended to cover both the operational loss and the inventory buildup was approximately $23,000 in total (see note 3 of Exhibit 4 for a more detailed explanation). When Marilyn looked at the exhibits, she could see better why she had to loan the firm money. She also recognized that the bottom line was that the numbers did not look good, and she wondered if the ad would help turn things around for 2001.

If the ad did not have its desired affect, she wondered what she should do next. She clearly had limited resources to work with. She had already pretty much decided that if this ad did not work, she would not run another one in the near future. She was also pretty wary of working with distributors. In addition to her own bad experience, she knew of others in the industry that had bad experiences with distributors, and she did not think she could afford to take another gamble on a distributor. She wondered if she should

EXHIBIT 4
Summary of 2000
Financial
Information
(Unaudited)

Revenues:	
Product Sales	$ 26,000
Revenue from Shipping	4,046 (see Note 1)
Total Revenues	**$ 30,046**
Expenses: (related to cost of sales)	
Chocolate (raw material)	$16,508
Caramel (raw material)	2,647
Packaging (bags, boxes, tins)	9,120
Printing (labels, cards, etc)	3,148
Subtotal	$31,423 (see Note 2)
Other Expenses	
Shipping and Postage	$ 4,046
Brokers	540
Travel (airfare, lodging, meals, gas)	5,786
Trade shows (promotions, etc.)	6,423
Website	1,390
Phone	981
Office Supplies	759
Photography	356
Insurance, Lawyers, Memberships	437
Charitable Contributions	200
Miscellaneous Other Expenses	1,071
State Taxes	35
Subtotal	$ 22,024
Total Expenses	**$ 53,447**
Cash needed to sustain operations	**$ 23,023** (see Note 3)
Estimated year-end inventory (12/31/00):	
Product Inventory	$ 9,848
Extra Packaging and Labels	7,000
Total Inventory	**$16,848**

Notes (1) The $4,046 Revenue from Shipping represents income received from customers who are charged shipping and postage up front as part of the order. Cowgirl then pays the shipping and postage when the order is delivered. The offsetting operating expense is noted in "Other Expenses."

(2) Of this amount, $14,575 is attributed to product actually sold and shipped. The remaining $16,848 represents leftover inventory and related supplies (i.e., $16848 + $14575 = $31,423).

(3) Marilyn made a personal loan to the firm in the year 2000 for approximately $23,000 to sustain the business's operations.

focus more attention on her online retail sales or on expanding her wholesale business to include more retailers. If she focused more on her own online sales, what exactly should she do? If she focused on expanding her wholesale business, where should she put her emphasis? Should she continue to pursue retailers that specialized in hot and spicy foods, try to get her product placed in more co-ops, expand her efforts to get the product positioned as a gift in museum gift shops and similar outlets, or focus her efforts on large, high-end retailers like Coldwater Creek and Dean & Delucca now that she had a non-spicy chocolate in her product mix? Or should she try to do something else entirely new? And what more should she do to create publicity for her product? Was the cookbook idea worth pursuing? As she thought about it, she began to wonder if things were beginning to spin out of control. Here she was, contemplating writing a cookbook to generate publicity for her chocolate company that she started to raise money to publish her arts magazine. Where would this end?

EXHIBIT 5   Cowgirl Chocolates Income Statement (Accountant's unaudited estimate for Year 2000)

			% of Sales
Revenues:			
Product Sales	$26,000		
Miscellaneous Income	$4,046		
Total Net Sales		**$30,046**	100%
Cost of Sales (shipped portion of chocolate, caramel, packaging, and printing)		$14,197	47%
Gross Margin		**$15,849**	53%
Operating Expenses:			
Advertising & Promotions:			
Trade Shows	6,423		
Website	1,390		
Charitable Contributions	200		
Subtotal		8,013	27%
Travel		5,786	19%
Miscellaneous		1,071	4%
Payroll Expense/Benefits @ 20%	(no personnel charges)	—	0%
Depreciation on Plant and Equipment	(no current ownership of PPE)	—	0%
Continuing Inventory (finished and unfinished)	(not included in income statement)	—	
Shipping & Postage		4,046	13%
Insurance, Lawyers, Professional Memberships		437	1.5%
Brokers		540	1.8%
Office Expenses (phone, supplies, photography, taxes)		2,131	7%
Total Operating Expenses		**22,024**	
Grand Total: All expenses		**$36,221**	
Profit before Interest & Taxes		**($6,175) [see note]**	
Interest Expense (short term)		—	
Interest Expense (long term)		—	
Taxes Incurred (Credit @ 18%, approximate tax rate)		($1,124)	
Net Profit After Taxes		**($5,051.15)**	
Net Profit After Taxes/Sales			−17%

Note: The ($6,175) loss plus the $16,848 in inventory build-up approximates the cash needed ($23,023—see Exhibit 4) to cover the total expenses for year 2000.

22

Clearwater Technologies

Susan F. Sieloff and Raymond M. Kinnunen *Northeastern University*

At 9:00 AM on Monday, May 2004, Rob Erickson, QTX Product Manager; Hillary Hanson, Financial Analyst; and Brian James, District Sales Manager; were preparing for a meeting with Mark Jefferies, Vice President of Marketing, at Clearwater Technologies. The meeting's objective was to establish the end-user pricing for a capacity upgrade to the QTX servers Clearwater offered.

No one was looking forward to the meeting because company pricing debates were traditionally long and drawn out. Because there had already been several meetings, everyone knew that that was no consensus on how to determine the appropriate price, but company policy insisted on agreement. Only one price proposal went forward, and it had to represent something everyone could accept.

When Jefferies called the meeting, he commented:

> We've struggled with this pricing issue for several months. We can't seem to all agree on the right price. Finance wants the price as high as possible to generate revenue. Sales wants it low to sell volume. Product management wants the price to be consistent with the current product margin model. We've debated this for quite a while, but we need to finalize the third quarter price book update before June in order to get it into print and out to the sales force. We need to get this done.

Clearwater Technologies, Inc. History

Clearwater Technologies, Inc. was a small, publicly traded technology firm outside Boston. It was the market share leader in customer relationship management (CRM) servers for sales staffs of small- to medium-sized companies. Four MIT graduates had founded the company when they saw an opportunity to meet a market need that larger firms ignored. Unlike the CRM systems from Oracle or SAP, Clearwater customized the QTX for companies with sales forces of 10 to 30 people. Clearwater had been first to market in this particular segment, and QTX sales represented $45 million of its $80 million sales in 2004.

The QTX product line represented Clearwater's core franchise. Clearwater's premium-priced products were renowned for high reliability in performance supported by free lifetime technical support. The QTX line held 70 percent of its mature market. To date, competition in this market had been minimal, because no competitor had been able to match Clearwater's general functionality, and Clearwater held a U.S. patent on a popular feature that directed faxed documents to a specific salesperson's e-mail rather than a central fax machine.

Since 1999, Clearwater had used the cash generated by the QTX line to support engineering-intensive internal product development and to buy four other companies. None of these other businesses had achieved a dominant market position or profitability, so maximizing the QTX cash flow remained a priority.

The QTX Product

QTX was a sales support server that allowed multiple users to simultaneously maintain their sales account databases. These databases covered contact information, quote histories, copies of all communications, and links to the customer's corporate database for shipping records. The basic QTX package consisted of a processor, chassis, hard drive, and network interface, with a manufacturing cost of $500. The package provided simultaneous access for 10 users to the system, referred to as 10 "seats." Each seat represented one accessing employee. The product line consisted of 10-, 20-, and 30-seat capacity QTX servers. Each incremental 10 seats required $200 of additional manufacturing cost. Yearly sales were at the rate of 4,000 units across all sizes. In initial sales, approximately 30 percent of customers bought the 30-seat unit, 40 percent bought the 20-seat unit, and 30 percent bought the 10-seat unit. Customers who needed more than 30 seats typically went to competitors servicing the medium-to-large company market segment.

Clearwater set a per-seat manufacturer's suggested retail price (MSRP) that decreased with higher quantity seat purchases, reflecting the customer perception of declining manufacturing cost per seat. Clearwater also saw this as advantageous because it encouraged customers to maximize their initial seat purchase.

Clearwater typically sold its products through value-added resellers (VARs). A VAR was typically a small local firm that provided sales and support to end users. The value added by these resellers was that they provided a complete solution to the end user/customer from a single point of purchase and had multiple information technology products available from various vendors. Using VARs reduced Clearwater's sales and service expense significantly and increased its market coverage.

These intermediaries operated in several steps. First, the VAR combined the QTX from Clearwater with database software from other suppliers to form a turnkey customer solution. Second, the VAR loaded the software with customer-specific information and linked it to the customer's existing sales history databases. Finally, the VAR installed the product at the customer's site and trained the customer on its use. Clearwater sold the QTX to resellers at a 50 percent discount from the MSRP, allowing the VARs to sell to the end user at or below the MSRP. The discount allowed the VARs room to negotiate with the customer and still achieve a profit (Table 1).

TABLE 1

Number of Seats	MSRP to End User	VAR Price	Unit Cost*	Unit Margin**
10	$8,000	$4,000	$500	87.5%
20	$14,000	$7,000	$700	90.0%
30	$17,250	$8,625	$900	89.6%

*Unit cost reflects additional $200 for memory capability for each additional 10 seats.

$$**\text{Margin} = \frac{\text{VAR Price} - \text{Unit Cost}}{\text{VAR Price}}$$

TABLE 2

Number of Seats	Original Unit Cost	Original Unit Margin	Actual Unit Cost	Actual Unit Margin
10	$500	87.5%	$900	77.5%
20	$700	90.0%	$900	87.1%
30	$900	89.6%	$900	89.6%

The Upgrade

Initially, the expectation had been that the 30-seat unit would be the largest volume seller. In order to gain economies of scale in manufacturing, reduce inventory configurations, and reduce engineering design and testing expense to a single assembly, Clearwater decided to manufacture only the 30-seat server with the appropriate number of seats "enabled" for the buyer. Clearwater was effectively "giving away" extra memory and absorbing the higher cost rather than manufacturing the various sizes. If a customer wanted a 10-seat server, the company shipped a 30-seat capable unit, with only the requested 10 seats enabled through software configuration. The proposed upgrade was, in reality, allowing customers to access capability already built into the product (Table 2).

Clearwater knew that many original customers were ready to use the additional capacity in the QTX. Some customers had added seats by buying a second box, but because the original product contained the capability to expand by accessing the disabled seats, Clearwater saw an opportunity to expand the product line and increase sales to a captive customer base. Customers could double or triple their seat capacity by purchasing either a 10- or a 20-seat upgrade and getting an access code to enable the additional number of seats. No other competitor offered the possibility of an upgrade. To gain additional seats from the competitor, the customer purchased and installed an additional box. Because customers performed a significant amount of acceptance testing, which they would have to repeat before switching brands, the likelihood of changing brands to add capacity was low.

The objective of this morning's meeting was to set the price for the two upgrades.

As QTX product manager Rob Erickson stopped to collect his most recent notes from his desk, he reflected:

> What a way to start the week. Every time we have one of these meetings, senior management only looks at margins. I spent the whole weekend cranking numbers and I'm going in there using the highest margin we've got today. How can anybody say that's too low?

He grabbed his notes, calculator, and coffee and headed down the hall.

From the other wing of the building, financial analyst Hillary Hanson was crossing the lobby towards the conference room. She was thinking about the conversation she had late

Friday afternoon with her boss, Alicia Fisher, Clearwater's CFO. They had been discussing this upcoming meeting and Alicia had given Hillary very clear instructions.

> I want you to go in and argue for the highest price possible. We should absolutely maximize the profitability on the upgrade. The customers are already committed to us and they have no alternative for an upgrade but with us. The switching costs to change at this point are too high since they've already been trained in our system and software. Let's go for it. Besides, we really need to show some serious revenue generation for the year-end report to the stockholders.

Hillary had not actually finalized a number. She figured she could see what the others proposed and then argue for a significant premium over that. She had the CFO's backing so she could keep pushing for more.

From the parking lot, Brian James, the district sales manager, headed for the rear entrance. He, too, was thinking about the upcoming meeting and anticipating a long morning.

> I wish marketing would realize that when they come up with some grandiose number for a new product, sales takes the hit in the field. It's a killer to have to explain to customers that they have to pay big bucks for something that's essentially built in. It's gonna be even tougher to justify on this upgrade. At least with the QTX, we have something the buyer can see. It's hardware. With the upgrade, there isn't even a physical product. We're just giving customers a code to access the capability that's already built into the machine. Telling customers that they have to pay several thousand dollars never makes you popular. If you think about it, that's a lot of money for an access code, but you won't hear me say that out loud. Maybe I can get them to agree to something reasonable this time. I spent the weekend working this one out, and I think my logic is pretty solid.

Price Proposals

Once everyone was settled in the conference room, Rob spoke first:

> I know we have to come up with prices for both the 10-seat and 20-seat upgrades, but to keep things manageable, let's discuss the 20-seat price first. Once that number is set, the 10-seat price should be simple. Because the margin on the 30-seat unit is the highest in the line, I think we should use that as the basis to the price for the upgrade.

He went to a whiteboard to show an example:

> If a customer is upgrading from a 10-seat unit to a 30-seat unit, they are adding two steps of capacity costing $200 each to us, or $400. $400 /1-0.90 = $4,000 to the reseller, and $8,000 to the end user. We keep the margin structure in place at the highest point in the line. The customer gets additional capacity, and we keep our margins consistent.

He sat down feeling pleased. He had fired the first shot, had been consistent with the existing margin structure, and had rounded up the highest margin point in the line.

Brian looked at Rob's calculations and commented:

> I think that's going to be hard for the customer to see without us giving away information about our margins, and we don't want to do that, since they are pretty aggressive to begin with. However, I think I have solved this one for us. I've finally come up with a simple, fair solution to pricing the upgrade that works for us and the customers.

He walked over to a whiteboard and grabbed a marker:

> If we assume an existing 10-seat customer has decided to upgrade to 30-seat capability, we should charge that customer the difference between what the buyer has already paid and the price of the new capacity. So . . .

New 30-seat unit	$17,250
Original 10-seat unit	$8,000
Price for 20-seat upgrade	$9,250

It's consistent with our current pricing for the QTX. It's fair to the customer. It's easy for the customer to understand and it still makes wads of money for us. It also is easy for the customer to see that we're being good to them. If they bought a 20-seat box in addition to the 10-seat box they already have, it would be costing them more.

He wrote:

| New 20-seat unit | $14,000 |

A new unit provides customers with redundancy by having two boxes, which they might want in the event of product failure, but the cost is pretty stiff. Upgrading becomes the logical and affordable option.

Hillary looked at the numbers and knew just what she was going to do.

That all looks very logical, but I don't see that either of you has the company's best interests at heart. Brian, you just want a simple sale that your sales people and the customers will buy into, and Rob, you are charging even less than Brian. We need to consider the revenue issue as well. These people have already bought from us; are trained on our hardware and software and don't want to have to repeat the process with someone else. It would take too long. They've got no desire to make a change and that means we've got them. The sky is really the limit on how much we can charge them because they have no real alternative. We should take this opportunity to really go for the gold, say $15,000 or even $20,000. We can and should be as aggressive as possible.

All three continued to argue the relative merits of their pricing positions, without notable success. Jefferies listened to each of them and after they finished, he turned to a clean whiteboard and took the marker.

I've done some more thinking on this. In order to meet the needs of all three departments, there are three very important points that the price structure for these upgrades must accomplish:

1. The pricing for the upgrades shouldn't undercut the existing pricing for the 30-seat QTX.
2. We want to motivate our buyers to purchase the maximum number of seats at the initial purchase. A dollar now is better than a potential dollar later. We never know for sure that they will make that second purchase. If we don't do this right, we're going to encourage customers to reduce their initial purchase. They'll figure they can add capacity whenever, so why buy it if they don't need it. That would kill upfront sales of the QTX.
3. We don't want to leave any revenue on the table when buyers decide to buy more capacity. They are already committed to us and our technology and we should capitalize on that, without totally ripping them off. Therefore, while Hillary says "the sky's the limit," I think there is a limit and we need to determine what it is and how close we can come to it.

If we assume that those are the objectives, none of the prices you've put together thus far answers all three of those criteria. Some come close, but each one fails. See if you can put your heads together and come to a consensus price that satisfies all three objectives. OK?

Heads nodded and with that, Jefferies left the conference room. The three remaining occupants looked at one another. Brian got up to wipe the previous numbers off the whiteboards and said:

OK, one more time. If our numbers don't work, why not and what is the right price for the 20-seat upgrade?

Social and Ethical Issues in Marketing Management

23

E. & J. Gallo Winery

A. J. Strickland III and Daniel C. Thurman *The University of Alabama*

In the mid-1980s, alcohol consumption in the United States had been declining in virtually every category except low-priced wines. A number of producers in the wine industry did not believe they should be producing what they called skid-row wines (wines fortified with additional alcohol and sweetener and sold in screwtop, half-pint bottles). Richard Maher, president of Christian Brothers Winery in St. Helena, California, who once was with E. & J. Gallo Winery, said he didn't think Christian Brothers should market a product to people, including many alcoholics, who were down on their luck. "Fortified wines lack any socially redeeming values," he said.

Major producers of the low-end category of wines, called "dessert" or "fortified" (sweet wines with at least 14 percent alcohol), saw their customers otherwise. Robert Hunington, vice president of strategic planning at Canandiaqua (a national wine producer whose product, Wild Irish Rose, was the number 1 low-end wine), said 60 percent to 75 percent of its "pure grape" Wild Irish Rose was sold in primarily black, inner-city markets. Hunington described Wild Irish Rose's customer in this $500 million market as "not super-sophisticated," lower middle-class, and low-income blue-collar workers and mostly men. However, Canandiaqua also estimated the annual national market for dessert category wine to be 55 million gallons; low-end brands accounted for 43 million gallons, with as much as 50 percent sold

Prepared by Daniel C. Thurman, doctoral student, under the supervision of A. J. Strickland III, both of The University of Alabama.

in pints (typically the purchase choice of winos—alcoholics with a dependency on wine). Daniel Solomon, a Gallo spokesman, said Gallo's Thunderbird had lost its former popularity in the black and skid-row areas and was consumed mainly by retired and older people who didn't like the taste of hard distilled products or beer.[1]

Tony Mayes, area sales representative for Montgomery Beverage Company, Montgomery, Alabama, said one-third of the total revenue from wine sales in the state of Alabama was from the sale of one wine product—Gallo's Thunderbird. Sales crossed all demographic lines. According to Mayes, a consumer developed a taste for wine through an education process that usually began with the purchase of sweet wines from the dessert category. He attributed the high sales of Thunderbird to the fact that the typical wine drinker in Alabama was generally not the sophisticated wine drinker found in California or New York.

Company History and Background

The E. & J. Gallo Winery, America's biggest winery, was founded by Ernest and Julio Gallo in 1933. More than 55 years later, the Gallo Winery was still a privately owned and family-operated corporation actively managed by the two brothers. The Gallo family had been dedicated to both building their brands and the California wine industry.

The Gallos started in the wine business working during their spare time in the vineyard for their father, Joseph Gallo. Joseph Gallo, an immigrant from the Piedmont region in northwest Italy, was a small-time grape grower and shipper. He survived Prohibition because the government permitted wine for medicinal and religious purposes, but his company almost went under during the Depression. During the spring of 1933, Joseph Gallo killed his wife and chased Ernest and Julio with a shotgun. He killed himself following their escape. Prohibition ended that same year, and the Gallos, both in their early 20s and neither knowing how to make wine, decided to switch from growing grapes to making wine. With $5,900 to their names, Ernest and Julio found two thin pamphlets on winemaking in the Modesto Public Library and began making wine.[2]

The Gallos had always been interested in quality and began researching varietal grapes in 1946. They planted more than 400 varieties in experimental vineyards during the 1950s and 1960s, testing each variety in the different growing regions of California for its ability to produce fine table wines. Their greatest difficulty was to persuade growers to convert from common grape varieties to the delicate, thin-skinned varietals because it took at least four years for a vine to begin bearing and perhaps two more years to develop typical, varietal characteristics. As an incentive, in 1967, Gallo offered long-term contracts to growers, guaranteeing the prices for their grapes every year, provided they met Gallo quality standards. With a guaranteed long-term "home" for their crops, growers could borrow the needed capital to finance the costly replanting, and the winery was assured a long-term supply of fine wine grapes. In 1965, Julio established a grower relations staff of skilled viticulturists to aid contract growers. This staff still counsels growers on the latest viticultural techniques.[3]

Private ownership and mass production were the major competitive advantages contributing to Gallo's success. Gallo could get market share from paper-thin margins and absorb occasional losses that stockholders of publicly held companies would not tolerate. Gallo was vertically integrated, and wine was its only business. While Gallo bought about 95 percent of its grapes, it virtually controlled its 1,500 growers through long-term

[1]Alix M. Freedman, "Misery Market—Winos & Thunderbird Are a Subject Gallo Doesn't Like to Discuss," *The Wall Street Journal,* February 25, 1988, pp. 1, 18.

[2]Jaclyn Fierman, "How Gallo Crushes the Competition," *Fortune,* September 1, 1986, pp. 24–31.

[3]"The Wine Cellars of Ernest & Julio Gallo, a Brief History," a pamphlet produced by Ernest & Julio Gallo, Modesto, Calif.

contracts. Gallo's 200 trucks and 500 trailers constantly hauled wine out of Modesto and raw materials in. Gallo was the only winery to make its own bottles (2 million a day) and screw-top caps. Also, while most of the competition concentrated on production, Gallo participated in every aspect of selling its product. Julio was president and oversaw production, while Ernest was chairman and ruled over marketing, sales, and distribution. Gallo owned its distributors in about a dozen markets and probably would have bought many of the more than 300 independents handling its wines if laws in most states had not prohibited it.

Gallo's major competitive weakness over the years had been an image associated with screwtops and bottles in paper bags that developed because of its low-end dessert wine, Thunderbird.[4] There were stories, which Gallo denied, that Gallo got the idea for citrus-flavored Thunderbird from reports that liquor stores in Oakland, California, were catering to the tastes of certain customers by attaching packages of lemon Kool-Aid to bottles of white wine to be mixed at home.[5]

Thunderbird became Gallo's first phenomenal success. It was a high-alcohol, lemon-flavored beverage introduced in the late 1950s. A radio jingle sent Thunderbird sales to the top of the charts on skid rows across the country: "What's the word? Thunderbird. How's it sold? Good and cold. What's the jive? Bird's alive. What's the price? Thirty twice." Thunderbird has remained a brand leader in its category ever since. In 1986, Ernest Gallo poured $40 million into advertising aimed at changing Gallo's image to one associated with quality wines.

Information on Gallo's finances was not publicly available, and the brothers maintained a tight lid on financial details. In a 1986 article, *Fortune* estimated that Gallo earned at least $50 million a year on sales of $1 billion. By comparison, the second leading winery, Seagram's (also the nation's largest distillery), had approximately $350 million in 1985 wine revenues and lost money on its best-selling table wines. *Fortune* stated that several of the other major Gallo competitors made money, but not much.[6]

Gallo produced the top-selling red and white table wines in the country. Its Blush Chablis became the best-selling blush-style wine within the first year of its national introduction. Gallo's award-winning varietal wines were among the top sellers in their classification. The company's Carlo Rossi brand outsold all other popular-priced wines. Gallo's André Champagne was by far the country's best-selling champagne, and E & J Brandy has outsold the number two and three brands combined. Gallo's Bartles & Jaymes brand was one of the leaders in the new wine cooler market.[7]

The U.S. Wine Industry

Wine sales in the United States grew from about 72 million gallons in 1940 to over 600 million gallons, accounting for retail sales in excess of $9 billion (see Exhibit 1). This retail sales volume had exceeded such major established grocery categories as detergents, pet foods, paper products, and canned vegetables. While wine consumption had grown at an astonishing rate, trends toward moderation and alcohol-free life-styles made this growth rate impossible to maintain. Nevertheless, annual growth was projected to be 3.2 percent through 1995.

Per capita consumption of wine was low in the late 1950s and early 1960s because wine drinking was perceived as either the domain of the very wealthy or the extreme opposite. "Fortified" dessert wines were the top-selling wines of the period. The first surge in consumption in the late 1960s was the result of the introduction of "pop" wines, such as

---

[4]Fierman, "How Gallo Crushes the Competition."

[5]Freedman, "Misery Market."

[6]Fierman, "How Gallo Crushes the Competition."

[7]"Gallo Sales Development Program," a pamphlet produced by Ernest & Julio Gallo, Modesto, Calif.

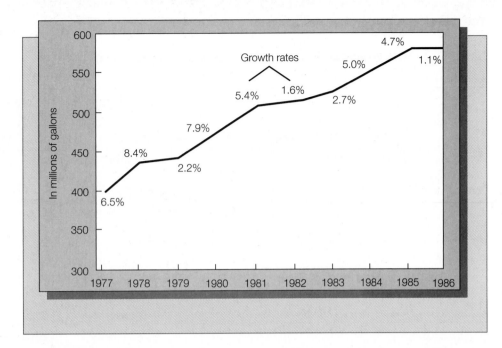

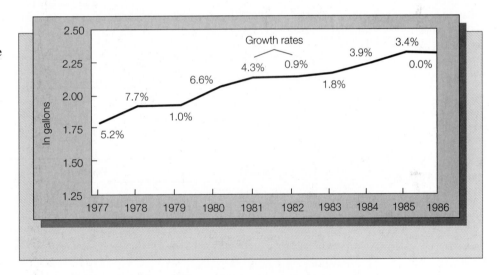

Boones Farm, Cold Duck, and Sangrias. These wines were bought by baby boomers, who were now young adults. Their palates were unaccustomed to wine drinking and these wines were suited to them. By the mid-1970s, the pop wine drinkers were ready to move up to Lambruscos and white wine "cocktails," and per capita consumption increased (see Exhibit 2). The wine spritzer became the trend, still the alternative to more serious wines for immature palates. Just as this surge began to wane, wine coolers were introduced in 1982 and exploded on the market in 1983. Wine coolers were responsible for a 5 percent market surge in 1984 and experienced four consecutive years of very high growth rates, rising 6 percent in 1987 to 72.6 million nine-liter cases.

The imported wines category enjoyed an upward growth rate from 6.6 percent of the market in 1960 to a high of 27.6 percent in 1985 (see Exhibits 3 and 4). The category lost market share to 23.1 percent in 1986 primarily because of the shift from Lambruscos to

511

EXHIBIT 3   Wine Production by Place of Origin (Millions of nine-liter cases)

Source: *Impact* 17, no. 11 (June 1, 1987), p. 4.

| Origin | 1970 | 1975 | 1980 | 1985 | 1986 | Average Annual Compound Growth Rate | | | Percent Change |
						1970–75	1975–80	1980–85	1985–86
California	82	115	139.5	133.2	133.3	7.0%	3.9%	−0.9%	−0.1%
Other states*	18	19	18.7	16.9	17.3	1.4	−0.3	−2.0	2.4
United States	100	134	158.2	150.1	150.6	6.1	3.3	−1.0	0.3
Imports	13	21	43.1	57.2	45.3	10.5	15.8	5.8	−20.8

*Includes bulk table wine shipped from California and blended with other state wines.

Note: Addition of columns may not agree because of rounding.

EXHIBIT 4   Market Share Trends in Wine Production

Source: *Impact* 17, no. 11 (June 1, 1987), p. 4.

| Place Produced | 1970 | 1975 | 1980 | 1985 | 1986 | Share Point Change | | |
						1970–80*	1980–85	1985–86
California	73%	74%	69.3%	64.3%	68.0%	4	−5.0	3.8
Other states	16	12	9.3	8.2	8.8	−7	1.1	0.7
United States	88	86	78.6	72.4	76.9	−10	−6.2	4.5
Imports	12	14	21.4	27.6	23.1	9	6.2	−4.5
Total†	100%	100%	100.0%	100.0%	100.0%	—	—	—

*1980 based on unrounded data.

†Addition of columns may not agree because of rounding.

EXHIBIT 5
1985 Share of U.S. Wine Market

Source: Jaclyn Fierman, "How Gallo Crushes the Competition," *Fortune*, September 1, 1986, p. 27.

Company	Percent
E. & J. Gallo Winery	26.1%
Seagram & Sons	8.3
Canandiaqua Wine	5.4
Brown-Forman	5.1
National Distillers	4.0
Heublein	3.7
Imports	23.4
All others	24.0
Total	100.0%

wine coolers. Additional factors were the weakening dollar and an overall improved reputation for domestic wines.

There were about 1,300 wineries in the United States. *Fortune* identified the major market-share holders in the U.S. market in a September 1986 article. It showed Gallo as the clear leader, nearly outdistancing the next five competitors combined (see Exhibit 5).

A number of threats had faced the wine industry, not the least of which had been the national obsession with fitness and the crackdown on drunken driving. Americans drank 6.5 percent less table wine in 1985 than in 1984 (see Exhibits 6 and 7), and consumption was

EXHIBIT 6   **Shipments of Wine Entering U.S. Trade Channels by Type (millions of nine-liter cases)**

Source: *Impact* 17, no. 11 (June 1, 1987), p. 3.

Type	1970	1975	1980	1984	1985	1986	Average Annual Compound Growth Rate			Percent Change*
							1970–75	1975–80	1980–85	1985–86
Table	55.9	88.9	150.8	170.9	159.2	147.1	9.9%	11.2%	1.1%	−7.4%
Dessert	31.1	28.2	19.1	15.5	14.3	14.7	−2.0	−7.5	−5.7	3.2
Vermouth	4.2	4.2	3.7	3.0	2.9	2.7	—	−2.5	−4.8	−6.9
Sparkling	9.3	8.4	12.7	19.7	19.4	18.7	−1.9	8.6	8.6	−4.5
Special natural	11.8	24.0	13.6	10.9	10.7	10.9	15.3	−10.7	−4.7	1.9
Imported specialty†	0.3	1.0	1.5	1.0	0.9	1.8	25.4	8.1	−9.7	104.7
Total‡	112.6	154.7	201.3	220.1	207.3	195.9	6.6%	5.4%	0.6%	−5.5%

*Based on unrounded data.

†Imported fruit wines and wine specialties (includes sangria and fruit-flavored wines).

‡Addition of columns may not agree because of rounding.

EXHIBIT 7   **Share of Market Trends in Shipments of Wine Entering U.S. Trade Channels, by Type**

Source: *Impact* 17, no. 11 (June 1, 1987), p. 3.

Type	1970	1975	1980	1984	1985	1986	Share Point Change		
							1970–80*	1980–85	1985–86
Table	50%	57%	74.9%	77.2%	76.8%	75.1%	25	1.9	−1.7
Dessert	28	18	9.5	7.0	6.9	7.5	−18	−2.6	0.6
Vermouth	4	3	1.8	1.4	1.4	1.4	−2	−0.4	‡
Sparkling	8	5	6.3	9.0	9.4	9.5	−2	3.0	0.2
Special natural	10	16	6.8	5.0	5.2	5.6	−3	−1.6	0.4
Imported specialty	‡	1	0.7	0.5	0.4	0.9	+	−0.3	0.5
Total†	100%	100%	100.0%	100.0%	100.0%	100.0%	—	—	—

*1980 based on unrounded data.

†Addition of columns may not agree because of rounding.

‡Less than 0.05%.

projected to be down another 5 percent in 1986. The industry answer to this problem had been introduction of wine coolers. Gallo's Bartles and Jaymes Coolers were number 1 until they lost the lead by only a slight margin to a Seagram's brand in 1987.

Another trend had been a shift toward a demand for quality premium wines made from the finest grapes. Premium wines increased market share from 8 percent in 1980 to 20 percent in 1986. Again, Gallo had sold more premium wine than any other producer, but Gallo's growth had been limited by its lack of snob appeal.[8]

Although more than 80 percent of the U.S. adult population enjoyed wine occasionally, Gallo's research indicated most Americans were still infrequent wine drinkers by global standards. Only about one in four Americans drank wine as often as once a week. Per capita consumption in the United States was less than 2.5 gallons per year, compared to about 20 gallons in some Western European countries.[9]

[8]Fierman, "How Gallo Crushes the Competition."

[9]"Gallo Sales Development Program."

EXHIBIT 8   Beverage Consumption Patterns

Source: *Impact* 17, no. 18 (September 15, 1987), pp. 3–4.

1986 National Beverage Consumption by Gender (Percent of volume):

Gender	Malt Beverages	Wine	Distilled Spirits	Coolers	Total Nonalcoholic Beverages	Total Beverages
Male	80.8%	51.6%	62.6%	44.9%	51.1%	52.7%
Female	19.2	48.4	37.4	55.1	48.9	47.3
Total	100.0%	100.0%	100.0%	100.0%	100.0%	100.0%

1986 National Alcoholic Beverage Consumption by Household Income (Percent of volume):

Household Income	Malt Beverages	Wine	Distilled Spirits	Coolers	Total Alcoholic Beverages
Under $15,000	26.1%	11.7%	19.7%	22.3%	26.5%
$15,000–$24,999	19.1	13.9	18.1	19.5	21.3
$25,000–$29,999	10.8	14.2	6.6	10.9	12.1
$30,000–$34,999	11.7	9.9	14.7	7.9	10.3
$35,000 & over	32.3	50.3	40.9	39.4	29.8
Total	100.0%	100.0%	100.0%	100.0%	100.0%

1986 National Beverage Consumption by Time of Day (Percent of volume):

Time of Day	Malt Beverages	Wine	Distilled Spirits	Coolers	Total Nonalcoholic Beverages	Total Beverages
Breakfast/morning	2.7%	2.1%	4.6%	1.5%	32.7%	30.6%
Lunch	6.8	5.8	4.2	4.4	20.8	19.8
Snack	27.5	19.0	31.9	27.0	10.9	12.0
Dinner	14.2	45.8	15.5	13.7	22.9	22.6
Evening	48.8	27.3	43.8	53.4	12.7	15.0
Total	100.0%	100.0%	100.0%	100.0%	100.0%	100.0%

1986 National Beverage Consumption by Location of Consumption (Percent of volume):

Location	Malt Beverages	Wine	Distilled Spirits	Coolers	Total Nonalcoholic Beverages	Total Beverages
Total home	64.6%	75.8%	61.4%	76.9%	76.1%	75.5%
Total away from home	35.4%	24.2%	38.6%	23.1%	23.9%	24.5%

Though the health-consciousness and alcohol-awareness of the 1980s had a moderating influence on wine growth patterns as consumers traded up in quality and drank less, long-term growth was expected to be steady but slower than that of the 1970s and early 1980s. Exhibit 8 provides drinking patterns for 1986. Personal disposable income was expected to grow in the United States through 1995; busy lifestyles contributed to more dining out; and sale of wine in restaurants was expected to increase. As the aging baby boomers grew in number and importance, their wine purchases were expected to increase. All these factors contributed to the projected average yearly increase in growth rate of 3.2 percent through 1995.[10]

[10]"Coolers Providing Stable Growth," *Beverage Industry Annual Manual,* 1987.

The Dessert Wine Industry

Dessert wine represented a 55 million-gallon, $500 million industry. The dessert wine category, also called fortified wines, included wines that contained more than 14 percent alcohol, usually 18 percent to 21 percent. They were called fortified because they usually contained added alcohol and additional sugar or sweetener. This category included a group of low-end priced brands that had been the brunt of significant controversy. Canandiaqua's Wild Irish Rose had been the leading seller in this category, with Gallo's Thunderbird claiming second place, followed by Mogen David Wine's MD 20/20.[11]

Dessert wines had shown a decreasing trend both in amount of wine consumed and in market share from 1970 through 1985. However, the trend changed in 1986 when dessert wine's market share rose six-tenths of a share point to 7.5 percent of the total wine market (see Exhibit 7). The rise was attributed in large measure to the 19 percent federal excise tax increase on distilled spirits. An additional factor in the increase in the dessert wine category was the shift to fruit-flavored drinks, which also affected the soft drink industry and wine coolers.[12]

A number of factors indicated that the growth trend would continue for the $500 million dessert wine category. The desire to consume beverages that contained less alcohol than distilled spirits and were less expensive than distilled spirits, the desire for fruit flavor, and the American trend toward eating out at restaurants more often contributed to the trend toward increased consumption of dessert wines. Additionally, the dessert wine category had survived relatively well with virtually no promotion or advertising. This had been possible because, of the category's 55 million gallons, low-end brands accounted for 43 million gallons, approximately 50 percent of which was sold in half pints; and this market had not been accessible by traditional advertising or promotion.

The dessert wine category had been a profitable venture because many of the wines in this category were made with less expensive ingredients, packaged in less expensive containers, and had usually been sold without promotion. Canandiaqua estimated that profit margins in this category were as much as 10 percent higher than those of ordinary table wines. Gallo said this was not true for its products, but it would not reveal the figures.

The low-end dessert wines were a solid business. *The Wall Street Journal* reported that, of all the wine brands sold in America, Wild Irish Rose was the number 6 best seller, Thunderbird was 10th, and MD 20/20 was 16th. In contrast to the growth expectations of other brands and categories, sales of these low-end brands were expected to be up almost 10 percent. Yet the producers of these top-selling wines distanced themselves from their products by leaving their corporate names off the labels, obscuring any link to their products. Paul Gillette, publisher of the *Wine Investor,* was quoted in a discussion of this unsavory market as saying: "Makers of skid-row wines are the dope pushers of the wine industry."[13]

[11]Freedman, "Misery Market."

[12]"U.S. News and Research for the Wine, Spirits and Beer Executive," *IMPACT* 17, no. 11 (June 1, 1987): and *IMPACT* 17, no. 18 (September 15, 1987).

[13]Freedman, "Misery Market."

24

Abercrombie & Fitch: An Upscale Sporting Goods Retailer Becomes a Leader in Trendy Apparel

Janet Rovenpor *Manhatten College*

On November 10, 2005, Abercrombie & Fitch (A&F) celebrated the opening of a new 36,000 square-foot, four-level flagship store on Fifth Avenue and 56th Street in Manhattan. The timing was perfect—right ahead of the busy Christmas shopping season during which the retailer hoped to sell large quantities of cashmere sweaters, Henley long-sleeved fleeces, hand-knit wool sweaters, polo shirts, and jeans. The Fifth Avenue store, considered a prototype for other flagship stores, featured dark interiors, oak columns, bronze fixtures and a central staircase with frosted glass-block flooring. A mural of muscular, skin-showing rope climbers in a setting from the 1930s by the artist Mark Beard, was prominently displayed. "We're really excited to be back on Fifth Avenue. We're really trying to build the character of the brand. We had a little store in Trump Tower that closed in 1986, and we have been looking on Fifth Avenue for a few years. This is a prestige location and great for the positioning of the brand," commented CEO Michael Jeffries.[1]

In an attempt to gauge customer reaction to the opening of the new store, *New York Magazine* surveyed 75 teenagers asking them what the A&F brand meant to them. Answers were varied: "It's gross"; "It's overpriced"; "It's stylish and sleek"; "It's very logotistical"; "It projects the typical image of the perfect American male—good at school and masculine;" "It

---

[1]J.E. Palmierie and D. Moin, "A&F Hits Fifth Avenue Fray," *DNR* 35 (November 14, 2005), p. 4. Retrieved April 19, 2006, from ABI/Inform (Proquest) database.

was cool up until we were 16. Then it got this dumb-jock-meathead image."[2] Perhaps such contradictory statements were just what A&F's senior executives wanted. Consumers either loved or hated the company, its products and its image. Part of the trendy retailer's competitive strategy, in fact, was to stir up controversy, go against convention and appeal emotionally to its youthful customers.

A&F's 5th Avenue store symbolized the values the retailer held: sensuality, a youthful lifestyle, a love for the outdoors and fun with friends. It was the culmination of the retailer's creative endeavors to design and implement an exciting store format that drew shoppers in and captivated them. The loud music, appealing visuals, and perfumed interiors encouraged teenagers to "hang out" and "browse." A&F had come a long way from its early beginnings in 1892. Back then, A&F was considered a luxury sporting goods retailer with conservative tastes that appealed to affluent clients, including adventurers, hunters, presidents, and heads of royal families. President Theodore Roosevelt, for example, purchased snake-proof sleeping bags for a 1908 African safari at an Abercrombie store. Admiral Richard Byrd bought equipment for his 1950s expedition to Antarctica.

A&F's competitive strategies seemed to be working. By February 2007, the retailer operated 944 stores in 49 states, the District of Columbia and Canada. It had 8,500 full-time and 77,900 part-time employees (including temporary staff hired during peak periods such as the back-to-school and holiday seasons). Its fiscal 2006 revenues were $3.32 billion and its net income was $422.2 million. It opened its first European store, in London, in March 2007. It expected to open a store in Tokyo in late 2009. *Apparel Magazine* ranked A&F number 3 in terms of profitability (net income as a percentage of sales) among apparel retailers in 2007 (up from number 4 in 2006).[3] In March 2007, A&F joined the S&P 500 stock index (replacing Univision Communications, Inc. which had been acquired by an investor group).

At the same time, questions existed regarding the retailer's long-term success. Would teenagers, A&F's primary target market, remain loyal to the company and its products? Could A&F bring back some of the shoppers it had alienated because of its treatment of minority employees and its racy slogans on its T-shirts? Would A&F be able to maintain its competitive advantage in a fragmented industry in which new entrants from both the US as well as from overseas markets were intent on imitating A&F's strategies? Should CEO Jeffries be concerned with the exodus of talented senior executives from his top management team? Who would eventually succeed Jeffries? Would the retailer's new corporate governance and diversity initiatives pay off?

The U.S. Specialty Apparel Industry

A&F was considered a "specialty retailer." Retailers in this category sold products in specific merchandise categories—apparel, footwear, office supplies, home furnishings, books, jewelry, or toys, among others. Numerous small to midsized firms existed. They survived by catering to local tastes and preferences. Sometimes, their financial performance was adversely affected when a competitor entered their niche or when the preferences, life-styles, and demographics of their target markets changed. As young people became interested in electronics and began spending more and more time playing video games, for example, the fortunes of retailers like Best Buy rose at the expense of retailers like Toys 'R Us.[4]

[2]D Penny, "The Abercrombie Report," *New York* 38 (November 21, 2005), p. 6. Retrieved April 19, 2006, from ABI/Inform (Proquest) database.

[3]"The Apparel Top 50," *Apparel Magazine* 48, no.11 (July 2007) pp. 12–20. Retrieved September 13, 2007, from EBSCOhost database.

[4]M. Souers and M. Normand, "Specialty Retailers Demonstrate Resilience in Face of Adversity," *Standard & Poor's Industry Surveys: Retailing: Specialty*, January 12, 2006.

Specialty apparel retailers opened stores in shopping malls and constructed free-standing units along major roadways. The firms enhanced their capabilities to sell products via direct mailings of catalogues and through Web sites equipped with shopping cart technologies. To compete with mass merchandiser and department stores, they tried to maintain high prices and high quality merchandise, cultivate customer loyalty through various membership programs, and promote their own private-label brands. J. Crew, for example, offered high-end, limited edition items (e.g., crocodile sling-backs and silk wedding dresses), which created excitement and enticed consumers to buy early at full prices. Chico's FAS Inc. offered a customer loyalty program, Passport Club, which gave customers discounts and other benefits when their purchases exceeded $500.

In 2007, consumer spending tightened as the economy slowed. Individuals spent more on gasoline and food and began to cut back on other purchases amid lower consumer confidence and a slump in the housing market. Retailers saw declines in customer traffic and sales in July, the start of the usually brisk back-to-school shopping season.[5] July same-store sales (that is, sales dollars generated by stores that have been open more than one year) at A&F, American Eagle Outfitters (AEOS), and the Gap fell 4 percent, 6 percent, and 7 percent, respectively.

Demographics began to shift; the children of the "baby boom" generation were getting older. Those specialty apparel retailers who appealed mostly to teenagers realized that they needed to hold on to their consumers as they entered their 20s. A&F, AEOS, and even the Gap began to open, with varying degrees of success, stores that targeted an older demographic. Rivals who already catered to an older consumer group, such as Ann Taylor Loft and Express LLC, were equally eager to lure such young adults away.[6] Specialty apparel retailers also faced increased competition from such department store chains as JC Penney and Kohl's which started offering more fashionable and exclusive private labeled goods.

There was some threat of being an acquisition target. Many private equity transactions were completed in 2007. Apollo Management LP acquired Claire's Stores Incorporated (a teen accessory retailer) for $3.1 billion; Golden Gate Capital acquired a 67 percent stake in The Limited's Express clothing chain. Private equity firms saw an opportunity to turn around struggling businesses and get them ready for resale. When retailers went private, they no longer had to report comparable same store sales or quarterly earnings to investors; they could concentrate on improving their business operations.[7]

Believing that "trend transcends age," A&F catered to cool, attractive, fashion-conscious consumers offering products to meet their needs through different life stages—from elementary school to postcollege.[8] The retailer managed four brands:

- A&F: a brand that was repositioned in 1992. It offered apparel that reflected the youthful lifestyle of the East Coast and Ivy League traditions for 18–22-year-old college students. In February 2007, there were 360 A&F brand stores in the United States (close to its capacity of 400 stores).
- abercrombie: a brand that was launched in 1998. It targeted customers aged 7–14 with fashions similar to the A&F line. There were 177 stores in early 2007.

---

[5] J. Covert, "Shoppers Held Back in July; Retailers' Weak Sales Show Impact of Tumult in the Housing Market," *The Wall Street Journal,* August 10, 2007, p. A2. Retrieved September 6, 2007, from ABI/Inform (Proquest) database.

[6] M. Souers & J. DeFoe, "Specialty Retailers Experience Mixed Results in 2007," *Standard & Poor's Industry Surveys: Retailing: Specialty,* August 2, 2007.

[7] Ibid.

[8] A&F, 10-K; J. Sheban, "Oh, Canada!" *Knight Ridder Tribune Business News.* February 26, 2006, p. 1. Retrieved April 18, 2006, from ABI/Inform (ProQuest) database.

- Hollister Company: a brand that was launched in 2000. It targeted 14–18-year-old high school students with lower priced casual apparel, personal care products, and accessories. It promoted the laid-back, California surf lifestyle. There were 393 stores in early 2007 (with potential for many more).

- Ruehl: a brand that was launched in 2004. It sold casual sportswear, trendy apparel, and leather goods to postcollege consumers aged 22–35 years. Its line of clothing was inspired by the lifestyle of New York City's Greenwich Village. The merchandise was more upscale and more expensive than the A&F line. There were 14 stores in early 2007.

A fifth store concept was on its way. A&F refused to reveal details, although Jeffries remarked that accessories—hats, totes, fragrances and jewelry—were a growing and important part of the business.[9] Rumors circulated that the retailer would launch either an accessories brand or an intimate apparel line with its own store locations.

A&F had three main competitors. Two were publicly held firms—American Eagle Outfitters, Incorporated (AEOS), and Gap Incorporated. A third firm, J. Crew Group, had been a privately held firm until June 2006. For basic comparative financial data, see Exhibit 1 (five-year data for JC are not reported because the retailer had operated at a loss when it was privately held; ratios, such as return on revenues and return on equity, are not meaningful).

Based in Warrendale, Pennsylvania, AEOS sold lower-priced casual apparel and accessories to men and women aged 15–25. The Schottenstein family (whom held interests in Value City Department and Furniture Stores) owned 14 percent of the retailer. AEOS operated over 900 stores in the US and Canada with approximately 40 percent of its stores located west of the Mississippi River. Revenues in fiscal 2006 were $2.8 billion (an increase of 21 percent from fiscal 2005); net income reached $387 million (an increase of 31.9 percent from fiscal 2005).

AEOS launched two new store concepts in 2006. Martin + Osa was a clothing store selling denim and active sportswear targeting men and women aged 24–40. It did not perform as well as expected. Efforts were underway in 2007 to make the women's merchandise more feminine, less outdoorsy, less expensive and of better quality. AEOS hired a former Liz Claiborne executive to become president of Martin + Osa (who replaced the previous president). Aerie was an intimate apparel subbrand that was launched adjacent to existing AEOS stores and as stand-alone stores. It was successful and plans were in place to expand upon its merchandise with fragrance and personal care items.

JC operated 227 retail and outlet stores in the United States. With a joint venture partner, it also had 45 stores in Japan. Millard "Mickey" Drexler, former CEO of the Gap, headed the retailer. He promised that JC would "be the best, not the biggest."[10] Revenues in fiscal 2006 were 1.15 billion (up 20.9 percent from fiscal 2005). Net income (applicable to common shareholders) in fiscal 2006 was $71.6 million (or $1.49 a diluted share) compared to a net loss of $9.7 million (or a loss of 39 cents a diluted share) in fiscal 2005. JC launched Madewell, a casual clothing store for women which sold merchandise at prices that were 20 percent to 30 percent lower than JC merchandise. Its initial public offering of common stock in June 2006 raised $402.8 million. At the time, this was the third largest apparel retailing IPO in history.

Whereas JC was the smallest of A&F's direct competitors, the Gap was the largest with 3,000 stores worldwide. The Gap sold basic casual clothing and accessories for children, men and women. Revenues in fiscal 2006 were $15.9 billion (a decrease of 0.5 percent

[9]J. Sheban, "Abercrombie & Fitch Plans Fifth Concept," *Knight Ridder Tribune Business News*, November 18, 2006, p. 1. Retrieved September 6, 2007, from ABI/Inform (ProQuest) database.

[10]D. Molin, "J. Crew Mission: Being Best, Not Biggest," *WWD*, 193, no 125 (June 13, 2007), p. 2. Retrieved September 13, 2007, from ABI/Inform (ProQuest) database.

EXHIBIT 1 Basic Comparative Financial Information for Abercrombie & Fitch (A&F), American Eagle Outfitters (AEOS), and the Gap

	A&F					AEOS					GAP				
	2006	2005	2004	2003	2002	2006	2005	2004	2003	2002	2006	2005	2004	2003	2002
Operating revenues (in millions $)	3,318.2	2,784.7	2,021.3	1,707.8	1,595.8	2,794.4	2,309.4	1,881.2	1,520.0	1,463.1	15,943.0	16,023.0	16,267.0	15,854.0	14,454.7
Net income (in millions $)	422.2	334.0	216.4	204.8	194.8	387.4	293.7	224.2	60.0	88.7	778.0	1,113.0	1,150.0	1,030.0	477.5
Return on revenues (%)	12.7	12.0	10.7	12.0	12.2	13.9	12.7	11.9	3.9	6.1	4.9	6.9	7.1	6.5	3.3
Return on assets (%)	20.9	21.3	15.8	17.2	22.1	21.6	20.3	20.8	7.5	12.6	9.0	11.8	11.3	10.2	5.4
Return on equity (%)	35.2	40.1	28.3	25.5	29	30.1	27.7	27.9	9.8	16.4	14.7	21.5	23.7	24.4	14.3
Current ratio	2.1	1.9	1.6	2.4	2.8	2.6	3.0	3.3	2.8	3.0	2.2	2.7	2.8	2.7	2.1
Debt/capital ratio (%)	0	0	0	0	0	0	0	0	2.1	2.8	3.5	8.6	27.6	34.2	44.2
Debt as a % of net working capital	0	0	0	0	0	0	0	0	4.1	5.7	6.8	15.6	46.4	59.3	96.1
Price/earnings ratio (high-low)	17-10	19-12	20-10	16-10	17-8	19-9	18-10	15-5	28-16	25-8	23-17	18-13	20-14	20-10	31-15
Earnings per share—basic ($)	4.79	3.83	2.33	2.12	1.99	1.74	1.29	1.03	.28	.41	.94	1.26	1.29	1.15	.55
Share price (high-low, $)	79.42- 49.98	74.10- 44.17	47.45- 23.07	33.65- 20.65	33.85- 14.97	33.01- 14.83	22.69- 12.97	15.92- 5.28	7.79- 4.40	10.15- 3.25	21.39- 15.91	22.70- 15.90	25.72- 18.12	23.47- 12.01	17.14- 8.35

Sources: Standard & Poor's Industry Surveys: Retailing Specialty; August 2007.

from fiscal 2005); net income was $778 million (a decrease of 30.1 percent from fiscal 2005). It operated Banana Republic (high quality, fashionable apparel) and Old Navy (low-priced trendy clothing). Its most recent entry, Forth&Towne (stylish apparel for women over 35), was open for 18 months before being shut down.

The Gap was struggling to turn around its performance which began to decline in 2000 when it overexpanded, assumed too much debt, and made a few fashion-related miscalculations. Under pressure from the board of directors, CEO Paul Pressler resigned in January 2007. Glenn Murphy, who had been the CEO of a large Canadian drug store chain, was hired to replace him. The firm also hired Goldman Sachs to explore strategic options for the retailer. Rumors circulated that the company intended to put itself up for sale or to spin off one of its divisions, most likely Banana Republic.

A&F's Early Beginnings

A&F was founded in 1892 by David T. Abercrombie (see Exhibit 2 for key milestones in A&F's history). Abercrombie was a civil engineer, topographer, and colonel in the Officers Reserve Corps. He was also an avid hunter and fisherman. The first store was located on Water Street in lower Manhattan. Ezra Fitch, a lawyer and one of Abercrombie's best customers, became a partner in 1900. The two men frequently argued. Fitch continued to run the company after Abercrombie resigned in 1907.

EXHIBIT 2
Key Milestones in A&F's Early History

1892:	A&F was founded by David T. Abercrombie, an engineer, topographer, outdoorsman and colonel.
1900:	Ezra Fitch, a lawyer from Kingston, NY, became Abercrombie's business partner.
1907:	Abercrombie resigned from the company.
1917:	A&F's 12-story building on Madison Avenue and 45th Street opened.
1928:	Ezra Fitch resigned as president. He was succeeded by James S. Cobb.
1929:	A&F acquired an interest in Von Lengerke & Detmold, a gun, camp, and fishing chain based in Chicago.
1935:	A&F earned a net profit of $148,123, up from $123,424 in the previous year.
1940:	Otis Guernsey was elected president and CEO.
1943:	A&F earned a net profit of $286,694.
1958:	A store in San Francisco opened.
1961:	John H. Ewing became president and CEO, succeeding Guernsey. Earl Angstadt became the president and CEO in the mid-1960s.
1962:	A&F opened a store in Colorado Springs, CO.
1963:	A&F's opened a store in Short Hills, NJ.
1967:	A&F acquired the Crow's Nest, a nautical supply store with a national mail order business.
1968:	Sales peaked at $28 million and net income rose to $866,000.
1970:	Angstadt resigned. He was replaced by William Humphreys. Henry Haskell, a major shareholder, soon replaced Humphreys as CEO. A&F lost money every year until 1977.
1972:	A store in a Chicago suburb opened.
1977:	A&F declared bankruptcy.
1978:	A&F was acquired by Oshman's Sporting Goods Incorporated.
1988:	The Limited acquired A&F from Oshman's.
1989:	Sally Frame-Kasaks was named president and chief executive of A&F. She left in 1992.
1992:	Michael Jeffries became president and chief executive of A&F.
1996:	A&F was spun off from the Limited.
1999:	A&F ran 186 A&F stores and 13 abercrombie stores.
2001:	A&F opened a new 260,000 square foot corporate office and a 700,000 square foot distribution center in New Albany, Ohio. It cost $130 million.

A&F's 12-story building on Madison Avenue and 45th Street opened in 1917. It featured a log cabin and casting pool on the roof and a rifle range in the basement. The store's location was excellent. By 1923, Madison Avenue and 45th Street had become the "heart" of the "specialized shop trade."[11] Near A&F's flagship store were Brooks Brothers, Tiffany Studios, Eastman Kodak, and Maillard's. The Roosevelt Hotel was just undergoing construction. Abercrombie died in 1931 at the age of 64; Fitch died of a stroke aboard his yacht in Santa Barbara, California in 1930 at the age of 65.

A&F's managers promoted it as "The Finest Sporting Goods Store in the World." An early advertisement announcing the opening of a new store on 36th Street appears in Exhibit 3. A&F was known for its expensive and exotic goods as well as for its affluent clientele. It was possible to buy an antique miniature cannon for $300, a custom-made rifle for $6,000 or a Yukon dog sled for $1,188. Presidents William Taft and Warren Harding purchased golf clubs at A&F. President Dwight Eisenhower bought hunting boots for $55 for his walks in the woods at Camp David. Other famous customers included Amelia Earhart, Greta Garbo, Charles Lindberg, Clark Gable, the Duke of Windsor, Howard Hughes, and Ernest Hemmingway.

A&F was not just a place to purchase sporting goods and rugged apparel. It was also a place where individuals could learn new skills and get involved in the community. In 1923, the Adirondack Club held its annual meeting in A&F's log cabin. Its members discussed whether or not an open season should be declared on beavers whose dam-building activities were causing floods which damaged timber and ruined trout streams. In 1966, A&F held a lecture on how to capture a musk ox bare-handed without harming it. In 1967, A&F ran a fishing clinic in which experts discussed tackle, knot tying, and trout angling techniques. In 1973, A&F served flambé quail, prepared in the log cabin's fireplace, in celebration of a talking cookbook it had produced. The cookbook contained two 40-minute cassettes and a booklet of recipes printed on waterproof and grease-proof plastic.

Throughout its early history, A&F did a good job keeping up with its customers and with changing fashions. During World War II, when activities such as parlor skeet and military board games were popular, A&F sold a wooden box that could be filled with water and used to blow sailboats from side to side. In the 1940s, barbeque picnics in fields outside country homes became the latest fad arriving from the West. A&F sold high quality BBQ equipment and insulated canvas bags to keep drinks cold. In 1964, A&F made a splash when it developed the capacity to produce a cashmere sweater with a lifelike reproduction of a color photograph of one's pet embroidered on it. It sold resort wear with a fruit motif in the 1940s and Bermuda length culottes in the 1960s. A&F had a clearly defined target market. CEO Anstadt said, "We aren't out for the teenage business. Our customers are on the go and have the time and the money to enjoy travel and sport."[12]

A&F had its share of problems. Some were typical of all retailers throughout the decades and some were atypical. During the early 1940s, A&F stores were low on inventory. Commerce had been disrupted by the war effort. It was difficult to import goods from abroad. Manufacturers were busy making binoculars, field glasses, saddles and marine clocks for use by the army and navy. A&F wrote to its customers, asking them if they would like to sell optical or sporting goods in satisfactory condition back to the retailer so that the items could be refurbished and resold to new customers. One year, the Office of Price Administration placed limitations on civilian consumption of rubber products. This caused a rush on golf balls sold by A&F. A&F joined other retailers in asking customers to do their

---

[11]"Rapid Growth in Specialized Shop Trade Madison Avenue in the Forties The Centre," *The New York Times*, February 18, 1923. Retrieved April 21, 2006, from ProQuest Historical Newspapers database.

[12]"New Face for Fashion at Abercrombie & Fitch," *The New York Times,* September 11, 1965, p. 14. Retrieved April 21, 2006, from ProQuest Historical Newspapers database.

EXHIBIT 3
An Early A&F Advertisement in the New York Times from 1912

Opening

We Cordially Invite You to Inspect Our New Store

We maintain at this address, the finest Sporting Goods Store in the world. We want you to visit the establishment—we are proud of it, and we are proud of the stock we have to show you. It comprises everything for the Great Out of Doors, each article the BEST for its purpose and most of them exclusive. You can't get them elsewhere.

For a good many years, this concern, The Abercrombie & Fitch Co., occupied a small, exclusive store at 57 Reade Street, in the dingy downtown district where buyers came only because they HAD to—because they could not buy elsewhere the things they bought from us. We have been known the world over not only as the one place where the big Nimrods, Explorers, Hunters, Trappers, Fishermen,—the whole Out-of-Door Brotherhood were outfitted, but as a sort of informal clearing house of information for them. We outfitted Col. Roosevelt for his trip into Africa—Stewart Edward White speaks of our outfits in his textbooks—our peculiar specialty of having the RIGHT thing, the CORRECT thing and finally the EXCLUSIVE thing was recognized by the adept many years ago. Our business grew by word of mouth—by talks over camp fires and at club tables, because when once a man or woman found us, they had found the ONLY one there was and took a pride in passing on the good news. We outgrew our store—we outgrew the building—and now we have our own building on 36th Street. So long as we

had to move, we moved to a place where you could get at us—right in the centre of your shopping district.

We have the finest store of its kind in the world. We have not merely the finest stock of our sort in the world, but we carry the ONLY correct things for the purpose. We have broadened our business and to bring this about, we have manufactured in quantities impossible before because of the restrictions of space in our old quarters. All the economies due to manufacturing and buying on a wholesale plan are reflected in the very low prices of the goods we offer you.

We want you to see our Out-of-Door Clothing for Men and Women and for Boys. We want you to see our complete outfits for camping, for canoeing, for fishermen, for golfers, for every one of the sports. We want you to see to what lengths we have gone to provide not only the best, but the exactly RIGHT and the EXCLUSIVE thing for your favorite sport, the thing you have always wanted but couldn't get elsewhere because it didn't EXIST elsewhere.

EZRA H. FITCH, President

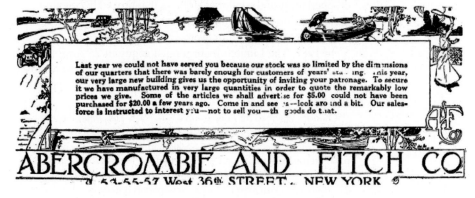

Last year we could not have served you because our stock was so limited by the dimensions of our quarters that there was barely enough for customers of years' standing. This year, our very large new building gives us the opportunity of inviting your patronage. To secure it we have manufactured in very large quantities in order to quote the remarkably low prices we give. Some of the articles we shall advertise for $5.00 could not have been purchased for $20.00 a few years ago. Come in and see us—look around a bit. Our sales-force is instructed to interest you—not to sell you—the goods do that.

ABERCROMBIE AND FITCH CO.

53-55-57 West 36th STREET. NEW YORK

Christmas shopping early—in November. A lack of manpower had overwhelmed the postal services and caused delays.

At least twice in A&F's history, a customer used one of the guns on display in an A&F shop to commit suicide. The first shooting occurred in 1932, when the son of a famous horse breeder killed himself. The second shooting occurred in 1968 when an immigrant from Czechoslovakia killed himself. Subsequently, extra care was taken to ensure that every gun was fitted with a trigger lock and kept in locked show cases. Customers were no longer handed guns or ammunition over the counter; upon purchase, the firearms were delivered to their homes.

Employee theft and shoplifting occurred. In 1915, for example, Gustave Touchard, Jr., a champion tennis player, was charged with stealing 48 dozen golf balls worth $288 from an A&F store on 36th Street. He had worked at the store as a manager of its sporting department. In 1923, a well-dressed woman was caught with 21 yards of Scotch tweed cloth hidden in the ulster (a bulky overcoat) she was wearing. The theft occurred a few weeks after two sisters who shopped at Macy's while carrying small dogs in their arms were caught with stolen items in their wide sleeves. In 1969, inventory shrinkage (from bookkeeping errors, internal theft and shoplifting) totaled $1 million (up from between $600,000 and $700,000 the previous year). This contributed to the retailer's pretax loss for the year.[13]

Between 1970 and 1976, A&F continued to incur financial losses. In the fiscal year ending January 31, 1976, A&F incurred a net loss of $1 million on sales of $23.8 million.[14] The loss followed annual deficits ranging from $287,000 to $540,000 every year since 1970.[15] A&F's best year had been in 1968 when it reported pretax earnings of $866,000 on sales of $28 million.[16] Managers began to search for a possible buyer of the firm. No one was seriously interested.

In August 1976, A&F filed for bankruptcy. It held a sale to liquidate its inventory of $8.5 million. A sign in the retailer's Madison Avenue store read: "They say we're stuffy so we're moving the stuff out at tremendous reductions on all floors."[17] After the sale, the stores were closed. A&F's difficulties were attributed to competition from mass marketers (e.g., Hermann's World of Sporting Goods) that sold discounted merchandise, the lack of professional managers and leadership turnover (the retailer had three different CEO's in its last six years), high overhead costs, and fewer customers who could afford its exotic, high-priced items.

In 1978, Oshman's Sporting Goods, Incorporated of Houston acquired A&F's name, trademark, and mailing list for $1.5 million. A&F's slogan was changed from "The Finest Sporting Goods Store in the World" to "The Adventure Goes On." The new owners had studied A&F's business model for two years. According to president Nanna, "We examined the original business, took it apart and retained the good qualities. We also retained some of the legendary old products that Abercrombie had and expanded their variety. But we dropped most of the tailored clothing that proved to be a drain."[18] The owners believed that they could bring A&F up-to-date to the styles of the 1980s. The chain expanded to 12 stores; sales of $20 million were expected in 1982.

In 1988, The Limited Incorporated acquired 25 A&F stores and its catalogue business for $47 million from Oshman's. Two additional stores were closed. At the time, the Limited operated a chain of 3,100 stores that sold women's apparel. In 1992, Michael Jeffries

[13]"Changes Weighed for Abercrombie," *The New York Times*, September, 1970, p. 73. Retrieved April 21, 2006, from ProQuest Historical Newspapers database.

[14]"Abercrombie Reports Loss of $1 Million in Fiscal Year," *The New York Times*, August 26, 1976, p. 68. Retrieved April 21, 2006, from ProQuest Historical Newspapers database.

[15]R. Hanley, "Abercrombie & Fitch Put Up for Sale," *The New York Times*, July 20, 1976. Retrieved April 21, 2006, from ProQuest Historical Newspapers database.

[16]I. Barmash, "Abercrombie & Fitch in Bankruptcy Step," *The New York Times*, August 7, 1976, p. 47. Retrieved April 21, 2006, from ProQuest Historical Newspapers database.

[17]C. G. Fraser, "'Stuffy' Abercrombie's Gets Sale Relief," *The New York Times*, August 29, 1976, p. 47. Retrieved April 21, 2006, from ProQuest Historical Newspapers database.

[18]I. Barmash. "New Guise for Abercrombie's," *The New York Times*, November 9, 1982, p. D1. Retrieved April 21, 2006, from ProQuest Historical Newspapers database.

became president and chief executive of A&F, a retailing unit of the Limited. A new format was introduced. The chain began to carry casual, classic American clothes for 20-year-old men and women. A&F became one of the Limited's fastest growing divisions. The number of stores grew from 40 in 1992 to 113 in 1996. Its sales increased at a compounded annual rate of 40.3 percent during those same years.[19] In 1996, the Limited spun off A&F. Jeffries stayed on as CEO.

Senior Executives and Corporate Governance

Michael Jeffries got his start in retailing at an early age when he helped his father select the toys that were sold in the family's chain of party supply stores. He also enjoyed organizing and designing the window and counter displays. Born in 1944, Jeffries received a BA in economics from Claremont McKenna College and an MBA from Columbia University. He entered the management training program of Abraham & Straus (a New York department store that belonged to Federated) in 1968. From there, he went on to start a women's clothing store, Alcott & Andrews, which later failed. He worked in merchandising at Paul Harris, which also went bankrupt.[20]

In his flip-flops, polo shirt, and torn jeans, Jeffries embodied the casual look of A&F more than any one else. He made sure that A&F's apparel reflected the life styles of college students. Teams of designers, merchandisers, and marketers visited college campuses once a month to talk to students and find out what they liked and how they spent their time. On one of those visits in 1998, Jeffries saw someone wearing nylon wind pants. A&F was quick to make its own version of the pants. Tom Lennox, A&F's director of corporate communications and investor relations once said, "We just believe that it is our job to position Abercrombie and Fitch as the coolest brand, the brand with the greatest quality, the aspirational brand of college students."[21]

A&F's success did not make Jeffries complacent. He was quoted as saying, "Every morning I'm scared. I'm superstitious. I come in every morning being afraid to look a yesterday's figures, and I want everyone else to have that same kind of fear."[22] He worked hard and constantly traveled from store to store. He was always thinking of ways to extend the A&F brand. Jeffries had a few eccentric habits. He went through revolving doors twice, parked his black Porsche at an odd angle in the company's parking lot and wore the same lucky shoes when he reviewed financial reports.[23] It was almost as if he felt that his firm's good fortune could change at any time. Perhaps he realized that his primary target audience—teenagers—was fickle and that trendy apparel quickly became outdated.

Between 2003 and 2006, A&F had three different chief financial officers and two different chief operating officers. The latter position remained unfilled. In July 2003, Wesley McDonald, who had been A&F's CFO for four years, left to become CFO of Kohl's Corporation. He was replaced in February 2004 by Susan Riley who had held CFO positions at Mount Sinai Medical Center, Dial Corporation, and Tambrands Incorporated. In August 2005, Riley resigned for family reasons and returned to her home in New York City.

---

[19]D. Canedy, "After Unbuttoning Its Image, A Retail Legend Comes to Market," *The New York Times*, September 1996, p. F3. Retrieved April 21, 2006, from ProQuest Historical Newspapers database.

[20]R. Berner, "Flip-Flops, Torn Jeans—And Control," *Business Week*, May 30, 2005, p. 68. Retrieved December 12, 2005, from ABI/Inform (ProQuest) database.

[21]M. Cole, "Facing a Brave New World," *Apparel*, 45 (July 2004), p. 22. Retrieved April 20, 2006, from ProQuest Historical Newspapers database.

[22]M. Pledger, "Abercrombie & Fitch Focuses on American College Audience," *The Plain Dealer*, June 22, 1999, p. 2S. Retrieved April 19, 2006, from Lexis/Nexis Acdemic database.

[23]Berner, "Flip-Flops."

Michael Kramer became A&F's new CFO. He had been the CFO of the retail unit of Apple Incorporated. He also had retail experience working for Gateway Inc., The Limited, and Pizza Hut. He had a BA in Business Administration and Accounting from Kansas State University and was a certified public accountant.

Seth Johnson was A&F's COO between 2000 and 2004. Before that, he had been its CFO. Johnson was credited with keeping costs down by reducing payroll and travel expenses. He was responsible for installing computer systems to help A&F's distribution system run more efficiently. He had aspired to a CEO position and was offered such an opportunity at Pacific Sunwear of California, Inc. Robert Singer, a former executive at Gucci, became the next president and COO in 2004. After 15 months on the job, Singer resigned to become the CEO of Barilla Holding SpA. Disagreements about international expansion were cited as the reason for his departure. Singer's duties were divided between John Lough (executive vice president of logistics and store operations) and Michael Kramer (CFO). Search for a replacement began.

Unlike other retailers, A&F did not have division presidents for its brands. Merchants from different businesses reported directly to the CEO. They did not work within a particular brand. Instead, they led categories—for example, denim or outerwear. They were responsible for these brands across each of the company's divisions. That way, their expertise and knowledge could best be leveraged and exploited.

A&F encountered criticism from shareholders regarding executive compensation and the composition of its board of directors. In February 2005, shareholders charged A&F directors with wasting corporate assets by paying CEO Jeffries $22.9 million in salary, bonus, and stock options. The company settled the lawsuit and Jeffries agreed to reduce his $12 million bonus to $6 million and to forgo new stock options for two years. The bonus was contingent on meeting specific earnings targets. Jeffries would receive the full $6 million bonus if A&F's earnings per share increased by 13.5 percent between February 1, 2005 to January 31, 2009.[24]

Shareholders also expressed concern over the independence of A&F's board of directors. John W. Kessler, chair of the compensation committee, had financial ties to the retailer. As chair of a real estate development firm owned by the Limited's CEO Wexner (Jeffries former boss), Kessler sold the land upon which A&F built its headquarters in 1999. He received a fee for finding the site. Kessler's son-in-law, Thomas D. Lennox, was A&F's director of investor relations and communications. Samuel Shahid, president and creative director of the advertising agency that received $2 million a year from A&F for its services, was a board member until May 2005. He was replaced by Allan A. Tuttle, an attorney for the luxury goods maker, Gucci Group. While Tuttle did not have financial ties to A&F, he was a friend of Robert Singer, who at the time was A&F's president and COO.

A&F denied wrongdoing and settled the lawsuits to "avoid the uncertainty, harm and expense of litigation."[25] As part of its agreement with shareholders, A&F promised to provide more public information about executive compensation and to add independent members to its board and compensation committee.

A&F faced a formal investigation by the U.S. Securities and Exchange Commission regarding insider selling of stock. In June and July of 2005, when A&F's stock price was high, Jeffries sold 1.6 million shares worth $120 million. In August, share prices declined after the company announced it would miss Wall Street expectations regarding its second quarter earnings. A&F was also sued for making false and misleading statements of monthly and quarterly sales figures and for failing to disclose that profit margins were

---

[24]"Abercrombie CEO Benefits Settlement OKd." *Los Angeles Times*, June 15, 2005. Retrieved May 18, 2006, from ABI/Inform (Proquest) database.

[25]"Abercrombie CEO Benefits."

declining and inventory rising. The company announced that it was cooperating with the SEC and that the shareholder lawsuit had no merit.

Store Concept and Marketing Strategies

When customers walked into an original A&F clothing store in a local mall, they were often greeted by a young, handsome salesperson wearing the latest fashion in casual attire. The store's lights were dimmed and posters of attractive models wearing its trademark cargo pants and polo shirts adorned the walls. In some stores, chandeliers made of fake deer antlers or whitewashed moose antlers hung from the ceilings. Apparel was neatly folded and placed on long wooden tables. The retailer's hip, trendy, and "All-American" look was reinforced by loud dance music and sprays of men's cologne. The intent was to provide a sensual experience that appealed to a shopper's sense of sight, smell, and sound. According to marketing expert, Pam Danziger, "Shoppers are rejecting the old concept of 'hunting and gathering' shopping in favor of a more involved, interesting, dynamic retail experience."[26] A&F was able to successfully implement an exciting store format.

Every A&F store was designed according to one of several specific models created at company headquarters. The retailer wanted to maintain complete control over its brand and to communicate a consistent message in all stores across the nation. Jeffries himself made sure the model stores were "perfect."[27] The prototypes were photographed and sent to the store managers of the individual outlets for replication. Jeffries was known for paying attention to every detail. He visited stores and made sure that the clothes were folded correctly. He approved of the background music to be played in the stores and selected the appropriate volume level for all locations. He even gave suggestions on how mannequins could be made to look more rugged and masculine.

A&F's website (www.abercrombie.com) was created to match the feel and aura of its stores as much as possible. It featured striking black and white images of young people in outdoor settings. A&F's low rise jeans for men and women were advertised. Was that shirtless young man lying on the grass placing his hand in a sexually suggestive position (see Exhibit 4)? The photograph appeared on the store locator Web page. Through its "A&F Lifestyle" link, Web surfers could download screen savers or send e-postcards to one another. According to *Forbes* magazine, the Web site's best feature is the photo gallery showing images of the models that made A&F famous. Its worst feature was that its line of clothing was not shown by the models.[28]

A&F extended its successful store concept and marketing ideas to its newer brand name stores, Hollister Company and Ruehl. Hollister stores were designed to look like beach houses with faux porches and house style layouts. The name came from a span of gated coastal property north of Santa Barbara where surfers liked to hang out. Surfboards leaned against the store walls. Fans blew constantly to mimic the breeze coming in from the ocean. Shoppers could sit in comfortable chairs and read surfing, skateboarding, and snowboarding magazines.

Ruehl (rhymes with "cool") stores imitated the architecture of Greenwich Village with red-brick facades, iron fences, flowerboxes, and small windows. They looked like brownstones. Ruehl was the name of a fictitious German family who had come to America in the

[26]M. Wilson, "The 'Pop' Factor," *Chain Store Age* 82 (April 2006), p. 78. Retrieved May 18, 2006, from ABI/Inform (Proquest) database.

[27]Denizet-Lewis, "The Man."

[28]"Web Site Reviews: Abercrombie & Fitch," Forbes.com. Retrieved May 1, 2006, from http://www.forbes.com/bow/b2c/review. jhtml?id=6833.

EXHIBIT 4
A Photograph from
A&F's Web Site

1850s and opened a leather-goods shop in Greenwich Village. Couches and armchairs were available for lounging. Copies of the *Village Voice* and *The New York Times* are found on coffee tables. The music playing was jazz. Signs were not posted outside. The shopper was expected to stumble upon the store just as if he or she were walking in a city neighborhood; the great "find" would be spread via word-of-mouth.[29] Experts reported that young people want to be part of a brand story.[30]

A&F had an enviable target market. It catered to teenagers, whose population in the United States was expanding. In 2003, 32 million teens lived in the United States. This number was expected to rise to 35 million by 2010. Moreover, teens spent approximately $170 billion on goods and services in 2002, with one-third going towards apparel.[31] Spending in 2005 was lower—$159 billion.[32] Teen retailing was considered to be somewhat recession-proof. Although teens worked for low wages, they had multiple revenue streams—babysitting, paper routes, part-time jobs, and assistance from parents.[33] They usually did not have financial obligations (no mortgages or bills to pay.) Parents, too, were more likely to spend money on their children than on themselves.

[29]J. Verdon. "Abercrombie Targets 20-Somethings with Coffeehouse-Style Store in Paramus, N.J.," *Knight Ridder Tribune Business News*, September 17, 2004, p. 1. Retrieved April 20, 2006, from ABI/Inform (Proquest) database.

[30]C. Collins. "Status of U.S. Brands Slips Globally Among Teens," *Christian Science Monitor*, February 16, 2006, p. 13. Retrieved June 11, 2006, from ABI/Inform (Proquest) database.

[31]J. Ablan, "Trend Setter," *Barron's* 83 (March 31, 2003), p. 21. Retrieved April 20, 2006, from ABI/Inform (Proquest) database.

[32]PB Erikson, "Companies Focus on Youthful Influence for Prosperity," *Knight Ridder Tribune Business News*, April 16, 2006, p. 1. Retrieved April 21, 2006, from ABI/Inform (Proquest) database.

[33]Ablan, "Trend Setter."

A&F's busy seasons were spring and fall. Forty percent of its sales were realized in the Spring and 60 percent in the fall (during the back to school and holiday season periods). It hired extra employees during those times. A&F was able to maintain its high prices without resorting to sales and discounts. It was afraid that cutting prices for a big sale would cheapen its brand. A&F saved money on promotions, relying frequently on word of mouth advertising. The retailer claimed that it spent less than 2 percent of net sales on marketing in 2004.[34] It also kept down its administrative expenses and negotiated lower fees from its suppliers. High prices and low costs comprised a formula that clearly worked.

In its A&F stores, the retailer tried to introduce two or three new items in its stores every week. It launched a new men's line, "Ezra Fitch," which featured high-quality apparel made from cashmere, velvet, and leather. A&F cultivated brand loyalty. Shoppers could join Hollister's Club Cali and receive gift cards based on how much they spent. Invitations to after-hours parties with new bands at the stores were also available. Instead of marking down items the day after Thanksgiving in 2004 (the start of the busy Christmas shopping season), preferred customers who spent $1,000 a year or more were invited to a live concert given by Ryan Cabrera. The concert was also shown on big screen televisions in 50 other Hollister stores around the nation.

A&F generated controversy. Adults often reacted negatively to its catalogues, revealing clothes, and racy slogans (see Exhibit 5 for some of its t-shirts). Some teenagers, however, might have responded positively to its advertising in a show of rebellion against the traditional values and lifestyles of their parents. Teens were reluctant to shop in the same stores as their parents. Some observers believed that A&F purposely created controversy and engaged in risky practices to attract attention, draw in shoppers, and sell more products. As an analyst with Midwest Research in Cleveland remarked, "Abercrombie is not a company that really cares about backing away from controversy. They use controversy as a free advertising gig and are successful in driving traffic into the stores."[35]

Here is a list of A&F's controversial moves:

- In July 1998, a story entitled, "Drinking 101," appeared in an A&F Fall back-to-school catalogue. It featured recipes for alcoholic beverages and a game for helping students decide which drink to mix. After being criticized by Mothers Against Drunk Driving (MADD), A&F deleted the story and sent postcards to students who received the publication by mail reminding them to "be responsible, be 21, and don't ever drink and drive."[36]

- In April 2002, A&F sold a line of T-shirts with Asian cartoon characters and matching ethnic slogans: "Wong Brothers Laundry Service, Two Wongs Can Make it White"; "Wok-N-Bowl"; "Buddha Bash, Get Your Buddha on the Floor." The retailer took the T-shirts off store shelves after protests from college students from campuses around the country. A&F's spokesperson, Hampton Carney apologized, saying "It is not, and never has been, our intention to offend anyone. These were designed to add humor and levity to our fashion line. Since some of our customers were offended by these T-shirts, we removed them from all our stores."[37]

[34]Presentation at the Merrill Lynch Retailing Leaders & Household Products & Cosmetics Conference, March 25, 2005; Retrieved April 22, 2006 from the World Wide Web: http://www.abercrombie.com.

[35]T. Turner, "Retailer Abercrombie & Fitch Angers West Virginia Residents with New T-Shirt," *Knight Ridder Tribune Business News*, March 24, 2004, p. 1. Retrieved November 8, 2004, from ABI/Inform (Proquest) database.

[36]"Abercrombie & Fitch Plans to Delete Drinking Section," *The Wall Street Journal*, July 30, 1998, p. 1. Retrieved November 8, 2004, from ABI/Inform (Proquest) database.

[37]G. Kim, "Racism Doesn't Belong on T-shirts," *Knight Ridder Tribune Business News*, April 28, 2002, p. 1. Retrieved April 21, 2006, from ABI/Inform (Proquest) database.

EXHIBIT 5
A&F's Controversial
T-Shirt Slogans

Source: http://www.click2houston.com/ money/3683643/detail.html

Source: http://news.bbc.co.uk/.../newsid_1938000/1938914.st

Source: http://www.80-20initiative.net/tshirts.html

• In May 2002, A&F sold thong underwear for girls 10 years and over with sexual phrases
such as "eye candy" and "wink, wink" printed on the front. Family-advocacy groups and
Christian organizations protested. The line was recalled in Washington, DC area stores.[38]

[38]D. DeMarco, "Abercrombie & Fitch Pulls Children's Thong," *Knight Ridder Tribune Business News*,
May 23, 2002, p. 1. Retrieved November 8, 2004, from ABI/Inform (Proquest) database.

- In December 2003, under heavy criticism from parents and consumer groups, A&F decided to stop publishing its provocative catalogue, *A&F Quarterly*. Its holiday issue featured nude models and articles about group sex and masturbation.[39]

- In March 2004, Bob Wise, Governor of West Virginia asked A&F to pull from its shelves T-shirts with the slogan, "It's All Relative in West Virginia." Wise explained that the slogan was offensive because it referred to a stereotype that West Virginia was a state that condoned incest.[40]

- In October 2004, officials of USA Gymnastics sought the immediate removal of a T-shirt depicting a male gymnast performing on the still rings alongside the phrase, "L is for Loser." They wrote a letter to Jeffries saying its members would be encouraged to withdraw their support of the chain.[41]

- In May 2005, A&F quietly pulled a line of T-shirts from its stores with slogans that read: "I Brews Easily," "Candy is Dandy but Liquor is Quicker," and "Don't Bother I'm Not Drunk Yet." The company was criticized for glorifying underage drinking and promoting a lifestyle that was illegal for its target audience. Pressure came from the International Institute for Alcohol Awareness, a public advocacy group that worked to reduce underage drinking. This time, A&F responded to criticism before the issue was reported in national newspapers.[42]

- In November 2005, 24 participants in the Allegheny County Girls as Grantmakers program, organized a "girlcott" of A&F stores to protest its "attitude T-shirts" which featured such slogans as: "Who needs brains when you have these?"; "Blondes are Adored, Brunettes Are Ignored';" "All Men Like Tig Old Bitties." Other groups, such as Peace Project, an antidiscrimination student club in Norwalk, Connecticut, and the Women & Girls Foundation of Southwestern Pennsylvania, joined in. A&F pulled two of the more offensive T-shirts and its executives agreed to meet with several of the protestors. The girls suggested that the retailer print more appropriate slogans such as: "All This and Brains to Match" and "Your Future Boss." They hoped the firm would launch such a line and donate a portion of revenues to groups like theirs.[43]

Logistics and Supply Chain Management

A&F operated solely as a retailer. It assumed responsibility for creating and managing its brands. Unlike other businesses, A&F did not distribute its apparel and accessories through wholesale channels, through licensing or through franchising. Abercrombie clothing could not be purchased in department stores or in discount stores. It could, however, be purchased online via the A&F's Web site. E-commerce transactions generated over $100 million in business a year.[44]

[39]J. Caggiano, "Abercrombie & Fitch Drops Racy Publication," *Knight Ridder Tribune Business News*, December 11, 2003, p. 1. Retrieved November 8, 2004, from ABI/Inform (Proquest) database.

[40]T. Turner, "Retailer Abercrombie & Fitch Angers West Virginia Residents with New T-Shirt."

[41]"USA Gymnastics Upset with Abercrombie & Fitch," *The Washington Post*, October 8, 2004, p. D2. Retrieved November 8, 2004, from ABI/Inform (Proquest) database.

[42]KS Shalett, "Shamed off Shelves," *Times-Picayune*, May 20, 2005, p. 1. Retrieved December 12, 2005, from ABI/Inform (Proquest) database.

[43]M. Haynes, "'Girlcott' Organizers Meet with Abercrombie & Fitch Execs over T-shirts," *Knight Ridder Tribune Business News*, December 6, 2005, p. 1. Retrieved December 12, 2005, from ABI/Inform (Proquest) database.

[44]"Abercrombie & Fitch Co. at Banc of America Securities Consumer Conference," *Fair Disclosure Wire*, March 17, 2005. Retrieved May 24, 2006, from ABI/Inform (Proquest) database.

During 2005, A&F purchased merchandise from approximately 246 factories and suppliers located around the globe, primarily in Southeast Asia and Central and South America. It did not source more than 50 percent of its apparel from any single factory or supplier. The design and development process for a garment took between six weeks to three months.[45] Retailers struggled to reduce this time so as not to get stuck with inventory of merchandise that had lost its fashion appeal. A&F made the process more efficient by centralizing its design services at its New Albany headquarters which reduced overseas travel of executives.

A&F also operated a distribution center in New Albany, Ohio. Merchandise was received and inspected and then distributed to stores via contract carriers. It was here that concepts for new divisions were created and prototypes for new stores were constructed. The new formats were kept secret until their launch dates.

A&F launched an anticounterfeiting program in an effort to protect its brand and prevent low-cost manufacturers in Asian factories from making imitations of its products. Local authorities seized 300,000 pairs of fake Abercrombie jeans (worth $20 million) in a raid of a Chinese warehouse in 2006. The retailer hired a former FBI agent to head a 10-person department to conduct investigations overseas and to work with foreign authorities.[46]

A&F began experimenting with radio frequency identification (RFID) technology in its Rhuel stores which sold higher priced and higher quality merchandise. Tags that could be monitored electronically were sewn into the seams of garments. The location of the garments could be tracked, enabling an employee to quickly return to the shelves garments that had been left in dressing rooms or placed in the wrong spots on the floor. The technology could be used to prevent theft and to differentiate between authentic products and counterfeit goods.

A&F's Financial Performance

In fiscal 2006, A&F achieved revenues of $3.32 billion, an increase of 19 percent from fiscal 2005. Its net income rose to $422.2 million, an increase of 26.4 percent from fiscal 2005 (see Exhibit 6). Earnings per share rose to $4.59 from $3.66. A&F opened 93 new stores and added 11,000 employees to its payroll. It had no long-term debt. It repurchased 1.8 million shares of common stock for $103.3 million in fiscal 2005, but it did not make additional purchases in fiscal 2006. It paid dividends of 70 cents a share for a total of $61.6 million.

Managers at the retailer considered Abercrombie & Fitch to be a maturing brand with opportunities for expansion in prime locations in the United States and with greater potential overseas. The Abercrombie brand might grow to 250 stores and seek locations in Canada. Hollister was seen as the fastest growing brand while Ruehl was building a strong customer base but still needed to prove itself (see Exhibit 7 for sales by brand).[47]

[45]K. Showalter, "A&F Readies $10 Million Expansion," *Business First of Columbus*, March 11, 2005. Retrieved April 29, 2006 from the World Wide Web: http://columbus.bizjournals.com/columbus/stories/ 2005/03/14/story5.html.

[46]J. Sheban, "Fighting Fakes: Abercrombie Enlists Expert to Help it Combat Counterfeiting," *Knight Ridder Tribune Business News*, February 3, 2006, p. 1. Retrieved April 23, 2006, from ABI/Inform (Proquest) database.

[47]A&F 10-K, 2006, p. 31.

EXHIBIT 6
Five Year Summary of A&F's Financial Performance

	2006*	2005	2004	2003	2002
Operating revenues (in thousands)	$3,318,158	$2,784,711	$2,021,253	$1,707,810	$1,595,757
Gross profit (in thousands)	$2,209,006	$1,851,416	$1,341,224	$1,083,170	$980,555
Operating income (in thousands)	$658,090	$542,738	$347,635	$331,180	$312,315
Net income (in thousands)	$422,186	$333,986	$216,376	$204,830	$194,754
Earnings per share—diluted	$4.59	$3.66	$2.28	$2.06	$1.94
Dividends declared per share	$.70	$.60	$.50	0	0
Total assets (in thousands)	$2,248,067	$1,789,718	$1,386,791	$1,401,369	$1,190,615
Capital expenditures (in thousands)	$403,476	$256,422	$185,065	$159,777	$145,662
Long-term debt (in thousands)	0	0	0	0	0
Shareholder's equity (in thousands)	$1,405,297	$995,117	$669,326	$857,764	$736,307
Number of stores	944	851	788	700	597
Gross square feet	6,693,000	6,025,000	5,590,000	5,016,000	4,358,000
Number of employees (average)	80,100	69,100	48,500	30,200	22,000

*Fiscal 2006 is a 53-week year.

Source: A&F 10-K

EXHIBIT 7
Three Year Summary of A&F's Financial Performance by Brand

	2006*	2005	2004
Net Sales by Brand (in thousands)	$3,318,158	$2,784,711	$2,021,253
Abercrombie & Fitch	$1,515,123	$1,424,013	$1,210,222
abercrombie	$405,820	$344,938	$227,204
Hollister	$1,363,233	$999,212	$579,687
RUEHL**	$33,982	$16,548	$4,140
	2006*	**2005**	**2004**
Increase (Decrease) in Comparable Store Sales * **	2%	26%	2%
Abercrombie & Fitch	(4)%	18%	(1)%
abercrombie	10%	54%	1%
Hollister	5%	29%	13%
RUEHL**	14%	N/A	N/A
	2006*	**2005**	**2004**
Net Retail Sales Per Average Store (in thousands)	$3,533	$3,284	$2,569
Abercrombie & Fitch	$3,945	$3,784	$3,103
abercrombie	$2,251	$1,957	$1,241
Hollister	$3,732	$3,442	$2,740
RUEHL**	$3,248	$2,903	$1,255

*Fiscal 2006 is a 53-week year.

**Data for RUEHL reflect the activity of 14 stores open in fiscal 2006, 8 stores open in fiscal 2005, and 4 stores open in fiscal 2004. Year to year comparisons may not be meaningful.

***A store is included in comparable store sales when it has been open as the same brand at least one year and its square footage has not been expanded or reduced by more than 20 percent within the past year.

Source: A&F 10-K

A&F's Socially Responsible Practices

A&F held fund-raising activities that benefited local charities and communities. Every Christmas holiday season, shoppers were invited into its stores to have their picture taken with its models. The fee was $1, which the retailer matched. The proceeds were donated to foundations such as Toys for Tots or the Juvenile Diabetes Research Foundation. It held the "A&F Challenge," an action-packed outdoor event, at its headquarters in New Albany, Ohio. Participants, who paid an entry fee of $25, went on a 20-mile cycling tour, a 5K in-line skating tour and a 5K run. They heard live music from a band, enjoyed food and drinks, and received a T-shirt. All proceeds went to the Center for Child and Family Advocacy in Columbus, Ohio. Its largest donation—$10 million—went to a Children's Hospital in Columbus, in June 2006. The hospital's new trauma center would bear the A&F name.

A&F also sometimes got involved in issues at the supplier end of its business. In 2004, it joined a boycott of Australian merino wool in an effort to force ranchers to end a cruel procedure that protected lambs from flies, mulesing. Even though A&F did not purchase much Australian wool, wool producers feared that the retailer would set a precedent and that other retailers would soon join the boycott. They agreed to end the practice of mulesing by 2010 or sooner.[48]

Organizational Culture and Human Resource Management

A&F's core corporate values were: "nature, friendships and having fun."[49] The values were reflected in everything from the decor of the retailer's stores and the casual attire of its employees to the layout of A&F's headquarters in New Albany, Ohio and to the firm's advertising messages. If there were no customers to serve, employees might throw a football to one another in the store. The retailer's home page on the World Wide Web featured a tree house that could be downloaded as wallpaper.

A&F's headquarters, built in 2001, was situated in the woods along Blacklick Creek in New Albany, Ohio. Its campus-like setting served as a continual reminder to employees that the firm's target audience was college students. It was also designed to encourage team work and creativity. Instead of using desks in individual cubicles, employees engaged in collaborative work situated at long tables in doorless conference rooms. Employees could walk along paths in the woods to relax, think, or seek inspiration for a new idea. There was no executive suite. Jeffries had no desk or office. He worked in a conference room with a view of the grounds from large windows.

Employees enjoyed healthy meals that included roast chicken, international dishes, salads, fruit juices, and gourmet coffees in the full-service cafeteria. They traveled from building to building on scooters and were allowed to bring their skateboards. A bonfire pit provided the atmosphere of an outdoors summer camp. Employees worked out in the gym. One of the architects said, "A&F wants to give back to the people who work there. That's why they can go to that rusty barn the first thing in the morning, or get sweaty in the gym and then go to work, have a great meal and then go back to work again. It reinforces the idea that this is community."[50]

[48]J. Sheban, " Abercrombie & Fitch's Wool Boycott Helps End 'Mulesing" Practice. *Knight Ridder Tribune Business News*, November 12, 2004, p. 1. Retrieved April 19, 2006, from ABI/Inform (Proquest) database.

[49]D. Gebolys, "Inside Abercrombie & Fitch," *Columbus Dispatch*, May 24, 2001, p. 1F. Retrieved April 19, 2006, from LexisNexis Academic database.

[50]K. Showalter, "Abercrombie & Fitch: Campus Reflects the True Nature of New Albany Firm's Culture," *Business First of Columbus*, August 24, 2001. Retrieved April 29, 2006 from http://columbus. bizjournals.com/ columbus/stories/2001/08/27/focus1.html?page=3.

Store managers visited nearby fraternities and sororities to recruit salespeople or "brand representatives." They were encouraged to ask attractive shoppers in their stores if they wanted to apply for a sales position. Lennox, A&F's investor relations and communications director, acknowledged that the firm liked to hire job candidates who looked great. "Brand representatives are ambassadors to the brand. We want to hire brand representatives that will represent the Abercrombie & Fitch brand with natural classic American style, look great while exhibiting individuality, project the brand and themselves with energy and enthusiasm, and make the store a warm, inviting place that provides a social experience for the customer," he said.[51] The company ran a manager-in-training program for seniors and graduates. Promotion to store manager could occur one year after completing the training.

Brand representatives were expected to adhere to a dress code outlined in an Abercrombie Associate's Handbook. Hair was to be neatly combed and attractive; makeup was to be worn to enhance natural features and create a fresh, natural appearance; fingernails were not to extend more than 1/4 inch beyond the tip of the finger and nail polish was to be a natural color; mustaches, goatees, and beards were unacceptable; jewelry was to be simple and classic (only women were allowed to wear earrings as long as they wore no more than two earrings in each ear and each earring was no larger than a dime and did not dangle).[52]

In 2000, the California Department of Industrial Relations received complaints from several A&F employees who said that they were forced to buy and wear the company's clothes on the job. One woman, in another part of the country, later claimed that she spent more on clothes for work than she earned at the store. Such company policy might have violated a state work uniform law which required employees to supply the clothing when they wanted workers to wear specific apparel. In 2003, A&F settled the lawsuit in California for $2.2 million without admitting wrongdoing. Employees received reimbursements ranging from $180 to $490 depending on their job status and the amount of money spent on clothing.[53] The case spurred other similar lawsuits across the state and the rest of the nation against The Limited, The Gap, Chico's, and Polo Ralph Lauren. In some states, lawyers used the federal Fair Labor Standards Act that required employers to pay minimum wage to argue that sales associates ended up with less than minimum wage after spending their earnings on store clothing.

A&F's legal problems were only just beginning. In July 2003, two former A&F employees filed a lawsuit accusing the company of failing to pay overtime wages when they were required to work 50–60 hours a week. The plaintiffs claim that they were sales associates, with no management responsibilities, but were classified as managers so that the retailer could avoid paying overtime. According to the Federal Fair Labor Standards Act and the Ohio Minimum Fair Wage Standards Act, nonexempt employees must be paid time and a half for work in excess of 40 hours a week.

In June 2003, lawyers for nine plaintiffs filed a lawsuit against the retailer for discriminating against minorities in its hiring practices and job placement. It allegedly cultivated an "overwhelmingly white work force" and steered minority applicants into less visible jobs.[54] Former A&F employees appeared on CBS's television program *60 Minutes* and said that A&F was interested in hiring employees who fit a certain look. Anthony Ocampo worked

---

[51]S. Greenhouse, "Going for the Look, But Risking Discrimination," *The New York Times*, July 13, 2003, p. 12. Retrieved November 9, 2004, from ABI/Inform (Proquest) database.

[52]B. Paynter, "Don't Hate Me Because I'm Beautiful," *Kansas City Pitch Weekly*, September 4, 2003. Retrieved February 12, 2005, from LexusNexis Academic database.

[53]"Abercrombie & Fitch Settles Dress Code Case," *Houston Chronicle*, June 25, 2003, p. 2. Retrieved November 4, 2004, from ABI/Inform (Proquest) database.

[54]T. Turner, "Cincinnati Suit Charges Abercrombie & Fitch with Failing to Pay Overtime," *Knight Ridder Tribune Business News*, July 9, 2003, p. 1.

at an Abercrombie store during his Christmas break from Stanford University. When he returned to get a summer job, he was told that he could not be rehired because the store already had too many Filipinos working there. Eduardo Gonzalez, another Stanford University student who was Latino, was told that he could only work as in the store's stock room or as part of the overnight crew. At Banana Republic, he was asked if he was applying for a management position. Carla Grubb, an African-American student at California State University at Bakersfield, felt she was not treated fairly because she was scheduled to work only during closing times and was asked to wash the front windows, vacuum, and clean the mannequins.

In November 2003, another lawsuit was filed against A&F on behalf of a New Jersey woman who claimed that her application for a sales associate position was denied because she was African-American. A&F denied that it discriminated against minorities. It claimed that minorities represented 13 percent of all its store associates (which exceeded national averages). The U.S. Equal Employment Opportunity Commission also initiated a lawsuit, claiming that A&F violated parts of the Civil Rights Act of 1964 (see Exhibit 8 for a summary of relevant laws and legal procedures). Store managers reported that they were instructed to discard job applications in the candidates did not possess the right look.

In November 2004, A&F paid $50 million (including legal fees) to settle the discrimination lawsuits. It agreed to hire a vice president of diversity, provide training in diversity and inclusion to its employees and managers, increase the number of minority employees in sales and store management positions, enhance its compliance and oversight processes, and use more minority models in its advertising. The retailer promised that within two years its sales force would be 9 percent African Americans, 9 percent Latinos, its current percentage of Asians, and 53 percent women.[55] A&F was told to stop recruiting from predominantly white fraternities and sororities. It agreed to hire 25 full-time diversity recruiters who would seek new hires from historically black colleges, minority job fairs, and

EXHIBIT 8
Summary of Workplace Discrimination Acts in the United States

a. Title VII of the Civil Rights Act of 1964 makes discrimination based on race, color, religion, sex, and natural origin, illegal. It applies to employers with 15 or more employees. Before a plaintiff can file a lawsuit, he or she must file a charge with the Equal Employment Opportunity Commission within 180 days of the discriminatory act. The EEOC will conduct an initial investigation and will attempt to reconcile the parties. If the EEOC decides not to sue, it will issue a right-to-sue letter, giving the complaining party 90 days to file a lawsuit on her own. A charging party can request the EEOC to issue a right-to-sue letter 180 days after filing the charge with the EEOC.

b. The Americans with Disabilities Act of 1990 prohibits discrimination against the disabled. It applies to employers with 15 or more employees. "Disability" is broadly defined. The same EEOC procedures must be followed under this Act as with a Title VII action as discussed above.

c. The Age Discrimination in Employment Act of 1967 prohibits discrimination against employees who are more than 40 years old. It pertains to employers with 20 or more employees. The complainant must file a charge with the EEOC but can file a lawsuit after waiting only 60 days after filing with the EEOC.

d. The Civil Rights Act of 1866, 42 U.S.C. Section 1981, protects against racial discrimination. This statute does not require any filing with the EEOC and applies to all employers, regardless of number of employees. An employer's practice is illegal if it treats one protected group of employees more harshly than others, unless the employer can prove the practice was justified because of "business necessity." This Act allows for unlimited compensatory and punitive damages as well as reimbursement of legal expenses.

Source: D. Kolber. "Knowledge of Discrimination Laws Vital," *Atlanta Business Chronicle*, May 27, 2005. Retrieved June 10, 2005, from http://atlanta.bizjournals.com/atlanta/stories /2005/05/30/ smallb7.html. For more information, go to: http://www.eeoc.gov/.

[55]J. Sheban, "Abercrombie & Fitch: The Face of Change," *Columbus Dispatch*, July 31, 2005, p. F1. Retrieved April 19, 2006, from ABI/Inform (Proquest) database.

minority recruiting events. Michael Jeffries issued a statement: "We have, and always have had, no tolerance for discrimination. We decided to settle this suit because we felt that a long, drawn-out dispute would have been harmful to the company and distracting to management."[56]

Todd Corley became A&F's new vice president of diversity. Due to his efforts, A&F established a $300,000 grant for scholarships for the United Negro College Fund, became a sponsor of the Organization of Chinese Americans' College Leadership Summit, became a sponsor of the National Black MBA Association, and offered internships for minority college juniors seeking retail-management careers through Inroads, Incorporated.

A&F's Future

Looking ahead, A&F was likely to face increased competition. One of its direct rivals, American Eagle Outfitters, was able to outperform A&F in terms of profitability and assume the number 1 rank (compared to A&F's third rank) among U.S. publicly traded apparel companies in 2007 as listed by *Apparel Magazine*. Newcomers to the specialty apparel industry, as well as large department stores, sought to imitate A&F's product offerings. Metropark, for example, a West Coast chain for 20-to 35-year-old shoppers, opened its 15th store in Atlanta, Georgia. It planned to open an additional 50 stores by 2007. The retailer sold brand name casual apparel made by such designers as True Religion and Joe's Jeans. It also tried to create a night club–like atmosphere in its stores with flat screen televisions playing music videos and a lounge offering energy drinks and magazines.

Department stores, too, began to diversify their lines by stocking merchandise from new suppliers and by promoting their own in-house labels. Oved Apparel launched Company 81 in 2005 as "an Abercrombie for department stores."[57] It began to sell distressed denim, chinos, shorts, golf jackets, blazers, and graphic T-shirts at the wholesale level. It provided department stores with in-store signage and imagery from its advertising campaign to complement its merchandise. Federated Department stores, which operated Macy's and Bloomingdales, created an in-house label called, "American Rag." Its merchandise was similar in style to A&F's but priced more moderately.

As if sensing the encroachment of competitors, A&F began an unusual effort to improve its customer service. In the past, brand representatives acted more like models than salespeople. They were known for their snobbish disregard of shoppers. They did not talk to customers until they were within five feet of each other.[58] Some customers felt intimidated. Under COO Singer, store greeters were positioned in the entrance to each store and salespeople were posted in every section. A vice president of training was hired to work with store staff. The number of employees was increased and hours of store operations were extended. The added attention helped reduce shrink of merchandise.[59] Nonetheless, progress in customer service may have been derailed by the departure of Singer from the company.

A&F also needed to be ever vigilant regarding the needs and preferences of its target markets. Teenagers were perceived as being fickle. According to experts on the reactions of millenials to pop culture, they were difficult to influence because they thought more

[56]S. Greenhouse, "Abercrombie & Fitch Bias Case is Settled," *The New York Times*, November 17, 2004, p. A16. Retrieved May 24, 2006, from ABI/Inform (Proquest) database.

[57]L. Bailey, "The New South: Young Men's & Streetwear," *DNR* 35 (August 22, 2005), p. 94. Retrieved June 1, 2006, from ABI/Inform (Proquest) database.

[58] Paynter, "Don't Hate."

[59]S. Kng, "Style and Substance: Abercrombie $ Fitch Tries to be Less Haughty," *The Wall Street Journal*, June 17, 2005, p. B1. Retrieved June 23, 2005, from ABI/Inform (Proquest) database.

independently and changed their minds more frequently than previous generations. They would find the "emphasis on the physicality of models" in A&F advertisements unappealing.[60] The emerging trend towards ethical consumption was also something to be watched. Young people began to purchase food products and clothing with "Fair Trade" labels. They were committed, for example, to purchasing coffee that was organically grown from suppliers who paid bean pickers higher wages than the going rate. They bought T-shirts that were not made in overseas sweatshops.

The challenges for A&F executives in 2007 and beyond were to anticipate competitor moves, to improve customer service, and to maintain consumer loyalty. They needed to hire talented top managers who could work well alongside CEO Jeffries. These domestic imperatives came at a critical time for the retailer. It was about to expand further into the European and Asian markets by opening stores in Italy, France, Germany, Spain, Denmark, Sweden and Japan. Pamela Quintiliano, a WR Hambrecht retail analyst, gave the expansion plan a nod of approval: "Abercrombie is an incredibly strong brand name, and there's a hunger for American brands around the world."[61]

[60]V. Seckler, "Brands' Challenge: Bridging Gap with Young People," *WWD 77* (April 12, 2006). Retrieved June 1, 2006, from ABI/Inform (Proquest) database.
[61]Sheban, "Oh Canada!"

25

Philip Morris Companies

Keith Robbins *George Mason University*

Philip Morris (PM) is best known as a manufacturer and marketer of cigarettes. In fact, PM is the largest cigarette company in the United States, with a 42 percent share of the $70 billion industry.[1] However, over the past 30 years the company has been pursuing such a systematic diversification strategy that, in addition to cigarettes, the company now ranks as the second largest beer brewer in the United States and the second largest food processing company in the world.[2] The company's brands include Clark Chewing Gum, Louis Kemp Seafood, Miller, Miller Lite, Lowenbrau, Jell-O, Oscar Mayer, Sealtest, Maxwell House, Oroweat Baked Goods, Light Touch Desserts, and Marlboro, Virginia Slims, Bucks, Benson & Hedges, Merit, and Parliament (see Exhibit 1).

Philip Morris Companies was incorporated in Virginia on March 1, 1985, as the holding company for the diverse businesses of Philip Morris, Inc.[3] Today, the company is the largest private employer in Richmond.[4,5] The company's ambition has been and remains to be the most successful consumer packaged goods company in the world.[6]

This ambition is reflected in the company's mission statement presented in its 1991 annual report to shareholders: "We are a global consumer products company, manufacturing and marketing tobacco, food, and beer brands around the world. Our broad-based operations generate strong and growing returns for investors by answering consumer needs with low-priced, high-volume, quality products. We are committed to the highest standards of ethics and fairness in all of our activities and operations."

Current CEO Michael Miles (the first nonsmoking CEO at Philip Morris in 145 years) describes the company's strategy for meeting its goal as developing new products to meet emerging consumer trends, expanding geographically, and manufacturing and marketing

This case was prepared by Keith Robbins of the School of Business Administration at George Mason University. Development of this case was made possible by a grant from the Funds for Excellence Program of the State Council of Higher Education in Virginia.

[1] Standard & Poor's, *Industry Survey*, 1992.

[2] P. Sellers, "Can He Keep Philip Morris Growing?" *Fortune* 125, no. 7 (1992), pp. 86–92.

[3] Moody's *Industrial Manual*, 1991.

[4] "The Forbes 500 Ranking," *Forbes* 149, no. 9 (April 29, 1992), pp. 190–396.

[5] "The Fortune 500 Largest Industrial Corporations," *Fortune* 125, no. 8, 1991.

[6] PM, annual report, 1991.

EXHIBIT 1
PM Brands

Cigarettes: *Philip Morris U.S.A., Philip Morris International*
   Marlboro Brands
   Virginia Slims
   Benson & Hedges
   Merit
   Parliament
Beer: *The Miller Brewing Company*
   Miller Lite
   Miller High Life
   Milwaukee's Best
   Lowenbrau
   Sharp's
Food: *Kraft General Foods, Kraft International, General Foods International*
   Kraft Cheeses
   Maxwell House Coffees
   Louis Rich Turkey
   Oscar Mayer Luncheon Meats, Hot Dogs, and Bacon
   Louis Kemp Seafood Products
   Post Cereals
   Jell-O Brand Gelatin
   Kool-Aid
   Sealtest Dairy Products
   Breyers Dairy Products
   Light'n Lively Dairy Products
Financial: *Philip Morris Capital Corporation*
   Major equipment leasing programs for customers and suppliers

globally.[7] The strategy appears to be working, as PM remains the largest and most profitable consumer products company in the world. In 1990, Philip Morris had risen to seventh on *Fortune*'s list of largest U.S. manufacturers, with sales approaching $50 billion.[8]

A History of Diversification Via Acquisition

The company has a distinct heritage among U.S. tobacco companies; it is the only major company that was not formed when the Supreme Court broke up the James Duke American Tobacco Trust in 1912.[9] Since its inception in England, Philip Morris has emphasized growth through acquisitions (see Exhibit 2). The success of Philip Morris in growing the purchased companies into industry leaders is legendary.

In 1957, Philip Morris was sixth and last in the U.S. cigarette market. Under the leadership of Joseph F. Cullman III and by emphasizing the Marlboro brand, the company climbed to first place by the end of 1983. In 1970, it bought Miller Brewing, which at the time ranked seventh among U.S. brewers. By 1977, the company had leapfrogged up to second place behind Anheuser-Busch.[10]

Philip Morris has been able to fund its numerous acquisitions through its high-margin tobacco products, which continue to contribute a disproportionate share of corporate earnings.

---

[7]Ibid.

[8]"The Fortune 500."

[9]R. Levering, M. Moskowitz, and M. Katz, *The 100 Best Companies to Work for in America* (Reading, Mass.: Addison-Wesley, 1984).

[10]Ibid.

EXHIBIT 2
PM's History of Acquisitions

Source: Moody's Industrial Manual, 1991.

June 1944	Purchased cigarette-producing assets from Axton-Fisher Tobacco Company, Louisville, Kentucky, for $8.9 million cash.
Feb. 1945	Acquired 99% interest in Benson & Hedges through common stock exchange on a share-for-share basis.
Dec. 1959	Acquired an interest in C.A. Tabacalera Nacional Venezuela.
Dec. 1963	Acquired a substantial interest in Fabriques de Tabac Reunies, S.A., Swiss cigarette manufacturer and licensee.
April 1967	Acquired an interest in Kwara Tobacco Company, Ilorin, Nigeria.
June 1969	Purchased 53% interest in Miller Brewing Company for $130 million.
Jan. 1970	Acquired control of Mission Viejo, Cal., new city and land developer for $20 million.
Feb. 1977	Acquired Wisconsin Tissue Mills, Menasha, Wis., for 314,000 shares of common stock.
Feb. 1977	Purchased 97% of common stock of The Seven-Up Company, a soft-drink extract manufacturer, for $520 million.
June 1978	Purchased the international cigarette business of Liggett Group, Inc., (consisting of rights to sell L&M, Lark, Chesterfield, Eve, and Decade outside of United States) for $45 million.
Nov. 1985	Purchased General Foods Corporation for $5.6 billion.
Dec. 1988	Acquired, through merger with a subsidiary, Kraft, Inc., for approximately $12.9 billion.
Aug. 1990	Acquired Swiss-based coffee and confectionery company Jacobs Suchard AG for $4.1 billion.

According to U.S. Labor Department statistics, retail tobacco prices have increased on average 10 percent over the past 11 years. This rate of increase exceeds that of any other product, including hospital rooms and prescription drugs, over this period.[11,12] Cigarette manufacturers have found demand for tobacco to be price inelastic—smokers do not seem to decrease consumption despite price increases.

The acquisition spree has been motivated by the company's desire to lessen its dependence on tobacco. Many senior executives openly express concern about the company's heavy dependence on tobacco.[13] Thus, the central issue facing management at Philip Morris is the careful selection of the correct portfolio of consumer packaged goods that will allow the company to protect and build upon global operations. This mixture of businesses must smooth the transition away from tobacco dependence to avoid adverse consequences in an increasingly hostile environment.

Industry Segments

Philip Morris's significant industry segments consist of tobacco products, food products, beer, and financial services, including real estate. Operating revenues and operating profits for each of the segments over the past three years are detailed in Exhibit 3.

The company's dependence on tobacco is evidenced by the fact that tobacco revenues account for 41 percent of the company's revenue and 68 percent of its income, though this dependence has lessened somewhat recently. Tobacco's profits represented 72 percent of the company's operating income in 1989. Food products accounted for approximately 27 percent of the company's operating profit in 1990, compared with 23 percent

[11]J. Dagnoli, "Philip Morris Keeps Smoking," *Advertising Age* 61, no. 48 (1990), p. 20.
[12]E. Giltenan, "Profits Keep Rollin' in . . . ," *Forbes* 146, no. 1 (1992), pp. 152–53.
[13]Sellers, "Can He Keep."

EXHIBIT 3
Company Income and Revenue Contribution by Industry Segment (in millions of dollars)

	1990	1989	1988
Operating revenues:			
Tobacco	$21,090 (41%)	$17,849 (40%)	$16,576 (53%)
Food	26,085 (51)	22,373 (51)	10,898 (35)
Beer	3,534 (7)	3,342 (7)	3,177 (10)
Financial services	460 (1)	516 (2)	622 (2)
Total operating revenues	$51,169	$44,080	$31,273
Operating profit:			
Tobacco	$ 5,596 (67%)	$ 5,063 (72%)	$ 3,846 (84%)
Food	2,205 (27)	1,580 (23)	392 (9)
Beer	285 (4)	226 (3)	190 (4)
Financial services	196 (2)	172 (2)	162 (3)
Total operating revenues	$ 8,282	$ 7,041	$ 4,590

in 1989. In 1990, beer accounted for 7 percent of company revenues and 4 percent of income from operations.[14]

Tobacco Products

Philip Morris U.S.A. is responsible for the manufacture, marketing, and sale of tobacco products in the United States (including military sales), and Philip Morris International is responsible for the manufacture, marketing, and sale of such products outside the United States and for tobacco product exports from the United States.

Domestic Tobacco

Philip Morris sold 220.5 billion units of cigarettes in 1990, an increase of 1 billion units over 1989. Industry sales decreased 0.3 percent in 1990, compared to 1989. Over the past three years, Philip Morris has increased its sales and market share in the United States even though industry revenues have declined:

Year	Industry (billions of units)	Philip Morris	Market Share (%)
1990	522.1	220.5	42.2%
1989	523.9	219.5	41.9
1988	558.1	219.3	39.3

Source: Wheat, First Securities, Inc.

The major industry rivals in domestic tobacco are American Brands; RJR Nabisco, Inc.; B.A.T. Industries (parent of Brown and Williamson); Loews Corporation (parent of Lorillard); and the Liggett Group. The tobacco companies typically are operated as a subsidiary of - diverse parent corporations. American Brands, in addition to its Pall Mall and Carlton cigarettes, markets Titleist golf balls, Jim Beam whiskey, and Master Locks. RJR Nabisco, in addition to its Winston, Salem, and Camel cigarettes, markets Oreos cookies, Planter's Peanuts, Del Monte Fruits, and Grey Poupon mustard. Loews Corporation, in addition to its Newport, Kent, and True cigarettes, owns CNA Financial Services, Inc.; Loews' theaters and hotels; and the Bulova Watch Company.

Philip Morris is the overwhelming leader in domestic market share, achieving 1.5 times the sales of its closest rival, RJR Nabisco (see Exhibit 4).

The Maxwell Consumer Report issued by Wheat, First Securities, Inc., has ranked Philip Morris U.S.A. as the leading cigarette company in the United States market since 1983. The

[14]Moody's *Industrial Manual,* 1990, 1991, and 1992.

EXHIBIT 4

Domestic Cigarette Producers' Market Shares (Percentage of industry units sold)

Source: Standard & Poor's *Industry Surveys,* 1991.

Company	1990	1989	1988	1987
Philip Morris	42.0%	42.2%	39.3%	37.8%
Reynolds	28.9	28.7	31.8	32.5
Brown & Williamson	10.8	11.4	10.9	11.0
Lorillard	7.8	7.1	8.2	8.2
American	6.8	7.0	7.0	6.9
Liggett	3.7	3.4	2.8	3.6

EXHIBIT 5

Top 10 Domestic Cigarette Brands, 1990

Sources: Moody's, Standard & Poor's.

Rank	Brand	Company	Units (billions)	Mkt. Share
1	Marlboro	Philip Morris	135.6	26%
2	Winston	Reynolds	46.4	9
3	Salem	Reynolds	32.0	6
4	Kool	Brown & Williamson	32.0	6
5	Newport	Lorillard	25.1	5
6	Camel	Reynolds	21.2	4
7	Benson & Hedges	Philip Morris	20.5	4
8	Merit	Philip Morris	20.3	4
9	Doral	Reynolds	19.2	4
10	Virginia Slims	Philip Morris	16.8	3

company's best-selling brands are Marlboro, Benson & Hedges, Merit, Virginia Slims, and Cambridge. Philip Morris produces 4 of the top 10 selling brands in the United States, including best-selling Marlboro, which garnered 26 percent of the market in 1990 (see Exhibit 5).

Cigarette Industry Segments

Premium and Discount Brands

Philip Morris premium brands consist of top 10 performers Marlboro, Benson & Hedges, Merit, and Virginia Slims. In the summer of 1991, PM spent a record $60 million to advertise Marlboro Medium, the first spinoff from the Marlboro brand in 20 years.[15] According to Marlboro VP Nancy Brennan Lund, the brand's 26 percent domestic market share should increase, though its volume probably will not.

A growing industry segment consists of the discount brands. After initially rejecting the idea of selling less-profitable brands, Philip Morris decided to enter the discount segment in 1985. This was prompted by the realization that many of its customers were switching to cheap cigarettes.[16,17] By 1991, Philip Morris became the market leader in the low-priced segment. Now, 17 percent of PM's U.S.A. sales are discount brands, such as Cambridge, Alpine, Bristol, and Bucks.

Industrywide discount brand sales have risen from 11 percent of sales in 1989 to 25 percent today and are expected to double again over the coming five years. Although Philip Morris is performing well in the discount segment, it is unable to put its formidable advertising might behind these brands for fear of cannibalizing its higher-margin premium brands. Recently tobacco companies have raised prices on the discount brands—for example, PM increased its prices by 20 percent on the discount brands.

[15]Sellers, "Can He Keep."
[16]C. Leinster, "Is Bigger Better for Philip Morris?" *Fortune* 119, no. 10 (1989), pp. 66–68+ .
[17]A. Farnham, "From Soup to Nuts," *Fortune* 119, no. 1 (1989), pp. 43–47.

According to industry analysts,[18,19,20] William Campbell, CEO of Philip Morris U.S.A., is determined to compete in every major cigarette category. The result is that the company now produces low-profit generic cigarettes. Generics, sometimes referred to as *black and whites,* are sold in places like Wal-Mart bearing such names as Best Buy, Basic, and Gridlock: The Commuter's Cigarette—a California brand. Campbell's predominant goal is to increase PM's domestic market share a point a year.

Low Tar

The low tar segment of the market consists of cigarettes delivering 15 milligrams (mg) or less of "tar" per cigarette. In 1990 and 1989, this market accounted for 57.4 percent and 55.5 percent of U.S. industry sales, respectively.[21,22] Philip Morris's low tar brands comprised 42.1 percent of the low tar market in 1990 and 42.8 percent in 1989. The low tar market includes a subsegment referred to as *ultra-low tar* that consists of brands that deliver 6 mg. or less of tar per cigarette. Ultra-low tar brands accounted for 11.3 percent of industry sales in 1990, compared with 10.8 percent in 1989. Philip Morris's ultra-low tar brands garnered 32.9 percent of this market in 1990 and 33.4 percent in 1989.

The low tar and ultra-low tar segments are growing, whereas the industry is in general decline. Philip Morris must ensure that its brands competing in these segments are able to achieve market share positions at least commensurate with its non-low tar cigarettes. This is currently not the case in the rapidly expanding ultra-low tar category, where Philip Morris lost market share during 1990.

International Tobacco

Worldwide tobacco industry sales have been growing at approximately 2 percent per year for the past several years. The United States exported $5 billion of tobacco products in 1990.[23] Philip Morris International's share of this market was 7.6 percent in 1990, compared with 6.7 percent in 1989. Marlboro is the leader. Its sales increased 13.2 percent in 1990. Its 206.9 billion units accounted for over 4.3 percent of the non-United States cigarette market. In particular, Philip Morris International has strong market share positions in Argentina, Australia, Finland, France, Germany, Hong Kong, Italy, Mexico, Saudi Arabia, and Switzerland, holding at least a 15 percent market share position in each.

Philip Morris is the leading cigarette exporter. Total cigarette exports to 111 foreign countries in 1990 were valued at $4.75 billion. The leading destinations were Asian (58 percent) and European (38 percent) countries. Two factors were primarily responsible for the growth in international sales: the lowering of trade barriers in Japan, Taiwan, and South Korea, and the weakened dollar.[24]

The market for cigarettes outside the United States in 1980 was 3.9 trillion units, with only 40 percent open to Western companies. Currently, international (non-U.S.) consumption stands at 4.9 trillion cigarettes a year, and Western companies now can deal with 95 percent of this market. PM sold 640 billion, or 11.6 percent of the world's cigarettes last year. That places PM second behind the Chinese government (1.5 trillion) in terms of total cigarette sales.

[18]S. Chakravraty, "Philip Morris Is Still Hungry," *Forbes* 145, no. 7 (1990).

[19]J. Dagnoli, "CEO Miles Sees International Growth for Philip Morris," *Advertising Age* April 8, 1991.

[20]Sellers, "Can He Keep."

[21]Moody's *Industrial Manual,* 1990 and 1991.

[22]S&P's *Industry Surveys,* 1990 and 1991.

[23]M. Levin, "U.S. Tobacco Firms Push Easily into Asian Markets," *Marketing News* 25, no. 2 (January 21, 1991), pp. 2, 14.

[24]Sellers, "Can He Keep."

It is interesting that the company's global perspective largely resulted from its inability to penetrate domestic markets. When it was number 6 among U.S. tobacco companies during the '50s, PM was the first U.S. manufacturer to begin selling its products in duty-free shops in foreign countries. It focused on those countries most frequented by U.S. travelers. Because many of these markets were closed to imports, the company was forced to license the sale of its cigarettes in the areas. The company reasoned that foreign-domestic managers could best oversee these foreign operations. As a result of this early emphasis on international operations, PM's management is more globally diverse than most: Miles and Mayer are Americans, Maxwell is a Scot, Campbell is Canadian, David Dangoor (PM U.S.A. marketing head) is Iranian. Two of the three bosses Miles vied with for the CEO position are Australian; the third is German.[25]

Though many foreign markets recently have opened access to U.S. firms, many protectionist policies are mitigating penetration. Many governments control prices, levy huge taxes, and even market state-owned brands (Taiwanese government's Long Life cigarettes; Japan's Dean cigarettes). Last year in Hong Kong, a 200 percent tax increase on imported cigarettes effectively doubled the price of a pack of Marlboros and cut PM's sales by 80 percent. The government later cut the tax in half after Philip Morris International employees and friends gathered 75,000 signatures.

In Italy, the company was implicated in a government investigation of cigarette imports that illegally avoided Italian taxes. Consequently, Italy imposed a one-month ban on Marlboro, Merit, and Muratti, a popular local blend.

International tobacco's profit margins are half those of the United States. These margins are improving—they rose 24 percent in 1991 on a 14 percent increase in revenues. In the European community, sales volume has risen 25 percent during the past three years. PM management views Turkey as the "gateway to the east," particularly the former Soviet Union and Central Asia. PM recently broke ground on a $400 million cigarette factory there.[26]

In 1990, PM bought three deteriorating East German factories that churn out the leading local cigarette, F6. In a recent year, PM shipped 22 billion cigarettes to the former Soviet Union.[27]

Food

CEO Miles was formerly head of Kraft General Foods (KGF), which was formed after PM bought Kraft. He was instrumental in the successful implementation of Hamish Maxwell's diversification strategy. Miles's promotion to chief executive helped ease the tension between PM and General Foods that had existed since the latter's hostile takeover. Miles's insight into the food business permitted him to ignore pessimistic forecasts for traditionally strong brands, such as Maxwell House and Post. Many insiders felt that these brands could expect, at best, marginal increases in volume. Miles reemphasized growth and, as a consequence, sales of such leading products as Kool-Aid, Jell-O, and Grape Nuts cereal are expanding again.[28,29] Operating profits in General Foods exceeded $700 million in 1991, versus $433 million in 1989.

Kraft's cheese division has not fared as well. Sales have stagnated. Analysts blame this on Miles's continued price hikes in the face of stable prices for private label cheeses. During 1991, Kraft began cutting prices in an attempt to regain lost market share from the private labels. However, the retailers—who profit quite nicely off their own private label

[25]Ibid.

[26]Moody's *Industrial Manual,* 1992.

[27]PM, annual reports, 1991 and 1992.

[28]Dagnoli, "CEO Miles Sees."

[29]Sellers, "Can He Keep."

brands—were naturally reluctant to pass the cuts on down to the consumers.[30] The division experienced a shortfall of $125 million between anticipated and realized cheese profits. The problems of the cheese division also have resulted from increased health consciousness among consumers. Cheese products are notoriously high in saturated fat and cholesterol. As more consumers become sensitive to nutritional guidelines espoused by leading health agencies, overall demand for cheese likely will continue to decline. Kraft's products in general and cheese products in particular typically are not purchased by health conscious consumers due to their high fat content.

Richard Mayer, president and CEO of KGF, has two primary ideas for stimulating the food division: (1) to get market research and computer people working in teams with brand managers to make better use of scanner-generated sales data and (2) to distribute all KGF products within a particular region from a single warehouse location to serve customers better.[31] Presently, grocers buy 10 percent of all their grocery items from KGF but draw from many warehouses. These strategies should help KGF respond more expeditiously to market trends and competitors' moves.

Philip Morris as an Employer

Philip Morris consistently is ranked as one of the more progressive employers in the United States. Levering, Moskowitz, and Katz included PM among their listing of *The 100 Best Companies to Work for in America.*

According to James Bowling, director of public relations and public affairs, caring about its employees is what distinguishes Philip Morris: "everybody bought tobacco competitively at auction; manufactured cigarettes in Kentucky, Virginia, and North Carolina; used essentially the same machinery; paid the same union wages; and sold through the same wholesalers and retailers. Therefore, they said that, if there is going to be a difference, it will have to be in the people. As simplistic and corny as that seems, it has been the guiding principle here since that day. We have always tried to treat our people better—by being the first or among the first with amenities and working pleasantries."

One survey of senior managers conducted by an independent auditor, showed very high satisfaction with the company. The benefits package includes long- and short-term disability compensation. Employees automatically are insured for twice their annual salary, and there is a survivor income benefit that, in the event of employee death, would start paying, after four years, 25 percent of last base pay to surviving spouses every month plus 5 percent of your last base pay to each surviving child. There is an employee stock ownership plan and employees who smoke—and the majority do—are entitled to one free carton of cigarettes per week.[32]

Philip Morris was one of the first companies to employ blacks in sales positions. One out of every four persons who works for the company is a minority-group member—and minorities hold 14 percent of positions classified as "officials and managers."[33]

The Richmond cigarette factory is a futuristic plant completed in 1974 at a cost of over $200 million—at the time the largest capital investment in the company's history. The plant boasts parquet floors and floor-to-ceiling windows overlooking elaborate ornamental gardens.[34]

---

[30]Ibid.

[31]Dagnoli, "CEO Miles Sees."

[32]Levering et al., *The 100 Best.*

[33]PM, annual report, 1991.

[34]Levering et al., *The 100 Best.*

EXHIBIT 6   **Philip Morris Companies, Inc: Consolidated Income (In millions of dollars)**

	1991	1990	1989	1988	1987
Operating revenues	$56,458	$51,169	$44,080	$31,273	$27,650
Cost of sales	25,612	24,430	21,868	13,565	12,183
Excise taxes on products	8,394	6,846	5,748	5,882	5,416
Gross profit	22,452	19,893	16,464	11,826	10,051
Marketing, admin., & research	13,331	11,499	9,290	7,304	5,956
Amortization of goodwill	499	448	385	125	105
Operating income	8,622	7,946	6,789	4,397	3,990
Interest & other debt expense	1,651	1,635	1,731	670	646
Earnings before income taxes	6,971	6,311	5,058	3,727	3,344
Provision for income taxes	3,044	2,771	2,112	1,663	1,502
Earnings before cumulative effect of acct. change	3,927	3,540	2,946	2,064	1,842
Cumulative effect of acct. change for income taxes	(921)			273	
Net earnings	3,006	3,540	2,946	2,337	1,842
Retained earnings (B.O.Y.)	10,960	9,079	7,833	6,437	5,344
Common dividends	(1,765)	(1,432)	(1,159)	(941)	(749)
Four-for-one stock split			(478)		
Exercise of stock options	(172)	(218)	(63)		
Other	9	(9)			
Retained earnings (E.O.Y.)	12,038	10,960	9,079	7,833	6,437

1991 Performance and Future Prospects

Philip Morris currently sells more than 3,000 items. The value of the shares of stock outstanding reached $74 billion in December 1991 (trading at $75 per share) exceeding the value of all other U.S. companies except Exxon. Among the 1991 highlights: revenues increased 10 percent to $56.5 billion; operating income grew 14 percent to $9.9 billion; unit sales increased nearly 200 million in the United States over 1990, whereas U.S. industry volume decreased by 13 billion units.

Despite many bright spots, particularly in fat-free products, beverages, and breakfast cereals, overall results in North American food businesses were lower than expected. Volume in the brewing business grew 0.4 percent despite a doubling of the federal excise tax at the beginning of the year. Performance in 1991 allowed the company to increase dividends by 22.1 percent to an annualized rate of $2.10 per share, the 24th consecutive year of dividend increases.[35]

According to Miles, the company will throw off free cash of more than $21 billion. This is the excess after capital expenditures, dividends, and taxes—and Philip Morris can use it either to pay for acquisitions or to buy back stock, or both. The company currently realizes $15 billion annually from international operations (more than Coca-Cola, PepsiCo, and Kellogg combined). Marlboro is especially strong internationally in Asia, Eastern Europe, and the former Soviet Union.[36]

As portrayed in the company's consolidated income statement (Exhibit 6), Philip Morris U.S.A.'s sales went up 9 percent to $9.4 billion in 1991, and operating profits rose even faster to reach $4.8 billion. Operating margin rose a fabulous 51 percent, up from 42 percent

[35]PM, annual report, 1992.
[36]Sellers, "Can He Keep."

EXHIBIT 7   Comparative Consolidated Balance Sheet as of December 31 (in millions of dollars)

	1991	1990	1989	1988	1987
Assets					
Consumer products:					
Cash & equivalents	$ 126	$ 146	$ 118	$ 168	$ 90
Receivables, net	4,121	4,101	2,956	2,222	2,065
Inventories	7,445	7,153	5,751	5,384	4,154
Other current assets	902	967	555	377	245
Total current assets	12,594	12,367	9,380	8,151	6,554
Property, plant, & equipment	15,281	14,281	12,357	11,932	9,398
Less accum. depreciation	5,335	4,677	3,400	3,284	2,816
Property account net	9,946	9,604	8,951	8,648	6,582
Other assets	20,306	20,712	17,251	16,992	5,411
Total consumer products assets	42,846	42,683	35,588	33,791	18,547
Total financial & real estate assets	4,538	3,886	3,440	3,169	2,890
Total assets	$47,384	$46,569	$39,028	$36,960	$21,437
Liabilities					
Total current liabilities	11,824	11,360	8,943	7,969	5,164
Total consumer products liabilities	31,344	31,460	26,108	26,664	12,234
Total financial & real estate assets	3,528	3,162	2,849	2,617	2,330
Stockholders' Equity					
Common stock ($1, par)		935	935	240	240
Additional paid-in capital				252	272
Earnings reinvested in business		10,960	9,079	7,833	6,437
Currency translation adj.		561	143	117	146
Net stockholders' equity	12,512	11,344	9,871	8,208	6,803
Total	$47,384	$45,956	$38,828	$37,489	$21,367

seven years ago. Philip Morris's gains in market share are impressive, too—43.3 percent of total U.S. cigarette sales today, versus 35.9 percent in 1985.

The primary objective at Philip Morris traditionally has been to achieve 20 percent annual earnings growth. Hamish Maxwell hit the mark each of the last five years, but Miles is facing a more maleficent marketplace.

The company is in a very solid financial position as it remains one of the more liquid U.S. companies. It often is referred to as the "King of Cash" (see Exhibit 7).

Threats To Philip Morris's Traditional Level of Performance

The Declining American Cigarette Industry

Domestic cigarettes contributed $4.8 billion in operating income last year, roughly half the corporate total. But the American cigarette industry is declining 2 to 3 percent per year. Additionally, the trend is toward budget brands with smaller profit margins and away from premium products, such as Marlboro, Merit, Virginia Slims, and Benson & Hedges. According to industry analysts, the bargain brands—including those marketed by Philip Morris—pose more of a threat to the 20 percent target than the product liability litigation now pending Supreme Court review.[37]

[37]S&P's *Industry Survey,* 1992.

Slowing Processed Food Sales

Recession intensifies price elasticity, so shoppers are moving toward less-costly private label brands. Increasing consumer awareness of ingredients has invited comparison between the private labels and national brands, such as Kraft General Foods (KGF). In many cases, there is no substantive difference. KGF's North American revenues rose only 1 percent last year. Excluding special charges, operating income increased a disappointing 8 percent.

Antismoking Litigation and Legislation

Investors remain concerned about tobacco's legal status. This hinged on a Supreme Court ruling expected during the summer of 1992. The court will decide whether the federally mandated warning labels on cigarette packs—required since 1966—insulate tobacco companies from liability claims in state courts.

Smoking and Health Related Issues

Since 1964, the Surgeon General of the United States and the Secretary of Health and Human Services have released reports alleging a correlation between cigarette smoking and numerous physical maladies, including cancer, heart disease, and chronic diseases of the respiratory system. Recent reports continue to emphasize the health warnings from the earlier studies and additionally focus on the addictive nature of smoking and the demographics of smokers. In particular, the prevalence and growth rates of smoking among women and African-Americans have received much publicity.[38]

Federal law requires marketers of cigarettes in the United States to include one of four warnings on a rotating basis on cigarette packages and advertisements:

> SURGEON GENERAL'S WARNING: Smoking Causes Lung Cancer, Heart Disease, Emphysema, and May Complicate Pregnancy.
>
> SURGEON GENERAL'S WARNING: Quitting Smoking Now Greatly Reduces Serious Risk to Your Health.
>
> SURGEON GENERAL'S WARNING: Smoking by Pregnant Women May Result in Fetal Injury, Premature Birth, and Low Birth Weight.
>
> SURGEON GENERAL'S WARNING: Cigarette Smoke Contains Carbon Monoxide.

In addition to the warnings, federal regulations require that cigarettes sold in the United States disclose the average tar and nicotine deliveries per cigarette.

A more recent concern has been the alleged health risks to nonsmokers from what is most often referred to as *passive smoking* or *environmental tobacco smoke* (ETS). In 1986, the U.S. Surgeon General issued a report claiming that nonsmokers were at increased risk of lung cancer and respiratory illness due to ETS. The Environmental Protection Agency is currently at work on a report detailing the risks of ETS. The findings concerning ETS have been instrumental in the passage of legislation that restricts or bans cigarette smoking in public places and places of employment.

Television and radio advertising of cigarettes has been prohibited in the United States since 1971. Since this time, regulatory agencies have acted to further restrict or prohibit smoking in certain public places, on buses, trains, and airplanes, and in places of employment.

Such restrictions are not exclusive to the United States. Many foreign countries have restricted or prohibited cigarette advertising and promotion, increased taxes on cigarettes, and openly campaigned against smoking. Thailand, Hong Kong, France, Italy, and Portugal all have

[38]Ibid.

implemented cigarette advertising bans. This virtually precludes successful introduction of new brands in these countries. The European Economic Community (EEC) is contemplating a ban on tobacco advertising in newspapers, magazines, and billboards.[39] More recently, the Asian Consultancy on Tobacco Control, a 14-nation consortium, has been formed to combat smoking in this region. Thus, some countries have tighter restrictions than the United States.

Litigation

Approximately 50 court cases are pending, wherein plaintiffs are seeking damages from leading United States cigarette manufacturers. The litigation involves alleged cancer and other health maladies directly resulting from cigarette smoking. Philip Morris was a defendant in 23 actions pending as of March 1, 1991, compared with 24 at the same point in 1990 and with 32 in 1989. The number of court cases appears to have stabilized.

Philip Morris's primary defense tactic has been based on seeking a preemption of liability based on the Federal Cigarette Labeling and Advertising Act. Five federal courts have ruled that the cigarette labeling act does protect cigarette manufacturers from some liability claims. Conversely, the Supreme Court of New Jersey and one of the Texas appellate courts ruled that the cigarette labeling act does not limit the liability of the cigarette manufacturers.

As with any court case the outcome is uncertain. A finding in favor of the plaintiff would have the effect of denying preemption of liability on the basis of the existence of the cigarette warning labels. This could entice additional litigation against cigarette manufacturers. Philip Morris remains confident that, even in this worst-case scenario, the lawsuits will not pose a substantive threat to its overall financial health.

The Company's Position

No tobacco company has ever lost a liability case or paid a penny to settle; juries thus far have ruled that smokers have been adequately warned cigarettes can ruin their health. According to John McMillin of Prudential Securities: "A Supreme Court ruling against the industry has limited downside for the stock because worries have already pulled down the price. A tobacco victory could mean the end of major litigation risk and take Philip Morris's stock up 15 to 20 percent."

Tobacco use is one of the most widely discussed health issues around the world. The company's position was stated by CEO Miles in a letter to shareholders in 1992: "Given the general availability of information concerning the health issue, we regard smoking as a voluntary lifestyle decision that need not be subjected to new marketing or use restrictions."

He added: "While we believe that consumers are aware of the claimed health risks of smoking, nonetheless in February 1992 we took actions to begin placing the U.S. Surgeon General's health warning on all our cigarette packages worldwide where warnings are not currently required. This initiative applies to brands manufactured in the United States for export, as well as to those produced overseas by our affiliates and affected licensees. We are taking these steps because the lack of warning on a relatively small number of packages—approximately 10 percent of our volume—has become an issue out of proportion to its importance."

Continuing, Miles stated: "Moreover in the United States we are acting to increase awareness and enforcement of minimum age purchase restrictions on our tobacco products through multimillion-dollar programs involving advertising, trade relations, and family education."

---

[39]P. Engardio, "Asia: A New Front in the War on Smoking," *BusinessWeek* (Industrial/Technical Edition), no. 3201 (February 25, 1991), p. 66.

Future Prospects

According to Miles, the company has no plans to diversify outside of packaged goods. Since acquisition opportunities in tobacco are limited, most analysts predict a major food acquisition, probably in Western Europe within the coming year or so. In 1990, PM bought one of Europe's largest coffee and chocolate companies, Jacobs Suchard, well known for Toblerone candy bars. The $4.1 billion deal made PM the third-largest food marketer in Europe, behind Nestlé and Unilever. The company's European revenues today are approaching $10 billion in food. Nestlé has about $15 billion in European sales but, with acquisitions, PM figures it will grow faster.

There is much speculation centered on acquisition targets. One is rumored to be H. J. Heinz, a European powerhouse. PepsiCo is not considered a likely target but Cadburry Schweppes is. Another suspected target is Paris-based BSN, which would help PM penetrate the lucrative French cheese market with its Velveeta, Cracker Barrel, and Kraft Natural brands.

For Miles to meet the company's goals, PM must reach $85 billion in sales by 1995, with net income of $9 billion.[40] The future of the tobacco industry, particularly domestically, is cloudy. With numerous product liability lawsuits pending and increasing antismoking sentiments, PM must face the increasingly realistic possibility that cigarette smokers will become virtually nonexistent. As pessimistic as this may sound, a more threatening though less-likely scenario exists: cigarette manufacturing could be banned by the FDA. Within the coming five years, Miles must reposition the firm so it may withstand the effects of declining tobacco income.

[40]Sellers, "Can He Keep."

Section VI

Strategic Marketing Cases

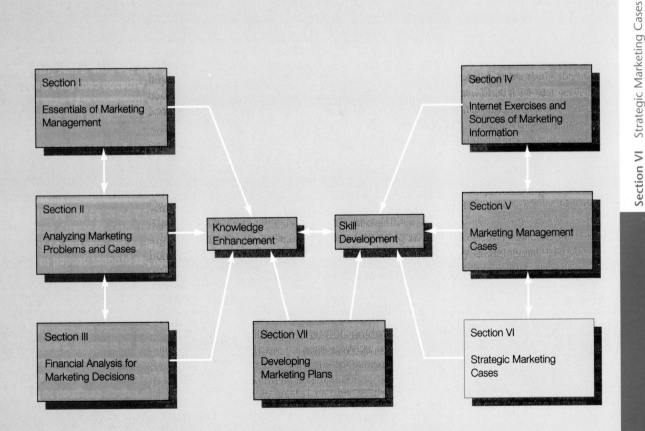

Note to the Student

The cases in this section emphasize the role of marketing in developing successful business or organizational strategies. While marketing is critical in these cases, successful analysis and strategy formulation will often involve other areas in the organization as well.

The knowledge and skills you've developed in the analysis of the cases in the previous section provide a useful foundation for analyzing the cases in this section. However, these cases are intended to broaden your knowledge of marketing and your skills at analyzing various strategic problems.

Case **1**

Yum! Brands, Pizza Hut, and KFC

Jeffrey A. Krug *Appalachian State University*

Yum! Brands, Inc., was the world's largest fast-food company in 2004. It operated more than 33,000 KFC, Pizza Hut, Taco Bell, Long John Silver's, and A&W restaurants worldwide. It was the market leader in the chicken, pizza, Mexican, and seafood segments of the U.S. fast-food industry. Yum! Brands also operated more than 12,000 restaurants outside the United States. KFC and Pizza Hut accounted for more than 96 percent of the company's international restaurant base and managed restaurants in 116 countries. Among the first fast-food chains to go international in the late 1950s and 1960s, KFC and Pizza Hut were two of the world's most recognizable brands. Both KFC and Pizza Hut expanded through the 1990s by growing their restaurants into as many countries as possible. However, Yum! Brands realized that different countries offered different opportunities to contribute to the company's worldwide operating profits.

By 2004 Yum! Brands began to focus more attention on portfolio management in individual countries. It increasingly focused its international strategy on developing strong market share positions in a small number of high-growth markets such as Japan, Canada, the United Kingdom, China, Australia, Korea, and Mexico. It also hoped to build strong positions in continental Europe, Brazil, and India. Consumer awareness in these markets, however, was still low and neither KFC nor Pizza Hut had strong operating capabilities there. China and India were appealing markets because of their large populations. From a regional point-of-view, Latin America was appealing because of its close proximity to the United States, language and cultural similarities, and the potential for a future World Free Trade Area of the Americas, which would eliminate tariffs on trade within North and South America. The most important long-term challenge for Yum! Brands was to strengthen its position in a set of core international markets while also developing new markets where consumer awareness and operating capabilities were weak.

Company History

Kentucky Fried Chicken Corporation

Fast-food franchising was still in its infancy in 1952 when Harland Sanders began his travels across the United States to speak with prospective franchisees about his "Colonel Sanders Recipe Kentucky Fried Chicken." By 1960, "Colonel" Sanders had granted Kentucky Fried Chicken (KFC) franchises to more than 200 take-home retail outlets and restaurants across the United States. Four years later, at the age of 74, he sold KFC to two Louisville businessmen for $2 million. In 1966 KFC went public and was listed on the New York Stock Exchange. In 1971 Heublein, Inc., a distributor of wine and alcoholic beverages, successfully approached KFC with an offer and merged KFC into a subsidiary. Eleven years later, R.J. Reynolds Industries, Inc., (RJR) acquired Heublein and merged it into a wholly owned subsidiary. The acquisition of Heublein was part of RJR's corporate strategy of diversifying into unrelated businesses such as energy, transportation, food, and restaurants to reduce its dependence on the tobacco industry. In 1985 RJR acquired Nabisco Corporation in an attempt to redefine RJR as a world leader in the consumer foods industry. As RJR refocused its strategy on processed foods, it decided to exit the restaurant industry. It sold KFC to PepsiCo, Inc., one year later.

Pizza Hut

In 1958 two students at Wichita State University—Frank and Dan Carney—decided to open a pizza restaurant in an old building at a busy intersection in downtown Wichita. To finance their new business, they borrowed $500 from their mother. They called the restaurant the "Pizza Hut," a reference to the old tavern beside the market that they renovated to open the new business. They opened four more restaurants during the next two years. The Pizza Hut concept was so well received by consumers that they were soon licensing the concept to franchises. By 1972 the Carneys had opened 1,000 restaurants and listed the firm on the New York Stock Exchange. In less than 15 years, Pizza Hut had become the number 1 pizza restaurant chain in the world in terms of sales and number of units. Internationally, Pizza Hut opened its first restaurant in Canada in 1968 and soon established franchises in Mexico, Germany, Australia, Costa Rica, Japan, and the United Kingdom. In 1977 it sold the business to PepsiCo, Inc. Pizza Hut's headquarters remained in Wichita and Frank Carney served as Pizza Hut's president until 1980. (It is interesting to note that Frank opened a Papa John's Pizza franchise in 1994. Today he is one of Papa John's largest franchisees).

PepsiCo, Inc.

PepsiCo believed the restaurant business complemented its consumer product orientation. The marketing of fast food followed many of the same patterns as soft drinks and snack foods. Pepsi-Cola and Pizza Hut pizza, for example, could be marketed in the same television and radio segments, which provided higher returns for each advertising dollar. Restaurant chains also provided an additional outlet for the sale of Pepsi soft drinks. In 1978 PepsiCo acquired Taco Bell. After acquiring KFC in 1986, PepsiCo controlled the leading brands in the pizza, Mexican, and chicken segments of the fast-food industry. PepsiCo's strategy of diversifying into three distinct but related markets created one of the world's largest food companies.

In the early 1990s, PepsiCo's sales grew at an annual rate of more than 10 percent. Its rapid growth, however, masked troubles in its fast-food businesses. Operating margins at Pepsi-Cola and PepsiCo's Frito-Lay division averaged 12 and 17 percent, respectively. Margins at KFC, Pizza Hut, and Taco Bell, however, fell from an average of 8 percent in 1990 to 4 percent in 1996. Declining margins reflected increasing maturity in the U.S. fast-food industry, intense competition, and the aging of KFC and Pizza Hut restaurants. PepsiCo's restaurant chains absorbed nearly one-half of PepsiCo's annual capital spending but generated less than one-third of its cash flows. Cash had to be diverted from PepsiCo's soft drink and snack food businesses to its restaurant businesses. This reduced PepsiCo's corporate return on assets, made it more difficult to compete effectively with Coca-Cola, and hurt its stock price. In 1997 PepsiCo decided to spin off its restaurant businesses into a new company called Tricon Global Restaurants, Inc.

Yum! Brands, Inc.

The spin-off created a new, independent, publicly traded company that managed the KFC, Pizza Hut, and Taco Bell franchises. David Novak became Tricon's new CEO. He moved quickly to create a new culture within the company. One of his primary objectives was to reverse the long-standing friction between management and franchisees that was created under PepsiCo ownership. Novak announced that PepsiCo's top-down management system would be replaced by a new management emphasis on providing support to the firm's franchise base. Franchises would have greater independence, resources, and technical support. Novak symbolically changed the name on the corporate headquarters building in Louisville to "KFC Support Center" to drive home his new philosophy.

The firm's new emphasis on franchise support had an immediate effect on morale. In 1997, the year of the divestiture, the company recorded a loss of $111 million in net income. In 2003 it recorded net income of $617 million on sales of $7.4 billion, a return on sales of 8.3 percent. In 2002 Tricon acquired Long John Silver's and A&W All-American Food Restaurants. The acquisitions increased Tricon's worldwide system to almost 33,000 units. One week later, shareholders approved a corporate name change to Yum! Brands, Inc. (Exhibit 1). The acquisitions signaled a shift in the company's strategy from a focus on individual to multibranded units. Multibranding combined two brands in a single

EXHIBIT 1   Yum! Brands, Inc.: Organizational Chart, 2004

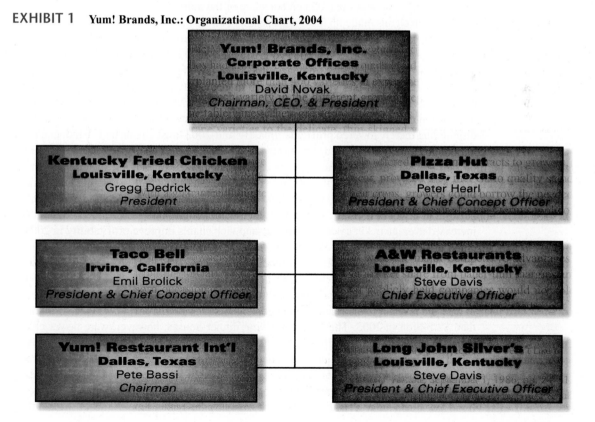

restaurant such as KFC and Taco Bell, KFC and A&W, Pizza Hut and Taco Bell, and Pizza Hut and Long John Silver's. Multibranded units attracted a larger consumer base by offering them a broader menu selection in one location. By 2004 the company was operating more than 2,400 multibrand restaurants in the United States.

Fast-Food Industry

The National Restaurant Association (NRA) estimated that U.S. food service sales increased by 3.3 percent to $422 billion in 2003. More than 858,000 restaurants made up the U.S. restaurant industry and employed 12 million people. Sales were highest in the full-service, sit-down sector, which grew 3.3 percent to $151 billion. Fast-food sales rose at a slower rate, 2.7 percent to $119 billion. The fast-food sector was increasingly viewed as a mature market. As U.S. incomes rose during the late 1990s and early 2000s, more consumers frequented sit-down restaurants that offered better service and a more comfortable dining experience. Together, the full-service and fast-food segments made up about 64 percent of all U.S. food service sales.

Major Fast-Food Segments

Eight major segments made up the fast-food segment of the restaurant industry: sandwich chains, pizza chains, family restaurants, grill buffet chains, dinner houses, chicken chains, nondinner concepts, and other chains. Sales data for the leading chains in each segment are shown in Exhibit 2. Most striking is the dominance of McDonald's, which had sales of more than $22 billion in 2003. McDonald's accounted for 14 percent of the sales of the top 100 chains. To put McDonald's dominance in perspective, the second largest chain—Burger King—held less than a 5 percent share of the market.

Sandwich chains made up the largest segment of the fast-food market. McDonald's controlled 35 percent of this segment, while Burger King ran a distant second with a 12 percent share. Sandwich chains struggled through early 2003 as the U.S. recession lowered demand and the war in Iraq increased consumer uncertainty. U.S. consumers were also trending away from the traditional hamburger, fries, and soft drink combinations and demanding more healthy food items and better service. Many chains attempted to attract new customers through price discounting. Instead of drawing in new customers, however, discounting merely lowered profit margins. By mid-2003 most chains had abandoned price discounting and began to focus on improved service and product quality. McDonald's, Taco Bell, and Hardee's were particularly successful. They slowed new restaurant development, improved drive-through service, and introduced a variety of new menu items. McDonald's and Hardee's, for example, introduced larger, higher-priced hamburgers to increase value perceptions and ticket prices. The shift from price discounting to new product introductions increased average ticket sales and helped sandwich chains improve profitability in 2004.

Dinner houses made up the second-largest and fastest-growing fast-food segment. Segment sales increased by almost 9.0 percent in 2003, surpassing the average increase of 5.5 percent in the other segments. Much of the growth in dinner houses came from new unit construction in suburban areas and small towns. Applebee's, Chili's, Outback Steakhouse, Red Lobster, and Olive Garden dominated the segment. Each chain generated sales of more than $2 billion in 2003. The fastest-growing dinner houses, however, were newer chains generating less than $700 million in sales, such as P. F. Chang's China Bistro, the Cheesecake Factory, Carrabba's Italian Grill, and LongHorn Steakhouse. Each chain was increasing sales at a 20 percent annual rate. Dinner houses continued to benefit from rising household incomes in the United States. As incomes rose, families were able to move up from quick-service restaurants to more upscale, higher-priced dinner houses. In addition,

EXHIBIT 2   **Top U.S. Fast-Food Restaurants (Ranked by 2003 sales, $ millions)**

Source: *Nation's Restaurant News*. Sales rankings for contract and hotel chains not included.

Sandwich Chains	Sales	Change	Dinner Houses	Sales	Change
McDonald's	$22,121	8.9%	Applebee's	$ 3,520	10.6%
Burger King	7,680	–2.8	Chili's	2,505	11.8
Wendy's	7,315	5.2	Outback Steakhouse	2,456	7.1
Subway	5,690	8.8	Red Lobster	2,315	–1.9
Taco Bell	5,346	2.8	Olive Garden	2,165	11.6
Arby's	2,710	0.6	TGI Friday's	1,791	2.6
Jack in the Box	2,360	5.4	Ruby Tuesday	1,450	14.8
Sonic Drive-In	2,359	7.0	Romano's	699	9.4
Dairy Queen	2,165	–1.1	Cheesecake Factory	689	20.6
Hardee's	1,662	–2.3	Hooter's	670	6.5
Other Chains	3,934	9.4	Other Chains	5,277	10.7
Total Segment	$63,342	5.2%	Total Segment	$23,537	8.8%
Pizza Chains			**Chicken Chains**		
Pizza Hut	$ 5,033	–1.3%	KFC	$ 4,936	2.8%
Domino's	3,003	2.6	Chick-fil-A	1,534	11.8
Papa John's	1,719	–2.4	Popeyes	1,274	1.6
Little Caesars	1,200	4.3	Church's	700	–2.5
Chuck E. Cheese's	476	3.5	Boston Market	646	0.8
CiCi's Pizza	380	13.9	El Pollo Loco	396	8.7
Round Table Pizza	378	1.1	Bojangles'	375	8.0
Total Segment	$12,189	0.7%	Total Segment	$ 9,861	3.8%
Family Restaurants			**Other Dinner Chains**		
Denny's	$ 2,132	0.6%	Panera Bread	$ 908	32.0%
IHOP	1,676	14.7	Long John Silver's	777	2.8
Cracker Barrel	1,480	5.3	Disney Theme Parks	707	0.4
Bob Evans	954	9.0	Old Country Buffet	548	–4.5
Waffle House	789	2.7	Captain D's Seafood	506	1.7
Perkins	787	–1.3	Total Segment	$ 3,446	7.0%
Other Chains	2,162	1.2	**Nondinner Concepts**		
Total Segment	$ 9,980	4.3%			
Grill Buffet Chains			Starbucks	$ 3,118	25.8%
			Dunkin' Donuts	2,975	10.2
Golden Corral	$ 1,247	7.8%	7-Eleven	1,410	5.6
Ryan's	814	0.2	Krispy Kreme	957	24.0
Ponderosa	537	–2.1	Baskin-Robbins	510	–2.5
Total Segment	$ 2,598	3.2%	Total Segment	$ 8,970	14.9%

higher incomes enabled many professionals to purchase more expensive homes in new suburban developments, thereby providing additional opportunities for dinner houses to build new restaurants in unsaturated areas.

Increased growth among dinner houses came at the expense of sandwich chains, pizza and chicken chains, grill buffet chains, and family restaurants. "Too many restaurants chasing the same customers" was responsible for much of the slower growth in these other fast-food categories. Sales growth within each segment, however, differed from one chain to another. In the family segment, for example, Denny's (the segment leader in sales), Shoney's, Perkins, and Big Boy shut down poorly performing restaurants. At the same time, IHOP, Bob Evans, and Cracker Barrel expanded their bases. The hardest-hit segment was grill buffet chains. Declining sales caused both Sizzlin' and Western Sizzlin' to drop out of

EXHIBIT 3
Leading Pizza,
Chicken, and
Sandwich
Chains, 2003

Source: *Nation's Restaurant
News.*

Pizza Chains	Sales ($ millions)	Growth Rate (%)	Units	Growth Rate (%)	Sales per Unit ($000s)
Pizza Hut	$ 5,033.0	(1.3)%	7,523	(1.0)%	$ 665.7
Domino's Pizza	3,003.4	2.6	4,904	1.2	616.0
Papa John's Pizza	1,718.5	(2.4)	3,035	(0.4)	661.5
Little Caesars Pizza	1,200.0	4.4	2,593	(0.2)	395.1
Chuck E. Cheese's	476.2	3.5	485	5.1	1,070.1
CiCi's Pizza	380.4	13.9	465	11.5	862.6
Round Table Pizza	378.4	1.1	456	(5.6)	757.6
Total	$12,189.9	3.1%	19,461	1.5%	$718.3
Chicken Chains					
KFC	$ 4,936.0	2.8%	5,524	1.0%	$ 897.8
Chick-fil-A	1,534.4	11.8	1,235	4.9	1,394.3
Popeyes Chicken	1,274.0	1.6	1,447	3.8	896.9
Church's Chicken	700.0	(2.5)	1,235	(1.0)	564.1
Boston Market	646.0	0.8	630	(3.1)	1,009.4
El Pollo Loco	395.7	8.7	314	2.6	1,276.5
Bojangles'	374.8	8.0	320	9.6	1,224.8
Total	$ 9,860.9	4.5%	10,705	2.6%	$1,037.7
Sandwich Chains					
McDonald's	$22,121.4	8.9%	13,609	0.9%	$1,632.6
Burger King	7,680.0	(2.8)	7,656	(3.1)	987.1
Wendy's	7,315.0	5.2	5,761	3.8	1,293.5
Subway	5,690.0	8.8	16,499	13.6	366.8
Taco Bell	5,346.0	2.8	5,989	(2.9)	879.7
Arby's	2,710.0	0.6	3,303	1.6	827.1
Jack in the Box	2,360.0	5.4	1,947	4.6	1,239.2
Total	$53,222.4	4.1%	54,764	2.6%	$1,032.3
Long John Silver's	777.0	2.8	1,204	(1.4)	640.8
A&W Restaurants	200.0	NA	576	(13.4)	NA
Yum! Brands Total	16,292.0	NA	20,822	(1.4)	NA

Note: Sales per unit are calculated based on a mathematical equation of annual systemwide sales growth and changes in the number of operating units.

the list of Top 100 chains, leaving only three chains in the Top 100 (Golden Corral, Ryan's, and Ponderosa). Each of these three chains shut down restaurants in 2003. Dinner houses, because of their more upscale atmosphere and higher-ticket items, were better positioned to take advantage of the aging and wealthier U.S. population.

Yum! Brands: Brand Leadership

Exhibit 3 shows sales and restaurant data for the pizza, chicken, and sandwich segments. Yum! Brands generated U.S. sales of $16.3 billion across its five brands. It operated close to 21,000 U.S. and 12,000 non-U.S. restaurants, or more than 33,000 restaurants worldwide. Four of its brands—Pizza Hut (pizza), KFC (chicken), Taco Bell (Mexican), and Long John Silver's (seafood)—were the market leaders in their segments. Taco Bell was the third most profitable restaurant concept behind McDonald's and Starbucks. Profitability at McDonald's was primarily driven by volume; each McDonald's restaurant generated an annual average of $1.6 million in sales compared to an industrywide average of $1.0 million. Starbucks, in contrast, generated less revenue per store—about $660 million each year—but premium pricing for its specialty coffee drinks drove high profit margins. Taco Bell was able to generate greater overall profits because of its lower operating costs. Products such as tacos, burritos, gorditas, and chalupas used similar ingredients. In addition, cooking machinery was simpler, less costly, and required less space than pizza ovens or chicken broilers.

Pizza Hut controlled the pizza segment with a 41 percent share, followed by Domino's (25 percent) and Papa John's (14 percent). As the pizza segment became increasingly mature, the traditional pizza chains were forced to close old or underperforming restaurants. Only relatively new pizza chain concepts such as CiCi's Pizza, which offered an inexpensive all-you-can-eat salad and pizza buffet, and Chuck E. Cheese's, which focused on family entertainment, were able to significantly grow their restaurant bases during 2003. Most chains could no longer rely on new restaurant construction to drive sales. Another problem was the proliferation of new diets. Many Americans were eating pizza less often as they pursued the Atkins Diet (low carbohydrates), "The Zone" (balanced meals containing equal parts of carbohydrates, protein, and unsaturated fat), or a traditional low-fat diet. Each diet discouraged users from eating pizza, which was high in both fat and carbohydrates.

Operating costs were also rising because of higher cheese and gasoline prices. Pizza chains were forced to develop unique strategies that attracted more customers but protected profit margins. Some chains raised pizza prices to offset higher-priced ingredients or raised home delivery charges to offset higher gasoline costs. Most chains, however, responded with new product introductions. Pizza Hut introduced a low-fat "Fit 'n Delicious" pizza that used one-half the cheese of normal pizzas and toppings with lower fat content. It also introduced a "4forAll" pizza that contained four individually topped six-inch square pizzas in the same box. Domino's introduced a Philly cheese steak pizza, its first new product introduction since 2000. Papa John's introduced a new barbeque chicken and bacon pizza. In addition, it began a campaign that allowed customers to choose one of three free DVDs with the purchase of a large pizza. By matching pizza and movies, Papa John's hoped to encourage customers to eat pizza more often. Pizza Hut quickly responded with its own offer for a free DVD with the purchase of any pizza at the regular price.

KFC continued to dominate the chicken segment with sales of $4.9 billion in 2003, more than 50 percent of sales in the chicken segment. Its nearest competitor, Chick-fil-A, ran a distant second with sales of $1.5 billion. KFC's leadership in the U.S. market was so extensive that it had fewer opportunities to expand its U.S. restaurant base. Despite its dominance, KFC was slowly losing market share as other chicken chains increased sales at a faster rate. Sales data indicated that KFC's share of the chicken segment fell from a high of 64 percent in 1993, a 10-year drop of 14 percent. During the same period, Chick-fil-A and Boston Market increased their combined share by 11 percent. On the surface, it appeared that these market share gains came by taking customers away from KFC. The growth in sales at KFC restaurants, however, had generally remained steady during the last two decades. In reality, the three chains competed for different market groups. Boston Market, for example, appealed to professionals with higher incomes and health-conscious consumers who didn't regularly frequent KFC. It expanded the chicken segment by offering healthy, "home-style" alternatives to nonfried chicken in a setting resembling an upscale deli. Chick-fil-A concentrated on chicken sandwiches rather than fried chicken and most of its restaurants were still located in shopping mall food courts.

The maturity of the U.S. fast-food industry intensified competition within the chicken segment. As in the pizza segment, chicken chains could not rely on new restaurant construction to build new sales. In addition, chicken costs, which represented about one-half of total food costs, increased dramatically in 2004. A boneless chicken breast, which cost $1.20 per pound in early 2001, cost $2.50 per pound in 2004, an increase of more than 100 percent. Profit margins were being squeezed from both the revenue and cost sides. All chains focused on very different strategies. KFC added new menu boards and introduced new products such as oven roasted strips and roasted twister sandwich wraps. Boston Market experimented with home delivery and began to sell through supermarkets. Chick-fil-A continued to build freestanding restaurants to expand beyond shopping malls. Church's focused on adding drive-through service. The intensity of competition led chicken chains to implement very different strategies for differentiating their product and brand.

Trends in the Restaurant Industry

A number of demographic and societal trends influenced the demand for food eaten outside the home. Rising income, greater affluence among a larger percentage of American households, higher divorce rates, and the marriage of people later in life contributed to the rising number of single households and the demand for fast food. More than 50 percent of women worked outside the home, a dramatic increase since 1970. This number was expected to rise to 65 percent by 2010. Double-income households contributed to rising household incomes and increased the number of times families ate out. Less time to prepare meals inside the home added to this trend. Countering these trends, however, was the slower growth rate of the U.S. population and a proliferation of fast-food chains that increased consumer alternatives and intensified competition.

Baby boomers (ages 35 to 50) constituted the largest consumer group for fast-food restaurants. Generation Xers (ages 25 to 34) and the "mature" category (ages 51 to 64) made up the second and third largest groups, respectively. As consumers aged, they became less enamored of fast food and were more likely to trade up to more expensive restaurants such as dinner houses and full-service restaurants. Sales for many Mexican restaurants, which were extremely popular during the 1980s, began to slow as Japanese, Indian, and Vietnamese restaurants became more fashionable. Ethnic foods were rising in popularity as U.S. immigrants, who constituted 13 percent of the U.S. population in 2004, looked for establishments that sold their native foods.

Labor was the top operational challenge of U.S. restaurant chains. Restaurants relied heavily on teenagers and college-age workers. Twenty percent of all employed teenagers worked in food service, compared to only 4 percent of all employed men over the age of 18 and 6 percent of all employed women over age 18. As the U.S. population aged, fewer young workers were available to fill food service jobs. The short supply of high school and college students meant they had greater work opportunities outside food service. Turnover rates were notoriously high. The National Restaurant Association estimated that about 96 percent of all fast-food workers quit within a year, compared to about 84 percent of employees in full-service restaurants.

Labor costs made up about 30 percent of a fast-food chain's total costs, second only to food and beverage costs. To deal with the decreased supply of employees in the age 16 to 24 category, many restaurants were forced to hire less reliable workers. This affected service and restaurant cleanliness. To improve quality and service, restaurants hired elderly employees who wanted to return to the workforce. To attract more workers, especially the elderly, restaurants offered health insurance, noncontributory pension plans, and profit-sharing benefits. To combat high turnover rates, restaurants turned to training programs and mentoring systems that paired new employees with experienced ones. Mentoring systems were particularly helpful in increasing the learning curve of new workers and providing better camaraderie among employees.

The Global Fast-Food Industry

As the U.S. market matured, more restaurants turned to international markets to expand sales. Foreign markets were attractive because of their large customer bases and comparatively little competition. McDonald's, for example, operated 48 restaurants for every one million U.S. residents. Outside the United States, it operated only one restaurant for every

EXHIBIT 4 The World's 35 Largest Fast-Food Chains in 2004

Source: Case author's research.

Franchise	Corporate Headquarters	Home Country	Number of Countries with Operations
1. McDonald's	Oak Brook, Illinois	U.S.	121
2. KFC	Louisville, Kentucky	U.S.	99
3. Pizza Hut	Dallas, Texas	U.S.	92
4. Subway Sandwiches	Milford, Connecticut	U.S.	74
5. TCBY	Little Rock, Arkansas	U.S.	67
6. Domino's Pizza	Ann Arbor, Michigan	U.S.	65
7. Burger King	Miami, Florida	U.S.	58
8. TGI Friday's	Dallas, Texas	U.S.	53
9. Baskin-Robbins	Glendale, California	U.S.	52
10. Dunkin' Donuts	Randolph, Massachusetts	U.S.	40
11. Wendy's	Dublin, Ohio	U.S.	34
12. Chili's Grill & Bar	Dallas, Texas	U.S.	22
13. Dairy Queen	Edina, Minnesota	U.S.	22
14. Little Caesars Pizza	Detroit, Michigan	U.S.	22
15. Popeyes	Atlanta, Georgia	U.S.	22
16. Outback Steakhouse	Tampa, Florida	U.S.	20
17. A&W Restaurants	Lexington, Kentucky	U.S.	17
18. PizzaExpress	London	U.K.	16
19. Carl's Jr.	Anaheim, California	U.S.	14
20. Church's Chicken	Atlanta, Georgia	U.S.	12
21. Taco Bell	Irvine, California	U.S.	12
22. Hardee's	Rocky Mount, North Carolina	U.S.	11
23. Applebee's	Overland Park, Kansas	U.S.	9
24. Sizzler	Los Angeles, California	U.S.	9
25. Arby's	Ft. Lauderdale, Florida	U.S.	7
26. Denny's	Spartanburg, South Carolina	U.S.	7
27. Skylark	Tokyo	Japan	7
28. Lotteria	Seoul	Korea	5
29. Taco Time	Eugene, Oregon	U.S.	5
30. Mos Burger	Tokyo	Japan	4
31. Orange Julius	Edina, Minnesota	U.S.	4
32. Yoshinoya	Tokyo	Japan	4
33. IHOP	Glendale, California	U.S.	3
34. Quick Restaurants	Brussels	Belgium	3
35. Red Lobster	Orlando, Florida	U.S.	3

five million residents. McDonald's, Pizza Hut, KFC, and Burger King were the earliest and most aggressive chains to expand abroad beginning in the 1960s. This made them formidable competitors for chains investing abroad for the first time. Subway, TCBY, and Domino's were more recent global competitors. By 2004 each was operating in more than 65 countries. Exhibit 4 lists the world's 35 largest restaurant chains.

The global fast-food industry had a distinctly American flavor. Twenty-eight chains (80 percent of the total) were headquartered in the United States. U.S. chains had the advantage of a large domestic market and ready acceptance by the American consumer. European firms had less success developing the fast-food concept because Europeans were more inclined to frequent midscale restaurants where they spent several hours enjoying multicourse meals in a formal setting. KFC had trouble breaking into the German market during the 1970s and 1980s because Germans were not accustomed to buying takeout or

EXHIBIT 5
Yum! Brands, Inc.—
Largest International
Markets, 2004

Source: Yum! Brands, Inc.

				Number of Restaurants		
	KFC	Pizza Hut	Taco Bell	Long John Silver's	A&W	Yum! Brands
United States	5,524	7,523	5,989	1,207	579	20,822
International	7,354	4,560	249	31	183	12,377
Worldwide	12,878	12,083	6,238	1,238	762	33,199
International Total (%)	57.1%	37.7%	4.0%	2.5%	24.0%	37.3%
Top Foreign Markets						
1. Japan	1,167	327	24			1,518
2. Canada	733	353	84			1,170
3. U.K.	591	556				1,147
4. China	979	127	1			1,107
5. Australia	516	319	7			842
6. Korea	209	299				508
7. Malaysia	329	106	32	6	26	499
8. Mexico	309	180	1		1	491
9. Thailand	299	77	28		28	432
10. Indonesia	198	85	69		74	426
11. South Africa	360	3				363
12. Philippines	128	113	6		6	253
Other Latin America						
Puerto Rico	95	60	32			187
Ecuador	45	20	4			69
Costa Rica	15	41	11			67
Brazil	3	63				66
Chile	30	28				58
Other Asia						
Taiwan	132	111				242
Singapore	73	34	24	24		155
Other Selected Markets						
France	24	126				150
Germany	45	77				122
Saudi Arabia	50	92	9		9	160
India	2	65				67

ordering food over the counter. McDonald's had greater success in Germany because it made changes to its menu and operating procedures to appeal to German tastes. German beer, for example, was served in all of McDonald's restaurants in Germany. In France, McDonald's used a different sauce that appealed to the French palate on its Big Mac sandwich. KFC had more success in Asia and Latin America where chicken was a traditional dish.

Yum! Brands operated more than 12,000 restaurants outside the United States (see Exhibit 5). The early international experience of KFC and Pizza Hut put them in a strong position to exploit the globalization trend in the industry. A separate subsidiary in Dallas—Yum! Brands International—managed the international activities of all five brands. As a result, the firm had significant international experience concentrated in one location and a well-established worldwide distribution network. KFC and Pizza Hut accounted for almost all of the firm's international restaurants. Yum! Brands planned to open 1,000 new KFC and Pizza Hut restaurants outside the United States each year, well into the future. This came at a time when both KFC and Pizza Hut were closing units in the mature U.S. market.

Of the KFC and Pizza Hut restaurants located outside the United States, 77 percent were owned by local franchisees or joint venture partners who had a deep understanding of local language, culture, customs, law, financial markets, and marketing characteristics. Franchising allowed firms to expand more quickly, minimize capital expenditures, and maximize return on invested capital. It was also a good strategy for establishing a presence in smaller markets like Grenada, Bermuda, and Suriname where the small number of consumers only allowed for a single restaurant. The costs of operating company-owned restaurants were prohibitively high in these markets. In larger markets such as China, Canada, Australia, and Mexico, there was a stronger emphasis on building company-owned restaurants. Fixed costs could be spread over a larger number of units and the company could coordinate purchasing, recruiting, training, financing, and advertising. This reduced per unit costs. Company-owned restaurants also allowed the company to maintain tighter control over product quality and customer service.

Country Evaluation and Risk Assessment

International Business Risk

Worldwide demand for fast food was expected to grow rapidly during the next two decades as rising per capita income made eating out more affordable for greater numbers of consumers. International business, however, carried a variety of risks not present in the domestic market. Long distances between headquarters and foreign franchises made it more difficult to control the quality of individual restaurants. Large distances also caused servicing and support problems, and transportation and other resource costs were higher. In addition, time, cultural, and language differences increased communication problems and made it more difficult to get timely and accurate information.

During the 1970s and 1980s, KFC and Pizza Hut attempted to expand their restaurant bases into as many countries as possible—the greater the number of countries, the greater the indicator of success. By the early years of the 21st century, however, it became apparent that serving a large number of markets with a small number of restaurants was a costly business. If a large number of restaurants could be established in a single market or region, then significant economies of scale could be achieved by spreading fixed costs of purchasing, advertising, and distribution across a larger restaurant base. Higher market share, as a result, was typically associated with greater cash flow and higher profitability.

Country analysis was an important part of the strategic decision-making process. Few companies had sufficient resources to invest everywhere simultaneously. Choices had to be made about when and where to invest scarce capital. Country selection models typically assessed countries on the basis of market size, growth rates, the number and type of competitors, government regulations, and economic and political stability. In an industry such as fast food, however, an analysis of economic and political variables was insufficient. As mentioned earlier, KFC had trouble establishing a presence in Germany because many consumers there didn't accept the fast-food concept. An analysis of Germany's large, stable economy would otherwise have indicated a potentially profitable market.

An important challenge for multinational firms was to accurately assess the risks of doing business in different countries and regions in order to make good choices about where to invest. A useful framework for analyzing international business risk was to separate risk into factors of country, industry, and firm. Country factors, for example, included risks associated with changes in a country's political and economic environment. These included political risk (e.g., war, revolution, changes in government, price controls, tariffs, and government regulations), economic risk (e.g., inflation, high interest rates, foreign exchange rate volatility, balance of trade movements, social unrest, riots, and terrorism), and natural risk (e.g., rainfall, hurricanes, earthquakes, and volcanic activity).

Industry factors addressed changes in industry structure that inhibited a firm's ability to compete successfully in its industry. These included supplier risk (e.g., changes in supplier quality and supplier power), product market risk (e.g., consumer tastes and the availability of substitute products), and competitive risk (e.g., rivalry among competitors, new market entrants, and new product innovations).

Last, firm factors examined a firm's ability to control its internal operations. They included labor risk (e.g., labor unrest, absenteeism, employee turnover, and labor strikes), supplier risk (e.g., raw material shortages and unpredictable price changes), trade secret risk (e.g., protection of trade secrets and intangible assets), credit risk (e.g., problems in collecting receivables), and behavioral risk (e.g., control over franchise operations, product quality and consistency, service quality, and restaurant cleanliness). Each of these factors— country, industry, and firm—had to be analyzed simultaneously to fully understand the costs and benefits of international investment.[1]

Country Risk Assessment in Latin America

Latin America is comprised of some 50 countries, island nations, and principalities that were settled by the Spanish, Portuguese, French, Dutch, and British during the 1500s and 1600s. Spanish is spoken in most countries, the most notable exception being Brazil where the official language is Portuguese. Despite commonalities in language, religion, and history, however, political and economic policies differ significantly from one country to another.

Mexico

Many U.S. companies considered Mexico to be one of the most attractive investment locations in Latin America in the 1990s. Its population of 105 million was more than one-third as large as the United States, and three times larger than Canada's population of 32 million. Prior to 1994, Mexico levied high tariffs on many goods imported from the United States. As a result, many U.S. consumers purchased less expensive products from Asia or Europe. In 1994 the North American Free Trade Agreement (NAFTA) was signed. NAFTA eliminated tariffs on goods traded between the United States, Canada, and Mexico. It created a trading bloc with a larger population and gross domestic product than the European Union. The elimination of tariffs led to an immediate increase in trade between Mexico and the United States. By 2004, 85 percent of Mexico's exports were purchased by U.S. consumers. In turn, 68 percent of Mexico's total imports came from the United States.

Most Mexicans (70 percent) lived in urban areas such as Mexico City, Guadalajara, and Monterrey. Mexico City's population of 18 million made it one of the most populated areas in Latin America. Many U.S. firms had operations in or around Mexico City. The fast-food industry was well developed in Mexico's cities. The leading U.S. fast-food chains already had significant restaurant bases in Mexico, most importantly KFC (274 restaurants), McDonald's (261), Pizza Hut (174), Burger King (154), and Subway (71). Mexican consumers readily accepted the fast-food concept. Chicken was also a staple product in Mexico and helped explain KFC's wide popularity. Mexico's large population and ready acceptance of fast-food represented a significant opportunity for fast-food chains. Competition, however, was intense.

Brazil

Brazil, with a population of 182 million, was the largest country in Latin America and the fifth largest country in the world. Its land base was almost as large as the United States and bordered 10 countries. It was the world's largest coffee producer and largest exporter of

---

[1]For an in-depth discussion of international business risk, see Kent D., Miller, "A Framework for Integrated Risk Management in International Business, *Journal of International Business Studies*, 21 (2): (1992), pp. 311–31.

sugar and tobacco. In addition to its abundant natural resources and strong export position in agriculture, Brazil was a strong industrial power. Its major exports were airplanes, automobiles, and chemicals. Its gross domestic product of $1.3 trillion was larger than Mexico's and the largest in Latin America (see Exhibit 6). Some firms viewed Brazil as one of the most important emerging markets, along with China and India.

The fast-food industry in Brazil was less developed than in Mexico or the Caribbean. This was partly the result of the structure of the fast-food industry that was dominated by U.S. restaurant chains. U.S. chains expanded further away from their home base as they gained experience operating in Latin America. As firms gained a foothold in Mexico and Central America, it was a natural progression to move into South America. McDonald's understood the importance of Brazil. It opened its first restaurant in 1979 and by 2004 was operating 1,200 restaurants, ice-cream kiosks, and McCafés there. Many restaurant chains such as Burger King, Pizza Hut, and KFC built restaurants in Brazil in the early- to mid-1990s but eventually closed them because of poor sales. Like Germany, many Brazilians were not quick to accept the fast-food concept.

One problem facing U.S. fast-food chains was eating customs. Brazilians ate their big meal in the early afternoon. In the evening, it was customary to have a light meal such as soup or a small plate of pasta. Brazilians rarely ate food with their hands, preferring to eat with a knife and fork. This included food like pizza, which Americans typically ate with their hands. They also were not accustomed to eating sandwiches; if they did eat sandwiches, they wrapped the sandwich in a napkin. U.S. fast-food chains catered to a different kind of customer who wanted more than soup but less than a full sit-down meal. U.S. fast-food chains were more popular in larger cities such as São Paulo and Rio de Janeiro where business people were in a hurry. Food courts were well developed in Brazil's shopping malls but included sit-down as well as fast-food restaurants. U.S. restaurant chains were, therefore, faced with the challenge of changing the eating habits of Brazilians or convincing Brazilians of the attractiveness of fast-food, American style.

Risks and Opportunities

Yum! Brands faced difficult decisions surrounding the design and implementation of an effective international strategy over the next 20 years. Its top seven markets generated more than 70 percent of its international profits. As a result, it planned to continue its aggressive investments in its primary markets. It was also important, however, to improve brand equity in other regions of the world such as continental Europe, Brazil, and India where consumer acceptance of fast food was still weak and the company had limited operational capabilities. Latin America as a region was of particular interest because of its geographic proximity to the United States, cultural similarities, and NAFTA. The company needed to sustain its leadership position in Mexico and the Caribbean but also looked to strengthen its position in countries such as Brazil, Venezuela, and Argentina. Limited resources and cash flow limited KFC's ability to aggressively expand in all countries simultaneously. Country evaluation and risk assessment would be an important tool for developing and implementing an effective international strategy.

EXHIBIT 6 Latin America: Selected Economic and Demographic Data

Source: U.S. Central Intelligence Agency, *The World Factbook*, 2002. Demographic data is 2003 estimate; economic data as of year-end 2002.

	United States	Canada	Mexico	Colombia	Venezuela	Peru	Brazil	Argentina	Chile
Population (millions)	290.3	32.2	104.9	41.7	24.7	28.4	182.0	38.7	15.7
Growth rate (%)	0.9%	0.9%	1.4%	1.6%	1.5%	1.6%	1.5%	1.1%	1.1%
Population Data: Origin									
European (non-French origin)	65.1%	43.0%	9.0%	20.0%	21.0%	15.0%	55.0%	97.0%	95.0%
European (French origin)		23.0%							
African	12.9%			4.0%	10.0%		6.0%		
Mixed African and European		6.0%		14.0%		37.0%	38.0%		
Latin American (Hispanic)	12.0%								
Asian	4.2%								
Amerindian or Alaskan native	1.5%	2.0%	30.0%	1.0%	2.0%	45.0%			3.0%
Mixed Amerindian and Spanish			60.0%	58.0%	67.0%				
Mixed African and Amerindian				3.0%					
Other	4.3%	26.0%	1.0%			3.0%	1.0%	3.0%	2.0%
Total	100.0%	100.0%	100.0%	100.0%	100.0%	100.0%	100.0%	100.0%	100.0%
GDP ($ billions)	$10,400	$ 923	$ 900	$ 268	$ 133	$ 132	$1,340	$ 391	$ 151
Per capita income (US$)	$37,600	$29,400	$9,000	$6,500	$5,500	$4,800	$7,600	$10,200	$10,000
Real GDP growth rate	2.5%	3.4%	1.0%	2.0%	-8.9%	4.8%	1.0%	-14.7%	1.8%
Inflation rate	1.6%	2.2%	6.4%	6.2%	31.2%	0.2%	8.3%	41.0%	2.5%
Unemployment rate	5.8%	7.6%	3.0%	17.4%	17.0%	9.4%	6.4%	21.5%	9.2%
Literacy rate	97.0%	97.0%	92.2%	92.5%	93.4%	90.9%	86.4%	97.0%	96.2%

Case 2

Caterpillar, Inc.

Sara L. Pitterle and J. Paul Peter *University of Wisconsin–Madison*

After a record year in 1988, Caterpillar's profits declined steadily, culminating in a $404 million loss ($4.00 per share of common stock) in 1991. The loss was attributed to a number of factors, including a prolonged global recession and one-time charges associated with facility closings, consolidation, and employment reductions. These cutbacks were designed to reduce Caterpillar's manufacturing costs over the long term. On April 23, 1992, Caterpillar announced a $132 million loss for the first quarter. Although a strike by the United Auto Workers had disrupted production for the entire quarter, management attributed the loss solely to lower sales. (Appendix A contains a summary of Caterpillar's recent financial performance.)

These losses were incurred by a company which had made unprecedented changes over the past decade in response to the changing industrial equipment market. These changes include a multibillion dollar plant modernization program begun in 1985 and a company reorganization undertaken in 1990. These two changes were designed to ensure Caterpillar's profitability for the 1990s and beyond. However, the 1991 and 1992 profit results led management to wonder whether the changes would be successful.

History

Caterpillar is a multinational corporation headquartered in Peoria, Illinois, that competes in three principal business segments. The company designs, manufactures, and markets engines for a wide range of applications including electrical power generation systems, on-highway trucks, and industrial machinery. The company also designs, manufactures, and markets earthmoving, construction, and materials-handling machinery. (See Appendix B for a complete listing of Caterpillar equipment.) In addition, Caterpillar provides financial products to assist customers in purchasing Caterpillar and noncompetitive related equipment.[1] The company has manufacturing facilities and/or marketing offices in 15 countries besides the United States.[2]

Caterpillar, the largest manufacturer of engines and construction equipment in the world, traces its origins to two inventors, Daniel Best and Benjamin Holt, who in the late

This case was prepared by Sara L. Pitterle, Nielson Fellow at the University of Wisconsin–Madison, under the supervision of J. Paul Peter.

[1] Caterpillar, Inc. Annual Report for 1991.

[2] Taken from speech by Ed Terrel, Manager of Human Resources for Caterpillar, Inc., at the University of Wisconsin–Madison, September 23, 1992.

1800s independently developed mechanized agricultural equipment. In February 1889, Daniel Best introduced the first steam-powered harvester, replacing the 40-horse-drawn combine with an 8-man, 11-ton, self-propelled tractor using wheels eight feet in diameter. Around the same time, Benjamin Holt began field testing the first crawler-type equipment, built simply by replacing the wheels on existing equipment with new "track" structures—pairs of treads comprised of wooden slats linked loosely together.

The two companies prospered, driven by increasing demand in agriculture, road building, military equipment, and industrial construction. The introduction of the internal-combustion engine provided yet another boost for the evolving heavy-equipment industry. In 1925, the Holt and Best companies merged to form Caterpillar Tractor Company, setting the stage for several decades of uninterrupted growth through technological leadership and a commitment to total quality.

In 1931, the first Caterpillar diesel tractor was introduced. This product initiated a six-year sales growth from $13 million to $63 million and launched the track-type tractor into prominence as the single largest user of diesel power. Caterpillar's growing reputation for industry leadership and technological superiority was further strengthened during World War II by U.S. government defense contracts. These contracts included demand for both existing equipment (e.g., bulldozers and graders) and special government requests for revolutionary and sophisticated equipment such as air-cooled diesel engines for advanced military operations.

Throughout the postwar years, and into the 1970s, Caterpillar generally concentrated on the development of large industrial-sized machines and engines. During this time the company purchased the Trackson Company of Milwaukee to produce hoists, pipe layers, and hydraulically operated tractor shovels for Caterpillar crawlers. Later, Towmotor Corporation was acquired to continue the company's expansion into heavy equipment with forklift trucks and straddle carriers for a wide range of materials-handling applications. By the early 1970s, Caterpillar had achieved at least foothold positions in a variety of heavy equipment product lines, with the objective of achieving industry leadership in each of the new areas.

In 1977, Caterpillar unveiled the single largest, most technologically advanced tractor in the world—the D-10. Foremost among its advantages were an elevated drive sprocket and modular-designed major components. The elevation of the drive sprocket removed it from high-wear and shock-load areas, reduced overall stress on the undercarriage, and produced a smoother ride. The modular design of major components not only permitted faster and more efficient servicing, but also provided the opportunity to pretest components before final assembly. Modular designs thereby reduced repair and overall downtime in some cases by as much as 80 percent.[3] Caterpillar rapidly introduced other new products which incorporated the modular design concept.

In the early 1980s, after 50 years of uninterrupted profits, Caterpillar appeared to be invincible because of its ability to continually introduce technologically superior machines that became the industry standard. The company built the biggest and the best equipment in the world for which customers were willing to pay hefty premiums. Then, during 1982, in the words of past Caterpillar chairman and chief executive officer George Schaefer, "Almost overnight the world changed for us."[4]

The construction industry collapsed. Oil and other commodity prices fell, eliminating demand for Caterpillar equipment in mining, logging, and other heavy equipment markets. The dollar strengthened against the yen, giving Japanese equipment makers, especially Komatsu, an opportunity to aggressively pursue the United States' equipment

---

[3]Donald Eckrich, "Caterpillar Tractor Company," in J. Paul Peter and James H. Donnelly, Jr., *Marketing Management: Knowledge and Skills,* 3rd ed. (Homewood, IL: Richard D. Irwin, 1991), pp. 702–4.

[4]Ronald Henkoff, "This Cat Is Acting Like a Tiger," *Fortune,* December 19, 1988, p. 72.

market with cost advantages of up to 40 percent.[5] If these factors were not enough to disrupt the "profits as usual" pattern at Caterpillar, the United Auto Workers, Caterpillar's largest union, went out on strike for seven months during 1982. After making record profits of $579 million in 1981, the company lost $953 million over the next three years.

Realignment Strategies

Some of Caterpillar's financial problems during the early '80s were a result of management's failure to react to the changing world environment. Caterpillar was increasing its plant capacity at a rate of 5 percent a year as late as 1982, even though expansion in the world heavy-equipment market ended in 1980. In fact, Caterpillar had pursued expansion until less than half of existing capacity was needed. As a result of this overcapacity, the company reduced plant space by one-third, closing 10 plants (8 in the United States) between 1983 and 1987. During this same time period, 28 percent of the company's equity and 40 percent of its labor force, more than 30,000 jobs, were eliminated.[6]

New Products

With the realization that world demand for large heavy equipment would expand only marginally in the future, the company began to consider other market opportunities. The company recognized that it had been ignoring small contractors who did not need such massive equipment, but who represented a growing market segment. The company responded by introducing new multipurpose products for the owner/operator or small construction contractor. These products included tractor mounted backhoes, front-end loaders, and even farm tractors.[7] While Caterpillar has gained market share in these segments quite successfully (11 percent by 1987), these smaller products also have smaller profit margins and more competition from both domestic manufacturers, such as Deere & Company and Tenneco's J. I. Case, and Japanese companies such as Komatsu, Kawasaki, and Kubota.[8]

Price Changes

Because of Caterpillar's leadership position in product quality and innovation, the company was able to obtain a premium price for its equipment. However, when Komatsu began offering comparable equipment at a 40 percent lower price in the early 1980s, Caterpillar was forced to cut prices to match those of a competitor for the first time in its history. The company decided to sacrifice profits to protect market share and ensure the company's long-term survival. Even using this strategy, Caterpillar's North American market share dropped 11 points from 1981 to 1986. Most analysts agree the figures would have been worse had the company not slashed prices and profits in response to its competitors.[9]

In addition, Caterpillar recognized that pricing was just one part of the overall revenue-generating strategy for the corporation. Caterpillar pursued other strategies to generate income. For example, the company capitalized on its recognized strength in distribution of products, and sold logistic services to a variety of corporations including Land Rover and Chrysler.[10]

---

[5]Allan J. Magrath, "Eight Ways to Avoid Marketing Shock," *Sales & Marketing Management,* April 1989, p. 55.

[6]Robert S. Eckley, "Caterpillar's Ordeal: Foreign Competition in Capital Goods," *Business Horizons,* March–April 1989, p. 80.

[7]Henkoff, p. 73.

[8]Kathleen Deveny, "For Caterpillar, the Metamorphosis Isn't Over," *BusinessWeek,* August 31, 1987, p. 73.

[9]Henkoff, p. 72.

[10]Allan J. MaGraph, "Ten Timeless Truths about Pricing," *Journal of Consumer Marketing,* Winter 1991, pp. 5–13.

Production Changes

In response to Japanese competition, Caterpillar also broke with its traditional policy of manufacturing everything it sells. The company's paving equipment, sold under the Cat name, was manufactured by CMI Corp. Caterpillar also began a joint venture with Mitsubishi Heavy Industries Ltd. to make excavation equipment in Japan, as well as light construction equipment and forklifts for the U.S. market. In addition, almost all of the equipment sold with the Caterpillar name in the Pacific Rim was manufactured jointly with Mitsubishi.

Plant with a Future Program

Although Caterpillar was profitable in 1985, management had no illusions about the company's ability to remain profitable for the long term with its historically high cost structure. For this reason, the company decided to concentrate on driving costs down and improving quality standards. To achieve these objectives, Caterpillar completed a massive six-year, $1.2 billion plant modernization program called *Plant with a Future (PWAF)*. At the heart of PWAF were automation, new factory layouts, and continuous work flow. The program meant a complete remake of Caterpillar's tooling and manufacturing methods, as well as a change to global sourcing to achieve the lowest possible costs on components.

The first priority for the Plant with a Future program was to simplify and integrate assembly-line processes. This objective was accomplished using a cell manufacturing concept in which plants and equipment are arranged to process families of components from start to finish. For example, machining, welding, heat treating, and painting might all be functions within a single cell. Work flow is continuous because all cells feed the assembly line just in time. Thus, the entire plant requires just-in-time (JIT) delivery schedules.

For Caterpillar to integrate just-in-time delivery to each cell, computer integrated manufacturing (CIM) was utilized. CIM links self-contained manufacturing cells (independent islands of automation) to a material tooling and information network. The program allows and enhances electronic communication between engineering, logistics, and the factory floor. At the completion of the modernization program, interplant communication flowed through a corporate information center coupled with global marketing and financial databases. All systems, from the plant's host computer to personal computers on the shop floor, were linked—resulting in unprecedented coordination and optimization of all manufacturing functions.

An example of what Plant with a Future accomplished can be found at the East Peoria, Illinois, transmission factory. Modernization took five years and cost $200 million. While workers put together gears and clutch assemblies, construction crews worked to build an underground chamber the size of a high school gymnasium. The chamber became a computer-controlled heat treatment system, just one part of the modernization program that touched every corner of this 20-acre factory. Transmission assembly, formerly performed in five different buildings, has been consolidated under one roof. Nearly every one of the 500 machine tools has been moved or replaced, and all of this modernization was accomplished without slowing down production lines.

Efficiency at the East Peoria plant increased even during modernization. By installing a computerized inventory control system, the time it took to run components through the plant was cut dramatically. The parts for a clutch housing used to take 20 days to assemble and ship under the old system. With the new system, this same process took just four hours. Quality standards were maintained by shifting quality-control responsibilities to the workers themselves. Costs at this plant were expected to drop 19 percent.[11]

---

[11]Henkoff, p. 74.

Company Reorganization

In addition to the plant modernization program, Caterpillar tried to reduce costs and maintain a competitive advantage by restructuring the entire company. In 1990, the company announced a plan to change the company from its functional structure to a modern product orientation. The new matrix revolves around 13 profit centers spread throughout the world. Each profit center is divided into specific product groups and four service divisions. This new structure has streamlined processes to such an extent that the company has been able to eliminate 1,000 positions that were no longer necessary.[12]

Caterpillar's new structure tied the entire company much more closely to its customers. For example, although Caterpillar has always had an impressive global dealer network, the old structure required countless phone calls to multiple functional areas in order to receive assistance from the company. Under the new structure, customers and dealers are able to contact each product group directly. The ability to effectively communicate with dealers and customers enabled Caterpillar to guarantee delivery of replacement parts in 48 hours or there was no charge.

This enhanced ability to communicate directly with customers and dealers enabled Caterpillar to respond to customer suggestions more rapidly, and allowed the company to exploit product niches. Under the new structure, decisions were pushed down to lower level management throughout the company. This simplification of the decision-making chains enabled the company to introduce new models every two years instead of every five as it had under the old system.[13]

Labor Agreements

Caterpillar's responses to foreign competitors and sliding market share in the '80s assumed that personnel, both salaried and hourly, would give full support to each new program. The plant-modernization program and the company's reorganization into strategic profit centers required unequivocal labor support to be successful. Caterpillar assumed personnel support through these changes. The company endured a decade of tumultuous relations with its largest union, the United Auto Workers.

The company weathered two prolonged strikes, a seven-month strike in 1982 and a five-month strike beginning in late 1991. In between these strikes, the company managed to increase its production flexibility by winning union approval to cut the number of union job classifications from 418 to 150 in 1986.

During the 1991 strike, Caterpillar steadfastly refused to accept another "pattern agreement" with the United Auto Workers as it has done since 1950.[14] The company maintained that such pattern agreements provided Japanese competitors with a 25 percent wage cost-advantage. While the union never accepted this position, the strike was broken when Caterpillar announced plans to replace all striking workers. The company hoped to gain productivity increases by avoiding job security clauses that were traditionally part of union contracts.

By breaking the union's strike, Caterpillar had an opportunity to negotiate favorable wage and benefit terms but also had to manage a disgruntled and disheartened workforce. The company, at this writing, has not been able to regain workers' trust. In November 1992, the union cancelled all worker involvement programs. These worker involvement programs

---

[12]Tracy E. Benson, "Caterpillar Wakes Up," *Industry Week,* May 20, 1991, p. 33.

[13]Gary Slutsker, "Cat Claws Back," *Forbes,* February 17, 1992, p. 46.

[14]Pattern bargaining is a potent negotiating tactic for the United Auto Workers, although it was abandoned long ago by unions in other industries like communications and steel. Under pattern bargaining, a union negotiates a new contract with one company and that contract then becomes the pattern for contracts with the company's competitors. In Caterpillar's case, its UAW contract would be patterned on contracts negotiated with both Deere and Tenneco's J. I. Case.

had been a successful and critical part of both the factory modernization and company reorganization programs. At a single plant in Aurora, Illinois, the worker involvement programs had saved the company in excess of $4 million. Now, many workers view these programs as management's attempt to weaken the influence of the UAW at Caterpillar.[15]

Dealers

While Caterpillar substantially changed its manufacturing systems, philosophy, and corporate structure, the company did not change its distribution system. Caterpillar's channel involved a network of independent dealers. Caterpillar's dealer network handled all sales and service worldwide, with the exception of direct sales to the U.S. government, the Soviet Union, and the People's Republic of China. Caterpillar's 215 independent dealers represented an enterprise almost as large as the company itself; it included operating, sales, parts, and service outlets in more than 140 countries, and employed approximately 72,000 people. A typical dealership sold and serviced Caterpillar equipment exclusively and was likely to be in a second- or third-generation affiliation with the company. Caterpillar's dealer network has long been recognized as the strongest in the industry.

In the early '80s, Caterpillar responded to Komatsu's entrance into the U.S. market by capitalizing on the area where it had a strong competitive advantage—its extensive global dealer network. Caterpillar chose to compete with a total product concept by providing the services that customers deemed most important, which included postsales support and responsiveness to equipment malfunction. Typically, the purchaser of industrial equipment can expect to spend three to four times the original investment on repair and maintenance costs over the life of the machine. While equipment breakdown is a normal part of using this equipment, customers expect quick service and replacement parts for machinery; downtime is extremely costly for them. Caterpillar, through its dealers, has been able to provide unequaled postsales service to the end users.

Caterpillar expects its dealers to be experts in the industry in which they compete. The dealers must know which Caterpillar equipment is required by what market segments and how best to reach these market segments in their own territories. Dealers decide on the best marketing strategy to reach potential customers in their territory. Dealers can elect to reach their customers through direct-mail campaigns, electronic media, trade shows, or some unique combination of the above. The company supports each dealer's marketing plans through merchandising plans, inventory plans, and assistance in pricing and advertising.

Caterpillar recognizes that to sustain its competitive advantage in the industry, it must provide an aggressive program of ongoing training and support for its dealers. Caterpillar provides training for dealership personnel, both sales and service, to make them more responsive to the market and to improve total product image. As the company's product line broadens and deepens, it has to ensure that dealers are aware of each new product and its potential market. In 1985, Caterpillar initiated a program known as the *Sales Team Development System (STDS)*. The aim of the program was to provide professional assistance in utilizing all the resources that are available through Caterpillar. The results from STDS were impressive: 80 percent of the participating dealers felt they significantly improved their planning skills, product/technical knowledge, and general marketing sales skills. Dealers participating in the program increased their net revenues by 102 percent during a time of contraction in global markets.[16]

[15]Robert L. Rose and Alex Kotlowitz, "Strife between UAW and Caterpillar Blights Promising Labor Idea," *The Wall Street Journal,* November 23, 1992, Section A: p. 1.

[16]S. Tamer Cavusgil, "The Importance of Distributor Training," *Industrial Marketing Management,* February 1990, p. 5.

Caterpillar also increased its support for dealers through improved information flow and communications. The company modernized its communications capabilities with the purchase of advanced computer equipment that allowed for more accurate record and inventory keeping. During the 1991 strike at Caterpillar's U.S. plants, the ability to communicate effectively with dealers enabled Caterpillar to meet the needs of the majority of customers. Equipment was moved between dealers as needed, and some used equipment was leased to customers until new equipment could be made available. Domestic dealers, who normally received most of their inventory from manufacturing plants in the United States, received equipment from Japan, Belgium, and Brazil to meet their customers' orders. Caterpillar management stated repeatedly that they could not identify a single sale lost due to the strike.[17]

Caterpillar's distinct advantage lies not only in its control of the largest market share in the United States, but also in having the most extensive and competent dealership organization in the industry. Its customer offering goes beyond the equipment to a complete package of unique benefits. Caterpillar was able to break away from the competition because of its stronger distribution network. Caterpillar's dealers compete directly and effectively with competitors' dealers, especially Komatsu's and Deere's, by being able to respond to individual customer needs more effectively.

Competition

Caterpillar is striving to remain the dominant manufacturer in a mature industry that has many competitors. One competitor, Japan's Komatsu, has aggressively pursued Caterpillar for the last decade. Its motto has been "Encircle Cat."[18] Long before the crisis in the early 1980s, management had identified Komatsu as deadly serious in its quest to become the new industry leader. While management had identified the risk, it failed to act upon this information. In 1982, Komatsu began to aggressively pursue market share in the United States. The strong dollar allowed Komatsu to offer prices 40 percent below Caterpillar's prices and still remain profitable.

In 1983, Komatsu continued its aggressive entry into Caterpillar's home market by adding five lines to the crawler tractor and loaders already being sold in the United States. Two years later, the company established a manufacturing plant in Tennessee and bought an old Caterpillar plant in England. In 1988, Komatsu and Dresser formed a 50/50 joint venture for their operations in the United States, Canada, and Latin America. The joint venture combined the two companies' manufacturing, financial, and distribution functions but maintained the companies' separate product lines. The joint venture did not change the dealership network of either company. Komatsu dealers still competed with Dresser dealers in most territories.

Komatsu's surge in the U.S. market slowed in 1987 when it lost its price advantage. Komatsu began to lose market share in the following year, and by 1991 its market share in the United States had fallen from a high of 20 percent to 18 percent. During this same period, Caterpillar increased its market share from 34.5 percent to 36.4 percent.[19]

In addition to losing its price advantage, Komatsu had problems with the Dresser joint venture from the beginning. After the joint venture was established, Dresser executives

[17]Robert L. Rose, "Caterpillar Reports First-Quarter Loss Plays Down Strike," *The Wall Street Journal,* April 23, 1992, Section A: p. 6.

[18]Robert L. Rose and Masayoshi Kanabayashi, "Corporate Focus: Komatsu Throttles Back on Construction Equipment; Japanese Company, Lagging Rival Caterpillar, Eyes Other Areas for Growth," *The Wall Street Journal,* May 13, 1992, Section B: p. 4.

[19]Ibid.

felt left out of decision making, and most U.S. employees could not understand the work ethic or culture of Japanese personnel. Another major problem for the Komatsu-Dresser venture was that the dealers of both companies struggled against each other for sales, instead of focusing on the major competition from Caterpillar dealers. As a solution to this problem, Komatsu-Dresser began encouraging dealers to combine operations and sell both lines of equipment. Currently, over 50 percent of dealers have combined operations. Komatsu-Dresser's 60 independent U.S. and Canadian dealers have a net worth of $300 million. In comparison, Caterpillar's 65 full-line U.S. dealers have a net worth of $1.72 billion.[20]

Komatsu reported its first annual loss of $14.4 million in 1990. It was followed by a $74 million operating loss in 1991. Both of these losses were attributed to low sales volume as a result of a severe recession. Komatsu began to diversify away from construction equipment, which accounted for 63 percent of the company's total sales. Company executives said publicly that they were no longer trying to overtake Caterpillar as industry leader and that Komatsu's future lies in robotics and machine tools. To underline this shift away from construction equipment, the bulldozer was removed from atop the corporate headquarters in Tokyo.[21]

While Komatsu states that it is no longer going head-to-head with Caterpillar, the companies are still arch rivals in all markets. Although Komatsu has lost many of its competitive advantages, the company has been able to maintain a better relationship with blue-collar workers in its North American factories. In addition, its per-unit labor costs are lower than Caterpillar's. In the international market arena, when Caterpillar was constrained by U.S. foreign policy from selling to many former communist countries, Komatsu was able to develop strong trading relationships with them. For example, when Caterpillar was prohibited by the Carter administration from making sales to the Soviet Union, Komatsu was able to provide the necessary equipment.

Major Domestic Competitors

While Caterpillar and Komatsu battle for the number 1 and 2 positions in the heavy equipment market around the world, Caterpillar also competes with a number of domestic manufacturers. These include Deere & Company and Tenneco's J. I. Case in selected product lines. While Deere is more commonly known for its major share of the farm equipment market, it does manufacture and market a line of industrial equipment. Caterpillar has met more competition from Deere & Company since introducing backhoes and front-end loaders for smaller construction companies. These are areas that have traditionally been serviced by Deere and others.

Deere & Company has gone through a turbulent decade much the same as Caterpillar. The company has survived strikes by its largest union and a decade-long slump in its farm-equipment markets. Deere responded by trimming its payroll by 29,000 jobs, which included both salaried and hourly positions. The company restructured and modernized its manufacturing facilities to be able to react more quickly and efficiently to changing customer requirements. Deere expects to compete aggressively in all market segments, but sees its best growth potential in the farm equipment segment of its business.

Tenneco's J. I. Case was primarily a manufacturer of tractors and industrial equipment until it acquired International Harvester and Steiger Tractor Company. Case now has a full line of agricultural equipment and has the number 2 position for the farm equipment market behind Deere & Company. Case competes with Caterpillar primarily in the smaller construction lines and the farm equipment segment.

[20]Kevin Kelly, "A Dream Marriage Turns Nightmarish," *BusinessWeek,* April 29, 1991, p. 94.

[21]Robert L. Rose and Masayoshi Kanabayashi, "Corporate Focus: Komatsu Throttles Back on Construction Equipment; Japanese Company, Lagging Rival Caterpillar, Eyes Other Areas for Growth," *The Wall Street Journal,* May 13, 1992, Section B: p. 4.

International Sales

Caterpillar has traditionally sold approximately 50 percent of its products in countries other than the United States. Sales outside of the United States are projected to increase in the future. Many of Caterpillar's greatest opportunities lie in developing countries that are not able to pay for products in hard currency. Caterpillar established the Caterpillar World Trade Corporation in response to these payment difficulties. The World Trade Corporation negotiates payment for Caterpillar equipment in commodities or other finished goods that are then resold to obtain hard currency.

An example of how the World Trade Corporation facilitates Caterpillar's equipment sales can be seen in a recent sale of mining equipment to a Brazilian corporation. Instead of paying for the equipment in an agreed-upon currency, the Brazilian company traded iron ore for it. Caterpillar's World Trade Corporation sold the iron ore to a company in Hungary for men's suits. These suits were then sold in London for hard currency. Although this is a complex means of receiving payment for construction equipment, it allows Caterpillar to take advantage of opportunities in developing countries.[22]

Africa

Caterpillar is one of the largest exporters to Africa. The company has been successful on this continent because it has exploited the expertise of its local dealers. In addition, the company has been extremely flexible in arranging sales terms. The company will sell to governments under existing international loans programs, or establish long-term leasing arrangements. Countertrade options have also been used with success.[23] The company has met with success on this continent on its own terms. While adopting the local business practices, it will not indulge in bribery or other kickbacks, which are a common means of facilitating business exchanges in many parts of this continent. In the future, Africa is expected to be an area of continued growth for mining equipment because of the continent's mineral wealth.

Brazil

The decline in the company's overall profits during 1990 was due in large part to difficulties in the Brazilian unit. The unit was profitable through 1989 and the first quarter of 1990, but incurred an operating loss for the year overall. The Brazilian government, in March 1990, introduced austerity programs that curtailed government spending and reduced sales volume for Caterpillar. The Brazilian currency weakened substantially, which meant that sales that were finalized translated into fewer dollars for the parent company.[24] In 1991, due to continuing economic turmoil in Brazil, Caterpillar Brasil S.A. announced the planned closing of its facility in São Paulo and the consolidation of all operations in Piracicaba. Business conditions are expected to continue to be affected by political and economic factors in the short term.

Eastern Europe and Countries of the Former Soviet Union

While there are definite opportunities for industrial equipment manufacturers in the countries that made up Eastern Europe and the former Soviet Union, in all these countries some means of payment for imported equipment must be established. Counter-trade arrangements and international loan programs are expected to play a major role in these countries.

---

[22]Taken from speech by Ed Terrel, manager of human resources for Caterpillar Inc., at the University of Wisconsin–Madison, September 23, 1992.

[23]Countertrade options are defined as the selling company accepting commodities in lieu of cash payment. Caterpillar's World Trade Corporation specializes in countertrade options.

[24]James P. Miller, "Caterpillar Shares Tumble as Firm Says Profit Will Drop Substantially in 1990," *The Wall Street Journal,* June 26, 1990, Section C: p. 15.

Caterpillar pursued these opportunities with caution because of continued political instability. The company has tried to extend its distribution network into these countries. However, establishing dealerships in these countries is difficult because most interested parties do not meet Caterpillar's criteria, which include a stable financial position and the ability to do business with Caterpillar in English.

Southeast Asia, China, and Pacific Rim Countries

Caterpillar has been quite successful in pursuing opportunities in these countries. The company has established a special Far East trading company to focus on the opportunities and special problems associated with transacting business in many of these countries. Caterpillar already has a manufacturing plant in Indonesia and has been successful in selling heavy equipment in China. To take advantage of many of these sales, the company has had to establish complex countertrade arrangements. In the future, there should be additional opportunities in Cambodia if the recently signed peace agreement is successful.

Countertrade has not been necessary when dealing with the developed countries of Australia and New Zealand. Caterpillar had been extremely successful in selling equipment, particularly large mining equipment, in these two countries. Recently, environmental concerns in both these countries have reduced sales. In Australia, large new mining developments in the Northern Territory have been rejected because of environmental concerns and complaints from indigenous people. In addition, the government has been prohibiting the expansion of even existing mining operations in all regions of the country.

Caterpillar's Future

Slow growth in the industrial equipment market is projected for the short term because of continued global recession. In the United States, industrial equipment market growth is closely linked to expansion in the national economy. The need to upgrade and maintain the public infrastructure in older cities is expected to increase and stimulate growth in the construction equipment segment of this market. In addition, highway and bridge repair may continue to provide a major source of market demand, as will the continued construction of new power plants and water supply facilities.

Environmental issues are affecting the demand of industrial equipment. Demand for products used primarily in large mining operations will be most affected by the increased awareness of environmental issues. The world's recent focus on the environment has forced many existing mining operations to downsize, and in some countries, mining projects which would utilize industrial equipment are not being approved.

The equipment market is expected to be stimulated by the growing versatility of products in which attachments are designed to be changed quickly. For example, excavators can now be equipped with bucket or rock-breaker attachments for a wide range of applications. In addition, higher productivity is being achieved through computerized power transmissions that automatically control the engine speed and hydraulic output to maximize productivity and achieve fuel savings. These product improvements promote higher product-replacement rates in the near term.[25]

Caterpillar responded to the challenges of the 1980s better than many other U.S. manufacturers. The company made unprecedented changes and learned from previous mistakes. Even with all these changes, the company still recorded losses in recent years and continues to be troubled by severe labor problems. The company must decide whether there is a profitable future for it as a U.S.–based manufacturer of heavy construction equipment and diesel engines.

[25]1991 U.S. Industrial Outlook.

APPENDIX A   Four-Year Financial Summary (Dollars in millions except per share data)*

Years Ended December 31

	1991	1990	1989	1988
Sales and revenues	$ 10,182	$ 11,436	$ 11,126	$ 10,435
Sales	9,838	11,103	10,882	10,255
Percent inside U.S.	41%	45%	47%	50%
Percent outside U.S.	59%	55%	53%	50%
Revenues	344	333	244	180
Profit (loss)	(404)	210	497	616
As a percent of sales and revenue	(4.0%)	1.8%	4.5%	5.9%
Profit (loss) per share of common stock	(4.00)	2.07	4.90	6.07
Dividends per share of common stock	1.05	1.20	1.20	.86
Return on average common stock equity	(9.4%)	4.7%	11.6%	16.0%
Capital expenditures:				
Land, buildings, etc.	653	926	984	732
Equipment leased to others	121	113	105	61
Depreciation and amortization	602	533	471	434
R&E expense	441	420	387	334
As a % of sales and revenue	4.3%	3.7%	3.5%	3.2%
Provision (credit) for income taxes	(152)	78	162	262
Wages, salaries, and employee benefits	3,051	3,032	2,888	2,643
Average number of employees	55,950	59,662	60,784	57,954
Total receivables:				
Trade and other	2,133	2,361	2,353	2,349
Finance	2,145	1,891	1,498	1,222
Inventories	1,921	2,105	2,120	1,986
Total assets:				
Machinery and engines	9,346	9,626	9,100	8,226
Financial products	2,696	2,325	1,826	1,460
Long-term debt due after one year:				
Machinery and engines	2,676	2,101	2,561	1,428
Financial products	1,216	789	491	525
Total debt:				
Machinery and engines	3,136	2,873	2,561	2,116
Financial products	2,111	1,848	1,433	1,144
Ratios—excluding financial products:				
Ratio of current assets to current liabilities	1.74 to 1	1.67 to 1	1.78 to 1	1.76 to 1
Percent of total debt to total debt and stockholders' equity	43.7%	38.8%	36.4%	34.0%

*Data taken from Caterpillar's 1991 Annual Report, pp. 28–29.

APPENDIX B
Caterpillar Product Line

Source: Tabulated from Caterpillar's 1991 Annual Report.

Type of Equipment	Number of Models
Wheel loaders	10
Integrated tool carriers	4
Backhoe loaders	5
Pavement profilers	4
Asphalt pavers	5
Road reclaimer/soil stabilizer	2
Compaction equipment	15
Wheel tractors	3
Compactors	2
Landfill compactors	4
Track loaders	10
Track-type tractors	22
Motor graders	6
Excavators	18
Pipelayers	4
Scrapers	12
Trucks	6
Tractors	4
Articulated trucks	8
Forest machines	4
Skidders	4
Engines	7
Lift trucks	8

Case 3

EMR Innovations

Kay M. Palan, *Iowa State University*

Eric Reynolds stood inside the door to his RV repair shop and surveyed the activities. He and his wife Mary were avid RVers and had combined their love of RVing with business by starting an RV repair business out of their home in 1995. In 1999, the business was large enough to allow them to open their own shop in Amana, Iowa. By 2002, the business had steadily grown, but he and Mary wanted more—they wanted to be "the" supplier of innovative RV products. To that end, they had developed their first product, the Lock-Awn antibillow device for RV patio awnings. In fact, Eric mused, he and Mary had invested about $10,000 of their own money to develop a prototype product. They had even sought assistance from an industry research center located at a nearby university with respect to developing the prototype. Now, in late fall 2003, Eric and Mary had a working prototype, and preliminary feedback from some of their RV repair customers who had seen the product was very positive.

However, even though potential customers seemed to like it, Eric and Mary were unsure about whether or not the Lock-Awn product would be successful. In the last several months, they had become aware of a potential competitor selling a similar product. While Eric and Mary believed the Lock-Awn was superior to the competitor's product, they were uncertain if potential customers would feel the same way. Money was too tight for the Reynolds to risk market entry without a better grasp of the Lock-Awn's market viability.

Mary, who did the bookkeeping for the RV repair shop in between caring for their three children, looked up from her desk and saw Eric. She walked over to him and placed her hand on his shoulder. "What are you thinking about?" she asked.

Eric turned and said, "I just wish I knew for certain if investing more money in the Lock-Awn is the right thing to do. I think we need to know more about how we would actually market it before we can seek additional funding. That manufacturing consultant we've talked with said the next step was to decide on a marketing strategy."

Mary nodded her agreement, stating, "I've been thinking the same thing. I know you've got your hands full with the shop right now, so I'll start reviewing the information we have about customers and competitors and start thinking about how we would market the Lock-Awn. Hopefully, in a few weeks we can make sense of it all and decide on a marketing strategy."

EXHIBIT 1
Estimated Breakdown of RV Ownership

[1] Estimated from data taken from 2001 RVIA industry survey.
[2] Based on 7.5 million estimated households owning RVs in 2002

Type of RV	Estimated ownership[1] (percent)	Estimated number in U.S.[2]
Folding camper trailers	24	1,800,000
Truck campers	5	375,000
Travel trailer (includes fifth-wheel trailers)	47	3,525,000
Class C motorhomes	8	600,000
Class A motorhomes	16	1,200,000

The RV Industry

Recreational vehicles (RVs) were vehicles that combined transportation and temporary living quarters for recreation, camping, and travel. According to Web sites that Mary found (RV Central and RV Hotline Canada), interest in RVs dated back to the early 1900s when nature enthusiasts customized their own vehicles with such accessories as bunks, storage lockers, and cooking capabilities, in order to see the country. When roads began to improve in the 1920s, RV enthusiasm grew and did not diminish during the Depression. After World War II, the RV industry flourished. Enthusiasts could build their own RVs with home kits or could purchase ready-made motor homes. However, it wasn't until the 1960s that the term *RV* was coined as a marketing tool.

By 2000, the RV industry consisted of 135 RV manufacturers and more than 200 suppliers of component parts and services. There were two main RV categories—motorhomes (motorized) and towables (towed behind the family car, van, or pickup). Purchased new, towables were the least expensive. Towables included folding camping trailers, ranging from $5,000 to $10,000, and truck campers, affixed to the bed or chassis of a truck, at an average sticker price of $10,500. Conventional travel trailers, which were also towed, cost about $13,000, while fifth-wheel trailers (towed by a vehicle equipped with a device known as a fifth-wheel hitch) ranged from $25,000 to over $80,000. Motorhomes were considerably more expensive than towables, ranging from $35,000 for Class C motorhomes (built on a van cutaway chassis) to over $500,000 for the most luxurious Class A motorhomes (built on a specially designed motor vehicle chassis).

According to the Recreational Vehicle Industry Association (RVIA), nearly 7.5 million households in the U.S. owned an RV in 2002, and RV sales were expected to hit a 25-year high in 2003. RV shipments, shown in Exhibit 1, had steadily grown, although there were occasional decreases in shipped units that tended to coincide with increases in gasoline prices. Although it was difficult to find hard-and-fast numbers detailing exactly how many of which types of RVs were owned by U.S. households, data from a 2001 survey suggested the breakdown of RV ownership, illustrated in Exhibit 2.

Nonetheless, the economic forecast for the RV industry was positive. There was renewed interest in domestic ground travel in the United States, resulting in more people taking driving vacations than ever before. The aging baby boom generation, which had greater buying power relative to previous generations, was buying more RVs as it neared retirement. Moreover, low interest rates since 2001 encouraged Americans to purchase big-ticket, leisure items.

The RV Culture

According to a 2001 University of Michigan study commissioned by the RVIA, RV enthusiasts were growing in numbers. In 2001, nearly 7 million U.S. households owned an RV, which translated to almost one RV in every 12 households, although the RVIA estimated

EXHIBIT 2
Total RV Shipments:
1986–2002 (Units in
Thousands)

Source: Recreation Vehicle
Industry Association (RVIA),
RVIA Facts, RV Shipments
Data, http://www.rvia.org/
media/ShipmentsData.htm

Year	Shipped Units
1986	189.8
1987	211.7
1988	215.8
1989	187.9
1990	173.1
1991	163.3
1992	203.4
1993	227.8
1994	259.2
1995	247.0
1996	247.5
1997	254.5
1998	292.7
1999	321.2
2000	300.1
2001	256.8
2002	311.0

that there were as many as 30 million RV enthusiasts in the U.S., which included RV renters. Although people of all ages owned RVs, the largest segment was the 55 and older crowd, with about 10 percent of the RVs, closely followed by the 35–54-year-olds, who owned 8.9 percent of the nation's RVs. The fastest growing segment of the RV market was the Baby Boomers. By 2010, the RVIA projected that there would be 8.5 million RV-owning households.

The same University of Michigan study identified the typical RV owner as 49 years old, married, owning his/her own home, and having an annual household income of $56,000. RV owners spent their disposable income on traveling an average of 4,500 miles and 28–35 days annually. The RVIA further noted several reasons why people chose RVs as a way to travel:

- Convenience, flexibility, and freedom to go where they wanted, when they wanted, without having to plan in advance.
- Comfort and amenities of home while on the road or at a campground.
- Enjoyment of traveling together as a family.
- Affordability—even factoring in RV ownership, a family of four spent up to 70 percent less when traveling by RV (according to a cost-comparison study conducted in 2000 by PKF Consulting).
- Accessibility to enjoying outdoor getaways—the beach, mountains, parks, tourist attractions.
- Versatility of vehicle—in addition to traveling, the RV was used for shopping, tailgating, and pursuing special hobbies.

Two-thirds of RV owners purchased a previously owned vehicle. RV owners tended to keep their RVs a long time—nearly 25 percent owned their RVs for 10 or more years. The average age of used RVs when purchased was 11.6 years.

RVers were an adventuresome group. From their own experience in the RV business, Mary knew that some RVers lived full-time on the road, traveling from place to place, absorbing the sights and sounds wherever they happened to be. Many of these people were retired couples who wanted to see the country. Others traveled for part of the year; for example, it was common for retirees in the Midwest to spend spring/summer in the Midwest, and fall/winter in warmer climes. They would use their RV as their residence during the fall and winter months. Still others took a week or two here or there for short vacations. In 2003, Workamper News, an RV publication, estimated that approximately 750,000 Americans lived and worked out of travel trailers, truck campers, or motor homes full-time—it called these people "workampers," individuals motivated to earn a living but without being tied down to either one address or to an employer.

RVers were well connected through a variety of networking groups and forums. In her research, Mary found countless Web sites devoted to members of RV clubs. Members formed clubs based on type of RV ownership (e.g., Gulf Streamers International RV Club), travel and leisure interests (e.g., Happy Camper Club), geographic location (e.g., Carolina Cruisers), or other demographics (e.g., The Handicapped Travel Club). Numerous Web sites were devoted to answering RVers' questions and also featured chat rooms, which encouraged informal networking among RVers.

Regardless of how many months of the year RVers lived on the road or what their specific purpose was, all of them wanted their accommodations to be as comfortable as possible and, Mary knew, were willing to spend money on products that improved their RVs. Dozens of companies manufactured and sold RV gadgets and accessories like auxiliary fuel tanks, power booster equipment, and antisway trailer hitches (RV-Info). Some RVers invented their own gadgets to improve RVs, and then peddled these inventions to other RVers they met on the road. In some instances, this led to substantive businesses. One such RVer, Richard Dahl of Roseburg, Oregon, invented a water filter for RV plumbing systems and subsequently sold the $30 filter, which he manufactured himself, at trailer parks, campgrounds, and motor-home shows. Eventually he expanded his product line to 300 items, created The RV Water Filter Store, and made more than enough to pay for his and his wife's travels, plus $30,000 or so left over each year for fun (Henricks 2003). What Dahl discovered was that RVers were more than willing to purchase accessories like his water filter when they appreciated the benefits.

EMR Innovations

Eric and Mary Reynolds hoped to be as successful as Richard Dahl had been. Being acquainted with RVs through both personal experience and through their repair business, Eric and Mary discovered that most RVs suffered from design flaws. Some were minor inconveniences, but others were dangerous.

One such problem was with patio awnings, which were standard equipment on virtually all RVs, including motor homes, fifth-wheel trailers, and travel trailers. A very small percentage of RVs had motorized awnings, but most RVs had manually operated awnings, which had a propensity to become unwound while the RV was in motion or parked. The awnings, which were 8 feet wide and up to 22 feet long, could billow in the wind, either startling the driver or causing the driver to lose control and cause accidents (Siuru, RV Awning Care). In fact, although Eric could not find specific numbers on exactly how many accidents the billowing problem had caused, he had found several RV Internet forums and chat rooms where the string of discussion focused on the awning billowing problem. Many RVers reported trying to fix the problem with things like duct tape and Velcro. Eric saw an opportunity to create a permanent and practical fix for the many RV owners who still had to deal with the awning problem.

Thus began the idea for EMR Innovations. Eric believed that he could design a product that would lock awnings in place and be affordable. Moreover, he readily identified several other RV design flaws that EMR Innovations could address: sewer hookups, a battery fluid indicator cap, an all-in-one tow tester, an RV essentials toolkit, and a streamlined brake control device. Some of these devices Eric had already designed for use on his own RV while others were just ideas. However, he was certain there was a market for all these products.

Both Eric and Mary thought that the best product to introduce first to the market was the Lock-Awn device. Given RVers' concerns about this problem, it made sense that the product would sell. They had invested $10,000 so far to design and perfect a prototype. In addition, they had invested a lot of their time. However, if they proceeded to introduce the product, they needed an infusion of cash, either from an investor or through a bank loan. Although they did not have a well-formulated business or marketing plan, they roughly estimated that they needed about $200,000 to begin production, distribution and promotion. The local bank estimated that the Reynolds' RV repair business was worth $800,000 to $900,000, so Eric and Mary planned to use that as collateral for a loan if necessary. Their credit history with the bank was excellent, and they had no outstanding debt other than their house mortgage. If they borrowed $200,000 from the bank, Eric and Mary wanted to repay the loan within two years, even though the bank would be willing to give them anywhere from three to seven years, because they just didn't want any debt hanging over their heads any longer than necessary.

Eric and Mary had talked with a nearby manufacturer about producing the Lock-Awn, although they had not formalized any agreement. To begin, they planned to manage EMR Innovations themselves with part-time workers to help with production—Mary would manage inventory and shipping, and Eric would manage sales. However, they thought that eventually, as the business grew, they would hire a full-time office manager and additional help for shipping. This would permit them to focus on marketing and sales, and would free up some of Eric's time to develop new products. However, they knew this would not happen right away. For the first year or two at least, they did not think they would need to hire additional help. The profits from the RV repair business, while not large, were sufficient to maintain their current modest lifestyle and support their involvement in EMR Innovations.

EMR Innovations was just an idea—it was not formalized into any type of organization (e.g., sole proprietorship or subchapter S corporation).

Now in their mid-30s, neither Eric nor Mary had attended college or taken business courses. High school sweethearts, they had married and started their family when they were young. Eric trained and worked as a mechanic and, given his love for RVs, had found it natural to begin an RV repair business. Mary had always been a stay-at-home mom, but had helped Eric by taking on the bookkeeping responsibilities. Now that their youngest child had started kindergarten, Mary found herself with more time to devote to beginning EMR Innovations. What Eric and Mary knew about business was what they had learned by owning the RV repair business, so they felt challenged by all of the details necessary to develop, manufacture, and sell a new product. Mary appreciated that they didn't know everything there was to know about operating a business, but she knew that both she and Eric had common sense, a strong work ethic, and the desire to succeed.

The Lock-Awn Antibillow Device

Manually operated patio awnings on RVs consisted of a long aluminum roller tube with two spring-loaded end-cap assemblies, the awning fabric, a locking cam or ratchet on the front spring, two vertical awning arms, and an awning rod. The awning rod or wand, separately stored, disengaged the awning's locking mechanism. The user pulled a strap attached to the

EXHIBIT 3 Components of the Lock-Awn Anti-Billowing Device

Source: Eric and Mary Reynolds

Figure A.
A catch that attaches to
the awning arm.

Figure B.
A lock rod with spring-loaded
handle.

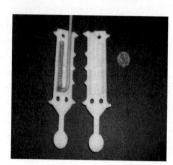

Figure C.
A two-piece roller tube collar.

awning fabric to extend the awning for use. In windy conditions, when the awning was stored or retracted, the force of the wind could cause the locking cam mechanism to fail by overcoming the spring tension. This, in turn, could cause the aluminum cam to break. The aluminum teeth could also become so worn that they no longer held. Or, the lock could break. Any of these scenarios caused the fabric roller tube to come loose, allowing the awning fabric to release and billow in the wind.

The Lock-Awn antibillow device consisted of three main components—a catch that attached to the awning arm, a lock rod with a spring-loaded handle, and a two-piece roller tube collar, shown in Exhibit 3. Eric had designed the spring-loaded handle to keep constant tension on the awning roller tube to minimize friction wear from the wind and road rattle; thus, the Lock-Awn would protect the internal awning mechanisms from wear and tear *and* would prevent billowing. Mary was especially excited because the Lock-Awn replaced the awning rod, which she (and all the RVers she knew) found to be very inconvenient to use and store. The Lock-Awn would operate the awning lock and pull the awning strap when extending the awning for use.

Eric had put great thought and care into designing and developing the Lock-Awn. The device had the following features:

- Heavy-duty injection molded U.V. and weather-resistant collar and handle.
- Nickel-plated steel lock rod.
- Ergonomically designed handle.
- Heavy-duty spring and rivet components.
- A 30-day, 100 percent satisfaction guarantee and a 90-day limited warranty against defects in parts or workmanship.
- Embossed company and product logo on the formed handle with contact information.

Moreover, the Lock-Awn took only a few minutes to install, would work on either the right or left spring assembly of RV awnings, and did not detract from the RV's appearance, as shown in Exhibit 4.

Production costs for the Lock-Awn included a one-time investment of $40,000 for the mold and tooling. In addition, material cost for each unit was $5.95, packaging cost per unit, $0.75, and labor cost per unit, $5.90. Labor cost was calculated by dividing monthly projected part-time payroll costs, including wages and taxes, for part-time production

EXHIBIT 4   **The Lock-Awn Antibillowing Device Installed on an RV**

Source: Eric and Mary Reynolds

workers by estimated Lock-Awn units produced per month. Eric and Mary thought of this as a variable cost because the workers' hours would fluctuate with demand. There would also be costs for packaging and assembly equipment ($3,500), office equipment ($1,000), product liability insurance ($5,000/year), building lease ($1,500/month), utilities (estimated to be $400/month), and standard commercial insurance ($1,000/year). Eric and Mary's time was also worth something, though that was more difficult for them to quantify. Mary figured she would eventually devote about half of her workweek (20 hours) to EMR, and to replace her would cost roughly $300/week. Mary further assumed that Eric would also put in about 20 hours a week into marketing the Lock-Awn, and to replace his time in the RV repair business would be about $600/week.

Eric had considered and rejected patenting the Lock-Awn because he didn't think patent protection was worth the $10,000 investment. He believed they could better protect their competitive advantage by penetrating the market.

Competitors

There were many do-it-yourself homemade versions of awning locks—Eric and Mary found many described on RV Internet chat sites, and they had seen some themselves on their RV travels. As one might expect, the homemade versions varied in sophistication, level of function, attractiveness, and ease of use. The most common homemade "fix" was to use rope to tie up the awning, which people did when their awnings had already been damaged by billowing. More sophisticated versions utilized dog-collar, metal-strap devices to secure the awning. Although some of these homemade devices provided protection, in Eric and Mary's opinion all of the do-it-yourself devices were lacking in some way, either in appearance, ease of installation, or ease of operation.

Eric found one commercial product designed to prevent billowing, the "AwningSaver" which a small company in Texas sold by mail order. The company had first offered the AwningSaver in 2001, but did not distribute it widely. However, some of the RV Internet chatters mentioned they had purchased the product. According to the company's materials, the AwningSaver worked by locking the awning roller tube to the awning arm. The device, shown in Exhibit 5, was permanently clamped to the awning arm, and a brake clamp gripped the roller tube end securely, preventing rotation of the tube. The user opened the brake clamp with the standard awning wand.

Neither Eric nor Mary believed the AwningSaver was a credible threat to the LockAwn. After examining one of the AwningSaver devices themselves, they believed that the product would prevent billowing. But, they found it difficult to operate, contrary to the company's claims, and they thought the AwningSaver had a "homemade" look to it when installed, which Eric and Mary found unappealing. As Mary said, "why would you want to put something that looks cheap on a motor home that cost $100,000?" In addition, Eric and Mary thought the AwningSaver was overpriced—it retailed at $59.95 plus $7.50 for shipping, for an assortment of bolts, nuts, washers, and clamps that could be purchased for under $5 from any hardware store.

Marketing and Distribution of the Lock-Awn

When Mary finished collecting information about RVers and competitors, she began to research information she could use to develop a marketing mix. Mary thought there were three viable distribution channels. First, they could sell the Lock-Awn as a mail-order

EXHIBIT 5
The Awning Saver

Source: www.awningsaver.com

product, much as the AwningSaver, passing the shipping costs on to the buyer. This would require a good Web site and knowledge about how to get the Web site highly ranked on search engines. Neither Eric nor Mary had that knowledge, but Mary thought that perhaps they could use the plethora of RV-related Web sites to direct Internet traffic to a Lock-Awn Web site. Mary contacted a regional company wellknown for its Web site design and management and discovered that a basic five-page Web site design and hosting would cost $600, while search engine optimization would cost a minimum of $1,795 per year. If they wanted customized features on their Web site, the cost could go as high as $2,000–$3,000.

A second possibility was to attract individual dealers from the Workampers group. This group, at 70,000 members, lived full time in their RVs and looked for business opportunities they could conduct from their RVs. "Who better to sell the Lock-Awn to RVers than people who live in their RVs all the time?" thought Mary. They could recruit Workampers through the Workamper publication and Web site (a one-time ad cost $100). They would advance qualified applicants 10 Lock-Awn units on 30-day net terms. EMR would also provide promotional materials and one free display unit for the dealers to install on their own awnings. Workampers would earn a 25 percent margin (a 25 percent discount off the retail price) on each Lock-Awn unit they sold. Mary thought that Workamper dealers could not only make money by selling the Lock-Awn devices, but they could also charge to install the Lock-Awn to earn some additional income. Dealers also had the option to sell the product to retail distributors, such as RV repair shops or campground stores.

EXHIBIT 6 **EMR Sales Projections in Units—Years 1 and 2**

Year 1													
Month	1	2	3	4	5	6	7	8	9	10	11	12	Total Unit Sales
Direct Sales	0	0	0	100	300	400	500	500	600	600	600	600	4,200
Indirect Sales	0	0	0	20	40	100	300	350	500	500	500	500	2,810
Total Sales	0	0	0	120	340	500	800	850	1,100	1,100	1,100	1,100	7,010
Year 2													
Month	1	2	3	4	5	6	7	8	9	10	11	12	Total Unit Sales
Direct Sales	650	650	650	650	650	675	675	675	675	675	675	675	7,975
Indirect Sales	550	550	550	550	550	575	575	575	575	575	575	575	6,775
Total Sales	1,200	1,200	1,200	1,200	1,200	1,250	1,250	1,250	1,250	1,250	1,250	1,250	14,750

Source: Eric and Mary Reynolds

A third distribution method was to use an established distributor that already sold RV accessories, such as Camping World. Camping World was the largest RV after-market retailer in the United States. Mary thought that without a strong sales record, it would be difficult to get Camping World to sell the Lock-Awn. Still, she recognized it as a possibility, if not right away, then at least in the future. Mary was not sure what kind of margin Camping World required, but she assumed that the distributor would dictate the terms, not the Reynolds.

As she considered the distribution options, Mary figured that she and Eric would probably use some combination of direct selling and the Workampers (indirect selling). She also assumed that for the first few months EMR Innovations was officially open, there would be no sales, as they implemented their distribution systems. Mary quickly projected what the sales of the Lock-Awn might be for the first couple of years (Exhibit 6), given that it would take a few months to establish the sales channels and that EMR Innovations was a small company. These projections were very modest, amounting to only 0.02 percent of the entire U.S. RV market (7.5 million households) by the end of the second year. Mary had no idea how many Lock-Awns would be returned under the 30-day satisfaction guarantee or 90-day warranty, but to be safe, she thought maybe a 0.5 percent return rate was a reasonable expectation.

To support selling efforts, Mary knew it was important to increase awareness for the Lock-Awn. She researched several different ways to do this:

- Advertise in popular RV magazines, such as *Motor Home* and *Trailer Life*. The combined circulation of these two publications was 1.5 million. A ⅓ page, black-and-white ad inserted four times would cost $25,000.
- Advertise on RV-related Web sites. Some would include links to other Web sites. Some would include ads on their sites for minimal or no cost.
- Develop promotional brochures detailing the awning billowing problem and the benefits of the Lock-Awn in addressing this problem. They would make the brochures available to dealers and RV parts distributors throughout the country. For high-quality 4-color brochures, design and printing costs would be about $1,500 for 10,000 brochures, according to some printing Web sites Mary consulted.
- Promote and demonstrate the Lock-Awn at RV shows and rallies. These types of shows attracted RV enthusiasts either for the purpose of learning more about RVs or for social

gathering (traveling) with other RVers. Virtually every state had an RV show every year, and numerous rallies were sponsored throughout the company by RV clubs and organizations. Mary estimated that registration and travel costs for each show would be approximately $1,800, and that they could go to four regional shows annually.

- Ask RV trade publications to evaluate and feature the Lock-Awn in new product spotlight columns.
- Generate discussion about the Lock-Awn in RV chat rooms.
- Use the networking systems of RV clubs to spread information about the Lock-Awn device.

Conclusion

Eric and Mary carved some time out of their busy schedules a few weeks later to look at the marketing information Mary had put together. As she summarized her findings, she explained, "We need to decide which RVers are most likely to buy the Lock-Awn. And we have to decide how much we want to charge and how to distribute it. Once we've done that, we should be able to have a better idea about whether or not we can make money selling the Lock-Awn."

Eric was quiet for a moment, sighed, and then replied, "I know the Lock-Awn is a good product, and I think all RV owners should install it on their RVs, but I guess we can't build a business on what I think. So, let's really look at this information and consider our options with respect to how we would market the Lock-Awn."

"Yes," Mary said, "we have to. Otherwise we can't really know if we should do this or not."

Focused on their decision-making task, Mary and Eric began to review the market data piece by piece. Both knew the future of EMR Innovations depended on what the data told them.

References

AwningSaver, retrieved from http://www.awningsaver.com, January 4, 2006.

Henricks, Mark, "RV-Based Businesses Can Be 'Going Concerns,'" *WSJ.com Startup Journal,* October 31, 2003, retrieved from http://www.startupjournal.com/startuplifestyle/20030910-lifestyle.html.

Recreation Vehicle Industry Association, *2001 National Survey of Recreation Vehicle Owners,* 2001, conducted by Dr. Richard Curtin, University of Michigan.

Recreation Vehicle Industry Association (RVIA) RVIA Facts, http://www.rvia.org/media/fastfacts.htm.

Recreation Vehicle Industry Association (RVIA) RVIA Facts, http://www.rvia.org/media/shipmentsdata.htm.

RV Central, RV History, retrieved from http://www.rvcentral.com/rv_history.htm, June 2, 2005.

RVHotlineCanada.com—From Past to Present, retrieved from http://www.rvhotlinecanada.com/rvhistory.asp, June 2, 2005.

RV-Info: Your RV News and Information Portal, RV gadgets and accessories, retrieved from http://www.rv-info.net/rvgadgets.html, February 26, 2006.

Siuru, William D., Jr., "RV Awning Care: Protect this Expensive Investment," *Woman Motorist,* retrieved from http://www.womanmotorist.com/index.php/news/man/3062/event=view, January 4, 2006.

Harley-Davidson, Inc.— Motorcycle Division

J. Paul Peter *University of Wisconsin–Madison*

Harley-Davidson, Inc., is a diversified company with corporate headquarters at 3700 Juneau Avenue, Milwaukee, Wisconsin. Its three major business segments include (1) motorcycles and related products, (2) transportation vehicles including both recreational and commercial vehicles, and (3) defense and other businesses. In 1990, the company experienced another record year of growth. In the *BusinessWeek 1,000* ranking of the top U.S. companies, Harley-Davidson, Inc., with a market value of $515 million, moved from the 973rd to the 865th largest U.S. company. Richard F. Teerlink, president and chief executive officer of the company, offered the following introduction to the company's 1990 annual report:

> Fellow Shareholder: I am again pleased to announce a record year at Harley-Davidson, Inc. in terms of revenues, profits and earnings. I'm especially proud this year because we were able to deliver very impressive results despite the fact that 1990—the third and fourth quarters, especially—was tough on most American manufacturers.
>
> Revenues for 1990 totaled $864.6 million, an increase of 9.3 percent over 1989. Net income was $37.8 million, a 14.8 percent increase and net earnings per share increased 11.0 percent to $2.12. Since 1987, revenues, net income, and net earnings per share have increased 33.8, 78.3, and 29.3 percent, respectively. Considering where we were as recently as five years ago, these are tremendous results.

Indeed, these were tremendous results given that the company is the only U.S. motorcycle manufacturer still in business, although there were once more than 140 competitors. In addition, the company had tremendous difficulties surviving the 1970s and early '80s and few analysts thought it would survive. In fact, the company would have gone bankrupt in 1985 had it not gotten refinancing with only days to spare.

Company Background and Operations

Harley-Davidson was established in 1903 and had a virtual monopoly on the heavyweight motorcycle market by the 1960s.[1] In the early '60s Japanese manufacturers entered the marketplace with lightweight motorcycles that did not directly compete with Harley-Davidson. The influx of the Japanese products backed by huge marketing programs caused the demand for motorcycles to expand rapidly.

Recognizing the potential for profitability in the motorcycle market, American Machine and Foundry (AMF, Inc.) purchased Harley-Davidson in 1969. AMF almost tripled production to 75,000 units annually over a four-year period to meet the increases in demand. Unfortunately, product quality deteriorated significantly as over half the cycles came off the assembly line missing parts and dealers had to fix them up in order to make sales. Little money was invested in improving design or engineering. The motorcycles leaked oil, vibrated, and could not match the excellent performance of the Japanese products. While hard-core motorcycle enthusiasts were willing to fix up their Harleys and modify them for better performance, new motorcycle buyers had neither the devotion nor skill to do so. If Harley-Davidson was to remain in business, it desperately needed to improve quality and update its engine designs. Japanese manufacturers also moved into the heavyweight motorcycle market and began selling Harley look-alike motorcycles. Yamaha was the first company to do so and was soon followed by the three other major Japanese manufacturers, Honda, Suzuki, and Kawasaki. Their products looked so similar to Harley's that it was difficult to tell the difference without reading the name on the gas tank. The Japanese companies also copied the style of the Harley advertisements. As one Harley executive put it, "We weren't flattered."

In late 1975, AMF appointed Vaughn Beals in charge of Harley-Davidson. He set up a quality control and inspection program that began to eliminate the worst of the production problems. However, the cost of the program was high. For example, the company had to spend about $1,000 extra per bike to get the first 100 into shape for dealers to sell at around $4,000. Beals along with other senior managers began to develop a long-range product strategy—the first time the company had looked 10 years ahead. They recognized the need to upgrade the quality and performance of their products to compete with the faster, high-performance Japanese bikes. However, they also recognized that such changes would require years to accomplish and a huge capital investment.

In order to stay in business while the necessary changes in design and production were being accomplished, the executives turned to William G. Davidson, Harley's styling vice president. Known as "Willie G." and a grandson of one of the company founders, he frequently mingled with bikers, and with his beard, black leather, and jeans was well accepted by them. Willie G. understood Harley customers and stated that:

> They really know what they want on their bikes: the kind of instrumentation, the style of bars, the cosmetics of the engine, the look of the exhaust pipes, and so on. Every little piece on a Harley is exposed, and it has to look just right. A tube curve or the shape of a timing case can generate enthusiasm or be a total turnoff. It's almost like being in the fashion business.[2]

Willie G. designed a number of new models by combining components from existing models. These included the Super Glide, the Electra Glide, the Wide Glide, and the Low Rider. Each model was successful and other Harley executives credit Davidson's skill with

---

[1]This section is based on "How Harley Beat Back the Japanese," *Fortune,* September 25, 1989, pp. 155–64.

[2]Ibid., p. 156.

saving the company. One senior executive said of Willie G., "The guy is an artistic genius. In the five years before we could bring new engines on-stream, he performed miracles with decals and paint. A line here and a line there and we'd have a new model. It's what enabled us to survive."

Still, Harley-Davidson was losing market share to its Japanese competitors, who continued to pour new bikes into the heavyweight market. By 1980, AMF was losing interest in investing in the recreational market and decided to focus its effort on its industrial product lines. Since AMF could not find a buyer for Harley-Davidson, it sold the company to 13 senior Harley executives in an $81.5 million leveraged buyout financed by Citicorp on June 16, 1981.

In 1982 things turned worse than ever for Harley-Davidson. Overall demand for motorcycles dropped dramatically and Harley's market share of this smaller market also continued to drop. The company had a large inventory of unsold products and could not continue in business with its level of production and expenses. Production was cut drastically, and more than 1,800 of the 4,000 employees were let go.

The Japanese manufacturers continued producing and exporting to the United States at rates well above what the market could endure. Harley-Davidson was able to prove to the International Trade Commission (ITC) that there was an 18-month finished-goods inventory of Japanese motorcycles that fell well below fair market value and asked for protection. The ITC can offer protection to a U.S. industry being threatened by a foreign competitor. In 1983, President Reagan increased the tariffs on large Japanese motorcycles from 4.4 percent to 49.4 percent, but these would decline each year and be effective for only five years. While this did decrease the imports somewhat and gave Harley some protection, Japanese manufacturers found ways to evade most of the tariffs, for example, by assembling more of their heavyweight bikes in their U.S. plants. Harley-Davidson's market share in the 1983 heavyweight motorcycle market slipped to 23 percent, the lowest ever, although it did earn a slight profit. By 1984, it had sales of $294 million and earned $2.9 million; it has continued to increase sales and profits through the early 1990s.

Manufacturing Changes

From the late 1970s Harley-Davidson executives recognized that the only way to achieve the quality of Japanese motorcycles was to adopt many of the manufacturing techniques they used. The manufacturing systems changes that were instituted included a just-in-time manufacturing program and a statistical operator control system.[3]

The just-in-time manufacturing program was renamed MAN, which stood for Materials As Needed. When the program was discussed with managers and employees at the York, Pennsylvania, manufacturing facility, many of them reacted in disbelief. The York plant already had a modern computer-based control system with overhead conveyors and high-rise parts store and the new system would replace all of this with push carts! However, the MAN system eliminated the mountains of costly parts inventory and handling systems, speeded up set-up time, and could solve other manufacturing problems. For example, parts at the York facility were made in large batches for long production runs. They were stored until needed and then loaded on a 3.5 mile conveyor that rattled endlessly around the plant. In some cases, parts couldn't be found, or when they were, they were rusted or damaged. In other cases, there had been engineering changes since the parts were made and they simply no longer fit. The MAN system consisted of containers that traveled between the place where the parts were made and where they were to be used. The containers served as a

---

[3]This section is based on Thomas Gelb, "Overhauling Corporate Engine Drivers Winning Strategy," *Journal of Business Strategy,* November/December 1989, pp. 8–12.

signal at each end to either "feed me" or "empty me." This system is credited with reducing work-in-process inventory by $22 million.

The statistical operator control (SOC) system allows continuous process improvements to reduce costs. The system involves teaching machine operators to use simple statistics to analyze measurements taken from parts to determine dimensional accuracy and quality. The system helps identify problems that occur during production early enough that they can be corrected before many parts are produced.

Human Resource Changes

In designing the new manufacturing processes, Harley executives recognized the importance of employee involvement.[4] In 1978 the company was among the first in the United States to institute a companywide employee involvement program. Harley-Davidson was the second U.S. company to begin a quality circles program, which permits employees to contribute their ideas, solve problems, and improve the efficiency and quality of their work. Prior to these changes, engineers would figure out how to improve the manufacturing process and then tell operating employees what changes they needed to make. Naturally, the engineering plans were not flawless but the operating employees would not lift a finger to help solve the problems and would simply blame the engineers for screwing up again.

The changes in manufacturing and human resource strategy were credited with a 36 percent reduction in warranty costs; a 46 percent increase in defect-free vehicles received by dealers since 1982; inventory turnover up 500 percent; and productivity per employee up 50 percent.

Marketing Changes

By 1983 Harley executives recognized that they had become too internally oriented and needed to pay greater attention to customers.[5] They recognized that they would not be able to compete effectively with the Japanese manufacturers by offering a complete product line of motorcycles but rather would have to find a niche and defend it successfully. They decided to focus all of their efforts on the superheavyweight motorcycle market (850cc or greater) and adopted a "close-to-the-customer" philosophy. This involved several unique marketing strategies. First, Harley executives actively sought out and discussed motorcycle improvement issues with customers. Second, it started the Harley Owner Group (HOG) to bring together Harley riders and company management in informal settings to expand the social atmosphere of motorcycling. The club is factory sponsored and is open to all Harley owners. It sponsors national rallies and local events and gives customers a reason to ride a Harley and involves them in a social group whose main activities revolve around the product.

Third, it began a Demo Ride program in which fleets of new Harleys were taken to motorcycle events and rallies and licensed motorcyclists were encouraged to ride them. This program was felt to be critical for convincing potential new customers that Harley-Davidson motorcycles were of excellent quality and not the rattling, leaking bikes of the 1970s. The program was renamed SuperRide and $3 million was committed to it. A series of TV commercials was purchased to invite bikers to come to any of Harley's over 600 dealers for a ride on a new Harley. Over three weekends, 90,000 rides were given to 40,000 people, half of whom owned other brands. While sales from the program did not immediately cover costs, many of the riders came back a year or two later and purchased a Harley.

Fourth, the company invited several manufacturing publications to visit the plant and publish articles on quality improvement programs. These articles reached the manufacturing trade audience and the national media as well. Finally, recognizing that many dealers

[4]Ibid.

[5]Ibid.

viewed their business as a hobby and did not know how to sell, the company increased its sales force by 50 percent to give sales representatives more time to train dealers in how to sell Harleys.

Financial Changes

Although Harley-Davidson was improving its quality, reducing its breakeven point, catching up with competitors in the superheavyweight market, and marketing more aggressively, Citicorp was concerned about the economy and what would happen to Harley-Davidson when the tariffs on Japanese bikes were lifted in 1988.[6] The bank decided it wanted to recover its loans and quit being a source of funds for the company. After a number of negotiations, Citicorp took a $10 million write-off which might have facilitated Harley obtaining new financing. However, other bankers felt that the company must have been in really bad shape if Citicorp took a write-off and refused financial assistance. While lawyers were drawing up a bankruptcy plan, Harley executives continued to seek refinancing. Finally, several banks did agree to pay off Citicorp and refinance the company with $49.5 million.

Harley-Davidson went public with a stock sale on the American Stock Exchange in 1986. The company hoped to raise an additional $65 million and obtained over $90 million with the sale of common stock and high-yielding bonds. It then was in an excellent cash position and purchased Holiday Rambler Corporation, at that time the largest privately held recreational vehicle company in the United States. Holiday Rambler is similar to Harley-Davidson in that it is a niche marketer that produces premium-priced products for customers whose lives revolve around their recreational activities. In 1987 the company moved to the New York Stock Exchange and made two additional stock market offerings. Selected financial data for Harley-Davidson is contained in Exhibits 1 through 4.

By 1987, Harley-Davidson was doing so well that it asked to have the tariffs on Japanese bikes removed a year ahead of schedule. On its 85th birthday in 1988, the company held a huge motorcycle rally involving over 40,000 motorcyclists from as far away as San Francisco and Orlando, Florida. All attenders were asked to donate $10 to the Muscular Dystrophy Association and Harley memorabilia was auctioned off. The event raised over $500,000 for charity. The final ceremonies included over 24,000 bikers whose demonstration of product loyalty is unrivaled for any other product in the world.

Motorcycle Division—Early 1990

Exhibit 5 shows the motorcycle division's growth in unit sales. In 1990, Harley-Davidson dominated the superheavyweight motorcycle market with a 62.3 percent share while Honda had 16.2 percent, Yamaha had 7.2 percent, Kawasaki had 6.7 percent, Suzuki had 5.1 percent, and BMW had 2.5 percent. Net sales for the division were $595.3 million with parts and accessories accounting for $110 million of this figure. Production could not keep up with demand for Harley-Davidson motorcycles although a $23 million paint center at the York, Pennsylvania plant was nearing completion and would increase production to 300 bikes per day.[7]

Approximately 31 percent of Harley-Davidson's 1990 motorcycle sales were overseas. The company worked hard at developing a number of international markets. For example, anticipating the consolidation of Western European economies in 1992, a European parts and accessories warehouse was established in Frankfurt, Germany, in 1990. After

[6]Ibid.
[7]Harley-Davidson, Inc. Annual Report 1990, p. 12.

EXHIBIT 1   Harley-Davidson, Inc., Selected Financial Data (In thousands, except share and per share amounts)

	1990	1989	1988	1987	1986
Income statement data:					
Net sales	$864,600	$790,967	$709,360	$645,966	$295,322
Cost of goods sold	635,551	596,940	533,448	487,205	219,167
Gross profit	229,049	194,027	175,912	158,761	76,155
Selling, administrative, and engineering	145,674	127,606	111,582	104,672	60,059
Income from operations	83,375	66,421	64,330	54,089	16,096
Other income (expense):					
Interest expense, net	(9,701)	(14,322)	(18,463)	(21,092)	(8,373)
Lawsuit judgment	(7,200)	—	—	—	—
Other	(3,857)	910	165	(2,143)	(388)
	(20,758)	(13,412)	(18,298)	(23,235)	(8,761)
Income from continuing operations before income taxes and extraordinary items	62,617	53,009	46,032	30,854	7,335
Provision for income taxes	24,309	20,399	18,863	13,181	3,028
Income from continuing operations before extraordinary items	38,308	32,610	27,169	17,673	4,307
Discontinued operation, net of tax	—	3,590	(13)	—	—
Income before extraordinary items	38,308	36,200	27,156	17,673	4,307
Extraordinary items	(478)	(3,258)	(3,244)	3,542	564
Net income	$ 37,830	$ 32,942	$ 23,912	$ 21,215	$ 4,871
Weighted average common shares outstanding	17,787,788	17,274,120	15,912,624	12,990,466	10,470,460
Per common share:					
Income from continuing operations	$ 2.15	$ 1.89	$ 1.70	$ 1.36	$ 0.41
Discontinued operation	—	0.21	—	—	—
Extraordinary items	(.03)	(.19)	(.20)	0.28	0.05
Net income	$ 2.12	$ 1.91	$ 1.50	$ 1.64	$ 0.46
Balance sheet data:					
Working capital	$ 50,152	$ 51,313	$ 74,904	$ 64,222	$ 38,552
Total assets	407,467	378,929	401,114	380,872	328,499
Short-term debt, including current maturities of long-term debt	23,859	26,932	33,229	28,335	18,090
Long-term debt, less current maturities	48,339	74,795	135,176	178,762	191,594
Total debt	72,198	101,727	168,405	207,097	209,684
Stockholders' equity	198,775	156,247	121,648	62,913	26,159

In December 1986, the company acquired Holiday Rambler Corporation. Holiday Rambler Corporation's results of operations are not included in the income statement data for 1986.

Source: Harley-Davidson, Inc., Annual Report 1990, p. 29.

entering a joint venture in 1989 with a Japanese distributor, the company bought out all rights for distribution in Japan in 1990. Revenue from international operations grew from $40.9 million in 1986 to $175.8 million in 1990.

Product Line

For 1991, Harley-Davidson offered a line of 20 motorcycles shown in Exhibit 6. Other than the XLH Sportster 883 and XLH Sportster 883 Hugger which had chain drives, all models were belt driven; all models had a five-speed transmission. Three of the Sportster models had an

EXHIBIT 2   Harley-Davidson, Inc., Consolidated Statement of Income (in thousands except per share amounts)

Years Ended December 31	1990	1989	1988
Net sales	$864,600	$790,967	$709,360
Operating costs and expenses:			
Cost of goods sold	635,551	596,940	533,448
Selling, administrative, and engineering	145,674	127,606	111,582
	781,225	724,546	645,030
Income from operations	83,375	66,421	64,330
Interest income	1,736	3,634	4,149
Interest expense	(11,437)	(17,956)	(22,612)
Lawsuit judgment	(7,200)	—	—
Other-net	(3,857)	910	165
Income from continuing operations before			
provision for income taxes and extraordinary items	62,617	53,009	46,032
Provision for income taxes	24,309	20,399	18,863
Income from continuing operations before extraordinary time	32,610	27,169	38,308
Discontinued operation, net of tax:			
Income (loss) from discontinued operation	—	154	(13)
Gain on disposal of discontinued operation	—	3,436	—
Income before extraordinary items	38,308	36,200	27,156
Extraordinary items:			
Loss on debt repurchases, net of taxes	(478)	(1,434)	(1,468)
Additional cost of 1983 AMF settlement, net of taxes	—	(1,824)	(1,776)
Net income	$ 37,830	$ 32,942	$ 23,912
Earnings per common share:			
Income from continuing operations	$ 2.15	$ 1.89	$ 1.70
Discontinued operation	—	.21	—
Extraordinary items	(.03)	(.19)	(.20)
Net income	$ 2.12	$ 1.91	$ 1.50

Source: Harley-Davidson, Inc., Annual Report 1990, p. 34.

883cc engine and one had a 1200cc engine; all of the remaining models had a 1340cc engine. The first five models listed in Exhibit 6 were touring models while the remaining bikes were standard and cruising types. All of the models exhibited impressive painting and classic styling attributes visually reminiscent of Harley-Davidson motorcycles from the '50s and '60s.

Motorcycle magazine articles commonly were favorable toward Harley-Davidson products but pointed out weaknesses in various models. For example, a review of the XLH Sportster 1200 in the December 1990 edition of *Cycle* reported that

> But Harley undeniably has its corporate finger on the pulse of Sportster owners, and knows what they want. All of the complaints—poor suspension, high-effort brakes, awkward riding position, short fuel range, engine vibration, and poor seat—have echoed through the halls of 3700 Juneau Ave. for more than a decade, yet have had seemingly little effect on XL sales. H-D sold 24,000 Sportsters over the past two years, and these complaints have been common knowledge to anyone who's cared enough to listen.[8]

The article, however, was very complimentary of the newly designed engine and new five-speed transmission and concluded that "This is the best Sportster ever to roll down an assembly line."

A review of the same model in *Cycle World's 1991 Motorcycle Buyer's Guide* pointed out a number of the same problems but concluded,

[8]"Harley-Davidson 1200 Sportster," *Cycle,* December 1990, p. 90.

EXHIBIT 3   **Harley-Davidson, Inc., Consolidated Balance Sheet (In thousands except share amounts)**

December 31	1990	1989
Assets		
Current assets:		
Cash and cash equivalents	$ 14,001	$ 39,076
Accounts receivable, net of allowance for doubtful accounts	51,897	45,565
Inventories	109,878	87,540
Deferred income taxes	14,447	9,682
Prepaid expenses	6,460	5,811
Total current assets	196,683	187,674
Property, plant and equipment, net	136,052	115,700
Goodwill	63,082	66,190
Other assets	11,650	9,365
	$407,467	$378,929
Liabilities and Stockholders' Equity		
Current liabilities:		
Notes payable	$ 22,351	$ 22,789
Current maturities of long-term debt	1,508	4,143
Accounts payable	50,412	40,095
Accrued expenses and other liabilities	72,260	69,334
Total current liabilities	146,531	136,361
Long-term debt	48,339	74,795
Other long-term liabilities	9,194	5,273
Deferred income taxes	4,628	6,253
Commitments and contingencies (Note 6)		
Stockholders' equity:		
Series A Junior Participating preferred stock, 1,000,000 shares authorized, none issued	—	—
Common stock, 18,310,000 and 9,155,000 shares issued in 1990 and 1989, respectively	183	92
Additional paid-in capital	87,115	79,681
Retained earnings	115,093	77,352
Cumulative foreign currency translation adjustment	995	508
	203,386	157,633
Less:		
Treasury stock (539,694 and 447,091 shares in 1990 and 1989, respectively), at cost	(771)	(112)
Unearned compensation	(3,840)	(1,274)
Total stockholders' equity	198,775	156,247
	$407,467	$378,929

Source: Harley-Davidson, Inc., Annual Report 1990, p. 33.

Yet the bike's appeal is undeniable. A stab at the starter button rumbles it into instant life, and as the engine settles into its characteristically syncopated idle, the bike is transformed into one of the best platforms anywhere from which to Just Cruise. And that means everything from cruising your immediate neighborhood to cruising (with appropriate gas and rest stops) into the next state.

This the bike is more than willing to do, with its premium tires and seemingly bullet-proof reliability. The important thing is to not ask the Sportster 1200 to be something it isn't. What it is, is a Sportster, much as Sportsters always have been.

This is merely the best one yet.[9]

[9]"Harley-Davidson Sportster 1200—Improving on Tradition," *Cycle World 1991 Motorcycle Buyer's Guide,* April–May 1991, p. 27.

EXHIBIT 4   **Harley-Davidson, Inc., Business Segments and Foreign Operations**

A. Business Segments (in thousands)			
	1990	**1989**	**1988**
Net sales:			
Motorcycles and related products	$595,319	$495,961	$397,774
Transportation vehicles	240,573	273,961	303,969
Defense and other businesses	28,708	21,045	7,617
	$864,000	$790,967	$709,360
Income from operations:			
Motorcycles and related products	$ 87,844	$ 60,917	$ 49,688
Transportation vehicles	825	12,791	20,495
Defense and other businesses	2,375	2,236	755
General corporate expenses	(7,699)	(9,523)	(6,608)
	83,375	66,421	64,330
Interest expense, net	(9,701)	(14,322)	(18,463)
Other	(11,057)	910	165
Income from continuing operations before provision for income taxes and extraordinary items	$ 62,617	$ 53,009	$ 46,032

	Motorcycles and Related Products	Transportation Vehicles	Defense and Other Businesses	Corporate	Consolidated
1988					
Identifiable assets	$180,727	$215,592	$2,863	$1,932	$401,114
Depreciation and amortization	10,601	6,958	3	396	17,958
Net capital expenditures	14,121	6,693	66	29	20,909
1989					
Identifiable assets	192,087	176,813	7,018	3,011	378,929
Depreciation and amortization	9,786	7,282	1,125	1,814	20,007
Net capital expenditures	18,705	3,524	1,190	200	23,619
1990					
Identifiable assets	220,656	177,498	7,163	2,150	407,467
Depreciation and amortization	13,722	6,925	1,166	618	22,431
Net capital expenditures	34,099	2,547	1,257	490	38,393

There were no sales between business segments for the years ended December 31, 1990, 1989, and 1988.

B. Foreign Operations			
	1990	**1989**	**1988**
Assets	$25,853	$18,065	$ 6,557
Liabilities	17,717	15,814	3,761
Net sales	82,811	39,653	22,061
Net income	5,555	2,281	1,941

Export sales of domestic subsidiaries to nonaffiliated customers were $93.0 million, $75.4 million and $56.8 million in 1990, 1989, and 1988, respectively.

Source: Harley-Davidson, Inc., Annual Report 1990, p. 43.

EXHIBIT 5
Harley-Davidson Motorcycle Unit Sales 1983–1990

Source: Adapted from Harley-Davidson, Inc., Annual Report 1990, p. 20.

Year	Total Units	Domestic Units	Exports Units	Export Percentage
1990	62,458	43,138	19,320	30.9
1989	58,925	43,637	15,288	25.9
1988	50,517	38,941	11,576	22.9
1987	43,315	34,729	8,586	19.8
1986	36,735	29,910	6,825	18.6
1985	34,815	29,196	5,619	16.1
1984	39,224	33,141	6,083	15.5
1983	35,885	31,140	4,745	13.2

EXHIBIT 6
Harley-Davidson, Inc., 1991 Product Line and Suggested Retail Prices

Source: Adapted from *Cycle World 1991 Motorcycle Buyer's Guide*, pp. 76–82.

Model	Suggested Retail Price
FLTC Tour Glide Ultra Classic	$13,895
FLHTC Electra Glide Ultra Classic	$13,895
FLTC Tour Glide Classic	$11,745
FLHTC Electra Glide Classic	$11,745
FLHS Electra Glide Sport	$10,200
FXDB Sturgis	$11,520
FLSTC Heritage Softail Classic	$11,495
FLSTF Fat Boy	$11,245
FXSTS Springer Softail	$11,335
FXSTC Softail Custom	$10,895
FXLR Low Rider Custom	$10,295
FXRT Sport Glide	$10,595
FXRS Low Rider Convertible	$10,445
FXRS SP Low Rider Sport Edition	$10,295
FXRS Low Rider	$10,195
FXR Super Glide	$ 8,995
XLH Sportster 1200	$ 6,095
XLH Sportster 883 Deluxe	$ 5,395
XLH Sportster 883 Hugger	$ 4,800
XLH Sportster 883	$ 4,395

Pricing

The suggested retail prices for 1991 Harley-Davidson motorcycles are also shown in Exhibit 6. These products were premium-priced although the low-end XLH Sportster 883 and XLH Sportster 883 Hugger were less so in order that new motorcyclists could buy them and then trade up at a later time to larger, more expensive models. In fact, in 1987 and 1988, the company offered to take any Sportster sold in trade on a bigger Harley-Davidson at a later time.

The prices for Harleys can be compared with competitive products.[10] For example, the three 1991 Honda Gold Wing touring models with larger 1520cc engines had suggested retail prices of $8,998, $11,998 and $13,998. A Harley look-alike, the Kawasaki Vulcan 88, had a 1470cc engine and a suggested retail selling price of $6,599; a Kawasaki Voyager XII with a 1196cc engine had a suggested retail selling price of $9,099. Another Harley look-alike, the Suzuki Intruder 1400, had a 1360cc engine and a suggested retail selling price of

[10]All prices are taken from the same reference as footnote 9.

$6,599. The Yamaha Virago 1100, another Harley look-alike, had a 1063cc engine and also had a suggested retail selling price of $6,599.

Promotional Activities

Kathleen Demitros, vice president of marketing for the Motorcycle Division, discussed a problem in designing advertising for Harley-Davidson motorcycles:

> One of the problems was that we had such a hard-core image out there that it was turning off a lot of people, even though people basically approved of Harley-Davidson. We had to find a way to balance our image more, without turning it into 'white bread' and making it bland. Our goal was to get as close to our Harley riders as possible and communicate with them very personally.[11]

In addition to print advertising in general magazines, and Harley's own quarterly magazine, called *Enthusiast,* Harley has its own catalogs with full color pictures and descriptions of each model and discussions of Harley-Davidson products. For example, following is an excerpt from the 1991 Harley-Davidson catalog:

> To the average citizen, it's a motorcycle. To the average motorcyclist, it's a Harley. To the Harley owner, it's something else entirely, something special. Once you've got your Harley, it's much more than a piece of machinery or a way to get around. In a sense, it actually owns you. It occupies you even when you're not riding it. It's part of your life. And while you might not ever be able to explain it to anyone who doesn't know, you know; the trip certainly doesn't end after the road does. Different? Most wouldn't have it any other way.

In 1990 the Harley Owner Group had 650 chapters and 134,000 members with expected growth in 1991 of 15 percent and an additional 55 chapters.[12] In addition to national, regional, and state rallies and other events, meetings between HOG members and Harley management continued to provide suggestions for product improvements. HOG groups have "adopted" various scenic highways and have taken responsibility for their upkeep. In the 10 years Harley-Davidson and its owner groups have been involved, they have raised over $8.6 million for the Muscular Dystrophy Association.

Dealer Improvements

Several years earlier Harley-Davidson instituted a Designer Store program to improve the appearance, image, and merchandising of its products at the retail level. By the end of 1990, more than 310 of the company's 851 domestic and international motorcycle dealerships had completed major store renovation projects or had agreed to do them in 1991. Some dealers reported receiving full return on the renovation investment within 12 to 18 months due to increased sales brought about by a more inviting shopping environment.

Market Information

The traditional U.S. motorcyclist is an 18- to 24-year-old male.[13] Since 1980, the number of men in this age group has declined from 42.4 million to 35.3 million. By 2000 the number is expected to be only slightly higher, at 36.1 million. Women are buying motorcycles in increasing numbers and sales to them have doubled. However, they still account for only 6 percent of the total motorcycles purchased. Motorcycle manufacturers have responded to this market, however, by designing bikes that are lower slung and easier for

[11]Kate Fitzgerald, "Kathleen Demitros Helps Spark Comeback at Harley-Davidson," *Advertising Age,* January 8, 1990, p. 3.

[12]This discussion is based on Harley-Davidson, Inc., Annual Report 1990, pp. 15–26.

[13]This discussion is based on Doron P. Levin, "Motorcycle Makers Shift Tactics," *The New York Times,* September 16, 1989.

EXHIBIT 7 U.S. Motorcycle Market Shares for Major Manufacturers

Source: R. L. Polk & Co., as reported in "That 'Vroom!' You Hear Is Honda Motorcycles," *BusinessWeek,* September 3, 1990, p. 74.

Company	1985	1987	1989
Honda	58.5	50.8	28.9
Yamaha	15.5	19.8	27.7
Kawasaki	10.2	10.2	15.6
Suzuki	9.9	11.6	14.2
Harley-Davidson	4.0	6.3	13.9

women to ride. The Harley-Davidson XLH Sportster 883 Hugger was designed in part for this market.

The sale of motorcycles, including three- and four-wheel off-road vehicles, peaked in 1984 at 1,310,240 units. Five years later sales had dropped to 483,005 units. Sales dropped in all categories, although dirt bikes had the largest sales losses. Sales of larger motorcycles, which tend to be purchased by older buyers for use on highways, represented 12.2 percent of sales in 1984 but increased to 21.3 percent of sales five years later.

As less affluent young men have drifted away from motorcycling, the sport has been taken up by professionals and businesspeople in their 40s and 50s. Likely, the late Malcolm S. Forbes, motorcycle enthusiast and wealthy magazine publisher, influenced this market which is older, more conservative, and often rides long distances with their spouses on luxury vehicles.

There is some evidence that many motorcycle owners do not use their bikes very often, some only for a ride or two in the summer. Although the number of fatal accidents involving motorcycles declined 9 percent in a recent year, this decrease was likely because of decreased usage. The Insurance Institute for Highway Safety reported that in a crash, a person was 17 times more likely to die on a motorcycle than in a car.

Competition

Exhibit 7 shows changes in overall market share percentages for the five major competitors in the U.S. motorcycle market.[14] Honda clearly lost the greatest share and its sales decreased from $1.1 billion in fiscal 1985 to $230 million in fiscal 1990. However, motorcycle sales represent less than 1 percent of Honda's worldwide revenues.

Honda's plan to battle its sagging sales involved the introduction of more expensive, technologically advanced bikes. However, with an increase in the value of the yen from 250 to the dollar in 1987 to 120 by 1988, all Japanese competitors had to raise prices. Honda had to raise its prices even more to cover its expensive new models and became less price competitive. In fact, nearly 600 Honda motorcycle dealers went out of business since 1985, leaving the company with 1,200 dealers in North America. Honda's Maryville, Ohio, plant had so much excess capacity that executives considered transforming much of it to production of auto parts.

Honda's 1990 strategy included cutting back prices and a $75 million advertising campaign to reintroduce the "wholesome" angle of cycling to reach new market segments. Promotional emphasis was also given to encouraging Americans to use motorcycles for commuting as an alternative to cars as is done in Europe and the Far East. High levels of air pollution, increased traffic, and rising fuel costs supported Honda's strategy. The advertising campaign was oriented less to selling individual products than to selling the idea that motorcycling is fun. Honda also offered free rides in shopping malls, sponsored races, and paid for Honda buyers to be trained at Motorcycle Safety Centers throughout the country.

[14]This discussion is based on "That 'Vroom!' You Hear Is Honda Motorcycles," *BusinessWeek,* September 3, 1990, pp. 74, 76.

In 1991, Honda's motorcycle product line included 25 models with displacements from 49 to 1520cc's including sportbikes, touring, cruisers, standards, and dual purpose types. It also included four models of four-wheel all terrain vehicles (ATVs). Kawasaki's line included 23 motorcycle models in a variety of types and 4 four-wheel models. Suzuki offered 24 models of motorcycles and 8 four-wheel models. Yamaha offered 25 motorcycle models and 7 four-wheel models. Other smaller competitors in the U.S. market included ATK, BMW, Ducati, Husqvarna, KTM, and Moto Guzzi.

The Future

Rich Teerlink and the other Harley executives have much to be proud of in bringing back the company to a profitable position. However, they must also plan for the future, a future that is uncertain and fraught with problems. For example, the company faces much larger, well-financed competitors in the industry. The company faces increasing legislation on motorcycle helmet use and noise abatement laws that could decrease industry sales.

The company clearly recognizes the fact that the motorcycle industry has contracted greatly since the mid-1980s. It faces the problem of judging how much to increase supply of Harley-Davidson motorcycles given that it is a mature product whose future is uncertain. It faces decisions concerning how much should be invested in such an uncertain market and what marketing approaches are the most appropriate given this situation.

Case 5

PepsiCo in 2007: Strategies to Increase Shareholder Value

John E. Gamble *University of South Alabama*

PepsiCo was the world's largest snack and beverage company with 2006 net revenues of approximately $35 billion. The company's portfolio of businesses in 2007 included Frito-Lay salty snacks, Quaker Chewy granola bars, Pepsi soft drink products, Tropicana orange juice, Lipton Brisk tea, Gatorade, Propel, SoBe, Quaker Oatmeal, Cap'n Crunch, Aquafina, Rice-A-Roni, Aunt Jemima pancake mix, and many other regularly consumed products. Gatorade, Propel, Rice-A-Roni, Aunt Jemima, and Quaker Oats products were added to PepsiCo's arsenal of brands through the $13.9 billion acquisition of Quaker Oats in 2001. The acquisition was the final component of a major portfolio restructuring initiative that began in 1997. Since the restructuring, the company had consistently increased value delivered to its shareholders through share price appreciation and growth in dividends. A summary of PepsiCo's financial performance is shown in Exhibit 1. Exhibit 2 tracks PepsiCo's market performance between 1997 and March 2007.

In 2007, the company's top managers were focused on sustaining the impressive performance that had been achieved since its restructuring through strategies keyed to product innovation, close relationships with distribution allies, international expansion, and strategic acquisitions. Newly introduced products generated an additional $1 billion in sales during 2006 and had accounted for 15 percent to 20 percent of all new growth in recent years. New product innovations that addressed consumer health and wellness concerns were the greatest contributors to the company's growth with PepsiCo's better-for-you and good-for-you products accounting for 15 percent of its 2006 snack sales in North America, 70 percent of net beverage revenues in North America during 2006, and 55 percent of its 2006 sales of Quaker Oats products in North America. The company also planned to increase the percentage of healthy snacks in markets outside North America since consumers in most developed countries wished to reduce their consumption of saturated fats, cholesterol, trans fats, and simple carbohydrates.

The company's Power of One retailer alliance strategy had been in effect for nearly 10 years and was continuing to help boost PepsiCo's volume and identify new product formulations desired by consumers. Under the Power of One strategy, PepsiCo marketers and

EXHIBIT 1   **Financial Summary for PepsiCo, Inc., 1997–2006 (in millions, except per share amounts)**

	2006	2005	2004	2003	2002	2001	2000	1999	1998	1997
Net revenue	$35,137	$32,562	$29,261	$26,971	$25,112	$23,512	$20,438	$20,367	$22,348	$20,917
Net income	5,642	4,078	4,212	3,568	3,000	2,400	2,183	2,050	1,993	1,491
Income per common share—basic, continuing operations	$3.42	$2.43	$2.45	$2.07	$1.69	$1.35	$1.51	$1.40	$1.35	$0.98
Cash dividends declared per common share	$1.16	$1.01	$0.85	$0.63	$0.60	$0.58	$0.56	$0.54	$0.52	$0.49
Total assets	29,930	31,727	27,987	25,327	23,474	21,695	18,339	17,551	22,660	20,101
Long-term debt	2,550	2,313	2,397	1,702	2,187	2,651	2,346	2,812	4,028	4,946

Source: PepsiCo 10-Ks, various years.

EXHIBIT 2

Monthly Performance of PepsiCo, Inc.'s Stock Price, 1997 to March 2007

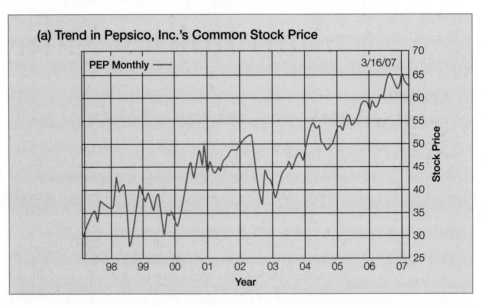

(a) Trend in Pepsico, Inc.'s Common Stock Price

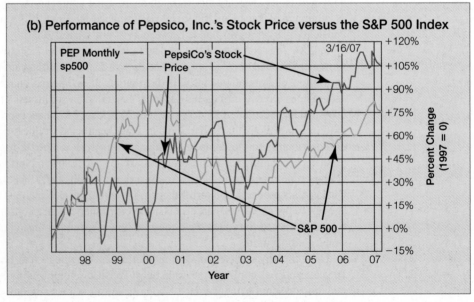

(b) Performance of Pepsico, Inc.'s Stock Price versus the S&P 500 Index

retailers collaborated in stores and during offsite summits to devise tactics to increase consumers' tendency to purchase more than one product offered by PepsiCo during a store visit. In addition, some of PepsiCo's most successful new products had been recommended by retailers.

PepsiCo's international sales had grown by 14 percent during 2006 and by 15% between 2004 and 2005, but the company had many additional opportunities to increase sales in markets outside North America. The company held large market shares in many international markets for beverages and salty snacks, but it had been relatively unsuccessful in making Quaker branded products available outside the United States. In 2006, 75 percent of Quaker Oats' international sales of $500 million was accounted for by just six countries.

For the most part, PepsiCo's strategies seemed to be firing on all cylinders in early 2007. If the company's current growth rates were sustained, projected free cash flows of approximately $15 billion would be generated between 2007 and 2009. PepsiCo had made only $1.2 billion in acquisitions between 2003 and 2005, which had allowed it to pay $4 billion in dividends and complete an $8 billion share buyback plan during that time. Going forward PepsiCo management would need to consider what strategy changes were still needed and how to best use its operating cash flows to further build shareholder value.

Company History

PepsiCo, Inc. was established in 1965 when Pepsi-Cola and Frito-Lay shareholders agreed to a merger between the salty snack icon and soft drink gaint. The new company was founded with annual revenues of $510 million and such well-known brands as Pepsi-Cola, Mountain Dew, Fritos, Lay's, Cheetos, Ruffles, and Rold Gold. PepsiCo's roots can be traced to 1898 when New Bern, North Carolina pharmacist, Caleb Bradham, created the formula for a carbonated beverage he named Pepsi-Cola. The company's salty snacks business began in 1932 when Elmer Doolin of San Antonio, Texas, began manufacturing and marketing Fritos corn chips and Herman Lay started a potato chip distribution business in Nashville, Tennessee. In 1961, Doolin and Lay agreed to a merger between their businesses to establish the Frito-Lay Company.

During PepsiCo's first five years as a snack and beverage company, it introduced new products such as Doritos and Funyuns, entered markets in Japan and Eastern Europe, and opened, on average, one new snack food plant per year. By 1971, PepsiCo had more than doubled its revenues to reach $1 billion. The company began to pursue growth through acquisitions outside snacks and beverages as early as 1968, but its 1977 acquisition of Pizza Hut significantly shaped the strategic direction of PepsiCo for the next 20 years. The acquisitions of Taco Bell in 1978 and Kentucky Fried Chicken in 1986 created a business portfolio described by Wayne Calloway (PepsiCo's CEO between 1986 and 1996) as a balanced three-legged stool. Calloway believed the combination of snack foods, soft drinks, and fast food offered considerable cost sharing and skills transfer opportunities and he routinely shifted managers between the company's three divisions as part of the company's management development efforts.

PepsiCo also strengthened its portfolio of snack foods and beverages during the 1980s and 1990s with acquisitions of Mug Root Beer, 7-Up International, Smartfood ready-to-eat popcorn, Walker's Crisps (UK), Smith's Crisps (UK), the Mexican cookie company Gamesa, and Sunchips. Calloway also added quick service restaurants Hot-n-Now in 1990, California Pizza Kitchens in 1992, and East Side Mario's, D'Angelo Sandwich Shops, and Chevy's Mexican Restaurants in 1993. The company expanded beyond carbonated beverages with a 1992 agreement with Ocean Spray to distribute single-serving juices, the introduction of Lipton ready-to-drink (RTD) teas in 1993, and the introduction of Aquafina bottled water and Frappucino ready-to-drink coffees in 1994.

By 1996 it had become clear to PepsiCo management that the potential strategic fit benefits existing between restaurants and PepsiCo's core beverage and snack businesses were difficult to capture. In addition, any synergistic benefits achieved were more than offset by the fast food industry's fierce price competition and low profit margins. In 1997, CEO Roger Enrico spun off the company's restaurants as an independent, publicly traded company to focus PepsiCo on food and beverages. Soon after the spin-off of PepsiCo's fast food restaurants was completed, Enrico acquired Cracker Jack, Tropicana, Smith's Snackfood Company in Australia, SoBe teas and alternative beverages, Tasali Snack Foods (the leader in the Saudi Arabian salty snack market) and the Quaker Oats Company.

The Quaker Oats Acquisition

At $13.9 billion, Quaker Oats was PepsiCo's largest acquisition and gave it the number 1 brand of oatmeal in the U.S. with a greater than 60 percent category share; the leading brand of rice cakes and granola snack bars; and other well known grocery brands such as Cap'n Crunch, Rice-A-Roni, and Aunt Jemima. However, Quaker's most valuable asset in its arsenal of brands was Gatorade.

Gatorade was developed by University of Florida researchers in 1965, but was not marketed commercially until the formula was sold to Stokley-Van Camp in 1967. When Quaker Oats acquired the brand from Stokely-Van Camp in 1983, Gatorade gradually made a transformation from a regionally distributed product with annual sales of $90 million to a $2 billion powerhouse. Gatorade was able to increase sales by more than 10 percent annually during the 1990s, with no new entrant to the isotonic beverage category posing a serious threat to the brand's dominance. PepsiCo, Coca-Cola, France's Danone Group, and Swiss food giant Nestlé all were attracted to Gatorade because of its commanding market share and because of the expected growth in the isotonic sports beverage category. PepsiCo became the successful bidder for Quaker Oats and Gatorade with an agreement struck in December 2000, but would not receive U.S. Federal Trade Commission (FTC) approval until August 2001. The FTC's primary concern over the merger was that Gatorade's inclusion in PepsiCo's portfolio of snacks and beverages might give the company too much leverage in negotiations with convenience stores and ultimately force smaller snack food and beverage companies out of convenience store channels. In its approval of the merger, the FTC stipulated that Gatorade with PepsiCo's soft drinks could not be jointly distributed for 10 years.

Acquisitions after 2001

After the completion of the Quaker Oats acquisition in August 2001, the company focused on integration of Quaker Oats' food, snack, and beverage brands into the PepsiCo portfolio. The company made a number of small, "tuck-in" acquisitions such as Stacey's bagel and pita chips, Izze carbonated beverages, Netherlands-based Duyvis nuts, and Star Foods (Poland) in 2006. Tuck-in acquisitions made during the first quarter of 2007 included Naked Juice fruit beverages and New Zealand's Bluebird snacks. Acquisitions in 2006 totaled $522 million, while PepsiCo had made acquisitions totaling $1.1 billion in 2005. The largest acquisition in 2005 was the $750 million acquisition of Generals Mills' minority interest in Snack Ventures Europe. The company's management sought to identify additional small, fast-growing food and beverage companies in the United States and internationally that could broaden its portfolio of brands. The combination of acquisitions with PepsiCo's core snacks and beverages business had allowed the company's revenues to increase from approximately $20 billion in 2000 to more than $35 billion in 2006. Exhibit 3 presents PepsiCo's consolidated statements of income for 2004–2006. The company's balance sheets for 2005–2006 are provided in Exhibit 4. The company's calculation of management operating cash flow for 2004–2006 is shown in Exhibit 5.

EXHIBIT 3   PepsiCo, Inc.'s Consolidated Statements of Income, 2004–2006 (in millions, except per share amounts)

	2006	2005	2004
Net Revenue	$35,137	$32,562	$29,261
Cost of sales	15,762	14,176	12,674
Selling, general and administrative expenses	12,774	12,314	11,031
Amortization of intangible assets	162	150	147
Restructuring and impairment charges	—	—	150
Operating profit	6,439	5,922	5,259
Bottling equity income	616	557	380
Interest expense	(239)	(256)	(167)
Interest income	173	159	74
Income from continuing operations before income taxes	6,989	6,382	5,546
Provision for income taxes	1,347	2,304	1,372
Income from continuing operations	5,642	4,078	4,174
Tax benefit from discontinued operations	—	—	38
Net Income	$5,642	$4,078	$4,212
Net income per common share—Basic			
Continuing operations	$3.42	$2.43	$2.45
Discontinued operations	—	—	0.02
Total	$3.42	$2.43	$2.47
Net income per common share—Diluted			
Continuing operations	$3.34	$2.39	$2.41
Discontinued operations	—	—	0.02
Total	$3.34	$2.39	$2.44

Source: PepsiCo, Inc., 2006 10-K.

EXHIBIT 4   PepsiCo, Inc.'s Consolidated Balance Sheets, 2005–2006 (in millions, except per share amounts)

	December 30, 2006	December 31, 2005
ASSETS		
Current Assets		
Cash and cash equivalents	$1,651	$1,716
Short-term investments	1,171	3,166
Accounts and notes receivable, net	3,725	3,261
Inventories	1,926	1,693
Prepaid expenses and other current assets	657	618
Total Current Assets	$9,130	$10,454
Property, Plant and Equipment, net	9,687	8,681
Amortizable Intangible Assets, net	637	530
Goodwill	4,594	4,088
Other nonamortizable intangible assets	1,212	1,086
Nonamortizable intangible assets	5,806	5,174
Investments in Noncontrolled Affiliates	3,690	3,485
Other assets	980	3,403
Total Assets	$29,930	$31,727
LIABILITIES AND SHAREHOLDERS' EQUITY		
Current liabilities		
Short-term obligations	$274	$2,889
Accounts payable and other current liabilities	6,496	5,971
Income taxes payable	90	546
Total Current Liabilities	6,860	9,406

(*continued*)

EXHIBIT 4   PepsiCo, Inc.'s Consolidated Balance Sheets, 2005–2006 (concluded)

	December 30, 2006	December 31, 2005
Long-term debt obligations	2,550	2,313
Other liabilities	4,624	4,323
Deferred income taxes	528	1,434
Total Liabilities	**$14,562**	**$17,476**
Commitments and contingencies		
Preferred stock, no par value	41	41
Repurchased preferred stock	(120)	(110)
Common shareholders' equity		
Common stock, par value 1²/₃¢ per share (issued 1,782 shares)	30	30
Capital in excess of par value	584	614
Retained earnings	24,837	21,116
Accumulated other comprehensive loss	(2,246)	(1,053)
	23,205	20,707
Less: repurchased common stock, at cost (144 and 126 shares, respectively)	(7,758)	(6,387)
Total Common Shareholders' Equity	**$15,447**	**$14,320**
Total Liabilities and Shareholders' Equity	**$29,930**	**$31,727**

Source: PepsiCo, Inc., 2006 10-K.

EXHIBIT 5   Net Cash Provided By PepsiCo's Operating Activities, 2004–2006

	2006	2005	2004
Net cash provided by operating activities	$6,084	$5,852	$5,054
Capital spending	(2,068)	(1,736)	(1,387)
Sales of property, plant and equipment	49	88	38
Management operating cash flow	$4,065	$4,204	$3,705

Source: PepsiCo, Inc 2006 10-K.

Building Shareholder Value in 2007

Three people had held the position of CEO since the company began its portfolio restructuring in 1997. Even though Roger Enrico was the chief architect of the business lineup as it stood in 2007, his successor Steve Reinemund and Indra Nooyi, the company's CEO in 2007, were both critically involved in the restructuring. Indra Nooyi joined PepsiCo in 1994 and developed a reputation as a tough negotiator who engineered the 1997 spin-off of Pepsi's restaurants, spearheaded the 1998 acquisition of Tropicana, and played a critical role in the 1999 IPO of Pepsi's bottling operations. After being promoted to chief financial officer, Nooyi, was also highly involved in the 2001 acquisition of Quaker Oats. Indra Nooyi was selected as the company's CEO upon Reinemund's retirement in October 2006. Indra Nooyi emigrated to the United States in 1978 to attend Yale's Graduate School of Business and worked with Boston Consulting Group, Motorola, and Asea Brown Boveri before arriving at PepsiCo in 1994.

In 2007 PepsiCo's corporate strategy had diversified the company into salty and sweet snacks, soft drinks, orange juice, bottled water, ready-to-drink (RTD) teas and coffees, purified and functional waters, isotonic beverages, hot and ready-to-eat breakfast cereals, grain-based products, and breakfast condiments. Many PepsiCo brands had achieved number 1 or number 2 positions in their respective food and beverage categories through strategies keyed to product innovation, close relationships with distribution allies, international expansion, and strategic acquisitions. A relatively new element of PepsiCo's corporate strategy was product reformulations to make snack foods and beverages less unhealthy. The company believed its efforts to develop good-for-you (GFY) or better-for-you (BFY) products would create growth opportunities from the intersection of business and public interests.

The company was organized into four business divisions, which all followed the corporation's general strategic approach. Frito-Lay North America manufactured, marketed, and distributed such snack foods as Lay's potato chips, Doritos tortilla chips, Cheetos cheese snacks, Fritos corn chips, Quaker Chewy granola bards, Grandma's cookies, and Smartfood popcorn. PepsiCo's North American beverage business manufactured, marketed, and sold beverage concentrates, fountain syrups, and finished goods under such brands as Pepsi, Gatorade, Tropicana, Lipton, Dole, and SoBe. PepsiCo International manufactured, marketed, and sold snacks and beverages in approximately 200 countries outside the United States. Quaker Foods North America manufactured and marketed cereals, rice and pasta dishes, and other food items that were sold in supermarkets. A full listing of Frito-Lay snacks, PepsiCo beverages, and Quaker Oats products is presented in Exhibit 6. Selected financial information for PepsiCo's four divisions is presented in Exhibit 7.

EXHIBIT 6   PepsiCo, Inc.'s Snack, Beverage, and Quaker Oats Brands, 2007

Frito-Lay Brands	PepsiCo Beverage Brands	Quaker Oats Brands
• Lay's potato chips	• Pepsi-Cola	• Quaker Oatmeal
• Maui Style potato chips	• Mountain Dew	• Cap'n Crunch cereal
• Ruffles potato chips	• Mountain Dew AMP energy drink	• Life cereal
• Doritos tortilla chips	• Mug	• Quaker 100% Natural cereal
• Tostitos tortilla chips	• Sierra Mist	• Quaker Squares cereal
• Santitas tortilla chips	• Slice	• Quisp cereal
• Fritos corn chips	• Lipton Brisk (Partnership)	• King Vitaman cereal
• Cheetos cheese flavored snacks	• Lipton Iced Tea(Partnership)	• Quaker Oh's! Cereal
• Rold Gold pretzels & snack mix	• Dole juices and juice drinks (License)	• Mother's cereal
• Funyuns onion flavored rings	• FruitWorks juice drinks	• Quaker grits
• Go Snacks	• Aquafina purified drinking water	• Quaker Oatmeal-to-Go
• Sunchips multigrain snacks	• Frappuccino ready-to-drink coffee (Partnership)	• Aunt Jemima mixes & syrups
• Sabritones puffed wheat snacks	• Starbucks DoubleShot (Partnership)	• Quaker rice cakes
• Cracker Jack candy coated popcorn	• SoBe juice drinks, dairy, and teas	• Quaker rice snacks (Quakes)
• Chester's popcorn	• SoBe energy drinks (No Fear and Adrenaline Rush)	• Quaker Chewy granola bars
• Grandma's cookies	• Gatorade	• Quaker Dipps granola bars
• Munchos potato crisps	• Propel	• Rice-A-Roni side dishes
• Smartfood popcorn	• Tropicana	• Pasta Roni side dishes
• Baken-ets fried pork skins	• Tropicana Twister	• Near East side dishes
• Oberto meat snacks	• Tropicana Smoothie	• Puffed Wheat
• Rustler's meat snacks	• Izze	• Harvest Crunch cereal
• Churrumais fried corn strips	• Naked Juice	• Quaker Baking Mixes
• Frito-Lay nuts	***Outside North America***	• Spudz snacks
• Frito-Lay, Ruffles, Fritos and Tostitos dips & salsas	• Mirinda	• Crisp'ums baked crisps
• Frito-Lay, Doritos and Cheetos snack crackers	• 7UP	• Quaker Fruit & Oatmeal bars
• Fritos, Tostitos, Ruffles and Doritos snack kits	• Pepsi	• Quaker Fruit & Oatmeal Bites
• Hickory Sticks		• Quaker Fruit and Oatmeal Toastables
• Hostess Potato		• Quaker Soy Crisps
		• Quaker Bakeries

(continued)

EXHIBIT 6   **PepsiCo, Inc.'s Snack, Beverage, and Quaker Oats Brands, 2007 (concluded)**

Frito-Lay Brands	PepsiCo Beverage Brands	Quaker Oats Brands
• Lay's Stax potato crisps	• Kas	*Outside North America*
• Miss Vickie's potato chips	• Teem	• FrescAvena beverage powder
• Munchies snack mix	• Manzanita Sol	• Toddy chocolate powder
• Stacy's Pita Chips	• Paso de los Toros	• Toddynho chocolate drink
• Flat Earth Fruit and Vegetable	• Fruko	• Coqueiro canned fish
Chips	• Evervess	• Sugar Puffs cereal
Outside North America	• Yedigun	• Puffed Wheat
• Bocabits wheat snacks	• Shani	• Cruesli cereal
• Crujitos corn snacks	• Fiesta	• Hot Oat Crunch cereal
• Fandangos corn snacks	• D&G (License)	• Quaker Oatso Simple hot cereal
• Hamka's snacks	• Mandarin (License)	• Scott's Porage Oats
• Niknaks cheese snacks	• Radical Fruit	• Scott's So Easy Oats
• Quavers potato snacks	• Tropicana Touche de Lait	• Quaker Bagged cereals
• Sabritas potato chips	• Alvalle gazpacho fruit juices and	• Quaker Mais Sabor
• Smiths potato chips	vegetable juices	• Quaker Oats
• Walkers potato crisps	• Tropicana Season's Best juices and	• Quaker oat flour
• Gamesa cookies	juice drinks	• Quaker Meu Mingau
• Doritos Dippas	• Loóza juices and nectars	• Quaker cereal bars
• Sonric's sweet snacks	• Copella juices	• Quaker Oatbran
• Wotsits corn snacks	• Frui'Vita juices	• Corn goods
• Red Rock Deli		• Magico chocolate powder
• Kurkure		• Quaker Vitaly Cookies
• Smiths Sensations		• 3 Minutos Mixed Cereal
• Cheetos Shots		• Quaker Mágica
• Quavers Snacks		• Quaker Mágica con Soja
• Bluebird Snacks		• Quaker Pastas
• Duyvis Nuts		• Quaker Frut

Source: Pepsico.com

Frito-Lay North America

In 2006, Frito-Lay brands accounted for 31 percent of the PepsiCo's total revenues and 51 percent of the company's profits. Frito-Lay also accounted for nearly 50 percent of the snack food industry's total sales in the United States, which had grown by 3 percent annually since 2000 to reach $24.6 billion in 2005. Three key trends that were shaping the industry were convenience, a growing awareness of nutritional content of snack foods, and indulgent snacking. A product manager for a regional snack producer explained, "Many consumers want to reward themselves with great-tasting, gourmet flavors and styles . . . The indulgent theme carries into seasonings as well. Overall, upscale, restaurant-influenced flavor trends are emerging to fill consumers' desires to escape from the norm and taste snacks from a wider, often global, palate."[1] Most manufacturers had developed new flavors of salty snacks such as jalapeño and cheddar tortilla chips and pepper jack potato chips to attract the interest of indulgent snackers. Manufacturers had also begun using healthier oils when processing chips and had expanded lines of baked and natural salty snacks to satisfy the demands of health conscious consumers. Snacks packaged in smaller bags also addressed overeating concerns and were, in addition, convenient to take along on an outing. In 2007 Frito-Lay owned the top-selling chip brand in each U.S. salty snack category and held nearly a two-to-one lead over

[1]As quoted in "Snack Attack," *Private Label Buyer,* August 2006, p. 26.

EXHIBIT 7   Selected Financial Data for PepsiCo, Inc.'s Business Segments, 2004–2006 (in millions)

Net Revenues

	2006	2005	2004
Frito-Lay North America	$10,844	$10,322	$9,560
Pepsi Bottling North America	9,565	9,146	8,313
Pepsi International	12,959	11,376	9,862
Quaker Foods North America	1,769	1,718	1,526
Total division	35,137	32,562	29,261
Corporate	—	—	—
Total	$35,137	$32,562	$29,261

Operating Profit

	2006	2005	2004
Frito-Lay North America	$2,615	$2,529	$2,389
Pepsi Bottling North America	2,055	2,037	1,911
Pepsi International	1,948	1,607	1,323
Quaker Foods North America	554	537	475
Total division	7,172	6,710	6,098
Corporate	(733)	(788)	(689)
	6,439	5,922	5,409
Restructuring and impairment charges	—	—	(150)
Total	$6,439	$5,922	$5,259

Capital Expenditures

	2006	2005	2004
Frito-Lay North America	$499	$512	$469
Pepsi Bottling North America	492	320	265
Pepsi International	835	667	537
Quaker Foods North America	31	31	33
Total division	1,857	1,530	1,304
Corporate	211	206	83
Total	$2,068	$1,736	$1,387

Total Assets

	2006	2005	2004
Frito-Lay North America	$5,969	$5,948	$5,476
Pepsi Bottling North America	6,567	6,316	6,048
Pepsi International	11,274	9,983	8,921
Quaker Foods North America	1,003	989	978
Total division	24,813	23,236	21,423
Corporate	1,739	5,331	3,569
Investments in bottling affiliates	3,378	3,160	2,995
Total	$29,930	$31,727	$27,987

Depreciation and Other Amortization

	2006	2005	2004
Frito-Lay North America	$432	$419	$420
Pepsi Bottling North America	282	264	258
Pepsi International	478	420	382
Quaker Foods North America	33	34	36
Total division	1,225	1,137	1,096
Corporate	19	21	21
Total	$1,244	$1,158	$1,117

(*continued*)

EXHIBIT 7   **Selected Financial Data for PepsiCo, Inc.'s Business Segments, 2004 – 2006 (in millions) (concluded)**

Amortization of Other Intangible Assets

	2006	2005	2004
Frito-Lay North America	$9	$3	$3
Pepsi Bottling North America	77	76	75
Pepsi International	76	71	68
Quaker Foods North America	—	—	1
Total division	162	150	147
Corporate	—	—	—
Total	$162	$150	$147

Source: PepsiCo, Inc., 2006 10-K.

then next largest snack food maker in the United States. The table below presents shares of the U.S. convenience food market for leading manufacturers in 2006. Convenience foods include chips, pretzels, ready-to-eat popcorn, crackers, dips, snack nuts & seeds, candy bars, cookies, and other sweet snacks.

Manufacturer	Market Share
PepsiCo	21%
Kraft Foods	12
Hershey	9
Kellogg	6
Master Foods	5
General Mills	2
Procter & Gamble	1
Private Label	7
Others	37
Total	100%

Note: The share information shown above excludes data from certain retailers such as Wal-Mart that do not report data to Information Resources, Inc. and A.C. Nielsen Corporation.
Source: PepsiCo, Inc. 2006 10-K.

Frito-Lay North America's (FLNA) revenues increased 5 percent during 2006 as a result of double-digit growth in sales of SunChips, Quaker Rice Cakes, and multipacks of other products. FLNA's better-for-you (BFY) and good-for-you (GFY) snacks also grew at double-digit rates during 2006 and represented 15 percent of the division's total revenue. Sales of Lay's and Doritos branded products declined slightly between 2005 and 2006. In 2007, improving the performance of the division's core salty brands and further developing health and wellness products were key strategic initiatives. The company had eliminated trans fats from all Lay's, Fritos, Ruffles, Cheetos, Tostitos, and Doritos varieties and was looking for further innovations to make its salty snacks more healthy. The company had introduced Lay's Classic Potato Chips cooked in sunflower oil that retained Lay's traditional flavor, but contained 50 percent less saturated fat. The company had also developed new multigrain and flour tortilla Tostitos varieties that appealed to indulgent snackers and were healthier than traditional Tostitos. Other new indulgent Doritos flavors included Fiery Habanero and Blazin' Buffalo & Ranch. FLNA had also expanded the number of flavors of SunChips to sustain the brand's double-digit growth. New SunChips flavors included Garden Salsa and Cinnamon Crunch. SunChips were also introduced in 100-calorie minipacks and 20-bag multipacks.

PepsiCo's 2006 acquisition of Flat Earth fruit and vegetable snacks offered an opportunity for the company to exploit consumers' desires for healthier snacks and address a deficiency in most diets. Americans, on average, consumed only about 50 percent of the U.S. Department of Agriculture's recommended daily diet of fruits and vegetables. Flat Earth

Cheddar, Tangy Tomato Ranch, Garlic Herb Garden Veggie Crisps and Peach Mango, Apple Cinnamon, Wild Berry Fruit Crisps were all launched in February 2007. Other GFY snacks included Stacy's Pita Chips, which was also acquired in 2006, and Quaker Chewy Granola Bars. In 2007, Stacy's Pita Chips came in Multigrain, Cinnamon Sugar, Whole Wheat, and Simply Cheese flavors. Quaker Chewy Granola Bars had achieved a number 2 rank in the segment with a 25 percent market share in 2006. Some of the success of Quaker Chewy Granola products was related to product innovations such as reduced calorie oatmeal and raisin bars. PBNA also distributed Quaker Rice Cakes, which had added chocolate drizzled and multigrain varieties in 2006.

PepsiCo Beverages North America

PepsiCo was the largest seller of liquid refreshments in the United States with a 26 percent share of the market in 2006. Coca-Cola was the second-largest nonalcoholic beverage producer with a 23 percent market share. Cadbury Schweppes and Nestle were the third and fourth largest beverage sellers in 2006 with market shares of 10 percent and 8 percent, respectively. Like Frito-Lay, PepsiCo's beverage business contributed greatly to the corporation's overall profitability and free cash flows. In 2006, PepsiCo Beverages North America (PBNA) accounted for 27 percent of the corporation's total revenues and 39 percent of its profits. Revenues for PBNA had increased by 7.5 percent annually between 2004 and 2006 as the company broadened its line of noncarbonated beverages like Gatorade, Tropicana fruit juices, Lipton ready-to-drink tea, Propel, Aquafina, Dole fruit drinks, Starbucks cold coffee drinks, and SoBe. Carbonated soft drinks (CSDs) were the most consumed type of beverage in the United States in 2006, with a 50.9 percent of share of the stomach, but carbonated soft drink volume declined by 1.1 percent between 2005 and 2006 as consumers searched for healthier beverage choices. In contrast, noncarbonated beverages grew by 7 percent and bottled water grew by 8 percent between 2005 and 2006. The table below presents U.S. liquid refreshment beverage volume and volume share by beverage category in 2006.

Beverage Category	Millions of Gallons		Volume Share	
	2005	2006	2005	2006
Carbonated soft drinks	15,271.6	15,103.6	52.9%	50.9%
Bottled water	7,537.1	8,253.1	26.1%	27.8%
Fruit beverages	4,119.0	4,020.1	14.3%	13.5%
Isotonic sports drinks	1,207.5	1,348.8	4.2%	4.5%
Ready-to-drink tea	555.9	701.5	1.9%	2.4%
Energy drinks	152.5	227.4	0.5%	0.8%
RTD coffee	38.9	43.0	0.1%	0.1%
Total	28,882.5	29,697.5	100.0%	100.0%

Source: Beverage Marketing Corporation.

PepsiCo's Carbonated Soft Drinks Business

During the mid-1990s, it looked as if Coca-Cola would dominate the soft drink industry, with every Pepsi-Cola brand except Mountain Dew losing market share to Coca-Cola's brands. Coca-Cola's CEO at the time, Roberto Goizueta, had stated that the company's strategic intent was to control 50 percent of U.S. cola market by 2000 and seemed convinced PepsiCo could do little to stop the industry leader. Goizueta summed up his worries about Pepsi as a key rival in an October 28, 1996 *Fortune* article entitled "How Coke Is Kicking Pepsi's Can" by saying "As they've become less relevant, I don't need to look at them very much anymore."

Pepsi-Cola management engineered a dramatic comeback in the late-1990s and early-2000s by launching new brands like Sierra Mist and new flavors of existing brands such as Mountain Dew Code Red and focused on strategies to improve local distribution. Among

Pepsi's most successful strategies to build volume and share in soft drinks was its Power of One strategy that attempted to achieve the synergistic benefits of a combined Pepsi-Cola and Frito-Lay envisioned by shareholders of the two companies in 1965. PepsiCo had found that even though Frito-Lay and Pepsi-Cola products were consumed together 58 percent of the time, they were purchased together only 22 percent of the time. The Power of One strategy called for supermarkets to place Pepsi and Frito-Lay products side by side on shelves. Roger Enrico visited the CEOs of the 25 largest supermarket chains to encourage their companies to participate in the plan, citing research finding that supermarket profit margins on PepsiCo's products were typically 9 percent, compared with an average profit margin of 2 percent on other items sold by supermarkets. In addition, Enrico stressed that PepsiCo products accounted for only 3 percent of supermarket sales, but 20 percent of retailers' cash flows. By 2001 Power of One and other PepsiCo strategies allowed Pepsi-Cola to draw within two percentage points of market leader Coca-Cola. In 2006, PepsiCo added "Innovation Summits" to its Power of One program whereby retailers could share their views on consumer shopping and eating habits. PepsiCo used the information gleaned from the summits in developing new products like SoBe Life Water and Lay's Potato Chips cooked in sunflower oil.

In 2007, PBNA was attempting to reinvent carbonated diet soft drinks as energy boosting drinks to better appeal to health conscious consumers, since market research had found that 43 percent of consumers wanted drinks that would invigorate them. Diet Mountain Dew's energy-boosting properties had helped its volume increase by 8.5 percent during 2006 and PBNA added Diet Pepsi Max energy drink to its product line in 2007. The company also expanded the Mountain Dew line in 2006 to include Mountain Dew Amp energy drinks. SoBe Essential Energy beverages were also launched in 2006.

The company was attempting to develop new types of sweeteners for its soft drinks that would lower their calorie content of nondiet drinks. PepsiCo also planned a packaging redesign for Diet Pepsi in 2007 and planned to launch as many as 35 new designs for Pepsi cans, bottles, cartons, vending machines, and fountain cups during the year. The company also hoped its 2006 acquisition of Izze lightly carbonated sparkling fruit drinks would prove popular with consumers. Tava was an additional sparking beverage PBNA scheduled for a U.S. launch in 2007.

PepsiCo's Noncarbonated Beverage Brands

Although carbonated beverages made up the largest percentage of PBNA's total beverage volume, much of the division's growth was attributable to the success of its noncarbonated beverages. In 2006, total case volume for the division increased by 4 percent, which was driven by a 14 percent increase in noncarbonated beverages. Carbonated soft drink volume declined by 2 percent during 2006.

Aquafina was the number 1 brand of bottled water in the United States and grew by 21.9 percent between 2005 and 2006. Bottled water was a particularly attractive segment for PepsiCo since U.S. bottled water consumption had from increased 4.6 billion gallons in 1999 to 6.8 billion gallons in 2004. PepsiCo's Frappucino RTD coffee and Lipton RTD teas made it the leader in the RTD tea and RTD coffee categories as well. The RTD tea category grew by 26.2 percent between 2005 and 2006, while RTD coffees grew by 10.4 percent during 2006. New flavors like Doubleshot Light and Italian Roast Iced Coffee were expected to contribute further growth for Starbucks RTD coffees. PBNA also introduced Starbucks RTD coffee vending machines in 2006.

In 2007, PBNA's Propel Fitness Water was the leading brand of functional water. In 2006, the company had also introduced SoBe Life Water and functional versions of Aquafina. The product lines for its water business were developed around customer type and lifestyle. Propel was a flavor and vitamin-enriched water marketed to physically active consumers, while Life Water was a vitamin-enhanced water that was marketed to image-driven consumers. The company targeted mainstream water consumers with unflavored Aquafina, Aquafina

FlavorSplash (offered in four flavors) and Aquafina Sparkling (a zero-calorie, lightly carbonated citrus or berry flavored water). Aquafina Alive was launched in 2007 and included vitamins and natural fruit juices. The company's strategy involved offering a continuum of healthy beverages from unflavored Aquafina to nutrient-rich Gatorade. In 2006, Gatorade, Propel, and Aquafina were all number 1 in their categories with market shares of 80 percent, 34 percent, and approximately 14 percent, respectively.

Gatorade's volume had grown by 21 percent in 2005 and by 12 percent in 2006 to reach sales of over $3 billion. Gatorade's impressive growth had come about through the introduction of new flavors, new container sizes and designs, new multipacks, world-class advertising, and added points of distribution. Analysts believed that Gatorade could achieve even stronger performance once the FTC's 10-year prohibition on bundled beverage contracts with retailers and joint Gatorade–soft drink distribution came to an end. Gatorade's broker-distribution system also allowed Tropicana and Lipton RTD teas to double sales volume between the 2001 acquisition of Quaker Oats and year-end 2006. Volume gains for Tropicana and Lipton were also aided by the addition of new flavors and packaging.

Tropicana was not only the number 1 brand in the $3 billion orange juice industry, it was also among the fastest growing beverage brands with 10.3 percent growth in 2006. Tropicana achieved double-digit volume growth during 2006 even though the fruit beverage category declined by 2.4 percent that year. Tropicana had achieved volume and revenue growth through the introduction of such new products as Tropicana Pure super-premium blended juice drinks, Tropicana Essentials Omega-3 fortified orange juice, and Tropicana Organic orange juice. The combined sales of PBNA's BFY and GFY beverages made up 70 percent of the division's net revenue in 2006.

PepsiCo International

All PepsiCo snacks, beverages, and food items sold outside North America were included in the company's PepsiCo International division. International snack volume grew by 9 percent in 2006, with double-digit growth in emerging markets such as Russia, Turkey, Egypt, and India. Beverage volume in international markets increased by 9 percent as well during 2006, with the fastest growth occurring in the Middle East, China, Argentina, Russia, and Venezuela. The company made three small acquisitions of snack brands in the Netherlands, Poland, and New Zealand in 2006.

PepsiCo's Sale of Beverages in International Markets

PepsiCo also found that it could grow international sales through its Power of One strategy. A Pepsi-Cola executive explained how the company's soft drink business could gain shelf space through the strength of Frito-Lay's brands. "You go to Chile, where Frito-Lay has over 90 percent of the market, but Pepsi is in lousy shape. Frito-Lay can help Pepsi change that."[2] PepsiCo's market share in carbonated soft drinks in its strongest international markets during 2006 is presented below.

Country/Region	PepsiCo's Carbonated Soft Drink Market Share
Middle East	75%+
India	49
Thailand	49
Egypt	47
Venezuela	42
Nigeria	38
China	36
Russia	24

Source: PepsiCo Investor Presentation by Mike White, CEO PepsiCo International, 2006.

[2]"PepsiCo's new formula," *BusinessWeek Online,* April 10, 2000.

PepsiCo International management believed further opportunities in other international markets existed. In 2006, the average consumption of carbonated soft drinks in the United States was 32 servings per month, while the average consumption of CSDs in other developed countries was 17 servings per month and was 5 servings per month in developing countries. The company also saw a vast opportunity for sales growth in the $70 billion market for noncarbonated beverages in international markets. In 2006, PepsiCo International recorded less than $1 billion in noncarbonated beverage sales outside North America. The company was rapidly rolling out Tropicana to international markets and had acquired two international juice brands to capture a larger share of the $37 billion international markets for juice drinks. Also, PepsiCo was making Gatorade available in more international markets to capture a share of the $5 billion isotonic sports drink market outside the United States. Sales of Gatorade in Latin America more than doubled between 2001 and 2006 to give the sports drink a 72 percent market share in the entire Latin American region in 2006. PepsiCo International was also moving into new markets with Lipton RTD tea to gain a share of the $15 billion international RTD tea market. In 2007, Gatorade was available in 42 international markets, Tropicana was in 27 country markets outside North America, and Lipton was sold in 27 international markets. Tropicana was the number 1 juice brand in Europe and had achieved a 100 percent increase in sales in the region between 2001 and 2006. By 2012, PepsiCo planned to launch Gatorade in 15 additional country markets, Tropicana in 20 new markets, and Lipton in 5 new international markets.

PepsiCo had moved somewhat slowly into international bottled water markets, with its most notable effort occurring in Mexico. In 2002, PepsiCo's bottling operations acquired Mexico's largest Pepsi bottler, Pepsi-Gemex SA de CV for $1.26 billion. Gemex not only bottled and distributed Pepsi soft drinks in Mexico, but was also Mexico's number 1 producer of purified water. After its acquisition of Gemex, PepsiCo shifted its international expansion efforts to bringing Aquafina to selected emerging markets in Eastern Europe, the Middle East, and Asia. In 2006, Aquafina was the number 1 brand of bottled water in Russia and Vietnam and the number 2 brand in Kuwait.

PepsiCo's Sales of Snack Foods in International Markets

Frito-Lay was the largest snack chip company in the world with sales of approximately $7 billion outside the U.S. and an over 40 percent share of the international salty snack industry in 2006. Frito-Lay held commanding shares of the market for salty snacks in many country markets. The table below presents PepsiCo's salty snack market share in selected countries in 2006.

Country	PepsiCo's Salty Snack Market Share
Mexico	75%
Holland	59
South Africa	57
Australia	55
Brazil	46
India	46
United Kingdom	44
Russia	43
Spain	41
China	16

Source: PepsiCo Investor Presentation by Mike White, CEO PepsiCo International, 2006.

PepsiCo management believed international markets offered the company's greatest opportunity for growth since per capita consumption of snacks in the United States averaged 13.9 servings per month, while per capita consumption in other developed countries averaged 8.8 servings per month, and per capita consumption averaged 1.9 servings per month in developing countries. PepsiCo executives expected that, by 2010, China and Brazil would be the two largest international markets for snacks. The UK was projected to be the third largest international market for snacks, while developing markets, Mexico and Russia, would be the fourth and fifth largest international markets, respectively.

Developing an understanding of consumer taste preferences was a key to expanding into international markets. Taste preferences for salty snacks were more similar from country to country than many other food items, which allowed PepsiCo to make only modest modifications to its snacks in most countries. For example, classic varieties of Lay's, Doritos, and Cheetos snacks were sold in Latin America. However, the company supplemented its global brands with varieties spiced to local preferences such as Lay's Artesanas chips sold in Latin America and Lay's White Mushroom potato chips sold in Russia. In addition, consumer characteristics in the United States that had forced snack food makers to adopt better-for-you or good-for-you snacks applied in most other developed countries as well. In 2007, PepsiCo was eliminating trans fats from its snacks and expanding the nutritional credentials of its snacks sold in Europe since demand for health and wellness products in Europe was growing by 10 percent to 13 percent per year. The annual revenue growth for core salty snacks in Europe was growing at a modest 4 percent to 6 percent per year. Among PepsiCo's fastest growing snacks in the United Kingdom was Walker's Low Fat Ready Salted potato chips that had 70 percent less saturated fat and 25 percent less salt than regular Walker's chips. The company's Potato Heads natural chip line, which also boasted less fat and reduced salt, became the number 1 food launch in the UK during 2005. In addition, Walker's Baked Potato Chips had outperformed forecasted sales in 2006 by 100 percent.

International Sales of Quaker Oats Products

PepsiCo International also manufactured and distributed Quaker Oats oatmeal and cereal in international markets. In 2006, just six countries accounted for 75 percent of Quaker Oats' international sales of $500 million. The United Kingdom was Quakers' largest market outside the United States, where it held more than a 50 percent market share in oatmeal. The company had launched new oatmeal products in the United Kingdom, including Organic Oats, OatSo Simple microwaveable oatmeal and oatmeal bars, and Oat Granola and Oat Muesli cereals. PepsiCo also added new varieties of Quaker Oatmeal products in Latin America to double the brand's sales in the region from the time of its acquisition by PepsiCo to year-end 2006. Exhibit 8 presents a breakdown of PepsiCo's net revenues and long-lived assets by geographic region.

Quaker Foods North America

Quaker Oats produced, marketed, and distributed hot and ready-to-eat cereals, pancake mixes and syrups, and rice and pasta side dishes in the United States and Canada. The division recorded sales of nearly $1.8 billion in 2006. Net revenues during 2006 increased by 3 percent during the year with Quaker Oatmeal, Life cereal, and Cap'n Crunch cereal volumes increasing at single digit rates. Sales of Aunt Jemima syrup and pancake mix and Rice-A-Roni rice and pasta kits declined slightly during 2006. Quaker Oats was the star product of the division with a 58 percent market share in North America in 2006. Rice-A-Roni held a 33 percent market share in the rice and pasta side dish segment of the consumer food industry. Although Quaker Foods was just the third largest ready-to-eat cereal maker with a 14 percent market share in 2005, it was the only cereal producer to increase volume during the year. Quaker sales increased by 3.1 percent during 2005, while Kellogg's sales declined by 0.8 percent and General Mills' sales declined by 6.1 percent during the year. Some of Quaker's gains were a result of new cereal varieties such as Take Heart cereal, which included heart-healthy Omega-3s, Oatmeal Crunch, Oatmeal Squares, Natural Granola, and Oat Bran cereals. In

EXHIBIT 8

PepsiCo, Inc.'s U.S. and International Sales and Long-Lived Assets, 2004–2006 (in millions)

Net Revenues

	2006	2005	2004
U.S.	$20,788	$19,937	$18,329
Mexico	3,228	3,095	2,724
United Kingdom	1,839	1,821	1,692
Canada	1,702	1,509	1,309
All other countries	7,580	6,200	5,207
	$35,137	$32,562	$29,261

Long-Lived Assets

	2006	2005	2004
U.S.	$11,515	$10,723	$10,212
Mexico	996	902	878
United Kingdom	1,995	1,715	1,896
Canada	589	582	548
All other countries	4,725	3,948	3,339
	$19,820	$17,870	$16,873

Source: PepsiCo, Inc., 2006 10-K.

2005, Kellogg's held a 30 percent share of the $6 billion ready-to-eat cereal market and General Mills held a 26 percent market share. Quaker grits and Aunt Jemima pancake mix and syrup competed in mature categories and all enjoyed market leading positions. Fifty-five percent of Quaker Foods' 2006 revenues was generated by BFY and GFY products.

Value Chain Alignment Between PepsiCo Brands and Products

PepsiCo's management team was dedicated to capturing strategic fit benefits within the business lineup throughout the value chain. The company shared marketed research information to better enable each division to develop new products likely to be hits with consumers, consolidated its purchasing to reduce costs, and manufactured similar products in common facilities whenever possible. The company had also consolidated sales and marketing functions of similar products to eliminate duplication of effort and to present "one face" to customers.

The efforts to achieve synergies undertaken upon the acquisition of Quaker Oats had delivered an estimated $160 million in cost savings by 2005 through the combined corporatewide procurement of product ingredients and packaging materials. Also, the combination of Gatorade and Tropicana hot fill operations saved an estimated $120 million annually by 2005. The joint distribution of Quaker snacks and Frito-Lay products reduced distribution expenses by an estimated $40 million by 2005.

PepsiCo's Investment Priorities in 2007

PepsiCo's financial managers expected the company's lineup of snack, beverage, and grocery items to generate cumulative management operating cash flows of $15 billion between 2007 and 2009. The company's priorities for free cash flow were to reinvest in its core businesses, provide cash dividends to shareholders, and identify strategic growth opportunities that would provide attractive returns. From the close of the Quaker Oats acquisition in 2001 through early 2007, the company had chosen to make only small "tuck-in" acquisitions.

The company's executives expected to continue to make additional "tuck-in" acquisitions totaling approximately $500 million per year. Future capital expenditures for existing businesses were expected to range from 5 percent to 7 percent of net revenues. Dividends to shareholders had grown at a compounded annual rate of 15 percent between 2001 and 2006 to reach $1.16 per share. Between 2003 and 2005, PepsiCo had completed $1.2 billion in acquisitions, made $4.5 billion in capital expenditures, paid $4 billion in dividends, and completed an $8 billion share repurchase program. In May 2006, the company's board announced a new $8.5 billion share repurchase program that would expire on June 30, 2009. The company repurchased shares totaling $1.1 billion in 2006, which left $7.4 billion remaining on the share repurchase program.

Case

6

Kikkoman Corporation in the Mid-1990s: Market Maturity, Diversification, and Globalization

Norihito Tanaka *Kanagawa University*

Marilyn L. Taylor *University of Missouri at Kansas City*

Joyce A. Claterbos *University of Kansas*

In early 1996 Mr. Yuzaburo Mogi, president of Kikkoman Corporation, faced a number of challenges. Analysts indicated concern with Kikkoman's slow sales growth and noted that the company's stock had underperformed on the Nikkei Exchange in relation to the market and to its peers for several years. Throughout the world ongoing changes in taste preferences and dietary needs presented threats to the company's traditional food lines. The company marketed its branded products in 94 countries and had to consider which products and

Reprinted by permission from the *Case Research Journal,* 21, no. 3. Copyright 2001 by Norihito Tanaka, Marilyn Taylor, Joyce A. Claterbos, and the North American Case Research Association. All rights reserved.

The authors express deep appreciation to Kikkoman Corporation, which provided encouragement to this study, including access to the U.S. manufacturing and marketing facilities in addition to time in the corporate offices in Japan. The authors also gratefully acknowledge the support for this study provided by the Japanese Department of Education and the Institute for Training and Development in Tokyo. Quotes and data in this case study were drawn from a variety of personal interviews in the United States and Japan, company documents, and public sources. Documents and public sources appear in the list of references at the conclusion of the case.

markets to emphasize as well as which new markets to enter. As Mr. Mogi described the company's focus, ". . . we are now concentrating on further enhancing our ability to serve consumers in Japan and overseas. The basic keynotes of this effort are expansion of soy sauce markets, diversification and globalization."

In Japan, Kikkoman had long dominated the soy sauce market, and its mid-1990s market share position of 27 percent was well beyond the 10 percent of its next closest competitor. However, its share of the soy sauce market had continued to decline from its high of 33 percent in 1983, falling from 28 percent in 1993 to 27.2 percent in 1994. Further, although the company's worldwide sales had increased slightly overall from 1994 to 1995, sales of soy sauce in Japan had decreased over 1 percent during that period.

The U.S. market had provided significant opportunity in the post–World War II period. However, the company's U.S. market share for soy and other company products was essentially flat. In addition, three competitors had built plants in the United States beginning in the late 1980s. Mr. Mogi was aware that Kikkoman's choices in the U.S. market would provide an important model for addressing higher income mature markets.

With a market capitalization of nearly ¥160 billion,[1] Kikkoman Corporation was the world's largest soy sauce producer, Japan's nineteenth largest food company, and also Japan's leading soy sauce manufacturer. The company was the oldest continuous enterprise among the 200 largest industrials in Japan. The company began brewing shoyu, or naturally fermented soy sauce, in the seventeenth century and had dominated the Japanese soy industry for at least a century. The company held 50 percent of the U.S. soy sauce market and 30 percent of the world market. Kikkoman had 13 manufacturing facilities in Japan and one each in the United States, Singapore, and Taiwan. The company was one of the few traditional manufacturers to successfully establish a presence worldwide. (Exhibits 1 and 2 have the locations of and information on the company's principal subsidiaries. Exhibits 3 and 4 list the consolidated financial statements.)

Kikkoman in Japan

The Beginnings in Noda

In 1615, the widow of a slain samurai warrior fled 300 miles from Osaka to the village of Noda near Edo (now called Tokyo). With her five children the widow Mogi embarked upon rice farming and subsequently began brewing shoyu, or soy sauce. The quality of the Mogi family's shoyu was exceptional almost from its beginnings. At the time, households produced shoyu for their own use, or local farmers made and sold excess shoyu as a side enterprise to farming. As more people moved to the urban areas in the seventeenth and eighteenth centuries, demand for nonhome production increased. Households developed preferences for the product of a particular brewer. (See Appendix A: The Making of Soy Sauce.)

Shoyu had come to Japan with the arrival of Buddhism in the sixth century. The teachings of Buddhism prohibited eating meat and fish. Residents of the Japanese islands turned from meat-based to vegetable-based flavorings. One of the favorites became a flavorful seasoning made from fermented soy beans. A Japanese Zen Buddist priest who had studied in China brought the recipe to Japan. The Japanese discovered that adding wheat gave the sauce a richer, more mellow flavor.

---

[1]In early 1996, the exchange rate was about 95 yen per U.S. dollar. Thus, in U.S. dollars, Kikkoman's market value was about $1.7 billion. Sales at year end 1995 for the consolidated company were 203 billion yen, or slightly less than $2 billion (See Exhibits 2 and 3 for consolidated financial data and Exhibits 8, 9, and 11 for parent company and domestic versus non-Japan revenues plus other selected financial information.)

EXHIBIT 1 **Locations of Principal Subsidiaries**

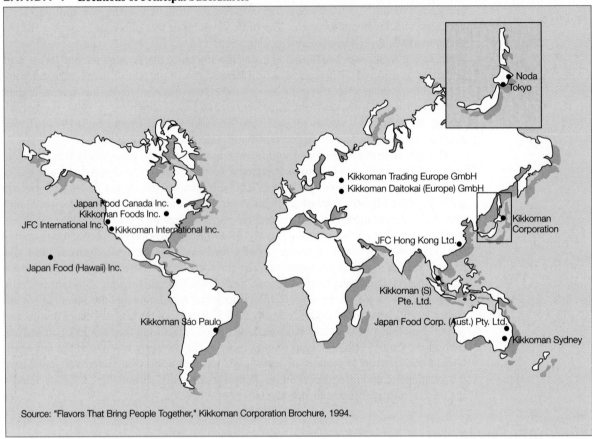

Source: "Flavors That Bring People Together," Kikkoman Corporation Brochure, 1994.

EXHIBIT 2 **Consolidated Subsidiaries as of FY 1995**

Source: Table 4: Consolidated Subsidiaries, UBS Securities Limited, May 28, 1996, as reported by *Investext*.

Subsidiary	Country	Paid-In Capital ((Y)m/$m)	Kikkoman Equity (%)
Japan Del Monte	Japan	900	99.7
Mann's Wine	Japan	900	100
Pacific Trading	Japan	72	66.7
Morishin	Japan	30	66.7
Kikkoman Foods, Inc.	US	US$6	100
Kikkoman International	US	US$3.5	92.6
JFC International	US	US$1.2	98
Kikkoman Trading Europe	Germany	DM1.5	75
Kikkoman Pte	Singapore	S$7.5	100
Kikkoman Trading Pte	Singapore	S$.4	100
Tokyo Food Processing	US	US$.02	100
Hapi Products	US	US$.05	100
Rex Pacific	US	US$1.5	100

EXHIBIT 3   Consolidated Profit and Loss Statement ((Y) m)

Sources: Table 9: UBS Securities Limited, May 28, 1996; *The World Almanac*, 1998 (original source: IMF).

	1989	1990	1991	1992	1993	1994	1995
Sales	195,851	196,925	206,861	211,671	203,491	200,976	203,286
COGS	117,062	118,808	122,872	124,882	118,504	117,809	119,656
Gross profit	78,789	78,117	83,989	86,789	84,987	83,167	83,629
Gross profit margin (%)	40.2	39.7	40.6	41	41.8	41.4	41.1
SG&A expenses	71,227	71,876	74,181	76,019	74,320	72,689	72,836
SG&A exp. (%)	36.4	36.5	35.9	35.9	36.5	36.2	35.8
Operating profit	7,562	6,240	9,807	10,769	10,666	10,477	10,792
Operating margin (%)	3.9	3.2	4.7	5.1	5.2	5.2	5.3
Net non-op. income	−572	−1,042	−1,564	−1,895	−2,282	−2,197	−2,305
Recurring profit	6,990	5,197	8,243	8,873	8,384	8,280	8,487
Recurring margin (%)	3.6	2.6	4	4.2	4.1	4.1	4.2
Net extraordinary income	181	1,165	1,317	59	108	1,434	−1,177
Pretax profit	7,170	6,363	9,559	8,932	8,493	9,714	7,310
Tax	3,327	3,299	4,726	5,178	4,597	4,157	3,569
Tax rate (%)	46.4	50.7	49.4	58	54.1	42.8	48.8
Minority interest	56	78	37	34	1	−52	46
Amortization of consol. dif.	0	0	−35	1	5	0	−314
Equity in earnings	1,097	1,464	1,188	1,245	887	1,002	996
Net profit	4,697	4,694	6,166	4,928	4,688	6,614	4,447
Shares outstanding (m)	169.08	169.71	169.97	178.61	187.62	187.77	197.2
EPS	27.8	27.7	31.3	25	23.8	33.5	22.6
EPS change (%_)	80	−0.4	13.3	−20.2	−4.9	41	−32.8
Cash flow per share	20.8	46.5	48	41.9	44.4	58.5	46.8
Average exchange rate (yen/USD)	137.96	144.79	134.71	126.65	111.20	102.21	94.06

Over the eighteenth century, Noda became a major center for shoyu manufacturing in Japan. Shoyu's major ingredients, soybeans and wheat, grew readily in the rich agricultural Kanto plain that surrounded Noda. The trip to the major market of Edo took only one day on the Edo River. The various shoyu-producing families in the Noda area actively shared their knowledge of fermentation. The Mogi family and another Noda area family, the Takanashi family, were especially active in the industry. By the late eighteenth century, the two families had become interrelated through marriage. Their various enterprises made considerable investment in breweries, and family members began ancillary enterprises such as grain brokering, keg manufacture, and transportation.

Japan's Shoyu Distribution System and Industry Structure

Japan's neophyte and fragmented shoyu industry had two distribution systems during this time. In the rural areas the shoyu breweries sold their products directly to households. In the cities, urban wholesalers distributed shoyu, vinegar, and sake. The wholesalers purchased bulk shoyu and established their own brands. The wholesalers controlled pricing, inventory, distribution, and marketing knowledge. They would distribute branded shoyu only on consignment. During the 1800s, the wholesalers formed alliances that gave them near monopolistic power over the Tokyo market. As the shoyu manufacturers became more efficient, they found it impossible to lower prices or make other adjustments to increase their market share.

The Mogi and Takanashi families took several steps to counteract the wholesalers' dominance. The Takanashi family had diversified into wholesaling some years prior and were

EXHIBIT 4   Consolidated Balance Sheet ((Y) m)

Source: Nikkei Needs as reported in Table 12: Consolidated Balance Sheet, UBS Securities Limited, May 28, 1996.

	1990	1991	1992	1993	1994	1995
Current Assets	81,611	88,092	89,705	103,152	105,220	107,339
Cash and deposits	13,254	17,570	18,261	28,826	36,381	37,366
Accounts receivable	43,579	44,661	44,503	46,009	44,246	44,439
Securities	315	1,012	1,316	3,310	3,306	3,307
Inventories	21,769	21,300	22,484	21,469	18,579	19,258
Fixed assets	94,631	97,999	105,231	113,940	112,183	119,411
Tangible assets	52,087	53,254	59,276	67,649	65,795	72,684
Land	11,768	12,011	11,910	15,156	15,613	11,540
Investments	26,371	29,597	31,771	33,051	34,083	35,006
Total Assets	177,583	187,316	195,955	218,561	218,805	228,308
Liabilities and Owner's Equity						
Current liabilities	48,040	52,626	54,014	50,272	46,663	63,400
Short-term borrowings	18,846	18,908	19,046	17,462	14,838	15,741
Fixed liabilities	58,374	58,850	62,351	85,532	85,143	71,710
Long-term borrowings	4,457	4,549	4,723	3,274	3,091	2,312
Bonds and CBs*	26,565	26,346	26,231	46,170	44,776	29,921
Minority interest	1,223	1,166	1,157	1,103	1,024	427
Total liabilities	107,638	112,643	117,522	136,909	132,832	135,538
Shareholders' equity	69,945	74,673	78,434	81,651	85,973	92,770
Total Liabilities and Equity	177,583	187,316	195,955	218,561	218,805	228,308

*There were two CBs issued Jan. 90 exercisable at (Y) 1,522. The other two were issued July 93 and were exercisable at (Y) 969. With the share price at approximately (Y) 100, the total dilution factor was about 18 percent, with 80 percent of that dependent on the two CBs exercisable at (Y) 969. Of 228 ((Y) m) in 1995, about 170 belonged to the parent (i.e., Japan corporation) company.

part of the wholesalers' alliance. One Mogi family intermarried with a wholesaler's family—a traditional strategy in Japan for cementing strategic alliances. In addition, the Mogi and Takanashi families worked to increase brand recognition and dominance. In 1838, Mogi Saheiji applied for and received the shogunate's recognition of his family's premier brand, named Kikkoman. He aggressively promoted the brand by sponsoring professional story-tellers and sumo wrestlers, embossing paper lanterns and umbrellas with the Kikkoman trademark, and putting ornate gold labels from Paris on his Kikkoman shoyu kegs. In the latter part of the nineteenth century, Kikkoman shoyu won recognition in several world's fairs.

In reaction to depressed market prices and fluctuating costs of inputs, a number of the Noda shoyu brewers formed the Noda Shoyu Brewers' Association in 1887. The association purchased raw materials, standardized wages, and regulated output quality. The members' combined efforts resulted in the largest market share at the time, 5 to 10 percent of the Tokyo market, and widespread recognition of the high quality of Noda shoyu.

Noda brewers, and especially the Mogi and Takanashi families, began research and development activities early. The Japanese government encouraged the Noda shoyu brewers to conduct research in the recovery and processing of the two by-products of shoyu manufacture, shoyu oil and shoyu cake. In the early 1900s, the association began to fund a joint research and development laboratory.

The Shoyu Industry in the Twentieth Century

In 1910, there were still 14,000 known makers of shoyu in Japan. However, a number of changes led to consolidation. Manufacturing shifted from a small-batch, brewmaster-controlled production process to a large-batch, technology-controlled process. Mogi families in Noda invested in modernized plants, and a fifth-grade Japanese geography reader featured a state-of-the-art Kikkoman facility. A national market also developed, thanks to the development of a railway system throughout most of the country. In addition, consumer tastes shifted to the Tokyo-style shoyu produced by eastern manufacturers such as the Noda Shoyu Brewers' Association.

Consumers also began to purchase shoyu in smaller glass bottles rather than in the traditional large wooden barrels that sometimes leaked and were expensive to build and difficult to store. Raw materials also became more expensive as the brewers increasingly sought higher quality imported soybeans (from Manchuria, China, and Korea) and salt (from England, Germany, and China). The association members controlled costs by purchasing in bulk and demanding high-quality materials from suppliers.

The Noda Shoyu Company: 1918–1945—A Family Zaibatsu[2]

In 1918, seven Mogi families and a related Takanashi family combined their various enterprises into a joint stock holding company called the Noda Shoyu Company. The merger was in reaction to the market upheaval caused by World War I. The new company was a small zaibatsu with nearly a dozen companies in manufacturing fermented grain-based products, transportation, and finance. Unlike early shoyu manufacturing where ownership, management, and operations were clearly separated, the Mogi and Takanashi families owned, managed, and operated their firm. Initially the family produced 34 different brands of shoyu at various price points. The Kikkoman brand had a history of heavy promotion for over 40 years, greater Tokyo market share, and a higher margin than the company's other brands. The Kikkoman brand became the company's flagship brand. The new corporation continued its long-standing emphasis on research and development and aggressively pursued new manufacturing processes, increased integration, and acquired other shoyu companies.

After the Mogi Takanashi coalition, the company aggressively pursued a strong nationwide sole agent system and direct distribution. The combined company also continued Kikkoman's well-known advertising activities. Kikkoman had carried out the first newspaper advertising in 1878. In 1922, the company carried out the firm's first advertising on the movie screen.

During the 1920s, the company aggressively modernized with machines such as hydraulic presses, boilers, conveyors, and elevators. The company's modernization efforts were emulated by competitors, and the results were increased supply and heightened industry competition. The changes brought about by increased automation led to severe labor unrest. One particularly long strike against the Kikkoman company in the late 1920s almost destroyed the participating labor union. After the strike ended, Kikkoman rehired about a third of the striking employees. The company centralized and reorganized the work processes to accommodate improved technology, restructured work practices, and established methods to monitor and reward workers for their performance. However, the company also established efforts to improve the identity of the workers with the company. Internal communications carried the message that all employees were members of one family, or *ikka,* united in a common purpose, that is the production of shoyu. The Noda Shoyu Company was also heavily involved in the city of Noda and supported many of its cultural and charitable activities as well as the local railroad, bank, town hall, cultural center, library, fire station, elementary school, hospital, recreation facilities and association, and much of the city's water system.

---

[2]*Zaibatsu:* Industrial and financial combines dissolved by occupation fiat after World War II, but which have reemerged as somewhat weaker entities. Some of these *zaibatsu* have developed into large conglomerates such as Mitsubishi. However, they should be distinguished from *keiretsu* (of which Mitsubishi is also one of the largest). *Keiretsu* are informal enterprise group-based associations of banks, industrials, and so forth.

Kikkoman's International Activities

Kikkoman's initial export activities began in the late seventeenth century with Dutch and Chinese traders. The Dutch began to export shoyu to Holland and the rest of Europe, while the Chinese served the southeast Asian markets. The shoyu brewers relied on agents for these early export transactions. During the nineteenth century, one Mogi patriarch opened a factory in Inchon, Korea. Demand for the increasing export, marketing, and direct investment continued to come primarily from Japanese and other peoples living abroad whose traditional cuisines called for shoyu. In 1910, the Noda city brewers' international activities were recognized when the Japanese government selected Noda shoyu to appear in a public relations publication introducing Japan's industries overseas.

Noda Shoyu Company continued to expand internationally between World War I and World War II. Acquisition of raw materials from abroad continued. The company added a manufacturing facility for shoyu and miso in Manchuria and two shoyu factories in North America. Other facilities in Japan were expanded or updated to support increasing international sales.

The company established sales offices in China and Korea to market shoyu, miso, and sake. By the late 1930s, the company exported 10 percent of its output, about half to the Asian region—especially Korea, China, and Indonesia—and half to Hawaii and California. Almost all of the exports were the Kikkoman brand and were sold through food import/export firms to the company's traditional customers.

Post–World War II Kikkoman in Japan

At the end of World War II, Kikkoman operated only in Japan. Activities elsewhere had been closed. To meet the need for capital, Kikkoman issued publicly traded stock in 1946, reducing family ownership markedly. (Exhibit 5 shows the changes in ownership from 1917 to 1993.) The post–World War II period brought a number of social changes to Japanese society. Japanese families began the change to nuclear rather than extended-family formation. Food tastes changed leading, among other trends, to a decline in per capita consumption of shoyu. Compared with other industries, demand for soy sauce grew very slowly. In 1942, demand for soy sauce in Japan was 1.7 times greater than in 1918. Demand in the 1960s was expected to be 2.2 times greater than that in 1918. However, modernization led to increased output.

Kikkoman had received considerable recognition for its advertising efforts prior to World War II. After the war, the company began to market even more aggressively in Japan. These efforts included establishing the company's strong nationwide distribution system throughout Japan; mounting aggressive activities in marketing research, advertising, and consumer education; and changing to a new and more Western image. As a result

EXHIBIT 5   **Noda Shoyu Company and Kikkoman Corporation Ownership**

Sources: W. Mark Fruin, *Kikkoman—Company, Clan, and Community* (Cambridge, MA, Harvard, University Press, 1983), pp. 98, 121, 249, *Japan Company Handbook,* Toyo Keizai, Inc., 1993, p. 207.

	Holdings (% of total shares or assets)			
Shareholder Name	**1917**	**1925**	**1955**	**1993**
Mogi-Takanashi-Horikiri Brewing Families	100%[a]	34.6%	15.0%[b]	2.3%
Senshusha Holding Company		62.0%	3.1%	3.4%
Insurance and Banking Companies			9.9%[c]	20.5%[c]
All Others		3.6%	71.1%	73.6%

[a]Eight holdings ranging from 1.4 percent to 29.3 percent.
[b]Five holdings ranging from 1.5 percent to 4.4 percent.
[c]In 1955 and 1993, including Meiji Mutual Insurance Co, Mitsubishi Trust Bank; in 1955, including Kofukan Foundation and Noda Institute of Industrial Science; in 1993, including Nitsuit Trust Bank, Nippon Life Insurance, Sumitomo Trust, and Yasuda Trust.

EXHIBIT 6
National Output and Company Market Share of Shoyu (in kiloliters)[a]

Source: W. Mark Fruin, *Kikkoman—Company, Clan, and Community* (Cambridge, MA, Harvard University Press, 1983), pp. 40–41.

Year	National Output (Japan)	Noda Shoyu Share
1893	230,360	3.5%
1903	317,500	4.5
1913	430,435	6.1
1923	624,764	5.1
1933	576,026	10.1
1943	680,955	12.0
1953	822,179	14.1
1963	1,051,730	21.4
1973	1,277,887	31.4
1983	n.a.	33.0
1993	n.a.	28.0[c]
1994	1,323,529[b]	27.2[c]

[a] 1 kiloliter = 264 gallons.
[b] Derived from Kikkoman's production of 360,000 kl and its 27.2 percent market share. Residents of Japan consumed about 2.6 gallons of soy sauce per capita yearly. In contrast, U.S. citizens consumed about 10 tablespoons.
[c] As reported by UBS Securities Limited, May 28, 1996 in *Investext*. This source also reported that demand for soy sauce was flat in Japan and production between 1984 and 1994 had declined about 5.1 percent.

of Kikkoman's marketing efforts, the company's market share rose sharply. (Exhibit 6 shows the national output of shoyu and the company's market share from 1893 to 1994.) By 1964 the company officially changed its name to Kikkoman Shoyu and in 1980 became Kikkoman Corporation. The word *Kikkoman* is a combination of *kikko* (the shell of a tortoise) and *man* (10,000). It was taken from an old Japanese saying, "A crane lives a thousand years and a tortoise 10,000 years." (Implying, in other words, "May you live as long!") In essence, the Kikkoman brand connotes a long-lasting living thing. Kikkoman had become well-known for its advertising skill in Japan and had found that the word *Kikkoman* was easy for Americans to pronounce.

The company also diversified its product line using its expertise in shoyu manufacture, fermentation, brewing, and foods marketing. This diversification included a 1963 venture to market Del Monte products in Japan. In 1990, the company bought the Del Monte assets and marketing rights for the Del Monte brand name in the Asia–Pacific region. (Exhibit 7 shows Kikkoman Corporation's product lists as of 1949, 1981, and 1993.) Kikkoman's R&D expertise led to activities in biotechnology and products such as enzymes, diagnostic reagents, and other biologically active substances used to test for microorganisms in water samples in hospitals, food processing factories, and semiconductor plants. The company also developed a number of patents at home and overseas. The company became involved in both the import and export of wines. It also undertook activities in food processing machinery. In spite of the diversification, Kikkoman's domestic sales were still about 55 percent soy-sauce related.

In the 1990s, soy sauce continued as a perennial favorite in Japan's cuisine, although demand was essentially flat. Among the remaining 3,000 shoyu companies in Japan, Kikkoman produced 360,000 kl in Japan, or about 27 percent of the country's output (Exhibit 6.) The company faced price pressures especially on its base product of soy sauce, mainly due to the competitive pressures at the retail level in Japan and the aggressive introduction of private brands. Sales in the Del Monte line also decreased in the early 1990s. To improve performance, Kikkoman began to reduce its product line from a high of 5,000 items to an expected eventual 2,500. One bright spot was the growth in wines and spirits. In addition, Kikkoman also introduced successful new soy-sauce related products in 1993, 1994, and 1995 in the form of two soup stocks and Steak Soy Sauce. Profit increases in the early 1990s came primarily from higher priced luxury products. (Exhibits 8 and 9 display the parent company financial statements.) The company recognized that continuing success in

EXHIBIT 7   Kikkoman Corporation Products and Product Lines

Sources: W. Mark Fruin, *Kikkoman—Company, Clan, and Community* (Cambridge, MA, Harvard University Press, 1983), pp. 275–276; "Flavors That Bring People Together," Kikkoman Corporation Brochure, 1994.

1949	1981	1994
Kikkoman Brand soy sauce, sauce, memmi and tsuyu (soup bases)	*Kikkoman Brand* soy sauce, mild soy sauce (lower salt, 8%), light color soy sauce (usu-kuchi), teriyaki barbecue marinade and sauce, Worcestershire sauce, tonkatsu sauce, memmi and tsuyu (soup bases), sukiyaki sauce, instant soy soup mix, instant osumono (clear broth soup mix)	*Kikkoman Brand* soy sauce, mild soy sauce (lower salt, 8%), light color soy sauce (usu-kuchi), teriyaki sauce, Worcestershire sauce, tonkatsu sauce, memmi (soup base), sukiyaki sauce, sashimi soy sauce, lemon flavored soy sauce, mirin (sweet rice wine), Aji-Mirin, plum wine, instant miso (soybean paste) soups, egg flower soup mixes, rice crackers, tofu, neo-genmai (puffed brown rice), genmai soups, oolong tea, tsuyudakono (soup base), ponzu soy sauce, soy sauce dressing, oyster sauce, bonito stock
Manjo Brand mirin (sweet rice wine), sake, shochu, whiskey	*Manjo Brand* mirin (sweet rice wine), shochu, plum wine	*Manjo Brand* triangle, komaki
	Yomonoharu Brand sake	*Yomonoharu Brand*
	Del Monte Brand tomato ketchup, juice, puree, paste, chili sauce, Mandarin orange juice	*Del Monte Brand* tomato ketchup, juice, fruit drinks, Mandarin orange juice
	Disney Brand fruit juice (orange, pineapple, grape), nectar (peach, orange)	
	Mann's Brand[a] wine and sparkling wine, brandy	*Mann's Brand* koshu, koshu (vintage), zenkoji, blush, brandy
	Higeta Brand shoyu, tsuyu, Worcestershire sauce	
	Ragu Brand spaghetti sauces	
	Kikko's Brand tomato ketchup	*Beyoung* protein powder, wheat germ
	Monet Brand cognac	*Imported wines* aujoux, chateau tatour, borie-manoux, franz reh and sohn, pol roger

[a]The company established its Mann Wine subsidiary in 1964.

EXHIBIT 8

Parent Company Revenues by Product Line

((Y) m)

Source: Table 5: UBS Securities Limited, May 28, 1996, as available on *Investext*.

	1994	1995	Percent Change	1996E	Percent Change
Soy Sauce	74,666	73,843	−1.1	75,000	1.6
Food	15,091	16,310	8.1	18,500	13.4
Del Monte	24,692	19,857	−19.6	19,000	−4.3
Alcohol	24,993	25,925	3.7	27,000	4.1
Others	4,159	4,285	3	4,500	5
Total	143,601	140,220	−2.4	144,000	2.7

EXHIBIT 9
Parent Company Balance Sheet ((Y) m)

Source: UBS Securities Limited, May 28, 1996. Table 11 as reported by *Investext*.

	1993	1994	1995
Current assets	78,463	81,805	80,749
Fixed assets	88,007	86,029	89,599
Total	166,802	168,000	170,348
Short-term liabilities	33,469	32,033	46,762
Long-term liabilities	79,898	79,527	66,567
Equity	53,434	56,440	57,019
Total liabilities and equity	166,802	168,000	170,348

its mature domestic market would depend on continuous development of new applications and variations of its older products as well as development of new products.

Kikkoman in the United States in the Post–World War II Era

U.S. Market Potential

The various Mogi family branches and Noda Shoyu Company had expanded company efforts beyond Japan since the early 1800s. By the end of World War II, the various family enterprises and the Noda Shoyu Company had ended all activities outside Japan. Japanese expatriates living in various countries and other peoples whose traditional cuisine used shoyu comprised the company's primary pre–World War II markets. In 1949, Kikkoman started to export soy sauce, mainly to the United States. In the 1950s, consumption of soy sauce began to decline in Japan. Noda Shoyu Company made the decision to invest heavily in expanding the international sales of Kikkoman brand shoyu to overseas markets. Prior to World War II, Noda Shoyu's major overseas markets were Asia and Hawaii. After the war, the company decided to focus on the mainland United States because (1) political and economic conditions in Asia were very unstable, (2) the Japanese community in Hawaii had relearned shoyu brewing during World War II, and there were many small Hawaiian shoyu breweries that would have made competition intense in that market, and (3) the United States had a healthy and rapidly growing economy.

Several changes in the U.S. market made that market attractive to Noda Shoyu Company. First, Americans who had been in Asia during or just after World War II developed a taste for Japanese goods, including food. Second, the company expected that as Asians in the United States became more Americanized, their consumption of traditional foods including soy sauce would decline. Third, American eating habits were shifting to more natural foods and to food that could be prepared quickly. Noda Shoyu Company moved to target both Asians and non-Asians in its marketing efforts.

During the 1956 U.S. presidential elections, Noda Shoyu bought air time to advertise Kikkoman brand products. Yuzaburo Mogi, son of the head of the company's planning department, urged this move to U.S. television advertising.

U.S. Distribution Activities

During the years immediately after World War II, Japanese companies in general relied on a small group of internationalized and entrepreneurial Japanese and Japanese-American individuals. Sale of food products in the United States involved a complex distribution system with heavy reliance on food brokers as promoters to local wholesalers and retailers. Food brokers required careful training by a knowledgeable sales team in how to use the product, especially where the product was unusual or unfamiliar to consumers. Food brokers marketed the product to wholesalers and large retailers, took orders for the product, and relayed the orders to the manufacturer or, in the case of foreign manufacturers, the manufacturer's agent. The manufacturer or agent then made delivery of the product to the wholesaler or retailer and handled all billing and accounts, paying the broker a commission for his/her marketing representation. The food broker was an important link between the manufacturer and the wholesaler or retailer. Food brokers were evaluated based on their ability to persuade retailers and wholesalers to carry products and to feature them prominently.

In 1957, the company formed Kikkoman International, Inc. (KII), a joint venture between Noda Shoyu Company in Japan and Pacific Trading of California. KII was incorporated in San Francisco to serve as the marketing and distribution center for Kikkoman products in the United States. Most of the products were produced by Noda Shoyu Company, but some were purchased from other manufacturers and sold under the Kikkoman label.

Over the next 10 years, sales grew 20 to 30 percent a year. In 1960, the Safeway grocery store chain agreed to have some of its stores carry Kikkoman Soy Sauce. Noda Shoyu opened regional sales offices for KII in Los Angeles (1958), New York City (1960), Chicago (1965), and Atlanta (1977). Retail marketing activities included in-store demonstrations, advertising campaigns in women's magazines that emphasized soy sauce use in American cuisine, and limited television commercials. The company used brokers as their distribution channels to supermarkets and wholesalers for the small oriental retail stores. The company encouraged food brokers through contests and training. For the food service and industrial market segments, the company carried out industrial magazine ad campaigns and special educational programs. The company also formed partnerships with the American Veal Manufacturers' Association and the Avocado Association to feature Kikkoman Soy Sauce in their product advertisements.

Other major international companies had to modify their products for the United States. However, Kikkoman marketed the same soy sauce in the United States as in Japan. The company's experience in its campaign to "westernize" soy sauce for the Japanese market applied to the campaign in the United States. In the United States Kikkoman provided the traditional, low-sodium preservative-free, and dehydrated soy sauce. The company also marketed tailor-made sauces, other food extracts, and agents.

Exploration of Potential U.S. Manufacturing Capacity

As early as 1965, Kikkoman Corporation began to explore the possibility of manufacturing in the United States. However, the company determined that sales in North America were insufficient to support the economies of scale required for a minimum efficient scale production facility. Instead, in 1968 Kikkoman Corporation contracted with a subsidiary of Leslie Salt Company of Oakland, California, to bottle the Kikkoman soy sauce shipped in bulk from Japan and to blend and bottle teriyaki sauce, a major ingredient of which was soy sauce. These bottling efforts constituted Kikkoman's first post–World War II manufacturing efforts in the United States. Bottling in the United States reduced customs and tariff costs. However, moving goods back and forth from the United States and Japan added considerably to the company's costs. In the mid 1980's Japan imported 95 percent and 88 percent of its soybeans and wheat respectively. The United States was Japan's major source of supply. Transportation of raw materials (e.g., soybeans and wheat) to Japan was between 5 percent and 20 percent of preproduction costs; transportation costs of brewed soy sauce from Japan to the United States was 25 percent of production costs. Various import/export restrictions and tariffs increased the risk and expense of importing raw materials to Japan and exporting finished goods to the United States.

The North American market was potentially much larger than the Japanese market, and Kikkoman had a greater share of the North American market than the company had in Japan. Yuzaburo Mogi hired a Columbia University classmate as a consultant, and the company formed a team to work with him to consider a U.S. plant. By 1970, the analyses, in spite of higher U.S. labor costs, favored construction of a U.S. manufacturing facility. As Yuzaburo Mogi put the company's motivation, "We made a decision to go after the American consumer."

Selection of Walworth, Wisconsin

The team considered over 60 potential sites in the east, west, and midwest. The team chose the midwest because of its central location and crop production. Ultimately, the team selected a 200-acre dairy farm site in Walworth, Wisconsin. Walworth provided the best fit with the five criteria established by the company: (1) access to markets (proximity to Milwaukee and Chicago, as well as the geographic convenience of a midway point between the east and west coasts made shipping relatively efficient); (2) ample supplies of wheat and soybeans (soybeans came from Wisconsin, wheat from North Dakota, and salt from Canada); (3) a dedicated workforce, (4) a strong community spirit; and (5) an impeccable supply of water. Kikkoman also appreciated Wisconsin's emphasis on a clean environment.

Walworth, Wisconsin, was situated about two hours northwest of Chicago and about one hour west of Milwaukee. A community of about 1,100, Walworth was surrounded by some of the most productive farmland in the United States. The area included a number of other smaller communities whose economies depended primarily on farming and summer vacation home residences. The company hired a local consultant, lawyer Milton Neshek, who ultimately became general counsel of Kikkoman Foods, Inc. Mr. Neshek described the original reaction to Kikkoman's purchase of prime farmland as mixed, "with a small faction on the town board opposed to the company coming in." Yuzaburo Mogi described the opposition as strong. Residents of the small, rural, close-knit farming community expressed concerns about the impact of a large, especially foreign, corporation in a small community, potential inflation of land values, and the possibility of industrial pollution.

One of Neshek's partners, Thomas Godfrey, visited Kikkoman facilities in Noda City, Japan. "When Kikkoman called me in 1971," said Godfrey, "and asked me to create a Wisconsin corporation for them so they could make soy sauce, I didn't even know what the hell soy sauce was. Nobody else around here did either." Walworth's plant manager, Bill Wenger, recalled his introduction to the company. In 1972, he was stationed with the U.S. Marines in Hawaii. His mother sent a newspaper clipping about the soy sauce plant, suggesting that it might be a good place to begin his return to civilian life. Wenger and his wife didn't know what soy sauce was either, but his wife went to the local grocery store and bought a bottle. As Wenger described it, the purchase was ". . . some horrible local Hawaiian brand. She brought it home and opened it. We looked at one another and said, '*@& . . ., this stuff is terrible.'" Another of the three American production managers employed at the plant had a similar tale. The production manager said, "The first year I worked here, we never had any soy sauce in my home. My wife wouldn't buy it, wouldn't even allow it in the house. I finally brought home a bottle and put it on some meatloaf. Now we use it on just about everything. I put it on peaches. And we even have a local minister who puts it on his ice cream . . . I do too. It's good."

No other Japanese-owned manufacturing facility had been constructed in the United States at the time. Neshek's partner, Godfrey, visited Noda because as he put it, "I had to see for myself what it was they were talking about. I had to make sure the factory wasn't going to pollute the air and water and stink up the place." Local Kikkoman representatives met with organizations such as the Local Grange, Farm Bureau groups, church groups, Rotary, and ladies' clubs. Wisconsin's governor, Patrick Lucey, came to one of the seven town meetings held to discuss the plant and explain the state's role and position. Yuzaburo Mogi described the process as "removing the fears of the local people and local council about the building of the new factory." The company was able to convince area residents that Kikkoman would not pollute the environment and would use local labor and other resources. The final vote of the county zoning board was 53 for, 13 against. The town board declined to oppose the zoning board's action. Among other issues, Kikkoman put a great deal of effort into reducing potential pollution. In talking about this process of "nemawashi" or root tending, Mr. Mogi emphasized the importance of a prosperous coexistence between the company and the local community. He said, "We've been doing business in Noda for 360 years. We learned a long time ago that to survive you need to coexist with the surrounding community."

Opening the New Plant

In January 1971, Kikkoman executives along with Japanese, Walworth, and Wisconsin officials held a ceremonial groundbreaking on the 200-acre site. A Cleveland, Ohio, design and construction firm built the plant. Other American companies, many located in the region, built many of the critical components. The initial investment in the 10,000 kiloliter facility was $8 million, and the plant was finished just in time to avoid the 1973 American embargo on the sale of soybeans to Japan. Kikkoman's Walworth plant was the first Japanese investment in production capacity in the United States in the post–World War II period and the first plant Kikkoman built outside Japan after World War II. Opening ceremonies included dignitaries and officials from Wisconsin, Kikkoman, Japan, and the United States. The 700 invited guests heard the texts of telegrams from the Japanese Prime Minister and President Richard Nixon. President Nixon referred to the plant as a ". . . visionary step (that) will mean meaningful trade relations and balance of trade and will enhance further friendships between our two countries."

From its opening in 1972 through the mid-1990s, the company expanded the Walworth facility eight times to 500,000 square feet. Kikkoman invested in facilities or equipment every year with production increasing 8 to 10 percent per year. Originally, the plant produced two products, soy sauce and teriyaki sauce. In the mid-1990s, the plant produced 18 products, including regular and light soy sauce, teriyaki steak sauce, sweet and sour sauce, and tempura dip. All but one used a soy base. The company had been very careful about pollution, treating its wastewater carefully so that there was no threat to nearby popular Lake Geneva. The Walworth town clerk said, "There's no noise, no pollution. I live about three-quarters of a mile from them, and once a day, I get a whiff of something that's like a sweet chocolate odor. It's no problem." The company marketed the plant's output in all 50 states plus Canada and Mexico. Soy sauce was shipped in many varieties, including bottles ranging from 5 to 40 ounces, 1- to 5-gallon pails, and sometimes in stainless steel tank trucks for large customers. McDonald's, for example, used soy sauce in one of the Chicken McNuggets condiments.

Management of the Walworth Plant

The company maintained a state-of-the-art laboratory at the Walworth facilities. However, plant management pointed out that the most accurate test during production was the human nose. "Our people have worked with the product for so long, a whiff can tell them something is not quite right," said one Kikkoman director. The venture was described as "a prime example of the best combination of Japanese and American business and industrial savvy." As the plant's general manager, Michitaro Nagasawa, a Ph.D in Biochemistry from the University of Wisconsin, put it, "The productivity of this plant is the highest of all our plants. . . . It's an exceptional case in Kikkoman history. We took the sons and daughters of farmers, trained them and taught them about total quality management. They were raw recruits with no experience in making soy sauce. People with farm backgrounds are very diligent workers. They will work seven days a week, 24 hours a day if necessary. They understand what hard work is."

The plant opened with 50 employees. Originally, 14 Japanese Kikkoman employees and their families came to Walworth to train employees and get the plant functioning. The Japanese families scattered in groups of two or three to settle in Walworth and various nearby communities. Local women's community organizations "adopted" the Japanese wives, formed one-to-one friendships, and helped the Japanese wives become acclimated to the communities, including learning to drive, using the local supermarkets, and hiring baby-sitters for their children. The Japanese husbands joined local service clubs. "That helped achieve an understanding between the Americans and Japanese and helped them to assimilate faster. It exposed Japanese people to a farming town that had had no Asian people before," noted Bill Nelson, Kikkoman Foods Vice President. Kikkoman established the practice of rotating its Japanese employees back to Japan after an average of five years in the United States. In the mid-1990s, only seven Japanese families remained in the Walworth area, still spread throughout the local communities.

Community Contributions

Kikkoman Foods, Inc., was an active and contributing member of the community. The company donated time and funds on three levels. At the local level the company established Kikkoman Foods Foundation in 1993. The foundation, which was to be ultimately funded at the $3 million level, was formed to support area charitable activities. The company supported as many as 30 local projects a year, including college scholarships for area students, local hospital activities, a vocational program that assisted people in developing employment-related skills, and a nearby facility that preserved circus-related items. As Walworth's town clerk put it, "They sponsor just about everything—Community Chest (an organization similar to the United Way), Boy Scouts, Girls Scouts, all the way down the line. They're very good neighbors." The clerk treasurer from a nearby town said, "You see their name in the paper almost every week helping out some organization."

At the state level, Kikkoman Foods, Inc., supported the University of Wisconsin educational system, established up to four Beloit College scholarships to honor Governor Lucey at his alma mater, and funded a Mogi Keizaburo scholarship at the Milwaukee School of Engineering. Members of the board of directors served on several public service boards and commissions. At the national level, Kikkoman Corporation, through its U.S. subsidiary Kikkoman Foods, Inc., supported Youth for Understanding exchange programs. At the fifth anniversary celebration, Kikkoman's chairman reported that the plant had developed better than had been anticipated. At the tenth anniversary celebration of the Kikkoman plant, the local Walworth paper reported, "In the 10 years that Kikkoman Foods, Inc., has been located here, it has become an integrated part of the community. The company has truly become a part of the Walworth community, and not only in a business sense." In 1987, reflecting Kikkoman's contributions, Wisconsin's governor appointed Yuzaburo Mogi as Wisconsin's honorary ambassador to Japan.

Kikkoman's Japanese–American Management in the United States

In the mid-1990s, Kikkoman operated its U.S. activities through two subsidiaries, Kikkoman Foods, Inc. (KFI), and Kikkoman International, Inc. (KII). KFI owned and operated the Walworth manufacturing plant. KII in San Francisco, California, undertook marketing responsibilities, including wholesaler and distributor activities throughout the United States. The boards of directors for both subsidiaries had several members from the parent corporation but were primarily Americans from among local operations officers or local Walworth citizens (for KFI) or the broader U.S. community (for KII). The KFI board met as a whole once a year and rotated the site of its annual stockholders' meeting between Japan and Wisconsin. An executive committee met monthly to consider operational decisions. The executive committee included Yuzaburo Mogi, who attended two to three meetings in the United States every year, and the head of Kikkoman Corporation's International Division. The remaining members of the executive committee included American and Japanese officers from the U.S. corporation. The KII Board operated in a similar manner but met only in the United States.

Yuzaburo Mogi believed that a long-term commitment was essential for international success. A 1961 alumnus of Columbia University's Graduate School of Business, Mr. Mogi was the first Japanese to graduate from a U.S. university with an MBA degree. In the years following graduation, he worked in various departments in Kikkoman, including accounting, finance, computers, long-range planning, and new product development. In time, he took on other roles, including member of Kikkoman's board of directors (1979), managing director of the company (1982), executive management director (1989), and executive vice president (1994). The seventeenth generation of his family to brew soy sauce, Mr. Mogi had become Kikkoman's president in early 1995. He explained his view regarding the necessity of a long-term perspective: "We should do business from a longer range viewpoint. It will be very difficult to expect fruitful results in the short run under different and difficult circumstances. Failure will be inevitable in foreign countries if one proceeds with a short-range view. In fact, it took Kikkoman 16 years to become established in the United States."

Of the five senior managers at the Walworth facility, three were Japanese and two were American. The plant manager, the finance manager, and the laboratory manager were Japanese. It was expected that these three positions would continue to be Japanese appointments. One American manager described the situation, "We know we will only attain a certain level, but that's OK, though. I can accept that. Soy sauce has been made in Japan for centuries. It's their product, their technology. They have the history, the research."

The general manager, that is, the plant manager, was the most senior person in authority at the plant and was responsible directly to headquarters in Japan. The appointment would be a person who had been with the company for many years. The finance manager's position required someone who was familiar with Japanese accounting systems and who was steeped in the Japanese emphasis on long-range profits. Japanese corporate headquarters controlled their foreign branches through their accounting and finance sections.

Mr. Mogi explained the Japanese appointment to the position of laboratory manager, "The production of soy sauce is very sophisticated. Normally, we recruit graduates with a master's degree in Japan who have gone to universities that have specialized programs in soy sauce production. In America, there is no university that teaches soy sauce production techniques, so it is difficult to promote Americans into general manager positions." As Dr. Magasawa, general manager at the Walworth plant, put it in explaining the discriminating tastes the Japanese have developed since childhood, "The sensory system, passion, feeling, or sensitivity can't transfer. That is based on just experience. Our vice president is a kind of god in this plant because he recognizes (even) a slight difference . . . I don't have that. That's why I can't be manufacturing vice president. I am a general manager—nothing special. I am a biochemist (with) 39 years in Kikkoman, mostly in research."

Decisions at the Walworth plant, when possible, were made by consensus. KFI vice president Bill Nelson described the plant management as American in content and Japanese in style, with decisions arrived at from the bottom up and most matters of importance needing a consensus of employees. "It's hard, really, to get at because of the fact that nothing . . . here should run in an American style or a Japanese style or what have you. It was just simply—let's see what happens when you have both parties participate," he said. Nelson gave the example of an idea for changing summer working hours to start at 7 A.M. instead of 8 A.M. so that workers could leave earlier and enjoy more daylight. It was, Nelson, pointed out, unusual for a company to even entertain the idea. Nelson explained the process: "Instead of simply exploring it on a management level, here we started the process of asking individual employees what personal inconvenience would be experienced if the hours were changed."

Milton Neshek observed that Japanese management and the middle management at the Walworth plant worked well together with long-range budgeting and strategic planning carried out by the Japanese executive team. He described the situation, "Our 30 employees feel like part of our family. That makes management more responsive to employees. Decisions, whenever possible, are made by consensus." The fact that the plant has no labor union was no surprise to Nelson. As he put it, a union "has never been an issue here."

Yuzaburo Mogi summarized Kikkoman's approach to its U.S. operations and, in particular, its Walworth plant as a five-point approach:

> Kikkoman has been successful doing business in the United States by adapting to American laws, customers, and most importantly, its culture . . . (An) important matter to consider, especially when establishing a manufacturing plant in a foreign country, is the maintenance of what has come to be called "harmony" with society and the local community. A foreign concern should try to prosper together with society and the local community. . . . It is important to try to localize the operation. . . . (Our) . . . first commitment is the employment of as many local people as possible. Second we try to participate in local activities . . . trying to be a good corporate citizen (in Wisconsin) and contributing to society through our business activities. Third, we have been trying to avoid the so-called "Japanese-village" . . . by advising our people from Japan not to live together in one single community, but to spread out and live in several separate communities in order to become more familiar with the local people. Fourth, we try to do business with American companies. The fifth commitment is our practice of delegating most authority to local management in order to better reflect local circumstances. Through this process we are better able to make the most responsible decision. If we have an opinion, for example, we discuss it with other members at a local meeting in our American plant before reaching a decision. Kikkoman attempts to avoid a remote-control situation with letters or telephone calls from Japan. . . . If we have an opinion, we discuss it with other members at a local meeting in our American plant before reaching a decision.

The plant did encounter intercultural issues, however. For example, plant manager Bill Wenger pointed out "Communication can be a problem sometimes. The language barrier is one reason. Then there's the problem of saving face. If a mistake is made, the Japanese tend to cover up for one another so the person who made the mistakes doesn't lose face."

The company was a popular local employer in Walworth. Local unemployment was phenomenally low at 2 percent, but the Walworth plant had over 1,000 active applications on file for the plant's total 136 positions. However, turnover among plant employees was negligible. "No one quits unless it is a move by a spouse. Our absenteeism is minimal and as for tardiness—we just don't have it. We offer competitive wages and good benefits . . . employees feel like part of our family," said general counsel Neshek. Company officials stated that they paid about 10 percent more than the state average of $9.71 per hour, and employees did not have to contribute to the cost of their health insurance. As the company's vice president Shin Ichi Sugiyama put it, "In management, our primary concern is always the employee." The employees reported, "We feel like they listen to us. Our opinion counts, and we have the ability to make change, to better the company."

Mr. Sugiyama pointed out that the Walworth plant's productivity and quality had been about equal to that of Japanese plants. Productivity improved following the plant opening and by 1993 was actually the best of all the company's plants.

The U.S. Market in the 1990s[3]

U.S. Demand in the 1990s

After the opening of the Walworth plant, Kikkoman's U.S. sales growth slowed somewhat. However, Ken Saito, Kikkoman's brand manager for the midwest, summarized the company's hopes: "Americans are more adventurous than Japanese when it comes to trying new

---

[3]Information on the market and competitors was drawn primarily from InfoScan.

foods. That's why we have developed some products only for the American market. But most Americans still are not familiar with how to use soy sauce." Thus, the company developed a number of nonoriental recipes that call for soy sauce and other Kikkoman products, for example, teriyaki chicken wings and Pacific Rim pizza with sweet and sour sauce, beef and chicken fajitas, and grilled salmon with confetti salsa flavored with "lite" soy sauce. Kikkoman clearly expected Americans to increasingly use soy sauce for applications beyond oriental foods and expected significant growth in the company's base product in the United States. According to Saito, "We figure the market in the United States will increase 100 times in the next decade." Kikkoman marketing coordinator, Trisha MacLeod, articulated the goal as ". . . to get consumers to realize soy sauce is the oldest man-made condiment, and that it can also be used in meatloaf, barbecue—across the spectrum."

MacLeod pointed out, "Americans eat a lot more soy sauce than they realize." However, America's per capita consumption was barely 10 tablespoons, translating into $300 million in North American sales. In contrast, Japanese per capita consumption was about 10.5 quarts per person, which translated into about $1.4 billion in annual sales in Japan.

The population of Asian immigrants and families of Asian descent was projected to grow significantly in the United States. The California population increased 127 percent to 2.8 million during the 1980s. The total population of Asian-Americans in the United States was estimated at 7.3 million in 1990, up 108 percent over the 1980s. Asian peoples represented the traditional mainstay market for oriental foods. Asians had higher income and educational levels than any other ethnic groups in the United States. However, each country represented a different cuisine, and the different Asian ethnic groups required different marketing approaches. Asian populations had spread throughout many parts of the United States, and retail outlets were learning how to highlight and display oriental foods to spur sales. Restaurants greatly influenced American food-buying habits. One industry executive observed that almost all U.S. restaurant kitchens in the 1990s had soy sauce. A 1996 National Restaurant Association study indicated that ethnic foods were increasing in popularity. Thus, oriental food manufacturers and distributors expected that oriental food sales would increase sharply.

Some information in the mid-1990s suggested strong and increasing popularity for oriental foods. U.S. sales of oriental foods had slowed considerably. The most recent aggregate information regarding the demand for oriental food in the United States in the mid-1990s is shown in Exhibit 10.

By the late 1980s consumers began to indicate dissatisfaction with canned entrees, at $81 million in sales the second largest subcategory of oriental foods. Sales of this subcategory had declined as much as 10 percent (1991 to 1992) and showed no signs of abating. Competition was intense, with a third of all products sold on the basis of feature, price, and/or display promotion.

U.S. Major Competitors

Kikkoman's two major competitors in the United States were Chun King and LaChoy. Both companies made soy sauce by hydrolyzing vegetable protein. This European derived method was faster and less expensive than the six-month fermentation process Kikkoman used. By 1971, Kikkoman had surpassed Chun King in supermarket sales of soy sauce, becoming number 2 in the American marketplace. In 1976, Kikkoman outsold LaChoy

EXHIBIT 10 U.S.
Oriental Food Sales
($000,000)

Year	1992	1993	1994
Sales	$275	$305	$301

Source: Information Resources, Inc., Chicago, IL.

brand soy sauce and became the number 1 retailer of soy sauce in the United States, a position it continued to hold in the mid-1990s. However, the company faced strong competitors in the oriental foods category and in the sauces and condiments subcategory.

The new consumer focus was on oriental food ingredients that individuals could add to home-cooked dishes. "People are cooking more oriental foods at home," said Chun King's vice president of marketing, "Over 40 percent of U.S. households stir-fry at least once a month. Sauces are an opportunity to get away from the canned image." Indeed, sauces were the only growth area on the oriental food category, with 1992 sales rising 11 percent over the previous year. Rivals Chun King and LaChoy were flooding the oriental foods aisle in American supermarkets with new products. LaChoy had about 40 percent of the shelf products in oriental foods and Chun King had about 20 percent.

However, there were more changes than just new products. In the early 1990s, LaChoy and Chun King had revved up their marketing efforts under new ownership. LaChoy was owned by ConAgra's Hunt-Wesson division. Among other initiatives, ConAgra, a major U.S. food company, hired a new advertising firm for LaChoy.

A Singapore-based firm purchased Chun King in 1989 and brought in a new management team. As one observer put it, "The brand had really been neglected as part of Nabisco (its previous owner). It was just a small piece of a big pie." The new management team introduced a line of seasoned chow mein noodles and another of hot soy sauces. The firm's marketing plan included consumer promotions and a print ad campaign in women's magazines. Chun King's 1992 oriental food sales were estimated at $30 million. In mid-1995, ConAgra purchased Chun King from the Singapore company and added the brand to its Hunt-Wesson division. ConAgra was no stranger to the Chun King brand. The large U.S. competitor had purchased Chun King's frozen food line in 1986 from Del Monte. It was expected that Hunt-Wesson would eventually consolidate manufacturing but continue to aggressively advertise the two brands separately. As a Hunt-Wesson executive put it, "They're both established leaders in their field, and they both have brand strength."

LaChoy advertised itself as "the world's largest producer of oriental foods created for American tastes." The company led the oriental foods category with sales (excluding frozen) of $87 million in 1992 and $104.4 million in 1994. Its products included chow mein noodles, bamboo shoots, sauces, and miscellaneous foods. About $28 million of the 1992 sales came from sauce and marinade sales. LaChoy's manager of corporate communications indicated that the Chicago-based firm planned no increase in marketing spending in reaction to the new Chun King initiatives. However, the company did plan to advertise two new lines—Noodle Entrees and Stir-Fry Vegetables 'N Sauce. The company expected to expend most of its marketing support for the latter product line, a set of vegetables in four sauces formulated for consumers to stir-fry with their choice of meat.

Kikkoman and Other Competitors

Kikkoman remained the one bright spot in the oriental food category of sauces and marinades. Kikkoman controlled $63 million of the $160 million sauces/marinades segment and supported its position with a moderate amount of advertising—$3.2 million in 1992, about the same as 1991. In its major product lines, Kikkoman controlled about two-thirds of the California market and had about one-third market share in other major U.S. sales regions. The company was test-marketing a new line of sauces for addition to the consumer's own vegetables and meat.

Kikkoman also had to consider recent moves by several other competitors. Yamasa Shoyu Co., Ltd., Japan's second-largest soy sauce maker, had announced plans to build a factory in Oregon in mid-1994. This multigenerational company was founded in 1645 in Choshi City, Japan. Estimates on the cost of the Oregon factory ranged from $15 million to $20 million, and the plant was expected to eventually employ 50 workers. Yamasa intended to produce soy sauce for the U.S. market by using soybeans shipped from the midwest. It took Yamasa four years to select the final site for its new plant. The company produced a number of products in addition to soy sauce, including other food and drugs made from biological raw materials such as soybean protein and wheat starch.

Hong Kong–based Lee Kum Kee was a producer and importer of Chinese-oriented sauces and condiments. Lee Kum Kee had opened a sauce manufacturing plant in Los Angeles in 1991 to keep up with rising U.S. demand and to reduce dependence on imports thus avoiding payment of import duties, which could be as high as 20 percent. The company was a Hong Kong subsidiary of one of Japan's leading soy sauce brewers. Lee Kum Kee retailed its sauces in big supermarket chains in all 50 states. Historically, the company imported its soy sauce through an independent U.S.-based importer of the same name. The U.S. importer also imported about 40 other food products, mostly marinades, curries, and sauces from the East. Lee Kum Kee found its sales propelled by the population doubling of Americans of Asian or Pacific Island descent.

Competitor San-J International of the San-Jirushi Corporation of Kuwana, Japan, built a soy sauce plant in Richmond, Virginia in 1988. Hawaiian competitor Noh Foods of Hawaii innovated a line of oriental dried seasonings and powdered mixes. In reaction, other manufacturers, including Kikkoman, produced copycat products. Noh Foods distributed its products in the United States, Europe, and Australia through distributors and trade show activities.

Kikkoman's International Position

The Kikkoman Vision

In the mid-1990s, Kikkoman manufactured in four countries and marketed its brand products in over 90 countries. (Exhibit 11 shows the comparison of domestic and non-Japan sales and operating profits.) Of the company's 3,200 employees, over 1,000 were in international subsidiaries, and only 5 percent of those were Japanese. The company saw at least part of its mission as contributing to international cultural exchange. Yuzaburo Mogi explained,

> Kikkoman believes that soy sauce marketing is the promotion of the international exchange of food culture. In order to create a friendlier world, I believe we need many types of cultural exchanges. Among these, there is one that is most closely related to our daily lives—the eating of food. Soy sauce is one of the most important food cultures in Japan. Hence, the overseas marketing of soy sauce means the propagation of Japanese food culture throughout the world.

As one U.S. scholar who had studied the company extensively in the 1980s put it, "There is an evident willingness on the part of Kikkoman to experiment with new products, production techniques, management styles, and operational forms in the international arena." Yuzaburo Mogi put it similarly when he said, "It should be understood that adjustment to different laws, customs, and regulations is imperative, instead of complaining about those differences."

EXHIBIT 11
Consolidated Results FY 1995 ((Y) m)

Source: UBS Securities Limited, May 28, 1996. Table 7 as reported by *Investext*.

	Domestic	Non-Japan
Sales	162,426	40,860
Operating Profit	6,640	4,152
Operating Margin	4.0	10.1

Kikkoman in Europe

Kikkoman began its marketing activities in Europe in 1972. Kikkoman found Europeans more conservative and slower to try new tastes than Americans. The firm found Germany the least conservative and opened restaurants there in 1973. By the early 1990s, the company had opened six Japanese steak houses in Germany. The restaurants gave their customers, over 90 percent of whom were non-Asian, the opportunity to try new cuisine. The Kikkoman trading subsidiary in Germany was the company's European marketing arm. Said the managing director for Kikkoman's European marketing subsidiary located in Germany, "Germany and Holland are big business for us, as both countries are very much into interesting sauces and marinades." Kikkoman's managing director of Europe made it clear that he had aggressive plans to grow sales both by increasing the sales of soy sauce as well as extending the markets in which the company operated. The massive ready-made meal business in both the United States and Europe had huge potential for Kikkoman. The firm would need to market to end consumers at the retail level as well as to food manufacturers.

The company established its second overseas manufacturing facility in 1983. This facility supplied soy sauce to Australian and European markets. By the early 1990s, Kikkoman had about 50 percent of the Australian soy sauce market. The United Kingdom brand debut occurred in 1986, and the 1992 U.K. market was estimated at 1 billion pounds. In 1993, the firm opened a 25,000-square-foot warehouse in London. With $1.66 billion (U.S.) in sales, Kikkoman had come a long way with "just" soy sauce. Overall, analysts noted that the United States had experienced about 10 percent annual growth in soy sauce demand and expected Europe to expand similarly.

Kikkoman in Asia

In Asia, the company opened a production facility in Singapore in 1983 and incorporated a trading company in 1990. Industry observers expected the company to enter the soy sauce market in China in the near future. In addition, other Asian countries offered various opportunities in sauces, condiments, and foods.

Kikkoman—The Challenges

The company the Mogi family had headed for nearly 400 years confronted a number of challenges on the global stage in the latter part of the 1990s. Kikkoman executives realized that the company's future could depend primarily on its mature domestic market. The multi-generation family firm would have to change its image as a maker of a mature product. As Mr. Mogi stated "We . . . take pride in our ability to contribute to the exchange of cultures by using some of the world's most familiar flavors. We are now concentrating on further enhancing our ability to serve consumers in Japan and overseas. Kikkoman continues as a company that is proud of its heritage, but nevertheless willing and able to adapt to the constantly evolving requirements of our customers and markets."

References

Allen, Sara Clark. "Kikkoman, a Good Neighbor in Wisconsin," *Business,* Tuesday, June 11, 1996.

Bergsman, Steve. "Patience and Perseverance in Japan," *Global Trade* 109, no. 8 (August 1989), pp. 10, 12.

Campbell, Dee Ann. "Del Monte Foods to See European Foods Business," *Business Wire,* April 17, 1990.

Demestrakakes, Pan. "Quality for the Ages," *Food Processing* 70, no. 6 (September 1996).

"Fireflies Help Kill Germs," *Times Net Asia,* January 1, 1996.

Forbish, Lynn. "Grand Oriental Celebration Held for Opening of Kikkoman Foods," *Janesville Gazette,* June 18, 1973.

Forrest, Tracy. "Kikkoman: a Way of Life," *Super Marketing,* January 28, 1994.

Fruin, W. Mark. *Kikkoman: Company, Clan, and Community* (Cambridge, Massachusetts: Harvard University Press, 1983).

Hewitt, Lynda. "Liquid Spice," *Food Manufacture,* February, 1993, p. 23.

Hostveldt, John. "Japan's Kikkoman Corp. Brews Success Story in Walworth," *Business Dateline: The Business Journal—Milwaukee* 3, no. 31, sec. 3 (May 19, 1986), p. 17.

"In-Store: Happy New Year's Feast," (Article on Kikkoman's In-Store Promotion), *Brandsweek* 37 (January 1, 1996), pp. 14–15.

Jensen, Debra. "Kikkoman Executive Lauds Wisconsin, Lucey," *Gazette,* January 13, 1989, p. 1B.

Jensen, Don. "A Stainless Success Story," *Kenosha News,* Business Section, August 1, 1993.

Jensen, Leah. "Kikkoman Spices Up Walworth's Quality of Life," *Janesville Gazette,* January 21, 1984.

Kikkoman Corporation: Flavors That Bring People Together (Company Brochure).

Kinugasa, Dean. "Kikkoman Corporation," 1979 (Private Translation by Norihito Tanaka and Marilyn Taylor, 1994).

LaChoy's Homepage (www.hunt-wesson.com/lachoy/main/mission/).

LaGrange, Maria L. "RJR Sells Del Monte Operations for $1.4 Billion," *Los Angeles Times* 108, no. 297, September 26, 1989, p. 2.

Mogi, Yuzaburo. "*Masatsunaki Kokusai Senryaku,*" (Tokyo, Japan: Selnate Publishing Co., Ltd., 1988—in English Translation).

Mogi, Yuzaburo. "The Conduct of International Business: One Company's Credo— Kikkoman, Soy Sauce and the U.S. Market," (Available from Company).

Ostrander, Kathleen. "Kikkoman's Success Tied to Proper Blend," *Business Datelines (Wisconsin State Journal),* March 1, 1992, p. 29.

Plett, Edith. "Kikkoman Foods Marks Fifth Year," *Janesville Gazette,* January 26, 1979.

Redman, Russell. "Hunt-Wesson Acquires Chun King," *Supermarket News* 45, no. 19 (May 8, 1995), p. 101.

SBA Homepage, Wisconsin Gallery.

Schoenburg, Lorraine. "Governor Supports Kikkoman," *Janesville Gazette,* September 14, 1989.

Shima, Takeshi. "Kikkoman's Thousand-Year History," *Business JAPAN,* January, 1989, p. 65.

"The Joy of Soy: How a Japanese Sauce Company Found a Happy Home in Walworth, Wisc.," *Chicago Tribune Magazine,* January 31, 1993, p. 13.

Wilkins, Mira. "Japanese Multinational in the United States: Continuity and Change, 1879–1990," *Business History Review* 64, no. 4 (Winter 1990), pp. 585–629.

Yates, Ronald E. "Wisconsin's Other Brew," *Chicago Tribune Magazine,* January 31, 1993, p. 14.

In addition to personal interviews in Tokyo, Walworth, Wisconsin, and San Francisco, information and quotations were also drawn from these references. This list is part of a much broader set of sources that the authors consulted.

The Making of Soy Sauce

The Chinese began making jiang, a precursor of soy sauce, about 2,500 years ago. The most likely story of soy sauce's origins relates how Kakushin, a Japanese Zen priest who studied in China, returned to Japan in the middle of the thirteenth century and began preparing a type of miso, or soybean paste produced through fermentation, that became a specialty of the area. By the end of the thirteenth century, the liquid was called *tamari* and sold commercially along with the miso. Experimentation with the raw ingredients and methods of fermentation began. Vegetarianism also became popular in Japan during this time, and people were eager for condiments to flavor their rather bland diet. Soldiers also found the transportability of the seasonings useful.

Soy sauce evolved from tamari and miso by adding wheat to the soybean fermentation mash. The Japanese modified the shoyu to include wheat to gentle the taste so that it did not overwhelm the delicate flavors of Japanese cuisine. Most households made their shoyu during the slack time in agricultural cycles. Families harvested grains in the fall and processed them into mash. The mash fermented beginning in October–December to January–March when the shoyu was pressed from the mash.

Regional differences among the soy sauces developed depending upon the mix of soybean, wheat, and fermentation techniques. Even in the last decade of the twentieth century, hundreds of local varieties of soy sauce were available commercially in Japan.

Produced in the traditional way, soy sauce was a natural flavor enhancer. In the latter part of the twentieth century, ingredient-conscious consumers shied away from artificial flavor enhancers. Soy sauce responded to the challenge of finding ingredients to flavor foods. For vegetarian manufacturers, the "beefy" taste provided by the soy sauce without any meat extract was highly desirable.

There were two methods of manufacturing soy sauce—the traditional fermentation process used by Kikkoman and the chemical method.

Soy Sauce through Fermentation— Kikkoman's Traditional Method

Kikkoman's process was the traditional one and involved processing soy and wheat to a mash. Kikkoman had developed an innoculum of seed mold that the company added. The seed mold produced a growth, the development of which was controlled by temperature and humidity. The resulting mash (koji) was discharged into fermentation tanks where selected microorganism cultures and brine were added. The product (moromi mash) was aerated and mixed, then aged. During this process, enzymes formed in the cells of the koji and provided the characteristics of the brewed sauce. The soybean protein changed to amino acid, and the enzymatic reaction that occurred between the sugar and amino acids produced the taste and color. Enzymes changed the wheat starch to sugars for sweetness, and a special yeast developed changing some of the sugars to alcohol. Fermentation changed other parts of the sugars to alcohol that produced tartness. The brewing process determined flavor, color, taste, and aroma. The brine added to the koji mixture stimulated the enzymes and produced the reddish brown liquid mash. This process resulted in umami—or flavor-enhancing—abilities, as well as the brewed flavor components. The final mash was pressed between layers of cloth under constant pressure. After a pasteurization process to intensify color and aromas, the shoyu was filtered again and bottled. There were no flavorings, coloring, additives, or artificial ingredients in the product. According to produce developers, these complex flavors were not present in brewed soy sauce.

Chemically Produced Soy Sauce

Nonbrewed soy sauce could be made in hours. Soybeans were boiled with hydrochloric acid for 15 to 20 hours. When the maximum amount of amino acid was removed from the soybeans, the mixture was cooled to end the hydrolysis action. The amino acid liquid was then neutralized, mixed with charcoal, and finally purified through filtration. Color and flavor were introduced via varying amounts of corn syrup, salt, and caramel coloring. The resulting soy sauce was then refined and bottled.

7

The Black & Decker Corporation

John E. Gamble *University of South Alabama*

Arthur A. Thompson *University of Alabama*

In 2000 Black & Decker Corporation was still struggling to get out from under the array of financial and strategic problems stemming from the company's $2.8 billion acquisition of Emhart Corporation in 1989. Black & Decker had long been the world's leading producer and marketer of power tools and power tool accessories. But it had begun a program of diversification in the 1980s that had produced mixed results for shareholders. The company's foray into small household appliances had been a success originally, but the small-appliance division acquired from General Electric in the early 1980s had recently been divested because of its drag on B&D's growth. The follow-on acquisition of Emhart, a conglomerate with very diverse business interests, had proved to be a significant impairment to the company's earnings and cash flow as well as a management burden, and during the past 11 years Black & Decker had achieved success in only a few of the businesses it obtained in the Emhart acquisition.

Black & Decker described itself as a diversified global manufacturer and marketer of household, commercial, and industrial products. Going into 2000, the company was the world's largest producer of power tools, power tool accessories, security hardware, and electric lawn and garden products. The company's Price Pfister kitchen and bathroom faucets subsidiary, a business acquired in the Emhart deal, had gained market share for 11 consecutive years to become the third largest brand of plumbing fixtures in North America. Black & Decker was also the worldwide leader in the market for certain types of mechanical fastening systems used in automobile assembly and in other industrial applications—fasteners had been one of Emhart's businesses as well. But while Black & Decker's business portfolio included a lineup of several competitively strong brands, the company's stock price had been a ho-hum performer throughout the unprecedented bull market of the 1990s, substantially lagging behind the performance of well-known indexes like the Dow Jones Industrials Average and the Standard & Poor's 500 Index. A graph of Black & Decker's stock performance between 1985 and January 2000 is presented in Exhibit 1. Exhibit 2 provides an 11-year summary of Black & Decker's financial performance.

EXHIBIT 1   **Market Performance of Black & Decker's Common Stock, by Quarter, 1985–January 2000**

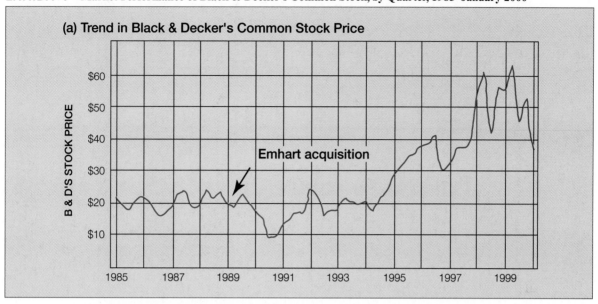

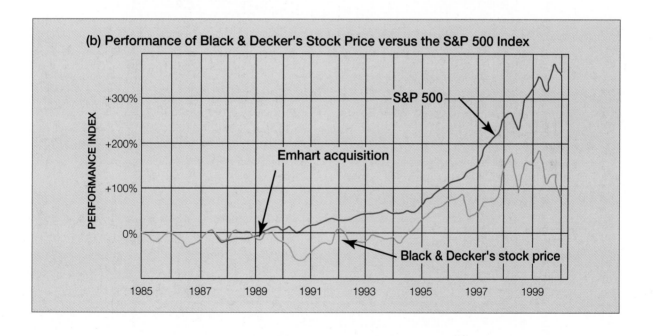

The Expectation of Better Times for Black & Decker

In late 1998 Black & Decker management celebrated the completion of an almost decade-long effort to divest nonstrategic businesses gained through its 1989 acquisition of Emhart Corporation and expected the company to enter a long-awaited period of growth as its entire management attention was refocused on its core power tools, plumbing, and security hardware businesses. Black & Decker's CEO, Nolan Archibald, told Wall Street analysts in

EXHIBIT 2 Summary of Black & Decker's Financial and Operating Performance, 1989–99 (in millions of dollars except per share and employee data)

Source: The Black & Decker Corporation annual reports.

	1999	1998	1997	1996	1995	1994	1993	1992	1991	1990	1989
Sales	$4,520.5	$4,559.9	$4,940.5	$4,914.4	$4,766.1	$4,365.2	$4,121.5	$4,045.7	$3,952.6	$4,313.2	$3,172.5
Operating income	536.3	(466.2)	489.3	356.9	426.1	351.9	302.7	177.1	365.2	458.1	259.2
Operating income excluding restructuring and goodwill amortization*	536.3	509.2	552.6	514.5	494.5	424.9	364.4	391.3	436.0	524.1	284.5
Income taxes	141.0	166.5	122.3	43.5	9.0	62.7	60.7	44.3	54.5	72.4	32.9
Earnings data:											
Earnings (loss) from continuing operations	300.3	(754.8)	227.2	159.2	216.5	89.9	64.1	(95.3)	16.1	19.7	30.0
Discontinued operations	—	—	—	70.4	38.4	37.5	31.1	22.0	36.9	31.4	—
Extraordinary item	—	—	—	—	(30.9)	—	—	(22.7)	—	—	—
Cumulative effects of accounting change	—	—	—	—	—	—	(29.2)	(237.6)	—	—	—
Net earnings (loss)	300.3	(754.8)	227.2	229.6	224.0	127.4	66.0	(333.6)	53.0	51.1	30.0
Total assets	4,012.7	3,852.5	5,360.7	5,153.5	5,545.3	5,264.3	5,166.8	5,295.0	5,456.8	5,829.7	6,258.1
Long-term debt	847.1	1,148.9	1,623.7	1,415.8	1,704.5	1,723.2	2,069.2	2,108.5	2,625.8	2,754.7	2,629.7
Total debt	1,243.5	1,360.6	1,862.5	1,705.8	2,351.7	2,393.3	2,564.6	2,563.8	2,870.3	3,266.2	4,057.5
Stockholders' equity	801.1	574.0	1,791.4	1,632.4	1,423.2	1,169.4	1,048.9	1,074.0	1,027.1	920.7	720.7
Capital expenditures	171.1	146.0	203.1	196.3	203.1	181.5	190.3	167.7	94.9	103.1	112.1
Depreciation and amortization	160.0	155.2	214.2	214.6	206.7	195.4	182.4	188.3	187.1	197.8	131.0
Number of employees	22,100	21,800	28,600	29,200	29,300	29,200	30,500	32,300	31,900	35,900	38,600
Number of shares outstanding	88.4	91.8	96.5	96.1	94.4	85.3	84.5	76.3	62.6	61.4	59.6
Dividends per share	$0.48	$0.48	$0.48	$0.48	$0.40	$0.40	$0.40	$0.40	$0.40	$0.40	$0.40

*For 1998 this figure also excludes goodwill write-off and gain on sale of businesses.

early 1998 that the pending elimination of nonstrategic businesses that manufactured and marketed such products as True Temper golf club shafts and Emhart glass-making machinery would allow the company to position itself for greater growth in 1999 and 2000. "This [portfolio restructuring] will allow us to focus on core operations that can deliver dependable and superior operating and financial results."[1] However, with the exception of a brief run up to $60 per share in mid-1999, the portfolio restructuring had done little to improve the market performance of the company's securities. In January 2000 Black & Decker's common shares traded at a 52-week low and at a price below the high for 1996 and 1997. Nevertheless, management continued to express confidence that the company's streamlined business portfolio would allow Black & Decker to achieve revenue and earnings growth that the market would find impressive. In commenting on the company's year-end 1999 financial performance, Nolan Archibald said, "We are extremely pleased with Black & Decker's performance this past year, which resulted in record earnings and clearly indicates that the strategic repositioning we undertook in 1998 has been successful."[2]

Company Background

Black & Decker was incorporated by Duncan Black and Alonzo Decker in 1910 and initially produced milk cap machines and candy dippers. In 1916 the company introduced its first power tool—a portable half-inch electric drill that was eventually placed on display in the Smithsonian Institution. Over the next 40 years, Duncan Black and Alonzo Decker undertook a number of actions that established the company as the dominant name in power tools and accessories. Black & Decker introduced the first portable screwdriver in 1922, the first electric hammer in 1936, finishing sanders and jigsaws in 1953, and the Dustbuster handheld vacuum in 1978. The company expanded internationally in 1919 when it began sales operations in Russia, Japan, and Australia and opened a production facility in Canada in 1922. It eventually became known worldwide for its power tools, particularly so in Europe. Black & Decker was managed by the two partners until they died—Black in 1951 and Decker in 1956. As managers, Black and Decker achieved growth by adding to the company's lineup of power tools and accessories and by increasing its penetration of more and more foreign markets. The company maintained a corporate growth strategy tied exclusively to product-line extensions and international expansion until the mid-1980s.

Diversification into Small Household Appliances

Black & Decker began to pursue diversification in the 1980s because of growing maturity of its core power tools business. In 1984 Black & Decker acquired General Electric's housewares business for $300 million. GE's brands had about a 25 percent share of the small-appliance market and generated annual revenues of about $500 million. GE sold its small-appliance division, despite its number 1 market position, because of the division's low profitability. GE's strong suit was in irons and toaster ovens, where its share was close to 50 percent; sales of GE irons alone totaled about $250 million. Among the other 150 GE products acquired by Black & Decker were coffeemakers, hair dryers, and hair curlers, food mixers and processors, toasters, electric skillets, can openers, waffle irons, and blenders. Also in 1984, Black & Decker purchased three European tool manufacturers to fill in product gaps and strengthen its manufacturing base; the acquisition involved a Swiss manufacturer of portable electric woodworking tools for professional users, the leading European manufacturer of drill bits, and a German producer of hobby and precision power tools.

---

[1]As quoted in *Knight-Ridder/Tribune Business News,* January 28, 1998.
[2]As quoted in *PR Newswire,* January 27, 2000.

The acquisition of GE's housewares division launched Black & Decker on a course to transform the company from a power tools manufacturer into a consumer products company. In early 1985, the firm changed its name from Black & Decker Manufacturing Company to Black & Decker Corporation to reflect its new emphasis on "being more marketing driven" rather than being merely engaged in manufacturing.

Black & Decker's CEO—Nolan D. Archibald

The chief architect of Black & Decker's foray into diversification was Nolan D. Archibald. Black & Decker hired Archibald as president and chief operating officer in 1985, shortly after the acquisition of GE's small household appliance business. Prior to joining Black & Decker, Archibald was president of the $1.7 billion consumer durables group at Beatrice Companies, where he was responsible for such business units as Samsonite luggage, Culligan water treatment products, Del Mar window coverings, Stiffel lamps, and Aristocraft kitchen cabinets. At the time he was hired, Archibald was 42 years old; he was chosen from a pool of some 50 candidates for the position and turned down offers to be president at two other companies to take the B&D job. Archibald had been at Beatrice since 1977 and was successful in engineering turnarounds in three of Beatrice's businesses. Prior to that, he had headed a turnaround of Conroy Inc.'s Sno-Jet Snowmobile business. Archibald spent two years of his youth winning converts as a Mormon missionary, was an All-American basketball player at Utah's Dixie College, became a standout player at Weber State College in Utah, earned his MBA degree at Harvard Business School, and tried out (unsuccessfully) for the Chicago Bulls professional basketball team. Corporate headhunters rated Archibald as a good strategic thinker who was personable, versatile, and sensitive to people.

Archibald's Early Successes at B&D

According to one Black & Decker dealer, prior to when Archibald took over as president in September 1985 "Black & Decker had been coasting along for quite a few years like a ship without a captain."[3] Archibald wasted little time in reorganizing Black & Decker's worldwide manufacturing operations. Within three months, Archibald initiated a restructuring plan to close older, inefficient plants and boost factory utilization rates by consolidating production within B&D's newest and biggest plants. Approximately 3,000 jobs were eliminated, including a number of high-level managerial jobs. In 1985, B&D took a $215 million write-off for plant shutdowns and other cost-saving reorganization efforts.

Prior to 1985, the company had pursued a decentralized, multicountry strategy. Each geographic area had its own production facilities, its own product-design centers, and its own marketing and sales organizations to better cater to local market conditions. Over the years, this had resulted in short production runs at scattered production sites, reduced overall manufacturing efficiency, and prevented achievement of scale economies—for example, there were about 100 different motor sizes in B&D's product line. Archibald set the company on a more globalized approach to product design and manufacturing, with much greater communication and coordination between geographic operating units. Production at plants was organized around motor sizes, the number of product variations was reduced, and production runs were lengthened. From 1984 to 1989 seven plants were closed and nearly 3,000 employees were let go. Archibald also insisted more emphasis be put on quality control—during the early 1980s, B&D's reputation in power tools had been tarnished by shoddy product quality.

Meanwhile, Archibald put additional resources into new product development and redesign of the company's power tools and small-appliance lines. Archibald set a goal for the tool division to come up with more than a dozen new products each year—more than B&D had introduced in the five years before his arrival. He also created panels of dealers

[3]As quoted in *BusinessWeek*, July 13, 1987, p. 90.

to suggest new products and features that consumers desired. The company introduced a number of highly successful products such as its Snakelight flashlights; a line of cordless power tools; Macho rotary hammers that could punch holes in stone, brick, and concrete; DeWalt professional power tools; and VersaPak rechargeable batteries that fit both Black & Decker power tools and household appliances.

One of Archibald's biggest marketing challenges was transferring consumers' brand loyalty for GE small appliances over to Black & Decker. Some observers believed Black & Decker would have trouble because B&D's traditional customers were men, and buyers of houseware products were usually women—as a *Wall Street Journal* article headline put it, "Would You Buy a Toaster from a Drillmaker?" B&D executives believed, however, that many women were familiar with the Black & Decker name because they bought power tools as gifts for men and because B&D had pioneered the development of household appliances powered by rechargeable batteries. Black & Decker's handheld DustBuster vacuum cleaner was the market leader, with a 45 percent share. B&D also had been marketing a cordless rotary scrub brush, a cordless rechargeable shoe shiner, and a rechargeable flashlight. Even before acquiring GE's housewares business, B&D had planned to introduce a line of cordless kitchen appliances, but gaining ample retail shelf space was often a hit-or-miss proposition. What made the GE acquisition attractive to B&D was the extra clout that being able to offer retailers a full line of housewares would have in competing for shelf space.

Black & Decker's competitors in small appliances saw the brand-name transition from GE to Black & Decker as an opportunity to gain market share that once was GE's. Sunbeam Appliance quadrupled its 1985 ad budget to $42 million because it wanted to replace GE as the best-known brand in small appliances. Norelco launched a new line of irons and a handheld can opener powered by rechargeable batteries to wrest share away from GE/Black & Decker. Hamilton Beach introduced a battery-operated carving knife. Nearly all small-appliance producers were rumored to be trying to develop cordless adaptations of irons, coffee makers, handheld mixers, and electric carving knives.

Archibald responded to the brand transfer challenge with a series of actions. Since Black & Decker had until 1987 to put its own name on all the GE products it acquired, it led off the transfer process by first putting its name on GE's innovative, expensive, high-margin Space-maker products, which were designed to be mounted under kitchen cabinets—a line that was not as strongly identified with the GE name. Then B&D introduced a new iron (invented by GE) that shut off automatically when it sat too long or was tipped over; B&D's TV ads for the iron showed an elephant walking away from an iron that had been left on, with a tag line: "Even elephants forget." The brand transfer was accomplished product by product, in each case accompanied by heavy advertising. Under Archibald, Black & Decker spent approximately $100 million during the 1985–87 period to promote the brand transition. The company also organized a large team of brand transition assistants to hang paper tags on display models of newly rebranded products in about 10,000 retail stores across the United States—the tags stated that GE previously sold products now made by Black & Decker. Most analysts regarded Archibald's brand transfer program as successful; a Harvard Business School professor stated, "It is almost a textbook example of how to manage a brand transition."[4]

Archibald was promoted to chairman, president, and chief executive officer in 1986. He was listed among *Fortune* magazine's 10 Most Wanted Executives that year and was named as one of the Six Best Managers of 1987 by *BusinessWeek*. By year-end 1988, Archibald was widely credited with engineering another impressive turnaround, having boosted Black & Decker's profits to $97.1 million—up sharply from the loss of $158.4 million posted in 1985. Archibald was also the recipient of the American Marketing Association's 1996 Edison Achievement Award for his accomplishments as Black & Decker chief executive.

[4]Ibid.

Failed Acquisition Attempts

In early 1988 Black & Decker began an unsolicited takeover bid for American Standard Inc., a diversified manufacturer of bathroom fixtures, air conditioning products, and braking systems for rail and automotive vehicles. American Standard had revenues of $3.4 billion and earnings of $127 million in 1987 (compared to revenues of $1.9 billion and earnings of almost $70 million for Black & Decker). After several months of negotiations, the takeover effort failed and B&D withdrew from the battle.

In January 1989, Black & Decker negotiated a deal with Allegheny International to purchase its Oster/Sunbeam appliance division for about $260 million. Oster/Sunbeam was a leading manufacturer and marketer of small household appliances—blenders, can openers, food mixers, electric skillets, steam irons, and other kitchen items. However, in February, Allegheny International backed out of the sale and merged with another company instead.

The Emhart Acquisition

A month later, in March 1989, Black & Decker agreed to acquire Emhart Corporation for $2.8 billion, rescuing the firm from a hostile takeover bid. Emhart had 1988 sales of $2.8 billion, earnings of $127 million, assets of $2.4 billion, and shareholders' equity of $971 million. Emhart was a diversified manufacturer of industrial products (1988 sales of $1.6 billion), information and electronic systems (1988 sales of $654 million), and consumer products (1988 sales of $547 million). Approximately 40 percent of Emhart's sales and earnings came from foreign operations, the majority of which were concentrated in Europe. Exhibit 3 provides a profile of Emhart's business portfolio. Exhibit 4 provides data on the financial performance of Emhart's business units.

In the days following the announcement of Black & Decker's friendly plan to acquire Emhart, B&D's stock price dropped about 15 percent. There was considerable skepticism over the wisdom of the acquisition, both from the standpoint of whether Emhart's businesses had attractive strategic fit with B&D's businesses and whether B&D could handle the financial strain of making such a large acquisition. Emhart was significantly larger than Black & Decker:

1988 Financials	Emhart	Black & Decker
Sales revenues	$2.76 billion	$2.28 billion
Net earnings	126.6 million	97.1 million
Assets	2.43 billion	1.83 billion
Stockholders' equity	970.9 million	724.9 million
Long-term debt	$674.3 million	$277.1 million

The acquisition agreement called for Black & Decker to purchase 59.5 million shares (95 percent) of Emhart Corporation common stock at $40 per share—a price almost three times book value per share ($14.32). Altogether, Black & Decker had to secure $2.7 billion in financing to acquire Emhart. To come up with the funds, Black & Decker entered into a credit agreement with a group of banks that consisted of term loans due 1992 through 1997 and an unsecured revolving credit loan of up to $575 million. The loans carried an interest rate of ¼ percent above whatever the prevailing prime rate was. Scheduled principal payments on the term loans were as follows:

1992	$201,217,000
1993	274,287,000
1994	275,221,000
1995	743,923,000
1996	401,318,000

EXHIBIT 3   **Emhart Corporation's Business Portfolio in 1989 (at the time of the company's acquisition by Black & Decker)**

Business and Product Categories	Trademarks/Names	Primary Markets/ Customers
Industrial Businesses (1988 sales of $1.6 billion)		
Capacitors, audible signal devices	Emhart, Mallory, Sonalert, Arcotronica	Telecommunications, computer, automotive, and electronic components industries
Electromechanical devices, solid-state control systems, hydrocarbon leak detection systems	Emhart, Mallory, Pollulert	Appliance, automotive, and environmental controls manufacturers
Commercial door hardware, electronic locking systems	Emhart, Carbin, Russwin	Commercial, institutional building construction, and original equipment manufacturers
Footwear materials (insoles, toe puffs, shanks, eyelets, tacks, and nails)	Emhart, Texon, Aquiline	Manufacturers of footwear
Fastening systems (rivets, locknuts, screw anchors, adhesive systems, sealants, and grouts)	Emhart, Molly, Warren, Gripco, Bostik, Kelox, Dodge, Heli-Coil, POP	Appliance, construction, electronics, furniture/ woodwork, packaging, automotive, and other transportation industries
Glass container machinery	Emhart, Hartford, Powers, Sundsvalls	Producers of glass containers for beverage, food, household, and pharmaceutical products
Printed circuit board assembling machinery	Emhart, Dynapert	Electronics industry
Information and Electronic Systems (1988 sales of $654 million)		
Technology-based systems and services (including computer-based systems), scientific research services, program management	Emhart, PRC, Planning Research Corp., PRC System Services, PRC Environmental Management, PRC Medic Computer Systems, Nova, Stellar	Governmental units and agencies, real estate multiple listing services, group medical practices, and public utilities
Consumer Products Businesses (1988 sales of $547 million)		
Door hardware, including lock sets, high-security locks, and locking devices	Emhart, Kwikset	Residential construction
Nonpowered lawn and garden equipment, landscape lighting	Garden America, True Temper	Do-it-yourself homeowners
Underground sprinkling and watering systems	Lawn Genie, Drip Mist, Irri-trol	Landscape specialists, do-it-yourself consumers
Golf club shafts, bicycle-frame tubing	True Temper, Dynamic Gold, Black Gold	Golf club manufacturers
Bathroom and kitchen faucets	Price Pfister, The Pfabulous Pfaucet with the Pfunny Name	Residential and commercial construction
Adhesive, sealants	Bostik, Thermogrip	Residential and commercial construction, do-it-yourself consumers
Fasteners, staplers, nailers	Blue-Tack, POP, Molly	Residential and commercial construction

EXHIBIT 4
Financial Performance of Emhart's Business Groups, 1986–88 (In millions of dollars)

Source: Emhart 1988 annual report.

	1988	1987	1986A*	1986B
Revenues				
Industrial				
Components	$ 641.8	$ 671.9		$ 653.9
Fastening systems	640.5	638.8		576.3
Machinery	279.0	291.1	———	419.2
	$1,561.3	$1,601.8		$1,649.4
Information and electronic systems	653.7	438.3		39.3
Consumer	547.5	414.4		405.6
Total	$2,762.5	$2,454.5		$2,094.3
Operating Income (Loss)				
Industrial				
Components	$ 63.8	$ 65.7	$ 48.2	$ (5.4)
Fastening systems	74.8	78.7	68.3	24.8
Machinery	42.7	34.1	44.4	3.9
	$ 181.3	$ 178.5	$160.9	$ 23.3
Information and electronic systems	37.2	22.3	2.0	2.0
Consumer	84.8	68.3	60.4	51.7
	$ 303.3	$ 269.1	$223.3	$ 77.0
Corporate expense	(35.0)	(32.9)	(30.3)	(34.0)
Total	$ 268.3	$ 236.2	$193.0	$ 43.0
Identifiable Assets				
Industrial				
Components	$ 457.8	$ 472.0		$ 400.3
Fastening systems	428.4	428.2		409.7
Machinery	167.8	164.8	———	297.2
	$1,054.0	$1,065.0		$1,107.2
Information and electronic systems	546.7	361.3		334.5
Consumer	702.7	225.1		266.1
	$2,303.4	$1,651.4		$1,707.8
Corporate	123.2	378.5	———	148.9
Total	$2,426.6	$2,029.9	$000.0	$1,856.7

*1986 before provision for restructuring.

The credit agreement included covenants that required Black & Decker to achieve certain minimum levels of cash flow coverage of its interest obligations and not to exceed specified leverage (debt-to-equity) ratios during the term of the loan:

Fiscal Year	Maximum Leverage Ratio	Minimum Cash Flow Coverage Ratio
1992	3.25	1.35
1993	2.75	1.50
1994	2.25	1.55
1995 and thereafter	1.50	1.60

Note: The leverage ratio was calculated by dividing indebtedness, as defined by the credit agreement, by consolidated net stockholders' equity. The cash flow coverage ratio was calculated by dividing earnings before interest, taxes, depreciation, and amortization of goodwill minus capital expenditures by net interest expense plus cash income tax payments and dividends declared.

Other covenants in the credit agreement limited Black & Decker's ability to incur additional indebtedness and to acquire businesses or sell assets.

Black & Decker also entered into factoring agreements with financial institutions where it sold its receivables at a discounted rate to avoid waiting 30 to 60 days to collect on its invoices. The company ended its sale of receivables program in December 1997 when it became able to meet its liquidity requirements without factoring receivables.

Black & Decker recorded the excess amount of its purchase price for Emhart over the book value of Emhart's net assets as goodwill to be amortized on a straight-line basis over 40 years. This resulted in Black & Decker's having increased depreciation and amortization charges of about $45 million annually.

Initial Divestitures of Emhart Businesses

Senior management at Black & Decker realized early on that as much as $1 billion of Emhart's business assets would have to be sold to reduce B&D's interest expenses and debt obligations and enable it to meet its covenant agreements. According to accounting rules, these assets had to either be sold within a year or be consolidated with the rest of B&D assets—a move that could cause B&D to fail to meet its maximum leverage covenant. The Emhart businesses that were identified for sale within one year from the acquisition date included footwear materials, printed circuit board assembly equipment (Dynapert), capacitors, chemical adhesives (Bostik), and the entire information and electronic systems business unit (PRC). During 1989 and early 1990, Black & Decker sold the Bostik chemical adhesives division to a French company for $345 million, the footwear materials business to the United Machinery Group for approximately $125 million, and its Arcotronics capacitors business to Nissei Electric of Tokyo for about $80 million; the net proceeds from these sales were used to reduce debt. In early 1990, when the one-year period expired, Black & Decker was forced to consolidate about $566 million of the unsold assets, boosting the goodwill on its balance sheet by $560 million, raising annual amortization charges by $14 million. To keep from violating the maximum debt/equity ratio allowed under its credit schedule, Black & Decker was forced to issue $150 million in new preferred stock, $47 million of which was purchased from its 401(K) employee thrift plan when no other buyers came forward.

Throughout 1991 Black & Decker continued to struggle to meet its covenant agreements. The company divested Emhart's Garden America business unit and the Mallory Controls operations in North America and Brazil for a combined total of about $140 million. The company also sold its True Temper Hardware unit, its PRC Medic unit, and its U.S. Capacitors business for a combined total of nearly $110 million. The prices B&D got for the Emhart businesses it sold were generally below management's expectations, partly because oncoming recessionary effects reduced what buyers were willing to pay.

Nonetheless, these divestitures (described by B&D management as "nonstrategic assets") and the sale of $150 million in preferred stock, allowed Black & Decker to reduce its total debt from a peak of $4 billion following the Emhart acquisition in April 1989 to $2.9 billion at year-end 1991. Even so, Black & Decker was still hard pressed to generate enough cash to meet its debt repayment schedule, a problem compounded by the 1990–91 recession, which hit the company's tool and household goods businesses fairly hard. The company's stock price fell from the mid-20s at the time of the Emhart acquisition to a low of $11–$12 in early 1991—many observers believed that the fundamental cause of B&D's financial plight was that it had paid too much for Emhart. There was also concern about whether there was enough strategic fit between Emhart and B&D. By early 1992, the stock price had recovered to the low 20s, partly because a decline in the prime rate from 10 percent to 6.5 percent had lowered B&D's interest burden substantially. (The credit agreement pegged the interest rate B&D paid at ¼ percent above the prevailing prime rate.)

Subsequent Divestitures: 1993–96

During the next six years, Black & Decker's corporate management sought to find buyers for several nonstrategic businesses acquired as part of the Emhart deal. Three were sold between 1993 and 1996.

Dynapert

The Dynapert business unit provided automated equipment for assembling printed circuit boards to electronics customers around the world. The equipment was among the most complex computer-controlled machinery being used in any industrial application. Dynapert had two manufacturing plants (one in the United States and one in England) and sales and service facilities throughout the world. The unit had launched a total quality program and implemented just-in-time manufacturing techniques.

Sales were made directly to users by an employee sales force and independent sales representatives. Dynapert faced competition from both U.S. and foreign manufacturers. Competition centered on technological and machine performance features, price, delivery terms, and provision of technical services. The Dynapert division, which generated 1991 sales of about $180 million, had been put on the market shortly after the Emhart acquisition, and was sold two years later to Dover Corporation's Universal Instrument division for an undisclosed amount.

Corbin Russwin

Emhart's Corbin Russwin manufactured locks and door hardware for the European commercial security hardware market. The unit employed 550 people at its plant in Berlin, Germany. Yale and Valour, Inc., the British manufacturer of Yale locks, purchased the Corbin Russwin unit from Black & Decker in 1994 for $80 million. Black & Decker recorded a gain of $18 million on the combined sales of the Corbin Russwin and Dynapert units.

PRC Information Systems and Services

This segment consisted of a single business unit known as PRC, Inc., headquartered in McLean, Virginia. PRC and its predecessors had been in business since the mid-1970s. A majority of PRC's business came from contracts with various agencies and units of the federal government. Approximately 40 percent of PRC's 1991 revenues were from contracts with the Department of Defense. In addition, PRC was the leading provider of (1) online printed residential real estate multiple listing systems and (2) computer-aided emergency dispatch systems. The types of services PRC provided were highly competitive, and strategic defense expenditures were expected to decline given the improvement of foreign relations. Many of PRC's competitors were large defense contractors with significantly greater financial resources. As the Department of Defense's expenditures for weapons programs continued to decline, these large contractors were expected to bid more aggressively for the types of contract work done by PRC. PRC had also been put on the market for sale following the Emhart acquisition. In 1991, PRC had sales of $684 million and pretax operating earnings of $32.3 million. In mid-1991 B&D appointed a new person to head PRC; shortly thereafter, PRC launched an initiative to pursue new markets. The objective was to shift PRC's business mix so that half came from U.S. customers and half from overseas customers. However, PRC management had great difficulty developing new nongovernment customers and was only growing at about one-third the rate of its closest competitors under Black & Decker ownership.

Black & Decker had little success in locating interested buyers for the PRC unit until 1995, when PRC Realty Systems and PRC Environmental Management, Inc., were sold for $60 and $35.5 million, respectively. Litton Industries agreed to purchase the remaining PRC operations in 1996 for $425 million. Prior to its sale to Litton, when it appeared that finding a buyer was becoming increasingly unlikely, Black & Decker management had considered a spinoff of the unit in 1992. The spinoff was never finalized because Wall

Street showed little interest in a $350 million public offering of PRC stock. PRC's 1995 sales and after-tax earnings were $800 million and $38.4 million, respectively.

Black & Decker's 1998 Divestitures

Black & Decker again initiated portfolio restructuring in 1998 when it divested its household products business and two businesses gained through the Emhart acquisition.

Household Products

Black & Decker's household products business had established itself as a worldwide leader in products used for home cleaning, garment care, cooking, and food and beverage preparation by 1990. It had the largest market share of any full-line producer of household appliance products in the United States, Canada, Mexico, and Australia and a growing presence in Europe, Southeast Asia, and Latin America. The household products division was using the worldwide distribution network and brand-name recognition that had been established by the tools division to gain greater global penetration in household appliances. However, by 1996, the company had lost substantial market share in almost every housewares product category. Its Toast-R-Ovens and irons were the only remaining Black & Decker products that held leading shares of their respective markets. (See Exhibit 5 for market shares of the major competitors by product category for 1990, 1993, and 1996.)

Like the market for power tools, the market for small household appliances was both mature and cyclical. Growth opportunities existed mainly in the form of creating innovative new products and in increasing market penetration in the countries of Eastern Europe and other developing nations where household appliance saturation rates were low. It was difficult to grow sales in the United States without introducing innovative new products since most small appliances had very high household saturation rates. In 1996 blenders were found in 80 percent of U.S. households, coffeemakers had a 74 percent saturation rate, and toasters were found in 90 percent of U.S. households. Many consumers clearly had both a toaster and toaster oven, since toaster ovens had a 42 percent U.S. household saturation rate.

Black & Decker's housewares business unit had been successful at launching new products that might entice a consumer into replacing an existing small appliance for one offering more features or better performance. The company's SnakeLight flexible flashlight was introduced in 1994 and quickly became one of the most popular small appliances ever developed by the company. In 1996 the company introduced a revamped Quick 'N Easy line of irons with a new Sure Steam system, and in 1998 it improved the glideability of its irons with a new proprietary coated soleplate. The company also introduced cordless products such as the ScumBuster, a submersible scourer and scrubber, and the FloorBuster, an upright vacuum cleaner that achieved rapid sales increases.

In late 1997 the company launched a designer line of small kitchen appliances, Kitchentools, which won five Industrial Design Excellence Awards in 1998. The Kitchentools line carried premium pricing; the stand mixer had a suggested retail price of $289.99, the thermal coffeemaker listed at $159.99, the blender was priced at $139.99, the food processor was priced at $229.99, the hand mixer's retail price was $69.00, and the Kitchentools can opener carried a suggested retail price of $34.99. Even though the Kitchentools line was praised for its quality and innovative styling, it did not sell as well as Black & Decker management had expected. The company also had some difficulty manufacturing the products and getting them to market by the planned launch date.

Black & Decker had lost substantial market share in recent years and had seen its profit margins erode despite its best efforts to maintain efficient operations. Between 1995 and 1997 the company had completely overhauled its supply chain management to reduce finished goods inventory and improve customer service and production planning. The company had eliminated $150 million from logistics costs during that time period but still only

EXHIBIT 5
Unit Volume for Selected Small Appliances and Market Shares of Leading Producers, 1990, 1993, and 1996 (unit volume in thousands)

Source: Compiled by case researchers from data presented in *Appliance,* April 1991 and April 1997.

Product/Leading Brands	1990	1993	1996
Can openers	6,200	6,380	6,910
Rival	33%	27%	26%
Hamilton Beach/Proctor Silex	13	15	24
Black & Decker	26	28	13
Oster/Sunbeam	11	13	13
Coffeemakers	17,740	14,390	15,000
Mr. Coffee	28%	31%	32%
Hamilton Beach/Proctor Silex	19	18	24
West Bend	—	3	9
Black & Decker	20	17	8
Food processors	4,760	1,916	1,525
Hamilton Beach/Proctor Silex	21%	19%	40%
Cuisinart	Unknown	13	18
Black & Decker	25	21	10
Oster/Sunbeam	18	19	8
Hand mixers	4,400	5,060	5,280
Hamilton Beach/Proctor Silex	14%	18%	24%
Black & Decker	34	28	15
Oster/Sunbeam	25	18	13
HPA/Betty Crocker	—	—	11
Irons	16,950	17,460	15,600
Black & Decker	50%	50%	38%
Hamilton Beach/Proctor Silex	24	30	29
Oster/Sunbeam	17	10	17
Rowenta	—	—	7
Toaster ovens	2,800	3,340	3,670
Black & Decker	57%	56%	56%
Toastmaster	13	16	17
Hamilton Beach/Proctor Silex	19	20	11
HPA/Betty Crocker	—	—	6
Toasters	8,900	9,850	10,760
Hamilton Beach/Proctor Silex	35%	50%	37%
Toastmaster	27	31	30
Rival	—	—	17
HPA/Betty Crocker	—	—	5
Black & Decker	16	13	4

averaged about 2 percent profit margins on its housewares products. The business unit was identified for divestiture by Nolan Archibald in January 1998 and was sold to Windmere-Durable in May 1998 for $315 million. The agreement allowed Black & Decker to retain its DustBuster, FloorBuster, ScumBuster, and SnakeLight product lines. In June 1998 Black & Decker announced the sale of its housewares operations in New Zealand and Australia to Gerard Industries, an Australian electrical products manufacturer. The company had also sold its consumer glue gun and stapler business to Longwood Industries for an undisclosed amount in July 1998.

Recreational Outdoor Products

In 1998 B&D's True Temper Sports business unit was the leading global designer, manufacturer, and marketer of steel golf club shafts; with over a 60 percent market share in the steel shaft segment, it was three times as large as its closest rival. True Temper also manufactured graphite shafts but had a very limited market share in that segment since it focused on the premium end of the market. The division supplied more than 800 golf club manufacturers around the world, including such industry leaders as Callaway Golf, Ping, Titleist, and Taylor Made. The sales of this unit had grown at a compounded annual rate of 12 percent between 1995 and 1997. True Temper Sport's growth rate reflected the overall growth in the golf equipment industry. The unit also manufactured specialty tubing for the bicycle and sporting goods industries. Many of the bicycles and kayak paddles used by U.S. Olympians were manufactured from True Temper precision tubing.

Black & Decker sold the business to Cornerstone Equity Investors in June 1998 for $178 million. The new owners stated that they intended for True Temper to remain the leader in golf club shafts and that they intended to expand into new product categories requiring specialty tubing. True Temper's president said that the new company would develop precision tubing products for such sporting goods industries as down-hill skiing and archery.

Glass-Container-Forming Machinery

In 1998 B&D's Emhart glass-container-forming machinery division was considered the global leader and offered the world's most complete line of glass-container-making equipment. Important competitive factors were price, technological and machine performance features, product reliability, and technical and engineering services. An increasing worldwide preference for plastic and other nonglass containers had led to a slowing growth rate for glass-container-forming equipment and inspection equipment. There was little seasonal variation in industry demand. Glass-container-making equipment was in 24-hour use in virtually all plants worldwide, creating a predictable need for servicing and rebuilding; nearly two-thirds of the unit's revenues came from rebuilding and repair services and technology upgrades. In January 1998 the business was identified as a nonstrategic asset that was to be divested; it was sold to Bucher Holding AG of Switzerland in September 1998 for $178 million.

Black & Decker's Business Portfolio in 2000

In 2000 Black & Decker Corporation was a diversified multinational enterprise with a business portfolio consisting of

- Power tools and accessories for both do-it-yourselfers and professional tradespeople.
- Lawn and garden equipment.
- Security hardware for residential markets in the United States and residential and commercial hardware in certain European countries.
- Cleaning and lighting products.
- Plumbing products.
- Commercial fastening systems.

Exhibit 6 provides a detailed listing of the products produced and marketed by B&D in these business areas. Exhibit 7 provides 1997–99 financial performance data by business group. A brief description of each business group follows.

Power Tools and Accessories

Black & Decker was the world's largest manufacturer, marketer, and servicer of power tools and accessories. The company's products were available at almost all retail outlets that sold power tools in the United States, Europe, and other developed countries. In fact, Black & Decker products were so popular in the United Kingdom that many British do-it-yourselfers referred to home improvement projects as "Black & Deckering." Black & Decker was named as the top-performing hardware brand by 6 out of every 10 U.S. retailers included in

EXHIBIT 6
Black & Decker's
Business Portfolio at
Year-End 1999

Power tools and accessories (1999 sales: $3.21 billion)	**Fastening and assembly systems** (1999 sales: $498 million)
• Drills	• Rivets and riveting tools
• Screwdrivers	• Threaded inserts
• Saws	• Stud welding fastening systems
• Sanders	• Lock nuts
• Grinders	• Self-drilling screws
• Tabletop saws	• Construction anchors
• Drill bits	
• Screwdriver bit	
• Saw blades	
• Cleaning and lighting products	

Hardware and home improvement
(1999 sales: $882 million)

• Lock sets
• Deadbolts
• Master keying systems
• Faucets and fixtures
• Lawn and garden care products

a 1997 survey conducted by *Discount Store News*. Other brands that were highly rated by hardware retailers were Stanley, General Electric, Skil, Rubbermaid, Makita, and Dutch Boy. Black & Decker's products were also highly rated in terms of performance by consumers, and most of its products carried a two-year warranty.

Industry Growth and Competition

Demand for power tools and accessories was regarded as mature and cyclical. Volume was influenced by residential and commercial construction activity, by consumer expenditures for home improvement, and by the overall level of manufacturing activity. (A number of manufacturers used power tools in performing certain production tasks—automotive and aerospace firms, for example, were heavy users of power tools.) Worldwide sales of power tools were an estimated $10 billion in 1999. The North American market for power tools was estimated at $3.5 billion, European sales were estimated at $4.0 billion, Asia/Pacific sales were an estimated $2.0 billion, and Latin American sales of power tools were approximately $500 million. The global market for power tools failed to grow significantly between 1997 and 1999, but was expected to grow at low- to mid-single-digit annual rates between 2000 and 2002. The industry's worldwide demand plateau during the late 1990s was attributable in large part to Asian financial and economic troubles. During 1998 and 1999 North America was the fastest-growing market for power tools as cordless and professional-grade power tools gained in popularity with consumers. Demand in Europe grew more slowly than in the United States during the late 1990s and was expected to continue to lag behind U.S. demand in the near future. Worldwide, the biggest percentage growth during the early and mid-1990s occurred in emerging Asian countries, where the use of power tools was quickly replacing the use of hand tools. Healthy demand for power tools was expected to return to Asian markets once the region had fully recovered from the effects of financial and economic instability that began in late 1997.

Market Segments

There were two distinct groups of buyers for power tools: professional users and do-it-yourselfers. Professional users included construction workers, electricians, plumbers, repair

EXHIBIT 7 **Black & Decker's Financial Performance by Business Segment, 1997–99**

Source: Black & Decker annual reports.

	Power Tools and Accessories	Hardware and Home Improvement	Fastening and Assembly Systems	All Others	Currency Translation Adjustments	Corporate Adjustments and Eliminations	Consolidated
1999							
Sales to unaffiliated customers	$3,209.3	$881.8	$497.7	—	($68.3)	$ —	$4,520.5
Operating income before restructuring and exit costs, write-off of goodwill, and gain on sales of businesses	377.3	124.0	84.3	—	(6.9)	(42.4)	536.3
Depreciation and amortization	87.7	31.1	15.4	—	(1.8)	27.6	160.0
Identifiable assets	1,836.0	508.2	273.2	—	2,617.4	1,395.3	4,012.7
Capital expenditures	$ 109.1	$ 38.3	$ 26.9	—	($ 3.5)	$ 0.3	$ 171.1
1998							
Sales to unaffiliated customers	$2,946.4	$851.1	$463.0	$333.6	($34.2)	$ —	$4,559.9
Operating income before restructuring and exit costs, write-off of goodwill, and gain on sales of businesses	293.4	125.2	76.6	16.5	(4.4)	(23.3)	484.0
Depreciation and amortization	88.2	27.1	13.4	—	(1.1)	27.6	155.2
Identifiable assets	1,631.3	507.8	246.7	—	(4.6)	1,471.3	3,852.5
Capital expenditures	$ 79.1	$ 36.5	$ 16.2	$ 13.3	($ 1.1)	$ 2.0	$ 146.0
1997							
Sales to unaffiliated customers	$2,936.4	$804.8	$451.3	$718.1	$29.9	$ —	$4,940.5
Operating income before restructuring and exit costs, write-off of goodwill, and gain on sales of businesses	290.7	121.3	69.7	61.7	(2.3)	(51.8)	489.3
Depreciation and amortization	87.5	24.7	11.9	24.4	(0.3)	66.0	214.2
Identifiable assets	1,635.4	476.5	248.2	438.6	8.0	2,554.0	5,360.7
Capital expenditures	$ 113.2	$ 47.3	$ 15.4	$ 25.3	($ 0.2)	$ 2.1	$ 203.1

and maintenance workers, auto mechanics, and manufacturing workers. Professional users were very conscious of quality and features; they tended to buy only those tools that were durable, functional, dependable, and capable of precision. They also tended to be very knowledgeable compared to do-it-yourselfers, many of whom were first-time buyers and used power tools infrequently.

Because the needs of professional users and do-it-yourself consumers tended to be sharply different, some manufacturers had a heavy-duty professional line and a consumer/do-it-yourself line and others catered to just one of the two segments. Professional users tended to purchase their tools through jobbers, contractor supply firms, industrial supply houses, building supply centers, and some home improvement centers. Tools for the consumer segment were sold at home improvement centers, building materials centers, mass merchandisers (Sears), discount chains (Wal-Mart, Kmart), and hardware stores.

Until the late 1980s, the consumer tool segment was growing at a faster clip than the professional segment. But narrowing price differentials and a rising interest on the part of gung-ho do-it-yourselfers in professional-quality tools had, in the U.S. market, spurred demand for heavy-duty professional tools. The sales of both consumer-grade and professional-grade cordless products were also becoming increasingly popular, with a compound annual growth rate of over 10 percent during the mid- and late 1990s.

Competition

Power tool manufacturers competed on such variables as price, quality, product design, product innovation, brand-name reputation, size and strength of retail dealer networks, and after-sale service. All makers were working to bring out new products that were lightweight, compact, cordless, quiet, less prone to vibration, strong, and easy to manipulate. The major manufacturers had sales forces whose main task was to expand and strengthen the network of retail dealers carrying their line of tools. Salespeople signed on new dealers and called on major accounts—wholesale distributors, discount chains, home improvement centers, and other mass merchandisers—to win better access to shelf space in their retail outlets, help with promotion and display activities, and upgrade dealers' product knowledge and sales skills. Some manufacturers offered training seminars and provided training videos to dealers/distributors. Manufacturers that concentrated on the professional segment engaged in limited advertising and promotion activities, spending their dollars for trade magazine ads, trade shows, and in-store displays. Those that concentrated on the consumer segment, like Black & Decker, spent comparatively heavily for TV and magazine ads and also for co-op ad programs with dealers.

Black & Decker's Global Competitive Position in Power Tools

In 2000 Black & Decker was the overall world leader in the world power tool industry, followed by Bosch/Skil Power Tools, a division of Robert Bosch Corporation (one of Germany's leading companies), and Japanese brands Makita and Hitachi. Other competitors were Atlas/Copco, Delta/Porter Cable, Hilti, Ryobi, and Electrolux. For most of the company's history, Black & Decker's greatest strength was in the consumer tools segment (see Exhibit 8); it was the market leader in the United States, Europe (where it had had a presence since the 1920s), and many other countries outside Europe. No other manufacturer came close to matching B&D's global distribution capabilities in the do-it-yourself segment. Makita and Ryobi were the leaders in Japan and several other Asian countries. Bosch was strongest in Europe.

In consumer tools Black & Decker's strongest U.S. competitor was Sears, which marketed tools under the Sears Craftsman label. Sears's longtime supplier of tools was Ryobi, which supplied Sears with 75 percent of its tool requirements. Skil's strength was in power saws; its 1992 joint venture with Robert Bosch Power Tools was contrived to give the two

EXHIBIT 8

Estimated U.S. Sales and Market Shares of Power Tool Manufacturers, 1979, 1991, and 1997 ($ millions)

Source: Compiled by the case researchers from a variety of sources, including telephone interviews with company personnel; data for 1979 are based on information in Skil Corporation, Harvard Business School, case #9–389–005.

	1979		1991		1997	
	Dollar Sales	Percent Share	Dollar Sales	Percent Share	Dollar Sales	Percent Share
Consumer Tools						
Black & Decker	$169	44.5%	$325	39.7	$460	43.1%
Sears/Ryobi	107	28.2	280	34.0	305	28.5
Milwaukee	6	1.5	4	0.5	6	0.6
Makita	2	0.5	43	5.2	32	3.0
Porter Cable	—	—	—	—	—	—
Delta	—	—	—	—	—	—
Skil	52	13.7	82	10.0	165	15.4
Others	44	11.6	86	10.6	102	9.4
Total	$380	100.0%	$820	100.0%	$1,070	100.0%
Professional Tools						
Black & Decker	$205	42.1%	$125	17.9%	$918	36.7%
Sears/Ryobi	9	1.8	50	7.1	285	11.4
Milwaukee	89	18.2	145	20.7	436	17.4
Makita	22	4.5	160	22.9	304	12.2
Porter Cable	NA	NA	50	7.1	240	9.6
Delta	NA	NA	40	5.7	209	8.4
Skil	54	11.1	40	5.7	32	1.3
Others	109	22.3	90	12.9	76	3.0
Total	$488	100.0%	$700	100.0%	$2,500	100.0%
Total Tools						
Black & Decker	$374	43.1%	$450	29.6%	$1,378	38.6%
Sears/Ryobi	116	13.4	330	21.7	590	16.5
Milwaukee	95	10.9	149	9.8	442	12.4
Makita	24	2.8	203	13.4	336	9.4
Porter Cable	NA	NA	50	3.3	240	6.7
Delta	NA	NA	40	2.6	209	5.9
Skil	106	12.2	122	8.0	197	5.5
Others	153	17.6	176	11.6	210	9.4
Total	$868	100.0%	$1,520	100.0%	$3,570	100.0%

NA = not available

brands more clout in gaining shelf space and greater global coverage capabilities. Black & Decker's consumer-grade power tools were also carried by Sears, and the company had developed a new Quantum line of power tools sold exclusively by Wal-Mart. Quantum was an intermediate line that was more durable than typical consumer lines but did not meet the performance of the company's professional power tools. Black & Decker's Mouse sander, WoodHawk circular saws, and FireStorm drills, along with its products that used the VersaPak interchangeable battery, were among the company's best-selling consumer tools.

Although surveys showed that consumers associated the Black & Decker name with durable power tools, trade professionals viewed Black & Decker products as products for do-it-yourselfers. During the late 1980s, the company's charcoal-gray professional tools line was not seen by professional users as sufficiently differentiated from B&D's traditional black line of consumer tools. Professionals preferred tools made by Makita, Skil, and Milwaukee (a U.S. tool manufacturer with a reputation for quality, heavy-duty tools). During the 1970s and 1980s, Makita had steadily increased its share of the professional segment and by 1991 had captured 53 percent of the U.S. professional handheld power tool segment.

In 1991 B&D executives formed a team, headed by the president of B&D's power tools division, to come up with a new strategy for the professional market segment. The team elected to create an entirely new line of industrial-grade tools for professional users under the DeWalt brand, a name borrowed from a 65-year-old maker of high-quality stationary saws acquired by B&D in 1960. The team changed the tools' color from gray to industrial yellow because the latter was easy to see, signaled safety, and was distinct from other leading brands of professional power tools. Every product in B&D's professional line was redesigned based on input from professionals, dealers, and B&D engineers. The redesigned versions were all tested by professional users; every item had to meet or beat Makita's tools in user tests before going into production. The new DeWalt line was introduced in March 1992. As part of the introduction of the DeWalt line, B&D created "swarm teams" of 120 young, high-energy marketers that visited construction sites to demonstrate DeWalt tools in their bright yellow-and-black Chevy Blazers. DeWalt swarm teams also promoted DeWalt tools at NASCAR events, vocational clubs, union apprenticeship programs, and retail locations. The company intended to double the number of swarm team members in the United States between 1998 and 1999. In 1996 DeWalt swarm teams invaded Europe with a fleet of yellow-and-black Range Rover Defenders with the charge of making DeWalt a leading brand on that continent. The company also instituted a policy of offering professional users the loan of a DeWalt power tool when waiting for their equipment to be fixed at any of the company's 135 U.S. service centers. There were also DeWalt demonstration booths at each of the service centers.

Initial response to the DeWalt line was excellent. As the brand began to gain in popularity with professional users, Black & Decker developed additional DeWalt tools. In 1997, newly introduced DeWalt products were awarded two Industrial Design Excellence Awards from the Industrial Designers Society of America. The success of the new DeWalt line exceeded Black & Decker management's expectations and surpassed its $200 million sales volume objective for 1995 by over $100 million. In 1999 DeWalt was one of the leading power tool brands for professionals and serious do-it-yourselfers.

Black & Decker was also the world leader in the market for such accessories as drill bits, saw blades, and screwdriver bits. Vermont American, Irwin Hanson/American Tool, Bosch, Freud, and Wolfcraft were B&D's closest competitors in the accessories market, but no other company had as broad a product line or geographic coverage as Black & Decker. Most of the company's growth in accessory sales was accounted for by accessory lines developed for the DeWalt brand and a line of new premium woodworking saw blades. The company intended to maintain its market leadership by expanding into more woodworking supply and industrial/construction distribution channels and continuing to introduce innovative products.

In 1998 Black & Decker launched a series of initiatives intended to strengthen its competitive position in power tools and accessories. First, it introduced a corporatewide six sigma quality program to bring about improvements in costs, defect rates, product quality, and customer satisfaction. Second, the company took a $164 million restructuring charge that involved the elimination of 2,900 positions; worldwide plant rationalization that resulted in plant closings in Canada, Singapore, and Italy; a reorganization of its European operations; and various reengineering projects in all plants. Third, it initiated a restructuring of its supply chain management to improve customer service while reducing inventories. Although Black & Decker's restructuring program cut across all business units, it was primarily focused on its global power tools business and was expected to yield more than $100 million annually in cost savings. Additional cost savings were achieved through the integration of Black & Decker's cleaning and lighting products like its DustBuster vacuum cleaner, ScumBuster wet scrubber, and SnakeLight flashlight with its power tool businesses after the sale of the housewares division to Windmere in 1998.

The April 21, 1999, exit of Joseph Galli, Black & Decker's president of its Worldwide Power Tools and Accessories group, shocked analysts and investors and caused a one-day

8 percent decline in the company's share price. Galli, age 41, was a rising star at Black & Decker and was thought to be the leading candidate to succeed Archibald as CEO. There was a widely held belief in the power tools industry that much of the DeWalt brand's success was attributable to Galli's strategic leadership and that Galli had been forced out of B&D as a result of his desire to become the company's CEO within the near future. Archibald, who had no immediate retirement plans, commented that Galli had "expressed an interest in advancing his management career to a higher level, and we have agreed it makes sense for him to pursue this goal outside of Black & Decker."[5] In June 1999 Joe Galli become president and chief operating officer of Amazon.com. Even though there was some initial concern by investors over Galli's departure, B&D's Power Tools and Accessories group continued to perform well in his absence; its sales increased by 11 percent and operating profit increased by 27 percent during the fourth quarter of 1999. The business unit's annual sales and operating profits increased by 9 percent and 29 percent, respectively, over 1998 sales and operating profits.

Lawn and Garden Equipment

Black & Decker's lawn and garden tools like Groom 'N' Edge, Vac 'N' Mulch, and Leaf-Buster were distributed through the same channels as the company's power tools. In addition, the buyers of B&D's hedge trimmers, string trimmers, lawn mowers, edgers, and blower/vacuums could get the items repaired at B&D's 150 company-owned service centers worldwide and several hundred other authorized service centers operated by independent owners. Where feasible, B&D's lawn and garden products had a global design. The company had recently begun to offer cordless electric string trimmers and hedge trimmers in North America and Europe. The cordless hedge trimmer could run continuously for about 30 minutes, and the cordless string trimmer could trim hard-to-reach areas from a half-acre lawn on a single battery charge. As of 2000, Black & Decker marketed its cordless lawn mowers only in Europe.

Security Hardware

B&D's security hardware business was the leader in the $2 billion global market for door hardware for homes and businesses. The company had developed good-better-best product lines that covered all major residential price points. The Kwikset brand was positioned as an affordable product targeted to do-it-yourselfers; B&D had boosted Kwikset's sales by providing retailers with a videotape that took the mystery out of changing household locks. Kwikset Plus was a midrange product, and the company's TITAN products were designed for the fine home market. TITAN NightSight handsets and deadbolts featured lighted keyways, and the TITAN AccessOne keyless entry deadbolt and handset systems allowed homeowners to use a remote control to unlock the door from as far away as 30 feet. The TITAN line also included the Society Brass Collection of solid brass designer door hardware. All TITAN products boasted a lifetime finish that was protected against tarnishing, rust, and corrosion.

This business, acquired from Emhart, had achieved significant cost savings by integrating its purchasing, distribution, and marketing activities with B&D's other consumer products businesses. B&D's worldwide distribution network was also providing the hardware group wider geographic sales opportunities. In many instances, door hardware was sold in the same retail channels as B&D's power tools and accessories. Black & Decker's restructuring and six sigma quality initiatives, begun in 1998, also affected its security hardware business—products and facilities were rationalized, high-cost operations were restructured, and automation was used where feasible. Black & Decker's major competitors in the North American

[5]As quoted in the *Baltimore Sun,* April 22, 1999.

security hardware market included Schlage, Weiser, Weslock, and a variety of Asian exporters. Major competitors in Europe included Williams, Assa Abloy, Cisa, Keso, and Abus.

Plumbing Products

B&D's plumbing products business, Price Pfister, had gained market share since the Emhart acquisition to become the third largest manufacturer and marketer of plumbing fixtures in North America by 2000. Price Pfister had benefited from access to B&D's retail distribution network by gaining more shelf space in home improvement centers. Price Pfister had also introduced fashionable, but affordably priced, new designs and new lines that had become popular with plumbing wholesalers and plumbing contractors. Price Pfister had increased its brand recognition through in-store merchandising activities and with TV ads using the theme "The Pfabulous Pfaucet with the Pfunny Name" in the early 1990s and "The Pfabulous Pfaucet. Pforever. No Drips, No Tarnish, No Worries" theme in the late 1990s.

Price Pfister's major competitors in the $1.9 billion North American market for sink, tub, shower, and lavatory plumbing hardware were American Standard, Kohler, Delta, and Moen. The industry had grown at a slow rate of 2 to 3 percent since 1995 and was expected to grow at a comparable rate over the next few years. Plumbing products with new styles and features were in the highest demand. Black & Decker expected new decorative faucets like Price Pfister's Georgetown and Roman lines, introduced during the late 1990s, to account for 20 percent of the unit's annual sales. Price Pfister expected to improve its performance with the addition of innovative and attractive new lines, better in-store merchandising, improved manufacturing efficiency, and better supply chain management.

Commercial Fastening Systems

Black & Decker was among the global leaders in the $2 billion fastening and assembly systems market. This business unit marketed fastening products under 26 different brands and trademarks to automotive, electronics, aerospace, machine tool, and appliance companies in the United States, Europe, and the Far East. The industry's recent growth rate had ranged between 3 and 5 percent, and future growth was expected to remain within that range. Some emerging markets did generate higher growth rates as new industries and companies emerged and plant capacity was added.

Products were sold directly to users and also through distributors and manufacturers' representatives. Competition centered on product quality, performance, reliability, price, delivery, and ability to provide customers with technical and engineering services. Competition came from many manufacturers in several countries. Major competitors included Textron, TRW, Eaton, and such regional companies as Raymond, Gesipa, Huck, and Fukui. Black & Decker was the global leader in commercial blind riveting and automotive stud welding systems, and its other fastening system categories held strong positions in various geographic regions. Black & Decker management intended to maintain its leadership in the automotive stud welding category with new product innovations. More than 30 percent of the unit's 1999 sales were accounted for by products introduced within the past five years. Black & Decker intended to improve the performance of the division through implementation of its six sigma quality initiative, reengineered operations, and plant rationalizations.

Black & Decker's Future Prospects

The year 2000 marked the beginning of Black & Decker's second year of operations with its streamlined portfolio of businesses following the 1998 divestiture of its small-appliance, True Temper recreational products, and Emhart glass-forming machinery businesses. Black & Decker had sold the three businesses for more than management's expected $500 million and was able to reduce operating expenses by more than $100 million annually, primarily as a result of the elimination of 3,000 jobs from its payroll. In addition, the series of divestitures had cut the company's amortization of goodwill associated with the Emhart acquisition by about $30 million annually for the next 30 years.

This last round of divestitures, coupled with the sale of businesses in earlier years, completed the divestiture of the nonstrategic Emhart assets gained in the 1989 acquisition. Price Pfister and Kwikset were two of the Emhart businesses that initially captured the attention of Black & Decker management and were now among the three remaining Emhart businesses still included in Black & Decker's portfolio. So far, the 1998 divestitures had not produced steady increases in the company's stock price, but Nolan Archibald was confident that the company's ability to focus solely on power tools and other closely aligned businesses would allow the company to begin to provide its shareholders with above-average returns.

Expresso Espresso

Calvin M. Bacon, Jr. *University of South Alabama*

"DAVID, WHATSUP?" Todd Sylvester bellowed as a regular customer entered. He believed the need to feel recognized and loved was part of the human condition and considered it part of his mission to provide those feelings. To make the customers feel welcome, Todd made a point of knowing their names and recognizing them as they came through the door. Years ago, when he drove a school bus through the same tollbooth every day, he made a point of knowing the tollbooth operators' names. Every day as he paid his toll, he gave them the biggest smile he could muster, greeted them by name, and wished them a happy day. "There is a real deprivation of joy in society. I think it is important to provide comfort and help people feel good," Todd noted.

Expresso Espresso coffee shop opened in March 2006 across the street from the University of South Alabama (South) in Mobile. The shop targeted the university's 13,000 students as well as the staff and faculty. Although the business had only been open for 12 weeks and was still operating at a loss, Todd, the owner, was already making plans to expand into the city's midtown area. He believed that the culture and values he instilled in the company would make it successful anywhere, and he believed growth was imperative to achieve his long-term goals. Todd wanted to use his first shop to prove the business concept so he could begin expanding as soon as possible.

Although he was optimistic about the business, he was worried about the changing dynamics of the coffee shop industry in the Mobile Bay area. Several other new shops were either in the planning or construction stage, and he wondered what impact those shops might have on Expresso. Moreover, he was concerned about the strategic position his shop would have once the dust settled from all the expansion. In addition, Todd was not sure if his marketing efforts would increase sales soon enough to avoid a financial hardship for his family. He and his wife, Angelle, had taken a $100,000 equity loan on their home to provide start-up funds for the new business. Exhibits 1 and 2 present income and profit and loss statements.

Copyright © 2007 by the *Case Research Journal* and Calvin M. Bacon, Jr.

The author is grateful to Todd Sylvester for his cooperation in preparing this case, to Robin Hayes for transcribing the interviews, and to the reviewers of the *Case Research Journal* who gave invaluable advice and suggestions for improving the case. This case is intended to stimulate class discussion rather than to illustrate the effective or ineffective handling of a managerial situation. All events and individuals in this case are real. I disguised the name of the company for competitive reasons and consolidated the financial statements to facilitate student analysis.

The Entrepreneur

Todd was born in Boston and raised in Connecticut. Upon graduating from high school, he entered Franciscan University in Ohio and majored in divinity with the intention of becoming a priest. Before his second year, he changed majors to theology. After graduating from college and getting married, Todd took a job at an electronics store while he waited for Angelle to graduate. Although the store offered him a management position, he turned it down because he felt it would be too much strain on his marriage. Within a year, he accepted a teaching job in Louisiana. There, he supplemented his income by driving a school bus.

While teaching, he became an active singer and recorded a couple of tapes. His music reached Nashville, where a recording company signed him to a contract. Soon Todd went on tour and became the small company's biggest act. However, one day while he was driving across the country in his tour bus, he realized that he was spending lots of time away from his family, and he noticed that he was the only person on the bus who was not divorced. He abruptly notified the record company that he was quitting.

Fortunately, Todd was able to begin working in his parents' business, Cool Wraps. The Connecticut-based company produced specialty CD cases. Todd was glad to get a position as the operations manager, but he was disillusioned. He observed that, "We had millions of dollars in sales, but it was all done over the phone—no personal contact, no shaking hands. So, to me it just wasn't human enough. Anyone can sit at a desk and crunch numbers. We couldn't even develop a relationship with the buyers because every two months they had different employees."

The experience at Cool Wraps helped Todd realize that he loved being with people and wanted to put his people skills to use. As a result, he decided to take an offer to become the youth minister in Mobile and move his family there. He and Angelle had eight children, and she spent her time home-schooling them. They had been in Mobile nine years when they started the business.

Motivation for Starting the Business

Having come from an entrepreneurial family Todd had considered opening a business for years. He had thought about a pizza restaurant because people could socialize there, but he was afraid that the concept might be too complicated. Finally, Todd and Angelle chose to open a coffee shop primarily because they saw it as a good family business, a place where their kids could work and learn certain life lessons they viewed as important. The Sylvesters envisioned their kids growing up and going off to college at the university across the street. Regardless of their children's future career directions, the Sylvesters wanted them to have business and management skills. In Todd's words:

> I want them to know how business works. To give you an example, we charge a dollar fifty for a muffin that costs us fifty cents. So when my son, Stephen, saw that, he thought it was great to make a dollar a muffin, but I told him that we certainly do not. The bakery case breaks even and doesn't make us any money. I explained that when you grab the muffin, you're using wax paper and a paper bag and a napkin and sometimes they want butter that we don't charge for. The labor costs us and the lights are on. Also, you throw away muffins when they are not fresh, and they're not free. Then my son said we need to charge more for the muffins. I explained that we can't charge more because the market has pretty much set that price. If you can go down the road, no one is going to pay more for a muffin. Now when my son comes in, he realizes that when he gets a drink for himself, that drink is not free.

The Vision and Core Values

Todd wanted a place where customers could find comfort. He relished the fact that some customers would visit a few times a week as a treat. Some would come in, sit down in one of the four black leather chairs placed about the store, and read while they sipped mocha lattes and frappes. Some customers drank one of Expresso Espresso's frothy delights instead of having dessert, and some would actually take their shoes off and relax as if they were at home. Todd saw this as "creating an environment of comfort."

Todd placed such an emphasis on comfort, that it was a major consideration when developing the business. The owner wanted customers to feel at home, even selecting the color scheme and furniture for the warm feeling they invoked. He wanted the interior to draw the customers in. Once in, Todd wanted them to linger. If students wanted to use the free Wi-Fi Internet connection, or if professors wanted to come in to grade papers, they had no pressure to buy anything.

The Specialty Coffee Industry

The specialty coffee industry had seen steady growth for years and the trend was expected to continue until at least 2015.[1] Of the various segments within the specialty coffee industry, most of the growth was attributable to beverage retailers (cafes and kiosks). In 1979, there were approximately 250 specialty coffee retailers. The number quadrupled by 1989 to approximately 1,000 outlets, and it exploded to roughly 15,000 by 2002. Nationally, specialty coffee sales totaled over $10 billion in 2005 (see Table 1).

For specialty coffee beverage services, including coffee, espresso, tea, chai, and granita (See Exhibit 5) the leading drinks in 2004 were espresso-based beverages with average

[1]"Specialty Coffee," *Encyclopedia of Emerging Industries.* Online Edition, Thomson Gale, 2005, http://galenet.galegroup.com/servlet/BCRC.

TABLE 1   Specialty Coffee Industry Locations and Sales for 2005

Segment	Description	Locations	Average Sales	Total Sales (in $ millions)
Cafes	Beverage retailer with seating	13,900	$550,000	$7,650
Kiosks	Beverage retailer without seating	3,300	$300,000	990
Carts	Mobile beverage retailers	2,500	$140,000	350
Roasters	Roasting on premise	1,700	$925,000	1,570
Total				$10,560

Source: Ferguson, "Specialty Coffee Retail in the USA 2005," Specialty Coffee Association of America, 2006.

sales of $50,395 per store.[2] The second best selling drinks were drip-brewed coffee beverages at $33,336 per store, and third were cold and iced coffee beverages with an average of $22,061 per store.

By May 2006, Starbucks Corporation was the premier coffee retailer in the United States. Industry analysts generally credited it for popularizing specialty coffee and legitimizing higher drink prices. Starbucks sold specialty coffee, food items, coffee-related equipment, and teas in about 37 countries.[3] The company, headquartered in Seattle, had roughly 115,000 employees and 2005 revenues of over $6.3 billion. Starbucks was changing its menu to add more food, and it was doubling the number of outlets selling hot breakfast sandwiches. The firm expected revenues to grow 20 percent per year and to increase its dominating 40 percent market share. Starbucks had strong profits and cash flow that it planned to use to open company-owned and licensed stores domestically and abroad.

Diedrich Coffee, Inc., roasted and sold various brands of coffee through company-owned retail stores and through distributors, restaurants, mail order, and specialty stores. Diedrich was headquartered in Irvine, California, and had 2005 revenues of more than $52.5 million with growth from 2004 of about 3 percent.[4] Its brands included Diedrich Coffee, Gloria Jean's, and Coffee People. Located in 33 states and 15 foreign countries, the firm operated 50 retail stores and franchised more than 420 others. Diedrich had been a small, family business with three locations until 1992 when it began expansion through acquisitions of other coffeehouses in Houston, Denver, and San Diego.

Caribou Coffee Co, Inc., went public in October 2005 and reported sales of $191 million in 2005.[5] The company expected the $67.7 million the IPO raised to fund growth of the 360-store chain.[6] By the end of 2005, the firm expected to add 40 new outlets and another 130 in 2006. While the company owned almost all of the current stores, management expected to franchise about 10 percent of the new stores. The company expected 6 to 7 percent in further growth to come from existing stores, largely due to the introduction of its Bou Gourmet brand of food products, which expanded and upgraded its previous food offerings.

Coffee Beanery was a coffee shop franchise with over 200 franchisees by the end of 2005.[7] During 2006, industry analysts expected about 40 new stores to open[8] with much of

---

[2]Laura Everage, Specialty Coffee Reasearch Results I, *Gourmet Retailer* 26, no. 5, (May 2005).

[3]"Starbucks Corporation Company Profile," Datamonitor, PLC, www.datamonitor.com, May 2006.

[4]"Diedrich Coffee, Inc., Company Profile," Datamonitor, PLC, www.datamonitor.com, February 2006.

[5]Caribou Coffee Company, Inc., Annual Report, Brooklyn Center, Minnesota, March 31, 2006.

[6]Caroly Walkup, IPO-enriched Caribou Coffee Brews Plans to Gain Ground on Starbucks, *Nation's Restaurant News,* November 28, 2005.

[7]"About Us," Coffee Beanery, http://www.coffeebeanery.com/company/default.htm, 2005.

[8]Walkup, "IPO-enriched Caribou Coffee."

TABLE 2   Common-Size Income Statement (Snack and Nonalcoholic Beverage Bars)

Net sales	100.0
Operating expenses	91.6
Operating profit	8.4
All other expenses	3.8
Profit before taxes	4.7

Source: RMA Annual Statement Studies, 2006.

this growth coming from existing franchisees in China, South Korea, and the Middle East. At the beginning of 2006, the private company was testing a co-branding concept with the Cinnabon bakery chain.

Peet's Coffee & Tea claimed the title "grandfather of specialty coffee" because it could trace its roots to Alfred Peet who opened his first store in 1966. The company roasted its beans "European Style" from processes developed by the family business in Holland. By January of 2006, the company operated 111 retail stores in six states and had revenues of $175 million.[9] Peet's sold coffee, coffee-based beverages, teas, pastries, and other related items, with an emphasis on freshness. In 1997, the company made the decision to increase distribution channels and currently distributes coffee beans through company-owned stores, direct sales, restaurants, specialty groceries, and gourmet food stores. (Common-size income statement for snack and nonalcoholic beverage bars is shown in Table 2.)

There were two trends in the specialty coffee industry. First, although convenience had been a key success factor within the industry for many years, specialty coffee retailers were adding new stores in suburban locations. Locating within buyers' communities not only provided convenience but also gave them places to meet friends and neighbors.

Second, while industry observers traditionally viewed specialty coffee as served by coffee shops and kiosks, large restaurants were trying to find ways to capitalize on the specialty coffee industry growth.[10] McDonald's, Krispy Kreme, and Dunkin' Donuts were modifying their menus to feature more upscale coffee. In February 2006, McDonald's introduced a new premium roast coffee that it priced 40 cents above the price of $1.19 for the previous large size and about 30 cents less than Starbucks. Analysts credited the premium roast coffee offered by McDonald's with increasing sales 5.2 percent.[11] At the same time, Starbucks was changing its menu to add more food. Between 2005 and 2006, the company doubled the number of outlets selling hot breakfast sandwiches from 300 to 600 stores.[12]

The Specialty Coffee Market

According to the National Coffee Association, 54 percent of adults in America consumed coffee daily with over 18 percent buying specialty coffee beverages.[13] Specialty coffee buyers were generally more affluent, well educated, and worked in urban areas.[14] Research indicated that individuals with college degrees purchased almost 50 percent more specialty

---

[9]Peet's Coffee & Tea, Inc., Annual Report, 2005. Peets Coffee & Tea, Inc., Berkeley, California.

[10]Elizabeth Fuhrman, "Brew Wars," *Beverage Industry,* March, 2006.

[11]"Coffee Culture: Making a Great Cup o' Joe," *The Breakfast Journal,* August 7, 2006.

[12]Fuhrman, "Brew Wars."

[13]"Coffee Culture."

[14]"Specialty Coffee."

FIGURE 2
Expresso Espresso
Seating Area

coffee than those without college degrees. The link to education was even greater for people with some postgraduate education. In addition to education, households with two working parents and kids were more likely to purchase specialty coffee. According to the Specialty Coffee Association of America, the market for specialty coffee was "an educated urban resident with the disposable income to spend on fine coffee."

Three factors heavily influenced purchasing decisions. About 70 percent of coffee drinkers thought the most important coffeehouse characteristic was coffee quality and convenient location.[15] The next most important was friendly and knowledgeable staff with a 40 percent response. The third most important characteristic was variety with 35 percent. The least important factor was price.

Expresso Espresso Marketing

Target Market

Because of the store location, Expresso Espresso necessarily targeted college students, staff, and faculty. Students at South Alabama were older than those at most four-year universities and Todd theorized that the older students would have more disposable income. According to him, the street in front of the store had between 24,000 and 27,000 cars a day, and these potential customers had a median income of about $45,000.

While talking with one of the business professors from the university, Todd asked how he might get more information about what the target market really wanted. The professor offered to allow the students in one of his classes to conduct a survey to find out more. Todd eagerly agreed. The survey was not scientific, as it was intended to be a demonstration of surveying methods. However, the professor shared the survey information with Todd anyway. The results of the survey are in Exhibit 8.

[15]G. Ferguson, Specialty Coffee Retail in the USA 2005, Specialty Coffee Association of America, 2006.

Products

Todd tried to remain a "purist" in developing his products. He did not brew drip coffee and then leave it sitting around in warming pots. In fact, he did not offer drip-brewed coffee at all although it cost substantially less to make. Instead, he preferred to make each drink fresh from espresso. If a customer asked for coffee, the barista would offer an Americano instead. An Americano was an espresso with water added. It did not taste the same as drip-brewed coffee, and Todd considered it better. Expresso's menu offered traditional European-style coffee drinks. Todd stated that, "Some people come in and they want a Snickerdoodle, which is half chocolate and half caramel. We don't put it up on the menu because if you write it up there, people are going to be like, what's a Snickerdoodle? It's too complicated."

Although he wanted a European-style shop, occasionally he bent to customer demand. One customer wanted iced tea. He really did not want to offer iced tea, but the customer was a close friend so he relented. It turned out to be a lot more popular than he expected. The other product pressure he got was from Starbucks. "You have Starbucks that just came out with a new green tea cappuccino. So we've already had people come and ask if we have a green tea blend," Todd said with amazement. He continued, "We will have to add it because they are selling so well over there. Just like before the holiday season, Starbucks comes out with the spiced cappuccino, the pumpkin cappuccino, and the eggnog cappuccino. We're going to have to have them. Even though I'll be pumping a bunch of sugar into people because that is what they are. I will try to make it as best I can. They set the market." Todd was trying to be sensitive to what his customers wanted, but he was concerned that if all he did was copy Starbucks, he would not be able to differentiate his business. Somehow, he sensed that he should not just make Starbucks drinks. However, he was not sure what alternatives he had.

In addition to traditional coffee drinks, the shop also sold teas, smoothies, and a limited variety of pastries (see Table 3 and Exhibit 3). No sandwiches or soups were available. The display case usually had some muffins, lemon bars, cookies, and brownies on hand. Prices for pastries that Todd bought from a nearby grocery store ranged from $.75 to $1.50. Todd was not keen on the idea of selling food. He thought the waste and overall cost of food was excessive. Although he kept a few food items, he did not expect to make a profit on them. In addition, the store offered other retail items such as T-shirts and coffee mugs with humorous coffee-related sayings on them. The idea was to get people smiling when thinking about Expresso Espresso.

Prices

When deciding on prices, Todd went around town looking at everyone else's prices (see Exhibit 4). He made sure that his were 10 percent lower than any competitor. He believed

TABLE 3   **Expresso Espresso's Sales By Type (5/14/2006–5/20/2006)**

Type	Amount	Tickets
Hot drinks	$605.95	552
Iced drinks	254.58	206
Iced blended drinks	415.74	236
Add-ons	40.38	91
Baked goods	81.56	80
Retail items	96.85	16
Total	$1,651.84	1,271

Source: Expresso Espresso POS data.

that having a low price was important in attracting new customers. He also considered it important to show that he was providing a good value.

Promotion

Some coffee shops used a "buyer card" to promote customer loyalty and to give the perception of offering more value. Commonly shops gave the customer a free coffee after they bought nine cups, which was similar to a 10 percent discount if you bought enough coffee. Todd considered it more of a "psychological tool" rather than a true discount. Buyer cards were often lost before customers used them, and he thought asking the customer to keep track of the card was a hassle. To Todd, pricing products at 10 percent less was a more direct and honest approach to serving the customer. He commented, "When people say 'Hey, do you have a buyer's card?' I'll say 'Hey, our prices are already 10 percent lower than everybody so I am giving you the discount now.'" Although he felt his approach was more honest, he was not sure it was the best approach. "Now, I don't know if that is generating more sales," he said. "I don't know if it is working against me, quite frankly, but I just feel personally—not that I'm some high moralist in the business world—but I feel like if I have 300 customers a day, I don't want to rip off 100."

Other promotions included a mix of media. Expresso Espresso advertised on 92-ZEW, a local radio station that Todd believed had a strong student audience. In addition, the company placed ads in the campus newspaper and distributed flyers at apartment complexes surrounding the campus. Flyers typically showed the menu and contained a 10 percent off coupon. The coupons were good for one day only. It was as close to a "grand opening" as the store had. According to Todd, Expresso Espresso used a "soft opening" approach. It could still have a grand opening, but most of the students would not be on campus until the fall semester began.

One idea that Todd considered for promoting the shop was having live music. He thought that local musicians would make Expresso Espresso a destination rather than simply a convenience. He expected that many people would drive across the Mobile Bay just

FIGURE 3
The Food Case

FIGURE 4
Product Display

to see popular performers. He intended to begin having bands play on Friday and Saturday nights during the summer. There would be no cover charge; the store would simply make money from the drink sales. News of the performers would be by word of mouth. It was not clear where the band would play. The only reasonable space was in front of the product display case shown in Figure 4.

Publicity

Todd wanted to run the store differently from other coffee shops. He did not like the idea that employees might argue over the shifts because some shifts may get better tips. He also wanted to make sure the business could help others. He decided to create a policy whereby he would give away all tips. A huge coffee cup sat on the front counter with a sign indicating the charity of the week. At the end of each week, Todd would collect whatever people chose to give and pass it on to a good cause (see Figure 5 and Table 4). In just a few weeks, the business had given thousands to other organizations. The local paper considered this approach so novel that it ran an article on the practice. However, Todd did not think it was a big deal, "I don't think it is a new concept. A lot of restaurants will have jars that are specifically for someone—saying so and so has leukemia and people will drop money in." The primary difference was that Todd's approach was more organized. He selected a different recipient each week and prominently placed the cup and sign so that customers were more aware. It was part of the comfort concept of the store. Customers had the opportunity to help others as they treated themselves. This not only benefited the community but also had considerable "feel-good" value for those participating.

FIGURE 5
The Tip Cup

Competitors

The nearest competitor was Satori Coffee House, an eclectic coffee house that also sold music and sold alcohol (see Mobile Area Map in Exhibit 10). It was located about a half mile east on Old Shell Road, the same street as Expresso Espresso, in an old residence converted into commercial property. None of the furniture matched, and dark, moody paint colored the walls. In general, Satori attracted an "edgier" crowd than other competitors. Occasionally, Satori offered live bands. It levied a cover charge to pay the band and generated a profit from selling drinks to the listeners.

Todd considered Carpe Diem to be a competitor although it was about two miles east of Expresso Espresso. It catered more to the students and teachers at Springhill College which was also on Old Shell Road. The shop was also a favorite of students from nearby St. Paul's High School. Like Satori, Carpe Diem did not have a drive-through window, and was a house that had been converted into a coffee shop. Unlike Satori, the atmosphere was a bit

TABLE 4 **Tip Charities (Year to Date)**

Recipient	Amount
St. Mary's Home	$165.01
American Cancer Society	165.01
2B Choices for Women	315.18
Ronald McDonald House	107.95
Little Sisters of the Poor	226.32
Penelope House	185.45
St Jude's Children's Hospital	223.01
Home of Grace	266.72
Camp Rap-A-Hope	242.85
Habitat for Humanity	193.96
Total	$2,004.44

Source: Expresso Espresso company records.

more "wholesome." It was rather busy when school was in session, and often the parking lot was full. Carpe Diem was the only coffee shop that roasted its own coffee on-site, and the company was the sole supplier of roasted beans to Expresso. The company provided the high-quality Arabica beans that Todd insisted on using.

Another competing coffee shop was the Daily Grind, which was in the cafeteria on campus at the University of South Alabama and operated by contract by the same company that ran the cafeteria. The facility was well kept and within convenient walking distance from most administration and classroom buildings. If students wanted to, they could read a free copy of the local newspaper or study in the cafeteria while waiting for their next class. Overall, the Daily Grind did not offer the cozy atmosphere of the other shops. It participated in the "Proudly Serving Starbucks Coffee" program.

Some patrons preferred Beaners, a franchise operation, because of its convenient location on Airport Boulevard, its gourmet coffee, and its unique atmosphere. It was in the end unit of a shopping center and provided tables outside for customers to enjoy the sunshine while they drank their coffee. Sometime people commented on Beaners' self-serve option. Customers could get coffee from the self-serve line and pay for it by placing their money in an "Honor Box." The system made customers feel the company trusted them and made it possible for customers to customize their coffee and still get fast service. Beaners was about a one-mile drive from Expresso.

Although Todd did not necessarily view them as "competitors," some local churches had opened coffee shops in town. Warm Heart Café and The Mug were both on Grelot Road close to the new Starbucks location. These shops did not have the look or feel of Starbucks, and mostly they catered to church members and their friends. The churches supported the shops financially so they did not have to make a profit. Some attributes of various Mobile coffee shops are provided in Table 5.

Perhaps the competitor that worried Todd the most was Starbucks. Starbucks had a free-standing store on Airport Boulevard—the busiest road in Mobile, a shop on Schillinger Road, and a shop in the Mobile County Government building downtown. It also had licensed stores in the Barnes and Noble by the interstate and in the new Target in the developing west side of town. Starbucks had started building four new freestanding stores—one by the mall, one by I-65, one on Airport Boulevard across form Beaners, and one on Grelot Road across from Warm Heart Cafe. Baldwin County, which was in the Mobile metropolitan statistical area, only had three coffee shops, but Starbucks had recently announced a new store on one of the busiest streets in the county.

As if that were not enough competition from Starbucks, the company had announced plans to build a drive-through store on Old Shell Road about 400 feet east of Expresso Espresso. One of Todd's biggest concerns was the ability of Mobile to support so many coffee shops. The warm, humid climate did not seem to match the typical city for coffee shops. Exhibit 6 shows coffee shop densities for the top coffee-shop cities. In addition, Todd was concerned that Starbucks would take customers from Expresso's drive-through window.

TABLE 5 **Attributes of Mobile Coffee Shops**

	Expresso Espresso	Carpe Diem	Satori	Daily Grind	Starbucks	Beaners
Seating Space	Moderate	High	High	Extra High	Low	High
Food Variety	Low	Moderate	High	Low	Moderate	Moderate
Drive-Through	Yes	No	No	No	Yes	No

Source: Case researcher observation of coffee shops.

Operations

Quality

Although Todd wanted patrons to feel comfortable, he also understood the importance of convenience and speed especially when individuals were getting coffee before going to work. He placed a priority on making orders quickly for the drive-through. The acceptable standard was to complete the order within 45 seconds. To give employees feedback, Todd often set a timer when customers placed their orders. Completing orders fast might not seem like a big deal to McDonald's or Krispy Kreme, but it was a bit more challenging for Expresso Espresso because all of the drinks were made to order. Before they made any coffee drink, baristas had to fill the espresso maker, tamp it, brew it, and pour it. These steps took more time than other restaurants but provided the consistent, high-quality drinks that Todd insisted on serving.

While there was a sensor that beeped to let baristas know when a drive-though customer was present, Todd often would be heard yelling, "DRIVE-THROUGH" to give the baristas advance warning and to reinforce the importance of fast service. Todd knew that the drive-through not only gave the store a differentiating factor but also contributed about 40 percent of its total revenues.

Costs

Quality was an important factor for Expresso Espresso. As a result, some of its costs were higher than those of competitors. Todd stated, "I don't compromise with making coffee. Like my espresso blend. It is not cheap because it is so good. You can get much cheaper." Other ingredients also are on the high end. "Most of my flavored syrups have reasonable costs, but my chocolate, caramel, and white chocolate syrups are from a high-end company in San Francisco, and they are very expensive. But they are so good! Any person can taste the difference. I refuse to compromise. I refuse to use powders. I hate the grittiness."

Another example of the cost/quality trade-off made by the company was the way it produced drinks. There were actually no coffee machines in the store; the staff made all

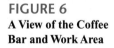

FIGURE 6
A View of the Coffee Bar and Work Area

TABLE 6 **Expresso Espresso's Sales By Hour**
(5/14/2006–5/20/2006)

Time	Amount	Tickets
6:00–6:59 A.M.	$ 20.00	7
7:00–7:59 A.M.	131.95	39
8:00–8:59 A.M.	108.25	32
9:00–9:59 A.M.	98.05	31
10:00–10:59 A.M.	126.50	36
11:00–11:59 A.M.	60.65	17
12:00–12:59 P.M.	101.75	25
1:00–1:59 P.M.	50.65	15
2:00–2:59 P.M.	122.25	36
3:00–3:59 P.M.	117.70	32
4:00–4:59 P.M.	108.10	30
5:00–5:59 P.M.	54.40	17
6:00–6:59 P.M.	58.15	16
7:00–7:59 P.M.	130.00	27
8:00–8:59 P.M.	213.15	61
9:00–9:59 P.M.	114.20	32
10:00–10:59 P.M.	53.00	17

Source: Expresso Espresso POS data.

coffee drinks from espresso. If a customer wanted a simple coffee, then the baristas made an Americano, a drink with two shots of espresso diluted in water. As for the espresso machines, Todd had to choose between a standard machine and a super-automatic machine as used by Starbucks. The super-automatic machines were faster and baristas needed less training to operate them. However, Todd believed manual machines produced a higher quality drink, although operating them required close monitoring. He observed, "With us, we're adjusting our grind all day long. The first thing I do when I come in is to ask the baristas how they are 'pulling.' What that means is: Are you timing them? Are you getting the essence of the coffee out? Does the coffee have a consistent taste? Is the espresso bitter?" Because manual machines were slower, and because the company made all coffee drinks from espresso, Expresso Espresso had installed two of them in the barista work area.

Operating Hours

Normal store hours were Monday–Friday, 6:30 A.M. to 11:00 P.M.; Saturday, 7:30 A.M. to 11:00 P.M.; and Sunday, 4:00 P.M. to 11:00 P.M. Expresso Espresso usually had two employees running the store. This provided plenty of help during the busy periods, but resulted in overstaffing during the slow times of the day (see Table 6). During the first few months after opening, the store had two days that were so busy Todd had to call in extra help. Both days were during spring semester final exams (see April 26 and 29 in Exhibit 7). During finals week, customers tended to linger more than usual. In fact, the store had to ask customers to leave when it closed at 11:00 P.M. No restaurant served specialty coffee past 11:00 P.M.; the best alternative was a nearby Waffle House.

Management and Organization

Todd was the only manager of the business. This caused some stress on his time because his primary job was youth minister of a local church. He worked in the shop on his days off, Tuesdays and Saturdays, and on some evenings. To supplement Todd's efforts, certain employees had the responsibility of opening and closing the shop. Todd did not think of himself as a manager. To him he was simply the one who trained employees to become baristas, and it was their job to work as good team members and to become self-managed. He believed that if people knew what to do, you just did not have to watch over them. Todd enjoyed developing people more than working with numbers. To assist him with the financials, he hired a bookkeeper to come in once a month. This was a big help because Todd did not want to spend his time on the books.

In general, employees were very happy working at Expresso Espresso. Because Todd had worked as a youth minister for nine years, he had a rich pool of high school and college students from which he could hire. He believed his employees were the cream of the crop—he could pick and choose from people he knew very well. In return, the employees were very loyal. He paid them a bit above minimum wage, but they often left higher-paying jobs to work for Todd. Expresso had higher operating costs, due in part to the fact that the company donated tips rather than giving them to employees. Other coffee shops used tips to supplement wages to reach the minimum wage requirements.

Todd did not believe in being what he called a "tyrannical boss." He created a family environment and even allowed employees to chat with their friends who came in while the baristas worked. Employees enjoyed the workplace so much they often hung out at the shop during their off-hours. Occasionally, when employees were off the clock, they would pitch in to help if needed. They felt a strong sense of responsibility to the company and to the other employees. In addition to nonfamily staff, Expresso Espresso also employed two of the Sylvesters' children.

The New Location

Todd wanted to find a midtown location where the target market would be young professionals. He wanted more space for seating and sufficient parking, which was at a premium in that area of Mobile. In addition, he expected the new store to have a kitchen that could support making items like breakfast foods and sandwiches. There was such a building about a mile east of the mall on Airport Boulevard; the owner was selling it for $500,000. It had a place where he could add a drive-through window. Todd planned to purchase the building so that he would get the full benefit from the upgrades he would make. The new store would allow customers to grab breakfast and an espresso drink on the way to work, and with a kitchen available, Todd could prepare food at the new store to send to the first store. Exhibit 9 presents start-up costs for the new location.

Decision Time

Although Todd was proud of the organization he had created, he knew that he needed to make some decisions about the future of his company. He felt he had developed a warm, friendly place for people to relax and socialize, but he was not sure what to do about the threat of Starbucks moving in and stealing his customers. Todd faced several nagging questions: Was the company positioned properly in the local specialty coffee industry? How high would sales need to go to reach profitability? What would he need to do to be successful? Todd was confident about the company's success but just was not sure of the best combination to get there quickly.

EXHIBIT 1 Expresso Espresso, Inc., Profit and Loss, 2006

Source: Expresso Espresso company records.
Note: Expresso Espresso was an S Corporation.

	February	March	April	May
Sales		$ 9,162.86	$ 10,970.67	$ 11,891.41
Cost of goods sold		6,821.18	6,128.68	6,897.02
Gross profit		2,341.68	4,841.93	4,994.39
Operating expenses				
Advertising	—	—	1,064.50	1,177.00
Automobile expenses	—	—	70.91	214.40
Credit card expenses	62.71	127.59	186.05	389.21
Contributions	—	315.18	—	—
Depreciation	—	122.05	122.05	122.05
Gift cards	—	—	—	685.00
Licenses and taxes	—	243.00	21.16	8.51
Postage	24.73	39.00	41.00	26.33
Professional fees	—	300.00	—	—
Rent	1,727.00	1,727.00	1,727.00	1,727.00
Repairs	8,109.45	3,243.76	1,091.64	655.62
Janitorial supplies	73.20	514.48	214.62	107.84
Miscellaneous	—	—	—	1,483.33
Office supplies	149.65	—	235.36	20.51
Telephone	47.93	64.86	243.59	367.83
Utilities	189.52	301.02	390.97	448.41
Payroll	1,330.59	5,054.49	5,322.36	5,011.89
Total operating expenses	$ 11,714.78	$ 12,052.43	$ 10,731.21	$ 12,444.93
Net income	$-11,714.78	$-9,710.75	$-5,889.28	$-7,450.54

EXHIBIT 2   Expresso Espresso, Inc., Ending Balance Sheet, 2006

Source: Expresso Espresso company records.

	February 28	March 31	April 30	May 31
ASSETS				
Current assets				
Cash	$ 5,187.49	$ 5,678.65	$ 5,788.33	$ 4,781.93
Accounts receivable	—	336.36	885.42	1,072.72
Other current assets	917.79	1,835.57	1,115.39	2,343.92
Total current assets	6,105.28	7,850.58	7,789.14	8,198.57
Fixed assets				
Fixtures, furniture, equipment	25,473.08	25,473.08	25,473.08	25,473.08
Accumulated depreciation	—	544.87	1,089.74	1,634.61
Total fixed assets	25,473.08	26,017.95	26,562.82	23,838.47
Total assets	$ 31,578.36	$ 33,868.53	$ 34,351.96	$ 32,037.04
LIABILITIES AND EQUITY				
Liabilities				
Current liabilities				
Payroll payable	$ —	$ 101.81	$ 276.54	$ 362.87
Sales tax payable	—	856.96	998.95	1,189.43
Total current liabilities	—	958.77	1,275.49	1,552.30
Total long-term liabilities	—	—	—	—
Total liabilities	$ —	$ 958.77	$ 1,275.49	$ 1,552.30
Equity				
Owner's contribution	$ 43,293.14	$ 54,335.29	$ 60,391.28	$ 65,250.09
Retained earnings	—	−11,714.78	−21,425.53	−27,314.81
Net income	−11,714.78	−9,710.75	−5,889.28	−7,450.54
Total equity	$ 31,578.36	$ 32,909.76	$ 33,076.47	$ 30,484.74
TOTAL LIABILITIES AND EQUITY	$ 31,578.36	$ 33,868.53	$ 34,351.96	$ 32,037.04

EXHIBIT 3 Expresso Espresso Menu

Source: Expresso Espresso menu.

Hot Drinks (espresso with hot steamed milk, some foam)	Small (12 oz.)	Medium (16 oz.)	Large (20 oz.)
Cafe Latte	$ 1.95	$ 2.50	$ 2.95
Vanilla Latte	2.25	2.75	3.25
Carmel Latte	2.25	2.75	3.25
Mocha Latte	2.25	2.75	3.25
Mocha Bianca (white chocolate Mocha)	2.50	3.00	3.50
Raspberry Mocha	2.50	3.00	3.50
Italian Style real Cappuccino (espresso with hot, mostly foamy milk)	1.95	2.50	—
Espresso (strong black "real taste" coffee, served in a small 1.5 oz. cup)	1.75	2.00	—
Hot Chocolate	1.75	2.00	2.50
Americano	1.25	1.50	1.75
Add a shot of espresso: add 50 cents			
Any drink made with soy or half and half: add 50 cents			

Iced Drinks	Small (16 oz.)	Medium (20 oz.)	Large (24 oz.)
Iced Latte	$ 1.95	$ 2.50	$ 2.95
Iced Vanilla Latte	2.25	2.75	3.25
Iced Carmel Latte	2.25	2.75	3.25
Iced Raspberry Mocha (or any other flavor)	2.50	3.00	3.50
Iced Chai Latte	2.25	2.75	3.25
Iced Tea (Lemon Blossom, Wild Raspberry, Ruby Mist, Mango Passionfruit)	1.25	1.50	1.75

Iced Blended Drinks	Small (16 oz.)	Medium (20 oz.)	Large (24 oz.)
Vanilla Frappe (a delightful blend of espresso and vanilla cream)	$ 3.25	$ 3.60	$ 3.95
Carmel Frappe	3.25	3.60	3.95
Mocha Frappe	3.25	3.60	3.95
Smoothies (Strawberry, Four Berry, Mango Tropics, Pineapple Paradise)			
Flavors: Vanilla, Almond, Hazelnut, Raspberry, Carmel, Irish Cream, Butterscotch, Peppermint	3.35	3.60	3.95

EXHIBIT 4   Price Comparison among Several Mobile Coffee Shops

Source: Case researcher observation of coffee shops. All medium size except where indicated.

	Beaners	Carpe Diem	Daily Grind	Expresso Espresso	Satori	Starbucks
Hot Drinks						
Espresso (small)	$ 1.69	$ 1.80	$ 1.45	$ 1.75	$ 1.75	$ 1.75
Cappuccino	3.09	3.05	3.10	2.50	2.50	3.20
Latte	3.09	2.85	3.10	2.50	3.00	3.20
Mocha	3.49	3.15	3.30	3.00	3.25	3.50
Hot Chocolate	3.29	2.50	3.00	2.00	2.75	2.60
Americano	2.06	1.80	2.15	1.50	2.00	2.15
Coffee	1.49	1.59	1.60	none	1.69	1.70
Chai Latte	3.30	3.10	3.10	2.75	3.00	3.30
Hot Tea	1.69	1.21	1.65	1.50	1.30	1.70
Iced Drinks						
Latte	3.59	2.95	3.50	2.50	3.25	3.20
Vanilla Latte	3.49	3.20	3.50	2.75	3.25	3.50
Iced Tea	1.69	1.30	none	1.50	1.30	1.70
Blended Drinks						
Frappe	4.39	3.60	3.50	3.60	3.50	3.80
Smoothies	4.39	3.60	none	3.60	3.75	none

EXHIBIT 5   Typical Coffee Beverages in Coffee Shops

Source: Adapted from http://www.espressotec.com and http://www.coffeeandteawarehouse.com.

Beverage	Description
Americano	A single shot of espresso with 6 to 8 ounces of hot water
Caffe Latte	A single shot of espresso with steamed milk (about 1:3 ratio)
Caffe au Lait	A 1:1 mixture of coffee and steamed milk
Cappucino	Equal parts espresso and steamed milk with milk froth on top
Cafe Breva	A cappuccino made with half-and-half instead of whole milk
Cafe Macchiato	A shot of espresso topped off with steamed milk
Cafe Mocha	A cappuccino or caffe latte with chocolate syrup
Espresso Breve	A single shot of espresso with heated half-and-half added
Espresso Con Panna	A shot of espresso with whipped cream
Espresso Mocha	An espresso with steamed milk and chocolate syrup
Espresso Romano	An espresso served with a twist of lemon
Iced Cappuccino	A double espresso with cold milk (1:1 ratio) over ice
Iced Latte	A double espresso with cold milk (1:3 ratio) over ice
Granita	An espresso that has been frozen and crushed
Macchiato	A single espresso topped with a dollop of frothed milk
Nienta	Decaffeinated cappuccino with nonfat milk

EXHIBIT 6 Coffee Shop Densities

Top Ten Cities For Coffee Restaurants Per Capita

MSA*	MSA Population	Units	Units per 10,000 Population
Anchorage, AK	274,398	77	2.8
Seattle, WA	2,494,976	628	2.5
San Francisco, CA	1,682,362	373	2.2
Bellingham, WA	179,262	37	2.1
Portland, OR	2,064,660	419	2.0
Bremerton, WA	241,570	45	1.9
Boulder, CO	302,622	55	1.8
Olympia, WA	225,373	40	1.8
San Luis Obispo, CA	254,929	41	1.6
Santa Rosa, CA	468,852	72	1.5

Source: "Anchorage Alaska Tops the List of Most Coffee Shops Per Capita in the U.S." NPD Press Release, The NPD Group, March 14, 2005, http://www.npd.com.
*Metropolitan Statistical Area

Top Ten Cities for Number of Coffee Restaurants

MSA*	MSA Population	Units	Units per 10,000 Population
Los Angeles, CA	9,980,242	801	0.8
Seattle, WA	2,494,976	628	2.5
Chicago, IL	8,558,311	568	0.7
New York, NY	9,434,917	525	0.6
Portland, OR	2,064,660	419	2.0
Minneapolis, WI	3,117,850	384	1.2
Washington, DC	5,326,702	379	0.7
San Francisco, CA	1,682,362	373	2.2
San Diego, CA	2,966,163	344	1.2
Orange County, CA	2,991,264	326	1.1

Source: "Anchorage Alaska Tops the List of Most Coffee Shops Per Capita in the U.S." NPD Press Release, The NPD Group, March 14, 2005, http://www.npd.com.
* Metropolitan Statistical Area

Mobile Area Population

Geographical Area	Population
City of Mobile	198,983
Mobile County	410,500
Baldwin County	158,944
Metropolitan Statistical Area	569,524

Source: Mobile Area Chamber of Commerce, viewed September 15, 2006, http://www.mobilechamber.com/faq.asp.

EXHIBIT 7   **Daily Sales for April 2006**

	Day	Sales	Tax	Total	Tickets
1	Saturday	$ 261.49	$ 26.41	$ 287.89	84
2	Sunday	157.35	15.77	173.12	47
3	Monday	313.84	31.47	345.31	94
4	Tuesday	351.65	35.14	386.78	106
5	Wednesday	361.56	36.41	397.97	122
6	Thursday	228.40	22.93	251.32	70
7	Friday	449.52	45.13	494.65	119
8	Saturday	396.53	39.94	436.47	103
9	Sunday	151.89	15.28	167.17	40
10	Monday	318.98	32.21	351.19	106
11	Tuesday	312.77	31.54	344.31	98
12	Wednesday	331.67	33.21	364.88	101
13	Thursday	359.72	35.86	395.58	97
14	Friday	319.68	32.09	351.77	86
15	Saturday	250.81	25.08	275.89	74
16	Sunday	—	—	—	—
17	Monday	301.61	30.43	332.04	105
18	Tuesday	355.96	35.69	391.65	105
19	Wednesday	418.29	41.88	460.16	104
20	Thursday	417.63	41.86	459.49	127
21	Friday	295.66	29.79	325.45	76
22	Saturday	314.26	31.67	345.93	93
23	Sunday	121.80	12.25	134.05	36
24	Monday	416.13	41.97	458.09	126
25	Tuesday	354.94	35.71	390.65	116
26	Wednesday	472.94	47.28	520.22	133
27	Thursday	446.57	44.54	491.11	128
28	Friday	402.29	40.24	442.52	114
29	Saturday	780.93	76.33	857.26	169
30	Sunday	306.79	30.90	337.69	86

Source: Expresso Espresso POS data.

EXHIBIT 8   Partial Student Survey Results

Favorite Coffee Shop		Importance of Features	
Barney's	4	Product Quality	4.52
Beaners	5	Convenient Location	4.16
Carpe Diem	9	Product Variety	3.86
Daily Grind	2	Low Price	3.85
Expresso Espresso	10	Drive-Through	3.10
Joe Mugs	2	Self-Service	2.85
Satori	5	Food	2.76
Starbucks	53	Wi-Fi Internet	2.77
Other	3	Frequent Buyer Card	2.71
None	31	Live Entertainment	2.16
Total	124		

Favorite Coffee Shop Drink	
Frappuccino	35
Coffee	17
Cappuccino	16
Latte	13
Tea	13
Other	27

Average Drink Price	
Cappuccino	4.23
Coffee	1.99
Espresso	3.64
Frappuccino	3.71
Latte	3.49
Tea	2.00
Other	2.99
Average	3.24

EXHIBIT 9   Some Projected Start-up Expenses for Expresso Espresso's New Location

Equipment

Espresso machines/Bunn brewing equipment/grinders	$4,000
Two-door refrigerator (used)	1,500
Two-door freezer (used)	1,800
Blenders	1,800
Convection oven	2,900
Under counter commercial dishwasher	3,000
Three compartment sink and prep tables	800
Tables and chairs (most used)	2,700
Refrigerated glass display case for desserts (used)	1,500
Two refrigerators for other cold beverages (used)	1,400
Total	**$21,400**

Construction

Drive-through window installation	$4,500
Architect costs/permits/contractor	7,000
Counters and counter tops including retail shelves	2,800
Cups/saucers/disposable stock	1,000
T-Shirts/light retail items (mugs)	600
Alarm system	500
Video surveillance system	1,500
POS computers and software	4,000
Office computer and software/office supplies	2,500
Sign on building	1,200
Sign at street	1,700
Total	**$27,300**

EXHIBIT 10   Mobile Area Map

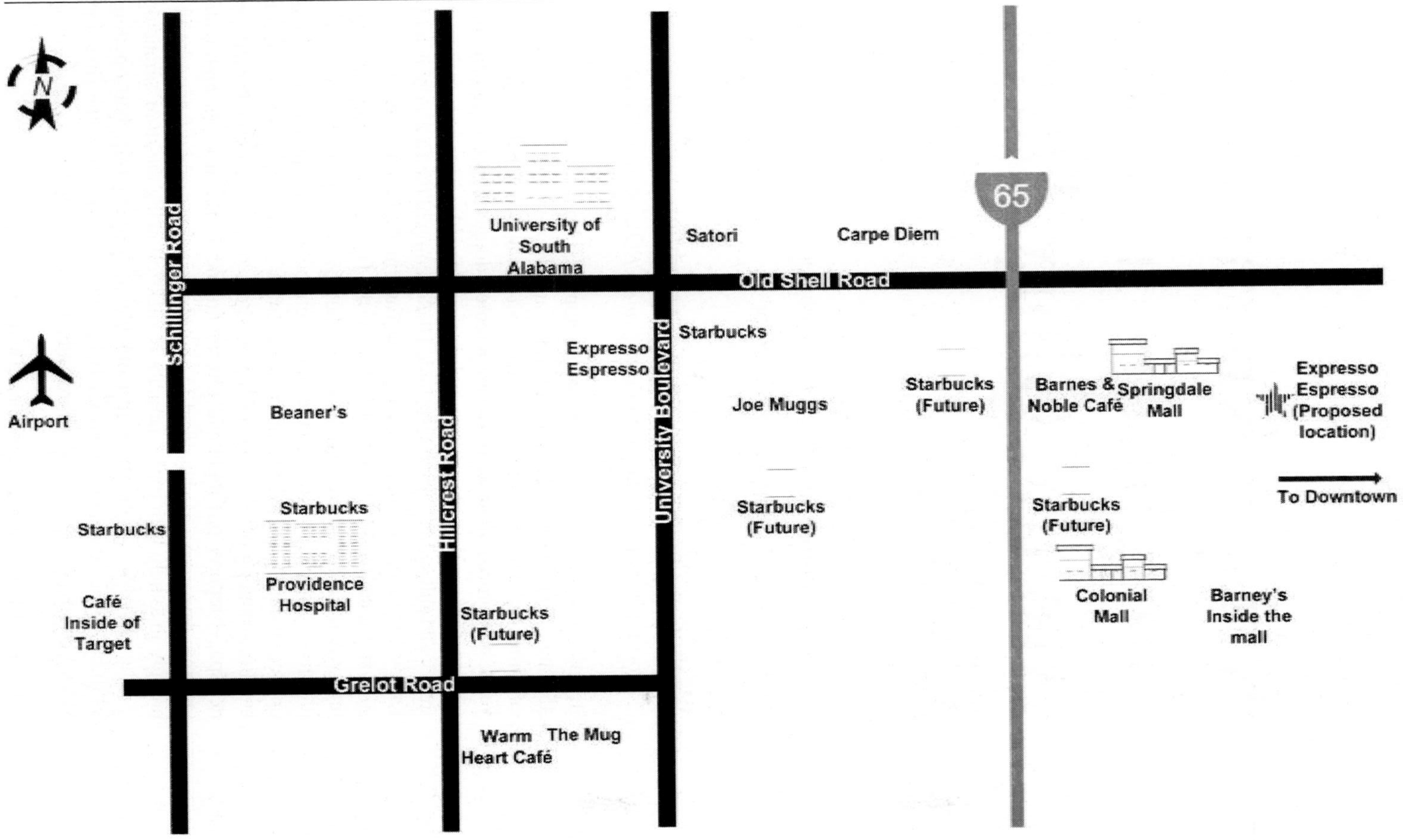

Krispy Kreme Doughnuts in 2005: Are the Glory Days Over?

Arthur A. Thompson *University of Alabama*

Amit J. Shah *Frostburg State University*

We think we're the Stradivarius of doughnuts.

—*Scott Livengood, president, chairman, and CEO of Krispy Kreme*

In early 2004, Krispy Kreme's prospects appeared bright. With 357 Krispy Kreme stores in 45 states, Canada, Great Britain, Australia, and Mexico, the company was riding the crest of customer enthusiasm for its light, warm, melt-in-your-mouth doughnuts. During the past four years, consumer purchases of Krispy Kreme's doughnut products had taken off, with sales reaching 7.5 million doughnuts a day. Considerable customer excitement—approaching frenzy and cult status—often surrounded the opening of the first store in an area. When a new Krispy Kreme opened in Rochester, New York, in 2000, more than 100 people lined up in a snowstorm before 5:00 A.M. to get some of the first hot doughnuts coming off the conveyor line; within an hour there were 75 cars in the drive-through lane. Three TV stations and a radio station broadcast live from the store site. The first Krispy Kreme store in Denver, which opened in 2001, grossed $1 million in revenues in its first 22 days of operation; commonly had lines running out the door with a one-hour wait for doughnuts; and, according to local newspaper reports, one night had 150 cars in line for the drive-through window at 1:30 A.M. Opening day was covered by local TV and radio stations, and off-duty sheriff's deputies were brought in to help with traffic jams for a week following the store's grand opening.

The first Minnesota store, just outside of Minneapolis, had opening-week sales of $480,693—the company record for fiscal 2002. In July 2003, the first store to open in the Massachusetts market—in Medford, outside Boston—had a record opening-day revenue of

$73,813 and a record opening-week sales volume of $506,917. Sales exceeded $2 million in the first seven weeks. At the June 2003 opening of the company's first store in Australia, in the outskirts of Sydney, some customers camped overnight in anticipation of the opening and others waited in line for hours to experience their first Krispy Kreme hot doughnut. The store, about an hour from downtown Sydney, attracted more than 500,000 customers from Sydney in its first six months of operations. In South Bend, Indiana, one exuberant customer camped out in the parking lot for 17 days to be the first in line for the grand opening of that city's first Krispy Kreme store.

To capitalize on all the buzz and customer excitement, Krispy Kreme had been adding new stores at a record pace throughout 2002–2003. The company's strategy and business model were aimed at adding a sufficient number of new stores and boosting sales at existing stores to achieve 20 percent annual revenue growth and 25 percent annual growth in earnings per share. In the just-completed 2004 fiscal year, total company revenues rose by 35.4 percent, to $665.6 million, compared with the $491.5 million in the fiscal 2003. Net income in fiscal 2004 increased by 70.4 percent, from $33.5 million to $57.1 million. Krispy Kreme's stock price had increased eightfold since the company went public in April 2000, giving the company a high profile with investors and Wall Street analysts. In February 2004, Krispy Kreme stock was trading at 30 times the consensus earnings estimates for fiscal 2005, a price/earnings ratio that was justified only if the company continued to grow 20 to 25 percent annually.

A number of securities analysts doubted whether Krispy Kreme's strategy and growth potential would continue to push the company's stock price upward. According to one analyst, "The odds are against this stock for long-term success." Another commented, "I think the market is overly optimistic about the long-term opportunities of the growth of the doughnut business." A third said, "Single-product concepts only have so many years to run." Indeed, restaurants with quick-service products presently had the slowest revenue growth of any restaurant type. The Krispy Kreme bears were particularly concerned about reports from franchisees that, as the number of Krispy Kreme stores expanded in choice markets, average-store sales were slowing and newly opened stores were not performing as well as the first one or two stores. After the initial buying frenzy at high-profile store openings in a major market, the buzz tended to fade as the fourth, fifth, and sixth outlets opened; moreover, new stores started to cannibalize sales from existing stores, thus moderating the potential for new stores to boost overall sales. Several franchisees in California, Michigan, New York, Canada, and a few other places were said to be in financial difficulty because of overexpansion and disappointing sales at newly opened stores.

Company Background

In 1933, Vernon Rudolph bought a doughnut shop in Paducah, Kentucky, from Joe LeBeau. His purchase included the company's assets and goodwill, the Krispy Kreme name, and rights to a secret yeast-raised doughnut recipe that LeBeau had created in New Orleans years earlier. Several years thereafter, Rudolph and his partner, looking for a larger market, moved their operations to Nashville, Tennessee; other members of the Rudolph family joined the enterprise, opening doughnut shops in Charleston, West Virginia, and Atlanta, Georgia. The business consisted of producing, marketing, and delivering fresh-made doughnuts to local grocery stores. Then, during the summer of 1937, Rudolph decided to quit the family business and left Nashville, taking with him a 1936 Pontiac, $200 in cash, doughnut-making equipment, and the secret recipe; after some disappointing efforts to find another location, he settled on opening the first Krispy Kreme Doughnuts shop in Winston-Salem, North Carolina. Rudolph was drawn to Winston-Salem because the city was developing into a tobacco and textiles hub in the Southeast, and he thought a doughnut shop would make a good addition to the thriving local economy. Rudolph and his two partners, who accompanied him from Nashville, used their last $25 to rent a building across from Salem College and Academy. With no money left to buy ingredients, Rudolph convinced a local grocer to lend them what they needed, promising payment once the first doughnuts were sold. To deliver the doughnuts, he took the backseat out of the 1936 Pontiac and installed a delivery rack. On July 13, 1937, the first Krispy Kreme doughnuts were made at Rudolph's new Winston-Salem shop and delivered to grocery retailers.

Soon afterward, people began stopping by the shop to ask if they could buy hot doughnuts. There were so many requests that Rudolph decided to cut a hole in the shop's wall so that he could sell doughnuts at retail to passersby. Krispy Kreme doughnuts proved highly popular in Winston-Salem, and Rudolph's shop prospered. By the late 1950s, Krispy Kreme had 29 shops in 12 states, with each shop having the capacity to produce 500 dozen doughnuts per hour.

In the early 1950s, Vernon Rudolph met Mike Harding, who was then selling powdered milk to bakeries. Rudolph was looking for someone to help grow the business, and Harding joined the company as a partner in 1954. Starting with six employees, the two began building an equipment department and a plant for blending doughnut mixes. They believed the key to Krispy Kreme's expansion was to have control over each step of the doughnut-making process and to be able to deliver hot doughnuts to customers as soon as they emerged from the frying and sugar-glazing process. In 1960, they decided to standardize all Krispy Kreme shops with a green roof, a red-glazed brick exterior, a viewing window inside, an overhead conveyor for doughnut production, and bar stools—creating a look that became Krispy Kreme's trademark during that era.

Harding focused on operations, while Rudolph concentrated on finding promising locations for new stores and getting bank financing to support expansion into other southeastern cities and towns. Harding became Krispy Kreme's president in 1958, and he became chief executive officer when Rudolph died in 1973. Under Rudolph and then Harding, Krispy Kreme's revenues grew from less than $1 million in 1954 to $58 million by the time Harding retired in 1974. Corporate headquarters remained in Winston-Salem.

In 1976, Beatrice Foods bought Krispy Kreme and proceeded to make a series of changes. The recipe was changed, and the company's script-lettered signs were altered to produce a more modern look. As customers reacted negatively to Beatrice's changes, business declined. A group of franchisees, led by Joseph McAleer, bought the company from Beatrice in 1982 in a $22 million leveraged buyout. The new owners quickly reinstated the original recipe and the original script-lettered signs. Sales rebounded, but with double-digit interest rates in the early 1980s, it took years to pay off the buyout debt, leaving little for expansion.

To grow revenues, the company relied mainly on franchising "associate" stores, opening a few new company-owned stores—all in the southeastern United States—and boosting store volume through off-premise sales. Associate stores operated under a 15-year licensing agreement that permitted them to use the Krispy Kreme system within a specific geographic territory. They paid royalties of 3 percent of on-premise sales and 1 percent of all other branded sales (to supermarkets, convenience stores, charitable organizations selling doughnuts for fund-raising projects, and other wholesale buyers); no royalties were paid on sales of unbranded or private-label doughnuts. The primary emphasis of the associate stores and many of the company stores was on wholesaling both Krispy Kreme doughnuts and private-label doughnuts to local groceries and supermarkets. Corporate revenues rose gradually to $117 million in 1989 and then flattened for the next six years.

New Leadership and a New Strategy

In the early 1990s, with interest rates falling and much of the buyout debt paid down, the company began experimenting cautiously with expanding under Scott Livengood, the company's newly appointed president and chief operating officer. Livengood, 48, joined Krispy Kreme's human relations department in 1978 three years after graduating from the

University of North Carolina at Chapel Hill with a degree in industrial relations and a minor in psychology. Believing strongly in the company's product and long-term growth potential, he rose through the management ranks, becoming president and chief operating officer in 1992, a member of the board of directors in 1994; president and CEO in 1998; and president, CEO, and chairman of the board in 1999.

Shortly after becoming president in 1992, Livengood became increasingly concerned about stagnant sales and shortcomings in the company's strategy: "The model wasn't working for us. It was more about selling in wholesale channels and less about the brand." He and other Krispy Kreme executives, mindful of the thousands of "Krispy Kreme stories" told by passionate customers over the years, concluded that the emphasis on off-premise sales did not adequately capitalize on the enthusiasm and loyalty of customers for Krispy Kreme's doughnuts. A second shortcoming was that the company's exclusive focus on southeastern U.S. markets unnecessarily handcuffed efforts to leverage the company's brand equity and product quality in the rest of the U.S. doughnut market. The available data also indicated that the standard 7,000-plus-square-foot stores were uneconomic to operate in all but very high-volume locations.

By the mid-1990s, with fewer than 100 franchised and company-owned stores and corporate sales stuck in the $110–$120 million range for six years, company executives determined that it was time for a new strategy and aggressive expansion outside the Southeast. Beginning in 1996, Krispy Kreme began implementing a new strategy to reposition the company, shifting the focus from a wholesale bakery strategy to a specialty retail strategy that promoted sales at the company's own retail outlets and emphasized the "hot doughnut experience" so often stressed in customers' Krispy Kreme stories. Doughnut sizes were also increased. The second major part of the new strategy was to expand the number of stores nationally using both area franchisees and company-owned stores. In preparing to launch the strategy, the company tested several different store sizes, eventually concluding that stores in the 2,400- to 4,200-square-foot range were better suited for the company's market repositioning and expansion plans.

The franchising part of the strategy called for the company to license territories, usually defined by metropolitan statistical areas, to select franchisees with proven experience in multiunit food operations. Franchisees were expected to be thoroughly familiar with the local area market they were to develop and also to have the capital and organizational capability to open a prescribed number of stores in their territory within a specified period. The minimum net worth requirement for franchise area developers was $750,000 per store or $5 million, whichever was greater. Area developers paid Krispy Kreme a franchise fee of $20,000 to $40,000 for each store they opened. They also were required to pay a 4.5 percent royalty fee on all sales and to contribute 1.0 percent of revenues to a company-administered advertising and public relations fund. Franchisees were expected to strictly adhere to high standards of quality and service.

By early 2000, the company had signed on 13 area developers operating 33 Krispy Kreme stores and committed to open another 130 stores in their territories within five years. In addition, the company was operating 61 stores under its own management. Sales had zoomed to $220 million, and profits were a record $6 million.

After a decision was made to take the company public in April 2000, Krispy Kreme spent much of late 1999 and early 2000 preparing for an initial public offering (IPO) of the company's stock. The old corporate structure, Krispy Kreme Doughnut Corporation, was merged into a new company, Krispy Kreme Doughnuts, Inc. The new company planned to use the proceeds from its IPO to remodel or relocate older company-owned stores, to repay debt, to make joint venture investments in franchised stores, and to expand its capacity to make doughnut mix.

The IPO of 3.45 million shares was oversubscribed at $21 per share, and when the stock began trading in April under the ticker symbol KREM, the price quickly rose. Krispy Kreme was the second-best-performing stock among all IPO offerings in the United States

EXHIBIT 1 **Financial Statement Data for Krispy Kreme Doughnuts, Fiscal Years 2000–2004 (Dollar amounts in thousands, except per share data)**

	Fiscal Years Ending				
	Jan. 30, 2000	Jan. 28, 2001	Feb. 3, 2002	Feb. 2, 2003	Feb. 1, 2004
Statement of operations data					
Total revenues	$220,243	$300,715	$394,354	$491,549	$665,592
Operating expenses	190,003	250,690	316,946	381,489	507,396
General and administrative expenses	14,856	20,061	27,562	28,897	36,912
Depreciation and amortization expenses	4,546	6,457	7,959	12,271	19,723
Arbitration award	—	—	—	9,075	(575)
Income from operations	10,838	23,507	41,887	59,817	102,086
Interest expense, (income), net, and other adjustments	1,232	(276)	(659)	5,044	7,409
Income (loss) before income taxes	9,606	23,783	42,546	54,773	94,677
Provision for income taxes	3,650	9,058	16,168	21,295	37,590
Net income	$ 5,956	$ 14,725	$ 26,378	$ 33,478	$ 57,087
Net income per share:					
Basic	$0.16	$0.30	$0.49	$0.61	$0.96
Diluted	$0.15	0.27	0.45	0.56	0.92
Shares used in calculation of net income per share:					
Basic	37,360	49,184	53,703	55,093	59,188
Diluted	39,280	53,656	58,443	59,492	62,388
Balance sheet data					
Current assets	$ 41,038	$ 67,611	$101,769	$141,128	$138,644
Current liabilities	29,586	38,168	52,533	59,687	53,493
Working capital	11,452	29,443	49,236	81,441	85,151
Total assets	104,958	171,493	255,376	410,487	660,664
Long-term debt, including current maturities	22,902	—	4,643	60,489	137,917
Total shareholders' equity	$ 47,755	$125,679	$187,667	$273,352	$452,207
Cash flow data					
Net cash provided by operating activities	$ 8,498	$ 32,112	$ 36,210	$ 51,036	$ 95,553
Net cash used for investing activities	(11,826)	(67,288)	(52,263)	(94,574)	(186,241)
Net cash provided by (used for) financing activities	(398)	39,019	30,931	53,837	79,514
Cash and cash equivalents at end of year	3,183	7,026	21,904	32,203	21,029

Source: Company SEC filings and annual reports.

in 2000. The company's stock began trading on the New York Stock Exchange in May 2001 under the symbol KKD.

Between early 2000 and early 2004, the company increased the number of Krispy Kreme stores from 144 to 357, boosted doughnut sales from an average of 3 million a day to an average of 7.5 million a day, and began the process of expanding internationally— opening its first factory store in Europe, located in the world-renowned department store Harrods of Knightsbridge, London (with plans for another 25 stores in Britain and Ireland by 2008), and continuing expansion in Australia, Canada, and Mexico. In fiscal 2004, Krispy Kreme captured an estimated 30.6 percent of the market for packaged doughnut sales, compared with 23.9 percent in fiscal 2003 and 6.4 percent in fiscal 2002.

Exhibit 1 presents a summary of Krispy Kreme's financial performance and operations for fiscal years 2000–2004.

EXHIBIT 2   **Krispy Kreme's Performance by Business Segment, Fiscal Years 2000–2003 (In thousands)**

	Fiscal Years Ending				
	Jan. 30, 2000	Jan. 20, 2001	Feb. 3, 2002	Feb. 2, 2003	Feb. 1, 2004
Revenues by business segment					
Company store operations	$164,230	$213,677	$266,209	$319,592	$441,868
Franchise operations	5,529	9,445	14,008	19,304	23,848
KK Manufacturing and Distribution	50,484	77,593	114,137	152,653	193,129
Total	$220,243	$300,715	$394,354	$491,549	$665,592*
Operating income by business segment (before depreciation and amortization)					
Company store operations	$ 18,246	$ 27,370	$ 42,932	$ 58,214	$ 83,724
Franchise operations	1,445	5,730	9,040	14,319	19,043
KK Manufacturing and Distribution	7,182	11,712	18,999	26,843	39,345
Total	$ 10,838	$ 23,507	$ 41,887	$ 59,817	$ 102,086*
Unallocated general and administrative expenses	$ (16,035)	$ (21,305)	$ (29,084)	$ (30,484)	$ (38,564)
Depreciation and amortization expenses					
Company store operations	$ 3,059	$ 4,838	$ 5,859	$ 8,854	$ 14,392
Franchise operations	72	72	72	108	173
KK Manufacturing and Distribution	236	303	507	1,723	3,006
Corporate administration	1,179	1,244	1,521	1,586	1,653
Total	$ 4,546	$ 6,457	$ 7,959	$ 12,271	$ 19,723*

*Totals include operations of Montana Mills, a business that was acquired in April 2004 and divested during fiscal 2005.

Source: Company SEC filings and annual reports.

EXHIBIT 3
Estimated Krispy Kreme Store Economics as of 2001

Store revenues	$3,600,000
Cash flow (after operating expenses)	960,000
Cash flow margin	27%
Owner's equity investment to construct store	$1,050,000
Cash flow return on equity investment	91%

Source: As estimated by Deutsche Bank Alex. Brown.

Krispy Kreme's Business Model and Strategy

Krispy Kreme's business model involved generating revenues and profits from three sources:

- Sales at company-owned stores.
- Royalties from franchised stores and franchise fees from new store openings.
- Sales of doughnut mixes, customized doughnut-making equipment, and coffees to franchised stores.

Exhibit 2 shows revenues, operating expenses, and operating income by business segment. The company was drawn to franchising because it minimized capital requirements, provided an attractive royalty stream, and put responsibility for local store operations in the hands of successful franchisees who knew the ins and outs of operating multiunit chains efficiently. Krispy Kreme had little trouble attracting top-quality franchisees because of the attractive economics of its new stores (see Exhibit 3).

Krispy Kreme had developed a vertically integrated supply chain whereby it manufactured the mixes for its doughnuts at company plants in North Carolina and Illinois and also manufactured proprietary doughnut-making equipment for use in both company-owned and franchised stores. The sale of mixes and equipment, referred to as "KK manufacturing and distribution" by the company, generated a substantial fraction of both revenues and earnings (Exhibit 2).

Many of the stores built prior to 1997 were designed primarily as wholesale bakeries, and their formats and site locations differed considerably from the newer stores being located in high-density areas where there were lots of people and high traffic counts. In order to improve on-premise sales at these older stores, the company was implementing a program to either remodel them or close and relocate them to sites that could better attract on-premise sales. In new markets, the company's strategy was to focus initial efforts on on-premise sales at its stores and then leverage the interest generated in Krispy Kreme products to secure supermarket and convenience store accounts and grow packaged sales.

So far, the company had spent very little on advertising to introduce its product to new markets, relying instead on local media publicity, product giveaways, and word of mouth. In almost every instance, local newspapers had run big features headlining the opening of the first Krispy Kreme stores in their area; in some cases, local radio and TV stations had sent news crews to cover the opening and conduct on-the-scene interviews. The grand opening in Austin, Texas, was covered live by five TV crews and four radio station crews (there were 50 people in line at 11:30 P.M. the night before the 5:30 A.M. store opening). At the first San Diego store opening, there were five remote TV trucks on the scene; radio reporters were out interviewing customers camped out in their pickup trucks in the parking lot; and a nationally syndicated radio show broadcast "live" at the site. It was common for customers to form lines at the door and at the drive-through window well before the initial day's 5:30 A.M. grand opening, when the HOT DOUGHNUTS NOW sign was first turned on. In a number of instances, there were traffic jams at the turn in to the store—a Buffalo, New York, traffic cop said, "I've never seen anything like this . . . and I mean it." As part of the grassroots marketing effort surrounding new-store openings, Krispy Kremes were typically given away at public events as a treat for participants— then, as one franchisee said, "the Krispy Kremes seem to work their own magic and people start to talk about them."

Krispy Kreme had originally financed its expansion strategy with the aid of long-term debt. However, the April 2000 IPO raised enough equity capital to completely pay off the long-term debt outstanding as of fiscal 2001. Since then the company had borrowed about $50 million on a long-term basis to help fund its rapid growth during 2002–2004. When the company went public, it ceased paying dividends to shareholders; currently all earnings were being retained and reinvested in growing the business.

Company Operations

Products and Product Quality

Doughnuts

Krispy Kreme produced nearly 50 varieties of doughnuts, including specialty doughnuts offered at limited times and locations. By far the biggest seller was the company's signature "hot original glazed" doughnut made from Joe LeBeau's original yeast-based recipe. Exhibit 4 shows the company's doughnut varieties as of September 2003. Exhibit 5 indicates the nutritional content for a representative selection of Krispy Kreme doughnuts.

EXHIBIT 4
Varieties of Krispy Kreme Doughnuts

- Original Glazed
- Chocolate Iced
- Chocolate Iced with Sprinkles
- Maple Iced
- Chocolate Iced Creme Filled
- Glazed Creme Filled
- Traditional Cake
- Apple Fritter
- Powdered Strawberry Filled
- Chocolate Iced Custard Filled
- Raspberry Filled
- Lemon Filled
- Cinnamon Apple Filled

- Powdered Blueberry Filled
- Chocolate Iced Cake
- Dulce de Leche
- Sugar Coated
- Glazed Cruller
- Powdered Cake
- Glazed Devil's Food
- Chocolate Iced Cruller
- Cinnamon Bun
- Glazed Blueberry
- Glazed Sour Cream
- Caramel Kreme Crunch

Source: www.krispykreme.com, September 22, 2003.

EXHIBIT 5   Nutritional Content of Selected Varieties of Krispy Kreme Doughnuts

Product	Calories	Calories from Fat	Total Fat Grams	% Daily Value*	Saturated Fat Grams	% Daily Value*	Carbohydrates Grams	% Daily Value*	Sugars (grams)
Original Glazed	200	110	12	18	3	15	22	7	10
Chocolate Iced Glazed	250	110	12	19	3	15	33	11	21
Maple Iced Glazed	240	110	12	18	3	15	32	11	20
Powdered Blueberry Filled	290	150	16	25	4	21	32	11	14
Chocolate Iced Creme Filled	350	190	21	32	5	25	39	13	23
Glazed Creme Filled	340	180	20	31	5	24	39	13	23
Traditional cake	230	120	13	20	3	15	25	8	9
Glazed Cruller	240	130	14	22	3.5	17	26	9	14
Cinnamon Bun	260	140	16	24	4	20	28	9	13
Glazed Devil's Food	340	160	18	28	4.5	21	42	14	27

*Based on a 2,000-calorie diet.
Source: www.krispykreme.com, September 22, 2003.

Company research indicated that Krispy Kreme's appeal extended across all major demographic groups, including age and income. Many customers purchased doughnuts by the dozen for their office, clubs, and family. According to one enthusiastic franchisee:

> We happen to think this is a very, very unique product which has what I can only describe as a one-of-a-kind taste. They are extremely light in weight and texture. They have this incredible glaze. When you have one of the hot original doughnuts as they come off the line, there's just nothing like it.

In 2003, Krispy Kreme ranked number 1 in Restaurants and Institutions' Choice in Chains category, beating number-2-ranked Starbucks.

The company received several thousand e-mails and letters monthly from customers. By all accounts, most were from customers who were passionate about Krispy Kreme products, and there were always some from people pleading for stores to be opened in their area.

EXHIBIT 6   Sample Comments from Krispy Kreme Customers and Franchisees

Customer comments:

- "I ate one and literally it brought a tear to my eye. I kid you not."
- "Oh my gosh, this is awesome. I wasn't even hungry, but now I'm going to get two dozen."
- "We got up at 3 o'clock this morning. I told them I would be late for work. I was going to the grand opening."
- "They melt in your mouth. They really do."
- "Krispy Kreme rocks."
- "It's hot, good and hot. The way a doughnut should be."
- "The doughnut's magnificent. A touch of genius."
- "I love doughnuts, but these are different. It's terrible for your weight because when you eat just one, you feel like you've barely tasted it. You want more. It's like popcorn."*
- "When you bite into one it's like biting into a sugary cloud. It's really fun to give one to someone who hasn't had one before. They bite into one and just exclaim."†

Franchisee comments:

- "Krispy Kreme is a 'feel good' business as much as it is a doughnut business. Customers come in for an experience which makes them feel good—they enjoy our doughnuts and they enjoy the time they spend in our stores watching the doughnuts being made."
- "We're not selling doughnuts as much as we are creating an experience. The viewing window into the production room is a theater our customers can never get enough of. It's fun to watch doughnuts being made and even more fun to eat them when they're hot off the line."
- "Southern California customers have responded enthusiastically to Krispy Kreme. Many of our fans first came to Krispy Kreme not because of a previous taste experience but rather because of the 'buzz' around the brand. It was more word of mouth and publicity that brought them in to sample our doughnuts. Once they tried them, they became loyal fans who spread the word that Krispy Kreme is something special. . . We witness the excitement everyday, especially when we're away from the store and wearing a hat or shirt with the Krispy Kreme logo. When people see the logo, we get the big smile and are always asked. 'When will we get one in our neighborhood?' . . . The tremendous local publicity coupled with the amazing brand awareness nationwide has helped us make the community aware of our commitment to support local charities. Our fundraising program, along with product donations to schools, churches, and other charitable organizations have demonstrated our real desire to give back. This commitment also impacts our employees who understand firsthand the value of supporting the needy as well as the worthy causes in our neighborhoods."
- "In all my many years of owning and operating multiple food franchise businesses, we have never been able to please—until Krispy Kreme—such a wide range of customers in the community. Its like an old friend has come to town when we open our doors: we're welcomed with open arms . . . Quite frankly, in my experience, publicity for Krispy Kreme is like nothing I have ever seen. It is truly unprecedented."

*As quoted in "Winchell's Scrambles to Meet Krispy Kreme Challenge," *Los Angeles Times,* September 30, 1999, p. C1.
†As quoted in Greg Sukiennik, "Will Dunkin' Donuts Territory Take to Krispy Kreme?" The Associated Press State & Local Wire, April 8, 2001.

Source: Krispy Kreme's 2000 and 2001 annual reports, except for two quotes noted above.

Exhibit 6 presents sample comments from customers and franchisees. According to Scott Livengood:

> You have to possess nothing less than a passion for your product and your business because that's where you draw your energy. We have a great product . . . We have loyal customers, and we have great brand equity. When we meet people with a Krispy Kreme story, they always do it with a smile on their faces.

Coffee

Krispy Kreme had recently launched strategic initiatives to improve the caliber and appeal of its on-premise coffee and beverage offerings, aligning them more closely with the hot doughnut experience in its stores. The first move came in early 2001 when Krispy Kreme acquired Digital Java, Inc., a small Chicago-based coffee company that sourced and roasted premium quality coffees and that marketed a broad line of coffee-based and noncoffee beverages. Scott Livengood explained the reasons for the acquisition:

> We believe the Krispy Kreme brand naturally extends to a coffee and beverage offering that is more closely aligned with the hot doughnut experience in our stores. Vertical integration of our coffee business provides the capability to control the sourcing and roasting of our coffee. Increasing control of our supply chain will help ensure quality standards, recipe formulation, and roast consistency. With this capability, one of our first priorities will be the research and benchmarking necessary to develop premier blends and roasts of coffee which will help make Krispy Kreme a coffee destination for a broader audience. Beyond coffee, we intend to offer a full line of beverages including espresso-based drinks and frozen beverages. We believe we can substantially increase the proportion of our business devoted to coffee specifically and beverages generally by upgrading and broadening our beverage offering.

Since the acquisition of Digital Java, coffee sales at Krispy Kreme stores had increased nearly 40 percent due to expanded product offerings and upgraded quality. In 2003, Krispy Kreme was marketing four types of coffee: Smooth, Rich, Bold, and Robust Decaf—all using coffee beans from the top 5 percent of the world's growing regions. Beverage sales accounted for about 10 percent of store sales, with coffee accounting for about half of the beverage total and the other half divided among milk, juices, soft drinks, and bottled water. In the years ahead, Krispy Kreme hoped to increase beverage sales to about 20 percent of store sales.

Store Operations

Each store was designed as a "doughnut theater" where customers could watch the doughnuts being made through a 40-foot glass window (see Exhibit 7). New stores ranged in size from 2,400 to 4,200 square feet. Stores had a drive-through window and a dining area that would seat 50 or more people—a few of the newer and larger stores had special rooms for hosting Krispy Kreme parties. Store decor was a vintage 1950s look with mint green walls and smooth metal chairs; some of the newest stores had booths (see Exhibit 8). A typical store employed about 125 people, including about 65 full-time positions. Approximately half of on-premise sales occurred in the morning hours and half in the afternoon and evening. Many stores were open 24 hours a day, with much of the doughnut making for off-premise sales being done between 6:00 P.M. and 6:00 A.M. Production was nearly always under way during peak in-store traffic times. In several large metropolitan areas, however, the doughnut making for off-premise sales was done in a central commissary specially equipped for large-volume production, packaging, and local-area distribution.

Each doughnut took about one hour to make. After the ingredients were mixed into dough, the dough was rolled and cut. The pieces went into a 12-foot-tall machine where each piece rotated on a wire rack for 33 minutes under high humidity and a low heat of 126 degrees to allow the dough to rise. When the rising process was complete, the doughnuts moved along a conveyor to be fried on one side, flipped, fried on the other side, and drained. Following all this came inspection. Doughnuts destined to be glazed were directed through a waterfall of warm, sugary topping; the others were directed to another part of the baking section to be filled and/or frosted. Exhibit 8 depicts the mixing, rising, frying, draining, and glazing parts of the process. Depending on store size and location, a typical day's production ranged between 4,000 and 10,000 dozen doughnuts.

Each producing store featured a prominent HOT DOUGHNUTS NOW neon sign (Exhibit 8) signaling customers that freshly made original glazed doughnuts were coming off the bakery conveyor belt and were available for immediate purchase. Generally, the signs glowed from 6:00 to 11:00 A.M. and then came on again during the late afternoon into the late-night hours.

Depending on the store location, Krispy Kreme's original glazed doughnuts sold for 60 to 75 cents each, or $4.50 to $7.50 per dozen; a mixed dozen usually sold for about 50 cents extra.

EXHIBIT 7   Making the Doughnuts

Mixing Ingredients

Rising

Frying and Flipping

Inspection and Draining

Drying and Entering Glazing

Inspection and Draining

Packaging

EXHIBIT 8   **Representative Krispy Kreme Stores and Store Scenes**

Some stores charged a small premium for hot doughnuts coming right off the production line. Customers typically got a $1.00-per-dozen discount on purchases of two or more dozen.

Stores generated revenues in three ways:

- On-premise sales of doughnuts.
- Sales of coffee and other beverages.
- Off-premise sales of branded and private-label doughnuts to local supermarkets, convenience stores, and fund-raising groups. Krispy Kreme stores actively promoted sales to schools, churches, and civic groups for fund-raising drives.

The company had developed a highly effective system for delivering fresh doughnuts, both packaged and unpackaged, to area supermarket chains and convenience stores. Route drivers had the capability to take customer orders and deliver products directly to retail accounts where they were typically merchandised either from Krispy Kreme–branded displays or from bakery cases (as unbranded doughnuts). The popularity of Krispy Kreme's stores had prompted many area supermarkets to begin stocking a selection of Krispy Kreme products in either branded display cases or in dozen and half-dozen packages.

The franchisee for Krispy Kreme stores in San Francisco had arranged to sell a four-pack of Krispy Kremes for $5 at San Francisco Giant baseball games at Pacific Bell Park—Krispy Kreme sold out of 2,100 packs by the third inning of the first game and, despite increasing supplies, sold out again after the fourth and sixth innings of the next two games; stadium vendors were supplied with 3,450 four-packs for the fourth game. The franchisee of the Las Vegas stores had a Web site that allowed customers to place orders online before 2:00 P.M. and have them delivered to their place of work by a courier service.

A Texas franchisee built a new 18,000-square-foot production and distribution center to supply Metroplex supermarkets, convenience stores, and other area retailers with Krispy Kreme 12-packs because newly opened Krispy Kreme stores did not have the baking capacity to keep up with both on-premise and off-premise demand; there were similar franchiser-operated wholesale baking and distribution centers in Nashville, Cincinnati, Atlanta, Chicago, and Philadelphia. Several of these centers had established delivery capability to supply Krispy Kremes to retailers in outlying areas deemed too small to justify a stand-alone Krispy Kreme store.

In 2004, about 20,000 supermarkets, convenience stores, truck stops, and other outside locations sold Krispy Kreme doughnuts. A growing number of these locations had special Krispy Kreme display cases, stocked daily with trays of different varieties for shoppers to choose from; these stand-alone cases could be placed in high-traffic locations at the end of an aisle or close to the check-out register.

The cost of opening a new store was around $2 million (including the standard package of equipment purchased from Krispy Kreme), but new store construction could range as high as $2.5 million in locations with high land and/or building costs. The initial franchise fee per unit was $40,000. Site selection was based on household density, proximity to both daytime employment and residential centers, and proximity to other retail traffic generators. A record number of new stores were opened in fiscal 2004—28 company-owned stores and 58 franchised stores (the net gain in stores was only 81 because 5 older stores were closed). Plans were in place to open 75 new stores in the upcoming fiscal 2005 year.

Weekly sales at newly opened stores could run anywhere from $100,000 to $500,000 the first couple of weeks a new store was open. Weekly sales tended to moderate to around $40,000 to $50,000 after several months of operation, but Krispy Kreme management expected new stores to have annual sales averaging more than $3 million in their first year of operation. In fiscal 2003, sales at all of the company's 276 stores (which included those open less than a year) averaged $2.82 million. In fiscal 2004, sales at all 357 stores averaged $2.76 million—slightly lower than in 2003, chiefly because of the larger number of

EXHIBIT 9   **Store Operations Data, Krispy Kreme Doughnuts, Fiscal Years 1998–2004**

	1998	2000	2001	2002	2003	2004
Systemwide sales	$203,439	$318,854	$448,129	$621,665	$778,573	$984,895
Number of stores at end of period:						
Company-owned	58	58	63	75	99	141
Franchised	62	86	111	143	177	216
Systemwide total	120	144	174	218	276	357
Increase in comparable store sales:						
Company-owned	11.5%	12.0%	22.9%	11.7%	12.8%	13.6%
Franchised	12.7%	14.1%	17.1%	12.8%	11.8%	10.2%
Average weekly sales per store:						
Company-owned (000s)	$42	$54	$69	$72	$76	$73
Franchised (000s)	$23	$38	$43	$53	$58	$56

Source: Company annual reports and 10K reports.

new store openings (roughly half of the 86 new stores were open less than six months). Exhibit 9 provides data on store operations.

Krispy Kreme Manufacturing and Distribution

All the doughnut mix and equipment used in Krispy Kreme stores was manufactured and supplied by the company, partly as a means of ensuring consistent recipe quality and doughnut making throughout the chain and partly as a means of generating sales and profits from franchise operations. Revenues of the Krispy Kreme Manufacturing and Distribution (KKM&D) unit had averaged about 30 percent of total Krispy Kreme revenues for the past three years and contributed 38 to 45 percent of annual operating income (Exhibit 2). The company's line of custom stainless-steel doughnut-making machines ranged in capacity from 230 to 600 dozen doughnuts per hour. Franchisees paid Krispy Kreme about $770,000 for the standard doughnut-making equipment package in 2003–2004 (up from about $500,000 In the late 1990s); the price increase was due partly to increased equipment capacity and partly to longer equipment durability. Increased doughnut sales at franchised stores also translated into increased revenues for KKM&D from sales of mixes, sugar, and other supplies to franchisees.

Krispy Kreme had recently opened a state-of-the-art 187,000-square-foot manufacturing and distribution facility in Effingham, Illinois, dedicated to the blending and packaging of prepared doughnut mixes and to distributing mixes, equipment, and other supplies to stores in the Midwest and the western half of North America. This facility had significantly lowered Krispy Kreme's unit costs and provided triple the production capacity of the older plant in Winston-Salem.

Training

Since mid-1999, Krispy Kreme had invested in the creation of a multimedia management training curriculum. The program included classroom instruction, computer-based and video training modules, and in-store training experiences. The online part of the training program made full use of graphics, video, and animation, as well as seven different types of test questions. Every Krispy Kreme store had access to the training over the company's intranet and the Internet; employees who registered for the course could access the modules from home using their Internet connection. Learners' test results were transferred directly to a Krispy Kreme human resources database; learners were automatically redirected to lessons where their test scores indicated that they had not absorbed the material well on the first attempt. The online course was designed to achieve 90 percent mastery from 90 percent of the participants and could be updated as needed.

The course for managers had been recast into a program suitable for hourly employees. The course could also be divided into small pieces and customized to fit individual needs. In 2003, Krispy Kreme intensified its focus on leadership development by establishing the Learning Initiative Program as well as the Performance Management System. In 2003, 18 employees attended the Krispy Kreme Leadership Institute to increase their capacities in senior management areas.

Growth Potential

In 2003 and continuing into early 2004, Krispy Kreme management expressed confidence that the company was still in its infancy. The company's highest priority was on expanding into markets with over 100,000 households; management believed these markets were attractive because the dense population characteristics offered opportunities for multiple store locations, gave greater exposure to brand-building efforts, and afforded multiunit operating economies. However, the company believed that secondary markets with fewer than 100,000 households held significant sales and profit potential—it was exploring smaller-sized store designs suitable for secondary markets. In 2002, Krispy Kreme CEO Scott Livengood stated, "We are totally committed to putting full factory stores in every town in the U.S." Krispy Kreme's management further believed the food-service and institutional channel of sales offered significant opportunity to extend the brand into colleges and universities, business and industry facilities, and sports and entertainment complexes. Management had stated that the company's strong brand name, highly differentiated product, high-volume production capability, and multichannel market penetration strategy put the company in a position to become the recognized leader in every market it entered.

Expansion into Foreign Markets

In December 2000, the company hired Donald Henshall, 38, to fill the newly created position of president of international development; Henshall was formerly managing director of new business development with the London-based Overland Group, a maker and marketer of branded footwear and apparel. Henshall's job was to refine the company's global strategy, develop the capabilities and infrastructure to support expansion outside the United States, and consider inquiries from qualified parties wanting to open Krispy Kreme stores in foreign markets. Outside of the United States, Krispy Kreme stores had opened in Canada, Australia, Mexico, and Great Britain. Krispy Kreme and its franchisees planned to open 39 new stores in Canada, 30 in Australia and New Zealand, 20 in Mexico, and 25 in Great Britain and Ireland in the coming years. So far, sales had been very promising at the foreign locations that had been opened, and franchise agreements were in the works for further global expansion.

As of May 2001, the company had stopped accepting franchise applications for U.S. locations, indicating that there were no open territories. By 2003, it had stopped accepting franchise applications in Canada, Mexico, Western Europe, and Australia, indicating that franchise contracts were already under way and that Krispy Kreme would be opening in these areas soon. According to Scott Livengood, "Krispy Kreme is a natural to become a global brand. Looking at our demographics, we appeal to a very broad customer base. We receive lots of interest on a weekly basis to expand into international locations and we are confident our brand will be received extremely well outside the U.S."

The Montana Mills Acquisition

Krispy Kreme's chief strategic move in 2003 was to acquire Montana Mills Bread Company, a Rochester, New York–based bakery operation with 11 retail locations. The acquisition price was 1.2 million shares of Krispy Kreme stock (worth roughly $50 million). The

Montana Mills chain of neighborhood bakeries featured fresh stone-ground flour, a highly visual presentation of the baking process in full view of the customer, and customer sampling with large slices of a variety of fresh-baked breads. In explaining why the acquisition was made, Scott Livengood, Krispy Kreme's Chairman and CEO, said:

> This acquisition is a natural outgrowth of the development of Krispy Kreme over the past five years. As I have indicated previously, we view Krispy Kreme Doughnuts, Inc., first and foremost as a set of unique capabilities which include the abilities to explore and nurture our customers' passion for and connection to a brand, create an effective franchise network, vertically integrate to provide a complete range of products and services to a system-wide store network serving flour-based, short shelf life products, and deliver these products daily across multiple channels. Applying these core organizational competencies to the development of a second concept has the potential to create significant leverage.
>
> The opportunity to create a wholesome, fresh-baked bakery and café concept the "Krispy Kreme way" is obviously unique to Krispy Kreme. I have long considered how to capitalize on this opportunity. In Montana Mills, we found the perfect foundation for this new concept—passionate bread bakers who have created a fiercely loyal customer following around a wide variety of fresh-baked goods, bread-baking theater, and sampling of large slices of bread. I have personally observed this passion that each Montana Mills employee carries for their customers and their breads. This is a great platform on which to build. We will work closely with the Montana Mills team as we try to add value to an already outstanding concept.
>
> I expect we will spend in the range of two years fully developing the concept I described. As we have indicated regarding our international expansion, we will always try to prepare for any type of expansion well before we need the growth. We want the time to do it right. For this concept, I think that time is now.

In fiscal 2004, Montana Mills generated revenues of $6.7 million and had operating expenses of $8.7 million, thus resulting in operating loss of $2.0 million.

Industry Environment

By some estimates, the U.S. doughnut industry was a $5 to $6 billion market in 2003–2004. Americans consumed an estimated 10 to 12 billion doughnuts annually—over three dozen per capita. In 2002, doughnut industry sales rose by about 13 percent. According to a study done by Technomic, a marketing research specialist in foods, doughnut shops were the fastest-growing dining category in the country in 2002–2003.

In 2002, estimated sales at outlets specializing in doughnuts rose by about 9 percent, to about $3.6 billion. Growth in packaged doughnut sales at supermarkets, convenience stores, and other retail outlets had been quite small in the past five years. The proliferation of bakery departments in supermarkets had squeezed out many locally owned doughnut shops and, to some extent, had constrained the growth of doughnut chains. Doughnuts were a popular item in supermarket bakeries, with many customers finding it more convenient to buy them when doing their regular supermarket shopping as opposed to making a special trip to local bakeries. Doughnut aficionados, however, tended to pass up doughnuts in the grocery store, preferring the freshness, quality, and variety offered by doughnut specialty shops. Most patrons of doughnut shops frequented those in their neighborhoods or normal shopping area; it was unusual for them to make a special trip of more than a mile or two for doughnuts.

Small independent doughnut shops usually had a devoted clientele, drawn from neighborhood residents and regular commuters passing by on their way to and from work. A longtime employee at a family-owned shop in Denver said, "Our customers are very loyal to us. Probably 80 percent are regulars."[1] Owners of independent shops seemed to believe

---

[1] As quoted in "Dough-Down at the Mile High Corral," *Rocky Mountain News,* March 25, 2001, p. 1G.

that new entry by popular chains like Krispy Kreme posed little competitive threat, arguing that the market was big enough to support both independents and franchisers, that the Krispy Kreme novelty was likely to wear off, and that unless a doughnut franchiser located a store close to their present location the impact would be minimal at worst. A store owner in Omaha said, "Our doughnut sales increased when Krispy Kreme came to town. We benefit every time they advertise because doughnuts are as popular as ever."[2]

As of early 2004, there was little indication the low-carbohydrate, weight-watching craze that had swept the United States and other countries in recent years had cut much into sales. Industry observers and company officials attributed this in part to doughnuts being an affordable indulgence, easy to eat on the run, and in part to the tendency of many people to treat themselves occasionally. Doughnuts were readily available almost anywhere.

The three leading doughnut chains were Krispy Kreme; Dunkin' Donuts, with worldwide 2002 sales of $2.7 billion, 5,200 outlets worldwide (3,600 in the United States), and close to a 45 percent U.S. market share based on dollar sales volume; and Tim Hortons (160 outlets and 2002 U.S. sales of $115 million, plus 2,300 Canadian outlets with 2002 sales of $536 million).

Krispy Kreme's Chief Competitors

Dunkin' Donuts

Dunkin' Donuts was the largest coffee and baked-goods chain in the world, selling 4.4 million donuts and 1.8 million cups of coffee daily. The quick-service restaurant chain was owned by British-based Allied Domecq PLC, a diversified enterprise whose other businesses included the Baskin-Robbins ice cream chain, ToGo's Eateries (sandwiches), and an assortment of alcoholic beverage brands (Kahlúa, Beefeater's, Maker's Mark, Courvoisier, Tia Maria, and a host of wines). In 2004, Allied Domecq's Dunkin' Donuts chain had total sales approaching $4 billion, almost 6,200 franchised outlets in 40 countries (including 4,418 in the United States), and comparable store sales growth of 4.4 percent in the United States. About 83 percent of the chain's total sales were in the United States. In New England alone, Dunkin' Donuts operated 1,200 stores, including 600 in the Greater Boston area, where the chain was founded in 1950. Starting in 2000, Dunkin' Donuts franchisees could open co-branded stores that included Baskin Robbins and ToGo. Dunkin' Donuts ranked ninth in *Entrepreneur* magazine's annual Franchise Top 500 for 2005.

The key thrust of Dunkin' Donuts' strategy was to expand into those geographic areas in the United States where it was underrepresented. In areas where there were clusters of Dunkin' Donuts outlets, most baked items were supplied from centrally located kitchens rather than being made on-site. Despite its name, Dunkin' Donuts put more emphasis on coffee and convenience than on doughnuts. According to one company executive, "People talk about our coffee first. We're food you eat on the go. We're part of your day. We're not necessarily a destination store." Roughly half of all purchases at Dunkin' Donuts included coffee without a doughnut.[3] Dunkin' Donuts menu included doughnuts (50 varieties), muffins, bagels, cinnamon buns, cookies, brownies, Munchkins doughnut holes, cream cheese sandwiches, nine flavors of fresh coffee, iced coffees, and a lemonade Coolatta.

In 2004, Coolatta was being promoted in collaboration with MTV in a campaign called "Route to Cool." Dunkin' Donuts also had a new "express donuts" campaign to promote the sale of boxed donuts—12-packs containing the top six flavors. This campaign was being supported by advertising based on the theme "Who brought the donuts?" In addition,

[2]As quoted in "Hole-ly War: Omaha to Be Battleground for Duel of Titans," *Omaha World Herald,* September 7, 1999, p. 14.

[3]According to information in Hermione Malone, "Krispy Kreme to Offer Better Coffee as It Tackles New England," *Charlotte Observer,* March 16, 2001.

the chain was emphasizing coffee sales by the pound and had recently broadened its coffee offerings to include cappuccino, latte, espresso, and iced coffees.

The nutritional content of Dunkin' Donuts' 50 doughnut varieties ranged between 200 and 340 calories, between 8 and 19 grams of fat, between 1.5 and 6 grams of saturated fat, and between 9 and 31 grams of sugars; its cinnamon buns had 540 calories, 15 grams of fat, 4 grams of saturated fat, and 42 grams of sugars. Whereas Krispy Kreme's best-selling original glazed doughnuts had 200 calories, 12 grams of fat, 3 grams of saturated fat and 10 grams of sugar, the comparable item at Dunkin' Donuts had 180 calories, 8 grams of fat, 1.5 grams of saturated fat, and 6 grams of sugar. Several Dunkin' Donuts customers in the Boston area who had recently tried Krispy Kreme doughnuts reported that Krispy Kremes had more flavor and were lighter.[4]

Dunkin' Donuts had successfully fended off competition from national bagel chains and Starbucks. When national bagel chains, promoting bagels as a healthful alternative to doughnuts, opened new stores in areas where Dunkin' Donuts had stores, the company responded by adding bagels and cream cheese sandwiches to its menu offerings. Dunkin' Donuts had countered threats from Starbucks by adding a wider variety of hot and cold coffee beverages—and whereas coffee drinkers had to wait for a Starbucks barista to properly craft a $3 latte, they could get coffee and a doughnut on the fly at Dunkin' Donuts for less money. Quick and consistent service was a Dunkin' Donuts forte. Management further believed that the broader awareness of coffee created by the market presence of Starbucks stores had actually helped boost coffee sales at Dunkin' Donuts. In markets such as New York City and Chicago where there were both Dunkin' Donuts and Krispy Kreme stores, sales at Dunkin' Donuts had continued to rise. In commenting on the competitive threat from Krispy Kreme, a Dunkin' Donuts vice president said:

> We have a tremendous number of varieties, a tremendous level of convenience, tremendous coffee and other baked goods. I think the differentiation that Dunkin' enjoys is clear. We're not pretentious and don't take ourselves too seriously, but we know how important a cup of coffee and a donut or bagel in the morning is. Being able to deliver a great cup of coffee when someone is on their way to something else is a great advantage.[5]

In 2003, Couche-Tard, Canada's largest convenience store operator, bought control of the Dunkin' Donuts name in Quebec as well as the 104 Dunkin' Donuts outlets located there. Couche-Tard planned to double the number of outlets within five years to better compete with Tim Hortons and Krispy Kreme.

Tim Hortons

Tim Hortons, a subsidiary of Wendy's International, was one of North America's largest coffee and fresh-baked-goods chains, with almost 2,400 restaurants across Canada and a steadily growing base of 200 locations in key markets within the United States. In April 2004, Tim Hortons acquired 42 Bess Eaton coffee and doughnut restaurants throughout Rhode Island, Connecticut, and Massachusetts, which it planned to convert to the Tim Hortons brand and format. Tim Hortons had systemwide sales of around $3.0 billion in 2003, equal to annual sales of about $1.3 million per store. Same-store sales were up about 4.7 percent in 2003 and, during the first nine months of 2004, were up 10.1 percent in the United States and 7.7 percent in Canada. In Canada, the Tim Hortons chain was regarded as something of an icon—it was named for a popular Canadian-born professional hockey player who played for the Toronto Maple Leafs, Pittsburgh Penguins, and Buffalo Sabers; Horton was born in 1930, started playing hockey when he was five years old, and died in

---

[4]"Time to Rate the Doughnuts: Krispy Kreme Readies to Roll into N.E. to Challenge Dunkin' Donuts," *Boston Globe,* February 21, 2001, p. D1.

[5]As quoted in Malone, "Krispy Kreme to Offer Better Coffee."

an auto accident while on the Buffalo Sabers. A recent survey of Canadian consumers rated Tim Hortons as the best managed brand in Canada.

The Tim Hortons division of Wendy's relied heavily on franchising—only 57 of the 2,527 Tim Hortons outlets at year-end 2003 were company-owned. Franchisees paid a royalty of 3 to 6 percent of weekly sales to the parent company, depending on whether they leased the land and/or buildings from Tim Hortons and on certain other conditions; in addition, franchisees paid fees equal to 4 percent of monthly gross sales to fund advertising and promotional activities undertaken at the corporate level. Franchisees were also required to purchase such products as coffee, sugar, flour and shortening from a Tim Hortons subsidiary; these products were distributed from five warehouses located across Canada and were delivered to the company's Canadian restaurants primarily by its fleet of trucks and trailers. In the United States, both company and franchised stores purchased ingredients from a supplier approved by the parent company.

Tim Hortons used outside contractors to construct its restaurants. The restaurants were built to company specifications as to exterior style and interior decor. The standard Hortons restaurant being built in 2003–2004 consisted of a freestanding production unit ranging from 1,150 to 3,030 square feet. Each included a bakery capable of supplying fresh baked goods throughout the day to several satellite Tim Hortons within a defined area. Tim Hortons locations ranged from full standard stores with in-store baking facilities, to combo units with Wendy's and Tim Hortons under one roof, to carts and kiosks in shopping malls, highway outlets, universities, airports, and hospitals. Most full-standard Tim Hortons locations offered 24-hour drive-through service. Tim Hortons promoted its full-standard stores as neighborhood meeting places and was active in promoting its products for group fund-raisers and community events.

The menu at each Tim Hortons unit consisted of coffee, cappuccino, teas, hot chocolate, soft drinks, soups, sandwiches, and fresh baked goods such as doughnuts, muffins, pies, croissants, tarts, cookies, cakes, and bagels. In recent years, the chain had expanded its lunch menu to include a bigger variety of offerings. One of the chain's biggest drawing cards was its special blend of fresh-brewed coffee, which was also sold in cans for customers' use at home. About half of the purchases at Tim Hortons included coffee without a doughnut. Tim Hortons was number 1 in market share in Canada during breakfast, was number 1 in the afternoon/early evening snack category, and had a strong number 2 position at lunch with a menu featuring six sandwiches.

Executives at Tim Hortons did not feel threatened by Krispy Kreme's expansion into Canada and those parts of the United States where it had stores (Michigan, New York, Ohio, Kentucky, Maine, and West Virginia). According to David House, Tim Hortons president, "We really welcome them. Anyone who draws attention to doughnuts can only help us. It is a big market and a big marketplace. I would put our doughnut up against theirs any day."[6] A Canadian retailing consultant familiar with Tim Hortons and Krispy Kreme said, "This is the Canadian elephant and the U.S. mouse. Listen, if there's anything where Canadians can kick American butt, it is in doughnuts."[7] Another Canadian retailing consultant said, "It [Krispy Kreme] is an American phenomenon. These things are sickeningly sweet."[8]

Canada was reputed to have more doughnut shops per capita than any other country in the world. Aside from Tim Hortons, other chains in Canada featuring doughnuts included Dunkin' Donuts, Robin's Donuts, Country Style, and Coffee Time. Tim Hortons management had a goal of opening 500 Tim Hortons stores in the United States over the next three years, mostly in the Northeast and Great Lakes regions, and a longer-term goal of growing to about 3,500 outlets in Canada.

---

[6]As quoted in "Can Krispy Kreme Cut It in Canada?" *Ottawa Citizen,* December 30, 2000, p. H1.
[7]As quoted in ibid.
[8]As quoted in ibid.

Winchell's Donut House

Winchell's, founded by Verne Winchell in 1948, was owned by Shato Holdings, Ltd., of Vancouver, Canada. In 2000, there were approximately 600 Winchell's units located in 10 states west of the Mississippi River, along with international franchises in Guam, Saipan, Korea, Egypt, Saudi Arabia, and New Zealand. Since then, Winchell's Doughnut House had lost steam and closed two-thirds of its locations. In 2003, there were 200 units in 12 states, plus locations in Guam, Saipan, New Zealand, and Saudi Arabia. Winchell's was the largest doughnut chain on the West Coast. To combat Krispy Kreme's entry into Southern California, where Winchell's had a brand awareness of 97 percent, Winchell's had launched a Warm 'n Fresh program for all outlets in 2000. The program entailed having fresh glazed doughnuts in display cases that were replaced every 15 to 20 minutes between 6:00 and 9:00 A.M. daily. A flashing red light on display cases signaled that a fresh batch of glazed doughnuts was available. Winchell's was offering customers a Warm 'n Fresh doughnut between 6:00 and 11:00 A.M. daily.

As of September 2003, a "Winchell's dozen" of 14 doughnuts sold for $5.99 and a double dozen (28) sold for $9.99. A single donut sold for about 60 cents, and many stores regularly ran a special of two donuts and a cup of coffee for $1.99. Winchell's bakery offerings included 20 varieties of doughnuts and 14 flavors of muffins, as well as croissants, bagels (breakfast bagel sandwiches were available at select locations), eclairs, tarts, apple fritters, and bear claws. It served three varieties of its "legendary" coffees—Dark Roast Supreme, Legendary Blend, and Legendary Decaf—all using only 100 percent arabica beans (considered by many to be the finest coffee beans in the world). Other beverages included regular and frozen cappuccino, soft drinks, milk, and juices.

Winchell's corporate goal for the next five years was to triple its sales. In 2003–2004 it was actively seeking franchisees in 14 western and midwestern states. Winchell's charged a franchise fee of $7,500 and required franchisee's to be able to invest $75,000 of unborrowed funds; the cost of new stores depended on such factors as store size, location, style of decor, and landscaping. A 5 percent royalty and a 3 percent advertising fee were charged on net sales.

LaMar's Donuts

Headquartered in Englewood, Colorado, LaMar's was a small, privately held chain that had 32 corporate-owned and franchised doughnut shops open or under development in 10 states; 8 stores were in the Denver area. Ray LaMar opened the original LaMar's Donuts in 1960 on Linwood Avenue in Kansas City and quickly turned the shop into a local institution. On a typical day, lines started forming before 6:00 A.M. and, by closing time about 11,000 donuts would be sold. Based on the doughnut shop's success and reputation, Ray and his wife, Shannon, decided in the early 1990s to franchise LaMar's. Hundreds of LaMar's devotees applied for the limited number of franchises made available in the Kansas City area; 15 were granted over a few months. But little became of the initial franchising effort and, in 1997, Franchise Consortium International, headed by Joseph J. Field, purchased a majority interest in LaMar's Franchising, renamed the company LaMar's Donuts International, moved the company's headquarters to a Denver suburb, and began laying the groundwork for a national expansion program.

LaMar's stores were typically located along neighborhood traffic routes. Average unit sales were $500,000 in 2003, and management expected that the average would increase to $750,000 in a few years. At one point, Fields expressed an objective of having 1,200 stores in operation by 2013, but so far LaMar's expansion was far slower than had been anticipated.

LaMar's utilized a secret recipe to produce "artisan quality" doughnuts that were handmade daily with all-natural ingredients and no preservatives. Day-old doughnuts were never sold at the shops but were donated at day's end to the needy. In addition to 75 varieties of doughnuts, LaMar's menu included gourmet coffee and cappuccino. LaMar's had recently partnered with Dazbog Coffee Company in Denver, Colorado, and created over a dozen customized specialty coffee blends under the LaMar's Old World Roast label. Beans were hand-picked from Costa Rica and then slow-roasted in an authentic Italian brick fire oven. Coffee products at LaMar's shops included cappuccinos, espressos, lattes, iced coffee drinks, and chai teas.

The company used the tag line "Simply a better doughnut." Joe Fields said, "People come in and try the product and they are surprised. They are wowed, in a very different way than Krispy Kreme. They say, 'Oh my God, this is the best doughnut I've had in my life.'" The Zagat Survey, a well-known rater of premier dining spots nationwide, described LaMar's doughnuts as "extraordinary; fit for kings." *Gourmet* magazine, in search of the country's favorite doughnut, conducted a nationwide poll; the winner was a LaMar's doughnut. LaMar's Donuts has been named Best in the Country by the John Walsh Show, a one-hour daily nationally syndicated television program. Several newspapers had named LaMar's doughnuts as tops in their market area.

Unexpected Developments at Krispy Kreme in 2004

In March 2004, Krispy Kreme's management announced that it expected the company to have diluted earnings per share of $1.16 to $1.18 for fiscal 2005 (up from $0.92 in fiscal 2004) and systemwide comparable store sales growth in the mid-to-high single digits. Executives estimated that systemwide sales would increase approximately 25 percent in fiscal 2005 (ending January 29, 2005) and that approximately 120 new stores would be opened systemwide, including 20 to 25 smaller doughnut-and-coffee-shop stores, during the next 12 months. But as 2004 progressed, Krispy Kreme's business prospects went from rosy to stark within a matter of months.

Developments at Krispy Kreme in May 2004

In a May 7, 2004, press release that caught investors by surprise, CEO Scott Livengood said:

> For several months, there has been increasing consumer interest in low-carbohydrate diets, which has adversely impacted several flour-based food categories, including bread, cereal and pasta. This trend had little discernable effect on our business last year. However, recent market data suggests consumer interest in reduced carbohydrate consumption has heightened significantly following the beginning of the year and has accelerated in the last two to three months. This phenomenon has affected us most heavily in our off-premises sales channels, in particular sales of packaged doughnuts to grocery store customers.

Sales at Krispy Kreme's franchised stores were approximately evenly split between on-premises and off-premises sales, while approximately 60 percent of company-owned store sales were off-premises. As a consequence of the falloff in sales at external outlets, sales at Krispy Kreme stores open at least 18 months grew only 4 percent, well below the 9 percent realized in the preceding quarter. Due to the lower-than-expected off-premise sales at company stores, Livengood said the company was lowering its earnings guidance for the first quarter of fiscal 2005 to about $0.23 per share, down from about $0.26 per share. The company went on to announce in the same press release that it was

- Divesting its recently acquired Montana Mills operation. The plan was to close the majority of the Montana Mills store locations, which were underperforming, and pursue a sale of the remaining Montana Mills stores. Management indicated the Montana Mills divesture would entail write-offs of approximately $35 to $40 million in the first quarter on its Montana Mills investment and would likely involve further write-offs of $2 to $4 million in subsequent quarters.

- Closing six underperforming factory stores—four in older retail locations in below-average retail trade areas and two commissaries.

- Lowering its guidance for fiscal 2005 diluted earnings per share from continuing operations, excluding asset impairment and other charges described below, to between $1.04 and $1.06, approximately 10 percent lower than prior forecasts. Including the Montana Mills charges, diluted earnings per share from continuing operations were estimated to be between $0.93 and $0.95 for fiscal 2005.

In the hours following the announcement, the company's stock price was hammered in trading—dropping about 20 percent.

On May 25, 2004, Krispy Kreme reported a $24.4 million loss for the first quarter of fiscal 2005, blaming (1) trendy low-carb diets such as Atkins and South Beach for a decline in its sales in grocery stores and (2) a $34 million write-off of its investment in Montana Mills. The stock price was down 37 percent since the May 7 lower earnings announcement and was trading at about $20.

At the company's annual stockholders' meeting on May 26, 2004, executives said the company was slowing down expansion plans and had plans to counter consumer interest in low-carbohydrate foods by adding a sugar-free doughnut to its product lineup. Management also announced that the company would soon (1) introduce a chocolate-flavored glazed doughnut; mini rings that were 40 percent smaller than regular doughnuts; and crushed-ice drinks in raspberry, latte, and double chocolate flavors and (2) begin selling bags of the company's own brand of coffee in whole-bean and ground form in grocery stores alongside Krispy Kreme doughnut displays. The company said it planned to go forward with overseas expansion. The overseas expansion was concentrated in Asia; 25 new stores were being planned for South Korea, and on the horizon were stores in Japan, China, Indonesia, the Philippines, and the Persian Gulf.

Developments at Krispy Kreme in July–August 2004

In late July 2004, the company announced that the U.S. Securities and Exchange Commission was launching an inquiry into the company's accounting practices regarding certain franchise buybacks. A *Wall Street Journal* article in May had detailed questionable accounting in the $32.1 million repurchase of a struggling seven-unit franchise in Michigan that was behind on its payments for equipment, ingredients, and franchise fees, along with questionable accounting for another reacquired franchise in southern California.

In late August 2004, Krispy Kreme reported its second-quarter fiscal 2005 results:

- Systemwide sales increases of 14.8 percent as compared with the prior year's second quarter.

- An 11.5 percent increase in company revenue to $177.4 million (versus $159.2 million in the second quarter of the prior year)—company store sales increased 18.7 percent to $123.8 million, revenues from franchise operations grew 13.7 percent to $6.8 million, and KKM&D revenues decreased 4.1 percent to $46.9 million (principally because of lower equipment sales to franchisees opening new stores).

- Very small comparable store sales increases—sales at company-owned increased 0.6 percent, and systemwide sales (at both company-owned and franchised stores) increased only 0.1 percent.

- A decline in operating income from continuing operations for the second quarter of fiscal 2005 to $6.2 million, or $0.10 per diluted share, versus $13.4 million, or $0.22 per diluted share, in the second quarter of fiscal 2004.

- Twenty-two new Krispy Kreme factory/retail stores in 12 new markets, and 10 new doughnut-and-coffee-shop stores. Six company-owned factory/retail stores and three doughnut-and-coffee shops were closed during the quarter.

Commenting on the Krispy Kreme's second quarter performance, Scott Livengood, said:

> Although we are disappointed with the second-quarter financial results, we are optimistic about the long-term growth potential of the business. We are focusing our efforts and resources on initiatives that improve long-term business prospects. We have core strategies with supporting initiatives, a leading consumer brand and great people to address the current challenges. Krispy Kreme has proven over its 67-year history an ability to overcome challenges, and I am confident in our ability to restore our business momentum.[9]

Top management indicated that systemwide sales should grow approximately 15 percent for fiscal 2005 and approximately 10 percent in the last two quarters of the year but declined to provide updated earnings estimates. The company said it had scaled back expansion plans and would only open approximately 75 new stores systemwide (60 factory/retail stores and 15 doughnut-and-coffee shops) during fiscal 2005.

Developments at Krispy Kreme in November–December 2004

In November 2004, Krispy Kreme reported that the company lost $3.0 million in the third quarter of fiscal 2005. Total revenues for the quarter, which included sales from company stores, franchise operations and KKM&D, were up only 1.4 percent to $170.1 million (versus $167.8 million in the third quarter of fiscal 2004). Third-quarter systemwide sales at both company-owned and franchised stores were up 4.7 percent over the third quarter of fiscal 2004. The sales increases were well below the 10 percent gains that management had forecast in August.

During the quarter, 13 company-owned factory/retail stores and two doughnut-and-coffee shop stores were opened, and seven company owned factory/retail stores and two doughnut-and-coffee shop stores were closed. There were total 429 Krispy Kreme stores systemwide at the end of October 2004, consisting of 393 factory/retail stores and 36 doughnut-and-coffee shops. There were plans to open approximately 10 new stores systemwide in the fourth quarter of fiscal 2005.

Exhibit 10 shows the declining performance of Krispy Kreme's stores during the first three quarters of fiscal 2005. Exhibits 11 and 12 shows selected financial statistics for Krispy Kreme Doughnuts during the first nine months of fiscal 2005 compared to the first nine months of fiscal 2004.

Management declined to provide systemwide sales and earnings guidance for the fourth quarter of fiscal 2005 and withdrew its previous estimates of 10 percent systemwide sales growth made in August. Commenting on the company's performance, Scott Livengood said, "Clearly we are disappointed with our third-quarter results. We are focused on addressing the challenges facing the Company and regaining our business momentum." Early in the fourth fiscal quarter, Krispy Kreme sold its remaining Montana Mills assets for what management described as "a modest amount."

In December 2004, Krispy Kreme announced that it had identified accounting errors related to its acquisition of two franchises that could reduce net income for fiscal 2004 by 2.7 percent to 8.6 percent. It was as yet unclear whether the company would have to restate its fiscal year 2004 results. A special committee of the company's board of directors was investigating the accounting problems. The company's outside auditor, Pricewaterhouse-Coopers LLP, said it refused to complete reviews of Krispy Kreme's financial performance for the first six months of 2005 until the special committee completed its probe of the bookkeeping problems.

In late December 2004, Krispy Kreme's stock was trading in the $10–$13 range, well below the $40 high attained in March 2004.

[9]Company press release, August 26, 2004.

EXHIBIT 10   Quarterly Operating Performance of Krispy Kreme Stores, Fiscal Years 2004–2005

	Fiscal Year 2004				Fiscal Year 2005		
	Q1	Q2	Q3	Q4	Q1	Q2	Q3
Average sales per week							
Company stores	$77.4	$74.4	$73.0	$69.1	$67.9	$63.1	$58.4
Area developer stores	58.0	61.2	60.3	58.7	59.2	54.3	49.9
Associate stores	52.4	48.7	45.9	42.6	46.7	43.9	41.7
Franchised store average	56.2	57.3	56.3	54.3	56.0	51.6	47.9
Systemwide average	64.1	63.7	62.7	60.1	60.7	56.3	52.2
Change in comparable store sales							
Company stores	15.4%	15.6%	13.3%	10.7%	5.2%	0.6%	−6.2%
Systemwide	11.2%	11.3%	9.5%	9.1%	4.0%	0.1%	−6.4%
Increase in systemwide sales	24.4%	27.6%	28.6%	25.5%	24.2%	14.8%	4.7%

Source: Company press releases of quarterly earnings results.

EXHIBIT 11   Financial Statement Data for Krispy Kreme Doughnuts, First Nine Months of Fiscal 2004 versus First Nine Months of 2005 (Dollar amounts in thousands, except per share)

	Nine Months ending November 2, 2003	Nine Months ending October 31, 2004
Statement of operations data		
Total revenues	$475,598	$531,941
Operating expenses	359,820	430,613
General and administrative expenses	27,362	34,928
Depreciation and amortization expenses	13,473	19,496
Arbitration award	(525)	—
Impairment charge and store closing costs	—	14,865
Income from operations	$ 75,468	$ 32,039
Interest expense, (income), net, and other expenses and adjustments	6,410	5,424
Income (loss) from continuing operations before income taxes	69,058	26,615
Provision for income taxes	27,488	11,543
Income from continuing operations	41,570	15,072
Discontinued operations	(907)	(36,741)
Net income (loss)	$ 40,663	$ (21,669)
Diluted earnings (loss) per share		
Income (loss) from continuing operations	$0.67	$0.24
Discontinued operations	(0.01)	(0.58)
Net income (loss) per share	$0.66	$(0.34)
Diluted shares outstanding	61,975	63,441
Balance sheet data		
Cash and cash equivalents	$ 39,287	$ 17,213
Receivables	62,454	73,416
Inventories	29,717	32,287
Payables and accrued expenses	52,101	67,820
Long-term debt and other long-term obligations, including current maturities	149,142	170,509
Total assets	$629,431	$675,897
Total shareholders' equity	$428,188	$437,568

Source: Company press releases, November 21, 2003, and November 22, 2004.

EXHIBIT 12   **Krispy Kreme's Performance by Business Segment, First Nine Months of Fiscal 2004 versus First Nine Months of 2005 (In thousands)**

	Nine Months ending November 2, 2003	Nine Months ending October 31, 2004
Revenues by business segment		
Company store operations	$317,158	$369,593
Franchise operations	17,555	20,060
KK Manufacturing and Distribution	140,885	142,288
Total	$475,598*	$531,941
Operating income by business segment (before depreciation and amortization)		
Company store operations	$ 61,969	$ 41,797
Franchise operations	13,721	14,694
KK Manufacturing and Distribution	27,824	26,706
Total	103,514*	83,197
Unallocated general and administrative expenses	$ (28,571)	$(36,293)

*Totals do not include operations of Montana Mills, a business which was acquired in April 2004 and divested during fiscal 2005; nine-month revenues for Montana Mills were $4,481,000, and the operating loss at Montana Mills was $1,408,000.

Source: Company press releases, November 21, 2003, and November 22, 2004.

Case

10

Dell, Inc., in 2005: A Winning Strategy?

Arthur A. Thompson *University of Alabama*

John E. Gamble *University of South Alabama*

In 1984, at the age of 19, Michael Dell invested $1,000 of his own money and founded Dell Computer with a simple vision and business concept—that personal computers (PCs) could be built to order and sold directly to customers. Michael Dell believed his approach to the PC business had two advantages: (1) bypassing distributors and retail dealers eliminated the markups of resellers, and (2) building to order greatly reduced the costs and risks associated with carrying large stocks of parts, components, and finished goods. Between 1986 and 1993 the company worked to refine its strategy, build an adequate infrastructure, and establish market credibility against better-known rivals. In the mid- and late 1990s, Dell's strategy started to click into full gear. By 2003, Dell's sell-direct and build-to-order business model and strategy had provided the company with the most efficient procurement, manufacturing, and distribution capabilities in the global PC industry and had given Dell a substantial cost and profit margin advantage over rival PC vendors. And by late 2004 Dell seemed well on its way to solidifying its market standing as the global leader in PCs.

Dell had a market-leading 33 percent share of PC sales in the United States in the first nine months of 2004, comfortably ahead of Hewlett-Packard (19.5 percent), IBM (5.1 percent), and Gateway (4.7 percent). Dell had moved ahead of IBM into second place during 1998 and then overtaken Compaq Computer as the U.S. sales leader in the third quarter of 1999. Its market share leadership in the United States had widened every year since 2000. Dell had overtaken Compaq as the global market leader in 2001. But when HP, the third-ranking PC seller in the world, acquired Compaq, the second-ranking PC vendor in 2002, Dell found itself in a tight battle with HP for the top spot globally. Dell was the world leader in unit sales in the first and third quarters of 2002, and HP was the sales leader in the second and fourth quarters. However, Dell opened a clear market share gap over HP in 2003–2004. In the United States, Dell had the number one PC market share in every customer segment in the three months ending October 2004. However, Dell trailed HP in PC sales outside the United States; HP's non-U.S. share had been in the 12.5 to 13.8 percent range since late 2001, with Dell's

EXHIBIT 1   U.S. And Global Market Shares of Leading PC Vendors, 1998–2004

		A. U.S. Market Shares of the Leading PC Vendors, 1998–2003					
		First Nine Months of 2004		2003		2002	
2003 Rank	Vendor	Shipments (in 000s)	Market Share	Shipments (in 000s)	Market Share	Shipments (in 000s)	Market Share
1	Dell	14,011	33.1%	16,319	30.9%	13,324	27.90%
	Compaq*	—	—	—	—	—	—
2	Hewlett-Packard*	8,256	19.5	10,851	20.6	8,052	16.8
3	IBM	2,170	5.1	2,748	5.2	2,531	5.3
4	Gateway	1,991	4.7	1,987	3.8	2,725	5.7
5	Apple	n.a.	n.a.	1,675	3.2	1,693	3.5
	Others	15,954	37.6	19,158	36.3	19,514	40.8
	All vendors	42,382	100.0%	52,739	100.0%	47,839	100.0%

		B. Worldwide Market Shares of the Leading PC Vendors, 1996–2003[†]					
		First Nine Months of 2004		2003		2002	
2003 Rank	Vendor	Shipments (in 000s)	Market Share	Shipments (in 000s)	Market Share	Shipments (in 000s)	Market Share
1	Dell	22,999	18.4%	25,833	16.9	20,672	15.2%
	Compaq*	—	—	—	—	—	—
2	Hewlett-Packard*	19,796	15.8	25,009	16.4	18,432	13.6
3	IBM	7,478	6.0	9,000	5.9	7,996	5.9
4	Fujitsu Siemens	5,142	4.1	6,375	4.2	5,822	4.3
5	Toshiba	n.a.	n.a.	5,080	3.3	n.a.	n.a
	Others	69,753	55.7	81,271	53.3	78,567	57.8
	All vendors	125,168	100.0%	152,568	100.0%	136,022	100.0%

n.a. = Not available.

*Compaq was acquired by Hewlett-Packard in May 2002. The 2002 data for Hewlett-Packard include both Compaq-branded and Hewlett-Packard-branded PCs for the last three quarters of 2002 plus only Hewlett-Packard-branded PCs for Q1 2002. Compaq's worldwide PC shipments during Q1 2002 totaled 3,367,000 units; its U.S. PC shipments during Q1 2002 totaled 1,280,000 units.

[†]Includes branded shipments only and excludes original equipment manufacturer (OEM) sales for all manufacturers; shipments of Compaq PCs for last three quarters of 2002 included in 2002 figures for Hewlett-Packard.

Source: International Data Corp.

share climbing from about 7.5 percent in late 2001 to 11 percent in 2004. Exhibit 1 shows the shifting domestic and global sales and market share rankings in PCs during 1998–2004.

Since the late 1990s, Dell had also been driving for industry leadership in servers. In 2004 Dell was the number 1 domestic seller of servers, with close to a 33 percent market share (up from about 3–4 percent in the mid-1990s). It was number 2 in the world in server shipments, with a 24.5 percent share in the third quarter of 2004, within striking distance of global market leadership. Dell was the leader in servers in the three largest server markets—the United States, Japan, and China. In the mid-to-late 1990s, a big fraction of the servers sold were proprietary machines running on customized Unix operating systems and carrying price tags ranging from $30,000 to $1 million or more. But a seismic shift in server technology, coupled with growing cost-consciousness on the part of server users, produced a radical shift away from more costly, proprietary, Unix-based servers during 1999–2004. In 2003–2004, about 8 out of 10 servers sold carried price tags below $10,000, were based on standardized components and technology, and ran on either Windows or Linux operating systems. The overall share of Unix-based servers shipped in

A. U.S. Market Shares of the Leading PC Vendors, 1998–2003

2001		2000		1999		1998	
Shipments (in 000s)	Market Share	Shipments (in 000s)	Market Share	Shipments (in 000s)	Market Share	Shipments (in 000s)	Market Share
10,817	23.5%	9,645	19.7%	7,492	16.6%	4,799	13.2%
5,341	11.6	7,761	15.9	7,222	16	6,052	16.7
4,374	9.5	5,630	11.5	3,955	8.8	2,832	7.8
2,461	5.3	2,668	5.5	3,274	7.2	2,983	8.2
3,219	7.0	4,237	8.7	4,001	8.9	3,039	8.4
1,665	3.6	n.a	n.a.	n.a	n.a.	n.a.	n.a.
23,509	51.0	18,959	38.8	19,248	42.6	16,549	45.6
46,051	100.0%	48,900	100.0%	45,192	100.0%	36,254	100.0%

B. Worldwide Market Shares of the Leading PC Vendors, 1996–2003[†]

2001		2000		1999		1998	
Shipments (in 000s)	Market Share	Shipments (in 000s)	Market Share	Shipments (in 000s)	Market Share	Shipments (in 000s)	Market Share
17,231	12.9%	14,801	10.6%	11,883	10.5%	7,770	8.5%
14,673	11	17,399	12.5	15,732	14	13,266	14.5
9,309	7	10,327	7.4	7,577	6.7	5,743	6.3
8,292	6.2	9,308	6.7	9,287	8.2	7,946	8.7
6,022	4.5	6,582	4.7	n.a.	n.a.	n.a.	n.a.
n.a.	n.a.	n.a.	n.a.	n.a.	n.a.	n.a.	n.a.
73,237	54.9	80,640	58	62,258	55.2	50,741	55.5
133,466	100.0%	139,057	100.0%	112,726	100.0%	91,442	100.0%

2003–2004 was under 10 percent, down from about 18 percent in 1997. Dell's rise to prominence in servers came from its focus on low- and mid-range servers that used standard technology.

In addition, Dell was making market inroads in other product categories. Its sales of data storage devices had grown to over $2 billion annually, aided by a strategic alliance with EMC, a leader in the data storage. In 2001–2002, Dell began selling low-cost data-routing switches—a product category in which Cisco Systems was the dominant global leader. In late 2002 Dell introduced a new line of handheld PCs—the Axim X5—to compete against the higher-priced products of Palm, HP, and others; the Axim offered a solid but not trend-setting design, was packed with features, and was priced roughly 50 percent below the best-selling models of rivals. Starting in 2003, Dell began marketing Dell-branded printers and printer cartridges, product categories that provided global leader HP with the lion's share of its profits—the company was on track to sell over 5 million printers and generate more than $1 billion in imaging and printing revenues in 2004. Also in 2003, Dell began selling flat-screen LCD TVs and retail-store systems, including electronic cash registers, specialized software, services, and peripherals required to link retail-store checkout lanes to corporate information systems. Dell's recently introduced MP3 player, the Dell DJ, was number 2 behind the Apple iPod. Dell added plasma screen TVs to its TV product line in 2004. Since the late 1990s, Dell had been marketing CD and DVD drives, printers, scanners, modems, monitors, digital cameras, memory cards, data storage devices, and speakers made by a variety of manufacturers.

So far, Dell's foray into new products and businesses had proved to be profitable. According to Michael Dell, "We believe that all our businesses should make money. If a business doesn't make money, if you can't figure out how to make money in that business, you shouldn't be in that business."[1] In 2003 and 2004, Dell earned a profit in each of its product categories, customer segments, and geographic markets. Dell products were sold in more than 170 countries, but sales in 60 countries accounted for about 95 percent of total revenues.

Company Background

At age 12, Michael Dell was running a mail-order stamp-trading business, complete with a national catalog, and grossing $2,000 a month. At 16 he was selling subscriptions to the *Houston Post,* and at 17 he bought his first BMW with money he had earned. He enrolled at the University of Texas in 1983 as a premed student (his parents wanted him to become a doctor), but he soon became immersed in computers and started selling PC components out of his college dormitory room. He bought random-access memory (RAM) chips and disk drives for IBM PCs at cost from IBM dealers, who at the time often had excess supplies on hand because they were required to order large monthly quotas from IBM. Dell resold the components through newspaper ads (and later through ads in national computer magazines) at 10–15 percent below the regular retail price.

By April 1984 sales were running about $80,000 per month. Michael decided to drop out of college and form a company, PCs Ltd., to sell both PC components and PCs under the brand name PCs Limited. He obtained his PCs by buying retailers' surplus stocks at cost, then powering them up with graphics cards, hard disks, and memory before reselling them. His strategy was to sell directly to end users; by eliminating the retail markup, Dell's new company was able to sell IBM clones (machines that copied the functioning of IBM PCs using the same or similar components) about 40 percent below the price of IBM's best-selling PCs. The discounting strategy was successful, attracting price-conscious buyers and generating rapid revenue growth. By 1985, the company was assembling its own PC designs with a few people working on six-foot tables. The company had 40 employees, and Michael Dell worked 18-hour days, often sleeping on a cot in his office. By the end of fiscal 1986, sales had reached $33 million.

During the next several years, however, PCs Ltd. was hampered by growing pains—specifically, a lack of money, people, and resources. Michael Dell sought to refine the company's business model; add needed production capacity; and build a bigger, deeper management staff and corporate infrastructure while at the same time keeping costs low. The company was renamed Dell Computer in 1987, and the first international offices were opened that same year. In 1988 Dell added a sales force to serve large customers, began selling to government agencies, and became a public company—raising $34.2 million in its first offering of common stock. Sales to large customers quickly became the dominant part of Dell's business. By 1990 Dell Computer had sales of $388 million, a market share of 2–3 percent, and a research and development (R&D) staff of over 150 people. Michael Dell's vision was for Dell Computer to become one of the world's top three PC companies.

Thinking its direct sales business would not grow fast enough, in 1990–93, the company began distributing its computer products through Soft Warehouse Superstores (now CompUSA), Staples (a leading office products chain), Wal-Mart, Sam's Club, and Price

---

[1]As quoted in "Dell Puts Happy Customers First," *Nikkei Weekly,* December 16, 2002.

Club (now Price/Costco). Dell also sold PCs through Best Buy stores in 16 states and through Xerox in 19 Latin American countries. But when the company learned how thin its margins were in selling through such distribution channels, it realized it had made a mistake and withdrew from selling to retailers and other intermediaries in 1994 to refocus on direct sales. At the time, sales through retailers accounted for only about 2 percent of Dell's revenues.

In 1993, further problems emerged: Dell reportedly lost $38 million in a risky foreign-currency hedging, quality difficulties arose with certain PC lines made by the company's contract manufacturers, profit margins declined, and buyers were turned off by the company's laptop PC models. To get laptop sales back on track, the company took a charge of $40 million to write off its laptop line and suspended sales of laptops until it could get redesigned models into the marketplace.

Because of higher costs and unacceptably low profit margins in selling to individuals and households, Dell did not pursue the consumer market aggressively until sales to individuals at the company's Internet site took off in 1996 and 1997. It became clear that PC-savvy individuals, who were buying their second and third computers, wanted powerful computers with multiple features; did not need much technical support; and liked the convenience of buying direct from Dell, ordering exactly what they wanted, and having it delivered to their door within a matter of days. In early 1997, Dell created an internal sales and marketing group dedicated to serving the individual consumer segment and introduced a product line designed especially for individual users.

By late 1997, Dell had become a low-cost leader among PC vendors by wringing greater and greater efficiency out of its direct sales and build-to-order business model. Since then, the company had continued driving hard to reduce its costs and, by late 2004, was considered the lowest-cost producer among all the leading vendors of PCs and servers. The company was a pioneer and an acknowledged world leader in incorporating e-commerce technology and use of the Internet into its everyday business practices. Michael Dell's goal was to stitch Dell's business together with its supply partners and customers in real time such that all three appeared to be part of the same organizational team.[2]

In its fiscal year ending January 30, 2004, Dell Computer posted revenues of $41.4 billion, up from $3.4 billion in the year ending January 29, 1995—a nine-year compound average growth rate of 32 percent. Over the same period, profits were up from $140 million to $2.62 billion—a 38.5 percent compound average growth rate. Dell expected to achieve close to $50 billion in sales in its fiscal year ending January 2005. A $100 investment in Dell's stock at its initial public offering in June 1988 would have been worth about $52,000 in December 2004. Based on 2003 data, Dell ranked number 31 on the Fortune 500, number 93 on the Fortune Global 500, and number 6 on the Fortune Global "most admired" list. In late 2004, Dell Computer had over 53,000 employees worldwide, up from 16,000 at year-end 1997; over 50 percent of Dell's employees were located in countries outside the United States, and this percentage was growing. The company's headquarters and main office complex was in Round Rock, Texas (an Austin suburb). The company changed its name from Dell Computer to Dell, Inc., in 2003 to reflect the company's growing business base outside of PCs. Exhibits 2 and 3 provide information about Dell's financial performance and geographic operations.

Michael Dell

In the company's early days Michael Dell hung around mostly with the company's engineers. He was so shy that some employees thought he was stuck up because he never talked

[2]Joan Magretta, "The Power of Virtual Integration: An Interview with Dell Computer's Michael Dell," *Harvard Business Review,* March–April 1998, p. 75.

EXHIBIT 2   **Selected Financial Statement Data for Dell Inc., Fiscal Years 1998–2004**
(In millions, except per share data)

	Fiscal Year Ended	
	January 30, 2004	**January 31, 2003**
Results of operations		
Net revenue	$41,444	$35,404
Cost of revenue	33,892	29,055
Gross margin	7,552	6,349
Operating expenses:		
Selling, general and administrative	3,544	3,050
Research, development and engineering	464	455
Special charges	—	—
Total operating expenses	4,008	3,505
Operating income	3,544	2,844
Investment and other income (loss), net	180	183
Income before income taxes, extraordinary loss, and cumulative effect of change in accounting principle	3,724	3,027
Provision for income taxes	1,079	905
Net income	$ 2,645	$ 2,122
Earnings per common share:		
Basic	$1.03	$0.82
Diluted	$1.01	$0.80
Weighted average shares outstanding:		
Basic	2,565	2,584
Diluted	2,619	2,644
Cash flow and balance sheet data		
Net cash provided by operating activities	$ 3,670	$ 3,538
Cash, cash equivalents, and investments	11,922	9,905
Total assets	19,311	15,470
Long-term debt	505	506
Total stockholders' equity	$ 6,280	$ 4,873

*Includes effect of $59 million adjustment due to the cumulative effect of a change in accounting principle.

Source: Dell, Inc., 2004 10-K and 1999 annual report.

to them. But people who worked with him closely described him as a likable young man who was slow to warm up to strangers.[3] He was a terrible public speaker and wasn't good at running meetings. But Lee Walker, a 51-year-old venture capitalist brought in by Michael Dell to provide much-needed managerial and financial experience during the company's organization-building years, became Michael Dell's mentor, built up his confidence, and was instrumental in turning him into a polished executive.[4] Walker served as the company's president and chief operating officer during the 1986–1990 period; he had a fatherly image, knew everyone by name, and played a key role in implementing Michael Dell's marketing ideas. Under Walker's tutelage, Michael Dell became intimately familiar with all parts of the business, overcame his shyness, learned to control his ego, and turned into a charismatic leader with an instinct for motivating people and winning their loyalty and respect.

[3]"Michael Dell: On Managing Growth," *MIS Week,* September 5, 1988, p. 1.
[4]"The Education of Michael Dell," *BusinessWeek,* March 22, 1993, p. 86.

	Fiscal Year Ended			
February 1, 2002	February 2, 2001	January 28, 2000	January 29, 1999	February 1, 1998
$31,168	$31,888	$25,265	$18,243	$12,327
25,661	25,455	20,047	14,137	9,605
5,507	6,443	5,218	4,106	2,722
2,784	3,193	2,387	1,788	1,202
452	482	374	272	204
482	105	194	—	—
3,718	3,780	2,955	2,060	1,406
1,789	2,663	2,263	2,046	1,316
(58)	531	188	38	52
1,731	3,194	2,451	2,084	1,368
485	958	785	624	424
$ 1,246	$ 2,177*	$ 1,666	$ 1,460	$ 944
$0.48	$0.84	$0.66	$0.58	$0.36
$0.46	$0.79	$0.61	$0.53	$0.32
2,602	2,582	2,536	2,531	2,631
2,726	2,746	2,728	2,772	2,952
$ 3,797	$ 4,195	$ 3,926	$ 2,436	$ 1,592
8,287	7,853	6,853	3,181	1,844
13,535	13,670	11,560	6,877	4,268
520	509	508	512	17
$ 4,694	$ 5,622	$ 5,308	$ 2,321	$ 1,293

When Walker had to leave the company in 1990 because of health reasons, Dell turned to Morton Meyerson, former CEO and president of Electronic Data Systems, for advice and guidance on how to transform Dell Computer from a fast-growing medium-sized company into a billion-dollar enterprise. Though sometimes given to displays of impatience, Michael Dell usually spoke in a quiet, reflective manner and came across as a person with maturity and seasoned judgment far beyond his age. His prowess was based more on an astute combination of technical knowledge and marketing know-how than on being a technological wizard. In 1992, at the age of 27, Michael Dell became the youngest CEO ever to head a Fortune 500 company; he was a billionaire at the age of 31.

By the late 1990s, Michael Dell had become one of the most respected executives in the PC industry. Media journalists had described him as "the quintessential American entrepreneur" and "the most innovative guy for marketing computers." He was a much-sought-after speaker at industry and company conferences. His views and opinions about the future of PCs, the Internet, and e-commerce practices carried considerable weight both in the PC industry and among executives worldwide. Once pudgy and bespectacled, in early 2005, 40-year-old Michael Dell was physically fit, considered good-looking, wore contact lenses,

EXHIBIT 3   **Dell's Geographic Area Performance, Fiscal Years 2000–2004 (In millions of dollars)**

	Fiscal Year Ended				
	January 30, 2004	January 31, 2003	February 1, 2002	February 2, 2001	January 28, 2000
Net revenues					
Americas					
Business	$21,888	$19,394	$17,275	$18,969	$15,160
U.S. consumer	6,715	5,653	4,485	3,902	2,719
Total Americas	28,603	25,047	21,760	22,871	17,879
Europe	8,495	6,912	6,429	6,399	5,590
Asia-Pacific-Japan	4,436	3,445	2,979	2,618	1,796
Total net revenues	$41,444	$35,404	$31,168	$31,888	$25,265
Operating income					
Americas					
Business	$ 2,124	$ 1,945	$ 1,482	$ 1,999	$ 1,800
U.S. consumer	400	308	260	253	204
Total Americas	2,594	2,253	1,742	2,252	2,004
Europe	637	388	377	347	359
Asia-Pacific-Japan	313	203	152	169	94
Special charges	—	—	(482)	(105)	(194)
Total operating income	$ 3,544	$ 2,844	$ 1,789	$ 2,663	$ 2,263

Source: Dell, Inc., 10-K reports, 2004 and 2001.

ate only health foods, and lived in a three-story 33,000-square-foot home on a 60-acre estate in Austin, Texas, with his wife and four children. He owned about 9 percent of Dell's common stock, worth over $9 billion.

Michael Dell was considered a very accessible CEO and a role model for young executives because he had done what many of them were trying to do. He delegated authority to subordinates, believing that the best results came from turning "loose talented people who can be relied upon to do what they're supposed to do." Business associates viewed Michael Dell as an aggressive personality, an extremely competitive risk taker who had always played close to the edge. He spent about 30 percent of his time traveling to company operations and meeting with customers. In a typical year, he would make two or three trips to Europe and two trips to Asia.

In mid-2004, Michael Dell, the company's first and only CEO, transferred his title of CEO to Kevin Rollins, the company's president and chief operating officer. Dell remained as chairman of the board. Dell and Rollins had run the company for the past seven years under a shared leadership structure. The changes were primarily ones of title, not of roles or responsibilities.

Dell Computer's Strategy

The core of Dell Computer's strategy during 2002–2004 was to use its strong capabilities in supply chain management, low-cost manufacturing, and direct sales capabilities to expand into product categories where it could provide added value to its customers in the form of lower prices. Its standard pattern of attack was to identify an IT product with good margins; figure out how to build it (or else have it built by others) cheaply enough to be able to significantly underprice competitive products; and then market the new product to Dell's steadily growing customer base and watch the market share points, incremental revenues, and incremental profits pile up.

Dell management believed it had the industry's most efficient business model. The company's strategy was built around a number of core elements: a cost-efficient approach to build-to-order manufacturing, partnerships with suppliers aimed at squeezing cost savings out of the supply chain, direct sales to customers, award-winning customer service and technical support, pioneering use of the Internet and e-commerce technology, and product-line expansion aimed at capturing a bigger share of the dollars its customers spent for IT products and services.

Cost-Efficient Build-to-Order Manufacturing

Dell built its computers, workstations, and servers to order; none were produced for inventory. Dell customers could order custom-equipped servers and workstations based on the needs of their applications. Desktop and laptop customers ordered whatever configuration of microprocessor speed, random-access memory, hard disk capacity, CD or DVD drives, fax/modem/wireless capabilities, graphics cards, monitor size, speakers, and other accessories they preferred. The orders were directed to the nearest factory. In 2004 Dell had assembly plants in Austin, Texas; Nashville, Tennessee; Limerick, Ireland; Xiamen, China; Penang, Malaysia; and El Dorado do Sul, Brazil; a seventh manufacturing plant was being constructed in North Carolina. At all locations, the company had the capability to assemble PCs, workstations, and servers; Dell assembled its data storage products at its Austin, Limerick, and Penang plants. In 2002–2004, typical orders were built and delivered in three to five days.

Until 1997, Dell operated its assembly lines in traditional fashion with workers performing a single operation. An order form accompanied each metal chassis across the production floor; drives, chips, and ancillary items were installed to match customer specifications. As a partly assembled PC arrived at a new workstation, the operator, standing beside a tall steel rack with drawers full of components, was instructed what to do by little red and green lights flashing beside the drawers. When the operator was finished, the drawers containing the used components were automatically replenished from the other side, and the PC chassis glided down the line to the next workstation. However, Dell had reorganized its plants in 1997, shifting to "cell manufacturing" techniques whereby a team of workers operating at a group workstation (or cell) assembled an entire PC according to customer specifications. The shift to cell manufacturing reduced Dell's assembly times by 75 percent and doubled productivity per square foot of assembly space. Assembled computers were first tested and then loaded with the desired software, shipped, and typically delivered five to six business days after the order was placed.

At Dell's newest plant on its Austin manufacturing campus, the cell manufacturing approach had been abandoned in favor of an even more efficient assembly-line approach. Workers at the new plant in 2004 could turn out close to 800 desktop PCs per hour on three assembly lines that took half the floor space of the older cell manufacturing process, where production had run about 120 units per hour. Although the new Austin plant was originally designed for production of 400 units per hour, management believed that it would be able to boost hourly production to 1,000 units per hour. The gains in productivity were being achieved partly by redesigning the PCs to permit easier and faster assembly, partly by innovations in the assembly process, and partly by reducing the number of times a computer was touched by workers during assembly and shipping by 50 percent. At both Dell's Austin plant and its plant in Ireland, workers could assemble a PC in two to three minutes. Moreover, just-in-time inventory practices that left pallets of parts sitting around everywhere had been tweaked to just-in-the-nick-of-time delivery by suppliers of the exact parts needed every couple of hours; double-decker conveyor belts moved parts and components to designated assembly points. Newly assembled PCs were routed on conveyors to shipping, where they were boxed and shipped to customers the same day.

Dell was regarded as a world-class manufacturing innovator and a pioneer in how to mass-produce a customized product—its methods were routinely studied in business schools worldwide. Most of Dell's PC rivals—notably IBM and HP/Compaq—had given up on trying to produce their own PCs as cheaply as Dell and shifted to outsourcing their PCs from contract manufacturers. Dell management believed that its in-house manufacturing delivered about a 6 percent cost advantage versus outsourcing. Dell's build-to-order strategy meant that the company had no in-house stock of finished goods inventories and that, unlike competitors using the traditional value chain model, it did not have to wait for resellers to clear out their own inventories before it could push new models into the marketplace—resellers typically operated with 30 to 60 days inventory of prebuilt models (see Exhibit 4). Equally important was the fact that customers who bought from Dell got the satisfaction of having their computers customized to their particular liking and pocketbook.

Quality Control

All assembly plants had the capability to run testing and quality control processes on components, parts, and subassemblies obtained from suppliers, as well as on the finished products Dell assembled. Suppliers were urged to participate in a quality certification program that committed them to achieving defined quality specifications. Quality control activities were undertaken at various stages in the assembly process. In addition, Dell's quality control program included testing of completed units after assembly, ongoing production reliability audits, failure tracking for early identification of problems associated with new models shipped to customers, and information obtained from customers through its service and technical support programs. All of the company's plants had been certified as meeting ISO 9002 quality standards.

Partnerships with Suppliers

Michael Dell believed that it made much better sense for the company to partner with reputable suppliers of PC parts and components than to integrate backward and get into parts and components manufacturing on its own. He explained why:

> If you've got a race with 20 players all vying to make the fastest graphics chip in the world, do you want to be the twenty-first horse, or do you want to evaluate the field of 20 and pick the best one?[5]

Dell management evaluated the various makers of each component; picked the best one or two as suppliers; and then stuck with those suppliers as long as they maintained their leadership in technology, performance, quality, and cost. Management believed that long-term partnerships with reputable suppliers had at least five advantages. First, using name-brand processors, disk drives, modems, speakers, and multimedia components enhanced the quality and performance of Dell's PCs. Because of varying performance among different brands of components, the brand of the components was quite important to customers concerned about performance and reliability. Second, because Dell partnered with suppliers for the long term and because it committed to purchase a specified percentage of its requirements from each supplier, Dell was assured of getting the volume of components it needed on a timely basis even when overall market demand for a particular component temporarily exceeded the overall market supply. Third, Dell's long-run commitment to its suppliers made it feasible for suppliers to locate their plants or distribution centers within a few miles of Dell assembly plants, putting them in position to make deliveries daily or

---

[5]As quoted in Magretta, "The Power of Virtual Integration," p. 74.

EXHIBIT 4   Comparative Value Chain Models of PC Vendors

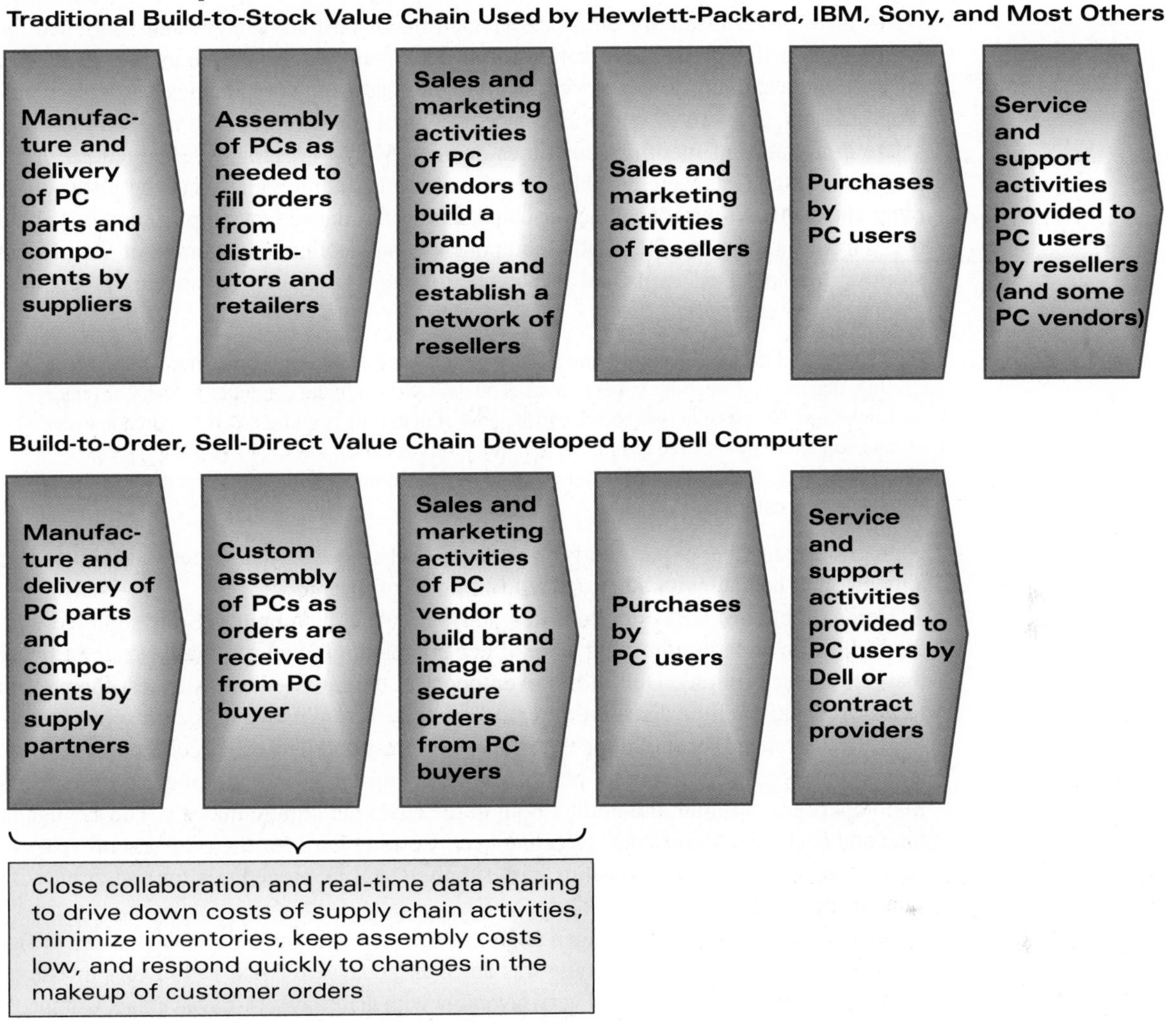

Traditional Build-to-Stock Value Chain Used by Hewlett-Packard, IBM, Sony, and Most Others

Manufacture and delivery of PC parts and components by suppliers	Assembly of PCs as needed to fill orders from distributors and retailers	Sales and marketing activities of PC vendors to build a brand image and establish a network of resellers	Sales and marketing activities of resellers	Purchases by PC users	Service and support activities provided to PC users by resellers (and some PC vendors)

Build-to-Order, Sell-Direct Value Chain Developed by Dell Computer

Manufacture and delivery of PC parts and components by supply partners	Custom assembly of PCs as orders are received from PC buyer	Sales and marketing activities of PC vendor to build brand image and secure orders from PC buyers	Purchases by PC users	Service and support activities provided to PC users by Dell or contract providers

Close collaboration and real-time data sharing to drive down costs of supply chain activities, minimize inventories, keep assembly costs low, and respond quickly to changes in the makeup of customer orders

every few hours, as needed. Dell supplied data on inventories and replenishment needs to its suppliers at least once a day—hourly in the case of components being delivered several times daily from nearby sources.

Fourth, long-term supply partnerships facilitated having some of the supplier's engineers assigned to Dell's product design teams and being treated as part of Dell. When new products were launched, suppliers' engineers were stationed in Dell's plants; if early buyers called with a problem related to design, further assembly and shipments were halted while the supplier's engineers and Dell personnel corrected the flaw on the spot.[6] Fifth, long-term partnerships enlisted greater cooperation on the part of suppliers to seek new ways to drive costs out of the supply chain. Dell openly shared its daily production schedules, sales forecasts, and new model introduction plans with vendors. Dell also did a three-year plan with each of its key suppliers and worked with suppliers to minimize the number of different stock-keeping units of parts and components in its products and to identify ways to drive costs down.

[6]Ibid., p. 75.

Commitment to Just-in-Time Inventory Practices

Dell's just-in-time inventory emphasis yielded major cost advantages and shortened the time it took Dell to get new generations of its computer models into the marketplace. New advances were coming so fast in certain computer parts and components (particularly microprocessors, disk drives, and wireless devices) that any given item in inventory was obsolete in a matter of months, sometimes quicker. Moreover, rapid-fire reductions in the prices of components were not unusual—for example, Intel regularly cut the prices on its older chips when it introduced newer chips, and it introduced new chip generations about every three months. In 2003–2004, component costs declined an average of 0.5 percent weekly.[7] Michael Dell explained the competitive and economic advantages of minimal component inventories:

> If I've got 11 days of inventory and my competitor has 80 and Intel comes out with a new chip, that means I'm going to get to market 69 days sooner. In the computer industry, inventory can be a pretty massive risk because if the cost of materials is going down 50 percent a year and you have two or three months of inventory versus eleven days, you've got a big cost disadvantage. And you're vulnerable to product transitions, when you can get stuck with obsolete inventory.[8]

For a growing number of parts and components, Dell's close partnership with suppliers was allowing it to operate with no more than two hours of inventory.

Dell's supplier of CRT monitors was Sony. Because the monitors Sony supplied with the Dell name already imprinted were of dependably high quality (a defect rate of fewer than 1,000 per million), Dell didn't even open up the monitor boxes to test them at its Reno, Nevada, monitor distribution center.[9] Utilizing sophisticated data exchange systems, Dell arranged for its shippers (Airborne Express and United Parcel Service) to pick up computers at U.S. assembly plants, then pick up the accompanying monitors at its Reno distribution center and deliver both to the customer simultaneously. The savings in time and cost were significant. Dell had been working hard for the past several years to refine and improve its relationships with suppliers and its procedures for operating with smaller inventories.

In fiscal year 1995, Dell averaged an inventory turn cycle of 32 days. By the end of fiscal 1997 (January 1997), the average was down to 13 days. In fiscal 1998 Dell's inventory averaged 7 days, which compared very favorably with Gateway's 14-day average, Compaq's 23-day average, and the estimated industrywide average of over 50 days. In fiscal years 1999 and 2000, Dell operated with an average of six days' supply in inventory; the average dropped to five days' supply in fiscal year 2001, four days' supply in 2002, and three days' supply in 2003 and 2004.

Dell's Direct Sales Strategy and Marketing Efforts

With thousands of phone, fax, and Internet orders daily and ongoing field sales force contact with customers, the company kept its finger on the market pulse, quickly detecting shifts in sales trends, design problems, and quality glitches. If the company got more than a few of the same complaints, the information was relayed immediately to design engineers who checked out the problem. When design flaws or components defects were found, the factory was notified and the problem corrected within a few days. Management believed Dell's ability to respond quickly gave it a significant advantage over PC makers that operated

---

[7]Speech by Michael Dell at University of Toronto, September 21, 2004; posted at www.dell.com and accessed December 15, 2004.

[8]Ibid., p. 76.

[9]Ibid.

on the basis of large production runs of variously configured and equipped PCs and sold them through retail channels. Dell saw its direct sales approach as a totally customer-driven system, with the flexibility to transition quickly to new generations of components and PC models.

Dell's Customer-Based Sales and Marketing Focus

Whereas many technology companies organized their sales and marketing efforts around product lines, Dell was organized around customer groups. Dell had placed managers in charge of developing sales and service programs appropriate to the needs and expectations of each customer group. Up until the early 1990s, Dell operated with sales and service programs aimed at just two market segments—high-volume corporate and governmental buyers, and low-volume business and individual buyers. But as sales took off in 1995–97, these segments were subdivided into finer, more homogeneous categories that by 2000 included global enterprise accounts, large and midsize companies (over 400 employees), small companies (under 400 employees), health care businesses (over 400 employees), federal government agencies, state and local government agencies, educational institutions, and individual consumers. Many of these customer segments were further subdivided—for instance, in education, there were separate sales and marketing programs for K–12 schools; higher education institutions; and personal-use purchases by faculty, staff, and students.

Dell's largest global enterprise accounts were assigned their own dedicated sales force—for example, Dell had a sales force of 150 people dedicated to meeting the needs of General Electric's facilities and personnel scattered across the world. Dell's sales to individuals and small businesses were made by telephone, fax, and the Internet. It had call centers in the United States, Canada, Europe, and Asia with toll-free lines; customers could talk with a sales representative about specific models, get information faxed or mailed to them, place an order, and pay by credit card. The Asian and European call centers were equipped with technology that routed calls from a particular country to a particular call center. Thus, for example, a customer calling from Lisbon, Portugal, was automatically directed to a Portuguese-speaking sales rep at the call center in Montpelier, France.

Dell in Japan

With a market share of about 10 percent, Dell was the number 3 provider of computer systems in Japan (behind NEC and Toshiba); in 2002 Dell had the fifth highest dollar market share, at 7.7 percent. Other competitors in Japan included Sony, Fujitsu, Hitachi, IBM, Sharp, and Matshusita. Counting units sold, however, Dell was number 1 in business desktop computers and was number 2 in entry-level and midrange servers. Dell's 2004 sales in Japan were up about 30 percent, in a market where overall sales were flat. Dell's technical and customer support for PCs, servers, and network storage devices was ranked the best in Japan in 2002 and 2003. Dell had 1,100 personnel in Japan and was tracking Japanese buying habits and preferences with its proprietary software. The head of Dell's consumer PC sales group in Japan had installed 34 kiosks in leading electronics stores around Japan, allowing shoppers to test Dell computers, ask questions of staff, and place orders—close to half the sales were to people who did not know about Dell prior to visiting the kiosk. Dell believed that it was more profitable than any other PC-server vendor selling in the Japanese market. Dell's profit margins in Japan were higher than those in the U.S. market, and sales were rising briskly.

Dell in China

Dell Computer entered China in 1998 and achieved faster growth there than in any other foreign market it had entered. The market for PCs in China was the third largest in the world, behind the United States and Japan, and was on the verge of being the second largest. PC sales in China were growing 20–30 percent annually and, with a population of 1.4 billion people (of which some 400 million lived in metropolitan areas where computer use was growing rapidly), the Chinese market for PCs was expected to become the largest in the world by 2010.

The market leader in China was Lenovo, a local company formerly called Legend, which had a 26.4 percent share in 2004. Other major local PC producers were Founder (10.3 percent share) and Great Wall (8.7 percent share). Dell had an 8.1 percent share and expected to overtake Great Wall and move into third place in 2004. Dell's shipments in China rose 60 percent in fiscal 2004 (four times the rest of the industry) and its revenues were up 40 percent, making China Dell's fourth largest market. Other competitors in China included IBM, Hewlett-Packard, Toshiba, Acer, and NEC Japan. All of the major contenders except Dell relied on resellers to handle sales and service; Dell sold directly to customers in China just as it did elsewhere.

Dell's primary target market in China consisted of large corporate accounts. Management believed that many Chinese companies would find the savings from direct sales appealing, that they would like the idea of having Dell build PCs and servers to their requirements and specifications, and that—once they became a Dell customer—they would like the convenience of Internet purchases and the company's growing array of products and services. Dell recognized that its direct sales approach put it at a short-term disadvantage in appealing to small business customers and individual consumers. According to an executive from rival Lenovo, "It takes two years of a person's savings to buy a PC in China. And when two years of savings is at stake, the whole family wants to come out to a store to touch and try the machine."[10] But Dell believed that over time, as Chinese consumers became more familiar with PCs and more comfortable with making online purchases, growing numbers of small business customers and consumers would become comfortable with placing Internet and telephone orders. In 2002, about 40 percent of Dell's sales in China were over the Internet.

Dell in Latin America

In 2002 PC sales in Latin America exceeded 5 million units. Latin America had a population of 450 million people. Dell management believed that in the next few years PC use in Latin America would reach 1 for every 30 people (one-tenth the penetration in the United States), pushing annual sales up to 15 million units. The company's plant in Brazil, the largest market in Latin America, was opened to produce, sell, and provide service and technical support for customers in Brazil, Argentina, Chile, Uruguay, and Paraguay.

Using Dell Direct Store Kiosks to Access Individual Consumers

In 2002 Dell began installing Dell Direct Store kiosks in a variety of retail settings. The kiosks did not carry inventory, but customers could talk face-to-face with a knowledgeable Dell sales representative, inspect Dell's products, and order them on the Internet while at the kiosk. The idea for using kiosks had begun in Japan, where Dell sales reps were encountering resistance to Dell's direct sales approach from individual buyers—Japanese consumers were noted for wanting to carefully inspect different PC brands in stores before making a purchase. When kiosks were installed in Japanese retail settings, they proved quite popular and helped generate a big boost in Dell's share of PC sales to consumers in Japan. The success of kiosks in Japan had inspired Dell to try them in the United States. About 60 kiosks were in place at U.S. locations during the 2002 holiday sales season. Dell began placing Dell Direct Store kiosks in selected Wal-Mart and Sears stores in 2003 and had a total of 80 kiosks at various locations in December 2004.

---

[10]Quoted in Neel Chowdhury, "Dell Cracks China," *Fortune,* June 21, 1999, p. 121.

Customer Service and Technical Support

Service became a feature of Dell's strategy in 1986 when the company began providing a year's free onsite service with most of its PCs after users complained about having to ship their PCs back to Austin for repairs. Dell contracted with local service providers to handle customer requests for repairs; on-site service was provided on a next-day basis. Dell also provided its customers with technical support via a toll-free phone number and e-mail. Dell received 500,000 to 600,000 e-mail messages and 6 to 8 million phone calls annually requesting service and support. Dell was aggressively pursuing initiatives to enhance its online technical support tools and reduce the number and cost of telephone support calls. The company was adding Web-based customer service and support tools to make a customer's online experience pleasant and satisfying. In 2003–2004, over 50 percent of Dell's technical support activities were conducted via the Internet.

Bundled service policies were a major selling point for winning corporate accounts. If customers preferred to work with their own service provider, Dell supplied the provider of choice with training and spare parts needed to service customers' equipment. Recently, Dell had instituted a First Call Resolution initiative to strengthen its capabilities to resolve customer inquiries or difficulties on the first call; First Call Resolution percentages were made an important measure in evaluating the company's technical support performance.

Value-Added Services

Dell kept close track of the purchases of its large global customers, country by country and department by department—and customers themselves found this purchase information valuable. Dell's sales and support personnel used their knowledge about a particular customer's needs to help that customer plan PC purchases, to configure the customer's PC networks, and to provide value-added services. For example, for its large customers Dell loaded software and placed ID tags on newly ordered PCs at the factory, thereby eliminating the need for the customer's IT personnel to unpack the PC, deliver it to an employee's desk, hook it up, place asset tags on the PC, and load the needed software from an assortment of CD-ROMs and diskettes—a process that could take several hours and cost $200–$300.[11] While Dell charged an extra $15 or $20 for the software-loading and asset-tagging services, the savings to customers were still considerable—one large customer reported savings of $500,000 annually from this service.[12]

Premier Pages

Dell had developed customized, password-protected Web sites called Premier Pages for close to 50,000 corporate, governmental, and institutional customers worldwide. These Premier Pages gave customers' personnel online access to information about all Dell products and configurations the company had purchased or that were currently authorized for purchase. Employees could use Premier Pages to (1) obtain customer-specific pricing for whatever machines and options the employee wanted to consider, (2) place an order online that would be electronically routed to higher-level managers for approval and then on to Dell for assembly and delivery, and (3) seek advanced help desk support. Customers could also search and sort all invoices and obtain purchase histories. These features eliminated paper invoices, cut ordering time, and reduced the internal labor customers needed to staff corporate purchasing and accounting functions. Customer use of Premier Pages had boosted the productivity of Dell salespeople assigned to these accounts by 50 percent. Dell was providing Premier Page service to thousands of additional customers annually and adding more features to further improve functionality.

[11]Magretta, "The Power of Virtual Integration," p. 79.
[12]"Michael Dell Rocks," *Fortune,* May 11, 1998, p. 61.

www.dell.com

Dell operated one of the world's highest-volume Internet commerce sites, with nearly 8 billion page requests annually at 81 country sites in 28 languages/dialects and 26 currencies. Dell began Internet sales at its Web site (www.dell.com) in 1995, almost overnight achieving sales of $1 million a day. By early 2003, over 50 percent of Dell's sales were Web-enabled—and the percentage was increasing, especially for sales to small businesses and consumers. Dell's Web site sales exceeded $60 million a day in 2004, up from $35 million daily in early 2000 and $5 million daily in early 1998. Its Web site averaged over 6 million visits weekly in the third quarter of 2004.

At the company's Web site, prospective buyers could review Dell's entire product line in detail, configure and price customized PCs, place orders, and track orders from manufacturing through shipping. The closing rate on sales at Dell's Web site was 20 percent higher than that on sales inquiries received via telephone. Management believed that enhancing www.dell.com to shrink transaction and order fulfillment times, increase accuracy, and provide more personalized content resulted in a higher degree of "e-loyalty" than traditional attributes like price and product selection.

On-Site Services

Corporate customers paid Dell fees to provide technical support, on-site service, and help with migrating to new IT technologies. Services were one of the fastest-growing part of Dell, accounting for almost $4 billion in sales in 2002 and close to $6 billion in fiscal 2003. Dell's service business was split about 50–50 between what Michael Dell called close-to-the-box services and management and professional services—but the latter were growing faster, at close to 25 percent annually. Dell estimated that close-to-the-box support services for Dell products represented about a $50 billion market, whereas the market for management and professional services (IT life-cycle services, deployment of new technology, and solutions for greater IT productivity) was about $90 billion. IT consulting services were becoming more standardized, driven primarily by growing hardware and software standardization, reduction in on-site service requirements (partly because of online diagnostic and support tools, growing ease of repair and maintenance, increased customer knowledge, and increased remote management capabilities), and declines in the skills and know-how that were required to perform service tasks on standardized equipment and install new, more standardized systems.

Dell's strategy in services, like its strategy in hardware products, was to bring down the cost of IT consulting services for its large enterprise customers. The providers of on-site service, technical support, and other types of IT consulting typically charged premium prices and realized hefty profits for their efforts. According to Michael Dell, customers who bought the services being provided by Dell saved 40 to 50 percent over what they would have paid other providers of IT services.

Top management expected services to play an expanding role in the company's growth. Kevin Rollins, Dell's president and CEO in 2004, indicated the company's business model "isn't just about making cheap boxes, it's also about freeing customers from overpriced relationships" with such vendors as IBM, Sun Microsystems, and Hewlett-Packard.[13] While a number of Dell's corporate accounts were large enough to justify dedicated on-site teams of Dell support personnel, Dell generally contracted with third-party providers to make the necessary onsite service calls. Customers notified Dell when they had problems; such notices triggered two electronic dispatches—one to ship replacement parts from Dell's factory to the customer sites, and one to notify the contract service provider to prepare to

---

[13]Quoted in Kathryn Jones, "The Dell Way," *Business 2.0,* February 2003.

make the needed repairs as soon as the parts arrived.[14] Bad parts were returned so that Dell could determine what went wrong and how to prevent such problems from happening again. Problems relating to faulty components or flawed components design were promptly passed along to the relevant supplier for correction.

Customer Forums

In addition to using its sales and support mechanisms to stay close to customers, Dell periodically held regional forums for its best customers. The company formed Platinum and Gold Councils composed of its largest customers in the United States, Europe, Japan, and the Asia-Pacific region; regional meetings were held every six to nine months.[15] Some regions had two meetings—one for chief information officers and one for technical personnel. At the meetings, which frequently included a presentation by Michael Dell, Dell's senior technologists shared their views on the direction of the latest technological developments, what the flow of technology really meant for customers, and Dell's plans for introducing new and upgraded products over the next two years. There were also breakout sessions on topics of current interest. Dell found that the information gleaned from customers at these meetings assisted the company in forecasting demand for its products.

Pioneering Leadership in Use of the Internet and E-Commerce Technology

Dell was a leader in using the Internet and e-commerce technologies to squeeze greater efficiency out of its supply chain activities, to streamline the order-to-delivery process, to encourage greater customer use of its Web site, and to gather and use all types of information. In a 1999 speech to 1,200 customers, Michael Dell said:

> The world will be changed forever by the Internet . . . The Internet will be your business. If your business isn't enabled by providing customers and suppliers with more information, you're probably already in trouble. The Internet provides a dramatic reduction in the cost of transactions and the cost of interaction among people and businesses, and it creates dramatic new opportunities and destroys old competitive advantages. The Internet is like a weapon sitting on a table ready to be picked up by either you or your competitors.[16]

Dell's use of its Web site and various Internet technology applications had proved instrumental in helping the company become the industry's low-cost provider and drive costs out of its business. Internet technology applications were a cornerstone of Dell's collaborative efforts with suppliers. The company provided order-status information quickly and conveniently over the Internet, thereby eliminating tens of thousands of order-status inquiries coming in by phone. It used its Web site as a powerful sales and technical support tool. Few companies could match Dell's competencies and capabilities in the use of Internet technology to improve operating efficiency and gain new sales in a cost-efficient manner.

Expansion into New Products

Dell's recent expansion into data storage hardware, switches, handheld PCs, printers, and printer cartridges represented an effort to diversify the company's product base and to use its competitive capabilities in PCs and servers to pursue revenue growth opportunities.

---

[14]Kevin Rollins, "Using Information to Speed Execution," *Harvard Business Review,* March–April 1998, p. 81.

[15]Magretta, "The Power of Virtual Integration," p. 80.

[16]Keynote speech given on August 25, 1999, in Austin, Texas, at Dell's DirectConnect Conference and posted at www.dell.com.

Michael Dell explained why Dell had decided to expand into products and services that complemented its sales of PCs and servers:

> We tend to look at what is the next big opportunity all the time. We can't take on too many of these at once, because it kind of overloads the system. But we believe fundamentally that if you think about the whole market, it's about an $800 billion market, all areas of technology over time go through a process of standardization or commoditization. And we try to look at those, anticipate what's happening, and develop strategies that will allow us to get into those markets. In the server market in 1995 we had a 2 percent market share, today we have over a 30 percent share, we're number 1 in the U.S. How did that happen? Well, first of all it happened because we started to have a high market share for desktops and notebooks. Then customers said, oh yes, we know Dell, those are the guys who have really good desktops and notebooks. So they have servers, yes, we'll test those, we'll test them around the periphery, maybe not in the most critical applications at first, but we'll test them here. [Then they discover] these are really good and Dell provides great support . . . and I think to some extent we've benefited from the fact that our competitors have underestimated the importance of value, and the power of the relationship and the service that we can create with the customer.
>
> And, also, as a product tends to standardize there's not an elimination of the requirement for custom services, there's a reduction of it. So by offering some services, but not the services of the traditional proprietary computer company, we've been able to increase our share. And, in fact, what tends to happen is customers embrace the standards, because they know that's going to save them costs. Let me give you an example . . . about a year ago we entered into the data networking market. So we have Ethernet switches, layer 2 switches. So if you have PCs and servers, you need switches; every PC attaches to a switch, every server attaches to a switch. It's a pretty easy sale, switches go along with computer systems. We looked at this market and were able to come up with products that are priced about 2 1/2 times less than the market leader today, Cisco, and as a result the business has grown very, very quickly. We shipped 1.8 million switch ports in a period of about a year, when most people would have said that's not going to work and come up with all kinds of reasons why we can't succeed.[17]

As Dell's sales of data-routing switches accelerated in 2001–2002 and Dell management mulled whether to expand into other networking products and Internet gear, Cisco elected to discontinue supplying its switches to Dell for resale as of October 2002. Dell's family of PowerConnect switches—simple commodity-like products generally referred to as layer 2 switches in the industry—carried a price of $20 per port, versus $70–$100 for comparable Cisco switches and $38 for comparable 3Com switches.

Michael Dell and Kevin Rollins saw external storage devices as a growth opportunity because the company's corporate and institutional customers were making increasing use of high-speed data storage and retrieval devices. Dell's PowerVault line of storage products had data protection and recovery features that made it easy for customers to add and manage storage and simplify consolidation. The PowerVault products utilized standardized technology and components (which were considerably cheaper than customized ones), allowing Dell to underprice rivals and drive down storage costs for its customers by about 50 percent. Dell's competitors in storage devices included Hewlett-Packard (HP) and IBM.

Some observers saw Dell's 2003 entry into the printer market as a calculated effort to go after HP's biggest and most profitable business segment and believed the Dell offensive was deliberately timed to throw a wrench into HP's efforts to resolve the many challenges of successfully merging its operations with those of Compaq. One of the reasons that Dell had entered the market for servers back in 1995 was that Compaq Computer, then its biggest rival in PCs, had been using its lucrative profits on server sales to subsidize charging lower prices on Compaq computers and thus be more price-competitive against Dell's

---

[17]Remarks by Michael Dell, Gartner Fall Symposium, Orlando, Florida, October 9, 2002; posted at www.dell.com.

PCs—at the time Compaq was losing money on its desktop and notebook PC business. According to Michael Dell:

> Compaq had this enormous profit pool that they were using to fight against us in the desktop and notebook business. That was not an acceptable situation. Our product teams knew that the servers weren't that complicated or expensive to produce, and customers were being charged unfair prices.[18]

Dell management believed that HP was doing much the same thing in printers and printer products, where it had a dominant market share worldwide and generated about 75 percent of its operating profits. Dell believed HP was using its big margins on printer products to subsidize selling its PCs at prices comparable to Dell's, even though Dell had costs that were about 8 percent lower than HP's. HP's PC operations were either in the red or barely in the black during most of 2003–2004, while Dell consistently had profit margins of 8 percent or more on PCs. Dell's entry and market success in printer products had put pricing pressure on HP in the printer market and had helped erode HP's share of the printer market world-wide from just under 50 percent to around 46 percent. Kevin Rollins believed that Dell's decision to enter the printer market as a head-to-head rival of HP served two purposes:

> Any strategist is going to try to develop a strategy that is going to help them and hurt competitors. Our whole vision here was to do both: improve the revenues and profits of our own business, and at the same time put our competitors at a disadvantage.[19]

To further keep the pricing pressure on HP in 2003, Dell had priced its new Axim line of handheld PCs at about 50 percent less than HP's popular iPaq line of handhelds, and Dell's storage and networking products also carried lower prices than comparable HP products. Dell management believed the company's entry into the printer market would add value for its customers. Michael Dell explained:

> We think we can drive down the entire cost of owning and using printing products. If you look at any other market Dell has gone into, we have been able to significantly save money for customers. We know we can do that in printers; we have looked at the supply chain all the way through its various cycles and we know there are inefficiencies there. I think the price of the total offering when we include the printer and the supplies . . . can come down quite considerably.[20]

When Dell announced it had contracted with Lexmark to make printers and printer and toner cartridges for sale under the Dell label beginning in 2003, HP immediately discontinued supplying HP printers to Dell for resale at Dell's Web site. Dell had been selling Lexmark printers for two years and since 2000 had resold about 4 million printers made by HP, Lexmark, and other vendors to its customers. Lexmark designed and made critical parts for its printers but used offshore contract manufacturers for assembly. Gross profit margins on printers (sales minus cost of goods sold) were said to be in single digits in 2002–2004, but the gross margins on printer supplies were in the 50–60 percent range—brand-name ink cartridges for printers typically ran $25 to $35.

Dell's Entry into the White-Box PC Segment

In 2002 Dell announced it would begin making so-called white-box (i.e., unbranded) PCs for resale under the private labels of retailers. PC dealers that supplied white-box PCs to small businesses and price-conscious individuals under the dealer's own brand name

[18]Remarks by Michael Dell at the University of Toronto, September 21, 2004; posted at www.dell.com.

[19]Quoted in Adam Lashinsky, "Where Dell Is Going Next," *Fortune,* October 18, 2004, p. 116.

[20]Quoted in the *Financial Times* Global News Wire, October 10, 2002.

accounted for about one-third of total PC sales and about 50 percent of sales to small businesses. According to one industry analyst, "Increasingly, Dell's biggest competitor these
days isn't big brand-name companies like IBM or HP, it's white-box vendors." Dell's thinking in entering the white-box PC segment was that it was cheaper to reach many small businesses through the white-box dealers that already served them than by using its own sales
force and support groups to sell and service businesses with fewer than 100 employees. Dell
believed its low-cost supply chain and assembly capabilities would allow it to build generic
machines cheaper than white-box resellers could buy components and assemble a customized machine. Management forecast that Dell would achieve $380 million in sales of
white-box PCs in 2003 and would generate profit margins equal to those on Dell-branded
PCs. Some industry analysts were skeptical of Dell's move into white-box PCs because they
expected white-box dealers to be reluctant to buy their PCs from a company that had a
history of taking their clients. Others believed this was a test effort by Dell to develop the
capabilities to take on white-box dealers in Asia and especially in China, where the sellers
of generic PCs were particularly strong.

Other Elements of Dell's Business Strategy

Dell's strategy had two other elements that assisted the company's drive for industry leadership: R&D and advertising.

Research and Development

Dell's R&D focus was to track and test new developments in components and software,
ascertain which ones would prove most useful and cost-effective for customers, and then
design them into Dell products. Management believed that it was Dell's job on behalf of its
customers to sort out all the new technology coming into the marketplace and help steer
customers to options and solutions most relevant to their needs. The company talked to its
customers frequently about "relevant technology," listening carefully to customers' needs
and problems, and endeavoring to identify the most cost-effective solutions.

Dell was a strong advocate of incorporating standardized components in its products so
as not to tie either it or its customers to one company's proprietary technology and components, which almost always carried a price premium and increased costs for its customers.
Dell actively promoted the use of industrywide standards and regularly pressed its suppliers of a particular part or component to agree on common standards. Dell executives saw
standardized technology as beginning to take over the largest part of the $800 billion spent
annually on IT—standardization was particularly evident in servers, storage, networking,
and high-performance computing. One example of the impact of standardized technology
was at the University of Buffalo, where Dell had installed a 5.6 teraflop cluster of about
2,000 Dell servers containing 4,000 microprocessors that was being used to decode the
human genome. The cluster of servers, which were the same as those Dell sold to its business
customers, had been installed in about 60 days at a cost of a few million dollars and represented the third most powerful supercomputer in the world. High-performance clusters of
PCs and servers were replacing mainframe computers and custom-designed supercomput-
ers because of their much lower cost. Amerada Hess, attracted by Dell's use of standardized
and upgradable parts and components, installed a cluster of several hundred Dell workstations and allocated about $300,000 a year to upgrade and maintain it; the cluster had
replaced an IBM supercomputer that cost $1.5 million a year to lease and operate. Studies
conducted by Dell indicated that, over time, products incorporating standardized technology
delivered about twice the performance per dollar of cost as products based on proprietary
technology.

Dell's R&D group included over 3,000 engineers, and its annual R&D budget was $450
to $470 million. The company's R&D unit also studied and implemented ways to control

quality and to streamline the assembly process. About 15 percent of Dell's 800 U.S. patents were ranked "elite."

Advertising

Michael Dell was a strong believer in the power of advertising and frequently espoused its importance in the company's strategy. His competitive zeal resulted in the company's being the first to use comparative ads, throwing barbs at Compaq's higher prices. Although Compaq won a lawsuit against Dell for making false comparisons, Michael Dell was unapologetic, arguing that the ads were very effective: "We were able to increase customer awareness about value."[21] He insisted that the company's ads be communicative and forceful, not soft and fuzzy. The company regularly had prominent ads describing its products and prices in such leading computer publications as *PC Magazine* and *PC World,* as well as in *USA Today, The Wall Street Journal,* and other business publications.

Dell's Performance in 2004

During the first nine months of 2004, Dell's revenues and unit shipments grew 2–3 times faster than the industry average. Despite steadily eroding average selling prices—$1,540 in fiscal 2004, down from $1,640 in 2003; $1,700 in 2002; $2,050 in 2001; $2,250 in 2000; and $2,600 in 1998—Dell's revenues were climbing as the company gained volume and market share in virtually all product categories and geographic areas where it competed. Worldwide revenues, which reached $35.7 billion in the first nine months of fiscal 2005, were expected to run about 20 percent higher than fiscal 2004 levels and total about $48–$50 billion for the full year. Dell's sales increases were strongest in Europe and in notebook PCs.

During the November 2002–January 2003 period (the fourth quarter of Dell's 2003 fiscal year), the company posted its best-ever quarterly product shipments, revenues, and operating profits. Management indicated that Dell's global market share in PCs in the last quarter of fiscal 2003 was almost 3 points higher than in its fiscal 2002 fourth quarter, and its U.S. share was 5 points higher—in servers, Dell's market share was over 3 points higher. Unit shipments were up by 25 percent, and shipments in China, France, Germany, and Japan increased a combined 39 percent, with server sales in those countries up by 47 percent.

Market Conditions in the Information Technology Industry in Late 2004

Analysts expected the $800 billion worldwide IT industry to grow roughly 10 percent in 2004, following a single-digit increase in 2003, a 2.3 percent decline in 2002, and close to a 1 percent decline in 2001—corporate spending for IT products accounted for about 45 percent of all capital expenditures of U.S. businesses. From 1980 to 2000, IT spending had grown at an average annual rate of 12 percent and then flattened. The slowdown in IT spending reflected a combination of factors: sluggish economic growth worldwide that was prompting businesses to delay IT upgrades and hold on to aging equipment longer, overinvestment in IT in the 1995–99 period, declining unit prices for many IT products (especially PCs and servers), and a growing preference for lower-priced, standard-component hardware that was good enough to perform a variety of functions using off-the-shelf Windows or Linux operating systems (as opposed to relying on proprietary hardware and customized

[21]"The Education of Michael Dell," p. 85.

EXHIBIT 5
Worldwide
Shipments of PCS,
1980–2005

Year	PCs Shipped (in millions)	Year	PCs Shipped (in millions)
1980	1	1999	113
1985	11	2000	139
1990	24	2001	133
1995	58	2002	136
1996	69	2003	153
1997	80	2004*	177
1998	91	2005*	195

*Forecast data.

Source: International Data Corp.

Unix software). The selling points that appealed most to IT customers were standardization, flexibility, modularity, simplicity, economy of use, and value.

Exhibit 5 shows actual and projected PC sales for 1980–2005 as compiled by industry researcher International Data Corporation (IDC). According to Gartner Research, the billionth PC was shipped sometime in July 2002; of the billion, an estimated 550 million were still in use. Nearly 82 percent of the 1 billion PCs that had been shipped were desktops, and 75 percent were sold to businesses. With a world population of 6 billion, most industry participants believed there was ample opportunity for further growth in the PC market. Computer usage in Europe was half of that in the United States, even though the combined economies of the European countries were a bit larger than the U.S. economy. Growth potential for PCs was particularly strong in China, India, several other Asian countries, and portions of Latin America. Forrester Research estimated that the numbers of PCs in use worldwide would approach 1.3 billion by 2010, up from 575 million in 2004, with the growth being driven by the emerging markets in China, India and Russia. IDC had predicted that notebook PC sales would grow from 26.9 percent of PC shipments in 2003 to 37.3 percent in 2007.

Currently, there was growing interest in notebook computers equipped with wireless capability; many businesses were turning to notebooks equipped with wireless data communications devices to improve worker productivity and keep workers connected to important information. The emergence of Wireless Fidelity (Wi-Fi) networking technology, along with the installation of wireless home and office networks, was fueling the trend. Wi-Fi systems were being used in businesses, on college campuses, in airports, and other locations to link users to the Internet and to private networks. Three other devices—flat-panel LCD monitors, DVD recorder drives, and portable music players like Apple's iPod—were also stimulating sales of new PCs.

The Server Market

At the same time, forecasters expected full global build-out of the Internet to continue, which would require the installation of millions of servers. But since 2000 IT customers had been switching from the use of expensive high-end servers running customized Unix operating systems to the use of low-cost servers running on standardized Intel/Windows/Linux technologies; the switch to stands-based servers had caused a slowdown in dollar revenues from server sales despite rapidly increasing unit volume. A number of industry observers believed that the days of using expensive, proprietary Unix-based servers were numbered. The Unix share of the server operating system market (based on unit shipments) was said to have decreased by nearly 50 percent over the past five years, whereas Windows and Linux servers had tripled in use. As of the third quarter of 2004:

- IBM held the number 1 spot in the worldwide server systems market based on dollar revenues, with a 31.7 percent market share. HP had the number two spot, with a 26.8 percent share.

- Sun and Dell tied for third place in server revenues, with 10.2 percent and 10.1 percent shares, respectively. Dell had experienced strong 14.1 percent year-over-year revenue growth while Sun's revenues were flat.

- In terms of unit shipments, HP was the number 1 vendor worldwide and Dell was number 2, with a 24.5 percent share. HP had been the unit volume leader in server shipments for 10 consecutive quarters, but Dell had narrowed the gap considerably.

- HP had the number 1 spot in Linux servers, with a 26.9 percent market share based on revenue, while IBM was second, with 20.5 percent, and Dell was third, with 17.4 percent. Overall, 31.7 percent of the servers shipped in the third quarter of 2004 were Linux-based.

Competing Value Chain Models in the Global PC Industry

When the personal computer industry first began to take shape in the early 1980s, the founding companies manufactured many of the components themselves—disk drives, memory chips, graphics chips, microprocessors, motherboards, and software. Subscribing to a philosophy that mandated in-house development of key components, they built expertise in a variety of PC-related technologies and created organizational units to produce components as well as handle final assembly. While certain noncritical items were typically outsourced, if a computer maker was not at least partially vertically integrated and produced some components for its PCs, then it was not taken seriously as a manufacturer. But as the industry grew, technology advanced quickly in so many directions on so many parts and components that the early personal computer manufacturers could not keep pace as experts on all fronts. There were too many technologies and manufacturing intricacies to master for a vertically integrated manufacturer to keep its products on the cutting edge.

As a consequence, companies emerged that specialized in making particular components. Specialists could marshal enough R&D capability and resources to either lead the technological developments in their area of specialization or else quickly match the advances made by their competitors. Moreover, specialist firms could mass-produce the component and supply it to several computer manufacturers far cheaper than any one manufacturer could fund the needed component R&D and then make only whatever smaller volume of components it needed for assembling its own brand of PCs. Thus, in the early 1990s, such computer makers as Compaq Computer, IBM, Hewlett-Packard, Sony, Toshiba, and Fujitsu-Siemens began to abandon vertical integration in favor of a strategy of outsourcing most components from specialists and concentrating on efficient assembly and marketing their brand of computers. They adopted the build-to-stock value chain model shown in the top section of Exhibit 4. It featured arm's-length transactions between specialist suppliers, manufacturer/assemblers, distributors and retailers, and end users. However, a few others, most notably Dell and Gateway, employed a shorter value chain model, selling directly to customers and eliminating the time and costs associated with distributing through independent resellers. Building to order avoided (1) having to keep many differently equipped models on retailers' shelves to fill buyer requests for one or another configuration of options and components, and (2) having to clear out slow-selling models at a discount before introducing new generations of PCs (for instance, HP's retail dealers had an average of 43 days of HP products in stock as of October 2004). Direct sales eliminated retailer costs and markups (retail dealer margins were typically in the range of 4 to 10 percent).

Because of Dell's success in using its business model and strategy to become the low-cost leader, most other PC makers in 2002–2004 were endeavoring to emulate various aspects of Dell's strategy, but with only limited success. Nearly all vendors were trying to cut days of inventory out of their supply chains and reduce their costs of goods sold and operating expenses to levels that would make them more cost-competitive with Dell. In an effort to cut their assembly costs, IBM, HP, and several others had begun outsourcing assembly to contract manufacturers and refocused their internal efforts on product design and marketing. Virtually all vendors were trying to minimize the amount of finished goods in dealer/distributor inventories and shorten the time it took to replenish dealer stocks. Collaboration with contract manufacturers was increasing to develop the capabilities to build and deliver PCs equipped to customer specifications within 7 to 14 days, but these efforts were hampered by the use of Asia-based contract manufacturers—delivering built-to-order PCs to North American and European customers within a two-week time frame required the use of costly air freight from Asia-based assembly plants.

While most PC vendors would have liked to adopt Dell's sell-direct strategy for at least some of their sales, they confronted big channel conflict problems: if they started to push direct sales hard, they would almost certainly alienate the independent dealers on whom they depended for the bulk of their sales and service to customers. Dealers saw sell-direct efforts on the part of a manufacturer whose brand they represented as a move to cannibalize their business and to compete against them. However, Dell's success in gaining large enterprise customers with its direct sales force had forced growing numbers of PC vendors to supplement the efforts of their independent dealers with direct sales and service efforts of their own. During 2003–2004, several of Dell's rivals were selling 15 to 25 percent of their products direct.

Profiles of Selected Competitors in the PC Industry

This section presents brief profiles of three of Dell's principal competitors. Exhibit 6 summarizes Dell's principal competitors in the various product categories where it competed and the sizes of these product markets.

Hewlett-Packard

In one of the most contentious and controversial acquisitions in U.S. history, Hewlett-Packard shareholders voted by a narrow margin in early 2002 to approve the company's acquisition of Compaq Computer, the world's second largest full-service global computing company (behind IBM) and a company with 2001 revenues of $33.6 billion and a net loss of $785 million. Compaq had passed IBM to become the world leader in PCs in 1995 and remained in first place until it was overtaken by Dell in late 1999. Compaq had acquired Tandem Computer in 1997 and Digital Equipment Corporation in 1998 to give it capabilities, products, and service offerings that allowed it to compete in every sector of the computer industry.[22] When Compaq purchased it, Digital was a troubled company with high operating costs, an inability to maintain technological leadership in high-end computing, and a nine-year string of having either lost money or barely broken even.[23]

The acquisitions gave Compaq a product line that included PCs, servers, workstations, mainframes, peripherals, and such services as business and e-commerce solutions, hardware and software support, systems integration, and technology consulting. In 2000, Compaq spent $370 million to acquire certain assets of Inacom Corporation that management believed would help Compaq reduce inventories, speed cycle time, and enhance its

[22]"Can Compaq Catch Up?" *BusinessWeek,* May 3, 1999, p. 163.

[23]More information on Digital's competitive position can be found in "Compaq-Digital: Let the Slimming Begin," *BusinessWeek,* June 22, 1998.

EXHIBIT 6 **Dell's Principal Competitors and Dell's Estimated Market Shares by Product Category, 2004**

Product Category	Dell's Principal Competitors	Estimated Size of Worldwide Market, 2003–2004 (in billions)	Dell's Worldwide Share, 2004
PCs	Hewlett-Packard (maker of both Compaq and HP brands); IBM, Gateway, Apple, Acer, Sony, Fujitsu-Siemens (in Europe and Japan), Legend (in China)	$175	18.5%
Servers	Hewlett-Packard, IBM, Sun Microsystems, Fujitsu	50	~10
Data storage devices	Hewlett-Packard, IBM, EMC, Hitachi	40	~10
Networking switches and related equipment	Cisco Systems, Enterasys, Nortel, 3Com	58	2–3
Handheld PCs	Palm, Sony, Hewlett-Packard, Toshiba, Casio	4	~2–3
Printers and printer cartridges	Hewlett-Packard, Lexmark, Canon, Epson	~50	~7
Cash register systems	IBM, NCR, Wincor Nixdorf, Hewlett-Packard, Sun Microsystems	4 (in North America)	~1–2
Services	Accenture, IBM, Hewlett-Packard, many others	350	~2–3

Source: Compiled by the case authors from a variety of sources, including International Data Corp. and www.dell.com.

capabilities to do business with customers via the Internet. Carly Fiorina, who became HP's CEO in 1999, explained why the acquisition of Compaq was strategically sound:

> With Compaq, we become No. 1 in Windows, No. 1 in Linux and No. 1 in Unix . . . With Compaq, we become the No. 1 player in storage, and the leader in the fastest growing segment of the storage market—storage area networks. With Compaq, we double our service and support capacity in the area of mission-critical infrastructure design, outsourcing and support . . . Let's talk about PCs . . . Compaq has been able to improve their turns in that business from 23 turns of inventory per year to 62—100 percent improvement year over year—and they are coming close to doing as well as Dell does. They've reduced operating expenses by $130 million, improved gross margins by three points, reduced channel inventory by more than $800 million. They ship about 70 percent of their commercial volume through their direct channel, comparable to Dell. We will combine our successful retail PC business model with their commercial business model and achieve much more together than we could alone. With Compaq, we will double the size of our sales force to 15,000 strong. We will build our R&D budget to more than $4 billion a year, and add important capabilities to HP Labs. We will become the No. 1 player in a whole host of countries around the world—HP operates in more than 160 countries, with well over 60 percent of our revenues coming from outside the U.S. The new HP will be the No. 1 player in the consumer and small- and medium-business segments . . . We have estimated cost synergies of $2.5 billion by 2004 . . . It is a rare opportunity when a technology company can advance its market position substantially and reduce its cost structure substantially at the same time. And this is possible because Compaq and HP are in the same businesses, pursuing the same strategies, in the same markets, with complementary capabilities.

However, going into 2005 the jury was still out on whether HP's acquisition of Compaq was the success that Carly Fiorina had claimed it would be. The company's only real bright spot was its $24 billion crown jewel printer business, which still reigned as the unchallenged world leader (largely because of a highly productive $1 billion investment in printer R&D). But the rest of HP's businesses were underachievers. Its PC and server businesses were struggling, losing money in most quarters and barely breaking even in others—and

HP was definitely losing ground to Dell in PCs and low-priced servers. In servers, HP was being squeezed on the low-end by Dell's low prices and on the high-end by strong competition from IBM. Most observers saw IBM as overshadowing HP in corporate computing—high-end servers and IT services. In data storage and technical support services, HP had been able to grow revenues but profit margins and total operating profits were declining. While HP had successfully cut annual operating costs by $3.5 billion—beating the $2.5 billion target set at the time of the Compaq acquisition, the company's operating margins in the first nine months of 2004 were a skimpy 5.3 percent, well below the 8–10 percent targets expected when the Compaq deal was finalized.[24] And the company had missed its earnings forecasts in 7 of the past 20 quarters.

With the company's stock price stuck in the $18–$23 price range, impatient investors had recently begun clamoring for the company to break itself up and create two separate companies, one for its printer business and one for all the rest of the businesses (PCs, servers, storage devices, digital cameras, calculators, and IT services). A Merrill Lynch analyst had estimated that the total value of HP's business would be 25–45 percent greater if split into printing and nonprinting operations.[25] In fact, HP's board of directors was actively considering breaking up the company into smaller pieces, but so far had taken no action. Carly Fiorina had expressed opposition to a breakup, arguing that HP's broad product/business lineup paid off in the form of added sales and lower costs. In an August 2004 speech, she said, "We think we have a unique opportunity, because we have leadership positions and intellectual property at every stage of the value chain."[26]

HP reported total revenues of $79.9 billion and net profits of $3.5 billion for fiscal 2004, versus total revenues of $73.1 billion and earnings of $2.5 billion in 2003. However, a substantial portion of the increase in net earnings in 2004 was due to cutbacks in R&D spending and a lower effective tax rate. Moreover, the company's EPS of $1.16 in 2004 was substantially below the EPS of $1.80 reported in 2000. Exhibit 7 shows the performance of HP's four major business groups.

IBM

IBM was seen as a "computer solutions" company and had the broadest and deepest capabilities in customer service, technical support, and systems integration of any company in the world. IBM's Global Services business group was the world's largest information technology services provider, with sales of $42.6 billion in 2003. In addition to its IT services business, IBM had 2003 hardware sales of $28.2 billion and software sales of $12.2 billion. IBM conducted business in 170 countries and had total sales of $89 billion and earnings of $7.6 billion in 2003. Once the world's undisputed king of computing and information processing, IBM was struggling to remain a potent contender in PCs, servers, storage products, and other hardware-related products. Since the early 1990s, IBM had been steadily losing ground to competitors in product categories it had formerly dominated. Its recognized strengths—a potent brand name, global distribution capabilities, a position as the longtime global leader in mainframe computers, and strong capabilities in IT consulting services and systems integration—had proved insufficient in overcoming buyer resistance to IBM's premium prices. Many of its former customers had turned to lower-priced vendors—the old adage "No one ever got fired for selecting IBM products" no longer applied. IBM's revenues had hovered in the $81 to $89 billion range for the past five years. The company's only remaining strength in IT hardware was in high-end servers.

[24]Ben Elgin, "Carly's Challenge," *BusinessWeek*, December 13, 2004, p. 101.
[25]Ibid.
[26]Ibid., p. 102.

EXHIBIT 7   **Performance of Hewlett-Packard's Four Major Business Groups, Fiscal Years 2001–2004**
(In billions of dollars)

	Printing and Imaging	Personal Computing Systems*	Enterprise Systems*	HP Services
2004 (fiscal year ending October 31)				
Net revenue	$24,199	$24,622	$16,074	$13,778
Operating income (loss)	3,847	(210)	28	1,263
2003 (fiscal year ending October 31)				
Net revenue	$22,623	$21,228	$15,379	$12,305
Operating income (loss)	3,570	19	(54)	1,372
2002 (fiscal year ending October 31)*				
Net revenue	$20,447	$21,895	$16,194	$12,326
Operating income (loss)	3,345	(372)	(664)	1,369
2001 (fiscal year ending October 31)*				
Net revenue	$19,602	$26,710	$20,205	$12,802
Operating income (loss)	2,103	(728)	(579)	1,617

*Results for 2001 and 2002 represent the combined results of both HP and Compaq Computer.

Source: 2003 10-K report and company press release, November 16, 2004.

IBM's Troubles in PCs

IBM's market share in PCs was in a death spiral—it had lost more market share in the 1990s than any other PC maker. Once the dominant global and U.S. market leader, with a market share exceeding 50 percent in the late 1980s and early 1990s, IBM was fast becoming an also-ran in PCs, with a global market share of only 6 percent in 2004 (see Exhibit 1). Its last stronghold in PCs was in laptop computers, where its ThinkPad line was a consistent award winner on performance, features, and reliability. The vast majority of IBM's laptop and desktop sales were to large enterprises that had IBM mainframe computers and had been long-standing IBM customers. IBM's PC group had higher costs than rivals, making it virtually impossible to match rivals on price and make a profit. IBM distributed its PCs, workstations, and servers through reseller partners, but used its own sales force to market to large enterprises. IBM competed against rival hardware vendors by emphasizing confidence in the IBM brand and the company's longstanding strengths in software applications, IT services and support, and systems integration capabilities. IBM had responded to the direct sales inroads Dell had made in the corporate market by allowing some of its resellers to economize on costs by custom-assembling IBM PCs to buyer specifications.

The Sale of IBM's PC Business to Lenovo in Late 2004

In December 2004, IBM agreed to sell its PC business to Lenovo Group Ltd., the number 1 computer maker in China, in a $1.75 billion business deal that made Lenovo the world's third biggest PC maker, with a global market share of about 8.7 percent, and that also gave IBM an 18.9 percent ownership interest in Lenovo. The head of IBM's PC operations was slated to become CEO of Lenovo, with Lenovo's current CEO (who did not speak English) assuming the role of chairman. Lenovo announced it would move its corporate headquarters from Beijing to New York City.

The new company was expected to have about $12 billion in annual sales and about 20,000 employees, including about 10,000 IBM employees who would be a part of the new company—about 2,500 of the IBM employees scheduled to become part of Lenovo were in North Carolina, about half were in China, and the rest were scattered around the world. Prior to the deal, Lenovo had annual sales of about $3 billion and IBM's PC business had annual sales close to $9 billion; IBM's PC business lost $258 million in 2003. IBM had about a 6 percent share of the PC market in China. The new company had the rights to use the IBM name on its PCs for a maximum of five years, but Lenovo indicated it would consider co-branding after 18 months. The new company planned to continue to sell its PCs through the efforts of an internal sales force for large accounts and its network of distributors and retail outlets.

Lenovo had little reputation for innovation, and it usually followed the technology lead of Intel and Microsoft, the PC industry's standard setters. It was regarded as a made-in-China-for-China producer of PCs. It had previously tried to enter the PC market outside China without success and was under competitive pressure in its home market, particularly from Dell (which was said to have lower costs). However, the company's original parent, the government's Chinese Academy of Sciences, was still a major shareholder, which gave Lenovo access to loans from state banks.

Some observers believed that one of management's major challenges would be integrating the cultures of the operations. Twice daily at Lenovo's headquarters, the sound system broadcast "Number Six Broadcast Exercises," a set of stretches and knee bends—participation was voluntary but highly encouraged.[27] The company song was played every morning at eight o'-clock and sung by workers at the start of widely attended meetings. Lenovo employees who were late to meetings had to stand behind their chairs for one minute (as an attempt to humiliate them into being punctual). Employees' activities were strictly monitored; time spent outside the work area during work hours had to be accounted for, and deductions were made from employees' paychecks if the explanations were unsatisfactory. Most employees were young and had worked at Lenovo since graduating from college; few spoke English and most had never met a foreigner.

Gateway

Gateway, a San Diego–based company (recently relocated from South Dakota), had 2003 revenues of $3.4 billion (down from $4.2 billion in 2002) and a net loss of $515 million (bigger than the loss of $298 million in 2002). It was the fourth largest seller of PCs in the U.S. market and one of the top 10 sellers worldwide. However, as shown in Exhibit 1, its unit sales and market share had been sliding since 2000. Gateway's all-time peak revenues were $9.6 billion in 2000 and its peak-year profits were $428 million.

In 2001–2002, Gateway's top management tried to reverse the company's deteriorating market position; the turnaround initiatives included

- Closing its retail stores in Canada, Europe, the Middle East, Africa, and the Asia-Pacific region, along with 70 underperforming U.S. retail locations.
- Combining its consumer and business sales organization into a single unit.
- Focusing its sales and marketing efforts on consumers, small and medium-sized businesses, educational institutions, and government.
- Consolidating its manufacturing operations and call center operations to pave the way for a 50 percent cutback in its workforce in 2001. Manufacturing operations in Ireland and Malaysia were closed, and all production was moved to the company's two existing plants in South Dakota and Virginia. Further cutbacks to reduce the workforce from 14,000 to 11,500 employees were announced in early 2002.

[27]Julie Chao, "Chinese Computer Maker Lenovo Shoots for Leadership in the World," *Atlanta Journal-Constitution*, December 14, 2004, pp. F1, F8.

- Supplementing its sell-direct distribution strategy by stocking a limited inventory of prebuilt Gateway PCs in its retail stores that customers could take home immediately.
- Improving its offering of digital cameras, music, and videos and actively marketing broadband Internet services to its customers via alliances with a number of cable broadband Internet access providers.
- Introducing a sleek new line of desktop and notebook PCs with industry-leading features.
- Refreshing its spotted-cow box logo, used since 1998.
- Selling consumer electronics products made by other manufacturers in its retail stores, including digital cameras, MP3 players, and high-end plasma-screen TVs.

The 2001–2002 initiatives failed to reverse the decline. In 2003, further efforts were made to stem Gateway's slide in the marketplace (which was mainly due to stiff competition from Dell):

- The entire product line was refreshed and expanded, with 118 Gateway-branded products in 22 categories being introduced.
- The company concentrated its sales efforts in PCs on the government and education segments.
- Back-office operations were streamlined to reduce costs.

Then in January 2004, Gateway acquired eMachines, Inc., for 50 million shares of Gateway common stock and $30 million in cash. A $1.1 billion producer of low-end computers, eMachines had distribution capabilities in Japan, Great Britain, and parts of western Europe. The two companies had combined sales of $4.5 billion in 2003. Gateway management believed the eMachines acquisition would allow Gateway to better compete in the low end of the PC market and also give it the resources and competitive strength to reenter markets outside the United States. As part of the deal, the founder and CEO of eMachines, Wayne Inouye, became the CEO of Gateway, with Ted Waitt, Gateway's founder and former CEO, functioning as chairman.

Gateway's revenue decline continued in the first half of 2004. The company had a net loss of $561 million on sales of $2.6 billion during the first nine months of 2004, but management expected that the company to become profitable in the fourth quarter on sales of about $1 billion. Gateway sold 931,000 units in the third quarter of 2004, its highest volume in 14 quarters. Management had forecast sales of $4 billion in 2005 and earnings of $50–$60 million.

Dell's Future Prospects

In a February 2003 article in *Business 2.0,* Michael Dell said, "The best way to describe us now is as a broad computer systems and services company. We have a pretty simple system. The most important thing is to satisfy our customers. The second most important thing is to be profitable. If we don't do the first one well, the second one won't happen."[28] For the most part, Michael Dell was not particularly concerned about the efforts of competitors to copy many aspects of Dell's build-to-order, sell-direct strategy. He explained why on at least two separate occasions:

> The competition started copying us seven years ago. That's when we were a $1 billion business . . . And they haven't made much progress to be honest with you. The learning curve for them is difficult. It's like going from baseball to soccer.[29]

[28]*Business 2.0,* February 2003; posted at www.business2.com.
[29]Comments made to students at the University of North Carolina and reported in the *Raleigh News & Observer,* November 16, 1999.

I think a lot of people have analyzed our business model, a lot of people have written about it and tried to understand it. This is an 18½-year process . . . It comes from many, many cycles of learning . . . It's very, very different than designing products to be built to stock . . . Our whole company is oriented around a very different way of operating . . . I don't, for any second, believe that they are not trying to catch up. But it is also safe to assume that Dell is not staying in the same place. You know, this past year we've driven a billion dollars of cost out of our supply chain, and certainly next year we plan to drive quite a bit of cost out as well.[30]

On two other occasions, Michael Dell spoke about the size of the company's future opportunities:

When technologies begin to standardize or commoditize, the game starts to change. Markets open up to be volume markets and this is very much where Dell has made its mark—first in the PC market in desktops and notebooks and then in the server market and the storage market and services and data networking. We continue to expand the array of products that we sell, the array of services and, of course, expand on a geographic basis. The way we think about it is that there are all of these various technologies out there . . . What we have been able to do is build a business system that takes those technological ingredients, translates them into products and services and gets them to the customer more efficiently than any company around.[31]

This year [2004], we're roughly a $50 billion business. We have only six percent market share in an $800 billion market. There are enormous opportunities for us to grow across multiple dimensions in terms of products, with servers, storage, printing and services, representing a huge realm of expansion for us. There's geographic expansion and market share expansion back in the core business. The primary focus for us is picking those opportunities, seizing on them, and making sure we have the talent and the leadership growing inside the company to support all that growth. We have the goal of reaching $60 billion and we're tracking about a year ahead of plan. And there's also a network effect here. As we grow our product lines and enter new markets, we see a faster ability to gain share in new markets versus ones we've previously entered. Printing is a great example; it's also a great example of a market where people are either underestimating us or wondering if we'll succeed. In the U.S. market where all-in-one inkjets are the fastest growing part of the market, we already have 20 percent of the market. We just introduced color laser printers. You can pay only $449 for a color networked laser printer that offers industry-leading price performance for both the hardware and printing supplies. That's a huge new opportunity for us that's highly-related to computing. Our first full year in [the printer] business, we hit a billion dollars of revenue— that's pretty good for a startup.[32]

Going into 2005, Dell Computer had a war chest of over $12 billion in cash and liquid investments that it could deploy in its pursuit of attractive revenue growth opportunities.

[30]Remarks by Michael Dell, Gartner Fall Symposium, Orlando, Florida, October 9, 2002; posted at www.dell.com.

[31]Remarks by Michael Dell, MIT Sloan School of Management, September 26, 2002, and posted at www.dell.com.

[32]Remarks by Michael Dell, University of Toronto, September 21, 2004, and posted at www.dell.com.

Section VII

Developing Marketing Plans

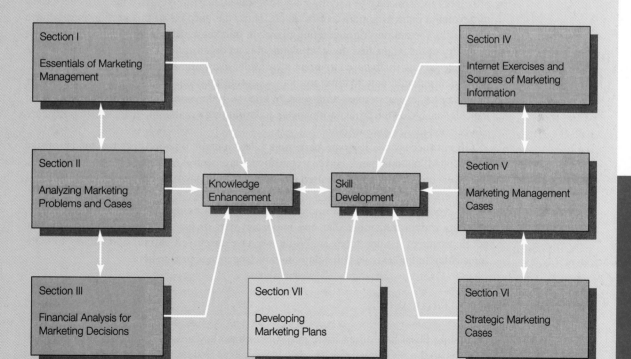

Section I — Essentials of Marketing Management

Section II — Analyzing Marketing Problems and Cases

Section III — Financial Analysis for Marketing Decisions

Section IV — Internet Exercises and Sources of Marketing Information

Section V — Marketing Management Cases

Section VI — Strategic Marketing Cases

Section VII — Developing Marketing Plans

Knowledge Enhancement

Skill Development

Imagine this scenario. After receiving your bachelor's or master's degree in marketing, you are hired by a major consumer goods company. Because you've done well in school, you are confident that you have a lot of marketing knowledge and a lot to offer to the firm. You're highly motivated and are looking forward to a successful career.

After just a few days of work you are called in for a conference with the vice president of marketing. The vice president welcomes you and tells you how glad the firm is that you have joined them. The vice president also says that, because you have done so well in your marketing courses and have had such recent training, he wants you to work on a special project.

He tells you that the company has a new product, which is to be introduced in a few months. He also says, confidentially, that recent new product introductions by the company haven't been too successful. Suggesting that the recent problems are probably because the company has not been doing a very good job of developing marketing plans, the vice president tells you not to look at marketing plans for the company's other products.

Your assignment, then, is to develop a marketing plan for the proposed product in the next six weeks. The vice president explains that a good job here will lead to rapid advancement in the company. You thank the vice president for the assignment and promise that you'll do your best.

How would you feel when you returned to your desk? Surely, you'd be flattered that you had been given this opportunity and be eager to do a good job. However, how confident are you that you could develop a quality marketing plan? Would you even know where to begin?

We suspect that many of you, even those who have an excellent knowledge of marketing principles and are adept at solving marketing cases, may not yet have the skills necessary to develop a marketing plan from scratch. Thus, the purpose of this section is to offer a framework for developing marketing plans. In one sense, this section is no more than a summary of the whole text. In other words, it is an organizational framework based on the text material that can be used to direct the development of marketing plans.

Students should note that we are not presenting this framework and discussion as the only way to develop a marketing plan. While we believe this is a useful framework for logically analyzing the problems involved in developing a marketing plan, other approaches can be used just as successfully.

Often, successful firms prepare much less detailed plans because much of the background material and current conditions are well known to everyone involved. However, our review of plans used in various firms suggests that something like this framework is not uncommon.

We would like to mention one other qualification before beginning our discussion. Students should remember that one important part of the marketing plan involves the development of a sales forecast. While we have discussed several approaches to sales forecasting in the text, we will detail only one specific approach here.

A Marketing Plan Framework

Marketing plans have three basic purposes. First, they are used as a tangible record of analysis so the logic involved can be checked. This is done to ensure the feasibility and internal consistency of the project and to evaluate the likely consequences of implementing the plan. Second, they are used as roadmaps or guidelines for directing appropriate actions. A marketing plan is designed to be the best available scenario and rationale for directing the firm's efforts for a particular product or brand. Third, they are used as tools to obtain funding for implementation. This funding may come from internal or external sources. For

FIGURE 1
A Marketing Plan Format

- Title page.
- Executive summary.
- Table of contents.
- Introduction.
- Situational analysis.
- Marketing planning.
- Implementation and control of the marketing plan.
- Summary.
- Appendix: Financial analysis.
- References.

example, a brand manager may have to present a marketing plan to senior executives in a firm to get a budget request filled. This would be an internal source. Similarly, proposals for funding from investors or business loans from banks often require a marketing plan. These would be external sources.

Figure 1 presents a format for preparing marketing plans. Each of the 10 elements will be briefly discussed. We will refer to previous chapters and sections in this text and to other sources where additional information can be obtained when a marketing plan is being prepared. We also will offer additional information for focusing particular sections of the plan as well as for developing financial analysis.

Title Page

The *title page* should contain the following information: (1) the name of the product or brand for which the marketing plan has been prepared—for example, Marketing Plan for Little Friskies Dog Food; (2) the time period for which the plan is designed—for example, 2008–2010; (3) the person(s) and position(s) of those submitting the plan—for example, submitted by Amy Lewis, brand manager; (4) the persons, group, or agency to whom the plan is being submitted—for example, submitted to Lauren Ellis, product group manager; and (5) the date of submission of the plan—for example, June 30, 2008.

While preparing the title page is a simple task, remember that it is the first thing readers see. Thus, a title page that is poorly laid out, is smudged, or contains misspelled words can lead to the inference that the project was developed hurriedly and with little attention to detail. As with the rest of the project, appearances are important and affect what people think about the plan.

Executive Summary

The *executive summary* is a two- to three-page summary of the contents of the report. Its purpose is to provide a quick summary of the marketing plan for executives who need to be informed about the plan but are typically not directly involved in plan approval. For instance, senior executives for firms with a broad product line may not have time to read the entire plan but need an overview to keep informed about operations.

The executive summary should include a brief introduction, the major aspects of the marketing plan, and a budget statement. This is not the place to go into detail about each and every aspect of the marketing plan. Rather, it should focus on the major market opportunity and the key elements of the marketing plan that are designed to capitalize on this opportunity.

It is also useful to state specifically how much money is required to implement the plan. In an ongoing firm, many costs can be estimated from historical data or from discussions with other executives in charge of specific functional areas. However, in many situations (such as a class project), sufficient information is not always available to give exact costs for every aspect of production, promotion, and distribution. In these cases, include a rough estimate of total marketing costs of the plan. In many ongoing firms, marketing cost elements are concentrated in the areas of promotion and marketing research, and these figures are integrated with those from other functional areas as parts of the overall business plan.

Table of Contents

The *table of contents* is a listing of everything contained in the plan and where it is located in the report. Reports that contain a variety of charts and figures may also have a table of exhibits listing their titles and page numbers within the report.

In addition to using the table of contents as a place to find specific information, readers may also review it to see if each section of the report is logically sequenced. For example, situational analysis logically precedes marketing planning as an activity, and this ordering makes sense in presenting the plan.

Introduction

The types of information and amount of detail reported in the *introduction* depend in part on whether the plan is being designed for a new or existing product or brand. If the product is new, the introduction should explain the product concept and the reasons it is expected to be successful. Basically, this part of the report should make the new idea sound attractive to management or investors. In addition, it is useful to offer estimates of expected sales, costs, and return on investment.

If the marketing plan is for an existing brand in an ongoing firm, it is common to begin the report with a brief history of the brand. The major focus here is on the brand's performance in the last three to five years. It is useful to prepare graphs of the brand's performance that show its sales, profits, and market share for previous years and to explain the reasons for any major changes. These exhibits can also be extended to include predicted changes in these variables given the new marketing plan. A brief discussion of the overall strategy followed in previous years also provides understanding of how much change is being proposed in the new marketing plan.

Also useful in the introduction is to offer a precise statement of the purpose of the report as well as a roadmap of the report. In other words, tell readers what this report is, how it is organized, and what will be covered in the following sections.

Situational Analysis

The *situational analysis* is not unlike the analysis discussed in Chapter 1 and Section II of this text. The focus remains on the most critical and relevant environmental conditions (or changes in them) that affect the success or failure of the proposed plan. While any aspect of the economic, social, political, legal, or cooperative environments might deserve considerable attention, there is seldom if ever a marketing plan in which the competitive environment does not require considerable discussion. In fact, the competitive environment may be set off as a separate section called *industry analysis*. The strengths and weaknesses of major competitors, their relative market shares, and the success of various competitive strategies are critical elements of the situation analysis.

Section V of the text offers some sources of information for analyzing the competitive environment, such as the *Audits and Surveys National Total-Market Index* and the *Nielsen Retail Index*. In addition, trade association publications, *Fortune, BusinessWeek,* and *The Wall Street Journal* frequently have useful articles on competitive strategies. Firms' annual reports often provide considerable useful information.

Marketing Planning

Marketing planning is, of course, a critical section of the report. As previously noted, it includes three major elements: marketing objectives, target markets, and the marketing mix.

Understanding an industry and the actions of competitors is critical to developing successful marketing plans. Below is a list of some questions to consider when performing competitive analysis. Thinking about these questions can aid the marketing planner in developing better marketing strategies.

1. Which firms compete in this industry and what is their financial position and marketing capability?
2. What are the relative market shares of various brands?
3. How many brands and models does each firm offer?
4. What marketing strategies have the market leaders employed?
5. Which brands have gained and which have lost market share in recent years, and what factors have led to these changes?
6. Are new competitors likely to enter the market?
7. How quickly do competitive firms react to changes in the market?
8. From which firms or brands might we be able to take market share?
9. What are the particular strengths and weaknesses of competitors in the industry?
10. How do we compare with other firms in the industry in terms of financial strength and marketing skills?

Marketing Objectives

Marketing objectives are often stated in plans in terms of the percentage of particular outcomes that are to be achieved: for example, 80 percent awareness of the brand in particular markets, increase in trial rate by 30 percent, distribution coverage of 60 percent, or increase in total market share by 3 percent over the life of the plan. Similarly, objectives may be stated in terms of sales units or dollars or increases in these. Of course, the reasons for selection of the particular objectives and rationale are important points to explain.

Target Markets

The *target markets* discussion explains the customer base and rationale or justification for it. An approach to developing appropriate target markets is contained in Chapter 5 of this text, and a useful source of secondary data for segmenting markets is the *National Purchase Diary Panel*.

This section also includes relevant discussion of changes or important issues in consumer or organizational buyer behavior: for example, what benefits consumers are seeking in this products class, what benefits does the particular brand offer, or what purchasing trends are shaping the market for this product. Discussions of consumer and organizational buyer behavior are contained in Chapters 3 and 4 of this text.

Marketing Mix

The *marketing mix* discussion explains in detail the selected strategy consisting of product, promotion, distribution and price, and the rationale for it. Also, if marketing research has been done on these elements or is planned, it can be discussed in this section.

Product   The *product* section details a description of the product or brand, its packaging, and its attributes. Product life-cycle considerations should be mentioned if they affect the proposed plan.

Of critical importance in this discussion is the competitive advantage of the product or brand. Here it must be carefully considered whether the brand really does anything better than the competition or is purchased primarily on the basis of brand equity or value. For example, many brands of toothpaste have fluoride, yet Crest has the largest market share primarily through promoting this attribute of its brand. Thus, does Crest do anything more than other toothpastes, or is it Crest's image that accounts for sales?

Discussion of product-related issues is contained in Chapters 6 and 7, and services are discussed in Chapter 12 of this text. For discussion of marketing plans for products marketed globally, see Chapter 13.

Promotion The *promotion* discussion consists of a description and justification of the planned promotion mix. It is useful to explain the theme of the promotion and to include some examples of potential ads as well as the nature of the sales force if one is to be used. For mass-marketed consumer goods, promotion costs can be large and need to be considered explicitly in the marketing plan.

Discussion of promotion-related issues is contained in Chapters 8 and 9 of this text. Secondary sources, such as *Standard Rate and Data, Simmons Media/Market Service, Starch Advertising Readership Service,* and the *Nielsen Television Index,* provide useful information for selecting, budgeting, and justifying media and other promotional decisions.

Distribution The *distribution* discussion describes and justifies the appropriate channel or channels for the product. This includes types of intermediaries and specifically who they will be. Other important issues concern the level of market coverage desired, cost, and control considerations. In many cases, the channels of distribution used by the firm, as well as competitive firms, are well established. For example, General Motors and Ford distribute their automobiles through independent dealer networks. Thus, unless there is a compelling reason to change channels, the traditional channel will often be the appropriate alternative. However, serious consideration may have to be given to methods of obtaining channel support, for example, trade deals to obtain sufficient shelf space.

Discussion of distribution-related issues is contained in Chapter 10 of this text. Useful retail distribution information can be found in the *Nielsen Retail Index* and the *Audits and Surveys National Total-Market Index.*

Price The pricing discussion starts with a specific statement of the price of the product. Depending on what type of channel is used, manufacturer price, wholesale price, and suggested retail price need to be listed and justified. In addition, special deals or trade discounts that are to be employed must be considered in terms of their effect on the firm's selling price.

Discussion of price-related issues is contained in Chapter 11. In addition to a variety of other useful information, the *Nielsen Retail Index* provides information on wholesale and retail prices.

Marketing Research For any aspect of marketing planning, there may be a need for marketing research. If such research is to be performed, it is important to justify it and explain its costs and benefits. Such costs should also be included in the financial analysis.

If marketing research has already been conducted as part of the marketing plan, it can be reported as needed to justify various decisions that were reached. To illustrate, if research found that two out of three consumers like the taste of a new formula Coke, this information would likely be included in the product portion of the report. However, the details of the research could be placed here in the marketing research section. Discussion of marketing research is contained in Chapter 2.

Implementation and Control of the Marketing Plan

This section contains a discussion and justification of how the marketing plan will be implemented and controlled. It also explains who will be in charge of monitoring and changing the plan should unanticipated events occur and how the success or failure of the plan will be measured. Success or failure of the plan is typically measured by a comparison of the results of implementing the plan with the stated objectives.

For the direction-setting purpose of objectives to be fulfilled, objectives need to meet five specifications:

1. An objective should relate to a single, specific topic. (It should not be stated in the form of a vague abstraction or a pious platitude—"we want to be a leader in our industry" or "our objective is to be more aggressive marketers.")
2. An objective should relate to a result, not to an activity to be performed. (The objective is the result of the activity, not the performance of the activity.)
3. An objective should be measurable (stated in quantitative terms whenever feasible).
4. An objective should contain a time deadline for its achievement.
5. An objective should be challenging but achievable.

Consider the following examples:

1. Poor: Our objective is to maximize profits.
   Remarks: How much is "maximum"? The statement is not subject to measurement. What criterion or yardstick will management use to determine if and when actual profits are equal to maximum profits? No deadline is specified.
   Better: Our total profit target in 2010 is $1 million.

2. Poor: Our objective is to increase sales revenue and unit volume.
   Remarks: How much? Also, because the statement relates to two topics, it may be inconsistent. Increasing unit volume may require a price cut, and if demand is price inelastic, sales revenue would fall as unit volume rises. No time frame for achievement is indicated.
   Better: Our objective this calendar year is to increase sales revenues from $30 million to $35 million; we expect this to be accomplished by selling 1 million units at an average price of $35.

3. Poor: Our objective in 2010 is to boost advertising expenditures by 15 percent.
   Remarks: Advertising is an activity, not a result. The advertising objective should be stated in terms of what result the extra advertising is intended to produce.
   Better: Our objective is to boost our market share from 8 percent to 10 percent by 2010 with the help of a 15 percent increase in advertising expenditures.

4. Poor: Our objective is to be a pioneer in research and development and to be the technological leader in the industry.
   Remarks: Very sweeping and perhaps overly ambitious; implies trying to march in too many directions at once if the industry is one with a wide range of technological frontiers. More a platitude than an action commitment to a specific result.
   Better: During the 2000–2010 decade, our objective is to continue as a leader in introducing new technologies and new devices that will allow buyers of electrically powered equipment to conserve on electric energy usage.

5. Poor: Our objective is to be the most profitable company in our industry.
   Remarks: Not specific enough by what measures of profit—total dollars, or earnings per share, or unit profit margin, or return on equity investment, or all of these? Also, because the objective concerns how well other companies will perform, the objective, while challenging, may not be achievable.
   Better: We will strive to remain atop the industry in terms of rate of return on equity investment by earning a 25 percent after-tax return on equity investment by 2010.

Source: Adapted from Arthur A. Thompson, Jr., and A. J. Strickland, *Strategic Management: Concepts and Cases,* 5th ed. (Burr Ridge, IL: Irwin/McGraw-Hill, 1990), pp. 23–34.

Knowledge of consumers is paramount to developing successful marketing plans. Below is a list of questions that are useful to consider when analyzing consumers. For some of the questions, secondary sources of information or primary marketing research can be employed to aid in decision making. However, a number of them require the analyst to do some serious thinking about the relationship between brands of the product and various consumer groups to better understand the market.

1. How many people purchase and use this product in general?
2. How many people purchase and use each brand of the product?
3. Is there an opportunity to reach nonusers of the product with a unique marketing strategy?
4. What does the product do for consumers functionally and how does this vary by brand?
5. What does the product do for consumers in a social or psychological sense and how does this vary by brand?
6. Where do consumers currently purchase various brands of the product?
7. How much are consumers willing to pay for specific brands and is price a determining factor for purchase?
8. What is the market profile of the heavy user of this product and what percentage of the total market are heavy users?
9. What media reach these consumers?
10. On average, how often is this product purchased?
11. How important is brand equity for consumers of this product?
12. Why do consumers purchase particular brands?
13. How brand loyal are consumers of this product?

For a marketing plan developed within an ongoing firm, this section can be quite explicit, because procedures for implementing plans may be well established. However, for a classroom project, the key issues to be considered are the persons responsible for implementing the plan, a timetable for sequencing the tasks, and a method of measuring and evaluating the success or failure of the plan.

Summary

This *summary* need not be much different than the executive summary stated at the beginning of the document. However, it is usually a bit longer, more detailed, and states more fully the case for financing the plan.

Appendix—Financial Analysis

Financial analysis is a very important part of any marketing plan. While a complete business plan often includes extensive financial analysis, such as a complete cost breakdown and estimated return on investment, marketing planners frequently do not have complete accounting data for computing these figures. For example, decisions concerning how much overhead is to be apportioned to the product are not usually made solely by marketing personnel. However, the marketing plan should contain at least a sales forecast and estimates of relevant marketing costs.

Sales Forecast

As noted, there are a variety of ways to develop sales forecasts. Regardless of the method, however, they all involve trying to predict the future as accurately as possible. It is, of

FIGURE 2

A Basic Approach to Sales Forecasting

Total number of people in target markets (*a*)	*a*
Annual number of purchases per person (*b*)	× *b*
Total potential market (*c*)	= *c*
Total potential market (*c*)	*c*
Percent of total market coverage (*d*)	× *d*
Total available market (*e*)	= *e*
Total available market (*e*)	*e*
Expected market share (*f*)	× *f*
Sales forecast (in units) (*g*)	= *g*
Sales forecast (in units) (*g*)	*g*
Price (*h*)	× *h*
Sales forecast (in dollars)(*i*)	= *i*

course, necessary to justify the logic for the forecasted figures, rather than offer them with no support.

One basic approach to developing a sales forecast is outlined in Figure 2. This approach begins by estimating the total number of persons in the selected target market. This estimate comes from the market segmentation analysis and may include information from test marketing and from secondary sources, such as *Statistical Abstracts of the United States*. For example, suppose a company is marketing a solar-powered watch that is designed not only to tell time but also to take the pulse of the wearer. The product is targeted at joggers and others interested in aerobic exercise. By reviewing the literature on these activities, the marketing planner, John Murphy, finds that the average estimate of this market on a national level is 60 million persons and is growing by 4 million persons per year. Thus, John might conclude that the total number of people in the target market for next year is 64 million. If he has not further limited the product's target market and has no other information, John might use this number as a basis for starting the forecast analysis.

The second estimate John needs is the annual number of purchases per person in the product's target market. This estimate could be quite large for such products as breakfast cereal or less than one (annual purchase per person) for such products as automobiles. For watches, the estimate is likely to be much less than one since people are likely to buy a new watch only every few years. Thus, John might estimate the annual number of purchases per person in the target market to be .25. Of course, as a careful marketing planner, John would probably carefully research this market to refine this estimate. In any event, multiplying these two numbers gives John an estimate of the *total potential market,* in this case, 64 million times .25 equals 16 million. In other words, if next year alone John's company could sell a watch to every jogger or aerobic exerciser who is buying a watch, the company could expect sales to be 16 million units.

Of course, the firm cannot expect to sell every jogger a watch for several reasons. First, it is unlikely to obtain 100 percent market coverage in the first year, if ever. Even major consumer goods companies selling convenience goods seldom reach the entire market in the first year and many never achieve even 90 percent distribution. Given the nature of the product and depending on the distribution alternative, John's company might be doing quite well to average 50 percent market coverage in the first year. If John's plans call for this kind of coverage, his estimate of the total available market would be 16 million times .5, which equals 8 million.

A second reason John's plans would not call for dominating the market is that his company does not have the only product available or wanted by this target market. Many of the people

Below is a brief list of questions about the marketing planning section of the report. Answering them honestly and recognizing both the strengths and weaknesses of the marketing plan should help to improve it.

1. What key assumptions were made in developing the marketing plan?
2. How badly will the product's market position be hurt if these assumptions turn out to be incorrect?
3. How good is the marketing research?
4. Is the marketing plan consistent? For example, if the plan is to seek a prestige position in the market, is the product priced, promoted, and distributed to create this image?
5. Is the marketing plan feasible? For example, are the financial and other resources (such as a distribution network) available to implement it?
6. How will the marketing plan affect profits and market share, and is it consistent with corporate objectives?
7. Will implementing the marketing plan result in competitive retaliation that will end up hurting the firm?
8. Is the marketing mix designed to reach and attract new customers or increase usage among existing users or both?
9. Will the marketing mix help to develop brand-loyal consumers?
10. Will the marketing plan not only be successful in the short run but also contribute to a profitable long-run position?

who will purchase such a watch will purchase a competitive brand. He must, therefore, estimate the product's likely market share. Of all the estimates made in developing a sales forecast, this one is critical because it is a reflection of the entire marketing plan. Important factors to consider in developing this estimate include (1) competitive market shares and likely marketing strategies; (2) competitive retaliation should the product do well; (3) competitive advantage of the product, such as lower price; (4) promotion mix and budget relative to competitors; and (5) market shares obtained by similar products in the introductory year.

Overall, suppose John estimates the product's market share to be 5 percent, because other competitive products have beat his company to the market and because the company's competitive advantage is only a slightly more stylish watch. In this case, the sales forecast for year one would be 8 million times .05, which equals 400,000 units. If the manufacturer's selling price was $50, then the sales forecast in dollars would be 400,000 times $50, which equals $20 million.

This approach can also be used to extend the sales forecast for any number of years. Typically, estimates of most of the figures change from year to year, depending on changes in market size, distribution coverage, and expected market shares. The value of this approach is that it forces an analyst to carefully consider and justify each of the estimates offered, rather than simply pulling numbers out of the air.

Estimates of Marketing Costs

A complete delineation of all costs, apportionment of overhead, and other accounting tasks are usually performed by other departments within a firm. All of this information, including expected return on investment from implementing the marketing plan, is part of the overall business plan.

However, the marketing plan should at least contain estimates of major marketing costs. These include such things as advertising, sales force training and compensation, channel de-

Implementation and control of a marketing plan require careful scheduling and attention to detail. While some firms have standard procedures for dealing with many of the questions raised below, thinking through each of the questions should help improve the efficiency of even these firms in this stage of the process.

1. Who is responsible for implementing and controlling the marketing plan?
2. What tasks must be performed to implement the marketing plan?
3. What are the deadlines for implementing the various tasks and how critical are specific deadlines?
4. Has sufficient time been scheduled to implement the various tasks?
5. How long will it take to get the planned market coverage?
6. How will the success or failure of the plan be determined?
7. How long will it take to get the desired results from the plan?
8. How long will the plan be in effect before changes will be made to improve it based on more current information?
9. If an ad agency or other firms are involved in implementing the plan, how much responsibility and authority will they have?
10. How frequently will the progress of the plan be monitored?

velopment, and marketing research. Estimates may also be included for product development and package design.

For some marketing costs, reasonable estimates are available from sources such as *Standard Rate and Data*. However, some cost figures, such as marketing research, might be obtained from asking various marketing experts for the estimated price of proposed research. Other types of marketing costs might be estimated from financial statements of firms in the industry. For example, Morris's *Annual Statement Studies* offers percentage breakdowns of various income statement information by industry. These might be used to estimate the percentage of the sales-forecast figure that would likely be spent in a particular cost category.

References

The *references* section contains the sources of any secondary information that was used in developing the marketing plan. This information might include company reports and memos, statements of company objectives, and articles or books used for information or support of the marketing plan.

References should be listed alphabetically using a consistent format. One way of preparing references is to use the same approach as is used in marketing journals. For example, the format used for references in *Journal of Marketing* articles is usually acceptable.

Conclusion

Suppose you're now sitting at your desk faced with the task of developing a marketing plan for a new product. Do you believe that you might have the skills to develop a marketing plan? Of course, your ability to develop a quality plan will depend on your learning experiences during your course work and the amount of practice you've had; for example, if you developed a promotion plan in your advertising course, it is likely that you could do a better job on the promotion phase of the marketing plan. Similarly, your experiences in analyzing cases should have sharpened your skills at recognizing problems and developing solutions to them. But inexperience (or experience) aside, hopefully you now feel that you understand the process of developing a marketing plan. You at least know where to start, where to seek information, how to structure the plan, and some of the critical issues that require analysis.

Additional Readings

Cohen, William A. *The Marketing Plan.* 4th ed. New York: John Wiley & Sons, 2005.

Cravens, David W., and Nigel F. Piercy, *Strategic Marketing,* 8th ed. Burr Ridge, IL: McGraw-Hill/Irwin, 2006.

Hiebing, Romon G., and Scott W. Cooper. *The Successful Marketing Plan,* Burr Ridge, IL: McGraw-Hill, 2003.

Hiebing, Roman G., and Scott W. Cooper. *The One-Day Marketing Plan: Organizing and Completing a Plan that Works.* 3rd ed. Burr Ridge, IL: McGraw-Hill, 2004.

Lehmann, Donald R., and Russell S. Winer. *Analysis for Marketing Planning.* 6th ed. Burr Ridge, IL: McGraw-Hill/Irwin, 2005.

Walker, Orville C., John Mullins, and Harper W. Boyd, Jr. *Marketing Strategy: A Decision Focused Approach.* 5th ed. Burr Ridge, IL: McGraw-Hill/Irwin, 2006.

Chapter Notes

Chapter 1

1. See Reinhard Angelmar and Christian Pinson, "The Meaning of Marketing," *Philosophy of Science,* June 1975, pp. 208–14.

2. "Marketing Redefined," *Marketing News,* September 15, 2004, p. 1.

3. Much of this section is based on J. H. Donnelly, Jr., J. L. Gibson, and J. M. Ivancevich, *Fundamentals of Management,* 9th ed. (Burr Ridge, IL: Irwin/McGraw-Hill, 1998), chap. 7.

4. The process may differ depending on the type of organization or management approach, or both. For certain types of organizations, one strategic plan will be sufficient. Some manufacturers with similar product lines or limited product lines will develop only one strategic plan. However, organizations with widely diversified product lines and widely diversified markets may develop strategic plans for units or divisions. These plans usually are combined into a master strategic plan.

5. For a discussion of this topic, see Gerald E. Ledford, Jr., Jon R. Wendenhof, and James T. Strahely, "Realizing a Corporate Philosophy," *Organizational Dynamics,* Winter 1995, pp. 4–19; and Stephan Cummings and John Davies, "Mission, Vision, Fusion," *Long Range Planning,* December 1994, pp. 147–50.

6. Philip Kotler and Gary Armstrong, *Principles of Marketing,* 6th ed. (Englewood Cliffs, NJ: Prentice Hall, 1994), chap. 2.

7. Philip Kotler, *Marketing Management: Analysis, Planning, Implementation and Control,* 8th ed. (Englewood Cliffs, NJ: Prentice Hall, 1994), chap. 3.

8. Norton Paley, "A Sign of Intelligence," *Sales & Marketing Management,* March 1995, pp. 30–31.

9. Peter Drucker, *Management: Tasks, Responsibilities, Practices* (New York: Harper & Row, 1974), pp. 77–89; Kotler, *Marketing Management,* chap. 3.

10. Much of the following discussion is based on Drucker, *Management,* pp. 79–87.

11. Noel B. Zabriskie and Alan B. Huellmantel, "Marketing Research as a Strategic Tool," *Long Range Planning,* February 1994, pp. 107–18.

12. Originally discussed in the classic H. Igor Ansoff, *Corporate Strategy* (New York: McGraw-Hill, 1965).

13. For complete coverage of this topic, see Michael E. Porter, *Competitive Advantage: Creating and Sustaining Superior Performance* (New York: The Free Press, 1985). Material in this section is based upon discussions contained in Steven J. Skinner, *Marketing,* 2nd ed. (Boston: Houghton Mifflin Co., 1994), pp. 48–50; and Thomas A. Bateman and Carl P. Zeithaml, *Management Function & Strategy,* 2nd ed. (Burr Ridge, IL: Irwin/McGraw-Hill, 1993), pp. 152–53.

14. For a complete discussion of this topic, see Michael Treacy and Fred Wiersema, *The Discipline of Market Leaders* (Reading, MA: Addison-Wesley, 1995); and Michael Treacy and Fred Wiersema, "How Market Leaders Keep Their Edge," *Fortune,* February 6, 1995, pp. 88–98.

15. Philip Kotler, *Marketing Management,* p. 13.

16. For a discussion of this issue and other mistakes marketers frequently make, see Kevin J. Clancy and Robert S. Shulman, "Breaking the Mold," *Sales & Marketing Management,* January 1994, pp. 82–84.

17. George S. Day and David B. Montgomery, "Diagnosing the Experience Curve," *Journal of Marketing,* Spring 1983, pp. 44–58.

18. P. Rajan Varadarajan, Terry Clark, and William M. Pride, "Controlling the Uncontrollable: Managing Your Market Environment," *Sloan Management Review,* Winter 1992, pp. 39–47.

19. Reed E. Nelson, "Is There Strategy in Brazil?" *Business Horizons,* July–August 1992, pp. 15–23.

20. Peter S. Davis and Patrick L. Schill, "Addressing the Contingent Effects of Business Unit Strategic Orientation on the Relationship between Organizational Context and Business Unit Performance," *Journal of Business Research,* 1993, pp. 183–200.

21. J. Scott Armstrong and Roderick J. Brodie, "Effects of Portfolio Planning Methods on Decision Making: Experimental Results," *International Journal of Research in Marketing,* January 1994, pp. 73–84.

22. Michel Roberts, "Times Change but Do Business Strategies?" *Journal of Business Strategy,* March–April 1993, pp. 12–15.

23. Donald L. McCabe and V. K. Narayanan, "The Life Cycle of the PIMS and BCG Models," *Industrial Marketing Management,* November 1991, pp. 347–52.

Chapter 2

1. Based on Peter D. Bennett, ed., *Dictionary of Marketing Terms,* 2nd ed. (Chicago: American Marketing Association, 1995), p. 77.

2. Gilbert A. Churchill, Jr., and J. Paul Peter, *Marketing: Creating Value for Customers,* 2nd ed. (Burr Ridge, IL: Irwin/McGraw-Hill, 1998), p. 116.

3. For a discussion of some general problems in marketing research, see Alan G. Sawyer and J. Paul Peter, "The Significance of Statistical Significance Testing in Marketing Research," *Journal of Marketing Research,* May 1983, pp. 122–33.

4. This section is based on Churchill and Peter, *Marketing,* pp. 114–16.

Chapter 3

1. Richard P. Coleman, "The Continuing Significance of Social Class to Marketing," *Journal of Consumer Research,* December 1983, pp. 265–80.

2. See William O. Bearden and Michael J. Etzel, "Reference Group Influence on Product and Brand Purchase Decisions," *Journal of Consumer Research,* September 1982, pp. 183–94; and Terry L. Childers and Akshay R. Rao, "The Influence of Familial and Peer-Based Reference Groups on Consumer Decisions," *Journal of Consumer Research,* September 1992, pp. 198–211.

3. See Rosann L. Spiro, "Persuasion in Family Decision Making," *Journal of Consumer Research,* March 1983, pp. 393–402.

4. See Janet Wagner and Sherman Hanna, "The Effectiveness of Family Life Cycle Variables in Consumer Expenditure Research," *Journal of Consumer Research,* December 1983, pp. 281–91. Also see Charles M. Schanninger and William D. Danko, "A Conceptual and Empirical Comparison of Alternative Household Life Cycle Models," *Journal of Consumer Research,* March 1993, pp. 580–94.

5. Russell W. Belk, "Situational Variables and Consumer Behavior," *Journal of Consumer Research,* December 1975, pp. 156–64. Also see Jacob Hornik, "Situational Effects on the Consumption of Time," *Journal of Marketing,* Fall 1982, pp. 44–55; C. Whan Park, Easwer S. Iyer, and Daniel C. Smith, "The Effects of Situational Factors on In-Store Grocery Shopping Behavior: The Role of Store Environment and Time Available for Shopping," *Journal of Consumer Research,* March 1989, pp. 422–33; and Mary Jo Bitner, "Servicescapes: The Impact of Physical Surroundings on Customers and Employees," *Journal of Marketing,* April 1992, pp. 57–71.

6. J. Paul Peter and Jerry C. Olson, *Consumer Behavior and Marketing Strategy,* 7th ed. (Burr Ridge, IL: Irwin/McGraw-Hill, 2005), chap. 4.

7. A. H. Maslow, *Motivation and Personality* (New York: Harper & Row, 1954); also see James F. Engel, Roger D. Blackwell, and Paul W. Miniard, *Consumer Behavior,* 8th ed. (Fort Worth, TX: Dryden Press, 1995), chap. 5, for further discussion of need recognition.

8. For a detailed review of research on external search, see Sharon E. Beatty and Scott M. Smith, "External Search Effort: An Investigation across Several Product Categories," *Journal of Consumer Research,* June 1987, pp. 83–95. Also see Narasimhan Srinivasan and Brian T. Ratchford, "An Empirical Test of a Model of External Search for Automobiles," *Journal of Consumer Research,* September 1991, pp. 233–42; and Julie L. Ozanne, Merrie Brucks, and Dhruv Grewal, "A Study of Information Search Behavior during the Categorization of New Products," *Journal of Consumer Research,* March 1992, pp. 452–63.

9. For further discussion of information processing, see J. Paul Peter and Jerry C. Olson, *Consumer Behavior and Marketing Strategy,* 8th ed. (Burr Ridge, IL: Irwin/McGraw-Hill, 2008), chap. 3.

10. For a summary of research on attitude modeling, see Blair H. Sheppard, Jon Hartwick, and Paul R. Warshaw, "The Theory of Reasoned Action: A Meta-Analysis of Past Research with Recommendations for Modification and Future Research," *Journal of Consumer Research,* December 1988, pp. 325–43.

11. For further discussion of postpurchase feelings, see Richard L. Oliver, "Cognitive, Affective, and Attribute Bases of the Satisfaction Response," *Journal of Consumer Research,* December 1993, pp. 418–30; and Haim Mano and Richard L. Oliver, "Assessing the Dimensionality and Structure of the Consumption Experience: Evaluation, Feeling, and Satisfaction," *Journal of Consumer Research,* December 1993, pp. 451–66.

Chapter 4

1. This discussion is based on Gilbert A. Churchill, Jr., and J. Paul Peter, *Marketing: Creating Value for Customers,* 2nd ed. (Burr Ridge, IL: Irwin/McGraw-Hill, 1998), pp. 182–84. Also see Michele D. Bunn, "Taxonomy of Buying Decision Approaches," *Journal of Marketing,* January 1993, pp. 38–56.

2. This discussion is based on Eric N. Berkowitz, Roger A. Kerin, Steven W. Hartley, and William Rudelius, *Marketing,* 8th ed. Irwin/McGraw-Hill (Burr Ridge, IL: 2006), p. 157.

3. For research on influence strategies in organizational buying, see Gary L. Frazier and Raymond Rody, "The Use of Influence Strategies in Interfirm Relationships in Industrial Product Channels," *Journal of Marketing,* January 1991, pp. 52–69; and Julia M. Bristor, "Influence Strategies in Organizational Buying," *Journal of Business-to-Business Marketing,* 1993, pp. 63–98.

4. For research on the role of organizational climate in industrial buying, see William J. Qualls and Christopher P. Puto, "Organizational Climate and Decision Framing: An Integrated Approach to Analyzing Industrial Buying Decisions," *Journal of Marketing Research,* May 1989, pp. 179–92.

Chapter 5

1. Russell I. Haley, "Benefit Segmentation: A Decision-Oriented Research Tool," *Journal of Marketing,* July 1968, pp. 30–35; Russell I. Haley, "Benefit Segmentation—20 Years Later," *Journal of Consumer Marketing,* 1983, pp. 5–13; and Russell I. Haley, "Benefit Segments: Backwards and Forwards," *Journal of Advertising Research,* February–March 1984, pp. 19–25.

2. Roger J. Calantone and Alan G. Sawyer, "The Stability of Benefit Segments," *Journal of Marketing Research,* August 1978, pp. 395–404; also see James R. Merrill and William A. Weeks, "Predicting and Identifying Benefit Segments in the Elderly Market," in *AMA Educator's Proceedings,* eds. Patrick Murphy et al. (Chicago: American Marketing Association, 1983), pp. 399–403; Wagner A. Kamakura, "A Least Squares Procedure for Benefit Segmentation with Conjoint Experiments," *Journal of Marketing Research,* May 1988, pp. 157–67; and Michel Wedel and Jan-Benedict E. M. Steenkamp, "A Clusterwise Regression Method for Simultaneous Fuzzy Market Structuring and Benefit Segmentation," *Journal of Marketing Research,* November 1991, pp. 385–96.

3. John L. Lastovicka, John P. Murry, Jr., and Eric Joachimsthaler, "Evaluating the Measurement Validity of Lifestyle Typologies with Qualitative Measures and Multiplicative Factoring," *Journal of Marketing Research,* February 1990, pp. 11–23.

4. This discussion is taken from J. Paul Peter and Jerry C. Olson, *Consumer Behavior and Marketing Strategy,* 8th ed. (Burr Ridge, IL: Irwin/McGraw-Hill, 2008), pp. 373–75.

5. Ibid, pp. 379–381.

6. See Al Ries and Jack Trout, *Positioning: The Battle for Your Mind* (New York: Warner Books, 1981); and Al Ries and Jack Trout, *Marketing Warfare* (New York: McGraw-Hill, 1986).

Chapter 6

1. Material for this section is based on discussions contained in Louis E. Boone and David L. Kurtz, *Contemporary Marketing,* 8th ed. (Fort Worth, TX: Dryden, 1995), Chap. 2; Gilbert A. Churchill, Jr., and J. Paul Peter, *Marketing: Creating Value for Customers* (Burr Ridge, IL: Irwin/McGraw-Hill, 1995), chap. 1, p. 634; James H. Donnelly, James L. Gibson, and John M. Ivancevich, *Fundamentals of Management,* 9th ed. (Burr Ridge, IL: Irwin/McGraw-Hill 1995), p. 501; Joseph M. Juran, "Made in the U.S.A.: A Renaissance in Quality," *Harvard Business Review,* July–August 1993, pp. 42–47, 50; and Valerie A. Zeithaml, "Consumer Perceptions of Price, Quality, and Value: A Means End Model and Synthesis of Evidence," *Journal of Marketing,* April 1988, pp. 35–48.

2. For a discussion on this topic, see Andrew J. Bergman, "What the Marketing Professional Needs to Know about ISO 9000 Series Registration," *Industrial Marketing Management,* 1994, pp. 367–70.

3. The material for this section comes from Glenn L. Urban and Steven H. Star, *Advanced Marketing Strategy* (Englewood Cliffs, NJ: Prentice Hall, 1991), chap. 16.

4. For a detailed discussion of this topic, see Anne Perkins, "Product Variety beyond Black," *Harvard Business Review,* November–December 1994, pp. 13–14; and "Perspectives: The Logic of Product-Line Extensions," *Harvard Business Review,* November–December 1994, pp. 53–62.

5. Mats Urde, "Brand Orientation—A Strategy for Survival," *Journal of Consumer Marketing,* 1994, pp. 18–32.

6. James Lowry, "Survey Finds Most Powerful Brands," *Advertising Age,* July 11, 1988, p. 31.

7. Peter H. Farquhar, "Strategic Challenges for Branding," *Marketing Management,* 1994, pp. 8–15.

8. Peter D. Bennett, ed., *Dictionary of Marketing Terms,* 2nd ed. (Chicago: American Marketing Association, 1995), p. 27.

9. Terance Shimp, *Promotion Management and Marketing Communications,* 2nd ed. (Hinsdale, IL: Dryden Press, 1990), p. 67.

10. David A. Aaker and Kevin Lane Keller, "Consumer Evaluations of Brand Extensions," *Journal of Marketing,* January 1990, pp. 27–41.

11. Ibid.

12. For a detailed discussion of brand equity, see David Aaker, *Managing Brand Equity* (New York and London: Free Press, 1991).

13. For a complete discussion of this topic, see Geoffrey L. Gordon, Roger J. Calantone, and C. A. Di Benedetto, "Brand Equity in the Business-to-Business Sector: An Exploratory Study," *Journal of Product & Brand Management,* 1993, pp. 4–16.

14. Jeffrey D. Zbar, "Industry Trends Hold Private-Label Promise," *Advertising Age,* April 3, 1995, p. 31.

15. Karen Benezra, "Frito Bets 'Reduced' Pitch Is in the Chips," *Brandweek,* January 23, 1995, p. 18.

16. Thomas Hine, "Why We Buy," *Worth,* May 1995, pp. 80–83.

17. For a discussion of problems related to this issue, see Geoffrey L. Gordon, Roger J. Calantone, and C. Anthony Di Benedetto, "Mature Markets and Revitalization Strategies: An American Fable," *Business Horizons,* May–June 1991, pp. 39–50.

18. Barry L. Bayus, "Are Product Life Cycles Really Getting Shorter?" *Journal of Product Innovation Management,* September 1994, pp. 300–308.

19. The discussion on benchmarking is based on Stanley Brown, "Don't Innovate—Imitate," *Sales & Marketing Management,* January 1995, pp. 24–25; Charles

Goldwasser, "Benchmarking: People Make the Process," *Management Review,* June 1995, pp. 39–43; and L. S. Pryor and S. J. Katz, "How Benchmarking Goes Wrong (and How to Do It Right)," *Planning Review,* January–February 1993, pp. 6–14.

Chapter 7

1. "Face Value: The Mass Production of Ideas, and Other Impossibilities," *The Economist,* March 18, 1995, p. 72.

2. Greg Erickson, "New Package Makes a New Product Complete," *Marketing News,* May 8, 1995, p. 10.

3. Zina Mouhkheiber, "Oversleeping," *Forbes,* June 15, 1995, pp. 78–79.

4. The material on the five categories of new products is from C. Merle Crawford and Anthony Di Benedetto, *New Products Management,* 6th ed. (Burr Ridge, IL: McGraw-Hill/Irwin, 2000), chap. 1.

5. H. Igor Ansoff, *Corporate Strategy* (New York: McGraw-Hill, 1965), pp. 109–10.

6. Richard Stroup, "Growing in a Crowded Market Requires Old and New Strategies," *Brandweek,* August 22, 1994, p. 19.

7. These two examples came from Justin Martin, "Ignore Your Customers," *Fortune,* May 1, 1995, pp. 121–26.

8. "Where Do They Get All Those Ideas?" *Machine Design,* January 26, 1995, p. 40.

9. This section is based on Daryl McKee, "An Organizational Learning Approach to Product Innovation," *Journal of Product Innovation Management,* September 1992, pp. 232–45.

10. The discussion on risk is from Thomas D. Kuczmarski and Arthur G. Middlebrooks, "Innovation Risk and Reward," *Sales & Marketing Management,* February 1993, pp. 44–51.

11. For a more complete discussion on the advantages and disadvantages of strategic alliances, see Richard N. Cardozo, Shannon H. Shipp, and Kenneth J. Roering, "Proactive Strategic Partnerships: A New Business Markets Strategy," *Journal of Business and Industrial Marketing,* Winter 1992, pp. 51–63; and Frank K. Sonnenberg, "Partnering: Entering the Age of Cooperation," *Journal of Business Strategy,* May/June 1992, pp. 49–52.

12. James Quinn, "Managing Innovation: Controlled Chaos," *Harvard Business Review,* May–June 1985, pp. 73–84; and Hirotaka Takeuchi and Ikujiro Nonaka, "The New New Product Development Game," *Harvard Business Review,* January–February 1986, pp. 137–46.

13. For a discussion of this issue, see Eric M. Olson, Orville C. Walker, Jr., and Robert W. Ruekert, "Organizing for Effective New Product Development: The Moderating Role of Product Innovativeness," *Journal of Marketing,* January 1995, pp. 48–62; and Cristopher

Meyer, "How the Right Measures Help Teams Excel," *Harvard Business Review,* May–June 1994, pp. 95–97.

14. For a detailed discussion on these stages, see Karl T. Ulrich and Steven D. Eppinger, *Product Design and Development* (New York: McGraw-Hill, 1995); and Glen Rifken, "Product Development: Emphatic Design Helps Understand Users Better," *Harvard Business Review,* March–April 1994, pp. 10–11.

15. Patricia W. Meyers and Gerald A. Athaide, "Strategic Mutual Learning between Producing and Buying Firms during Product Innovation," *Journal of Product Innovation Management,* September 1991, pp. 155–69.

16. For a discussion of this issue, see Christina Brown and James Lattin, "Investigating the Relationship between Time in Market and Pioneering Advantage," *Management Science,* October 1994, pp. 1361–69; Robin Peterson, "Forecasting for New Product Introduction," *Journal of Business Forecasting,* Fall 1994, pp. 21–23; and Tracy Carlson, "The Race Is On," *Brandweek,* May 9, 1994, pp. 22–27.

17. For a discussion of reasons why products fail, see Betsy Spellman, "Big Talk, Little Dollars," *Brandweek,* January 23, 1995, pp. 21–29.

Chapter 8

1. This discussion is adapted from material contained in Gilbert A. Churchill, Jr., and J. Paul Peter, *Marketing: Creating Value for Customers,* 2nd ed., (Burr Ridge, IL: Irwin/McGraw-Hill, 1998), chap. 18.

2. Material for this section is largely based on the discussion of advertising tasks and objectives contained in William Arens and Courtland Bovèe, *Contemporary Advertising,* 5th ed. (Burr Ridge, IL: Irwin/McGraw-Hill, 1994), chap. 7.

3. For more comprehensive coverage of this topic, see George E. Belch and Michael A. Belch, *Advertising and Promotion: An Integrated Marketing Communications Perspective,* 7th ed. (Burr Ridge, IL: Irwin/McGraw-Hill, 2007), chap. 12.

4. For a fuller explanation of the pros and cons associated with push marketing strategies, see Betsy Spellman, "Trade Promotion Redefined," *Brandweek,* March 13, 1995, pp. 25–34; and John McManus, "'Lost' Money Redefined as 'Found' Money Won't Connect the Disconnects," *Brandweek,* March 25, 1995, p. 16.

5. This discussion is based on Donald R. Glover, "Distributor Attitudes toward Manufacturer-Sponsored Promotions," *Industrial Marketing Management,* August 1991, pp. 241–49.

6. For a discussion of this topic, see Murray Raphel, "Frequent Shopper Clubs: Supermarkets' Newest Weapon," *Direct Marketing,* May 1995, pp. 18–20; Richard G. Barlow, "Five Mistakes of Frequency Marketing,"

Direct Marketing, March 1995, pp. 16–17; and Alice Cuneo, "Savvy Frequent-Buyer Plans Build on a Loyal Base," *Advertising Age,* March 20, 1995, pp. S10–11.

Chapter 9

1. Warren Keegan, Sandra Moriarty, and Thomas Duncan, *Marketing,* 2nd ed. (Englewood Cliffs, NJ: Prentice Hall, 1994), p. 654.

2. Material for this discussion came from Ronald B. Marks, *Personal Selling: An Interactive Approach,* 5th ed. (Boston, MA: Allyn and Bacon, 1994), pp. 12–13.

3. Material for the discussion of objectives is adapted from Joel R. Evans and Barry Berman, *Marketing,* 6th ed. (New York: Macmillan, 1994), pp. 640–42.

4. Unless otherwise noted, the discussion on the relationship-building process is based largely on material contained in Barton A. Weitz, Stephen B. Castleberry, and John F. Tanner, Jr., *Selling: Building Partnerships,* 3rd ed. (Burr Ridge, IL: Irwin/McGraw-Hill, 1998); and Rolph Anderson, *Essentials of Personal Selling: The New Professionalism* (Englewood Cliffs, NJ: Prentice Hall, 1995). For an in-depth discussion of this topic, readers should consult these references.

5. The discussion of aftermarketing is based on the work of Terry Vavra, *Aftermarketing: How to Keep Customers for Life through Relationship Marketing* (Burr Ridge, IL: McGraw-Hill, 1995).

6. Ibid.

7. The discussion on national account management is from James S. Boles, Bruce K. Pilling, and George W. Goodwyn, "Revitalizing Your National Account Marketing Program," *Journal of Business & Industrial Marketing,* no. 1 (1994), pp. 24–33.

8. Based on a survey by the National Industrial Conference Board: "Forecasting Sales," *Studies in Business Policy,* no. 106.

9. Much of the discussion in this section is based on material contained in Gilbert A. Churchill, Jr., Neil M. Ford, and Orville C. Walker, Jr., *Sales Force Management,* 4th ed. (Burr Ridge, IL: Irwin/McGraw-Hill, 1993); and William J. Stanton, Richard H. Buskirk, and Rosann L. Spiro, *Management of a Sales Force,* 9th ed. (Burr Ridge, IL: Irwin/McGraw-Hill, 1995), pp. 319–20.

10. For a complete discussion of the skills and policies successful sales leaders use in motivating salespeople, see David W. Cravens, Thomas N. Ingram, Raymond W. LaForge, and Clifford E. Young, "Hallmarks of Effective Sales Organizations," *Marketing Management,* Winter 1992, pp. 57–66; Thomas R. Wortruba, John S. Mactie, and Jerome A. Colletti, "Effective Sales Force Recognition Programs," *Industrial Marketing Management,* February 1991, pp. 9–15; and Ken Blanchard, "Reward Salespeople Creatively," *Personal Selling Power,* March 1992, p. 24.

Chapter 10

1. Peter D. Bennett, *Dictionary of Marketing Terms,* 2nd ed. (Chicago: American Marketing Association, 1995), p. 242.

2. For further discussion of relationship marketing, see Jan B. Heide, "Interorganizational Governance in Marketing Channels," *Journal of Marketing,* January 1994, pp. 71–85; Robert M. Morgan and Shelby D. Hunt, "The Commitment-Trust Theory of Relationship Marketing," *Journal of Marketing,* July 1994, pp. 20–38; and Manohar U. Kalwani and Narakesari Narayandas, "Long-Term Manufacturer-Supplier Relationships: Do They Pay Off for the Supplier Firm?" *Journal of Marketing,* January 1995, pp. 1–16.

3. This section is based on Donald J. Bowersox and M. Bixby Cooper, *Strategic Marketing Channel Management* (New York: McGraw-Hill, 1992), pp. 104–7; Bert Rosenbloom, *Marketing Channels: A Management View,* 4th ed. (Hinsdale, IL: Dryden Press), pp. 440–65; and Roger A. Kerin, Eric N. Berkowitz, Steven W. Hartley, and William Rudelius, *Marketing,* 8th ed. (Burr Ridge, IL: Irwin/McGraw-Hill, 2006), pp. 405–407.

4. This section is based on Gilbert A. Churchill, Jr., and J. Paul Peter, *Marketing: Creating Value for Customers,* 2nd ed. (Burr Ridge, IL: Irwin/McGraw-Hill, 1998), pp. 392–98.

5. www.naics.com, April 6, 2007.

6. This classification is based on Michael Levy and Barton A. Weitz, *Retailing Management,* 8th ed. (Burr Ridge, IL: Irwin/McGraw-Hill, 2007), chap. 2.

7. For an excellent discussion of electronic exchange, see David W. Stewart and Qin Zhao, "Internet Marketing, Business Models, and Public Policy," *Journal of Public Policy & Marketing,* Fall 2000, pp. 287–96.

Chapter 11

1. Kent B. Monroe, "Buyers' Subjective Perceptions of Price," *Journal of Marketing Research,* February 1973, pp. 70–80; also see Donald R. Lichtenstein and Scot Burton, "The Relationship between Perceived and Objective Price—Quality," *Journal of Marketing Research,* November 1989, pp. 429–43.

2. For research concerning the effects of price and several other marketing variables on perceived product quality, see Akshay R. Rao and Kent B. Monroe, "The Effect of Price, Brand Name, and Store Name on Buyers' Perceptions of Product Quality: An Integrative Review," *Journal of Marketing Research,* August 1989, pp. 351–57; and William B. Dodds, Kent B. Monroe, and Dhruv Grewal, "Effects of Price, Brand, and Store Evaluations on Buyers' Product Evaluations," *Journal of Marketing Research,* August 1991, pp. 307–19.

3. For further discussion of price elasticity, see Stephen J. Hoch, Byung-Do Kim, Alan L. Montgomery, and Peter Rosi, "Determinants of Store-Level Price Elasticity," *Journal of Marketing Research,* February 1995, pp. 17–29.

4. For further discussion of legal issues involved in pricing, see Louis W. Stern and Thomas L. Eovaldi, *Legal Aspects of Marketing Strategy* (Englewood Cliffs, NJ: Prentice Hall, 1984), chap. 5.

5. For more detailed discussions, see Frederick E. Webster, *Marketing for Managers* (New York: Harper & Row, 1974), pp. 178–79; also see Thomas T. Nagle and Reed K. Holden, *The Strategy and Tactics of Pricing* (Englewood Cliffs, NJ: Prentice Hall, 1995); and Kent B. Monroe, *Pricing: Making Profitable Decisions,* 3rd ed. (Burr Ridge, IL: McGraw-Hill/Irwin, 2003).

Chapter 12

1. Much of the material for this introduction came from Ronald Henkoff, "Service Is Everybody's Business," *Fortune,* June 27, 1994, pp. 48–60; and Tim R. Smith, "The Tenth District's Expanding Service Sector," *Economic Review,* Third Quarter 1994, pp. 55–66.

2. Peter D. Bennett, ed., *Dictionary of Marketing Terms,* 2nd ed. (Chicago: American Marketing Association, 1995), p. 261.

3. The material in this section draws from research performed by Leonard L. Berry, Valerie A. Zeithaml, and A. Parasuraman, "Quality Counts in Services, Too," *Business Horizons,* May–June 1985, pp. 44–52; A. Parasuraman, Valerie A. Zeithaml, and Leonard L. Berry, "A Conceptual Model of Service Quality and Its Implications for Future Research," *Journal of Marketing,* Fall 1985, pp. 41–50; Leonard L. Berry, A. Parasuraman, and Valerie A. Zeithaml, "The Service-Quality Puzzle," *Business Horizons,* September–October 1988, pp. 35–43; Stephen W. Brown and Teresa A. Swartz, "A Gap Analysis of Professional Service Quality," *Journal of Marketing,* April 1989, pp. 92–98; Leonard L. Berry, Valerie A. Zeithaml, and A. Parasuraman, "Five Imperatives for Improving Service Quality," *Sloan Management Review,* Summer 1990, pp. 29–38; A. Parasuraman, Leonard L. Berry, and Valerie A. Zeithaml, "Understanding Customer Expectations of Service," *Sloan Management Review,* Spring 1991, pp. 39–48; and Leonard L. Berry, *On Great Service: A Framework for Action* (New York: Free Press, 1995).

4. Rick Berry, "Define Service Quality So You Can Deliver It," *Best's Review,* March 1995, p. 68.

5. Material for this section is drawn from John T. Mentzer, Carol C. Bienstock, and Kenneth B. Kahn, "Benchmarking Satisfaction," *Marketing Management,* Summer 1995, pp. 41–46; and Alan Dutka, *AMA Handbook for Customer Satisfaction: A Complete Guide to Research, Planning and Implementation* (Lincolnwood,

IL: NTC Books, 1994). For detailed information on this topic, readers are advised to consult these sources.

6. Much of the material for this section was taken from Karl Albrecht and Ron Zemke, *Service America* (Burr Ridge, IL: Irwin/McGraw-Hill, 1985); and Ron Zemke and Dick Schaaf, *The Service Edge 101: Companies That Profit from Customer Care* (New York: New American Library, 1989).

7. Chip R. Bell and Kristen Anderson, "Selecting Super Service People," *HR Magazine,* February 1992, pp. 52–54.

8. James A. Schlesinger and James L. Heskett, "Breaking the Cycle of Failure in Services," *Sloan Management Review,* Spring 1991, pp. 17–28.

9. Leonard L. Berry and A. Parasuraman, "Services Marketing Starts from Within," *Marketing Management,* Winter 1992, pp. 25–34.

10. Ibid.

11. Leonard L. Berry and A. Parasuraman, "Prescriptions for a Service Quality Revolution in America," *Organizational Dynamics,* Spring 1992, pp. 5–15.

12. Bob O'Neal, "World-Class Service," *Executive Excellence,* September 1994, pp. 11–12.

13. This example is from David E. Bowen and Edward E. Lawler III, "The Empowerment of Service Workers: What, Why, How, and When," *Sloan Management Review,* Spring 1992, pp. 31–39.

14. Howard Schlossberg, "Study: U.S. Firms Lag in Using Customer Satisfaction Data," *Marketing News,* June 1992, p. 14.

15. Andrew E. Serwer, "The Competition Heats Up in Online Banking," *Fortune,* June 26, 1995, pp. 18–19.

16. John Labate, "Chronimed," *Fortune,* February 20, 1995, p. 118.

17. Elaine Underwood, "Airlines Continue Flight to E-Ticketing," *Brandweek,* May 8, 1995, p. 3.

18. Peter L. Ostrowski, Terrence V. O'Brien, and Geoffrey L. Gordon, "Determinants of Service Quality in the Commercial Airline Industry: Differences between Business and Leisure Travelers," *Journal of Travel & Tourism Marketing* 3, no. 1 (1994), pp. 19–47.

Chapter 13

1. Jason Vogel, "Chicken Diplomacy," *Financial World,* March 14, 1995, pp. 46–49.

2. For a full explanation on cultural differences, see Rose Knotts, "Cross-Cultural Management: Transformations and Adaptations," *Business Horizons,* January–February 1989, pp. 29–33.

3. Claudia Penteado, "Pepsi's Brazil Blitz," *Advertising Age,* January 16, 1995, p. 12.

4. Karen Benezra, "Fritos 'Round the World,'" *Brandweek,* March 27, 1995, pp. 32, 35.

5. Material for this section is from Craig Mellow, "Russia: Making Cash from Chaos," *Fortune,* April 17, 1995, pp. 145–51; and Peter Galuszka, "And You Think You've Got Tax Problems," *Business Week,* May 29, 1995, p. 50.

6. Mir Magbool Alam Khan, "Enormity Tempts Marketers to Make a Passage to India," *Advertising Age International,* May 15, 1995, p. 112.

7. This section was taken from James F. Bolt, "Global Competitors: Some Criteria for Success," *Business Horizons,* January–February 1988, pp. 34–41.

8. This section is based on George S. Yip, Pierre M. Loewe, and Michael Y. Yoshino, "How to Take Your Company to the Global Market," *Columbia Journal of World Business,* Winter 1988, pp. 37–48.

9. Ibid.

10. The introductory material on foreign research is based on Michael R. Czintoka, "Take a Shortcut to Low-Cost Global Research," *Marketing News,* March 13, 1995, p. 3.

11. Donald B. Pittenger, "Gathering Foreign Demographics Is No Easy Task," *Marketing News,* January 8, 1990, pp. 23, 25.

12. This discussion is based on John Burnett, *Promotion Management* (Boston: Houghton-Mifflin Co., 1993), chap. 19.

13. The material for this section on market entry and growth approaches is based on Philip R. Cateora, *International Marketing,* 8th ed. (Burr Ridge, IL: Irwin/McGraw-Hill, 1993), pp. 325–34; Charles W. L. Hill, *International Business: Competing in the Global Marketplace* (Burr Ridge, IL: Irwin/McGraw-Hill, 1994), pp. 402–8; and William M. Pride and O. C. Ferrell, *Marketing: Concepts and Strategy,* 9th ed. (Boston: Houghton-Mifflin Co., 1995), pp. 111–14.

14. Bruce A. Walters, Steve Peters, and Gregory G. Dess, "Strategic Alliances and Joint Ventures: Making Them Work," *Business Horizons,* July–August 1994, pp. 5–10.

15. Material in this section is based on Subhash C. Jain, "Standardization of International Marketing Strategy: Some Research Hypotheses," *Journal of Marketing,* January 1989, pp. 70–79.

Section II

1. Michael E. Porter, *Competitive Strategy* (New York: Free Press, 1980). Also see Michael E. Porter, *Competitive Advantage: Creating and Sustaining Superior Performance* (New York: Free Press, 1985); and Michael E. Porter, *The Competitive Advantage of Nations* (New York: Free Press, 1990).

Section III

1. For methods of estimating the cost of capital, see Charles P. Jones, *Introduction to Financial Management* (Burr Ridge, IL: Irwin/McGraw-Hill, 1992), chap. 14.

2. See Eugene F. Brigham, *Fundamentals of Financial Management* (Hinsdale, IL: Dryden Press, 1986).

3. It is useful to use average inventory rather than a single end-of-year estimate if monthly data are available.

4. For a discussion of ratio analysis for retailing, see Michael Levy and Barton A. Weitz, *Retailing Management* (Burr Ridge, IL: McGraw-Hill/Irwin, 2007), chap. 5.

Index

NAME INDEX

SUBJECT INDEX